PALMYRENE SARCOPHAGI

STUDIES IN PALMYRENE ARCHAEOLOGY AND HISTORY

VOLUME 10

FOUNDING EDITOR

Professor **Rubina Raja**, *Centre for Urban Network Evolutions, Aarhus University, Denmark*

ADVISORY BOARD

Professor **Nathanael Andrade**, *Binghamton University, New York, USA*
Dr **Olympia Bobou**, *Aarhus University, Denmark*
Professor **Maura K. Heyn**, *University of North Carolina, Greensboro, USA*
Dr **Emanuele Intagliata**, *Università degli Studi di Milano, Italy*
Professor **Ted Kaizer**, *Durham University, UK*
Professor **Eivind Heldaas Seland**, *University of Bergen, Norway*
Dr **Jean-Baptiste Yon**, *Laboratoire HiSoMA, CNRS, Lyon*

Previously published volumes in this series are listed at the back of the book.

Palmyrene Sarcophagi

Volume 1

OLYMPIA BOBOU and RUBINA RAJA

BREPOLS

British Library Cataloguing in Publication Data
A catalogue record for this book is available from the British Library.

© 2023, Brepols Publishers n.v., Turnhout, Belgium.

All rights reserved. No part of this publication may be reproduced,
stored in a retrieval system, or transmitted, in any form or by any means,
electronic, mechanical, photocopying, recording, or otherwise without
the prior permission of the publisher.

D/2023/0095/19
ISBN: 978-2-503-60466-4 (2 volumes)
eISBN: 978-2-503-60754-2 (2 volumes)
10.1484/M.SPAH-EB.5.134891

Printed in the EU on acid-free paper.

Table of Contents

List of Figures — 7

Colour Plates — 9

Acknowledgements — 37

Chapters

1. Palmyra and its Funerary Sphere — 39

2. The Portrait Habit in Palmyra and the Funerary Sphere — 53

3. Dated Objects — 81

4 In situ Contexts — 93

5. Iconography — 125

   Appendix: The Costume of Reclining Figures — 141

6. Conclusion: Sarcophagi as Vehicles of Elite Identity — 145

Works Cited — 149

Catalogue

Dated by Inscription (Cat. 1–12) — 177

Objects from Tower Tombs (Cat. 13–59) — 209

Objects from Hypogea (Cat. 60–179) — 246

Objects from Temple Tombs (Cat. 180–277) — 441

Credits

Text Image Credits — 556

Catalogue Image Credits — 558

List of Figures

Figure 1.	Map of Palmyra and the region.	42
Figure 2.	Map of Palmyra and the surrounding area.	43
Figure 3.	Cassas' drawing of the founder relief from the tower tomb of Kîtôt.	45
Figure 4.	Sarcophagus with the triumph of Dionysos, marble. From Rome, A.D. 260–270.	48
Figure 5.	Strigillated sarcophagus. Probably from Rome, made of Proconnesian marble, ca. A.D. 220.	48
Figure 6.	Sarcophagus with scenes from the life of Achilles on the box and reclining couple on the lid. From Athens, A.D. 180–220.	49
Figure 7.	The Amathus sarcophagus, limestone. From Amathous, Cyprus, 475–450 B.C.	50
Figure 8.	Loculus relief depicting a priest, limestone. From Palmyra, A.D. 200–220.	51
Figure 9.	Loculus relief depicting a female, limestone. From Palmyra, A.D. 50–150.	51
Figure 10.	Relief with veiled women, limestone. From Palmyra, Temple of Bel, A.D. 32–100.	54
Figure 11.	Statue of togate man, marble. From near the Agora of Palmyra, A.D. 200–273.	54
Figure 12.	Statue of togate man with priestly hat by his feet, limestone. From the Great Colonnade of Palmyra, A.D. 200–220.	55
Figure 13.	Statue of seated man in chiton and himation, marble. From the Agora of Palmyra, A.D. 150–200.	55
Figure 14.	Statue of standing female of the Large Herculaneum Woman type, marble. Either from the Agora or the Senate of Palmyra, A.D. 200–225.	56
Figure 15.	Relief of Ur-Nanshe, limestone. King Ur-Nanshe of Lagash (r. ca. 2550–2500 B.C.) is the only one seated in the banquet.	59
Figure 16.	Guests at a banquet, illustration by Nina de Garis Davies, facsimile of wall-painting from the tomb of Nebamun and Ipuky (TT181), Thebes, tempera on paper.	60
Figure 17.	Guests at a banquet, illustration by Nina de Garis Davies, facsimile of wall-painting from the tomb of Rekhmire (TT 100), Thebes, tempera on paper.	60
Figure 18.	Tessera with reclining priest, terracotta.	61
Figure 19.	Stele with reclining female at banquet, marble. From Heraclea Pontica, A.D. 100–200.	62
Figure 20.	Kline monument with a reclining girl, marble. From Rome, A.D. 120–140.	63
Figure 21.	Plate with the king Yazdgard I (r. 399–420) slaying a stag, silver. From Iran, A.D. 399–420.	63
Figure 22.	Julius Terentius performing a sacrifice, wall-painting. From Dura-Europos, Temple of Bel, ca. A.D. 200–220.	64

Figure 23.	Map of the west necropolis, Palmyra, with the locations of the tombs. The tombs are named following Schnädelbach 2010.	68
Figure 24.	Tower tombs in the landscape.	68
Figure 25.	Map of the north necropolis, Palmyra, with the locations of the tombs. The tombs are named following Schnädelbach 2010.	69
Figure 26.	Map of the south-west necropolis, Palmyra, with the locations of the tombs. The tombs are named following Schnädelbach 2010.	70
Figure 27.	Map of the south-east necropolis, Palmyra, with the locations of the tombs. The tombs are named following Schnädelbach 2010.	71
Figure 28.	Plan and elevation of tower tomb of Kîtôt.	74
Figure 29.	Temple tomb no. 86, reconstructed elevation of the façade.	79
Figure 30.	Stele with depiction of god Šadrafâ, limestone. From Palmyra, A.D. 55.	88
Figure 31.	Fragment of loculus relief depicting a female, limestone. From Palmyra, A.D. 65/66.	88
Figure 32.	Loculus relief with female portrait bust, limestone. From Palmyra, A.D. 113/114.	88
Figure 33.	Loculus relief with male portrait bust, limestone. From Palmyra, A.D. 133/134.	88
Figure 34.	Loculus relief with female portrait bust, limestone. From Palmyra, A.D. 150.	90
Figure 35.	Loculus relief with male bust, limestone. From Palmyra, A.D. 154/155.	90
Figure 36.	Loculus relief with male and female bust, limestone. From Palmyra, A.D. 218/219.	90
Figure 37.	Loculus relief with bust of female holding a child, limestone. From Palmyra, A.D. 240/241.	90
Figure 38.	Distribution map of the tombs with sarcophagi according to type of tomb.	93
Figure 39.	Distribution map of the tombs with sarcophagi and other funerary sculptures.	94
Figure 40.	Distribution map of the tombs with documented sarcophagi.	95
Figure 41.	Painted arch of exedra of Julius Aurelius Maqqaî, in the hypogeum of ʿAtenatan.	101
Figure 42.	Decorated ceiling of exedra in hypogeum of ʿAbdʿastôr.	102
Figure 43.	Interior of ground floor of tower tomb of Elahbel.	104
Figure 44.	Niches in the hypogeum of Yarḥaî.	105
Figure 45.	Reconstruction of the exedra with the sarcophagi from the hypogeum of Yarḥaî. The reconstruction includes more objects than were found in the exedra.	105
Figure 46.	Painted exedra in hypogeum of the Three Brothers.	113
Figure 47.	Detail with standing child, from sarcophagus cat. 10.	126
Figure 48.	Stele with funerary banquet, marble. From Thessaloniki, A.D. 75–100.	127
Figure 49.	Fulcrum with horse's head, bronze, 100 B.C.–A.D. 100.	128
Figure 50.	Attic sarcophagus with undecorated mattress and cushion, marble. Found in Thessaloniki, ca. A.D. 180.	130
Figure 51.	Stele with funerary banquet: in memory of Menophilos, set up by his wife, Synete, marble. From Cyzicus, 25 B.C.–A.D. 25.	133
Figure 52.	Dionysus, from the tomb of Dionysus.	140

COLOUR PLATES 9

Plate 1. Sarcophagus with the triumph of Dionysos, marble. From Rome, A.D. 260–270.

Plate 2. Strigilated sarcophagus. Probably from Rome, made of Proconnesian marble, ca. A.D. 220.

Plate 3. Sarcophagus with scenes from the life of Achilles on the box and reclining couple on the lid. From Athens, A.D. 180–220.

Plate 4. The Amathus sarcophagus, limestone. From Amathous, Cyprus, 475–450 B.C.

Plate 5. Loculus relief depicting a priest, limestone.
From Palmyra, A.D. 200–220.

Plate 6. Loculus relief depicting a female, limestone.
From Palmyra, A.D. 50–150.

COLOUR PLATES 13

Plate 7. Statue of togate man, marble.
From near the Agora of Palmyra, A.D. 200–273.

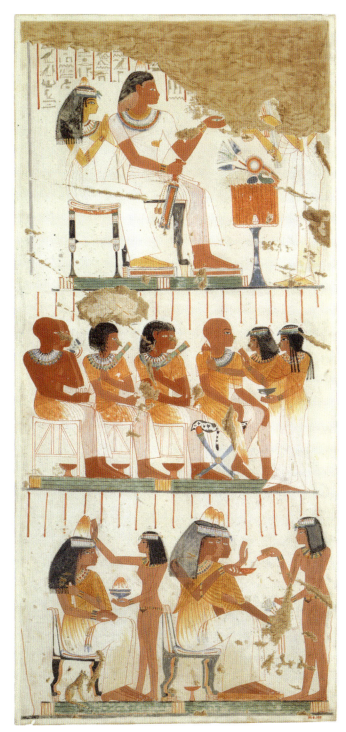

Plate 8. Guests at a banquet, illustration by Nina de Garis Davies, facsimile of wall-painting from Tomb of Nebamun and Ipuky (TT181), Thebes, tempera on paper.

14 COLOUR PLATES

Plate 9. Guests at a banquet, illustration by Nina de Garis Davies, facsimile of wall-painting from Tomb of Rekhmire (TT 100), Thebes, tempera on paper.

Plate 10. Tessera with reclining priest, terracotta.

Plate 11. Kline monument with a reclining girl, marble. From Rome, A.D. 120–140.

Plate 12. Julius Terentius performing a sacrifice, wall-painting. From Dura-Europos, temple of Bel, ca. A.D. 200–220.

Plate 13. Plate with the king Yazdgard I (r. 399-420) slaying a stag, silver. From Iran, A.D. 399–420.

Plate 14. Mummy from Palmyra.

Plate 15. Tower Tombs in the landscape.

Plate 16. Tower tomb of Elahbel.

Plate 17. Exedra with three sarcophagi in underground tomb of Three Brothers.

Plate 18. Temple tomb no. 86, reconstructed elevation of the façade.

Plate 19. Fragment of loculus relief depicting a female, limestone.
From Palmyra, A.D. 65/66.

Plate 20. Loculus relief with male portrait bust, limestone.
From Palmyra, A.D. 133/134.

Plate 21. Loculus relief with female portrait bust, limestone.
From Palmyra, A.D. 150.

COLOUR PLATES 19

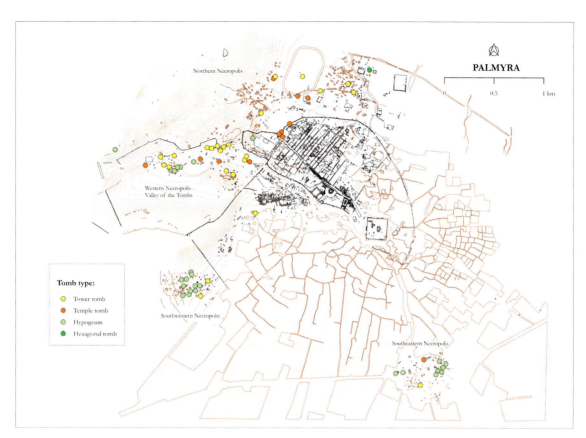

Plate 22. Distribution map of the tombs with sarcophagi according to type.

Plate 23. Distribution map of the tombs with sarcophagi and other funerary sculptures.

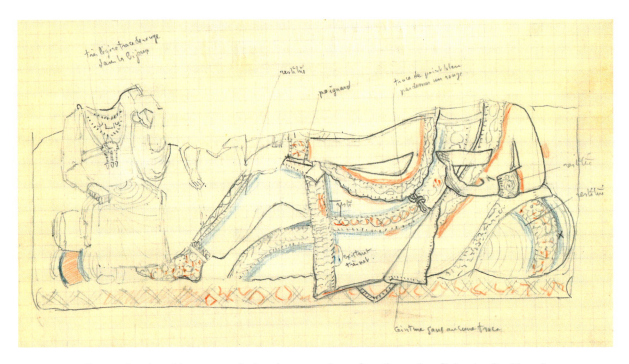

Plate 24. Drawing with remnants of colour from sarcophagus from the exedra of Julius Aurelius Maqqaî.

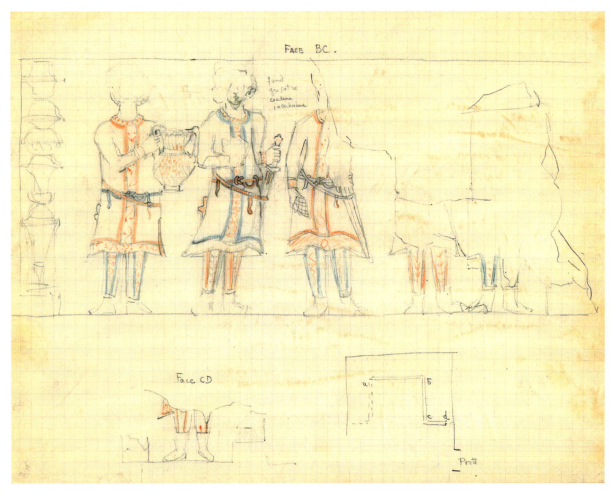

Plate 25. Drawing with remnants of colour from sarcophagus from the exedra of Julius Aurelius Maqqaî.

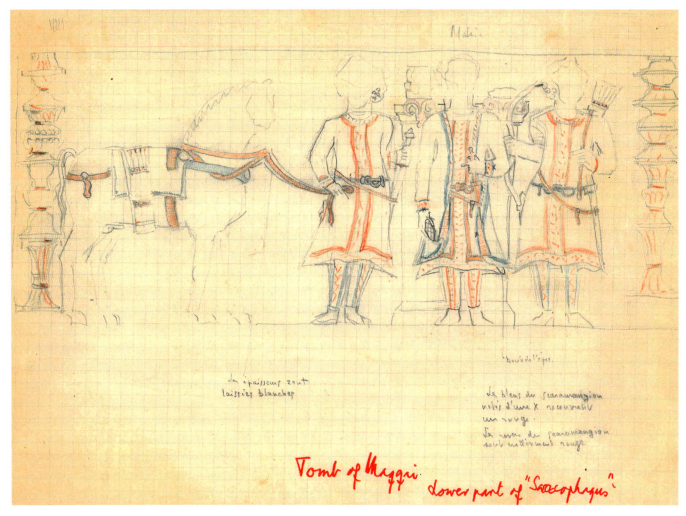

Plate 26. Drawing with remnants of colour from sarcophagus from the exedra of Julius Aurelius Maqqaî.

Plate 27. Drawing of painting on back of arch of exedra of Julius Aurelius Maqqaî.

Plate 28. Painted arch of exedra of Julius Aurelius Maqqaî, in the hypogeum of ʿAtenatan.

Plate 29. Interior of ground floor of tower tomb of Elahbel.

Plate 30. Detail of ceiling of tower tomb of Elahbel.

Plate 31. Niches in the hypogeum of Yarḥaî.

Plate 32. Attic sarcophagus with undecorated mattress and cushion, marble. Found in Thessaloniki, ca. A.D. 180.

Plate 33. Tomb of Three brothers, the painted exedra.

Plate 34. Tomb of Three brothers, ceiling detail of the painted exedra.

Plate 35. Painted eagle from hypogeum of Ḥairan.

Plate 36. Painted portrait from hypogeum of Ḥairan.

Plate 37. Painted portrait from hypogeum of Ḥairan.

Plate 38. Dionysus, from Tomb of Dionysus.

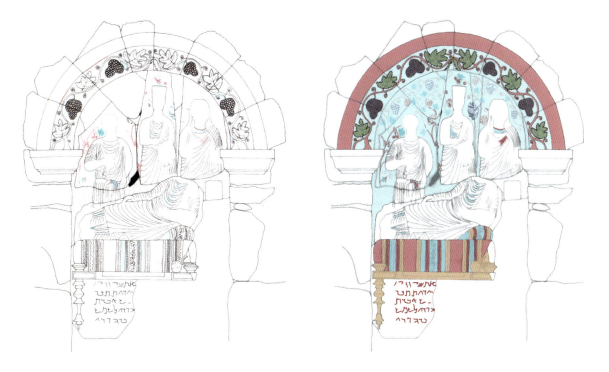

Plate 39. Drawing of founder banqueting relief from tower tomb of Kitôt, cat. no. 1.

Plate 40. Sarcophagi in tower tomb no. N206, A.D. 128, cat. no. 4.

Plate 41. Fragment of sarcophagus box with female portrait, A.D. 140/141, cat. no. 5.

COLOUR PLATES 29

Plate 42. Complete sarcophagus relief with banqueting scene from hypogeum of Three Brothers, A.D. 142/143, cat. no. 6.

Plate 43. Fragments of banqueting relief, A.D. 146/147, cat. no. 7.

Plate 44. Sarcophagus box relief with portrait busts, A.D. 148, cat. no 8.

Plate 45. Banqueting relief belonging with sarcophagus box relief from A.D. 148, cat. no. 9.

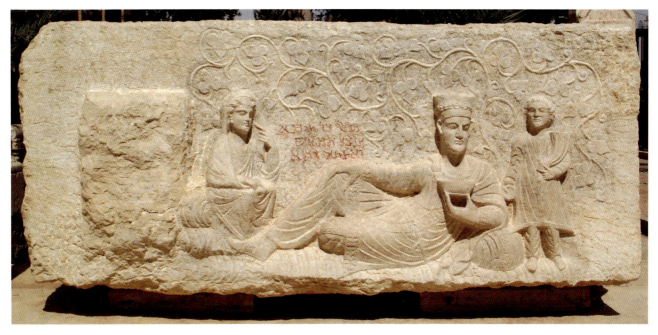

Plate 46. Sarcophagus box with banqueting scene, cat. no. 103.

Plate 47. Banqueting relief, cat. no. 104.

Plate 48. Sarcophagus box with portrait busts, cat. no. 114.

Plate 49. Sarcophagus lid with banqueting scene, cat. no. 123.

Plate 50. Sarcophagus lid with banqueting scene, cat. no. 124.

Plate 51. Sarcophagus lid relief with banqueting scene, cat. no. 128.

Plate 52. Sarcophagus box relief with portrait busts, cat. no. 173.

COLOUR PLATES 35

Plate 53. Complete sarcophagus relief with banqueting scene and portrait busts, cat. no. 177.

Plate 54. Detail of fulcrum, cat. no. 178.

Acknowledgements

The Palmyra Portrait Project, which was initiated in January 2012, has provided the framework for this publication. During the project it became clear that the corpus of limestone sarcophagi from Palmyra constitutes a unique group of material from outside of Rome and can cast new light on local funerary traditions and portrait sculpture in the Roman world. Therefore, it was decided to publish the sarcophagi in monograph form. Since 2012 the Palmyra Portrait Project directed by Rubina Raja has been supported by the Carlsberg Foundation (2012–2020). We are grateful for the funding, which has allowed for a corpus of all known funerary sculpture from Palmyra to be collected. Numerous publications have come out of the Palmyra Portrait Project, and a full list can be found on Figshare[1]. We are also grateful to the Danish National Research Foundation, who presented Rubina Raja with the opportunity to establish the Centre for Urban Network Evolutions at Aarhus University in 2015 (DNRF grant 119). Through this grant, it has been possible to take research on urban matters far further than would otherwise have been possible — research which also has provided new insights about Palmyra and its surroundings. We are also grateful to the Augustinus Foundation and the Carlsberg Foundation for funding the project Circular Economy and Urban Sustainability in Antiquity: Comparative Perspectives from the Ancient World with a Point of Departure in Roman Palmyra (2020–2023) and to the ALIPH Foundation for financing the project Archive Archaeology: Preserving and Sharing Palmyra's Cultural Heritage through Harald Ingholt's Digital Archives (2020–2023).

This book would not have been possible without the expertise input by Jean-Baptiste Yon. Yon, who is also in charge of all inscriptions of the forthcoming corpus, translated the inscriptions on the sarcophagi, and offered valuable epigraphic insights on the Palmyrene material, as well as photographs of published and unpublished material. We would also like to thank the colleagues at the DAI – Orient Abteilung, in particular its former director Karin Bartl, for giving us the opportunity to study Palmyrene material in their photographic collection and to reproduce the images. A large thank you also goes to Michał Gawlikowski, Agnes Henning, Annie Sartre-Fauriat, and Jean-Baptiste Yon for generously sharing their images with us for reproduction. We also thank Andreas Schmidt-Colinet for letting us acquire against payment the rights to reprint images from his publications. We also offer our deepest gratitude to numerous colleagues who shared their insights both during conferences and workshops as well as on a one to one basis.

The help of the various fantastic research assistants who have worked in the Palmyra Portrait Project and UrbNet was invaluable for completing this book: Jesper Vestergaard Jensen, Joan Campmany Jiménez, Ditte Kvist Johnson, Nathalia Breintoft Kristensen, Mette Lang, Katarína Mokránová, Julia Steding, and Rikke Randeris Thomsen.

Olympia Bobou and Rubina Raja
Aarhus, December 2022

---

[1] Raja 2021c.

CHAPTER 1

Palmyra and its Funerary Sphere

Structure of the Book

This monograph presents the limestone sarcophagi, banqueting reliefs, founder reliefs, and sarcophagus reliefs from Palmyra, Syria. Several of them have been discussed by scholars in the past[2], but only now, through the work of the Palmyra Portrait Project, is it possible to present a comprehensive corpus of the material. The Palmyra Portrait Project, initiated and headed by Rubina Raja since 2012, set out to collect all known Palmyrene funerary sculptural representations. This quest has led to the project having collected presently 3976 funerary portraits that were depicted on 2902 objects[3]. Early in the project it became clear that the locally produced limestone sarcophagi made up a significant part of the corpus, and almost all of them have the same iconographic motif, that of the banquet. In addition to them, the motif is shown on the founder reliefs placed outside tower tombs, as well as on reliefs that imitated sarcophagi, and smaller reliefs that were used as sarcophagi lids. Therefore it seemed appropriate to present these collectively, since they should be accessible to scholars in such a format in order to provide a comparative basis to sarcophagus material from other sites of the ancient world, for example, Rome, Athens, Aphrodisias, Tyros, and Sidon, to name but a few.

The sarcophagi found in Palmyra were almost exclusively produced in the local limestone. A few imported pieces are known (appendix 4, cat. 1–4), but they are outliers within the corpus of the 745 sarcophagi or sarcophagi fragments in total that we know of[4]. We do not claim to have been exhaustive in our work, but we have been as thorough as the situation has allowed us to be. When considering the history of research at Palmyra and the accounts of travellers from the 19th cent., it is clear that the spoliation and vandalism of the monuments in Palmyra, also in the graves of the city, was a process which had been taking place for a long time[5]. The heads of the sculptural representations were easy to cut off and to export, legally or illegally — just as it is the case still today — and unfortunately, due to the conflict in Syria which has now been ongoing for more than ten years, we have seen several pieces — both heads but also large-scale pieces such as banqueting reliefs and sarcophagi lids — in recent years ending up on the antiquities market without any firm provenance[6].

The monograph is divided into two parts. The first part presents the material, sets the chronological framework for it, places the objects whose provenance is known within the context of the individual tombs, and gives an overview of the iconography of the sarcophagi. The second part is the comprehensive catalogue of all the objects.

The first chapter presents the history of Palmyra, the exploration of the city from the early modern period onwards, and the historiography of research on Palmyrene sarcophagi and other objects with the banqueting motif from the funerary sphere. Indeed, as the earliest scholars had already noticed, sarcophagi cannot be discussed separately from the foundation reliefs outside tower tombs or the larger and smaller reliefs placed inside the tombs. They all have the banqueting imagery in common, and the interest in Palmyra from a period before the development of proper archaeological methods and techniques, as well as recent events, no longer make it possible to separate the objects into neat, typological categories[7]. This

---

2   For example, the sarcophagi from the tomb of Yarḥaî had been published in Amy – Seyrig 1936, those from the hypogeum of ʿAlaînê in Sadurska 1977, the founder reliefs were discussed in Henning 2013b, 49–51. See also below, section on literature survey.
3   For summaries of the results of the project, see Romanowska et al. 2021; Raja et al. 2021c; Bobou et al. 2021a.
4   The number does not include the small reliefs with frame that, despite having a banqueting scene, were not placed over sarcophagi.

5   Østrup 1894; Østrup 1895; Raja 2019c; Raja 2019d.
6   See, among others, Terril 2017; Brodie et al. 2019; Hashemi – Shelley 2022; Jacobs – Mashberg 2022.
7   This will be discussed more in this and the following chapters. For Palmyra and its history, see recently Sommer 2020; Gawlikowski 2021; Raja 2022b.

chapter also presents a brief overview of sarcophagi in the Roman world.

The second chapter offers an introduction to the banqueting motif in Palmyra, the burial customs of the city, the types of funerary monuments, as well as the portrait habit in Palmyra and the place of sarcophagi within the corpus of Palmyrene portraiture. The production of sarcophagi is only one part of the sculptural production of the city and cannot be understood without a brief introduction to the portraits produced and displayed in the city. This chapter also presents the iconography within the context of the broader iconographic traditions in the Roman province of Syria and the Near East, in order to highlight similarities and differences and, ultimately, the iconographic choices of the Palmyrenes compared to that of the inhabitants of other areas. The persistence of the banqueting motif for use in the funerary sphere is perhaps the biggest difference between the Palmyrenes and their neighbours, as the evidence shows. In addition to that, the Palmyrenes also distinguished themselves by their burial customs and their choices of tomb types. These are also presented in this chapter.

The third chapter is a discussion of the objects and portraits that can be dated securely thanks to epigraphic evidence. It is possible to distinguish between portraits dated with precision and the portraits that can be dated within a certain timeframe. The first group consists of inscribed portraits that mention either the year of construction and creation of the monument, as is the case with founder reliefs, or the date of death of the depicted individual. The second group includes portraits that were found within tombs or sections of tombs whose construction date is known, providing scholars with a *terminus post quem* for their creation. These dated portraits provide valuable information about the styles, fashions, and objects popular in the period of their creation, and have been used for the construction of the chronological framework on which the remaining objects are based, especially those whose provenance is completely lost. Compared to previous chronological divisions of Palmyrene portraits, especially that devised by Harald Ingholt[8] who had distinguished three periods: (1) between A.D. 50–150, (2) between A.D. 150–200, and (3) between A.D. 200–250, and Malcolm A. R. Colledge[9], who had separated the artworks into four groups: (1) between 50 B.C.–A.D. 50, (2) between A.D. 50–150, (3) between A.D. 150–200, and (4) between A.D. 200–273, the portraits in this publication are divided into five groups: (1) between A.D. 1–100, (2) between A.D. 100–150, (3) between A.D. 150–200, (4) between A.D. 200–240, and (5) between A.D. 240–273. This division follows the stylistic trends and fashions observed in the corpus of the sarcophagi. Of course, we are aware that these chronological categories are somewhat artificial. They, however, reflect choices which we have made when we reworked the dating of the portraits in general and more information on these choices can also be found in two major publications from 2021[10].

Of all the sarcophagi documented in the corpus, 325 can be connected to seventy-one specific tombs: 293 objects with portraits, eight without portraits, and twenty-five that are known through publications. A short survey of the finds of these tombs is presented in the fourth chapter, with the aim to contextualize the 325 sarcophagi and fragments thereof as much as possible and show the range of choices that every Palmyrene was faced with when planning their tomb and commemoration.

The fifth chapter discusses the iconographic motifs of the sarcophagi. The banqueting motif is only one of the motifs and images presented on the sarcophagi, and this chapter aims to examine all the different elements that were used in the composition of these funerary monuments. Thus, individual elements are seen within a Palmyrene and a broader context, in order to elucidate questions of influence, local traditions, and personal choices.

The last chapter brings together the various points of discussion raised by the different chapters and presents concluding remarks on the sarcophagi, their use, and their place within Palmyrene society.

The catalogue presents all the sarcophagi and fragments thereof known from Palmyra[11]. The first objects (cat. 1–12) are the ones that are dated with precision, thanks to their accompanying inscriptions. These are followed by objects whose provenance is known (cat. 13–277). These are divided first according to the type of monument they come from: tower tombs, hypogea, and temple tombs; secondly according to their typology; and thirdly according to their chronology. Sarcophagi proper consisting of lid and box are arranged first, followed

---

8 Ingholt 1928. For Harald Ingholt, his involvement with Palmyrene archaeology and his legacy, see Raja – Sørensen 2015b; Raja 2019c; Raja 2019d; Raja 2021a; Bobou et al. 2022a; Bobou et al. 2022b.
9 Colledge 1976.
10 Raja et al. 2021c; Romanowska et al. 2021.
11 The number of the object in the Palmyra Portrait Project database has also been included. While the fate of some objects that have been recorded on site in Palmyra (and assigned an 'insitu' number in the database) is known (for example, relief cat. 1 that was located on the now destroyed tower tomb of Kitôt), the fate of most in-situ objects is not known and the location 'Palmyra, in situ' reflects the status of the object as it was before 2011.

by isolated, single lids and boxes. Reliefs in the shape of sarcophagi are catalogued next, followed by sarcophagi lid reliefs and box reliefs. The reliefs with banqueting scenes are the third large group, while fragments are catalogued last. Fragments that could belong either to sarcophagi proper, sarcophagi reliefs, or banqueting reliefs are catalogued separately within the group of fragments. Heads belonging to portraits have been grouped according to gender and size, with the heads of priests forming a separate subgroup of male heads. Within each group, the objects are arranged according to their state of preservation (for example, between two sarcophagi lids of the same period, the more complete one is presented first). Even though most of the sarcophagi in the corpus could be assigned to one of the five chronological groups mentioned above, there are several sarcophagi whose date is broader or falls between two groups. These have been arranged according to their end date in the catalogue (for example, cat. 191, dating between A.D. 150–225 has been placed after cat. 190, dating between A.D. 150–200, and before cat. 192, dating between A.D. 150–240). Objects whose area of provenance is known are catalogued next (cat. 278–288). These were found close to tombs but cannot be associated with them with certainty, or only the necropolis in which they were found is known. The next group consists of all the objects that have no other known provenance except for Palmyra (cat. 289–729). They are arranged firstly according to type, following the division outlined above, and secondly according to chronology. Sarcophagi that were documented in the 18th cent. but are now lost are presented in appendix 1 (securely dated sarcophagus relief), and appendices 2 and 3 (sarcophagus reliefs with provenance). The four fragments of imported Athenian sarcophagi form their own group (appendix 4), as do the sarcophagi without portraits (appendix 5), the sarcophagi known only from publications (appendix 6), and the small reliefs with frame but without any portraits (appendix 7). All the inscriptions have been transcribed and translated by Jean-Baptiste Yon.

History of Palmyra

Palmyra or Tadmor, as was the name of the city in antiquity and also in modern Arabic, is an oasis city located in the Syrian steppe desert[12]. The city and its hinterland, the Palmyrena, were occupied from the Palaeolithic period, as the archaeological evidence shows (Figs. 1–2)[13]. Flint tools and human remains testify that the area was settled already from the Middle Palaeolithic[14], while marine shells indicate that already from 30,000 B.C., the site was on a trade route connecting the Mediterranean to the Euphrates[15]. The evidence from Palmyra, slim though it may be[16], indicates the establishment of a settlement between Tell ez-Zor and the spring Efqa already from ca. 8500 B.C. that continued into the Bronze Age[17]. These two focal points represented what was essential in the lives of the early occupants of Palmyra: life-giving water and a centre of ritual significance[18]. The first textual evidence for the site of Tadmor come from the site of Kanesh (modern Kültepe, Turkey) and Mari (modern Syria), dating from the 19th and 18th cent. B.C.: one is a contract made by Puzur-Ishtar, the »Tadmorean« at Kanesh, one of the Mari letters mentions the arrival of four Tadmoreans, and another the attacks of nomads against Tadmor[19]. These early sources hint at the presence of an established community, whose inhabitants undertook long-distance travel[20]. Tadmor is next mentioned in the records of Tiglath-Pileser I (r. 1114–1076 B.C.). The city was conquered by the Assyrian king during his campaigns against the Arameans[21]. References to a city called Tadmor (Ταδάμορα) that was built by King Solomon and called Palmyra by the Greeks[22] and a reference to Marc Antony's troops trying to loot the city of Palmyra but without success[23] have proven unreliable and can only be used as testament to the importance of Palmyra at the times when Josephus and Appian were writing[24]. The archaeological exploration of the city has not shed much light on the settlement in the pre-Roman periods either, since the focus of most archaeologists has been on the impressive Roman remains. Mud-brick walls suggest the need to fortify the settlement[25]. Unlike other

---

12 Raja 2022b, 1. For the history of Palmyra, see also the recent book by Michał Gawlikowski: Gawlikowski 2021. Still useful accounts are Gawlikowski – Starcky 1985; Will 1992; Sommer 2017; Sommer 2018.

13 Bonacossi – Iamoni 2012, 33 f. For the later occupation of the Palmyrena, see the Syrian-Norwegian project *Palmyrena*. See also Campmany Jiménez et al. 2022, for a study of the carrying capacity of Palmyra's hinterland and its connection to the city in the Roman period.
14 Muhesen 2012; Sommer 2017b, 14; Raja 2022b, 7.
15 Muhesen 2012, 25.
16 Bonacossi – Iamoni 2012, 34 f.
17 Sartre – Sartre 2016, 20; Raja 2022b, 7.
18 Hammad 2010, 8–15; Raja 2022b, 7.
19 Starcky 1952, 27 f.; Raja 2022b, 7. See also Veenhof 2013 for the Kanesh archives, and Sasson 2017 for an introduction to the Mari archives and a selection of representative letters.
20 Raja 2022b, 8. This travel could be related to trade or diplomatic activities, according to Dalley 1995, 139.
21 Starcky 1952, 28; Sommer 2017b, 24. For the texts relating to the reign of Tiglath-Pileser I, see Grayson 1976.
22 Josephus, Ant. 8. 145.
23 Appian, Civil Wars V. 9.
24 See Sommer 2017b, 24; Hekster – Kaizer 2004.
25 Raja 2022b, 8 f. with further bibliography.

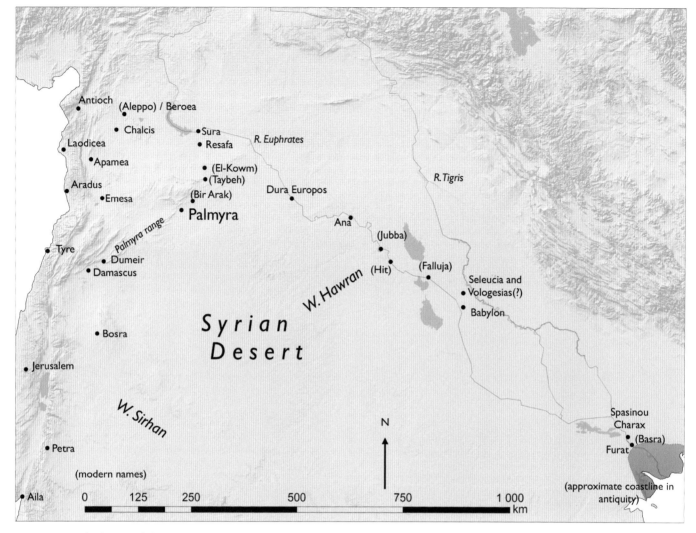

Figure 1. Map of Palmyra and the region.

cities in the Near East, Palmyra does not appear to have been refounded by one of the Seleucid kings who ruled the region after the death of Alexander the Great. One fragmentary, honorific inscription, however, indicates that there were diplomatic relations and perhaps even political connections between the Palmyrenes and the Seleucids, while all the later inscriptions show that the Palmyrenes had adopted the Seleucid calendar[26]. The Hellenistic settlement has been located in the south area of the city, and pottery and glass finds from there indicate trade links with the Graeco-Roman and the Parthian worlds[27]. The two sanctuaries of Bel and Allat were also established in this period, possibly thanks to benefactions[28]. The evidence from the funerary sphere also indicates the presence of a wealthy stratum in Palmyrene society[29].

The earliest dated inscription from Palmyra, from 44 B.C., shows that already by that time, the Temple of Bel and the tribal organization of Palmyra had been established in the city[30]. Whether Palmyra was a city in the Greek sense of the word, however, a *polis*, at this time, is a matter of debate. In addition, a matter of debate is the question of Palmyra's connection to the Roman Empire and the degree of autonomy that Palmyra enjoyed in the late Republican period. In A.D. 18, Germanicus made three decrees on the taxation of goods, while a funerary inscription dating to A.D. 27 testifies to the presence of an auxiliary unit in Palmyra. These texts indicate that by the time of Tiberius (r. A.D. 14–37), the

---

26 Kaizer 2020, 25; Raja 2022b, 8.
27 Schmidt-Colinet – al-Asʿad 2013; Gawlikowski 2019a, 79.
28 Gawlikowski 2019a, 81 f.

29 Fellmann 1970; Sommer 2017b, 54; Saito 2018, 192.
30 Kaizer 2020, 25 f.

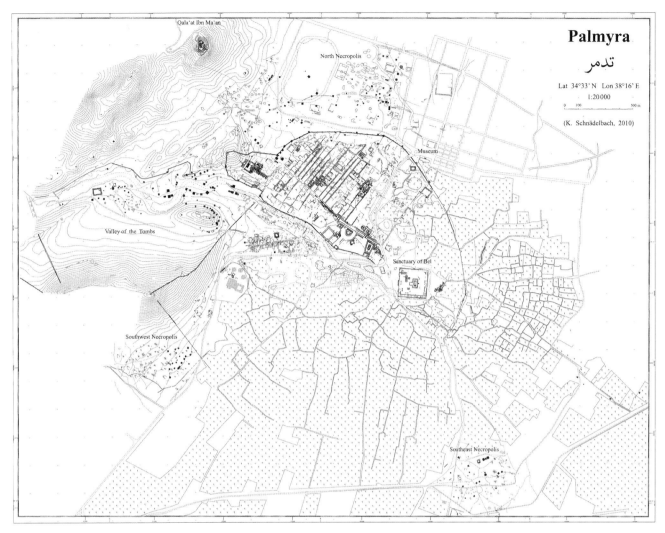

Figure 2. Map of Palmyra and the surrounding area.

Roman presence and involvement were felt in internal Palmyrene politics[31]. The 1st cent. A.D. is the period where the city of Palmyra also begins to acquire its monumental architecture in both the public and the funerary sphere, with the construction and rebuilding of tower tombs and major sanctuaries, including the Temple of Bel, consecrated in A.D. 32, and the Temples of Allat and Nabu[32]. By the time of Hadrian (r. A.D. 117–138), when the emperor visited the city in A.D. 129, Palmyra was fully integrated into the Roman Empire, and even acquired a new name during Hadrian's visit: Hadriane Palmyra or ›hdryn' tdmr‹[33]. The first half of the 2nd cent. A.D. was a period of intense building activity with the aggrandizement of the existing sanctuaries of the city, the construction of the Sanctuary of Baalshamin, the theatre, the Great Colonnade, more monumental tower tombs, and the appearance of the underground hypogea, a new type of burial monument[34]. By the 3rd cent. A.D., when Palmyra acquired the status of *colonia*, most of the grand architectural monuments of the city were built, and most of the building activities in the second half of the 2nd cent. and the 3rd cent. A.D., are connected to the funerary sphere, both hypogea and the newly introduced temple tombs, while the public structures were built on a much smaller scale[35]. Palmyra's geographical position, at the edge of the

---

31 See Kaizer 2020, 26–29; Raja 2022b, 11.
32 Temple of Bel: Kaizer 2002, 67–69. Temple of Allat: Kaizer 2002, 99–108. Temple of Nabu: Kaizer 2002, 89–91. Temple of Arsu: Kaizer 2002, 116–121. See also Gawlikowski 2017; Gawlikowski 2019a, 81.
33 Smith II 2013, 25 f.; Kaizer 2020, 29.
34 Gawlikowski 2019a, 82–85.
35 Inscriptions testifying to the construction of public buildings: Yon 2012, nos. 96–98. 110–112. Expansion of the Great Colonnade: Sartre 2001, 667 f.

Roman Empire and next to the Parthian Empire, up to the early 3rd cent. A.D., had helped the Palmyrenes play an important role in the international trade between the two ancient superpowers[36]. With the overthrow of the Arsacid dynasty by Ardashir I in A.D. 224, Palmyra's trade activities were disrupted and reduced, while soon after the middle of the century, Odainath rose to a position of great power in the East thanks to his military skills, especially after the defeat of the Roman emperor Valerian by Shapur I at the battle of Edessa (A.D. 260)[37]. In A.D. 267, Odainath was assassinated, and his widow Zenobia took control of Palmyra in the name of their son, declaring him emperor. Zenobia expanded the territory of Palmyra and created an empire that spanned from the heart of modern Turkey in Ankara to the western part of modern Egypt by the shore of the Red Sea[38]. This was considered a threat to Roman interests and led to her fall in A.D. 272 and that of the city in A.D. 273[39]. Destruction layers have been found in the Agora, the Sanctuary of Allat, the Great Colonnade, and other locations within the city and have been associated with the looting of the city by the troops of Aurelian reported in the sources[40]. The city continued to exist after the destruction of the Palmyrene Empire; however, it never recovered its former wealth or glory[41].

The Exploration of Tadmor-Palmyra

Palmyra has captivated the imagination of early travellers and explorers, partly because of its legendary Queen Zenobia who was defeated by the Roman emperor Aurelian[42]. The first detailed exploration of the site can be attributed to James Dawkins and Robert Wood in 1751, while Louis-François Cassas visited the site in 1785. The inscriptions and funerary portraits of the city began receiving scholarly attention in the middle of the 19th cent., while the first surveys of the archaeological site took place in 1902 and 1917[43]. Syria was under French mandate between the two world wars. During that time, the archaeological service was reorganized[44], the site of Palmyra was plotted systematically[45], the early modern village was moved away from the Temple of Bel to a neighbouring site, and serious and systematic clearing and restorations began at the site[46]. At the same time, foreign archaeologists also started getting concessions to work in Palmyra. Ingholt excavated between 1924 and 1928, and again in 1935, in the area of the south-west necropolis[47].

After the end of the French mandate in 1943 and the establishment of the Syrian republic in 1946, the directorship and management of the archaeological sites of the country, including Palmyra, passed to the Syrian government. In 1946, the newly established Directorate-General of Antiquities and Museums continued the archaeological exploration and management of Palmyra[48]. It also allowed non-Syrian archaeological missions and teams to work in Palmyra, resulting in the exploration of tombs in the south-east necropolis[49], the north necropolis[50], the city itself[51], as well as the continuation of work in important sanctuaries of the city[52]. The civil war in Syria put an end to the exploration, excavation, and management of the site, while numerous tombs were either destroyed or looted[53].

Literature Survey

When, in 1758, Gavin Hamilton painted the portraits of James Dawkins and Robert Wood discovering the ruins of Palmyra in 1751[54], he placed the monumental tower tombs of the city at a distance and framed by the monumental arch of Palmyra that linked two sections of the grand colonnade[55]. The view in Hamilton's painting is not an exact copy from real life, but it references the

---

36 For Palmyrene trade, see Seland 2016; Seland 2019.
37 For Odainath, see Hartmann 2001, 129 f.
38 For Zenobia, see the recent monograph by Andrade 2018, with critical examination of previous scholarship.
39 See Andrade 2018, 191–212.
40 Intagliata 2018, 97.
41 For the history of Palmyra after Zenobia, see Intagliata 2018.
42 For Palmyra, its history, and archaeology, see Raja 2022b, with further bibliography.
43 Wiegand 1932, 1; Raja 2019c; Sartre-Fauriat 2019.
44 Delplace, Syria. Maqdissi forthcoming.
45 Gabriel 1926.

46 Sartre-Fauriat 2019, 72.
47 Sartre-Fauriat 2019, 72. For Ingholt and Palmyra, see recently Raja 2019a, 38–41; Raja 2019c; Raja 2021a.
48 Maqdissi forthcoming.
49 Most notably by the Nara-Palmyra Archaeological Mission: see Saito 2018 especially for their work between 2000–2011.
50 Most notably by the Polish Archaeological Mission, whose work has been published in a series of volumes and articles by the Polish Centre of Mediterranean Archaeology, University of Warsaw.
51 See Schmidt-Colinet 2018a and Schmidt-Colinet 2018b for the work of Syrian-German-Austrian archaeological research between 1981 and 2011.
52 For example, the Sanctuary of Allat was excavated by the Polish Archaeological Mission: Gawlikowski 2017; the Sanctuary of Baalshamin by the Swiss Archaeological Mission: Collart – Vicari 1969; Fellmann 1970; Dunant 1971; Dunant – Stucky 2000.
53 Ali 2015; Cuneo et al. 2015.
54 Now at the Scottish National Gallery, Edinburgh, acc. no. NG 2666. For the expedition of Dawkins and Wood, see Raja 2019a, 17.
55 For the arch, see Gawlikowski 2019a, 85 with further bibliography.

view from plate 26 in the 1753 publication by Wood on Palmyra[56]. Giovanni Battista Borra, who was working for Dawkins and Wood, recorded several of the funerary monuments of Palmyra in his drawings used in their publication, but they did not discuss them in great detail[57]. Louis-François Cassas was the next draughtsman and architect to visit the site of Palmyra in 1785. During his stay, he surveyed and measured the monuments of the city, and created more than a hundred drawings of buildings, including of their architectural and sculpted decoration[58]. His drawings show that he was trained using material from the classical Roman world: the figures he drew belong more to a monument from the area of Rome than Palmyra; however, they do preserve reliefs that are now lost (Fig. 3).

The next major archaeological expeditions in Palmyra took place in 1902 under Otto Puchstein and in 1917 under Theodor Wiegand. Wiegand led a German-Turkish expedition aiming to protect and record the monuments of Palmyra, and as members of this team Carl Watzinger and Karl Wulzinger surveyed and catalogued the funerary monuments, numbered them, and created the first major reference point for the documentation and study of Palmyrene necropoleis that is still used to this day. The results of this survey were published in 1932[59]. The monuments and burial types were not treated in detail, since the focus was the recording of the monuments and the documentation of their architecture, decoration, and the funerary monuments they contained, including the sarcophagi, was described with brevity. Most of the sarcophagi are not illustrated in their publication; however, they did record and draw details that are now lost: for example, details and inscriptions on cat. 180 are known only from their publication.

In 1924, Ingholt undertook his first excavation campaign in the south-west necropolis of the city, after gaining a permit from the French Antiquities Authority that was in charge of Syrian antiquities and sites, since Syria was under the French mandate. During the following four years, he conducted two more excavation campaigns, while he conducted two more campaigns in 1935 and 1937 that were focused on specific tombs[60]. At the same period, Ingholt was studying Palmyrene portraits on loculus reliefs aiming to establish their chronology and typology as

Figure 3. Cassas' drawing of the founder relief from the tower tomb of Kîtôt.

part of his higher doctoral dissertation on Palmyrene sculpture. The result of his successful defence was a monograph published in 1928 that is still in use today[61]. In his publication, Ingholt uses the sarcophagi in order to check his chronological system: since they carried multiple portraits of men and women, it was possible to examine and compare their typological and stylistic details instead of seeing them in isolation, as was the case with almost all the portraits on loculus reliefs[62]. In later articles, presenting the best-preserved tombs and their finds among those he had excavated during his campaigns, Ingholt discussed specific sarcophagi in depth and connected their iconographic motifs to the imagery found in other types of Palmyrene reliefs, such as stelai (for example, cat. 81. 82).

The first to discuss sarcophagi as a distinct category was Ernest Will, in his 1951 publication that had the

---

56 Wood 1753, pl. 26.
57 Wood 1753, 47–50 pls. 36–57.
58 For Cassas' journey and drawings of Palmyra, see Schmidt-Colinet 1996; Terpak – Bonfitto; Cassas and the Legacy of Palmyra.
59 Wiegand 1932, 1.
60 His diaries from the campaigns were published by Raja et al. 2021a.

61 This significant work for Palmyrene studies was only translated into English in 2021: Bobou et al. 2021b.
62 Ingholt 1928, 94.

founder relief of the tower tomb of Kithôt as its starting point[63]. He pointed out that the banquet motif appeared fully formed early in the 1st cent. A.D. in Palmyra, and he suggested that the origins of the motif were to be found in the Macedonian funerary klinai, and that was transmitted through Seleucid monuments that have not survived but must have existed: »oeuvres seleucides hypothetiques«[64]. Will was also the first to acknowledge that the term »klinè funéraire«[65] was used for multiple types of monuments, and to classify them in: (1) simple klinai and (2) sarcophagus klinai[66]. Founder reliefs, banqueting reliefs, and sarcophagus reliefs constituted the first group[67], while the sarcophagi in the round formed the second group[68]. He further divided the second group into (a) complete sarcophagi in the shape of a kline and (b) sarcophagi covers in the shape of a kline[69]. Will was also the first to underline the importance of the banquet motif in Palmyra's funerary sphere and how it was repeated throughout the monuments, in the founder reliefs, the sarcophagus reliefs covering burials in loculus niches, as well as on the sarcophagi in the round[70].

In 1976, Malcolm A. R. Colledge published the first monograph treating Palmyrene art since Ingholt's 1928 *Studier over Palmyrensk Skulptur*[71]. Sarcophagi were discussed together with other funerary monuments in the chapter on funerary sculpture[72]. Colledge divided the monuments according to their placement. Thus, reliefs placed outside the tomb, such as stelai[73], were discussed next to the founder reliefs[74], while the reliefs and sculptures from inside the tomb were discussed in the following sections. Furthermore, he divided the objects inside the tomb into (1) large reliefs with banqueting scenes[75], (2) sarcophagi[76], and (2) small reliefs with banqueting scenes[77]. According to Colledge, this last group had a decorative function in the tomb[78]. The reliefs with solitary standing males were also treated as a separate category, whose function might have been decorative as well[79]. Each section is effectively a short survey presenting changes and continuities across the three centuries during which the monuments were constructed.

Sarcophagi and reliefs with banqueting motifs were also treated within presentations of funerary monuments, such as Michał Gawlikowski's 1970 publication of the *Monuments funéraires de Palmyre*[80]. There, they were treated within the context of each individual tomb. Similarly, in the 1977 publication of the excavation of the hypogeum of ʿAlaînê, Anna Sadurska discusses in detail the sarcophagi and reliefs with banqueting scenes found in the tomb[81], but does not offer a general survey of the banqueting motif or sarcophagi in Palmyra. This was also the case in the publication of the groups of sculptures found in fourteen hypogea by Anna Sadurska and Adnan Bounni: the sarcophagi were presented within their context but were not discussed as a separate category of Palmyrene sculpture[82]. Similarly, Agnes Henning treated the sarcophagi found in tower tombs as part of the whole of the sculptural assemblage within each individual tomb in her 2013 publication of this type of funerary monuments[83]. Another very important publication is the 1992 monograph on tomb no. 36 by Andreas Schmidt-Colinet, where several sarcophagi and reliefs with banqueting scenes were found. Schmidt-Colinet discusses their typology, as well as their iconography, in detail[84]. These publications are particularly valuable, since they offer insight into the placement of sarcophagi and how they related to the other funerary monuments within the tomb.

Sarcophagi and reliefs with banqueting motifs were also treated in separate articles. Klaus Parlasca, a prolific scholar of Roman art in the Near East, treated in depth several issues connected to the development of the iconography of sarcophagi in Palmyra in two articles, the first published in 1984 and the second in 1998. In his 1984 paper, he connected the production in Palmyra with that of sarcophagi in the Roman Empire[85], examined the various theories about the origins of the banqueting motif[86], and its development in Palmyra[87]. He suggested that the type was of a hybrid form, combining the so-called Totenmahl with the sarcophagus proper[88]. He also traced the development and transmission of

---

63 Will 1951.
64 Will 1951, 77.
65 Will 1951, 77.
66 Will 1951, 77.
67 Will 1951, 77 f.
68 Will 1951, 77–84.
69 Will 1951, 77.
70 Will 1951, 84–89.
71 Colledge 1976.
72 Colledge 1976, 58–82.
73 Colledge 1976, 63 f.
74 Colledge 1976, 64 f.
75 Colledge 1976, 73–77.
76 Colledge 1976, 77 f.
77 Colledge 1976, 78 f.
78 Colledge 1976, 78 f.

79 Colledge 1976, 79.
80 Gawlikowski 1970a.
81 Sadurska 1977, 36–48. 76–166.
82 Sadurska – Bounni 1994.
83 Henning 2013b.
84 Schmidt-Colinet 1992, esp. 105–110. 133–138.
85 Parlasca 1984, 283.
86 Parlasca 1984, 283–285.
87 Parlasca 1984, 285–294.
88 Parlasca 1984, 285; Parlasca 1998, 314.

the banqueting motif from the founder reliefs to the banqueting reliefs, the sarcophagi, and finally the sarcophagi reliefs[89]. Like Colledge, he also identified the small reliefs with banqueting scenes as decorative objects within the tomb[90].

Three more articles worth mentioning in this brief and non-exhaustive survey are two published by Krzysztof C. Makowski in 1985[91] and one by Lucy Audley-Miller in 2016[92]. In the first of the two 1985 articles, Makowski discussed funerary sculpture with banqueting iconography within its context, by examining objects with known provenance[93]. He divided the objects into five groups: (1) stelai where both kline and reclining figures are sculpted on the same plaque — with founder reliefs forming part of this group; (2) banquets carved in high relief and often in the round — this group is subdivided into (a) stand-alone reliefs, (b) reliefs with a kline carved below the banqueting scene, (c) reliefs forming part of a sarcophagus; (3) small reliefs with banqueting scenes; (4) lids carved in the round; and (5) sarcophagi boxes with a banqueting scene[94]. Makowski proposed that the banquet motif had a dual function, both decorative and commemorative[95], before examining the different objects with the banqueting iconography known from Palmyrene tombs[96] and tracing the changes in placement within funerary contexts[97]. In his second paper, Makowski discussed the reliefs with banqueting scenes[98], and divided them into three categories: (1) banquet scenes carved in high relief imitating lids in the round; (2) banquet scenes carved in high relief; and (3) banquet scenes carved in low relief, sometimes with a frame[99]. Despite the categorization into three groups, the meaning of the banquet motif was the same in all three: a display of the main, honoured figure's prestige and status[100]. Audley-Miller focuses on the local and contemporary perceptions of the banqueting iconography and proposes that it was not a static, unchanged imagery but rather a dynamic one that could be used by different patrons in ways that suited their needs and could express personal status and individuality[101].

Sarcophagi in the Roman Empire

It is not possible to conduct a study on any corpus of sarcophagi without looking at the already published corpora of sarcophagi from the Roman world. It is not our intention to conduct a comparative study of sarcophagi in the Roman world in this publication. This undertaking, however, is even more desirable with the publication of the corpus from Palmyra. Here, we only give a brief overview of the most important corpora and material groups of sarcophagi known from various regions of the Roman Empire, which provide a comparative basis for future studies and are considered as general comparanda in our publication[102].

The sarcophagi from three areas of the ancient world have been studied the most: Rome, Athens, and Asia Minor[103]. Each city and region had workshops that produced sarcophagi, often for centuries, and these can be distinguished from each other thanks to their iconography and decoration, but also choice of marble type. Sarcophagi from the city of Rome were perhaps the most diverse in their shape (the most common being rectangular boxes with flat lids, or lids with reclining figures, or boxes in the shape of a tub, *lenos*), while their iconography could include decorative motifs such as garlands, mythological scenes, or scenes from daily life. Most often, they would be decorated only on the sides meant for display (Figs 4–5, Pls 1–2)[104]. Attic sarcophagi, on the other hand, were tall rectangular boxes with a gabled lid or a lid with reclining figures, and they were decorated in the round, almost exclusively with mythological scenes (Fig. 6, Pl. 3)[105]. Marble sarcophagi from Asia Minor can be connected to specific sites, such as Dokimeion, where sarcophagus boxes with architectural articulation (columnar decoration) and single figures between the intercolumniations were commonly produced, or Prokonnesos, where the garland

---

89 Parlasca 1984, 290.
90 Parlasca 1984, 285.
91 Makowski 1985a and 1985b.
92 Audley-Miller 2016.
93 Makowski 1985b.
94 Makowski 1985b, 70 f.
95 Makowski 1985b, 73.
96 Makowski 1984b, 73–107.
97 Makowski 1985b, 107–116.
98 Makowski 1985a.
99 Makowski 1985a, 119.
100 Makowski 1985a, 130.
101 Audley-Miller 2016.

102 The motifs on sarcophagi from the Roman world will be discussed in the chapter on iconography wherever they are relevant.
103 The bibliography on sarcophagi is long, and constantly expanding, so these are just a few recent and important contributions to their study: Elsner – Hung 2012; Koch – Baratte 2012; Zanker – Ewald 2012; Koortbojian 2015; Koiner – Porod 2015; Dally et al. 2018; Hallett 2019a; The publications of the series *Die antiken Sarkophag-Reliefs*, edited by Guntram Koch and others remain invaluable. Koch – Sichtermann 1982 and Koch 1993 remain among the standard reference books on the matter.
104 In addition to the literature mentioned above, for sarcophagi from Rome and its environs see also Wrede 2001; Bielfeldt 2004; Birk 2013; Borg 2013; Meinecke 2014; Huskinson 2015; Russenberger 2015.
105 For Attic sarcophagi, see recently Rogge 1995; Oakley 2011; Kintrup 2016; Papagianni 2016; Katakes 2018.

48 CHAPTER 1

Figure 4. Sarcophagus with the Triumph of Dionysos, marble. From Rome, A.D. 260–270.

Figure 5. Strigillated sarcophagus. Probably from Rome, made of Proconnesian marble, ca. A.D. 220.

Figure 6. Sarcophagus with scenes from the life of Achilles on the box and reclining couple on the lid. From Athens, A.D. 180–220.

decoration of sarcophagi was often left unfinished[106]. Both Athens and the sites in Asia Minor that had sarcophagi workshops were close to marble quarries and so made use of local resources. In contrast, workshops in Rome, but in other locations as well, had to import the marble for their sarcophagi[107].

In addition to these well-studied marble sarcophagi that were exported and could be found in different areas of the Roman Empire[108], sarcophagi made of locally sourced stones were also produced and used in different sites across the Roman world. As one example, in the city of Rome, in the Republican period, sarcophagi were made almost exclusively of the local tuff[109]. Only

---

106 For sarcophagi from Asia Minor, see the recent works by Işık et al. 2007; Koch 2011; Alexandridis 2014. See also Waelkens 1982, specifically for the Dokimeion sarcophagi, and Öğüş-Uzun 2018 for the sarcophagi from Aphrodisias.
107 Russell 2013, 260–262.
108 For trade and distribution patterns of marble objects in general, see Russell 2013. See also Waelkens 2021.
109 Meinecke 2014, 14–16. For locally quarried stones in Rome, see Heiken et al. 2013, and for the tuffs used in the city see esp. 38–47.

Figure 7. The Amathus sarcophagus, limestone. From Amathous, Cyprus, 475–450 B.C.

in three out of all the known Republican tombs were sarcophagi made of limestone[110]. In the early Imperial period (A.D. 1–100), the majority of the sarcophagi were made of marble; however, travertine, a local type of limestone, and peperino stone, a type of tuff, were also used in sarcophagi documented in five metropolitan burials[111]. The popularity of marble continued into the later Imperial periods, with limestone or locally sourced tuff used as the material in only forty-nine out of 220 studied sarcophagi (all the others were made of marble)[112]. Unlike marble sarcophagi, stone sarcophagi had minimal or no decoration[113].

In Greece, with its abundance of marble quarries, the use of limestone for sarcophagi was limited[114]. Limestone sarcophagi were associated with elite burials in classical

110 Meinecke 2014, 16.
111 Meinecke 2014, 30 f.
112 Meinecke 2014, 45–47.
113 Meinecke 2014, in passim.

114 On the whole, limestone sarcophagi are understudied, but more so those from Greece. Limestone has been used for sarcophagi from the Minoan period (for example, the well-studied sarcophagus from Hagia Triada: Heraklion Archaeological Museum 396: Burke 2005 with previous bibliography), and in archaic sculpture and architecture (see Spivey 2013, 64–74. 153–158), but it was used sparingly for sarcophagi. Some examples: early geometric monolithic sarcophagi from the Corinth region: Sanders et al. 2014, 10–13. 35; middle geometric monolithic sarcophagus from Corinth: Sanders et al. 2014, 35; archaic sarcophagi from the area of Vassiloudi, near Thessaloniki: Misailidou-Despotidou et al. 2017, 447; early Hellenistic tomb with sarcophagi made of limestone plaques and plastered so as to give the impression of being monolithic at Thessaloniki: Tsimpidou-Aulonitou 1986, 124–126; monolithic sarcophagi from the late 6th to the 5th cent. B.C. at Demetrias-Pagasai: Batziou-Eustathiou – Triantafyllopoulou 2012, 213. 215 f. 223. Roman-period limestone sarcophagi have been found at the west necropolis of Eleusis: Mylonas 1975, in passim, as well as

Cyprus (Fig. 7, Pl. 4)[115]; however, in the Roman period, sarcophagi in general were rare, and then often imported and made of marble[116]. Limestone sarcophagi seem to be more popular in areas away from the immediate coastline, such as North Africa[117], some sites in Asia Minor such as Ariassos in Pisidia[118], and the Near East[119]. There, they have been discovered, among other sites, in Sidon[120], Tyre[121], Baalbek[122], and the Bekaa valley[123], the Decapolis, especially at the city of Jerash[124], and various sites in Israel[125]. At Chhim, in Lebanon, sarcophagi were »cut directly into the limestone bedrock, and covered by typical sarcophagi lids«[126]. The evidence shows that the practice of using limestone sarcophagi was widespread in the Middle and Near East, in areas that did not have marble quarries and were far from the coast — making importing marble sarcophagi prohibitively expensive[127] — but where people were still familiar with the popularity of burials in sarcophagi in Rome, Athens, and important cities in Asia Minor. Furthermore, sarcophagi of materials such as lead or clay, as well as limestone and imported marble, were already in use in the regions from earlier periods and were also popular in Mesopotamia. A comprehensive study of the local limestone sarcophagi traditions of these regions is still missing, and it is yet another desideratum in research in order to understand the relationship between these regions and their knowledge of traditions in other parts of the empire.

Most of the sarcophagi have been published in excavation reports, rather than collected in corpora; yet, enough material has been published that it is possible to identify local variations in the decoration and the placement of these sarcophagi. At Jerash, where over 100 sarcophagi have been examined, it was possible to divide them into four groups depending on their decoration: (1) sarcophagi with the depiction of an

Figure 8. Loculus relief depicting a priest, limestone. From Palmyra, A.D. 200–220.

Figure 9. Loculus relief depicting a female, limestone. From Palmyra, A.D. 50–150.

---

in Fiskardo, Cephalonia; unpublished and on display in the Archaeological Museum of Sami.
115 Parks 2002; Petit 2004; Stylianou – Schollmeyer 2007; Satraki 2013.
116 Vessberg 1956, 18–33; Parks 2002, 11 f. 19.
117 Barate – de Chaisemartin 2015, 515.
118 Cormack 1996.
119 For a brief overview of the sarcophagi from the Near East, see Ebeling 2011.
120 Contenau 1914.
121 De Jong 2010. They have not received as much attention as the imported Attic sarcophagi from the same site. See de Bellefonds 1985.
122 Hitzl – Petersen 2001; de Jong 2015.
123 Newson 2015.
124 Lichtenberger – Raja 2019, 144 f. for the Decapolis, and Jerash in particular; Pogoda 2018 for Jerash.
125 Masarwa 2007; Sion – Rapuano 2010.
126 Waliszewski – Wicenciak 2015.
127 Russell 2013, 35; Russell 2015, 201.

Amazon shield (*pelta*), a type common in the city but only recorded in a few other sites[128]; (2) sarcophagi with handles depicted on the sides[129]; (3) undecorated sarcophagi[130]; and (4) sarcophagi with other decorative elements, such as garlands[131]. Sarcophagi with depictions of Amazon shields, garlands, and other such elements, or undecorated, have also been recorded in the Bekaa valley[132]. Only a few sarcophagi have mythological scenes[133]. Two sarcophagi from northern Lebanon are even more distinct in their iconography, one showing a row of faces and a single, armless bust and the other a male and female reclining and taking part in a banquet[134]. Without a corpus of the limestone sarcophagi from Lebanon, however, it is not possible to say whether this differentiation is because of individual choices of the commissioners of the monuments, or because of different iconographic trends to the north. Most of these sarcophagi were placed inside the tombs with one side against the wall; however, they could also be displayed on podia, either in the burial buildings or even in the open air. These free-standing sarcophagi could be placed in a triclinium arrangement, or next to each other on their pedestals[135].

---

128   Pogoda 2018, 143. They are also found at Baalbek, Nablus, and Sachnin.
129   Pogoda 2018, 143–147.
130   Pogoda 2018, 147.
131   Pogoda 2018, 147.
132   De Jong 2017.
133   Newson 2015, 358 f.
134   Annan 2019, 187–189.
135   De Jong 2017, 46.

CHAPTER 2

The Portrait Habit in Palmyra and the Funerary Sphere

It is not possible to understand the role of sarcophagi in Palmyra without surveying first the city's portraiture and burial customs and practices. Sarcophagi as carriers of multiple portraits cannot be separated from the now-lost portraits from the public sphere and the thousands of loculus reliefs with portrait busts that were placed inside tombs, sometimes side by side or facing sarcophagi. At the same time, almost all the sarcophagi, reliefs that functioned as sarcophagus lids, reliefs recording the foundation of tombs, and smaller, mostly rectangular, reliefs with or without frame from monumental tombs, share a common iconographic motif, that of the banquet[1]. That creates a clear distinction between this material and other funerary portraits as well as the portraits from the public sphere. This chapter offers a brief introduction to the city's portrait habit.

The Portrait Habit in Palmyra

As mentioned in the first chapter, the Palmyra Portrait Project has collected 2902 objects with 3976 portraits. The earliest known securely dated portraits were on the relief depicting Kîtôt, the founder of the tower tomb no. 44, together with members of his family (cat. 1). They are dated to A.D. 41, thanks to the inscription that records the creation of the portrait[2]. A votive relief, which may have had a portrait of the dedicant, is dated even earlier, to A.D. 21/22[3]. The latest securely dated portrait from Palmyra dates from A.D. 258[4].

Therefore, the portrait habit in Palmyra starts from the earliest phases of the city's integration into the Roman Empire[5]. Even though the city has the largest number of portraits outside of Rome[6], the majority of the portraits that have survived come from the funerary sphere. The evidence from the public sphere (inscriptions as well as consoles on columns that served as statue bases) testifies to a rich tradition of honorific statues[7], while votives also carried portraits of dedicants, ranging from objects with simple representations of figures, with only the basic details that could gender the figures[8], or with carefully crafted images of god and dedicant[9]. Most of these, however, have been lost, either because they were made of valuable and reusable bronze, or on account of the weathering of the soft limestone with which they had been carved, or because they were deliberately destroyed[10].

In the surviving limestone reliefs and statues, men are often depicted in their roles as priests, wearing a himation that was often tied around the waist, and wearing the Palmyrene priestly hat (Fig. 8, Pl. 5)[11]. Women almost

---

1 The few exceptions of objects without the banqueting motif are discussed in chapter 5, on iconography.
2 The tower tomb was blown up in 2015 by ISIL: Cuneo et al. 2015.
3 Gawlikowski 2017, 245 f. cat. 15.
4 It is a votive relief to the god Abgal, dedicated by a servant of Odainath. This object only appeared on the art market in 2002. According to the auction house, it belonged to a »European Private Collection«. The lack of acquisition history makes this object problematic, even though it is important because of its inscription: Christie's, New York, sale of 12th December 2002, lot.

304: <https://www.christies.com/lot/lot-4026241/?from=sale summary&intObjectID=4026241> (26.04.2022); Yon 2013, 360 cat. 157.
5 We do not know of any Hellenistic portraits from the city, even though it had a Hellenistic phase: see Raja 2017e; Raja 2019a, 24 f. For Hellenistic Palmyra, see Schmidt-Colinet – al-Asʿad 2000; Schmidt-Colinet – al-Asʿad 2013. For Palmyra's integration see recently Kaizer 2020. See also Smith II 2013.
6 Raja 2019i, 283 f.
7 Raja 2019a, 24.
8 For example, altar with mother and child, Copenhagen, Ny Carlsberg Glyptotek, inv. no. IN 1080: Raja 2019a, 352 f. cat. 136, with previous bibliography.
9 For example, the relief dedicated by Worod, Ingholt 1936, 93 pl. 19, 1.
10 Raja 2019i, 283 f.; Gawlikowski 2021, 95, 205; Raja 2022b, 31.
11 See, for example, the relief with three priests from the Sanctuary of Nabu: Palmyra, Palmyra Museum, inv. no. B 2228/7957: Colledge 1976, 29. 126. 131. 135. 140. 146 f. 157. 210 fig. 21; Raja 2017g, 81. 83 fig. 7; Raja 2017h, 81. 83 fig. 7. On the iconography of priests see Stucky 1973; Raja 2017j; Raja 2018b.

Figure 10. Relief with veiled women, limestone. From Palmyra, Temple of Bel, A.D. 32–100.

Figure 11. Statue of togate man, marble. From near the Agora of Palmyra, A.D. 200–273.

always appear in tunic and himation, and very often with a veil, headband, and turban as well. This can be considered the typical Palmyrene dress (Fig. 9, Pl. 6)[12]. The tunic is sometimes decorated, while the himation is fastened over the left shoulder with a brooch; it falls diagonally across the chest and is wrapped around the body[13]. In two examples from the religious sphere, the women are completely covered with their veil while taking part in a religious procession (Fig. 10)[14].

There is also evidence of marble statues that had to be imported at what we expect to have been great cost to the city. The fragments and the few almost complete statues that have survived demonstrate that the Palmyrenes participated in the culture of importing expensive marble statuary[15]. They were also familiar with the motifs appropriate for good citizens and citizen wives: two of the almost complete statues of men show them wearing the toga[16], a costume appropriate for the location where the statues had been placed: the Agora of Palmyra (Fig. 11, Pl. 7)[17]. Another man

12 For women without the veil, see Krag – Raja 2018. For female headdresses, see Krag 2018, 106–109.
13 For the costume of Palmyrene women see Krag 2018, 27–29 with previous bibliography.
14 Relief on the peristyle beam of the Temple of Bel, now lost. One of the most important discussions remains Drijvers 1976, 11. 36 pls. 5. 6. See recently: Klaver 2019, 161 fig. 2, and Fowlkes-Childs and Seymour 2019, 148 fig. 59, with previous bibliography. Relief from the Temple of Allat, Palmyra, Palmyra Museum, inv. no. B 2310/8504 or A 182/75: see recently Gawlikowski 2017, 212 fig. 177 and Krag 2018, 35 n. 105; 111 n. 1; 115 n. 57. 65; 407 cat. 903, with previous bibliography.

15 For the marble fragments from Palmyra, see Wielgosz 2010; Gawlikowski 2021, 221; Raja 2022b, 14.
16 Damascus, National Museum of Damascus, inv. nos. C4024–C4025: Wielgosz 2010, cat. 20. 21 figs. 14. 15, respectively.
17 Balty 2005, 321 f. figs. 427–429 and Balty 2005, 323 f. figs. 430–432, respectively.

THE PORTRAIT HABIT IN PALMYRA AND THE FUNERARY SPHERE 55

Figure 12. Statue of togate man with priestly hat by his feet, limestone. From the Great Colonnade of Palmyra, A.D. 200–220.

was depicted with the toga and the Palmyrene priestly hat; his statue was placed on a console on one of the columns of the Great Colonnade of Palmyra (Fig. 12)[18]. A fourth togatus statue that was found in the Baths of Diocletian could also have been created earlier in the 3rd cent. A.D. and moved to the baths from its original position[19]. The Palmyrenes were also familiar with the ›Greek‹ citizen costume of the period, the chiton and himation, as demonstrated by the statue of a seated man

18 Colledge 1976, 91. 105. 125. 134. 146–148. 224 pl. 127.
19 Palmyra, Palmyra Museum, inv. no. B2062/7390: Wielgosz 2010, 79. 101 cat. 22 fig. 16.

Figure 13. Statue of seated man in chiton and himation, marble. From the Agora of Palmyra, A.D. 150–200.

(Fig. 13)[20]. Marble female statues also conformed to the empire-wide trend that wanted respectable female citizens to be depicted wrapped in their himatia, in types that were instantly recognizable. One female statue follows the so-called Pudicitia type[21], another the Large Herculaneum Woman type[22], and two more follow the Small Herculaneum Woman (Fig. 14)[23]. The

20 Damascus, National Museum of Damascus, inv. no. C4129: Colledge 1976, 91. 135. 157. 240 pl. 125.
21 Damascus, National Museum of Damascus, inv. no. 4022: Balty 2005, 324–326 figs. 433–435; Wielgosz 2010, 79–81. 102 cat. 24 fig. 19; Krag 2018, 62 n. 346; 111 n. 1; 114 n. 39–42. 47; 404 cat. 893.
22 Damascus, National Museum of Damascus, inv. no. C4021: Balty 2005, 326 cat. 4 figs. 436 f.; Wielgosz 2010, 79. 81. 102 cat. 25 fig. 20; Krag 2018, 62 n. 346; 111 n. 1; 114 n. 39. 40. 42. 43. 47; 404 cat. 891.
23 Damascus, National Museum of Damascus, inv. no. C4023: Balty 2005, 327 f. figs. 438–440; Wielgosz 2010, 77. 80 f. 100 cat. 12 fig. 10; Krag 2018, 62 n. 346; 111 n. 1; 114 n. 39–43. 47; 403 cat. 890, and Damascus, National Museum of Damascus, inv. no. C4020: Balty 2005, 329; Wielgosz 2010, cat. 13 fig. 11; Krag 2018, 62 n. 346; 111 n. 1; 114 n. 39. 42. 43. 47. 404 cat. 892.

Figure 14. Statue of standing female of the Large Herculaneum Woman type, marble. Either from the Agora or the Senate of Palmyra, A.D. 200–225.

(mostly epigraphic) evidence from the public sphere shows that the emphasis was on an individual's role in society[24], while the iconographic evidence shows knowledge of and participation in the empire-wide, Roman portrait habit that presented an instantly recognizable image of the Roman citizen.

This stands in contrast to both the epigraphic and iconographic evidence from the funerary sphere, where the Palmyrenes privileged their place in their immediate and extended families, as well as their local traditions[25]. In the inscriptions, a person is identified primarily through their family ties. This is more obvious in the case of females, since men were identified through the formula >X, son of Y, son of Z< in the public sphere as well. Females are described as daughters and wives, as well as mothers[26]. Iconographically, only in two sarcophagi do men appear dressed in toga (cat. 290

---

24 Raja 2019h, 150.

25 Raja 2019h, 145–150.
26 Cussini 2019a.

and cat. 304). In all the other reliefs from the funerary sphere, they are dressed in either tunic and himation, or in Parthian-inspired costume: trousers, over-trousers on occasion, a Parthian tunic worn with or without a coat[27]. Women appear in the typical Palmyrene dress, described briefly above[28]. In a few cases, mourning women are shown wearing only a himation and with their chest bare[29]. Only in very few cases do we see women dressed in the Graeco-Roman manner (cat. 220. 304), while in other cases, their costume and posture seem influenced by Greek and Roman statuary (for example, cat. 295. 485)[30]. In a couple of examples, the main elements of the type are preserved, but there are variations in the posture or exact rendering of the dress, for example, in cat. 485 the figure is modelled after the Large Herculaneum Woman, but she is facing frontally[31].

From the little evidence that has survived from the public sphere, and the numerous examples of funerary portraiture, it is possible to ascertain that the Palmyrenes prioritized their local traditions and Palmyrene identity[32]. In the public sphere, however, wealthy Palmyrenes also showed participation in the empire-wide culture of civic representation.

The Sarcophagi within the Portrait Corpus

Out of the 2902 objects recorded in the Palmyra Portrait Project's database, 440 are complete or large fragments of sarcophagi and banqueting reliefs that carry portraits. Another 315 objects represent small fragments, such as heads. In addition to those 755 sarcophagi, this study presents another twenty-one objects that did not have portraits, but either had mythological scenes (appendix 4, cat. 1–4. appendix 5, cat. 10), or were undecorated (appendix 5, cat. 1–3), or their portraits were weathered and/or completely lost by the time of the object's discovery (appendix 5, cat. 4–7. 9. 11), or it is not possible to identify them based on the information published (appendix 6, cat. 4. 5. 7–20). Of the objects known only from publications, only those that are accompanied by their precise measurements, as well as distinctive inscriptions when published, have been included in the database, since those can allow identification with pieces that may one day be published accompanied by images. One sarcophagus only (appendix 5, cat. 8) was decorated with garlands. Therefore, sarcophagi and related material represent 26% of the whole corpus of Palmyrene sculptures known so far, so a little over a quarter of all the known Palmyrene sculptures, and 36% of all the documented portraits: 1440 portraits come from sarcophagi[33] out of 3976 portraits. As the material shows[34], the production of sarcophagi was concentrated in the period A.D. 150–240 and represents one option of elite families for their burials. This means that, despite the relatively short span of their production, they represent considerable expenditure and use of resources, as well as a substantial part of the funerary, sculptural production of Palmyra.

The Typology and Iconography of Palmyrene Sarcophagi

The iconography of Palmyrene sarcophagi will be discussed in greater detail in a later chapter, but it is important to stress from the beginning that it differs markedly from all the other sarcophagi in Syria in its iconography but also its typology[35]. They can be divided into two main groups: sarcophagi proper and sarcophagus reliefs. The first comprises separate boxes and lids that were carved in the round, though, almost always only the front and the sides that were visible were decorated. Their lids are either monolithic or L-shaped, with the figures taking part at the banquet carved in full or in a high relief respectively. The second is a type unique to Palmyra and not known from other sites either in Syria or the Roman world: in a rock-cut tomb, where the burial could take place in a recess, the front of the recess could be carved in the shape of a sarcophagus box, usually with a lid. In other cases, low reliefs in the shape of lids could be carved separately and placed over the box relief, or even a proper sarcophagus box in the round. In essence, both sarcophagus lid reliefs and lids in the round served the same purpose within the burial complex[36]. The most important difference, however, with sarcophagi of other regions is that the majority of the surviving sarcophagi from the site have

---

27 For the Parthian-style dress, see Curtis 2017.
28 For women without the veil, see Krag – Raja 2018. For female headdresses, see Krag 2018, 106–108.
29 Krag 2018, 90–92.
30 See also a statue last seen in Beirut by Ingholt: Krag 2018, 34 n. 89–90. 94; 230 cat. 24.
31 See also a loculus relief at the Istanbul Arkeoloji Müzesi, inv. no. 3806/ O.M 265, where the woman's posture is influenced by the Pudicitia type, but she also wears a typical Palmyrene combination of headdress, turban, and veil: Krag 2018, 36 n. 109; 50 n. 234; 103 n. 74; 277 cat. 413.
32 See Raja 2015b.

33 These 1440 portraits are the 1125 portraits from the better-preserved sarcophagi and banqueting reliefs and the 315 fragments thereof.
34 This will be discussed further in the next two chapters.
35 De Jong 2017, 53.
36 Makowski 1985a offers the most detailed discussion of the typology of the monuments on which banqueting scenes could be placed.

portraits. This is in stark contrast to the rest of the Near East, where sarcophagi were commonly undecorated[37], or they had motifs such as peltai or garlands but rarely portraits[38].

The gable lids common in sarcophagi in Syria also do not appear in Palmyra[39]. A typical Palmyrene sarcophagus lid was decorated with a banquet scene: a reclining male surrounded by his closest relatives, and his wife seated at the other end. The lid was rarely fully carved in the round; usually it was a relief placed at the edge of the box, but there are exceptions where the banqueting scene is fully carved (for example, cat. 290). What makes the iconography unique is that in the Palmyrene banquet, the entire family is taking part[40]; in Roman and Attic sarcophagi, as well as in sarcophagi inspired by them, only the husband and wife were shown participating in the banquet[41]. These couples' representations were perhaps inspired by Etruscan sarcophagi where the deceased was shown reclining with a drinking vessel in their hand, sometimes accompanied by their spouse[42].

Decorative schemes or motifs such as Amazon shields or handles that appear in the sarcophagi boxes from Jerash or Baalbek do not appear in Palmyra. So far, no sarcophagi have been found decorated with such motifs or other isolated representations. Only one garland sarcophagus is known from the city (appendix 5, cat. 8), while another sarcophagus with a panther's head placed inside a garland may have carried portraits as well (appendix 5, cat. 16), since lion heads have been attested in sarcophagi boxes placed between busts (cat. 302. 403). Palmyrene sarcophagi boxes are often decorated with armless busts (for example, cat. 90), rarely placed within garlands (for example, cat. 181) or, more often, within clipei (for example, cat. 134); armless busts between single rosettes; or, more rarely, with figurative scenes from life, such as caravan scenes with camels (for example, cat. 228), scenes of men with weapons (for example, cat. 81), sacrifice scenes (for example, cat. 290, Pl. 56), scenes of banqueting (for example, cat. 103, Pl. 46)[43].

Mythological scenes or motifs are almost completely absent from Palmyrene sarcophagi, in contrast to marble sarcophagi created in Rome, Athens, or Asia Minor, or limestone sarcophagi from other Syrian sites[44], where scenes from myths cover the most prominent areas of the monument and can take up the entirety of the boxes[45]. When they appear in Palmyra, they are relegated to secondary areas of decoration, such as fulcra, the sides of the bed, or panels on the stretchers, and show isolated figures rather than scenes with multiple figures depicting episodes from myths (for example, cat. 290, Pl. 58). There are also no >biographical< sarcophagi in Palmyra as known from Rome. In the few cases where we have the depiction of scenes from life, for example, sacrifices or caravan-related imagery, these take up the entire surface available (for example, cat. 81. 290. 306, Pl. 57), while in Roman >biographical< sarcophagi, these are inserted in the sequence of important milestones in a person's life and the >snapshots< demonstrating his virtues (birth, military success, wedding, participation in religious life).

Another difference from sarcophagi in other regions, including metropolitan Rome, the great urban centres of Asia Minor, and Athens, is that Palmyrene sarcophagi carry numerous inscriptions. Often, each person depicted in a sarcophagus is named, and their relationship to the other figures is given. Almost always, the persons are connected by family ties: sons, husbands, fathers, mothers, sisters, wives. Only in five sarcophagi is there mention of people belonging to the household (as opposed to the family): three sarcophagi with three reclining men identified as freedmen from the inscriptions accompanying their names (cat. 108. 109. 169); one foundation relief, where a servant is mentioned in the inscription (cat. 1, Pl. 39); and a lid fragment where a standing male figure is named as a trusted confidant (cat. 282). In the foundation relief, it is not possible to say if the servant was depicted; perhaps he was the standing person to the far left of the relief (if that figure was not one of the two sons mentioned in the inscription)[46]. Inscriptions mentioning the

---

37 De Jong 2017, 53.
38 Lichtenberger – Raja 2019, 144 f. See also Pogoda 2018; Al-Gonmeen – Khries 2020.
39 For gable lids see Newson 2015, 359.
40 There are family banquets depicted in other regions, but not on sarcophagi.
41 Koch 1993, 19–22.
42 Koch 1993, 53–55. See also Cameron 2019, 34 f. For Etruscan sarcophagi see Meer 2004.
43 For these, see chapter on iconography.

44 Cf. >Adonis sarcophagus< from Baalbek: Newson 2015, 359.
45 See Hallett 2019b for mythological sarcophagi and the uses of myth.
46 It must be noted that in all five examples, the figures are not depicted in any way that could set them apart from other adult or young males in Palmyrene iconography: the reclining males in the sarcophagi wear >Parthian-style< attire (decorated tunic, chlamys, trousers, and over-trousers in cat. 108. 109) and a combination of >Parthian-style< tunic and himation (cat. 169); the standing male in the foundation relief wears a belted tunic; and the standing male from the lid or banqueting relief wears a tunic and himation. A tunic tied at the waist with a belt, sometimes worn with other pieces of clothing underneath, is worn by young men in several sarcophagi and banqueting reliefs (for example, cat. 178. 224. 440. 441. 447). Whether these young men were servants or younger sons of the family is still a matter of debate: Albertson 2019.

profession of the deceased are also almost completely absent from Palmyrene sarcophagi, as they are in the whole corpus of Palmyrene inscriptions[47]. There is only one mention of a man identified as a »craftsman« in the inscription next to his name (cat. 8) among the 113 inscriptions recorded.

Inscriptions denoting who had the right to be buried in the sarcophagus, and that violators would pay a fine, so common in other areas[48], are absent in the Palmyrene sarcophagi. The Palmyrene practice of displaying sarcophagi indoors, as opposed to in the open air[49], would have made unnecessary the use of formulas against secondary burials. Two more factors may have made the use of such inscriptions unnecessary: (1) the practice of multiple burials in the same loculus or sarcophagus within tombs that were to be used by the same family; and (2) the practice of selling or conceding parts of the tomb, where the sarcophagus was placed. So, the place of burial was a place of dynamic changes either by members of the same family group or of the new owners/occupants of the tomb, and the practice of secondary burial that was so abhorrent to owners of sarcophagi at other sites was not considered problematic.

Everything in a Palmyrene sarcophagus highlighted the local cultural identity of its commissioners and makers. The emphasis on the family banqueting motif as well as the persistence of using epigraphy almost exclusively for recording genealogies and an individual's place within the family group are both elements that set apart Palmyrene sarcophagi from those of other regions, and are in use from the earliest foundation reliefs to the very end of sarcophagi production.

The Banqueting Motif

The representation of banquets has a long history in the eastern Mediterranean and the Near East, and its meaning and function in society have been studied intensely, especially in the last fifty years[50]. Representations from

Figure 15. Relief of Ur-Nanshe, limestone. King Ur-Nanshe of Lagash (r. ca. 2550–2500 B.C.) is the only one seated in the banquet.

across this area, dating from 3400 B.C. to the middle of the 7th cent. B.C. are consistent in showing the host and the most important guests as seated. One early image of a feast comes from Čoğā Mīš, a prehistoric town in the area below the Zagros mountains, and is preserved on a door sealing, showing a figure banqueting among musicians and depictions of bowls and plates[51]. In the so-called Standard of Ur, the host and the guests are all depicted seated and holding a drinking cup in one hand[52], while in a slightly later relief from ancient Girsu, king Ur-Nanshe is seated at a banquet in the same way, illustrating that it was the norm for the host or honoured person to be seated in the region (Fig. 15)[53]. In Egypt, banquet scenes are known from images decorating the walls of tombs, but it is thought that the painters take inspiration for their depictions from the way banquets were conducted: the hosts and guests of honour are shown seated on chairs that are more or less elaborately decorated, depending on the importance of the guest, and with the least important guests sitting on mats on the ground. The food is often placed on tables in front of the banqueters (Figs 16–17, Pl. 9)[54]. In the same period,

---

47 Long – Sørensen 2017, 9 f.; Cussini 2017.
48 For example, for formulae forbidding secondary burials from Aphrodisias, see IAph2007 1.140, 1.188, 2.309, 2.322: Reynolds et al. 2007. For such formulae from Kyzikos, see Harter-Uibopuu 2014a; for such formulae from Ephesos, see Harter-Uibopuu 2014b.
49 Cf. Öğüş 2014, 114; Öğüş-Uzun 2018 for the sarcophagi at Aphrodisias; de Jong 2017, in passim.
50 The scholarship on the topic is too great to cover in this volume. Dentzer 1982 is perhaps one of the most influential books written on the subject. For other significant contributions, see the collection of essays by Oswyn Murray around the topic of the *symposion*, Murray 2017, and more recently, Draycott – Stamatopoulou 2016.

51 Kantor 1992.
52 Collins 2015.
53 Hansen 2003, 31 fig. 16.
54 While in earlier depictions, married men and women are shown seated side by side, from the period of the New Kingdom onwards, men and women are usually shown seated separately: Sherif-Shaban 2014, 475; Robins 2016, 111. Unmarried men and women are depicted seated apart always, though it is not certain if that is a pictorial convention: Harrington 2016, 129.

Figure 16. Guests at a banquet, illustration by Nina de Garis Davies, facsimile of wall-painting from the tomb of Nebamun and Ipuky (TT181), Thebes, tempera on paper.

Figure 17. Guests at a banquet, illustration by Nina de Garis Davies, facsimile of wall-painting from the tomb of Rekhmire (TT 100), Thebes, tempera on paper.

representations of feasting also appear in Mycenaean art[55]. In Syro-Hittite monuments, the banqueting figure is also shown seated in an elaborately wrought chair, while the food is placed on a table in front of him[56]. In around 645 B.C., with the representation of king Ashurbanipal in a banquet after his victory over the Elamites, this changed. The image of the king reclining on an elaborately carved kline while holding a drinking vessel is considered the first image of a person reclining in a banquet. From this period, this became the canonical representation of someone enjoying a banquet in the eastern Mediterranean[57].

The banquet motif in Palmyra appears mainly on two iconographic spheres: on the tesserae, small tokens granting entry to religious banquets[58], and on the reliefs presented in this monograph. On the

---

55 Wright 2004, 155–167.
56 Bonatz 2016.
57 For the motif of the reclining banqueter and its various local adaptations, see Dentzer 1982. The relief with Ashurbanipal's banquet has been studied extensively. For a recent contribution with previous bibliography, see Ataç 2018, 151–178. Dentzer's book treats the motif until the 4th cent. B.C., but the motif of the reclining banqueter continues to be used in the Hellenistic and Roman period. For Hellenistic banquets, one of the most important contributions is Fabricius 1999. For Roman-period banquets, see Dunbabin 2010. See also Draycott – Stamatopoulou 2016 for a cross-cultural investigation of the banquet in art. If the history of the iconography of the banquet can be traced broadly from the 4th millennium B.C. to the 4th cent. A.D., the same cannot be said about the meaning of the scene. The popularity of the banquet motif in the funerary sphere has especially spurred scholars to examine its meaning. See Draycott 2016 for an overview of the different theories proposed as to the meaning of the funerary banquet.
58 The most comprehensive collection of tesserae remains the RTP. For the role of the tesserae in Palmyrene society, see Raja 2015a; Raja 2015c; Raja 2016a; Raja 2019b; Raja 2019h.

Figure 18. Tessera with reclining priest, terracotta.

tesserae, the iconography focuses on the reclining figure, usually a priest, who is depicted either alone or with another reclining figure by his side (Fig. 18, Pl. 10)[59]. Rarely is he accompanied by a standing figure, perhaps a servant[60], or a god shown in bust form[61]. The kline is rudimentary, often portrayed as a simple, thick line, perhaps indicating its mattress[62], while the pillow on which the reclining figure rests is depicted as a round mass, when it is shown[63]. The background features schematically depicted vines[64], crescents[65], and stars[66], often in combination[67]. Compared to the iconography on the funerary reliefs, the imagery on the tesserae presents a synoptic view of the banquet, reducing it to its most essential element: the person sponsoring the feast.

All the known representations of banquets from the funerary sphere have been collected here: founder reliefs; reliefs with or without a frame, that were used as sarcophagus lids; as well as on sarcophagus lids carved in the round. Their study shows that there are several elements that are consistent throughout the three centuries of documented Palmyrene sculptural production. The reclining person takes pride of place and is surrounded by family members. The banqueter is depicted reclining in such a manner that his upper body is always on the left side of the relief, closing off the composition[68]. That person is almost always male, and together with his relatives, he rests on a kline with one or two mattresses and one or more pillows. He holds a drinking cup in one hand, usually the left[69]. The most important female in the family unit is depicted on the right side of the relief, providing the other end to the composition. On almost all the reliefs, she is shown seated. Only in the earliest recorded founder relief (cat. 1, Pl. 39) is she depicted standing. Between the reclining male and the seated female, the other family members are depicted standing and in smaller scale.

The imagery invites the viewer to consider the contemporary images of Roman banquets. Both Palmyrene and Roman depictions, after all, show a reclining person enjoying a drink. Banquet images in the Roman Empire appear on a wide range of objects and materials, and they can be divided according to the areas where they were used: domestic, religious, or funerary. Leaving aside the imagery from the domestic and religious spheres, in the funerary sphere there are different ways of representing a banquet, depending on the medium. On stelai, urns, or altars, the banqueter, almost always a man, may be shown either alone on a kline, or with his wife seated on a chair beside him, with a table of food in front of him and one or more attendants at the side. In some cases, the wife may be shown reclining next to her husband[70], or women may even be represented alone (Fig. 19)[71]. In another category of monuments, the so-called kline monuments, the deceased is represented reclining on the banqueting couch. These klinai are low and relatively unadorned. Men were the first to be shown reclining in this manner. Sometimes they hold a drinking vessel that could sometimes function as a libation bowl[72]. From the early 1st cent. A.D., adult women and young boys and girls are also represented on a kline; however, they are never shown banqueting, but rather half-seated or lying back without any drinking vessels[73] (Fig. 20, Pl. 11). The kline monuments were originally free-standing and set up on podia or in niches[74], but when the burial practice changed from cremation to inhumation, the motif of the reclining

---

59 For example, Raja 2019a, 364 f. cat. 140–141.
60 For example, RTP 12.
61 For example, Raja 2019a, 374 cat. 150.
62 For example, Raja 2019a, 366 cat. 142.
63 For example, Raja 2019a, 368 cat. 144.
64 For example, Raja 2019a, 370 cat. 146.
65 For example, Raja 2019a, 368 cat. 144.
66 For example, Raja 2019a, 369 cat. 145.
67 For example, Raja 2019a, 371 cat. 147.

68 There is one example (appendix 3.1) where the banqueter is shown reclining framed by standing figures, but since the relief does not survive, it is not possible to ascertain whether Cassas recorded the true arrangement of the figures on the relief.
69 There are forty-seven examples where he holds a drinking cup in the left hand, and only ten where he holds it in the right.
70 Dunbabin 2010, 114 f.
71 Dunbabin 2010, 115–120.
72 Ewald 2015, 397.
73 Dunbabin 2010, 110–113.
74 Ewald 2015, 397.

Figure 19. Stele with reclining female at banquet, marble. From Heraclea Pontica, A.D. 100–200.

figure, in a schematically rendered kline, was used for the covers of sarcophagi. Unlike the kline monuments, in the sarcophagi the deceased could be represented either alone or with his/her spouse[75]. Banquets with attendants as well as the main participants, the man reclining, his wife seated usually, could also appear on the sarcophagi boxes[76]. The funerary banquet on wall-paintings inside funerary chambers or catacombs is yet of a different type, as it shows numerous reclining men, or women, on the beds arranged around a table[77].

This brief survey of the motif in the Roman funerary sphere shows that, even though the banquet as a motif was, by this period, accepted as one of the most important motifs associated with the funerary sphere across the empire, in Palmyra, the local elements are predominant[78]. Only the idea of a person shown reclining on a kline with a drinking vessel is taken from Rome[79]. The first obvious difference is the presence of the whole family, a rare iconographic feature in Rome. Secondly, the manner that everyone in the family group — husband, wife, and children — is shown on the mattress of the kline has no comparanda, to our knowledge. Finally, the kline itself is elaborately decorated with multiple panels, the fulcrum may be carved with various mythological figures, and it has tall, turned legs, unlike the plain and short klinai of the Roman world. No tables with food or drink ever appear, even when there are attendants carrying plates laden with fruit or other comestibles.

In addition to these differences in what is represented, there are also differences in how the deceased and their family were represented. In the rest of the Roman Empire, the banqueters, both male and female, could appear in a chiton, maybe a himation as well, the women with little jewellery, if any[80]. In Palmyra, men may appear in a tunic and himation or a Parthian-inspired costume comprised of decorated tunics, trousers, and boots, and could also include coats and over-trousers. The women appear dressed in a tunic and himation, as well as the typical headdresses (headband, turban, veil), but they are shown wearing various pieces of jewellery — at least a pair of earrings and an elaborate brooch. Children appear wearing tunics, but they could also appear wearing jewellery. In addition to those figures, in Palmyrene banqueting reliefs, young men dressed in decorated tunics, trousers, and often with a decorated cap attend to the reclining figure[81].

This elaborate costume is named after Palmyra's neighbours, the Parthians; however, it appears long before the Parthians. Evidence from the Persian Empire shows that the combination of trousers and tunic was already used by certain populations living under the control of the Great King. The earliest record is perhaps on the Bisitun relief, where three of the defeated rebels wear a tunic tied with a belt at the waist and trousers. The inscription identifies two of them as kings, one of Media and one of Sagartia, while the third is a Scythian[82]. In slightly later reliefs, in the tomb of Darius and the great staircase of the Palace of Darius at Persepolis (Apadana reliefs), the combination of trousers and tunic or coat is worn with variations by representatives of several nations, and members of Darius' court[83]. In the tomb of Darius, the tunic tied with a belt and worn with trousers is worn by Aspathines,

---

75 Dunbabin 2010, 122–126; Ewald 2015, 397.
76 Dunbabin 2010, 120–122.
77 Dunbabin 2010, 176–191.
78 Audley-Miller 2016.
79 Audley-Miller 2016, 567 f. with previous bibliography.

80 See, for example the female on a marble sarcophagus lid wearing a bracelet: <https://www.metmuseum.org/art/collection/search/256163> (26.04.2022).
81 Their identity is still under debate. Some consider them servants, see Curtis 2017, 59 f.; Albertson 2019 has suggested they are sons of the family.
82 Curtis 1988, 332 f.
83 Curtis 1988, 333 f.

Figure 20. Kline monument with a reclining girl, marble. From Rome, A.D. 120–140.

»the chamberlain carrying king Darius' quiver«[84]. Among the representatives, it is worn by the Mede, Bactrian, Armenian, Cappadocian, and Parthian envoys. The Parthian representative, in particular, wears his trousers »tucked inside low boots«[85] while he wears »a twisted fillet«[86]. The »belted cut-away coat«[87] is worn by the Sogdian, Chorasmian, Saka Haumavarga, Saka Paradraya, and Skudra envoys[88]. In the Apadana reliefs, where the identity of the representatives is debated by scholars since, unlike the tomb of Darius, they are not identified by inscriptions, the combination of tunic and trousers, or coat and trousers is worn by members of several delegations[89].

Archaeological evidence shows how widespread this costume was in Achaemenid Persia[90], and how it was later worn by nobles and kings at the fringes of the various Hellenistic kingdoms[91] as well as by peoples to the east[92]. The costume, therefore, had a long presence in the East, and was associated in particular with nomadic people[93]. In Parthia, the combination of tunic and trousers became the favourite costume for nobles and royalty, to the point that by the 3rd cent. A.D. this had become so closely associated with elite status that it remained the costume of choice for the Sasanian nobility and royalty, especially but not only for ceremonies (Fig. 21, Pl. 13)[94].

Figure 21. Plate with the king Yazdgard I (r. 399–420) slaying a stag, silver. From Iran, A.D. 399–420.

To the west of the Parthian Empire, the costume choice of tunic-trouser or coat-trouser combination, is seen primarily in the art of Hatra, Dura-Europos, and Palmyra. In neighbouring Hatra, a small kingdom to the north-east of Palmyra that flourished in approximately the same period as Palmyra and was close politically and culturally to the Parthian Empire[95],

---

84 Curtis 1988, 333; Lecoq 1997, 225, inscription DNd.
85 Curtis 1988, 334.
86 Curtis 1988, 334.
87 Curtis 1988, 334.
88 Curtis 1988, 334.
89 Curtis 1988, 335–341.
90 Curtis 1988, 341–353.
91 Curtis 1988, 353–359.
92 Curtis 1988, 359–371.
93 Curtis 1988, 381 f.
94 Curtis 1988, 381. 383 f.

95 Curtis 1988, 183–207. For Hatra, see Hauser 1996; Dirven 2013.

Figure 22. Julius Terentius performing a sacrifice, wall-painting. From Dura-Europos, Temple of Bel, ca. A.D. 200–220.

the tunic-trouser combination was the most popular costume choice among the various other garment combinations for the depiction of males[96]. Several of these statues represented kings or members of the local aristocracy[97], thus showing the connection of this costume with elite culture[98]. In Dura-Europos, a city that was under Parthian control until A.D. 165, when it was taken by the Romans, and remained a part of the Roman Empire until its destruction by the Sasanians in A.D. 265[99], the tunic-trouser combination is seen mostly in wall-paintings either from the houses or the religious buildings of the city, although it also appears in sculptural depictions[100]. There, it is worn by gods in the Aphlad stele[101] and on a painting in the Temple of Bel[102], in the depictions of Mithras from the city's Mithraeum[103], as well as by attendants or worshippers in paintings in the Temple of Bel[104] (Fig. 22, Pl. 12), the Temple of Azzanatkhona[105], and the Synagogue. In the last place of worship, the Synagogue, biblical figures are also shown wearing this costume[106]. It is also worn by male figures depicted in various media and found in houses[107]. The tunic-trouser combination in the representations from Dura-Europos is thus associated both with noble figures and deities, but also with worshippers, indicating that the elite costume choices were widely disseminated among the population and, based on it being worn by attendants or worshippers, could be considered a costume for special occasions.

In Palmyra, there are 214 figures represented with the main elements of the Parthian costume, a pair of trousers and a tunic[108]. The majority of these figures are

96 Rosenfield 1967, 170–173; Curtis 1988, 186 f.; Anderson 2017.
97 Curtis 1988, 188 f.; Dirven 2008.
98 See also Ellerbrock 2021, 214.
99 For Dura-Europos, see Curtis 1988, 208–234; Baird 2018.
100 Curtis 1988, 210.
101 Curtis 1988, 210 f.
102 Curtis 1988, 215. 216.

103 Curtis 1988, 219–225.
104 Curtis 1988, 212–216.
105 Curtis 1988, 216 f.
106 Curtis 1988, 225–232.
107 Curtis 1988, 217–219.
108 Curtis 2017, 52.

in funerary reliefs: twelve in loculus reliefs, eighteen in stelai, fifty-three in banqueting reliefs, ninety-seven in sarcophagi, two in statues found in tombs, and only thirty-two portraits can be connected to the public/religious sphere, or they were found in secondary contexts and their original function cannot be identified. The costume of trousers worn with a coat or tunic, but also a himation, appears worn by riders on reliefs from the Temple of Bel[109] and the Temple of Allat[110]; in depictions of priests on reliefs from the Temple of Bel[111], the Temple of Allat[112], the Temple of Baalshamin[113], and the Sanctuary of Nabu[114]; standing figures that may represent attendants or worshippers from the Temple of Baalshamin[115], the Temple of Allat[116], the Temple of Bel[117]; in reliefs or statues in the round found out of context[118]; and in seated figures, possibly free-standing honorific statues[119]; in addition to the depictions from the funerary sphere: in stelai, banqueting reliefs, sarcophagi, and loculus reliefs.

The trousers may be undecorated or decorated with a wide band that runs along the centre front of each trouser leg, while the tunic is long-sleeved and may be decorated on the neckline as well as on the edge of the sleeves and the lower hem, and may have a wide band running along the centre of the front piece. In addition to these garments, the Palmyrenes were represented most often wearing a chlamys that was fastened over the right shoulder with a brooch. This is a contrast to the depictions of the costume in Parthia, where the tunic-trousers combination may be supplemented by a long coat or a mantle[120]. This combination of trousers, Parthian-style tunic, and chlamys, is the most common for men reclining in a banquet, whether they are depicted as priests (seventy-nine examples in total) or not. Trousers may be worn in other combinations of garments, such as long coats (cat. 82. 199. 200) or with over-trousers (cat. 29. 108. 109. 699). In total, there are 150 reclining men wearing at least one Parthian-inspired garment, in contrast to eighty-one reclining men wearing a plain tunic and himation.

Standing men and children in the art of Palmyra are usually represented wearing tunic and trousers, sometimes worn with over-trousers as well. The tunic may be worn with a belt, creating an overfold to the garment. There are five representations of children in this costume on sarcophagi (cat. 72. 107. 115. 351. 390), eleven on loculus reliefs[121], and nine on stelai[122], as

---

109 Palmyra, Palmyra Museum, unknown inv. number: Seyrig 1937, pl. 3, 1; Curtis 1988, 239.
110 (1) Palmyra, Palmyra Museum, inv. no. A 141/75: Gawlikowski 2017, 204 cat. 4 fig. 169; (2) Palmyra, Palmyra Museum, inv. no. CD 37/74: Gawlikowski 2017, 231 cat. 30 fig. 200; (3) Palmyra, Palmyra Museum, inv. no. AL 2/06: Gawlikowski 2017, 215 cat. 15 fig. 180; (4) Palmyra, Palmyra Museum, inv. no. AL 1/06: Gawlikowski 2017, 224 cat. 22 fig. 192.
111 Temple of Bel: Seyrig et al. 1975, 24 pl. 15 fig. 32.
112 Temple of Allat: Gawlikowski 2017, 87 fig. 69.
113 (1) Palmyra, Palmyra Museum, inv. no. B 1865: Dunant – Stucky 2000, 96 cat. 42 pls. 15–16; (2) Palmyra, Palmyra Museum, inv. no. 1057: Collart – Vicari 1969, 161 pl. 96, 6. These fragments of standing figures may also represent priests: (1) Palmyra, Palmyra Museum, unknown inv. no: Dunant – Stucky 2000, 98 cat. 50 pl. 18; (2) Palmyra, Palmyra Museum, unknown inv. no: Dunant – Stucky 2000, 98 cat. 51 pl. 19.
114 Palmyra, Palmyra Museum, inv. no. B 2228/7957: Tanabe 1986, 28 pl. 173; Raja 2017f, 81. 83 fig. 7; Raja 2017g, 81. 83 fig. 7.
115 (1) Damascus, National Museum of Damascus, unknown inv. no.: Dunant – Stucky 2000, 102 cat. 70 pl. 21; (2) Palmyra, Palmyra Museum, inv. no. B 1919: Dunant – Stucky 2000, 113 cat. 125 pl. 29, 125.
116 Palmyra, Palmyra Museum, inv. no. CD 11/77: Gawlikowski 2017, 214 cat. 14 fig. 179.
117 Damascus, National Museum of Damascus, unknown inv. no.: Drijvers 1976, 19. 32 pl. 52, 2; Tanabe 1986, 24 pl. 132.
118 (1) Palmyra, Palmyra Museum, inv. no. A453: Ingholt 1936, 93 pl. 19, 1; (2) Palmyra, Palmyra Museum, inv. no. CD 18/77: Gawlikowski 1984, 101 f. cat. 35 pl. 81, 170; (3) Palmyra, Palmyra Museum, unknown inv. no.: Tanabe 1986, 44 pl. 445; (4) Palmyra, Palmyra Museum, inv. no. CD 36: Michalowski 1960, 116 f. cat. 39 fig. 128; (5) Palmyra, Palmyra Museum, inv. no. CD 33: Michalowski 1960, 114 f. cat. 38 fig. 127.
119 Palmyra, Palmyra Museum, unknown inv. no: Ingholt Archives, PS 1128.
120 Curtis 2017, 52.
121 (1) Loculus relief with male and standing child, Istanbul, Istanbul Arkeoloji Müzesi, inv. no. 3745/O.M.200: Long 2017, 76 f. fig. 8; (2) loculus relief with female and standing child, Antakya, Hatay Arkeoloji Müzesi, inv. no. 9044: Meischner – Cussini 2003, 98 f. 102 f. fig. 3; (3) loculus relief with male and standing child, London, British Museum, inv. no. BM 125046: Ingholt 1935, 69 n. 59 pl. 31, 1; (4) loculus relief with female holding child, Bibel und Orient Museum, Universität Fribourg, inv. no. 2001.8: Keel 2008, 34 cat. 20; (5) loculus relief with female and standing child, Museo Nazionale d'Arte Orientale, inv. no. 6011/6827: Krag 2018, 355 cat. 721; (6) loculus relief with female and standing child, Copenhagen, Ny Carlsberg Glyptotek, inv. no. IN 1075: Raja 2019a, 192 f. cat. 54; (7) loculus relief with male and two standing children, Copenhagen, Ny Carlsberg Glyptotek, inv. no. IN 2763: Raja 2019a, 222–225 cat. 66; (8) loculus relief with female holding child, Krag 2018, 365 cat. 753; (9) loculus relief with female and standing child, Palmyra, Palmyra Museum, inv. no. 1777/6601: Sadurska – Bounni 1994, 164 f. cat. 218 fig. 205; (10) loculus relief with female and standing child, private collection: Krag 2018, 285 cat. 439.
122 (1) Stele with standing child, Istanbul, Istanbul Arkeoloji Müzesi, inv. no. 3826/329: Ingholt 1928, 154 PS 526; (2) stele with standing female and child, seen in Beirut: Teixidor 1966, 178 f. no. 7 pl. 2, 7; (3) stele with standing child, seen by Ingholt in Damascus: Ingholt Archives, PS 559; (4) stele with standing child, Beirut, Musée National de Beyrouth, inv. no. 37: Ingholt 1928, 153 PS 519; (5) stele with two children: Copenhagen, Ny Carlsberg Glyptotek, inv. no. IN 2776: Raja 2019a, 98–101 cat. 13; (6) stele with standing female and child, private collection: Krag 2018, 375 cat. 785. One stele was confiscated by the Turkish authorities at the Syrian borders and is unpublished, and another was sold through Christie's New York, sale of 7th December 2011, lot 24. The given acquisition history of the last object mentioned

well as one of a male figure on a stele[123]. The tunic may also be worn without a belt. This is more common in adult male representations: there are only two children wearing an unbelted tunic together with trousers and over-trousers[124], while all the other figures are adults. Thirty-six are depicted on sarcophagi (cat. 23. 68. 69. 82. 86. 103. 179. 198. 204. 205. 224. 290. 386. 427. 430. 433–435. 439. 440. 459. 465. 691. 705. 711. 713. 714. 716. 726–729)[125], and there are five representations on other monuments[126]. Far less common are depictions of standing men with: (1) tunic, trousers, and over-trousers, with only three representations known so far (cat. 108. 109. 280); (2) with tunic, trousers, and chlamys, with five representations known, four from sarcophagi (cat. 441. 447. 479), and one from a stele[127]; (3) five representations of men wearing tunic, trousers, chlamys, and over-trousers, three from sarcophagi (cat. 60. 315. 477) and two from other monuments[128]; (4) one male shown wearing tunic, trousers, and mantle[129]; (5) two males shown with tunic, trousers, and himation[130]; and (6) one male wearing tunic, trousers, and long coat[131]. Just as rare is the wearing of a himation over the tunic and the trousers, and it seems to have been reserved for priests, as there are eight representations shown wearing this combination with the himation wrapped around their body in the ›arm-sling‹ type[132]. Riding males are also shown with the tunic and trousers costume[133], usually with a mantle[134] or over-trousers[135]. There are also two rare representations of seated figures with trousers, tunic, and himation, one male[136], and a female one[137]. All the figures wear their trousers tucked into their boots. The great variation in combining garments shown in Palmyra justifies the name ›Parthian-inspired‹ for this type of costume choice.

The survey above shows that the Parthian-inspired costume was the costume of choice for reclining men, that is, men who took pride of place in sarcophagi and banqueting reliefs. This is confirmed by the comparison with reclining men appearing in tunic and himation (151 compared to eighty-one). In most of these representations of men in tunic and himation, the lower part of the figure is not preserved, however, in almost all the cases where it is preserved, it is possible to distinguish either the outline of a closed boot or identify the footwear as a boot with certainty (cat. 68. 71. 72. 98. 104. 110. 124. 129. 168. 169. 182. 293. 715. 717. 721. 727). Only in one relief (cat. 9) is the figure shown wearing sandals. The presence of the boots indicates they, too, probably wore a pair of trousers under the himation. Standing males were also more often represented in the Parthian-inspired costume than in the tunic and himation combination. This is also corroborated by the almost complete absence of men represented in

---

by the auction house in the catalogue is suspicious and highlights the problem of antiquities that appear on the art market without good documentation that proves their existence in collections that were created before 1970. Such antiquities are likely products of illicit excavations, and when they are not, they may have been created by forgers.

123 Stele with standing male: Beirut, Musée National de Beyrouth, inv. no. 692: Starcky 1955, 33 pl. 17, 3.
124 (1) Stele with standing child at Hypogeum C: Higuchi – Izumi 1994, 77 f. 130–132 pl. 48, 9; (2) loculus relief with female holding child: Paris, Musée du Louvre, inv. no. AO 4147: Krag 2018, 365 cat. 756.
125 Two males are depicted on fragments, possibly from sarcophagi that were sold through Christie's, New York, sale of 5th–6th December 2001, lot 724, and sale of 9th December 2010, lot 62. The auction house only gave the information that they were both in private collections. Again, the lack of documentation makes the acquisition history suspicious and the objects problematic.
126 (1) Votive relief: Ingholt 1936, 93 pl. 19, 1; (2) loculus relief with female and standing male: Palmyra, Palmyra Museum, inv. no. 2149/7611: Sadurska – Bounni 1994, 131 f. cat. 175 fig. 190; (3) stele with male: Palmyra, Palmyra Museum, inv. no. unknown: Michalowski 1963, 111 f. cat. 2; (4) stele with male: Ingholt Archives, IA_NCG_Portrait2016_032. A fifth object was a votive relief sold through Christie's, sale of 12th December 2002, lot 304. The object's acquisition history from a »European private collection« is suspicious and makes the object problematic, as with other objects that have appeared on the art market since 1970.
127 Palmyra, Palmyra Museum, inv. no. CD 36: Michalowski 1960, 116 f. cat. 39 fig. 128.
128 Two statues: (1) Palmyra, Palmyra Museum, inv. no. A29/1231: Raja – Sørensen 2015a, 444. 448 f. fig. 6; (2) Palmyra, Palmyra Museum, inv. no. unknown: Raja – Sørensen 2015a, 446. 449 fig. 7.
129 Stele with caravan scene: Palmyra, Palmyra Museum, inv. no. 9708: Al-Hariri 2013, 149 f. fig. 5.
130 Votive relief: Palmyra, Palmyra Museum, inv. no. A1121: Tanabe 1986, 24 pl. 132.
131 Stele with male: Colledge 1976, 67. 147. 240 fig. 38.
132 None of the portraits is on a sarcophagus. One stele, possibly funerary: Istanbul, Istanbul Arkeoloji Müzesi, inv. no. 3825: Ingholt Archives, PS 554; three religious reliefs: (1) Palmyra, once in the Temple of Bel: Tanabe 1986, 16 pl. 53; (2) Palmyra, Palmyra Museum, inv. no. B 2228/7957: Tanabe 1986, 28 pl. 173; (3) Palmyra, Palmyra Museum, inv. no. B 449: Collart – Vicari 1969, 161 pl. 96, 6. One more fragment of a statue may represent a priest as well: Palmyra, Palmyra Museum, inv. no. 7224: Sadurska – Bounni 1994, 141 cat. 187 fig. 206.
133 Relief with horseman: Palmyra, Palmyra Museum, inv. no. AL 2/06: Gawlikowski 2017, 215 cat. 15 fig. 180.
134 (1) Relief with camel rider: Palmyra, Palmyra Museum, inv. no. A 141/75: Gawlikowski 2017, 204 cat. 4 fig. 169; (2) relief with horse rider: Palmyra, Palmyra Museum, inv. no. unknown: Colledge 1976, 43 pl. 32.
135 Relief with horse rider: Palmyra, Palmyra Museum, inv. no. AL 1/06: Gawlikowski 2017, 224 cat. 22 fig. 192.
136 Statue depicting a seated male: Palmyra, Palmyra Museum, inv. no. unknown: Ingholt Archives, PS 1128.
137 Fragment of banqueting relief sold through Gorny and Mosch, sale of 16th December 2008, lot 273.

the Parthian-inspired costume in the funerary reliefs that covered loculus burials[138].

This costume, in all its variations, was the most elaborate and richly decorated costume of all the costumes represented in Palmyrene art. In addition to the complicated decoration, reflecting embroidered or woven fabrics, the wearers also appear carrying an *akinakes*, the dagger popular in the East from the time of the Persian Empire, suspended from a belt. The belts that were worn around the tunics are usually simple, thin bands, reproducing possibly leather belts[139], but some are elaborate belts, decorated with attachments, presumably replicating metal fittings[140], or made out of elements indicating that the original belts would have been made of metal almost completely[141]. The most striking part of the costume, however, apart from the clothes themselves, was the pair of boots worn by the banqueters. Several of them are plain, but there are examples with stars, rosettes, or other motifs indicating that the originals would have been made of worked leather. The banqueters also held bowls in their hands, which can be broadly divided into (1) two-handled cups (*skyphoi*) or (2) shallow cups without handles[142]. They have parallels in other areas that show that the originals could have been made in metal or glass[143].

It has been suggested that the Parthian-inspired costume was worn because it carried connotations of exoticism and wealth through trade. Wearing such a costume would have signalled to viewers of the person — and the artefacts — that the wearer belonged to the elite class and enjoyed a life of luxury[144]. The costume, however, was not chosen to be worn outside the imagined and/or represented banquet[145]. Therefore, even when it did carry connotations of luxury, it was a costume particularly appropriate for the banquet, the intimate gathering of friends and family members, both for men reclining and for their attendants. At the same time, both costume and setting reinforced the wearer's status.

The survey of the banqueting scenes brings another aspect of Palmyrene sarcophagi into sharp focus: the evolution and development of the iconography of the sarcophagi. From the beginning, sarcophagi and banqueting reliefs were multi-figural compositions, but the earliest examples represent men and women without many attributes and plainly attired. From A.D. 150, the complexity of the decoration and the presence of jewellery grows, and in the last two phases of Palmyrene sculpture from A.D. 220–240, and A.D. 240–273, men and women compete in the richness of their clothes and attributes. This will be discussed in detail in chapter 3 (chronology), but suffice to write here that the elaborate carving and multiple attributes and decorations can serve as a dating criterion in the absence of other evidence such as inscriptions and context.

Burial Customs

Palmyra's most iconic monuments may be the tower tombs that rose in the landscape around the city, but they were not the only funerary buildings that the Palmyrenes used. In addition to tower tombs, they built hypogea and temple/house tombs, the latter also marking the landscape[146]. In this chapter, the discussion is limited to the structures that contained sarcophagi with figural representation, that is, to all the monumental tombs[147].

The tombs were located along the main roads to and from Palmyra, leading to the creation of five main necropoleis that are today named conventionally according to their geographic location around Palmyra. Of these, the most impressive was the western one, with numerous tower tombs rising on the low hills on either side of the road towards Emesa (Figs. 23–24). There were two routes leading to the Euphrates; the first was to the north of the city where several temple

---

138 Only seven reliefs: (1) relief at Beirut, American University Museum, inv. no. 32.25: Ingholt 1934, 36–38 cat. 3 pl. IX, 1; (2) relief at hypogeum of TYBL: <https://www.facebook.com/103105249750926/photos/pcb.758083210919790/758082734253171/?type=1&theate> (12.05.2022); (3) relief with two busts at Mainz, Prinz Johann Georg-Sammlung, inv. no. PJG835: Schollmeyer 2004, 63 f. 77 fig. 1; (4) Atlanta, Michael C. Carlos Museum, inv. no. 2019.014.001; (5) Palmyra, Palmyra Museum, inv. no. B 1764/6588: Sadurska – Bounni 1994, cat. 197 fig. 25; (6) Palmyra, Palmyra Museum, inv. no. unknown: Tanabe 1986, 37 pl. 324; (7) Palmyra, Palmyra Museum, inv. no. A 1225/6312: Tanabe 1986, 37 pl. 318; (8) Palmyra, Palmyra Museum, inv. no. unknown: al-Asʿad et al. 2012, 167 f. cat. 10.
139 For example, the belt on the reclining male in cat. 6.
140 For example, the belt on the reclining male in cat. 133.
141 For example, the belt on the reclining male in cat. 290.
142 Miyashita 2016, 136.
143 Miyashita 2016, 142–145.
144 Curtis 2017, 65 f.
145 For the meaning of the Palmyrene banquet scenes, see Audley-Miller 2016.
146 A detailed examination of the monument types is beyond the scope of this monograph. While tower tombs were the object of a detailed study by Agnes Henning (Henning 2013b), hypogea and temple tombs have not received the same attention, although specific tombs have been the subject of monographs or articles (see, for example, Sadurska 1977 and Schmidt-Colinet 1992). Also, the tombs of Palmyra have rarely been placed within the wider context of funerary monuments of Roman Syria: see de Jong 2017 and Blömer – Raja 2019 for two exceptions.
147 There are also simple burials in Palmyra, but they have not been investigated well. For these, see Cantineau 1932, 4; Colledge 1976, 58.

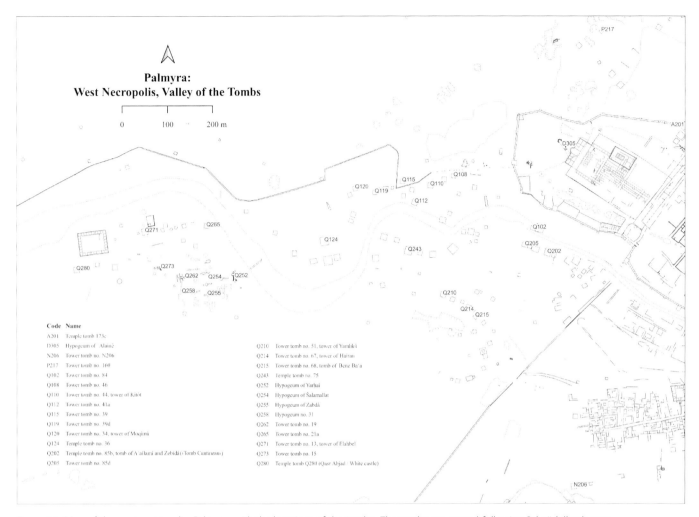

Figure 23. Map of the west necropolis, Palmyra, with the locations of the tombs. The tombs are named following Schnädelbach 2010.

Figure 24. Tower tombs in the landscape.

tombs were located (Fig. 25). Along the southern route to the Euphrates was the eastern necropolis, where only a few isolated tombs have been explored and which, so far, seems the least monumental of all the necropoleis. Two more necropoleis have been identified in the south of Palmyra, the south-west necropolis, along the route to Damascus, and the south-eastern one, along the route to Hit (Figs. 26–27)[148]. Over 400 monumental tombs have been documented in these necropoleis[149]. A characteristic of all the monumental tombs of Palmyra is that they were built in order to house successive generations of a family. This is made clear in the foundation inscriptions placed on the exterior of the monuments and that consistently refer

---

148 Henning 2019a, 158.
149 Henning 2019a, 157. See also Schnädelbach 2010 and Raja et al. 2021b for the documented tombs.

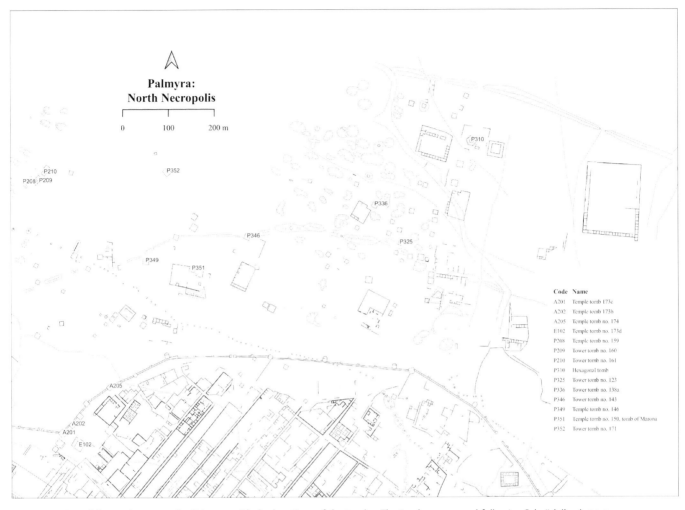

Figure 25. Map of the north necropolis, Palmyra, with the locations of the tombs. The tombs are named following Schnädelbach 2010.

to the tomb as a structure meant to house the builder and his descendants for all time[150].

Throughout the Roman period, the burial habit in Palmyra was inhumation, a practice that effectively created the need for spacious tombs. In combination with the need to build tombs for housing the dead of an entire family, this led to solutions for saving space and accommodating as many of a family's deceased as possible. One of these solutions was the creation of towers, where the tomb was expanded vertically. Another solution was the horizontal expansion of the tomb, by digging an underground tomb that had the potential to be expanded *ad infinitum*[151]. Another solution was the burial of the deceased (most likely relatives) within the same loculus niches or sarcophagi[152]. That this attitude towards the tomb was in some cases more ambitious rather than realistic is evident from the so-called concession texts: inscriptions that document the sale of part of a tomb to another family. Most of these come from hypogea, sometimes recording the sale of different sections of the same tomb, but there are two from tower tombs, and one from a temple/house tomb[153].

---

150 Henning 2019a, 157–161. There is some variation in the phrases used, but the meaning is always the same: that the tomb is meant to house the founder and his family forever. Cf. Yon 2012, 313–369, for bilingual inscriptions from tombs and the variety of expressions used in them. See also Gawlikowski 1970a, 184–204, for a corpus of eighty-one foundation inscriptions.

151 Gawlikowski 2021, 170–172, proposes that the tower tombs and temple tombs of Palmyra were tombs created by the elite, while hypogea were constructed by middle-class Palmyrenes.

152 Henning 2019a, 161 f.

153 Gawlikowski 1970a, 204–219 has collected fifty-two of these concession inscriptions, nine of which were found in secondary contexts: Gawlikowski 1970a, 25–27. 40. 43. 48. 51. 52 cat. 7; Gawlikowski 1970a, cat. 38. 39 were found in tower tomb no. 70; Gawlikowski 1970a, cat. 50 was from tower tomb no. 50, and

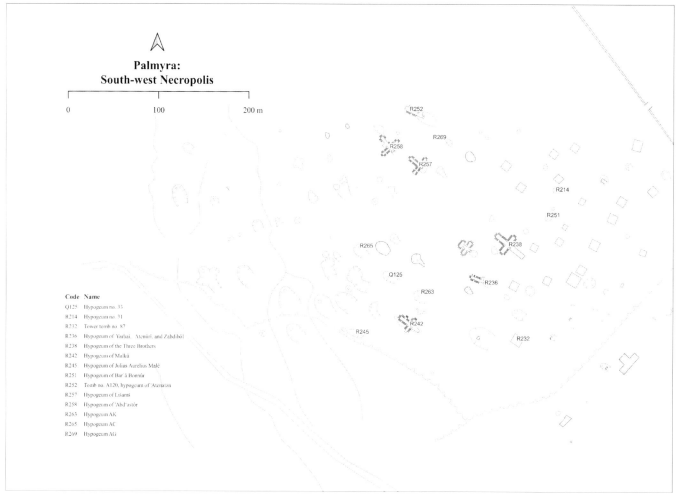

Figure 26. Map of the south-west necropolis, Palmyra, with the locations of the tombs. The tombs are named following Schnädelbach 2010.

The evidence from the tombs, scant though it may be, reveals a variety of attitudes towards the deceased. Mummies were found in five tower tombs, all constructed in the 1st cent. A.D. In the same tombs, however, non-mummified skeletal remains were also found[154]. Skeletal remains, mostly disarticulated, were found in the hypogea excavated by the Japanese Archaeological Mission, but no mummies[155], as well as in tomb no. 36[156]. This shows that mummification and inhumation were practised at the same time in Palmyra, with mummification perhaps being limited to the period of the first two centuries A.D. (Pl. 14)[157] From the evidence of those mummies, it is possible to see how mummification was practised in Palmyra. The body was first allowed to dry, and no organs were removed. After this preparatory period, it was covered in a clean and new cloth, myrrh paste was applied, and two more layers of fabric were used, one made of linen strips and one of finer materials, which was the last layer. Face, hands, and feet in particular were the focus of special attention, with silk fabrics often used to cover them[158]. Most of the skeletal material found in the tombs of Palmyra was disturbed because of looting, which had most likely already taken place in antiquity[159]. Where it was possible to ascertain that the burials had not been disturbed, it was evident that

Gawlikowski 1970a, cat. 49 from temple/house tomb no. 150. To these can be added the texts from hypogeum of Bôlḥâ and Borpa, excavated by the Japanese Archaeological Mission from the Research Centre of Silk Roadology at Palmyra: Higuchi – Saito 2001, 199 f. It is important to note here the work of Eleonora Cussini on these texts, especially Cussini 1995.

154 De Jong 2017, 111.
155 Higuchi – Izumi 1994, 147–155; Nakahashi et al. 2001, 145–164.
156 Caselitz 1988–1990; Caselitz 1992.
157 De Jong 2017, 111.
158 Schmidt-Colinet et al. 2000, 56 f.; de Jong 2017, 111.
159 Cantineau 1929, 13–15; Caselitz 1988–1990; Caselitz 1992; Higuchi – Izumi 1994, 41–70; Nakahashi et al. 2001, 145–164.

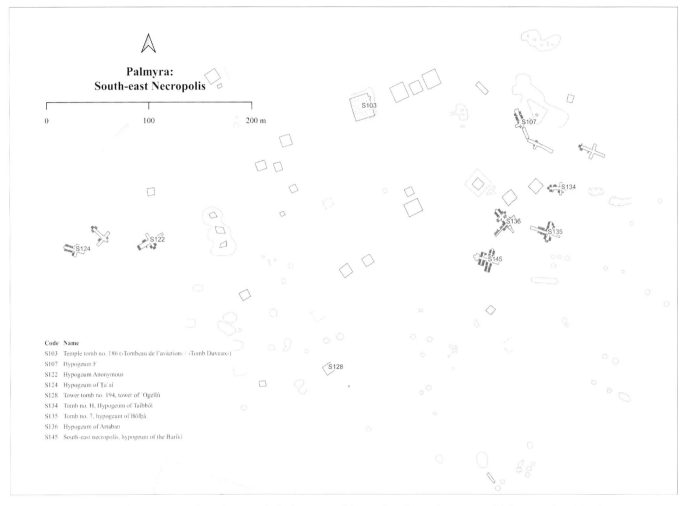

Figure 27. Map of the south-east necropolis, Palmyra, with the locations of the tombs. The tombs are named following Schnädelbach 2010.

multiple burials had taken place in the same loculus[160]. In addition, it seems that the graves of the founders of the monumental tombs, or the burial niches next to them, were the ones that were used for multiple burials, most often in the same monument[161].

Apart from the rituals associated with the preparation of the deceased, there is evidence for rituals associated with the burials[162]. Wells for drawing water, basins for holding liquids, incense bowls, and burnt remains have been excavated in the hypogea, while lamps have been found inside loculi. All these have been connected to rituals that could have taken place during or after the burial[163]. The presence of cooking pots, in particular, suggests that a communal meal must have taken place at some point[164]. With the absence of written evidence that could illuminate these rituals and meals, it is not possible to determine how they formed part of funerary cult rituals, let alone whether they indicated a belief in the afterlife, as it has been suggested. This, with the present evidence, must remain a matter of conjecture[165].

As part of the research conducted within the Palmyra Portrait Project, the information relating to all the published Palmyrene burials was collected. In total, remains of 769 humans have been recorded in the publications[166]. Of these, however, very few burials can be associated with sarcophagi. All the other adult burials were in loculi. Most of the older children were buried together with an adult, while the younger children and

---

160 Higuchi – Izumi 1994, 41–70; Nakahashi et al. 2001, 150.
161 De Jong 2017, 114–119.
162 De Jong 2017, 146–174 contains the best discussion on funerary beliefs and rituals in Roman Syria. Especially for Palmyra, see de Jong 2017, 150–154. 160–163. 166 f. 169–174.
163 De Jong 2017, 152.
164 Higuchi – Saito 2001, 135–144, for cooking pots and other vessels that could have been used in ritual activities.
165 See Kaizer 2010, 26; Yon 2018.
166 Romanowska et al. 2021, funerary dataset.

infants were often placed in pit graves on the ground[167]. The few burials associated with sarcophagi show a variety of practices. Two of the deceased were mummified before burial[168]. In the hypogeum of Yarḥaî, there is evidence of both cremation and inhumation, in the east and the west niches: one inhumation was found with cremated human remains between their feet, while two inhumations were found under the east niche. On the tombs placed behind the niche of the west exedra, there were more inhumations[169]. In hypogeum F, two adult burials were found in the central sarcophagus in the main exedra[170], three adults, one child, and one person of undetermined age and gender were buried in the east sarcophagus of the main exedra[171], and two adults in the west sarcophagus of the main exedra[172]. Two inhumations were found disturbed in one sarcophagus from the hypogeum of ʿAlaînê (cat. 135)[173], and two more inhumations were in one sarcophagus (cat. 76 for the lid) at the west exedra of the hypogeum of Ṭaʿaî, divided originally by terracotta plaques[174].

The lack of burials from sarcophagi is to be expected, though, the same way that the known burials from the site are relatively few. The ruins of Palmyra have been attracting looters and explorers from antiquity. An iconic drawing of the tower tomb of Kîtôt by early explorer Louis-Francois Cassas, engraved by Simon Charles Miger, shows local guides entering the tomb under the light of torches[175]. The scene is evocative of the fascination of the tombs exerted on early travellers, but also shows a hole through which the explorers enter, possibly a hole that had been created by looters in the past in an attempt to find treasures. Ingholt, who excavated in Palmyra between 1924 and 1928, as well as in 1935, recorded the presence of such holes, as well as reporting how they used them to enter the tombs[176]. The main reason, however, why there are relatively few burials recorded from Palmyra is that systematic archaeological exploration and excavation took place before the Second World War. In that period, archaeologists rarely analysed or collected bones systematically, either human or animal ones, or remains of plants and seeds[177]. Even though the importance of botanical and zoological material had been recognized from the middle of the 19th cent., it was only in the 1960s that it became standard excavation practice to collect and analyse these remains[178]; however, one that was practised most by prehistoric archaeologists rather than archaeologists working on classical sites[179].

The introduction above makes clear that sarcophagi in Palmyra had their own distinct typology and trajectory of use. In fact, the earliest sarcophagi that can be identified from the site are not connected either with specific tombs, as far as we know, or the typology of sarcophagi from the Graeco-Roman world. They are the so-called slipper-shaped coffins, named after their distinctive tapering shape with an opening at the upper, wider part. This type of coffin was prevalent in neighbouring Parthia[180].

Inscriptions

Palmyrene Aramaic was the language of the funerary sphere. Almost all of the inscriptions on funerary portrait busts closing off loculus burial niches were in Palmyrene Aramaic. The same can be seen in sarcophagi. The only exceptions are three inscriptions associated with founder reliefs that were both in Palmyrene Aramaic and Greek (cat. 3. appendix 1, cat. 1. appendix 3, cat. 1), and six from sarcophagi and banqueting reliefs that are either bilingual or in Greek (cat. 180. 193. 194. 365. 446. 469)[181].

Whereas in funerary busts the location of the inscriptions was fairly standardized, to the left or right

---

167 Romanowska et al. 2021, funerary dataset.
168 Remains of one mummy were found in an undecorated built sarcophagus in tomb no. 46: Henning 2013b, 189. The remains of a second were found in one of the sarcophagi of tower tomb no. 46, possibly in one of the sarcophagi in the catalogue, although it is now impossible to ascertain which: Henning 2013b, 189.
169 Amy – Seyrig 1936, 256 f.
170 Higuchi – Saito 2001, 56 f.
171 Higuchi – Saito 2001, 58–60.
172 Higuchi – Saito 2001, 57 f.
173 Sadurska 1977, 66.
174 Abdul-Hak 1952, 200.
175 Tower tomb of Kîtôt, Simon Charles Miger after Louis-François Cassas. Etching. From Voyage pittoresque de la Syrie, de la Phoénicie, de la Palestine, et de la Basse Egypte (Paris, ca. 1799), vol. I, pl. 102. The Getty Research Institute, 840011: <https://artsandculture.google.com/asset/tower-of-kitot-simon-charles-miger-after-louis-francois-cassas/kAE9i6MVJAxkRg> (12.05.2022).

176 For example, Ingholt 1935, 78. 108. Ingholt's excavation diaries and his archive have been published, and they are invaluable sources for the study of Palmyrene art and archaeology: Raja et al. 2021a; Raja 2021b.
177 De Jong 2017, 5.
178 Landon 2005; Fuller – Lucas 2014.
179 For example, Pease writing on »ancient botany« in the Graeco-Roman world, refers only to depictions of plants when mentioning »archaeological remains«: Pease 1952, 44, and advocates for an ethnographic approach in order to identify plants mentioned in literary sources: Pease 1952, 50 f.
180 There are only reports of these coffins, without drawings or photographs: Gawlikowski 1970a, 34; de Jong 2017, 55. For Parthian slipper-shaped coffins, see Middleton et al. 2007; Olbrycht 2017.
181 Raja – Yon 2022.

of the head, in sarcophagi there was greater variation. The most common location for the inscriptions naming the represented figures, who were also identified as the primary occupants of the sarcophagi, were the areas next to the heads of the figures on the lid (for example, cat. 9. 10) or the portrait busts on the box (for example, cat. 5. 8. 10). Inscriptions could, however, also be placed on the mattress of the kline (for example, cat. 12), on the clothes (for example, cat. 12), the base on which the sarcophagus could be placed (for example, cat. 4), or on the frame of the relief (for example, cat. 7. 33). Some sarcophagi, such as cat. 11, had inscriptions in several locations: next to the figures, on the clothes, and on the podium. Rarely, inscriptions were placed on attributes (cat. 355 on skyphos; cat. 365 on keys; cat. 469 on the writing tablet). Thus, it seems that the primary consideration of Palmyrenes when placing an inscription was the direct association between text and portrait, and they used whatever area of the sarcophagus would suit their purpose best. Despite the diversity in location, the inscriptions, however, were standardized in terms of their content: they give the name of the deceased as well as their genealogy and family relations (for example, cat. 4. 7).

Just as standardized were the foundation inscriptions placed on the tomb's façade or entrance: they gave the name and genealogy of the tomb's founder, recorded the construction of the tomb for eternity, and stipulated who had the right to be buried there. Often, the text was written both in ancient Greek, the official language of the Roman Near East[182], and Palmyrene Aramaic. In total, there are eighty-one recorded foundation inscriptions, of which thirty-six (including the ones in cat. 1. 3. appendix 1, cat. 1) that are bilingual, so less than half of them[183]. Even rarer was the use of bilingual inscriptions in the cession texts: only eight out of fifty-two were bilingual[184].

The evidence from some of the other bilingual inscriptions in Greek or Latin from Palmyra indicates that the use of Greek in the funerary sphere was most likely connected to specific families and their tombs[185], and was not a wider cultural phenomenon but rather yet another marker of elite identity. That Greek was used for highlighting participation in the »broader cultural koine of the Roman Near East«[186] is made more evident when considering how it was used more often in the foundation texts that were publicly displayed compared to cessions and commemorative inscriptions that completed the corpus of funerary inscriptions.

Tower Tombs

The earliest of the monumental funerary buildings are the tower tombs (Pl. 15). Foundation inscriptions testify to their creation between 9 B.C.–A.D. 128[187]. It is likely, however, that their construction started before the first known foundation inscription, probably even before the last quarter of the 1st cent. B.C.[188], and it is certain that they continued being in use after the last tower tomb was constructed. Testifying to that continuous and extended use is a graffito inside tower tomb no. 98 that shows that the tomb was used until the 3rd cent. A.D.[189].

These foundation inscriptions were placed on the wall with the highest visibility (in the case of the earliest tombs) or facing the road[190]. Inscribed on slabs with moulded frames, they proclaimed the name of the person who had built the tomb, his genealogy (no tower tomb was built by a woman, as far as the inscriptions testify), and that he had built it for his descendants[191]. In some cases, the foundation inscription was placed under a relief within a niche[192]. The foundation reliefs show a bed with a reclining figure, sometimes accompanied by family members. The relief on the tower tomb of Kîtôt is the earliest of these and shows the founder together with his wife, his sons, and his servant (cat. 1). Its early date (A.D. 41) might explain the differences between the imagery on this relief and all the other reliefs with banqueting scenes: the wife is shown standing behind her husband, while in the other reliefs, she is shown seated at the other end of the relief. The relief on the tower tomb of Elahbel (cat. 3) probably also had a relief with a banqueting scene on the kline, but that was lost[193] (Pl. 16).

In the earliest tower tombs, dating from before or around the 1st half of the 1st cent. A.D., the deceased were deposited in loculi that were in the exterior of the pedestal of the tower, rather than inside it. These were the only burials associated with the tombs[194]. A stairwell led to the roof of the tower from the pedestal[195]. This

---

182 Mazzilli 2020, 105. See also Sartre 2001, 269–304.
183 Gawlikowski 1970a, 184–204.
184 Gawlikowski 1970a, 204–219.
185 Raja – Yon 2022.
186 Raja – Yon 2022.
187 Henning 2013b, 3; Henning 2019a, 162.
188 Henning 2013b, tombs nos. 2, 5. 6. 10. 12a. 24–27. 29. 62a. 71a.
189 Henning 2013b, 92.
190 Henning 2019a, 158.
191 Henning 2019a, 158–161.
192 Henning 2013b, tower tombs nos. 13. 44. 51.
193 Henning 2013b, 153.
194 Will 1949, 90–93, tower tombs nos. 2. 4–6. 10. 12a. 24. 29. 52; Gawlikowski 1970a, 57–60; Henning 2013a, 160.
195 Henning 2013a, 160.

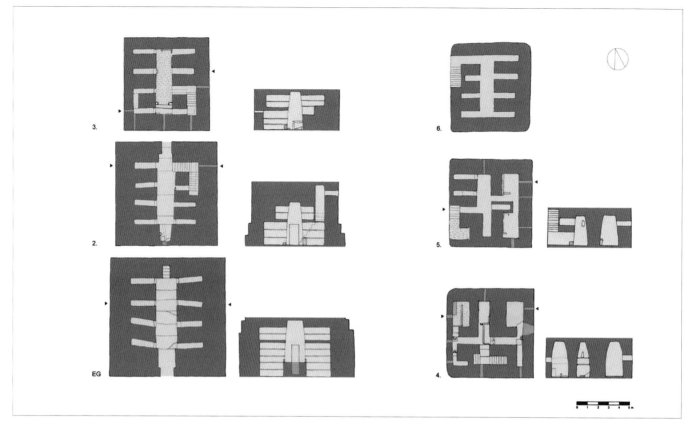

Figure 28. Plan and elevation of tower tomb of Kîtôt.

feature has led scholars to suggest that it was the necessity for conducting rituals at a high location that led to the creation of the tower tombs[196].

From the first half of the 1st cent. A.D. onwards, however, the tower tombs acquire their canonical form and are characterized by uniformity in the way they were constructed: they have a »square ground plan«[197] and are set on a podium. A tower tomb could have up to seven floors[198], reaching a height of up to thirty metres[199]. A stairwell beginning from the base of the tomb led to the upper floors. The floors had tapered rather than straight walls for stability reasons, although the inclination is very slight in the first floors (Fig. 28)[200].

In the 1st cent. A.D., a few tower tombs were expanded horizontally also, with the addition of a subterranean tomb, a hypogeum, that was accessible through a staircase on the ground floor[201]. The earliest of these composite tombs was tower tomb no. 19[202]. It had a hypogeum that was constructed between the end of the 1st cent. B.C. and the first three decades of the 1st cent. A.D.[203]. In form, it had a corridor with two narrow side chambers and three bays with spaces for loculi between them on each side[204]. These hypogea could be richly decorated with architectural details rendered by plaster and painted[205]. The construction of these tombs seems to be limited in the period between the last decades of the 1st cent. B.C. and the first decades of the 2nd cent. A.D.[206].

From this period, the burials are located inside the monument, rather than on the exterior of the pedestal. Most of the deceased were placed inside bays. The earliest tombs chronologically held two burials per bay, with a stone slab dividing them. Soon, but still within the first half of the 1st cent. A.D., the bays started being divided into loculi with the use of thinner stone plaques while the height of the floors increased, resulting in

196 Henning 2013b, 89 f.
197 Henning 2019a, 164.
198 Henning 2019a, 164.
199 Henning 2013a, 45.
200 Henning 2019a, 164.
201 Gawlikowski 1970a, 60–74; Henning 2013b, 37 f.

202 Gawlikowski 1970a, 61–63.
203 Gawlikowski 1970a, 64; Henning 2013b, 162, tower tomb no. 15.
204 Henning 2013b, 161.
205 Henning 2013b, 38, tower tomb no. 62.
206 Henning 2013b, tower tombs nos. B. TT. 9a. 9b. 14. 19. 44. 46. 62. 64–71. 73d. 83. 155.

greater numbers of burials in the same bay. Thus, a bay could now hold up to five burials in the lower floors of a tower tomb, as was the case in the tower tomb of Kîtôt. In the upper floors, where the walls receded, only two burials could be placed per bay[207]. This practice was partly abandoned in the second half of the 1st cent. A.D.: while stone slabs continued dividing the bays into burial loculi niches on the ground floors of the tower tombs, in the upper tombs, the niches were divided by either terracotta plaques, or stone slabs. These early loculi were closed with combined mortar and stones with the name of the deceased inscribed on the smooth, outer surface[208].

In the first half of the 1st cent. A.D., sarcophagi also appear for the first time in tower tombs. These early sarcophagi were simple, undecorated structures made of plaster in the shape of rectangular boxes that were built against the walls of the rooms[209]. Henning has catalogued thirty or thirty-four of these plaster sarcophagi: twelve in tower tomb no. 13[210], one in tower tomb no. 15[211], two in tower tomb no. 20[212], either five or nine in tower tomb no. 44[213], two in tower tomb no. 46[214], two in tower tomb no. 50[215], four in tower tomb no. 51[216], and two in tower tomb no. 98[217]. These plaster sarcophagi were placed within rooms on the first floors of the tower tombs, and so the sarcophagi are dated together with the construction of the monument. The first such rooms appear in the tower tomb of Kîtôt[218]. These rooms sometimes had elaborate painted decoration or vaulted roofs[219]. It is likely that the founder as well as other important members of his family were buried in these separate rooms[220]. Only a few tombs, however, had such sarcophagus chambers: out of 178 tower tombs catalogued by Henning, only six had separate sarcophagus rooms or chambers[221].

Their construction within the tomb meant that they could be placed in any floor of the tower. In tower tombs no. 15, 50, and 98, they were placed in the ground-floor area, but in all the other cases documented by Henning, they were placed in the upper floors of the tower[222]. In tower tomb 13, where twelve such sarcophagi were documented, they are found in the ground, second, and sixth floor of the building. Each floor of the same tower also contained loculus bays, with numerous burial niches[223]. This was also the case with the four plaster sarcophagi in tower tomb no. 51, which were also placed in separate sarcophagus rooms in the upper floors of a building otherwise containing multiple loculus burials[224]. Their placement in sarcophagus chambers in a building with numerous loculus burials gives credence to the suggestion that only the most important family members were buried there.

Their construction method and material, of plaster that could be easily carried up the narrow stairwells of the tower tombs, gave these sarcophagi an advantage over the more elaborate and ornamented sarcophagi made of limestone. It also ensured their continuity, even after the introduction of limestone sarcophagi, as these were too cumbersome to move in the narrow staircases of the tower tombs.

There is little evidence for the covers of the very first plaster sarcophagi; from the second half of the 1st cent. A.D., though, these sarcophagi were covered with reliefs with banqueting scenes[225]. The banqueting scene relief was aligned with the front of the box, thus leaving a space between the relief and the wall against which the sarcophagus was placed[226]. The relief was also narrow and could be carried to the upper floors of the tower tomb, unlike a proper limestone sarcophagus box.

Sarcophagus boxes and lids made of limestone started being used in the 2nd cent. A.D.[227]. There are very few sarcophagi from the first half of the 2nd cent.; however, the existence of three boxes dated by inscription shows that already by A.D. 128, limestone sarcophagi were in use[228]. Of these, cat. 4 and appendix 5, cat. 2. 3 come from a tower tomb (N206) and are the earliest securely dated sarcophagi so far[229].

Unlike plaster sarcophagi, all the limestone sarcophagi were located on the ground floors of the tower tombs, since they were too cumbersome to

---

207 Henning 2013b, 34.
208 Colledge 1976, 59; Henning 2013b, 34 f.
209 Will 1949, 104; Colledge 1976, 63. 77; Henning 2013a, 162; Henning 2013b, 35.
210 Henning 2013b, 153.
211 Henning 2013b, 157.
212 Henning 2013b, 163.
213 Henning 2013b, 186.
214 Henning 2013b, 188.
215 Henning 2013b, 192.
216 Henning 2013b, 193.
217 Henning 2013b, 240.
218 Henning 2013b, 35.
219 Will 1949, 104; Colledge 1976, 63; Henning 2013a, 162; Henning 2013b, 35.
220 Henning 2013b, 35.
221 Henning 2013b, tower tombs nos. 13 (ten chambers). 44 (five chambers). 51 (two chambers). 61 (possibly one chamber). 91 (possibly one chamber). 98 (one chamber).
222 Henning 2013b, tower tombs nos. 20. 44. 46. 51.
223 Henning 2013b, 153. She catalogued 285 loculus burial niches.
224 Henning 2013b, 19. She catalogued 217 loculus burial niches.
225 Henning 2013a, 163; Henning 2013b, 35.
226 Colledge 1976, 77; Makowski 1985a, 112 f.; Henning 2013b, 70 f. Colledge and Makowski suggest that this method of covering the sarcophagi boxes was introduced in the 2nd cent. A.D. contra Henning.
227 Colledge 1976, 77.
228 Cat. 4. 5. 8.
229 al-Asʿad 2013, 16.

move to the upper floors[230]. Of the tombs studied by Henning, only three tombs contained more than one sarcophagus[231]. The two sarcophagi in tower tomb 46 (cat. 50 and 51) were placed in front of bays with burial niches, testifying to the continuous use of the tomb[232]. The multiple sarcophagi in temple tomb no. 159 and tower tomb no. 161, were arranged in the form of a triclinium[233], that is, with two of the sarcophagi placed left and right of the third one and at a right angle to it, thus recreating the formal arrangement of the dining couches in a Graeco-Roman house[234].

This is an unusual arrangement for sarcophagi in tower tombs, as Henning observes[235]; however, this was often the way that sarcophagi were displayed in hypogea. This form of arrangement in tower tombs shows the awareness of the sponsors of these monuments of trends in contemporary funerary architecture.

Hypogea

Underground tombs appear early in Palmyra[236]. The oldest of them was located in the area of the Sanctuary of Baalshamin and dates from the 2nd cent. B.C.[237]. Its type is unique among the tombs of Palmyra: a rectangular building with a long corridor (*dromos*), with bays with loculi opening on either side of it. Fellmann had cautiously suggested that its structure could be considered an early precursor to the so-called house or temple tombs[238].

The earlier hypogea of Palmyra's Roman period were the above-mentioned ones that were associated with tower tombs. Hypogea started being constructed independently of tower tombs from at least A.D. 81/82, when there is the first epigraphic evidence for their construction[239]. These were dug into the soil, and thus could only be constructed where the geological conditions were suitable[240]. The last dated foundation inscription is from the hypogeum of Julius Aurelius Hermes, from A.D. 232[241]. Cession texts, however, testify to the continuation of burials in hypogea and perhaps also construction of new loculus bays as late as A.D. 274[242].

Because the tomb was cut into the soil, rather than built, a hypogeum had the potential to be expanded as much as necessary. From what we can see from the tomb plans and the concession inscriptions on the lintels, individual families had different strategies for dealing with the space[243]. While all were dug with the intention to house successive generations of the same family, some families cut into the soil as many burial bays as they thought they would need[244], while others left spaces that allowed for cutting into the soil later[245]. The concession inscriptions inform us that burial bays[246], exedrae[247], and spaces[248] could be sold off. In some cases, we know that the bays had been created by the previous owner of the tomb, but never used[249], and in another the new owner was given the right to enlarge the tomb[250].

Unlike other tomb types, only the corridor and the door of the hypogeum would have been visible to passers-by. The door had an elaborate frame, where the foundation text was inscribed. Texts recording the sale of parts of the tomb (»cession texts«) were also inscribed there[251]. In some hypogea, the foundation

---

230 Henning 2013b, tower tombs nos. 34. 39. 39d. 46. 68. 84. 85d. 123. 159. 161. 168. 171.
231 Henning 2013b, tower tomb no. 46: two sarcophagi; temple tomb no. 159: three sarcophagi; tower tomb no. 161: two sarcophagi.
232 Henning 2013b, tower tomb no. 46.
233 Henning 2013b, tower tomb nos. 159 and 161.
234 For dining in the Roman period, see Dunbabin – Slater 2011, with suggested reading. See also Draycott – Stamatopoulou 2016.
235 Henning 2013b, 272. 274.
236 The concept of an underground tomb was not unique to Palmyra. The catacombs documented in Rome and other locations are, perhaps, the most famous underground tombs of the Roman world. Even though they too are cut into the soft rock, tuff in the case of Rome, their layout and arrangement of the loculi differs from that of the Palmyrene hypogea. The underground tombs of Alexandria also differ in their layout and the arrangement of spaces around a central courtyard. The underground tombs at Kibyra are closer in layout but they are much smaller in scale. Another parallel may be found at the Beit She'arim necropolis. The bibliography on catacombs is large. The most recent publication is Bertolino 2022; for the tombs of Alexandria, still important is Venit 2002; for the Kibyra tombs, see: Şimşek 2013; for the Beit She'arim tombs see Mazar 1973.
237 Gawlikowski 1970a, 48. Fully published in Fellmann 1970.
238 Fellmann 1970, 130; Fellmann 1976, 215.

239 Gawlikowski 1970a, 48; Henning 2019a, 166.
240 Henning 2019a, 161.
241 Gawlikowski 1970a, 50.
242 Gawlikowski 1970a, 210 f. cat. 24.
243 See Cussini 1995 for the transfer of property in Palmyra.
244 This was the case with the hypogeum of the Three Brothers, Gawlikowski 1970a, concession nos. 1–5, where the owners of the tomb sell off already dug-out exedrae and burial bays.
245 This was the case with the hypogeum of Yarḥai, where the archaeological investigation showed that not all of the 219 loculi dug in the soil were used: Amy – Seyrig 1936, 256; Gawlikowski 1970a, 113.
246 Gawlikowski 1970a, concession nos. 2–5. 9. 10. 16. 17. 19. 21–24. 31–33. 35. 47: already dug bays; Gawlikowski 1970a, concession nos. 14. 20. 44: bays of exedra.
247 Gawlikowski 1970a, concession nos. 12. 13. 15. 28. 29. 41. 42. 46: exedra; Gawlikowski 1970a, concession nos. 1. 8: already-dug exedra with bays.
248 Gawlikowski 1970a, concession nos. 11. 18. 30. 34. 36. 37: space.
249 Gawlikowski 1970a, concession nos. 1. 16. 19.
250 Gawlikowski 1970a, concession no. 18.
251 Henning 2019a, 164.

text was in a separate plaque[252]. In the hypogeum of the Three Brothers, the only inscription relating to the foundation of the tomb was placed inside the monument, while the inscriptions on the external door lintel all record cessions of sections of the tomb[253].

Beyond the door was the tomb proper. Hypogea have a relatively uniform layout: they have a long corridor, with spaces branching out of it. Gawlikowski separated them in three subgroups, depending on whether the space opening to the left and right of the corridor was an exedra[254], a lateral corridor[255], or a chamber[256]. An exedra is a recess dug into the soil, while a chamber is a whole room accessible via a corridor[257]. All three subgroups, however, follow the same basic scheme of having an inverted T-shaped structure, although the size of the two lateral branches differs, depending on whether they are formed of corridors, exedrae, or chambers[258]. In some cases, exedrae and chambers could coexist, and a hypogeum could have more than two lateral branches[259].

The structure of the hypogeum places great emphasis on axiality and visibility from the entrance, much more so than in other tombs, where the ground floor contains a single chamber that can be surveyed at a glance, thus having competing high-visibility areas. In hypogea, the area facing the entrance directly is the most prominent in the structure and the one usually emphasized by the architecture. In the hypogeum of Yarḥaî, the exedra at the end of the corridor leading across the structure was richly decorated and reminiscent of architecture in the public sphere[260]. In the hypogeum of the Three Brothers, the exedra one first saw from the entrance was richly painted, with a mythological scene on the lunette on the wall and Victories carrying busts within wreaths on the pillars separating the loculus bays[261].

The burial bays were cut into the tomb's walls, with the loculi separated by terracotta plaques. In most cases, the loculi covers were either plain slabs that were inscribed with the name of the deceased[262], like the ones used in tower tombs, or limestone reliefs carrying portraits of the deceased. Most of these portraits were in the form of busts; however, there are a few stelai that were used more often for the depiction of single children[263].

The space of the exedrae, however, offered other opportunities. The bays could be closed with reliefs depicting whole sarcophagi, or even with sarcophagi proper[264]. As will be discussed in detail later, the lids of these sarcophagi or sarcophagi reliefs carried images of the deceased and his family participating in a banquet. Commonly, these sarcophagi or sarcophagi reliefs in the exedrae were arranged in the form of a triclinium (Pl. 17). Thus, the funerary banquet reflected the banquet of the living, with the three couches arranged around a table[265].

Other arrangements were also possible. In the hypogeum of Yarḥaî, where there are multiple exedrae, the south exedra, that belonged to the tomb's first phase, had two niches with architectural decoration that were closed with banqueting reliefs[266]. Burials were located both left and right of the niches, but also behind the banqueting reliefs[267]. The west exedra, which was constructed at the end of the 2nd cent., had been dug into a recess of the wall that was slightly over one metre above ground. The recess had the form of a small chamber with three sarcophagi placed in the form of a triclinium. Loculi burials were located both below and to the sides of the exedra[268].

In the earlier hypogea, those dating from the early 2nd cent. A.D., only sarcophagi reliefs can be documented with certainty. The first sarcophagi proper that can be securely connected to a hypogeum are those from hypogeum F. The tomb was constructed in A.D. 128 and thus gives us a date *post quem* for the sarcophagi (cat. 105–109). The first sarcophagus proper that is securely dated is cat. 6 from the hypogeum of the Three Brothers, dating from A.D. 142–143. So, we can trace the presence of complete sarcophagi proper in hypogea already from the second quarter of the 2nd cent. A.D.

In hypogeum F, we see again the coexistence of loculi and sarcophagi. The three sarcophagi, arranged in a triclinium, were placed over four burial bays, each with three loculi, at a height of 1.27 m above ground[269]. Because the hypogeum is well published, it is possible to see how the sarcophagi were incorporated into this particular tomb's design and structure. They were

---

252 Gawlikowski 1970a, 111.
253 Yon 2019a.
254 Gawlikowski 1970a, 111–117: type A.
255 Gawlikowski 1970a, 117–121: type B.
256 Gawlikowski 1970a, 121–123: type C.
257 Gawlikowski 1970a, 107–128.
258 Henning 2019a, 164.
259 For example, hypogeum of ʿAbdʿastôr: Ingholt 1938, 119–140.
260 Amy – Seyrig 1936, 235–243.
261 Eristov et al. 2019, pl. 8.3.
262 Gawlikowski 1970a.
263 Forty-five stelai showing single children (number according to PPP database, 12.11.2021).
264 Nikitine 2019, pl. 4, 9.
265 Gawlikowski 2019b, 90; Gawlikowski 2021, 249.
266 Amy – Seyrig 1936, 235–243.
267 Amy – Seyrig 1936, 237.
268 Amy – Seyrig 1936, 243–252.
269 Higuchi – Saito 2001, 28.

carved out of limestone, the middle one of hard[270] limestone and the one to the west side of the chamber of soft limestone[271], and both were plastered at the side abutting the walls[272]. The terracotta plaques covering the middle sarcophagus were preserved, showing that, at least in this tomb, the lid was not made of a single stone slab[273]. The front of the sarcophagi was carved in the shape of a bed with portrait busts between the legs[274]. Over this part, a separate relief with a family banqueting scene was placed[275].

Of the three sarcophagi in the main exedra, the middle one contained two burials[276]. The two sarcophagi to the sides, however, were internally divided by terracotta plaques. They were divided horizontally in two tiers by terracotta plaques, mimicking the arrangement of loculi burial niches in bays. Furthermore, the area of the box was further divided by vertical plaques that effectively created a second sarcophagus in each[277]. The remains of the deceased in the west sarcophagus were disturbed, and the excavators have suggested that at least one of them must have »come from another loculus«[278]. The remains of multiple bodies were found disturbed also in the tiers and second sarcophagus at the east of the exedra[279].

Temple Tombs

The third type of monumental tomb that was built in Palmyra was that of the so-called temple or house tomb. The type derives its names from its form: an overground structure on a podium that had a façade reminiscent of temple architecture, with columns and other embellishments (hence ›temple tomb‹), and an interior courtyard, like domestic buildings (thus, the name ›house tomb‹). The name most commonly used, however, is that of temple tomb (Fig. 29, Pl. 18)[280]. This is the smallest category of the three, with only sixty-eight examples[281], most of which are only partly and badly preserved[282].

The earliest surviving foundation text from a temple tomb can be dated to A.D. 143[283]. Watzinger and Wulzinger, in their survey of Palmyrene funerary monuments, had also included a foundation text that is now lost, that of tomb no. 191, that was dated to A.D. 104[284]. This would mean that temple tombs appeared as funerary monuments roughly at the same time as hypogea and continued to be built until the middle of the 3rd cent. A.D.

Gawlikowski divides temple tombs into four types: (1) tombs with a single chamber (*cella*), with either a plain or more elaborate façade, where the deceased were buried in built loculi niches[285]; (2) tombs with a single chamber and a bench running along the inner walls, where sarcophagi were placed[286]; (3) tombs with an inner peristyle court, with benches for sarcophagi, as well as built loculus bays[287]; and (4) tombs with burials in both loculi and sarcophagi, sometimes with a crypt, an inner courtyard, prostyle façades, and second stories[288]. This is but one way of subdividing the tomb types, however. Schmidt-Colinet divides the tombs into two large groups, based on their plan: (1) buildings without columns, both inside the chamber and on the façade, and (2) buildings with columns[289]. The last group can be further subdivided depending on the location of the columns: (1) only in the façade, (2) only in the interior of the building, (3) both inside and in the façade[290]. He also suggests a division according to the form of the roof: (1) with horizontal roof, and (2) with pediment[291]. Furthermore, he identifies the following as essential components of a temple tomb: (1) an almost square funerary chamber, (2) podium with pilasters highlighting the corners of the building, (3) use of architectural ornamentation to emphasize the structure of the building[292]. Henning, in her overview of Palmyrene tomb tombs, emphasizes the podium, the architecturally ornate façade, and the inner peristyle courtyard as the main elements of temple tombs[293].

This tomb type is the least studied of the three, and there is little information on how sarcophagi were placed in the buildings. The evidence so far shows great variation: they could be placed on benches[294], on

---

270 Higuchi – Saito 2001, 56.
271 Higuchi – Saito 2001, 57.
272 Higuchi – Saito 2001, 56–60. No information is given whether plaster had been used in the sarcophagus at the east side of the chamber.
273 Higuchi – Saito 2001, 56.
274 Higuchi – Saito 2001, 31.
275 Higuchi – Saito 2001, 31.
276 Higuchi – Saito 2001, 56–60.
277 Higuchi – Saito 2001, 57–60.
278 Higuchi – Saito 2001, 57.
279 Higuchi – Saito 2001, 58–60.
280 Henning 2019a, 166–170.
281 Based on the information provided in Schnädelbach 2010.
282 Gawlikowski 1970a, 129; Henning 2019a, 166.

283 Gawlikowski 1970a, 51 tomb no. 188; Gawlikowski 1970a, 170.
284 Watzinger – Wulzinger 1932, 70; Gawlikowski 1970a, 51.
285 Gawlikowski 1970a, 130–133.
286 Gawlikowski 1970a, 133–135.
287 Gawlikowski 1970a, 135–140.
288 Gawlikowski 1970a, 140.
289 Schmidt-Colinet 1992, 47.
290 Schmidt-Colinet 1992, 47.
291 Schmidt-Colinet 1992, 50.
292 Schmidt-Colinet 1992, 52, point (3) conflating the last two details in Schmidt-Colinet's publication.
293 Henning 2019a, 166.
294 For example, Gawlikowski 1970a, 133 tomb no. 174.

Figure 29. Temple tomb no. 86, reconstructed elevation of the façade.

exedrae[295], or covering loculus bays[296], while the evidence from tomb no. 36 shows that they were located on the upper floor of the building (*Hauptgeschoss*), against the wall[297]. This also shows that, unlike hypogea or tower tombs, the most prominent locations were not necessarily the ones directly visible from the entrance, as was the case with tomb no. 36, where they were placed on the upper floor. There is also little information about burials in sarcophagi. In tomb no. 36, no burial was associated with the sarcophagi. All the burials were in loculi[298]. This was also the case with tomb no. 85b, excavated by Cantineau[299].

This brief survey of the portrait and burial habit in Palmyra forms the background for the following chapters. The next chapter focuses on the dated sarcophagi, and their role in defining and refining the chronology of Palmyrene sculpture, and chapter 4 forms a survey of the tombs for which we have documentation of their holding sarcophagi.

---

295 For example, Gawlikowski 1970a, 137 tomb no. 186.
296 For example, Gawlikowski 1970a, 136 tomb no. 85b.
297 Schmidt-Colinet 1992, 23.
298 Caselitz 1988–1990; Caselitz 1992; Schmidt-Colinet 1992, 12.
299 Cantineau 1929, 13–15.

CHAPTER 3

Dated Objects

Introduction

Securely dated objects are of primary importance to archaeology since they permit scholars to place objects in relative order to each other, constructing a sequence, and gain insight into the economic, political, and cultural life of a site at a specific moment in time or period. In a historical society that is keeping written records of its activities and events[1], any text can provide scholars with the date when an event took place. This text may be in a literary format, like the work of a historian[2], but it may also be written on an object, for example, an inscription carved on a marble base, or a graffito on a wall. In Palmyra, where no literary textual evidence written by the Palmyrenes themselves has survived[3], inscriptions on objects from the public and the funerary sphere are the only Palmyrene source for fixing points in time in the chronology of the city and its art. It is thanks to such inscriptions that most of the major religious and funerary monuments of the city are dated, allowing scholars to trace periods of growth and decline in its history[4]. Ingholt, when was working on his higher doctoral dissertation on Palmyrene sculpture in the 1920s[5], used fifty-five votive reliefs, stelai, and loculus reliefs with an inscription giving the date either of the dedication of the object or of the death of the depicted figure or figures as the basis for his system of arranging all the portraits within a chronological sequence[6]. In this monograph, the objects that can be securely dated through an inscription, as well as the objects that can be relatively dated because they were found in a securely dated context, are used as the basis for establishing stylistic period traits and subsequently constructing the chronological sequence of the numerous sarcophagi without known provenance (cat. 278–729).

Of the 786 complete or fragmentary sarcophagi or banqueting reliefs known from Palmyra, only eleven can be dated with absolute certainty (cat. 1–8. 10–12) through their accompanying inscriptions. These objects are three founder reliefs (cat. 1–3), two sarcophagus boxes (cat. 4. 5), three complete sarcophagi (cat. 6. 10. 11), one banqueting relief (cat. 7), one sarcophagus box relief (cat. 8), and one sarcophagus lid (cat. 12). To these, a relief with a banqueting scene (cat. 9) can be added, since several scholars have argued convincingly that it joins the securely dated sarcophagus box at the National Museum in Damascus (cat. 8), a suggestion that the authors of this volume find likely[7]. Furthermore, Louis François Cassas recorded the presence of a founder banqueting relief on the tower of Yamlikû (tower tomb no. 51) during his trip to Palmyra in 1785 (appendix 1, cat. 1). Therefore, only 1.5% of all the known sarcophagi and sarcophagi fragments are precisely dated, a percentage that is too small and can be of limited use when considering the development of Palmyrene funerary sculpture and the establishment of chronological criteria for dating the other surviving artefacts[8].

---

1 See Sauer 2004, 20 for a definition of ›historical‹ versus ›pre-historical‹ periods based on existence or not of textual evidence.
2 For example, the work of Thucydides recording the events of the Peloponnesian War.
3 Palmyra is discussed or mentioned in Roman textual sources, which are biased or full of misunderstandings: see Hekster – Kaizer 2004; Kaizer 2020.
4 Raja et al. 2021c.
5 Ingholt 1928, 5 writes that the project was conceived in 1922. His higher doctoral dissertation was finished by 1928, when it was defended and published.
6 Ingholt 1928, 19–93 PS 1–54.

7 Contra Parlasca 1984, 288: he argues that the two objects differ in size and cat. 9 should be identified with a foundation relief placed on a tower tomb façade; however, the cushion on the lower left side of cat. 9 aligns neatly with the left end of the mattress of cat. 8, and as the examples of cat. 10. 11. 133. 134 show, discrepancies between the width of the lid and the width of the box were possible.
8 Traditional art-historical methods of dating, such as stylistic seriation, have been used effectively in the study of Palmyrene sculpture already in the 1920s; see Ingholt 1928. Since most of the excavations that brought to light these artefacts took place in the period before the application of more scientific methods of dating, there are no such data about Palmyra, while the current situation does not allow re-examination of the archaeological material.

In addition to these pieces, it is possible to use objects from tombs whose construction date is known thanks to the presence of a foundation inscription. As mentioned in the previous chapter, the inscriptions on the exterior of the tombs proudly proclaimed who the founders of these »houses for eternity« were[9]. This particular practice allows us to date with precision several of the tombs, since the inscriptions followed set formulas and always ended with the date of construction of the monument. Within the framework of the Palmyra Portrait Project, information on 329 tombs known from publications has been recorded, of which fifty-seven carry foundation inscriptions, giving us their date of construction, and twenty-five of these tombs contained sarcophagi or sarcophagi reliefs[10] that can be used for re-evaluating the chronology of the reliefs. As with everything else in Roman-period Palmyra, the last possible date for their creation is A.D. 273, the year of the final fall of the city to Aurelian's troops[11].

Of the pieces that can be dated either with absolute or relative precision, only the best-preserved are useful for re-examining the chronology of the sarcophagi and Palmyrene sculpture in general. First of all, the relief drawn by Cassas (appendix 1, cat. 1) can be immediately discarded. Cassas' drawings are not always reliable: in some cases, they present a mixture of elements from different tombs all in the same monument[12], and in others he misinterpreted what he was recording[13]. When one looks at individual drawings, such as that of the relief on the tower of Yamlikû (appendix 1, cat. 1), it is clear that his knowledge of Graeco-Roman art led him to produce works that look Roman rather than Palmyrene. This would not have been apparent to his contemporaries, and perhaps not even to him, as there are several examples of drawings or paintings done by artists from the Renaissance onwards that show that, rather than accurate renditions, the artists often reinterpreted ancient paintings, motifs, and sculptures in the style of their period[14]. The comparison between surviving artefacts and Cassas' drawings limits the usefulness of Cassas' testimony. It is possible to accept his drawing as evidence of the existence of a relief on the façade of the tower tomb, as well as of the general motif and number of figures, but not as a drawing that could help with the establishment of a chronology of Palmyrene sarcophagi. Of the other pieces, cat. 2 and cat. 4, dated to A.D. 73 and A.D. 128, respectively, are poorly preserved and thus cannot be helpful either.

Chronological Criteria

When Ingholt in 1928 published *Studier over Palmyrensk Skulptur*[15], he used fifty-five reliefs that were dated with absolute certainty as the basis of his chronological division of Palmyrene sculpture. Ingholt examined the rendition of facial features and of folds of garments, as well as the types of attributes in the dated reliefs, and determined their common features. He only used sarcophagi in his book as a means of checking whether his groupings were correct, since portraits of men and women appear on those monuments together[16], but also because he was aware of very few sarcophagi, as has been noted by other scholars[17]. In his publication, Ingholt divided Palmyrene portraits into three groups:[18]

1. Group I (A.D. 50–150)
2. Group II (A.D. 150–200)
3. Group III (A.D. 200–250)

Since Ingholt's publication, another fifty objects have been discovered that are dated to a specific date thanks to their accompanying inscriptions. That brings the total number of precisely dated objects to 104[19], and they can be used as comparanda to the dated sarcophagi.

Like Ingholt, the authors of this volume have used the following criteria for the chronology: the rendering of hair, facial features, folds of clothes, the number (rather than the types) of jewellery, and the degree of ornamentation in the different parts of the sculpture: attributes, mattresses, clothes, and jewellery. These criteria allowed the authors to observe (1) changes in style and fashion, for example, from plain, undecorated garments to garments with decorated strips, or from trapezoidal to circular brooches; and (2) technical changes, for example, from fully carved to partially carved faces. These changes then could be associated with specific periods thanks to the securely and relatively

---

9 Neither the construction of monumental tombs, nor the inscriptions honouring tomb founders were unique to Palmyra. Toynbee's work on burial practices of the Roman period remains a classic reference work (Toynbee 1966). For similar founder inscriptions in tombs in the region of Syria, see de Jong 2017, 112.
10 Palmyra Portrait Project; Raja 2021a; Raja et al. 2021c.
11 For a brief history of Palmyra, see Sommer 2017a; Sommer 2017b; Raja 2022b.
12 For examples of such composite drawings, see Schmidt-Colinet 1996, figs. 201–204.
13 For example, he drew the sarcophagus box relief inside the tower tomb of Elahbel with male busts, while in reality the relief only had female representations (Schmidt-Colinet 1996, fig. 186).
14 See for example, Dacos 1969.
15 Ingholt 1928. Recently translated into English: Bobou et al. 2021b.
16 Ingholt 1928, 94.
17 Parlasca 1984, 284; Krag 2018, 12.
18 Ingholt 1928; Bobou et al. 2021b (for the English translation of Ingholt's book). For a summary of the main characteristics of each group, see Raja et al. 2021c.
19 Raja et al. 2021c.

dated portraits. Hair, facial features, clothes, jewellery, and attributes, so the elements used for the creation of the chronological criteria, were studied first in the group of dated sarcophagi (cat. 1–12). The unequal state of preservation and publication of each object, especially for the objects that it was not possible to study in Syria since the project started after the eruption of the Syrian civil war in 2011, necessitated the comparison of each element (hair, jewellery, etc.) on sarcophagi or banqueting reliefs to their depictions in the other dated funerary reliefs. This comparison showed that there are trends shared across the range of funerary objects[20], like the move from linearity to plasticity and an increased elaboration of the decorative patterns on jewellery and clothes. The rendering of hair, clothes, attributes, etc. was then studied in the group of sarcophagi with a secure and dated provenance (cat. 13–277). This examination led to the creation of five chronological groups (see below for a detailed description of the features of each group): (1) A.D. 1–100, (2) A.D. 100–150, (3) A.D. 150–200, (4) A.D. 200–240, and (5) A.D. 240–273.

In addition to stylistic criteria, the amount of human remains as well as evidence of burials, and the construction of public buildings were used in a different publication in order to examine periods of growth and decline in Palmyra's history. There, the evidence led to the creation of seven distinct chronological groups: (1) A.D. 1–100, (2) A.D. 100–135, (3) A.D. 135–160, (4) A.D. 160–175, (5) A.D. 175–220, (6) A.D. 220–240, and (7) A.D. 240–273[21]. It is obvious that there are overlaps and differences between the two divisions, reflecting the different evidence used as well as the different aims of each investigation: stylistic changes in the corpus of sarcophagi in this publication, changes in Palmyra's history, especially economic, in the other.

In cases where it was possible to subdivide a group further because of external criteria (for example, knowing the date of the foundation of a tomb), we have done so in the catalogue. For example, even though Group II spans the period between A.D. 100 and A.D. 150, cat. 71 has been dated to the period A.D. 100–130 because the evidence points to the construction of the tomb in A.D. 75–100[22], so the relief must date soon after. Stylistically, the rendering of the folds is more >doughy< rather than linear, hence the date A.D. 100–130 was assigned to it. The mixture of features was also used as a criterion for assigning an object to the earlier or the later part of a chronological group in the catalogue. For example, cat. 298 is broadly dated to the period A.D. 200–240 because the hair of the figures is voluminous, and the eyes are partly carved, both features of that period, yet, in the catalogue, it was assigned in the period A.D. 220–240 because of the additional rich decoration of the background, since it was observed that later sarcophagi were more elaborately decorated.

Groups

Group I: A.D. 1–100

There are only nineteen objects belonging to this group, since the use of sarcophagi was not a widespread practice in this period. Their most prominent characteristic is the linear and schematic rendering of features and folds alike.

In both men and women, the hair is rendered schematically, giving the impression of locks and curls without details. Men have short hair (for example, cat. 13)[23], the eyebrows are depicted by thin ridges (for example, cat. 13. 14) or thin grooves (for example, cat. 15)[24]; the eyes are large; the irises and the pupils are indicated by concentric, incised circles (for example, cat. 13. 15)[25]; both upper and lower eyelids are thick; and they are beardless[26]. The most common garment is the tunic that can be either long- or short-sleeved and can be worn in different costume combinations: long-sleeved tunic, himation, and >Parthian-style< trousers (cat. 1 and cat. 2); >Parthian-style< tunic and trousers as well as chlamys and over-trousers (for example, cat. 60); plain, long-sleeved, long tunic (for example, cat. 61); or short-sleeved tunic and himation (for example, cat. 71). Priests have the same facial features as other men, appear beardless, and wear a tunic and himation (cat. 1). Their priestly hat (tall, cylindrical, flat-topped) is undecorated in this period (for example, cat. 21). Women wear a veil that falls behind their head and over their shoulders with vertical folds (for example, cat. 1. 21), a headband that may be undecorated with a groove in the middle (for example, cat. 18), and a turban that is coiled (for example, cat. 18). The hair is almost completely covered by the headdress, except for a single lock of hair that falls down the shoulder (for example, cat. 21). Like the men of the period, they have large eyes and thick upper and lower eyelids (for example, cat. 18). They wear jewellery: earrings in the shape of bunches of grapes (for example, cat. 21) or as a series of small hoops (for example, cat. 18). Their costume

---

20 This was also observed by Krag 2018, 12.
21 Raja et al. 2021c.
22 Sadurska – Bounni 1994, 137.
23 Heyn 2016.
24 Long 2016.
25 Long 2016.
26 Heyn 2010; Heyn 2016.

is simple: a tunic and a himation fastened over the left shoulder with a brooch (for example, cat. 1. 21). Only the brooch of cat. 21 survives: it is trapezoidal, and a key is suspended from it. The trend for simple clothes and jewellery can be compared with the better-documented fashions seen in loculus reliefs and stelai[27]. The folds of the garments are often widely spaced. There is little effort to create the effect of depth through shading that would result from deeply carved or drilled folds, producing garments that look two-dimensional and relatively flat (cat. 1).

Only five depicted klinai that can be dated based on context or inscription survive from this period (cat. 1. 2. 19. 21. 22). They have carved legs (cat. 1. 19), and the mattress is thick. In the two earliest reliefs, the mattress is flat (cat. 1. 19), while in the later reliefs, the mattress is plastically rendered and has a curved profile (cat. 2. 22).

Group II: A.D. 100–150

During this period, the use of sarcophagi becomes more prevalent in both tower tombs and hypogea. Eighty-three sarcophagi have been assigned to this group.

Men have short hair that is rendered with simple, wavy grooves, giving a schematic impression of locks and curls (cat. 8. 9. 71). The eyebrows are rendered either by curving grooves (cat. 7) or by thin ridges (cat. 8). Their eyes are relatively large compared to the rest of the face with thick upper and lower eyelids. The pupils and the irises are rendered by concentric circles (cat. 7–9). Men are shown beardless (cat. 8. 13–17). When they appear as priests, the priestly hat can be decorated with a wreath that has a central ornament, for example, a bust (cat. 7). The tunic continues to be the most common garment for men, including priests, worn either alone (cat. 1) or in combination with a himation (cat. 71. 75. 105). The tunic can have long (cat. 72) or short sleeves (cat. 71). The himation is usually worn over the left shoulder and wrapped around the waist, although standing men can be depicted with the himation in the ›arm-sling‹ type (see cat. 104 for two men wearing the himation in both above-mentioned ways).

A Parthian-inspired costume also becomes popular, both for reclining and for standing males, including priests (cat. 103). It is composed of several elements, but a decorated tunic and trousers are its essential components. In this period, men in ›Parthian-style‹ costume wear over-trousers: these can be compared to cowboy chaps in form, and they probably served a similar purpose when riding (for example, cat. 7. 60. 80. 72). The Parthian-inspired clothes are decorated with bands that have geometric patterns or motifs inspired by nature. These bands always appear in the same areas of the garment: the neckline, the middle of the tunic, the cuffs and the hem, and the middle of the trouser legs (cat. 80), although not all of them need to be in the same garment (for example, tunics without the central band and without a decorated neckline: cat. 93. 94). The top part of the over-trousers is also decorated (cat. 80. 93. 94). Standing men can appear with or without the over-trousers (cat. 103). The men wear plain, closed shoes (cat. 71).

The women have their hair mostly covered up. They can have hair brushed back over the temples (cat. 71), and they usually have two long locks of hair that fall on their shoulders on either side of the neck (cat. 7. 8. 71). Their headdress is plainly decorated with alternating panels that may carry simple, geometric decoration (cat. 7. 9. 71) or be left empty (cat. 5. 9). These blank panels could have been decorated with paint, but no analyses have been done on most of the portraits in the catalogue. The turban is relatively simply constructed with a few coiling bands (cat. 5. 7. 9), twisted bands (cat. 71), or in two layers (cat. 8). The veil falls over behind the head in long, vertical folds (cat. 71).

The women are shown with a few pieces of jewellery: apart from the brooch that holds their himation in place over the left shoulder, and earrings, they usually wear one necklace (cat. 9) or no other jewellery (cat. 5. 78. 71. 93). Ingholt had identified the following types of earrings: a series of hoops along the outer shell of the ear, earrings with round beads or pearls attached to horizontal bars, or earrings in the shape of clusters of grapes. In addition to these, some pairs of earrings were in the shape of dumbbells (cat. 9) or the ears could be covered completely by the hair (cat. 5. 8. 94). Women wear a tunic and himation fastened over the shoulder (cat. 71). The tunic can have short sleeves (cat. 71). It is not always possible to understand whether the himation is short or tied at the middle with an overfold (cat. 71).

Reclining men are depicted holding drinking cups. These are often left plain (cat. 71. 94) or have simple decorations consisting of geometric patterns (for example, cat. 70. 74. 75). Seated women are depicted with spindle and distaff (cat. 71. 72) or with no attributes (cat. 93). Standing males are shown with objects associated with drinking, such as a rhyton (cat. 103).

Children also appear in this period. They have short hair (cat. 72). Boys appear wearing either a Parthian-inspired costume with tunic, trousers, and over-trousers (cat. 72), or a tunic that may be fastened at the waist with a belt (cat. 93). The tunic can be long (cat. 93) with short sleeves (cat. 93). They hold the attributes known from other types of funerary monuments: bunches of grapes (cat. 72) or bunches of dates (cat. 93).

---

27 Earrings: Krag 2018. Trapezoidal brooches with keys: Krag 2017a; Krag 2017b; Krag 2018; Thomsen 2021.

What is particular with the rendering of the folds of the costume of both men and women in this period is its plasticity, a certain flowing quality of the curves of the folds. They are still relatively schematic and flat, but they are rendered in a softer, rather than linear, manner, almost as if they were made of dough.

The depiction of the beds and mattresses does not differ greatly from that of the later klinai of the previous group. All the beds have carved legs (cat. 105–107. 115. 118). They can be either left plain (cat. 105–107) or be decorated (cat. 115). The stretcher may have small, rectangular panels with depictions of animals (cat. 105–107. 115), and the fulcrum is decorated (cat. 105–107. 115. 118). The mattress has a curved profile. It is shown as covered by a fabric that has oblique grooves to show the folds and is decorated with two (cat. 105. 106) or three (cat. 107. 115) bands that have rosettes in running scrolls (cat. 105–107) or rosettes in running scrolls and branches with leaves (cat. 115). The cushions on which the reclining men rest are round and decorated with beaded bands (cat. 115), geometric patterns (cat. 105), or rosettes (cat. 105–107).

Group III: A.D. 150–200

In this period, the first temple or house tombs are constructed and sarcophagi can be found in every type of monumental tomb. In total, 178 sarcophagi belong to this group. The first partly carved sarcophagi appear in this period: figures appear either carved only roughly or in outline (cat. 123. 124. 132. 193) or combining detailed carving for the body and rough carving for the face (cat. 131).

Men can appear either reclining or standing. They have short hair that is rendered with multiple locks in rows (cat. 129). Like in the previous and the following periods, men who appear wearing a priestly hat, are shown beardless (cat. 10. 125). Men also appear with beards from this period onwards (cat. 129).

The costume is the same both for reclining and for standing men: either a tunic and himation (cat. 129) or a ›Parthian-inspired‹ costume (cat. 133). The tunic is long-sleeved (cat. 129. 132. 133). The decoration in Parthian-inspired tunics can vary. The tunic can have only a decorated neckline with beaded band (cat. 132) or only a decorated hem (cat. 133). It is tied around the waist with a thin band belt (cat. 133). The trouser legs are decorated with a band along the middle (cat. 133). Reclining men often wear the himation wrapped over the shoulder and the arm resting on the cushion or cushions and around the lower body (cat. 129. 70. 182). In one case, the himation is decorated with a pleated edge (cat. 132). Standing men can be shown wearing the himation in the ›arm-sling‹ type (cat. 129). The chlamys worn by men, including priests, is fastened over the right shoulder with a button-like brooch (cat. 125. 131. 133). Men wear plain, undecorated boots tied at the front (cat. 133).

When the men are shown as priests, the priestly hat may be undecorated (cat. 125) or decorated with a wreath with a central decoration. This may be a medallion with a bust (cat. 10) or a bust alone (cat. 130). Priests can appear dressed in a tunic and himation (cat. 125) or in a tunic and chlamys (cat. 125. 130). The himation can be shown in the ›arm-sling‹ type when they are standing (cat. 125).

Reclining men hold drinking vessels with (cat. 76. 133. 182) or without a foot (cat. 132. 133). When a drinking cup has a foot, it often has handles and the man holds it by one of them (cat. 76. 182) but when it has no foot and no handles, it is usually held with the fingertips (cat. 133). They are also shown carrying a dagger (cat. 133).

Women appear wearing multiple headdresses: a headband, a turban, and a veil. The headband may be undecorated and divided into rectangular panels (cat. 130). The turban is coiled (cat. 125. 130. 131), while the veil is long, sometimes falling to the ground (cat. 125. 129). They have most of their hair covered up by the headdresses. The hair of the figures starts becoming more complex and realistic: often the locks are divided into smaller locks through the use of incised lines. The hair is brushed back over the temples (cat. 125. 129–130). Rarely is their hair centrally parted and shown under the turban (cat. 131).

The female costume still consists of a tunic and a himation. The tunic can have short sleeves (cat. 125), while the himation is fastened over the left shoulder with a brooch. The brooch can be trapezoidal (cat. 129. 130. 182). When the women are depicted on sarcophagi boxes in the form of armless busts, the veil falls over the chest, covering most of the torso (cat. 131. 167). The rendering of the garments in some cases shows that the himation was long and covered the whole body (cat. 125. 182). The folds of clothes of men and women are beginning to be more naturalistic and follow the shape of the body more. They are often widely spaced.

Klinai and mattresses seem to be depicted and decorated in the same way as in the previous period. The beds have carved legs (cat. 33. 108. 109. 115. 118. 125), and the fulcrum may be decorated with a resting animal (cat. 108. 109) or a portrait bust (cat. 115). The mattresses usually have a curved profile (cat. 33. 108. 109. 115), although flat mattresses still appear (cat. 118). They are decorated with bands that carry vegetal or floral motifs, such as scrolls with rosettes (cat. 108. 109. 115. 131) or leaves (cat. 115. 131), or they may have continuous decoration (cat. 79. 193). In a few instances, two mattresses are depicted instead of the usual one: a thick mattress placed directly on the bed, and a thinner one, on which the figures are resting (cat. 118. 129).

Group IV: A.D. 200–240

This is the group with by far the greatest number of sarcophagi: 287 objects have been dated to this period. Only one sarcophagus lid from this period is partly carved (cat. 127), but the survival of several partly carved heads testifies that the practice continued from the previous phase, and had probably even gained in popularity.

The hair of male and female figures can be voluminous (cat. 169. 170. 119. 178. 262–266. 268) with the hair divided into numerous locks or curls (cat. 262–264. 266. 268). The eyebrows are rendered plastically with raised surfaces for the shape and small, oblique grooves for the hair (cat. 262. 264. 266). They may also be depicted by ridges (cat. 263) or grooves (cat. 264). In this period, the eyes are partly carved: the upper eyelids are carved, but the eyeballs may be blank, and the lower eyelid is not depicted (cat. 169–171. 178. 244. 229. 254) or has no inner details (cat. 255. 263. 265). Other examples, however, have surviving traces of polychromy and detailed rendering of the eyes (cat. 119) or have carved irises (cat. 257. 261. 264. 269) or carved irises and pupils indicated by punch holes (cat. 258. 271. 272). In one example, the whole iris is rendered by a hole (cat. 259). Facial hair is also rendered in great detail with multiple incised lines (cat. 262–264. 268).

Standing and reclining men appear in tunic and himation (cat. 168. 240. 234). The tunic can have short sleeves (cat. 168. 178. 240) and be undecorated (cat. 168. 178. 237) or be decorated (>Parthian-style<) (cat. 119. 120. 169. 178. 240). The himation is wrapped around the left shoulder and arm and around the lower body of reclining (cat. 119. 120. 168. 172. 231) and standing men (cat. 169. 240) or around both arms and the lower body of reclining men (cat. 169. 237). Standing men and priests appear wearing the >arm-sling< type of himation (cat. 120. 128. 178), and standing men also appear in tunics only (cat. 74. 237. 241). Rarely does a reclining man appear in tunic alone (cat. 244).

The Parthian-inspired costume remains popular: it consists of a tunic, chlamys, and trousers (cat. 11. 74. 171. 224. 227). The tunic can have multiple decorated bands in different areas: along the neckline, along the middle, cuffs, and along the hem (cat. 11. 74. 89. 178. 233), or on the neckline and along the middle alone (cat. 169. 234), or along the middle and the hem (cat. 224), or on the hem (cat. 227), or along the middle only (cat. 231). The trouser legs are decorated with a band along the centre of each leg (cat. 178. 233). Regardless of whether it is worn under a chlamys or a himation, the tunic is tied around the waist with a thin band belt (cat. 89. 178. 224. 227. 231. 233. 234). The chlamys is fastened over the right shoulder with a circular brooch (cat. 178. 233). Men wear either decorated boots (cat. 119. 232. 249) or plain boots (cat. 74. 128. 178).

Priests appear beardless (cat. 168. 171. 231. 240), while other men may appear either beardless (cat. 169. 170. 178) or with a beard (cat. 119. 171. 177. 178. 244). The priestly hat is decorated with a wreath (cat. 168. 171. 231), with a bust (cat. 168. 171), or a medallion (cat. 178. 231. 255. 257).

Reclining men hold drinking vessels. When they have no foot, they also have no handles and they are held by the fingertips (cat. 74. 119. 120. 169. 170. 178. 231. 233. 234. 244). Drinking cups with a foot have handles, and they are held by them (cat. 89. 170. 171. 178. 227). Standing men may appear with jugs (cat. 74. 224. 231). Reclining men appear with other attributes as well: pinecones (cat. 178. 233) or fruit (cat. 231). Standing men, including priests, may appear with a branch of leaves (cat. 74. 245), a pinecone (cat. 231), or even a small bird (cat. 178). Reclining men are shown carrying a dagger (cat. 178. 227), while standing men can be portrayed with daggers (cat. 224) and swords (cat. 224).

Women are usually shown seated or standing, but reclining women appear also in this period (cat. 225. 236. 243)[28]. They usually wear multiple headdresses: a headband, a turban, and a veil. The headband can be decorated with geometric patterns (cat. 270). The turban is coiled (cat. 171. 178) and the veil is long, sometimes covering most of the body or falling to the ground (cat. 120. 128. 171. 178. 231. 235). There are a few exceptions, however, with women shown with their hair up in the >Faustina-hairstyle< (cat. 178. 247)[29], in a topknot (cat. 271. 273), or with a turban and veil only (cat. 272). Women can wear multiple pieces of jewellery in this period (cat. 171. 225. 231. 232. 235. 242. 246).

The costume of women still consists of a tunic and a himation. The tunic can have long (cat. 11. 74. 169) or short sleeves (cat. 231. 232. 242), while the himation is fastened over the left shoulder with a brooch. The brooch can be circular (cat. 11. 171. 231. 233) or triangular (cat. 169). When women are depicted on sarcophagi boxes in the form of armless busts, the veil falls over the chest, covering most of the torso (cat. 11. 119. 120. 168. 171). The rendering of the garments in some cases shows that the himation was long and covered the whole body (cat. 11. 178. 231. 232). In some cases, they are shown wearing sandals (cat. 231. 232).

Children can appear in a tunic and himation wrapped around the shoulder and lower body in the manner of adult men (cat. 169. 170) or just with a tunic (cat. 172).

---

28 For reclining women, see Raja 2022a.
29 See Krag – Raja 2019 for this hairstyle.

They may be standing (cat. 169. 170) or seated next to the adult figure (cat. 172).

The bed, mattress, and cushions continue to be rendered and decorated as in Group V. There is one example, however, where the mattress is decorated with faces, hinting at greater decorative variety in this period (cat. 233).

The folds of the garments continue to be more natural and follow the shape of the body, but the grooves used for carving them are deeper, creating the impression of depth. The play of light and shadow thus gives a stronger impression of three-dimensionality in the portraits of this period. Clothes become more elaborately decorated, especially the Parthian-inspired garments.

Group V: A.D. 240–273

The last group has the shortest span of the five; yet, a relatively high number of sarcophagi for its duration have been assigned to it: seventy-eight sarcophagi, compared to eighty-three in Group II, which has a relatively similar chronological span (A.D. 100–150).

The hair of the figures of this period can be characterized as voluminous (cat. 275–277). The eyebrows are rendered plastically with raised surfaces for the shape and small, oblique grooves for the hair (cat. 275–277). The eyes can be left blank (cat. 179). The facial hair is also rendered with great detail (cat. 275–277). In addition to the Palmyrene priestly hat, there are a few examples of men wearing a type of diadem decorated with a bust (cat. 275. 277) or decorated with a medallion (cat. 276). Priestly hats can be undecorated (cat. 90) or decorated (cat. 90) with a wreath with a bust (cat. 90).

The costume choices remain the tunic and himation or the ›Parthian-style‹ costume. Reclining men, including priests, are shown with ›Parthian-style‹ costume: tunic, chlamys, and trousers (cat. 90). These may be combined with the himation, as is the case with one reclining priest shown wearing a tunic and himation (cat. 90), with his himation wrapped around the whole body (cat. 90). Another reclining man is depicted wearing a ›Parthian-style‹ tunic and trousers together with a himation (cat. 228). The tunic is decorated on the neckline, the centre, and the cuffs (cat. 228). His himation is wrapped over the left shoulder and arm and the lower body (cat. 228). In other cases, the tunic may be decorated on the neckline, the centre, the cuffs, and the hem (cat. 179), while the trousers are decorated along the centre with a band (cat. 179). The tunic can be tied with a thin band belt (cat. 12. 179). Standing priests are depicted with a tunic and himation. The tunic can have long sleeves, and the himation is worn wrapped around the left arm and lower body (cat. 90), or it can be wrapped in the ›arm-sling‹ type (cat. 90). Men, including priests, are shown with the chlamys fastened over the right shoulder with a circular brooch (cat. 90. 179). The men can be shown wearing plain boots (cat. 90. 179) or decorated boots (cat. 228).

The attributes of reclining men, including priests, continue to be the drinking vessels and the dagger. As in the previous periods, the drinking cup with foot and handles is held by the handles (cat. 90. 228), while the footless drinking cup is held with the fingertips (cat. 90. 179). A reclining man, most likely one who had served as priest[30], is shown with a dagger (cat. 179). A standing male with a ›Parthian-style‹ costume (cat. 179) is shown carrying a priestly hat (cat. 179).

Women wear several headdresses, as in the previous periods, and the same clothes. The veil can be long and falling to the ground (cat. 90), and the women can be depicted wearing multiple pieces of jewellery (cat. 179). The costume of choice is the tunic and the himation. The tunic can have short sleeves (cat. 179), while the himation may be long, fastened over the left shoulder and covering the body (cat. 90. 228). When the women are depicted on sarcophagi boxes in the form of armless busts, the veil falls over the chest, covering most of the torso (cat. 90). The trend for natural-looking garments and elaborate jewels known from the previous period continues.

The beds and mattresses are shown as in the previous groups. In addition to sarcophagus boxes with busts, boxes with trading or caravan scenes (cat. 179. 274) or standing figures (cat. 238. 239) also appear in this period. These new iconographic motifs are characteristic of this group. Even though objects in this group do not have particularly distinct features, as for example, the partly carved facial features that appear in A.D. 150–200, what characterizes objects in this group is the richness of decoration and the high degree of elaborateness in all the parts.

Other Sarcophagi

In addition to these 651 sarcophagi that can be dated neatly within one of the above-discussed groups, there are another 129 sarcophagi whose date cannot be assigned to one group so easily. Most of these objects are badly preserved, and so it is not possible to distinguish stylistic features to the degree that would allow for a more precise dating. A total of ninety-six objects have ranges that are as broad as 123 years (cat. 672 dated between A.D. 150–273). Nine are dated between A.D. 100–200, eight are dated between A.D. 180–240, and sixty-six have been broadly dated to the period A.D. 200–273. Even more broadly dated are eleven objects: (1) appendix 3, cat. 2, dated between A.D. 33–170; (2) cat. 20–21. 525.

---

30 For men with a priestly hat on the side, see Raja 2017h.

Figure 30. Stele with depiction of god Šadrafâ, limestone. From Palmyra, A.D. 55.

Figure 31. Fragment of loculus relief depicting a female, limestone. From Palmyra, A.D. 65/66.

Figure 32. Loculus relief with female portrait bust, limestone. From Palmyra, A.D. 113/114.

Figure 33. Loculus relief with male portrait bust, limestone. From Palmyra, A.D. 133/134.

594. 659 dated between A.D. 50–150; (3) appendix 5, cat. 1 and appendix 6, cat. 6 dated between A.D. 75–150; (4) cat. 44 dated between A.D. 140–200; (5) cat. 192 dated between A.D. 150–225; and (6) cat. 653. 662 dated between A.D. 175–225. The other thirty-three sarcophagi have dates that fall between two groups. This may be because the object is not well preserved, and so it is not possible to assign it to a specific group (for example, cat. 50. 51, dated between A.D. 135–170), or because they have characteristics of two groups (for example, cat. 118 is dated between A.D. 140–160 because the garments worn by the figures combine sharply rendered and naturalistic folds).

Comparison with Palmyrene Dated Pieces outside the Sarcophagi Corpus

The comparison with the pieces not belonging to the sarcophagi corpus of Palmyra in the list of 104 securely dated objects shows that similar features can be seen in Palmyrene sculpture more broadly[31]. The earliest known Palmyrene object, a votive relief from the Sanctuary of Allat from A.D. 21/22[32], shows the same flat and linear treatment of the folds seen later in the foundation relief from the tower of Kîtôt (cat. 1). A votive to the god Shadrafa, dated to A.D. 55[33], also shows similar treatment of the garments. In addition, the god is depicted wearing his chlamys fastened over the left shoulder with a circular brooch like the Palmyrene men in reliefs and sarcophagi (Fig. 30). The fragment of a slightly later loculus relief from A.D. 65/66, now at the Ny Carlsberg Glyptotek, shows a woman with a plain headband, a coiled turban, and a heavy veil, with eyes that are too large in proportion to the face, and wearing a series of hoop earrings (Fig. 31, Pl. 19)[34]. The features and plain garments can be compared with those of women on sarcophagi in the period A.D. 1–100. This is also the case with a loculus relief at the Ny Carlsberg Glyptotek from A.D. 96 that shows a female bust[35].

Objects dating between A.D. 100–150 show similar treatment of the figures as observed in the sarcophagi pieces of this period. The tunic and himation are the most popular costume choice for men and women. Men usually wear the himation in the arm-sling type.

The folds are still mostly linear and widely spaced, the men are beardless, and the hair is still not shown in great detail. Priestly hats are decorated with wreaths, but they can also appear plain and undecorated. The eyes continue to be relatively large in proportion to the face, and the garments, especially of the women, are not highly decorated (Figs. 32–33, Pl. 20). Children are shown with grapes and dressed in tunics[36].

The next phase is A.D. 150–200. The non-sarcophagi pieces from this period show greater naturalism in the facial features (for example, the eyes are proportionate to the face), and the folds follow the shape of the body. Tunic and himation remain popular costumes for men and women, while children appear in tunics. Men usually wear the himation in the arm-sling type. Men appear sporting a beard. Priestly hats continue to be decorated with a wreath. Women may appear with more jewellery: bracelets in addition to earrings and brooches. Their headbands are also often decorated in this period (Figs. 34–35, Pl. 21)[37].

---

31 See Raja et al. 2021c for an overview of these features according to the sculptural phases.
32 Palmyra, Palmyra Museum, inv. no. CD 11/77: Gawlikowski 2017, 214. 245 f.
33 London, British Museum, inv. no. 125206: Ingholt 1928, PS 1.
34 Copenhagen, Ny Carlsberg Glyptotek, inv. no. IN 2816: Raja 2019a, 66 f. cat. 1, with previous bibliography.
35 Copenhagen, Ny Carlsberg Glyptotek, inv. no. IN 1057: Raja 2019a, 68 f. cat. 2, with previous bibliography.
36 Compare with relief in the hypogeum of Bôlḥâ: Sadurska – Bounni 1994, 75 cat. 98 fig. 21 (A.D. 103/104); London, British Museum, inv. no. 125695: Krag 2018, cat. 89 (A.D. 113/114); Copenhagen, Ny Carlsberg Glyptotek, inv. no. IN 1079: Raja 2019a, 70 f. cat. 3, with previous bibliography (A.D. 113/114); St Petersburg, State Hermitage Museum, inv. no. ДВ-4177: Ingholt 1928, 20–22 PS 2 (A.D. 114); Toronto, Royal Ontario Museum, inv. no. 953.94.1: Krag 2018, cat. 90, with previous bibliography (A.D. 123); Copenhagen, Ny Carlsberg Glyptotek, inv. no. IN 1155: Raja 2019a, 72 f. cat. 4, with previous bibliography (A.D. 125/126); Beirut, Musée National de Beyrouth, unknown inv. no.: Krag 2018, cat. 216, with previous bibliography (A.D. 130); Copenhagen, Ny Carlsberg Glyptotek, inv. no. IN 1049: Raja 2019a, 74 f. cat. 5, with previous bibliography (A.D. 133/134); unknown collection in Damascus: Ingholt 1928, 28 PS 5 (A.D. 133/134); Beirut, American University Museum, inv. no. 2740: Krag 2018, cat. 92 (A.D. 134/135); Palmyra, Palmyra Museum, inv. no. B 2687/9088: Yon 2012, cat. 524 (A.D. 138); Beirut, Robert Mouawad Private Museum, inv. no. 0149: Forge 2004, 88 cat. 31 (A.D. 138); Brussels, Musée Art & Histoire, inv. no. A 1620: Ingholt 1928, 28 f. PS 6 (A.D. 138/139); St. Louis, Saint Louis Art Museum, inv. no. 24:1960: Ingholt 1928, 29–31 PS 7; Rome, Musei Vaticani, inv. no. VII 61/ MV 15029: Krag et al. 2019, cat. 13 (A.D. 145); New York, Metropolitan Museum of Art, inv. no. 02.29.3: Fowlkes-Childs – Seymour 2019, 166–168 cat. 113 (A.D. 146); Copenhagen, Ny Carlsberg Glyptotek, inv. no. IN 2794: Raja 2019a, 80 f. cat. 7 (A.D. 149).
37 Compare with loculus reliefs at: Beirut, Syriac Catholic Patriarchate, unknown inv. no.: Krag 2018, cat. 302 (A.D. 150); Beirut, American University Museum, inv. no. 2739: Krag 2018, cat. 15 (A.D. 150); Beirut, American University Museum, inv. no. 2739: Krag 2018, cat. 306 (A.D. 151); Beirut, Robert Mouawad Private Museum, inv. no. 0101: Forge 2004, 90 cat. 32 (A.D. 151); Damascus, National Museum of Damascus, inv. no. 2842: Teixidor 2001, 268 cat. 160 (A.D. 154); St. Petersburg, State Hermitage Museum, inv. no. ДВ-8841: Raja 2019g, 69 f. cat. 35 (A.D. 154/155); unknown collection: Ingholt 1934, 42 f. cat. 6 pl. 10.2 (A.D. 154/155); Paris, Musée du Louvre, inv. no. AO 2201: Dentzer-Feydy – Teixidor 1993, 185 cat. 186 (A.D. 155).

90 CHAPTER 3

Figure 34. Loculus relief with female portrait bust, limestone. From Palmyra, A.D. 150.

Figure 35. Loculus relief with male bust, limestone. From Palmyra, A.D. 154/155.

Figure 36. Loculus relief with male and female bust, limestone. From Palmyra, A.D. 218/219.

Figure 37. Loculus relief with bust of female holding a child, limestone. From Palmyra, A.D. 240/241.

In the period between A.D. 200 and A.D. 240, clothes and facial features continue to be rendered in a more naturalistic manner. Tunic and himation remain popular costume choices for men and women. The men wear their himation in the ›arm-sling‹ type. Men appear both with and without beards. Their hair and facial hair are treated with greater detail. There is greater variation in the jewellery options and decoration for women: some appear with the minimum amount of jewellery and headbands with simple, geometric decorations, while others wear bracelets or rings, and their headbands are richly decorated (Fig. 36)[38].

In the last phase, between A.D. 240 and A.D. 273, there is continuity of motifs from the previous phase. Perhaps the most obvious change is the increased plasticity and detail in the modelling of the facial features and the greater naturalism of the folds. Men and women still appear dressed in tunic and himation, and the ›arm-sling‹ type remains a popular choice for men. Women may appear wearing multiple pieces of jewellery (Fig. 37)[39].

Conclusion

The survey of the securely dated sarcophagi pieces shows that there are certain features that appear in all the periods. The banqueting motif is one that first appears in A.D. 41 and continues to be used until A.D. 273. This is the primary motif used on sarcophagi, with only a few exceptions. Other iconographic elements that are in use throughout the period are the use of tunic and himation for men and women, as well as a Parthian-inspired costume for men. Women are shown with multiple headdresses, and they always wear jewellery. When women wear the himation, the brooch is always placed over the left shoulder, while men wearing a chlamys always wear their brooch over the right shoulder. Beds, cushions, and mattresses are shown in the same way throughout the period. In the last two phases, however, one sees some distinct features: reclining women, partly carved eyes, and boxes showing figural scenes and not just busts[40].

Thus, uniformity and adherence to tradition seem to characterize Palmyrene sculpture; yet, there are two major trends that show how even when the motifs were traditional, the sculpture itself changed. First of all, a general trend from linearity and flat treatment of surfaces to greater naturalism and plasticity can be observed. This is particularly obvious in the rendering of hair, facial features, and the folds of the garments. Second, a move from simplicity to greater elaboration and love of details in all the components of the sculptural composition is clear (hair, facial features, clothes, attributes) (compare cat. 1. 19. 60. 125. 178. 232. 275). These changes took place gradually, resulting in several sarcophagi having features that can be categorized into more than one chronological group, as mentioned above.

In addition to those two trends, it is possible to trace changes in the way that men and women were depicted. In the first two phases (A.D. 1–150), both men and women have large eyes with thick upper and lower eyelids, and their pupils and irises are rendered by concentric circles. Men are always shown beardless. In the first group (A.D. 1–100), men who are shown as priests have an undecorated priestly hat, while in the second group (A.D. 100–150), the priestly hat is decorated with a wreath with a central ornament. The Parthian-inspired costume becomes more popular from A.D. 100 onwards. For women, the trapezoidal brooch is popular for both groups. Women have their hair almost completely covered, with one lock falling on the shoulder in the period A.D. 1–100, and two locks in the period A.D. 100–150. The women of the first group also wear few pieces of jewellery: earrings in the shape of clusters of grapes or a series of small hoops. In the second group, women are shown with a greater variety in the types of earrings: in addition to the earrings worn by women of the first group, they wear earrings with suspended round beads, or in the shape of dumbbells. They can also be shown with a necklace in the second group. Children also appear for the first time on sarcophagi during the period A.D. 100–150.

From the period A.D. 150–200 onwards, men also appear sporting a beard. When they are depicted as priests, their priestly hat can be either undecorated or decorated with a wreath with various central ornaments. Women have their hair mostly covered, with only locks of hair shown brushed back behind the temples. In the last two periods (A.D. 200–273), men and women are

---

38 Loculus relief once in Baron Poche's collection: Ingholt 1928, 40 f. PS 20 (A.D. 201/202); Gołuchów, Gołuchów Castle Museum, unknown inv. no.: Sadurska 1972, 57 f. cat. 59 pl. 46 (A.D. 204); Charlottesville, the Fralin Museum of Art at the University of Virginia, inv. no. 2001.16.2: Krag 2018, cat. 25 (A.D. 211); Warsaw, Muzeum Narodowe w Warszawie, inv. no. 199576: Krag 2018, cat. 579 (A.D. 211); Baalbek, Baalbek Museum, unknown inv. no.: Krag 2018, cat. 580 (A.D. 215).

39 Compare with loculus reliefs at: Berlin, Vorderasiatisches Museum, inv. no. VA 16754: Ingholt 1928, 48 f. PS 25 (A.D. 240/241); private collection of Henri Marcopoli: Ingholt 1928, 49 f. PS 26 (A.D. 241/242); Oslo, Kulturhistorisk museum, Universitetet i Oslo, inv. no. C42231: Ingholt 1928, 50 PS 27 (A.D. 243/244); Oslo, Kulturhistorisk museum, Universitetet i Oslo, inv. no. C42237: Ingholt 1928, 86 f. PS 53 (A.D. 240/241); Washington, DC, Freer Gallery of Art, inv. no. F1908.236: Ingholt 1928, 87–89 PS 54 (A.D. 241/242).

40 These will be discussed in detail in the chapter on iconography.

shown with voluminous hair, while their eyes can be partly carved, or have carved irises and pupils indicated by punch holes. Hair, both for men and women, and beards are rendered in detail. Women also appear with their hair uncovered, usually worn in the ›Faustina-hairstyle‹ or a topknot, and they wear multiple pieces of jewellery. Men of the last group (A.D. 240–273) are sometimes shown wearing a type of diadem.

Other changes that can be observed are of a more technical nature. Already mentioned is the change from incised grooves for depicting pupils and irises to pupils indicated by punch holes in the 3rd cent. A.D. From A.D. 150–200 onwards, the appearance of partly carved sarcophagi can also be observed, and can range from sarcophagi where most of the monument is partly carved to sarcophagi where only the faces or details are left partly carved. The lack of finished portraits in sarcophagi from other areas of the Roman world has given rise to several theories[41], but with only five partly carved lids (cat. 123. 124. 127. 132. 193) and several detached heads surviving, it is not certain whether any of the theories proposed for other Roman-period sarcophagi can be applied to the Palmyrene material. What may be of interest, however, is that partly carved sarcophagi appear at Palmyra in the same period as in the rest of the Roman world, again highlighting the connections between the city and the empire[42].

Another change is in the total number of sarcophagi that gradually increases from the middle of the 2nd cent. onwards. Sarcophagi never replaced loculus burials, but their growing popularity shows that they were becoming a favourite alternative among Palmyra's wealthier strata. They allowed for a family to be depicted together, and its members immediately associated with each other, in contrast to loculus reliefs that depicted usually one, rarely two or more individuals at the same time, and whose relationships are not always clear to scholars now[43]. At the same time, the deliberate choices of costume, posture, and attributes created the impression of similarity or diversity, thus hinting at customer desires and wishes now lost to us (compare cat. 92. 178).

---

41 For these, see recently Birk 2013, 55–58; Russell 2013, 303–308; Birk 2014; Huskinson 2015, 56 f.; Platt 2017, 356 f.

42 The sarcophagi with ›unfinished‹ or ›blank‹ portraits, as they are often described, appear in the later 2nd cent. A.D.: Russell 2013, 304.

43 See Krag 2019 for the difficulties in establishing genealogies of particular families.

CHAPTER 4

In situ Contexts

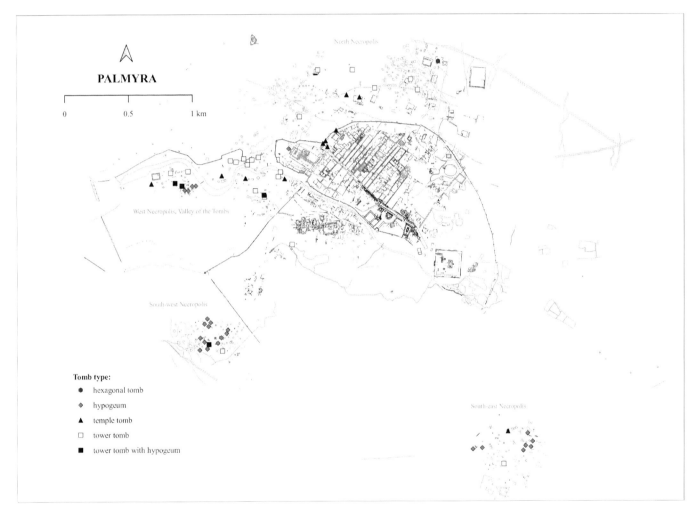

Figure 38. Distribution map of the tombs with sarcophagi according to type of tomb.

Just as securely dated objects are of primary importance to archaeologists, so are objects with a provenance, since they can give answers to questions of function, use, and significance. In order to better understand how Palmyrene sarcophagi were used, it is important to examine their placement in tombs. In this chapter, the various funerary sculptures and paintings of each tomb are presented, in order to place the sarcophagi within the context of each tomb, and to explore the relation between sarcophagi and the other forms of funerary commemoration.

Out of the 473 documented tombs in Palmyra[1], only seventy-one tombs are known to have contained sarcophagi (Fig. 38, Pl. 22). This is not surprising, considering the history of research in Palmyra and the

---

1 After Schnädelbach 2010.

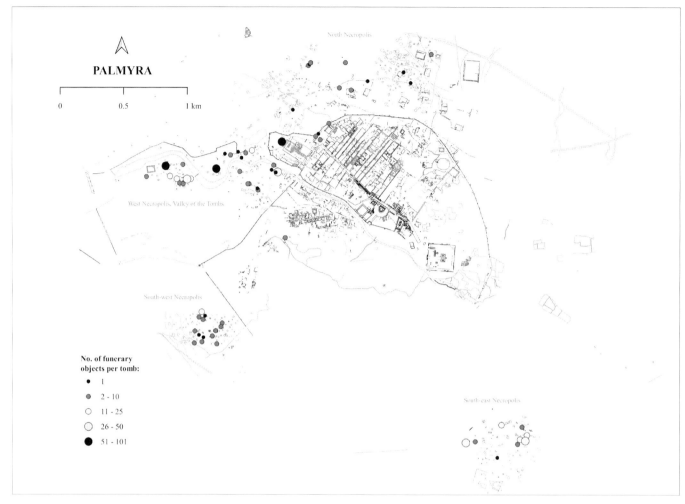

Figure 39. Distribution map of the tombs with sarcophagi and other funerary sculptures.

state of preservation of the tombs. Tower and temple tombs were visible, and so they provided people living in Palmyra with ready-made building materials from the early 4th cent. onwards[2]. All types of tombs were also susceptible to looting before the introduction of laws protecting Syrian antiquities in the late 19th cent.[3] and despite them afterwards[4]. Furthermore, the material from which the reliefs were carved is a type of soft limestone[5], while sarcophagi boxes were also constructed of plaster, and so are prone to weathering and deterioration. These factors have led to the poor preservation of tombs and their assemblages; already in 1902 and 1917, when Watzinger and Wulzinger surveyed the tombs, they had documented several in poor state of preservation, in some cases with only their foundations remaining[6].

The evidence shows that sarcophagi were used in all the types of elite Palmyrene tombs: they were found in seventeen tower tombs, thirty-one hypogea, thirteen temple tombs, and one of unusual shape (the hexagonal tomb). The total number of tower tombs and hypogea with sarcophagi is close, however, the total number of sarcophagi or fragments thereof that were found in the respective tomb types, shows that

---

2 Intagliata 2018, 31.
3 See Al Khabour 2018, 1–3 for Ottoman laws regarding Syrian antiquities.
4 Ingholt documents the presence of holes in the underground tombs he excavated through which looters entered the monuments: for example, see Ingholt 1935, 108.
5 See Abdul Massih 2021 for the types of limestone quarried in Palmyra. For the quarries of Palmyra, see also Schmidt-Colinet 1990; Schmidt-Colinet 1995; Schmidt-Colinet 2005; Schmidt-Colinet 2017; Steding 2022, 39 f.

6 Watzinger – Wulzinger 1932, nos. 8. 9a. 9b. 13a. 26. 34a. 35a. 38b. 41a. 43a. 71b. 71c. 72. 74. 78. 84. 84a. 85. 92. 94. 98a. 104. 115. 115a. 116. 116a. 120. 124–126a. 127. 129. 129a. 136. 138. 139. 142. 148a. 149d. 151–154a. 155a. 157. 158. 163. 165. 180. 183. 188a. 189. 190. 193. 196. 198. 199.

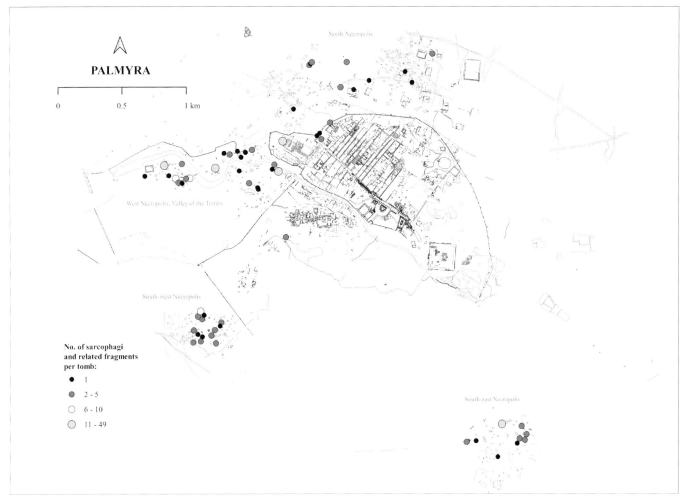

Figure 40. Distribution map of the tombs with documented sarcophagi.

sarcophagi were not as common in tower tombs as they were in hypogea, and that temple tombs also had a high number of sarcophagi: seventy-two sarcophagi in various states of preservation were found in tower tombs (cat. 1–4. 13–59. appendix 1, cat. 1. appendix 2, cat. 1. 2. appendix 5, cat. 1–3. appendix 6, cat. 4–6. 8–12. 14–19) in contrast to 128 from hypogea (cat. 10–12. 60–178. appendix 5, cat. 8. appendix 6, cat. 1–3. 13. 20), and 106 from temple tombs (cat. 180–274, appendix 5, cat. 4–7. appendix 6, cat. 7. 21–23. 28). Three large heads were found in the hexagonal tomb, suggesting the presence of a sarcophagus (cat. 275–277).

Out of 786 known sarcophagi and banqueting reliefs[7], only 274 have a known context (cat. 1–4. 6. 10–277. appendix 1, cat. 1. appendix 2, cat. 1. 2) while another eleven (cat. 278–288) were found close to tombs and could have been placed there originally. Another thirty-two sarcophagi without portraits (appendix 5, cat. 1–8) or that have not been illustrated in publications (appendix 6, cat. 1–23. 28) also have a known and secure provenance (Figs. 39 and 40, Pl. 23). This means that only 39.1% of all the objects in the catalogue has a context. Four of the objects with a provenance are founder reliefs. They are dated to A.D. 40 (cat. 1), A.D. 73 (cat. 2), A.D. 83 (appendix 1, cat. 1), and A.D. 103 (cat. 3), and they all come from tower tombs. The early dates of the reliefs are connected to their placement on those funerary monuments that were more prevalent in the 1st cent. A.D. and the first half of the 2nd cent. A.D. Underscoring the paucity of the founder reliefs is the low number of foundation inscriptions known: only fourteen inscriptions can be

---

7 This number represents all the fragments and full sarcophagi known so far, including those without figural representation, and documented in the catalogue.

connected securely with a funerary monument out of 165 known tower tombs[8].

The other reliefs and sarcophagi proper were found inside the tombs. Most of these objects are sarcophagus lids or fragments showing banqueting scenes: 110 in total, which include eighteen from tower tombs, forty-four from hypogea, and forty-eight from temple tombs. Thirty-eight are sarcophagus boxes or fragments thereof: nine from tower tombs, ten from hypogea, and nineteen from temple tombs. It is not surprising that there are more lids compared to boxes, since boxes could be made of plaster, as was the case in several tower tombs, or the burials could take place in built spaces, like benches, as was the case in temple tombs. The others are fragments that could have belonged either to lids or boxes or banqueting reliefs, among which there are seventy-two heads, eighty-three fragments that could have belonged either to sarcophagus lids, lid reliefs, or banqueting reliefs, and six sarcophagus fragments. A special category is that of reliefs depicting a sarcophagus that were placed on walls without covering burials, such as cat. 33.

Sarcophagi were sometimes placed on their own, in separate rooms within the tomb, for example, the sarcophagi from the tomb N206 (cat. 4. appendix 5, cat. 2. 3), but in most cases, they were in the same areas as loculus burials covered with plaques in the form of stelai or reliefs, and painted decoration on the walls. Furthermore, they were usually placed in groups of three, their arrangement replicating that of the triclinium. The arrangement of a single sarcophagus in a room was rare: out of the 786 sarcophagi and fragments thereof in the catalogue, only forty-five (cat. 21. 22. 52–59. 70–72. 74. 76. 80. 103. 116. 117. 118. 167. 173. 177. 179. 191. 192. 222–227. 274. appendix 5, cat. 8. appendix 6, cat. 4–12. 19) were found alone in the rooms or tombs in which they were placed.

The following section offers a brief survey of the information relating to the tombs where sarcophagi were found, including mentions of the other sculptural or painted decoration in them.

Late 1st cent. B.C. / Early 1st cent. A.D.: Tower Tomb no. 19

Tower tomb no. 19 is located in the west necropolis. It had been recorded by Carl Watzinger and Karl Wulzinger during their campaign of 1917[9], and was further explored by Kazimierz Michalowski in 1961, who identified it as a tower tomb with a hypogeum, surviving to the height of two floors[10]. Without a foundation inscription, the date of the tomb is based on building technique and stylistic criteria to the late 1st cent. B.C. or the early 1st cent. A.D.[11]. The tomb was in use until the middle of the 2nd cent. A.D.[12]. The tower tomb has a chamber with a loculus burial on the ground floor and loculus burials on the upper floors[13]. The hypogeum is accessible through a separate entrance[14] that was covered by a vault decorated with painted coffers with busts and stars[15]. Its plan consists of a long corridor with four galleries facing each other, two to the north and two to the south. The loculus bays were dug between the galleries[16].

Several fragments of sculpture were found in the tomb that have been assigned to either banqueting or sarcophagus reliefs because of their size (cat. 13–18). Cat. 13 was found at the threshold of the tower tomb, and cat. 14–18 were found in the hypogeum. In addition to cat. 13–18, several pieces of sculpture were found in the tomb: from the entrance and the area of the ground floor of the tower tomb come a lion's head[17], the fragment of a garment[18], and the fragment of an inscription[19]. On the steps leading up from the ground floor to the upper floors, Michalowski's team found two fragments of loculus reliefs[20]. A male head and small fragments of statues depicting different human

---

8   The number of tower tombs is based on Schnädelbach 2010. The known foundation inscriptions are: (1) tower tomb 7: Gawlikowski 1970a, 184 cat. 1; (2) tower tomb 67: Gawlikowski 1970a, 185 cat. 5; (3) tower tomb 44: Gawlikowski 1970a, 185 cat. 6 (with foundation relief, cat. 1); (4) tower tomb 194: Gawlikowski 1970a, 187 cat. 13 (with foundation relief, cat. 3); (5) tower tomb 63: Gawlikowski 1970a, 188 cat. 14; (6) tower tomb 155: Gawlikowski 1970a, 188 cat. 15; (7) tower tomb 51: Gawlikowski 1970a, 188 f. cat. 17 (with foundation relief, cat. app. 1. cat. 1); (8) tower tomb 68: Gawlikowski 1970a, 189 cat. 18; (9) tower tomb 169: Gawlikowski 1970a, 189 f. cat. 20; (10) tower tomb 13: Gawlikowski 1970a, 191 cat. 28; (11) tower tomb 164: Gawlikowski 1970a, 193 cat. 36; (12) tower tomb 34: Gawlikowski 1970a, 194 cat. 41 (with foundation relief, cat. 2); (13) tower tomb 145: Gawlikowski 1970a, 203 cat. 73; (14) tower tomb 118: Gawlikowski 1970a, 203 cat. 74.

9   Watzinger – Wulzinger 1932, 49.
10 Michalowski 1963, 197–250.
11 Michalowski 1963, 204–208; Henning 2013b, 162.
12 Michalowski 1963, 207.
13 Henning 2013b, 161.
14 Michalowski 1963, 197.
15 Michalowski 1963, 198.
16 Henning 2013b, 161.
17 Palmyra, Palmyra Museum, inv. no. T 22.19: Michalowski 1963, 201. 224 fig. 264.
18 Palmyra, Palmyra Museum, inv. no. T 33.19: Michalowski 1963, 201. 226 cat. 22 fig. 266.
19 Palmyra, Palmyra Museum, inv. no. T 25.19: Michalowski 1963, 201. 247 cat. 20 fig. 282.
20 Palmyra, Palmyra Museum, inv. no. T 34.19: Michalowski 1963, 202. 225 cat. 20 fig. 265 and Palmyra, Palmyra Museum, inv. no. T 39.19: Michalowski 1963, 202. 225 f. cat. 21 fig. 266.

and animal figures were found in the hypogeum of the tomb[21]. The extremely fragmentary state of preservation and the find locations led Michalowski to suggest that the fragments on the ground floor probably came from reliefs originally located in the upper floors of the tomb[22].

Late 1st cent. B.C. / Early 1st cent. A.D.: Tower Tomb no. 15

Tower tomb no. 15 is located near tower tomb no. 19 in the west necropolis. It is a tower tomb with a hypogeum with a separate entrance. Like tower tomb no. 19, it had been recorded by Watzinger and Wulzinger[23], and investigated further by Michalowski in 1962[24]. Its construction is dated to the end of the 1st cent. B.C. and the beginning of the 1st cent. A.D. based on technical and stylistic reasons in the absence of a foundation inscription[25]. The ground floor of the tower has a loculus burial to the north and a chamber to the south that is partly covered by a vault and where the remains of a plaster sarcophagus were found[26]. The upper floors are accessible via staircases and contained loculus burials. The hypogeum has a long corridor with two galleries near the entrance, one to the north and one to the south, two small exedrae to the north and south near the middle of the corridor, and one at its end. The loculus bays were dug into the sides of the galleries and of the corridor[27]. Together with cat. 20, another male head, possibly from a statue, was found under the tower tomb's threshold[28]. From the rubble of the tower come seven fragments[29], and from the hypogeum five fragments of pieces of sculpture[30], mainly showing hands or parts of garments of figures.

A.D. 33: Tower tomb no. 67, Tower of Ḥaîran

The tomb of Ḥaîran is situated in the west necropolis. It survives to a height of eleven metres and has five floors[31]. The tomb was documented by Watzinger and Wulzinger[32]. Its foundation inscription survives and records the date of the construction of the tomb in A.D. 33[33]. The façade was decorated with reliefs showing masks[34]. The first three floors of the tower tomb had chambers with loculus burials, while in the upper two floors the burial bays were built into the structure[35]. The hypogeum has a long corridor with five loculus bays on either side[36]. Cat. 19 was found in the hypogeum. No other reliefs or pieces of sculptural decoration were found inside the tomb. One of the loculus bays (»W III 5«) was decorated with painted garlands. A graffito on the same wall gives the date A.D. 129/130, indicating that the tomb was in use at least until the early 2nd cent. A.D.[37].

A.D. 35–70: Tower Tomb no. 46

Tomb no. 46 is located in the west necropolis, and only three floors survive. It was recorded by Watzinger and Wulzinger[38]. In the absence of a foundation inscription, the date of the construction is based on technical considerations and is placed between A.D. 35–70[39]. The ground floor has two chambers with two sarcophagi (cat. 50. 51) and loculus bays, while the upper floors only have loculus bays[40]. In addition to the two limestone sarcophagi in the ground-floor rooms, Henning recorded two more plaster sarcophagi on the second floor[41]. The two ground floor sarcophagi were placed in front of the lower sections of the loculus bays at the west of the chamber, and so Henning suggests that they were not contemporary with the construction and first phases of the tomb, but rather reflect later use[42]. In addition to these, the following pieces of sculpture come from the tomb: (1) a miniature altar; (2–3) two fragments of two different, inscribed loculus reliefs; (4) a loculus relief with a female portrait; (5) a sarcophagus fragment (app. 2, cat. 3); and (6–7) two male heads[43].

---

21 Male head: Palmyra, Palmyra Museum, inv. no. T 4.19: Michalowski 1963, 210 f. cat. 2 figs. 249–250; small fragments of funerary statues: Michalowski 1963, 217–221 cat. 8–15; fragments of animals: Michalowski 1963, 222–224 cat. 16–19.
22 Michalowski 1963, 207.
23 Watzinger – Wulzinger 1932, 49.
24 Michalowski 1964, 147–199.
25 Henning 2013b, 157.
26 Michalowski 1964, 150; Henning 2013b, 156.
27 Michalowski 1964, 154–157; Henning 2013b, 157.
28 Michalowski 1964, 159 f. cat. 1 fig. 189.
29 Michalowski 1964, 163 cat. 5; 165–169 cat. 8–10. 12–14.
30 Michalowski 1964, 161–168 cat. 3. 4. 6. 7. 11.
31 Henning 2013b, 207.
32 Watzinger – Wulzinger 1932, 56 f.; Henning 2013b, 207.
33 Henning 2013b, 207.
34 Henning 2013b, 207–209.
35 Henning 2013b, 208.
36 Henning 2013b, 208.
37 Henning 2013b, 208.
38 Watzinger – Wulzinger 1932, 53.
39 Henning 2013b, 188 f.
40 Henning 2013b, 188.
41 Henning 2013b, 188; Pfister 1940, 8 records only one.
42 Henning 2013b, 189.
43 Pfister 1940, 7–8; Henning 2013b, 189.

A.D. 41: Tower Tomb no. 44, Tower of Kîtôt

The tower tomb of Kîtôt was located in the west necropolis of Palmyra and was built on a slope of the wadi. It had survived in a good condition from the time of its construction to its destruction in 2015 by ISIL, preserved to a height of eighteen metres[44]. As such, the tomb was well known to travellers and scholars, documented in drawings by Cassas, and the inscription of the relief was first published in 1868 by Vogüe (cat. 1). Its first study, however, was undertaken by Watzinger and Wulzinger in April 1917[45]. Will, who published the first systematic study of the Palmyrene tower tombs[46], suggested that the tomb was representative of type B of his classification: tomb with loculi on the interior and a turning staircase[47]. Each floor had a chamber with rows of loculi, although the number of loculi was different from chamber to chamber[48]. The inner arrangement of the chambers is further described by Henning. In the upper floors, between five and nine sarcophagi built of plaster were to be found[49]. No lids can be associated with the remains of the sarcophagi from the upper chambers. The loculus reliefs were closed with stone plaques and plaster[50].

A.D. 70–100: Tower Tomb no. 41a

Tower tomb no. 41a is located in the west necropolis, and only one floor survives. The foundation inscription is not preserved, and so the building is dated to the period A.D. 70–100 based on technical observations. The tomb had a chamber on the ground floor[51]. Only the sarcophagus cat. 53 is known from this tomb, and its precise location within it is uncertain: it could have been placed either against a long wall of the ground-floor chamber or been built into the end wall of the same chamber[52].

A.D. 73: Tower Tomb no. 194, Tower of 'Ogeîlû

The tower tomb of 'Ogeîlû is located in the south-east necropolis of Palmyra. Only the ground floor survives. Burials took place in loculus niches[53]. Despite the destruction of the upper floors, the relief with the reclining founder and his family survived (cat. 2) and was placed by the left side of the tomb[54]. No other remains of sculptural or painted decoration were found in the tomb.

A.D. 83: Tower Tomb no. 51, Tower of Yamlikû

Tomb no. 51 was located in the west necropolis, Valley of the Tombs. It was the tallest of the tower tombs with five floors surviving to a height of twenty-eight metres[55]. The tomb was destroyed in 2015[56]. This was another tomb documented by early travellers. The foundation inscription gives the date of its construction in A.D. 83, and the drawing of Cassas shows that a relief with a banqueting scene had been placed above it (app. 1, cat. 1). Even though Cassas could be an unreliable witness, this drawing has been accepted as conforming to reality by scholars[57]. The floors had chambers with loculus niches[58], but the presence of sarcophagi can be determined by the survival of plaster sarcophagi remains on the third and fourth floor[59], and reliefs with banqueting scenes (cat. 12. 54. 55). No loculus reliefs can be associated with the tomb. The reliefs with banqueting scenes illustrate well the problem of the survival of Palmyrene sculpture. When Watzinger and Wulzinger surveyed Palmyra, they noted a relief with a reclining man and three standing figures behind him[60]. Relief cat. 54 may be this relief; however, by the time it was studied by Agnes Henning, only part of the figure of the reclining man survived[61]. Additionally, if Watzinger and Wulzinger and Henning refer to the same relief, it is possible to trace its state of preservation further, from its original location above the entrance and between two pilasters, to the floor of the chamber

---

44 Cuneo et al. 2016. The most recent study of the tower tomb is Henning 2013b, 185 f. with previous bibliography.
45 Watzinger – Wulzinger 1932, 54 f.
46 Will 1949.
47 Will 1949, 93–96.
48 Will 1949, 94 f.
49 Henning 2013b, 185 f. It is interesting that Watzinger – Wulzinger 1932, 54 f. ascribe three floors to the building, Will 1949, 94–96 five, and Henning 2013b, 185 f. six floors. Gawlikowski 1970a, 71–73 also writes that the tomb has six floors.
50 Henning 2013b, 186.
51 Henning 2013b, 184.
52 Henning 2013b, 184 f.

53 Watzinger – Wulzinger 1932, 70; Henning 2013b, 286.
54 Watzinger – Wulzinger 1932, 70. Contra Henning 2013b, 186, who writes that it was »in das Mauerwerk eingefügt«. See Gawlikowski 1970b, 81 fig. 13.
55 Henning 2013b, 192. For the tomb, see also Gawlikowski 2021, 159.
56 Cuneo et al. 2016.
57 Gawlikowski 1970a, 84. 86.
58 Watzinger – Wulzinger 1932, 54 f.; Gawlikowski 1970a, 84; Henning 2013b, 193–195.
59 Henning 2013b, 193 f.
60 Watzinger – Wulzinger 1932, 54.
61 Henning 2013b, 193.

when Henning studied the object, indicating that the object was removed from its original location[62]. The other two banqueting reliefs from the tomb (cat. 12. 55) reveal the tomb's history of use. Cat. 55 was found on the fourth floor, where the remains of plaster sarcophagi were found[63], while cat. 12 was found on the ground floor, and its inscription reveals that the tomb, or part of the tomb, stopped being used by the family of Yamlikû in the 3rd cent. A.D. The construction of the entrance and the »higher part that is inside« as well as the »higher part of the three« mentioned in the inscription on the relief indicate that this part of the tomb was sold off to a family that was not related to the family of the founder Yamlikû, as the names indicate[64], and that the banqueting relief was one of three, arranged in the form of a triclinium[65].

A.D. 83: Tower Tomb no. 68 of the Bene Ba'a

The tomb is located in the west necropolis. It was recorded by Watzinger and Wulzinger[66], and its foundation inscription gives its construction date in A.D. 83. It survives to the height of four floors. Each floor had chambers with loculus bays. In addition to the loculus bays, the sarcophagus in appendix 6, cat. 9 was recorded inside the ground-floor chamber. A loculus relief with five portraits in two registers[67], a stele with one standing female between two standing males[68], and a stele with two children dated to A.D. 114[69], are associated with this tomb because of the names mentioned in the inscriptions on the reliefs.

A.D. 88/89: Hypogeum of 'Aštôr

The hypogeum is located in the south-west necropolis, and was excavated in 1956 by Obaida Taḥa and Nazmi Kḫeir. The foundation inscription records its construction by 'Aštôr, son of Malikû, in A.D. 88/89. It has the ›canonical‹ inverted-T plan, with two long galleries leading to exedrae placed immediately after the vestibule, to its east and west, and a long gallery on the axis of the door that ends in another exedra. The loculus bays are dug into the walls of the exedrae and the galleries. According to Sadurska and Bounni, it was looted at some point before the excavations, since the pieces of sculpture were found broken and in disarray[70].

Two small banqueting reliefs (cat. 68–69) were found in the vestibule, as well as a loculus relief with a male bust[71], and an inscribed stele depicting a hanging cloth[72]. It is likely that the banqueting reliefs had formed a pair[73]. In the east exedra, in front of loculus bay 9 in the plan by Sadurska and Bounni[74], the loculus relief with the busts of a couple was found[75]. In the west exedra, in front of loculus bay 33[76], the excavators found a stele with a standing man[77]. The sarcophagi lid fragments from this tomb (cat. 60–65. 67) were all found in the central gallery of the tomb. They were arranged on the long sides of the main corridor, near the exedra (cat. 60. 64–67 on the east side, and cat. 61–63 on the west). The absence of female participants led Sadurska and Bounni to suggest that the reliefs replicated a religious or cultic banquet, rather than a family one[78]. Apart from these reliefs with banqueting scenes, this section of the hypogeum also yielded two loculus reliefs with a female bust each, one in front of loculus bay 22[79], and one in front of loculus bay 25[80], a stele with a standing female in front of loculus bay 16[81], and a small lion head in front of loculus bay 14, that must have come either from a statue or the architectural decoration of the tomb[82]. Based on the style of the sculptural pieces, the hypogeum continued to be in use until the 3rd cent. A.D.[83].

A.D. 89: Tomb no. 7, Hypogeum of Bôlḥâ

The hypogeum is located in the south-east necropolis and was excavated in 1958 by O. Taḥa and N. Kḫeir[84]. The

---

62 Watzinger – Wulzinger 1932, pl. 34 reproducing Cassas' drawing; Henning 2013b, pl. 52, a.
63 Henning 2013b, 193 f.
64 The names of Moqîmaî, and Našumaî, the sons of Rodônâ, are not attested elsewhere, unlike those of their brothers 'Oggâ and Nûrbel: Gawlikowski – al As'ad 1997, 32 f. cat. 17.
65 Gawlikowski – al As'ad 1997, 32 f. cat. 17; Yon 2013, 350 cat. 84.
66 Watzinger – Wulzinger 1932, 57.
67 Henning 2013b, 211.
68 Henning 2013b, 211.
69 Henning 2013b, 211.

70 Sadurska – Bounni 1994, 14.
71 Sadurska – Bounni 1994, 19 cat. 12 fig. 118.
72 Sadurska – Bounni 1994, 20 f. cat. 15 fig. 1. For this type of stele, see Raja 2019g, with previous bibliography.
73 Sadurska – Bounni 1994, 20.
74 Sadurska – Bounni 1994, pl. 4.
75 Sadurska – Bounni 1994, 15 f. cat. 4 fig. 36.
76 Sadurska – Bounni 1994, pl. 4.
77 Sadurska – Bounni 1994, 21 cat. 16 fig. 5.
78 Sadurska – Bounni 1994, 14 f. 16.
79 Sadurska – Bounni 1994, 17 f. cat. 9 fig. 132.
80 Sadurska – Bounni 1994, 18 cat. 10 fig. 133.
81 Sadurska – Bounni 1994, 21 f. cat. 17 fig. 12.
82 Sadurska – Bounni 1994, 22 cat. 18 fig. 254.
83 Sadurska – Bounni 1994, 15.
84 Sadurska – Bounni 1994, 70.

foundation inscription gives the date of construction as A.D. 89[85]. According to Sadurska and Bounni, four branches of the family of the founder were buried in the tomb[86]. It has two exedrae on either side of the main chamber immediately after the entrance, and the beginning of a third exedra at the end of the main chamber.

One branch was buried in the main gallery and the north exedra. Since the position of the reliefs found in the tomb is known, it is possible to arrange them according to their find location: a female bust from the main chamber, loculus bay 1, loculus 3[87]; a female bust from loculus bay 17, loculus 1[88]; and one stele with a standing male from the same loculus bay, loculus 2[89]; two male busts from loculus bay 18, loculi 1 and 2[90]; a male bust from the north exedra, loculus bay 29, loculus 3[91]; a male bust from the north exedra, loculus bay 30, loculus 2[92]; a stele with a standing male from the north exedra, loculus bay 31, loculus 2[93]; a male bust from the north exedra, loculus bay 31, loculus 3[94]; a stele with a male and female figure in the north exedra, loculus bay 31, loculus 4[95]; and a male and a female bust from loculus 1 and the central loculus of the podium niche, respectively[96].

Another branch of the family was buried in the triclinium of the north exedra: cat. 168–170. From the south exedra come: a stele with two standing boys, from loculus bay 4, loculus 3[97]; a female bust from loculus bay 32, loculus 1[98]; a male bust from loculus bay 36, loculus 1[99]; a female bust from loculus bay 36, loculus 2[100]; and a male bust from loculus bay 36, loculus 3[101]; a male bust from loculus bay 44, loculus 1[102]; a relief with two male busts from loculus bay 44, loculus 2[103]; a bust of a priest from loculus bay 45, loculus 1[104]; a female bust from loculus bay 45, loculus 2[105]; a male bust from loculus bay 46, loculus 1[106]; and a male bust from the base of podium, loculus 1[107]. The fourth branch of the family was buried in the sarcophagus in the south exedra: cat. 171.

Late 1st cent. / Early 2nd cent. A.D.: Tower Tomb no. 39d

The tower tomb is located in the west necropolis, and only one floor is preserved. The foundation inscription is not preserved, and so the date of the tomb in the end of the 1st or the beginning of the 2nd cent. A.D. is based on architectural/technical observations. The ground floor had a chamber, on the north side of which sarcophagus cat. 59 was placed[108]. Henning has recorded the following sculptural fragments that were either from the ground or the upper floor: (1) part of a relief with the bust of a priest in a medallion that could possibly be from a ceiling coffer, (2) fragment of a reclining man in rich dress[109].

Late 1st cent. / Early 2nd cent. A.D.: Hypogeum of 'Aqraban

The hypogeum is located in the south-west necropolis. It was discovered accidentally in 2007 and explored soon after[110]. The tomb is dated to the end of the 1st–early 2nd cent. A.D. based on the style of the reliefs found inside[111]. It has a long gallery, with two lateral galleries on either side, each with loculus bays, and an exedra at the end of the main gallery. The exedra gallery had six loculus bays and a sarcophagus (appendix 6, cat. 19). The find location of the two banqueting reliefs cat. 123. 124 is not given[112], nor is that of the other finds: an inscribed relief with camel riders[113], a relief with a male bust[114], a stele with a standing female[115], and the lower part of a stele with a hanging piece of cloth[116], since they were all published in a preliminary report.

---

85 Sadurska – Bounni 1994, 70 pl. 6.
86 Sadurska – Bounni 1994, 70–72.
87 Sadurska – Bounni 1994, 75 f. cat. 99 fig. 142 pl. 6.
88 Sadurska – Bounni 1994, 76 cat. 100 fig. 143 pl. 6.
89 Sadurska – Bounni 1994, 74 f. cat. 97 fig. 13 pl. 6.
90 Male bust from loculus 1: Sadurska – Bounni 1994, 75 cat. 98 fig. 21 pl. 6; male bust from loculus 2: Sadurska – Bounni 1994, 76 f. cat. 101 fig. 40 pl. 6.
91 Sadurska – Bounni 1994, 79 cat. 106 fig. 127 pl. 6.
92 Sadurska – Bounni 1994, 79 f. cat. 107 fig. 73 pl. 6.
93 Sadurska – Bounni 1994, 80 f. cat. 109 fig. 16 pl. 6.
94 Sadurska – Bounni 1994, 80 cat. 108 fig. 106 pl. 6.
95 Sadurska – Bounni 1994, 81 cat. 110 fig. 11 pl. 6.
96 Male bust: Sadurska – Bounni 1994, 78 cat. 104 fig. 26 pl. 6. Female bust: Sadurska – Bounni 1994, 78 f. cat. 105 fig. 163 pl. 6.
97 Sadurska – Bounni 1994, 85 f. cat. 119 fig. 19 pl. 6.
98 Sadurska – Bounni 1994, 85 cat. 118 fig. 174 pl. 6.
99 Sadurska – Bounni 1994, 81 cat. 111 fig. 79 pl. 6.
100 Sadurska – Bounni 1994, 77 f. cat. 102 fig. 203 pl. 6.
101 Sadurska – Bounni 1994, 77 f. cat. 103 fig. 107 pl. 6.
102 Sadurska – Bounni 1994, 84 f. cat. 117 fig. 105 pl. 6.
103 Sadurska – Bounni 1994, 84 cat. 116 fig. 104 pl. 6.
104 Sadurska – Bounni 1994, 83 cat. 114 fig. 94 pl. 6.
105 Sadurska – Bounni 1994, 82 f. cat. 113 fig. 191 pl. 6.
106 Sadurska – Bounni 1994, 82 cat. 112 fig. 27 pl. 6.
107 Sadurska – Bounni 1994, 83 f. cat. 115 fig. 119 pl. 6.
108 Henning 2013b, 181.
109 Henning 2013b, 181 f.
110 Al-Hariri 2013, 149.
111 Al-Hariri 2013, 151.
112 Al-Hariri 2013, 150 f.
113 Al-Hariri 2013, 149 f. fig. 5.
114 Al-Hariri 2013, 150 fig. 8.
115 Al-Hariri 2013, 150 fig. 7.
116 Al-Hariri 2013, 150 fig. 9.

Ca. A.D. 90: Hypogeum of Barîkî

The hypogeum was excavated in 1958 by O. Taḥa an N. Kḫeir and is located in the south-east necropolis. No foundation inscription is associated with the tomb, and the date of use is based on stylistic criteria and its proximity to two more tombs is between A.D. 90 and A.D. 200. It has a long gallery divided into three sections that culminates in an exedra[117].

The precise find location of the fifteen reliefs from this tomb, and cat. 129. 130 is known: one male bust in front of loculus bay 27[118]; one male bust in loculus bay 3, loculus 1[119]; one female bust between loculus bays 3 and 4[120]; one male bust between loculus bays 5 and 6[121]; one female bust between loculus bays 5 and 6[122]; one male bust in loculus bay 21, loculus 1[123]; and one male bust from central exedra, loculus bay 12, loculus 2[124]. Loculus bay 14 in the central exedra yielded three male busts: one in loculus 1[125], one in loculus 2[126], and one in loculus 3[127]. A female bust was found in the central exedra, loculus bay 13 loculus 1[128]; a male bust was from exedra, loculus bay 12, loculus 1[129]; a male and a female bust were found in loculus bay 10, loculus 1[130] and loculus 2, respectively[131]; and a male bust was found in the exedra, loculus bay 15, loculus 1[132]. Relief cat. 129 was found against the west wall, and cat. 130 against the east wall of the main gallery.

A.D. 98: Tomb no. A120, Hypogeum of ʿAtenatan

The tomb is located in the south-west necropolis and was excavated by Ingholt in 1924[133], although Robert Amy conducted the final clearing of the tomb[134]. The tomb was constructed in A.D. 98, according to its

Figure 41. Painted arch of exedra of Julius Aurelius Maqqaî, in the hypogeum of ʿAtenatan.

foundation inscription[135]. In A.D. 229, Julius Aurelius Maqqaî built with his own funds the exedra to the right of the entrance, according to the inscription recording the fact[136]. The layout is simple: it has two consecutive chambers, both with loculus bays dug out of the walls, and one exedra immediately after the vestibule[137]. The evidence of cat. 80 shows that there were more exedrae in the tomb[138].

Cat. 80, which is dated based on stylistic criteria to A.D. 100–150, perhaps belonged to the first phase of use of the tomb by ʿAtenatan and his family. The objects from the exedra of Julius Aurelius Maqqaî were made after A.D. 229 (Pls 24–26). In addition to cat. 81. 88, Ingholt recorded that he found (1–3) three headless male busts[139], (4–6) three fragments of female busts[140], as well as fragments of reclining figures from sarcophagi and a painting at the back of the wall (Pl. 27)[141]. The arch of the exedra also had painted decoration: two Victories on globes carrying garlands and palms on either end, and a floral design across it (Fig. 41, Pl. 28)[142].

---

117 Sadurska – Bounni 1994, 102–104.
118 Sadurska – Bounni 1994, 104 f. cat. 139 fig. 49 pl. 8.
119 Sadurska – Bounni 1994, 105 cat. 140 fig. 80 pl. 8.
120 Sadurska – Bounni 1994, 105 f. cat. 141 fig. 167 pl. 8.
121 Sadurska – Bounni 1994, 106 cat. 142 fig. 98 pl. 8.
122 Sadurska – Bounni 1994, 106 f. cat. 143 fig. 137 pl. 8.
123 Sadurska – Bounni 1994, 107 cat. 144 pl. 8.
124 Sadurska – Bounni 1994, 107 f. cat. 145 fig. 50 pl. 8.
125 Sadurska – Bounni 1994, 108 cat. 146 fig. 38 pl. 8.
126 Sadurska – Bounni 1994, 108 cat. 147 fig. 48 pl. 8.
127 Sadurska – Bounni 1994, 108 f. cat. 148 fig. 46 pl. 8.
128 Sadurska – Bounni 1994, 109 f. cat. 149 fig. 149 pl. 8.
129 Sadurska – Bounni 1994, 110 cat. 150 fig. 72 pl. 8.
130 Sadurska – Bounni 1994, 110 cat. 151 fig. 28 pl. 8.
131 Sadurska – Bounni 1994, 110 f. cat. 152 fig. 150 pl. 8.
132 Sadurska – Bounni 1994, 111 cat. 154 fig. 47 pl. 8.
133 Ingholt 1935, 58. Raja et al. 2021a, Diary 1, 30. 73. 86 f. 123 f. Diary 2, 87. Diary 3, 45. 69. 72. Diary 5, 76–82.
134 Seyrig 1937, 15 n. 2.
135 Ingholt 1935, 59 f. cat. 1.
136 Ingholt 1935, 60–62 cat. 2.
137 Ingholt 1935, pl. 23.
138 Seyrig 1937, 15.
139 (1) Raja et al. 2021a, Diary 5, 79 no. A; (2) Raja et al. 2021a, Diary 5, 79 no. B; (3) Raja et al. 2021a, Diary 5, 79 no. c.
140 (4) Raja et al. 2021a, Diary 5, 79 no. e. 3; (5) Raja et al. 2021a, Diary 5, 80 no. f; (6) Raja et al. 2021a, Diary 5, 80 no. g.
141 He does not record their number. It is likely that at least one of them may be identified in cat. 77.
142 Ingholt 1935, 62 f.

Figure 42. Decorated ceiling of exedra in hypogeum of ʿAbdʿastôr.

A.D. 98: Hypogeum of ʿAbdʿastôr

The tomb is located in the south-west necropolis and was excavated by Ingholt in 1924 and investigated again in 1937[143]. The foundation inscription of the tomb records its construction in A.D. 98[144]. His great-granddaughter, Julia Aurelia Šalmat, ceded the left chamber except for two niches in A.D. 239[145]. The tomb is composed of three sections, two placed laterally to and near the entrance of the main gallery, and each section is divided into two chambers. The first central chamber also has an exedra on the left side[146].

Inside the tomb were found the relief with the bust of a male[147], and a relief with two busts of a female and a male[148]. The presence of an inscribed female bust in the Musée des Antiquités[149] in Istanbul[150] indicates that the tomb had been looted at some point before Ingholt's excavations[151]. These three reliefs depict members of the immediate family of ʿAbdʿastôr[152]. Two reliefs at the İstanbul Arkeoloji Müzeleri represent more distant relatives of ʿAbdʿastôr: the relief of Julia Aurelia Šalmat, to be identified with ʿAbdʿastôr's descendant who ceded the left chamber, together with her daughter[153], and a relief depicting a male, possibly her father, according to Ingholt[154]. One more relief, depicting the bust of a boy was found during the 1937 investigations. The name indicates that the child was not related to any of the families that owned the sections of the tomb[155].

The three sarcophagi cat. 173–175 were found in the exedra of the first chamber of the vertical (main) section of the tomb, arranged in the form of a triclinium. The wall behind the sarcophagi had paintings, possibly two winged figures carrying a medallion[156], while the ceiling had architectural decorations (mouldings) and a scene of birds among grapevines was carved in relief and painted (Fig. 42)[157].

A.D. 98: Hypogeum of the Barîkî

The tomb is located in the south-west necropolis and was excavated between 1988 and 1992 in campaigns led by Khaled al-Asʿad[158], Director of Antiquities and the Palmyra Museum[159]. Its foundation text gives the date of its construction in A.D. 98[160], and the inscription on the bust of a priest that was found in the tomb (A.D. 137) indicates that the tomb was in use for at least two generations[161]. Apart from cat. 131 and the relief of a priest, a relief with a female bust with a seated child behind her is associated with this tomb[162]; their find location has not been published, since the tomb has not received a full publication yet.

Around A.D. 100: Hypogeum of the Bôlbarak Family

The hypogeum is located in the west necropolis, in the Valley of the Tombs, and was excavated by Adnan Bounni and Obaida Taḥa in 1958[163]. No foundation inscription is associated with the tomb, but the A.D. 239 date on the sarcophagus found inside the central exedra (cat. 11) indicates that the tomb was constructed before then. The stylistic dating of four of the reliefs found there, as well as the epigraphic evidence, makes a construction date

---

143 Ingholt 1938, 120.
144 Ingholt 1938, 120–123.
145 Ingholt 1938, 124–133.
146 Ingholt 1938, pl. 45.
147 Ingholt 1938, 123, pl. 46, 4.
148 Ingholt 1938, 123, pl. 46, 4.
149 As the İstanbul Arkeoloji Müzeleri was known when Ingholt was writing in the 1930s.
150 Ingholt 1928, PS 350; Ingholt 1938, 123 pl. 46, 3.
151 The relief was in the possession of the Musée Ottoman since 1896: Bobou et al. 2021b, 547 app. 2: Acquisition Histories, PS 350.
152 Ingholt 1938, 123.
153 Ingholt 1938, 126 pl. 47, 2.
154 Ingholt 1938, 126 pl. 48, 1.
155 Ingholt 1938, 138 pl. 49, 3.
156 Ingholt 1938, 139.
157 Ingholt 1938, 139 f.
158 al-Asʿad 2018, 25.
159 al-Asʿad 2018, 20.
160 al-Asʿad 2018, 25.
161 al-Asʿad 1993, cat. 234; Yon 2013, 343 no. 30.
162 al-Asʿad 1993, cat. 236; Yon 2013, 343 no. 32.
163 Sadurska – Bounni 1994, 142.

of the tomb around or soon after A.D. 100 plausible[164]. The hypogeum has a simple plan: a covered entrance[165]; a vestibule with four loculus bays, two on either side, and a chamber with an unfinished exedra to the north facing three loculus bays; and an exedra to the west, with a podium and four loculus bays[166].

The reliefs that were dated based on epigraphic evidence (onomastics) and stylistic criteria between A.D. 100 and A.D. 150 were found in the vestibule bays: three loculus reliefs depicting females, each one from a separate loculus bay[167]. The other reliefs from the tomb come from the area of the exedra and must be dated around or after A.D. 239: they are a loculus relief with a male figure[168], a banqueting relief (cat. 179), and a loculus relief with a female figure[169]. A statuette of a winged Victory was also found in that exedra[170]. The exact arrangement of the reliefs on the exedra is not known.

Around A.D. 100: Hypogeum of Zabdâ

The hypogeum, located in the west necropolis, was excavated by Michalowski in 1959. No foundation inscription is associated with the tomb, but cat. 71 preserves the name of the tomb's founder in the inscription. The stylistic dating of the sculptural pieces found in the tomb supports a construction date at the end of the 1st cent. A.D. and the end of its use at around A.D. 150[171]. The hypogeum has two side chambers and a long central chamber, with only a few niches cut into the rock, and so it has a relatively simple plan[172]. Apart from cat. 71, a female[173] and a male statuette[174] were found in the main chamber, and a loculus relief with a male bust was found in the north side exedra[175].

A.D. 103: Tower Tomb no. 13, Tower of Elahbel

It was one of the best-preserved tower tombs in Palmyra, rising to a height of five floors (twenty-five metres), and recorded by the early modern travellers at Palmyra[176]. The tomb was destroyed in 2015[177]. Thanks to the foundation inscription, it is known that the tomb was founded in A.D. 103[178]. The drawings by Cassas show both the façade and interior views of the building; their accuracy, however, varies[179]. Each floor had chambers with loculus bays. The chambers also contained remains of twelve plaster sarcophagi located in ten sarcophagi chambers (»Sarkophagkammern«)[180], which were in the different floors of the tomb[181]. The tomb offered one of the richest assemblages of funerary portraits from a tower tomb: fifty-four fragments of sculptural decoration have been associated with it[182]. The first of the fragments was found in an underground chamber that was attached to the tower and had a separate entrance[183]. It is a fragment of a banqueting scene showing a reclining man (cat. 35).

Most of the portraits or other sculptures that can be associated with a floor or chamber within the tomb come from the ground floor (Pl. 29). On the walls of the ground floor were located: (1) a relief with the bust portrait of a man above the entrance[184]; (2) a relief depicting three bust portraits of two women on either side of a priest[185]; (3) a relief with two bust portraits of women[186], both above the entrance of the staircase leading to the upper floors[187], and on the wall across the

---

164 Sadurska – Bounni 1994, 142 f.
165 Gawlikowski 1970a, 123 n. 64.
166 Sadurska – Bounni 1994, 142 pl. 12.
167 (1) Loculus relief with single female: Palmyra, Palmyra Museum, inv. no. 1789/6638: Sadurska and Bounni 1994, 144 cat. 189 fig. 130; Krag 2018, 181 cat. 60; (2) loculus relief with female and two children, one standing, one in her arm: Palmyra, Palmyra Museum, inv. no. 1788/6637: Sadurska and Bounni 1994, 143 f. cat. 188 fig. 159; Krag 2018, 225 cat. 220; (3) loculus relief with female holding child: Palmyra, Palmyra Museum, inv. no. B 1790/6639: Sadurska and Bounni 1994, 144 f. cat. 190 fig. 158; Krag 2018, 220 cat. 198.
168 Palmyra, Palmyra Museum, inv. no. 1794/6643: Sadurska and Bounni 1994, 146 cat. 194 fig. 129; Raja 2019e, 97. 111 cat. 23.
169 Palmyra, Palmyra Museum, inv. no. 1791/6640: Sadurska and Bounni 1994, 145 cat. 191 fig. 198; Krag 2018, 348 cat. 683.
170 Palmyra, Palmyra Museum, inv. no. 1792/6641: Sadurska and Bounni 1994, 145 cat. 192 fig. 255.
171 Sadurska – Bounni 1994, 137 f.
172 Sadurska – Bounni 1994, plan 11.
173 Sadurska – Bounni 1994, 140 f. cat. 186 fig. 206.
174 Sadurska – Bounni 1994, 141 cat. 187 fig. 206.
175 Sadurska – Bounni 1994, 139 f. cat. 185 fig. 41.
176 Schmidt-Colinet 1996, 364 f. For the tomb, see also Gawlikowski 2021, 159–162.
177 Cuneo et al. 2016.
178 Henning 2013b, 152.
179 Schmidt-Colinet 1996, 364 f.
180 Henning 2013b, 153.
181 In her description of the tomb, Henning only mentions explicitly the location of two of the chambers on the second floor, Henning 2013b, 153.
182 Henning 2013b, 153 f. 292–309. Of these, fifteen are fragments of inscribed plaques: Henning 2013b, 300–309, cat. S 24–S 35, S 52–S 54.
183 Gawlikowski 1970a, 87–90; Henning 2013b, 46. 153.
184 Gawlikowski 1970a, 90; Colledge 1976a, 72 pl. 57; Tanabe 1986, 29 cat. 183 pl. 183; Henning 2013b, pl. 13, b.
185 Krag 2018, 34 n. 96; 75 n. 62; 79 n. 99; 227 cat. 224, with previous bibliography; Henning 2019b, 29–31.
186 Krag 2018, 34 n. 96; 44 n. 175; 79 n. 100; 227. cat. 225, with previous bibliography; Henning 2019b, 29–31.
187 Henning 2019b, 30.

104 CHAPTER 4

Figure 43. Interior of ground floor of tower tomb of Elahbel.

door; (4) a relief with five female bust portraits[188]; (5) a relief depicting a sarcophagus, with four bust portraits on the box (cat. 33); and (6) a reclining figure resting on a kline (app. 2. cat. 1). There is no evidence that the reliefs on the wall of the chamber covered loculus bays for burials[189]. In addition to these, several fragments showing reclining (cat. 28–30. 32) or standing figures from banqueting reliefs (cat. 27) were found there, as were the fragment from a kline showing a pillow[190]. Of these reliefs, only cat. 32 was found inside a loculus bay

(O III). The others probably were placed against the wall[191]. The ceiling coffers of the ground-floor chamber were decorated with painted busts of priests and male figures (Fig. 43, Pl. 30)[192].

The upper floors contained the remains of plaster sarcophagi[193]. Henning mentions explicitly only the chambers with plaster sarcophagi on the second floor[194], but no lids or banqueting reliefs were found on this floor. The third floor has yielded evidence of five banqueting scenes (cat. 23–26. 31) as well as the fragments from a kline from the south sarcophagus chamber[195]. All five of them are long enough to have functioned as covers of single sarcophagi boxes, although only cat. 23 has enough of the background and the edges surviving to indicate that it covered a single plaster sarcophagus. Finally, two heads (cat. 43. 48) belonging to a male and a female figure, respectively, come from the fifth floor of the tomb. All the other fragments of reliefs do not have a precise provenance. Eleven heads and the fragment of a torso can be associated with sarcophagi or banqueting reliefs because of their size (cat. 34. 36–39. 40–42. 44–47)[196], while others possibly belonged to loculus reliefs[197], others to architectural decorations[198]. Thirteen fragments of inscriptions can also be connected to the tomb[199]. Three more reliefs[200], and a head most likely from a sarcophagus because of its size (cat. 49) have also been associated with the tomb.

In total, there are seven large banqueting reliefs, two from the ground floor (cat. 28. 29), and five from the third floor (cat. 23–26. 31), that could have functioned

---

188 Krag 2018, 34 n. 96; 44 n. 175; 75 n. 62; 78 n. 89; 79 n. 98. 107; 226. cat. 223, with previous bibliography; Henning 2019b, 29–31.
189 Henning 2019b, 30.
190 Henning 2013b, cat. S 42.
191 Henning 2019b, 31.
192 Schmidt-Colinet 1996, 366.
193 Gawlikowski 1970a, 91; Henning 2013b, 153.
194 Henning 2013b, 153.
195 Henning 2013b, 307 cat. S 48.
196 To these the fragment of a relief showing a garment of a reclining figure can be added: Henning 2013b, 304 cat. S 39.
197 (1) Female head: Palmyra, Palmyra Museum, inv. no. A 262/1465: Krag 2018, 202 cat. 132 with previous bibliography; (2) two hand fragments: Palmyra, Palmyra Museum, inv. no. A 45: Henning 2013b, 293 f. cat. S 4; (3) a fragment showing a child: Palmyra, Palmyra Museum, inv. no. A 274: Henning 2013b, 297 cat. S 15.
198 Two reliefs showing Dionysiac masks: (1) Palmyra, Palmyra Museum, inv. no. A 260: Henning 2013b, 294 cat. S 5; (2) Palmyra, Palmyra Museum, inv. no. A 261: Henning 2013b, 294 cat. S 6. Two reliefs showing lion heads: (1) Palmyra, Palmyra Museum, inv. no. A 275: Henning 2013b, 297 cat. S 16; (2) Palmyra, Palmyra Museum, inv. no. A 276: Henning 2013b, 298 cat. S 17.
199 Henning 2013b, 300–303 cat. S 25–35 and 308 f. cat. 52. 53.
200 (1) Palmyra, Palmyra Museum, inv. no. A 208/A 137: loculus relief depicting a male: Henning 2013b, 308 cat. S 51; Raja 2019b, 70. 108 cat. 115; (2) Paris, Musée du Louvre, inv. no. AO 4086: loculus relief depicting a priest: Henning 2013b, 309 cat. S54; (3) Palmyra, Palmyra Museum, inv. no. A 280/1483: loculus relief depicting a male: Henning 2013b, 299 cat. S 21.

as covers of sarcophagi, and several heads and other fragments indicating the presence of additional reliefs that did not survive as well (cat. 34. 36–39. 40–42. 44–47). In addition to those, three fragments from loculus reliefs[201], and probably three well-preserved loculus reliefs[202], show that the funerary niches were closed off with plaques with funerary portraits.

A.D. 108: Hypogeum of Yarḥaî

The hypogeum is located in the west necropolis. It was excavated in 1934/1935 by Robert Amy and Henri Seyrig, who discovered that, despite being looted in the past, the looters had left behind the sculptures as they had held no value for them[203]. The foundation text of the tomb gives the date of construction in A.D. 108[204]. In A.D. 240, the east side of the tomb with the unused exedra was ceded to Julius Aurelius Theophilus[205]. The plan of the tomb is relatively simple: it has a vestibule that opens to a long corridor with two exedrae on the east and west sides near the entrance, and an exedra at the end of the corridor[206]. Cat. 93 and cat. 94 belong to the earlier phase of the hypogeum, and they were found at the south exedra within a richly decorated, structured setting with niches and columns reminiscent of public architecture (Fig. 44, Pl. 31)[207]. Eleven reliefs or fragments thereof covering loculus burials were also found in the south exedra: four reliefs depicting female busts, one female head, and six reliefs depicting male busts. Their exact find location is not given[208]. Cat. 95 was also found in the east exedra. The west exedra belonged to the phase after the concession to Julius Aurelius Theophilus[209]. It contained the three sarcophagi cat. 90–92. They were placed on an elevated

Figure 44. Niches in the hypogeum of Yarḥaî.

Figure 45. Reconstruction of the exedra with the sarcophagi from the hypogeum of Yarḥaî. The reconstruction includes more objects than were found in the exedra.

---

201 (1) Female head: Palmyra, Palmyra Museum, inv. no. A262/ 1465: Krag 2018, 202 cat. 132 with previous bibliography; (2) two hand fragments: Palmyra, Palmyra Museum, inv. no. A 45: Henning 2013b, 293 f. cat. S 4; (3) a fragment showing a child: Palmyra, Palmyra Museum, inv. no. A 274: Henning 2013b, 297 cat. S 15.
202 (1) Palmyra, Palmyra Museum, inv. no. A 208/A 137: Loculus relief depicting a male: Henning 2013b, 308 cat. S 51; Raja 2019b, 70. 108 cat. 115; (2) Paris, Musée du Louvre, inv. no. AO 4086: Loculus relief depicting a priest: Henning 2013b, 309 cat. S54; (3) Palmyra, Palmyra Museum, inv. no. A 280/1483: Loculus relief depicting a male: Henning 2013b, 299 cat. S 21.
203 Amy – Seyrig 1936, 229.
204 Amy – Seyrig 1936, 242. 258 f.
205 Amy – Seyrig 1936, 259 f.
206 Amy – Seyrig 1936, pls. 26. 27.
207 Amy – Seyrig 1936, 236–238.
208 Amy – Seyrig 1936, 241–243.
209 Parlasca 1998, 311 f. The west exedra was reconstructed in the National Museum of Damascus, Amy – Seyrig 1936, 230. The reconstruction gives the impression of a Palmyrene tomb; however, it is not accurate, see Parlasca 1998, 311 f.

construction that covered burials and were arranged in a triclinium[210]. In addition to these sarcophagi, three reliefs were found there: cat. 97, a relief with two female busts[211], and one with a male bust (Fig. 45)[212].

A.D. 109: Hypogeum of Julius Aurelius Malê

The hypogeum is located in the south-west necropolis and was investigated by Ingholt in 1924[213]. It had been looted in antiquity, but part of the foundation inscription was preserved, recording the year A.D. 109[214]. Part of the tomb was ceded in A.D. 160[215], another in A.D. 215[216], a third in A.D. 219[217]. Three sarcophagi, arranged in a triclinium were found in the chamber, but only their inscriptions were published by Ingholt[218]. In A.D. 234, Julius Aurelius Malê ceded another part of the tomb[219]. More space was sold off in A.D. 235[220] and A.D. 237[221].

A.D. 113: Tomb no. H, Hypogeum of Taîbbôl

Tomb H is located in the south-east necropolis. It was excavated between 2002 and 2004 by the Nara-Palmyra Archaeological Mission[222]. The foundation inscription records its construction date in A.D. 113, while on the door lintel there are several cession texts[223]. The hypogeum has a long, main gallery, two side chambers near the entrance, one exedra on the north side of the main gallery, and a second side chamber to the south side of the main gallery, near the main exedra.

In the north exedra, cat. 98–100 were found. One loculus relief with a male bust may also be from the area of the exedra[224]. In the exedra at the end of the main gallery, cat. 101 and a relief with a female bust were found[225]. Two loculus reliefs, one with a male[226], one with a female bust[227], were found in the side chamber to the south, in the middle loculus bay, one above the other in the second and third burial niches, respectively. Seven more reliefs were found in the south side chamber near the entrance. Two reliefs were found in situ, a relief with a female bust[228], and a relief with a male bust[229] covering the third and second loculi niches in loculus bay 2 (beginning the numbering from the entrance of the side chamber)[230]. Another five reliefs were found in the chamber, and they were restored in their places: in loculus bay 1, two reliefs with female busts on the lower two burial niches[231], and a relief with a male bust on the upper burial niche[232]; and in loculus bay 3, a relief with a male bust on the second burial niche[233], and a relief with a female bust on the third burial niche[234].

A.D. 114: Hypogeum of Zabd'ateh and Moqîmû

The hypogeum is located in the south-west necropolis and was first discovered by Ludovic de Contenson in 1891, explored by Wiegand in 1902, and excavated in 1961 by Khaled al-As'ad and O. Taḥa. The date of its construction in A.D. 114 is recorded in its foundation inscription. In A.D. 131, the north exedra of the hypogeum was ceded to Bar'ateh[235]. The epigraphic evidence shows that two more families were also buried in this tomb, the family of Sî'ôna in the north exedra, and the family

---

210 Amy – Seyrig 1936, 243–252.
211 Amy – Seyrig 1936, 251 cat. 2 pl. 47, 2.
212 Amy – Seyrig 1936, 251 cat. 3 pl. 48, 2.
213 Ingholt 1935, 75.
214 Ingholt 1935, 75 f.
215 Ingholt 1935, 76 f.
216 Ingholt 1935, 77.
217 Ingholt 1935, 78 f.
218 Ingholt 1935, 79–82.
219 Ingholt 1935, 82–84.
220 Ingholt 1935, 84–86.
221 Ingholt 1935, 86–90.
222 Miyashita 2016, 132.
223 Saito 2016, 351.
224 Miyashita 2016, 132 fig. 11.
225 <https://www.facebook.com/permalink.php?story_fbid=758083210919790&id=103105249750926> (26.04.2022).
226 <https://www.facebook.com/103105249750926/photos/pcb.758083210919790/758082734253171/?type=1&theater> (26.04.2022).
227 Saito 2007, 92 fig. 15.
228 Krag 2018, 333 cat. 625 with previous bibliography.
229 <https://www.facebook.com/103105249750926/photos/pcb.758083210919790/758082780919833/?type=1&theater> (26.04.2022).
230 Saito 2016, 352.
231 Loculus relief in the first row: <https://www.facebook.com/permalink.php?story_fbid=758083210919790&id=103105249750926> (26.02.2022); loculus relief in the second row: <https://www.facebook.com/103105249750926/photos/pcb.758083210919790/758082757586502/?type=1&theater> (26.04.2022).
232 <https://www.facebook.com/103105249750926/photos/pcb.758083210919790/758082757586502/?type=1&theater> (26.04.2022).
233 <https://www.facebook.com/103105249750926/photos/pcb.758083210919790/758082780919833/?type=1&theater> (26.04.2022).
234 <https://www.facebook.com/103105249750926/photos/pcb.758083210919790/758082757586502/?type=1&theater> (26.04.2022).
235 Sadurska – Bounni 1994, 122.

of Corbulon in the south exedra[236]. The layout of the hypogeum is canonical, with a long, main gallery and two lateral ones near the entrance[237].

The reliefs from the main exedra, a male[238] and a female bust[239], show that this area was first used by the founders of the tomb and was kept in their possession until the end of the tomb's use. Barʿateh's family was buried in the north exedra. There, a relief with a male and a female bust[240], and three more male busts were found[241], in addition to cat. 115. The second family that was buried in the north exedra was that of Sîʿôna: three male busts[242] and a female bust[243] were found representing members of his family. Corbulon's family was buried in the south exedra: four male busts[244], a relief with a female bust and a standing boy[245], and a female bust[246] were found there. One male bust[247] and three female busts[248] were also found in the hypogeum, but their location is not specified, and the evidence of the names does not allow the figures to be connected to any of the above-mentioned four families.

A.D. 115–125: Hypogeum of Šalamallat

The hypogeum is located in the west necropolis and was excavated by Adnan Bounni and Nasib Saliby in 1957. The precise date is not preserved in the foundation inscription, but since half of the tomb was ceded in A.D. 147 to the family of the cousin of the founder, the construction date of the tomb was between A.D. 89 and A.D. 147[249], most likely between A.D. 115–125[250]. The tomb was used by the extended family of Šalamallat until the second half of the 3rd cent. A.D., possibly A.D. 260–268[251]. Its plan is tripartite, but instead of two long galleries placed near the entrance area of the main gallery, it is composed of three exedrae[252].

Apart from cat. 110–112 that were found in the vestibule, and cat. 113, found in the staircase, thirty-two reliefs were found in the tomb. Two male busts were found in the staircase to the hypogeum[253], and one female bust was found in the hypogeum without another indication of the find location[254]. All the other reliefs from the tomb, however, were found in the central exedra and depicted the founder and his immediate family, as well as members of the extended family that later took over the hypogeum. These are: two busts depicting priests[255], twelve male busts[256], fifteen female busts[257], and one relief with a male and a female bust[258]. The family tree can be reconstructed thanks to the numerous inscribed reliefs from the tomb (sixteen out of thirty-two) but since the reliefs were

---

236 Sadurska – Bounni 1994, 122–125.
237 Sadurska – Bounni 1994, pl. 10.
238 Sadurska – Bounni 1994, 125 cat. 163 fig. 45 pl. 10.
239 Sadurska – Bounni 1994, 126 cat. 165 fig. 196 pl. 10.
240 Sadurska – Bounni 1994, 131 cat. 174 fig. 42 pl. 10.
241 Three male busts: 1) Sadurska – Bounni 1994, 132 cat. 176 fig. 123 pl. 10; (2) Sadurska – Bounni 1994, 132 f. cat. 177 fig. 121 pl. 10; (3) Sadurska – Bounni 1994, 133 cat. 178 fig. 111 pl. 10.
242 Three male busts: (1) Sadurska – Bounni 1994, 133 f. cat. 179 fig. 78 pl. 10; (2) Sadurska – Bounni 1994, 135 f. cat. 182 fig. 110 pl. 10; (3) Sadurska – Bounni 1994, 136 cat. 183 fig. 124 pl. 10.
243 Sadurska – Bounni 1994, 134 cat. 180 fig. 189 pl. 10. The onomastics do not allow the assignment of this bust to a specific family, but the proximity to the male portraits of the Sîʿôna family make it likely that she belonged to it.
244 Four male busts (1) Sadurska – Bounni 1994, 126 f. cat. 166 fig. 108 pl. 10; (2) Sadurska – Bounni 1994, 128 cat. 169 fig. 112 pl. 10; (3) Sadurska – Bounni 1994, 129 cat. 171 fig. 125 pl. 10; (4) Sadurska – Bounni 1994, 129 f. cat. 172 fig. 109 pl. 10. The last two have no precise find location given, but onomastics indicate that they must have been placed in the south exedra.
245 Sadurska – Bounni 1994, 128 f. cat. 170 fig. 193 pl. 10.
246 Sadurska – Bounni 1994, 130 f. cat. 173 fig. 194 pl. 10. It has no precise find location given, but onomastics indicate that it must have been placed in the south exedra.
247 Sadurska – Bounni 1994, 125 f. cat. 164 fig. 62 pl. 10.
248 Three female busts: (1) Sadurska – Bounni 1994, 127 cat. 167 fig. 197 pl. 10; (2) Sadurska – Bounni 1994, 127 f. cat. 168 fig. 162 pl. 10; (3) Sadurska – Bounni 1994, 131 f. cat. 175 fig. 190 pl. 10.
249 Sadurska – Bounni 1994, 149 f.
250 Sadurska – Bounni 1994, 150.
251 Sadurska – Bounni 1994, 150 f.
252 Gawlikowski 1970a, 122 f.; Sadurska – Bounni 1994, 149.
253 Two male busts: (1) Sadurska – Bounni 1994, 156 f. cat. 203 fig. 90 pl. 13; (2) Sadurska – Bounni 1994, 160 cat. 210 fig. 95 pl. 13.
254 Sadurska – Bounni 1994, 168 f. cat. 226 fig. 172 pl. 13.
255 Priests: (1) Sadurska – Bounni 1994, 152 f.cat. 196 fig. 34 pl. 13; (2) Sadurska – Bounni 1994, 154 f. cat. 200 fig. 84 pl. 13.
256 Males: (1) Sadurska – Bounni 1994, 153 cat. 197 fig. 35 pl. 13; (2) Sadurska – Bounni 1994, 155 cat. 201 fig. 86 pl. 13; (3) Sadurska – Bounni 1994, 155 f. cat. 202 fig. 57 pl. 13; (4) Sadurska – Bounni 1994, 156 cat. 203 fig. 37 pl. 13; (5) Sadurska – Bounni 1994, 157 cat. 205 pl. 13; (6) Sadurska – Bounni 1994, 159 cat. 208 fig. 89 pl. 13; (7) Sadurska – Bounni 1994, 160 f. cat. 211 fig. 113 pl. 13; (8) Sadurska – Bounni 1994, 166 cat. 221 fig. 88 pl. 13; (9) Sadurska – Bounni 1994, 166 f. cat. 222 fig. 77 pl. 13; (10) Sadurska – Bounni 1994, 167 cat. 223 fig. 39 pl. 13; (11) Sadurska – Bounni 1994, 167 f. cat. 224 fig. 121 pl. 13; (12) Sadurska – Bounni 1994, 170 cat. 230 fig. 85 pl. 13.
257 Females: (1) Sadurska – Bounni 1994, 161 f. cat. 212 fig. 126 pl. 13; (2) Sadurska – Bounni 1994, 153 f. cat. 198 fig. 153 pl. 13; (3) Sadurska – Bounni 1994, 154 cat. 199 fig. 154 pl. 13; (4) Sadurska – Bounni 1994, 157 f. cat. 206 fig. 187 pl. 13; (5) Sadurska – Bounni 1994, 158 f. cat. 207 fig. 176 pl. 13; (6) Sadurska – Bounni 1994, 159 f. cat. 209 fig. 160 pl. 13; (7) Sadurska – Bounni 1994, 162 cat. 213 fig. 202 pl. 13; (8) Sadurska – Bounni 1994, 162 f. cat. 214 fig. 204 pl. 13; (9) Sadurska – Bounni 1994, 163 cat. 215 fig. 177 pl. 13; (10) Sadurska – Bounni 1994, 163 f. cat. 216 fig. 195 pl. 13; (11) Sadurska – Bounni 1994, 164 cat. 217 fig. 181 pl. 13; (12) Sadurska – Bounni 1994, 164 f. cat. 218 fig. 205 pl. 13; (13) Sadurska – Bounni 1994, 165 f. cat. 219 fig. 182 pl. 13; (14) Sadurska – Bounni 1994, 166 cat. 220 fig. 155 pl. 13; (14) Sadurska – Bounni 1994, 168 cat. 225 fig. 161 pl. 13.
258 Sadurska – Bounni 1994, 161 f. cat. 212 fig. 126 pl. 13.

found out of place, it is not possible to say how they were arranged in the tomb[259].

A.D. 116: Hypogeum of Malkû

The hypogeum, located in the south-west necropolis, was identified by Ingholt in 1924, but its excavation proper only took place in 1937[260]. Thanks to its foundation inscription, it is known that it was founded in A.D. 116 by Malkû, son of Nûrbel[261]. Several cession inscriptions on the door lintel make it possible to trace further the history of the tomb, as well as connect the various funerary sculptures found there to the different phases of occupation and use[262]. In A.D. 186, both the south and north exedrae of the tomb were given to new owners by the heirs of Malkû. The northern was given to Naḥasṭab and Rauḥibel, two freedmen[263]. In A.D. 213, one of the heirs of either Naḥasṭab or Rauḥibel ceded part of the exedra to Attetan[264]. Two pieces of sculpture that were found in the area can be associated with these two phases: a loculus relief with two busts depicting a man and a boy is probably connected to the cession of the exedra to Naḥasṭab and Rauḥibel[265], and a loculus relief with the bust of a bearded man, Attetan, is connected with the A.D. 213 cession[266]. The southern exedra was ceded to Baʿalaî in A.D. 186[267], who had a sarcophagus made for him and his family there in A.D. 188 (cat. 10)[268]. The same year, A.D. 188, Baʿalaî ceded »three niches in the exedra to the right« to Saʿarona[269]. The central chamber of the tomb was divided into two parts by archways: in the first part, there were six niches to the south, and three niches to the north followed by a recess with four niches. The six south niches were sold in A.D. 213 to Bassē and Risqā, sons of Saʿarona, who had already acquired three of the niches of the south exedra[270]. Four more niches, »two to the right … two to the left as you enter the exedra« were ceded to Ammô, daughter of the above-mentioned Bassē in A.D. 267. The cession text indicates that, in antiquity, there was one more sarcophagus located in this section[271]. Apart from the sarcophagus of Baʿalaî (cat. 10), two more reliefs were found in the southern exedra: a loculus relief depicting a female[272] and a loculus relief with two busts portraying a married couple, Balaî and Martî[273]. According to Ingholt, each one of these reliefs is associated with a different phase of the tomb: the relief of the single female is the earliest, and perhaps predated the sale of the exedra, the sarcophagus is associated with the cession of A.D. 186, and the loculus relief with the busts of the couple represented the parents of Saʿarona, who acquired part of the exedra in A.D. 188[274].

The first three niches to the north were sold in A.D. 214 to Julius Aurelius Agrippa[275], and the recess was sold in A.D. 214 to Julius Aurelius ʿOgeîlû. This was supposed to contain three niches but its new owner (Julius Aurelius ʿOgeîlû) had four niches dug out[276]. Two sculptures are associated with this area of the tomb: a stele depicting a boy in Parthian-inspired clothes that was found »in the westernmost niche of the back wall«[277]. The inscription identifies the figure as Afraḥat, son of ʿOgeîlû[278]. A relief depicting a full sarcophagus was also found in this section of the tomb, »along the eastern wall of the recess« (cat. 178)[279]. The find location of the relief prompted Ingholt to identify the figures with members of the family of Julius Aurelius Agrippa[280].

The second part of the tomb had a chamber with four niches on each side. This area yielded the following sculptures: a loculus relief depicting Malkû, son of Malkû[281]; a loculus relief depicting Malkû, son of Nûrbel, the physician[282]; a stele depicting Nûrbel[283]; and a loculus relief showing a female, Nûrbel's wife[284].

---

259 Sadurska – Bounni 1994, 150–152.
260 Ingholt 1935, 90–108; Ingholt 1941; Ingholt 1962, 102 f.; Ingholt 1966, 457.
261 Ingholt 1935, 90 f. no. 1. Ingholt 1970–1971, 174, gives the foundation date as A.D. 121.
262 For the inscriptions, see Ingholt 1935, 90–108.
263 Ingholt 1935, 91–93 no. 2.
264 Ingholt 1935, 96 f. no. 5.
265 Present whereabouts unknown: Ingholt 1970–1971, 175. Ingholt had suggested that the adult male was either Naḥasṭab or Rauḥibel portrayed with his son.
266 Palmyra, Palmyra Museum, inv. no. A 903/903: Ingholt 1970–1971, 176 f. pl. 1, 2; Yon 2013, 339 no. 9.
267 Ingholt 1935, 93–105 no. 3; Ingholt 1970–1971, 178–181.
268 Ingholt 1962, 102.
269 Ingholt 1935, 95 f. no. 4; Ingholt 1970–1971, 178 f.
270 Ingholt 1935, 97 f. no. 6; Ingholt 1962, 103.
271 Ingholt 1935, 102–104 no. 11; Ingholt 1970–1971, 179.
272 Palmyra, Palmyra Museum, inv. no. unknown: Ingholt 1970–1971, 179 f. pl. 2, 1; Krag 2018, 223 cat. 209.
273 Palmyra, Palmyra Museum, inv. no. A 904: Ingholt 1970–1971, 180–182 pl. 1, 2; Yon 2013, 339 no. 10; Krag 2018, 284 cat. 436.
274 Ingholt 1970–1971, 179–192.
275 Ingholt 1935, 99 f. no. 8; Ingholt 1962, 103.
276 Ingholt 1962, 103–119.
277 Ingholt 1962, 104.
278 Palmyra, Palmyra Museum, inv. no. unknown: Ingholt 1962, 104; PAT 1623.
279 Ingholt 1962, 104.
280 Ingholt 1962, 118 f.
281 Palmyra, Palmyra Museum, inv. no. A 902/902: Ingholt 1962, 101 f.; Ingholt 1966, 467 fig. 9.
282 Damascus, National Museum of Damascus, inv. no. unknown: Ingholt 1966, 463 fig. 5.
283 Palmyra, Palmyra Museum, inv. no. A 901: Ingholt 1966, 459 f. fig. 2.
284 Present whereabouts unknown: Ingholt 1962, 102.

The epigraphic evidence makes clear that this was the first chamber used in the tomb, contemporary with its foundation, and holding the burials of the founder's family[285].

A.D. 116: Hypogeum AK

The hypogeum is located in the south-west necropolis and was excavated by Ingholt during his campaigns in Palmyra. No foundation inscription was found on the door lintel. The tomb has a central chamber and two side chambers[286]. In his excavation diaries, he compared the entrance to that of the tomb of Malkû that was founded in A.D. 116[287], and together with the stylistic dating of cat. 70, these may indicate that tomb AK was also founded in the early part of the 2nd cent. A.D. Apart from cat. 70, Ingholt associated no other sculpture with the tomb.

Early 2nd cent. A.D.: Hypogeum of Arṭaban

The hypogeum is located in the south-west necropolis and was excavated in 1958 by O. Taḥa and N. Kheir[288]. The name of the founder is given by the inscription on the monument to the founder's family inside the tomb (cat. 72). Since there is no foundation inscription associated with the monument, the date of the construction is based on stylistic criteria to the early 2nd cent. A.D.[289]. The tomb has a relatively complex plan: a long vestibule leads to the main gallery, and it has two galleries at almost right angles to the main gallery, which are cut into the rock immediately after the vestibule (the one to the south notably longer than the one to the north), and two exedrae cut into the rock on either side of the middle of the main gallery[290]. Thanks to the numerous inscribed loculus reliefs, it is possible to reconstruct the genealogy of the founder and estimate the end of use of the tomb to the beginning of the 1st cent.[291].

Apart from the relief cat. 72, placed on the back wall of the main gallery facing the entrance[292], and the sarcophagus relief cat. 73, twenty-two loculus reliefs and one stele were found in the tomb: three busts of priest, one in loculus bay 4[293], one in loculus bay 16[294], one in loculus bay 14[295]; twelve male busts, one in loculus bay 12[296], one in loculus bay 10[297], one in loculus bay 14[298], two in loculus bay 24[299], one from loculus bay 26[300], two from loculus bay 38[301], one from loculus bay 39[302], one from loculus bay 28[303], one from loculus bay 55[304], and one whose precise location is not known[305]. There were also seven female busts, one in loculus bay 1[306], one in loculus bay 24[307], one in loculus bay 27[308], one from loculus bay 36[309], two from loculus bay 37[310], one from loculus bay 54[311]; as well as one a stele with a standing boy[312].

Early 2nd cent. A.D.: Hypogeum of Ṭaʿaî

The hypogeum is located in the south-east necropolis and was discovered and excavated in 1952 by O. Taḥa, Sélim Abdul-Hak, and N. Kheir[313]. No foundation inscription is associated with the tomb, but the stylistic dating of the sculptures found there, date the period of the use of the tomb to the 2nd cent. A.D.[314]. The tomb has a main, long gallery that ends in an exedra, and

---

285 Ingholt 1962, 103 f.
286 See Raja et al. 2021a, Diary 1, 119, Diary 5, 137 f.
287 Ingholt 1935, 90 f. no. 1. Ingholt 1970–1971, 174 gives the foundation date as A.D. 121. Raja et al. 2021a, Diary 1, 119, Diary 3, 63. 73, Diary 5, 137 f.
288 Sadurska – Bounni 1994, 23.
289 Sadurska – Bounni 1994, 23.
290 Sadurska – Bounni 1994, pl. 4.
291 Sadurska – Bounni 1994, 24–26.
292 Sadurska – Bounni 1994, 37–39 do not record if there were burials placed behind the monument, even though there is a loculus bay depicted behind it on their plan.
293 Sadurska – Bounni 1994, 26 cat. 19 fig. 83 pl. 4.
294 Sadurska – Bounni 1994, 28 f. cat. 23 fig. 70 pl. 4.
295 Sadurska – Bounni 1994, 29 cat. 25 fig. 120 pl. 4.
296 Sadurska – Bounni 1994, 26 f. cat. 20 fig. 29 pl. 4.
297 Sadurska – Bounni 1994, 27 cat. 21 fig. 32 pl. 4.
298 Sadurska – Bounni 1994, 29 cat. 24 fig. 59 pl. 4.
299 Sadurska – Bounni 1994, 29 f. cat. 26 fig. 115 pl. 4 and cat. 27 fig. 30 pl. 4.
300 Sadurska – Bounni 1994, 31 cat. 29 fig. 93 pl. 4.
301 Sadurska – Bounni 1994, 33 f. cat. 34 fig. 25 and 34 cat. 35 fig. 116 pl. 4.
302 Sadurska – Bounni 1994, 35 cat. 37 fig. 65 pl. 4.
303 Sadurska – Bounni 1994, 35 f. cat. 38 fig. 30 pl. 4.
304 Sadurska – Bounni 1994, 36 f. cat. 40 fig. 117 pl. 4.
305 Sadurska – Bounni 1994, 36 cat. 39 fig. 43 pl. 4.
306 Sadurska – Bounni 1994, 27 f. cat. 22 fig. 151 pl. 4.
307 Sadurska – Bounni 1994, 30 f. cat. 28 fig. 175 pl. 4.
308 Sadurska – Bounni 1994, 31 f. cat. 30 fig. 152 pl. 4.
309 Sadurska – Bounni 1994, 32 cat. 31 fig. 134 pl. 4.
310 Sadurska – Bounni 1994, 33 cat. 32 fig. 135 pl. 4 and cat. 33 fig. 136 pl. 4.
311 Sadurska – Bounni 1994, 34 f. cat. 36 fig. 178 pl. 4.
312 Sadurska – Bounni 1994, 39 f. cat. 42 fig. 3 pl. 4.
313 Abdul-Hak 1952, 193.
314 Abdul-Hak 1952, 194.

two lateral exedrae placed on either side of the area near the entrance[315].

The west exedra had a niche with an undecorated sarcophagus box in the shape of a kline (appendix 6, cat. 13)[316]. This was covered by cat. 76, and later cat. 79 was placed over cat. 76. Cat. 77. 78 were also found in the west exedra. The west exedra was divided into two sections, A and B.[317]. In section A of the south side, the following reliefs were found: in front of the first loculus bay (a): relief with bust of priest[318], in front of the second loculus bay (b): two reliefs with male busts[319], in front of the third loculus bay (c): relief with male bust[320] and cat. 79, and in front of the fourth loculus bay (d): a relief with a female bust[321]. In the north side of section A, the following reliefs were found: in front of the first loculus bay (e): a relief with female bust[322] and a relief with bust of priest[323], in front of the second loculus bay (f): two reliefs with male busts[324], and a fragment of a bust[325], in front of the third loculus bay (g): a relief with female bust[326] and a relief with male bust[327], and in front of the fourth loculus bay (h): a relief with a female bust[328] and a relief with the bust of a priest[329]. In section B of the south side, in front of the second loculus bay (n): were found relief fragments[330], in front of the third loculus bay (o): a relief with a male bust[331] and a relief with a standing child[332], in front of the fourth loculus bay (p): a relief with a standing child[333], a relief with a standing girl[334], and the fragment of a bust[335], and in front of the fifth loculus bay (q): a relief with a female bust[336], a relief with a male bust[337], and a fragment from another relief[338]. In the north side of section B, a relief with female bust was found in front of first loculus bay (i)[339], a relief with a male bust in front of second loculus bay (j)[340], and cat. 78 in front of the third loculus bay (k).

Four reliefs were found in the south exedra: (1) in front of first loculus bay (s) a relief with the bust of a priest[341], (2) in front of the second loculus bay (t) a relief with the bust of a man[342], (3) in front of the third loculus bay (u) a relief with two standing children[343], and (4) in front of the fourth loculus bay (v) a relief with a standing child[344]. A relief with two standing children was found in the north exedra[345].

A.D. 100–125: Tower Tomb no. 85d

The tower tomb is located in the west necropolis. Only the ground floor survives. Technical considerations and stylistic reasons date the tomb in the first quarter of the 2nd cent. A.D.[346]. The ground floor has a chamber with at least one loculus bay[347]. Only cat. 21 survives from the tomb's sculptural decoration, and its original location was probably on the ground floor[348].

A.D. 100–130: Tower Tomb no. 39

The tomb is located in the west necropolis, and only two floors are preserved. Since no foundation inscription survives, the tomb is dated by Henning based on the building techniques and the style of the architectural decoration to the period A.D. 100–130[349]. Each floor had chambers with loculus bays[350]. Only the sarcophagus cat. 22 survives from the reliefs that must have been located inside the tomb. Henning suggests that it is uncertain whether it had a decorative or a funerary function[351]. The only other sculpture from the tomb is a pediment with the bust of a priest that was on the tomb's façade, over a ground floor entrance[352].

---

315 Abdul-Hak 1952, 194–217.
316 Abdul-Hak 1952, 200.
317 Abdul-Hak 1952, 200.
318 Abdul-Hak 1952, 215. 226–228 cat. 8.
319 Abdul-Hak 1952, 215. 228 cat. 17 and Abdul-Hak 1952, 215. 228 f. cat. 18.
320 Abdul-Hak 1952, 215. 238 f. cat. 24.
321 Abdul-Hak 1952, 215. 239 f. cat. 27.
322 Abdul-Hak 1952, 215. 225 f. cat. 6.
323 Abdul-Hak 1952, 215. 226 cat. 7.
324 Abdul-Hak 1952, 215. 225 cat. 5 and Abdul-Hak 1952, 215. 237 f. cat. 22.
325 Abdul-Hak 1952, 215. 232 cat. 14.
326 Abdul-Hak 1952, 215. 235–237 cat. 21.
327 Abdul-Hak 1952, 215. 239 cat. 26.
328 Abdul-Hak 1952, 215. 239 cat. 25.
329 Abdul-Hak 1952, 215 cat. 00.
330 Abdul-Hak 1952, 216. 244 f. cat. 10. 36.
331 Abdul-Hak 1952, 216. 241 cat. 30.
332 Abdul-Hak 1952, 216. 242 cat. 31.
333 Abdul-Hak 1952, 216. 242 cat. 32.
334 Abdul-Hak 1952, 216. 243 cat. 34.
335 Abdul-Hak 1952, 216. 231 f. cat. 13.
336 Abdul-Hak 1952, 216. 244 cat. 35.
337 Abdul-Hak 1952, 216. 245 f. cat. 37.
338 Abdul-Hak 1952, 216 cat. 30.
339 Abdul-Hak 1952, 216. 240 cat. 28.
340 Abdul-Hak 1952, 216. 240 f. cat. 29.
341 Abdul-Hak 1952, 212 f. 221 f. cat. 1.
342 Abdul-Hak 1952, 213. 222 f. cat. 2.
343 Abdul-Hak 1952, 213. 224 f. cat. 4.
344 Abdul-Hak 1952, 214. 223 f. cat. 3.
345 Abdul-Hak 1952, 214 cat. 10.
346 Henning 2013b, 233.
347 Henning 2013b, 233.
348 Henning 2013b, 233.
349 al-Asʿad – Schmidt-Colinet 2005a, 41 figs. 52–54; Henning 2013b, 178 f.
350 Henning 2013b, 178 f.
351 Henning 2013b, 179.
352 Henning 2013b, 179.

A.D. 100–130: Tower Tomb no. 168

The tower tomb is located in the north necropolis and only one floor is preserved. In the absence of a foundation inscription, the stylistic dating of the sarcophagus and the technical aspects of the construction support a date of construction in A.D. 100–130. There is one poorly preserved chamber on the ground floor, where cat. 58 was found. No other piece of sculpture is associated with the tomb[353].

A.D. 100–150: Hypogeum of Lišamš

The hypogeum is located in the south-west necropolis, and it was excavated by Ingholt during his 1924 campaign[354]. It was looted in antiquity[355], and one inscription taken out of the tomb was recorded in neighbouring Qaryatein (modern Al-Qaryatayn)[356], while a second found its way to Istanbul, at the then Musée Imperial Ottoman[357]. Even though the foundation inscription was not found, the evidence from the various cession texts on the door lintel or removed from the tomb reveal the history of the tomb after its construction. In A.D. 181, Lišamš ceded part of the central chamber to Sirai[358], and a few years later, in A.D. 186, Lišamš and his half-brother Amdai, ceded yet another part of the central chamber with its niches to Wardan[359]. Two years later (A.D. 188), Lišamš alone ceded the eight lateral niches of the second central chamber to Bonnê[360], and in A.D. 228, Wardan sold part of his property from the tomb to Aurelius Malkû[361]. The graffiti in the individual niches shed more light on the division of the interior of the tomb[362]. The tomb has the ›canonical‹ layout with two chambers along the vertical axis and two side chambers to the left and right of the vestibule. Loculus bays were dug into the rock walls of all the chambers[363].

A few pieces of sculpture were found inside the tomb. Two of these, the fragment of an inscribed stele with a standing male[364], and cat. 75 are dated on stylistic criteria to the period A.D. 100–150, thus indicating that the tomb's construction must have taken place in this period. The exact find location of cat. 75 is not recorded[365]. Cat. 74 was found inside the central chamber, on the right[366]. Ingholt's picture shows that it was placed in front of and to the side of loculus bays, so it had been placed at the end of the second part of the central chamber, directly facing the tomb's entrance. According to the inscriptions in the tomb, this area had been ceded to Bonnê in A.D. 188, but it is not possible to connect the family of Shalam, daughter of ʿOggâ, mentioned in the inscription of cat. 74 to that of Bonnê[367].

A.D. 100–150: Hypogeum no. 31

The hypogeum is located in the south-west necropolis and was excavated by Ingholt in 1924 and 1925[368]. No foundation inscription is associated with it. The tomb had a central chamber and two lateral chambers. Two reliefs were found there, cat. 116 and 117[369].

A.D. 100–150: Hypogeum no. 33

The hypogeum is located in the south-west necropolis and was first excavated by Ingholt in 1924, and then explored further during the 1925 campaign[370]. An inscription on the door, possibly the foundation inscription, was badly preserved[371]. Ingholt recorded the discovery of one relief: cat. 118, found at the left wall of the right lateral chamber.

Before A.D. 128: Tower Tomb no. N206

Tower tomb no. N206 is located in the west necropolis. The tomb was noticed by Schnädelbach and excavated between 2007–2010, within the wider framework of an excavation project led by the Palmyra Museum and the Syrian Directorate General of Antiquities

---

353 Henning 2013b, 278 f.
354 Ingholt 1938, 106. For the tomb, see also Raja et al. 2021a, Diary 3, 7, Diary 5, 26–26b.
355 Ingholt 1938, 106.
356 CIS 4194; Ingholt 1938, 109.
357 There is no information about its acquisition by the museum in the early publications: Musée Imperial Ottoman 1895, 74 f. cat. 193; CIS 4195. Perhaps it was confiscated at the borders, and was then sent to Istanbul, as was the case with several reliefs. See Bobou et al. 2021b, appendix 2; Bobou – Randeris Thomsen 2021, 534.
358 CIS 4194; Ingholt 1938, 109.
359 Ingholt 1938, 106–109 cat. 1.
360 Ingholt 1938, 109 f. cat. 2.
361 Ingholt 1938, 110–112 cat. 3.
362 Ingholt 1938, 113–117.
363 Ingholt 1938, pl. 39.

364 Ingholt 1938, 116 f. pl. 42, 2.
365 Raja et al. 2021a, Diary 5, 34.
366 Raja et al. 2021a, Diary 5, 27.
367 Ingholt 1938, 118.
368 Ingholt recorded the tomb under two names in his diaries: E and 31, see Raja et al. 2021b.
369 Raja et al. 2021a, Diary 1, 103. 131 f.
370 Raja et al. 2021a, Diary 1, 109 f. 119, Diary 3, 43. 72, Diary 5, 108–108b.
371 Raja et al. 2021a, Diary 1, 110.

and Museums[372]. Only the ground floor of the tomb survived. No foundation inscription can be associated with the tomb, but an inscription on the podium of sarcophagus cat. 4 dated to A.D. 128 indicated that the tomb was constructed before that date. The sarcophagus was found at the end of a narrow chamber, together with two more sarcophagi without figural decoration that were placed along the long wall of the chamber (appendix 5, cat. 2. 3). Fragments of two standing statues were also found in the tomb[373].

A.D. 123: Hypogeum of Ḥennibel

The hypogeum of Ḥennibel is located in the south-west necropolis. It was discovered accidentally and excavated between 2007–2010, within the wider framework of an excavation project led by the Palmyra Museum and the Syrian Directorate General of Antiquities and Museums[374]. The foundation inscription of the tomb recorded its construction date in A.D. 123. It had the ›canonical‹ plan with »three galleries arranged in the form of an inverted T«[375]. In addition to cat. 103. 104, al-Asʿad records that they found a loculus relief with a female bust representing Ḥanna, daughter-law of Ḥennibel. The inscriptions on the reliefs as well as the low number of burial niches (twelve in total), indicate that the tomb was only used briefly[376].

A.D. 128: Tower Tomb no. 34, Tower of Moqîmû

Tower tomb no. 34 is located in the west necropolis, and only one floor survives. The date of construction is known thanks to the foundation inscription: A.D. 128. The ground floor had a chamber, where sarcophagus cat. 52 was found. Its exact location is not known: Henning suggests that it was placed either against one of the long walls of the ground-floor chamber, or that it was incorporated into the back wall of the same chamber[377].

A.D. 130/131: Hypogeum of Ḥatrai

The hypogeum is located in the north-west necropolis. It was excavated in 2009[378], within the wider framework of an excavation project led by the Palmyra Museum and the Syrian Directorate General of Antiquities and Museums[379]. The foundation inscription records its construction by the sons of Ḥatrai in A.D. 130/131. One of Ḥatrai's grandsons ceded an exedra several years later[380]. The plan of the tomb shows that it had a main gallery with two lateral galleries with loculus bays extending from the area near its entrance and two exedrae near the end of the main gallery, on either side of the area near the back wall of the tomb[381]. The tomb contains painted decoration showing a banqueting scene across the three walls of one of the lateral exedrae[382], in addition to cat. 177 and the loculus reliefs recorded by al-Asʿad[383].

A.D. 133/134: Hypogeum of Yarḥaî, ʿAtenûrî, and Zabdibôl

The hypogeum is located in the south-west necropolis and was excavated by Ingholt in 1925 and then investigated again in 1928[384]. The foundation inscription on the door lintel records the construction date in A.D. 133/134[385]. A second text on the door lintel records the cession of part of the tomb in A.D. 194 by Moqîmû and Aqamate to Šalman and Taimû[386]. The hypogeum is composed of two chambers joined by a narrow, wide corridor, and a lateral exedra near its entrance. The burial bays were dug into the sides of the chambers.

Ingholt records the discovery of cat. 132 near the entrance of the central chamber[387] and of cat. 133 within it[388]. As Ingholt observes, none of the names inscribed on cat. 133 appear on the inscriptions of the door lintel[389]. The date of the relief in the later part of the 2nd cent. A.D. makes the association with the family of Moqîmû likely[390].

---

372 al-Asʿad 2013, 15.
373 al-Asʿad 2013, 16 fig. 1.
374 al-Asʿad 2013, 19.
375 al-Asʿad 2013, 19.
376 al-Asʿad 2013, 19 f.
377 Henning 2013b, 174 f.
378 Eristov et al. 2019, 163–167 pl. 78, 1.
379 al-Asʿad 2013, 18 f.
380 al-Asʿad 2013, 18.
381 Eristov et al. 2019, pl. 78, 1.
382 al-Asʿad 2013, 18 f.; Eristov et al. 2019, 163–167 pl. 78, 3–6.
383 al-Asʿad 2013, 19.
384 Ingholt 1938, 95–103; Raja et al. 2021a, Diary 2, 53 f., Diary 3, 9. 66. 73, Diary 5, 0–5.
385 Ingholt 1938, 94.
386 Ingholt 1938, 95.
387 Raja et al. 2021a, Diary 5, 2.
388 Raja et al. 2021a, Diary 3, 9, Diary 5, 1 f.
389 Ingholt 1938, 102.
390 Ingholt 1938, 102 f.

A.D. 138: Hypogeum of ʿAlaînê

The hypogeum was excavated by the Polish Archaeological Mission in Palmyra by Wiktor Andrzej Daszewski and Anna Sadurska under the direction of K. Michalowski between 1969 and 1971, over the duration of three campaigns. The foundation inscription dates the construction of the tomb to A.D. 138, and the stylistic assessment of the sculptures found there indicates that the tomb was in use until the middle of the 3rd cent[391]. The hypogeum's plan is simple: a long, main gallery with one side exedra to the north of the entrance and three exedrae at the end in the shape of a T. In addition to the sarcophagi burials, there were numerous burials in loculus bays in all the exedrae of the tomb.

Numerous pieces of sculpture were found in a fragmentary state in the tomb[392], but the best-preserved pieces are cat. 134–136, and the following reliefs: from the podium of the central exedra, a female statue[393]; a male bust from the main exedra, loculus bay 30, loculus 3[394]; a female bust from loculus bay 28, loculus 3[395]; and a female bust from loculus bay 27, loculus 3[396]. The sarcophagi were arranged at the end of the main gallery: four sarcophagi were placed on the podium of the central exedra, two on each side (cat. 134–137), and one was near the base of the podium (cat. 137).

Before A.D. 142:
Hypogeum of the Three Brothers

The hypogeum of the Three Brothers, located in the south-west necropolis, is one of the best-studied Palmyrene tombs[397]. It first drew the attention of scholars in 1899 and was the focus of study in subsequent expeditions[398]. The tomb was constructed slightly before A.D. 142, according to the earliest inscription in the tomb that records the construction of an aedicula with a sarcophagus within the building (cat. 6). Already in A.D. 160, parts of the tomb were ceded to others by the three brothers who had built it, with the inscriptions recording the concessions written on the tomb's door

Figure 46. Painted exedra in hypogeum of the Three Brothers.

lintel[399]. On the same lintel, a series of other concession inscriptions shows how parts of the tomb were further sold off in A.D. 191[400] and in A.D. 241[401], while a partially preserved inscription may indicate another sale in A.D. 259[402]. The tomb has the canonical, inverted T-shape plan, formed by two consecutive exedrae divided by a small, wide corridor on the east side and two lateral exedrae to the north and south. All the walls of the four exedrae have dug-out loculus bays. The sarcophagi associated with the tomb were found in the north and south exedrae. Cat. 6 was placed inside an aedicula at the south exedra of the tomb[403], and cat. 122 was found inside in one of the loculus bays across cat. 6[404]. Cat. 119–121 were located in the north exedra[405]. All the sarcophagi were placed in front of bays with loculi; the loculus bays of the south exedra were the most carefully cut into the rock[406]. The second exedra at the east of the tomb carries painted scenes: there are full-figure painted portraits on the side pillars at the entrance of the exedra, Victories holding up medallions with bust portraits on the pillars between the burial bays, the discovery of Achilles at Skyros on the lunette of the east wall, and a medallion with the Rape of Ganymede on the vault. The vault and architectural details of the exedra are also painted (Fig. 46)[407].

---

391 Sadurska – Bounni 1994, 172–174.
392 Seventy-one in total, all fully published in Sadurska 1977.
393 Sadurska – Bounni 1994, 177 cat. 235 fig. 235 pl. 14.
394 Sadurska – Bounni 1994, 178 cat. 236 fig. 128 pl. 14.
395 Sadurska – Bounni 1994, 178 f. cat. 237 fig. 200 pl. 14.
396 Sadurska – Bounni 1994, 179 f. cat. 238 fig. 201 pl. 14.
397 See the recent monograph on the tomb, edited by Eristov et al. 2019.
398 Eristov – Vibert-Guigue 2019, 26 f. It was mistakenly identified with a tomb with painted decoration seen by Johannes Elith Østrup, but recent research has shown that Østrup must have seen a different tomb: Raja – Sørensen 2019, 60–62.
399 Yon 2019, 315 f. nos. 2. 3.
400 Yon 2019, 316 nos. 4. 5.
401 Yon 2019, 316 f. no. 6.
402 Yon 2019, 319 no. 18.
403 Vibert-Guigue 2019, 77.
404 Loculus bay 58 in the plan in Eristov et al. 2019, pl. 81.
405 Vibert-Guigue 2019, 76 f.
406 Vibert-Guigue 2019, 78.
407 Eristov – Vibert-Guigue 2019, 96–133.

A.D. 149: Temple Tomb no. 85b, Tomb of Aʿaîlamî and Zebîdâ (›Tomb Cantineau‹)

The tomb is located in the west necropolis. It was excavated and published in 1929 by Jean Cantineau[408]. The foundation inscription of the tomb was already published; it recorded the date of the construction of the tomb in A.D. 149 as well as the names of the founders[409]. The tomb was a square building with an ornamented prostyle façade with pilasters in the corners and an inner peristyle courtyard, around which were the burials bays and the exedrae where the sarcophagi were located[410]. The sarcophagi cat. 193. 194. 196 have been associated with the east exedra[411], and cat. 195. 197. 206. 207 with the west exedra[412]. Thanks to Makowski's work[413] and the photographs of the tomb preserved in the Library of Congress[414], it was possible to associate also cat. 198. 199. 202. 205. 215–217 with the east side of the tomb, and cat. 203. 212–214. 219 with the south side of the tomb. It was not possible to connect the other fragments known to have been found in the tomb to a specific side or location within it[415].

Ca. A.D. 150: Tower Tomb no. 87

The tower tomb is located in the south-west necropolis and has two surviving floors. The stylistic dating of the sarcophagus fragment (cat. 56) supports a date for the construction of the tomb around A.D. 150. The tomb has a chamber with loculus burial bays on each floor[416]. Watzinger and Wulzinger reported that they had seen a relief with a reclining figure with an altar and a Victory (app. 2, cat. 4), but only cat. 56 survived when Henning surveyed the tomb[417].

A.D. 150–200: Hypogeum AN

The tomb was excavated by Ingholt[418]. Ingholt records the finding of cat. 125–127, possibly all stemming from a chamber. From the archive photo, cat. 126 seems to have formed part of a triclinium (the ends of sarcophagi boxes in the shape of klinai are visible). If that is the case, then cat. 125 and cat. 127 most likely formed part of the burials of another chamber of the same tomb. Another sheet in the archive shows that the sarcophagus lid, cat. 128, was also found in this tomb, and not in the tomb of Malkû, as it had been reported in the guide of the National Museum of Damascus[419].

A.D. 186: Hypogeum of Barʿâ Bonnûr

The hypogeum is located in the south-west necropolis and was excavated by Ingholt in 1924 and 1925[420]. The foundation inscription gives the construction date of A.D. 186[421]. The tomb's plan has not been published. Apart from sarcophagus cat. 167, three reliefs can be associated with the tomb: two with male portraits in the Musée du Louvre[422], and a female portrait in the National Museum of Damascus[423]. Sarcophagus cat. 167 was found in an exedra in the main chamber of the tomb. Originally, it formed part of a triclinium[424].

2nd cent. A.D.: Hypogeum AC

The hypogeum is located in the south-west necropolis and was excavated by Ingholt in 1924. Stylistic criteria allow for a dating of the tomb in the 2nd cent. A.D. He recorded two sarcophagi that are unique so far for Palmyra: the first, a sarcophagus with »two dog-like creatures [placing their paws] onto a bowl at the centre of the sarcophagus« (app. 6, cat. 21)[425], and a sarcophagus with garland decoration (appendix 5, cat. 8).

---

408 Cantineau 1929.
409 Cantineau 1929, 4 f.
410 Cantineau 1929. See also Makowski 1983 for a reconsideration and re-evaluation of the tomb, its plan, and its sculptures.
411 Makowski 1983, 180.
412 Makowski 1983, 180 f.
413 Makowski 1983.
414 Interior of the tomb. American Colony, P. D., photographer. (1920) Palmyra. Remains of a tomb temple. Palmyrene type of reclining figures. Syria Tadmur, 1920. [Approximately to 1933] [Photograph] Retrieved from the Library of Congress, <https://www.loc.gov/item/mpc2010000996/PP/> (26.04.2022); Interior of the tomb. American Colony. Photo Dept, photographer. (1929) Palmyra, May. Syria Tadmur, 1929. May. [Photograph] Retrieved from the Library of Congress, <https://www.loc.gov/item/mpc2005008584/PP/> (26.04.2022).
415 Thirty-six objects in total.
416 Henning 2013b, 234.
417 Henning 2013b, 234 f.
418 It does not seem to be recorded in his excavation diaries, however, five sheets from his archive contain his notes on the tomb. These are catalogued as IA_NCG_Portrait2016_016, IA_NCG_Portrait2016_065, IA_NCG_Portrait2016_066, IA_NCG_Portrait2016_085, and IA_NCG_Portrait2016_124.
419 Abdul Hak – Abdul Hak 1951, 42 cat. 37.
420 Ingholt 1935, 13.
421 Ingholt 1935, 115 f.
422 Ingholt 1935, 116.
423 Ingholt 1935, 116.
424 Ingholt 1935, 116.
425 Raja et al. 2021a, Diary 1, 100. In Raja et al. 2021a, Diary 5, 121, the creatures are identified with panthers.

2nd cent. A.D.: Temple Tomb no. 146

The tomb was recorded by Watzinger and Wulzinger in 1917[426], and was re-investigated between 2007 and 2010 within the wider framework of an excavation project led by the Palmyra Museum and the Syrian Directorate General of Antiquities and Museums[427]. It had one chamber with loculus bays and the sarcophagi. Only the sarcophagi cat. 191, and appendix 5, cat. 4–6 survive, and they were placed in front of the loculus bays, two at the right and two at the left of the chamber[428]. When Watzinger and Wulzinger surveyed the tomb, the fragment of a reclining figure was also in the chamber[429].

Before A.D. 220: Hypogeum F

The hypogeum is located in the south-east necropolis. It was discovered in 1992 and excavated by the Nara — Palmyra Archaeological Mission during the campaigns of 1992, 1994, 1995, 1996, and 1997[430]. The foundation date of the tomb is not known, but two inscriptions record the concession of two sections of the tomb in A.D. 220 and A.D. 222[431]. The hypogeum has a vestibule leading to a long, main gallery that ends in an exedra and two lateral side chambers placed near the entrance[432]. The sarcophagi cat. 105–107 were found in the main exedra, at the end of the main gallery. They were arranged in a triclinium. The sarcophagi cat. 108. 109 were found in the east and west niches of the main gallery respectively. Only one more portrait relief, a stele with a standing boy that was found near the tomb, has been associated with it[433].

Late 2nd cent. A.D.: Hypogeum Anonymous

The tomb is located in the south-east necropolis and was excavated by O. Taḥa and N. Kheir in 1956. No foundation inscription was found. The tomb is composed of a main gallery with loculus bays on the north, west, and east walls, a lateral gallery without loculus bays to the north, and a lateral gallery to the south with loculus bays on all three walls. All the sculptures were found in the north side of the main gallery: a female bust in the loculus bay 3[434], a male bust in loculus bay 4[435], and the sarcophagus cat. 172 against the north wall.

2nd / 3rd cent. A.D.? Tower Tomb no. 101

The tower tomb is located in the south-west necropolis and has one surviving floor. It is not possible to date the construction of the tomb, as it is not very well preserved, but the stylistic dating of the sarcophagus fragment found inside it (cat. 57) indicates that it was in use in the 3rd cent. A.D. The ground floor has a badly preserved chamber[436].

Watzinger and Wulzinger had reported seeing in the ground-floor chamber a sarcophagus box in the shape of a kline with five busts, and the lid with a reclining man and a seated woman in front of it placed in the north-west corner. They also recorded two large sculptural fragments around the tower: (1) a reclining man with a drinking vessel in his hand (app. 2, cat. 5), and (2) a relief with a female bust, both headless. These were not seen by Henning when she surveyed the tombs[437].

Late 2nd cent. A.D.: Temple Tomb no. 186 (›Tombeau de l'aviation‹ / ›Tomb Duvaux‹)

The tomb is located in the south-east necropolis and was first explored by Captain Duvaux in 1923 and then by the team led by architect Albert Gabriel and Ingholt in 1925[438]. It was also investigated in 1988 by Andreas Schmidt-Colinet and his team[439]. No foundation inscription is associated with the tomb, and the date of the tomb is based on stylistic criteria. The tomb was a square building; inside, it had a peristyle courtyard in the centre, and thirty-eight loculus bays built into six sections of the walls of the tomb. The layout of the tomb, but especially the presence of a well in the north-east corner of the building, led Gabriel to suggest that the building was originally a house[440]. Several sarcophagus fragments are associated with the tomb[441], but Gabriel writes that probably only cat. 184 belonged to the original sculpture of the tomb, while

---

426 Watzinger – Wulzinger 1932, 64.
427 al-Asʿad 2013, 17.
428 al-Asʿad 2013, 17.
429 Watzinger – Wulzinger 1932, 64.
430 Higuchi – Saito 2001, 5–8.
431 Higuchi – Saito 2001, 15 f.
432 Higuchi – Saito 2001, 9–12.
433 Higuchi – Saito 2001, 104 cat. 3 fig. 72, S2.
434 Sadurska – Bounni 1994, 11 f. cat. 1 fig. 180 pl. 1.
435 Sadurska – Bounni 1994, 12 cat. 2 fig. 61 pl. 1.
436 Henning 2013b, 243.
437 Watzinger – Wulzinger 1932, 61; Henning 2013b, 243–245.
438 Gabriel 1926, 90; Ingholt 1935, 73. The tomb was located close to the camp of the aviation corps of Palmyra, and so got its name: Cantineau 1930c, 533–534.
439 Schmidt-Colinet 1992, 79 n. 185.
440 Gabriel 1926, 91.
441 Gabriel 1926, 90–92.

the others were brought there by Captain Duvaux from neighbouring tombs[442]. The photograph showing cat. 183 shows another sarcophagus to the right side from the viewer's point of view (cat. 181). According to Parlasca, this sarcophagus also belonged to the tomb's original sculptures[443]. Several of the sarcophagi associated with the tomb, however, present a unique iconographic feature: busts placed over or within garlands. This feature does not appear in other sarcophagi and may indicate that all the sarcophagi with this type of decoration had been placed originally inside tomb no. 186 or that they stem from a single, neighbouring tomb (cat. 180. 181. 187–190)[444]. The period of the tomb's use is dated from the end of the 2nd to the 3rd cent. A.D. based on the stylistic dating of the sculptures[445].

Late 2nd / Early 3rd cent. A.D.: Temple Tomb Q280, ›Qasr Abjad / White castle‹

The tomb is located in the west necropolis and was excavated by Ingholt in 1928[446]. No foundation inscription is associated with the tomb, and the tomb is dated based on the stylistic examination of the finds. The tomb structure was on a podium and has a plain, square plan, with loculus bays for burials[447]. Apart from cat. 192, several other reliefs and fragments of statues were found there. On the right of the entrance the following fragments were found: (1) torso from the statue of a standing male, (2) legs from the statue of a standing male, (3) head of a priest, (4) a second torso from the statue of a standing male[448]. The find location of the other fragments from the tomb has not been recorded: (1) the ›Beauty of Palmyra‹, (2) the »upper body of a figure«[449], (3) a female bust, (4) the head of a male figure, (5) the head of a female figure[450]. The tomb was probably in use between the second half of the 2nd cent. A.D. and the beginning of the 3rd cent. A.D.[451]

Late 2nd / Early 3rd cent. A.D.: Temple Tomb 173c

The tomb is located in the north necropolis and was recorded by Watzinger and Wulzinger after being documented by early travellers. It was incorporated into the late Justinian wall of Palmyra. No foundation inscription is associated with the tomb, and the date of construction and use is inferred from the finds. It had a prostyle façade. Inside the tomb, there were pillars with Victories on globes holding wreaths[452]. Only cat. 227 was found in the tomb.

Early 3rd cent. A.D.: Temple Tomb no. 173d

The tomb is located in the north necropolis and was recorded by Watzinger and Wulzinger. It was incorporated into the late Justinian wall of Palmyra. Fragments of a foundation inscription have been associated with the tomb, but neither the date nor the names of the founders are preserved[453]. It has rich architectural decoration, but apart from cat. 222, no other funerary sculpture is preserved[454].

Early 3rd cent. A.D.: Hypogeum AG

The tomb is located in the south-west necropolis and was excavated by Ingholt in 1925[455]. No foundation inscription is associated with the tomb. The plan shows that the tomb had a long, main gallery ending in an exedra, and two lateral galleries with two chambers each[456]. Ingholt writes that there were two sarcophagi inside the niche at the exedra at the end of the main gallery, one behind the other[457]. The relief cat. 172 was found in the main gallery[458].

Early 3rd cent. A.D.: Temple Tomb no. 174

The temple tomb was located in the north necropolis and was incorporated into the city walls during late antiquity. The tomb was recorded but not explored by

---

442 Gabriel 1926, 91.
443 Parlasca 1984, 290–292 fig. 7.
444 In this publication, all the sarcophagi that were inside the tomb are presented together, even if they do not belong, in order to facilitate further research on them.
445 Parlasca 1984, 290–292.
446 Raja – Sørensen 2015a, 439.
447 Raja – Sørensen 2015a, 440–443. For the tomb, see also Gawlikowski 1970a, 130–132; Parlasca 1989a.
448 Raja – Sørensen 2015a, 445 f.
449 Raja – Sørensen 2015a, 447.
450 Raja – Sørensen 2015a, 447–450.
451 Raja – Sørensen 2015a, 450.

452 Watzinger – Wulzinger 1932, 68. See also Schmidt-Colinet 1992, 47. 50. 53. 58 f.
453 Watzinger – Wulzinger 1932, 68.
454 For the architectural decoration, see Schmidt-Colinet 1992, 47. 68 n. 160. 80–88.
455 Raja et al. 2021a, Diary 3, 23. 72, Diary 5, 128–134.
456 Raja et al. 2021a, Diary 3, 23.
457 Raja et al. 2021a, Diary 3, 23, Diary 5, 128.
458 Raja et al. 2021a, Diary 5, 128.

Watzinger and Wulzinger[459], and was only investigated between 2007 and 2010 within the wider framework of an excavation project led by the Palmyra Museum and the Syrian Directorate General of Antiquities and Museums[460]. No foundation inscription is associated with the tomb, and the date of the construction and use of the tomb is inferred from the finds (stylistic criteria). It had a prostyle façade[461]. The chamber of the tomb contained ten loculus bays, but no reliefs were found there[462]. The sarcophagi cat. 223 and appendix 5, cat. 7 were placed over the loculi[463].

Early 3rd cent. A.D.: Temple Tomb 173b

The tomb is located in the north necropolis and was recorded by Watzinger and Wulzinger. It was incorporated into the late Justinian wall of Palmyra. No foundation inscription is associated with the tomb, and the date of the construction and use of the tomb is inferred from the finds (stylistic criteria). Watzinger and Wulzinger write that inside the chamber was a »male statue«[464]. No foundation inscription was associated with this tomb, and only cat. 226 is known from its sculptural decoration.

Early 3rd cent. A.D.: Temple Tomb no. 75

The tomb is located in the west necropolis and was recorded by Watzinger and Wulzinger. No foundation inscription is associated with the tomb, and the date of the construction and use of the tomb is inferred from the finds (stylistic criteria). It stood on a podium and had corner pilasters in the façade, while the inner chamber was also divided with pilasters. Inside, they recorded »a lot of fragments of recently broken up sculptures«[465]. Only cat. 224 is associated with this tomb.

Early 3rd cent. A.D.: Temple Tomb no. 159

The tomb is located in the north necropolis and was recorded by Watzinger and Wulzinger as a tower tomb[466]. No foundation inscription is associated with the tomb, and the date of the construction and use of the tomb is inferred from the finds and the architecture. There is only a badly preserved chamber on the ground floor[467]. They also recorded cat. 225 and appendix 6, cat. 13 inside the tomb.

Early 3rd cent. A.D.: Temple Tomb no. 36

Temple tomb no. 36 is located in the west necropolis. It was recorded in the survey by Watzinger and Wulzinger in 1917, who had noticed that it was destroyed, and still contained a lot of architectural fragments. They only recorded a sarcophagus box in the shape of a kline inside, with five figures between the legs[468]. Between 1981 and 1990, it was investigated and re-excavated again by the Syro-German/Austrian Archaeological Research led by Andreas Schmidt-Colinet[469]. The results of this new examination and documentation of the tomb were published in 1992[470], and since then, tomb no. 36 remains the best-published Palmyrene tomb[471]. The tomb has a rich architectural and sculptural decoration, with 101 surviving fragments of sculpture including mythological figures such as Victories, Attis, and sea creatures[472]. According to Schmidt-Colinet, only the find location of the architectural decorations and of certain sarcophagi and banqueting reliefs could be determined; that of the other sculptures could not[473]. The funerary sculptures whose location could be determined came from the main floor (»Hauptgeschoss«) at the north side of the building, and Schmidt-Colinet proposes that all the sculpture came from the main floor[474]. Cat. 238. 239 and the fragments of a third sarcophagus[475] were found in the »west niches of the north wing«[476], cat. 228. 231 were found in the »east niche of the north wing«[477], cat. 230 was found in the »west niche ending of the

---

459 Watzinger – Wulzinger 1932, 68.
460 al-Asʿad 2013, 18.
461 Schmidt-Colinet 1992, 55 fig. 24.
462 There are no images of the interior of the tomb but it is likely that the bays were meant for single burials, as was the case with the loculi bays in temple tomb 175.
463 al-Asʿad 2013, 18.
464 Watzinger – Wulzinger 1932, 68.
465 Watzinger – Wulzinger 1932, 58.
466 Watzinger – Wulzinger 1932, 65. Henning 2013b, 272, also accepts this classification, contra Gawlikowski 1970a, 143, who classifies this tomb under temple tombs.
467 Henning 2013b, 272.
468 Watzinger – Wulzinger 1932, 51.
469 Schmidt-Colinet 1992, 4.
470 Schmidt-Colinet 1992.
471 For a recent summary of the finds and the relation of the art of the tomb with that of Rome, see Gawlikowski 2021, 173 f.
472 Schmidt-Colinet 1992, 89–104.
473 Schmidt-Colinet 1992, 22 f.
474 Schmidt-Colinet 1992, 105.
475 Schmidt-Colinet 1992, 146 cat. S 3.
476 Schmidt-Colinet 1992, 105.
477 Schmidt-Colinet 1992, 105.

north corridor«[478], and cat. 236 and cat. 244 were found in the »west and east ends of the south corridor«[479].

A.D. 236: Temple Tomb no. 150, Tomb of Marona

The tomb is located in the north necropolis. It is a temple tomb, founded in A.D. 236 by Julius Aurelius Marona according to the foundation inscription on the door lintel[480]. A text on the door records the cession of the entire tomb and its hypogeum to Julius Aurelius Theodorus[481]. Perhaps on account of the good preservation of the tomb itself, very little remains of the sarcophagi or other funerary reliefs that might have been placed there: only cat. 274 is securely associated with the tomb, while cat. 281 may also come from there[482].

3rd cent. A.D.: Hexagonal Tomb

The so-called hexagonal tomb is located in the north necropolis of Palmyra. It was discovered by Khaled al-Asʿad, possibly between 2000–2010, and it was badly preserved[483]. Only the three heads from the tomb (cat. 275–277) are known from the tomb.

In addition to these, eight more tombs contained sarcophagi but no other sculptural decoration is associated with them: (1) tower tomb no. 21a (appendix 6, cat. 4. 8); (2) tower tomb no. 84 (appendix 5, cat. 1. appendix 6, cat. 5); (3) tower tomb no. 160 (appendix 6, cat. 6); (4) temple tomb no. 171 (appendix 6, cat. 7. 19); (5) tower tomb no. 123 (appendix 6, cat. 10); (6) tower tomb no. 138a (appendix 6, cat. 11); (7) tower tomb no. 143 (appendix 6, cat. 12); (8) tower tomb no. 161 (appendix 6, cat. 17. 18).

Discussion

Fifteen objects (cat. 1. 2. 13–19. 60–67) are dated to the period A.D. 50–100. Apart from the two foundation reliefs (cat. 1. 2), cat. 13–19 come from two tower tombs, while the others all come from the same hypogeum, that of ʿAštôr: cat. 60–67. The number of sarcophagi rises in the period A.D. 100–150: thirty-one objects in total.

Nine were found in tower tombs: cat. 3. 4. 22. 33. 43. 47. 48, appendix 2, cat. 1. 2, and twenty-two in hypogea: cat. 6. 70–72. 75. 77. 78. 80. 93–97. 101. 102. 104–107. 111. 112. 115. A small increase in numbers happens in the period A.D. 150–200 with forty-one objects: twenty from tower tombs (cat. 23–30. 34. 35. 40–42. 45. 46. 52–56), sixteen from hypogea (cat. 10. 73. 108. 109. 113. 123–125. 129–133. 150. 167) and five from temple tombs (cat. 184. 191. 193–195). In the period between A.D. 200–240, the increase in numbers is significant: 137 in total. Of these, only four were found in tower tombs (cat. 28. 31. 37. 59); sixty were found in hypogea (cat. 11. 68. 69. 74. 79. 89. 98–100. 110. 114. 119–121. 126. 127. 128. 134–166. 168–178) and seventy-four were found in temple tombs (cat. 180. 181. 183. 185–187. 196–218. 220. 222. 224–229. 231–250. 252. 254–265. 267–273). In the last period, A.D. 240–273, fifteen objects have a known provenance: one from a tower tomb (cat. 12), four from hypogea (cat. 90–92. 179), seven from temple tombs (cat. 188–190. 219. 230. 251. 266), and three from the hexagonal tomb (cat. 275–277). Not every object can be dated so neatly: cat. 50. 51 are dated between A.D. 135 and A.D. 170, cat. 20. 21 are dated between A.D. 50 and A.D. 150, cat. 39. 116. 118. 122. 182 are dated between A.D. 140 and A.D. 170, and cat. 46 is dated between A.D. 140 and A.D. 200. One object from a temple tomb, cat. 192, has an even broader date span: A.D. 150–225. Eleven objects are dated between A.D. 200 and A.D. 273: cat. 32. 36. 49. 57. 58. 209–211. 221. 223. appendix 3, cat. 1.

Leaving aside all the objects with ranges that do not fit within those of the five groups (20. 21. 32. 36. 38. 39. 49–51. 57. 58. 76. 81–88. 103. 116. 118. 122. 182. 192. 209–211. 221. 223. 253. 274), it is possible to see that there is a steady increase in the number of sarcophagi between A.D. 1 and A.D. 200, a steep increase in the period between A.D. 200 and A.D. 240, and a drop in the period A.D. 240–273. When examining the sarcophagi according to the type of monument where they were found, it seems that the number of sarcophagi remains steady in tower tombs between A.D. 1–150, rises in the period A.D. 150–200, and then drops again. The number of sarcophagi in hypogea rises between the periods A.D. 1–100 and A.D. 100–150, drops slightly in the period A.D. 150–200, and then increases sharply in the period A.D. 200–240, before falling again in the period A.D. 240–273. There are not many sarcophagi from temple tombs in the period A.D. 150–200, but their number rises significantly in the period A.D. 200–240, before dropping again.

The short survey above makes clear that the information gained from the tombs is uneven. It is possible to distinguish between (1) tombs that have been investigated, documented, and fully published, like temple tomb no. 36; (2) tombs like N206 that have been fully investigated, but published only in preliminary

---

478 Schmidt-Colinet 1992, 105.
479 Schmidt-Colinet 1992, 105.
480 Gawlikowski 1970a, 145 f.
481 Gawlikowski 1970a, 218 no. 49.
482 For the remaining architectural decoration of the tomb, see Schmidt-Colinet 1992, 65 n. 138.
483 Gawlikowski 2016a, 127 describes it as »a fairly recent discovery«.

reports; (3) tombs whose sculptural decoration has been published but the funerary complexes have been published in preliminary reports[484]; and (4) tombs known only from excavation diaries, like hypogeum AC. This means that the information one can have from each tomb varies. The information gained can also vary depending on the preservation of the tomb; for example, tomb no. 36 is one of the best documented and published; however, because of its state of preservation, the location of only seven sarcophagi is known (cat. 228. 230. 231. 236. 238. 239. 244). In addition to the state of preservation of the buildings and assemblages, the activity of looters has also had an impact on the information available to scholars, since they had managed to break into the tombs before archaeologists were able to investigate them properly[485]. The evidence from the undisturbed and systematically excavated tombs shows the range of sculptural and decorative choices for their founders and users.

Depending on the amount of contextual information that can be gained through the publication for each tomb, then, it is possible to divide the tombs further: (1) those where the precise find location of the sarcophagi and the other funerary sculptures is known, (2) those where the find location of the sarcophagi is known but not of the other funerary sculptures, and (3) those where only the provenance from a specific tomb is known (Table 1).

Tombs in Group 1 are those that have been well published or whose publications offer enough information to reconstruct the context of the sarcophagi. Of the sixty-seven tombs briefly discussed above, the first two (tower tomb no. 44 and no. 194) had founder reliefs on their façade, and so offer invaluable information for this category of funerary sculpture and the use of the banqueting motif in Palmyrene sculpture. Almost all the other tombs in this group are hypogea (seventeen out of twenty-one). This is not surprising, considering how hypogea were the least prominent of Palmyrene tombs, and so could escape the attention of looters. Furthermore, with the exception of five tombs (hypogeum no. 33, hypogeum of the Three Brothers, temple tomb no. 146, tomb AG, temple tomb no. 174), all the others were excavated from the middle of the 20th cent. onwards, thus following modern documentation techniques. Additionally, their funerary sculptures were also published in detail, with the exception of four tombs (hypogeum no. 33, hypogeum H, of Taîbbôl, temple tomb no. 174 and temple tomb no. 146). The first of these was excavated and documented by Ingholt, and the relevant information is kept in the Ingholt Archive. The publication of the archive and his diaries have allowed the contextualization of cat. 118[486]. Hypogeum H has not been fully published yet, but the photos from the press releases and preliminary publications give insight into the arrangement of the sculptures within the tomb. Finally, the re-investigation of temple tomb no. 174 and temple tomb no. 146 also allowed the reconstruction of their funerary contexts.

The second group is comprised of tombs that offer some information about the placement of the sarcophagi, but not of the other finds. It includes well-published hypogea that were looted in antiquity (hypogeum of ʿAštôr, hypogeum of Zabdâ, hypogeum of Lišamš), hypogea whose contexts are reconstructed to some degree thanks to the material in the Ingholt Archive (hypogeum of ʿAtenatan, hypogeum AK, hypogeum no. 31, hypogeum AN, hypogeum of Barʿâ Bonnûr, hypogeum AC, and hypogeum AG), tombs that were re-investigated since the middle of the 20th cent. (tower tomb no. 51, tower tomb no. 46, tower tomb no. 13, temple tomb no. 85b, temple tomb no. 186, temple tomb no. 36), and recently excavated tombs that were published in preliminary reports (hypogeum of ʿAqraban, tower tomb no. N206, hypogeum of Ḥennibel, and hypogeum of Ḥatrai).

The last group is composed of the tombs that are either too poorly preserved or where it was not possible to identify the original find locations of the sculptures associated with them. It is not surprising that most of the tower and temple tombs belong to this group, since they were always visible and so they were used as building material or as sources of easily found antiquities to be sold on the black market.

The reliefs accompanying the foundation inscriptions of the first two tombs of Group 1 (tower tomb no. 44 and tower tomb no. 194) show that from A.D. 41 the banqueting motif was in use in Palmyra and was used in a funerary context. The earliest tomb with a securely documented sarcophagus is the tower tomb no. 15[487]. It contained a plaster sarcophagus in a separate

---

484 Most of the tombs whose sculptures were published in Sadurska – Bounni 1994 belong to this category.
485 Sarcophagi boxes were too heavy to transport, but smaller reliefs functioning as covers (like cat. 9), and fragments that could be removed easily, such as single, statue-like figures, sarcophagi lids (like cat. 409, and possibly cat. 307. 317. 348), and heads (for example, cat. 504. 505. 512), as well as loculus reliefs were easy to remove from their original contexts. This activity is exemplified by the records concerning two reliefs: the relief depicting a male, Istanbul, Istanbul Arkeoloji Müzesi, inv. no. 3821/O.M.323: Chabot 1922, 126 cat. 31, and the stele depicting a child, Istanbul, Istanbul Arkeoloji Müzesi, inv. no. 3826/329: Ingholt 1928, 154 PS 526. Both were confiscated in Damascus in 1902 and moved to the then Musée Ottoman Impérial. See Parlasca 1995, 69 f.

486 Raja 2021b; Raja et al. 2022a.
487 The presence of sarcophagi in tower tomb no. 19, which may be earlier, is not secure, since the fragments from there (cat. 13–18)

Table 1.

Group 1	Group 2	Group 3
Tower tomb no. 44	Tower tomb no. 51	Tower tomb no. 19
Tower tomb no. 194	Tower tomb no. 46	Tower tomb no. 15
Hypogeum of Bôlḥâ	Hypogeum of ʿAštôr	Tower tomb no. 67
Hypogeum of Barîkî (SE)	Hypogeum of ʿAqraban	Tower tomb no. 41a
Hypogeum of ʿAbdʿastôr	Hypogeum of ʿAtenatan	Tower tomb no. 68
Hypogeum of Yarḥaî	Hypogeum of Zabdâ	Tower tomb no. 39d
Hypogeum of the Bôlbarak family	Tower tomb no. 13	Hypogeum of the Barîkî (SW)
Hypogeum H, of Taîbbôl	Hypogeum AK	Tower tomb no. 85d
Hypogeum of Zabdʿateh and Moqîmû	Hypogeum of Lišamš	Tower Tomb no. 39
Hypogeum of Šalamallat	Hypogeum no. 31	Tower tomb no. 168
Hypogeum of Malkû	Tower tomb no. N206	Tower tomb no. 34
Hypogeum of Arṭaban	Hypogeum of Ḥennibel	Tower tomb no. 87
Hypogeum of Ṭaʿaî	Hypogeum of Ḥatrai	Tower tomb no. 101
Hypogeum no. 33	Temple tomb no. 85b	Temple tomb Q280, ›Qasr Abjad / White castle‹
Hypogeum of Yarḥaî, ʿAtenûrî, and Zabdibôl	Hypogeum AN	Temple tomb 173c
Hypogeum of ʿAlaînê	Hypogeum of Barʿâ Bonnûr	Temple tomb no. 173d
Hypogeum of the Three Brothers	Hypogeum AC	Temple tomb 173b
Temple tomb no. 146	Hypogeum AG	Temple tomb no. 75
Hypogeum F	Temple tomb no. 186	Temple tomb no. 159
Hypogeum anonymous	Temple tomb no. 36	Tomb of Marona
Temple tomb no. 174		Hexagonal tomb
		Tower tomb no. 21a
		Tower tomb no. 84
		Tower tomb no. 160
		Temple tomb no. 171
		Tower tomb no. 123
		Tower tomb no. 138a
		Tower tomb no. 143
		Tower tomb no. 161
		Hypogeum of Julius Aurelius Malê

chamber of the ground floor that was partly covered by a vault. The sculptural fragments from the tomb indicate the presence of other funerary sculptures, but also that the sarcophagus was likely covered by a separately made limestone relief. The other fragments in the tomb, however, were found in the rubble[488] and the hypogeum of the tower[489], suggesting that the sarcophagus had been placed alone in the ground floor chamber. Furthermore, the vaulted ceiling of the sarcophagus chamber indicates the intent of the tomb owners to emphasize and ennoble the space of the sarcophagus. Plaster sarcophagi were found in tower

have been attributed to sarcophagi because of their size. For the tomb's date, see Michalowski 1963, 204–208; Henning 2013b, 162.
488 Michalowski 1964, 163 cat. 5; 165–169 cat. 8–10. 12–14.
489 Michalowski 1964, 161–168 cat. 3. 4. 6. 7. 11.

tombs no. 13[490], no. 20[491], no. 44[492], no. 46[493], no. 50[494], no. 51[495], no. 62[496], but with the exception of the plaster sarcophagi in tower tomb no. 50 that were placed on the ground floor, the others were located in the upper floors of the tombs[497]. None of the chambers with plaster sarcophagi in these tombs (13. 20. 44. 46. 50. 51. 62) seems to have been differentiated from the chambers with loculus bays either through painted decoration or vaulted ceilings, but this could be a result of the poor state of preservation of most of the tower tombs rather than an intentional choice of the owners. This is also the case for the tower tombs where limestone sarcophagi have been recorded. They were placed in chambers of the ground floor that did not have any distinctive decoration[498]. Very few sarcophagi associated with tower tombs were found in the same chamber: three in tomb N206[499], three in tomb no. 159[500], and two in tomb no. 161[501]. Cat. 12, from tower tomb no. 51, may also have been placed in the same chamber as two more reliefs and the sarcophagi they covered[502].

Only in the placement of the two sarcophagi from tomb no. 46 (cat. 50. 51), is it possible to observe reuse of space: both sarcophagi were found in front of loculus burials, indicating that they belonged to a later phase of use of the tomb. No cession text has been found associated with the tomb, however, so it is not possible to determine whether this addition was made by descendants of the original founder or by members of a different family[503].

The brief survey above shows that the coexistence of different types of funerary monuments (banqueting reliefs, statuettes, sarcophagi, loculus reliefs) was not unusual for hypogea. The sarcophagi, in particular, were not placed in separate chambers but in exedrae. These small recesses were often articulated by arches or other architectural elements that were richly decorated, thus creating an elaborate frame for the sarcophagi reminiscent of theatrical buildings with niches and aediculae within which statues would be placed[504]. Not every exedra was so elaborate, though[505]. Even though the architectural decoration was usually sculpted, painted decorations were also used in some cases[506]. The sarcophagi could also close off previously dug out loculus bays[507]. In addition to being used for closing off sarcophagi boxes and burial spaces, banqueting reliefs[508] and full sarcophagi reliefs[509] could be placed directly on the walls of hypogea. Thus, the hypogea present scholars with variety not only in the types of funerary sculptures found there, but also in the ways that objects that belong to the same type could be used differently — the full sarcophagi reliefs being the best example of that, as they could be used both for covering burial spaces, but also as pseudo-sarcophagi.

The examination of the finds of the hypogea of the first group also shows that persons belonging to the same family branch tended to be buried in the same area. Members of the same immediate family could be buried in the same or neighbouring loculus bays, or in the same sarcophagus[510]. In eight of the thirty hypogea (hypogeum of ʿAbdʿastôr, hypogeum of Yarḥaî, hypogeum of the Three Brothers, hypogeum AN, hypogeum of Barʿâ Bonnûr, hypogeum H, hypogeum F, exedra of Iulius Aurelius Maqqaî in the hypogeum of ʿAtenatan), the sarcophagi were arranged in a triclinium, while in the hypogeum of ʿAlaînê they were arranged in a pentaclinium. The others were placed alone in the exedrae or against the walls. In only eight of the thirty-four hypogea (hypogeum H, hypogeum of Lišamš, hypogeum of Zabdâ, hypogeum of the Bôlbarak family, hypogeum of ʿAlaînê, hypogeum of Arṭaban, hypogeum of Ṭaʿaî, hypogeum of Julius Aurelius Malê) were sarcophagi or banqueting reliefs placed across the entrance. Thus, the most prominent locations of most

---

490 Henning 2013b, 153 f. No attempt was made to match the seven surviving reliefs with banqueting scenes to the remains of the twelve plaster sarcophagi boxes in the tomb.
491 Henning 2013b, 163 f.
492 Henning 2013b, 185 f.
493 Henning 2013b, 188 f.
494 Henning 2013b, 192.
495 Henning 2013b, 193 f.
496 Henning 2013b, 199.
497 The location of the sarcophagus chambers of tomb no. 98 is not given by Henning: Henning 2013b, 240 f.
498 Tomb no. 41a: Henning 2013b, Henning 2013b, 184 f.; tomb no. 34: Henning 2013b, 174 f.; tomb no. 39: Henning 2013b, 179; tomb no. 39d: Henning 2013b, 181; tomb no. 68: Henning 2013b, 210; tomb no. 84: Henning 2013b, 231; tomb no. 85d: Henning 2013b, 233; tomb no. 123: Henning 2013b, 252; tomb no. 143: Henning 2013b, 262; tomb no. 159: Henning 2013b, 272; tomb no. 161: Henning 2013b, 274; tomb no. 168: Henning 2013b, 278 f.; tomb no. 171: Henning 2013b, 281.
499 al-Asʿad 2013, 15 f.
500 Watzinger – Wulzinger 1932, 65; Henning 2013b, 272.
501 Watzinger – Wulzinger 1932, 66; Henning 2013b, 274.
502 Gawlikowski – al Asʿad 1997, 32 f. cat. 17; Yon 2013, 350 cat. 84.
503 Henning 2013b, 188 f.
504 See, for example, the decoration for the exedrae at (1) the hypogeum of Yarḥaî: Amy – Seyrig 1936; (2) hypogeum F: Higuchi – Saito 2001.
505 See, for example, the south exedra of the hypogeum of the Three Brothers: Tanabe 1986, 257–259 pl. 224–226.
506 As, for example, the exedra of Julius Aurelius Maqqaî in the hypogeum of ʿAtenatan: Ingholt 1935, 62 f.
507 See, for example, the south exedra of the hypogeum of the Three Brothers: Tanabe 1986, 257–259 pl. 224–226.
508 As, for example, in the hypogeum of ʿAštôr: Sadurska – Bounni 1994, 14.
509 As, for example, in the hypogeum of Shalamallat: Sadurska – Bounni 1994, 169–171.
510 See the introductory sections to the finds from each of the hypogea published in Sadurska – Bounni 1994.

hypogea were occupied by loculus bays rather than sarcophagi, and despite the popularity of the banqueting motif, the arrangement of the kline-like sarcophagi in a triclinium was not as popular as one might expect.

Of the temple tombs that have given enough evidence as to the location of the sarcophagi (temple tombs of Group 1), it seems that sarcophagi could be placed over loculus bays and to the sides of the monument. Since the burials were arranged around a central courtyard, there were no obvious ›prominent‹ locations.

Conclusion

The evidence of the hypogea and the temple tombs in particular, but also of tower tombs such as that of Elahbel, shows that the presence of sarcophagi and monuments with the banqueting motif together with the statues, stelai, and funerary loculus reliefs contributed to the creation of a ›stacking aesthetic‹ within the tombs and the impression of a family gallery. The sheer number of sculpted objects from single tombs makes that obvious even when it is impossible to determine the exact location of the objects in the tombs[511]. This ›stacking aesthetic‹ can be observed best in these hypogea: (1) of ʿAštôr, (2) of Arṭaban, (3) of Yarḥaî, (4) F, (5) of Zabdʿateh and Moqîmû, (6) of ʿAlaînê, (7) of Barîkî (in the south-east necropolis), (8) of Ṭaʿaî, (9) of Ḥatrai, and (10) of Bôlḥâ. Out of the tombs with the objects that form the first part of the catalogue, these ten are the only ones that preserved almost (if not all) of the sculptured pieces that covered loculus burials as well as the sarcophagi, in their original locations, together with inscriptions that allow for reconstructing the history of use of the tombs. The evidence from these tombs shows how reliefs covering loculus burials would be placed one over the other, and gives a better impression of the galleries of funerary portraits and how they grew within the span of years of the tomb's use.

In hypogea, the position of sarcophagi within the Palmyrene tombs becomes more important: in all the tombs where the location of the sarcophagi is known, it is clear that sarcophagi, visually more complex and striking than the stelai or the loculus reliefs, were placed in such positions that could emphasize their predominance in the tomb, whether against the walls, set within recesses, or facing the entrance. When the sarcophagi are associated with the foundation and early phases of a tomb's use, then they are placed in exedrae directly facing the doors of the tomb. When they are associated with the following phases, sarcophagi take pride of place within the chambers (this is obvious in the tombs from the later 2nd cent. A.D. onwards, such as the tomb of ʿAlaînê, but it could appear in some of the earlier hypogea, such as that of Zabdâ or of the family of Bôlbarak) or the exedrae where they were placed (especially obvious in the cases where the exedrae are built by buyers of already existing sections of tombs, for example the exedra in the tomb of Yarḥaî and that of Iulius Aurelius Maqqaî). It is perhaps significant that, in ceded tomb sections, the new owners often preferred to place their burials or those of their families in sarcophagi rather than loculus bays, indicating that in the 3rd cent. A.D., sarcophagi had become a more prestigious form of burial, or perhaps one that offered greater opportunity for depicting the family as a coherent whole — in contrast to the fragmentation shown in funerary reliefs, where the different family members were shown separately, even when the inscriptions made their relationships clear.

To modern viewers of these reliefs, the loculus plaques with the funerary busts placed on rows within the space of the tomb, create the impression of a picture gallery, while the sarcophagi in the exedrae seem to recreate the most public space of the house where the banquets took place. To an ancient, non-Palmyrene viewer, however, the first impression would be of the unique way that the Palmyrenes dealt with the tomb. Picture galleries such as that created by the succession and placement of reliefs in multiple rows did not exist: the usual manner of display was paratactic, whether in the open air or in the villas of the elite[512]. Statues in the round, rather than paintings or reliefs, were preferred for the depictions of ancestors, benefactors, heroes, or deities. In the Near East, sarcophagi were often placed in the open air, whereas in Rome, they could be displayed, but they could also be permanently hidden from view at the end of the funerary ritual[513]. The Palmyrene tomb thus expressed a concept of funerary space that was reminiscent of private and public space at the same time, without imitating either.

---

511 On ›stacking aesthetics‹ see Raja 2019i.

512 For displays in public spaces, see, for example, Rutledge 2012. For displays in villas, see Zarmakoupi 2014; Lapatin 2019.

513 See Borg 2013; Meinecke 2014; Borg 2019 for the ways of displaying – or not – sarcophagi in Rome.

List of tombs with sarcophagi that are securely dated by a foundation inscription

1. A.D. 33: Tomb no. 67, tower of Ḥaîran
2. A.D. 40: Tower tomb no. 44, tower of Kîtôt
3. A.D. 73: Tower tomb no. 194, tower of ʿOgeîlû
4. A.D. 83: Tower tomb no. 51, tower of Yamlikû
5. A.D. 83: Tower tomb no. 68
6. A.D. 88/89: Hypogeum of ʿAštôr
7. A.D. 89: Tomb no. 7, hypogeum of Bôlḥâ
8. A.D. 98: South-west necropolis, hypogeum of the Barîkî
9. A.D. 98: Hypogeum of ʿAbdʿastôr
10. A.D. 103: Tower tomb no. 13, tower of Elahbel
11. A.D. 108: Hypogeum of Yarḥaî
12. A.D. 113: Tomb no. H, hypogeum of Taîbbôl
13. A.D. 114: Hypogeum of Zabdʿateh and Moqîmû
14. A.D. 116: Hypogeum of Malkû
15. A.D. 123: Hypogeum of Ḥennibel
16. A.D. 128: Tower tomb no. 34, tower of Moqîmû
17. A.D. 130/131: North-west necropolis. Hypogeum of Ḥatrai
18. A.D. 186: Hypogeum of Barʿâ Bonnûr
19. A.D. 236: Temple tomb no. 150, tomb of Marona

List of tombs with sarcophagi whose dates are established through inscriptions or cession texts

1. Before A.D. 128: Tower tomb no. N206
2. Before A.D. 142: Hypogeum of the Three Brothers
3. Before A.D. 147: Hypogeum of Šalamallat
4. Before A.D. 181: Hypogeum of Lišamš
5. Before A.D. 220: Hypogeum F
6. Before A.D. 229: Tomb no. A120, hypogeum of ʿAtenatan

CHAPTER 5

Iconography

Iconography is of primary importance to art historians, archaeologists, and social historians[1]. The study of the iconography of sarcophagi shows how different scholars can ask different questions of the same sets of images. It has been calculated that around 750,000 sarcophagi were created across the Roman Empire between the 1st and the 4th centuries A.D.[2]. Of these, only 12,000 to 15,000 have survived, most of them decorated[3]. The iconography of marble sarcophagi from Rome and Italy has attracted the attention of artists from the Middle Ages and the Renaissance in particular[4], while Roman sarcophagi regardless of place of manufacture became the focus of scholarly studies from the 19th cent., with the creation of a dedicated corpus in 1870[5]. Highlighting the importance of figural scenes on sarcophagi, the first volumes of the corpus of the ancient sarcophagus reliefs were dedicated to mythological cycles[6] and myths focusing on single figures[7]. Earlier scholars have focused on the typology of the scenes[8], while from the 1940s, the meaning of the iconography has attracted as much, if not more attention. The sarcophagi were seen as vehicles for ideas about the afterlife, or the ›personal beliefs‹[9] of the deceased by scholars working around the middle of the 20th cent.[10], but it is possible to observe a paradigm shift around the end of the 20th cent., with the imagery on sarcophagi interpreted through the lens of cultural history[11]. All the approaches, however, have the same starting point: the imagery on the sarcophagi, and so they feed into each other.

The iconography of Palmyrene sarcophagi has been the focus of several articles by Klaus Parlasca[12], two by Krzysztof C. Makowski[13], and one by Lucy Audley-Miller[14], while it has been treated briefly by Harald Ingholt[15] and Malcolm R. Colledge[16]. Furthermore, it has been discussed in Andreas Schmidt-Colinet's publication of the finds from tomb no. 36[17], as well as in publications of tomb assemblages, most notably that of tomb of Yarḥaï[18], the publication of the tomb of ʿAlaînê[19], and the presentation of the sculptures from fourteen hypogea by Anna Sadurska and Adnan Bounni[20]. Of these, the most comprehensive is the discussion in the 1992 publication by Schmidt-Colinet, but, naturally, the focus is on the sarcophagi from tomb no. 36 and not in presenting a history of the motifs on the sarcophagi found in Palmyra.

This chapter will present the iconographic subjects and motifs on the sarcophagi of Palmyra and discuss their typology, history, and comparanda. The most remarkable feature of Palmyrene sarcophagi is the iconographic continuity in the motifs used on the lids and the boxes[21]. The banqueting motif, as it was formulated in Palmyra[22], remained the most suitable motif for sarcophagus lids throughout the period. There is more variation on the boxes: portrait busts are the most common motif used, but scenes relating to trade can be identified on five sarcophagi (82. 228. 274. 447. appendix 5, cat. 11), eight sarcophagi have religious

---

1 See Taylor 2020 for a brief introduction to the topic as well as for further reading.
2 Koch 1993, 1.
3 Koch 1993, 1; Hallett 2019b, 1.
4 Koch 1995, 374 f.
5 Koch 1995, 375 f.
6 Robert 1890.
7 Robert 1897; Robert 1904; Robert 1919.
8 This has been of great interest already from the first volume of the corpus of ancient sarcophagi reliefs. See, for example, Robert 1890, 1, who immediately starts his discussion of the sarcophagi with depictions from the myths surrounding the Trojan War with a typological division.
9 Hallett 2019b, 1.
10 Hallett 2019b, 1 f.
11 Ewald 1999; Hallett 2019b, 1–3.
12 Especially Parlasca 1984; Parlasca 1989b; Parlasca 1998.
13 Makowski 1985a; Makowski 1985b.
14 Audley-Miller 2016.
15 Ingholt 1928, 94–97.
16 Colledge 1976, 77 f.
17 Schmidt-Colinet 1992, 105–140.
18 Amy – Seyrig 1936.
19 Sadurska 1997, 76–166.
20 Sadurska – Bounni 1994, in passim.
21 Parlasca 1984, 284 f.; Audley-Miller, 554.
22 Audley-Miller 2016, 554.

Figure 47. Detail with standing child, from sarcophagus cat. 10.

scenes (cat. 81. 86. 185. 186. 230. 290. 306. 430), while four boxes show banqueting scenes (cat. 74. 103. 200. 201). A small but distinct category shows a reclining female banqueting or in the process of being adorned. The motif appears on eight sarcophagus lids (cat. 31. 180. 193. 194. 206. 207. 225. 236), and four small reliefs with frame (cat. 79. 718–720). A related motif appears on the side of one of the few monumental sarcophagi of Palmyra (cat. 290) and shows two female attendants with objects relating to female beautification.

Banqueting Motif

The banqueting motif has been attested on (1) foundation reliefs; (2) sarcophagus lids; (3) the so-called banqueting reliefs, which are square reliefs with an architectural frame; (4) as well as on four sarcophagus boxes (cat. 74. 103. 200–201). These have been discussed together in scholarship on Palmyrene sculpture[23], although Malcolm Colledge tried to separate the first three[24]. The motif, as scholars have already observed, and the collected material in the catalogue shows, did not change between categories of reliefs: it is composed of a figure reclining on a bed with other figures attending or being present. The reclining figure is always shown larger than the other figures on the relief. Instead of trying to separate the reliefs according to where they might have been placed within Palmyrene tombs, something that cannot be proven in most cases, it is best to discuss the reliefs as one group, following their iconographic unity[25].

The motif can be shown in a full or a simplified form. The full form shows usually one or rarely two reclining figures on a bed with turned legs and covered with one or two mattresses. The figure is accompanied by standing attendants who are members of the household, a seated child, and a seated female. In the simplified form, the reclining figure is shown on the mattress, with or without other attending figures. The reclining figure is usually male; however, there are a few reliefs where the figure is female[26]. The attending figures may be depicted carrying objects related to the banquet, such as rhyta or jugs, or with attributes relevant to their age group; for example, children can be depicted with birds or grapes (Fig. 47). The earliest reliefs with the banqueting motif omit the seated female at one end, and all the figures attending the reclining male(s) are shown standing (cat. 1. 2. 13. 60. 61; to these, appendix 1, cat. 1 may be added). From the beginning of the 2nd cent. A.D., however, the motif of the seated female appears, and becomes a permanent element of the composition (the earliest dated seated females appear in cat. 71. 93. 95). The motif, therefore, appears almost fully formed in Palmyra, allowing questions as to how it arrived in the city, and from where.

Klaus Parlasca is the scholar who studied the question of the emergence of the motif the most[27], and in his articles he has suggested several incentives behind the use of the banqueting motif on sarcophagi: (1) an existing local tradition; (2) the import of Attic sarcophagi, so popular in the coastal towns of Syria, that offered the impetus for the reformulation of the local banqueting motif and its use on sarcophagi[28]; and (3) the Italian kline sarcophagi and the ›Totenmahl‹ reliefs[29]. It is possible that all three influenced the use of the motif in reliefs; however, the evidence for the manner of transmission is slim. There is no iconographic evidence of banqueting from Hellenistic Palmyra, although fine ware that would have been used in banquets was found in Palmyra[30]. Only four fragments of Attic sarcophagi were found in Palmyra (appendix

23 See, among others, Parlasca 1984; Audley-Miller 2016.
24 Colledge 1976, 73–79.

25 The survey of find locations presented in chapter 2, shows that only foundation reliefs placed outside the tomb, and some of the small reliefs with architectural frame were not used as sarcophagi lids or as sarcophagi markers.
26 Krag 2018, 64–66; Raja 2022a.
27 Will 1951; Makowski 1985a; Makowski 1985b had examined the development of the banqueting reliefs within their Palmyrene context.
28 Parlasca 1984, 294; Parlasca 1995, 68 f. For the popularity of Attic sarcophagi in Syria see de Jong 2017, in passim.
29 Parlasca 1998, 315.
30 Römer-Strehl 2013. For Hellenistic Palmyra, see Schmidt-Colinet – al-Asʿad 2013.

4), and even though a community of Palmyrenes in Rome had been established around the beginning of the 2nd cent. A.D.[31], it is not possible to know which of the attested Palmyrenes in Rome still had relatives in Palmyra and were in close touch with them[32]. The ›Totenmahl‹ reliefs, so popular in Hellenistic and Roman Asia Minor[33], are not that well attested in Seleucid Asia, although figures in banquets are depicted in both large-scale[34] and small-scale monuments (Fig. 48)[35]. In neighbouring Parthia, the political successor of the Seleucid Empire, the banquet only appears in large-scale sculpture between A.D. 150 and A.D. 190, and even then, it is not a common subject[36]. Banquet scenes, however, become far more popular in Sasanian art, and reflected high-status real banquets, known from literary sources[37]. They also appear on rock-cut funerary reliefs in the areas of modern Urfa (ancient Edessa)[38] and in the caves of Hilar[39], testifying to the strong banqueting tradition in the wider region that was not always reflected in artistic production[40], and perhaps there is little reason trying to establish from where the banqueting motif originated in Palmyra. It could reflect actual banqueting practices, or it could have

Figure 48. Stele with funerary banquet, marble. From Thessaloniki, A.D. 75–100.

been imported by sculptors who had been commissioned to produce reliefs such as those in the Roman East[41].

Lids

Kline and Mattress

Some individual elements of the iconography of the Palmyrene banqueting motif, as well as the banqueting motif itself, have been treated in detail in previous scholarship[42]. As mentioned above, the primary element of the banqueting motif is the reclining figure. The figure is shown on a bed that is always elaborately carved, from the depiction on the first securely dated banqueting relief (cat. 1) to that on the latest securely dated reliefs (cat. 11. 82. 90–92). Even though there is variation in the degree of elaboration of the stretchers of the bed, with some appearing with plain, carved bands (for example, cat. 1. 33), others with decorated bands (for example, cat. 8 has scrolls and rosettes in panels), others with plain bands and decorated panels (for example, cat. 10. 11), all the beds have turned

---

31 At least, that is the date of the earliest religious dedications of Palmyrenes from Rome: Ensoli 2001. For the religious community of the Palmyrenes in Rome, see also Fowlkes-Childs 2016.
32 Piersimoni 1995, 651, only writes »One of the numerous Palmyrenes in Rome« for Yarḥai and Piersimoni 1995, 808, »He is one of the Palmyrenes living in Rome« for T. Claudius Felix. Only one inscription in the Agora of Palmyra set up in honour of the commander of an auxiliary unit of Palmyrenes enlisted in Porolissum in Dacia Superior indicates contact between Palmyrene expatriates and Palmyra: Seyrig 1941, 231–233 no. 4; Starcky 1949, no. 79. The authors would like to thank the reviewers for this reference. A much later example of how families could remain connected even though they were living in different cities is provided by the Rothschilds, see Morton 1998.
33 Dentzer 1978; Fabricius 1999; Fabricius 2016.
34 The most famous and well-studied example is of the reclining Heracles at Behistun: Callieri – Askari-Chaverdi 2013, 693 with previous bibliography.
35 Langin-Hooper 2016.
36 Mathiesen 1993, 34–51. It only appears in the rock-cut relief at Tang-i Sarvak, Mathiesen 1993, cat. 18.
37 Canepa 2009, 183–186; Masia-Radford 2013.
38 For the rock-cut tombs and their reliefs, see Pognon 1907, 179–183; Segal 1970, 27; Drijvers – Healey 1999, As 12–19; Blömer 2022, 164.
39 For the reliefs at Hilar, see Equini Schneider 1992a; Spanu et al 1992–1993; Blömer 2022, 170.
40 For example, Mathiesen 1993, 29 suggested economic, cultural, or political reasons behind the reduced production of sculpture in the middle Parthian period (A.D. 1–150). Similar reasons could explain the gaps in the production of banqueting scenes in neighbouring regions, as well as the selection of particular motifs in certain areas. For example, naked female banqueting figures are common in Seleucid-Parthian Babylon, as opposed to male reclining figures: for these see Langin-Hooper 2016.

41 Audley-Miller 2016, 567 f.
42 Banqueting bowls and vessels: Miyashita 2016; Heyn 2021. Women and children: Krag – Raja 2017. For the motif, see Will 1951; Seyrig 1951; Dentzer 1971; Makowski 1985a; Makowski 1985b; Audley-Miller 2016.

Figure 49. Fulcrum with horse's head, bronze, 100 B.C.–A.D. 100.

legs composed of numerous separate elements (for example, concave quarters, bell-shaped elements, scotias, balls, and tori) that are arranged in such a manner as to avoid repetitions and create contrasts: so, a ball is never preceded or succeeded by another round element, but rather by conical or square elements[43]. The most elaborate element of the bed is the fulcrum, the headrest support. The fulcrum of the Palmyrene beds has similarities to that of the expensive Roman couches[44]: it is decorated on both ends, but the main element can be more linear compared to the more sinuous, or even s-shaped form of the Roman fulcra[45] (for example, cat. 8. 10. 72. 90–92. 98. 105. 107. 115. 119. 171. 173. 304. 305. 307. 308. 345. 417. 443. 445) or just as sinuous (for example, cat. 110. 121. 169.)[46]. The central element may be decorated with rosettes (cat. 8. 105. 107. 169), a reclining figure, most likely mythological (cat. 10. 345. 443. 444), a branch with leaves (cat. 173. 445), or,

in one particular case, decorated with two reclining figures, one placed above the other (cat. 290). In other cases, however, it remained undecorated (cat. 106. 110. 115. 305. 308. 417). The upper end is usually decorated with a lion head (cat. 8. 72. 90–91. 105–107. 307. 417. 445). Two are decorated with a horse's head (cat. 110. 443). The lower end is usually decorated with a bust in a medallion, commonly that of a priest (cat. 91. 105. 115. 304. 307. 308. 417. 443), or of a male not shown in a priestly role (cat. 8. 10. 72. 90. 106. 107. 290. 305). In three reliefs, the bust is placed directly at the end of the fulcrum and not in a medallion (cat. 3. 345. 444), while in three other reliefs, the lower end is decorated with a rosette within a medallion (cat. 171. 173. 445).

Some elements of the depicted Palmyrene fulcra have parallels to the bronze fittings of fulcra surviving from the Roman Empire[47], while others are unique to Palmyra. Couches of the Roman period followed Hellenistic examples, and some of the decorative elements have a long tradition: for example, already in the Hellenistic period, busts in medallions decorated the lower end of fulcra[48], and this practice continued in the Roman period[49]. Most of the figures in these

---

43 For turned legs in Roman furniture, see Ulrich 2007, 233 f.
44 Dunbabin 2003, 38 for couches made with fittings of expensive materials.
45 For Roman-period fulcra, see Richter 1966, 57 f.; Faust 1989; Dunbabin 2003, 38. The shape of the fulcrum fitting probably derived from Hellenistic models, but these earlier examples were longer: Richter 1966, 58.
46 There are more fulcra carved in the reliefs of the catalogue; however, these, and the ones mentioned below, are the ones that are depicted well enough in the publications to allow for further study.

47 Parlasca 1992, 260.
48 See Richter 1966, 57, with examples.
49 Richter 1966, 57 f.

medallions were mythological[50], although there are a few Hellenistic examples with portrait busts[51]. Therefore, the representation of the busts of priests or beardless males in medallions at the lower end of the fulcra is part of a long tradition, but at the same time, unique to Palmyra for the Roman period. The decoration of the upper end with animal heads also forms part of a tradition of decorating that area with an animal head[52], although the mule or horse heads that were common in other parts of the Roman world were not as common in Palmyra, where lion heads were more popular (Fig. 49)[53]. The decoration of the central element with leaves also finds parallels in other areas of the Roman world[54]; however, in Palmyra, the decoration with mythological figures seems to have been most prevalent. Two examples, in particular, highlight the inventiveness and ability of Palmyrene sculptors: the first is the fulcrum of the kline on cat. 290, and the other is appendix 5, cat. 12. The fulcrum fitting of cat. 290 shows a reclining male figure, while a female is seated above him, while in appendix 5, cat. 12, a male figure is seated on a panther, and a female figure is seated on the panther above him, possibly Dionysos and a maenad[55]. In the medallion closing the fitting, there is a bearded Silenus with a cup, reinforcing the Dionysian theme. Both fulcra show two figures: the presence of multiple figures is a feature that seems to be unique to Palmyra, and in contrast to the single figure known from other areas[56]. A third fulcrum (cat. 193) is partly carved and shows three figures, one placed over the other. It is not possible to determine their exact iconography, but it is very likely that they too belonged to the mythological sphere.

The klinai on the Palmyrene sarcophagi reliefs have one or two mattresses and cushions. Compared to the mattresses depicted on reliefs and paintings from other areas of the Roman world, the depiction of two mattresses is a distinctly Palmyrene element, and it is relatively common in Palmyra (cat. 6. 11. 90–92. 98–100. 110. 118–121. 126. 129. 168. 170. 171. 174. 180. 181. 290), unlike the depictions of klinai in other areas, where one mattress is the norm. When two mattresses are depicted, the lower mattress is thicker than the upper one, and has wide bands that have floral or vegetal decorative motifs. This can be compared to depictions of mattresses in other types of sarcophagi, for example, from Rome or Athens or Asia Minor, where the fabric has multiple bands, however, without carrying any decoration[57]. The upper mattress is thinner and carries a continuous decoration, usually rosettes or other flowers within lozenges[58]. Another distinctly Palmyrene element is the richly decorated cushion (or cushions), on which the banqueter rests. They have one wide band with vegetal or floral motifs that is framed by two narrow beaded bands, in contrast to cushions in other sarcophagi that were blank (Fig. 50, Pl. 32)[59].

One thing that is absent from the Palmyrene banqueting imagery is the table[60]. It only appears in one sarcophagus relief (cat. 446). It is in the form of a tripod with legs with animal heads, possibly panthers, and has two different bowls and what may be a rhyton on top. Next to the table are a jug and a two-handled vase with a conical foot.

---

50 See Richter 1966, 57 for Hellenistic examples of mythological figures in medallions. For Roman examples, see two busts of Silenoi at the Art Institute of Chicago, inv. nos. 1997.554.1–2: Raff 2017, cat. 139. 140.

51 Barr-Sharrar 1985 for a portrait of Arsinoe III; Faust 1989, 127–129 for more portraits in medallions, this time in profile.

52 The two examples at the British Museum, inv. no. 1784,0131.4, are perhaps the most famous ones, but they were not unique: <https://www.britishmuseum.org/collection/object/G_1784-0131-4> (26.04.2022). See discussion in Raff 2017.

53 One such example is the couch at the Walters Art Gallery, inv. no. 54.2365, where the fulcra fittings end in lions' heads: <https://art.thewalters.org/detail/29041/banquet-couch/> (26.04.2022). See also Kent Hill 1963, for examples of the use of busts of mythological figures. For the use of figures of tigers, dogs, and elephants on fulcra, see Vendries 2016, 280 n. 6. 7.

54 The fulcrum fittings at the British Museum, inv. no. 1784,0131.4, are two good examples of decoration with leaves, in this case formed of silver and copper inlays: <https://www.britishmuseum.org/collection/object/G_1784-0131-4-1> (26.04.2022).

55 Parlasca 1992, 260 had identified both figures as maenads.

56 Cf. Hellenistic bronze fulcrum fitting now in the British Museum, 1908,0410.2: <https://www.britishmuseum.org/collection/object/G_1908-0410-2> (26.04.2022); part of a fulcrum fitting, possibly Roman, in unknown location: <https://arachne.dainst.org/entity/723909> (26.04.2022); a bronze fulcrum fitting, now in unknown location: <https://arachne.dainst.org/entity/723915> (26.04.2022).

57 Sarcophagi with mattresses with figural scenes separated by bands have not been found in Palmyra so far, such as the Attic sarcophagus at Musei Capitolini: Dunbabin 2003, 124; Fittschen-Zanker 2014, cat. 61; a sarcophagus in the Museum of Antiquities in Cyrene: <https://arachne.dainst.org/entity/1069768> (26.04.2022); a sarcophagus in the National Museum of Athens: <https://arachne.dainst.org/entity/1254199> (26.04.2022). Also absent from Palmyra are the plain mattresses seen in funerary reliefs with single banqueting figures (›Totenmahl‹). These mattresses may have been painted, but the colours have not survived. For earlier, Hellenistic, examples of reliefs with plain but painted mattresses, see Stamatopoulou 2016.

58 It is likely that several objects in the catalogue that now appear with a single, thin mattress with continuous decoration originally had a second, thicker, lower mattress.

59 These cushions may have been painted originally, as the (earlier) examples from Demetrias show: Stamatopoulou 2016.

60 See also Colledge 1976, 77.

Figure 50. Attic sarcophagus with undecorated mattress and cushion, marble. Found in Thessaloniki, ca. A.D. 180.

The Reclining Figure

The reclining figure is almost always male. In the earlier reliefs, men are depicted beardless regardless of whether they are depicted as priests (who were always beardless when wearing their priestly hat). Bearded men appear from the beginning of the 2nd cent. A.D. in funerary loculus reliefs[61], but in sarcophagi they only seem to appear near the end of the same century. The drawings of Cassas showing the now-lost founder reliefs from the tower of Yamlikû (appendix 1, cat. 1) and from the tower of Elahbel (appendix 2, cat. 1) are the only testimonies for the depiction of bearded men in sarcophagi reliefs from the beginning of the 2nd cent.

---

61 Heyn 2010; Albertson 2016.

A.D. In some reliefs, the beard seems to be used as a way for representing the reclining man as older from the standing male figures on the relief (for example, cat. 11. 68. 69. 101. 129), but in other reliefs, the beard may be used as a way of differentiating one male from another: in cat. 110, for example, a beardless priest is reclining next to a bearded male, in cat. 173 and cat. 177 beardless and bearded busts are placed side by side on the boxes, while there are also reliefs where both reclining men sport a beard, for example, on cat. 102. In addition to beards that could function as markers of age, furrows on the forehead could be used to indicate the age and maturity of the depicted male. For example, in cat. 60, of the three figures, the one on the proper left has two lines across his forehead, indicating that he is older than the two other males on the relief, or on cat. 244, where the male has both a beard and a wrinkled forehead. Cat.

591 shows also the use of nasolabial folds for indicating that the man is of mature age.

The costume choices of the reclining males as well as the different combinations of garments that they could wear were mentioned in the introduction already (see also appendix at end of the chapter for a comprehensive list of all the costume choices seen on reclining males). The main combinations, however, were (1) the >Parthian-style< costume and (2) the tunic and himation. The most popular combination of garments for the >Parthian-style< costume was the Parthian-style tunic, worn together with trousers and chlamys (seventy-seven examples). In four portraits, the figure also wore over-trousers. The second most popular combination was that of the >Parthian-style< tunic worn under a himation (twenty-nine examples). The other combinations appear less frequently: eight figures with >Parthian-style< tunic and chlamys; six with >Parthian-style< tunic and trousers; four with >Parthian-style< tunic, trousers, and over-trousers; four with >Parthian-style< tunic, trousers, and himation; three with >Parthian-style< tunic, trousers, and long coat; three with plain tunic worn with chlamys; two with plain tunic worn with trousers and himation; and one with plain tunic, trousers, and chlamys. The combinations of >Parthian-style< tunic, himation and chlamys, and of plain tunic, chlamys, trousers, over-trousers, or plain tunic, chlamys and himation, are also rare, with one example each. In addition to these, there are ten reclining figures that are not fully preserved but also wore the >Parthian-style< costume. The plain, undecorated tunic worn with a himation is the other combination of garments that is often worn by reclining men (eighty-one examples). Extremely rare is the representation of a tunic with two clavi (two examples). In addition to these, there are thirteen examples where only the himation survives, four where only the tunic survives, and another eleven portraits whose garments cannot be determined.

The costume choices can be further nuanced if one looks at two more variables: the first is that of men who were represented as priests either wearing the Palmyrene priestly hat, or by having it placed beside them, and the dates of the reliefs. Of the 261 reclining men in total, thirty-eight are depicted as priests. Of these, only five wear the priestly hat while also wearing a plain tunic and himation. All the other priests, wear >Parthian-style< garments. The role of priest was the highest a Palmyrene man could aspire to, and it was hereditary. The choice of the >Parthian-style< garments, therefore, highlighted his high status in local society. Furthermore, the dates of the reliefs are revealing as well. Leaving aside reliefs that are either dated within a very broad range (for example, A.D. 100–200) or between the periods mentioned in chapter 2 (for example, A.D. 140–160), there are 232 portraits that can be dated within the Groups I–V. Only eleven portraits of reclining men are dated between A.D. 1–100, and all of them wear either the plain tunic and the himation, or just a himation. So, this type of garment combination, known from other Palmyrene reliefs, is the oldest to appear in the sarcophagi. Thirty-four portraits belong in the second group, A.D. 100–150. Of these, the majority (twenty-five portraits) wear the plain tunic and himation combination. In the next groups, however, the majority of the reclining males appear wearing a >Parthian-style< combination of garments: out of fifty-three portraits in the period A.D. 150–200, twenty-nine wear >Parthian-style< clothes, sixty-five out of 103 in the period A.D. 200–240, and twenty-six out of thirty-two in the period A.D. 240–273. It is clear that from the middle of the 2nd cent. A.D., the majority of reclining men are depicted in >Parthian-style< garments, while the number of men in plain tunics and himatia declines steadily. The >Parthian-style< clothes, therefore, become not only the most appropriate for banqueters, but also the ones that best reveal the wearers' high status.

The usual attribute of reclining men is the drinking vessel. There are three main types seen on the reliefs: shallow, handleless bowls, deep bowls with handles, and the rhyta[62]. There is great variation in their decoration, from plain cups to elaborately carved ones[63]. The handleless bowls are most likely phialae, and they are held with the fingertips of the upturned hand[64], while the deep bowl with handles closely resembles the skyphos[65] and what is depicted in Palmyrene art, probably a local variation of the type. The skyphoi are always held by the handles, while the rhyta are carried. Earlier reliefs (between A.D. 89–150) depict simpler, undecorated skyphoi, whose profiles are round or rounded (cat. 60–62. 71. 72. 75. 93. 104–107), but from around the middle of the 2nd cent. A.D., skyphoi appear decorated, either in continuous patterns or in distinct registers, and with angular profiles (cat. 7. 9 are two of the earliest examples). At the same time, the phialae held with the fingertips also appear: they are usually decorated with continuous patterns (for example, cat. 23. 69. 110), or undecorated (for example, cat. 74). That the shallow bowls did not replace the skyphoi but could be used for giving greater variety to the scene is demonstrated by examples such as cat. 90, and ultimately, the use of a skyphos or a bowl was a matter

---

62 For drinking vessels in banqueting reliefs, see Miyashita 2016; Heyn 2021.
63 See especially Miyashita 2016 for the types and decoration of bowls shown in banqueting scenes.
64 Heyn 2021, 67.
65 Heyn 2021, 67.

of preference by the commissioner of the monument (see, for example, cat. 110 where both figures hold a shallow bowl). The third drinking vessel shown is the rhyton: only in one example is it held by the reclining male (cat. 727). In all the other examples, it is carried by a standing male figure. Of the three, the skyphos has long been associated with the Graeco-Roman cultural sphere and was depicted in the hands of banqueters and comasts from the classical period[66]. The shallow bowl and the rhyton, however, are connected with the East[67]. The other attribute that often appears together with reclining males is the dagger. This is a typical *akinakes*, the dagger seen in Persian art and found in the East[68]. In Palmyra, it is shown placed against the thigh, defying gravity. It is held in place by a plain belt and, in reality, it would have fallen to the side the moment one reclined. In the reliefs, however, it is always represented, as it was an important status symbol.

Reclining women also appear in the reliefs functioning as sarcophagus lids. They are incredibly few compared to the depictions of reclining men, only nine (cat. 31. 79. 180. 193. 194. 206. 207. 225. 236) compared to over 200 reclining males[69]. It is possible to distinguish between women shown reclining together with reclining men (cat. 79. 193), usually assumed to be their husbands, though in one case, it is the brother of the woman that is depicted (cat. 79); women reclining next to a seated female (cat. 194); women next to a reclining male and a seated female (cat. 180); and women shown alone, though this could be due to the fragmentary preservation of the relief (cat. 31. 206. 207. 225. 236). They are all dressed in a tunic and himation and wear multiple headdresses (when they are preserved): headband, turban, and veil. These clothes are typical for women, regardless of whether they are depicted reclining, seated, or standing. They also wear multiple pieces of jewellery: earrings, several necklaces, bracelets, as well as the brooch that keeps their himation fastened. A hexagonal box with a lock, possibly a jewellery box, is prominently placed on a pedestal beside the female on cat. 76. It is worth noting that these few reclining women are among those carrying the most jewellery in Palmyra. All these reliefs date from the end of the 2nd cent. A.D. and the 3rd cent. A.D., indicating that there was a phenomenon particular to this period, and possibly also tied to particular families, since four of the reliefs stem from the same tomb (cat. 193. 194. 206. 207)[70].

Women appeared reclining alone in Etruscan art, but they are rare in the art of the Roman period, and they usually appear on urns or reliefs, rather than sarcophagi[71], while a kline monument shows a young girl on the cusp of adolescence reclining on a bed (Fig. 20)[72]. Like the Palmyrene reliefs, these particular examples seem to be tied to the wishes of specific families, adjusting rather than following empire-wide iconographic trends.

Seated Females

Females, almost always seated at the proper right end of the relief[73], were the second most important figure on the relief after the reclining banqueter. They are dressed in a tunic and himation. All seated women wear a veil, almost always with both headband and turban underneath. Only in nine reliefs do they wear only a turban (cat. 76. 98. 100. 102. 104. 168. 171. 694) or a headband under the veil (cat. 91)[74]. In addition to the textile head coverings, twenty-five females wear head ornaments, such as chains and pendants (cat. 136. 158. 159. 163. 164. 232. 235. 246. 429. 616. 622. 624. 625. 632. 638. 642. 644. 653. 655. 657. 660. 665–677. 682). The standing female on cat. 388 probably also wears head ornaments. The age of the women is subtly indicated through nasolabial folds (cat. 7. 48. 125. 633). Sunken cheeks in addition to the nasolabial folds can also be used to indicate the maturity of the female (cat. 272). In female portraits, however, physical markers of age are not shown as often as in male portraits; the maturity of the women is indicated through the wearing of the veil, multiple pieces of jewellery, as well as attributes such as the spindle and distaff. The tunic has either long or short sleeves, and the himation is always fastened over the upper left side of the torso with a brooch. The type of the brooch changes from period to period. It is not always clear whether the himation covers only the

---

66 Heyn 2021, 67. Schreiber 1999, 243. See, for example, the vase at Paris, Musée du Louvre, inv. no. CP10889, BAPD no. 1385. See also the humorous (by Greek male standards) scene of a woman drinking from a skyphos, depicted on a skyphos: <http://www.getty.edu/art/collection/objects/12040/unknown-maker-attic-red-figure-skyphos-greek-attic-460-450-bc/> (26.04.2022).

67 Heyn 2021, 67 f. For shallow bowls, see Pfrommer 1993, 21 f.; Raubitschek 1998, 21; Treister 2007. For rhyta, see Pfrommer 1993, 47–49.

68 For *akinakes*, see Miller 1997, 46–48; Minasyan 2021.

69 For a detailed discussion of reclining females, see Raja 2022a.

70 Raja 2022a, 77.

71 Dunbabin 2003, 114–120. See also Rose-Greenland 2007 and Aristodemou 2014. For the reclining posture of women, see Roller 2003.

72 Now at the J. P. Getty Museum, inv. no. 73.AA.11: Wrede 1990.

73 Only in cat. 11. 71. 98. 176. 390 are women seated to the proper left of the lid relief, and in the sarcophagi boxes cat. 74. 201. 285.

74 Krag 2018, 47. It has been suggested for the headdresses of other regions that they refer to tribal identities, Rumscheid 2019. Rumscheid 2019 also references Finlayson's unpublished dissertation, in which she tried to prove this for Palmyra: Rumscheid 2019, 74.

torso and upper legs or falls to the ground. Women in earlier reliefs hold the spindle and distaff (for example, cat. 71), but in later reliefs, they hold the edge of the veil (for example, cat. 74)[75].

These figures have parallels in the seated women seen so often in the so-called Totenmahl reliefs, and, like the women in those reliefs, they too usually were the wives or mothers of the reclining males (Fig. 51). There is one main difference, however, in their iconography: the Palmyrene women are seated on the mattress as if their chair itself is placed on the mattress. In the so-called Totenmahl reliefs, the women are seated either next to the banqueting couch or on it. This mode of representation, on a chair on the mattress, is particular to Palmyra.

Standing Figures

Standing figures were placed between the seated female to the right and the reclining figure on the left. Unlike standing figures in the so-called Totenmahl-reliefs, they too must have stood with their feet on the mattress, rather than on the ground next to the banqueting couch, from the way they are portrayed standing behind the feet of the reclining figure[76]. Males wear either a plain tunic with a belt (for example, cat. 1. 9. 61), plain tunic and himation (for example, cat. 10. 11. 19. 81), or a combination of Parthian-inspired garments (for example, cat. 23. 60. 68. 69. 81). That the clothes were probably chosen in order to differentiate the figures, rather than for imparting a certain meaning or denoting social status can be seen from sarcophagi such as cat. 81, where the reclining male and one of the standing figures both wear the >Parthian-style< garment combination that denotes elite status; yet, the other standing figure is shown wearing a plain tunic and himation. In other cases, though, the same garment combination was used to denote close relationship between the two family members depicted with them (for example, cat. 90–92). The combination of standing figures in plain tunic and himation together with reclining men in >Parthian-style< garments on sarcophagi from the 3rd cent. A.D. highlights that individual family preferences were more important than >fashion< trends when it came to the costume choices of standing figures, even in the period during which >Parthian-style< costume was the costume of choice for denoting elite status. That some of these standing males did not have lower status compared to the reclining men is made clear

Figure 51. Stele with funerary banquet: in memory of Menophilos, set up by his wife, Synete, marble. From Cyzicus, 25 B.C.–A.D. 25.

by such representations as in cat. 91. 92, where the standing figures are depicted as priests and so were definitely members of the same family as the reclining male who had pride of place in the relief[77]. In fact, without inscriptions mentioning the relationships of the standing figures to the reclining ones, it is not possible to determine their role within the household. Only one standing male is clearly described as a confidant (cat. 282), and thus it may be possible to understand that he was a non-free member of the household[78]. He

---

75 For a detailed discussion of female costume and jewellery in Palmyra, see Krag 2018, 27–29. 95–110. See also, Heyn 2019.
76 Unless one assumes that they stood on a podium behind the kline.
77 Priesthood was hereditary in Palmyra: see Kaizer 2002, 240; Raja 2016b.
78 The only detailed study of slavery and freedmen in Palmyra is Yon 2002, 165–196.

is shown wearing the plain tunic and himation, and so, without the inscription it would not be possible to determine his status, since that is a common garment combination for standing males.

Standing males hold a variety of attributes: ladles (cat. 60. 280. 691), wreaths (cat. 61. 84. 88), jugs of different types (cat. 74. 691), shallow bowls (cat. 103. 69. 424. 691.), and rhyta (cat. 103. 424. 493. 488. 721), either alone or in combination. They may also carry bowls with fruit (cat. 55) or even animals (cat. 371). The attributes carried by them are not determinant of status either. In cat. 1, a standing male is depicted carrying a jug and ladle, the banquet attributes that are so common in later reliefs (for example, in cat. 60. 74). The inscription mentions both the son of Kîtôt and his servant, so this figure could be either. In cat. 91, a standing priest is depicted with a shallow bowl, while in cat. 134, a priest is carrying a jug while a man in a ›Parthian-style‹ tunic and himation carries another jug and two men in tunics carry libation pitchers. In another relief, a standing male with a drinking bowl is clearly identified as »Malkû, son of Zabdâ« (cat. 347), and in a third one, a standing male shown holding a wreath, another attribute commonly associated with the banquet, is again identified as a son of the family (cat. 72). These last two reliefs are the only ones where the standing male with the banqueting attributes is clearly identified as a relative of the reclining male, however, several of the banqueting reliefs, especially the ones with frame, which show reclining men together with standing males carrying objects relating to the banquet carry no inscriptions (for example, cat. 68. 69. 687. 711. 713. 714. 716. 717. 722. 726–728), or inscriptions identifying only the reclining male (for example, cat. 691. 709).

Standing females wear tunic and himation (for example, cat. 9. 11), or simply a tunic (for example, cat. 72). Most standing women are veiled and wear a headband and a turban underneath, but there are three portraits where they only wear one headdress under the veil (232. 235. 306), and nine where they wear no headdress (72. 101. 387. 299. 306. 718. 719. 720). Rarer still is the so-called Faustina hairstyle, where the hair is piled up high on the head (cat. 247)[79]. Perhaps a variation of the so-called Faustina hairstyle is that worn by the standing female in cat. 388. Five of the women without headdresses are also shown carrying objects and they are placed next to a reclining female, attending to her (387. 306. 718–720): boxes (387. 718) that, when open, display the contained jewellery (55. 719), and mirrors (55. 720). One of the women carries a bowl of fruit (72). She is identified as a daughter of the family by the inscription on the relief. The depiction of standing women with boxes, jewellery, and mirrors attending seated females has a long tradition in the eastern Mediterranean, especially the Graeco-Roman world[80]. One cannot be certain, though, if these were servant women, as in Roman reliefs, or young relatives, as was the case with the female in cat. 72.

Seated Children

In addition to these figures, seated children also appear in the reliefs. They are wearing ›Parthian-style‹ clothes and hold birds or grapes, that is, the attributes typical for children in Palmyrene art (for example, cat. 72). Seated children are shown next to (cat. 107) or even in the lap of adult figures (cat. 390), highlighting their close relationship to the adults, presumably their parents[81].

Boxes

Portrait Busts

The iconography of the boxes remains almost always consistent until the late 2nd cent. A.D. The most common motif is that of armless bust portraits; however, since A.D. 150, sarcophagus boxes appear where the busts are placed inside clipei, while the background may also be embellished with garlands. From A.D. 200, boxes appear whose iconography seems to reflect Palmyrene life: caravan protection, trade, religious, and domestic activities.

The armless busts, ranging from two (cat. 8) to six (cat. 173. 177) are depicted between the legs of the kline. Most portraits are not accompanied by inscriptions, but when they are, the inscriptions reveal that they belong to the same family (for example, cat. 10. 173). In one case, the standing figure of a child is depicted between the busts (cat. 10), while in another sarcophagus box, the bust of a female is placed between two full figures of standing children (cat. 115). The busts are relatively uniform: the men in earlier sarcophagi appear beardless (for example, cat. 8), but from the 3rd cent. A.D. busts of bearded men also appear (for example, cat. 173. 177. 178). Priests are depicted beardless during all periods. Men wear the tunic and himation, while in their priestly role, they wear a tunic with a chlamys fastened over the right shoulder with a brooch. The women wear a veil, under which they have two or three headdresses (for example, in cat. 131). One end of the veil always falls over the shoulder, crosses over the chest, covering it, and then falls across the other shoulder, making it

---

79 Krag – Raja 2018. See also Parlasca 1987b.

80 See, for example, Blundell – Rabinowitz 2008.
81 For children in Palmyrene sarcophagi, see Krag – Raja 2017.

impossible to know if they, too, were meant to wear a himation like the females depicted on the sarcophagus lids. From around A.D. 130, portrait busts are placed inside clipei. It is not a very common motif, appearing only on thirty-three sarcophagus boxes (cat. 50. 51. 111. 112. 114. 134–136. 167. 171. 174–176. 178. 181. 188. 203. 223. 252. 298. 303. 308. 403. 406. 412. 419–423. 426. 431. 445). Of these, only nine date from around and after the middle of the 2nd cent. A.D. (cat. 50. 51. 111. 112. 167. 303. 403. 406. 412); the others date from the 3rd cent. A.D., the same period that portraits in clipei appear in funerary monuments in Italy and other areas of the Roman Empire[82]. Another rare motif is that of the lion's or panther's head with a ring in its mouth that is placed between the busts (cat. 302. 403). In one fragment the panther's head is placed inside a garland held up by eagles (appendix 5, cat. 16); the sarcophagus box may have carried portraits as well; in any case, this is, so far, another unique iconographic motif from Palmyra.

Sarcophagi boxes with busts are rare outside Palmyra, but they do exist. One example from Thessaloniki has four busts: two younger figures, a beardless male with his chest uncovered next to a female with uncovered hair, and an older, veiled female next to a beaded man in tunic and himation[83]. Much less detailed are the busts in a sarcophagus now in Tripoli[84]. The representation of busts over garlands was more common in the Roman Empire[85], but in Palmyra, almost all the busts were placed paratactically between the kline legs. Only the sarcophagi from temple tomb no. 186 had busts placed within garlands (cat. 180. 181. 187–190), indicating that these sarcophagi most likely came from the same tomb.

›Daily Life‹: Caravan/Trade, Religious, and Domestic Iconography

The rare scenes from ›daily life‹ have received much more attention in scholarship than the humble busts, to the extent that one might think that they were the norm in Palmyra rather than the exception. They can be divided into two broad categories: trade/caravan scenes, on five sarcophagus boxes (cat. 82. 228. 274. 447. appendix 5, cat. 11), and religious scenes, on eight sarcophagus boxes (cat. 81. 86. 185. 186. 230. 290. 306. 430). To these, four sarcophagus boxes and one banqueting relief with frame with men taking part in a banquet may be added (cat. 74. 103. 200. 201. 728). A third category, known only from two sarcophagus boxes (cat. 290. 306) and three small banqueting reliefs with frame (cat. 718–720), is that of female adornment. There are also nine sarcophagi with rows of standing figures. In eight of them, the figures are not preserved well enough (cat. 202. 238. 239. 285. 309–312), while the ninth sarcophagus is now lost (appendix 1, cat. 1) and so it is not possible to identify the scenes depicted on them.

Trade or caravan scenes show one (cat. 228) or more (cat. 82. 447) standing figures together with animals associated with trade: horses and camels. The figures wear Parthian-inspired costume comprised of tunic and trousers and they are armed (cat. 82. 228. 447). Camels appear more often: in four out of the five sarcophagus boxes (cat. 228. 274. 447. appendix 5, cat. 11), while the depiction of horses is not as common: they are depicted only in two out of the five sarcophagus boxes (cat. 82. 228). Both horses (cat. 82. 228) are shown with a quiver that is suspended next to the saddle, while the camels that are well preserved (cat. 228. 274. 447) are shown with a shield, with one exception (appendix 5, cat. 11). Even that last one, however, is shown with the same trappings as the others, and is not loaded with goods, thus indicating that this is another camel trained for military use. Four out of the five scenes, therefore, refer more to the activities of Palmyrene men who protected caravans rather than Palmyrene traders, and the camels are animals trained for military use[86]. The only trade scene is probably the one in cat. 274: the camel has not been preserved, but it is shown walking away from a ship, with a male standing between the camel and the ship[87]. The only comparable parallel to these scenes is the depiction of tradesmen and craftsmen practising their professions in Roman funerary reliefs, or the scenes of military action shown in sarcophagi, but clearly, the Palmyrenes only adopted the concept of portraying a scene from ›real life‹ rather than the iconographic motifs known from other areas of the Roman Empire[88].

The religious scenes can be divided broadly into two categories: scenes of ritual activity: making offerings to an altar (cat. 290. 306), and scenes where the figures are shown carrying objects that are connected to ritual activities: shallow bowls, possibly paterae, jugs, sacrificial animals, wreaths (cat. 81. 86. 185. 186. 230. 430). In the two scenes that show ritual activity, the men performing

---

82 Koch et al. 1982, 63 f.
83 Thessaloniki, Archaeological Museum of Thessaloniki, inv. no. 1942: Maniatis et al. 2010.
84 Annan 2019, 187 figs. 11. 22.
85 Annan 2019, 186.

86 For the iconography of camels in Palmyra, see Seland 2017; Raja 2020; Raja – Seland 2021. For the role of Palmyrene elites as caravan escorts, see recently Yon 2019b, with previous bibliography.
87 For Palmyrene trade, see Seland 2015; Gawlikowski 2016b; Seland 2017; Schörle 2017.
88 For funerary reliefs with trade scenes, see Clarke 2003, 181–220; for sarcophagi with military scenes, see Koch 1993, 66 f.

the activity are wearing togas, thus highlighting their participation in Roman civic culture[89]. In cat. 290, the men around them (one leading an animal and holding a dagger, one with patera and jug, one with a box, likely of incense, one with bowl of fruit, one with a bird in his hands, and one with a jug) are wearing simple tunics, with undergarments whose edges can be seen under the tunics. In cat. 306, where ritual activity is shown on both long sides of the sarcophagus, again the male figures performing the rite wear togas, while the other standing males wear tunics with undergarments with a fringed end (side A: one standing male with a box, one standing male with bowl of fruit; side B: standing male leading calf and holding dagger, standing male with patera and jug, standing male with box, standing male with bowl of fruit, standing male with small animal in hands, and standing male with jug). Two females wrapped in chiton and himation are also shown attending the ritual activity on side A of cat. 306, making the scene one of the few rare representations of women engaging in religious activities in Palmyra[90]. The other reliefs show standing men wearing ›Parthian-style‹ garments and even carrying swords and daggers, in addition to amphorae (cat. 81), jugs (cat. 230), cups (cat. 230), shallow bowls or paterae (cat. 86. 185. 186), bowls with possibly fruit (cat. 86), and wreaths (cat. 86. 185. 430). In addition to these, one male is shown leading an animal (cat. 230) and one holds a pinecone (cat. 81). All these objects are associated with the sphere of ritual activities. Sacrifice scenes were part of the iconography of the so-called ›biographical‹ Roman imperial sarcophagi, demonstrating the piety of the deceased. In Palmyra, however, these scenes cover the entire long side of the sarcophagus, and, in the case of cat. 306, both long sides.

Two more iconographic subjects appear even more rarely in Palmyrene sarcophagus boxes: the banqueting motif and the motif of the female with attendant. One sarcophagus box from the tomb of Lišamš (cat. 74) shows two males reclining side by side, with a seated female to the left end of the box and three standing figures to the right, partly covered by one of the reclining males. The sarcophagus box from the hypogeum of Ḥennibel shows a reclining priest with a standing male attendant to his left and a seated female to his right. Two sarcophagus boxes (cat. 200. 201) from tomb no. 85b show priests taking part in a banquet together with seated females. The banqueting motif is the same as the motif used on lids, with the male reclining while a female is seated by his side. In cat. 201, one of the women is shown seated at the left of the reclining male, no doubt for reasons of creating a symmetrical composition: two reclining men framed by the seated females.

One sarcophagus box also has a rare scene: a reclining female with a standing female attendant (cat. 290). The motif is also known from three small banqueting reliefs with frame (cat. 718–720). In almost all the reliefs, the reclining female is facing the viewer (cat. 290. 718. 719), while in cat. 720, she is depicted with her eyes closed and her head resting on her hand. The attendant figure holds a necklace in the side of the sarcophagus box relief (cat. 290), a jewellery box (closed in cat. 718, open in cat. 719), or a mirror (cat. 720). A jewellery box is placed on a pedestal between the female and the attendant (cat. 290), or a calathos with wool on the table between them (cat. 718. 719). Finally, in the sarcophagus box cat. 306, two standing females are depicted: one with an open jewellery box and one with a mirror and an object that is possibly a closed perfume bottle.

The motif of the woman reclining in banquet is rare on sarcophagi[91]. There are two examples from Tripolis, Lebanon, both at the İstanbul Arkeoloji Müzesi: one where the woman is reclining together with her husband[92] and one where she is shown reclining alone[93], and a few examples from Rome, where she is shown reclining together with her husband[94]. The Palmyrene examples are closer to the one from Tripolis where the female is shown alone on the kline, but in the Tripolis sarcophagus, the woman is dressed in a chiton and himation in the Roman manner and wears her hair in the hairstyle made fashionable by Julia Domna (reigned

---

89 For that see in particular Schmidt-Colinet 2004; Schmidt-Colinet 2009.
90 For women in the religious sphere, see Klaver 2019. See also Krag 2018, 115–122.
91 Koch et al. 1982, 126. 381 f. for scenes from daily life on sarcophagi from Rome and Athens. Women on klinai may appear on death scenes, cf. stele from Verona, Museo Maffeiano, inv. no. 28286: <https://arachne.dainst.org/entity/1107125> (26.04.2022); cf. side of sarcophagus of Crepereia Tryphaena: Rome, Musei Capitolini, inv. no. AC 459: <https://www.centralemontemartini.org/it/collezioni/percorsi_per_sale/sala_colonne/crepereia_tryphaena/sarcofago_di_crepereia_tryphaena> (26.04.2022); probable mythological scenes, cf. urn possibly from Volterra, Berlin, Staatliche Museen, Antikensammlung, inv. no. Sk 1277: <https://arachne.dainst.org/entity/1188455> (26.04.2022); or on ›Totenmahl‹ reliefs: Vienna, Kunsthistorisches Museum inv. no. I 1081: <https://arachne.dainst.org/entity/1101370> (26.04.2022).
92 Istanbul, Istanbul Arkeoloji Müzesi, inv. no. 2247: Annan 2019, 171.
93 Istanbul, Istanbul Arkeoloji Müzesi, inv. no. 345: Mendel 1914, cat. 1170.
94 For example, Rome, Museo Gregoriano Profano, inv. no. unknown: <https://arachne.dainst.org/entity/1250381> (02.12.2021); Catacombs of Pretextaetus: <https://arachne.dainst.org/entity/1250955> (26.04.2022).

A.D. 193–211), whereas the Palmyrene women flaunted their own local styles of dress and jewellery.

The motif of adornment, of choosing and/or wearing jewellery, is associated with women in the Graeco-Roman world since at least the classical period[95]. The motif, however, is very rare on sarcophagi[96]; it appears mostly on funerary stelai[97], funerary altars[98], and rarely on banqueting reliefs (›Totenmahl‹)[99]. In contrast to the Graeco-Roman depiction of the motif, where the female is depicted seated on her chair, the women of Palmyra are depicted reclining, their representations conflating the banqueting and the adornment motifs.

The sarcophagus appendix 5, cat. 10, with the series of statues of deities[100] seems to have no known parallels.

The Horse Sarcophagus

One unique sarcophagus has a horse in the place where one would find usually the seated female (cat. 290). The horse's saddle and tack are richly decorated, setting it apart from the other horses in Palmyrene art[101]. The choice of giving the horse pride of place has no comparisons in or outside Palmyra. The only possible comparison with the horse occupying an important place in a relief is with certain so-called Totenmahl reliefs from the late classical and Hellenistic period where a horse's head appears as if through an opening in the background. It has been suggested that the horse on those reliefs indicated the heroization of the deceased[102], but whether this Palmyrene horse had a similar meaning is debatable. The understanding of the so-called Totenmahl reliefs as depicting scenes from the afterlife, especially one showing the dead as a hero, is connected to evidence for heroization of the deceased in contemporary society[103]. Such evidence is absent from Palmyra, leaving us to wonder as to why this particular man chose to have his horse depicted with him; that is, if the sarcophagus was made during his lifetime[104], or if his descendants and heirs chose it for him.

The peculiarities of this sarcophagus are not limited to the horse in the location usually reserved for the wife of the sitter. On the side of the lid, there are two registers with two rows of figures in architectural frames, comparable to those in Dokimeion sarcophagi. This is, so far, the only attestation of this motif in Palmyra. The figures are badly preserved, but it seems likely that they represented statues[105]. On one of the short sides of the box, there is a female leading a camel, perhaps Astarte[106]. This is yet another unique representation in Palmyra.

Sarcophagi from Other Regions and their Influence

Only four fragments have been found that testify to the import of sarcophagi from other regions to Palmyra (appendix 4). They are made of white marble, badly preserved, and their subject matter is not clearly identifiable. Three must depict a mythological battle scene, as the men are shown in heroic nudity[107] (appendix 4, cat. 2–4), and the fourth depicts another mythological scene. Michalowski interprets this as a hunting scene, perhaps Hippolytus and Atalanta, although he acknowledges that there are no direct parallels to the iconography of the Palmyrene fragment, and so the identification is not certain[108]. Wielgosz recognizes these as fragments of Attic sarcophagi[109], popular in the coastal sites of the Levant[110].

Mythological scenes, however, that were the hallmark of Attic sarcophagi, did not become part of the repertory of Palmyrene sculptors[111]. The second characteristic feature of Attic and other kline sarcophagi, the motif of the reclining couple on the lid, also did not get adopted by Palmyrenes. The influence of sarcophagi from other regions can be seen in the use of garlands and clipei in the sarcophagi from temple tomb no. 186, and the use of niches as decorative elements framing representations of figures, possibly mythological, and statues (cat. 211. 221. 290). In cat. 290, in particular, the

---

95 Cf. the stele of Hegeso: Athens, Athens National Museum, inv. no. 3624: Kaltsas 2001, 156 cat. 309 with previous bibliography.
96 Koch et al. 1982, 126. 381 f. for scenes from daily life on sarcophagi from Rome and Athens.
97 For example, stele in the Museo Maffeiano, inv. no. 28685: <https://arachne.dainst.org/entity/1107068> (26.04.2022).
98 Altar from Rhodes: Vienna, Kunsthistorisches Museum inv. no. I 433: <https://arachne.dainst.org/entity/1101338> (26.04.2022).
99 For example, a ›Totenmahl‹ relief from Smyrna: Berlin, Staatliche Museen, Antikensammlung, inv. no. Sk 831: <https://arachne.dainst.org/entity/1122110> (26.04.2022).
100 Michalowski 1963, 53.
101 For the horses in Palmyrene art, see Raja – Seland 2021.
102 See the discussion in Draycott 2016, 4 with relevant bibliography.
103 See, especially Dentzer 1982, and Murray 1988. Against this view, Fabricius 1999.

104 This seems to be suggested by the inscription formula ›made by X for himself‹ in cat. 6. 11. 12. 71. 172.
105 Schmidt-Colinet 2009, 224, recognizes Victoria, Ariadne, and Dionysos among the figures.
106 Schmidt-Colinet 2004, 193.
107 For heroic nudity in Roman art, see Hallett 2005.
108 Michalowski 1962, 141 f. cat. 14 fig. 156.
109 Wielgosz 2001; Wielgosz 2010, 84 f.
110 De Jong 2017, 53. See, for example, de Bellefonds 1985 for the Attic sarcophagi from Tyre.
111 Even Astarte and the mythological figures in cat. 290 are not shown within the framework of a myth.

use of alternating niches and figures is reminiscent of the decorative pattern of Dokimeion sarcophagi, without copying it directly[112].

In addition to these, one sarcophagus decorated with roughly carved garlands (appendix 5, cat. 8) seems to indicate the influence of unfinished garland sarcophagi, such as those from Prokonnesos[113], or the sarcophagi from Jerash with that motif[114].

Conclusion

The individual elements of the iconography of Palmyrene sarcophagi indicate the following: (a) the commissioners of these monuments were keen to display their elite status; (b) they wanted to emphasize their roles as heads of families; (c) they promoted their local, Palmyrene identity; and (d) even when they were familiar with trends in the decoration of sarcophagi in the Roman Empire, they still preferred the local adaptations of motifs, rather than to imitate them.

Elite status was perhaps the easiest to demonstrate: commissioning a sarcophagus[115], either built by plaster and covered with a separate lid, or carved into the soft bedrock, or in the round, must have been a considerable expense, compared to the other burial option available to them: inside a loculus bay covered with a loculus relief with a portrait bust[116]. The details on the figures made the elite status even clearer. For men, the elaborate ›Parthian-style‹ costume, often worn with a dagger, probably a high-status symbol as well as part of a man's costume, the decorated boots, the chlamys fastened with a brooch, as well as the use of decorated drinking vessels (shallow bowls, skyphoi, and rhyta), and for women, the multiple pieces of jewellery, all indicated the elite status and luxurious lifestyle that the depicted figures enjoyed during their lifetime. For some men, in particular, high status was also displayed through the wearing of the priestly hat, since being a priest meant being in the upper rank of Palmyrene society. For children, who usually wear a simple tunic in the reliefs, it is details such as their jewellery or their attributes (birds or grapes or dates) that point to a life that is carefree and without burdens[117].

The iconography also shows the importance of the head of the family, almost always male. He, or rarely she, is shown reclining, his or her figure taking up most of the relief's surface, and larger than the other participants in the banquet. In most cases, the reclining figure's higher status is also demonstrated through the use of the elaborate Parthian-inspired costume (see appendix at end of chapter), but also through the acts of the attendants, where usually one[118], but sometimes more[119], individuals are approaching him bringing jugs or other objects for the banquet. In twenty sarcophagi lids, however, two men share pride of place (cat. 12. 60–61. 90. 94. 97. 98. 106. 115. 119–121. 126. 132. 133. 170. 174–178. 201. 294. 297. 389), as well as in two boxes (cat. 74. 201), and two banqueting reliefs (cat. 102. 728). Of these, two come from the hypogeum of ʿAštôr (cat. 60–61), three from the hypogeum of ʿAbdʿastôr (cat. 174–176), three from the hypogeum of the Three Brothers (cat. 119–121), and two from the hypogeum of Yarḥaî, ʿAtenûrî, and Zabdibôl (cat. 132. 133), indicating that family preferences and choices could override social trends. Individual family choices and decisions can also be detected in the three cases where females are shown in pride of place together with a man: cat. 180. 193 on the sarcophagus lids, and cat. 79. Of these, only cat. 79 has an inscription informing the viewers that the two are brother and sister.

Another aspect of the social fabric of Palmyrene society that is revealed through the iconography is the connection between the individual members of the same family, and how, even though the head of family had pride of place, the presence of his family members was important as it highlighted the continuity of the family, but also their close ties. This was demonstrated through proximity: even without inscriptions, one can assume that the reclining figure and the other figures on the lids or boxes were related since they were placed next to each other, and the box usually carried busts of other family members. How exactly they were related, however, is now lost to us without inscriptions. For contemporaries (and perhaps the next two generations of family members) of the families buried in and depicted on the sarcophagus, these relationships would have been known and obvious

---

112 For Dokimeion sarcophagi, see Waelkens 1982; Koch 1993, 113–122.
113 Koch 1993, 163–164. For good examples of such sarcophagi, see Stefanidou-Tiveriou 2014.
114 Pogoda 2018, 147.
115 Of course, being a tomb founder was the most prestigious and expensive way of showing elite status; however, not every sarcophagus commissioner founded or bought a tomb, and so this will not be discussed here.
116 See Steding 2022, esp. 119–121 on the costs of carving funerary portraits in Palmyra.
117 There is no data for Palmyrene child workers; however, when looking at the evidence from across the Roman Empire, it is unlikely that Palmyrene children, except those belonging in the upper classes, had a life free of manual labour. For child workers in the Roman period, see Bradley 1995; Laes 2011, 148–221; Sigismund-Nielsen 2013; Pudsey 2016.
118 Usually in the banqueting reliefs with frame.
119 Especially in sarcophagi, such as cat. 181.

without the need for inscriptions. For modern scholars, however, only the inscriptions can shed light on the relationships between the depicted figures, and some of them (cat. 1. 282) indicate that the Palmyrene family was much broader than modern, nuclear families. Most of the sarcophagi with inscriptions, however, show that the depicted persons did belong to the small, nuclear family unit, and so the sarcophagi burials formed discreet, separate groups within the large, extended family group represented by all the burials in the tomb (or section of the tomb).

The local, Palmyrene identity could be expressed in a variety of ways: the monuments themselves are particular to Palmyra, and so were the first and obvious sign of the distinct cultural identity of the city. Attributes, such as the priestly hat and the types of headdresses worn by the women, are also distinctive and unique to Palmyra[120]. The inscriptions also demonstrate the use of particular theophoric names that honoured the important gods of the city as well as the practice of naming male grandchildren after their paternal grandparents[121]. In the iconography of sarcophagi, the local identity was expressed through the use of the Parthian-inspired costume, which did not reproduce slavishly the garments worn in neighbouring Parthia, the Palmyrene costume and headdresses for women, and primarily through the use of the banqueting motif.

Even though the motif with its long history both East and West seems to originate outside Palmyra, it was transformed and adapted within the city. In other parts of the Roman Empire, only one figure, the honoured male, or rarely female, was shown reclining on a kline in front of a table with foodstuff, while (in the case of males), a female was shown seated on a chair beside their bed. Sometimes, attendants frame the scene, either bringing objects for the banquet, or by merely standing attentively, ready to serve, or as mourners. In Palmyra, the table is almost always absent; furthermore, the entire family of the reclining figure is using the mattress as if it were the ground floor, in a manner unlikely to derive from actual practice. Even the chairs of the seated females are placed on the mattress, and, in one unique occasion, a horse is standing next to the reclining figure, again, on the bed (cat. 290). In fact, the closest parallels to the Palmyrene reliefs come from the necropoleis of Edessa and Hilar: like in Palmyra, the deceased is shown reclining alone without a table in front of him and with other family members to his side,

when present[122]. These reliefs, however, were cut on the rock, so, they were not free-standing or movable, the way that most Palmyrene banqueting reliefs are; they were carved over the entrances or over the burials places, thus they functioned as markers of the grave, similar to the foundation reliefs on the façades of Palmyrene tower tombs. These reliefs demonstrate the existence of common visual cultural motifs in the area of greater northern Mesopotamia that were locally reinterpreted and adapted in each of the cities of the wider region[123].

The sarcophagi boxes are also peculiar to Palmyra: the armless, portrait busts that are so common on them, rarely appear outside the city. There are no figures framed in architectural settings, as seen in several of the sarcophagi from Asia Minor, and only one sarcophagus so far has been discovered that carries a non-figural, garland decoration (appendix 5, cat. 8). Furthermore, unlike the celebration of a person's whole life through a series of significant events, such as birth, marriage, victory at war, so often seen on Roman sarcophagi, in Palmyra, one scene only is chosen as worthy of commemoration, and even that is a very rare phenomenon of the 3rd cent. A.D. Mythological scenes, so prevalent outside Palmyra, are extremely rare in the city, attested only in the imported sarcophagi (appendix 4), one sarcophagus that is badly preserved (appendix 5, cat. 10) and perhaps on the sides of sarcophagus cat. 290. Even in the tombs themselves, mythological scenes are hardly ever painted, appearing only in the Painted Exedra of the tomb of the Three Brothers (Achilles at Skyros and Rape of Ganymede)[124], the tomb of Dionysus (Dionysus)[125], and the tomb of Ḥaîran (Victories) (Fig. 52, Pls 33–38)[126].

The iconography sets Palmyrene sarcophagi apart from the sarcophagi from the rest of the Roman Empire and highlights that the persons using these monuments were members of the local elite, showing the families at the peak of their splendour under the guidance of a benevolent and wealthy *pater familias*[127]. Instead of a focus on the afterlife, as has been suggested for the so-called Totenmahl reliefs that also have the banquet as central motif[128], the imagery of the Palmyrene sarcophagi refers to a moment in time in which the family members were present. This is more obvious on the lids, but it appeared on the boxes as well, as,

---

120 For the conical hats worn by priests of Dura-Europos and Hierapolis, see Millar 1993, 245; Butcher 2003, 331; Kaizer 2008, 224 f.
121 This practice was known from other areas of the ancient world. For Palmyrene onomastic practices, see Yon 2002, in passim.
122 For the reliefs, see Pognon 1907, 179–183; Equini Schneider 1992a; Spanu et al. 1992–1993; Segal 1970, 27; Drijvers – Healey 1999, As 12–19; Blömer 2022, 164. 170.
123 Equini Schneider 1992a, 30 f.; Blömer 2022, 172 f.
124 Eristov – Vibert-Guigue 2019, 96–133.
125 Ingholt 1932, 14–20.
126 Ingholt 1932, 1–13.
127 Seyrig 1951.
128 Draycott 2016, 3, with previous bibliography.

Figure 52. Dionysus, from the tomb of Dionysus.

for example, the inscriptions on cat. 173 show: the sarcophagus was created by Šoraîkû, and members of his family spanning two generations are depicted on the surface[129].

Trade, which was the source of Palmyrene wealth, is rarely commemorated in the sarcophagi, with only five objects giving testimony to it (cat. 82. 228. 274. 447. appendix 5, cat. 11). One could suggest that, like members of the Roman elite[130], the Palmyrenes had a negative attitude towards trade, but the various inscriptions from the public sphere commemorating merchants and caravan protectors show that this was not the case[131]. It is far more likely that the Palmyrene elites took seriously the formula >house of eternity< that they used for their tombs, and so perpetuated the image of their families within those spaces: either by placing members of the same family on the same or neighbouring loculus bays, or by burial in the same sarcophagus. The iconography, so focused on the family, its wealth, status, and cohesion, emphasized the private nature of the funerary space and perpetuated the image of the elite family at a moment of pleasure and enjoyment, during a banquet in which all the family members took part.

---

129   Sadurska – Bounni 1994, 11.
130   For the laws prohibiting members of the senatorial class and how they utilized >loopholes< in order to participate in trade, see d'Arms 1981, still a seminal study.
131   For these, see Yon 2002, in passim; Yon 2019b.

Appendix: The Costume of Reclining Figures

›Parthian-Style‹ Costume

Trousers, ›Parthian-Style‹ Tunic, and Chlamys (79)

1. Cat. 80: A.D. 100–150
2. Cat. 94: A.D. 108–150
3. Cat. 93: A.D. 108–150
4. Cat. 76: over-trousers too: A.D. 100–200 (priest)
5. Cat. 102: A.D. 113–200
6. Cat. 107: over-trousers too: A.D. 128–150 (priest)
7. Cat. 291: over-trousers too: A.D. 130–150 (priest)
8. Cat. 292: over-trousers too: A.D. 140–160 (priest)
9. Cat. 118: A.D. 140–160
10. Cat. 6: A.D. 142–143
11. Cat. 7: A.D. 146/147 (priest)
12. Cat. 123: A.D. 150–170 (priest)
13. Cat. 295: A.D. 170–200 (priest)
14. Cat. 687: A.D. 170–200
15. Cat. 350: A.D. 170–200
16. Cat. 684: A.D. 170–200
17. Cat. 688: A.D. 180–200
18. Cat. 25: A.D. 170–200
19. Cat. 355: A.D. 170–200
20. Cat. 23: A.D. 170–200
21. Cat. 24: A.D. 170–200
22. Cat. 108: A.D. 170–200
23. Cat. 109: A.D. 170–200
24. Cat. 133: A.D. 170–200
25. Cat. 195: A.D. 180–200
26. Cat. 200: A.D. 180–200 (priest)
27. Cat. 10: A.D. 188 (priest)
28. Cat. 171: A.D. 200–220 (priest)
29. Cat. 69: A.D. 200–220
30. Cat. 74: A.D. 200–220
31. Cat. 99: A.D. 200–240 (priest)
32. Cat. 201: A.D. 200–240 (priest)
33. Cat. 175: A.D. 200–240
34. Cat. 175: A.D. 200–240
35. Cat. 174: A.D. 200–240
36. Cat. 126: A.D. 200–240
37. Cat. 99: A.D. 200–240
38. Cat. 127: A.D. 200–240.
39. Cat. 201: A.D. 200–240 (priest)
40. Cat. 424: A.D. 200–250
41. Cat. 711: A.D. 200–273
42. Relief with seated female and banqueting male: A.D. 200–273[132]
43. Cat. 128: A.D. 220–240 (priest)
44. Cat. 445: A.D. 220–240 (priest)
45. Cat. 135: A.D. 220–240 (priest)
46. Cat. 135: A.D. 220–240 (priest)
47. Cat. 716: A.D. 220–240 (priest)
48. Cat. 136: A.D. 220–240 (priest)
49. Cat. 297: A.D. 220–240
50. Cat. 227: A.D. 220–240
51. Cat. 713: A.D. 220–240
52. Cat. 692: A.D. 220–240
53. Cat. 714: A.D. 220–240
54. Cat. 136: A.D. 220–240
55. Cat. 233: A.D. 220–240
56. Cat. 228: A.D. 220–240
57. Cat. 177: A.D. 220–240
58. Cat. 183: A.D. 220–240
59. Cat. 249: A.D. 220–240
60. Cat. 691: A.D. 220–240
61. Cat. 197: A.D. 220–240
62. Cat. 199: A.D. 220–240
63. Cat. 198: A.D. 220–240
64. Cat. 196: A.D. 220–240
65. Cat. 181: A.D. 220–240
66. Relief with banqueting priest: A.D. 220–240[133]
67. Cat. 103: A.D. 220–250 (priest)
68. Cat. 81: A.D. 229–250
69. Cat. 11: A.D. 239
70. Cat. 700: A.D. 240–273 (priest)
71. Cat. 90: A.D. 240–273 (priest)
72. Cat. 728: A.D. 240–273 (priest)
73. Cat. 700: A.D. 240–273
74. Cat. 179: A.D. 240–273
75. Cat. 26: A.D. 240–273
76. Cat. 290: A.D. 240–273
77. Cat. 446: A.D. 240–273

---

[132] Christies New York, sale of 4th June 2008, lot 98. Its acquisition history and lack of context make the object problematic.
[133] Christies New York, sale of 12th December 2002, lot 303. No acquisition history is given for the object, thus making it very problematic.

›Parthian-Style‹ Tunic and Himation (29)

78. Relief with bust of banqueting male: A.D. 120–140[134]
79. Cat. 333: A.D. 150–170
80. Cat. 346: A.D. 170–200
81. Cat. 132: A.D. 170–200
82. Cat. 119: A.D. 200–220
83. Cat. 119: A.D. 200–220
84. Cat. 689: A.D. 200–220
85. Cat. 120: A.D. 200–220
86. Cat. 135: A.D. 220–240 (priest)
87. Cat. 89: A.D. 220–240
88. Cat. 715: A.D. 220–240
89. Cat. 722: A.D. 220–240
90. Cat. 234: A.D. 220–240
91. Cat. 228: A.D. 220–240
92. Cat. 694: A.D. 220–240
93. Cat. 79: A.D. 220–240
94. Cat. 231: A.D. 220–240
95. Cat. 166: A.D. 220–240
96. Cat. 219: A.D. 240–273
97. Cat. 12: A.D. 240–273
98. Cat. 12: A.D. 240–273
99. Cat. 389: A.D. 240–273
100. Cat. 390: A.D. 240–273
101. Cat. 251: A.D. 240–273 (priest?)
102. Cat. 725: A.D. 240–273
103. Cat. 727: A.D. 240–273 (priest)
104. Cat. 91: A.D. 240–273 (priest)
105. Cat. 92: A.D. 240–273 (priest)
106. Cat. 299: A.D. 240–273

›Parthian-Style‹ Tunic and Chlamys (8)

107. Cat. 702: A.D. 170–200
108. Cat. 703: A.D. 170–200
109. Cat. 708: A.D. 200–220
110. Cat. 281: A.D. 220–240
111. Cat. 83: A.D. 229–250
112. Cat. 85: A.D. 229–250
113. Cat. 395: A.D. 240–273
114. Cat. 396: A.D. 240–273

›Parthian-Style‹ Tunic and Trousers (6)

115. Cat. 165: A.D. 200–240
116. Cat. 374: A.D. 200–240
117. Cat. 384: A.D. 200–273
118. Cat. 729: A.D. 240–273
119. Cat. 400: A.D. 240–273
120. Cat. 401: A.D. 240–273

›Parthian-Style‹ Tunic, Trousers, and Over-Trousers (4)

121. Cat. 108: A.D. 170–200
122. Cat. 109: A.D. 170–200
123. Cat. 119: A.D. 170–200
124. Cat. 699: A.D. 220–240

›Parthian-Style‹ Tunic, Trousers, and Himation (4)

125. Cat. 101: A.D. 113–200
126. Cat. 294: A.D. 150–200
127. Cat. 690: A.D. 200–220
128. Cat. 134: A.D. 220–240

›Parthian-Style‹ Tunic, Trousers and Long Coat (3)

129. Cat. 200: A.D. 180–200 (priest)
130. Cat. 201: A.D. 200–240 (priest)
131. Cat. 82: A.D. 229–250

Tunic and Chlamys (3)

132. Cat. 193: A.D. 170–190
133. Cat. 712: A.D. 200–220
134. Cat. 216: A.D. 220–240

Plain Tunic, Trousers, and Himation (2)

135. Cat. 1: A.D. 40
136. Cat. 693: A.D. 220–240

Plain Tunic, Trousers, and Chlamys (1)

137. Cat. 99: A.D. 200–240

Chlamys, ›Parthian-Style‹ Tunic and Himation (1)

138. Cat. 717: A.D. 220–240

Trousers and Over-Trousers (1)

139. Cat. 335: A.D. 150–170

Tunic, Chlamys, Trousers, and Over-Trousers (1)

140. Cat. 289: 150–200

Tunic, Chlamys, Trousers, and Himation (1)

141. Cat. 28: A.D. 170–200

Parthian-style — at Least One Garment Is Known

142. Cat. 705: A.D. 180–240: ›Parthian-style‹ trousers (upper garments unknown)

---

134 Palmyra, Palmyra Museum, inv. no. 1964/7056: Sadurska – Bounni 1994, 58 cat. 72 fig. 216.

143. Cat. 379: A.D. 200–273: ›Parthian-style‹ trousers (upper garments unknown)
144. Cat. 381: A.D. 200–273: ›Parthian-style‹ trousers (upper garments unknown)
145. Cat. 382: A.D. 200–273: ›Parthian-style‹ tunic (other garments unknown)
146. Cat. 217: A.D. 220–240: garment (details unclear) and a chlamys
147. Cat. 698: A.D. 220–240: ›Parthian-style‹ tunic (other garments unknown)
148. Cat. 685: A.D. 220–240: ›Parthian-style‹ tunic (other garments unknown)
149. Cat. 388: A.D. 240–273: ›Parthian-style‹ tunic (other garments unknown)
150. Cat. 393: A.D. 240–273: ›Parthian-style‹ trousers (upper garments unknown)

Himation

Tunic and Himation (81)

1. Cat. 313: A.D. 50–100
2. Cat. 60: A.D. 89–100
3. Cat. 60: A.D. 89–100
4. Cat. 61: A.D. 89–100
5. Cat. 61: A.D. 89–100
6. Cat. 62: A.D. 89–100
7. Cat. 63: A.D. 89–100
8. Cat. 64: A.D. 89–100
9. Cat. 70: A.D. 100–120
10. Cat. 71: A.D. 100–130
11. Cat. 72: A.D. 100–150 (priest)
12. Cat. 75: A.D. 100–150
13. Cat. 75: A.D. 100–150
14. Cat. 75: A.D. 100–150
15. Cat. 316: A.D. 100–150
16. Cat. 97: A.D. 108–150
17. Cat. 97: A.D. 108–150
18. Cat. 324: A.D. 120–140
19. Cat. 96: A.D. 120–140
20. Cat. 104: A.D. 123–140
21. Cat. 105: A.D. 128–150
22. Cat. 105: A.D. 128–150
23. Cat. 105: A.D. 128–150 (priest)
24. Cat. 106: A.D. 128–150
25. Cat. 106: A.D. 128–150
26. Cat. 106: A.D. 128–150 (priest)
27. Cat. 326: A.D. 130–150
28. Cat. 327: A.D. 130–150
29. Cat. 330: A.D. 130–150
30. Cat. 115: A.D. 131–150
31. Cat. 115: A.D. 131–150
32. Cat. 115: A.D. 131–150
33. Cat. 115: A.D. 131–150
34. Cat. 9: A.D. 130–170
35. Cat. 182: A.D. 140–160
36. Cat. 122: A.D. 140–160
37. Cat. 334: A.D. 150–170 (priest)
38. Cat. 124: A.D. 150–170 (priest)
39. Cat. 117: A.D. 150–200
40. Cat. 342: A.D. 150–200
41. Cat. 54: A.D. 150–200
42. Cat. 55: A.D. 150–200
43. Cat. 293: A.D. 150–200
44. Cat. 354: A.D. 170–200
45. Cat. 26: A.D. 170–200
46. Cat. 129: A.D. 170–200
47. Cat. 353: A.D. 170–200
48. Cat. 356: A.D. 170–200
49. Cat. 296: A.D. 180–200
50. Cat. 296: A.D. 180–200
51. Cat. 296: A.D. 180–200
52. Cat. 296: A.D. 180–200
53. Cat. 172: A.D. 200–220
54. Cat. 68: A.D. 200–220
55. Cat. 367: A.D. 200–220
56. Cat. 278: A.D. 200–220
57. Cat. 366: A.D. 200–220
58. Cat. 370: A.D. 200–220
59. Cat. 110: A.D. 200–220 (priest)
60. Cat. 110: A.D. 200–220
61. Cat. 169: A.D. 200–220
62. Cat. 170: A.D. 200–220
63. Cat. 121: A.D. 200–220
64. Cat. 168: A.D. 200–220 (priest)
65. Cat. 98: A.D. 200–240
66. Cat. 100: A.D. 200–240
67. Cat. 709: A.D. 200–240
68. Cat. 208: A.D. 200–240
69. Cat. 222: A.D. 200–240
70. Relief with bust of reclining male: A.D. 200–240[135]
71. Cat. 213: A.D. 220–240
72. Cat. 230: A.D. 220–240
73. Cat. 212: A.D. 220–240
74. Cat. 721: A.D. 220–240
75. Cat. 237: A.D. 220–240
76. Cat. 178: A.D. 220–240
77. Cat. 180: A.D. 220–240
78. Cat. 389: A.D. 240–273
79. Cat. 392: A.D. 240–273
80. Cat. 446: A.D. 240–273
81. Cat. 725: A.D. 240–273

---

135 The object is only known from photographs and there is no information as to its current location.

Tunic with Two Clavi

1. Cat. 226: A.D. 220–240
2. Cat. 446: A.D. 240–273

Only Himation (No Tunic Survives, or Cannot Be Determined) (13)

1. Cat. 2: A.D. 73
2. Cat. 19: A.D. 50–100: himation (upper garments unknown)
3. Cat. 332: A.D. 150–170: himation (upper garments unknown)
4. Cat. 338: A.D. 150–170: himation (other garments unknown)
5. Cat. 706: A.D. 180–240: himation (upper garments unknown)
6. Cat. 707: A.D. 180–240: himation (upper garments unknown)
7. Cat. 369: A.D. 200–220: himation (other garments unknown)
8. Cat. 207: A.D. 200–240: himation (other garments unknown)
9. Cat. 215: A.D. 220–240
10. Cat. 214: A.D. 220–240: possibly himation (other garments unknown)
11. Cat. 243: A.D. 220–240: himation
12. Cat. 32: A.D. 200–273: possibly himation
13. Cat. 391: A.D. 240–273

Only Tunic Survives (4)

1. Cat. 125: A.D. 150–200: tunic
2. Cat. 132: A.D. 170–200: tunic
3. Cat. 35: A.D. 170–200: tunic (other garments unknown)
4. Cat. 362: A.D. 180–200: tunic (other garments unknown)

Unknown or Unclear (11)

1. Cat. 30: A.D. 170–200: garments unclear
2. Cat. 380: A.D. 200–273: unknown garments
3. Cat. 285: A.D. 200–273: badly preserved
4. Cat. 57: A.D. 200–273: garments unclear
5. Cat. 209: A.D. 200–273: garments unclear
6. Cat. 385: A.D. 200–273: unknown garments
7. Cat. 245: A.D. 220–240: garments unclear
8. Cat. 229: A.D. 220–240: no garments preserved
9. Cat. 232: A.D. 220–240: garments unclear
10. Cat. 137: A.D. 220–240: garments unclear
11. Cat. 394: A.D. 240–273: unknown garments

CHAPTER 6

Conclusion: Sarcophagi as Vehicles of Elite Identity

Even though limestone was a commonly used material for funerary monuments, only a few monographs have focused on Roman-period monuments created with this material: the studies of Rahmani, Meyers, Hachlili, and Figueras on Jewish ossuaries from the 1st cent. B.C. – 1st cent. A.D.[1], and the study of Taner Korkut, who examined the ossuaries from Pamphylia and Cilicia[2]. A publication of the more than 100 limestone sarcophagi of Gerasa has been in preparation for a while[3]. Most of the scholarly focus has been on marble sarcophagi, especially those decorated with mythological scenes[4]. This publication is the first comprehensive — but not exhaustive — overview of the locally produced Palmyrene limestone sarcophagi.

The beginning of the use of limestone sarcophagi in Palmyra has been connected to the tradition of banqueting reliefs in Palmyra but also to the art of the Roman Empire[5]. Colledge had observed that full sarcophagi do not seem to appear before the middle of the 2nd cent. A.D.[6]. However, the publication of material from excavations conducted between 2007 and 2010, right before the Syrian civil war[7], demonstrated that already in A.D. 128, full sarcophagi were in use in Palmyra (cat. 4). The evidence from the tower tombs as well as the early appearance of the banqueting motif in the funerary towers point to the emergence of sarcophagi in Palmyra as a more complex phenomenon. Krag has suggested that their appearance may be a Palmyrene phenomenon independent from the western traditions, even though she does not state this explicitly[8]. Sarcophagi, however, were in use in neighbouring regions from the Hellenistic period[9], and so it has been hypothesized that the practice was brought to the region together with other elements of elite culture by the Seleucids[10]. Full sarcophagus reliefs already appear in the first half of the 2nd cent. A.D. (cat. 6. 8. 9 are the earliest dated ones). They were used to close niches with burials in loculus bays, therefore functioning as a much more elaborate version of the loculus portrait plaques that could depict the entire family occupying the niches (cat. 6 is a good example of this). That the practice of burials in loculus bays coexisted with burials in sarcophagi is shown by several sarcophagi being placed in front of bays (for example, cat. 119–121), as well as by the presence of sarcophagi in the same tombs as loculus bays used by the same family, as, for example, in the hypogeum of Šalamallat, where cat. 110–113 were found together with numerous loculus reliefs[11].

The overview of the material from Palmyra shows that, while burials in sarcophagi did not replace those in loculus niches, they became increasingly popular with the Palmyrene elite during the course of the first two and a half centuries of documented sculptural

---

1   Rahmani 1994; Meyers 1971; Hachlili 1988; Figueras 1983. See also Hachlili 2004 and Kloner – Zissu 2007 for Jewish burial practices in this period.
2   Korkut 2006.
3   Study undertaken by Cathrin Pogoda, with an article published in 2018 summarizing her observations on the typology and history of use of the sarcophagi: Pogoda 2018.
4   See, for example, the influential publication of Zanker and Ewald (Zanker – Ewald 2004), that was translated into Italian in 2008 and English in 2012, and the published proceedings of a recent conference on mythological sarcophagi: Hallett 2019a.
5   Parlasca, who has written extensively on the subject, connects the motif with Roman art and specifically with: Athenian sarcophagi: Parlasca 1984, 294; Roman art: Parlasca 1995, 68 f.; Italian kline monuments and ›Totenmahl‹ reliefs: Parlasca 1998, 315. Audley-Miller 2016, 554 associates it with Roman art but emphasizes its local reformulation. The Roman burial practices, including use of sarcophagi, have been connected to earlier Etruscan customs: Toynbee 1966, 11–32. Will 1951, 77 has proposed it had Hellenistic antecedents, now lost.
6   Colledge 1976, 62.
7   al-Asʿad 2013.
8   Krag 2018, 32–34.
9   These sarcophagi were of the slipper type, see Olbrycht 2017.
10 Will 1951, 77. For Hellenistic Seleucid elite culture, see Haubold 2016. See also Sartre 2001, 84–114.
11 For the sculptures from the hypogeum, see esp. Sadurska – Bounni 1994, 149–171.

production (A.D. 1–240). Based on contextual evidence, they were never common in tower tombs. Although there was never a gap in their production and display in hypogea, they were far more popular between the periods A.D. 100–150 and A.D. 200–240, and their numbers rose significantly in temple tombs in the period A.D. 200–240. The data shows a drop in the numbers of sarcophagi in all tomb types in the period A.D. 240–273, which reflects the Palmyrene elite's decrease of financial resources spent in the funerary sphere and may be related either to the so-called Plague of Cyprian, or, more likely, the wars against the Sasanians[12], which would have drained economic resources and most likely also craftsmen from the city. The end of production is connected with the fall of the city. Some of the old members of Palmyra's elite retained financial and social power, as can be seen from epigraphic evidence[13], but the practice of building new monumental tombs or commissioning new funerary monuments seemed to have ended by A.D. 273. Thus, the sarcophagi represent a particular habit of only a part of the Palmyrene elites that was more prevalent in the period A.D. 150–240, with some variations depending on the tomb type, and that did not replace the more traditional form of commemorating the deceased in relief portraits, usually single, less often double or multiple, that served as covers for the loculus niches.

The iconography of the sarcophagi and the reliefs with banqueting scenes shows that, already from the earliest foundation reliefs, elite Palmyrene identity was constructed along two axes: participation in the banquet, priesthood, as well as display of wealth. A priest was identified through the wearing of a cylindrical tall hat, particular to the city, and being one was a hereditary privilege[14]. One of their duties that also highlighted their wealth was sponsoring banquets for members of religious associations[15]. However, banquets could also be financed by other male elite members. The two roles of priest and benefactor are neatly joined in the numerous surviving tesserae that allowed entrance to these banquets and that showed reclining priests[16], as well as in the sarcophagi and reliefs with banqueting scenes known from the city (for example, cat. 90), but in other cases, the two may be separate. In the earliest dated foundation relief from the tower of Kîtôt (A.D. 41,

cat. 1), the reclining banqueter may or may not have been depicted as a priest (the head is missing), but one of his two sons mentioned in the inscription can be identified as one even though the face is broken off: the outline of the Palmyrene priestly hat is unmistakable. In other reliefs, the priest is clearly differentiated from his co-banqueters by the use of the hat, as for example, in cat. 105, where only one of the three reclining men is represented as priest.

The second element for constructing and representing elite identity was the banquet. In Palmyra, the banquet formed part of the life of the household, but was also an activity tied to special occasions, like religious or public feasts, and the tribes[17]. Little information is known about the banquets that took place in houses. Albert Gabriel, who surveyed Palmyra in 1925, observed that the houses that he cleared all had a room that was larger than the others facing the central courtyard, and named that ›oikos‹, like that identified by archaeologists at the houses of Priene and Delos[18]. In literature, however, the ›oikos‹ of the classical Greek houses was differentiated from the symposion room (›andron‹)[19], even though this distinction often does not appear in the archaeological record[20]. Gabriel did not recognize any of the rooms in the houses he investigated as the banqueting room. Only in the house of Cassiopeia, the excavators identified the room with the mosaic that gave its name to the residence, as one for the reception and gathering of visitors, and so possibly as a space for banquets[21]. There is more evidence for banquets in the civic and religious sphere. In Basilica I, the Polish Archaeological Mission in Palmyra excavated a banquet hall with mosaics that may refer to Odainath's victory over the Sasanians[22]. Furthermore, there were several banquet halls associated with sanctuaries in Palmyra[23]. There, members of cultic or tribal or other associations took part in feasts after presenting an entry token (›tesserae‹), often with the image of a reclining priest[24]. So, a Palmyrene could have participated in a number of banquets organized by different people during his lifetime and at different locations[25]. Furthermore, a

---

12 Raja et al 2021c; Romanowska et al 2021; Bobou et al 2021b.
13 Cantineau 1933, no. 28; Gawlikowski 1971, 412–421; Intagliata 2018, 99.
14 Kaizer 2002, 240–242; Raja 2016b. See, for example, cat. 10, for such a family of priests.
15 For these religious associations, see Kaizer 2002, 220–229; Gnoli 2016; for the priests as benefactors and banquet sponsors, see Raja 2016a.
16 See, in particular, Raja 2016a; Raja 2019h.
17 Kaizer 2002, 220–229; Raja 2016a; Raja 2019h.
18 Gabriel 1926, 85 f.
19 Vitruvius, De Architectura 6.7.5.
20 Nevett 1995; Trümper 1998.
21 Balty 2014, 2.
22 Gawlikowski 2014; Gawlikowski 2021, 69 f.
23 Four of these halls have been excavated, while several others are known only through the epigraphic record. See Raja 2016a, 349–351, with further bibliography.
24 For the tesserae, see Raja 2015c; Raja 2019b; Raja 2019h.
25 Apart from the imagery on sarcophagi or banqueting reliefs (both from the funerary sphere), we have no evidence for the participation of women in public banquets, either religious or civic, from Palmyra. From Dura-Europos, however, a series of

rich Palmyrene would have organized banquets himself, often in connection with his role as symposiarch, but perhaps also as part of other benefactions to the city[26]. The iconography of the banquet, as it is known from the funerary monuments and tesserae of the city, emphasizes a person's status and wealth. In the miniature images of the tesserae, where it was not possible to give as many details as in a sarcophagus, the reclining males are often shown under vines[27]. Only in one case, though, is this dual manifestation of elite identity obvious in the epigraphy of the sarcophagi: in cat. 193, a Greek inscription informs the viewers that one of the figures shown is that of Bolanos, who had been chosen as symposiarch of the priests of Zeus. The head of Bolanos, however, is missing, and so it is not possible to say whether he was depicted wearing the priestly hat or not[28].

The Greek inscription on cat. 193 is an added marker of elite identity. Of the 102 reliefs with inscriptions, there are only nine that have Greek inscriptions, three on foundation reliefs (cat. 3. appendix 1, cat. 1. appendix 3, cat. 1), two on the keys held by a figure (cat. 180. 365), one on a writing tablet held by a figure (cat. 469), and three commemorating figures on sarcophagi or sarcophagus reliefs (cat. 193–194. 446). Two of these (cat. 193–194) are on objects from the same tomb, while three on the foundation reliefs were particularly prominent because of their location on the exterior of the tombs. That Greek was used as a marker of status in Palmyra is evident from where it was used: there are eighty foundation inscriptions known from the city, of which thirty-six are in Greek[29]. In contrast to these inscriptions placed outside the tomb, there are more than 1100 objects with inscriptions associated with funerary portraits, of which only thirty-seven carry inscriptions in a language other than Palmyrene Aramaic: seventeen are bilingual, nine are Greek, and five are Latin[30]. So, there was a deliberate choice for the use of Palmyrene Aramaic on the commemorative reliefs, while Greek was mostly reserved for the more prominent and public areas of the funerary sphere, the foundation reliefs and inscriptions on tomb façades and door lintels.

These features (emphasis on a single socially important role, that of the priest, and a single event, that of the banquet, as well as Greek for highlighting participation in common elite culture of the Roman Near East) show that the Palmyrenes promoted a locally constructed and understood elite identity. The distinctive character of their culture and their choices for funerary monuments become even more apparent when one compares the sarcophagi from Palmyra to those from the rest of the Roman world. The Palmyrene reliefs differ from them on two main points. The first is that the visual focus was not on the box, but on the lid. The boxes of Palmyrene sarcophagi, with a few exceptions, carried busts of ancestors or family members, so a relatively simple and repetitive form of decoration, whereas in other areas of the Roman Empire, the box was often elaborately carved with multi-figural scenes either from mythology or covering aspects of daily life. The lids, however, carried banqueting scenes, drawing the viewer's attention towards the top of the monument. Furthermore, the Palmyrene sarcophagi are characterized by uniformity: the majority have depictions of banqueting families on their lids, while a few lids have a reclining figure and an attendant, who may have been a close relative (that is, a child of the depicted reclining, main figure) or a member of the figure's extended household (that is, a trusted servant). This makes them different from decorated lids of sarcophagi from other areas, where they preferred to depict couples rather than family groups[31].

In addition to these, Palmyrene sarcophagi also differed in the way they were positioned in the tomb itself. The first sarcophagi boxes were made of plaster; they were undecorated; and they were built in the monument, rather than free-standing monuments in the round that could be placed against walls. This early

---

paintings from the ›House of the banquet‹, shows on one wall a group of men and a group of women taking part in a banquet, and in the next wall, a group of men reclining while taking part in a banquet with a woman seated beside them. Kaizer 2019, 85 f. The imagery of the last painting is reminiscent of the sarcophagi, while some of the inscriptions identify the participants as Palmyrenes. It is likely, therefore, that women participated in banquets in Palmyra as well, despite the lack of evidence from the public or religious sphere from the site.

26 For the role of symposiarchs in Palmyra, see Yon 2002.
27 For example, see Raja 2019a, cat. 146. 147. 149. 151. There has not been a study of wine production in Palmyra, but there is epigraphic evidence for local production and the consumption of wine in the city: see Ingholt 1926 and Maraqten 1993, 104 f. for an inscription differentiating between local and wine »bought from the West«. See also Palmyrene tax tariff panel II, column 2, line 9: Shifman 2014, 116.
28 Although rare, some priests were depicted with their priestly hat on the side, and sporting a beard, so not immediately recognizable as members of the elite class who had held priestly office, see Raja 2017h; Raja 2017i; Raja 2017j. Only in one single relief known so far, was a priest shown without the priestly hat but identified through an inscription: Sadurska – Bounni 1994, 27 cat. 21.

29 Gawlikowski 1970a, cat. 7. 10–12. 15. 17–18. 20. 25. 26. 28. 29. 35. 36. 38. 48–51. 53–58. 60. 61. 63. 65. 69. 77. 79. 80.
30 Raja – Yon 2022.
31 In one sarcophagus from Phaselis, the lid is decorated with a series of busts depicting a family group, but this type of iconography is rare: Çelik et al. 2018.

type of sarcophagus appears in tower tombs, and in most cases, only the lowest part of the box has survived. The lid was carved separately out of limestone and carried a banqueting scene. The second type, which appeared together with the underground tombs and thus came into use from the 2nd cent. A.D., was that of sarcophagi carved into the bedrock. In some cases, the carved recess was covered with separately carved reliefs that imitated the exterior of a sarcophagus with a box with portrait busts and a lid with a family banqueting scene. In other cases, the busts and banqueting scene were carved directly onto the outer wall of the carved recess. These two types are unique to Palmyra and represent most of the sarcophagi found in the tombs of the city. Free-standing sarcophagi that were carved outside, in a workshop, and moved inside the tomb, formed the third type observed in Palmyrene tombs. These were found in the hypogea associated with tower tombs or the ground floors of tower tombs, in separate niches or exedrae in the hypogea that were constructed as independent tombs (that is, without forming part of a tower tomb complex) and in niches in the temple tombs. Only this last type is common in other regions of the Roman world[32].

The material from the city is clear: even though Palmyrenes were aware of cultural trends in their neighbouring areas, as the use of the Parthian-inspired costume and drinking vessels indicates, and the metropolitan centres of the Roman Empire, testified through imported Attic sarcophagi, sculpted fulcra reminiscent of those used in Rome, and Greek mythological scenes on mosaics and tombs, they only used specific elements that fit with their local, socially agreed concept of what it meant to be a member of the elite and participate in Palmyrene culture in almost all the objects used for commemorating the dead. Reliefs with banqueting scenes used in the tombs provided the best vehicle for commemorating family members as well as participation in the local Palmyrene elite culture, showing a wealthy family united under the benevolent rule of the patriarch and participating in a joyful occasion that allowed them to show off their wealth.

Abbreviations

BAPD: Beazley Archive Pottery Database
CIS: Corpus Inscriptionum Semiticarum
PAT: D. R. Hillers – E. Cussini, Palmyrene Aramaic texts (Baltimore 1996)
RTP: H. Ingholt – H. Seyrig – J. Starcky, Recueil des tessères de Palmyre (Paris 1955)
SEG: Supplementum Epigraphicum Graecum

---

[32] For the various ways that sarcophagi could be displayed in the Roman world, see Meinecke 2014; Borg 2013; Dally et al. 2018.

Works Cited

Abamelek-Lazarev 1897. S. S. Abamelek-Lazarev, Dzherash. arkheologicheskoe izsledovanie (Jerash. Archaeological Research) (Saint Petersburg 1897)

Abdul-Hak 1952. S. Abdul-Hak, L'hypogée de Taai à Palmyre, AAS 2, 1952, 193–251. Abdul-Hak – Abdul-Hak 1951. S. Abdul-Hak – A. Abdul-Hak, Catalogue illustré du Département des antiquités gréco-romaines au Musée de Damas (Damascus 1951)

Abdul Massih 2021. J. Abdul Massih, Quarrying in the Roman Near East: Palmyra and Baalbek — A Comparative Study, in: R. Raja – J. Steding (eds.), Production Economy in Greater Roman Syria. Trade Networks and Production Processes (Turnhout 2021) 71–86

Abousamra 2015. G. Abousamra, Palmyrene Inscriptions on Seven Reliefs, Semitica 57, 2015, 217–242

al-Asʿad 1993. K. al-Asʿad, Palmyre, in: S. Cluzan – E. Delpont – J. Mouliérac (eds.), Syrie. Mémoire et civilisation (Paris 1993) 276–279, 294–310

al-Asʿad 2013. W. al-Asʿad, Some Tombs Recently Excavated at Palmyra, Studia Palmyreńskie 12, 2013, 15–24

al-Asʿad 2018. W. al-Asʿad, A Tribute to the Late Khaled al-Asʿad, Martyr of Palmyra, in: J. Aruz (ed.), Palmyra. Mirage in the Desert (New York 2018) 20–27

al-Asʿad – Gawlikowski 1997. K. al-Asʿad – M. Gawlikowski, The Inscriptions in the Museum of Palmyra. A Catalogue (Warsaw 1997)

al-Asʿad – Schmidt-Colinet 1985. K. al-Asʿad – A. Schmidt-Colinet, Das Tempelgrab Nr. 36 in der Westnekropole von Palmyra. Ein Vorbericht, DaM 2, 1985, 17–35

al-Asʿad – Schmidt-Colinet 1995. K. al-Asʿad – A. Schmidt-Colinet, Zur Einführung, in: A. Schmidt-Colinet (ed.), Palmyra. Kulturbegegnung im Grenzbereich (Mainz 1995) 28–53

al-Asʿad – Schmidt-Colinet 2005. K. al-Asʿad – A. Schmidt-Colinet, Kulturbegegnung im Grenzbereich, in: A. Schmidt-Colinet (ed.), Palmyra. Kulturbegegnung im Grenzbereich (Mainz 2005) 36–63

al-Asʿad – Taha 1965. K. al-Asʿad – O. Taha, The Tomb of Zabdʿateh (in Arabic), AAS 15, 1965, 29–46

al-Asʿad – Taha 1968. K. al-Asʿad – O. Taha, Madfan Zabd-ʿAtah al-Tudmurî (The Tomb of Zabdʿateh), AAS 18, 1968, 83–108

al-Asʿad et al. 2012. K. al-Asʿad – M. Gawlikowski – J.-B. Yon, Aramaic Inscriptions in the Palmyra Museum: New Acquisitions, Syria 89, 2012, 163–184

al-Gonmeen – Khries 2020. T. Al-Gonmeen – Hashem Khries, Roman Sarcophagi at the Lower Terrace of Amman Citadel, Palestine Exploration Quarterly 152:2, 170–175: <https://doi.org/10.1080/00310328.2020.1759285>

al-Hariri 2013. K. al-Hariri, The Tomb of ʿAqraban, Studia Palmyreńskie 12, 2013, 149–157

Al Khabour 2018. A. Al Khabour, Il ruolo della Legge sulle Antichità Siriane per la protezione del patrimonio culturale fino allo scoppio della guerra civile in Siria nel 2011, Astarté. Estudios del Oriente Próximo y el Mediterráneo 1, 2018, 1–13

al-Ush et al. 1980. M. al-Ush – A. Judi – B. Zuhdi, A Concise Guide to the National Museum of Damascus (Damascus 1980)

Albertson 2000. F. C. Albertson, Three Palmyrene Reliefs in the Colket Collection, University of Wyoming, Syria 77, 2000, 159–168

Albertson 2014. F. Albertson, A Distribution Scene on a Palmyran Funerary Relief, AntK 57, 2014, 25–37

Albertson 2019. F. Albertson, So-Called Servants or Pages in Palmyran Funerary Sculpture, oral presentation in: Palmyra and the East, Getty Villa, 18–19 April 2019

Alexandridis 2014. A. Alexandridis, Death and the City. Asiatic Columnar Sarcophagi in Context (Albany 2014)

Ali 2015. C. Ali, Palmyra: Heritage Adrift. Detailed Report on All Damage Done to the Archaeological Site between February 2012 and June 2015, The Association for the Protection of Syrian Archaeology / The American Schools of Oriental Research Cultural Heritage Initiatives: 1–59: <http://www.asor-syrianheritage.org/wp-content/uploads/2015/06/Palmyra_Heritage_Adrift.pdf> (05.05.2022)

Altmann 1902. W. Altmann, Architectur und Ornamentik der antiken Sarkophage (Berlin 1902)

Amy – Seyrig 1936. R. Amy – H. Seyrig, Recherches dans la nécropole de Palmyre, Syria 17, 1936, 229–266

Anadol 2008. S. Anadol, Palmyra – Identity Expressed through Architecture and Art, in: M. Lönnqvist, Jebel Bishri in Context. Introduction to the Archaeological Studies and the Neighbourhood of Jebel Bishri in Central Syria. Proceedings of a Nordic Research Training Seminar in Syria, May 2004, BAR International Series 1817 (Oxford 2008) 59–72

Anderson 2017. B. Anderson, Beyond Rome/Parthia: Intersections of Local and Imperial Traditions in the Visual Record of Hatra, in: J. Schulde – B. Reubin (eds.), Arsacids, Romans and Local Elites. Cross-Cultural Interactions of the Parthian Empire (Oxford 2017) 137–158

Anderson – Ousterhout 2016. B. Anderson – R. G. Ousterhout, Palmyra 1885: The Wolfe Expedition and the Photographs of John Henry Haynes (Edinburgh 2016)

Andrade 2013. N. J. Andrade, Syrian Identity in the Greco-Roman World (Cambridge 2013)

Andrade 2018. N. Andrade, Zenobia. Shooting Star of Palmyra (Oxford 2018)

Annan 2019. B. Annan, Petrified Memories: On Some Funerary Portraits from Roman Phoenicia, in: M. Blömer – R. Raja (eds.), Funerary Portraiture in Greater Roman Syria, Studies in Classical Archaeology 6 (Turnhout 2019) 165–196

Aristodemou 2014. G. Aristodemou, Representations of Women and Children in Roman Banquet Scenes, in: I. Koncani Uhač (ed.), Proceedings of the 12th International Colloquium on Roman Provincial Art. The Dating of Stone Monuments and Criteria for Determination of Chronology, Pula, 23–28 May 2011, Archaeological Museum of Istria (Pula 2014) 123–128

Arnold 1905. W. R. Arnold, Additional Palmyrene Inscriptions in the Metropolitan Museum of Art, New York, JAOS 26, 1905, 105–112

Ataç 2018. M.-A. Ataç, Art and Immortality in the Ancient Near East (Cambridge 2018)

Audley-Miller 2016. L. Audley-Miller, The Banquet in Palmyrene Funerary Contexts, in: C. M. Draycott — M. Stamatopoulou (eds.), Dining and Death. Interdisciplinary Perspectives on the ›Funerary Banquet‹ in Ancient Art, Burial and Belief (Leuven 2016) 553–590

Bäärnhielm 1988. G. Bäärnhielm, Palmyra – en bakgrundsteckning, in: H. Pontus (ed.), Palmyra. Öknens drottning (Stockholm 1988) 11–30

Baird 2018. J. Baird, Dura-Europos (London 2018)

Balty 2005. J.-C. Balty, La sculpture, in: C. Delplace – J. Dentzer-Feydy (eds.), L'Agora de Palmyre (Bordeaux 2005) 321–341

Balty 2010. J.-C. Balty, Deux reliefs palmyréniens du Musée Saint-Raymond, Musée des Antiques de Toulouse, in: B. Bastl – V. Gassner – U. Muss (eds.), Zeitreisen. Syrien, Palmyra, Rom. Festschrift für Andreas Schmidt-Colinet zum 65. Geburtstag (Vienna 2010) 23–28

Balty 2014. J. Balty, Les mosaïques des maisons de Palmyre, BAH 206 (Beirut 2014)

Baratte – de Chaisemartin 2015. F. Baratte – N. de Chaisemartin, North Africa, in: E. A. Friedland – M. Grunow Sobocinski – E. K. Gazda (eds.), The Oxford Handbook of Roman Sculpture (Oxford 2015) 504–522

Barr-Sharrar 1985. B. Barr-Sharrar, The Anticythera Fulcrum Bust: A Portrait of Arsinoë III, AJA 89, 1985, 689–692

Bates 1911. W. N. Bates, Archaeological News, AJA 15:3, 1911, 403–443

Batziou-Eustathiou – Triantafyllopoulou 2012. A. Batziou-Eustathiou – P. Triantafyllopoulou, Από τα νεκροταφεία της αρχαίας Δημητριάδος-Παγασών, ADelt 58–64, 2003–2009, 211–324

Bernard 2015. S. Bernard, Musée de Grenoble. Guide des collections, Antiquité-XIXe siècle (Lyon 2015)

Bertolino 2022. A. Bertolino, Dagli ipogei alle catacombe. Organizzazione e funzionamento dei cimiteri sotterranei in epoca romana (Rome 2022)

Beyer 1998. K. Beyer, Die aramäischen Inschriften aus Assur, Hatra und dem übrigen Ostmesopotamien (Göttingen 1998)

Bielfeldt 2004. R. Bielfeldt, Orestes auf römischen Sarkophagen (Berlin 2004)

Birk 2013. S. Birk, Depicting the Dead. Self-Representation and Commemoration on Roman Sarcophagi with Portraits, Aarhus Studies in Mediterranean Antiquity 11 (Aarhus 2013)

Birk 2014. S. Birk, Using Images for Self-Representation on Roman Sarcophagi, in: S. Birk – T. Myrup Kristensen – B. Poulsen, Using Images in Late Antiquity (Oxford 2014) 33–47

Blömer 2022. M. Blömer, Edessa and the Sculpture of Greater North Mesopotamia in the Romano-Parthian Period, in: K. Lapatin – R. Raja (eds.), Palmyra and the East (Turnhout 2022) 155–178

Blundell – Rabinowitz 2008. S. Blundell – N. Sorkin Rabinowitz, Women's Bonds, Women's Pots: Adornment Scenes in Attic Vase-Painting, Phoenix 62, 2008, 115–144

Bobou – Randeris Thomsen 2021. O. Bobou – R. Randeris Thomsen, Appendix 1. Collecting Then and Now, in: O. Bobou – J. Vestergaard Jensen – N. Breintoft Kristensen – R. Raja – R. Randeris Thomsen (eds.), A Translation of Harald Ingholt's Studier over Palmyrensk Skulptur. Edited and with Commentary, Studies on Palmyrene Sculpture 1 (Turnhout 2021) 533–536

Bobou et al. 2021a. O. Bobou – I. Romanowska – R. Raja, Historical Trajectories of Palmyra's Elites through the Lens of Archaeological Data, JUA 4, 2021: <https://doi.org/10.1484/J.JUA.5.126598>

Bobou et al. 2021b. O. Bobou – J. V. Jensen – N.B. Kristensen – R. Raja – R. R. Thomsen (eds.), A Translation of Harald Ingholt's Studier over Palmyrensk Skulptur Published 1928. Commented and Edited by Olympia Bobou, Jesper V. Jensen, Nathalia B. Kristensen, Rubina Raja, and Rikke R. Thomsen, Studies on Palmyrene Sculpture 1 (Turnhout 2021)

Bobou et al. 2022a. O. Bobou – R. Raja – J. Steding, Excavating Archives. Narratives from 20th-Century Palmyra (Aarhus 2022)

Bobou et al. 2022b. O. Bobou – R. Raja – J. Steding, Excavating Archives: Narratives from 20th-Century Palmyra. An Online Exhibition: <https://projects.au.dk/archivearchaeology/cultural-heritage-resources/virtual-exhibition-excavating-archives-narratives-from-20th-century-palmyra> (30.06.2022)

Böhme – Schottroff 1979. A. Böhme – W. Schottroff, Palmyrenische Grabreliefs (Frankfurt 1979)

Bonacossi – Iamoni 2012. D. Morandi Bonacossi – M. Iamoni, The Early History of the Western Palmyra Desert Region. The Change in the Settlement Patterns and the Adaptation of Subsistence Strategies to Encroaching Aridity: A First Assessment of the Desert-Kite and Tumulus Cultural Horizons, Syria 89, 2012, 31–58

Bonatz 2016. D. Bonatz, Syro-Hittite Funerary Monuments Revisited, in: C. Draycott – M. Stamatopoulou (eds.), Dining and Death. Interdisciplinary Perspectives on the ›Funerary Banquet‹ in Ancient Art, Burial and Belief (Leuven 2016) 173–194

Bonicatti 1964. M. Bonicatti, Criteri di indagine sulla continuità della cultura provincial nel primo medioevo, 1. La ritrattistica, ArchCl 16, 1964, 272–283

Borg 2013. B. Borg, Crisis and Ambition. Tombs and Burial Culture in Third Century C.E. Rome (Oxford 2013)

Borg 2019. B. Borg, Hidden Splendour: The Display Context of Metropolitan Sarcophagi, in: C. Hallett (ed.), Flesheaters. An International Symposium on Roman Sarcophagi. University of California at Berkeley 18–19 September 2009, Sarkophag Studien 11 (Wiesbaden 2019) 145–160

Bossert 1930. H. Th. Bossert, Geschichte des Kunstgewerbes aller Zeiten und Völker (Berlin 1930)

Bossert 1951. H. Th. Bossert, Altsyrien (Tübingen 1951)

Bounni 1967. A. Bounni, En mission à Palmyre. Bilan de dix années d'explorations et découvertes, Archeologia 16, 1967, 40–49

Bounni – Saliby 1957. A. Bounni – N. Saliby, Madfan šalam allât (The Tomb of Shallamallat), AAS 7, 1957, 25–52

Bounni – Teixidor 1975. A. Bounni – J. Teixidor, Inventaire des inscriptions de Palmyre, Fascicule 12 (Damascus 1975)

Bradley 1995. K. Bradley, Child Labour in the Roman World, Historical Reflections / Réflexions historiques 12, 1985, 311–330

Brodie et al. 2019. N. Brodie et al., Countering Looting of Antiquities in Syria and Iraq, Final Report: <https://traccc.schar.gmu.edu/wp-content/uploads/2020/10/Final-TraCCC-CTP-CTAQM-17-006-Report-Jan-7-2019.pdf> (14.12.2022)

Brody – Hoffman 2011. L. R. Brody – G. L. Hoffman, Dura-Europos. Crossroads of Antiquity (Chestnut Hill 2011)

Browning 1979. I. Browning, Palmyra (London 1979)

Brykczynski 1975. P. Brykczynski, Astrologia w Palmyrze, Studia Palmyreńskie 6–7, 1975, 47–109

Budde – Nicholls 1964. L. Budde – R. Nicholls, A Catalogue of the Greek and Roman Sculpture in the Fitzwilliam Museum: Cambridge (Cambridge 1964)

Burke 2005. B. Burke, Materialization of Mycenaean Ideology and the Ayia Triada Sarcophagus, AJA 109, 403–422

Butcher 2003. K. Butcher, Roman Syria and the Near East (Los Angeles 2003)

Callieri 1986. P. Callieri, Rilievi funerari palmireni nella collezione Zeri, AnnAStorAnt 8, 1986, 223–244

Callieri – Askari-Chaverdi 2013. P. Callieri – A. Askari-Chaverdi, Media, Khuzestan, and Fars between the End of the Achaemenids and the Rise of the Sasanians, in: D. T. Potts (ed.), The Oxford Handbook of Ancient Iran (Oxford 2013): <https://doi.org/10.1093/oxfordhb/9780199733309.013.0020>

Cameron 2019. A. Cameron, Why Mythology?, in: C. Hallett (ed.), Flesheaters. An International Symposium on Roman Sarcophagi. University of California at Berkeley 18–19 September 2009, Sarkophag Studien 11 (Wiesbaden 2019) 27–41

Campmany Jiménez et al. 2022. J. Campmany Jiménez – I. Romanowska – R. Raja – E. H. Seland, Food Security in Roman Palmyra (Syria) in Light of Paleoclimatological Evidence and Its Historical Implications, Plos One 21st September 2022: <https://doi.org/10.1371/journal.pone.0273241>

Canepa 2009. M. P. Canepa, Two Eyes of the Earth. Art and Ritual of Kingship between Rome and Sasanian Iran (Oakland 2009)

Cantineau 1929. J. Cantineau, Fouilles à Palmyre, Mélanges de l'Institut français de Damas. Section des Arabisants 1, 1929, 3–15

Cantineau 1930a. J. Cantineau, Inscriptions palmyréniennes, RAssyr 27:1, 1930, 27–51

Cantineau 1930b. J. Cantineau, Inventaire des inscriptions de Palmyre, Fascicule 4. Le Vallée des Tombeaux (Beirut 1930)

Cantineau 1930c. J. Cantineau, Textes funéraires palmyréniens, Revue biblique 39:4, 1930, 520–551

Cantineau 1931. J. Cantineau, Inventaire des inscriptions de Palmyre, Fascicule 7. Les nécropoles nord-ouest et nord (Beirut 1931)

Cantineau 1932. J. Cantineau, Inventaire des inscriptions de Palmyre, Fascicule 8. Le dépôt des antiquités (Beirut 1932)

Cantineau 1933. J. Cantineau, Inventaire des inscriptions de Palmyre, Fascicule 9. Le Sanctuaire de Bêl (Beirut 1933)

Cantineau 1936. J. Cantineau, Tadmorea, Syria 17, 1936, 346–355

Cantineau 1938. J. Cantineau, Tadmorea, Syria 19, 1938, 153–171

Cappozzo 2017. M. Cappozzo, Frammento di rilievo funerario / Fragment of Funerary Relief, in: M. Novello – C. Tiussi (eds.), Volti di Palmira ad Aquileia/Portraits of Palmyra in Aquileia (Rome 2017) 101

Caselitz 1988–1990. P. Caselitz, Eine Palmyrenische Familie. Erste Ergebnisse der Untersuchung der menschlichen Skelettfunde aus dem Tempelgrab 36 von Palmyra/Syrien, Hamburger Beiträge zur Archäologie 15–17, 1988–1990, 251–267

Caselitz 1992. P. Caselitz, Die Skelettfunde aus Tempelgrab 36, in: A. Schmidt-Colinet, Das Tempelgrab Nr. 36 in Palmyra. Studien zur Palmyrenischen Grabarchitektur und ihrer Ausstattung I–II (Mainz 1992) 144–145

Caskey 1910. L. D. Caskey, Department of Classical Art, MFA Annual Report 1910, 58–67

Cassas and the Legacy of Palmyra: <https://archeologie.culture.fr/palmyre/en/cassas-and-legacy-palmyra> (05.05.2022)

Caubet 1990. A. Caubet, Aux sources du monde arabe. L'Arabie avant l'islam. Collections du Musée du Louvre (Paris 1990)

Chabot 1922. J. B. Chabot, Choix d'inscriptions de Palmyre (Paris 1922)

Chamay – Maier 1989. J. Chamay – J.-L. Maier, Art romain. Sculptures en pierre du Musée de Genève (Mainz 1989)

Champdor 1953. A. Champdor, Les ruines de Palmyre (Paris 1953)

Charles-Gaffiot et al. 2001. J. Charles-Gaffiot – H. Lavagne – J.-M. Hofman, Moi, Zénobie reine de Palmyre (Milan 2001)

Ciliberto 2017. F. Ciliberto, La scultura funeraria di Palmira/The Funerary Sculpture of Palmyra, in: M. Novello – C. Tiussi (eds.), Volti di Palmira ad Aquileia/Portraits of Palmyra in Aquileia (Rome 2017) 47–57

Clarke 2003. J. R. Clarke, Art in the Lives of Ordinary Romans. Visual Representation and Non-Elite Viewers in Italy, 100 B.C. – A.D. 315 (Berkeley 2003)

Clauss 2002. P. Clauss, Morire ai tempi di Zenobia, in: A. Gabucci (ed.), Zenobia. Il sogno di una regina d'Oriente (Milan 2002) 75–99

Clermont-Ganneau 1884. C. Clermont-Ganneau, Mission en Palestine et en Phénicie, entreprise en 1881 (Paris 1884)

Clermont-Ganneau 1886. C. Clermont-Ganneau, Antiquités et inscriptions inédites de Palmyre, Revue archéologique 8, 1886, 14–32

Clermont-Ganneau 1903. C. Clermont-Ganneau, Recueil d'archéologie orientale (Paris 1903)

Collart 1961. P. Collart, Le rôle de Palmyre à l'époque hellénistique et romaine d'après les découvertes récentes, in: Atti del settimo Congresso internazionale di archeologia classica (Rome 1961) 427–435

Collart – Vicari 1969. P. Collart – J. Vicari, Le Sanctuaire de Baalshamîn à Palmyre. Topographie et architecture, Le Sanctuaire de Baalshamîn à Palmyre I–II, Bibliotheca Helvetica Romana 10, 1–2 (Rome 1969)

Colledge 1967. M. A. R. Colledge, The Parthians (London 1967)

Colledge 1976. M. A. R. Colledge, The Art of Palmyra (London 1976)

Colledge 1977. M. A. R. Colledge, Parthian Art (London 1977)

Colledge 1986. M. A. R. Colledge, The Parthian Period, Iconography of Religions 14, 3 (Leiden 1986)

Colledge 1992. M. A. R. Colledge, La perle du désert de Syrie. Palmyre, Le Monde de la Bible 74, 1992, 44–50

Collins 2015. S. Collins, The Standard of Ur (London 2015)

Comstock – Vermeule 1976. M. B. Comstock – C. C. Vermeule, Sculpture in Stone. The Greek, Roman and Etruscan Collections of the Museum of Fine Arts Boston (Boston 1976)

Contenau 1914. G. Contenau, Mission archéologique à Sidon (1914), Syria 1, 1920, 16–55

Cormack 1996. S. H. Cormack, The Roman-Period Necropolis of Ariassos, Pisidia, Anatol. Stud. 46, 1996, 1–25

Cuneo et al. 2015. A. Cuneo – S. Penacho – L. Barnes Gordon, Asor Cultural Heritage Initiatives. Update on the Situation in Palmyra (2015): <https://www.asor.org/wp-content/uploads/2019/09/Palmyra_UpdateReport_FINAL4reduced.pdf> (06.05.2022)

Cuneo et al. 2016. A. Cuneo – S. Penacho – M. Danti – M. Gabriel – J. O'Connell – B. al Issa – B. Rouhani – K. Kaercher, The Recapture of Palmyra: <https://www.asor.org/wp-content/uploads/2019/09/NEW2_PalmyraSpecialReport3-FINAL.pdf> (06.05.2022)

Curtis 1988. V. Curtis, A Study of Parthian Costumes: Their Origin and Distribution (Ph.D. diss. University College London 1988)

Curtis 2017. V. S. Curtis, The Parthian Haute-couture at Palmyra, in: A. H. Sørensen – T. Long (eds.), Positions and Professions in Palmyra, Palmyrene Studies 2, Scientia Danica, Series H, Humanistica 4, 9 (Copenhagen 2017) 52–67

Cussini 1995. E. Cussini, Transfer of Property at Palmyra, ARAM 7, 1995, 233–250

Cussini 2012. E. Cussini, What Women Say and Do (in Aramaic Documents), in: G. B. Lanfranchi – D. M. Bonacossi – C. Pappi – S. Ponchia (eds.), LEGGO! Studies Presented to Prof. Frederick Mario Fales on the Occasion of his 65th Birthday, Leipziger Altorientalische Studien 2 (Wiesbaden 2012) 161–172

Cussini 2016a. E. Cussini, Family Banqueting at Palmyra: Reassessing the Evidence, in: P. Corò et al. (eds.), Libiamo ne' lieti calici. Ancient Near Eastern Studies Presented to Lucio Milano on the Occasion of His 65th Birthday by Pupils, Colleagues, and Friends (Münster 2016) 139–159

Cussini 2016b. E. Cussini, Reconstructing Palmyrene Legal Language, in: A. Kropp – R. Raja (eds.), The World of Palmyra, Palmyrene Studies 1, Scientia Danica, Series H, Humanistica 4, 6 (Copenhagen 2016) 84–96

Cussini 2017. E. Cussini, The Pious Butcher and the Physicians. Palmyrene Professions in Context, in: A. H. Sørensen – T. Long (eds.), Positions and Professions in Palmyra, Palmyrene Studies 2, Scientia Danica, Series H, Humanistica 4, 9 (Copenhagen 2017) 84–96

Cussini 2018. E. Cussini, Out of a Palmyrene Family: Notes on the Metropolitan Museum of Art's Palmyra Collection, in: J. Aruz (ed.), Palmyra. Mirage in the Desert (New York 2018) 90–99

Cussini 2019a. E. Cussini, Daughters and Wives: Defining Women in Palmyrene Inscriptions, in: S. Krag – R. Raja (eds.), Women, Children and the Family in Palmyra, Palmyrene Studies 3, Scientia Danica, Series H, Humanistica 4, 10 (Copenhagen 2019) 67–81

Cussini 2019b. E. Cussini, Images of Individual Devotion in Palmyrene Sources, in: R. Raja (ed.), Revisiting the Religious Life of Palmyra, Contextualizing the Sacred 9 (Turnhout 2019) 51–65

Dacos 1969. N. Dacos, La découverte de la Domus Aurea et la formation des grotesques à la Renaissance (Leiden 1969)

Dalley 1995. S. Dalley, Bel at Palmyra and Elsewhere in the Parthian Period, ARAM 7, 1995, 137–151

Dally et al. 2018. O. Dally – J. Fabricius – H. v. Hesberg (eds.), Bilder und Räume. Antike Sarkophage im Kontext, Sarkophag Studien 10 (Wiesbaden 2018)

Danti 2001. M. Danti, Palmyrene Funerary Sculptures at Penn, Expedition 43:3, 2001, 33–40

d'Arms 1981. J. H. d'Arms, Commerce and Social Standing in Ancient Rome (Cambridge MA 1981)

Daszewski 1972. W. A. Daszewski, Les fouilles polonaises a Palmyre en 1968 et 1969, AAS 22, 1972, 129–150

Davies 2017. G. Davies, The Body Language of Palmyra and Rome, in: A. H. Sørensen – T. Long (eds.), Positions and Professions in Palmyra, Palmyrene Studies 2, Scientia Danica, Series H, Humanistica 4, 9 (Copenhagen 2017) 20–51

Degeorge 2001. G. Degeorge, Palmyre. Métropole Caravanière (Paris 2001)

Degeorge 2002. G. Degeorge, Palmyra (Munich 2002)

Delplace, Syria. C. Delplace, Syria, in: BnF, Bibliothèques d'Orient, des patrimoines partagés en ligne: <https://heritage.bnf.fr/bibliothequesorient/en/archeology-syria-art> (06.05.2022)

Dentzer 1971. J.-M. Dentzer, L'Iconographie iranienne du souverain couché et le motif du banquet, AAS 21, 39–50

Dentzer 1978. J.-M. Dentzer, Reliefs au banquet dans la moitié orientale de l'empire romain: iconographie hellénistique et traditions locales, RA 1, 1978, 63–82

Dentzer-Feydy – Teixidor 1993. J. Dentzer-Feydy – J. Teixidor, Les antiquités de Palmyre au Musée du Louvre (Paris 1993)

Deonna 1929. W. Deonna, Marbres antiques du Musée de Genève, Genava 7, 1929, 213–215

Deonna 1931. W. Deonna, Sculptures antiques. Musée de Genève et Collections privées, Genava 9, 1931, 85–115

Dentzer 1982. J.-M. Dentzer, Le motif du banquet couché dans le Proche-Orient et le monde grec du VIIe au IVe siècle avant J.-C. (Rome 1982)

de Bellefonds 1985. P. Linant de Bellefonds, Sarcophages attiques de la nécropole de Tyr. Une étude iconographique (Paris 1985)

de Jong 2010. L. de Jong, Performing Death in Tyre: The Life and Afterlife of a Roman Cemetery in the Province of Syria, AJA 114, 597–630

de Jong 2015. L. de Jong, The Tombs of Roman Baalbek, BAAL 15, 2015, 239–256

de Jong 2017. L. de Jong, The Archaeology of Death in Roman Syria (Cambridge 2017)

Dirven 2008. L. Dirven, Aspects of Hatrene Religion: A Note on the Statues of Kings and Nobles from Hatra, in: T. Kaizer (ed.), The Variety of Local Religious Life in the Near East in the Hellenistic and Roman Periods, Religions in the Graeco-Roman World 164 (Leiden 2008) 209–246

Dirven 2013. L. Dirven (ed.), Hatra. Politics, Culture and Religion between Parthia and Rome, Oriens et Occidens 21 (Stuttgart 2013)

Dirven 2018. L. Dirven, Palmyrene Sculpture in Context: Between Hybridity and Heterogeneity, in: J. Aruz (ed.), Palmyra. Mirage in the Desert (New York 2018) 120–129

Draycott 2016. C. Draycott, Introduction: What Lies Beyond?, in: C. Draycott – M. Stamatopoulou (eds.), Dining and Death. Interdisciplinary Perspectives on the ›Funerary Banquet‹ in Ancient Art, Burial and Belief (Leuven 2016) 1–32

Draycott – Stamatopoulou 2016. C. Draycott – M. Stamatopoulou (eds.), Dining and Death. Interdisciplinary Perspectives on the ›Funerary Banquet‹ in Ancient Art, Burial and Belief (Leuven 2016)

Drijvers 1976. H. J. W. Drijvers, The Religion of Palmyra (Leiden 1976)

Drijvers 1982. H. J. W. Drijvers, Afterlife and Funerary Symbolism in Palmyrene Religion, EPRO 92, 1982, 709–733

Drijvers – Healey 1999. H. J. W. Drijvers – J. F. Healey, The Old Syriac Inscriptions of Edessa and Osrhoene (Leiden 1999)

du Mesnil du Buisson 1962. R. du Mesnil du Buisson, Les tessères et les monnaies de Palmyre (Paris 1962)

Dunant 1971. C. Dunant, Le Sanctuaire de Baalshamîn à Palmyre III. Les Inscriptions, Bibliotheca Helvetica Romana 10, 3 (Rome 1971)

Dunant – Stucky 2000. C. Dunant – R. A. Stucky, Le Sanctuaire de Baalshamîn à Palmyre IV. Les Sculptures, Bibliotheca Helvetica Romana 10, 4 (Rome 2000)

Dunbabin 2003. K. M. D. Dunbabin, The Roman Banquet. Images of Conviviality (Cambridge 2003)

Dunbabin 2010. K. M. D. Dunbabin, The Roman Banquet. Images of Conviviality, 2nd ed. (Cambridge 2010)

Dunbabin – Slater 2011. K. M. D. Dunbabin – W. J. Slater, Roman Dining, in: M. Peachin (ed.), The Oxford Handbook of Social Relations in the Roman World (Oxford 2011) <https://doi.org/10.1093/oxfordhb/9780195188004.013.0021>

Dussaud 1896. R. Dussaud, Voyage en Syrie (oct. nov. 1895), RA 28, 1896, 299–326

Dussaud 1932. R. Dussaud, Antiquités orientales. Bas-relief palmyrénien, Bulletin des musées de France 4:9, 1932, 149–151

Ebeling 2011. P. Ebeling, Hellenistic and Roman Sarcophagi in the Levant, in: Cultural Background, Agora 8, 2011, 12–18: <https://usercontent.one/wp/www.vox-populi.dk/wp-content/uploads/2021/03/Cultural_Background.pdf> (06.05.2022)

Edwell 2008. P. M. Edwell, Between Rome and Persia. The Middle Euphrates, Mesopotamia and Palmyra under Roman Control (London 2008)

Eisenberg 2000. J. M. Eisenberg, Syria. Land of Civilisations, Minerva 11:1, 2000, 8–17

el-Chehadeh 1972. J. el-Chehadeh, Untersuchungen zum antiken Schmuck in Syrien (Berlin 1987)

el-Chehadeh 1987. J. el-Chehadeh, Zu Schmuckdarstellungen auf palmyrenischen Grabreliefs, in: E. M. Ruprechtsberger (ed.), Palmyra: Geschichte, Kunst und Kultur der syrischen Oasenstadt (Linz 1987) 193–199

Ellerbrock 2021. U. Ellerbrock, The Parthians. The Forgotten Empire (London 2021)

Elsner – Hung 2012. J. Elsner (ed.), Sarcophagi, RES: Anthropology and Aesthetics 61/62, Spring/Autumn 2012

Ensoli 2001. S. Ensoli, Communauté et cultes syriens à Rome: les sanctuaires de la regio XIV Transtiberim, in: J. Charles-Gaffiot – H. Lavagne – J.-M. Hofman (eds.), Moi, Zénobie reine de Palmyre (Milan 2001) 123–128

Equini Schneider 1992a. E. Equini Schneider, Rilievi funerari dalla necropoli di Hilar, Rivista di archeologia 16, 1992, 28–35

Equini Schneider 1992b. E. Equini Schneider, Scultura e ritrattistica onorarie a Palmira. Qualche ipotesi, Archeologia classica 44, 1992, 113–145

Equini Schneider 1993. E. Equini Schneider, Septimia Zenobia Sebaste (Rome 1993)

Equini Schneider 2002. E. Equini Schneider, Zenobia e il suo tempo, in: A. Gabucci (ed.), Zenobia. Il sogno di una regina d'Oriente (Milan 2002) 23–37

Eristov – Vibert-Guigue 2019. H. Eristov – C. Vibert-Guigue, Introduction générale, in: H. Eristov – C. Vibert-Guigue – W. al-Asʿad – N. Sarkis (eds.), Le tombeau des trois frères à Palmyre. Mission archéologique franco-syrienne 2004–2009 (Beirut 2019) 25–30

Eristov et al. 2019. H. Eristov – C. Vibert-Guigue – W. al-Asʿad – N. Sarkis (eds.), Le tombeau des trois frères à Palmyre. Mission archéologique franco-syrienne 2004–2009 (Beirut 2019)

Ewald 1999. B. C. Ewald, Review Article: Death and Myth: New Books on Roman Sarcophagi, AJA 103, 1999, 344–348

Ewald 2015. B. C. Ewald, Funerary Monuments, in: E. A. Friedland – M. Grunow Sobocinski – E. K. Gazda (eds.), The Oxford Handbook of Roman Sculpture (Oxford 2015) 390–406

Exhibition of Treasures 1977. Exhibition of Treasures of Syrian Antiquity (Tokyo 1977)

Eydoux 1964. H.-P. Eydoux, Les grandes dames de l'archéologie (Paris 1964)

Fabricius 1999. J. Fabricius, Die hellenistischen Totenmahlreliefs. Grabrepräsentation und Wertvorstellung in ostgriechischen Städten (Munich 1999)

Fabricius 2016. J. Fabricius, Hellenistic Funerary Banquet Reliefs – Thoughts on Problems Old and New, in: C. M. Draycott — M. Stamatopoulou (eds.), Dining and Death. Interdisciplinary Perspectives on the ›Funerary Banquet‹ in Ancient Art, Burial and Belief (Leuven 2016) 33–70

Farjamirad 2016. M. Farjamirad, Burial Customs during the Seleuco-Parthian Period of Iran; Greek or Local Culture?, in: E. Foietta et al. (eds.), Cultural and Material Contacts in the Ancient Near East (= Proceedings of the International Workshop 1–2 December 2014), Torino (Florence 2016) 129–135

Faust 1989. S. Faust, Fulcra. Figürlicher und ornamentaler Schmuck an antiken Betten (Mainz 1989)

Fejfer 2009. J. Fejfer, Roman Portraits in Context (Berlin 2009)

Fellmann 1970. R. Fellmann, Le sanctuaire de Baalshamin à Palmyre 5: Die Grabanlage, Bibliotheca Helvetica Romana 10, 5 (Rome 1970)

Fellmann 1976. R. Fellmann, Le tombeau près du temple de Baʿalšamên, témoin de deux siècles d'histoire palmyrénienne, in: E. Frézouls (ed.), Palmyre. Bilan et perspectives. Colloque de Strasbourg 18–20 Octobre 1973 (Strasbourg 1976) 213–231

Fellmann – Dunant 1975. R. Fellmann – C. Dunant, Le sanctuaire de Baalshamin à Palmyre 6: Kleinfunde = Objets divers, Bibliotheca Helvetica Romana 10, 6 (Rome 1975)

Figueras 1983. P. Figueras, Decorated Jewish Ossuaries. Documenta et monumenta orientis antiqui 20 (Leiden 1983)

Finlayson 2002–2003. C. Finlayson, Veil, Turban, and Headpiece: Funerary Portraits and Female Status at Palmyra, AAS 2002–2003, 2002–2003, 221–235

Finlayson 2004. C. Finlayson, Textile Exchange and Cultural and Gendered Cross-Dressing at Palmyra, Syria (100 BC-AD 272), in: Appropriation, Acculturation, Transformation. Textile Society of America Symposium Proceedings, 2004 (Los Angeles 2004) 60–70

Finlayson 2008. C. Finlayson, Mut'a Marriage in the Roman Near East: The Evidence from Palmyra, Syria, in: B. A. Nakhai (ed.), The World of Women in the Ancient and Classical Near East (Newcastle upon Tyne 2008) 99–138

Fittschen – Zanker 2014. K. Fittschen – P. Zanker, Katalog der Römischen Porträts in den Capitolinischen Museen und den anderen kommunalen Sammlungen der Stadt Rom IV, 1. Kinderbildnisse. Nachträge zu den Bänden I–III. Neuzeitliche oder neuzeitlich verfälschte Bildnisse. Bildnisse an Reliefdenkmälern (Berlin 2014)

Forge 2004. O. Forge, Antiquities, in: The Future of the Past. The Robert Mouawad Private Museum (Beirut 2004) 76–111

Fortin 1999. M. Fortin, Syrien – Wiege der Kultur (Mainz 1999)

Fowlkes-Childes 2016. B. Fowlkes-Childes, Palmyrenes in Transtiberim: Integration in Rome and Links to the Eastern Frontier, in: D. Slootjes – M. Peachin (eds.), Rome and the Worlds beyond Its Frontiers, Impact of Empire 21 (Leiden 2016) 193–212

Fowlkes-Childs – Seymour 2019. B. Fowlkes-Childs – M. Seymour. The World Between Empires. Art and Identity in the Ancient Middle East (New Haven 2019)

Fuller – Lucas 2014. D. Q. Fuller – L. Lucas, Archaeobotany, Encyclopedia of Global Archaeology: <https://doi.org/10.1007/978-1-4419-0465-2_2273>

Gabriel 1926. A. Gabriel, Recherches archéologiques à Palmyre, Syria 7, 71–92

Gawlikowski 1966. M. Gawlikowski, Problemy Ikonografii Kapłanów Palmyreńskich, Studia Palmyreńskie 1, 1966, 74–95

Gawlikowski 1968. M. Gawlikowski, Die polnischen Ausgrabungen in Palmyra 1959–1967, AA 2, 1968, 289–307

Gawlikowski 1969. M. Gawlikowski, Rodzina Elahbela, Studia Palmyreńskie 3, 1969, 47–58

Gawlikowski 1970a. M. Gawlikowski, Monuments funéraires de Palmyre (Warsaw 1970)

Gawlikowski 1970b. M. Gawlikowski, Palmyrena, Berytus 19, 1970, 65–94

Gawlikowski 1971. M. Gawlikowski, Inscriptions de Palmyre, Syria 48, 1971, 407–426

Gawlikowski 1974a. M. Gawlikowski, Le tadmoréen, Syria 51, 1974, 91–103

Gawlikowski 1974b. M. Gawlikowski, Recueil d'inscriptions Palmyréniennes provenant de fouilles syriennes et polonaises récentes à Palmyre, Mémoires présentés par divers savants à l'Académie des Inscriptions et Belles-Lettres de l'Institut de France 16, 1974, 261–377 (1–115)

Gawlikowski 1984. M. Gawlikowski, Palmyre VIII. Les principia de Dioclétien. Temple des Enseignes (Warsaw 1984)

Gawlikowski 1987. M. Gawlikowski, Objektbeschreibungen, nr. 1–76, in: E. M. Ruprechtsberger (ed.), Palmyra. Geschichte, Kunst und Kultur der syrischen Oasenstadt (Linz 1987) 287–339

Gawlikowski 2001a. M. Gawlikowski, Funerary Bust of a Banqueting Youth, in: J. M. Padgett (ed.), Roman Sculpture in the Art Museum, Princeton University (Princeton 2001) 350–352

Gawlikowski 2001b. M. Gawlikowski, Funerary Slab with Male Bust in High Relief, in: J. M. Padgett (ed.), Roman Sculpture in the Art Museum, Princeton University (Princeton 2001) 352–353

Gawlikowski 2001c. M. Gawlikowski, Head of a Banquet Attendant, in: J. M. Padgett (ed.), Roman Sculpture in the Art Museum, Princeton University (Princeton 2001) 359

Gawlikowski 2005. M. Gawlikowski, The City of the Dead, in: E. Cussini (ed.), A Journey to Palmyra. Collected Essays to Remember Delbert R. Hillers (Leiden 2005) 44–73

Gawlikowski 2010a. M. Gawlikowski, Palmyra (Warsaw 2010)

Gawlikowski 2010b. M. Gawlikowski, The Roman Army in Palmyra under Tiberius, Studia Palmyreńskie 11, 2010, 49–54

Gawlikowski 2010c. M. Gawlikowski, The Royalty from Palmyra Once Again, in: B. Bastl – V. Gassner – U. Muss (eds.), Zeitreisen. Syrien, Palmyra, Rom. Festschrift für Andreas Schmidt-Colinet zum 65. Geburtstag (Vienna 2010) 67–72

Gawlikowski 2014. M. Gawlikowski, Palmyra: Season 2003, Preliminary Report, PAM 15, 2014, 313–324

Gawlikowski 2016a. M. Gawlikowski, The Portraits of the Palmyrene Royalty, in: A. Kropp – R. Raja (eds.), The World of Palmyra, Palmyrene Studies 1 (Copenhagen 2016) 126–134

Gawlikowski 2016b. M. Gawlikowski, Trade across Frontiers: Foreign Relations of a Caravan City, in: J. C. Meyer – E. H. Seland – N. Anfinset (eds.), Palmyrena. City, Hinterland and Caravan Trade between Orient and Occident. Proceedings of the Conference Held in Athens, December 1–3, 2012 (Oxford 2016) 19–28

Gawlikowski 2017. M. Gawlikowski, Le Sanctuaire d'Allat à Palmyre, PAM Monograph Series 8 (Warsaw 2017)

Gawlikowski 2019a. M. Gawlikowski, The Making of a City, in: A.-M. Nielsen – R. Raja (eds.), The Road to Palmyra (Copenhagen 2019) 77–90

Gawlikowski 2019b. M. Gawlikowski, La nécropole sudouest, in: H. Eristov – C. Vibert-Guigue – W. al-Asʿad – N. Sarkis (eds.), Le tombeau des trois frères à Palmyre. Mission archéologique franco-syrienne 2004–2009 (Beirut 2019) 89–92

Gawlikowski – al-Asʿad 1997. M. Gawlikowski – K. al-Asʿad, Inscriptions de Palmyre nouvelles et revisitées, Studia Palmyreńskie 10, 1997, 23–38

Gawlikowski – Starcky 1985. M. Gawlikowski – J. Starcky, Palmyre (Paris 1985)

Ghirshman 1962. R. Ghirshman, Persian Art. The Parthian and Sassanian Dynasties, 249 B.C.-A.D. 651 (New York 1962)

Gnoli 2016. T. Gnoli, Banqueting in Honour of the Gods. Notes on the *Marzēaḥ* of Palmyra, in: A. Kropp – R. Raja (eds.), The World of Palmyra, Palmyrene Studies 1 (Copenhagen 2016) 31–41

Grayson 1976. A. K. Grayson, Assyrian Royal Inscriptions 2: From Tiglath-pileser I to Ashur-nasir-apli II, Records of the Ancient Near East 2 (Wiesbaden 1976)

Hachlili 1988. R. Hachlili, Jewish Ornamented Ossuaries of the Late Second Temple Period (Haifa 1988)

Hachlili 2004. R. Hachlili, Jewish Funerary Customs, Practices and Rites in the Second Temple Period (Leiden 2004)

Hallett 2005. C. H. Hallett, The Roman Nude. Heroic Portrait Statuary 200 BC – AD 300 (Oxford 2005)

Hallett 2019a. C. Hallett (ed.), Flesheaters. An International Symposium on Roman Sarcophagi. University of California at Berkeley 18–19 September 2009, Sarkophag Studien 11 (Wiesbaden 2019)

Hallett 2019b. C. Hallett, Introduction. Roman Decorated Sarcophagi as a Source for the Cultural Historian, in: C. Hallett (ed.), Flesheaters. An International Symposium on Roman Sarcophagi. University of California at Berkeley 18–19 September 2009, Sarkophag Studien 11 (Wiesbaden 2019) 1–8

Hansen 2003. D. P. Hansen, Art of the Early City-States, in: J. Aruz (ed.), Art of the First Cities. The Third Millennium B.C. from the Mediterranean to the Indus (New York 2003) 21–37

Hansen – Croll 2010. M. Hansen – E. Croll, Worlds to Discover. Bryn Mawr College (Pennsylvania 2010)

Harrington 2016. N. Harrington, The Eighteenth Dynasty Egyptian Banquet: Ideals and Realities, in: C. Draycott – M. Stamatopoulou (eds.), Dining and Death. Interdisciplinary Perspectives on the ›Funerary Banquet‹ in Ancient Art, Burial and Belief (Leuven 2016) 129–172

Harter-Uibopuu 2014a. K. Harter-Uibopuu, How to Protect Your Grave — Funerary Inscriptions from Greco-Roman Asia Minor: <https://www.academia.edu/6078270/How_to_protect_your_grave_Funerary_inscriptions_from_Greco_Roman_Asia_Minor> (06.05.2022)

Harter-Uibopuu 2014b. K. Harter-Uibopuu, Tote soll man ruhen lassen … Verbote und Strafen zur Sicherung von Gräbern am Beispiel der Inschriften von Ephesos, in: J. Fischer (ed.), Der Beitrag Kleinasiens zur Kultur- und Geistesgeschichte der griechisch-römischen Antike (Vienna 2014) 157–180

Hartmann 2001. U. Hartmann, Das palmyrenische Teilreich, Oriens et Occidens 2 (Stuttgart 2001)

Hashemi – Shelley 2022. L. Hashemi – L. Shelley, Antiquities Smuggling in the Real and Virtual World (London 2022)

Haubold 2016. J. Haubold, Hellenism, Cosmopolitanism, and the Role of Babylonian Elites in the Seleucid Empire, in: M. Lavan – R. E. Payne – J. Weisweiler (eds.), Cosmopolitanism and Empire. Universal Rulers, Local Elites, and Cultural Integration in the Ancient Near East and Mediterranean (Oxford 2016) 89–101

Hauser 1998. St R. Hauser, Hatra und das Königreich der Araber, in: J. Wiesehöfer (ed.), Das Partherreich und seine Zeugnisse. Beiträge des Internationalen Colloquiums, Eutin, Juni 27–30, 1996 (Stuttgart 1998) 493–428

Heiken et al. 2005. G. Heiken – R. Funiciello – D. de Rita, The Seven Hills of Rome. A Geological Tour of the Eternal City (Princeton 2005)

Hekster 2008. O. Hekster, Rome and Its Empire, AD 193–284 (Edinburgh 2008)

Hekster – Kaizer 2004. O. Hekster – T. Kaizer. 2004. Mark Antony and the Raid on Palmyra: Reflections on Appian, ›Bella Civilia‹ v, 9, Latomus 63: 70–80

Henning 2013a. A. Henning, The Tower Tombs of Palmyra: Chronology, Architecture and Decoration, Studia Palmyreńskie 12, 2013, 159–176

Henning 2013b. A. Henning, Die Turmgräber von Palmyra. Eine lokale Bauform im kaiserzeitlichen Syrien als Ausdruck kultureller Identität (Rahden 2013)

Henning 2019a. A. Henning, Houses of Eternity, in: A.-M. Nielsen – R. Raja (eds.), The Road to Palmyra (Copenhagen 2019) 155–172

Henning 2019b. A. Henning, The Representation of Matrimony in the Tower Tombs of Palmyra, in: S. Krag – R. Raja (eds.), Women, Children and the Family in Palmyra, Palmyrene Studies 3, Scientia Danica, Series H, Humanistica 4, 10 (Copenhagen 2019) 19–37

Heyn 2008. M. K. Heyn, Sacerdotal Activities and Parthian Dress in Roman Palmyra, in: C. S. Colburn – M. K. Heyn, Reading a Dynamic Canvas. Adornment in the Ancient Mediterranean World (Newcastle upon Tyne 2008) 170–193

Heyn 2010. M. K. Heyn, Gesture and Identity in the Funerary Art of Palmyra, AJA 114:4, 2010, 631–661

Heyn 2016. M. Heyn, Status and Stasis: Looking at Women in the Palmyrene Tomb, in: A. Kropp — R. Raja (eds.), The World of Palmyra, Palmyrene Studies 1, Scientia Danica, Series H, Humanistica 4, 6 (Copenhagen 2016) 194–206

Heyn 2018. M. K. Heyn, Embodied Identities in the Funerary Portraiture of Palmyra, in: J. Aruz (ed.), Palmyra. Mirage in the Desert (New York 2018) 110–119

Heyn 2019. M. K. Heyn, Valuable Impressions of Women in Palmyra, in: A.-M. Nielsen – R. Raja (eds.), The Road to Palmyra (Copenhagen 2019) 173–192

Heyn 2021. M. K. Heyn, The Significance of the Drinking Attributes in Palmyrene Banquet Scenes, in: M. K. Heyn – R. Raja (eds.), Individualizing the Dead. Attributes in Palmyrene Funerary Sculpture (Turnhout 2021) 63–74

Heyn – Raja 2019. M. K. Heyn – R. Raja, Male Dress Habits in Roman Period Palmyra, in: M. Cifarelli (ed.), Fashioned Selves. Dress and Identity in Antiquity (Oxford 2019) 41–53

Higuchi – Izumi 1994. T. Higuchi – T. Izumi, Tombs A and C, Southeast Necropolis, Palmyra, Syria. Surveyed in 1990–92, Publication of Research Center for Silk Roadology 1 (Nara 1994)

Higuchi – Saito 2001. T. Higuchi – K. Saito, Tomb F: Tomb of BWLH and BWRP, Southeast Necropolis, Palmyra, Syria (Nara 2001)

Hitzl – Petersen 2001. K. Hitzl – L. Petersen, Die Sarkophage aus Baalbek, in: G. Koch, Akten des Symposiums des Sarkophag-Corpus 2001. Marburg, 2. – 7. Juli 2001 (Mainz 2001) 299–308

Howarth 1969. J. L. Howarth, A Palmyrene Head at Bryn Mawr College, AJA 74:4, 1969, 441–446

Huskinson 2015. J. Huskinson, Roman Strigillated Sarcophagi. Art and Social History (Oxford 2015)

Hvidberg-Hansen 1998. F. O. Hvidberg-Hansen, The Palmyrene Inscriptions. Ny Carlsberg Glyptotek (Copenhagen 1998)

Hvidberg-Hansen 2002. F. O. Hvidberg-Hansen, Zenobia – byen Palmyra og dens dronning (Aarhus 2002)

Hvidberg-Hansen – Ploug 1993. F. O. Hvidberg-Hansen – G. Ploug, Katalog. Palmyra Samlingen – Ny Carlsberg Glyptotek (Copenhagen 1993)

Ingholt Archives. H. Ingholt, Ingholt Archives, Copenhagen, Ny Carlsberg Glyptotek

Ingholt 1926. H. Ingholt, Un nouveau Thiase à Palmyre, Syria 7, 1926, 128–141

Ingholt 1928. H. Ingholt, Studier over Palmyrensk Skulptur (Copenhagen 1928)

Ingholt 1930. H. Ingholt, The Oldest Known Grave-Relief from Palmyra, ActaArch 1, 1930, 191–195

Ingholt 1934. H. Ingholt, Palmyrene Sculptures in Beirut, Berytus 1, 1934, 32–43

Ingholt 1935. H. Ingholt, Five Dated Tombs from Palmyra, Berytus 2, 1935, 58–120

Ingholt 1936. H. Ingholt, Inscriptions and Sculptures from Palmyra, Berytus 3, 1936, 83–125

Ingholt 1938. H. Ingholt, Inscriptions and Sculptures from Palmyra, Berytus 5, 1938, 93–140

Ingholt 1951. H. Ingholt, Additions, in: D. Schlumberger (ed.), La Palmyrène du nord-ouest (Paris 1951) 176–177

Ingholt 1954. H. Ingholt, Palmyrene and Gandharan Sculpture. An Exhibition Illustrating the Cultural Interrelations between the Parthian Empire and Its Neighbors West and East, Palmyra and Gandhara, Oct. 14 through Nov. 14, 1954 (New Haven 1954)

Ingholt 1962. H. Ingholt, Palmyrene Inscription from the Tomb of Malkû, MelBeyrouth 38:4, 1962, 99–120

Ingholt 1966. H. Ingholt, Some Sculptures from the Tomb of Malkû at Palmyra, in: M. L. Bernhard (ed.), Mélanges offerts à Kazimierz Michalowski (Warsaw 1966) 457–476

Ingholt 1970–1971. H. Ingholt, The Sarcophagus of Be'elai and Other Sculptures from the Tomb of Malkû, Palmyra, MelBeyrouth 46, 1970–1971, 171–200

Ingholt 1974. H. Ingholt, Two Unpublished Tombs from the Southwest Necropolis of Palmyra, Syria, in: D. K. Kouymjian (ed.), Near Eastern Numismatics, Iconography, Epigraphy and History. Studies in Honor of George C. Miles (Beirut 1974) 37–54

Ingholt 1976. H. Ingholt, Varia Tadmorea, in: E. Frézouls (ed.), Palmyre. Bilan et perspectives. Colloque de Strasbourg 18–20 Octobre 1973 (Strasbourg 1976) 101–137

Ingholt – Starcky 1951. H. Ingholt – J. Starcky, Recueil des inscriptions sémitiques de la Palmyrène du nord-ouest (Paris 1951)

Intagliata 2018. E. E. Intagliata, Palmyra after Zenobia (273–750). An Archaeological and Historical Reappraisal (Oxford 2018)

Işık et al. 2007. F. Işık – J. M. Reynolds – C. Roueché, Girlanden-Sarkophage aus Aphrodisias (Mainz 2007)

Jacobs – Mashberg 2022. J. Jacobs – T. Mashberg, Investigators Say Collector Had Suspect Art and Lots of Chutzpah. The New York Times, 8th August 2022: <https://www.nytimes.com/2022/08/08/arts/design/antiquities-looting-warrant-georges-lofti.html> (30.11.2022)

Jucker 1967. H. Jucker, Kunst der Antike aus Privatbesitz Bern – Biel – Solothurn (Solothurn 1967)

Jucker – Willers 1983. H. Jucker – D. Willers, Gesichter. Griechische und römische Bildnisse aus Schweizer Besitz (Bern 1983)

Kaim 2005. B. Kaim, Palmyrenes and Parthian Costume, in: P. Bielinski – F. M. Stepniowski (eds.), Aux pays d'Allat. Mélanges offerts à Michal Gawlikowski (Warsaw 2005) 113–122

Kaizer 2002. T. Kaizer, The Religious Life of Palmyra. A Study of the Social Patterns of Worship in the Roman Period (Stuttgart 2002)

Kaizer 2008. T. Kaizer, The Variety of Local Religious Life in the Near East in the Hellenistic and Roman Periods (Leiden 2008)

Kaizer 2010. T. Kaizer, Funerary Cults at Palmyra, in: O. Hekster (ed.), Cultural Messages in the Graeco-Roman World. Acta of the BABESCH 80th Anniversary Workshop Radboud University Nijmegen, September 8th 2006 (Leuven 2010) 23–31

Kaizer 2018. T. Kaizer, ›Ich bin ein Palmyrener‹ or ›Je suis Tadmor‹: On How to be a Proper Citizen of the Queen of the Desert, in: J. Aruz (ed.), Palmyra. Mirage in the Desert (New York 2018) 76–89

Kaizer 2019. T. Kaizer, Family Connections and Religious Life at Palmyra, in: S. Krag and R. Raja (eds.), Women, Children and the Family in Palmyra, Palmyrene Studies 3, Scientia Danica, Series H, Humanistica 4, 10 (Copenhagen 2019) 82–94

Kaizer 2020. T. Kaizer, Oasis-polis: Tadmur-Palmyra as a Greek City in the Roman World (or Not) in Five Episodes, in: M. Sommer (ed.), Inter duo imperia. Palmyra between East and West, Oriens et Occidens 31 (Stuttgart 2020) 23–36

Kaltsas 2001. N. Kaltsas, Sculpture in the National Archaeological Museum, Athens (Los Angeles 2001)

Kammerer 1929. A. Kammerer, Pétra et la nabatène (Paris 1929)

Kantor 1992. H. J. Kantor, Čogā Miš, Encyclopædia Iranica: <https://iranicaonline.org/articles/coga-mis-protohistoric-site> (06.05.2022)

Kaspar 1969–1970. D. Kaspar, Vier palmyrenische Grabporträts in Schweizer Sammlungen, JbBernHistMus 49, 1969–1970, 275–304

Katakes 2018. S. Katakes, Athens, National Archaeological Museum I. Attic Sarcophagi with Garlands, Erotes and Dionysiac Themes (Athens 2018)

Keel 2008. O. Keel, Gott weiblich. Eine verborgene Seite des biblischen Gottes (Gütersloh 2008)

Kelman 1908. J. Kelman, From Damascus to Palmyra (London 1908)

Kent Hill 1963. D. Kent Hill, Ivory Ornaments of Hellenistic Couches, Hesperia 32, 1963, 293–300

Kingley 2002. S. Kingley, Queen Zenobia and the Arts of Palmyra, Minerva 13:3, 2002, 3–4

Kintrup 2016. K. Kintrup, Die attischen Sarkophage, Fascicule 2. Amazonomachie – Schlacht – Epinausimachie, Die Antiken Sarkophagreliefs 9, 1, 2 (Berlin 2016)

Kitzinger 1938. E. Kitzinger, VI. – Notes on Early Coptic Sculpture, Archaeologia 87, 1938, 181–215

Klaver 2019. S. Klaver, The Participation of Palmyrene Women in the Religious Life, in: S. Krag – R. Raja (eds.), Women, Children and the Family in Palmyra, Palmyrene Studies 3, Scientia Danica, Series H, Humanistica 4, 10 (Copenhagen 2019) 157–167

Kloner – Zissu 2007. A. Kloner – B. Zissu, The Necropolis of Jerusalem in the Second Temple Period (Leuven 2007)

Koch 1993. G. Koch, Sarkophage der römischen Kaiserzeit (Darmstadt 1993)

Koch 1995. G. Koch, 125 Jahre Sarkophag-Corpus. Ein großes deutsches Forschungsvorhaben feiert Jubiläum, Antike Welt 26, 1995, 365–377

Koch 2011. G. Koch, Sarcofagi di età imperiale romana in Asia Minore: una sintesi, JRA 24, 2011, 9–29

Koch – Baratte 2012. G. Koch – F. Baratte (eds.), Akten des Symposiums ›Sarkophage der Römischen Kaiserzeit: Produktion in den Zentren–Kopien in den Provinzen‹ / ›Les sarcophages romains: Centres et périphéries‹, Paris, 2.–5. November 2005, Sarkophag-Studien 6 (Ruhpolding 2012)

Koch – Sichtermann 1982. G. Koch and H. Sichtermann, Römische Sarkophage, Handbuch der klassischen Altertumswissenschaft 6 (Munich 1982)

Koch – Wight 1988. G. Koch – K. Wight, Roman Funerary Sculpture. Catalogue of the Collections (Malibu 1988)

Koiner – Porod 2015. G. Koiner – B. Porod, Römische Sarkophage. Akten des internationalen Werkstattgesprächs, 11. – 13. Oktober 2012 (Graz 2015)

Koortbojian 2015. Koortbojian, M. 2015. Roman Sarcophagi, in: B. Borg (ed.), Blackwell Companion to Roman Art (Malden 2015) 286–300

Koustrup Høj 2017a. A. D. Koustrup Høj, Palmyrenske portrætter og kunstmarkedet, in: R. Raja (ed.), Palmyra. Ørknenes perle (Aarhus 2017) 30–37

Koustrup Høj 2017b. A. D. Koustrup Høj, Palmyrene Portraiture and Illegal Trade in Art and Antiquities, in: R. Raja (ed.), Palmyra. Pearl of the Desert (Aarhus 2017) 30–37

Kraeling 1961–1962. C. H. Kraeling, Color Photographs of the Paintings in the Tomb of the Three Brothers at Palmyra, AAS 11–12, 1961–1962, 13–18

Krag 2015. S. Krag, The Secrets of the Funerary Buildings in Palmyra during the Roman Period, in: E. Mortensen – S. Grove Saxkjær (eds.), Revealing and Concealing in Antiquity. Textual and Archaeological Approaches to Secrecy (Aarhus 2015) 105–118

Krag 2016. S. Krag, Females in Group Portraits in Palmyra, in: A. Kropp – R. Raja (eds.), The World of Palmyra, Palmyrene Studies 1, Scientia Danica, Series H, Humanistica 4, 6 (Copenhagen 2016) 180–193

Krag 2017a. S. Krag, Kvinder i Palmyra, in: R. Raja (ed.), Palmyra. Ørknens perle (Aarhus 2017) 57–64

Krag 2017b. S. Krag, Women in Palmyra, in: R. Raja (ed.), Palmyra. Pearl of the Desert (Aarhus 2017) 57–64

Krag 2018. S. Krag, Funerary Representations of Palmyrene Women from the First Century BC to the Third Century AD (Turnhout 2018)

Krag 2019. S. Krag, Palmyrene Funerary Buildings and Family Burial Patterns, in: S. Krag – R. Raja (eds.), Women, Children and the Family in Palmyra, Palmyrene Studies 3, Scientia Danica, Series H, Humanistica 4, 10 (Copenhagen 2019) 38–66

Krag – Raja 2017. S. Krag – R. Raja, Representations of Women and Children in Palmyrene Banqueting Reliefs and Sarcophagus Scenes, ZOrA 10, 2017, 196–227

Krag – Raja 2018. S. Krag – R. Raja, Unveiling Female Hairstyles: Markers of Age, Social Roles, and Status in the Funerary Sculpture from Palmyra, ZOrA, 11, 2018, 242–277

Krag et al. 2019. S. Krag – R. Raja – J. B. Yon, The Collection of Palmyrene Funerary Portraits in Musei Vaticani. Notes and Observations, with an introduction by Alessia Amenta (Vatican 2019)

Künzl 2001. E. Künzl, Römerzeitliche Skulpturen aus Kleinasien und Syrien in Römisch-Germanischen Zentralmuseum, Jahrbuch des RGZM 48, 2001, 499–529

Laes 2011. C. Laes, Children in the Roman Empire. Outsiders Within (Cambridge 2011)

Landon 2005. D. B. Landon, Zooarchaeology and Historical Archaeology: Progress and Prospects, J Archaeol Method Theory 12, 2005, 1–36

Langin-Hooper 2016. S. Langin-Hooper, Seleucid-Parthian Figurines from Babylon in the Nippur Collection: Implications of Misattribution and Re-evaluating the Corpus, Iraq 78, 2016, 49–77

Lapatin 2019. K. Lapatin, Buried by Vesuvius. The Villa dei Papiri at Herculaneum (Los Angeles 2019)

Lecoq 1997. P. Lecoq, Les inscriptions de la Perse achéménide (Paris 1997)

Legrain 1886. E. Legrain, Notice sommaire des monuments araméens et himyarites du Musée du Louvre (Paris 1886)

Legrain 1927. L. Legrain, Tomb Sculptures from Palmyra, The Museum Journal 18:4, 1927, 325–350

Liberati 2002. A. M. Liberati, La conquista dell'Oriente e la lotta contro Roma, in: A. Gabucci – A. Benotto – F. Palazzo Bricherasio (eds.), Zenobia. Il sogno de una regina d'Oriente (Milan 2002) 117–136

Lidzbarski 1898. M. Lidzbarski, Handbuch der nordsemitischen Epigraphik (Weimar 1898)

Lichtenberger – Raja 2019. A. Lichtenberger – R. Raja, Portrait Habit and the Funerary Portraiture of the Decapolis, in: M. Blömer – R. Raja (eds.), Funerary Portraiture in Greater Roman Syria, Studies in Classical Archaeology 6 (Turnhout 2019) 133–150

Long 2016. T. Long, Facing the Evidence: How to Approach the Portraits, in: A. Kropp – R. Raja (eds.), The World of Palmyra, Palmyrene Studies 1, Scientia Danica, Series H, Humanistica 4, 6 (Copenhagen 2016) 135–149

Long 2017. T. Long, The Use of Parthian Costume in Funerary Portraiture in Palmyra, in: A. H. Sørensen – T. Long (eds.), Positions and Professions in Palmyra, Palmyrene Studies 2, Scientia Danica, Series H, Humanistica 4, 9 (Copenhagen 2017) 68–83

Long – Sørensen 2017. T. Long – A. H. Sørensen, Introduction, in: T. Long – A. H. Sørensen (eds.), Positions and Professions in Palmyra. Palmyrene Studies 2, Scientia Danica, Series H, Humanistica 4, 9 (Copenhagen 2017) 7–19

Mackay 1949. D. Mackay, The Jewellery of Palmyra and Its Significance, Iraq 11:2, 1949, 160–187

Majcherek 2012. G. Majcherek, Polish Archaeological Mission to Palmyra. Seasons 2008 and 2009, Polish Archaeology in the Mediterranean 21, 2012, 459–479

Makowski 1983. C. Makowski, Recherches sur le tombeau de A'ailamî e Zebîdâ, DaM 1, 1983, 175–187

Makowski 1985a. K. C. Makowski, La sculpture funéraire palmyrénienne et sa fonction dans l'architecture sépulcrale, Studia Palmyreńskie 8, 1985, 69–117

Makowski 1985b. K. C. Makowski, Recherches sur le banquet miniaturisé dans l'art funéraire de Palmyre, Studia Palmyreńskie 8, 1985, 119–130

Maniatis et al. 2010. Y. Maniatis – D. Tambakopoulos – E. Dotsika – Th. Stefanidou-Tiveriou, Marble Provenance Investigation of Roman Sarcophagi from Thessaloniki, Archaeometry 2009: <https://doi.org/10.1111/j.1475-4754.2009.00469.x>

Maqdissi forthcoming. M. Maqdissi, Documents pour l'histoire de l'archéologie au temps du mandat français en Syrie. III. Le ›Service des Antiquités‹ de la République Française au Levant durant ses premières phases. ›Histoire d'une réussite archéologique‹ (forthcoming)

Maraqten 1993. M. Maraqten, Wine Drinking and Wine Prohibition in Arabia before Islam, Proceedings of the Seminar for Arabian Studies 23, 1993, 95–115

Masarwa 2007. M. Masarwa, Mishmarot, the Cemetery, Hadashot Arkheologiyot: Excavations and Surveys in Israel, חדשות ארכיאולוגיות: חפירות וסקרים בישראל 119, 2007

Masia-Radford 2013. K. Masia-Radford, Luxury Silver Vessels of the Sasanian Period, in: D. T. Potts (ed.), The Oxford Handbook of Ancient Iran (Oxford 2013): <https://doi.org/10.1093/oxfordhb/9780199733309.013.0031>

Masner 1893. K. Masner, Katalog der archäologischen Ausstellung (im) k.k. österreichschen Museum für Kunst und Industrie. 22. Mai – 31. August 1893 (Vienna 1893)

Mathiesen 1993. H. E. Mathiesen, Sculpture in the Parthian Empire (Aarhus 1993)

Mazar 1973. B. Mazar, Beth She'arim I. Catacombs 1–4 (Jerusalem 1973)

Mazzilli 2020. F. Mazzilli, Consciousness of Connectivity. Roman Temples in Southern Syria, in: A. W. Irvin (ed.), Community and Identity at the Edges of the Classical World (Hoboken 2020) 97–117

Mendel 1914. G. Mendel, Musées Impériaux Ottomans. Catalogue des sculptures grecques, romaines et byzantines III (Istanbul 1914)

Meer 2004. L. B. van der Meer, Myths and More on Etruscan Stone Sarcophagi (c. 350 – c. 200 B.C.) (Leuven 2004)

Meinecke 2014. K. Meinecke, Sarcophagum posuit. Römische Steinsarkophage im Kontext, Sarkophag Studien 7 (Ruhpolding 2014)

Meischner – Cussini 2003. J. Meischner – E. Cussini, Vier Palmyrenische Grabreliefs im Museum von Antakya, Archäologischer Anzeiger 2, 2003, 97–105

Meyers 1971. E. M. Meyers, Jewish Ossuaries. Reburial and Rebirth. Secondary Burials in Their Ancient Near Eastern Setting, Biblica et orientalia: sacra scriptura antiquitatibus orientalibus illustrata 24 (Rome 1971)

Michalowski 1960. K. Michalowski, Palmyre I. Fouilles Polonaises 1959 (Warsaw 1960)

Michalowski 1962. K. Michalowski, Palmyre II. Fouilles Polonaises 1960 (Warsaw 1962)

Michalowski 1963. K. Michalowski, Palmyre III. Fouilles Polonaises 1961 (Warsaw 1963)

Michalowski 1964. K. Michalowski, Palmyre IV. Fouilles Polonaises 1962 (Warsaw 1964)

Michalowski 1966. K. Michalowski, Palmyre V. Fouilles Polonaises 1963 et 1964 (Warsaw 1966)

Middleton et al. 2007. A. Middleton – St John Simpson – A. P. Simpson, The Manufacture and Decoration of Parthian Glazed ›Slipper Coffins‹ from Warka, The British Museum Technical Research Bulletin 2, 2007, 29–37

Milik 1972. J. T. Milik, Dédicaces faites par des dieux (Palmyre, Hatra, Tyr) et des thiases sémitiques à l'époque romaine (Paris 1972)

Millar 1993. F. Millar, The Roman Near East, 31 B.C.–A.D. 337 (London 1993)

Miller 1997. M. C. Miller, Athens and Persia in the Fifth Century BC. A Study in Cultural Receptivity (Cambridge 1997)

Minasyan 2021. R. S. Minasyan, Scythian and Sarmatian Weapons with Gold Decoration, in: S. Pankova – St. J. Simpson (eds.), Masters of the Steppe. The Impact of the Scythians and Later Nomad Societies of Eurasia (Oxford 2021) 320–326

Misailidou-Despotidou et al. 2017. V. Misailidou-Despotidou – M. Farmaki – C. Moustadami – E. Gkatzogia, Βασιλούδι. 2012. Η αρχαιοκαπηλία και η ανασκαφή: χρονικό, in: P. Adam-Veleni – K. Tzanavari, Το Αρχαιολογικό Έργο στη Μακεδονία και στη Θράκη [The Archaeological Work in Macedonia and Thrace] (Thessaloniki 2017) 447–456

Miyashita 2016. S. Miyashita, The Vessels in Palmyrene Banquet Scenes: Tomb BWLH and BWRP and Tomb TYBL, in: J. C. Meyer – E. H. Seland – N. Anfinset (eds.), Palmyrena. City, Hinterland and Caravan Trade between Orient and Occident. Proceedings of the Conference Held in Athens, December 1–3, 2012 (Oxford 2016) 131–146

Morehart 1956–1957. M. Morehart, Early Sculpture at Palmyra, Berytus 12, 1956, 53–83

Morton 1998. F. Morton, The Rothschilds. A Family Portrait (New York 1998)

Mouterde 1926. R. Mouterde, Dieux cavaliers de la région d'Alep (Collections Guillaume Poche et François Marcopoli), MelBeyrouth 11, 1926, 307–323

Muhesen 2012. S. Muhesen, Aperçu sur le paléolithique de Syrie, Syria 89, 2012, 7–29

Müller 1885. D. H. Müller, Vier Palmyrenische Grabinschriften im Besitze des Ministerial-Concipisten Herrn Dr J. C. Samson, SBWien 108, 1885, 973–977

Müller 1892. D. H. Müller, Palmyrenica aus dem British Museum, WZKM 6, 1892, 317–326

Müller 1898. D. H. Müller, Palmyrenische Inschriften nach Abklatschen des Herrn Dr Alois Musil (Vienna 1898)

Murray 2017. O. Murray, The Symposion. Drinking Greek Style. Essays on Greek Pleasure 1983–2017 (Oxford 2018)

Musée Impérial Ottoman 1895. Musée Impérial Ottoman, Antiquités Himyarites et Palmyréniennes. Catalogue sommaire (Istanbul 1895)

Mylonas 1975. G. Mylonas, Το δυτικόν νεκροταφείον της Ελευσίνος, BAE 81 (Athens 1975)

Myśliwiec 1974. K. Myśliwiec, Sculptures trouvées à Palmyre par la mission archéologique polonaise en 1968 et 1969, Studia Palmyreńskie 5, 1974, 83–96

Nakahashi et al. 2001. T. Nakahashi – K. Funahashi – H. Koga – K. Yoshimura, Human Skeletal Remains, in: T. Higuchi – K. Saito, Tomb F. Tomb of BWLH and BWRP, Southeast Necropolis, Palmyra, Syria (Nara 2001) 145–164

Nevett 1995. L. Nevett, Gender Relations in the Classical Greek Household: The Archaeological Evidence, BSA 90, 1995, 363–381

Newson 2015. P. Newson, Greco-Roman Burial Practices in the Bekaa Valley, Lebanon, and Its Adjacent Uplands, J. East. Mediterr. Archaeol. 3, 2015, 349–371

Nigro 2002. L. Nigro, I rilievi palmireni di Federico Zeri nei Musei Vaticani, in: A. Gabucci (ed.), Zenobia. Il sogno di una regina d'Oriente (Milan 2002) 38–43

Nikitine 2019. A. Nikitine, Palmyre dans les travaux des savants russes (trans. A. Nercessian), in: H. Eristov – C. Vibert-Guigue – W. al-Asʿad – N. Sarkis (eds.), Le tombeau des trois frères à Palmyre. Mission archéologique franco-syrienne 2004–2009 (Beirut 2019) 55

Oakley 2011. J. H. Oakley, Die attischen Sarkophage I. Einzelmythen. Dritter Faszikel Andere Mythen (Berlin 2011)

Öğüş 2014. E. Öğüş, Columnar Sarcophagi from Aphrodisias: Elite Emulation in the Greek East, AJA 118, 2014, 113–136

Öğüş-Uzun 2018. E. Öğüş-Uzun, Columnar Sarcophagi from Aphrodisias, Aphrodisias 9 (Wiesbaden 2018)

Olbrycht 2017. M. J. Olbrycht, Slipper Coffins and Funerary Practices in Parthia, in: M. J. Olbrycht (ed.), Collectanea Iranica et Asiatica. Iran and Western Asia in Antiquity. New Perspectives, Anabasis. Studia classica et orientalia 8, 2017, 301–313

Østrup 1894. J. Østrup, Skiftende Horizonter. Skildringer og Iagttagelser fra et Ridt gennem Ørkenen og Lille-Asien (Copenhagen 1894)

Østrup 1895. J. Østrup, Historisk-topografiske Bidrag til Kendskabet til den syriske Ørken, Det Kongelige Danske Videnskabernes Selskabs Skrifter 6, Historisk og filosofisk afdeling 4, 61–91

Palaz Erdemir 2013. H. Palaz Erdemir, Mystery of the Funerary Reliefs of Palmyra (Tadmor) in the Desert of Syria, Turkish Studies, 8.7, 2013, 507–518

Palmyra Portrait Project. Aarhus University / Centre for Urban Network Evolutions. Available at <https://projects.au.dk/palmyraportrait/> (06.05.2022)

Palmyrena: City, Hinterland and Caravan Trade between Orient and Occident: <https://org.uib.no/palmyrena/index.htm> (06.05.2022)

Papagianni 2016. E. Papagianni, Attische Sarkophage mit Eroten und Girlanden, Sarkophag Studien 9 (Wiesbaden 2016)

Parks 2002. D. Parks, Epitaphs and Tombstones of Hellenistic and Roman Cyprus, in: C. Callaway (ed.), Ancient Journeys. A Festschrift in Honor of Eugene Numa Lane: <https://hdl.handle.net/10355/70113> (06.05.2022)

Parlasca 1969–1970. K. Parlasca, A New Grave Relief from Syria, Brooklyn Museum Annual 11, 1969–1970, 169–185

Parlasca 1976. K. Parlasca, Probleme palmyrenischer Grabreliefs – Chronologie und Interpretation, in: E. Frézouls (ed.), Palmyre. Bilan et perspectives. Colloque de Strasbourg 18–20 Octobre 1973 (Strasbourg 1976) 33–44

Parlasca 1982a. K. Parlasca, Römische Kunst in Syrien, in: K. Kohlmeyer – E. Strommenger (eds.), Land des Baal. Syrien, Forum der Völker und Kulturen (Mainz 1982) 186–226

Parlasca 1982b. K. Parlasca, Syrische Grabreliefs hellenistischer und römischer Zeit (Mainz 1982)

Parlasca 1984. K. Parlasca, Probleme der palmyrenischen Sarkophage, MarbWPr 1984, 1984, 283–296

Parlasca 1985. K. Parlasca, Roman Art in Syria, in: H. Weiss (ed.), Ebla to Damascus. Art and Archaeology of Ancient Syria (Washington, DC 1985) 386–440

Parlasca 1987a. K. Parlasca, Aspekte der palmyrenischen Skulpturen, in: E. M. Ruprechtsberger (ed.), Palmyra. Geschichte, Kunst und Kultur der syrischen Oasenstadt (Linz 1987) 276–282

Parlasca 1987b. K. Parlasca, Ein antoninischer Frauenkopf aus Palmyra in Malibu, in: Ancient Portraits in the J. Paul Getty Museum 1 (Los Angeles 1987) 107–114

Parlasca 1988. K. Parlasca, Ikonographische Probleme palmyrenischer Grabreliefs, DaM 3, 1988, 215–221

Parlasca 1989a. K. Parlasca, Beobachtungen zur palmyrenischen Grabarchittektur, DaM 4, 1989, 181–190

Parlasca 1989b. K. Parlasca, La sculpture grecque et la sculpture d'époque romaine Impériale en Syrie, in: J.-M. Dentzer – W. Orthmann (eds.), Archéologie et histoire de la Syrie II (Saarbrücken 1989) 537–556

Parlasca 1990. K. Parlasca, Palmyrenische Skulpturen in Museen an der amerikanischen Westküste, in: M. True – G. Koch (eds.), Roman Funerary Monuments in the J. Paul Getty Museum 1 (Malibu 1990) 133–144

Parlasca 1994. K. Parlasca, Eine palmyrenische Tierkopffibel in Privatbesitz. Ein Beitrag zur Kulturgeschichte Palmyras, AKorrBl 24, 1994, 299–310

Parlasca 1995. K. Parlasca, Some Problems of Palmyrene Plastic Art, ARAM 7, 1995, 59–71

Parlasca 1998. K. Parlasca, Palmyrenische Sarkophage mit Totenmahlreliefs – Forschungsstand und ikonographische Probleme, Sarkophag Studien 1, 1998, 311–320

Parlasca 2000. K. Parlasca, Ein syrischer Kopf der römischen Kaizerzeit in Mariemont, DaM 12, 2000, 135–222

Parlasca 2001a. K. Parlasca, Personnage portant un costume parthe (fragment de sarcophage), in: J. Charles-Gaffiot – H. Lavagne – J.-M. Hofman (eds.), Moi, Zénobie reine de Palmyre (Milan 2001) 341

Parlasca 2001b. K. Parlasca, Portrait d'un homme barbu, in: J. Charles-Gaffiot – H. Lavagne – J.-M. Hofman (eds.), Moi, Zénobie reine de Palmyre (Milan 2001) 367

Parlasca 2001c. K. Parlasca, Tête d'un jeune homme, in: J. Charles-Gaffiot – H. Lavagne – J.-M. Hofman (eds.), Moi, Zénobie reine de Palmyre (Milan 2001) 336

Parlasca 2005. K. Parlasca, Zu Palmyrenischen Inschriften auf Reliefs, in: E. Cussini (ed.), A Journey to Palmyra: Collected Essays to Remember Delbert R. Hillers (Leiden 2005) 137–149

Pease 1952. A. S. Pease, A Sketch of the Development of Ancient Botany, Phoenix 6, 1952, 44–51

Petit 2004. T. Petit, Images de la royauté amathousienne: Le sarcophage d'Amathonte, in: Y. Perrin – T. Petit (eds.), Iconographie impériale, iconographie royale, iconographie des élites dans le monde gréco-romain (Saint-Étienne 2004) 49–96

Piersimoni 1995. P. Piersimoni, The Palmyrene Prosopography (Ph.D. diss. University College London 1995)

Pierson 1984. F. Pierson, Recherches sur le costume des enfants dans l'iconographie palmyrénienne, RAArtLouv 17, 1984, 85–111

Pfister 1940. R. Pfister, Textiles de Palmyre III (Paris 1940)

Pfrommer 1993. M. Pfrommer, Metalwork from the Hellenized East. Catalogue of the Collections (Los Angeles 1993)

Platt 2017. V. Platt, Framing the Dead on Roman Sarcophagi, in: V. Platt – M. Squire (eds.), The Frame in Classical Art. A Cultural History (Cambridge 2017) 353–381

Plattner 2010. A. G. Plattner, Palmyrenische Reliefs im Kunsthistorischen Museum Wien, in: B. Bastl – V. Gassner – U. Muss (eds.), Zeitreisen. Syrien, Palmyra, Rom. Festschrift für Andreas Schmidt-Colinet zum 65. Geburtstag (Vienna 2010) 159–184

Ploug 1995. G. Ploug, Catalogue of Palmyrene Sculptures Ny Carlsberg Glyptotek (Copenhagen 1995)

Ploug 1996. G. Ploug, Kvinder i Palmyra, Sfinx 1996:2, 60–65

Pognon 1907. H. Pognon, Inscriptions sémitiques de la Syrie de la Mésopotamie et de la région de Mossoul (Paris 1907)

Pogoda 2018. C. Pogoda, Limestone Sarcophagi from Gerasa/Jerash, Jordan, in: C. Eger – M. Mackensen (eds.), Death and Burial in the Near East from Roman to Islamic Times. Research in Syria, Lebanon, Jordan and Egypt (Wiesbaden 2018) 139–148

Polish Centre of Mediterranean Archaeology, University of Warsaw: <https://pcma.uw.edu.pl/en/about-us> (06.05.2022)

Poulsen 1921. F. Poulsen, De Palmyrenske Skulpturer, in: E. Wrangel – F. Hazelius (eds.), Tidskrift för Konstvetenskap 6, 1921, 79–105

Post 1891. G. E. Post, Narrative of a Trip to Palmyra in April, 1890, Palestine Exploration Quarterly 23:1, 1891, 20–49

Provenzali 2017. A. Provenziali, Ritratto femminile da rilievo funerario, in: M. Novello – C. Tiussi (eds.), Volti di Palmira ad Aquileia/Portraits of Palmyra in Aquileia (Rome 2017) 102

Pudsey 2016. A. Pudsey, Children's Cultures in Roman Egypt, in: L. Grig, Popular Culture in the Ancient World (Cambridge 2016) 208–234

Rachmani 1994. L. Y. Rahmani, A Catalogue of Jewish Ossuaries. In the Collections of the State of Israel (Jerusalem 1994)

Raff 2017. K. A. Raff (ed.), Roman Art at the Art Institute of Chicago (Chicago 2017): <https://www.artic.edu/digital-publications/5/roman-art-at-the-art-institute-of-chicago> (06.05.2022)

Raja 2015a. R. Raja, Cultic Dining and Religious Patterns in Palmyra: The Case of the Palmyrene Banqueting Tesserae, in: S. Faust – M. Seifert – L. Ziemer (eds.), Antike. Architektur. Geschichte. Festschrift für Inge Nielsen zum 65. Geburtstag (Berlin 2015) 181–200

Raja 2015b. R. Raja, Palmyrene Funerary Portraits in Context: Portrait Habit between Local Traditions and Imperial Trends, in: J. Fejfer – M. Moltesen – A. Rathje (eds.), Tradition. Transmission of Culture in the Ancient World (Copenhagen 2015) 329–362

Raja 2015c. R. Raja, Staging >Private< Religion in Roman >Public< Palmyra: The Role of the Religious Dining Tickets (Banqueting Tesserae), in: C. Ando – J. Rüpke (eds.), Public and Private in Ancient Mediterranean Law and Religion (Berlin 2015) 165–186

Raja 2016a. R. Raja, In and out of Contexts: Explaining Religious Complexity through the Banqueting Tesserae from Palmyra, Religion in the Roman Empire 2:3, 2016, 340–371

Raja 2016b. R. Raja, Representations of Priests in Palmyra: Methodological Considerations on the Meaning of the Representation of Priesthood in Roman Period Palmyra, Religion in the Roman Empire, 2:1, 2016, 125–146

Raja 2017a. R. Raja, Between Fashion Phenomena and Status Symbols. Contextualising the Dress of the So-Called >Former Priests< of Palmyra, in: C. Brøns – M.-L. Nosch (eds.), Textiles and Cult in the Mediterranean Area in the 1st Millennium BC (Oxford 2017) 209–229

Raja 2017b. R. Raja, Networking beyond Death: Priests and Their Family Networks in Palmyra Explored through the Funerary Sculpture, in: E. H. Seland – H. F. Teigen (eds.), Sinews of Empire. Networks in the Roman Near East and Beyond (Oxford 2017) 121–135

Raja 2017c. R. Raja, Palmyra: Pearl of the Desert, in: R. Raja (ed.), Palmyra. Pearl of the Desert (Aarhus 2017) 10–19

Raja 2017d. R. Raja, Palmyra: Ørknens perle, in: R. Raja (ed.), Palmyra. Ørknens perle (Aarhus 2017) 10–19

Raja 2017e. R. Raja, Powerful Images of the Deceased. Palmyrene Funerary Portrait Culture, in: D. Boschung – F. Queyrel (eds.), Bilder der Macht. Das griechische Porträt und seine Verwendung in der antiken Welt (Paderborn 2017) 319–348

Raja 2017f. R. Raja, Præster I Palmyra: Et embede eller en social status?, in: R. Raja (ed.), Palmyra. Ørknens perle (Aarhus 2017) 77–85

Raja 2017g. R. Raja, Priesthood in Palmyra: Public Office or Social Status?, in: R. Raja (ed.), Palmyra. Pearl of the Desert (Aarhus 2017) 77–85

Raja 2017h. R. Raja, Representations of the So-Called >Former Priests< in Palmyrene Funerary Art. A Methodological Contribution and Commentary, Topoi 21:1, 2017, 51–81

Raja 2017i. R. Raja, To Be or Not to Be Depicted as a Priest in Palmyra. A Matter of Representational Spheres and Societal Values, in: A. H. Sørensen – T. Long (eds.), Positions and Professions in Palmyra, Palmyrene Studies 2, Scientia Danica, Series H, Humanistica 4, 9 (Copenhagen 2017) 115–130

Raja 2017j. R. Raja, ›You Can Leave Your Hat on‹: Priestly Representations from Palmyra: Between Visual Genre, Religious Importance and Social Status, in: R. Gordon – G. Petridou – J. Rüpke (eds.), Beyond Priesthood. Religious Entrepreneurs and Innovators in the Roman Empire (Berlin 2017) 417–442

Raja 2018a. R. Raja, Compilation and Digitisation of the Palmyrene Corpus of Funerary Portraits, Antiquity 92:365, 2018, 1–7

Raja 2018b. R. Raja, The Matter of the Palmyrene ›Modius‹. Remarks on the History of Research into the Terminology of the Palmyrene Priestly Hat, in: R. Raja – J. Rüpke (eds.), Religious Terminology, Religion in the Roman Empire 2:4 (Tübingen 2018) 237–259

Raja 2018c. R. Raja, Palmyrene Funerary Portraits: Collection Histories and Current Research, in: J. Aruz (ed.), Palmyra. Mirage in the Desert (New York 2018) 90–99

Raja 2019a. R. Raja, Catalogue. The Palmyra Collection, Ny Carlsberg Glyptotek (Copenhagen 2019)

Raja 2019b. R. Raja, Dining with the Gods and the Others: The Banqueting Tickets from Palmyra as Expressions of Religious Individualization, in: M. Fuchs – A. Linkenbach – M. Mulsow – B.-C. Otto – R. B. Parson – J. Rüpke (eds.), Religious Individualisation. Historical Dimensions and Comparative Perspectives (Berlin 2019) 243–256

Raja 2019c. R. Raja, Harald Ingholt and Palmyra, in: A.-M. Nielsen – R. Raja (eds.), The Road to Palmyra (Copenhagen 2019) 42–64

Raja 2019d. R. Raja, Harald Ingholt – og Palmyra, oasen i den syriske ørken, in: E. Mortensen – R. Raja, Store danske arkæologer. På jagt efter fortidens byer (Aarhus 2019) 105–131

Raja 2019e. R. Raja, It Stays in the Family: Palmyrene Priestly Representations and Their Constellations, in: S. Krag – R. Raja (eds.), Women, Children and the Family in Palmyra, Palmyrene Studies 3, Scientia Danica, Series H, Humanistica 4, 10 (Copenhagen 2019) 95–156

Raja 2019f. R. Raja, Portrait Habit in Palmyra, in: A.-M. Nielsen – R. Raja (eds.), The Road to Palmyra (Copenhagen 2019) 137–154

Raja 2019g. R. Raja, Reconsidering the Dorsalium or ›Curtain of Death‹ in Palmyrene Funerary Sculpture: Significance and Interpretations in Light of the Palmyra Portrait Project Corpus, in: R. Raja (ed.), Revisiting the Religious Life of Palmyra, Contextualizing the Sacred 9 (Turnhout 2019) 67–151

Raja 2019h. R. Raja, Religious Banquets in Palmyra and the Palmyrene Banqueting Tesserae, in: A.-M. Nielsen – R. Raja (eds.), The Road to Palmyra (Copenhagen 2019) 221–234

Raja 2019i. R. Raja, Stacking Aesthetics in the Syrian Desert: Displaying Palmyrene Sculpture in the Public and Funerary Sphere, in: C. Draycott – R. Raja – K. Welch – W. Wootton (eds.), Visual Histories of the Classical World. Essays in Honour of R. R. R. Smith (Turnhout 2019) 281–298

Raja 2020. R. Raja, Men of the Desert or Men of the World? Revisiting the Iconography of Palmyrene Men and Their Camels, in: I. B. Mæhle – P. B. Ravnå – E. H. Seland (eds.), Methods and Models in Ancient History. Essays in Honor of Jørgen Christian Meyer (Athens 2020) 129–150

Raja 2021a. R. Raja, Harald Ingholt and Palmyrene Sculpture: Continuing a Lifelong Relationship a Century Later, in: O. Bobou – J. Vestergaard Jensen – N. Breintoft Kristensen – R. Raja – R. Randeris Thomsen (eds.), A Translation of Harald Ingholt's Studier over Palmyrensk Skulptur. Edited and with Commentary, Studies on Palmyrene Sculpture 1 (Turnhout 2021) 1–28

Raja 2021b. R. Raja, Ingholt Archive: <https://doi.org/10.6084/m9.figshare.c.5509725.v1>

Raja 2021c. R. Raja, Palmyra Portrait Project – Project Publications. Aarhus University / Centre for Urban Network Evolutions: <https://figshare.com/articles/Palmyra_Portrait_Project_full_bibliography_2013-2020_MAY_pdf/1227271> (15.11.2022)

Raja 2022a. R. Raja, Palmyrene Funerary Art between East and West: Reclining Women in the Funerary Sculpture, in: K. Lapatin – R. Raja (eds.), Palmyra and the East (Turnhout 2022) 71–96

Raja 2022b. R. Raja, Pearl of the Desert. A History of Palmyra (Oxford 2022)

Raja – Seland 2021. R. Raja – E. H. Seland, Horses and Camels in Palmyrene Art: Iconography, Contexts and Meanings, ZOrA 13, 2021, 300–329

Raja – Sørensen 2015a. R. Raja – A. Højen Sørensen, The ›Beauty of Palmyra‹ and Qasr Abjad (Palmyra): New Discoveries in the Archive of Harald Ingholt, JRA 28, 2015, 439–450

Raja – Sørensen 2015b. R. Raja – A. Højen Sørensen. Harald Ingholt & Palmyra (Aarhus 2015)

Raja – Sørensen 2019. R. Raja – A. H. Sørensen, Danish Research from Johannes Østrup to the Palmyra Portrait Project, in: H. Eristov – C. Vibert-Guigue – W. al-Asʿad – N. Sarkis (eds.), Le tombeau des trois frères à Palmyre. Mission archéologique franco-syrienne 2004–2009 (Beirut 2019) 59–64

Raja – Yon 2022. R. Raja – J.-B. Yon, Palmyrene Funerary Sculptural Representations with Greek, Latin and Bilingual Inscriptions, ZOrA 14 (2021), 2022, 170–229

Raja et al. 2021a. R. Raja – J. B. Yon – J. Steding, Excavating Palmyra. Harald Ingholt's Excavation Diaries. A Transcript, Translation, and Commentary (Turnhout 2021)

Raja et al. 2021b. R. Raja – K. Schnädelbach – J. Steding, A New Map of Palmyra's Southwest Necropolis Based on the Excavation Diaries of Harald Ingholt, ZOrA 14, 2021, 230–273

Raja et al. 2021c. R. Raja – O. Bobou – I. Romanowska, Three Hundred Years of Palmyrene History. Unlocking Archaeological Data for Studying Past Societal Transformations, PLOS One 16:11, 2021: e0256081: <https://doi.org/10.1371/journal.pone.0256081>

Raja et al. 2022. Bobou, O. – A. Miranda – R. Raja – J.-B. Yon, The Ingholt Archive. The Palmyrene Material, Archive Archaeology 2 (Turnhout 2022)

Raja et al. forthcoming. R. Raja – O. Bobou – J.-B. Yon, The Palmyrene Funerary Portraits (Turnhout, forthcoming)

Raubitchek 1998. K. Raubitchek, The Metal Objects, 1952–1989, Isthmia 7 (Athens 1998)

Reynolds et al. 2007. J. Reynolds – C. Roueché – G. Bodard, Inscriptions of Aphrodisias: <https://insaph.kcl.ac.uk/insaph/iaph2007/> (15.11.2022)

Richter 1966. G. M. A. Richter, The Furniture of the Greeks, Etruscans and Romans (London 1966)

Robert 1890. C. Robert, Die antiken Sarkophagreliefs II. Mythologische Cyklen (Berlin 1890)

Robert 1897. C. Robert, Die antiken Sarkophagreliefs III, 1. Einzelmythen. Actaeon-Hercules (Berlin 1897)

Robert 1904. C. Robert, Die antiken Sarkophagreliefs III, 2. Einzelmythen. Hippolytos-Meleagros (Berlin 1904)

Robert 1919. C. Robert, Die antiken Sarkophagreliefs III, 3. Einzelmythen. Niobiden-Triptolemos Ungedeutet (Berlin 1919)

Robins 2016. G. Robins, Meals for the Dead: The Image of the Deceased Seated before a Table of Offerings in Ancient Egyptian Art, in: C. Draycott – M. Stamatopoulou (eds.), Dining and Death. Interdisciplinary Perspectives on the ›Funerary Banquet‹ in Ancient Art, Burial and Belief (Leuven 2016) 111–128

Rogge 1995. S. Rogge, Die attischen Sarkophage, Fascicule 1. Achill und Hippolytos (Berlin 1995)

Roller 2003. M. Roller, Horizontal Women: Posture and Sex in the Roman Convivium, Am. J. Philol. 124, 2003, 377–422

Römer-Strehl 2013. C. Römer-Strehl, Keramik, in: A. Schmidt-Colinet – W. al-Asʿad (eds.), Palmyras Reichtum durch weltweiten Handel (Vienna 2013) 7–80

Romano 2006. I. B. Romano, Classical Sculpture. Catalogue of the Cypriot, Greek, and Roman Stone Sculpture in the University of Pennsylvania Museum of Archaeology and Anthropology (Philadelphia 2006)

Romanowska et al. 2021. I. Romanowska – O. Bobou – R. Raja, Reconstructing the Social, Economic and Demographic Trends of Palmyra's Elite from Funerary Data, JAS 133, 2021: <https://doi.org/10.1016/j.jas.2021.105432>

Rose-Greenland 2007. F. Rose-Greenland, Table for One: Drinking Alone on Women's Grave Monuments from Roman Celtiberia, AWE 6, 2007, 113–134

Rosenfield 1967. J. M. Rosenfield, The Dynastic Arts of the Kushans (Berkeley 1967)

Rostovstzeff 1932. M. Rostovstzeff, Caravan Cities (Oxford 1932)

Rumscheid 2000. J. Rumscheid, Kranz und Krone. Zu Insignien, Siegespreisen und Ehrenzeichen der römischen Kaiserzeit (Tübingen 2000)

Rumscheid 2019. J. Rumscheid, Different from the Others: Female Dress in Northern Syria Based on Examples from Zeugma and Hierapolis, in: M. Blömer – R. Raja (eds.), Funerary Portraiture in Greater Roman Syria (Turnhout 2019) 65–82

Ruprechtsberger 1987. E. M. Ruprechtsberger, Antikes Palmyra – Topographie und Denkmäler, in: E. M. Ruprechtsberger (ed.), Palmyra. Geschichte, Kunst und Kultur der syrischen Oasenstadt (Linz 1987) 44–114

Russell 2013. B. Russell, The Economics of the Roman Stone Trade (Oxford 2013)

Russell 2015. B. Russell, Transport and Distribution, in: E. A. Friedland – M. Grunow Sobocinski – E. K. Gazda (eds.), The Oxford Handbook of Roman Sculpture (Oxford 2015) 189–208

Russenberger 2015. C. Russenberger, Der Tod und die Mädchen. Amazonen auf römischen Sarkophagen, Image & Context 13 (Berlin 2015)

Rutledge 2012. S. H. Rutledge, Ancient Rome as a Museum. Power, Identity, and the Culture of Collecting (Oxford 2012)

Ruxer – Kubczak 1972. M. S. Ruxer – J. Kubczak, Naszyjnik grecki w okresach hellenistycznym i rzymskim (Warsaw 1972)

Sabeh 1953. J. Sabeh, Sculptures palmyréniennes inédites du Musée de Damas, AAS 3, 1953, 3–26

Sachau 1881. E. Sachau, Palmyrenische Inschriften, ZDMG 35, 1881, 728–748

Sadurska 1972. A. Sadurska, Corpus signorum imperii romani. Pologne I. Les portraits romains dans les collections polonaises (Warsaw 1972)

Sadurska 1975. A. Sadurska, Une nouvelle tessère de Palmyre, Studia Palmyreńskie 6–7, 1975, 121–126

Sadurska 1976. A. Sadurska, Nouvelles recherches dans la nécropole ouest de Palmyre, in: E. Frézouls (ed.), Palmyre. Bilan et perspectives. Colloque de Strasbourg 18–20 Octobre 1973 (Strasbourg 1976) 11–32

Sadurska 1977. A. Sadurska, Palmyre VII. Le tombeau de famille de ʿAlainê (Warsaw 1977)

Sadurska 1982. A. Sadurska, Portrait funéraire de Palmyre – problèmes et méthodes de recherches, WissZBerl 31, 1982, 269–368

Sadurska 1988. A. Sadurska, Die palmyrenische Grabskulptur, Altertum 34, 1988, 14–23

Sadurska 1994. A. Sadurska, L'art et la société: Recherches iconologiques sur l'art funéraire de Palmyre, ArcheologiaWarsz 45, 1994, 11–23

Sadurska 1995. A. Sadurska, La famille et son image dans l'art de Palmyre, in: F. E. Koenig – S. Rebetez (eds.), Arculiana. Ioanni Boegli anno sexagesimo Quinto feliciter peracto amici discipuli college socii dona dederunt A.D. XIIII Kalendas Decembris MDCCCCLXXXXV (Avenches 1995) 583–589

Sadurska – Bounni 1994. A. Sadurska – A. Bounni, Les sculptures funéraires de Palmyre (Rome 1994)

Saito 2007. K. Saito, Sheep Bones Accompanying the Dead from an Underground Tomb in Palmyra: Especially on Metacarpal Bones (in Japanese), Rāfidān 28, 2007, 83–94

Saito 2016. K. Saito, Palmyra, Japanese Archaeological Research (Homs), in: Y. Kanjou – A. Tsuneki (eds.), A History of Syria in One Hundred Sites (Oxford 2016) 349–354

Saito 2018. K. Saito, Japanese Archaeological Work in Palmyra from 1990 to 2010, in: J. Abdul Massih – S. Nishiyama – H. Charaf – A. Deb (eds.), Archaeological Explorations in Syria 2000–2011. Proceedings of ISCACH-Beirut 2015 (Oxford 2018) 189–197

Sanders et al. 2014. G. Sanders – S. A. James – I. Tzonou-Herbst – J. Herbst, The Panayia Field Excavations at Corinth: The Neolithic to Hellenistic Phases, Hesperia 83, 1–79

Sarre 1923. F. Sarre, Ein palmyrenische Relieffigur und der Typus des guten Hirten, in: H. Glück (ed.), Studien zur Kunst des Ostens. Josef Strzygowski zum sechzigsten Geburtstage von seinen Freunden und Schülern (Vienna 1923) 69–71

Sartre 2001. M. Sartre, D'Alexandre à Zénobie. Histoire du Levant antique IVe siècle av. J.-C.- IIIe siècle ap. J.-C. (Paris 2001)

Sartre-Fauriat – Sartre 2008. A. Sartre-Fauriat – M. Sartre, Palmyre. La cité des caravanes (Paris 2008)

Sartre – Sartre 2016. A. Sartre – M. Sartre, Palmyre. Vérités et légendes (Paris 2016)

Sartre-Fauriat 2019. A. Sartre-Fauriat, The Discovery and Reception of Palmyra, in: A.-M. Nielsen – R. Raja (eds.), The Road to Palmyra (Copenhagen 2019) 65–76

Sasson 2017. J. M. Sasson, From the Mari Archives. An Anthology of Old Babylonian Letters (University Park 2017)

Satraki 2013. A. Satraki, The Iconography of Basileis in Archaic and Classical Cyprus: Manifestations of Royal Power in the Visual Record, BASOR 370, 2013, 123–144

Sauer 2004. E. W. Sauer, The Disunited Subject: Human History's Split into ›History‹ and ›Archaeology‹, in: E. W. Sauer (ed.), Archaeology and Ancient History. Breaking down the Boundaries (London 2004) 17–46

Savignac 2001. M. R. Savignac, Mission épigraphique à Palmyre (juillet 1914), in: J. Charles-Gaffiot – H. Lavagne – J.-M. Hofman (eds.), Moi, Zénobie reine de Palmyre (Milan 2001) 163–170

Schmidt-Colinet 1987. A. Schmidt-Colinet, Das Tempelgrab einer Aristokratenfamilie (Neue deutsche Ausgrabungen in Palmyra), in: E. M. Ruprechtsberger (ed.), Palmyra. Geschichte, Kunst und Kultur der syrischen Oasenstadt (Linz 1987) 228–243

Schmidt-Colinet 1990. A. Schmidt-Colinet, Considérations sur les carrières de Palmyre en Syrie, in: M. Waelkens (ed.), Pierre éternelle du Nilau Rhin. Carrières et préfabrication (Brussels 1990) 88–92

Schmidt-Colinet 1992. A. Schmidt-Colinet, Das Tempelgrab Nr. 36 in Palmyra. Studien zur Palmyrenischen Grabarchitektur und ihrer Ausstattung I–II (Mainz 1992)

Schmidt-Colinet 1995. A. Schmidt-Colinet, The Quarries of Palmyra, ARAM 7, 1995, 53–58

Schmidt-Colinet 1996. A. Schmidt-Colinet, Antike Denkmäler in Syrien. Die Stichvorlagen von Louis-Francois Cassas (1756-1827) im Wallraf-Richartz-Museum in Köln, KölnJb 29, 1996, 343–548

Schmidt-Colinet 1997. A. Schmidt-Colinet, Aspects of ›Romanization‹: The Tomb Architecture at Palmyra and Its Decoration, in: S. E. Alcock (ed.), The Early Roman Empire in the East (Oxford 1997) 157–177

Schmidt-Colinet 2004. A. Schmidt-Colinet, Palmyrenische Grabkunst als Ausdruck lokaler Identität(en): Fallbeispiele, in: A. Schmidt-Colinet (ed.), Lokale Identitäten in Randgebieten des Römischem Reiches. Akten des Internationalen Symposiums in Wiener Neustadt 2003 (Vienna 2004) 189–198

Schmidt-Colinet 2005. A. Schmidt-Colinet, Die Steinbrüche von Palmyra, in: F. Meynersen (ed.), Orte und Zeiten. 25 Jahre archäologische Forschungen in Syrien 1980–2005 (Damascus 2005) 92–93

Schmidt-Colinet 2009. A. Schmidt-Colinet, Nochmal zur Ikonographie zweier palmyrenischer Sarkophage, in: M. Blömer – M. Facella – E. Winter (eds.), Lokale Identität im Römischen Nahen Osten (Stuttgart 2009) 223–233

Schmidt-Colinet 2017. A. Schmidt-Colinet, Die Steinbrüche von Palmyra. Ein Vorbericht, MDOG 149, 2017, 159–196

Schmidt-Colinet 2018a. A. Schmidt-Colinet, Palmyra. 30 Years of Syrian-German-Austrian Archaeological Research (1981–2010), in: J. Abdul Massih – S. Nishiyama – H. Charaf – A. Deb (eds.), Archaeological Explorations in Syria 2000–2011. Proceedings of ISCACH-Beirut 2015 (Oxford 2018) 251–258

Schmidt-Colinet 2018b. A. Schmidt-Colinet, Thirty Years of Syro-German/Austrian Archaeological Research at Palmyra in Memory of Khaled al-Asʿad, in: J. Aruz (ed.), Palmyra. Mirage in the Desert (New York 2018) 66–75

Schmidt-Colinet – al-Asʿad 2000. A. Schmidt-Colinet – K. al-Asʿad, Zur Urbanistik des hellenistischen Palmyra. Ein Vorbericht, DM 12, 61–93

Schmidt-Colinet – al-Asʿad 2007. A. Schmidt-Colinet – K. al-Asʿad, Zwei Neufunde Palmyrenischer Sarkophage, in: G. Koch (ed.), Akten des Symposiums des Sarkophag-Corpus. Marburg 2.-7. Juli 2001 (Mainz 2007) 271–278

Schmidt-Colinet – al-Asʿad 2013. A. Schmidt-Colinet – W. al-Asʿad (eds.), Palmyras Reichtum durch weltweiten Handel (Vienna 2013)

Schmidt-Colinet et al. 2000. A. Schmidt-Colinet – A. Stauffer – K. al-Asʿad, Die Textilien aus Palmyra (Mainz 1990)

Schnädelbach 2010. K. Schnädelbach, Topographia Palmyrena I. Topography (Damascus 2010)

Schnapp et al. 2008. A. Schnapp et al. Rodin, Freud, collectionneurs. La passion à l'œuvre (Paris 2008)

Schollmeyer 2004. P. Schollmeyer, Die Antiken des Prinzen Johann Georg, in: B. Heide – A. Thiel (eds.), Sammler – Pilger – Wegbereiter. Die Sammlung des Prinzen Johann Georg von Sachsen. Katalog zur Ausstellung herausgegeben vom Landesmuseum Mainz und dem Arbeitsbereich christliche Archäologie und byzantinische Kunstgeschichte am Institut für Kunstgeschichte der Johannes Gutenberg-Universität Mainz (Mainz 2004) 62–69

Schörle 2017. K. Schörle, Palmyrene Merchant Networks and Economic Integration in Competitive Markets, in: E. H. Seland – H. F. Teigen (eds.), Sinews of Empire. Networks in the Roman Near East and Beyond (Oxford 2017) 147–154

Schreiber 1999. T. Schreiber, Athenian Vase Construction. A Potter's Analysis (Los Angeles 1999)

Schröder 1885. P. Schröder, Palmyrenische Inschriften, Zeitschrift der Deutschen Morgenländischen Gesellschaft 39, 1885, 352–361

Scrase 2005. D. Scrase, Treasures of the Fitzwilliam Museum (Cambridge 2005)

Segal 1970. J. B. Segal, Edessa. The Blessed City (Oxford 1970)

Seipel 1996. W. Seipel, Weihrauch und Seide. Alte Kulturen an der Seidenstrasse (Milan 1996)

Seland 2010. E. H. Seland, Palmyra—Karavanehandel og geopolitikk i romersk Syria, Klassisk Forum 2, 2010, 54–69

Seland 2015. E. H. Seland, Camels, Camel Nomadism and the Practicalities of Palmyrene Caravan Trade, ARAM 27, 2015, 45–54

Seland 2016. E. H. Seland, Ships of the Desert and Ships of the Sea. Palmyra in the World Trade of the First Three Centuries CE (Wiesbaden 2016)

Seland 2017. E. H. Seland, The Iconography of Caravan Trade in Palmyra and the Roman Near East, in: A. H. Sørensen – T. Long (eds.), Positions and Professions in Palmyra, Palmyrene Studies 2, Scientia Danica, Series H, Humanistica 4, 9 (Copenhagen 2017) 106–114

Seland 2019. E. H. Seland, The Trade of Palmyra, in: A.-M. Nielsen – R. Raja (eds.), The Road to Palmyra (Copenhagen 2019) 127–136

Seyrig 1934. H. Seyrig, Antiquités syriennes: 17. Bas-reliefs monumentaux du temple de Bêl à Palmyre, Syria 15, 1934, 155–186

Seyrig 1937. H. Seyrig, Antiquités syriennes, Syria 18, 1937, 1–53

Seyrig 1940. H. Seyrig, Antiquités syriennes, Syria 21, 1940, 277–337

Seyrig 1941. H. Seyrig, Antiquités syriennes, Syria 22, 1941, 218–270

Seyrig 1950. H. Seyrig, Palmyra and the East, JRS 40, 1950, 1–7

Seyrig 1951. H. Seyrig, Le repas des morts et le ›Banquet Funèbre‹ a Palmyre, AAS 1, 1951, 1–11

Seyrig et al. 1975. H. Seyrig – R. Amy – E. Will, Le temple de Bel à Palmyre (Paris 1975)

Sherif-Shaban 2014. K. Sherif-Shaban, Banquets in Ancient Egypt, Heritage. Journal of Multidisciplinary Studies in Archaeology 2, 2014: 474–480: <http://www.heritageuniversityofkerala.com/JournalPDF/Volume2/474-480.pdf> (06.05.2022)

Shifman 2014. I. S. Shifman, The Palmyrene Tax Tariff, trans. by S. Khobnya and ed. by J. F. Healey, Journal of Semitic Studies Supplement 33 (Oxford 2014)

Sigismund-Nielsen 2013. H. Sigismund-Nielsen, Slave and Lower-Class Roman Children, in: J. Evans Grubbs – Tim Parkin, The Oxford Handbook of Childhood and Education in the Classical World: <10.1093/oxfordhb/9780199781546.013.014> (18.11.2021)

Silver et al. 2018. M. Silver, G. Fangi, and A. Denker. Reviving Palmyra in Multiple Dimensions. Images, Ruins and Cultural Memory (Dunbeath 2018)

Simonsen 1889. D. Simonsen, Skulpturer og Indskrifter fra Palmyra i Ny Carlsberg Glyptotek (Copenhagen 1889)

Şimşek 2013. M. Şimşek, Kibyra Yer Alti Oda Mezarlari: Mimari Ve Tipoloji (unpublished doctoral thesis Süleyman Demirel Üniversitesi 2013): <https://tez.yok.gov.tr/UlusalTezMerkezi/tezDetay.jsp?id=FNoWoie5JsV05lfEE0cXZQ&no=_TvUDChrGnfWego JfySU1A> (16.12.2022)

Sion – Rapuano 2010. O. Sion – Y. Rapuano, Ono: Final Report, Hadashot Arkheologiyot: Excavations and Surveys in Israel / 1002–997, 2010, 122, חדשות ארכיאולוגיות: חפירות וסקרים בישראל

Smith II 2013. A. M. Smith II, Roman Palmyra. Identity, Community, and State Formation (Oxford 2013)

Sokolowski 2014. L. Sokolowski, Portraying the Literacy of Palmyra. The Evidence of Funerary Sculpture and Its Interpretation, EtTrav 27, 2014, 375–403

Sollberger 1950. E. Sollberger, Les stèles de Palmyre, Les Musées de Genève. Bulletin mensuel des musées et collections de la ville de Genève 7, 1950, 2

Sommer 2005. M. Sommer, Roms orientalische Steppengrenze. Palmyra – Edessa – Dura-Europos – Hatra. Eine Kulturgeschichte von Pompeius bis Diocletian (Stuttgart 2005)

Sommer 2017. M. Sommer, Palmyra. Biographie einer verlorenen Stadt (Darmstadt 2017)

Sommer 2018. M. Sommer, Palmyra. A History (London 2018)

Sommer 2020. M. Sommer, Inter duo imperia. Palmyra between East and West, Oriens et Occidens, 31 (Stuttgart 2020)

Spanu et al. 1992–1993. M. Spanu – G. Bejor – E. Equini Schneider, Nuove ricerche nella Mesopotamia settentrionale, Scienze dell Antichità 6–7, 1992–1993, 343–385

Spivey 2013. N. Spivey, Greek Sculpture (Cambridge 2013)

Stamatopoulou 2016. M. Stamatopoulou, The Banquet Motif on the Funerary Stelai from Demetrias, in: C. M. Draycott — M. Stamatopoulou (eds.), Dining and Death. Interdisciplinary Perspectives on the ›Funerary Banquet‹ in Ancient Art, Burial and Belief (Leuven 2016) 405–480

Starcky 1941. J. Starcky, Palmyre: Guide archéologique, MelBeyrouth 24, 1941, 5–68

Starcky 1949. J. Starcky, Inventaire des inscriptions de Palmyre, Fascicule 10. L'Agora (Damascus 1949)

Starcky 1955. J. Starcky, Inscriptions palmyréniennes conservés au Musée de Beyrouth, Bulletin du Musée de Beyrouth 12, 1955, 29–44

Stark 1971. J. K. Stark, Personal Names in Palmyrene Inscriptions (Oxford 1971)

Stauffer 2010. A. Stauffer, Kleidung in Palmyra: Neue Fragen an alte Funde, in: B. Bastl – V. Gassner – U. Muss (eds.), Zeitreisen. Syrien, Palmyra, Rom. Festschrift für Andreas Schmidt-Colinet zum 65. Geburtstag (Vienna 2010) 209–218

Stauffer 2012. A. Stauffer, Dressing the Dead in Palmyra in the Second and Third Centuries AD, in: M. Carroll – J. P. Wild (eds.), Dressing the Dead in Classical Antiquity (Stroud 2012) 89–98

Stauffer 2013. A. Stauffer, Kleidung und Tracht in Palmyra, in: M. Tellenbach – R. Schulz – A. Wieczorek (eds.), Die Macht der Toga. DressCode im Römischen Weltreich (Regensburg 2013) 127–131

Steding 2022. J. Steding, Carvers and Customers in Roman Palmyra. The Production Economy of Limestone Loculus Reliefs (Turnhout 2022)

Stefanidou-Tiveriou 2014. Th. Stefanidou-Tiveriou, Die lokalen Sarkophage aus Thessaloniki (Ruhpolding 2014)

Stoneman 1992. R. Stoneman, Palmyra and Its Empire. Zenobia's Revolt against Rome (Ann Arbor 1993)

Strzygowski 1901. J. Strzygowski, Orient oder Rom. Beitrag zur Geschichte der spätantiken und frühchristlichen Kunst (Leipzig 1901)

Stucky 1973. R. A. Stucky, Prêtres syriens. 1. Palmyre, Syria 50, 1973, 163–180

Stylianou – Schollmeyer 2007. A. Stylianou – P. Schollmeyer, Dynastensarkophage mit Szenischen Reliefs aus Byblos und Zypern II. Der Sarkophag aus Amathous al Beispiel kontaktinduzierten Wandels (Andreas Stylianou), Der Sarkophag aus Golgoi zur Grabreprasentation eines zyprischen Stadtkonigs (Patrick Schollmeyer) (Mainz 2007)

Taha 1982. A. Taha, Men's Costume in Palmyra, AAS 32, 1982, 117–132

Tanabe 1986. K. Tanabe, Sculptures of Palmyra I (Tokyo 1986)

Taylor 2001. G. K. Taylor, An Annotated Index of Dated Palmyrene Aramaic Texts, Journal of Semitic Studies 46:2, 2001, 203–219

Taylor 2020. P. Taylor, Iconology and Iconography, in: Oxford Bibliographies: <https://doi.org/10.1093/OBO/9780195399301-0161>

Teixidor 1966. J. Teixidor, Monuments palmyréniens divers, Mélanges de l'Université Saint-Joseph 42:2, 1966, 177–179

Teixidor 2001. J. Teixidor, Bas-relief d'Abgal et Achar, in: J. Charles-Gaffiot – H. Lavagne – J.-M. Hofman (eds.), Moi, Zénobie reine de Palmyre (Milan 2001) 268

Terpak – Bonfitto. Terpak, F. – P. L. Bonfitto, The Legacy of Ancient Palmyra: <https://www.getty.edu/research/exhibitions_events/exhibitions/palmyra/exhibition.html> (06.05.2022)

Terrill 2017. W. A. Terrill, Antiquities Destruction and Illicit Sales as Sources of ISIS Funding and Propaganda (Carlisle 2017)

Thomsen 2021. R. Randeris Thomsen, Unlocking a Mystery? The Keys in Palmyrene Funerary Portraiture, in: M. K. Heyn – R. Raja (eds.), Individualizing the Dead. Attributes in Palmyrene Funerary Sculpture (Turnhout 2021) 51–62

Toynbee 1966. J. M. C. Toynbee, Death and Burial in the Roman World (Baltimore 1966)

Treister 2007. M. Y. Treister, The Toreutics of Colchis in the 5th–4th Centuries BC. Local Traditions, Outside Influences, Innovations, in: A. I. Ivanchik – V. Lič'eli, Achaemenid Culture and Local Traditions in Anatolia, Southern Caucasus and Iran (Leiden 2007) 67–108

Trümper 1998. M. Trümper, Wohnen in Delos. Eine baugeschichtliche Untersuchung zum Wandel der Wohnkulture in hellenistischer Zeit, Internationale Archäologie 46 (Rahden 1998)

Tsimpidou-Aulonitou 1986. M. Tsimpidou-Aulonitou, Ένας νέος μακεδονικός τάφος στη Θεσσαλονίκη, Μακεδονικά [Makedonika] 25, 117–142

Ulrich 2007. R. B. Ulrich, Roman Woodworking (New Haven 2007)

Uspensky 1902. E. I. Uspensky, Archaeological Monuments Syria (in Russian), Bulletin de l'institut archéologique russe de Constantinople 7, 1902, 93–207

van der Lans et al. 2017. B. van der Lans – E. H. Seland – H. F. Teigen, Journeys to Tadmor. History and Cultural Heritage in Palmyra and the Middle East (Bergen 2017)

Veenhof 2013. K. R. Veenhof, The Archives of Old Assyrian Traders: Their Nature, Functions and Use, in: M. Faraguna (ed.), Archives and Archival Documents in Ancient Societies. Legal Documents in Ancient Societies IV, Trieste 30 September – 1 October 2011 (Trieste 2013) 27–71

Vendries 2016. C. Vendries, Les Romains et l'image du rhinoceros les limites de la resemblance, Archeol. Class. 67, 2016, 279–340

Venit 2002. M. S. Venit, Monumental Tombs of Ancient Alexandria. The Theater of the Dead (Cambridge 2002)

Vessberg 1956. O. Vessberg, The Swedish Cyprus Expedition. The Hellenistic and Roman Periods in Cyprus (Stockholm 1956)

Vermeule 1964. C. C. Vermeule, Greek and Roman Portraits in North American Collections Open to the Public: A Survey of Important Monumental Likeness in Marble and Bronze Which Have Not Been Published Extensively, PAPS 108:2, 1964, 99–134

Vermeule 1981. C. C. Vermeule, Greek and Roman Sculpture in America. Masterpieces in Public Collections in the United States and Canada (Berkeley 1981)

Vibert-Guigue 2019. C. Vibert-Guigue, Nouvelles bases d'approche, in: H. Eristov – C. Vibert-Guigue – W. al-Asʿad – N. Sarkis (eds.), Le tombeau des trois frères à Palmyre. Mission archéologique franco-syrienne 2004–2009 (Beirut 2019) 74–78

Vigneau 1936. A. Vigneau, Encyclopédie photographique de l'art. Le Musée du Louvre II. Mésopotamie (suite), Canaan, Chypre, Grèce (Paris 1936)

Vogüe 1868. M. de Vogüe, Syrie Centrale. Inscriptions sémitiques (Paris 1868)

Waddington 1870. W.-H. Waddington, Inscriptions grecques et latines de la Syrie (Paris 1870)

Wadeson 2014. L. Wadeson, Funerary Portrait of a Palmyrene Priest, Records of the Canterbury Museum 28, 2014, 49–59

Waelkens 1982. M. Waelkens, Dokimeion. Die Werkstatt der repräsentativen kleinasiatischen Sarkophage. Chronologie und Typologie ihrer Produktion (Berlin 1982)

Waelkens 2021. M. Waelkens, The Trade in Marble and Other Stone in the Eastern Mediterranean, in: R. Raja – J. Steding (eds.), Production Economy in Greater Roman Syria. Trade Networks and Production Processes (Turnhout 2021) 123–154

Waliszewski – Wicenciak 2015. T. Waliszewski – U. Wicenciak, Chhim, Lebanon: A Roman and Late Antique Village in the Sidon Hinterland, J. East. Mediterr. Archaeol. 3, 2015, 372–395

Wartke 1991. R.-B. Wartke, Palmyrenische Plastik im Vorderasiatischen Museum, FuB 31, 1991, 67–100

Watzinger 1932. C. Watzinger, Zur Geschichte des Grabturms, in: T. Wiegand (ed.), Palmyra. Ergebnisse der Expeditionen von 1902 und 1917 (Berlin 1932) 77–84

Watzinger – Wulzinger 1932. C. Watzinger – K. Wulzinger, Die Nekropolen, in: T. Wiegand (ed.), Palmyra. Ergebnisse der Expeditionen von 1902 und 1917 (Berlin 1932) 44–76

Wenning 2001. R. Wenning, Hauranite Sculpture, in: J. M. Padgett (ed.), Roman Sculpture in the Art Museum Princeton University (Princeton 2001) 312–347

White et al. 2002. D. White – A. B. Brownlee – I. B. Romano – J. M. Turfa, Guide to the Etruscan and Roman Worlds at the University of Pennsylvania Museum of Archaeology and Anthropology (Philadelphia 2002)

Wiegand 1932. T. Wiegand (ed.), Palmyra. Ergebnisse der Expeditionen von 1902 und 1917 (Berlin 1932)

Wielgosz 1997. D. Wielgosz, Funeralia Palmyrena, Studia Palmyreńskie 10, 1997, 69–75

Wielgosz 2001. D. Wielgosz, Sarcofagi attici a Palmira, RdA 25, 2001, 167–176

Wielgosz 2010. D. Wielgosz, Les sculptures en marbre à Palmyre, Studia Palmyreńskie 11, 2010, 75–106

Wielgosz-Rondolino 2016a. D. Wielgosz-Rondolino, Orient et Occident unis par enchantement dans la pierre sculptée. La sculpture figurative de Palmyre, in: M. al-Maqdissi – E. Ishag (eds.), La Syrie et le désastre archéologique du Proche-Orient. ›Palmyre cité martyre‹ (Beirut 2016) 66–82

Wielgosz-Rondolino 2016b. D. Wielgosz-Rondolino, Palmyrene Portraits from the Temple of Allat: New Evidence, in: A. Kropp – R. Raja (eds.), The World of Palmyra, Palmyrene Studies 1, Scientia Danica, Series H, Humanistica 4, 6 (Copenhagen 2016) 116–179

Will 1949. E. Will, La tour funéraire de Palmyre, Syria 26, 1949, 87–116

Will 1951. E. Will, Le relief de la tour de Khitôt et le banquet funéraire à Palmyre, Syria 28, 1951, 70–100

Will 1992. E. Will, Les Palmyréniens. La Venise des sables (Paris 1992)

Wood 1753. R. Wood, The Ruins of Palmyra. Otherwise Tedmor, in the Desart (London 1753)

Wrede 1990. H. Wrede, Der Sarkophagdeckel eines Mädchens in Malibu und die frühen Klinensarkophage Roms, Athens und Kleinasiens, Roman Funerary Monuments in the J. Paul Getty Museum 1. Occasional Papers on Antiquities 6 (Malibu 1990) 15–46

Wrede 2001. H. Wrede, Senatorische Sarkophage Roms. Der Beitrag des Senatorenstandes zur römischen Kunst der hohen und späten Kaiserzeit, Monumenta artis Romanae 29 (Mainz 2001)

Wright 2004. J. C. Wright, A Survey of Evidence for Feasting in Mycenaean Society, Hesperia 73, 2004, 133–178

Yale University Art Gallery 1992. Yale University Art Gallery, Handbook of the Collections Yale University Art Gallery (New Haven 1992)

Yatsenko 2013. S. Yatsenko, Some Notes on Parthian Costume Studies, Parthica 15, 2013, 117–125

Yon 2001a. J.-B. Yon, Banquet funéraire, in: J. Charles-Gaffiot – H. Lavagne – J.-M. Hofman (eds.), Moi, Zénobie reine de Palmyre (Milan 2001) 343–344

Yon 2001b. J.-B. Yon, Femme assise sur une cathèdre, in: J. Charles-Gaffiot – H. Lavagne – J.-M. Hofman (eds.), Moi, Zénobie reine de Palmyre (Milan 2001) 355

Yon 2001c. J.-B. Yon, Stèle funéraire de Malê et Bôlayâ, in: J. Charles-Gaffiot – H. Lavagne – J.-M. Hofman (eds.), Moi, Zénobie reine de Palmyre (Milan 2001) 367–368

Yon 2002. J.-B. Yon, Les notables de Palmyre (Beirut 2002)

Yon 2012. J.-B. Yon, Inscriptions grecques et latines de la Syrie XVII, 1 (Beirut 2012)

Yon 2013. J.-B. Yon, L'epigraphie palmyrénienne depuis PAT, 1996–2011, Studia Palmyreńskie 12, 2013, 333–379

Yon 2018. J.-B. Yon, Les tombes palmyréniennes étaient-elles des lieux de culte? Éléments de réponse archéologiques et épigraphiques, in: M.-D. Nenna – S. Huber – W. Van Andringa (eds.), Constituer la tombe, honorer les défunts en Méditerranée antique (Alexandria 2018) 201–218

Yon 2019a. J.-B. Yon, Inscriptions araméennes, in: H. Eristov – C. Vibert-Guigue – W. al-Asʿad – N. Sarkis (eds.), Le tombeau des trois frères à Palmyre, Mission archéologique franco-syrienne 2004–2009 (Beirut 2019) 134–140

Yon 2019b. J.-B. Yon, Palmyra and Its Elites, in: A.-M. Nielsen – R. Raja (eds.), The Road to Palmyra (Copenhagen 2019) 91–108

Zahran 2004. Y. Zahran, Zenobia between Reality and Legend, Minerva 15:1, 2004, 29–32

Zanker 2010. P. Zanker, Roman Art (Los Angeles 2010)

Zanker – Ewald 2012. P. Zanker – B. C. Ewald, Living with Myths. The Imagery of Roman Sarcophagi (Oxford 2012)

Zarmakoupi 2014. M. Zarmakoupi, Designing for Luxury on the Bay of Naples Villas and Landscapes (c. 100 BCE – 79 CE) (Oxford 2014)

Zimmermann 1991. J.-L. Zimmermann, Ancient Art from the Barbier-Mueller Museum (New York 1991)

Zouhdi 1983. B. Zouhdi, La femme dans l'art de Palmyre, DaM 1, 1983, 315–316

Catalogue

Tombs Dated by Inscription

A.D. 41

TOWER TOMB NO. 44, TOWER OF KÎTÔT

1. FOUNDER BANQUETING RELIEF

DATABASE NUMBER: InSitu043.
LOCATION: Palmyra, in situ. Destroyed in 2015.
CONTEXT: West necropolis, Valley of the Tombs. Tower tomb no. 44, tower of Kîtôt.
ACQUISITION HISTORY: —
MEASUREMENTS: Height: 280 cm. Width: 153 cm.
MATERIAL: Limestone.
PRESERVATION: The lower left side of the relief is broken off. The surface is weathered. Portrait A: The neck and head of the figure are broken off. The arms are chipped. Portrait B: The face and torso are heavily chipped. The surface is weathered. Portrait C: The head and the lower arms of the figure are heavily chipped. The surface is weathered. Portrait D: The neck and head, the left arm, and the feet of the figure are broken off. The left shoulder is chipped.
TECHNICAL DESCRIPTION: Traces of red, turquoise, and black pigment have been detected on the vines, on the background, and on the kline.
DATE: A.D. 41 (dated by inscription).
REFERENCES: Will 1949, 94 f. fig. 8; Will 1951, 70 f. 74 f. fig. 1 pls. 7. 8; Morehart 1956–1957, 65–68 cat. 24 fig. 22; Gawlikowski 1970a, 71 f. fig. 36; Colledge 1976, 74. 83. 101. 114. 120. 131. 135 f. 146 f. 158. 209 f. 233. 239 fig. 37; Parlasca 1984, 284; Tanabe 1986, 29 pl. 177; Ruprechtsberger 1987, 112 fig. 95; Schmidt-Colinet 1996, 366 f. 475 cat. 62 fig. 198; Wielgosz 1997, 74 pl. 9, 2; Gawlikowski 2005, 46. 48. 53 f. fig. 6; Gawlikowski 2010a, 67; Henning 2013a, 161. 163 f. figs. 4. 15; Henning 2013b, 185 f. 312 f. cat. W 8 pl. 41, a. b; Wadeson 2014, 50 f. pl. 7; Audley-Miller 2016, 568 fig. 5; Wielgosz-Rondolino 2016a, 74 fig. 11; Krag 2018, 21 n. 132; 32 n. 61; 407 cat. 905. Inscription: Vogüe 1868, 29 cat. 33; Will 1951, 70 n. 1; Krag 2018, 407 cat. 905; Taylor 2001, 209; Yon 2002, 218.

OBJECT DESCRIPTION

The object is placed inside a niche and is a rectangular plaque with an arched top. The edge of the niche is decorated with a vine scroll with grapes and leaves. The relief has four figures: a male figure reclining on a kline, and three standing figures behind him; two males and a female. The kline has turned legs. The foot is broken off. Above is a stem-like element, a reeded bell-shaped element, a neck, a thin torus, a ball, a thin torus, a bell-shaped element, and above the kline stretcher is a reversed bell-shaped finial. The frame of the kline is decorated with rectangular panels. Over the kline is a mattress decorated with three wide bands divided by beaded borders. The reclining figure rests on a round cushion decorated with wide bands (details unclear).

Note: The tower tomb was destroyed in 2015 (Cuneo et al. 2015, 6).

INSCRIPTION

SCRIPT: Palmyrene Aramaic.
LOCATION ON RELIEF: Between the legs of the kline.
TRANSCRIPTION: [BYRḤ SYWN] ŠNT 352 | [ṢLMY ʾLN] DY KYTWT BR | [TYMRṢW WDY MYŠ]ʾ BRT | [MLKW ʾTT]H WDY LŠMŠ | [BRH WDY ŠLMN] BRH WDY | MLKW ʿLYMH.
TRANSLATION: In the month Sîwan year 352, these statues of Kîtôt son of Taîmarṣû and of Maîšâ daughter of Malkû, his wife, and of Lišamš, his son, and of Šalman, his son, and of Malkû, his servant/slave (A.D. 41).

CIS no. 4115bis; PAT no. 0464.

PORTRAIT A: STANDING MALE

The figure is shown frontally. The right arm is bent and held to the torso; the left arm falls along the side. The lower legs are obscured by the reclining figure.

He wears a tunic. The tunic has a wide, round neckline. The tunic has a band belt at the waist, knotted at the centre with the ends looped under on either side of the waist. The belt creates a slight overfold. The folds of the tunic are indicated by curving grooves over the chest, oblique grooves over the arms, and vertical ones over the legs.

He carries a small jug in his right hand in front of the chest, and a ladle in his lowered left hand (both visible in outline).

PORTRAIT B: STANDING PRIEST

The figure is shown frontally. The right arm is bent in front of the torso, the left falls along the side. The legs are obscured by the reclining figure.

He wears a tall, cylindrical, flat-top headdress: a Palmyrene priestly hat (visible in outline).

He wears a tunic and a himation. The himation's folds are rendered by oblique grooves over the chest and legs, and horizontal over the waist, indicating the wrapping of the himation around

Cat. 1

the waist. He wears a narrow band belt at the waist, knotted at the centre.

PORTRAIT C: STANDING FEMALE, MAÎŠÂ

The figure is shown frontally. The lower body is obscured by the reclining figure.

She wears a veil that falls over both shoulders.

She wears a tunic and a himation. The tunic has a long, tight-fitting sleeves. The himation crosses the chest diagonally and covers the waist and legs. It is fastened at the left shoulder. The folds of the himation are rendered by oblique grooves.

PORTRAIT D: RECLINING MALE

The figure's torso is shown in a three-quarter view. The arms and right leg are shown in profile. The left leg is shown frontally. The right arm is extended along the side; the left arm is bent and held in front of the torso. The legs are extended along the mattress.

He wears a tunic, a himation, and ›Parthian-style‹ trousers. The tunic has a wide, round neckline and long, tight-fitting sleeves. The folds of the tunic are rendered by curving grooves. Over the tunic, he wears a himation that is wrapped around the waist and covers the upper legs and knees. One end of the himation falls over the left leg in a zigzag-shaped fold. He wears trousers with a central, plain band extending downwards in the middle.

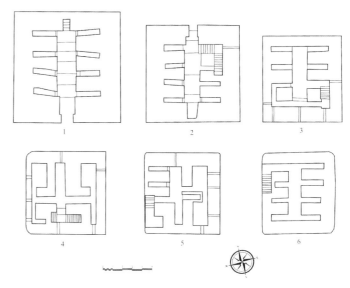

Plan of tower tomb no. 44, tower of Kîtôt.

Tower tomb no. 44, tower of Kîtôt, graphic reconstruction of relief, Pl. 39.

Tower tomb no. 44, tower of Kîtôt.

A.D. 73

TOWER TOMB NO. 194, TOWER OF ʿOGEÎLÛ

2. FOUNDER BANQUETING RELIEF

DATABASE NUMBER: InSitu174.
LOCATION: Palmyra, in situ.
CONTEXT: South-east necropolis. Tower tomb no. 194, tower of ʿOgeîlû.
ACQUISITION HISTORY: —
MEASUREMENTS: Height: 66 cm. Width: 108 cm.
MATERIAL: Limestone, white/yellow.
PRESERVATION: The upper part of the relief is broken off. The head, neck, shoulders, and right hand of the figure are broken off. The surface is weathered.
TECHNICAL DESCRIPTION: —
DATE: A.D. 73 (dated by inscription).
REFERENCES: Watzinger 1932, 77; Will 1951, 84 fig. 3; Gawlikowski 1970b, 81 fig. 13; Wielgosz 1997, 74 pl. 10, 1; Henning 2013b, 286. Inscription: Gawlikowski 1970a, 187 cat. 13; Taylor 2001, 210.

OBJECT DESCRIPTION
The object is rectangular in shape with a hemispherical upper edge. The relief depicts a male figure reclining on a kline with a mattress. The fabric and texture of the mattress are indicated by curving grooves. On the left side of the kline there is a fulcrum decorated with a figure (portrait B). The details of the kline, both stretcher and legs are unclear. There appear to be figures on the relief ground, but the details are unclear, and it is impossible to determine the number of figures.

INSCRIPTION
SCRIPT: Palmyrene Aramaic.
LOCATION ON RELIEF: Between the legs of the kline.
TRANSCRIPTION: ṢLMYʾ ʾLN DY ʿGYLW BR ʿGʾ BR MQYMW | BR ḤDWDN WDY ʾMTḤʾ BRT BWNʾ ʾTTH | TDMRY[ʾ] WDY ʿGʾ BRH DY BN ʾ [B]ḤYWHY LYQRH | WLY[QR B]NWHY DY BT ʿLMʾ BYRḤ NYSN ŠNT | [3]84.
TRANSLATION: These images of ʿOgeîlû son of ʿOggâ son of Moqîmû son of Ḥaddûdan and of Amataḥâ daughter of Bônnê, his wife, the Palmyrenes, and of ʿOggâ his son who built during his life, in his honour and in the honour of his sons, the house of eternity, in the month of Nîsan, year 384 (A.D. 73).

Cat. 2

CIS no. 4193; PAT no. 0549.

PORTRAIT A: RECLINING MALE

The figure's torso is shown in a three-quarter view. The arms and legs are shown in profile. The right arm is bent and extended to the side. The right leg is bent and raised; the left leg is extended and rests along the mattress. The right foot is obscured by the left leg.

He wears a tunic and a himation. The folds of the tunic are rendered by curving grooves. Over the tunic, he wears a himation that is wrapped around the waist and covers the legs.

The right hand rests on the right knee.

PORTRAIT B: BUST IN FULCRUM

The figure is an armless bust in the fulcrum (details unclear).

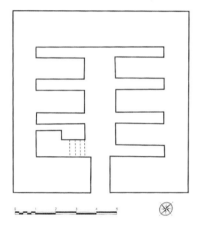

Plan of tower tomb no. 194, tower of ʿOgeîlû.

A.D. 103

TOWER TOMB NO. 13, TOWER OF ELAHBEL

3. FOUNDER BANQUETING RELIEF

DATABASE NUMBER: InSitu114.
LOCATION: Palmyra, in situ. Destroyed in 2015.
CONTEXT: West necropolis. Valley of the Tombs. Tower tomb no. 13, tower of Elahbel.
ACQUISITION HISTORY: —
MEASUREMENTS: —
MATERIAL: Limestone.
PRESERVATION: Only the kline and the mattress are preserved. The upper right corner and a part of the upper side of the mattress are chipped. The stretcher of the kline and the left kline leg are chipped.
TECHNICAL DESCRIPTION: —
DATE: A.D. 103 (dated by inscription).
REFERENCES: Kammerer 1929, 310 n. 2 pl. 116, 3; Watzinger 1932, 48; Will 1949a, 97 f. 104. 111 f. 115; Gawlikowski 1970a, 41. 87–91. 106 fig. 46; Milik 1972, 182; Parlasca 1984, 284 f.; Yon 2002, 204; Henning 2013a, 152–154 pl. 10, a; 11, c; Silver et al. 2018, 177 f. fig. 9.25. Inscription: Vogüé 1868, 41 cat. 37; Gawlikowski 1970a, 191 cat. 28; Milik 1972, 163. 245 fig. 1; Yon 2012, 319 f. cat. 407.

OBJECT DESCRIPTION

The object is placed inside a niche and is rectangular in shape. The edge of the niche is decorated with a vine scroll with grapes and leaves. The object depicts a kline with a thick mattress. The mattress has four wide bands decorated with running scrolls and rosettes. Curving grooves indicate the texture of the fabric. On the left side, the kline has a fulcrum with a bust (portrait A). The left end of the stretcher of the kline is decorated with a rectangular panel. The kline legs are turned. The legs are composed of a plinth and above is a concave quarter, a bell-shaped element, a concave quarter, a thin torus, a ball, a thin torus, and above the stretcher is a thin torus finial. Between the kline legs, five large rosettes are depicted. On top of the mattress, on the left side, two oblong, plain objects are preserved, possibly pillows.

Parlasca 1984 writes that there is evidence for a lid relief with a banquet scene on top of the kline.

NOTE: The tower tomb was destroyed in 2015 (Cuneo et al. 2015, 6).

INSCRIPTIONS

INSCRIPTION 1

SCRIPT: Ancient Greek.
LOCATION ON RELIEF: On a tabula ansata, on the façade of the tomb, approximately two–three metres below relief.
TRANSCRIPTION: Τὸ μνημεῖον ἔκτισαν Ελαβηλος Μ- | ανναιος Σοχαιεις Μαλιχος Οθαβαλ- | λαθου τοῦ Μανναιου τοῦ Ελαβηλου αὐτ- | οῖς καὶ υἱοῖς ἔτους διυʹ μηνὸς Ξανδικοῦ.
TRANSLATION: This monument was built by Elabelos, Mannaios, Sochaieis, Malichos, the sons of Ouaballathos son of Mannaios son of Elabelos, for him and for his sons, in the year 414, month of Xandikos.

INSCRIPTION 2

SCRIPT: Palmyrene Aramaic.
LOCATION ON RELIEF: On a tabula ansata, on the façade of the tomb, approximately two–three metres below relief.
TRANSCRIPTION: QBRʾ DNH BNʾ ʾLHBL WMʿNY WŠKYY | WMLKW BNY WHBLT BR MʿNY ʾLHBL | LHWN WLBNYHWN BYRḤ NYSN ŠNT 414.
TRANSLATION: This tomb was built by Elahbel and Maʿnaî and Šokaîaî and Malikû, the sons of Wahballat son of Maʿnaî Elahbel, for him and for his sons, in the month of Nîsan, year 414.

CIS no. 4134; PAT no. —.

PORTRAIT

The figure is an armless bust in the fulcrum (details unclear).

TOMBS DATED BY INSCRIPTION 183

Cat. 3

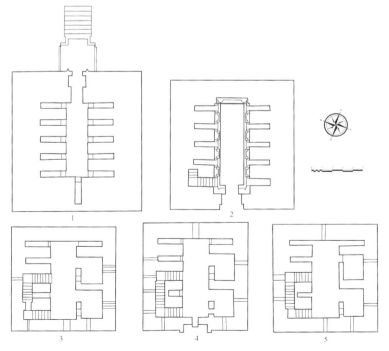

Plan of tower tomb no. 13, tower of Elahbel.

Tower tomb no. 13, tower of Elahbel.

A.D. 128

TOWER TOMB NO. N206

4. SARCOPHAGUS BOX WITH PORTRAIT BUSTS AND STANDING FIGURES

Cat. 4

Tower tomb no. N206, Pl. 40.

DATABASE NUMBER: InSitu095.
LOCATION: Palmyra, in situ.
CONTEXT: West necropolis. Tower tomb no. N206.
ACQUISITION HISTORY: —
MEASUREMENTS: Height: 80 cm. Width: 206 cm.
MATERIAL: Limestone.
PRESERVATION: The box is weathered. The upper part of the front side of the box has broken off. Portrait A: The head is broken off. The surface of the chest is weathered. Portrait B: The head is broken off. The surface is weathered. Portrait C: The surface is weathered. Portrait D: The surface is heavily weathered. Portrait E: The head is broken off. The surface is weathered.
TECHNICAL DESCRIPTION: —
DATE: A.D. 128 (dated by inscription).
REFERENCES: al-As'ad 2013, 16 fig. 1. Inscription: al-As'ad 2013, 16.

OBJECT DESCRIPTION
The sarcophagus box is rectangular in shape and is rendered as a kline. The kline legs appear to be turned (details unclear). Five figures are depicted on the box: a bust, a standing figure, a bust, a standing figure, and a bust.

INSCRIPTION
SCRIPT: Palmyrene Aramaic.
LOCATION ON RELIEF: On the podium that supports the sarcophagus box.
TRANSCRIPTION: —
TRANSLATION: —

CIS no. —; PAT no. —; al-As'ad 2013, 16.

COMMENT: According to al-As'ad 2013, 16, the inscription »is dated to November AD 128. The text consists of a long genealogy of the sarcophagus owner«.

PORTRAIT A: BUST
Folds of a tunic are rendered.

PORTRAIT B: STANDING FIGURE

PORTRAIT C: BUST
Fold of garments are visible, possibly from a tunic and a chlamys. The figure holds two objects against the chest, possibly a flask and a circular box.

PORTRAIT D: STANDING FIGURE

PORTRAIT E: BUST
The figure holds two objects against the chest, possibly a flask and a circular box.

A.D. 140/141

CONTEXT UNKNOWN

5. FRAGMENT OF SARCOPHAGUS BOX WITH PORTRAIT BUST

Cat. 5, Pl. 41

DATABASE NUMBER: PrivDeratiyeh001.
LOCATION: Deratiyeh, private collection.
CONTEXT: —
ACQUISITION HISTORY: —
MEASUREMENTS: —
MATERIAL: Limestone, white/yellow.
PRESERVATION: The left side and a small fragment of the right side of the relief are broken off. The upper part of the relief is very fragmented. A large crack runs diagonally across the relief from the right to the left side at the height of the neck of the portrait. The surface is weathered. The neck is fragmented. The left shoulder, brooch, and clothing are chipped.
TECHNICAL DESCRIPTION: —
DATE: A.D. 140/141.
REFERENCES: Personal communication with Annie Sartre.

OBJECT DESCRIPTION

The object is polygonal in shape with a rectangular main body and a triangular top and depicts a female bust. A cyma recta moulding at the upper and lower part of the rectangular main body creates a frame for the figure. The triangular top is decorated with a projecting moulding.

INSCRIPTION
SCRIPT: Palmyrene Aramaic.
LOCATION ON RELIEF: To the left of the portrait at the height of the head.
TRANSCRIPTION: 4 | +50 | +2.
TRANSLATION: 452.

CIS no. —; PAT no. —.

PORTRAIT

The figure is shown frontally. Her head is turned slightly to her right. The right arm is bent and raised to the height of the shoulder, while the left arm is bent and held in front of the torso. The arms appear small in relation to the body.

She wears three headdresses: a headband, a turban, and a veil. The headband is placed low on the forehead and is divided into rectangular, undecorated panels by vertical grooves. The turban is coiled. It is composed of three coiling bands, the folds indicated by oblique grooves. The veil is heavy. It falls over both shoulders and it is wrapped around her left arm. The folds of the veil are indicated by oblique grooves. Part of the hair is covered by the headdress: several strands of hair above the ears are brushed back over the headband and the edge of the turban and disappear under the veil. The individual strands of hair are indicated by incised lines. Her face is round. The eyebrows are curving, depicted as thin ridges, and starting from the root of the nose. The eyes are close-set, almond-shaped, and slanting with thick eyelids. The upper eyelids extend beyond the end of the lower ones. The irises and the pupils are indicated by concentric, incised circles. Only the earlobes are visible under the hair. The nose is straight and narrow with a wide base, incised alae, and carved nostrils. The mouth is small with thin lips. The chin is small and pointed. The neck is wide.

She wears a tunic and a himation. The tunic has a small, round neckline and long, tight-fitting sleeves. The folds of the tunic are indicated by wide, oblique grooves. Over the tunic, she wears a himation. It falls over the left shoulder, crosses the chest diagonally, and runs under the right arm. The folds of the himation are indicated by wide, oblique grooves. It is fastened at the shoulder with a brooch (details unclear). From the lower edge of the brooch, an L-shaped key is suspended by a band. The body and the bit are decorated with an incised X.

With her right hand, she holds the edge of the veil. The index finger is extended. With the left hand, she holds a conical object incised with fine, oblique lines, with a bowl-shaped tip, and a thick, short staff topped by a projecting disc and a round mass with a pattern of oblique, incised lines, and a small cylinder. These are reduced versions of a spindle and a distaff. The thumb, index, and middle finger are extended. The nails on both hands are indicated by fine, incised lines.

A.D. 142/143

HYPOGEUM OF THE THREE BROTHERS

6. COMPLETE SARCOPHAGUS RELIEF WITH BANQUETING SCENE

DATABASE NUMBER: InSitu031.
LOCATION: Palmyra, in situ.
CONTEXT: South-west necropolis. Hypogeum of the Three Brothers, south exedra, west wall.
ACQUISITION HISTORY: —
MEASUREMENTS: Height: 76 cm. Width: 174 cm.
MATERIAL: Limestone, white.
PRESERVATION: The lower mattress has been partly restored. The kline legs are fragmented. Portrait A: The head is broken off at the base of the neck. The right forearm and hand are broken off. A large crack runs diagonally across her chest and another one horizontally through the waist. Portrait B: Only a small piece of the lower body is preserved. Portrait C: The head is broken off at the base of the neck. The left arm and shoulder are broken off.
TECHNICAL DESCRIPTION: —

DATE: A.D. 142–143.
REFERENCES: Will 1951, 88 fig. 10; Kraeling 1961–1962, 15; Tanabe 1986, 31 pls. 224–226; Sadurska – Bounni 1994, 120 f. cat. 162 fig. 230; Krag – Raja 2017, 199 n. 24; 204 n. 72. 73; 205 n. 75. 76; 210 n. 107; 215 cat. 14; Krag 2018, 28 n. 9; 33 n. 78. 79. 84; 36 n. 112; 46 n. 198; 66 n. 382; 67 n. 4; 98 n. 28; 103 n. 74; 315 cat. 563. Inscription: Cantineau 1936, 354 f. cat. 27; Gawlikowski 1970a, 195 cat. 47; Sadurska – Bounni 1994, 120 f.; Krag 2018, 315 cat. 563; Yon 2019a, 135 cat. 1 pl. 57, 1.

OBJECT DESCRIPTION

The sarcophagus lid is rectangular in shape and depicts a seated female, a standing figure, and a reclining male. Beneath these figures is a box in the shape of a kline and two mattresses. The thin mattress at the top is decorated with an intersecting lozenges pattern with flowers in the lozenges. The lower one has three bands. The band in the middle is decorated with a floral motif between bands with lozenges. The bands at either end are decorated with a running scroll with rosettes with four or five petals, set between beaded bands, and bands with incised waves. Curving grooves indicate the texture of the lower mattress. The reclining figure rests along two cushions. The upper cushion is decorated with a central band with a

Cat. 6, Pl. 42

running scroll with five-petal rosettes. The lower cushion is decorated with a floral motif, set between beaded bands. The central stretcher of the kline is decorated with one rectangular indentation to the right. The kline has turned legs. Only the lower part of the kline legs is preserved: it is composed of a plinth and above is a convex quarter, a reversed bell-shaped element, a cyma recta, a concave quarter, and a thin torus. All the elements are decorated with diagonal reeding. The seated female sits on a cushion.

INSCRIPTION

SCRIPT: Palmyrene Aramaic.
LOCATION ON RELIEF: Above the sarcophagus, on the surrounding architrave.
TRANSCRIPTION: MQBRTʾ DH ʿBD MLʾ BR ṢʿDY BR MLʾ LH WLʾ<Ḥ>TH | WLBNWHY WLBNTH WLBNY BNWHY LʿLMʾ ŠNT 454.
TRANSLATION: This tomb which was made by Malê son of Ṣaʿadaî son of Malê for himself and for his sister? and for his sons and for his daughters and for the sons of his sons, for ever, year 454 (A.D. 142/143).

CIS no. —; PAT no. 2776.

COMMENTS: L.1: On the stone WLʾDTH (or WLʾRTH), but both words are unknown. ʾDTH could mean »his lady« (see PAT, p. 335, s.v.). With the correction ʾ<Ḥ>TH »his sister«, the meaning is at least probable.

SARCOPHAGUS LID

PORTRAIT A: SEATED FEMALE

The figure is shown frontally. The right arm is held along the body, the left arm is raised next to her shoulder. The legs are bent, slightly set apart with the knees rendered under the drapery. The right foot rests on the mattress, the left is obscured by the reclining figure to her left.

She wears a tunic. The ankle-length tunic has a wide, round neckline which leaves the upper part of the chest bare, and wide sleeves that reach to the elbows. The folds of the tunic are rendered by vertical and curving grooves. Another garment, possibly a fold of a veil, is visible in a diagonal line from her right side of the waist to her left side of the neck. One edge of the garment is scalloped. The toes of the right foot are visible under the garments. The nails are rendered by fine, incised lines.

With the left hand, she lightly pulls a diagonal fold of a garment. The nails are rendered by fine, incised lines.

PORTRAIT B: STANDING FIGURE

The figure is shown frontally. The legs are obscured by the reclining figure to the left.

The figure wears two garments. One garment, possibly a tunic, covers the lower body and legs. The folds are rendered by oblique grooves. Another garment, possibly a himation,

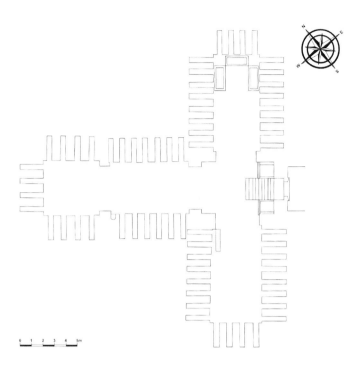

Plan of hypogeum of the Three Brothers.

is visible falling downwards on the right side of the figure. The folds of the garment are rendered in zigzag-shaped folds.

PORTRAIT C: RECLINING MALE, MALÊ

The figure is shown in frontal to three-quarter view. The feet appear large in relation to the body. The right arm is extended and rests on his raised right knee. The left arm may have rested against the cushions. The right leg of the figure is bent and the foot rests on the mattress. The left leg is bent under the right, with the knee pointing outwards. The lower left leg is obscured by the right leg.

He wears a ›Parthian-style‹ tunic, a chlamys, and ›Parthian-style‹ trousers. The tunic has long, tight-fitting sleeves and a small, round neckline decorated with a narrow, beaded band. The cuffs of the sleeves have a border decorated with a floral motif (details unclear). At the centre, the tunic has a wide band extending downwards and set between beaded bands. The central band is decorated with serrated leaves in an opposite arrangement on the stem. The tunic ends above the knees and has a lower border decorated with a running scroll with five-petal rosettes, set between two beaded bands at the hem. The folds of the tunic are rendered by curving, deep grooves. Over the tunic, he wears a chlamys that falls over both shoulders, and covers the upper part of his chest. One edge of the chlamys has a scalloped border decorated with five-petal rosettes, visible at the uppermost fold across the chest. The chlamys is fastened at the right shoulder with a circular brooch with a rosette within it (Colledge classification: g). A zigzag-shaped fold falls from under the brooch. A wide fold of the chlamys is falling across the cushion and on the mattress. The fold divides into two zigzag-shaped folds, with each edge tied into a small knot with tassels. The folds of the chlamys are indicated by deep, curving and oblique grooves. He also wears a plain band belt across the lower torso that is knotted at the centre with the ends looped under on either side of the waist. Along the right leg he has an object with a pointed end, a rectangular main body, and a lateral circle: a sheathed dagger. The trousers are visible from above the knees. Each trouser leg has a band that extends downwards in the middle, decorated with vine leaves that meander on the stem, set between beaded bands. The folds are rendered by wide, diagonal grooves. The trousers are tucked into his boots. The upper edge of the boot has a beaded band followed by a section decorated with an incised, wave line. The laces are tied into a knot. Three beaded lines extend out from under the knot. One extends towards the ankle joint and encircles a six-petal rosette. The other beaded line extends in a slightly curving line to the lower edge of the foot, while the last band extends to the toes. Incised circles, squares, and rhombi decorate the surface of the boot.

He holds a branch made up of lobed leaves, in his right hand. The midribs of the leaves are rendered by incised lines. The nails are rendered by fine, incised lines. The outline of an object, possibly a bowl, is visible at the centre of his chest.

A.D. 146/147

CONTEXT UNKNOWN

7. FRAGMENTS OF BANQUETING RELIEF

DATABASE NUMBER: NCG004 (7a) + NCG003 (7b).
LOCATION: Copenhagen, Ny Carlsberg Glyptotek, inv. no. IN 1160 and IN 1159.
CONTEXT: —
ACQUISITION HISTORY: Acquired by Puttmann in Syria.
MEASUREMENTS: 7a: Height: 80 cm. Width: 52 cm. Depth: 26.5 cm. Portrait A: Height of figure: 66 cm. Width of figure: 33.5 cm. Depth of figure: 12 cm. Height of head: 14 cm. Width of head: 13 cm. Depth of head: 12 cm. 7b: Height: 72.5 cm. Width: 84 cm. Depth: 22 cm. Portrait B: Height of figure: 67 cm. Width of figure: 84 cm. Depth of figure: 18 cm. Height of head: 24 cm. Width of head: 18.4 cm. Depth of head: 15 cm.
MATERIAL: Limestone, white/grey.
PRESERVATION: Composed of two non-joining fragments. 7a: There are small horizontal cracks on the surface of the background. A horizontal crack runs through the torso and there are several horizontal cracks running through the chair. The surface is lightly chipped, especially on the sides of the relief, the chair, the clothes, the face, and the foot of the male figure. 7b: The lower, right, and left part of the relief are missing. There are small horizontal cracks on the surface of the background of the relief. The surface is lightly chipped, especially on the arms and left hand, the face, and the top right side of the relief.
TECHNICAL DESCRIPTION: —
DATE: A.D. 146/147 (dated by inscription).
REFERENCES: 7a: Ingholt Archives, PS 38; Chabot 1922, 111. 121 cat. 50 pl. 27, 10; Ingholt 1928, 63 f. 93. f. 97. pl. 12, 1; Ingholt 1934, 35; Ingholt 1935, 68 n. 51; 109 n. 332; Will 1951, 89 n. 2; Champdor 1953, 55; el-Chehadeh 1972, 76 f. 96 n. 13; Colledge 1976, 63. 73 f. 124–126. 129. 131. 140. 142. 147. 155. 212. 217. 240. 246 pl. 98; Makowski 1985b, 122; Parlasca 1994, 304 fig. 5; Ploug 1995, 56–65 cat. 8; Wielgosz 1997, 71; Krag 2015, 109 fig. 2; Raja 2015b, 343–347 figs. 12. 15–16; Raja – Sørensen 2015b, 33. 35; Krag 2016, 188 f. fig. 5; Raja 2016a, 352 fig. 5; Krag – Raja 2017, 201 fig. 4; Raja 2017a, 213 fig. 19, 10; Raja 2017b, 125 fig. 8, 2; Raja 2017c, 15 fig. 9; Raja 2017d, 15 fig. 9; Raja 2017e, 334 f. fig. 7; Raja 2017i, 121 fig. 10; Raja 2017j, 420 fig. 4; Raja 2018a, 3 fig. 5; Raja 2018c, 91 fig. 3; Krag 2018, 16 n. 73; 33 n. 75. 77. 78; 41 n. 142. 143; 65 n. 377; 66 n. 382; 87 n. 182; 89 n. 204. 206; 240 cat. 278; Heyn – Raja 2019, 47 fig. 3.5; Raja 2019a, 76–79 cat. 6. 7b: Ingholt Archives, PS 8; Chabot 1922, 111. 121 cat. 50 pl. 27, 10; Ingholt 1928, 31–33. 94. 97. 107. 128 pl. 3, 1; Ingholt 1934, 35; Ingholt 1935, 68 n. 51; 109 n. 332; Seyrig 1937, 36; Will 1951, 89 n. 2; Champdor 1953, 55; Colledge 1976, 63. 73 f. 124–126. 129. 131. 140. 142. 147. 155. 212. 217. 240. 246 pl. 98; Makowski 1985b, 122; Hvidberg-Hansen – Ploug 1993, 50 f. cat. 8; Parlasca 1994, 302. 304 fig. 5; Ploug 1995, 56–65 cat. 8; Wielgosz 1997, 71; Krag 2015, 109 fig. 2; Raja 2015b, 343–347 figs. 12–16; Raja – Sørensen 2015b, 33. 35; Krag 2016, 188 f. fig. 5; Raja 2016a, 352 fig. 5; Krag 2017a, 60 fig. 3; Krag 2017b 60 fig. 3; Krag – Raja 2017, 201 fig. 4; Raja 2017a, 213 fig. 19, 10; Raja 2017b, 125 fig. 8, 2; Raja 2017c, 15 fig. 9; Raja 2017d, 15 fig. 9; Raja 2017e, 334 f. fig. 7; Raja 2017i, 121 fig. 10; Raja 2017j, 420 fig. 4; Raja 2018a, 3 fig. 5; Raja 2018c, 90. 101 f. fig. 3; Krag 2018, 16 n. 73; 33 n. 75. 77. 78; 41 n. 142. 143; 65 n. 377; 66 n. 382; 87 n. 182; 89 n. 204. 206; 240 cat. 278; Heyn – Raja 2019, 47 fig. 3.5; Raja 2019a, 76–79 cat. 6. Inscription: Chabot 1922, 121 cat. 50; Ingholt 1928, 32 f. 64; Ingholt 1930, 193; Hvidberg-Hansen – Ploug 1993, 50 f. cat. 8; Hvidberg-Hansen 1998, 33 f. cat. 8; Krag 2018, 240 cat. 278; Raja 2019a, 79 cat. 6.

OBJECT DESCRIPTION

The relief is rectangular in shape. It depicts a seated female and a reclining male figure. 7a: She sits on a high-backed chair with armrests. The back of the chair is curving and the border running from the back to the armrest is curving. A crisscross pattern is incised on the whole surface of the chair except along the edges where there is a narrow band. The top and the right side of relief are crowned by an ovolo moulding divided into two zones: a plain, upper one, where an inscription is located, and a lower one with an egg-and-dart motif. 7b: The top of relief is crowned by an ovolo moulding divided into two zones: a plain, upper one, and a lower one with an egg-and-dart motif. A lion's head with a ring in its mouth is placed at the upper right corner.

INSCRIPTION ON 7A
INSCRIPTION 1
SCRIPT: Palmyrene Aramaic.
LOCATION ON RELIEF: On the frontal surface of the upper part of the frame.
TRANSCRIPTION: [- - -] ŠMʿWN BR ḤYRN PRDŠY ʾTTH.
TRANSLATION: [- - - daughter of] Šimʿôn son of Ḥairân Firdušî, his wife.

CIS no. 4458; PAT no. 0818.

INSCRIPTION ON 7B
INSCRIPTION 2
SCRIPT: Palmyrene Aramaic.
LOCATION ON RELIEF: On the frontal surface of the upper part of the frame.
TRANSCRIPTION: [- - -] MLKW BR LŠMŠ BR ḤNBL ʾᶜBY ŠNT 58.
TRANSLATION: - - - Malkû son of Lišamš son of Ḥennibel ʾAʿabeî, year 58.

CIS no. 4458; PAT no. 0818.

COMMENT: If 4 is restored before 58 as it almost certain, the date is A.D. 146/147.

PORTRAIT A: SEATED FEMALE
The figure is shown in three-quarter view. Both arms are bent, the right raised to the shoulder, and the left held along the side. The hands appear large in relation to the body. Her feet are obscured by the foot of the reclining figure.

She wears three headdresses: a headband, a turban, and a veil. The headband is placed low on the forehead. It is divided into alternating square and rectangular panels by vertical grooves. Only the central, rectangular panel is decorated with a crisscross pattern. The turban is coiled, with grooves indicating the coiling of the fabric. Over the turban she wears a veil that falls over the shoulders, covers the left arm, except for the left hand, and then falls over the left thigh. Her hair is mostly covered by her headdress, except for three strands of hair over the ears that are pushed back under the veil, and two wavy locks that fall down her neck and shoulders. The individual strands of hair are indicated by incised lines. Her face is round. The eyebrows are rendered by low, curving grooves that start from the root of the nose. The eyes are deep-set, large, and almond-shaped with thick upper eyelids that extend beyond the end of the lower ones. The irises and pupils are indicated by concentric, incised circles. The ears are visible, with the tragus, helix, and scapha carved. She wears earrings in the shape of miniature bunches of grapes (Colledge classification: E). Her nose is straight. Nasolabial lines are indicated. Her mouth is small with full lips. Her chin is wide, and the neck is wide and short.

Cat. 7, Pl. 43

She wears a tunic and a himation. The tunic has a small, round neckline, long, tight-fitting sleeves, and it reaches the ankles. The folds are indicated by curving grooves. Over the tunic she wears a himation fastened at the left shoulder with a trapezoidal brooch with an incised border and an animal head finial (Colledge classification: a). The himation falls diagonally over the torso and covers the legs of the female to the middle of the lower leg. The folds of the himation are indicated by vertical and curving grooves.

With her right hand, she lightly pulls the veil over her shoulder. Her left arm rests on her left thigh. With her left hand, she holds a fold of the veil. She is wearing a finger ring with an oval bezel with an indication of a central inlay on her left little finger. The nails are indicated by fine, incised lines.

At the left bottom corner of the relief there is a foot, belonging to the male reclining on the belonging fragment NCG003 (cat. 47b). His foot is extended, and the edge of his trousers is visible. He is wearing a sandal.

PORTRAIT B: RECLINING PRIEST

The body is shown frontally, but the head is in a three-quarter view, turned slightly to the right. Both arms are bent; the right resting on his raised right knee, the left resting against an object (a cushion?). His right leg is bent. The right foot is visible. The left arm appears small in relation to the body, and the eyes large.

He wears a tall, cylindrical, flat-top headdress divided into three sections by two vertical grooves: a Palmyrene priestly hat. A wreath with three rows of elliptical leaves is depicted at the lower part of the headdress. The leaves point towards an armless bust of a figure wearing a chlamys and a Palmyrene priestly hat. The midribs of the leaves are indicated by incised lines. Small, oval-shaped elements project from between the leaves (berries?). His face is oblong. There are two horizontal grooves on his forehead. The eyebrows are rendered by curving, incised lines. The eyes are deep-set and almond-shaped with heavy upper eyelids. The irises and pupils are indicated by concentric, incised circles. The ears are protruding with large earlobes; the helix and scapha are depicted. The nose is straight with a wide base. Nasolabial lines are indicated subtly. The mouth is small with full lips, and the chin is pointed. His neck is long and wide.

He wears a ›Parthian-style‹ tunic, chlamys, over-trousers, and ›Parthian-style‹ trousers. The tunic has a round neckline with a beaded border and long, tight-fitting sleeves. A beaded band, followed by a band with a running spiral motif decorates the cuff of the right sleeve. The tunic ends above the knees and has a scalloped edge with a narrow border at the hem. The folds of the tunic are indicated by wide-spaced curving grooves over the torso, and curving grooves over the arms. Over the tunic, he wears a chlamys that is folded across the torso and over both shoulders. One edge of the chlamys has a border with a running scroll and rosettes pattern, visible on the fold extending towards the left shoulder. The chlamys is fastened at the right shoulder with a circular brooch with three concentric, incised circles (Colledge classification: i).

A zigzag-shaped fold falls from under the brooch. The folds of the chlamys are indicated by narrow, deep grooves. He wears trousers and over-trousers: the trousers are visible above the knee, and they have a decorated band with a running scroll and rosettes motif extending downwards in the middle. The over-trousers cover the knee, and their folds are indicated by wide, vertical grooves. He wears sandals.

With his right hand, he holds a branch of elliptical leaves and berries (?), similar to those seen on the headdress. With his left hand, he holds a skyphos: it has a conical foot; the lower part of the body is conical, the upper part of the body is trapezoidal, decorated with broad, diagonal grooves, the lip is rectangular, and has small loop-handles. He wears a ring with an oval bezel and a concentric incised oval, indicating the setting of the stone, on the little finger of the left hand.

Headdress: Ingholt suggests that the wreath of leaves on the Palmyrene priestly hat is a laurel wreath (Ingholt 1928, 32) where Hvidberg-Hansen and Ploug suggest that it is an olive wreath (Hvidberg-Hansen – Ploug 1993, 50). Left hand attribute: Ingholt suggests that the branch is a laurel branch (Ingholt 1928, 32) where Hvidberg-Hansen and Ploug suggest that it is an olive branch (Hvidberg-Hansen – Ploug 1993, 50).

A.D. 148

TOMB OF ZABDIBÔL, LOCATION UNKNOWN

8. SARCOPHAGUS BOX RELIEF WITH PORTRAIT BUSTS

DATABASE NUMBER: NMD101.
LOCATION: Damascus, National Museum of Damascus, inv. no. 15028.
CONTEXT: —
ACQUISITION HISTORY: —
MEASUREMENTS: Height: 51 cm. Length: 77 cm.
MATERIAL: Limestone, white/yellow.
PRESERVATION: Broken in two and joined vertically through the middle. The surface is chipped at the centre of the mattress and at the centre of the stretcher. Portrait B: The nose is chipped. Portrait C: The surface is chipped.
TECHNICAL DESCRIPTION: —
DATE: A.D. 148 (dated by inscription).
REFERENCES: Sabeh 1953, 18–21 pl. 1, 2; Parlasca 1984, 288 fig. 5; Cussini 2012, 166; Cussini 2017, 88 f.; Krag 2018, 32 n. 63; 47 n. 214; 51 n. 241; 55 n. 281; 87 n. 182; 98 n. 23; 103 n. 74; 246 cat. 295; Cussini 2018, 93 f. fig. 3; Fowlkes-Childs – Seymour 2019, 168. Inscription: Sabeh 1953, 19 f.; Taylor 2001, 212; Cussini 2012, 166; Cussini 2017, 88; Krag 2018, 246 cat. 295.

OBJECT DESCRIPTION

The object is rectangular in shape and is rendered as a kline. Two busts are depicted between the kline legs: a female and a male. Above the kline is a mattress. It has three wide bands:

the central band is decorated with lobed leaves set between beaded bands, and the two on either side are decorated with vine scrolls set between bands with crisscross pattern. The fulcrum is decorated with an animal's head on the upper part, and the bust of a male in a chlamys inside a tondo on the lower part (portrait C). The central stretcher of the kline is decorated on either side with a rectangular panel with vine scroll, followed by a small square panel with a four-petal rosette, and then a square with an unclear pattern. The legs are turned. They are composed of a plinth and above is a neck, a long, concave quarter, a bell-shaped element, a scotia, a reversed bell-shaped element, a ball decorated with two horizontal, incised lines, a square torus, a neck, and above the kline stretcher is a thin torus finial.

INSCRIPTIONS
INSCRIPTION 1
SCRIPT: Palmyrene Aramaic.
LOCATION ON RELIEF: Between the portraits.
TRANSCRIPTION: ḤBL | TDMR | ᾽TT | MQYMW | BR NWRBL | BR ZBD᾽ | ᾽MN᾽.
TRANSLATION: Alas, Tadmor wife of Moqîmû son of Nûrbel son of Zabdâ, the craftsman.

INSCRIPTION 2
SCRIPT: Palmyrene Aramaic.
LOCATION ON RELIEF: On the left of the male portrait.
TRANSCRIPTION: ḤBL | MQYMW | ᾽MN᾽ | BR NWRBL | BR ZBD᾽.
TRANSLATION: Alas, Moqîmû the craftsman son of Nûrbel son of Zabdâ.

INSCRIPTION 3
SCRIPT: Palmyrene Aramaic.
LOCATION ON RELIEF: To the left of the female head.
TRANSCRIPTION: MYTT | YWM 29 | BSYWN | ŠNT | 440+ | 19.
TRANSLATION: She died the 29th day of Sîwan, year 459 (A.D. 148).

CIS no. —; PAT no. 0005.

COMMENTS: Inscription 2: L.3: As often, name of occupation or nickname? Inscription 3: L.2–3: The signs for Y and W are almost identical.

PORTRAIT A: ARMLESS FEMALE BUST, TADMOR
The figure is shown frontally.
She wears three headdresses: a headband, a turban, and a veil. The headband falls in a curve to either side of the forehead from the centre. The turban is placed high on the head, and is rendered in two layers looped into each other, creating a knot

Cat. 8, Pl. 44

at the centre. The coiling of the fabric is indicated by three horizontal grooves. The veil has a scalloped edge. It is placed over the turban, falls onto the neck and shoulders and in a curving fold across the chest. The hair is mostly covered by the headdresses, except for four locks of hair over each ear that are brushed backwards over the turban, and two wavy locks of hair that fall down the neck and onto the shoulders. The individual strands of hair are indicated by incised lines. Her face is oval. The eyebrows are depicted as thin, curving ridges. The eyes are large and almond-shaped with thick eyelids. The irises and pupils are indicated by concentric, incised circles. The nose is straight. The mouth is small, with thin lips, the lower lip slightly fuller than the upper. Her chin is round. The neck is long.

She wears a tunic. Only the small, round neckline of the tunic is visible.

PORTRAIT B: ARMLESS MALE BUST, MOQÎMÛ
The figure is shown frontally.

His hair is arranged in three rows of s-shaped curls. Incised lines indicate the individual strands of hair. His face is oval. The eyebrows are depicted as thin, curving ridges. The eyes are large and almond-shaped with thick eyelids. The irises and the pupils are indicated by concentric, incised circles. The ears are protruding. The cheeks are fleshy. The mouth is wide with full lips. The chin is round. The neck is wide with a v-shaped groove indicating the jugular notch.

He wears a tunic and a himation. The tunic has a small, round neckline. Its folds are indicated by narrow, curving grooves. The himation falls diagonally from the left shoulder across the chest. It covers half his chest and is folded under the right shoulder. The folds of the himation are indicated by oblique grooves.

PORTRAIT C: ARMLESS MALE BUST IN FULCRUM
The figure is shown frontally, rendered in a clipeus.

His face is oval. The ears are large and protruding.

He wears a tunic and a chlamys. The tunic has a wide, round neckline. The folds of the tunic are rendered by curving grooves. Over the tunic, he wears a chlamys that falls over both shoulders, and covers most of the chest. It is fastened at the right shoulder with a brooch (details unclear).

A.D. 130–170

TOMB OF ZABDIBÔL, LOCATION UNKNOWN

9. BANQUETING RELIEF

DATABASE NUMBER: MET013.
LOCATION: New York, Metropolitan Museum of Art, inv. no. 02.29.1.
CONTEXT: —

ACQUISITION HISTORY: Purchased in 1902 from the antiquities dealer Azeez Khayat.
MEASUREMENTS: Min. height: 35 cm. Max. height: 50 cm. Width: 62 cm. Depth: 16 cm. Depth of figure: 8 cm. Portrait A: Height: 40 cm. Width: 14 cm. Depth: 3 cm. Head height: 8 cm. Head width: 8 cm. Head depth: 5 cm. Portrait B: Height: 23 cm. Width: 11 cm. Depth: 3 cm. Head height: 7 cm. Head width: 7 cm. Head depth: 5 cm. Portrait C: Height: 21 cm. Width: 10 cm. Depth: 5 cm. Head height: 9 cm. Head width: 7 cm. Head depth: 5 cm. Portrait D: Height: 35 cm. Width: 18 cm. Depth: 8 cm. Head height: 10 cm. Head width: 10 cm. Head depth: 9.5 cm.
MATERIAL: Limestone, yellow.
PRESERVATION: The lower left corner is broken off. The surface of the right side of the mattress is chipped. Portrait A: The lower right arm is chipped. Portrait D: The surface of the right hand and of the left foot is chipped.
TECHNICAL DESCRIPTION: There are traces of red pigment in the inscriptions. Traces of drill work are visible between the two folds under the left hand of portrait D.
DATE: A.D. 130–170 (Ingholt 1954: A.D. 150–200).
REFERENCES: Ingholt Archives, PS 67; Arnold 1905, 106 f. cat. 2 fig. 2; Chabot 1922, 112 f. pl. 27, 11; Ingholt 1928, 95 f.; Ingholt 1938, 103; Sabeh 1953, 21; Ingholt 1954, cat. 6; Parlasca 1984, 285 fig. 1; Albertson 2000, 160 n. 3; Ciliberto 2017, 51. 55 fig. 4; Cussini 2018, 90–96 figs. 1. 3; Krag 2018, 28 n. 9; 66 n. 382; 87 n. 182. 186; 88 n. 190. 193. 195; 89 n. 204. 207; 312 f. cat. 551; Fowlkes-Childs – Seymour 2019, 166 cat. 112; <https://www.metmuseum.org/art/collection/search/322375?sortBy=Relevance&ft=palmyra&offset=0&rpp=20&pos=1> (06.05.2022). Inscription: Arnold 1905, 106 f. cat. 2; Chabot 1922, 112 f.; Krag 2018, 312 f. cat. 551.

OBJECT DESCRIPTION
The relief is rectangular in shape with a round left side. It depicts a standing female, a standing male, a standing female again, and a reclining male. Beneath these figures is a mattress. It is decorated with an intersecting lozenges pattern with central four-petal flowers inside the lozenges. The veins of the petals are indicated by incised lines. The reclining male rests on a cushion. It is decorated with a wide band extending downwards. The band is decorated with a running scroll and rosettes and is set between two beaded bands. Curving grooves indicate the fabric of the cushion.

According to Sabeh (1953), Cussini (2018), and Fowlkes-Childs – Seymour (2019) this object belongs together with cat. 8.

INSCRIPTIONS
INSCRIPTION 1
SCRIPT: Palmyrene Aramaic.
LOCATION ON RELIEF: Between standing female to the right and standing male, at the height of their heads.
TRANSCRIPTION: ʿLYT | BRTH.
TRANSLATION: ʿAliyat his daughter.

INSCRIPTION 2
SCRIPT: Palmyrene Aramaic.
LOCATION ON RELIEF: Between standing male and standing female to the left, at the height of their heads.
TRANSCRIPTION: MQYMW | BRH.
TRANSLATION: Moqîmû his son.

INSCRIPTION 3
SCRIPT: Palmyrene Aramaic.
LOCATION ON RELIEF: Between standing female to the left and reclining male, at the height of their heads.
TRANSCRIPTION: TDMWR | BRTH.
TRANSLATION: Tadmôr his daughter.

INSCRIPTION 4
SCRIPT: Palmyrene Aramaic.
LOCATION ON RELIEF: To the left of the reclining male, at the height of his upper arm.
TRANSCRIPTION: ZBDBWL | BR MQYMW | BR NWRBL | BR ZBD' | [B]R 'BDY | [ZBD]BWL.

TRANSLATION: Zabdibôl son of Moqîmû son of Nûrbêl son of Zabdâ son of 'Abdaî [Zabdi]bôl.

CIS no. 4259; PAT no. 0615.

PORTRAIT A: STANDING FEMALE, 'ALIYAT
The figure is shown in frontal view. The head is turned slightly to the right. The head appears large. The right arm is bent and held in front of the torso. The left arm is bent and held in front of the waist. The knees are visible under the drapery. Her feet are obscured by the reclining figure to her left.

She wears three headdresses: a headband, a turban, and a veil. The headband is placed low on her forehead. It is decorated by three rectangular, horizontal panels, separated by two narrow, rectangular vertical panels. A narrow band runs horizontally along the lower border. The turban is coiled and divided into one twisting layer with oblique grooves indicating the coiling of the fabric. The veil is heavy. It falls over her shoulders, covers her left arm and continues down along the sides of her body. It ends at the ankles. The hair is

Cat. 9, Pl. 45

visible over her ears. It is brushed back over the headband and disappears under the veil. The individual locks of hair are indicated by incised, curving lines. Her face is square. The eyebrows are curving. The eyes are almond-shaped with thick eyelids. The upper eyelids extend beyond the end of the lower ones. The irises are indicated by incised circles. Her ears are partly covered by hair, the tail of the helix, scapha, and earlobe are depicted. She wears dumbbell-shaped earrings (Colledge classification: H). Her nose is short with a wide base. The alae are incised, and the nostrils are carved. The mouth is small with full lips. The chin is oval and prominent. The neck is long and wide. She wears a necklace: a beaded necklace with an oval, incised pendant suspended from the centre and two smaller, oval pendants suspended on each side. It is worn at the base of the neck.

She wears a tunic and a himation. The tunic falls to the ankles. It has a wide, round neckline. The folds of the tunic are rendered by curving grooves on her chest. The himation crosses the chest diagonally from the left shoulder to the right side and covers the left breast. It is fastened at the left shoulder with a circular brooch with three concentric circles and a beaded band along the outer circle (Colledge classification: f). The himation covers the lower body and ends diagonally above the knees, revealing the tunic underneath. The folds of the himation are rendered by curving, diagonal grooves.

Her left hand holds a fold of the veil.

PORTRAIT B: STANDING MALE, MOQÎMÛ

The figure is shown in frontal view. The head appears large. The arms appear short in relation to the body. The right arm is bent and held in front of his waist. The left arm is bent and held in front of his torso. His lower legs are obscured by the reclining figure to his left.

His hair is arranged in a single row of long s-shaped curls, each lock of hair rendered by incised lines. His face is oval. The eyebrows are slightly curving. The eyes are almond-shaped and slightly slanting. The eyelids are thick, and the upper eyelids extend beyond the end of the lower ones. The irises are indicated by incised circles. The ears are protruding and the helix, scapha, concha, and earlobe are depicted. The nose is wide. The alae are incised, and the nostrils carved. The mouth is small with thin lips. The chin is oval. The neck is wide. He wears a necklace: a loop-in-loop chain with a central, large, tubular bead. An incised, oval pendant is suspended from the central bead, and three vertical, rectangular pendants are suspended from the oval pendant. It is worn at the base of the neck.

He wears a tunic. The tunic has a wide, round neckline and long, tight-fitting sleeves. The tunic covers his lower body and upper legs, possibly continuing to the ankles. The folds of the tunic are rendered by curving grooves on the torso and at the legs, and vertical grooves between the legs. He wears a plain band belt, knotted at the centre with the ends looped tightly under either side of the waist.

His right hand is in front of the waist, and he holds a round object with smaller, round elements: a bunch of grapes. The fingers are slightly extended. The left hand is in front of the torso and holds a bird. The beak, head, and body are depicted, and the wing and feathers are indicated by incised lines. His left index finger is extended.

PORTRAIT C: STANDING FEMALE, TADMÔR

The figure is shown in frontal view, with the head turned slightly to the right. The head appears large. The arms appear short in relation to the body. Both arms are bent and held in front of her torso. The legs are obscured by the reclining figure to her left.

She wears three headdresses: a headband, a turban, and a veil. The headband is placed low on her forehead. It is decorated by three rectangular, horizontal panels separated by two narrow, rectangular, vertical panels. A narrow band runs horizontally along the lower border. The turban is coiled. It is divided into a single twisting layer with oblique grooves indicating the coiling of the fabric. The veil is heavy. It falls back over her right shoulder, over the left shoulder, and is folded around the left arm. Her face is round, and the eyebrows are slightly curving. The eyes are almond-shaped with thick upper eyelids. The irises are indicated by incised lines. The ears are protruding and the helix, scapha, and earlobe are depicted. She wears dumbbell-shaped earrings (Colledge classification: H). Her nose is narrow and pointed. The alae are incised, and the nostrils carved. The mouth is small with a full lower lip. The chin is prominent and oval. The neck is short and wide. She wears a necklace: a string of round beads worn at the base of her neck.

She wears a tunic and a himation. The tunic has a wide, v-shaped neckline and long sleeves. The folds of the tunic are rendered by curving grooves on her chest and oblique and vertical grooves on her right arm. The himation crosses the chest diagonally from the left shoulder to the right side and covers the left breast. It is fastened at the left shoulder with a circular brooch with three concentric circles and a beaded band along the outer circle (Colledge classification: f). The himation covers her lower body and legs. The folds of the himation are rendered by oblique grooves.

The right hand is in front of her torso and holds an oval element, possibly a fold of the garment. The thumb is extended. The left hand is in front of her torso and lightly holds a fold of the veil.

PORTRAIT D: RECLINING MALE, ZABDIBÔL

The body is shown in frontal view. His right arm appears short in relation to the body. The right arm is slightly bent and rests on his raised right knee. The left arm is bent in front of the torso and rests against a cushion. The right leg is bent and the right foot rests on the mattress. The left leg is slightly bent and rests on the mattress. The left knee is visible under the drapery.

His hair is arranged in a single row of long, s-shaped curls, each lock of hair is rendered by incised lines. His face is oval.

The eyebrows are slightly curving. The eyes are almond-shaped and slightly slanting. The upper eyelids are thick, and they extend beyond the end of the lower ones. The irises and pupils are indicated by concentric, incised circles. The ears are protruding and the helix, scapha, concha, and lobe are depicted. The nasal bridge is narrow, and the nose has a wide base. The alae are incised, and the nostrils carved. The mouth is small with thin lips. The chin is oval and prominent. The neck is wide and long.

He wears a tunic and a himation. The tunic has a wide, round neckline and short sleeves. The border of the sleeves is scalloped. The folds of the tunic are rendered by curving grooves along the middle of the torso and oblique grooves on the sleeve. The himation falls over his left shoulder and left arm and is wrapped around the left wrist. The end of the himation continues under his left wrist onto the mattress in two long, s-shaped folds. The himation falls along the left side of his body and is wrapped over the waist. It covers the legs and ends at the ankles. The folds of the himation are rendered by curving grooves. His feet are bare, with the toes depicted. Incised lines indicate the toenails.

He rests his right hand on his right knee and holds a branch with diamond-shaped leaves that falls down from his hand. The left hand holds a skyphos. The skyphos has a conical base and a tongues pattern on the lower part of the body. On the body, there is a wide band with a running scroll with rosettes. The rim is indicated by a horizontal, incised line. A handle is depicted on the right side. The thumb and the left index finger are extended.

A.D. 188

HYPOGEUM OF MALKÛ

10. COMPLETE SARCOPHAGUS RELIEF WITH BANQUETING SCENE AND PORTRAIT BUSTS

DATABASE NUMBER: PM325.
LOCATION: Palmyra, Palmyra Museum, inv. no. A 910/10.
CONTEXT: South-west necropolis. Hypogeum of Malkû, south exedra.
ACQUISITION HISTORY: —
MEASUREMENTS: Height 178 cm. Width: 207 cm.
MATERIAL: Limestone.
PRESERVATION: There are small breaks on the left side of the lid. The upper right corner is broken off. Large segments on the right side and between the figures are broken off and filled in. Portrait A: The portrait is badly fragmented with sections missing, especially across the top of the head, chest, and left leg. Portrait B: The head is broken off at the base of the neck. Portrait C: A crack runs from the right shoulder to the left of the face. Portrait D: Only a small part of both shoulders and the left arm is preserved. Portrait E: There are several large cracks across the body and the attribute in the left hand is chipped. Portrait F: A crack runs down the left side of the face. The body is fragmented, and the right arm and chest are chipped.
TECHNICAL DESCRIPTION: Light tool marks. Portrait C: There are traces of pigment in the eyes.
DATE: A.D. 188 (dated by inscription).
REFERENCES: Ingholt Archives, PS 1391; Ingholt 1970–1971, 182–192 pls. 3. 4; Makowski 1985a, 94 f. fig. 10; Tanabe 1986, 41 pls. 400–403; Anadol 2008, 70 fig. 11; Palaz Erdemir 2013, 510 f. 514 fig. 7; Krag – Raja 2017, 199 n. 24; 204 n. 72. 73; 205 n. 75. 78. 83; 206 n. 85; 207 n. 95; 208 n. 97. 99; 209 n. 100–102. 105; 210 n. 107–111. 113; 211. 215 f. cat. 15 fig. 7; Krag 2018, 23 n. 160; 28 n. 9; 32 n. 63; 33 n. 79. 82–84; 41 n. 143. 145. 146; 46 n. 198; 47 n. 214; 50 n. 234; 51 n. 241; 52 n. 248; 65 n. 377; 66 n. 382; 67 n. 4; 87 n. 181–184. 186. 187; 88 n. 189. 190. 193. 195. 197; 89 n. 201. 204. 206. 207. 210; 98 n. 28; 103 n. 74; 315 f. cat. 564; Silver et al. 2018, 109 fig. 6.6. Inscription: Ingholt 1970–1971, 182–192; Ingholt 1976, 102–115 pls. 1. 2; al-Asʿad – Gawlikowski 1997, 52 f. cat. 73 fig. 73, a–d; Yon 2013, 340 cat. 11; Krag 2018, 315 f. cat. 564.

OBJECT DESCRIPTION

The object is rectangular in shape and depicts a sarcophagus with a banquet scene on the lid and five armless busts and a full-length figure on the box. There are five portraits on the lid: a seated female, three standing females, a reclining male, and a standing male. The reclining figure is the largest of the group, and he rests on a mattress decorated with an intersecting lozenge pattern with four-petal rosettes inside the lozenges. His left arm rests on a cylindrical cushion that is decorated along its length with a wide band of four-petal rosettes between lozenges set between beaded bands.

The box of the sarcophagus has the depiction of a kline in relatively low relief. The kline has a fulcrum decorated with a male bust inside a tondo with a beaded border at the lower end (portrait M), a reclining figure on the body, and an animal at the upper end. The kline has a low mattress decorated with three bands: the central band is decorated with a running scroll with rosettes set between two beaded bands, and ones at the sides are decorated with four-petal rosettes between lozenges, set between beaded bands. The fabric of the mattress is indicated by curving grooves. The frame has a small, rectangular panel over the legs followed by two longer rectangles, and then another small, rectangular panel. At the centre is a rectangular panel, which is divided along its width in two parts: an upper part with diagonal, incised lines that fan out to the left and right from the centre, and a lower part with palm leaf moulding. The small, rectangular panels are decorated (depictions of animals?). The legs are turned. They are composed of a plinth and above is a convex quarter, a reversed bell-shaped element, a concave quarter, a reversed bell-shaped element, a thin torus, a ball, a thin torus, a concave quarter, and above the stretcher is a thin torus finial. All elements are decorated with a tongues pattern. There are five armless busts and a full-length figure between the legs of the kline: a female, two males, a female, a standing male figure, and a female bust.

Cat. 10

INSCRIPTIONS

INSCRIPTION 1
SCRIPT: Palmyrene Aramaic.
LOCATION ON RELIEF: To the left of portrait B, at the height of the head.
TRANSCRIPTION: ḤBY | BRTH.
TRANSLATION: Ḥabbaî, his daughter.

INSCRIPTION 2
SCRIPT: Palmyrene Aramaic.
LOCATION ON RELIEF: To the left of portrait C, at the height of the head.
TRANSCRIPTION: NBY | BRTH.
TRANSLATION: Nabbaî his daughter.

INSCRIPTION 3
SCRIPT: Palmyrene Aramaic.
LOCATION ON RELIEF: Between portraits C and E.
TRANSCRIPTION: ŠLY.
TRANSLATION: Šullaî.

INSCRIPTION 4
SCRIPT: Palmyrene Aramaic.
LOCATION ON RELIEF: To the right of the reclining figure, at the height of the head.
TRANSCRIPTION: ṢLM BʿLY BR | DYWN BR MLKW | ŠLY BRTH | BYRḤ ʾYR ŠNT | 480+ | 19.
TRANSLATION: Image of Baʿlaî son of Dayyôn son of Malkû. Šullaî his daughter. In the month Iyyar, year 499 (A.D. 188).

INSCRIPTION 5
SCRIPT: Palmyrene Aramaic.
LOCATION ON RELIEF: To the right of the standing male on the lid, at the height of the head.
TRANSCRIPTION: ŠLMN | GLYDH.
TRANSLATION: Šalman the?

INSCRIPTION 6
SCRIPT: Palmyrene Aramaic.
LOCATION ON RELIEF: To the left of the female bust at the right end, at the height of the head.
TRANSCRIPTION: BRBRH BT ḤYRN | ʾTT DYWN KLTH.
TRANSLATION: Barbarah daughter of Ḥaîran, wife of Dayyôn, his daughter-in-law.

INSCRIPTION 7
SCRIPT: Palmyrene Aramaic.
LOCATION ON RELIEF: Between the two male busts, at the height of their priestly hats.
TRANSCRIPTION: DYWN BR BʿLY BRH | BYRḤ ʾYR ŠNT 4- | 99.
TRANSLATION: Dayyôn son of Baʿlaî his son, in the month Iyyar, year 499 (A.D. 188).

INSCRIPTION 8
SCRIPT: Palmyrene Aramaic.
LOCATION ON RELIEF: Between the left priest bust and the female bust, at the height of their head.
TRANSCRIPTION: BʿLY BR DYWN | RMY BT NBY | BT BRTH.
TRANSLATION: Baʿlaî son of Dayyôn, Ramî daughter of Nabbaî, daughter of his daughter.

INSCRIPTION 9
SCRIPT: Palmyrene Aramaic.
LOCATION ON RELIEF: On the lid.
TRANSCRIPTION: ʾMTʾ BRT | ḤBY BRTH.
TRANSLATION: Amatâ daughter of Ḥabbaî, his daughter.

CIS no. —; PAT no. —.

COMMENTS: Inscriptions 1 and 2: Ingholt (1970–1971, 186) has inverted Ḥabbaî and Nabbaî. Inscription 3: According to Ingholt (1970–1971, 186), »Immediately to Beʿelai's right there had been a female figure which, however, was almost completely demolished«. Inscription 5: L.2: »Caravan-leader« Ingholt 1970, 183. See DNSWI, p. 223, s.v. gld2 and gldgyml. Inscription 9: L.2: Ingholt 1970 (followed by Yon 2013) has ʾḤBY but translates Ḥabbaî. Obviously a mistake, as ḤBY is already attested on the same monument. No photograph available for this last inscription.

SARCOPHAGUS LID

PORTRAIT A: SEATED FEMALE

The figure is shown in full-length and frontally. Both arms are bent; the right raised to the shoulder, and the left is held in front of the waist. The arms appear short and the left hand large in relation to the body. The feet are obscured by the reclining figure to her left.

She wears three headdresses: a headband, a turban, and a veil. The turban is coiled. It is rendered in two layers, which are lopped into each other, creating a knot at the centre. Curving grooves indicate the coiling of the fabric. The veil is heavy and falls over the neck and shoulders and covers the left arm. Most of the hair is covered by the headdresses except a series of overlapping locks over the ears that cover the sides of the headband and disappear under the veil. The individual strands of hair are indicated by incised lines. Her face is oval. The eyes are almond-shaped. The eyeballs appear blank. She is wearing dumbbell-shaped earrings (Colledge classification: H). The nose bridge is narrow. The mouth is small with thin lips. The chin is pointed.

She wears a tunic and a himation. The ankle-length tunic has short sleeves and a small, round neckline. The folds of the tunic are indicated by angular grooves on the chest. The himation falls over the left shoulder, crosses diagonally over the torso and covers the lower body, leaving the hemline of the tunic and the feet exposed. The folds of the himation are indicated by oblique grooves. She wears closed shoes (visible on the right foot).

With the left hand, she holds a fold of the veil over her lap, and with the right hand, she lightly pulls the veil at the height of the shoulder. She wears a wide hoop ring on the little finger of the left hand.

PORTRAIT B: STANDING FEMALE, ḤABBAÎ

The figure is shown in full-length and frontally. Her arms are bent; the right in front of the chest, the left in front of her waist. The arms appear short in relation to the body. The left leg and the lower part of the right leg are obscured by the reclining figure to her left.

A part of the veil is preserved, covering the left shoulder and upper arm, and along the right side. The folds of the veil are indicated by oblique grooves.

She wears a tunic. The tunic has a wide, v-shaped neckline and short sleeves. The folds of the tunic are indicated by curving grooves.

With her right hand, she pulls the veil over her left shoulder and breast. With her left hand, she holds the veil over her lower torso. She wears a bracelet on each wrist, each depicted as a plain, thick hoop.

PORTRAIT C: STANDING FEMALE, NABBAÎ

The figure is shown in full-length and frontally. Her arms are bent; the right is held in front of the chest, the left in front of her waist. The arms appear short in relation to the body. Her body from the waist down is obscured by the reclining figure.

She wears three headdresses: a headband, a turban, and a veil. The headband is placed high on the forehead and is divided into panels separated by beaded bands. The central panel is decorated with a vegetal motif. The turban is coiled. The lower part of the turban is indicated by a horizontal groove, while the upper two layers are looped into each other creating a central knot. The veil falls over the neck and shoulders. It covers the arms. She also wears a head-chain. It is fastened under the turban, at either side of the central panel of the headband, and runs to the sides. It is composed of round elements with incised borders, linked by beaded elements. Most of the hair is covered by the headdresses, except for a series of overlapping locks over the ears that cover the sides of the headband and disappear under the veil. The individual strands of hair are rendered by incised lines. Her face is round. The eyebrows are rendered by incised lines. The eyes are wide. The irises are indicated by incised circles, the pupils by punch holes. The ears are not visible; she wears dumbbell-shaped earrings (Colledge classification: H). The nose is thin. The mouth is small with full lips. The chin is small and pointed. The neck is smooth and slender. She wears a necklace at the base of the neck consisting of small, round beads.

She wears a tunic and a himation. The tunic has short sleeves and a small, round neckline. The folds of the tunic are indicated by curving grooves on the chest. The himation is fastened at the left shoulder with a circular brooch with an outer geometrical border. The outer border is decorated with a pentagon with curving sides meeting in flat ends. Circular elements are set between the curving sides. The central, circular bezel has a small round depression. The himation falls diagonally across the chest. The folds of the himation are indicated by oblique grooves.

With the left hand, she holds the veil over the right shoulder. With the right hand, she holds the veil at the waist. She wears a bracelet, composed of twisted beaded and plain bands, on each wrist. On the little finger of the left hand, she wears two rings: wide, thick hoops with small, circular bezels.

PORTRAIT D: STANDING FEMALE, ŠULLAÎ

The figure is shown in full-length and frontally. Her lower body is obscured by the reclining figure.

She wears a tunic (details unclear).

Her hand is resting on the right shoulder of the reclining male figure.

PORTRAIT E: RECLINING PRIEST, BAʿLAÎ

The figure is shown in full-length, with his upper body depicted frontally and the head turned slightly to his left. The head appears small in relation to the body. He is reclining with his right leg bent and the right foot resting on the mattress and the left leg bent under the right leg, leaving only the thigh and knee visible. The lower left leg is obscured. His left arm is bent in front of the middle of the torso, and his right arm is extended.

He wears a high, cylindrical, flat-top headdress divided into three sections by two vertical grooves: a Palmyrene priestly hat. Depicted at the lower part of the hat is a wreath with the leaves pointing towards a medallion. The medallion has the bust of a male figure with short hair and wearing a himation. The lowest part of the headdress has a horizontal, incised line and recedes slightly, suggesting a liner. His face is oval. The eyebrows are rendered by incised lines. The eyes are almond-shaped with thick eyelids. The irises are rendered by incised circles and the pupils by punch holes. The ears are protruding with the helix, scapha, and lobe depicted. The nose is thin. The mouth is small with full lips. The chin is pointed. The neck is slender.

He wears >Parthian-style< tunic, chlamys, and >Parthian-style< trousers. The tunic has a wide, round neckline and long, tight-fitting sleeves. The cuffs of the sleeves are decorated with a wide band with a vegetal motif and a beaded band at the hem. At the middle, the tunic has a wide band with a floral pattern between two beaded bands extending downwards. The tunic ends above the knees and has a decorated lower border with a running scroll with rosettes and a beaded band at the hem. The folds of the tunic are indicated by curving grooves. The chlamys is fastened at the right shoulder with a round brooch with a geometrical outer border. The outer border is composed of a hexagon with curved sides meeting in flat ends. The central bezel has an incised border. The chlamys is folded over the upper part of the torso. It falls over the left shoulder and one edge is wrapped around the left elbow, with a wide fold falling from under the left forearm. The edge of the chlamys is decorated with a band with floral motifs, visible at the folds over the torso. One fold of the chlamys falls under the brooch in a zigzag-shape. He wears a plain band belt, knotted at the centre with the ends looped under on either side of the waist. Each trouser leg is decorated in the middle with a wide band with vegetal motifs set between beaded bands extending downwards (visible from above the knees to above the hem). The folds of the garments are indicated by wide, curving grooves. The trousers are tucked into the boots with an overhang at the back of the ankle. Only the right boot is visible. It is decorated over the whole surface with circles enclosing rosettes. Just above the ankle is a plain band with an incised circle and a small hanging end. The shaft is decorated with a wave scroll and has a beaded border at the top.

His right hand is resting on his knee and lower leg, holding a schematically rendered pinecone. With his left hand, he holds a vessel. The nails are indicated. He wears a thick hoop ring with an oval bezel on the left little finger.

PORTRAIT F: STANDING MALE, ŠALMAN

The figure is shown in full-length and frontally. The left arm is slightly bent and falls to the side. The right arm is raised towards the right. The right side of his torso, the right leg, and the lower part of the left leg are obscured by the reclining figure to his right.

His hair is arranged in three rows of snail-shell curls. The individual strands of hair are indicated by incised lines. His face is round. The eyebrows are rendered by incised lines. The eyes are wide, almond-shaped, and slanting with thick upper eyelids. The upper eyelids extend beyond the end of the lower ones. The irises are rendered by incised circles and the pupils by punch holes. The ears are small and protruding with the helix and lobe depicted. The nose is thin. The mouth is small with full lips. The chin is pointed.

He wears a tunic and a himation. The tunic has a narrow, v-shaped neckline and long sleeves. The folds of the tunic are indicated by curving grooves. The himation covers the left shoulder and arm. The folds of the himation are indicated by oblique grooves.

He holds a rectangular object with his left hand, possibly a schedula. With his right hand, he reaches towards the Palmyrene priestly hat.

SARCOPHAGUS BOX

PORTRAIT G: ARMLESS FEMALE BUST, BARBARAH

The figure is shown frontally.

She wears three headdresses: a headband, a turban, and a veil. The headband has a central panel with a floral motif between two beaded bands. The turban is coiled, indicated by oblique grooves. The veil falls over the neck and shoulders, it crosses the chest in a curving fold, and falls behind the left shoulder. Most of the hair is covered by the headdresses, except for a series of curving locks over the ears that cover the sides of the headband and disappear under the veil. The individual strands of hair are rendered by incised lines. Her face is oval. The eyes are almond-shaped and slanting with thick eyelids. The irises are indicated (details unclear). The earlobes are visible beneath the hair, and she wears earrings with a single round bead suspended by a bar (Colledge classification: L). The nose is straight and wide. The mouth is small with thin lips. Her chin is small. She wears a string of round beads at the base of her neck.

She wears a tunic with a narrow, v-shaped neckline. The folds of the tunic are indicated by curving, wide grooves.

PORTRAIT H: ARMLESS BUST OF A PRIEST, DAYYÔN

The figure is shown frontally.

He wears a high, cylindrical, flat-top headdress divided into three sections by two vertical grooves: a Palmyrene priestly hat. Depicted at the lower part of the headdress is a wreath with the leaves pointing towards a medallion with the bust of a male (?) figure. The lowest part of the headdress has a horizontal, incised line and recedes slightly, suggesting a liner. His face is oval. The eyes are large, almond-shaped, and slanting with thick eyelids. The irises are indicated (details unclear). The ears are protruding. The nose is straight with a wide base. The mouth is small with a full lower lip. The chin is pointed.

He wears a tunic and a chlamys. The tunic has a narrow, v-shaped neckline, and the folds are indicated by vertical grooves on the sleeves and angular grooves on the chest. The chlamys is fastened at the right shoulder with a circular brooch (details unclear). A fold of the chlamys falls under the brooch in a zigzag-shape. The other end of the chlamys is folded over the torso and falls behind the left shoulder.

PORTRAIT I: ARMLESS BUST OF A PRIEST, BAʿLAÎ

The figure is shown frontally.

He wears a high, cylindrical, flat-top headdress divided into three sections by two vertical grooves: a Palmyrene priestly hat. Depicted at the lowest part of the headdress is a wreath with the leaves pointing towards a medallion with the bust of a male (?) figure. The lowest part of the headdress has a horizontal, incised line and recedes slightly, suggesting a liner. His face is oval. The eyes are large, almond-shaped, and slanting with thick eyelids. The irises are indicated (details unclear). The ears are protruding. The nose is straight with a wide base. The mouth is small with a full lower lip. The chin is pointed.

He wears a tunic and a chlamys. The tunic has a narrow, v-shaped neckline, and the folds are indicated by vertical grooves on the sleeves and angular grooves on the chest. The chlamys is fastened at the right shoulder with a circular brooch (details unclear). A fold of the chlamys falls under the brooch in a zigzag-shape. The other end of the chlamys is folded over the torso and falls behind the left shoulder.

PORTRAIT J: ARMLESS FEMALE BUST, RAMÎ

The figure is shown frontally.

She wears three headdresses: a headband, a turban, and a veil. The headband has a central panel with a floral motif. The turban is coiled. The coiling of the fabric is indicated by oblique grooves. The veil is heavy and falls over the neck and shoulders, and it crosses the chest in a curving fold, falling behind the left shoulder. Most of the hair is covered by the headdresses, except for a series of curving locks over the ears that cover the sides of the headband and disappear under the veil. The individual strands of hair are rendered by incised lines. Her face is oval. The eyes are almond-shaped and slanting, with thick eyelids. The irises are indicated (details unclear). The earlobes are visible beneath the hair, and she wears earrings with three juxtaposed beads (Colledge classification: K); a round bead at the top, a small oval bead at the centre, and a large round bead at the end. The nose is straight with a wide base. The mouth is small with a full lower lip. Her chin is small. She wears a string of round beads at the base of the neck.

She wears a tunic with a narrow, v-shaped neckline. The folds of the tunic are indicated by curving, wide grooves.

PORTRAIT K: STANDING MALE

The figure is shown frontally. Both arms are bent in front of the torso. The right and left side of his lower body are obscured by the two busts on either side.

His hair is short and voluminous. His face is round. The eyes are almond-shaped and slanting. The nose is straight.

He wears a knee-length tunic with a small, round neckline and long sleeves.

He holds a bunch of grapes with both hands.

PORTRAIT L: ARMLESS FEMALE BUST, AMATÂ

The figure is shown frontally.

She wears three headdresses: a headband, a turban, and a veil. The headband appears plain (details unclear). The turban is coiled, indicated by oblique grooves. The veil falls over the neck and shoulders, and crosses the chest in a curving fold, falling behind the left shoulder. Most of the hair is covered by the headdresses, except for a series of curving locks over the ears that cover the sides of the headband and disappear under the veil. The individual strands of hair are rendered by incised lines. Her face is oval. The eyes are almond-shaped and slanting with thick eyelids. The irises are indicated (details unclear). The earlobes are visible beneath the hair, and she wears earrings with three juxtaposed beads (Colledge classification: K); a small round bead at the centre with two larger round beads above and below. The nose is straight with a wide tip. The mouth is small with a full lower lip. Her chin is small. She wears a string of round beads at the base of the neck.

She wears a tunic with a narrow, v-shaped neckline. The folds of the tunic are indicated by curving, wide grooves.

PORTRAIT M: ARMLESS BUST IN FULCRUM

The figure is shown frontally.

He is wearing a chiton and a himation (details unclear).

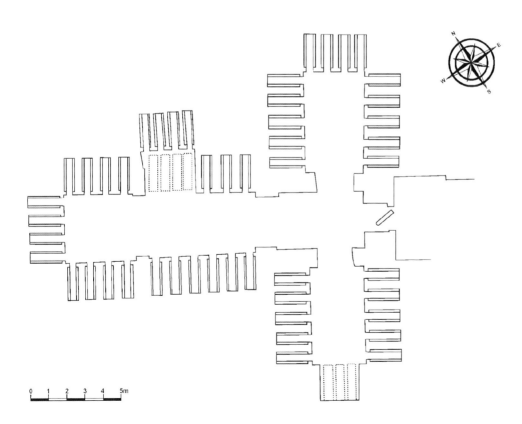

Plan of the hypogeum of Malkû.

A.D. 239

HYPOGEUM OF THE BÔLBARAK FAMILY

11. COMPLETE SARCOPHAGUS WITH BANQUETING SCENE AND PORTRAIT BUSTS

DATABASE NUMBER: PM274.
LOCATION: Palmyra, Palmyra Museum, inv. no. 1795/6644 (lid) and B 1796/6645 (box).
CONTEXT: West necropolis. Valley of the Tombs. Hypogeum of the Bôlbarak family, central exedra, on podium.
ACQUISITION HISTORY: —
MEASUREMENTS: Height: 143 cm. Width: 199 cm. Depth: 12 cm. Depth of figure: 2 cm.
MATERIAL: Limestone, white.
PRESERVATION: The lower corners of the box are broken off and restored; the top of the pedestal is broken off. The surface is lightly chipped. Portrait A: A crack runs across the neck. Portrait B: The surface is weathered. Portrait C: The surface is weathered. Portrait D: The surface is weathered. Portrait E: The surface is weathered. Portrait G: The nose is chipped. Portrait H: The nose is chipped. Portrait J: The nose is chipped, and the face is weathered.
TECHNICAL DESCRIPTION: Traces of pigment in the eyes of portrait G. There are traces of pigment in the inscriptions.
DATE: A.D. 239 (dated by inscription).
REFERENCES: Ingholt Archives, PS 1262/1264; Tanabe 1986, 41 pls. 393–395; Sadurska 1988, 16 f. fig. 1; Sadurska 1994, 16 fig. 3; Sadurska – Bounni 1994, 146–148 cat. 195 fig. 247; Sadurska 1995, 587 f. fig. 11; Palaz Erdemir 2013, 510 f. 514 fig. 8; Audley-Miller 2016, 557. 579 fig. 2; Krag – Raja 2017, 199 n. 24; 204 n. 72. 73; 205 n. 75. 76. 82. 83; 206 n. 87; 207 n. 95; 208 n. 99; 209 n. 100. 101; 210 n. 107. 109. 110; 211 n. 122. 123; 218 f. cat. 29 fig. 13; Raja 2017i, 121. 124 fig. 11; Raja 2017a, 213. 220 f. 227 cat. 20 fig. 19.11; Raja 2017e, 327 f. fig. 4; Raja 2017h, 64 f. 75 f. cat. 20 fig. 11; Raja 2017j, 421 fig. 5; Krag 2018, 28 n. 9; 32 n. 63; 53 n. 258; 58 n. 300; 59 n. 323; 61 n. 332; 62 n. 349. 353; 65 n. 377; 66 n. 382. 385; 67 n. 4; 83 n. 144. 146; 87 n. 181. 182. 184. 186; 88 n. 190. 192. 193. 195. 197; 89 n. 204–208. 210; 103 n. 74; 394 f. cat. 849; Silver et al. 2018, 61 fig. 4.1; <https://virtual-museum-syria.org/palmyra/40-sarcophagus-from-the-hypogeum-of-the-bolbarak/> (06.05.2022). Inscription: Bounni – Teixidor 1975, 10–12 cat. 2–11; Sadurska – Bounni 1994, 147 f.; al-Asʿad – Gawlikowski 1997, 46 f. cat. 65 fig. 65; Krag 2018, 394 f. cat. 849.

OBJECT DESCRIPTION

The sarcophagus relief is rectangular in shape and depicts a banqueting scene on the lid with two seated females, a standing male, a reclining male, and a seated female. Between portraits D and E is a pedestal; rectangular, with a cylindrical headdress with a wreath made of three rows of leaves and a central medallion at its lower part. Under these figures is a box in the shape of a kline with five busts between the kline legs: two female busts, a male bust, a female bust, and a male bust. On top of the kline are two mattresses. The upper mattress is decorated with an intersecting lozenge pattern with flowers in the lozenges. Portrait D is the largest figure of the group, and he rests the left arm on a cylindrical cushion that has a central band with a floral motif. The lower mattress has three bands decorated with rosettes. Curving grooves indicate the texture of the fabric. The stretcher is depicted with a rectangular panel over the legs, a longer, rectangular panel, and a square panel on either side. At the centre is a large, rectangular panel with diagonal, incised lines that fan out to the left and right from the centre. The legs are turned. They are composed of a thin plinth and above is a concave quarter, a reversed, long, concave quarter, a bell-shaped element, a thin torus, a reversed concave quarter, a thin torus, two opposed convex quarters, and an upper bell-shaped element. All elements are decorated with a tongues pattern.

INSCRIPTIONS

INSCRIPTION 1
SCRIPT: Palmyrene Aramaic.
LOCATION ON RELIEF: On the pedestal.
TRANSCRIPTION: ṢLMʾ DNH DY BWLBRK | BR MQYMW BWLBRK | DY ʿBD ʾKSDRʾ WTMLʾ | DQDMWHY NYSN ŠNT 550.
TRANSLATION: This image of Bôlbarak son of Moqîmû Bôlbarak, who made the exedra and the platform in front of it, Nîsan year 550 (A.D. 239).

INSCRIPTION 2
SCRIPT: Palmyrene Aramaic.
LOCATION ON RELIEF: On the dress of the seated female on outer left side, next to the pedestal.
TRANSCRIPTION: ʾTʾ BRT GDʾ ʾMH.
TRANSLATION: Attâ daughter of Gaddâ, his mother.

INSCRIPTION 3
SCRIPT: Palmyrene Aramaic.
LOCATION ON RELIEF: On the dress of the seated female on the outer right side.
TRANSCRIPTION: ʾMTDʿTH BRT BWLBRK | ʾTT BWLBRK.
TRANSLATION: Amatdʿateh daughter of Bôlbarak, wife of Bôlbarak.

INSCRIPTION 4
SCRIPT: Palmyrene Aramaic.
LOCATION ON RELIEF: Between the two seated women on the right side.
TRANSCRIPTION: ŠLMT BRT BWRPʾ ʾTT BWLBRK.
TRANSLATION: Šalmat daughter of Bôrrofâ, wife of Bôlbarak.

INSCRIPTION 5
SCRIPT: Palmyrene Aramaic.
LOCATION ON RELIEF: To the right of the standing boy, at his right elbow.
TRANSCRIPTION: MQYMW | BRH.

TRANSLATION: Moqîmû his son.

INSCRIPTION 6
SCRIPT: Palmyrene Aramaic.
LOCATION ON RELIEF: To the right of the outermost female bust.
TRANSCRIPTION: ŠLMT | BRTH.
TRANSLATION: Šalmat, his daughter.

INSCRIPTION 7
SCRIPT: Palmyrene Aramaic.
LOCATION ON RELIEF: To the right of the second female bust from the right.
TRANSCRIPTION: ʾMTNNY | BRTH.
TRANSLATION: Amatnannaî his daughter.

INSCRIPTION 8
SCRIPT: Palmyrene Aramaic.
LOCATION ON RELIEF: To the right of the central male bust.
TRANSCRIPTION: BWLBRK | BRH.
TRANSLATION: Bôlbarak his son.

INSCRIPTION 9
SCRIPT: Palmyrene Aramaic.
LOCATION ON RELIEF: To the right of the female bust on the left side.
TRANSCRIPTION: ʾTʾ | BRTH.
TRANSLATION: Attâ his daughter.

INSCRIPTION 10
SCRIPT: Palmyrene Aramaic.
LOCATION ON RELIEF: To the right of the male bust on the left side.
TRANSCRIPTION: WHBLT | BRH.
TRANSLATION: Wahballat his son.

Inscription 1: CIS no. —; PAT no. 1526.
Inscription 2: CIS no. —; PAT no. 1527.
Inscription 3: CIS no. —; PAT no. 1530.
Inscription 4: CIS no. —; PAT no. 1529.
Inscription 5: CIS no. —; PAT no. 1528.
Inscription 6: CIS no. —; PAT no. 1535.
Inscription 7: CIS no. —; PAT no. 1534.
Inscription 8: CIS no. —; PAT no. 1533.

Cat. 11

Inscription 9: CIS no. —; PAT no. 1532.
Inscription 10: CIS no. —; PAT no. 1531.

COMMENTS: Inscriptions 1–10: Vertical inscription. Dotted reš. Inscriptions 3 and 4: This is the only case in Palmyrene epigraphy where a male is described as having two wives. Inscriptions 6–10: Painted, not engraved.

SARCOPHAGUS LID

PORTRAIT A: SEATED FEMALE, AMATDʿATEH

The figure is shown frontally. Both arms are bent; the left raised to the shoulder, and the right is held at the waist. The head appears large, and the arms and legs appear short in relation to the body. She sits with her feet apart on the mattress, and the knees are rendered under the drapery.

She wears three headdresses: a headband, a turban, and a veil. The headband is divided into panels by vertical beaded bands. The central panel is decorated with a flower with serrated petals. The turban is coiled. The coiling of the fabric is rendered with horizontal grooves. The veil is heavy and falls over the neck and shoulders. It is wrapped around the right arm and covers the left upper arm. Most of the hair is covered by the headdresses, except for a series of overlapping locks above the ears that cover the sides of the headband and disappear under the veil. The individual strands of hair are rendered by incised lines. Her face is round. The eyebrows are indicated by curving ridges and the eyes are round and large with thick upper eyelids. The irises are rendered by incised circles. The end of the upper eyelids extends beyond the end of the lower ones. Only the earlobes are visible, and she is wearing dumbbell-shaped earrings (Colledge classification: H). The nose is wide and straight. The mouth is small, with thin lips. The chin and neck are wide. She wears three necklaces: a plain hoop around the base of the neck, with a pendant suspended by a thin sleeve from the centre. The pendant has an incised outer border. Below that, she wears a necklace composed of alternating round and square pendants, with incised borders, linked by beaded elements. She also wears a long necklace with large round beads, with a crescent-shaped pendant with a round bead between the horns, suspended from the centre with a narrow sleeve.

She wears a tunic and a himation. The tunic has long, wide sleeves and ends at the ankles. The folds of the tunic are lightly indicated by oblique, incised lines. The himation is fastened at the left shoulder with a circular brooch with an incised border (Colledge classification: h). It falls diagonally across the torso and covers the lower body, leaving only the hemline of the tunic and the feet exposed. The folds of the himation are indicated by oblique grooves.

With the right hand, she holds a fold of the veil over her lap, and with the left hand, she pulls the veil at the height of her shoulder.

PORTRAIT B: SEATED FEMALE, ŠALMAT

The figure is shown frontally. Both arms are bent; the left is held at the height of the shoulder, the right to the right thigh. The head appears large, and the arms appear short in relation to the body. The left leg and right foot are obscured by the reclining figure.

She wears three headdresses: a headband, a turban, and a veil. The headband is divided into panels by vertical lines. The turban is coiled. The coiling of the fabric is rendered with horizontal grooves. The veil falls over the neck and shoulders with the right end of the veil crossing the chest in a curving fold and falling behind the left shoulder. Most of the hair is covered by the headdresses, except for a series of overlapping locks over the ears that cover the sides of the headband and disappear under the veil. The individual strands of hair are rendered by incised lines. Her face is round. The eyebrows are indicated by curving ridges, and the eyes are almond-shaped and large, with thick upper eyelids. The eyeballs appear blank. Only the earlobes are visible, and she is wearing earrings (details unclear). The nose is short and wide. The mouth is small with thin straight lips. The chin and neck are wide. She wears a necklace at the base of the neck; a plain hoop with a circular pendant with an incised border, suspended from the centre by a narrow sleeve.

She wears a tunic with a small, round neckline and long, wide sleeves. The folds of the tunic are indicated by curving grooves.

Her right hand rests on her right thigh. She holds a fold of the veil in her hand. The left hand is raised in front of the left shoulder, and she pulls the veil. She wears a bracelet around the left wrist, depicted as a wide, plain hoop with a central incision. She wears a ring with an oval bezel on the ring finger of the right hand.

PORTRAIT C: STANDING MALE, MOQÎMÛ

The figure is shown frontally. His right arm is bent in front of the middle of the torso, and the left falls to the side. His lower body is obscured by the reclining figure. The head appears large, and the arms appear short in relation to the body.

He has short hair arranged in curling locks. The individual strands of hair are rendered with curving, incised lines. His eyes are large and almond-shaped with thick eyelids. The end of the upper eyelids extends beyond the end of the lower ones. The irises are indicated by incised circles. The ears are protruding with the helix and scapha depicted. The nose is wide. The mouth is small with straight, thin lips. The chin and cheeks are wide. He wears a necklace at the base of the neck; a plain hoop with a circular pendant suspended from the centre.

He wears a tunic and a himation. The tunic is only visible at the upper area of the chest. The folds of the tunic are indicated by curving grooves. The himation covers the upper body almost completely. It covers the right shoulder and arm, and the edge of the himation crosses the chest diagonally and falls behind the left shoulder (›arm-sling‹ type). The left shoulder and arm are covered by the himation. The folds of the himation are indicated by oblique grooves.

The right hand lightly holds a fold of the himation. The thumb and the index finger are extended. The left hand appears to rest on the shoulder of the reclining figure (details unclear).

PORTRAIT D: RECLINING MALE, BÔLBARAK

The figure is depicted with his upper body frontally, and the head turned slightly to his left. He is reclining with his left leg bent under the right leg, leaving only the thigh and knee visible, and the right leg bent and depicted in profile. The lower left leg is obscured by the right leg. His right arm is bent and held at the torso, and his left arm is extended.

His face is square. He has short hair arranged in individual, crescent-shaped locks around the head. The eyebrows are depicted as curving grooves. The eyes are large and almond-shaped, with thick eyelids. The end of the upper eyelids extends beyond the end of the lower ones. The irises are indicated by incised circles and the pupils by punch holes. The ears are protruding, with the helix, scapha, and concha depicted. The nose is prominent and wide. The mouth is small, with full lips. He has a full beard that starts at the temples and covers the cheeks, the upper lip, and the chin. The facial hair is rendered by wavy locks indicated by diagonal, incised lines.

He wears a >Parthian-style< tunic, a chlamys, and >Parthian-style< trousers. The tunic has a wide, round neckline with a beaded border. The sleeves are long and tight-fitting, and the cuffs are decorated with rosettes. The tunic has a wide band along the middle with square panels, each decorated with a rosette separated by beaded bands, extending downwards. The tunic ends above the knees and has a decorated lower border with floral motifs at the hem. The chlamys is fastened at the right shoulder with a round brooch (details unclear) and is folded over the upper part of the torso. It falls over the left shoulder and one edge is wrapped around the left elbow, with a wide fold falling from under the left forearm. Along his right thigh, he has an object with a pointed end, rectangular main body, and two lateral circular elements: a sheathed dagger. The band belt is tied around the waist with a large central knot and the ends are looped under on either side of the waist. The trousers are visible from above the knees, and each trouser leg is decorated in the middle with a wide band with floral motifs that extends downwards. The trousers are tucked into the boots. The folds of the garments are indicated by wide, curving grooves. He wears a plain ankle-boot.

His right hand is resting against his knee and lower leg, and he holds an oblong object. With the upturned palm of the left hand, he holds an undecorated bowl with his fingers. The bowl has a defined rim indicated by an incised line, and a conical foot.

PORTRAIT E: SEATED FEMALE, ATTÂ

The figure is depicted frontally. Both arms are bent; the right is held at the height of the shoulder, the left at the left thigh. The head and the right forearm appear large in relation to the body.

She wears three headdresses: a headband, a turban, and a veil. The headband is divided into decorated panels by vertical lines (details unclear). The turban is coiled with two layers looped into each other creating a knot at the centre. The veil is heavy and falls over the neck and shoulders, covering the left arm. Most of the hair is covered by the headdresses, except for a series of overlapping locks over the ears that cover the sides of the headband and disappear under the veil. The individual strands of hair are rendered by curving, incised lines. Her face is square. The eyebrows are curving, and the eyes are large, almond-shaped, and slanting with thick eyelids. The irises are indicated (details unclear). Only the earlobes are visible, and she is wearing dumbbell-shaped earrings (Colledge classification: H). The nose has a wide base. The mouth is small, with full lips. The chin and neck are wide.

She wears a tunic and a himation. The ankle-length tunic has long, wide sleeves and a wide, angular neckline. The folds of the tunic are indicated by curving grooves. The himation is fastened at the left shoulder with a circular brooch (Colledge classification: i). It falls diagonally across the torso and covers the lower body, leaving only the hemline of tunic and the feet exposed. The folds of the himation are indicated by oblique grooves.

With the right hand, she pulls the veil at the height of the shoulder. With the left hand, she holds a fold of the veil that comes from under her left forearm.

SARCOPHAGUS BOX

PORTRAIT F: ARMLESS FEMALE BUST, ŠALMAT

The figure is shown frontally. The head and eyes appear large in relation to the body.

She wears two headdresses: a headband and a veil. The headband is decorated (other details unclear). The veil falls over the neck and shoulders, and crosses the chest in a curving fold, falling behind the left shoulder. Most of the hair is covered by the headdresses, except for three locks over the ears that cover the sides of the headband and disappear under the veil. The individual strands of hair are rendered by incised lines. Her face is round. The eyebrows are indicated by curving ridges and start from the top of the nose. The eyes are almond-shaped and slanting. The irises are indicated by incised circles, and the pupils are marked. Only the earlobes are visible, and she is wearing earrings (details unclear). The nose is wide and flat, and the mouth is small, with a thin upper lip. Her chin is wide.

She wears a tunic with a wide, v-shaped neckline visible under the veil. The folds of the tunic are indicated by oblique grooves.

PORTRAIT G: ARMLESS FEMALE BUST, AMATNANNAÎ
The figure is shown frontally.

She wears two headdresses: a headband and a veil. The band is placed low on the forehead. The veil falls over the neck and shoulders, crosses the chest in a curving fold, and falls over the left shoulder. Most of the hair is covered by the headdresses, except for a series of curving locks over the ears that cover the sides of the headband and disappear under the veil. The individual strands of hair are rendered by incised lines. Her face is round. The eyes are small, almond-shaped, and slanting with thick upper eyelids that extend beyond the end of the lower ones. The irises are indicated by incised circles and the pupils are marked. The nose is short and wide at the tip. The mouth is wide with full lips. Her chin is wide and pointed.

She wears a tunic with a wide, v-shaped neckline. The folds of the tunic are indicated by curving, wide grooves.

PORTRAIT H: ARMLESS MALE BUST, BÔLBARAK
The figure is shown frontally. The head appears large in relation to the body.

He has voluminous hair, arranged in three rows. The individual strands of hair are indicated by vertical, incised lines. His face is oval. The eyebrows are rendered as slightly curving ridges. The eyes are large and round, with the upper eyelids extending beyond the end of the lower ones. The irises are indicated by incised circles. The ears are slightly protruding and the helix and scapha are depicted. The nose is long and narrow. The mouth is wide with thin lips. The neck and chin are wide.

He wears a tunic and a himation. The tunic has a wide, v-shaped neckline. The folds of the tunic are indicated by curving grooves. The himation is wrapped around both shoulders, with the left end falling down the left shoulder. The folds of the himation are indicated by oblique grooves.

PORTRAIT I: ARMLESS FEMALE BUST, ATTÂ
The figure is shown frontally. The head appears large in relation to the body.

She wears two headdresses: a headband and a veil. The band is placed high on the forehead. The veil falls over the neck and shoulders, crosses the chest in a curving fold, and falls back over the left shoulder. Most of the hair is covered by the headdresses, except for three locks over the ears that are brushed over the sides of the headband and disappear under the veil. The individual strands of hair are rendered by incised lines. Her face is oval. The eyebrows are depicted as curving ridges. The eyes are small and almond-shaped. The irises are indicated by incised circles and the pupils are marked. Only the earlobes are visible. The nose is short and flat. The mouth is small with thin lips. The chin and neck are wide.

She wears a tunic with a wide, v-shaped neckline. The folds of the tunic are indicated by curving, wide grooves.

PORTRAIT J: ARMLESS MALE BUST, WAHBALLAT
The figure is shown frontally. The head appears large in relation to the body.

He has voluminous hair, arranged in three rows of curling locks. The individual strands of hair are indicated by incised lines. His face is round. The eyebrows are rendered as slightly curving ridges. The eyes are large and round. The irises are indicated (details unclear). The ears are slightly protruding, and the helix and concha are depicted. The nose is long and narrow. The mouth is wide with thin lips. The neck and chin are wide.

He wears a tunic and a himation. The tunic has a wide, v-shaped neckline. The folds of the tunic are indicated by curving grooves. The himation is wrapped around both shoulders, with the left end falling down the left shoulder. The folds of the himation are indicated by oblique grooves.

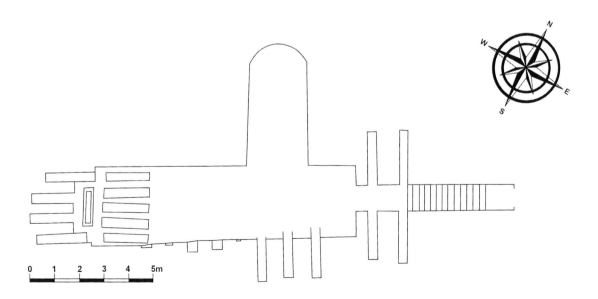

Plan of the hypogeum of the Bôlbarak family.

TOMBS DATED BY INSCRIPTION 207

A.D. 243–247

TOWER TOMB NO. 51, TOWER OF YAMLIKÛ

12. FRAGMENT OF SARCOPHAGUS LID WITH BANQUETING SCENE

DATABASE NUMBER: InSitu175.
LOCATION: Palmyra, Palmyra Museum, inv. no. unknown.
CONTEXT: West necropolis. Valley of the Tombs. Tower tomb no. 51, tower of Yamlikû, second floor. Possibly destroyed.
ACQUISITION HISTORY: —
MEASUREMENTS: Height: 185 cm. Width: 240 cm.
MATERIAL: Limestone.
PRESERVATION: Broken on right and upper side. Portrait A: The right side is broken off vertically from the lower torso and through the left thigh and the upper part is broken off horizontally through the upper chest. Portrait B: The upper part is broken off vertically through the upper chest, and at the lower left arm.
TECHNICAL DESCRIPTION: There are traces of red pigment in the inscription.

DATE: A.D. 243–247 (dated by inscription).
REFERENCES: Gawlikowski – al Asʿad 1997, 32 f. cat. 17 pl. 5, 2; Henning 2013b, 192–194 cat. 51 pl. 52, c. Inscription: Gawlikowski – al-Asʿad 1997, 32 f. cat. 17 pl. 5, 2; Yon 2013, 350 cat. 84.

OBJECT DESCRIPTION
The object is rectangular in shape and depicts two reclining males. The figures are resting on a mattress decorated with an intersecting lozenge pattern with flowers in the lozenges, visible below portrait A. Both reclining figures rest their left arm on a cushion. The cushions are decorated with a wide band with leaves set on a stem set between beaded bands. Curving grooves indicate the texture of the fabric.

NOTE: The tower of Yamlikû was destroyed in 2015 (Cuneo et al. 2015, 6).

INSCRIPTIONS
INSCRIPTION 1
SCRIPT: Palmyrene Aramaic.
LOCATION ON RELIEF: On the mattress.

Cat. 12

TRANSCRIPTION: ʿR[S]ʾ DNH WʿLYTʾ DY ṢʿPYʾ | TLTʾ WʿLYTʾ DYBGWʾ WMʿLYʾ ʿBD MQYMY | WNŠMY WʿGʾ WNWRBL BNY RDWNʾ BR MQYMY LYQRHWN | WLQYR BNYHWN WBNʾ BNYHWN LʿLM BYRḤ KNWN 55[---].

TRANSLATION: This couch and the higher part of the three --- (?) and the higher part which is inside and the entrance were made by Moqîmaî and Našumaî and ʿOggâ and Nûrbel, the sons of Rodônâ, son of Moqîmaî, in their honour and in the honour of their sons and the sons of their sons, for ever, in the month of Kanûn 55(5+) (A.D. 243–247).

INSCRIPTION 2
SCRIPT: Palmyrene Aramaic.
LOCATION ON RELIEF: On the fold of the tunic on the right reclining figure.
TRANSCRIPTION: ṢLM NŠMY [BR RDWNʾ] | Ḥ[BL].
TRANSLATION: Image of Našumaî son of Rodônâ, alas!

INSCRIPTION 3
SCRIPT: Palmyrene Aramaic.
LOCATION ON RELIEF: On the fold of the tunic on the left reclining figure.
TRANSCRIPTION: ṢLM MQYMY BR RDWNʾ ḤBL.
TRANSLATION: Image of Moqîmaî son of Rodônâ, alas!

CIS no. —; PAT no. —.

PORTRAIT A: RECLINING MALE, NAŠUMAÎ
The figure is shown in frontal view. The left arm is bent and held in front of the torso.

He wears a ›Parthian-style‹ tunic and a himation. At the middle, the tunic has a wide band with a running spiral motif between beaded bands. The folds of the tunic are rendered by curving, wide grooves. Over the tunic, he wears a himation. It is wrapped around his left lower arm and proceeds in a wide fold that ends in two s-shaped folds on the mattress. The folds of the himation are rendered by wide grooves. He wears a plain band belt, knotted at the centre with the ends looped under on either side of the waist.

PORTRAIT B: RECLINING MALE, MOQÎMAÎ
The figure is shown frontally. The arms appear short in relation to the body. The index and little finger of the right hand appear large in relation to the hand. The right arm is bent and held to the torso. The left is bent and held to the chest. The legs are obscured by the figure to his right.

He wears a tunic and a himation. The tunic has short sleeves. The folds of the tunic are rendered by curving, wide grooves. Over the tunic, he wears a himation. It is wrapped around his left arm and proceeds in a wide fold that ends in an s-shaped fold on the mattress. The folds of the himation are rendered by wide grooves. He wears a plain band belt, knotted at the centre with the ends looped under on either side of the waist.

He rests his right hand on the stomach. The thumb, index, and the little fingers are extended.

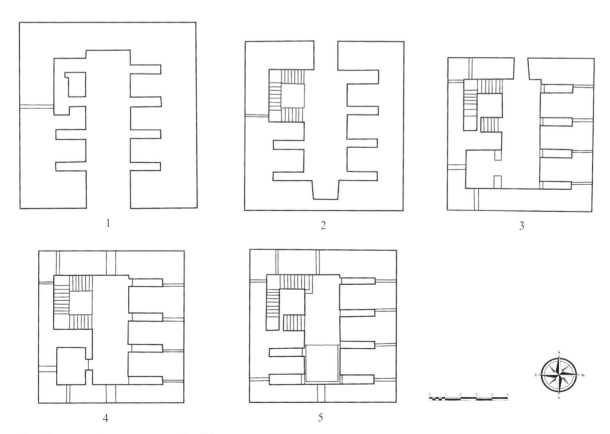

Plan of tower tomb no. 51, tower of Yamlikû.

Objects from Tower Tombs

A.D. 50–100

TOWER TOMB NO. 19

MALE HEADS

10–20 CM

13. MALE HEAD

Cat. 13

DATABASE NUMBER: PM322.
LOCATION: Palmyra, Palmyra Museum, inv. no. T 13.19.
CONTEXT: West necropolis. Valley of the Tombs. Tower tomb no. 19. Found at the threshold of the tower tomb (06.05.1961).
ACQUISITION HISTORY: —
MEASUREMENTS: Height: 15 cm. Width: 13 cm. Depth: 7.5 cm.
MATERIAL: Limestone, grey.
PRESERVATION: The figure is broken off at the top of the neck. The surface of the hair, eyes, and cheeks is chipped.
TECHNICAL DESCRIPTION: There are tool marks on the surface of the left cheek. There are traces of red colour on the hair, pupils, and face.
DATE: A.D. 50–100.

REFERENCES: Michalowski 1963, 209 f. cat. 1 figs. 247–248; Wielgosz-Rondolino 2016b, 172 fig. 7; <https://virtual-museum-syria.org/palmyra/honorific-portrait-head-of-a-young-man/> (06.05.2022).

OBJECT DESCRIPTION
The fragment depicts a male head.

PORTRAIT
The hair is arranged in one row of crescent-shaped curls. The individual strands of hair are rendered by incised lines. The face is oval and fleshy. The eyebrows are curving, rendered by thin ridges. The eyes are large, almond-shaped and slanting, with thick eyelids. The irises and pupils are plastically rendered with protruding, concentric circles. The nose is straight with a wide base. The mouth is small with a thin upper, and a full lower lip. The chin is round with a cleft.

14. MALE HEAD

Cat. 14

DATABASE NUMBER: PM454.
LOCATION: Palmyra, Palmyra Museum, inv. no. T 5.19.
CONTEXT: West necropolis. Valley of the Tombs. Tower tomb no. 19. Found in the main corridor of the tomb (03.05.1961).

ACQUISITION HISTORY: —
MEASUREMENTS: Height: 11.5 cm. Width: 11.5 cm. Depth: 9 cm.
MATERIAL: Limestone, grey.
PRESERVATION: The lower part of the figure is broken off at the neck. The face is chipped and weathered.
TECHNICAL DESCRIPTION: —
DATE: A.D. 50–100.
REFERENCES: Michalowski 1963, 213 f. cat. 5 fig. 253.

OBJECT DESCRIPTION
The fragment depicts the head of a male figure.

PORTRAIT
The hair is arranged in a row of s-shaped curls around his head. His face is oval. The eyebrows are curving, rendered by thin ridges. The eyes are close-set, large, round, with thick eyelids. The irises and pupils are depicted by concentric, incised circles. The nose is straight. The mouth is small with a thin upper lip and a full lower lip. The chin is round. The neck is wide.

15. MALE HEAD

Cat. 15

DATABASE NUMBER: PM455.
LOCATION: Palmyra, Palmyra Museum, inv. no. T 17.19.
CONTEXT: West necropolis. Valley of the Tombs. Tower tomb no. 19. Found in the vestibule of the tomb (06.05.1961).
ACQUISITION HISTORY: —
MEASUREMENTS: Height: 12 cm. Width: 8 cm. Depth: 11 cm.
MATERIAL: Limestone, grey.

PRESERVATION: The lower part of the figure is broken off at the neck. The left side of the face is broken off.
TECHNICAL DESCRIPTION: —
DATE: A.D. 50–100.
REFERENCES: Michalowski 1963, 215 cat. 6 fig. 254.

OBJECT DESCRIPTION
The fragment depicts the head of a male figure.

PORTRAIT
The hair is arranged in a row of s-shaped curls around his head. His face is oval. The eyebrows are curving, rendered by grooves. The eyes are large, round, with thick eyelids. The irises and pupils are depicted by concentric, incised circles. The mouth is small with a thin upper lip and a full lower lip. The chin is round. The neck is wide.

16. MALE HEAD

Cat. 16

DATABASE NUMBER: PM452.
LOCATION: Palmyra, Palmyra Museum, inv. no. T 14.19.
CONTEXT: West necropolis. Valley of the Tombs. Tower tomb no. 19. Found in the vestibule to the main gallery of the tomb (06.05.1961).
ACQUISITION HISTORY: —
MEASUREMENTS: Height: 12 cm. Width: 7 cm. Depth: 10.5 cm.
MATERIAL: Limestone, grey.
PRESERVATION: The lower part of the figure is broken off at the neck. The face is chipped, especially in the areas of the hair, right side of the forehead and eye, nose, and chin.

TECHNICAL DESCRIPTION: —
DATE: A.D. 75–100.
REFERENCES: Michalowski 1963, 213 f. cat. 4 fig. 252; Wielgosz-Rondolino 2016b, 170 fig. 5; <https://virtual-museum-syria.org/palmyra/head-of-a-statue-of-a-young-man/> (06.05.2022).

OBJECT DESCRIPTION
The fragment depicts the head of a male figure.

PORTRAIT
The hair is arranged in at least two rows of s-shaped curls around his head. His face is triangular. The eyebrows are curving, indicated by incised lines starting from the root of the nose. The eyes are close-set, large, round, with thick eyelids. The irises and pupils are depicted by concentric, incised circles. The nose is straight. The mouth is small with full lips.

20–30 CM

17. MALE HEAD

Cat. 17

DATABASE NUMBER: PM451.
LOCATION: Palmyra, Palmyra Museum, inv. no. T 7.19.
CONTEXT: West necropolis. Valley of the Tombs. Tower tomb no. 19 with hypogeum, main corridor, near north gallery.
ACQUISITION HISTORY: —
MEASUREMENTS: Height: 23 cm. Width: 19 cm. Depth: 13.5 cm.
MATERIAL: Limestone, white/grey.

PRESERVATION: The head is broken off just above the shoulders. The upper part of the head is broken off. The nose, mouth, and chin are chipped. The surface is heavily weathered.
TECHNICAL DESCRIPTION: —
DATE: A.D. 50–100.
REFERENCES: Michalowski 1963, 211 f. cat. 3 fig. 251.

OBJECT DESCRIPTION
The object depicts a male head.

PORTRAIT
His hair is arranged in a single row of s-shaped locks brushed from the top of the head towards the forehead. The individual strands of hair are indicated by incised lines. His face is long and oval. The eyebrows are curving, rendered by incised lines. The eyes are large and almost round with thick eyelids. The irises are indicated by incised circles. The ears are large and protruding, with the helix, scapha, and earlobe indicated. The neck is slender with a curving groove.

FEMALE HEADS

10–20 CM

18. FEMALE HEAD

Cat. 18

DATABASE NUMBER: PM453.
LOCATION: Palmyra, Palmyra Museum, inv. no. T 15.19.

CONTEXT: West necropolis. Valley of the Tombs. Tower tomb no. 19. Found in the vestibule of the tomb (06.05.1961).
ACQUISITION HISTORY: —
MEASUREMENTS: Height: 10.7 cm. Width: 8.5 cm. Depth: 7.6 cm.
MATERIAL: Limestone, grey.
PRESERVATION: The lower part of the figure is broken off at the neck. The left side of the forehead and the left, lower part of the face are broken off. The left side of the veil is chipped.
TECHNICAL DESCRIPTION: There are traces of red colour on the face and of black colour on the eyebrows and pupils.
DATE: A.D. 50–100.
REFERENCES: Michalowski 1963, 216 cat. 7 fig. 255; Wielgosz-Rondolino 2016b, 168 fig. 6; Krag 2018, 107 n. 109; 167 cat. 17; <https://virtual-museum-syria.org/palmyra/damaged-females-head-part-of-a-funerary-scene/> (06.05.2022).

OBJECT DESCRIPTION
The fragment depicts the head of a female figure.

PORTRAIT
She wears three headdresses: a headband, a turban, and a veil. The headband is placed low on the forehead. It is undecorated and a deep groove in the middle indicates the folding of the fabric. The turban is coiled. Oblique grooves indicate the coiling of the fabric. The veil is heavy. It falls over the back of the head down to the shoulders. The face is square. The eyebrows are curving, rendered by incised lines. The eyes are large, round, with thick eyelids. The irises are depicted by incised circles and the pupils by punch holes. The nose is straight with a wide base. The mouth is wide. The neck is slender with two curving grooves.

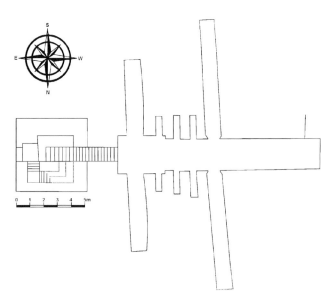

Plan of tower tomb no. 19.

TOWER TOMB NO. 67, TOWER OF ḤAÎRAN

BANQUETING RELIEFS

19. FRAGMENT OF BANQUETING RELIEF

DATABASE NUMBER: PM631.
LOCATION: Palmyra, Palmyra Museum, inv. no. unknown.
CONTEXT: West necropolis, Valley of the Tombs. Tomb no. 67, tower of Ḥaîran. The relief was found in the hypogeum of the tower.
ACQUISITION HISTORY: —
MEASUREMENTS: Height: 57 cm. Width: 59 cm.
MATERIAL: Limestone.
PRESERVATION: The upper, right, and left side of the relief are broken off. The lower left side of the relief is heavily chipped. The surface is weathered. Portrait A: The head and arms of the figure are broken off. The torso and right leg are chipped. Portrait B: The head and the right side of the torso are broken off. The arms and right knee are chipped. Portrait C: Most of the body, except for the lower right leg of the figure, is broken off.
TECHNICAL DESCRIPTION: —
DATE: A.D. 50–100 (Gawlikowski 1970b: soon after A.D. 33).
REFERENCES: Gawlikowski 1970b, 81–83 fig. 12; Colledge 1976, 73. 131. 136. 239 fig. 39; Henning 2013b, 208 pl. 59, a. Inscription: Gawlikowski 1970b, 82.

OBJECT DESCRIPTION
The object is rectangular in shape and depicts two standing male figures next to a male reclining on a kline with a mattress. The texture and fabric of the mattress are indicated by curving grooves. A small corner of the kline is depicted, with the uppermost turning of the kline leg and a part of the stretcher.

INSCRIPTIONS
INSCRIPTION 1
SCRIPT: Palmyrene Aramaic.
LOCATION ON RELIEF: Above the left shoulder of the male on the left, over the dividing line.
TRANSCRIPTION: [- - - BLŠWRY BR] ḤYRN BR | [BLŠWRY - - -]H LYQR.
TRANSLATION: - - - Belšûrî son of Ḥaîran son of Belšûrî - - - for his honour.

INSCRIPTION 2
SCRIPT: Palmyrene Aramaic.
LOCATION ON RELIEF: Above the left shoulder of the male on the left, below the dividing line.
TRANSCRIPTION: ṢLM | ḤYRN | BRH.
TRANSLATION: Image of Ḥaîran his son.

INSCRIPTION 3
SCRIPT: Palmyrene Aramaic.
LOCATION ON RELIEF: Between the two standing figures.
TRANSCRIPTION: ṢLM | ŠBY | BRH.

TRANSLATION: Image of Šabî his son.

INSCRIPTION 4
SCRIPT: Palmyrene Aramaic.
LOCATION ON RELIEF: Between the legs of the kline.
TRANSCRIPTION: [- - -]YT.
TRANSLATION: —

Inscription 1: CIS no. —; PAT no. 0127.
Inscription 2: CIS no. —; PAT no. 0128.
Inscription 3: CIS no. —; PAT no. 0129.
Inscription 4: CIS no. —; PAT no. 0130.

PORTRAIT A: STANDING MALE
The figure is shown frontally. The left arm falls along the side. He wears a tunic and a himation. The tunic has a wide, v-shaped neckline. The folds of the tunic are indicated by oblique, incised lines. Over the tunic, he wears a himation that covers the left shoulder and side of the figure, is wrapped around the waist, and covers the legs. The folds of the himation are indicated by horizontal, incised lines over the waist and oblique grooves over the legs.

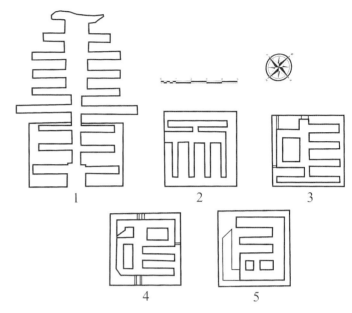

Plan of tomb no. 67, tower of Ḥaîran.

Cat. 19

His left hand rests on the left thigh, possibly holding a fold of the himation (visible in outline).

PORTRAIT B: STANDING MALE

The figure is shown in a three-quarter view. The right arm is bent and raised in front of him and to the side, and the left arm falls to the side.

He wears a tunic and a himation. The tunic has short, wide sleeves. Over the tunic, he wears a himation that covers the left shoulder and side of the figure, is wrapped around the waist, and covers the legs. The folds of the himation are indicated by horizontal, incised lines over the waist and curving and oblique grooves over the legs.

With his raised right hand, he holds a wreath. With his lowered left hand, he holds an object with an oblong body, possibly a libation pitcher.

PORTRAIT C: RECLINING MALE

The right leg of the figure is raised and bent. The figure's torso is shown in a three-quarter view. The arms and right leg are shown in profile. The left leg is shown frontally.

He is dressed. The oblique grooves indicate that he wears a garment that covers the legs.

A.D. 50–150

TOWER TOMB NO. 15

MALE HEADS

20. MALE HEAD

DATABASE NUMBER: PM713.
LOCATION: Palmyra, Palmyra Museum, inv. no. T 2.
CONTEXT: West necropolis. Valley of the Tombs. Tower tomb no. 15. Found at the threshold of the tower tomb (25.04.1962).
ACQUISITION HISTORY: —
MEASUREMENTS: Height: 18.5 cm. Width: 12 cm. Depth: 16 cm.
MATERIAL: Limestone, grey.
PRESERVATION: The figure is broken off at the top of the neck. The surface of the face is chipped.
TECHNICAL DESCRIPTION: There are traces of plaster on the left cheek and head and of red colour in the hair.
DATE: A.D. 50–150.
REFERENCES: Michalowski 1964, 160 f. cat. 2 fig. 190.

OBJECT DESCRIPTION

The fragment depicts a male head.

PORTRAIT

The hair is arranged in one row of crescent-shaped curls. The individual strands of hair are rendered by incised lines. The face is oval. The eyebrows are curving, rendered by grooves starting from the root of the nose. The eyes are small and round with thick eyelids. The irises are indicated by incised circles. The nose is straight. The alae are carved. The mouth is small with a thin upper, and a full lower lip. The chin is pointed.

Cat. 20

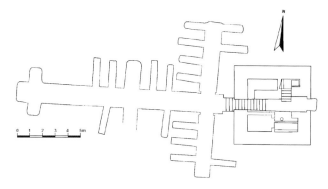

Plan of tower tomb no. 15.

TOWER TOMB NO. 85D

SARCOPHAGUS BOXES

21. FRAGMENT OF SARCOPHAGUS BOX WITH PORTRAIT BUSTS

DATABASE NUMBER: InSitu188.
LOCATION: Palmyra, in situ.
CONTEXT: West necropolis. Valley of the Tombs. Tower tomb no. 85d.
ACQUISITION HISTORY: —
MEASUREMENTS: —
MATERIAL: Limestone.
PRESERVATION: The right, lower, and left side are broken off. The object is heavily weathered and is broken vertically between the portraits. Portrait A: The head is broken off. The hands are chipped. Portrait B: The head is heavily chipped. The surface of the left shoulder and lower arms are chipped.
TECHNICAL DESCRIPTION: —
DATE: A.D. 50–150.
REFERENCES: Henning 2013b, 233.

OBJECT DESCRIPTION

The box is rectangular in shape and depicts a kline with two busts between the kline legs; a female and a priest. Above the figures is a thick mattress decorated with two wide bands decorated with a vegetal motif set between beaded bands (details unclear). Curving grooves indicate the texture of the fabric. On the right side, an oval part is preserved, possibly depicting a part of the kline leg.

PORTRAIT A: FEMALE BUST

The figure is shown frontally. The arms are bent and held to the torso.

She wears a heavy veil that falls over both shoulders and is wrapped around both arms. The folds are indicated by oblique grooves. A single curving lock of hair falls along the left side of the neck. The individual strands of hair are indicated by incised lines. She wears earrings shaped like miniature a bunch of grapes (Colledge classification: E).

She wears a tunic and a himation. The tunic has a wide, round neckline. The folds of the tunic are indicated by curving grooves. The himation falls diagonally from the left shoulder to the right side. It is fastened at the left shoulder with a trapezoidal brooch with an incised border and a round finial (Colledge classification: a/b). From the brooch, a P-shaped key and two circular rings are suspended. The key is decorated with an X-shaped incision, and the right ring is larger than the left ring. The folds of the himation are indicated by curving grooves.

With the left hand she holds a conical object incised with fine wavy lines, with a bowl-shaped tip, and a thick, round staff topped by a circular element, with a pattern of crisscrossing, incised lines. These are reduced versions of a spindle and a distaff.

PORTRAIT B: BUST OF A PRIEST

The figure is shown frontally. The arms are bent and held to the torso.

He wears a tall, cylindrical, flat-top headdress: a Palmyrene priestly hat.

He wears a tunic (according to Henning 2013b he also wears a chlamys). The tunic has short sleeves. The folds are indicated by vertical grooves.

Cat. 21

A.D. 100–150

TOWER TOMB NO. 39

SARCOPHAGUS BOXES

22. SARCOPHAGUS BOX WITH PORTRAIT BUSTS

DATABASE NUMBER: InSitu116.
LOCATION: Palmyra, in situ.
CONTEXT: West necropolis. Tower Tomb no. 39, ground floor.
ACQUISITION HISTORY: —
MEASUREMENTS: —
MATERIAL: Limestone.
PRESERVATION: The surface is heavily weathered and chipped.
TECHNICAL DESCRIPTION: —
DATE: A.D. 100–150 (Henning 2013b: A.D. 100–130).
REFERENCES: Watzinger – Wulzinger 1932, 52; Gawlikowski 1970a, 106; Henning 2013b, 178 f. pl. 38, c.

OBJECT DESCRIPTION

The sarcophagus box is rectangular in shape and is rendered as a kline. Three busts are depicted between the legs of the kline (details unclear).

PORTRAIT A: BUST
The figure is shown frontally.

PORTRAIT B: BUST
The figure is shown frontally.

PORTRAIT C: BUST
The figure is shown frontally.

A.D. 103–273

TOWER TOMB NO. 13, TOWER OF ELAHBEL

SARCOPHAGUS LIDS

A.D. 170–200

23. FRAGMENT OF SARCOPHAGUS LID WITH BANQUETING SCENE

DATABASE NUMBER: InSitu238.
LOCATION: Palmyra, Palmyra Museum, inv. no. unknown.
CONTEXT: West necropolis. Valley of the Tombs. Tower tomb no. 13, tower of Elahbel, third floor.
ACQUISITION HISTORY: —
MEASUREMENTS: Height: 75 cm. Width: 130 cm. Depth: 35 cm.
MATERIAL: Limestone, yellow.
PRESERVATION: The upper part of the object is broken off. Portrait A: The upper part of the figure is broken off at the waist. The right foot is chipped. Portrait B: The head is broken off. The surface of the left arm and of the attribute is chipped.

Cat. 22

TECHNICAL DESCRIPTION: —
DATE: A.D. 170–200 (Henning 2013b: A.D. 150–200).
REFERENCES: Seyrig 1937, 16 n. 2; Henning 2013a, 164 fig. 17; Henning 2013b, 306 f. cat. S 46 pl. 27, c; Silver et al. 2018, 177 f. fig. 9.34.

OBJECT DESCRIPTION

The object is rectangular in shape and depicts a standing male and a reclining male. Beneath the figures is a mattress. It is decorated with an intersecting lozenges pattern with beaded elements at the points of the intersections. In the centre of these squares are four-petal flowers, with incised veins at the petals.

PORTRAIT A: STANDING MALE

The figure is shown in frontal view. He stands with his feet on the mattress. The left lower leg is obscured by the reclining figure to his right.

He wears a >Parthian-style< tunic and >Parthian-style< trousers. The tunic ends at the knees and the lower border is decorated with a band of lanceolate leaves on a stem. The folds of the tunic are indicated with curving and vertical grooves. The folds of the trousers are rendered by curving grooves. He also wears a plain band belt, knotted at the centre with the ends looped under on either side of the waist. He wears closed-toe ankle boots. The shaft is decorated with a beaded band.

PORTRAIT B: RECLINING MALE

The chest is shown in frontal view, the lower body and legs in three-quarter view. The right arm is extended and rests on his raised right knee. The left arm is bent in front of the chest, and rests on a cushion. The cushion is folded in a snail-shell curl and decorated with a wide band with floral motifs. Curving grooves indicate the texture of the fabric. His right leg is bent and the right foot rests on the mattress. The left leg is bent under the right, and the knee is pointing forwards. The left lower leg is obscured by the right leg.

He wears a >Parthian-style< tunic, a chlamys, and >Parthian-style< trousers. The tunic has a round neckline decorated with a beaded band. The tunic has long, tight-fitting sleeves. The cuffs are decorated with a wide band with floral motifs between two narrow bands. The tunic has a wide band decorated with leaves on a stem extending downwards from the middle of the neckline. The tunic ends above the knees, and the lower border is decorated with a band of crossing lines with floral motifs. The folds of the tunic are rendered by oblique and vertical grooves. He wears a plain band belt, knotted at the centre

Cat. 23

with the ends looped under on either side of the waist. Over the tunic, he wears a chlamys: it falls over both shoulders and the left arm and continues down the left side of the body until the mattress, where it ends in two large zigzag-shaped folds. The chlamys is fastened at the left shoulder with a polygonal brooch with curved sides meeting in flat ends. There is a single bead between each curved side and an incised circle at the centre of the brooch (Colledge classification: i). A small zigzag-shaped fold falls from the brooch. The edge of the chlamys is decorated with a band with a floral motif, visible at the diagonal fold across the chest. The trousers are visible from the knee: each trouser leg is decorated in the middle with a wide band with vegetal motifs extending downwards. The folds of the garments are indicated by curving grooves. He wears closed-toe ankle boots. They are decorated with running scrolls and rosettes, rendered by incised lines. Around the ankle is a plain strap with a knot. The shaft is decorated with a band with a running scroll.

He rests his right hand on his right knee. In his right hand, he holds an oblong oval object with an incised diamond-pattern, possibly a pinecone. With the upturned palm of the left hand, he holds a bowl (visible in outline).

24. FRAGMENT OF SARCOPHAGUS LID WITH BANQUETING SCENE

DATABASE NUMBER: InSitu237.
LOCATION: Palmyra, Palmyra Museum, inv. no. unknown.
CONTEXT: West necropolis. Valley of the Tombs. Tower tomb no. 13, tower of Elahbel.
ACQUISITION HISTORY: —
MEASUREMENTS: Height: 77 cm. Width: 115 cm. Depth: 32 cm.
MATERIAL: Limestone.
PRESERVATION: The head is broken off at the base of the neck, and the lower part is broken off diagonally at the right thigh and left knee. The right arm is broken off. The left lower arm is chipped.
TECHNICAL DESCRIPTION: —
DATE: A.D. 170–200 (Henning 2013b: A.D. 150–200).
REFERENCES: Ingholt Archives, PS 1333; Starcky 1941, 34 fig. 27; Stauffer 2012, 90. 94 pls. 14–15; Henning 2013b, 305 cat. S 43 pl. 26, a.

OBJECT DESCRIPTION

The object depicts a reclining male. The figure rests on a thin mattress decorated with an intersecting lozenge pattern with rosettes in the lozenges. The left arm is resting on two cushions: the lower cushion is decorated with a band with a vegetal motif between beaded bands, the upper cushion is decorated with

Cat. 24

a wide band and a beaded band (details unclear). Curving grooves indicate the texture of the fabric.

PORTRAIT

The figure is shown frontally. The left arm appears short in relation to the body. The left arm is bent in front of the chest.

He wears a >Parthian-style< tunic, a chlamys, >Parthian-style< trousers, and over-trousers. The tunic has a small, round neckline. The tunic covers his body and ends at his thighs, where the border is decorated with a band (details unclear). The folds of the tunic are rendered by oblique and curving grooves. He also wears a plain band belt across the lower torso. It is knotted at the centre with the ends looped under either side of the waist. Over the tunic, he wears a chlamys that falls over both shoulders, and covers the upper chest. The edge of the chlamys has a scalloped border decorated with rosettes and a beaded band, visible on the fold across the chest. The chlamys is folded around his left arm and proceeds in one s-shaped fold over the cushions and his left side. The edge of the fold has a band with a vegetal motif. The folds of the chlamys are rendered by oblique and curving grooves. The trousers are visible at the knees. At the middle, the trouser leg is decorated with bands extending downwards: a wide, central one with a vegetal motif set between beaded bands. The over-trousers are indicated by curving grooves under the knee.

He holds an object in his left hand, possibly a skyphos.

25. FRAGMENT OF SARCOPHAGUS LID WITH BANQUETING SCENE

DATABASE NUMBER: InSitu096.
LOCATION: Palmyra, in situ.
CONTEXT: West necropolis. Valley of the Tombs. Tower tomb no. 13, tower of Elahbel, found on the third floor.
ACQUISITION HISTORY: —
MEASUREMENTS: Height: 90 cm. Width: 125 cm. Depth: 34 cm.
MATERIAL: Limestone, white/yellow.
PRESERVATION: The head is broken off at the base of the neck. The right arm is broken off at the shoulder and the left arm just below the shoulder. Only the torso and legs are preserved.
TECHNICAL DESCRIPTION: —
DATE: A.D. 170–200 (Henning 2013b: A.D. 150–200).
REFERENCES: Henning 2013b, 306 cat. S 45 pl. 26, c; Silver et al. 2018, 177 f. fig. 9.33.

Cat. 25

OBJECT DESCRIPTION
The sarcophagus lid depicts a reclining male.

PORTRAIT
The body is shown in three-quarter view.

He wears two ›Parthian-style‹ tunics, a chlamys, and ›Parthian-style‹ trousers. The innermost tunic has a small, round neckline decorated with a beaded band. The folds are indicated by curving grooves. On top he wears a tunic that has a low, round neckline decorated with two bands: a band of squares and a beaded band. The tunic ends above his knees and has a decorated lower border with a running scroll with rosettes. The folds of the tunic are rendered by curving, wide grooves. He also wears a band belt across the lower torso. It is knotted at the centre with the ends looped under either side of the waist. The ends of the belt have fringes. Over the tunic, he wears a chlamys that falls over both shoulders, and covers most of the chest. The upper edge of the chlamys has a border with a running scroll with rosettes and a beaded band. The chlamys is fastened at the right shoulder with a circular brooch with a hollowed centre as indication of an inlay (Colledge classification: i). A zigzag-shaped fold falls from under the brooch and on the left side of the torso. The folds of the chlamys are rendered by curving grooves. He wears trousers that have a wide band (details unclear), set between bands with squares, extending downwards. The folds of the trousers are indicated by curving grooves.

26. FRAGMENT OF SARCOPHAGUS LID WITH BANQUETING SCENE

DATABASE NUMBER: InSitu236.
LOCATION: Palmyra, Palmyra Museum, inv. no. unknown.
CONTEXT: West necropolis. Valley of the Tombs. Tower tomb no. 13, tower of Elahbel.
ACQUISITION HISTORY: —
MEASUREMENTS: Height: 60 cm. Width: 92 cm. Depth: 32 cm.
MATERIAL: Limestone.
PRESERVATION: The head is broken off at the base of the neck and the right and lower part are broken off at the right shoulder and at the waist.
TECHNICAL DESCRIPTION: —
DATE: A.D. 170–200 (Henning 2013b: A.D. 100–150).
REFERENCES: Henning 2013b, 307 cat. S 47 pl. 27, a.

OBJECT DESCRIPTION
The object depicts a reclining male figure. He rests the left arm against a cushion. It is decorated with a band with a crisscross design between beaded bands.

PORTRAIT
The figure is shown frontally. The left arm appears short in relation to the body. The left arm is bent in front of the torso.

He wears a tunic and a himation. The tunic has a wide, round neckline. The folds of the tunic are rendered by curving grooves. Over the tunic, he wears a himation. It is folded over his left shoulder and arm, leaving most of the chest and hand free. The folds of the himation are rendered by vertical grooves. He holds a skyphos in his left hand. It has a conical foot and a straight body decorated with a tongues pattern.

Cat. 26

Cat. 27

27. FRAGMENT OF SARCOPHAGUS LID WITH BANQUETING SCENE

DATABASE NUMBER: InSitu137.
LOCATION: Palmyra, in situ.
CONTEXT: West necropolis. Valley of the Tombs. Tower tomb no. 13, tower of Elahbel, found on the ground floor.
ACQUISITION HISTORY: —
MEASUREMENTS: Height: 26 cm. Width: 35 cm. Depth: 17 cm.
MATERIAL: Limestone.
PRESERVATION: The upper part of the figure is broken off at the collarbone. The left arm and the lower right arm are broken off. The lower part of the body is broken off at the waist.
TECHNICAL DESCRIPTION: —
DATE: A.D. 170–200 (Henning 2013b: A.D. 150–200).
REFERENCES: Henning 2013b, 233 cat. S 41 pl. 13, a.

OBJECT DESCRIPTION
The object depicts a standing male.

PORTRAIT
The figure is shown frontally. The right arm is bent and held in front of the torso.

He wears a tunic, possibly also a chlamys and another garment, perhaps a mantle. The tunic has short, wide sleeves. The folds are rendered by oblique grooves. A zigzag-shaped fold that falls over the right side of the chest and curving folds over the centre of the chest may indicate a chlamys. Another garment, perhaps a mantle, may be indicated by the decorated piece of fabric that is shown over the upper waist of the figure, that shows a band with a running scroll and rosettes between beaded bands.

28. FRAGMENTS OF SARCOPHAGUS LID WITH BANQUETING SCENE

DATABASE NUMBER: InSitu138.
LOCATION: Palmyra, in situ.
CONTEXT: West necropolis. Valley of the Tombs. Tower tomb no. 13, tower of Elahbel.
ACQUISITION HISTORY: —
MEASUREMENTS: Fragment 1: Height: 42 cm. Width: 30 cm. Fragment 2: Height: 42 cm. Width: 53 cm. Fragment 3: Height: 70 cm. Width: 53 cm. Depth of fragments: 25–30 cm.
MATERIAL: Limestone.
PRESERVATION: The object is preserved in three fragments. The surface is weathered. The feet are broken off and the upper part of the body is broken off at the waist. The head is broken off at the base of the neck; the lower part of the body is broken off at the waist. The left hand and left shoulder are chipped. The surface is weathered.
TECHNICAL DESCRIPTION: —
DATE: A.D. 170–200 (Henning 2013b: A.D. 150–200).
REFERENCES: Henning 2013b, 233 cat. S 36 pl. 13, a.

OBJECT DESCRIPTION
The object shows a reclining male. The figure rests on a thin mattress decorated with a running scroll with alternating central rosettes and trefoils. He rests one arm on two cushions. There is a band on each cushion: the band on the upper cushion is decorated with a running scroll with central rosettes set between beaded bands, the one on the lower cushion is decorated with a crisscross pattern set between beaded bands. Curving grooves indicate the texture of the fabric.

PORTRAIT
The figure is shown frontally. The left arm is bent and held in front of the torso. The legs are shown in three-quarter view. The right leg is bent upwards, the left is bent under the right leg.

He wears a tunic, a chlamys, and a himation. The tunic has a small, scalloped neckline decorated with a thin, beaded band. The tunic reaches the ankles, and the folds of the tunic are indicated by curving grooves. The chlamys falls over both shoulders and is folded over the left arm. The chlamys continues along the left side of the figure, along the mattress. It is fastened at the right shoulder with a circular brooch with an outer beaded band (Colledge classification: f). The fold of the chlamys that crosses the chest and falls along the mattress, is decorated with a running scroll with central rosettes. The folds of the chlamys are indicated by curving grooves. The himation is folded around the waist in a large fold and covers the legs. The folds of the himation are indicated by curving grooves.

With the left hand, he holds an object, possibly a skyphos.

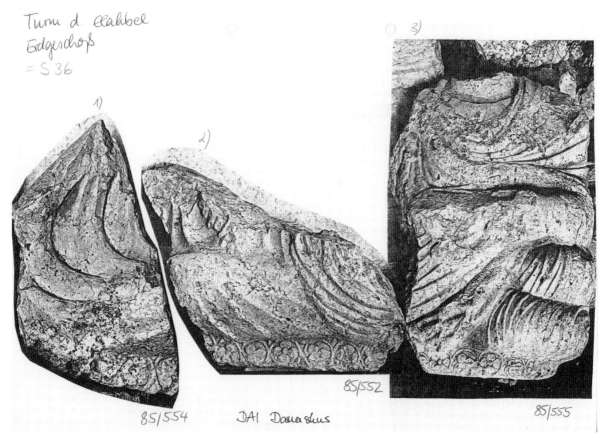

Cat. 28

29. FRAGMENT OF SARCOPHAGUS LID WITH BANQUETING SCENE

Cat. 29

DATABASE NUMBER: InSitu140.
LOCATION: Palmyra, in situ.
CONTEXT: West necropolis. Valley of the Tombs. Tower tomb no. 13, tower of Elahbel, ground floor.
ACQUISITION HISTORY: —
MEASUREMENTS: Height: 35 cm. Width: 41 cm. Depth: 26 cm.
MATERIAL: Limestone.
PRESERVATION: The upper part of the body is broken off below the waist. The right leg and lower left leg are broken off. The surface of the mattress is chipped.
TECHNICAL DESCRIPTION: —
DATE: A.D. 170–200 (Henning 2013b: A.D. 150–200).
REFERENCES: Henning 2013b, 304 cat. S 38.

OBJECT DESCRIPTION
The object shows the lower torso and part of the left leg of a reclining figure. Underneath the figure, is a thin mattress (details unclear).

PORTRAIT
The figure is shown frontally. The left leg is bent.

He wears a ›Parthian-style‹ tunic, ›Parthian-style‹ trousers, and over-trousers. The tunic ends at the knees and the border is decorated with a beaded band and a running scroll with central rosettes. The folds of the tunic are indicated by curving grooves. He also wears a plain band belt, where one end is looped under at the side. The end of the belt is decorated with a beaded band and vegetal motifs (details unclear). The trousers are visible from below the tunic to the knees. They have a band extending downwards in the middle, decorated with a vegetal motif (details unclear). Over the trousers, from the knees, he wears over-trousers. The upper border has a band decorated with a crisscross pattern. Curving grooves indicate the folds of the fabric.

30. FRAGMENT OF SARCOPHAGUS LID WITH BANQUETING SCENE

Cat. 30

DATABASE NUMBER: InSitu139.
LOCATION: Palmyra, in situ.
CONTEXT: West necropolis. Valley of the Tombs. Tower tomb no. 13, tower of Elahbel.
ACQUISITION HISTORY: —
MEASUREMENTS: Height: 39 cm. Width: 18 cm. Depth: 25 cm.
MATERIAL: Limestone.
PRESERVATION: The fragment is broken off on the right, upper, and left side.
TECHNICAL DESCRIPTION: —
DATE: A.D. 170–200 (Henning 2013b: A.D. 100–200).
REFERENCES: Henning 2013b, 233 cat. S 37 pl. 13, a.

OBJECT DESCRIPTION
The fragment shows part of a reclining figure. The figure rests on a thin mattress decorated with a running scroll with alternating central rosettes and trefoils.

Henning (2013b) suggests that because of the size and style the object may join either with cat. 20 or with cat. 28.

PORTRAIT
The figure wears a garment, where the folds are indicated by curving grooves. A small tassel is depicted along the mattress.

A.D. 200–220

31. FRAGMENTS OF SARCOPHAGUS LID WITH BANQUETING SCENE

DATABASE NUMBER: InSitu185.
LOCATION: Palmyra, in situ.
CONTEXT: West necropolis. Valley of the Tombs. Tower tomb no. 13, tower of Elahbel, third floor.
ACQUISITION HISTORY: —
MEASUREMENTS: Height: 76 cm. Width: 130 cm. Depth: 28 cm.
MATERIAL: Limestone.
PRESERVATION: The head is broken off at the base of the neck and the lower part of the figure is broken off below the knees. A large crack runs vertically at the waist. The surface is weathered.
TECHNICAL DESCRIPTION: —
DATE: A.D. 200–220 (Schmidt-Colinet 1992: A.D. 150–200).
REFERENCES: Makowski 1983, 181 n. 22; Schmidt-Colinet 1992, 110; Schmidt-Colinet 1996, 471 fig. 188; Henning 2013b, 305 f. cat. S 44 pl. 26, b; Krag 2018, 49 n. 229; 64 n. 361. 362; 65 n. 374; 98 n. 28; 103 n. 75; 314 cat. 557.

OBJECT DESCRIPTION

The object shows a reclining figure. The figure lies on a mattress decorated with a floral motif and rests the left arm on two cushions. Each of the cushions has a band decorated with a floral motif set between beaded bands. Curving grooves indicate the texture of the fabric.

PORTRAIT

The figure is shown in frontal to three-quarter view. The arms appear short in relation to the body. The right arm is slightly bent and held along the body. The left arm is bent and rests along her side.

She wears a tunic and a himation. The tunic has a wide, v-shaped neckline and short, wide sleeves that reach to the elbow. The tunic covers her torso. The folds of the tunic are indicated by curving grooves. Over the tunic, she wears a himation. It is wrapped around her left shoulder and arm, leaving the chest and the hand free. It falls along the left side of his torso where it is folded over the tunic, across her waist and legs. A zigzag-shaped fold falls from under her left hand. The folds of the himation are indicated by curving and oblique grooves. She holds a branch with her right hand. The individual leaves are rendered by incised lines. She holds a fold of the himation with her left hand.

Cat. 31

A.D. 200–273

32. FRAGMENT OF SARCOPHAGUS LID WITH BANQUETING SCENE

DATABASE NUMBER: InSitu189.
LOCATION: Palmyra, in situ.
CONTEXT: West necropolis. Valley of the Tombs. Tower tomb no. 13, tower of Elahbel, ground floor, loculus bay O III.
ACQUISITION HISTORY: —
MEASUREMENTS: Height: 80 cm. Width: 100 cm. Depth: 30–15 cm.
MATERIAL: Limestone.
PRESERVATION: The right and upper sides are broken off. The surface is weathered. The upper part of the figure is broken off horizontally at the waist and the lower part of the legs is broken off at the thighs. The left lower arm is chipped.
TECHNICAL DESCRIPTION: —
DATE: A.D. 200–273.
REFERENCES: Henning 2013b, 307 f. cat. S 50.

OBJECT DESCRIPTION

The object depicts a reclining male. Beneath the figure, is a thin mattress (details unclear). He rests the left arm on two cushions; the lower cushion is decorated with a band with a vegetal motif (details unclear). Curving grooves indicate the texture of the fabric.

PORTRAIT

The figure is shown frontally. The left arm is bent and held in front of the torso.

He wears a long garment, possibly a himation. The himation falls in a zigzag-shaped fold underneath the left arm and along the cushions and mattress. The folds of the himation are indicated by curving grooves.

With the left hand, he holds a skyphos. The skyphos has a conical foot.

SARCOPHAGI RELIEFS

A.D. 103–150

33. SARCOPHAGUS BOX RELIEF WITH PORTRAIT BUSTS

DATABASE NUMBER: InSitu077.
LOCATION: Palmyra, in situ.
CONTEXT: West necropolis. Valley of the Tombs. Tower tomb no. 13, tower of Elahbel.
ACQUISITION HISTORY: —
MEASUREMENTS: —
MATERIAL: —
PRESERVATION: The surface of the relief is severely weathered. The central part of the mattress and the right kline leg are chipped.

Cat. 32

TECHNICAL DESCRIPTION: —
DATE: A.D. 103–150.
REFERENCES: Chabot 1922, 89 pl. 11, 1; Watzinger – Wulzinger 1932, 48; Gawlikowski 1969, 49 f. figs. 2–3; Gawlikowski 1970a, 41. 90 f. 96. 175. fig. 48; Tanabe 1986, 29 pl. 182; Schmidt-Colinet 1996, 365. 471 cat. 57a fig. 187; Gawlikowski 2005, 49 fig. 7; Henning 2013b, 153 f. pls. 13, a. 15, b. 19, a; Palaz Erdemir 2013, 514 fig. 5; Raja 2017i, 119 f. fig. 7; Krag 2018, 32 n. 63; 34 n. 96; 45 n. 193; 46 n. 194; 87 n. 182. 184; 89 n. 205; 98 n. 23; 246 cat. 298; Silver et al. 2018, 177 f. fig. 9.30. Inscription: Chabot 1922, 91–93; Cantineau 1930b, 37 f. cat. 27, m–p; Gawlikowski 1969, 55; Milik 1972, 245 fig. 1; Yon 2002, 178 f. 204 f.; Krag 2018, 246 cat. 298.

OBJECT DESCRIPTION

The sarcophagus relief box is rectangular in shape and is rendered as a kline. Four female busts are depicted between the kline legs. On top of the kline is a mattress. The central stretcher of the kline is decorated (details unclear). On either end are two rectangular indentations. The legs of the kline are turned. The feet of the legs are broken off, but above they are composed of a reversed bell-shaped element, a ball, a concave quarter, and above the stretcher is a torus finial.

Cat. 33

INSCRIPTIONS

INSCRIPTION 1
SCRIPT: Palmyrene Aramaic.
LOCATION ON RELIEF: On the plinth.
TRANSCRIPTION: ʾMTʾ BRT | ʾLHBL BR WHBLT | ʾTT ŠKYY BR WHBLT.
TRANSLATION: Amatâ daughter of Elahbel son of Wahballat, wife of Šokaîaî son of Wahballat.

INSCRIPTION 2
SCRIPT: Palmyrene Aramaic.
LOCATION ON RELIEF: On the plinth.
TRANSCRIPTION: ʿTY BRT ŠLMLT | BR MʿNY ʾTT MLKW | BR WHBLT.
TRANSLATION: ʿAttaî daughter of Šalamallat son of Maʿnaî, wife of Malkû son of Wahballat.

INSCRIPTION 3
SCRIPT: Palmyrene Aramaic.
LOCATION ON RELIEF: On the plinth.
TRANSCRIPTION: HDYRT BRT MʿNY | BR WHBLT.
TRANSLATION: Hadîrat daughter of Maʿnaî son of Wahballat.

INSCRIPTION 4
SCRIPT: Palmyrene Aramaic.
LOCATION ON RELIEF: On the plinth.
TRANSCRIPTION: ŠGL BRT ŠKY[Y BR] | WHBLT ʾTT BL[ʿQB] | BR ʾLHBL WHBLT.
TRANSLATION: Šegel daughter of Šokaîaî son of Wahballat, wife of Belʿaqab son of Elahbel Wahballat.

Inscription 1: CIS no. 4145; PAT no. 0497.
Inscription 2: CIS no. 4146; PAT no. 0498.
Inscription 3: CIS no. 4147; PAT no. 0499.
Inscription 4: CIS no. 4148; PAT no. 0500.

PORTRAIT A: FEMALE BUST
The figure is shown frontally. The arms are bent and held to the chest.
She wears a heavy veil that falls over her shoulders. She wears a tunic and a himation.

PORTRAIT B: FEMALE BUST
The figure is shown frontally. The arms are bent and held to the chest.
She wears a heavy veil that falls over her shoulders. She wears a tunic and a himation.

PORTRAIT C: FEMALE BUST
The figure is shown frontally. The arms are bent and held to the chest.
She wears a heavy veil that falls over her shoulders. She wears a tunic and a himation.

PORTRAIT D: FEMALE BUST
The figure is shown frontally. The arms are bent and held to the chest.
She wears a heavy veil that falls over her shoulders. She wears a tunic and a himation.

FRAGMENTS FROM LIDS, LID RELIEFS, OR BANQUETING RELIEFS

A.D. 150–200

34. FRAGMENT OF MALE BUST

DATABASE NUMBER: PM053.
LOCATION: Palmyra, Palmyra Museum, inv. no. A 265 (1468).
CONTEXT: West necropolis. Valley of the Tombs. Tower tomb no. 13, tower of Elahbel.
ACQUISITION HISTORY: —
MEASUREMENTS: Height: 17 cm. Width: 11 cm.
MATERIAL: Limestone, white.

PRESERVATION: The head, the right arm and the left side of the figure are broken off.
TECHNICAL DESCRIPTION: —
DATE: A.D. 150–200 (Henning 2013b: A.D. 150).
REFERENCES: Henning 2013b, 295 f. cat. S 10 pl. 22, d.

OBJECT DESCRIPTION
The object depicts a male figure.

PORTRAIT
The figure is shown frontally.

He wears a tunic. The tunic has a wide, round neckline and short, wide sleeves. The folds of the garment are indicated by wide, curving grooves. A rectangular object, with a groove creating a frame around a rectangular depression is at the lower part, probably a tabula.

Cat. 34

A.D. 170–200

35. FRAGMENT OF BANQUETING RELIEF

Cat. 35

DATABASE NUMBER: InSitu141.
LOCATION: Palmyra, in situ.
CONTEXT: West necropolis. Valley of the Tombs. Tower tomb no. 13, tower of Elahbel, hypogeum.
ACQUISITION HISTORY: —
MEASUREMENTS: Height: 30 cm. Width: 60 cm. Depth: 15 cm.
MATERIAL: Limestone.
PRESERVATION: The upper part of the figure is broken off just above the waist. The legs are broken off at the middle of the thighs. The surface is weathered.
TECHNICAL DESCRIPTION: —
DATE: A.D. 170–200 (Henning 2013b: A.D. 150–200).
REFERENCES: Henning 2013b, 307 cat. S 49.

OBJECT DESCRIPTION
The object depicts the torso and part of the legs of a reclining figure.

PORTRAIT
The figure is shown frontally.
He wears a tunic. The folds of the tunic are indicated by curving grooves. He also wears a plain band belt, knotted at the centre with the ends looped under on either side of the waist.

HEADS OF PRIESTS

1–10 CM

36. HEAD OF PRIEST

Cat. 36

DATABASE NUMBER: PM061.
LOCATION: Palmyra, Palmyra Museum, inv. no. A 273/1476.
CONTEXT: West necropolis. Valley of the Tombs. Tower tomb no. 13, tower of Elahbel.
ACQUISITION HISTORY: —
MEASUREMENTS: Height: 10 cm. Width: 8 cm. Depth: 6.5 cm.
MATERIAL: Limestone.
PRESERVATION: The head is broken off at the neck. The surface is weathered. A large crack runs across the headdress and the right eye. The tip of the nose is broken off. The left eyebrow, ears, nose, left cheek, mouth, and chin are chipped.
TECHNICAL DESCRIPTION: —
DATE: A.D. 200–273.
REFERENCES: Henning 2013b, 297 cat. S 14 pl. 23, d.

OBJECT DESCRIPTION
The object depicts a priest.

PORTRAIT
The figure is shown frontally. The head is turned to his left. He wears a tall, plain, cylindrical, flat-top headdress divided into three sections by two vertical grooves: a Palmyrene priestly hat. His face is oval and fleshy. The eyebrows are curving. The eyes are large, deep-set, and almond-shaped. The ears are small. The nose is short with a wide base. The mouth is small with a full lower lip. The chin is wide. The neck is short and wide. Part of a garment is visible on the left side of the neck.

37. HEAD OF PRIEST

Cat. 37

DATABASE NUMBER: PM084.
LOCATION: Palmyra, Palmyra Museum, inv. no. A 281 (1484).
CONTEXT: West necropolis. Valley of the Tombs. Tower tomb no. 13, tower of Elahbel.
ACQUISITION HISTORY: —
MEASUREMENTS: Height: 9.5 cm. Width: 6.5 cm. Depth: 8 cm.
MATERIAL: Limestone.
PRESERVATION: The head is broken off at the neck. The surface of the head is weathered. The top of the headdress and the tip of the nose are broken off. The right ear and the chin are chipped.
TECHNICAL DESCRIPTION: —
DATE: A.D. 220–240.
REFERENCES: Henning 2013b, 300 cat. S 22 pl. 25, c.

OBJECT DESCRIPTION
The object depicts a priest.

PORTRAIT

The figure is shown frontally. The head is turned slightly to his left.

He wears a tall, plain, cylindrical, flat-top headdress divided into three sections by two vertical grooves: a Palmyrene priestly hat. His face is oval and fleshy. The eyebrows are curving. The eyes are large and round with thick upper eyelids. The eyeballs are blank. The ears are small and slightly protruding. The mouth is small with a full lower lip. The chin is round. The neck is wide with a curving groove.

31–40 CM

38. HEAD OF PRIEST

Cat. 38

DATABASE NUMBER: PM066.
LOCATION: Palmyra, Palmyra Museum, inv. no. A 279 (1482).
CONTEXT: West necropolis, Valley of the Tombs, Tomb no. 13, tower of Elahbel.
ACQUISITION HISTORY: —
MEASUREMENTS: Height: 36 cm. Width: 22 cm. Depth: 22 cm.
MATERIAL: Limestone.
PRESERVATION: The head is broken off at the neck. The surface of the face is weathered. The upper frontal part of the headdress is broken off. The wreath, the bust on the headdress, the left eyebrow, the nose, the ears, and the chin are chipped.
TECHNICAL DESCRIPTION: —
DATE: A.D. 220–240 (Henning 2013b: A.D. 100–150).
REFERENCES: Starcky 1941, 34 fig. 27; Henning 2013b, 299 cat. S 20 pl. 25, a–b.

OBJECT DESCRIPTION

The object depicts a priest.

PORTRAIT

The figure is shown frontally. The head is turned slightly to his left.

He wears a tall, cylindrical, flat-top headdress divided into three sections by two vertical grooves: a Palmyrene priestly hat. A wreath with three rows of small, pointed leaves pointing towards an armless bust of a male figure is depicted at the lower part of the hat. Two berries or fruits project from the leaves on either side of the medallion/bust. His face is oval and fleshy. The eyebrows are curving, rendered as thin ridges. The eyes are large and round with thick upper eyelids. The irises and the pupils are indicated by concentric, incised circles. The ears are small with the helix and lobe depicted. The mouth is small with full lips. The chin is round. He has a double chin. The neck is wide with two curving grooves.

The head was attached to cat. 24 in 1941.

MALE HEADS

1–10 CM

39. FRAGMENT OF A MALE HEAD

DATABASE NUMBER: PM065.
LOCATION: Palmyra, Palmyra Museum, inv. no. A 278 (1481).
CONTEXT: West necropolis. Valley of the Tombs. Tower tomb no. 13, tower of Elahbel.
ACQUISITION HISTORY: —
MEASUREMENTS: Height: 10 cm. Width: 6 cm. Depth: 7.5 cm.
MATERIAL: Limestone, white.
PRESERVATION: The head is broken off at the top, the left side of the face, and the base of the neck.
TECHNICAL DESCRIPTION: —
DATE: A.D. 140–170.
REFERENCES: Henning 2013b, 298 cat. S 19 pl. 24, e.

OBJECT DESCRIPTION

The object depicts a male figure.

PORTRAIT

The figure is shown frontally.

The hair is voluminous, arranged in three alternating rows of curls. At the centre, there is a plait ending in a round ornament. The eyebrows are rendered by thin, incised lines. The eyes are large, almond-shaped, with thick eyelids. The irises are indicated by incised circles and the pupils by punch holes. The nose is wide. The alae are carved. Nasolabial lines are indicated by incised lines. The mouth is small, with a full lower lip. The chin is pointed.

Cat. 39

40. FRAGMENT OF HEAD OF FIGURE

Cat. 40

DATABASE NUMBER: PM063.
LOCATION: Palmyra, Palmyra Museum, inv. no. A 277 (1480) 4.
CONTEXT: West necropolis. Valley of the Tombs. Tower tomb no. 13, tower of Elahbel.
ACQUISITION HISTORY: —
MEASUREMENTS: Height: 6 cm. Width: 6 cm. Depth: 7 cm.
MATERIAL: Limestone.
PRESERVATION: The figure is broken off at the top of the neck. The upper part of the head is broken off.
TECHNICAL DESCRIPTION: —
DATE: A.D. 150–200.
REFERENCES: Henning 2013b, 298 cat. S 18 pl. 24, d.

OBJECT DESCRIPTION

The object depicts a head. It could belong either to a male or a female figure.

PORTRAIT

The figure is shown frontally.

The face is oval and fleshy. The eyebrows are curving, rendered by thin grooves. The eyes are large, almond-shaped, with thick, upper eyelids. The irises are indicated by incised circles. The cheeks are fleshy. The nose is straight. The alae are indicated by incised lines. The mouth is small, with a full lower lip.

41. FRAGMENT OF A MALE HEAD

Cat. 41

DATABASE NUMBER: PM055.
LOCATION: Palmyra, Palmyra Museum, inv. no. A 263.
CONTEXT: West necropolis. Valley of the Tombs. Tower tomb no. 13, tower of Elahbel.
ACQUISITION HISTORY: —
MEASUREMENTS: Height: 8 cm. Width: 4.5 cm. Depth: 5 cm.
MATERIAL: Limestone, white.
PRESERVATION: The head is broken off at the top, the right side, and the base of the neck. The forehead, mouth, and the chin are heavily chipped.
TECHNICAL DESCRIPTION: —
DATE: A.D. 150–200 (Henning 2013b: A.D. 150).
REFERENCES: Henning 2013b, 295 cat. S 8 pl. 22, b.

OBJECT DESCRIPTION
The object depicts a male figure.

PORTRAIT
The figure is shown frontally.
 The eyes are large, almond-shaped, with thick eyelids. The irises are indicated by incised semicircles and the pupils by punch holes. The nose is straight. The alae are carved.

42. FRAGMENT OF A MALE HEAD

Cat. 42

DATABASE NUMBER: PM059.
LOCATION: Palmyra, Palmyra Museum, inv. no. A 271/1474.
CONTEXT: West necropolis. Valley of the Tombs. Tower tomb no. 13, tower of Elahbel.
ACQUISITION HISTORY: —
MEASUREMENTS: Height: 9 cm. Width: 7 cm. Depth: 7 cm.
MATERIAL: Limestone, yellow.
PRESERVATION: The head is broken off at the top, the right side of the face, and the base of the neck. The left side of the face is chipped.
TECHNICAL DESCRIPTION: —
DATE: A.D. 150–200.
REFERENCES: Henning 2013b, 296 cat. S 12 pl. 23, b.

OBJECT DESCRIPTION
The object depicts a male figure.

PORTRAIT
The figure is shown frontally.
 The hair is short and voluminous, arranged in two rows of curls. The face is oval. The eyebrows are rendered by thin

ridges. The eyes are large, round, with thick eyelids. The cheeks are fleshy. The neck is short and wide. A v-shaped groove indicates the sternocleidomastoid muscles.

11–20 CM

43. MALE HEAD

Cat. 43

DATABASE NUMBER: NMD043.
LOCATION: Damascus, Damascus National Museum, inv. no. C4979.
CONTEXT: West necropolis. Valley of the Tombs. Tower tomb no. 13, tower of Elahbel, fifth floor.
ACQUISITION HISTORY: —
MEASUREMENTS: Height: 29 cm. Width: 21 cm. Depth: 27 cm.
MATERIAL: Limestone, white/yellow.
PRESERVATION: The figure is broken off diagonally at the neck. The top of the head, the right ear, the left eye, and the left ear are chipped. The surface is lightly weathered. A crack runs across the lower part of the face.
TECHNICAL DESCRIPTION: —
DATE: A.D. 103–150.
REFERENCES: Abdul-Hak – Abdul-Hak 1951, 44 cat. 46; Al-Ush et al. 1980, 123; Parlasca 1984, 286. 288 fig. 4; Tanabe 1986, 44 pl. 457; Henning 2013b, 292 cat. S 1 pl. 20, a–b.

OBJECT DESCRIPTION
The object depicts a male figure.

PORTRAIT
The figure is shown frontally.
   The hair is voluminous, arranged in two alternating rows of crescent-shaped curls. The eyebrows are rendered by thin ridges. The eyes are large, almond-shaped, with thick upper eyelids. The irises and pupils are indicated by concentric, incised circles. The ears are large and protruding, with the helix indicated (other details unclear). The nose is thin. The alae are indicated by incised lines. Nasolabial lines are indicated by the carving of the planes of the face. The mouth is small, with full lips. The chin is round. The neck is slender.

44. FRAGMENT OF A MALE HEAD

Cat. 44

DATABASE NUMBER: PM057.
LOCATION: Palmyra, Palmyra Museum, inv. no. A 268.
CONTEXT: West necropolis. Valley of the Tombs. Tower tomb no. 13, tower of Elahbel.
ACQUISITION HISTORY: —
MEASUREMENTS: Height: 24 cm. Width: 23 cm. Depth: 25 cm.
MATERIAL: Limestone.
PRESERVATION: The head is broken off at the neck. The lower frontal part of the face is broken off at the nose. The forehead and the nose are chipped.
TECHNICAL DESCRIPTION: —
DATE: A.D. 140–200.
REFERENCES: Henning 2013b, 296 cat. S 11 pl. 23, a.

OBJECT DESCRIPTION
The object depicts a male.

PORTRAIT
His hair is arranged in comma-shaped locks around his head in an unruly manner. The individual strands of hair are indicated by incised lines. The eyebrows are curving and plastically rendered. The eyes are large and almond-shaped, with thick upper eyelids. The upper eyelids extend beyond the corner of the eyes. The irises and pupils are indicated by concentric, incised circles. The ears are large and protruding, with the helix and scapha rendered.

45. FRAGMENT OF A MALE HEAD

Cat. 45

DATABASE NUMBER: PM105.
LOCATION: Palmyra, Palmyra Museum, inv. no. B 340.
CONTEXT: West necropolis. Valley of the Tombs. Tower tomb no. 13, tower of Elahbel.
ACQUISITION HISTORY: —
MEASUREMENTS: Height: 17 cm. Width: 17 cm. Depth: 15 cm.
MATERIAL: Limestone, white.
PRESERVATION: The head is broken off diagonally at the middle of the face and the base of the neck.
TECHNICAL DESCRIPTION: —
DATE: A.D. 150–200.
REFERENCES: Henning 2013b, 300 cat. S 23 pl. 25, d.

OBJECT DESCRIPTION
The object depicts a male figure.

PORTRAIT
The figure is shown frontally.

The hair is straight, with individual strands of hair indicated by incised lines. The ears are long. The nose is thin. The alae are indicated by incised lines. Nasolabial lines are indicated by incised lines. The mouth is wide, with thin lips. The chin is square. The neck is short.

46. MALE HEAD

Cat. 46

DATABASE NUMBER: PM060.
LOCATION: Palmyra, Palmyra Museum, inv. no. A 272 (1475).
CONTEXT: West necropolis. Valley of the Tombs. Tower tomb no. 13, tower of Elahbel.
ACQUISITION HISTORY: —
MEASUREMENTS: Height: 12 cm. Width: 7.5 cm. Depth: 5.5 cm.
MATERIAL: Limestone, yellow.
PRESERVATION: The head is broken off at the top and the base of the neck. The face is chipped.
TECHNICAL DESCRIPTION: —
DATE: A.D. 150–200.
REFERENCES: Henning 2013b, 296 cat. S 13 pl. 23, c.

OBJECT DESCRIPTION
The object depicts a male figure.
Henning (2013b) recognizes a female figure in the head.

PORTRAIT
The figure is shown frontally.

The hair is voluminous, arranged in rows of curls. The face is round and fleshy. The eyebrows are rendered by thin ridges. The eyes are large and round. The eyeballs appear blank. The cheeks are fleshy. The nose is wide. The mouth is large with thin lips. The chin is pointed. The neck is short and wide with a curving groove.

FEMALE HEADS

1–10 CM

47. FEMALE HEAD

Cat. 47

DATABASE NUMBER: PM052.
LOCATION: Palmyra, Palmyra Museum, inv. no. A 264.
CONTEXT: West necropolis. Valley of the Tombs. Tower tomb no. 13, tower of Elahbel.
ACQUISITION HISTORY: —
MEASUREMENTS: Height: 7 cm. Width: 7 cm.
MATERIAL: Limestone.
PRESERVATION: The lower part of the figure is broken off at the base of the neck. The upper right part of the head, as well as the edges of the veil, are broken off. The face is heavily chipped.
TECHNICAL DESCRIPTION: —
DATE: A.D. 103–150.
REFERENCES: Henning 2013b, 295 cat. S 9 pl. 22, c.

OBJECT DESCRIPTION
The fragment depicts the head of a female figure.

PORTRAIT
The figure is shown frontally.
She wears three headdresses: a headband, a turban, and a veil. The headband is placed low on her forehead: it is decorated with plain panels divided by plain bands. The turban is coiled. Oblique grooves indicate the coiling of the fabric. The veil is heavy, and the edge is scalloped. Her face is round and fleshy. The eyebrows are curving, rendered by thin ridges. The eyes are large and round. The eyeballs are blank. The nose is straight. The mouth is small, with a thin upper lip and a full lower lip. The chin is pointed.

21–30 CM

48. FEMALE HEAD

Cat. 48

DATABASE NUMBER: NMD015.
LOCATION: Damascus, National Museum of Damascus, inv. no. C4980.
CONTEXT: West necropolis. Valley of the Tombs. Tower tomb no. 13, tower of Elahbel, fifth floor.
ACQUISITION HISTORY: —
MEASUREMENTS: Height: 30 cm. Width: 32 cm. Depth: 22 cm.
MATERIAL: Limestone, white/yellow.
PRESERVATION: The lower part of the figure is broken off at the base of the neck. The chin is broken off. The upper part of the face is chipped.
TECHNICAL DESCRIPTION: —
DATE: A.D. 103–150.

REFERENCES: Abdul-Hak – Abdul-Hak 1951, 44 cat. 45; Al-Ush et al. 1980, 115; Parlasca 1984, 295; Tanabe 1986, 45 pl. 468; Henning 2013b, 292 f. cat. S 2 pl. 20, c; Krag 2018, 208 cat. 153.

OBJECT DESCRIPTION
The fragment depicts the head of a female figure.

PORTRAIT
The figure is shown frontally.

She wears two headdresses: a turban and a veil. The turban is coiled. Oblique grooves indicate the coiling of the fabric. Two ends of the turban are looped into each other at the centre. The veil is heavy and falls to the back of the head. The hair is wavy and centrally parted. Three locks of hair are brushed back over the ears, and one lock falls on either side of the neck. Her face is oval and fleshy. The eyebrows are curving, rendered by thin grooves. The eyes are large and almond-shaped, with thick upper eyelids. The irises and the pupils are indicated by concentric, incised circles. Only the earlobes are visible under the hair. The nose has a wide base. Nasolabial lines are indicated by the carving of the planes of the face. The mouth is small, with full lips. The neck is wide.

31–40 CM

49. FEMALE HEAD

Cat. 49

DATABASE NUMBER: NMD014.
LOCATION: Damascus, National Museum of Damascus, inv. no. C4981.
CONTEXT: West necropolis. Valley of the Tombs. Tower tomb no. 13, tower of Elahbel.
ACQUISITION HISTORY: —
MEASUREMENTS: Height: 37 cm. Width: 29 cm. Depth: 29 cm.
MATERIAL: Limestone.
PRESERVATION: The lower part of the figure is broken off at the base of the neck. The edges of the veil, the eyebrows, the nose, and the chin are chipped. Cracks run across the surface of the face.
TECHNICAL DESCRIPTION: —
DATE: A.D. 200–273.
REFERENCES: Abdul-Hak – Abdul-Hak 1951, 44 cat. 43; al-Ush et al. 1980, 115; Parlasca 1984, 295; Tanabe 1986, 45 fig. 469; Finlayson 2002–2003, 227 pl. 4; Henning 2013b, 293 cat. S 3 pl. 20, d; Krag 2018, 56 n. 291; 101 n. 63; 106 n. 101; 342 cat. 657.

OBJECT DESCRIPTION
The fragment depicts the head of a female figure.

For the tomb plan, see cat. 3

Cat. 50

PORTRAIT
The figure is shown frontally.

She wears two headdresses: a headband and a veil. The headband is placed high on her forehead: it is wide and divided into two registers. The lower register is decorated with rectangular panels divided by beaded bands. The upper register is decorated with crisscrossing, beaded bands surrounding flowers. The flower in the central lozenge has six round petals and the one inside the right has serrated petals. The veil is heavy, and the edge is scalloped. Part of the hair is covered by the headdress: several strands of hair at the sides are brushed back over the headband and disappear under the veil. The individual strands of hair are indicated by incised lines. Her face is long. The eyebrows are curving, rendered by thin, incised lines. The eyes are large and almond-shaped, with thin eyelids. The eyeballs are blank. She wears earrings composed of three juxtaposed, round beads (Colledge classification: K). The nose is straight. The mouth is small with full lips. The chin is pointed. The neck is long and slender, with three curving grooves.

A.D. 135–170

TOWER TOMB NO. 46

SARCOPHAGUS BOXES

50. FRAGMENT OF SARCOPHAGUS BOX WITH PORTRAIT BUSTS

DATABASE NUMBER: InSitu142.
LOCATION: Palmyra, in situ.
CONTEXT: West necropolis. Tower Tomb no. 46, ground floor.
ACQUISITION HISTORY: —
MEASUREMENTS: —
MATERIAL: Limestone.
PRESERVATION: The surface is weathered. All the heads of the portraits are broken off.
TECHNICAL DESCRIPTION: —
DATE: A.D. 135–170.
REFERENCES: Pfister 1940, 8; Gawlikowski 1970a, 97 f.; Wielgosz 1997, 73; Henning 2013b, 188 f.

OBJECT DESCRIPTION
The sarcophagus box is rectangular in shape and depicts three busts inside clipei (according to Henning 2013b, 189).

The clipei have a narrow, plain outer border and the inside is decorated with a tongues pattern.

PORTRAIT A: ARMLESS BUST
Armless bust shown frontally. Curving grooves across the chest indicate drapery (details unclear).

PORTRAIT B: ARMLESS BUST
Armless bust shown frontally. The figure wears a garment with short, wide sleeves. Curving grooves across the chest indicate another garment (details unclear).

PORTRAIT C: ARMLESS BUST
Armless bust. The details are unclear.

51. SARCOPHAGUS BOX WITH PORTRAIT BUSTS

Cat. 51

DATABASE NUMBER: InSitu118.
LOCATION: Palmyra, in situ.
CONTEXT: West necropolis. Tower Tomb no. 46, ground floor.
ACQUISITION HISTORY: —
MEASUREMENTS: —
MATERIAL: Limestone.
PRESERVATION: The upper part of the sarcophagus box is broken off. The surface is weathered. Portrait B: The head, neck, and shoulders are broken off.

TECHNICAL DESCRIPTION: —
DATE: A.D. 135–170.
REFERENCES: Pfister 1940, 8; Gawlikowski 1970a, 97 f.; Wielgosz 1997, 73; Henning 2013b, 188 f. pl. 43, c.

OBJECT DESCRIPTION
The sarcophagus box is rectangular in shape and three busts are depicted. Curving and vertical grooves behind the central bust indicate a cloth. Henning (2013b, 189) writes that portraits A and C were inside clipei.

Note: According to Pfister (1940) there were several small fragments associated with the two sarcophagi. Gawlikowski (1970a) mentions a banqueting relief associated with one of the sarcophagi, while Wielgosz (1997) mentions three sarcophagi decorated with busts in clipei. Henning (2013b) mentions three fragments, once in the Palmyra Museum, that perhaps can be connected to the two sarcophagi: a sarcophagus fragment (inv. no. B 366), a small male head (inv. no. B 367), and another male head (inv. no. unknown). She was unable to locate these fragments when she conducted her study of tower tombs.

PORTRAIT A: BUST

PORTRAIT B: ARMLESS MALE BUST
The figure is shown frontally.

He wears a tunic and a chlamys. The tunic has short, wide sleeves. The chlamys is folded over the chest. A small zigzag-shaped fold can be seen on the right side of the torso.

PORTRAIT C: BUST

A.D. 150–200

TOWER TOMB NO. 34, TOWER OF MOQÎMÛ

SARCOPHAGUS BOXES

52. SARCOPHAGUS BOX WITH PORTRAIT BUSTS

DATABASE NUMBER: InSitu190.
LOCATION: Palmyra, in situ.
CONTEXT: West necropolis. Valley of the Tombs. Tower tomb no. 34, tower of Moqîmû, ground floor.
ACQUISITION HISTORY: —
MEASUREMENTS: —
MATERIAL: Limestone.
PRESERVATION: The object is heavily chipped and weathered. Only the outlines of the figures are preserved.
TECHNICAL DESCRIPTION: —
DATE: A.D. 150–200.
REFERENCES: Henning 2013b, 175.

Cat. 52

OBJECT DESCRIPTION
The box is rectangular in shape and depicts three busts (Henning 2013b describes four busts, but this is not visible from the picture).

PORTRAIT A: ARMLESS BUST
The figure is shown frontally.

PORTRAIT B: ARMLESS BUST
The figure is shown frontally.

PORTRAIT C: ARMLESS BUST
The figure is shown frontally.

TOWER TOMB NO. 41A

SARCOPHAGUS BOXES

53. FRAGMENT OF SARCOPHAGUS BOX WITH PORTRAIT BUSTS

DATABASE NUMBER: InSitu191.
LOCATION: Palmyra, in situ.
CONTEXT: West necropolis. Valley of the Tombs. Tower tomb no. 41a, ground floor.
ACQUISITION HISTORY: —
MEASUREMENTS: —
MATERIAL: Limestone.
PRESERVATION: The object is heavily chipped and weathered. The upper part of the figures is broken off.
TECHNICAL DESCRIPTION: —
DATE: A.D. 150–200.
REFERENCES: Henning 2013b, 184.

OBJECT DESCRIPTION
The box is rectangular in shape and depicts four armless busts.

PORTRAIT A: ARMLESS BUST
The figure is shown frontally.
The figure wears a garment, with curving grooves on the chest indicating the folds of the fabric.

PORTRAIT B: ARMLESS BUST
The figure is shown frontally.
The figure wears a tunic with a v-shaped neckline. Oblique and curving grooves indicate the folds of the fabric.

PORTRAIT C: ARMLESS BUST
The figure is shown frontally.
The figure wears a tunic with a v-shaped neckline. Oblique and v-shaped grooves indicate the folds of the fabric.

PORTRAIT D: ARMLESS BUST
The figure is shown frontally.

Cat. 53

TOWER TOMB NO. 51, TOWER OF YAMLIKÛ

BANQUETING RELIEFS

54. FRAGMENT OF BANQUETING RELIEF

DATABASE NUMBER: InSitu226.
LOCATION: Palmyra, Palmyra Museum, inv. no. unknown.
CONTEXT: West necropolis. Valley of the Tombs. Tower tomb no. 51, tower of Yamlikû, fourth floor.
ACQUISITION HISTORY: —
MEASUREMENTS: —
MATERIAL: Limestone.
PRESERVATION: The object is broken on all sides. Portrait A: The head and shoulders are broken off diagonally from the right to the left shoulder. The surface around the chest and at the legs is chipped. The surface is weathered. Portrait B: The head is broken off horizontally at the base of the neck, and the lower left arm is broken off. The surface at the right lower arm and the lower torso is chipped. The surface is weathered.

TECHNICAL DESCRIPTION: —
DATE: A.D. 150–200.
REFERENCES: Henning 2013b, 194 pl. 52, b; Krag 2018, 28 n. 9; 33 n. 78. 84; 43 n. 164; 66 n. 382; 313 cat. 552; Henning 2019b, 35 fig. 27.

OBJECT DESCRIPTION
The object depicts a seated female and a reclining male.

PORTRAIT A: SEATED FEMALE
The figure is shown in three-quarter view. The arms appear short in relation to the torso. Her right arm is held to the body. The right is raised to the neck. Her legs are bent and visible under the drapery.

She wears a veil that falls over her right shoulder.

She wears an ankle-length tunic and a himation. The tunic has short, loose sleeves. The folds of the tunic are rendered by curving grooves. Over the tunic, she wears a himation. The himation crosses the chest diagonally from the left shoulder to the right side and covers the left breast.

Cat. 54

PORTRAIT B: RECLINING MALE
The figure is shown frontally. The arms are bent. The lower part of the figure is obscured by the seated figure to his right. The arms appear short in relation to the body.

He wears a tunic and a himation. The tunic has short, loose sleeves. The folds of the tunic are rendered by curving grooves. Over the tunic, he wears a himation. The himation covers only part of the upper torso. It is wrapped around the left shoulder and arm and falls in a thick fold along his left side. The folds of the himation are rendered by diagonal grooves.

He holds a bowl in his right hand (details unclear).

55. FRAGMENT OF BANQUETING RELIEF

DATABASE NUMBER: InSitu235.
LOCATION: Palmyra, Palmyra Museum, inv. no. unknown.
CONTEXT: West necropolis. Valley of the Tombs. Tower tomb no. 51, tower of Yamlikû, ground floor.
ACQUISITION HISTORY: —
MEASUREMENTS: —
MATERIAL: Limestone.
PRESERVATION: The head is broken off at the neck, and the lower part of the body is broken off diagonally at the thighs. The left arm is chipped.
TECHNICAL DESCRIPTION: —
DATE: A.D. 150–200.
REFERENCES: Henning 2013b, 192–194 cat. 51 pl. 52, a.

OBJECT DESCRIPTION
The object depicts the torso and part of the lower body of a reclining male figure. He rests the left arm on a cushion. The cushion is decorated with a running scroll with rosettes between beaded bands. Curving grooves indicate the texture of the fabric.

PORTRAIT
The figure is shown in frontal view. The left arm appears short in relation to the body. The left arm is bent in front of the torso. He wears a tunic and a himation. The tunic has a small, round neckline. The folds of the tunic are indicated by curving grooves. Over the tunic, he wears a himation. It is wrapped around his left shoulder and arm, leaving the chest and the

Cat. 55

hand free. It falls along the left side of his torso where it is folded over the tunic, across his waist. A zigzag-shaped fold falls along his right side.

TOWER TOMB NO. 87

SARCOPHAGUS LIDS

56. FRAGMENT OF SARCOPHAGUS LID WITH BANQUETING SCENE

DATABASE NUMBER: InSitu192.
LOCATION: Palmyra, in situ.
CONTEXT: South-west necropolis. Tower tomb no. 87.
ACQUISITION HISTORY: —
MEASUREMENTS: —
MATERIAL: Limestone.
PRESERVATION: The upper and right sides are broken off. The lower and left side are chipped. The surface is heavily weathered. Portrait: The head is broken off at the base of the neck. The lower part of the body and the lower arms are broken off.
TECHNICAL DESCRIPTION: —
DATE: A.D. 150–200.
REFERENCES: Henning 2013b, 234.

OBJECT DESCRIPTION
The object depicts a reclining male. He rests the left arm on a curving object, possibly formed by a cushion and a fold of the garment.

PORTRAIT: RECLINING MALE
The figure is shown in frontal view. The right arm is extended away from the body, the left arm is bent.

He wears a tunic and an over-garment, possibly a chlamys. The tunic has a rounded neckline. The folds of the tunic are indicated by curving grooves. The garment over the tunic falls over the left shoulder and arm (details unclear). The folds of the garment are indicated by vertical grooves on the left shoulder.

Cat. 56

A.D. 200–273

TOWER TOMB NO. 101

BANQUETING RELIEFS

57. FRAGMENT OF BANQUETING RELIEF

DATABASE NUMBER: InSitu193.
LOCATION: Palmyra, in situ.
CONTEXT: South-west necropolis. Tower tomb no. 101.
ACQUISITION HISTORY: —
MEASUREMENTS: —
MATERIAL: Limestone.
PRESERVATION: The lower, right, and upper sides of the object are chipped. The left side is not visible. Portrait A: The head is heavily chipped. The lower legs, right knee, and right hand are chipped. Portrait B: The foot is weathered.
TECHNICAL DESCRIPTION: —
DATE: A.D. 200–273.
REFERENCES: Henning 2013b, 243.

OBJECT DESCRIPTION

The object depicts a seated female and a reclining male. Between the two figures is a vertical, rectangular object, possibly a pedestal. Henning (2013b) writes that there is a Palmyrene priestly hat on the pedestal. A thin mattress with decoration is rendered underneath the figures (details unclear).

PORTRAIT A: SEATED FEMALE

The figure is shown in three-quarter view, turned to the left. The right arm is extended along her side; the left arm is bent and raised to the neck. The head and upper body appears large in relation to the body. The feet are obscured by the reclining figure.

She wears a veil that falls over both shoulders and back at the upper arms. A fold of the veil is wrapped around the left arm. She wears at least two necklaces: a plain chain necklace at the centre of the chest and a wide plain necklace with three medallions at the lower part of the torso. The medallions are circular with an incised centre (details unclear).

She wears a tunic and a himation. The tunic has a v-shaped neckline and short, wide sleeves that reach below the elbows.

The himation falls diagonally from the left shoulder to the right side and is fastened by a circular brooch with a small, incised circle (Colledge classification: h). The himation reaches the ankles, and a fold runs diagonally from the feet to the right hand. The folds of the himation are indicated by oblique grooves.

With the right hand, she holds a fold of the himation. With the left hand, she lightly pulls a fold of the veil. She wears plain, wide hoop bracelets on both wrists.

PORTRAIT B: RECLINING MALE
The figure is shown in three-quarter view. The left leg is extended along the mattress; the right leg is bent and the foot rests on the mattress. The right foot is obscured by the left leg.

He wears a garment that reaches the ankles. The folds of the garment are indicated by oblique grooves on the legs. He wears a closed-toe shoe or boot. Tower Tomb no. 168

Cat. 57

SARCOPHAGUS BOXES

58. FRAGMENT OF SARCOPHAGUS BOX WITH PORTRAIT BUSTS

DATABASE NUMBER: InSitu143.
LOCATION: Palmyra, in situ.
CONTEXT: North necropolis. Tower tomb no. 168, ground floor.
ACQUISITION HISTORY: —
MEASUREMENTS: —
MATERIAL: Limestone.
PRESERVATION: The right, left, and upper sides of the object are broken off. The lower side is heavily chipped. The surface is heavily chipped and weathered. Portraits: The heads of the busts are broken off.
TECHNICAL DESCRIPTION: —
DATE: A.D. 200–273.
REFERENCES: Henning 2013b, 278.

OBJECT DESCRIPTION
The object is rectangular in shape and depicts four armless busts. There is a lower protruding edge.

PORTRAIT A: ARMLESS BUST
The figure is shown frontally.

PORTRAIT B: ARMLESS BUST
The figure is shown frontally.

PORTRAIT C: ARMLESS BUST
The figure is shown frontally.

PORTRAIT D: ARMLESS BUST
The figure is shown frontally.

Plan of tower tomb no. 168.

Cat. 58

A.D. 220–240

TOWER TOMB NO. 39D

SARCOPHAGUS BOXES

59. SARCOPHAGUS BOX WITH PORTRAIT BUSTS

DATABASE NUMBER: InSitu105.
LOCATION: Palmyra, in situ.
CONTEXT: West necropolis. Valley of the Tombs. Tower tomb no. 39d, ground floor.
ACQUISITION HISTORY: —
MEASUREMENTS: —
MATERIAL: Limestone.
PRESERVATION: The upper part of the sarcophagus box is broken off on all sides. The lateral sides are broken off diagonally. The front side of the box is broken off horizontally at the height of the neck of the busts. The surface is weathered. Portrait A: The head is broken off at the base of the neck. Portrait B: The head is broken off at the base of the neck. Portrait C: The head is broken off at the base of the neck.
TECHNICAL DESCRIPTION: —
DATE: A.D. 220–240.
REFERENCES: Watzinger – Wulzinger 1932, 52; Gawlikowski 1970a, 133 fig. 78; Gawlikowski 2005, 57 fig. 16; Henning 2013b, 181 f.

OBJECT DESCRIPTION
The sarcophagus box is rectangular in shape and depicts three male busts.

PORTRAIT A: ARMLESS MALE BUST
The figure is depicted frontally.
He wears a tunic and a chlamys. The tunic has wide sleeves. The chlamys is folded across the chest and falls over the left shoulder. The folds of the chlamys are rendered by deep, curving grooves.

PORTRAIT B: ARMLESS MALE BUST
The figure is depicted frontally.
He wears a tunic and a chlamys. The tunic has wide sleeves. The chlamys is folded across the chest and falls over the left shoulder. The folds of the chlamys are rendered by deep, curving grooves.

PORTRAIT C: ARMLESS MALE BUST
The figure is depicted frontally.
He wears a tunic and a chlamys. The tunic has wide sleeves. The chlamys is folded across the chest and falls over the left shoulder. The folds of the chlamys are rendered by deep, curving grooves.

Cat. 59

Objects from Hypogea

A.D. 89–220

HYPOGEUM OF ʿAŠTÔR

SARCOPHAGUS LID RELIEFS

A.D. 89–100

60. BANQUETING RELIEF

DATABASE NUMBER: PM130.
LOCATION: Palmyra, Palmyra Museum, inv. no. 1720/6391.
CONTEXT: South-east necropolis. Hypogeum of ʿAštôr, central gallery, in front of sections 19 and 21. Excavation number: 2–6.
ACQUISITION HISTORY: —
MEASUREMENTS: Height: 65 cm. Width: 84 cm. Depth: 16 cm.
MATERIAL: Limestone, yellow.
PRESERVATION: A crack runs horizontally through the figures. The lower left edge of the cushion to the left has been broken off and reattached. Portrait A: The edge of the right foot is chipped. The top of the attribute held in the right hand is chipped. Portrait B: His forehead and the lower part of his nose are chipped. Portrait C: The left index finger is chipped.
TECHNICAL DESCRIPTION: It has been restored: the crack was fixed with glue.
DATE: A.D. 89–100.
REFERENCES: Colledge 1976a, 277 n. 232; Tanabe 1986, 42 pl. 420; Sadurska – Bounni 1994, 16 cat. 5 fig. 208; Curtis 2017, 60 fig. 12a; <https://virtual-museum-syria.org/palmyra/base-relief-of-two-men-and-a-child/> (06.05.2022).

OBJECT DESCRIPTION
The sarcophagus lid relief depicts a standing male and two reclining males. Both reclining males rest their left arm on a cushion. The cushions have a wide, plain band set between beaded bands. Curving grooves indicate the texture of the fabric.

PORTRAIT A: STANDING MALE
The figure is shown frontally. The right arm is held along the body. The left is bent and held to the chest. The legs are slightly set apart.

His hair is long and arranged in snail-shell curls around the head, and it covers his ears and proceeds to his shoulders. The individual strands of hair are indicated by incised lines. His face is square. The eyebrows are curving, depicted by thin ridges. The eyes are close-set and almond-shaped with thick eyelids. The upper eyelids extend beyond the end of the lower ones. The irises are indicated. The nose is straight with incised alae. The mouth is small, with thin lips. The cheeks are fleshy, and the chin is round and almost double. The neck is wide, with two curving grooves.

He wears a >Parthian-style< tunic, chlamys, >Parthian-style< trousers, and over-trousers. The tunic has a small, round neckline decorated with a beaded band, and long, tight-fitting sleeves. The tunic ends above the knees where the lower edge is decorated with a beaded band. The folds of the tunic are rendered by oblique and curving grooves. He wears a plain band belt across the waist. He also wears a chlamys that falls over both shoulders and covers most of the upper chest. It is fastened at the right shoulder with a circular brooch with an incised outer border (Colledge classification: h). A zigzag-shaped fold falls from under the brooch. The folds of the chlamys are indicated by narrow grooves. The trousers are visible above the knees. Each trouser leg is decorated in the middle with a broad band extending downwards. The over-trousers are fastened on either side of the waist, fall in a curving fold that ends at the knees, and cover the lower legs. The folds of the garments are rendered by wide, curving grooves.

With his right hand, he holds the handle of a libation pitcher. With his left hand he holds a ladle. The left thumb, index, and the middle fingers are extended.

PORTRAIT B: RECLINING MALE
The figure is shown frontally. The eyes appear large. The right arm is obscured by the figure to his right. The left arm is bent and held in front of the torso. The legs are not rendered.

His hair is arranged in flame-shaped curls around the head. The individual strands of hair are indicated by incised lines. His face is oval. The eyebrows are curving, rendered by thin ridges starting from the root of the nose. The eyes are wide-set and almond-shaped, with thick eyelids. The upper eyelids extend beyond the end of the lower ones. The irises and pupils are indicated by concentric, incised circles. The ears are large and protruding, with the helix, scapha, concha, and tragus carved. The mouth is small, with a full lower lip. The cheeks are fleshy, and the chin is round and almost double. The neck is wide with two curving grooves.

He wears a tunic and a himation. The tunic has a wide, v-shaped neckline leaving the upper part of the chest bare. The folds of the tunic are rendered by curving grooves. Over the tunic, he wears a himation. It is wrapped around the left shoulder and arm, leaving most of the upper torso and hand free. It proceeds in a curving fold across the waist and falls over the right side. The folds of the himation are rendered by oblique and curving grooves.

With his left hand, he holds the left handle of an undecorated skyphos. It has a conical foot and body. The lip is straight with opposing vertical looped handles. He wears a ring composed of a thin plain hoop with a circular bezel on the little finger. The thumb, index, and the little fingers are extended.

PORTRAIT C: RECLINING MALE

The figure is shown frontally. The eyes appear large. The right arm is obscured by the figure to his right. The left arm is bent and held in front of the torso. The legs are not rendered.

His hair is arranged in one row of flame-shaped curls around the head. The individual strands of hair are indicated by incised lines. His face is oval. There are two furrows along his forehead. The eyebrows are curving, rendered by thin ridges starting from the root of the nose. The eyes are wide-set and almond-shaped with thick eyelids. The upper eyelids extend beyond the end of the lower ones. The irises and pupils are indicated by concentric, incised circles. The ears are large and protruding with the helix, scapha, concha, and tragus carved. The mouth is small, with a full lower lip. The chin is oval and almost double. The neck is wide with two curving grooves.

He wears a tunic and a himation. The tunic has a wide, round neckline leaving the upper part of the chest bare. The folds of the tunic are rendered by curving grooves. Over the tunic, he wears a himation. It is wrapped around the left shoulder and arm, leaving most of the upper torso and hand free. The folds of the himation are rendered by oblique and curving grooves.

With his left hand, he holds the left handle of an undecorated skyphos. It has a conical foot and body. The lip is straight with opposing vertical looped handles. The thumb, index, and the little fingers are extended. He wears a ring composed of a thin plain hoop on the little finger.

Cat. 60

61. BANQUETING RELIEF

DATABASE NUMBER: PM131.
LOCATION: Palmyra, Palmyra Museum, inv. no. 1724/6395.
CONTEXT: South-east necropolis. Hypogeum of ʿAštôr, central gallery. Excavation number: 10.
ACQUISITION HISTORY: —
MEASUREMENTS: Height: 60 cm. Width: 80 cm. Depth: 16 cm.
MATERIAL: Limestone, yellow.
PRESERVATION: The lower corners are broken off. Portrait A: The nose, part of the hair, and the left hand are chipped.
TECHNICAL DESCRIPTION: —
DATE: A.D. 89–100.
REFERENCES: Colledge 1976, 232; Tanabe 1986, 42 pl. 421; Sadurska – Bounni 1994, 17 cat. 7 fig. 209.

OBJECT DESCRIPTION

The sarcophagus lid is rectangular in shape and depicts two reclining males and a standing male. Both reclining males rest their left arm on a cushion. Each of the cushions has a wide, plain band set between beaded bands.

PORTRAIT A: RECLINING MALE

The figure is shown frontally. The eyes appear large. The left arm is bent and held in front of the torso.

His hair is arranged in two rows of crescent-shaped curls around the head. The individual strands of hair are indicated by incised lines. His face is oval. The eyebrows are curving, depicted as thin ridges. The eyes are close-set and almond-shaped with thick eyelids. The upper eyelids extend beyond the end of the lower ones. The irises and pupils are indicated by concentric, incised circles. The ears are large and protruding with the helix, scapha, concha, and tragus depicted. The mouth is small, with a full lower lip. The chin is small. The neck is wide, with two horizontal grooves.

He wears a tunic and a himation. The tunic has a wide, v-shaped neckline leaving the upper part of the chest bare. The folds of the tunic are rendered by curving grooves. Over the tunic, he wears a himation. It is wrapped around the left shoulder and arm, leaving most of the upper torso and hand free. It proceeds in a fold over the cushion. The folds of the himation are rendered by oblique and curving grooves.

With his left hand, he holds the left handle of a skyphos. It has a conical foot and an ovoid body. The lip is straight

Cat. 61

with opposing vertical looped handles. The body has two horizontal, incised lines. The thumb, index, and the little finger are extended. He wears a plain, thick hoop ring on his left little finger. The nails are indicated by fine, incised lines.

PORTRAIT B: RECLINING MALE

The figure is shown frontally. The left forearm appears short in relation to the torso. The eyes appear large. The right arm is obscured by the figure to his right. The left arm is bent and held in front of the torso. The legs are not rendered.

His hair is arranged in crescent-shaped curls around the head. The individual strands of hair are indicated by incised lines. His face is square. The eyebrows are curving, depicted as thin ridges. The eyes are close-set and round with thick eyelids. The upper eyelids extend beyond the end of the lower ones. The irises and pupils are indicated by concentric, incised circles. The nose is straight with incised alae. The ears are large and protruding with the helix, scapha, concha, and tragus depicted. The mouth is small, with thin lips. The chin is small. The neck is wide, with two horizontal grooves.

He wears a tunic and a himation. The tunic has a wide, v-shaped neckline leaving the upper part of the chest bare. The folds of the tunic are rendered by curving grooves. Over the tunic, he wears a himation. It is wrapped around the left shoulder and arm, leaving most of the upper torso and hand free. It proceeds in a curving fold over the cushion. The folds of the himation are rendered by oblique and curving grooves.

With his left hand, he holds the handle of a skyphos. It has a conical foot and body. The lip is straight with opposing vertical looped handles. The thumb, index, and the little fingers are extended. He wears a plain, thick hoop ring on his left little finger. The nails are indicated by fine, incised lines.

PORTRAIT C: STANDING MALE

The figure is shown frontally. The right arm is bent and held to the torso. The left is held along the body. The right leg is obscured by the figure to his right.

His hair is curly. It is centrally parted and brushed away on either side of the forehead, arranged in s-shaped curls around the head, covering the ears and proceeding to his neck. The individual strands of hair are indicated by incised lines. His face is oval. The eyebrows are curving, rendered by thin ridges. The eyes are close-set and almond-shaped with heavy upper eyelids. The upper eyelids extend beyond the end of the lower ones. The nose is straight, with incised alae. The mouth is small, with thin lips. The chin is oval. The neck is wide, with two curving grooves.

He wears an ankle-length tunic with a wide, round neckline and long, tight-fitting sleeves. The folds of the tunic are rendered by oblique and curving grooves and vertical grooves between the legs. At the waist, there is a large overfold, possibly indicating a belt.

With his right hand, he holds a libation pitcher. He holds a round object in his left hand, possibly a wreath.

62. FRAGMENT OF BANQUETING RELIEF

Cat. 62

DATABASE NUMBER: PM069.
LOCATION: Palmyra, Palmyra Museum, inv. no. 1726/6397.
CONTEXT: South-east necropolis. Hypogeum of ʿAštôr, central gallery in front of the sections 26 and 28. Excavation number: 12–15.
ACQUISITION HISTORY: —
MEASUREMENTS: Height: 66 cm. Width: 44 cm. Depth: 17 cm.
MATERIAL: Limestone, white/yellow.
PRESERVATION: A crack runs horizontally across his right arm and torso. The cracked fragment has been restored and glued back on.
TECHNICAL DESCRIPTION: —
DATE: A.D. 89–100.
REFERENCES: Sadurska – Bounni 1994, 17 cat. 8 fig. 211.

OBJECT DESCRIPTION

The fragment depicts a reclining male figure. He rests the left arm on a cushion, with curving grooves indicating the texture of the fabric.

The object is said to belong together with cat. 63.

PORTRAIT

The figure is shown in a frontal to three-quarter view. The head is turned slightly to the left. The eyes appear large in relation to the head. The arms appear short in relation to the body. The right arm is bent and held to the torso. The left arm is bent and rests along his side.

His hair is arranged in two rows of crescent-shaped curls around the head. The individual strands of hair are indicated by incised lines. His face is square. The eyebrows are curving, rendered by thin ridges. The eyes are close-set and round with thick eyelids. The upper eyelids extend beyond the end of the lower ones. The irises and pupils are indicated by concentric, incised circles. The ears are large and protruding with the helix, scapha, concha, and earlobe depicted. The nose is large, with carved nostrils. The mouth is small, with full lips. The cheeks are fleshy. The chin is wide, and the neck is long, with two curving grooves.

He wears a tunic and a himation. The tunic has a wide, v-shaped neckline, leaving a part of the upper chest bare and long, tight-fitting sleeves. The folds of the tunic are rendered by curving and oblique grooves. Over the tunic, he wears a himation. It is wrapped around the left shoulder and arm, leaving most of the torso and the hand free. The folds of the himation are indicated by oblique grooves.

He holds a skyphos in his right hand. It has a conical foot and a convex body. The lip is straight with opposing vertical looped handles. The thumb, index, and the little fingers are extended.

63. FRAGMENT OF BANQUETING RELIEF

DATABASE NUMBER: PM121.
LOCATION: Palmyra, Palmyra Museum, inv. no. 1726/6397, 1725/6396.
CONTEXT: South-east necropolis. Hypogeum of ʿAštôr, in front of the sections 26 and 28. Excavation number: 11.
ACQUISITION HISTORY: —
MEASUREMENTS: Height: 64 cm. Width: 46 cm. Depth: 18 cm.
MATERIAL: Limestone, white/yellow.
PRESERVATION: The surface is weathered. The right side is broken off at the right shoulder. A large crack runs diagonally from his neck to his left arm. The two separated pieces have been glued together. The nose and hand are chipped.
TECHNICAL DESCRIPTION: The object has been restored. The two pieces are glued together.
DATE: A.D. 89–100.
REFERENCES: Sadurska – Bounni 1994, 17 cat. 8 fig. 210.

OBJECT DESCRIPTION

The fragment depicts a reclining male figure. The left arm rests against a cushion with a beaded band.
The object is said to belong together with cat. 62.

PORTRAIT A

The figure is shown in frontal to three-quarter view. The head is turned slightly to the left. The eyes appear large. The arms appear short in relation to the body. The left arm is bent and held in front of the torso.

His hair is arranged in two rows of crescent-shaped curls around the head. The individual strands of hair are indicated by incised lines. His face is square. The eyebrows are curving, depicted as thin ridges. The eyes are close-set and round, with thick eyelids. The upper eyelids extend beyond the end of the lower ones. The irises are indicated by incised circles. The ears are large and protruding, with the helix, concha, tragus, and earlobe depicted. The mouth is small, with a full lower lip and a thin upper lip. The chin is round, and the neck is long, with two horizontal grooves.

He wears a tunic and a himation. The tunic has a wide, round neckline, leaving part of the upper chest bare. The folds of the tunic are rendered by curving and oblique grooves. Over the tunic, he wears a himation. It is wrapped around the left shoulder and arm, leaving most of the torso and the hand free. The folds of the himation are indicated by oblique and curving grooves.

He holds a skyphos in his left hand. It has a conical foot and a convex body. The lip is straight with opposing vertical looped handles. The thumb, index, and the little fingers are extended.

Cat. 63

64. FRAGMENT OF BANQUETING RELIEF

Cat. 64

DATABASE NUMBER: PM120.
LOCATION: Palmyra, Palmyra Museum, inv. no. 1721/6392.
CONTEXT: South-east necropolis. Hypogeum of ʿAštôr, central gallery between the sections 21 and 20. Excavation number: 9.
ACQUISITION HISTORY: —
MEASUREMENTS: Height: 57 cm. Width: 37 cm. Depth: 16 cm.
MATERIAL: Limestone, yellow.
PRESERVATION: The surface is weathered and chipped. The right side is broken off at the shoulder; the lower part is broken off under the cushion. The nose is chipped.
TECHNICAL DESCRIPTION: —
DATE: A.D. 89–100 (Sadurska – Bounni 1994: A.D. 89–110).
REFERENCES: Sadurska – Bounni 1994, 16 f. cat. 6 fig. 212.

OBJECT DESCRIPTION

The object depicts a reclining male figure. He rests the left arm on a cushion. The cushion has a wide, plain band set between beaded bands. Curving grooves indicate the texture of the fabric.

The object is said to belong together with cat. 65 and cat. 67.

PORTRAIT

The figure is shown frontally. The eyes appear large. The arms appear short in relation to the body. The left arm is bent and held in front of the torso.

His hair is arranged in one row of crescent-shaped curls around the head. The individual strands of hair are indicated by incised lines. His face is square. There are two furrows along his forehead. The eyebrows are curving, depicted as thin ridges. The eyes are close-set and round, with thick eyelids. The upper eyelids extend beyond the end of the lower ones. The irises are indicated by incised circles. The ears are large and protruding, with the helix, scapha, tragus, and earlobe depicted. The nose is wide at the base. The mouth is small with a full lower lip and a thin upper lip. The cheeks are fleshy. The chin is pointed, and the neck is long with two horizontal grooves.

He wears a tunic and a himation. The tunic has a wide, round neckline, leaving part of the upper chest bare. The folds of the tunic are rendered by curving and diagonal grooves. Over the tunic, he wears a himation. It is wrapped around the left shoulder and arm, leaving most of the torso and the hand free. The folds of the himation are indicated by oblique grooves.

He holds a skyphos in his left hand. It has a conical foot and a convex body. The lip is straight with opposing vertical looped handles. The thumb, index, and the little fingers are extended.

65. FRAGMENT OF MALE FIGURE

DATABASE NUMBER: PM119.
LOCATION: Palmyra, Palmyra Museum, inv. no. 1722/6393.
CONTEXT: South-east necropolis. Hypogeum of ʿAštôr, central gallery between the sections 21 and 20. Excavation number: 8.
ACQUISITION HISTORY: —
MEASUREMENTS: Height: 22 cm. Width: 12 cm. Depth: 12 cm.
MATERIAL: Limestone, yellow.
PRESERVATION: The surface is very weathered. The lower and right sides are broken off diagonally from the top of the right ear to the left upper arm.
TECHNICAL DESCRIPTION: —
DATE: A.D. 89–100.
REFERENCES: Sadurska – Bounni 1994, 16 f. cat. 6 fig. 213.

OBJECT DESCRIPTION

The object depicts the head and left shoulder of a male figure. The object is said to belong together with cat. 64 and cat. 67.

PORTRAIT

His hair is arranged in one row of snail-shell curls around the head. His face is round. The eyebrows are curving, depicted as thin ridges. The eyes are close-set and round, with thick eyelids. The upper eyelids extend beyond the ends of the lower ones. The pupils are rendered by punch holes. The nose is wide at the base and the nostrils are carved. The mouth is small, with full lips. The cheeks are fleshy. The chin is wide, and the neck is wide with two horizontal grooves.

He wears a tunic. The folds of the tunic are rendered by oblique grooves. Over the tunic, he wears another garment where a thick fold falls over the left shoulder.

Cat. 65

HEADS: MALE

A.D. 89–100

66. MALE HEAD

DATABASE NUMBER: PM117.
LOCATION: Palmyra, Palmyra Museum, inv. no. 1732/6403.
CONTEXT: South-east necropolis. Hypogeum of ʿAštôr, central gallery, in front of the wall between sections 18 and 19. Excavation number: 22.
ACQUISITION HISTORY: —
MEASUREMENTS: Height: 25 cm. Width: 17 cm. Depth: 16 cm.
MATERIAL: Limestone, yellow.
PRESERVATION: The surface is weathered.
TECHNICAL DESCRIPTION: —
DATE: A.D. 89–100.

REFERENCES: Sadurska – Bounni 1994, 18 f. cat. 11 fig. 215.

OBJECT DESCRIPTION
The fragment depicts the head of a male figure, from a sarcophagus lid.

PORTRAIT
The figure is shown frontally. The eyes appear large in relation to the head.

His hair is arranged in one row of crescent-shaped curls around the head. His face is square. The eyebrows are curving, rendered by thin ridges. The eyes are close-set and round, with thick eyelids. The irises are indicated by incised circles. The ears are large and protruding, with the helix, scapha, and concha depicted. The nose is straight. The mouth is small, with a full lower lip. The thin upper lip has an accentuated curving. The cheeks are fleshy. The chin is wide, and the neck is wide with two curving grooves.

Cat. 66

67. MALE HEAD

Cat. 67

DATABASE NUMBER: PM118.
LOCATION: Palmyra, Palmyra Museum, inv. no. 1723/6394.
CONTEXT: South-east necropolis. Hypogeum of ʿAštôr, central gallery between the sections 21 and 20. Excavation number: 7.
ACQUISITION HISTORY: —
MEASUREMENTS: Height: 28 cm. Width: 16 cm. Depth: 12 cm.
MATERIAL: Limestone, yellow.
PRESERVATION: The surface is weathered. The right side is broken off across the hair and diagonally across the cheek. The left side of the hair is chipped.
TECHNICAL DESCRIPTION: —
DATE: A.D. 89–100.
REFERENCES: Sadurska – Bounni 1994, 16 f. cat. 6 fig. 214.

OBJECT DESCRIPTION
The fragment depicts a male head.
The object is said to belong together with cat. 64 and cat. 65.

PORTRAIT
His hair is arranged in two rows of crescent-shaped curls around the head. His face is round. The eyebrows are curving, rendered by incised lines, starting from the root of the nose. The eyes are close-set and round, with thick eyelids. The upper eyelids extend beyond the ends of the lower ones. The irises are indicated by incised circles. The ears are large and protruding, with the helix, scapha, concha, and tragus depicted. The nose is small, with carved nostrils. The mouth is small, with full lips. The cheeks are fleshy. The chin is wide, and the neck is wide with two curving grooves.

BANQUETING RELIEFS

A.D. 200–220

68. BANQUETING RELIEF

DATABASE NUMBER: PM129.
LOCATION: Palmyra, Palmyra Museum, inv. no. 1731/6402.
CONTEXT: South-east necropolis. Hypogeum of ʿAštôr, vestibule. Excavation number: 26.
ACQUISITION HISTORY: —
MEASUREMENTS: Height: 52 cm. Width: 51 cm. Depth: 8 cm.
MATERIAL: Limestone, white.
PRESERVATION: The outer edges are slightly chipped. Portrait A: The surface of the forehead and nose is chipped. Portrait B: The surface of the nose, the mouth, the left ear, the right hand, and the left upper leg is chipped.
TECHNICAL DESCRIPTION: —
DATE: A.D. 200–220 (Sadurska – Bounni 1994: A.D. 180–200).
REFERENCES: Tanabe 1986, 43 pl. 432; Sadurska – Bounni 1994, 19 f. cat. 14 fig. 252.

OBJECT DESCRIPTION

The relief is rectangular in shape and depicts a standing male and a reclining male. The relief is framed on all sides by a plain band and has an inner frame on the right, upper, and left sides composed of a leaf-and-dart band with incised midribs in the leaves, a plain, narrow band, and a beaded band. Beneath the figures is a mattress, decorated with three bands. The central band is decorated with a running scroll and rosettes, set between two beaded bands. The bands on either side have leaves on a stem. Curving grooves indicate the texture of the fabric. The reclining male rests against a round cushion. The cushion is decorated with a band decorated with lobed leaves. Curving grooves indicate the texture of the fabric.

PORTRAIT A: STANDING MALE

The figure is shown in frontal view; the head is turned slightly to his left. The head appears small in relation to the body. The right arm is extended and falls alongside his body. The left arm is bent and held towards the left. He stands with the right foot on the relief ground, the left leg is obscured by the mattress and the reclining figure to his left.

His hair is arranged in two rows of crescent-shaped curls around his head. His face is oval. The eyebrows are slightly curving. The eyes are almond-shaped, with the upper eyelid depicted. The eyeballs are blank. The ears are protruding and the helix, tragus, concha, scapha, and lobe are depicted. The nose has a wide base. The mouth is small, with full lips. The chin is oval and prominent. The neck is wide, and there are two horizontal grooves.

He wears a ›Parthian-style‹ tunic and ›Parthian-style‹ trousers. The tunic has a round neckline decorated with a beaded band. The tunic has long, tight-fitting sleeves. The cuffs are decorated with beaded bands. The tunic has a band of lanceolate leaves extending downwards from the middle of the neckline. The tunic ends above the knees and the hem is decorated with a beaded band. The folds of the tunic are rendered by oblique grooves. He also wears a plain band belt. The trouser leg is decorated in the middle with a beaded band extending downwards. The folds of the trousers are indicated by oblique grooves. He wears a round, closed-toe shoe.

The thumb and index finger of the right hand are extended. The outline of an object is visible at his right hand, possibly a pitcher with conical foot. With the upturned palm of the left hand, he holds a plain bowl with a bird inside (visible in outline). The beak and head are pointed to the left.

PORTRAIT B: RECLINING MALE

The reclining figure is shown in three-quarter view; the head is turned slightly to the left. The head appears large. The arms and legs appear short in relation to the body. The right arm is bent and raised in front of the chest. The left arm is bent and rests on a cushion. The right leg is bent and raised, and the right foot rests on the mattress. The left leg is bent under the right leg, and the left leg is obscured by the right leg and the himation.

His hair is arranged in three rows of snail-shell curls around the head. His face is oval. There are two horizontal furrows on the forehead. The eyebrows are curving. The eyes are small and almond-shaped, with thick upper eyelids. The eyeballs are blank. The ears are protruding and the helix, tragus, concha, scapha, and lobe are depicted. The nose has a wide base and the alae are incised. He has a beard that starts from the temples and covers the outer side of the cheeks and the chin. The facial hair is rendered by crescent-shaped curls. The mouth is small. The chin is square, and the neck is wide. A v-shaped depression indicates the sternocleidomastoid muscles.

He wears a tunic and a himation. The tunic has a small, angular neckline and short, wide sleeves that reach to the elbows. The folds of the tunic are rendered by vertical and curving grooves. Over the tunic, he wears a himation. The himation falls over his left shoulder and arm and is folded around the left wrist. The himation continues along the left side of the body and is wrapped across his waist. The folds of the himation are rendered by curving grooves on the sleeves and waist, and oblique grooves at the legs. He wears a closed-toe shoe.

He holds a bowl in the right hand (visible in outline). The left hand rests on the cushion and holds a fold of the himation. The index finger is extended.

OBJECTS FROM HYPOGEA 255

Cat.68

69. BANQUETING RELIEF

DATABASE NUMBER: PM128.
LOCATION: Palmyra, Palmyra Museum, inv. no. 1730/6401.
CONTEXT: South-east necropolis. Hypogeum of ʿAštôr, vestibule. Excavation number: 25.
ACQUISITION HISTORY: —
MEASUREMENTS: Height: 52 cm. Width: 51 cm. Depth: 7 cm.
MATERIAL: Limestone.
PRESERVATION: The outer edges of the relief are slightly chipped. The lower left corner is chipped. The object is badly weathered. Portrait A: The surface of the nose and a part of mouth is chipped.
TECHNICAL DESCRIPTION: —
DATE: A.D. 200–220 (Sadurska – Bounni 1994: A.D. 180–200).
REFERENCES: Tanabe 1986, 43 pl. 433; Sadurska – Bounni 1994, 19 cat. 13 fig. 251.

OBJECT DESCRIPTION

The relief is square in shape and depicts a standing male and a reclining male. The relief is framed by a plain band on all four sides. The inner frame is on the right, upper, and left sides, and is composed of a leaf-and-dart band with incised midribs in the leaves, a plain, narrow band and a beaded band. Beneath the figures is a mattress, decorated with three bands. The central one is decorated with a running scroll with rosettes, set between two beaded bands. The bands on either side have leaves set between two beaded bands. Curving grooves indicate the texture of the fabric. The reclining male rests against a round cushion. Curving grooves indicate the texture of the fabric.

PORTRAIT A: STANDING MALE

The figure is shown in frontal view. The arms appear short in relation to the body. The arms are bent and crossed in front of his chest. He stands with the right foot on the relief ground; the left leg and foot are obscured by the mattress and reclining figure to his left.

His hair is arranged in a row of snail-shell curls around his head. His face is round. The eyebrows are curving. The eyes are almond-shaped, with thick upper eyelids. The eyeballs are blank. The ears are not visible under the hair. The nose has a wide base. The mouth is small, with a full lower lip. The chin is pointed and prominent. The neck is short and wide.

He wears a ›Parthian-style‹ tunic and ›Parthian-style‹ trousers. The tunic has a round neckline, decorated with a plain band and it has long, tight-fitting sleeves. The tunic has a beaded band extending downwards from the middle of the neckline. It ends at the knees and the hem is decorated with a beaded band. He also wears a plain band belt, knotted at the centre with the ends looped under on either side of the waist. The trouser leg is decorated in the middle with a beaded band extending downwards. The folds of the tunic are indicated by vertical grooves. He wears an ankle boot.

His arms are crossed in front of the chest. He holds a shallow bowl in his hands.

PORTRAIT B: RECLINING MALE

The reclining figure is shown in three-quarter view; the head is shown in frontal view. The head appears large. The arms and legs appear short in relation to the body. The right arm is bent and rests on his right knee. The left arm is bent in front of the chest and rests on a cushion. The right leg is bent and raised, and the right foot rests on the mattress. The left leg rests on the mattress, slightly bent under the right leg, and the left foot is obscured by the right leg.

His hair is arranged in two rows of snail-shell curls around the head. His face is oval. The eyebrows are curving. The eyes are almond-shaped, with thick upper eyelids. The eyeballs are blank. The earlobes are visible under the hair. The nose is short, and the nasal bridge is narrow. He has a beard that starts at the temples and covers his outer cheeks, chin, and upper lip. Incised, curving lines render the facial hair. The mouth is small, with a full lower lip. The chin is oval and prominent. The neck is wide.

He wears a ›Parthian-style‹ tunic, a chlamys, and ›Parthian-style‹ trousers. The tunic has a round neckline decorated with a beaded band. The tunic has long sleeves; the cuffs are decorated with a beaded band. The tunic has a wide band decorated with leaves on a stem extending downwards from the middle of the neckline. The tunic ends above the knees and has a hem decorated with leaves on a stem. The folds of the tunic are rendered by oblique grooves. He also wears a plain band belt across the lower torso, knotted at the centre with the ends looped under on either side of the waist. Over the tunic, he wears a chlamys, which falls over his shoulders and around the left arm. It is fastened at the right shoulder with a circular brooch with an incised outer border (Colledge classification: h). A small fold of the chlamys falls under the brooch. The edge of the chlamys is decorated with a beaded band, visible on the edge that crosses the chest. The folded edge of the chlamys continues under his left arm onto the pillow in small zigzag-shaped folds. The folds of the chlamys are rendered by curving grooves on the left arm. He wears trousers: each trouser leg is decorated in the middle with a beaded band extending downwards. The folds of the garments are indicated by oblique grooves. He wears round ankle boots, without decoration.

He rests his right hand on the right knee, and holds a round object, possibly fruit. The fingers are extended. With the upturned palm of the left hand, he holds a bowl with his fingertips. The bowl is low and plain.

OBJECTS FROM HYPOGEA 257

Cat. 69

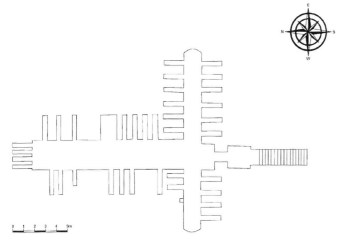

Plan of the hypogeum of ʿAštôr.

A.D. 100–120

HYPOGEUM AK

FRAGMENTS FROM LIDS, LID RELIEFS, OR BANQUETING RELIEFS

70. FRAGMENT OF BANQUETING RELIEF

DATABASE NUMBER: PM577.
LOCATION: Palmyra, Palmyra Museum, inv. no. unknown.
CONTEXT: South-west necropolis. Hypogeum AK.
ACQUISITION HISTORY: —
MEASUREMENTS: —
MATERIAL: Limestone.
PRESERVATION: The head is broken off at the base of the neck. The shoulders and the hands are broken off. The surface is weathered.
TECHNICAL DESCRIPTION: —
DATE: A.D. 100–120.
REFERENCES: Ingholt Archives, PS 1008.

OBJECT DESCRIPTION

The fragment depicts a reclining male. He rests his left arm against a cushion. Curving grooves indicate the texture of the fabric.

PORTRAIT

The figure is shown frontally. The right arm is bent and held to the torso. The left arm is bent.

He wears a tunic and a himation. The tunic has a wide, v-shaped neckline. The folds of the tunic are rendered by curving grooves. Over the tunic, he wears a himation. It is wrapped around the shoulders and arms and covers most of his chest. The folds are rendered by curving grooves.

Cat. 70

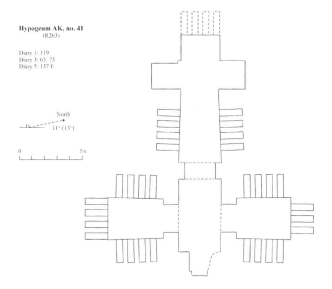

Plan of hypogeum AK.

A.D. 100–130

HYPOGEUM OF ZABDÂ

BANQUETING RELIEFS

71. FRAGMENTS OF BANQUETING RELIEF

DATABASE NUMBER: PM132 (71a) + PM133 (71b).
LOCATION: Palmyra, Palmyra Museum, inv. no. B 2024/7222 and B 2025/7223.
CONTEXT: West necropolis. Valley of the Tombs. Hypogeum of Zabdâ, central exedra in front of sections 2 and 3 (11.05.1959).
ACQUISITION HISTORY: —
MEASUREMENTS: 71a: Height: 60 cm. Width: 104 cm. Depth: 17.5 cm. Head height: 17.5 cm. 71b: Height: 55 cm. Width: 25 cm. Depth: 18 cm. Field depth: 3.5 cm.
MATERIAL: Limestone, grey.
PRESERVATION: 71a: The upper and lower edges of the relief are chipped. 71b: The upper right corner is broken off. The lower corners are chipped. The surface of the lower part of clothing and feet is chipped.

TECHNICAL DESCRIPTION: There are tooth chisel marks on the relief background. There are traces of red pigment in the inscriptions.
DATE: A.D. 100–130.
REFERENCES: 71a: Ingholt Archives, PS 1378; Michalowski 1960, 161. 178–180 cat. 1 figs. 186. 197. 198; Colledge 1976, 62. 66. 132. 150. 216 pl. 69; Tanabe 1986, 42 pl. 423; Sadurska 1994, 15 f. fig. 6; Sadurska – Bounni 1994, 138 f. cat. 184 fig. 220; Parlasca 1995, 68 f. fig. 11; al-Asʿad – Gawlikowski 1997, 49 cat. 68; Parlasca 1998, 315; Palaz Erdemir 2013, 515 fig. 9; Cussini 2016a, 144; Krag 2018, 23 n. 161; 25 n. 178. 179; 33 n. 75. 77; 39 n. 122; 43 n. 164; 44 n. 174. 175; 45 n. 193; 46 n. 194. 195; 47 n. 208; 65 n. 377; 66 n. 382; 83 n. 144; 87 n. 182. 185; 89 n. 204. 206; 90 n. 210; 240 cat. 277; <https://virtual-museum-syria.org/palmyra/a-relief-from-the-tomb-of-zabda/> (06.05.2022). 71b: Michalowski 1960, 161. 178–180 cat. 1 figs. 186. 197. 198; Tanabe 1986, 34 pl. 275; Sadurska – Bounni 1994, 138 f. cat. 184 fig. 220; Parlasca 1995, 68 f. fig. 11; al-Asʿad – Gawlikowski 1997, 49 f. cat. 69; Parlasca 1998, 315; Cussini 2016a, 144; Krag 2018: 23 n. 161; 25 n. 178. 179; 33 n. 75. 77; 39 n. 122; 43 n. 164; 44 n. 174. 175; 45 n. 193; 46 n. 194. 195; 47 n. 208; 65 n. 377; 66 n. 382;

Cat. 71a

83 n. 144; 87 n. 182. 185; 89 n. 204. 206; 90 n. 210; 240.
Inscription: Michalowski 1960, 219 f. cat. 15; Gawlikowski
1974b, 276 cat. 22; al-Asʿad – Gawlikowski 1997, 49 cat. 68;
Krag 2018, 240 cat. 277.

OBJECT DESCRIPTION

The relief cat. 71a is rectangular in shape and depicts a reclining male. Beneath the figure, is a mattress. It is decorated with four wide bands. The bands are undecorated and set between narrow, beaded bands. Curving grooves indicate the texture of the fabric. The male rests against a cushion. The cushion is decorated with a band with a wide, plain band set between narrow, beaded bands. Curving grooves indicate the texture of the fabric. The relief 71b is rectangular in shape and depicts a female sitting in a chair. The chair has a square plain back, which supports the figure up to the height of her head. The seat and legs are undecorated.

INSCRIPTION ON 71A
INSCRIPTION 1
SCRIPT: Palmyrene Aramaic.
LOCATION ON RELIEF: To the right of the reclining figure, at the height of the head.
TRANSCRIPTION: ṢLMY ʾLN DY ZBDʾ BR MQYMW BKRY WDY | BLTYḤN BRT ʾTPNY ʾTTH DY ʿBD BT ʿLM' | DNH WBNYNʾ DY LʿL MNH WQBYRYN LGW MN | ṢLMYʾ ʾLN.
TRANSLATION: These images are of Zabdâ, son of Moqîmû Bakrî, and of Beltîḥan, daughter of Etpenî, his wife, he who made this house of eternity and the construction which is above it. And they are buried behind these images.

CIS no. —; PAT no. 1812.

INSCRIPTION ON 71B
INSCRIPTION 2
SCRIPT: Palmyrene Aramaic.
LOCATION ON RELIEF: To the left of the figure, at the height of the neck.
TRANSCRIPTION: BLTYHtN ʾTTH.
TRANSLATION: Beltîḥan, his wife.
CIS no. —; PAT no. 1813.

PORTRAIT A: RECLINING MALE, ZABDÂ

The figure is shown in frontal view. The arms appear small in relation to the body. The right arm is slightly bent and rests on the right raised knee. The left arm is bent and rests on a cushion. His right leg is bent and the right heel rests on the mattress. The left leg is slightly bent and rests on the mattress. The knees are visible under the drapery.

His hair is arranged in two rows of crescent-shaped curls around his head, with individual strands of hair indicated by incised lines. His head is round, and there is a horizontal furrow on his forehead. The eyebrows are curving. His eyes are large and almond-shaped, with the eyelids depicted. The irises and pupils are indicated by concentric, incised circles.

Cat. 71b

The ears are protruding, and the helix, tragus, concha, scapha, and lobe are depicted. The nose is straight, with a wide base. The alae are incised, and the nostrils carved. The mouth is small, with full lips. The chin is oval and prominent. The neck is wide, and there are two curving grooves.

He wears a tunic and a himation. The tunic has a round neckline and short, loose sleeves. The folds of the tunic are rendered by curving grooves. Over the tunic, he wears a himation. It falls over his left shoulder and arm and is wrapped around the left wrist. A fold of the himation falls under his left hand in a single, wide fold. The himation continues along the left side of his body and is wrapped across the waist. The himation covers his legs and ends at the ankles. The folds of the himation are rendered with oblique grooves on the shoulder and arm and curving grooves on the legs. He wears round, closed-toe shoes.

His right hand rests on the right knee, and nails are indicated by incised lines. The left hand is resting on the mattress and holds a skyphos. The skyphos has a conical foot and a plain body with raised horizontal bands. Handles are depicted. The rim is indicated with a horizontal, incised line. The left index finger and thumb are extended. The nails are indicated with incised lines.

PORTRAIT B: SEATED FEMALE, BELTÎḤAN

The figure is shown frontally. The arms appear short in relation to the body. The right arm is bent and rests on her right thigh. The left is bent and held to the torso. She sits with her legs apart with the knees rendered under the drapery. Both feet rest on a protruding plinth.

She wears three headdresses: a headband, a turban, and a veil. The headband is placed low on the forehead and is decorated with horizontal rectangular panels, each separated by two vertical, incised lines. The turban is coiled. It is divided into two layers and the ends are looped into each other creating a knot in the middle. Curving grooves indicate the coiling of the fabric. The veil is heavy. It falls behind her right shoulder and is folded around the left shoulder and arm. It continues along both sides of the body until the protruding plinth. Part of the hair is covered by the headdress: several strands of hair above the ears are pushed back over the headband and the corners of the turban and disappear under the veil. Two thick, wavy locks of hair fall down her neck. The individual strands of hair are indicated by incised lines. Her face is oval. The eyebrows are curving. The eyes are almond-shaped, with thick upper eyelids. The irises and pupils are indicated by incised, concentric circles. The nose is straight, with a wide base. The alae are incised. The mouth is small, with full lips. The chin is oval. On the neck are three curving grooves.

She wears a tunic and a himation. The ankle-length tunic has a wide, round neckline and short sleeves. The folds of the tunic are rendered by curving grooves on the chest, oblique grooves on the sleeves, and vertical grooves over the feet. The himation crosses the chest diagonally from the left shoulder to the right side and covers the left breast. It is fastened at the shoulder with a trapezoidal brooch with an animal finial (Colledge classification: a). The himation covers the lower body and legs and ends at the shins, revealing the tunic underneath. The folds of the himation are rendered by oblique grooves on the body and thighs, and curving grooves on the lower legs.

She rests her right hand on the right thigh and holds a fold of the veil. The right index finger and thumb are extended. With the left hand she holds a conical object incised with fine, wavy lines, with a bowl-shaped tip, and a thick, short staff topped by a polygonal mass with a pattern of crisscrossing, incised lines, and a small cylinder. These are reduced versions of a spindle and a distaff.

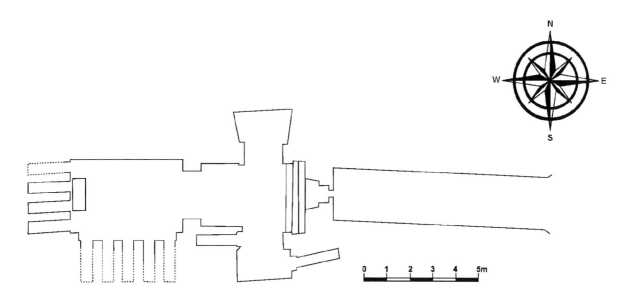

Plan of hypogeum of Zabdâ.

A.D. 100–200

TOMB NO. 5, HYPOGEUM OF ARṬABAN

SARCOPHAGI

A.D. 100–150

72. COMPLETE SARCOPHAGUS RELIEF WITH BANQUETING SCENE AND PORTRAIT BUSTS AND ASSOCIATED LOCULUS RELIEF

DATABASE NUMBER: InSitu086 (72a) + InSitu087 (72b).
LOCATION: Palmyra, in situ.
CONTEXT: South-east necropolis. Tomb no. 5, hypogeum of Arṭaban, back wall of the central exedra. Excavation number: 23, 23a.
ACQUISITION HISTORY: —
MEASUREMENTS: 72a: Height: 60 cm. Width: 125 cm. Depth: 10 cm. 72b: Height: 197 cm. Width: 217 cm. Depth: 15 cm.
MATERIAL: Limestone, yellow/white.
PRESERVATION: 72a: The upper right corner is broken off. The background has several cracks. Portrait A: Small areas on the lower right arm and on the left hand are chipped. Portrait B: The left side of the face and the hands are slightly chipped. Portrait C: The left hand is slightly chipped. 72b: Portrait D: The surface is weathered. Portrait I: The surface is weathered and chipped. Portrait J: The surface is weathered. Portrait K: The surface is weathered and there is a crack over the right elbow.
TECHNICAL DESCRIPTION: 72a: The background is roughly finished, except for the cloth. Portrait B: Tool marks are visible on the surface of the face, and the portrait is carved in high relief. Portrait C: The head is carved in very high relief. 72b: There may have been some restorations. Portrait D: The top half of the figure is in high relief. Portrait E: The figure is carved in high relief and is undercut behind the head and upper body. The left leg appears to merge with the right leg of the reclining figure. Portrait F: The area behind the arms and head is undercut. Portrait H: The head is undercut; the rest of the figure is in low relief. Tool marks are visible on the surface of the face. Portrait I: Carved in low relief.
DATE: A.D. 100–150 (Sadurska – Bounni 1994: A.D. 120–140).
REFERENCES: 72a: Tanabe 1986, 31 pls. 229–232; Parlasca 1987a, 281 fig. 3; Sadurska – Bounni 1994, 37–39 cat. 41 figs. 222–224; Raja 2018a, 3 fig. 6. 72b: Tanabe 1986, 31 pls. 229–232; Parlasca 1987a, 281 fig. 3; Sadurska 1994, 15 fig. 8; Sadurska – Bounni 1994, 37–39 cat. 41 figs. 222–224; Parlasca 1995, 68 f. fig. 10; Heyn 2010, 640 fig. 8; Krag – Raja 2017, 199 n. 24; 204 n. 72. 73; 205 n. 75. 76. 78. 83; 206 n. 87; 208 n. 97. 99; 209 n. 105. 106; 210 n. 107. 110. 116; 214 f. cat. 10; Krag 2018, 28 n. 9; 32 n. 63; 33 n. 77. 78. 80. 82; 45 n. 183; 49 n. 229; 65 n. 377; 66 n. 382; 67 n. 4; 73 n. 47. 56; 83 n. 144; 86 n. 178; 87 n. 182–185; 88 n. 190. 192. 193. 195. 197; 89 n. 204–208; 93 n. 242. 245; 98 n. 23; 103 n. 73; 244 cat. 289; Raja 2018a, 3 fig. 6. Inscriptions: Sadurska – Bounni 1994, 37 f.; Krag 2018, 244 cat. 289.

OBJECT DESCRIPTION

At the top of the relief, above the sarcophagus, there is a loculus relief (72a). It is rectangular in shape and depicts three male busts. Behind the two outermost figures, there is a cloth depicted hanging from two circular medallions rendered by concentric, incised circles at the height of the neck. A branch of leaves projects upwards and inwards from the side and below each medallion. The midribs of the leaves are incised. The folds of the cloth are indicated by curving and oblique grooves. The sarcophagus lid is rectangular in shape and depicts a seated female, a seated boy, a standing girl, a standing male, and a reclining priest. On each side of the relief are two projecting edges with carved architectural pilasters on moulded plinths. Beneath these figures are a mattress and a kline. Three bands decorate the mattress. The central is decorated with vines. The bands on either side are decorated with a running scroll with rosettes, set between beaded bands. Vertical curving grooves indicate the texture of the fabric. The reclining figure rests the left arm against two cushions. The upper cushion is decorated with a wide band with a vegetal motif, set between bands with squares. Curving grooves indicate the texture of the fabric. The left side of the kline is decorated with a fulcrum, where a small armless bust of a priest is shown (portrait I). The end of the fulcrum is decorated with a lion head. The central stretcher of the kline is decorated with two rectangular indentations on either end. On each side of these are two square inlays or appliqués with geometric patterns. The legs are turned. They are composed of a plinth, and above is torus, a reversed concave quarter, a bell-shaped element, a thin torus, a ball, a bell-shaped element, a torus, and above the stretcher is a torus finial. Between the kline legs, two busts, a female and male, are depicted. Flanking them are two animal heads, each carrying a ring in their mouths. The seated female sits in a high-backed chair that is woven, as is indicated by a crisscross pattern and an incised line just below the seat. There is an armrest visible below the figure's right elbow. She sits on a round cushion that is decorated with two beaded bands.

INSCRIPTIONS

INSCRIPTION 1
SCRIPT: Palmyrene Aramaic.
LOCATION ON RELIEF: To the left of the bust on the right side on the loculus.
TRANSCRIPTION: ḤBL | YRḤY | BR ʾRṬBN | BR ʿGʾ.
TRANSLATION: Alas, Yarḥaî son of Arṭaban son of ʿOggâ.

INSCRIPTION 2
SCRIPT: Palmyrene Aramaic.
LOCATION ON RELIEF: To the left of the central bust on the loculus.
TRANSCRIPTION: ḤBL | ʾRṬBN BR | YRḤY BRH.
TRANSLATION: Alas, Arṭaban son of Yarḥaî his son.

Cat. 72

INSCRIPTION 3
SCRIPT: Palmyrene Aramaic.
LOCATION ON RELIEF: To the left of the bust on the left side.
TRANSCRIPTION: ḤBL ʿGʾ | BR YRḤY | ʾRṬBN BRH.
TRANSLATION: Alas, ʿOggâ son of Yarḥaî Arṭaban, his son.

INSCRIPTION 4
SCRIPT: Palmyrene Aramaic.
LOCATION ON RELIEF: Next to seated female.
TRANSCRIPTION: BRTʾ BRT | YRḤY BRʾ | ʾTTH.
TRANSLATION: Bartê daughter of Yarḥaî Barâ, his wife.

INSCRIPTION 5
SCRIPT: Palmyrene Aramaic.
LOCATION ON RELIEF: Next to seated male.
TRANSCRIPTION: ʾRṬBN BR | ʿGʾ BRH.
TRANSLATION: Arṭaban son of ʿOggâ, his son.

INSCRIPTION 6
SCRIPT: Palmyrene Aramaic.
LOCATION ON RELIEF: Next to standing female.
TRANSCRIPTION: BRTʾ BRT | ʿGʾ BR[Ṭ]H.

TRANSLATION: Bartê daughter of ʿOggâ, his daughter.

INSCRIPTION 7
SCRIPT: Palmyrene Aramaic.
LOCATION ON RELIEF: Next to standing male.
TRANSCRIPTION: ʾRṬBN BR | YRḤY BRʾ.
TRANSLATION: Arṭaban son of Yarḥaî Barâ.

INSCRIPTION 8
SCRIPT: Palmyrene Aramaic.
LOCATION ON RELIEF: Next to reclining priest.
TRANSCRIPTION: [ʾRT]BN BR | [ʿGʾ ʾ]BWHY.
TRANSLATION: Arṭaban son of ʿOggâ, his father.

INSCRIPTION 9
SCRIPT: Palmyrene Aramaic.
LOCATION ON RELIEF: Next to female bust on box.
TRANSCRIPTION: MRTBW BRT | BRʾ ʾMH.
TRANSLATION: Martabû daughter of Barâ, his mother.

INSCRIPTION 10
SCRIPT: Palmyrene Aramaic.
LOCATION ON RELIEF: Next to male bust on box.
TRANSCRIPTION: ʿGʾ BR ʾRṬBN BR | ʿGʾ ḤBL DY LʾBWHY | WLʾḤWHY ʿL ḤYWHY.
TRANSLATION: ʿOggâ son of Arṭaban son of ʿOggâ, alas! Who (made this) for his father and for his brother, for his life?.

Inscription 1: CIS no. —; PAT no. 2671.
Inscription 2: CIS no. —; PAT no. 2672.
Inscription 3: CIS no. —; PAT no. 2673.
Inscription 4: CIS no. —; PAT no. 2667.
Inscription 5: CIS no. —; PAT no. 2670.
Inscription 6: CIS no. —; PAT no. 2669.
Inscription 7: CIS no. —; PAT no. 2668.
Inscription 8: CIS no. —; PAT no. 2666.
Inscription 9: CIS no. —; PAT no. 2665.
Inscription 10: CIS no. —; PAT no. 2664.

COMMENT: Inscription 10: One would rather expect BḤYWHY »while still alive«.

LOCULUS RELIEF

PORTRAIT A: MALE BUST, ARṬABAN

The figure is shown frontally. The arms are bent and held to the torso.

His hair is arranged in two rows of snail-shell curls around the head. The individual strands of hair are indicated by incised lines. His face is rectangular. The eyebrows are indicated by curving ridges, starting from the root of the nose. The eyes are large and almond-shaped with thick upper eyelids. The eyeballs are blank. The ears are large and protruding, with the helix, scapha, and earlobe depicted. The nose is long and wide, and the alae are incised. The mouth is small, with thin lips. The chin is square and prominent. The neck is long.

He wears a tunic and a himation. The tunic has a small, v-shaped neckline. The folds of the tunic are indicated by oblique and curving grooves on the chest. Over the tunic, he wears a himation. The himation is wrapped around the right shoulder and arm, leaving the upper torso and the hands free. One bunched end of the himation crosses the chest diagonally and falls over the left shoulder (›arm-sling‹ type). The folds of the himation are rendered by oblique, wide grooves over the arms and curving grooves over the left side of the chest.

With his right hand, he holds the diagonal fold of the himation. The thumb and the index finger are extended. With his left hand he holds a small oblong object, possibly a scroll. The thumb, index, and the little fingers are extended. The nails are indicated by fine, incised lines. On the little finger of the left hand, he wears a thin hoop ring.

PORTRAIT B: MALE BUST, YARḤAÎ

The figure is shown frontally. The arms are bent and held to the torso.

His hair is arranged in two rows of crescent-shaped curls around the head. The individual strands of hair are indicated by incised lines. His face is oval. The eyebrows are indicated by curving ridges, starting from the root of the nose. The eyes are almond-shaped, with thick eyelids. The eyeballs are blank. The ears are large and protruding, with the helix, scapha, and earlobe depicted. The nose is long and wide, and the alae are incised. The nostrils are carved. The mouth is small, with thin lips. The chin is square and fleshy and prominent. The neck is wide.

He wears a tunic and a himation. The tunic has a small, v-shaped neckline. The folds of the tunic are indicated by oblique and curving grooves on the chest. Over the tunic, he wears a himation. The himation is wrapped around the right shoulder and arm, leaving the upper torso and the hands free. One bunched end of the himation crosses the chest diagonally and falls over the left shoulder (›arm-sling‹ type). The folds of the himation are rendered by oblique, wide grooves over the arms and curving grooves over the left side of the chest.

With his right hand he holds the diagonal fold of the himation. The index finger is extended. With his left hand, he holds two small, rectangular objects one on top of the other, possibly a double schedula. The thumb, index, and the little fingers are extended.

PORTRAIT C: MALE BUST, ʿOGGÂ

The figure is shown frontally. The arms are bent and held to the torso.

His hair is arranged in two rows of comma-shaped curls around the head. The individual strands of hair are indicated by incised lines. His face is oval. The eyebrows are indicated by curving ridges, starting from the root of the nose. The eyes are large and almond-shaped, with thick eyelids. The eyeballs are blank. The ears are large and protruding, with the helix, scapha, and earlobe depicted. The nose is long and wide, and the alae are incised. The nostrils are carved. The mouth is small, with thin lips. The chin is square and fleshy. The neck is long.

He wears a tunic and a himation. The tunic has a small, v-shaped neckline. The folds of the tunic are indicated by oblique and curving grooves on the chest. Over the tunic, he wears a himation. The himation is wrapped around the right shoulder and arm, leaving the upper torso and the hands free. One bunched end of the himation crosses the chest diagonally and falls over the left shoulder (>arm-sling< type). The folds of the himation are rendered by oblique, wide grooves over the arms and curving grooves over the left side of the chest.

With his right hand he holds the diagonal fold of the himation. The thumb and the index finger are extended. With his left hand, he holds a small, triangular object, a roll according to Sadurska – Bounni (1994, 37). The thumb, index, and the little fingers are extended.

SARCOPHAGUS LID

PORTRAIT D: SEATED FEMALE, BARTÊ

The figure is seen in three-quarter view. The head appears large, and the arms appear short in relation to the body. Both arms are bent to the torso. The legs are bent with the knees rendered under the drapery. The left foot is obscured by the reclining figure to her left.

She wears three headdresses: a headband, a turban, and veil. The band is placed low on the forehead (details unclear). The turban is coiled. It is divided into two layers and the ends are looped into each other, creating a knot in the middle. Curving grooves indicate the coiling of the fabric. The veil is heavy. It falls over the shoulders and is wrapped around her arms. On either side of the body, the veil proceeds to her ankles. Part of the hair is covered by the headdresses: two thick locks of hair above the ears are pushed back over the headband. Her face is oval. The eyebrows are curving. The eyes are wide-set and round, with thick upper eyelids. The irises are indicated (details unclear). Only the earlobes are visible under the hair. She wears bell-shaped earrings (Colledge classification: D). The nose is straight, with carved alae and nostrils. The mouth is small, with thin lips. The cheeks are fleshy, and the chin is round and almost double. The neck is wide with a curving groove.

She wears a tunic. The tunic has a wide, round neckline, and it proceeds to her ankles. The folds of the tunic are rendered by curving and oblique grooves, and vertical grooves between the legs. She wears plain, round, closed-toe shoes.

The right hand is clenched around the edge of the veil. She holds an oblong object, possibly a spindle, in her left hand (details unclear).

PORTRAIT E: SEATED BOY, ARṬABAN

The figure is seen in three-quarter view. The head appears large. The arms and legs appear short. The right arm is bent and held to the torso. The left arm is extended away from the body. His legs are bent and indicated in the drapery. The left foot is obscured by the reclining figure to his left.

The hair is arranged in one row of crescent-shaped curls around the head. His face is oval. The eyebrows are curving. The eyes are close-set, with thick upper eyelids. The irises are indicated (details unclear). The ears are large, with the helix, scapha, tragus, and lobe carved. The nose is straight, with carved alae and nostrils. The cheeks are fleshy. The mouth is small. The chin is prominent and almost double. The neck is wide, with two curving grooves.

He wears a tunic, >Parthian-style< trousers, and over-trousers. The tunic has long, tight-fitting sleeves and it ends just below the waist. The folds of the tunic are rendered by curving and oblique grooves. He also wears a plain band belt at the waist, possibly knotted at the centre, as one lace is looped under the right side of the waist. The trousers are visible above the knees. Each trouser leg has a band extending downwards at the middle (details unclear). The over-trousers cover the shins and are fastened at the waist. The folds of the garments are rendered by curving and oblique grooves. He wears round-toe shoes.

He holds the stem of a bunch of grapes with his right hand. The index and the middle finger are extended. The left hand is resting on the right hand of the reclining figure to his left.

PORTRAIT F: STANDING GIRL/FEMALE, BARTÊ

The figure is shown frontally. The head is turned slightly to her left. The head appears large. The arms appear short. Both arms are bent to the torso. Her left leg and the lower right leg are obscured by the legs of the reclining figure to her left.

Her hair is straight, centrally parted and brushed to each side of the forehead, covering the ears, and reaching the neck. The individual locks of hair are rendered by incised lines. Her face is oval. The eyebrows are curving. The eyes are close-set and round, with thick eyelids. The irises are indicated by incised circles. Only the earlobes are visible, and she wears earrings with a large round ball (Colledge classification: J). The nose is narrow with carved alae and nostrils. The cheeks are fleshy, and the mouth is small with full lips. The chin is round and almost double. The neck is wide. She wears a necklace composed of large, round beads on a string. The necklace is worn at the base of the neck.

She wears a tunic with a wide, round neckline and long, tight-fitting sleeves. The folds of the tunic are rendered by vertical and curving grooves.

In front of her chest, she holds a large, wide bowl or basket with a broad, flat rim in her hands. The bowl contains round objects, possibly fruit. She wears bracelets composed of twisted wires at her wrists.

PORTRAIT G: STANDING MALE, ARṬABAN

The figure is shown in three-quarter view. The head is shown frontally. The arms appear short in relation to the body. The right arm is extended across the body towards the reclining figure to his left. The left arm is bent and held to the torso. His legs are obscured by the reclining figure to his left.

His hair is straight, brushed backwards and to each side of the forehead. The individual locks of hair are rendered by incised lines. His face is round. The eyebrows are curving. The eyes are close-set and round, with thick eyelids. The irises are indicated by incised circles. The nose is large and straight.

The ears are large and protruding, with the helix and concha depicted. The mouth is small, with thin lips. The chin is round, and the neck is wide with two horizontal grooves.

He wears a tunic and a himation. The tunic has a wide, round neckline and long, tight-fitting sleeves. The folds of the tunic are rendered by vertical and curving grooves. Over the tunic, he wears a himation. It is wrapped around his left shoulder and arm, leaving most of the chest and the hand free. It proceeds in a curving fold across his waist and falls back at his right side. The folds of the himation are rendered by vertical and curving grooves. His right hand is clenched around a wreath composed of lanceolate leaves. With the left hand, he holds a fold of the himation.

PORTRAIT H: RECLINING PRIEST, ARṬABAN
The figure is shown in frontal to three-quarter view. The arms appear short in relation to the body. The right arm is slightly bent and rests on his raised right leg. The left arm is bent and held to the torso. The right leg is bent. The left leg is extended along the mattress. The right foot is obscured by the left leg.

He wears a plain, high, cylindrical, flat-top headdress divided into three sections by two vertical grooves: a Palmyrene priestly hat. His face is oval. The eyebrows are curving. The eyes are close-set and round, with thick eyelids. The irises and pupils are indicated by concentric, incised circles. The ears are large and protruding, with the helix, scapha, tragus, and the lobe depicted. The nose is long, with carved alae and nostrils. The mouth is small, with thin lips. The chin is prominent and oval. The neck is long, with two curving grooves.

He wears a tunic and a himation. The tunic has a wide, round neckline and long, tight-fitting sleeves. The folds of the tunic are rendered by oblique and curving grooves. Over the tunic, he wears a himation. It is wrapped around his left shoulder and arm leaving most of the chest and the hand free. It proceeds in a wide fold onto the cushion and along his left side. Another fold of the himation crosses his waist, falls back at his right side, and covers his legs. The folds of the himation are rendered by curving and oblique grooves.

His right hand rests flat on his raised knee. With the left hand, he holds a skyphos. It has a conical foot, the body is straight, and the lip is straight. It has small, looped handles. The index and the little finger are extended. He wears a thin hoop ring on his left little finger.

SARCOPHAGUS BOX

PORTRAIT I: ARMLESS BUST OF A PRIEST ON FULCRUM
The figure is shown frontally, rendered in clipeus.

He wears a plain, high, cylindrical, flat-top headdress divided into three sections by two vertical grooves: a Palmyrene priestly hat. His face is oval. The eyebrows are curving. The eyes are wide-set and almond-shaped, with thick upper eyelids. The irises are indicated by incised circles. The ears are large and protruding, with the helix rendered. The nose is straight, with carved alae. The mouth is narrow, with thin lips. The chin is oval, and the neck is wide.

He wears a tunic and a chlamys. The tunic has a wide, round neckline. The folds of the tunic are rendered by curving grooves. Over the tunic, he wears a chlamys that falls over both shoulders, and covers most of the chest. It is fastened at the right shoulder with a circular brooch with an incised border (Colledge classification: h). A zigzag-shaped fold falls from under the brooch. The folds of the chlamys are indicated by curving and oblique grooves.

PORTRAIT J: FEMALE BUST, MARTABÛ
The figure is shown frontally. The arms appear short in relation to the body. The arms are bent and held to the torso.

She wears three headdresses: a headband, a turban, and a veil. The details of the headband are unclear. The turban is rendered in one thick layer. The veil is heavy. It falls over her shoulders and arms. Her face is round. The eyebrows are curving. The eyes are close-set. The eyeballs are blank. Oval elements, possibly earrings, are recognizable at the ears (details unclear). The nose is thin. The cheeks are fleshy, and the mouth is small with a full lower lip. The chin is oval, and the neck is wide.

She wears a tunic and a himation. The tunic has a wide, round neckline. The folds of the tunic are rendered by curving grooves. The tunic crosses the chest diagonally from the left shoulder to the right side (details unclear).

She holds an object in her right hand (details unclear). The index finger is extended. The left hand is clenched (details unclear).

PORTRAIT K: MALE BUST, ʿOGGÂ
The figure is shown frontally. The arms are bent and held to the torso. The head is slightly displaced to the left of the torso.

His hair is straight and brushed from the top of the head and to the forehead. The individual locks of hair are rendered by curving, incised lines. His face is oval. The eyebrows are slightly curving. The eyes are wide-set and round with thick upper eyelids. The eyeballs are blank. The ears are large and protruding with the helix depicted. The nose is small and crooked. The cheeks are fleshy, and the mouth is very small with a full lower lip. The chin is wide and double. The neck is wide.

He wears a ›Parthian-style‹ tunic and a chlamys. The tunic has a wide, round neckline decorated with a beaded band, and short, wide sleeves. The folds of the tunic are rendered by curving grooves. The chlamys falls over his shoulders and covers the lower part of the chest. It is fastened at the right shoulder with a circular brooch with an incised border (Colledge classification: h). A zigzag-shaped fold falls from under the brooch. The folds of the chlamys are rendered by oblique, curving grooves.

He holds an oblong flask, possibly an unguentarium in his right hand. It has a conical foot and neck, and the body is ellipse-shaped. He holds a small bowl in his left hand.

SARCOPHAGUS BOXES

A.D. 150–200

73. SARCOPHAGUS BOX WITH PORTRAIT BUSTS

DATABASE NUMBER: InSitu085.
LOCATION: Palmyra, in situ.
CONTEXT: South-east necropolis. Tomb no. 5, hypogeum of Arṭaban, along section 35. Excavation number. 25.
ACQUISITION HISTORY: —
MEASUREMENTS: Height: 38 cm. Width: 192 cm. Depth: 6 cm.
MATERIAL: Limestone, white/yellow.
PRESERVATION: The surface is weathered. There may be patches of restoration between the two right busts. Portrait A: The surface is crazed, especially across the middle of the face. Portrait B: The surface is crazed, crossing the face and body. Portrait C: There are multiple cracks on the surface especially across the himation over the left arm. Portrait D: There are multiple surface cracks especially across the face.
TECHNICAL DESCRIPTION: The finish of the portraits is quite smooth, but the limestone is crazed. Portrait A: Tool marks are visible on the surface of the face and neck. The top of the head is shaped to resemble a support for the above frame. Portrait B: The hair at the top of the head has been shaped to resemble a support for the above frame. Tool marks are visible on the neck. Portrait C: The hair at the top of the head is shaped to resemble a support to the above frame. Portrait D: The top of the veil is shaped as to resemble a support for the above frame. Tool marks are visible on the face and neck.
DATE: A.D. 150–200.
REFERENCES: Sadurska – Bounni 1994, 40 cat. 43 fig. 227; Krag 2018, 47 n. 214; 32 n. 63; 51 n. 241; 98 n. 23; 103 n. 74; 111 n. 8; 244 f. cat. 291. Inscription: Sadurska – Bounni 1994, 40; Krag 2018, 244 f. cat. 291.

OBJECT DESCRIPTION
The relief is rectangular in shape and depicts four armless busts, two males and two females. The relief is set in a recessed frame that surrounds the entire object.

INSCRIPTIONS
INSCRIPTION 1
SCRIPT: Palmyrene Aramaic.
LOCATION ON RELIEF: At the right end of the sarcophagus box.
TRANSCRIPTION: —
TRANSLATION: —

INSCRIPTION 2
SCRIPT: Palmyrene Aramaic.
LOCATION ON RELIEF: At the left end of the sarcophagus box.
TRANSCRIPTION: —
TRANSLATION: —

CIS no. —; PAT no. 2675.

COMMENT: Only slight traces of an inscription remain. There are two inscriptions at the extremities, next to the women (Sadurska – Bounni 1994).

PORTRAIT A: ARMLESS FEMALE BUST
The figure is shown frontally.
She wears three headdresses: a headband, a turban, and a veil. The band is placed high on the forehead and is divided into rectangular panels: the central panel is decorated with a flower with serrated petals, the details of the other panels are unclear. The turban is coiled. It is rendered in one twisted layer with oblique grooves indicating the coiling of the fabric. The veil is heavy. It falls over her right shoulder, proceeds in a curving fold across the chest, and falls back over her left shoulder. Oblique grooves indicate the folds of the veil. The headdress covers part of the hair. Several strands of hair above the ears are brushed back over the edge of the headband and disappear under the veil. The individual strands of hair are rendered by fine, incised lines. Her head is oval. The eyebrows are curving, rendered by thin ridges, starting from the root of her nose. The eyes are close-set and almond-shaped. The

Cat. 73

upper eyelids extend beyond the end of the lower ones. The irises are indicated with incised circles. Only the earlobes are visible, and she is wearing earrings with a horizontal bar from where two round beads are suspended by thin vertical bars (Colledge classification: F). The nose is straight with carved nostrils. The mouth is narrow, with thin lips. The chin is wide, and the neck is short.

She wears a tunic with a round neckline. The folds are indicated by curving, wide grooves.

PORTRAIT B: ARMLESS MALE BUST

The figure is shown frontally. The head appears large.

The hair is arranged in two rows of crescent-shaped curls around the head. The upper part is rendered as a row of circles, possibly a wreath. The individual strands of hair are indicated by incised lines. His face is round. His eyebrows are curving, rendered by incised lines, starting from the root of the nose. The eyes are close-set and almond-shaped, with thick eyelids. The upper eyelids extend beyond the end of the lower ones. The irises are indicated by incised circles. The ears are large and protruding, with helix, scapha, and lobe indicated. The nose is long with carved nostrils. The mouth is small, with full lips. The chin is wide, and the neck is long.

He wears a tunic and a himation. The tunic has a low, v-shaped neckline. The folds of the tunic are rendered by curving grooves. Over the tunic, he wears a himation. It is folded over his left shoulder and falls in a diagonal fold across the chest. The folds are indicated by curving grooves.

PORTRAIT C: ARMLESS MALE BUST

The figure is shown frontally.

The hair is arranged in rows of crescent-shaped curls around the head. The individual strands of hair are indicated by incised lines. His face is oval. His eyebrows are curving, rendered by incised lines, starting from the root of the nose. The eyes are close-set and almond-shaped, with thick eyelids. The upper eyelids extend beyond the end of the lower ones. The irises are indicated by incised circles. The ears are large and protruding, with helix, concha, scapha, and lobe indicated. The nose is straight with carved nostrils. The mouth is small with full lips. The chin is wide. The neck is long with a curving, incised line.

He wears a tunic and a himation. The tunic has a low, v-shaped neckline. The folds of the tunic are rendered by curving grooves. Over the tunic, he wears a himation. It is folded over his left shoulder and falls in a diagonal fold across the chest. The folds are indicated by curving grooves.

PORTRAIT D: ARMLESS FEMALE BUST

The figure is shown frontally.

She wears three headdresses: a headband, a turban, and a veil. The band is placed high on the forehead and has a central rectangular panel with a rosette. The turban is coiled. It is rendered in one twisted layer, with oblique grooves indicating the coiling of the fabric. The veil is heavy. It falls over her right shoulder, proceeds in a curving fold across the chest, and falls back over her left shoulder. The headdresses cover part of the hair. Several strands of hair above the ears are brushed back over the edge of the headband and disappear under the veil. A single wave-shaped lock falls onto her right shoulder. The individual strands of hair are rendered by incised lines. The folds of the veil are indicated by oblique grooves. Her face is round. The eyebrows are curving, depicted as thin ridges, starting from the root of her nose. The eyes are close-set and almond-shaped. The upper eyelids extend beyond the end of the lower ones. The irises are indicated by incised circles. Only the earlobes are visible, and she is wearing earrings in the shape of horizontal bars with two globular pendants (Colledge classification: F). The nose is straight, with carved nostrils. The mouth is narrow, with thin lips. The chin is wide, and the neck is short.

She wears a tunic with a low, round neckline. The folds are indicated by curving, wide grooves.

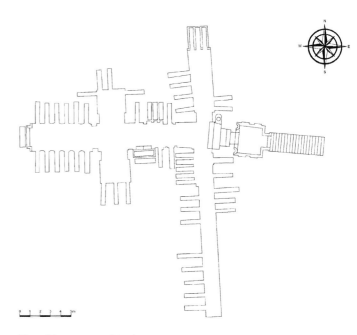

Plan of hypogeum of Arṭaban.

A.D. 100–220

HYPOGEUM OF LIŠAMŠ

SARCOPHAGUS BOXES

A.D. 200–220

74. SARCOPHAGUS BOX WITH BANQUETING SCENE

DATABASE NUMBER: PM783.
LOCATION: Palmyra, Palmyra Museum, inv. no. unknown.
CONTEXT: South-west necropolis. Hypogeum of Lišamš, inner central chamber.
ACQUISITION HISTORY: Excavated in 1924.
MEASUREMENTS: Height: 125 cm; Width: 245 cm.
MATERIAL: Limestone, white/yellow.
PRESERVATION: The upper edge of the sarcophagus box has broken off. The surface is weathered. The heads of the portraits are broken off.
TECHNICAL DESCRIPTION: Portrait A: There are traces of red pigment on her necklace. Portrait C: There are traces of red pigment on the brooch.
DATE: A.D. 200–220.
REFERENCES: Ingholt 1938, 117–119 pl. 43, 2; Krag – Raja 2017, 199 n. 24; 204 n. 72. 73; 205 n. 75. 76; 207 n. 94; 208 n. 99; 209 n. 100; 211 n. 117; 218 cat. 26; Krag 2018, 32 n. 63; 58 n. 304; 62 n. 349. 353; 87 n. 182; 103 n. 74; 397 cat. 861. Inscription: Ingholt 1938, 118; Krag 2018, 397 cat. 861.

OBJECT DESCRIPTION
The sarcophagus box is rectangular in shape and depicts a standing female, a standing male, two reclining males, and a seated female. The figures are resting on a mattress. Curving grooves indicate the texture of the fabric. The reclining figures rest their arms on cushions: the cushion to the right is decorated with a wide band (details unclear). The cushion at the left has a wide band with a vegetal motif between beaded bands. Curving grooves indicate the texture of the cushions.

INSCRIPTION
SCRIPT: Palmyrene Aramaic.

Cat. 74

LOCATION ON RELIEF: To the right of the head of the standing female.
TRANSCRIPTION: SLM BRT ʿGʾ ḤBL.
TRANSLATION: Shalam, daughter of ʿOggâ, alas!

CIS no. —; PAT no. 0093.

PORTRAIT A: STANDING FEMALE, SHALAM

The figure is shown frontally. The right arm is slightly bent and held to the waist. The left arm is bent and held to the chest. She stands with the legs slightly apart. Her feet are obscured by the reclining male to her left.

She wears a veil. It is falling in a wide, curving fold across the chest and falls back at the left shoulder. She wears one necklace composed of round beads with a central, round pendant.

She wears a tunic. The tunic has long sleeves, leaving only the hands free. The folds of the tunic are rendered by curving and oblique grooves. According to Ingholt (1938, 117), she also wears a himation.

With the right hand, she lightly pulls the tunic. The index and the little fingers are extended. With the left hand, she holds the wide fold of the over-garment. She wears a plain hoop bracelet at her wrist.

PORTRAIT B: STANDING MALE

The figure is seen in three-quarter view. Both arms are bent. His left leg and lower right leg are obscured by the reclining figure to his left.

He wears a tunic. The tunic has long sleeves. There is an overfold at the waist. The folds of the tunic are rendered by curving and oblique grooves.

He holds a jug in his hands. The body of the vessel is decorated with a pattern of hollowed-out lozenges.

PORTRAIT C: RECLINING MALE

The figure is shown in frontal to three-quarter view. The right arm is slightly bent and rests on his right knee. The left arm is bent. The right leg is bent, and he rests his foot on the mattress. The left leg is bent under the right, with the knee pointing forwards. The left lower leg is obscured by the right leg.

He wears a ›Parthian-style‹ tunic, a chlamys, and ›Parthian-style‹ trousers. The tunic has a wide, round neckline decorated with a vegetal motif bordered by rosettes. The tunic has long, tight-fitting sleeves with decorated cuffs (details unclear). At the middle, the tunic has a wide band decorated with a vegetal motif extending downwards. The tunic ends above the knees and has a decorated lower border (details unclear). The folds of the tunic are rendered by curving and oblique grooves. He

View of the central chamber of the hypogeum of Lišamš.

wears a plain band belt, knotted at the centre with the ends looped under on either side of the waist. Over the tunic, he wears a chlamys that falls over both shoulders, and covers most of the chest. A wide fold falls from under his left arm and along his side. The chlamys is fastened at the right shoulder with a circular brooch with an incised border (Colledge classification: h). A zigzag-shaped fold falls from under the brooch. The folds of the chlamys are indicated by narrow, deep grooves. The trousers are tucked into his boots. Each trouser leg is decorated in the middle with a band extending downwards (details unclear). The folds of the garment are rendered by curving and oblique grooves. His boots are plain with a pointed toe.

With the right hand resting on the raised knee, he holds a branch. With the upturned palm of the left hand, he holds a circular bowl near the chest with his fingertips. A horizontal groove indicates the rim of the bowl.

PORTRAIT D: RECLINING MALE

The figure is shown in frontal to three-quarter view. The left arm is bent. The right arm and lower body are extended behind the reclining figure to his right.

He wears a tunic and himation. The tunic has a wide, v-shaped neckline, and short, loose sleeves. The folds of the tunic are rendered by curving grooves. Over the tunic, he wears a himation. It falls over his shoulders, leaving most of the chest free, and is wrapped around the left upper arm. A wide fold falls from under the arm and over the cushion. The folds of the himation are rendered by curving and oblique grooves.

With the upturned palm of the left hand, he holds a circular bowl near the chest with his fingertips. The rim is indicated by an incised, horizontal line.

PORTRAIT E: SEATED FEMALE

The figure is shown frontally. The right arm is bent and rests on her right thigh. The left arm is bent and raised to the neck. She sits with the legs apart and the knees are rendered under the drapery. She rests her feet on the mattress.

She wears a veil. It falls over her right shoulder and arm.

She wears a tunic and a himation. The ankle-length tunic is short-sleeved. The folds of the tunic are rendered by curving and oblique grooves. Over the tunic, she wears a himation. It falls across her torso and covers the thighs. It ends at the knees. She wears pointed shoes.

Her right hand rests in her lap holding a fold of the veil. The thumb and the index finger are extended. With the left hand, she pulls the veil from the opposite site.

View of the central chamber of the hypogeum of Lišamš.

Plan of the hypogeum of Lišamš.

FRAGMENTS OF LIDS, LID RELIEFS, OR BANQUETING RELIEFS

A.D. 100–150

75. FRAGMENT OF BANQUETING RELIEF

DATABASE NUMBER: PM910.
LOCATION: Palmyra, Palmyra Museum, inv. A 92, A 93, A 94.
CONTEXT: South-west necropolis. Hypogeum of Lišamš.
ACQUISITION HISTORY: —
MEASUREMENTS: —
MATERIAL: Limestone.
PRESERVATION: The background is broken off. Portrait A: The head and the right arm are broken off. Portrait B: The head is broken off and the right arm is chipped. Portrait C: The head is broken off.
TECHNICAL DESCRIPTION: —
DATE: A.D. 100–150.
REFERENCES: Ingholt 1938, 117 pl. 43, 1; Makowski 1985b, 124 f. fig. 3.

OBJECT DESCRIPTION

The object depicts the upper torso of three reclining males.

PORTRAIT A: RECLINING MALE

The figure is shown frontally. The left arm is bent and held in front of the chest.

He wears a tunic and himation. The tunic has a wide, v-shaped neckline. The folds of the tunic are rendered by curving grooves. The himation is folded over the left shoulder and covers the left arm. The folds of the himation are rendered by vertical grooves.

He holds a drinking vessel in his left hand (details unclear).

PORTRAIT B: RECLINING MALE

The figure is shown frontally. The left arm is bent and held in front of the chest.

He wears a tunic and himation. The tunic has a wide, round neckline and long sleeves. The folds of the tunic are rendered by curving grooves. The himation is folded over the left shoulder. The folds of the himation are rendered by vertical grooves.

He holds a drinking vessel in his left hand, perhaps a skyphos (details unclear).

PORTRAIT C: RECLINING MALE

The figure is shown frontally. The left arm is bent and held in front of the chest.

He wears a tunic and himation. The tunic has a wide, v-shaped neckline. The folds of the tunic are rendered by curving grooves. The himation is folded over the left shoulder and covers the left arm. The folds of the himation are rendered by vertical grooves.

He holds a drinking vessel in his left hand, perhaps a skyphos (details unclear).

A.D. 100–240

HYPOGEUM OF ṬAʿAÎ

SARCOPHAGUS LIDS

A.D. 100–200

76. SARCOPHAGUS LID WITH BANQUETING SCENE

DATABASE NUMBER: NMD031.
LOCATION: Damascus, National Museum of Damascus, inv. no. unknown.
CONTEXT: South-east necropolis. Hypogeum of Ṭaʿaî, west exedra.
ACQUISITION HISTORY: —
MEASUREMENTS: Height: 130 cm. Width: 200 cm.
MATERIAL: Limestone, white/yellow.
PRESERVATION: The relief ground is only partly preserved. The lower left side is chipped. The surface is weathered. Portrait B: A crack runs diagonally through the lower torso and the right foot is chipped.
TECHNICAL DESCRIPTION: —
DATE: A.D. 100–200: body A.D. 100–120; head: 180–200 (Abdul-Hak 1952: relief: A.D. 100–150; head: A.D. 150–200).
REFERENCES: Abdul-Hak 1952, 201 f. 218. 229 f. 231–234 cat. 19; Makowski 1985a, 85 fig. 7; Krag 2018, 28 n. 9; 33 n. 77; 64 n. 365; 66 n. 382; 98 n. 28; 314 cat. 558.

OBJECT DESCRIPTION

The sarcophagus lid is rectangular in shape and depicts a seated female and a reclining male. Beneath the figures is a mattress (details unclear). The female sits on two cushions and the reclining male rests the left arm on two cushions. Curving grooves indicate the texture of all cushions.

Found adjacent to object cat. 79.

PORTRAIT A: SEATED FEMALE

The figure is shown frontally. The right arm falls along the body. The left arm is bent and rests on her thighs. Her legs are bent with the knees rendered under the drapery. Her feet are obscured by the reclining figure.

She wears two headdresses: a turban and a veil. The turban is coiled. Horizontal grooves indicate the coiling of the fabric. The veil is heavy. It falls over her shoulders and is wrapped around her left arm leaving the hand free. Her hair is visible under the veil. It is centrally parted and brushed away on each side of the forehead. It is arranged in thick locks, brushed back at the ears, and disappears under the veil. Her face is oval. Her eyebrows are slightly curving. The eyes are close-set and round with thick eyelids. Her nose is large. The mouth is small, with full lips. The cheeks are fleshy, and the chin is wide. The neck is wide.

She wears a tunic and a himation. The folds of the tunic are indicated by curving grooves. The ankle-length himation crosses her chest diagonally from the left shoulder to the right side, and covers the lower chest, body, and legs. It is fastened at the left shoulder with a brooch (details unclear). The folds of the himation are rendered by diagonal and curving grooves. The folds between the legs are rendered by curving grooves.

Her right hand rests on the cushions and the left hand on her right thigh.

PORTRAIT B: RECLINING PRIEST

The figure is shown in frontal to three-quarter view. The torso appears disproportional. The head appears small in relation to the body. The right arm is bent and held to the torso. The left arm is bent in front of the torso. The right leg is bent and the foot rests on the mattress; the left leg is bent under the right leg with the knee pointing outwards. The left foot is obscured by the right leg.

He wears a high, cylindrical, flat-top headdress divided into three sections by two vertical grooves: a Palmyrene priestly hat. A wreath is depicted at the lower part of the hat. It has three rows of leaves pointing towards an armless bust of a male wearing a Palmyrene priestly hat. His face is diamond-shaped. The eyebrows are curving. The ears are protruding, with the helix and lobe depicted. The nose is straight and wide at the base. The mouth is small with full lips. The chin is wide, and the neck is wide.

He wears a ›Parthian-style‹ tunic, a chlamys, ›Parthian-style‹ trousers, and over-trousers. The tunic has long, slightly loose sleeves. The chlamys ends above the knees and has a wide decorated border (details unclear). The folds of the tunic are rendered by curving and oblique grooves. Over the tunic, he wears a chlamys that falls over both shoulders, and covers most of the chest and body. It falls along the left side of the torso and over the cushions. It is fastened at the right shoulder with a circular brooch with an incised border (Colledge classification: h). The folds of the chlamys are rendered by curving and oblique grooves. He wears a band belt with laces across the lower torso. The belt is knotted at the centre and the ends are looped under on either side of the waist. The trousers are visible above the knees, and they have a central decorated band extending downwards. The over-trousers are visible under the knees and their folds are indicated by wide, vertical grooves.

He holds a skyphos in his right hand. It has a conical foot and a conical lower body. The neck is concave and has an undecorated field. It has small, looped handles.

The head was added at a later date. According to Abdul-Hak (1952, 231 f. cat. 13), the fragment of a priestly hat could have belonged to the first head of the reclining priest.

HEADS: MALES

A.D. 100–150

77. MALE HEAD

Cat. 77

DATABASE NUMBER: NMD024.
LOCATION: Damascus, National Museum of Damascus, inv. no. unknown.
CONTEXT: South-east necropolis. Hypogeum of Ṭaʿaî, west exedra, section A.
ACQUISITION HISTORY: —
MEASUREMENTS: Height: 20 cm. Width: 15 cm.
MATERIAL: Limestone, white/yellow.
PRESERVATION: The head is broken off at the top of the neck. Small areas on the forehead, the right eye, and the mouth are chipped. Many small cracks run horizontally and diagonally across the face. The surface is weathered.
TECHNICAL DESCRIPTION: —
DATE: A.D. 100–150.
REFERENCES: Abdul-Hak 1952, 230. 233 cat. 33 fig. 13.

OBJECT DESCRIPTION

The object depicts a male figure.
The object is possibly from the relief cat. 76 (according to Abdul-Hak 1952, 233).

PORTRAIT

His hair is arranged in a single row of large, comma-shaped locks around his head. The individual strands of hair are indicated by incised lines. His face is round. The eyebrows are curving and indicated by ridges. The eyes are large and almond-shaped, with thick eyelids. The irises and pupils are indicated by concentric, incised circles. The ears are small and protruding, with the helix, scapha, and earlobe rendered. The nose is short with a wide base. The alae are incised, and the nostrils are carved. The mouth is small, with a full lower lip. The chin is pointed and fleshy.

HEADS: FEMALES

A.D. 100–150

78. FEMALE HEAD

Cat. 78

DATABASE NUMBER: NMD016.
LOCATION: Damascus, National Museum of Damascus, inv. no. unknown.
CONTEXT: South-east necropolis. Hypogeum of Ṭaʿaî, west exedra.
ACQUISITION HISTORY: —
MEASUREMENTS: Height: 23.5 cm.
MATERIAL: Limestone.

PRESERVATION: The background is broken off. The lower part of the figure is broken off at the neck. The lower lip and part of the chin are broken off. The surface of the veil is chipped.
TECHNICAL DESCRIPTION: —
DATE: A.D. 100–150.
REFERENCES: Abdul-Hak 1952, 216. 231 cat. 11 pl. 12, 2; Tanabe 1986, 45 fig. 466; Krag 2018, 196 cat. 108.

OBJECT DESCRIPTION

The object depicts a female head.

PORTRAIT

The figure is shown frontally.

She wears three headdresses: a headband, a turban, and a veil. The headband is placed low on the forehead and is divided into rectangular panels separated by vertical, beaded bands. The central panel has a cruciform flower with eight petals. The centre of the petals has an incised line, indicating the central vein. The outer panels have a geometric crisscross design. The turban is divided into three layers. The lower is a coiling band, and the upper two are coiled and looped into each other creating a knot in the middle. Curving grooves indicate the coiling of the fabric. The veil is heavy. It falls over the back of the head. Part of the hair is covered by the headdress: several strands of hair above the ears are brushed back over the headband and disappear under the veil. The individual strands of hair are indicated by incised lines. Her face is oval. The eyebrows are indicated by thin ridges. The eyes are large, round, with thick eyelids. The eyeballs are blank. Only the earlobes are visible under the hair. She wears earrings shaped like a miniature bunch of grapes (Colledge classification: E). The nose is narrow. The philtrum is carved. The mouth is small. The chin is round.

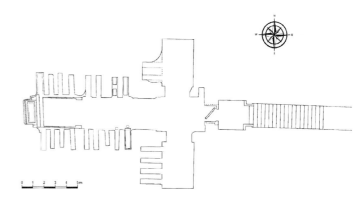

Plan of the hypogeum of Ṭaʿaî.

BANQUETING RELIEFS

A.D. 220–240

79. BANQUETING RELIEF

DATABASE NUMBER: NMD005.
LOCATION: Damascus, National Museum of Damascus, inv. no. 18802.
CONTEXT: South-east necropolis. Hypogeum of Ṭaʿaî, west exedra, south section A3.
ACQUISITION HISTORY: —
MEASUREMENTS: Height: 55.5 cm. Width: 82 cm. Depth: 11 cm.
MATERIAL: Limestone, yellow.
PRESERVATION: The right and the upper side of the relief are slightly chipped. Portrait A: The surface of the left knee is chipped.
TECHNICAL DESCRIPTION: Portrait B: The left hand is undercut.
DATE: A.D. 220–240 (Abdul-Hak 1952: A.D. 180–250).
REFERENCES: Abdul-Hak 1952, 215. 225. 228 n. 2. 230 f. 233–235. 246 cat. 20 pls. 2, 2; Gawlikowski 1974b, 270 f. cat. 11; Parlasca 1982a, 198 cat. 178; Exhibition of Treasures 1977, cat. 183; Parlasca 1985, 399 cat. 190; Tanabe 1986, 42 pl. 424; Yon 2001c, 367 f. cat. 255; Clauss 2002, 92 cat. 105; Finlayson 2002–2003, 228 pl. 7; Zahran 2004, 31 fig. 8; Finlayson 2008, 113 fig. 6, 5; Miyashita 2016, 133 fig. 18; Krag 2018, 28 n. 9; 32 n. 62; 56 n. 291; 62 n. 353; 63 n. 354; 64 n. 361. 362. 365; 65 n. 372. 373. 377; 87 n. 182. 186; 88 n. 192; 89 n. 203; 90 n. 210; 101 n. 63; 102 n. 66; 103 n. 75; 377 cat. 792. Inscription: Abdul-Hak 1952, 234; Gawlikowski 1974b, 270 f. cat. 11; Yon 2001c, 368 cat. 255; Krag 2018, 377 cat. 792.

OBJECT DESCRIPTION

The relief is rectangular in shape and depicts a reclining female and a reclining male. Beneath these figures is a mattress. It is decorated with an intersecting lozenges pattern with beaded elements at the intersections. The lozenges have four-petal flowers, with the veins of the petals incised. Behind the reclining male, there is a cloth depicted hanging from two six-petal rosettes. A branch of palm leaves projects upwards and inwards from each rosette. The midribs of the leaves are incised. The folds of the cloth are indicated by curving grooves. The female rests against a cushion. The cushion is decorated with a wide band extending downwards with leaves on a stem. Curving grooves indicate the fabric of the cushion. The male rests on a cushion. The cushion is decorated with a vertical band with lanceolate leaves closely arranged. Curving grooves indicate the fabric of the cushion. To the right of the two figures is a chest on a pedestal. The chest appears to be polygonal (four sides are visible) and has a stepped lid. The upper part of the box is decorated with four horizontal panels decorated, with leaves pointing towards a central rosette. The central part has three coffered rectangles. The middle rectangle has a circular incision with a horizontal and vertical rectangular depression, possibly a rendering of a lock or keyhole. The chest has disc-shaped feet.

Found adjacent to object cat. 76.

INSCRIPTIONS

INSCRIPTION 1
SCRIPT: Palmyrene Aramaic.
LOCATION ON RELIEF: To the right of reclining female, at the height of her head.
TRANSCRIPTION: ṢLMT BWLYʾ BRT | ʿGʾ BR BWRPʾ.
TRANSLATION: Image of Bôlayâ daughter of ʿOggâ Bôrrofâ.

INSCRIPTION 2
SCRIPT: Palmyrene Aramaic.
LOCATION ON RELIEF: To the right of reclining male, at the height of his head.
TRANSCRIPTION: ṢLM MLʾ | BR ʿGʾ | BWRPʾ.
TRANSLATION: Image of Malê son of ʿOggâ Bôrrofâ.

CIS no: —; PAT no. 1802.

PORTRAIT A: RECLINING FEMALE, BÔLAYÂ

The torso of the reclining female is shown in frontal view, with her head turned slightly to her right. The lower body and legs are in three-quarter view. The head and left arm appear large. The right arm is bent across the chest. The left is bent and raised to the head, and rests on a cushion. The right leg is bent and the right foot rests on the mattress. The left leg is bent under the right, and the knee is visible under the drapery, pointing forwards. The left lower leg is obscured by the right leg.

She wears three headdresses: a headband, a turban, and a veil. The headband is placed high on her forehead. It is decorated by a central square panel with four-petal flowers with incised midribs, set between two beaded bands. A narrow, plain band runs along the lower border. She also wears a head-chain that is attached under the centre of the turban and runs to the sides disappearing under the veil. It is composed of circular bezels linked by beaded elements. The turban is coiled. It is in a single layer with horizontal grooves indicating the coiling of the fabric. The veil is heavy. It falls behind her shoulders. The hair is visible over her ears, where it is brushed back under the head-chain, over the headband, and disappears under the veil. Individual strands of hair are indicated with incised lines. A row of single comma-shaped curls is under the headband. Her face is oval. The eyebrows are slightly curving, rendered by incised grooves, and starting from the root of the nose. The eyes are almond-shaped, with thick upper eyelids. The irises are indicated by incised circles. The earlobes are visible under the hair, and she wears dumbbell-shaped earrings (Colledge classification: H). The nose is straight and wide. The alae are incised, and the nostrils carved. The mouth is small, with a full lower lip. The chin is pointed. The neck is long, with three curving grooves. She wears four necklaces: a string of small, round beads worn at the base of the neck. A plain hoop necklace with a round pendant with an incised border, perhaps indicating the setting of a stone, suspended

Cat. 79

from a narrow sleeve, worn at the base of the neck. A chain of alternating square and circular bezels, all with an incised border, perhaps indicating the setting of a stone, joined by beaded elements, worn below the collarbone. A loop-in-loop chain with a circular pendant with an incised border, perhaps indicating the setting of a stone, suspended by a narrow sleeve at the centre, is worn below the collarbone.

She wears a tunic and a himation. The tunic has a small, angular neckline, and short sleeves. The folds of the tunic are rendered by oblique grooves on the chest and sleeve. The himation crosses the chest diagonally from the left upper arm to the right side and covers most of the left breast. It is folded around the left arm and two edges fall from under the arm onto the mattress in two large, zigzag-shaped folds. The himation covers the lower body and legs and ends at the ankles, with a scalloped edge. The folds of the himation are rendered by curving and oblique grooves. She wears sandals (visible on the right foot). The sandal has a plain strap between the first two toes that runs on either side of the foot. The sole is indicated by a horizontal, incised line. Incised lines indicate the toenails.

Her right hand rests on the cushion, with the fingers slightly extended. She wears a bracelet on her right wrist, composed of plain and beaded wires twisted together. The left hand is held to her face, with the fingers resting against the cheek. The left index finger is extended to the forehead. She wears a bracelet on her left wrist, composed of plain and beaded wires twisted together. She wears a ring on the left little finger: it has a round bezel with an incised border, perhaps indicating the setting of a stone.

PORTRAIT B: RECLINING MALE, MALÊ
The figure is shown in frontal view. The head appears large. The right arm is slightly bent and held in front of the waist. The left hand is bent in front of the chest and rests on a cushion. His legs are obscured by the reclining figure to his right.

His hair is arranged in three rows of snail-shell curls around his head. The individual strands of hair are indicated by incised lines. He wears a wreath high on the head. It has three rows of leaves pointing towards a central rosette. His face is diamond-shaped. The eyebrows are slightly curving, indicated with incised lines, and starting from the root of the nose. The eyes are almond-shaped, with thick upper eyelids. The irises and pupils are depicted, with concentric, incised circles. The ears are protruding, and the tail of the helix, scapha, and lobe are depicted. The nose is straight and wide. The alae are incised, and the nostrils carved. He has a beard: it starts at the temples, covers the outer side of the cheeks, the chin, and the upper lip. The facial hair is rendered by snail-shell curls in the beard, and incised vertical lines in the moustache. The mouth is small, with a full lower lip. The chin is round. The neck is wide.

He wears a >Parthian-style< tunic and a himation. The tunic has a round neckline decorated with a beaded band. The sleeves are long, the cuffs are decorated with a band of alternating incised circles and squares. The tunic has a wide band with leaves on a curving stem set between two beaded bands, extending downwards from the middle of the neckline. The folds of the tunic are rendered by vertical and oblique grooves. He wears a plain band belt, with a single strap looped under the side. The himation falls over his left shoulder and arm and along the left side of his body. It is folded around his left arm and the edge of the himation continues onto the cushion and mattress in two large, zigzag-shaped folds.

With his right hand, he holds an oblong oval object, with a pointed end and diamond-shaped pattern, possibly a pinecone. The right index finger and thumb are extended. With the upturned palm of the left hand, he holds a bowl with his fingertips. The bowl has a round base indicated by an incised, horizontal line. The body is decorated with hollowed circles, and the rim is indicated with a horizontal, incised line. The upper surface is plain. The nails are indicated with fine, incised lines.

A.D. 100–250

TOMB NO. A120, HYPOGEUM OF ʿATENATAN

BANQUETING RELIEF

A.D. 100–150

80. FRAGMENT OF BANQUETING RELIEF

DATABASE NUMBER: InSitu172.
LOCATION: Palmyra, in situ.
CONTEXT: South-west necropolis. Tomb no. A120, hypogeum of ʿAtenatan.
ACQUISITION HISTORY: —
MEASUREMENTS: —
MATERIAL: Limestone.
PRESERVATION: Broken on all sides. Only part of the torso, the lower left arm, and the upper thighs survive.
TECHNICAL DESCRIPTION: —
DATE: A.D. 100–150 (Seyrig 1937: A.D. 100–150).
REFERENCES: Seyrig 1937, 15 fig. 5.

OBJECT DESCRIPTION

The object depicts a reclining male. He rests his left arm on a round cushion, decorated with a beaded band at the centre.

Note: Excavated by M. Amy and attributed to an exedra other than Julius Aurelius Maqqai's (Seyrig 1937, 15 n. 2).

PORTRAIT

The figure is shown in three-quarter view. The left arm is bent and held in front of the torso. His right leg is bent. The left leg is extended.

He wears a >Parthian-style< tunic, a chlamys, >Parthian-style< trousers, and over-trousers. At the middle, the tunic has a wide band that extends downwards. It is decorated with a running scroll enclosing four-petal flowers, set between two beaded bands. The tunic ends above the knees, and has a decorated border: a beaded band on either side of a series of rectangles with a crisscross pattern divided by small, beaded bands. The folds of the tunic are rendered by curving, wide grooves. He wears a plain band belt across the lower torso. It is knotted at the centre, with the ends looped under on either side of the waist. Over the tunic, he wears a chlamys that is wrapped around the left arm and falls over the cushion. The folds of the chlamys are indicated by narrow grooves. Each trouser leg has a wide band that extends downwards: it is set between two beaded bands and is decorated with a leaf motif. The folds of the trousers are indicated by wide, curving grooves. Over the trousers he wears over-trousers: they are decorated with a wide band with a leaf motif set between two beaded bands on the edges.

With his left hand, he holds a two-handled skyphos in front of his chest. The index finger is extended.

TOMB NO. A120, HYPOGEUM OF ʿATENATAN, EXEDRA OF JULIUS AURELIUS MAQQAÎ

SARCOPHAGI

A.D. 229–250

81. FRAGMENTS OF COMPLETE SARCOPHAGUS WITH BANQUETING SCENE AND RELIGIOUS SCENE

DATABASE NUMBER: PM749 (81a) + InSitu094 (81b).
LOCATION: Palmyra. 81a: Palmyra Museum, inv. no. unknown. 81b: In situ.
CONTEXT: South-west necropolis. Tomb no. A120, hypogeum of ʿAtenatan, exedra of Julius Aurelius Maqqaî.
ACQUISITION HISTORY: —
MEASUREMENTS: —
MATERIAL: Limestone, white.
PRESERVATION: The upper left corner and side of the box are broken off. Portrait A: The upper part is broken off diagonally through the right elbow and horizontally at the waist. A large crack in the stone runs through the legs above her right foot. Portrait B: The head of the figure is broken at the base of the neck, vertically across the right side, and at the right wrist. A piece of the left arm has broken off. A large crack runs diagonally through his torso. Portrait C: The head is broken off at the base of the neck. A large crack runs vertically through the torso. The surface of the torso is chipped. Portrait D: The head is broken off at the base of the neck, and the area on the right side of the waist is broken off. A large crack runs diagonally through the upper chest. Another crack runs horizontally through the right shin. Portrait E: The head and left foot are chipped. Portrait F: The head, the right arm, and the hand are chipped. Portrait G: The head and the upper left side of the torso are broken off. Portrait H: Only the lower part of the legs and feet are preserved. Portrait I: Only a small part of the lower right leg and the heel of the left leg is preserved.
TECHNICAL DESCRIPTION: —
DATE: A.D. 229–250 (Schmidt-Colinet 1992: A.D. 200–273).
REFERENCES: 81a: Ingholt Archives, PS 1048; Ingholt 1935, 67 pl. 26; Seyrig 1937, 15 n. 3. 22 pl. 4; Starcky 1941, 28

Cat. 81

fig. 21; Seyrig 1951, 39; Colledge 1976a, 60. 63. 77 f. 87. 120. 124–126. 129. 131. 145–148; Parlasca 1984, 283; Parlasca 1989b, 547 fig. 204; Schmidt-Colinet 1992, 106 n. 373. 377. 380d; 108 n. 391; 111 n. 408. 410; 112 n. 415; 125 n. 470. 476; 130 n. 479; 133 f. n. 509 pl. 69, b; Parlasca 1998, 311. 81b: Ingholt Archives, PS 985; Ingholt 1935, 67 pls. 27, 2; Seyrig 1937, 15 n. 3. 22. 27. 41 n. 2 fig. 18 pl. 4; Starcky 1941, 28 fig. 21; Colledge 1976a, 60. 63. 87. 120. 125 f. 129. 131 f. 155; Parlasca 1984, 283; Parlasca 1989b, 547 fig. 204; Schmidt-Colinet 1992, 106 n. 373. 377. 380d; 108 n. 391; 111 n. 408. 410; 112 n. 415; 125 n. 470. 476; 130 n. 479; 133 f. n. 509 pl. 69, b; Parlasca 1998, 311; Krag – Raja 2017, 199 n. 24; 204 n. 72. 73; 205 n. 75; 208 n. 99; 209 n. 100; 219 cat. 32 fig. 10; Krag 2018, 28 n. 9; 32 n. 63; 59 n. 325; 62 n. 349. 352. 353; 66 n. 382. 385; 391 cat. 845.

OBJECT DESCRIPTION

The sarcophagus lid is rectangular in shape and depicts a seated female, two standing males, and a reclining male (81a). The figures are resting on a mattress decorated with an intersecting lozenge pattern with flowers inside them. The reclining figure rests on a cushion decorated with a wide band with a floral motif between beaded bands. The seated female sits in a chair covered by a cloth. The folds are rendered by vertical grooves. The sarcophagus box is rectangular in shape and is rendered as a kline. A fragment of a mattress is preserved in the upper right corner. It is decorated with an intersecting lozenges pattern with flowers in the lozenges. The right leg is preserved, and it is turned. It is composed of a plinth, and above is a long, reversed concave quarter, a bell-shaped element, a torus, a ball, a bell-shaped element, and a torus. The elements are decorated with a tongues pattern. Between the legs there are five standing males (81b). The figures are standing on a flat relief ground.

The sarcophagus was found next to object cat. 82.

SARCOPHAGUS LID

PORTRAIT A: SEATED FEMALE

The figure is shown in three-quarter view. She sits with her legs apart. Her thighs, knees, and shins are visible under the drapery. Her right arm is held along the side. Her feet are obscured by the reclining figure to her left.

A wide, s-shaped fold falls downwards from under her right hand. Another wide fold falls diagonally from her waist to her right foot. She wears an ankle-length himation. The folds of the himation are rendered by curving, wide grooves.

PORTRAIT B: STANDING MALE

The figure is shown frontally. The right arm is held along the body. The left arm is bent and held to the torso. His legs are obscured by the reclining figure to his left.

He wears a ›Parthian-style‹ tunic and a himation. The tunic has a wide, round neckline decorated with a beaded band. At the middle, the tunic has a wide band decorated with four-petal flowers separated by horizontal, beaded bands, extending downwards. The folds of the tunic are rendered by oblique grooves. Over the tunic, he wears a himation. It is folded around his left shoulder and arm, covering a small part of the chest. A wide edge of the himation is folded from his lower right side and up towards the waist. The folds of the himation are rendered by vertical and oblique, wide grooves. He wears a plain band belt, knotted at the centre with the ends looped under on either side of the waist.

His right hand rests at his right side. His left hand is holding a fold of the himation. The index finger is extended.

PORTRAIT C: STANDING MALE

The figure is shown frontally. The legs are obscured by the reclining figure to his left.

He wears a tunic and himation. The tunic has a narrow, v-shaped neckline. The folds of the tunic are rendered by curving grooves. Over the tunic, he wears a himation. It is folded around his right upper arm. The folds of the himation are rendered by wide grooves.

PORTRAIT D: RECLINING MALE

The figure is shown in frontal to three-quarter view. Both arms are bent to the sides, the right resting on his raised right knee, the left is resting against the cushion. His right leg is bent, and his foot is resting on the mattress. The left leg is bent under the right leg, and the left foot is obscured.

He is wearing a ›Parthian-style‹ tunic, a chlamys, and ›Parthian-style‹ trousers. The tunic has a small, round neckline and long, tight-fitting sleeves. The neckline is decorated with squares and rhombi between beaded bands. The cuffs of the sleeves are decorated with four-petal flowers in squares with a beaded band at the hem. At the middle, the tunic has a wide, decorated band with leaves extending downwards. The tunic ends above the knees and has a decorated border with flowers and vines between beaded bands. Over the tunic, he wears a chlamys that falls over both shoulders, and covers most of the chest. One edge of the chlamys has a border decorated with a beaded band. A wide fold falls from under his left arm and over the cushion, where it is further divided into two s-shaped folds. The chlamys is fastened at the right shoulder with a circular brooch with a beaded border (Colledge classification: f). A zigzag-shaped fold falls from under the brooch. The folds of the chlamys are indicated by narrow, deep grooves. He wears a plain band belt, knotted at the centre, with the ends looped under on either side of the waist. Each trouser leg is decorated in the middle with a wide band with leaves set between beaded bands. The folds of the trousers are rendered by curving, wide grooves. The trousers are tucked into his boots. The boots are decorated with flowers in squares separated by beaded bands. The upper edge of the boots is decorated with a band with waves and a clasp.

With his right hand, he holds a pinecone between his index and thumb. The outline of the scales is rendered by fine, incised lines. He holds the left handle of a skyphos in his left hand. The index and the little finger are extended.

SARCOPHAGUS BOX

PORTRAIT E: STANDING MALE

The figure is shown frontally. The right arm is bent and held over the chest. The left arm is obscured by a vessel. The legs are slightly set apart. The right leg is slightly turned to the right.

He wears a ›Parthian-style‹ tunic and ›Parthian-style‹ trousers. The tunic has a small, round neckline decorated with a beaded band and long, tight-fitting sleeves. The cuffs of the sleeves are decorated with a wide band. At the middle, the tunic has a wide band with vines extending downwards. The tunic ends above the knees and has a decorated lower border with a floral motif and a central six-petal rosette. The folds of the tunic are rendered by vertical and curving grooves. He also wears a plain band belt, knotted at the centre with the ends looped under on either side of the waist. Another band belt runs diagonally across the waist. Each trouser leg is decorated in the middle with a beaded band. The folds are indicated by vertical and oblique grooves. He is wearing plain ankle boots.

With the right hand, he holds the right handle of a decorated amphora. It has a wide mouth and tall handles. The neck is decorated with oblique grooves and the neck ring has a beaded band. The body of the vessel is decorated with hollowed-out lozenges. The foot is conical.

PORTRAIT F: STANDING MALE

The figure is shown frontally. The right arm is bent and held at the chest. The left arm is bent and held at his left side. His legs are slightly set apart. The weight is set on his left leg, resulting in a slight s-curve posture.

His neck is short.

He wears a ›Parthian-style‹ tunic and ›Parthian-style‹ trousers. The tunic has a small, round neckline decorated with a beaded band and long, tight-fitting sleeves. The cuffs of the sleeves are decorated with a wide band. At the middle, the tunic has a wide, decorated band with four-petal rosettes set between beaded bands, extending downwards. The tunic ends above the knees and has a decorated lower border with flowers in squares. The folds of the tunic are rendered by vertical and curving grooves. He also wears a plain band belt, knotted at the centre, with the ends looped under on either side of the waist. Another band belt runs diagonally across the waist. Each trouser leg is decorated in the middle with a band with leaves, extending downwards. The folds are indicated by

Cat. 81

vertical and oblique grooves. The trousers are tucked into his plain ankle boots.

With his palm turned outwards, he holds a large sword in his left hand. The pommel is round with a sharp point. The cross-guard is rendered by a curving line. At the blade, the fuller is rendered by a wide indentation. The scabbard is visible hanging from his belt at his lower right side.

PORTRAIT G: STANDING MALE

The figure is shown frontally. The right arm is held along the body. His legs are slightly set apart. The weight is set on his right leg, resulting in a slight s-curve posture.

He wears a >Parthian-style< tunic and >Parthian-style< trousers. The tunic has a small, round neckline decorated with a beaded band and long, tight-fitting sleeves. At the middle, the tunic has a wide decorated band with a pattern of six-petal rosettes placed between four-petal flowers set between two narrow bands, extending downwards. The tunic ends at the knees and has a decorated lower border with flowers pointing towards a central rosette. He also wears a plain band belt, knotted at the centre with the ends looped under on either side of the waist. Another band belt runs diagonally across the waist. It has an oblong element attached to it. Each trouser leg is decorated in the middle with a band with incised circles. The folds are indicated by vertical and oblique grooves. The trousers are tucked into his plain ankle boots.

He holds a pinecone in his right hand.

PORTRAIT H: STANDING MALE

The figure is shown frontally. The weight is set on his right leg, resulting in a contrapposto.

He wears a >Parthian-style< tunic and >Parthian-style< trousers. The tunic ends above the knees and has a decorated lower border with flowers. Each trouser leg is decorated in the middle with a band with leaves. The folds are indicated by oblique grooves. The trousers are tucked into his plain boots.

PORTRAIT I: STANDING MALE

The figure is shown frontally. His legs are slightly set apart. He wears trousers that are tucked into his plain boots.

82. COMPLETE SARCOPHAGUS WITH BANQUETING SCENE AND TRADE SCENE

DATABASE NUMBER: InSitu066.
LOCATION: Palmyra, in situ.
CONTEXT: South-west necropolis. Tomb no. A120, hypogeum of ʿAtenatan, exedra of Julius Aurelius Maqqaî.
ACQUISITION HISTORY: —
MEASUREMENTS: —
MATERIAL: Limestone, white.
PRESERVATION: The upper right corner of the box is broken off. A part of the stretcher of the kline is chipped. The head of the horse is chipped. Portrait A: The head is broken off at the base of the neck, and the right hand is broken off. Small areas of the left arm and of the clothing are chipped. Portrait B: The upper part of the figure is broken off at the waist. Portrait C: Only a small part of the torso has been preserved. Portrait D: The head is broken off at the base of the neck. Small areas of the hands and of the clothing are chipped. Portrait E: Only a small part of the lower body is preserved. Portrait F: The head is broken off from above the nose. Portrait G: The head is chipped.
TECHNICAL DESCRIPTION: Portrait A: There are traces of a red pigment on the cushions. Portrait D: There are traces of a red pigment on the coat and a blue pigment on the tunic, while the bands of the tunic have traces of a red pigment. Portrait F: There are traces of red pigment in the garment. Portrait G: There are traces of blue and red pigments on the clothing. Portrait H: The clothing has traces of red and blue pigments.
DATE: A.D. 229–250.
REFERENCES: Ingholt Archives, PS 984; Ingholt 1935, 63. 67 pls. 26. 27, 1; Seyrig 1937, 22 pl. 4; Starcky 1941, 28 fig. 21; Bossert 1951, 38 f. cat. 555 fig. 555; Seyrig 1951, 39 fig. 4; Colledge 1967, 91. 94. 221 pl. 4; Colledge 1976a, 60. 63. 77 f. 87. 120. 124–126. 129. 131 f. 134. 136. 145–148. 155; Parlasca 1984, 283; Schmidt-Colinet 1992, 106 n. 373. 377. 380d; 108 n. 391; 111 n. 408. 410; 112 n. 415; 125 n. 470. 476; 130 n. 479; 133 f. n. 509 pl. 69, b; Equini Schneider 1993, 116 fig. 24; Long 2017, 71 f. 78 fig. 3; Krag – Raja 2017, 199 n. 24; 204 n. 72. 73; 205 n. 75. 76; 217 cat. 22; Krag 2018, 28 n. 9; 32 n. 63; 59 n. 325; 62 n. 349. 352. 353; 63 n. 355; 66 n. 382. 385; 87 n. 182; 89 n. 210; 391 cat. 844. Inscription: Krag 2018, 391 cat. 844.

OBJECT DESCRIPTION

The sarcophagus lid is rectangular in shape and depicts a seated female, two standing figures, and a reclining male. Beneath these figures is a box in the shape of a kline with a standing male leading a horse and two standing males between the kline legs. The full-length horse is standing with the weight on the straight right foreleg, indicated by the tensed muscles at the torso. The mane is short, rendered by fine, incised lines. The neck and the chest are modelled with folds of the flesh leading to the forelegs. The two legs closest to the relief ground are carved in low relief, thereby differentiating them from the two legs closer to the viewer, where the skin is more carefully textured. The fetlock joint and the pastern are rendered over the hoofs. The tail is small, and the locks of hair are rendered by curving grooves. The horse is equipped with a harness, reins, and a plain saddle. The reins are placed around the neck and knotted at the mouthpiece. The figure to the left of the horse holds one of the reins, while the other is looped under the harness. The harness is composed of a broad chest collar and a breeching at the back. It also has a girth around the belly. A quiver is attached and hanging alongside the centre of the saddle. A row of arrows is rendered in the quiver. Between portraits E and F, a tall altar is shown. The outline of a tall, cylindrical object, possibly a headdress (Palmyrene priestly hat), is recognizable on top of the altar. Two volute-shaped folds of a garment are hanging from under the headdress. To the left of portrait F is a similar object with volute-shaped folds rendered. Above the kline is a mattress. The mattress is decorated with an intersecting lozenge pattern with flowers in the lozenges. The reclining figure rests the left arm against a cushion and a blanket. The cushion is decorated with a wide band with a sequence of rosettes and flowers, separated by horizontal, beaded bands. The blanket is also decorated, but the details are unclear. The central stretcher of the kline is decorated. The wide, rectangular central panel is divided into two horizontal sections by a thin line. The upper section is decorated with oblique grooves and the lower with a vegetal motif and a central rosette. On either end of the stretcher are two rectangular indentations decorated with a wave pattern. On each side of these are two square inlays or appliqués with animals. The legs of the kline are turned. They are composed of a plinth, and above is a convex quarter, a reversed bell-shaped element, a convex quarter, a small ball, a reversed bell-shaped element, a neck, a ball, a bell-shaped element, and a torus. All elements are decorated with a tongues pattern, rendered diagonally on the balls. The seated female sits on two cushions, each decorated with a wide band (details unclear).

The sarcophagus was found next to object cat. 81.

INSCRIPTION
SCRIPT: Palmyrene Aramaic.
LOCATION ON RELIEF: On the mattress to the right.
TRANSCRIPTION: ṢLM MQY BR ZBDBWL DY BN' | 'KSDR' DNH.
TRANSLATION: Image of Maqqaî son of Zabdibôl, who built this exedra.

CIS no. —; PAT no. 0025.

COMMENT: Inscription taken from Ingholt 1935. No photograph shows the inscription.

SARCOPHAGUS LID

PORTRAIT A: SEATED FEMALE
The figure is shown in three-quarter view. The left arm and legs appear short in relation to the body. The right arm is bent and rests on her right thigh. The left arm is raised to the neck. Her legs are bent, and the knees are rendered under the drapery. Her left foot is obscured by the reclining figure to her left.

She wears a veil that falls over her shoulders. She wears three necklaces. One composed of round beads with a central, oval pendant, worn at the base of the neck. One composed of a loop-in-loop chain with a central, oval pendant, worn high on the chest. One worn below the collarbone, composed of a loop-in-loop chain with a central, circular pendant. The pendant has a beaded border and three spirally wrapped wires ending with a round bead descending from the pendant. She also wears a bracelet on her right wrist. It is composed of twisted plain and beaded wires.

She wears a tunic and a himation. The tunic has a small, round neckline and short, loose sleeves. The folds of the tunic are indicated by curving grooves. The ankle-length himation crosses her chest diagonally from the left shoulder to the right side and covers the left breast and the lower body. It is fastened at the left shoulder with a circular brooch with an outer beaded border (Colledge classification: f). The folds between the legs are rendered by curving grooves. She also wears pointed shoes.

The right hand is placed on her right thigh and she is holding a fold of the veil. The outline of the left hand is recognizable, and she appears to hold a fold of the veil.

PORTRAIT B: STANDING FIGURE
The figure is shown frontally. The right arm is held along the body. The legs are obscured by the reclining figure to the left.

The figure wears a long garment, possibly a himation. The folds are indicated by oblique grooves. When photographed by Colledge, the upper torso was reattached, and the figure was wearing a tunic with short sleeves.

PORTRAIT C: STANDING FIGURE
The figure is shown frontally. The lower body and legs are obscured by the reclining figure.

The figure wears a garment, rendered by oblique and curving grooves. When photographed by Colledge, the upper torso was reattached, and the figure was wearing a tunic. Another garment, possibly a himation, running in a curving line across the chest, was visible. The left arm of the figure was raised to the neck and the hand holding the fold of the garment.

PORTRAIT D: RECLINING MALE, MAQQAÎ
The figure is shown in frontal to three-quarter view. The arms appear short in relation to the body. The right arm is extended and rests on his raised right knee. The left arm is bent and held to the torso. His right leg is bent, and his foot is resting on the mattress. The left leg is bent under the right leg with the knee pointing outwards. The left foot is obscured by the right leg.

The neck is wide.

He wears a >Parthian-style< tunic, a >Parthian-style< coat, and >Parthian-style< trousers. The tunic has a wide, round neckline decorated with a beaded band and long, tight-fitting sleeves. The cuffs of the sleeves are decorated with a running scroll with rosettes. At the middle, the tunic has a wide band with a running scroll with rosettes set between beaded bands, extending downwards. The tunic ends above the knees and has a lower border decorated with serrated leaves in an opposite arrangement on the stem. The folds of the tunic are rendered by curving, wide grooves. Over the tunic, he wears an open coat without sleeves. It has a wavy edge running along the torso, proceeding to his thighs. The edges along the torso are decorated with bands with vines and grapes followed by a beaded band. At his lower left side, the coat is folded open, revealing the interior. The inner edge is decorated with a beaded band at the hem. The folds of the coat are rendered by curving and oblique grooves. He also wears a plain band belt, knotted at the centre. Along the right thigh, there is an object with a round end, a rectangular main body, and a lateral rectangle:

a sheathed dagger. He wears trousers that are tucked into his boots. Each trouser leg is decorated in the middle with a wide band extending downwards (details unclear). He also wears boots. The upper edge of the shaft is decorated with a beaded band followed by two bands (details unclear). The lower part of the boot is decorated with rosettes within circles.

The outline of a bowl is recognizable at the centre of the chest.

SARCOPHAGUS BOX

PORTRAIT E: STANDING MALE

The figure is shown frontally. The arms appear short in relation to the body. Both arms are bent to the torso. His legs are slightly set apart. The weight is set on his left leg, resulting in a slight s-curve posture.

The hair is curly. Individual strands of hair are indicated by incised lines. His face is oval. The ears are protruding. The mouth is small with thin lips. The neck is short.

He wears a ›Parthian-style‹ tunic and ›Parthian-style‹ trousers. The tunic has a small, round neckline decorated with a beaded band and long, tight-fitting sleeves. At the middle, the tunic has a wide band decorated with a floral motif between beaded bands, extending downwards (details unclear). The tunic ends at the knees and has a decorated lower border with a floral motif. The folds of the tunic are rendered by oblique and curving grooves. He wears a broad band belt, around the waist, knotted at the centre. Another band belt runs diagonally across the waist with the ends knotted at the left lower side. The trousers are visible from the knees. Each trouser leg is decorated in the middle with a band with a floral motif. The trousers are tucked into his plain and pointed boots. The folds are indicated by vertical grooves.

He holds the end of the reins in his right hand. The index finger is extended. With his palm turned outwards, he holds a sword by the hilt with his left hand. The pommel is round with a sharp point. The cross-guard is rendered by a curving line.

PORTRAIT F: STANDING MALE

The figure is shown frontally. The right arm is held along the body and the left is bent and held to the torso. He stands with the legs set slightly set apart.

He wears a ›Parthian-style‹ tunic, a ›Parthian-style‹ coat, and ›Parthian-style‹ trousers. The tunic has a small, round neckline decorated with a beaded band. At the middle, the tunic has a wide band decorated with a floral motif extending downwards. The tunic ends at the knees and has a lower border decorated with a floral motif (details unclear). The folds of the tunic are rendered by curving, wide grooves. Over the tunic, he wears an open coat with long, tight-fitting sleeves. The coat proceeds to his thighs. The edges along each side of the torso are decorated with bands with vegetal motifs. The folds of the coat are rendered by oblique and curving grooves. He also wears a band belt that runs diagonally across the waist with the ends knotted at the left lower side. Each trouser leg is decorated in the middle with a band with a floral motif. The trousers are tucked into his plain boots. The folds are indicated by vertical grooves.

He holds a pinecone in his right hand. The ovules of the pinecone are rendered by incised lines. He holds a sword by its hilt with his left hand. The pommel is round with a sharp point. The cross-guard is rendered by a curving line.

PORTRAIT G: STANDING FIGURE
The figure is shown frontally. The head is turned to his left. Both arms are bent to the torso. His legs are slightly set apart. The weight is set on his right leg, resulting in a slight s-curve posture.

The hair is curly. Individual locks of hair are rendered by incised lines. His face is long. The eyebrows are curving, indicated by incised lines starting from the top of the nose. The eyes are almond-shaped. The nose is long. He has a moustache that covers the upper lip. The facial hair is rendered by small, snail-shell curls. The neck is long.

He wears a ›Parthian-style‹ tunic and ›Parthian-style‹ trousers. The tunic has a small, round neckline, decorated with a beaded band, and long, tight-fitting sleeves. At the middle, the tunic has a wide band decorated with a vegetal motif. The tunic ends at the knees and has a decorated border with a running scroll with rosettes. The folds of the tunic are rendered by oblique and curving grooves. He wears a broad band belt around the waist. Another band belt runs diagonally across the waist. Each trouser leg is decorated in the middle with a band with a floral motif. The trousers are tucked into his plain boots. The folds are indicated by vertical grooves.

With his palm turned outwards, he holds a bow in his right hand. He holds the strap from a quiver in his left hand. The upper part of the quiver is visible over his left shoulder. It is decorated with a vertical, beaded line at the edge, and the individual arrows are indicated by deep grooves. A sword is hanging from the belt on his left side. The pommel is round, and the cross-guard is rendered by a straight line.

SARCOPHAGUS LIDS

A.D. 229–250

83. FRAGMENT OF SARCOPHAGUS LID WITH BANQUETING SCENE

Cat. 83

DATABASE NUMBER: InSitu184.
LOCATION: Palmyra, in situ.
CONTEXT: South-west necropolis. Tomb no. A120, hypogeum of ʿAtenatan, exedra of Julius Aurelius Maqqaî.
ACQUISITION HISTORY: —
MEASUREMENTS: —
MATERIAL: Limestone.
PRESERVATION: The relief is composed of numerous fragments. Portrait A: Only the torso and the right arm of the figure survive. Portrait B: Only the lower part of the torso and

the left hand of the figure survive. The skyphos is partly broken off.
TECHNICAL DESCRIPTION: —
DATE: A.D. 229–250.
REFERENCES: Ingholt Archives, PS 986.

OBJECT DESCRIPTION

The object is composed of two main fragments, one depicting a standing and one a reclining male. The figure is resting on a mattress decorated with an intersecting lozenge pattern with flowers inside them. The reclining figure rests on a cushion decorated with a wide band with a vegetal motif between beaded bands.

PORTRAIT A: STANDING MALE

The figure is depicted standing. The right arm is bent and held in front of the chest.

He wears a tunic and himation. The tunic has a wide, round neckline. The folds of the tunic are rendered by curving grooves. Over the tunic, he wears a himation. One end of the himation crosses the chest diagonally and falls over the left shoulder (>arm-sling< type). The part of the himation that crosses the chest is decorated with a pleated band. The folds of the himation are rendered by wide grooves.

With his right hand, he holds the diagonal fold of the himation. The index finger is extended.

PORTRAIT B: RECLINING MALE

The figure is shown in frontal view. The left arm is resting against the cushion.

He is wearing a >Parthian-style< tunic and a chlamys. The tunic has long, tight-fitting sleeves (details unclear). At the middle, the tunic has a wide, decorated band with leaves extending downwards. The folds of the tunic are indicated by lightly curving grooves. Over the tunic, he wears a chlamys. A wide fold falls from under his left arm and over the cushion, where it is further divided into two s-shaped folds. The folds of the chlamys are indicated by narrow, deep grooves. He wears a plain band belt, knotted at the centre with the ends looped under on either side of the waist.

He holds the left handle of a skyphos in his left hand. The rim is decorated with a beaded band and the body with a tongues pattern set beneath a plain, horizontal band. The foot is stemmed and is decorated with a tongues pattern. The index and the little finger are extended. On the little finger, he wears a ring. It has an oval bezel with an inscribed border.

84. FRAGMENT OF MALE FIGURE

Cat. 84

DATABASE NUMBER: InSitu196.
LOCATION: Palmyra, in situ.
CONTEXT: South-west necropolis. Tomb no. A120, hypogeum of ʿAtenatan, exedra of Julius Aurelius Maqqaî.
ACQUISITION HISTORY: —
MEASUREMENTS: —
MATERIAL: Limestone.
PRESERVATION: The upper part is broken diagonally from the left shoulder to the right side. The lower part is broken off horizontally at the knees.
TECHNICAL DESCRIPTION: —
DATE: A.D. 229–250.
REFERENCES: Ingholt Archives, PS 987.

OBJECT DESCRIPTION

The object depicts a standing male.

PORTRAIT

The left arm is bent and held to the torso.

He wears a >Parthian-style< tunic with long, tight-fitting sleeves. The cuffs of the sleeves are decorated with four-petal flowers, separated by vertical, beaded bands. The midribs of the leaves are rendered by fine, incised lines. On the left side of the body, the tunic has a band decorated with a running scroll with rosettes extending downwards. The tunic ends at the knees and has a lower border decorated with a sequence of four-petal flowers followed by a six-petal rosette. The midribs of the leaves are rendered by incised lines. The folds of the tunic are rendered by vertical and curving grooves. He wears a plain band belt running from above the waist at his right side and below the waist at his left side. On the left side, the belt has a round button with a drop-shaped lace hanging from it. An object with a round lateral element is depicted along his right side, possibly a dagger.

He holds a wreath with a cloth beneath in his left hand. The wreath is composed of one row of lanceolate leaves pointing towards a central oval. The cloth is coiled in two snail-shell folds.

85. FRAGMENT OF BANQUETING RELIEF

Cat. 85

DATABASE NUMBER: PM584.
LOCATION: Palmyra, Palmyra Museum, inv. no. unknown.
CONTEXT: South-west necropolis. Tomb no. A120, hypogeum of ʿAtenatan, exedra of Julius Aurelius Maqqaî.
ACQUISITION HISTORY: —
MEASUREMENTS: —
MATERIAL: Limestone.
PRESERVATION: Broken on all sides. Portrait A: The upper part is broken off diagonally from the left shoulder to the right side and the lower part is broken off at the thighs. Portrait B: Only a knee and lower arm is preserved.

TECHNICAL DESCRIPTION: —
DATE: A.D. 229–250.
REFERENCES: Ingholt Archives, PS 988; Raja et al. 2021a, Diary 5, 79 no. d.

OBJECT DESCRIPTION
The object depicts a standing figure and a reclining male.

PORTRAIT A: STANDING FIGURE
The figure is shown frontally. The right arm is held in front of the waist; the left arm is bent and held to the torso.

He wears a ›Parthian-style‹ tunic and a chlamys. The tunic has long sleeves, and the cuffs of the sleeves are decorated with a band with a vegetal motif. At the middle, the tunic has a wide band extending downwards and decorated with four-petal flowers in squares separated by vertical, beaded bands. The folds of the tunic are rendered by diagonal grooves. He wears a plain band belt, knotted at the centre with the ends looped under on either side of the waist. Over the tunic, he wears a chlamys. It is folded around his left arm and wrist. The folds of the chlamys are rendered by curving, wide grooves.

He lightly holds a wide fold of the chlamys with his right hand. He also pulls a fold of the chlamys from the opposite side with his left hand, thus resulting in a wide curve across the waist.

PORTRAIT B: RECLINING MALE
He rests his right hand on his right knee.

He wears a ›Parthian-style‹ tunic and ›Parthian-style‹ trousers. The tunic has long sleeves, and the cuffs of the sleeves are decorated with flowers in squares between beaded bands. The trouser leg is decorated in the middle with a wide band extending downwards with a vegetal motif between beaded bands.

SARCOPHAGUS BOXES

A.D. 229–250

86. FRAGMENT OF SARCOPHAGUS BOX WITH RELIGIOUS SCENE

DATABASE NUMBER: MBA007.
LOCATION: Baalbek, Baalbek Museum, inv. no. unknown.
CONTEXT: South-west necropolis. Tomb no. A120, hypogeum of ʿAtenatan, exedra of Julius Aurelius Maqqaî.
ACQUISITION HISTORY: Bought by Michel Alouf from an antique dealer in Aleppo, and then donated to Baalbek Museum.
MEASUREMENTS: —
MATERIAL: Limestone.
PRESERVATION: Broken on all sides. Portrait A: His right hand has been reattached. The lower part of the face and of the left hand is chipped. A crack runs diagonally through his

OBJECTS FROM HYPOGEA 287

Cat. 86

neck. Portrait B: The left foot has broken off. The surface of the left hand is chipped. A crack runs from the upper right thigh to the left knee.

TECHNICAL DESCRIPTION: —
DATE: A.D. 229–250.
REFERENCES: Ingholt Archives, PS 564; Ingholt 1935, 72; Seyrig 1937, 16. 28 f. 40–43 pl. 5; Starcky 1941, 31 fig. 22; Seyrig 1950, 2 f. pl. 1, 1.

OBJECT DESCRIPTION

The object is rectangular in shape and depicts two standing males. At the bottom of the object is a protruding plinth.

PORTRAIT A: STANDING MALE

The figure is shown frontally. The right arm is bent and held out from the body and raised to the height of the head. The left arm is held along the body. He stands with the legs slightly apart. The left leg is slightly bent with the knee rendered under the drapery.

His hair is arranged in curving locks brushed to each side of the centre. The hair covers the ears and reaches the upper part of the neck and is arranged in snail-shell curls. His face is oval. The eyebrows are curving, rendered as thin ridges. The eyes are almond-shaped, and the eyeballs are blank. The neck is wide with a curving groove.

He wears a ›Parthian-style‹ tunic and ›Parthian-style‹ trousers. The tunic has a small, round neckline decorated with a beaded band and long, tight-fitting sleeves. The cuffs of the sleeves are decorated with lanceolate leaves in an opposite arrangement on the stem. At the middle, the tunic has a wide band extending downwards and decorated with a sequence of four-petal flowers followed by six-petal rosettes. The tunic ends at the knees and has a decorated border with lanceolate leaves pointing towards a central rosette at the hem. The folds of the tunic are rendered by vertical and curving grooves. He wears a plain band belt, knotted at the centre with the ends looped under on either side of the waist. He also wears another band belt that runs in a diagonal line from above the right side of the waist to below the waist at his left side. A large sword with a pointed pommel, oblong handle, narrow cross-guard, and long blade is attached to the belt. At the middle, each trouser leg has a band extending downwards and decorated with squares separated by horizontal, beaded lines. The folds of the trousers are rendered by shallow, diagonal grooves. The trousers are tucked into his high boots.

He holds a wreath in each hand. The wreaths are composed of lanceolate leaves.

PORTRAIT B: STANDING MALE

The figure is shown frontally. The head is turned slightly to his left. The right arm is slightly bent and held along the body. The left arm is slightly bent and held to the torso. He stands with legs set apart. The left leg is slightly bent, with the knee visible under the drapery.

His hair is arranged in two rows of snail-shell curls around the head. His face is oval. The eyebrows are curving, rendered as thin ridges. The eyes are close-set and almond-shaped. The eyeballs are blank. The nose is straight and narrow. The mouth is wide with thin lips. The chin is prominent with a cleft. The neck is slender.

He wears a ›Parthian-style‹ tunic and ›Parthian-style‹ trousers. The tunic has a small, round neckline decorated with a beaded band and long, tight-fitting sleeves. The cuffs of the sleeves are decorated with a floral motif (details unclear). At the middle, the tunic has a band extending downwards and decorated with serrated leaves in an opposite arrangement on the stem. The tunic ends at the knees and has a border decorated with four-petal flowers separated by vertical, beaded bands and a rosette in the centre. The midribs of the leaves are rendered by incised lines. The folds of the tunic are rendered by vertical and curving grooves. He wears a plain band belt, knotted at the centre with the ends looped under on either side of the waist. At the middle, each trouser leg has a band extending downwards decorated with floral motifs (details unclear). The folds of the trousers are decorated with shallow, vertical grooves. The trousers are tucked into his high boots.

He holds a wide bowl or patera in his right hand, with the interior facing outwards. The thumb is extended. With the left hand, he holds a rhyton. The upper and lower body of the vessel are decorated with a tongues pattern, separated by a beaded band.

FRAGMENTS

A.D. 229–250

87. FRAGMENT OF BANQUETING RELIEF

DATABASE NUMBER: PM913.
LOCATION: Palmyra, Palmyra Museum, inv. no. A 142.
CONTEXT: South-west necropolis. Tomb no. A120, hypogeum of ʿAtenatan, exedra of Julius Aurelius Maqqaî.
ACQUISITION HISTORY: —
MEASUREMENTS: —
MATERIAL: Limestone.
PRESERVATION: Only part of the background to the right of the figure, and the upper part of the figure are preserved. The face of the figure is broken off.
TECHNICAL DESCRIPTION: —
DATE: A.D. 229–250.
REFERENCES: Ingholt Archives, PS 989; Raja et al. 2021a, Diary 5, 79 no. e, 2.

OBJECT DESCRIPTION

The object is rectangular and preserves part of a standing figure.

PORTRAIT

The figure is depicted standing. The arms are crossed over the chest.

He wears a ›Parthian-style‹ tunic. The tunic has a wide, round neckline and long, tight sleeves. The neckline is decorated with a beaded band. At the middle, the tunic has a wide, decorated band extending downwards. At the top, there is a four-petal flower within a square border. The cuffs of the tunic are decorated with bands with vegetal motifs. Two bands seem to descend from the right end of the neckline downwards. The folds of the tunic are rendered by curving grooves over the arms, and oblique grooves over the chest.

Cat. 87

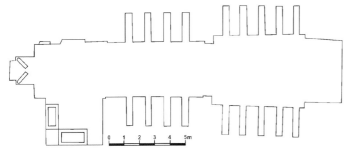

Plan of hypogeum of ʿAtenatan.

88. FRAGMENT OF MALE FIGURE

Cat. 88

DATABASE NUMBER: PM836.
LOCATION: Palmyra, Palmyra Museum, inv. no. A 145.
CONTEXT: South-west necropolis. Tomb no. A120, hypogeum of ʿAtenatan, exedra of Julius Aurelius Maqqaî.
ACQUISITION HISTORY: —
MEASUREMENTS: —
MATERIAL: Limestone.
PRESERVATION: Only the left hand of the figure with a wreath is preserved. The wreath is heavily chipped.
TECHNICAL DESCRIPTION: —
DATE: A.D. 229–250.
REFERENCES: Ingholt Archives, PS 989; Raja et al. 2021a, Diary 5, 79 no. e, 1.

OBJECT DESCRIPTION

The object is rectangular and preserves part of a standing male, holding a wreath.

PORTRAIT

The figure is depicted standing. The left arm is extended and held to the side.

He wears a ›Parthian-style‹ tunic. The tunic has long sleeves, and the cuffs are decorated with a band with vegetal motifs.

With the left hand, he holds a wreath of leaves (details unclear). The fingers of the hand are bent.

A.D. 109–273

HYPOGEUM OF JULIUS AURELIUS MALÊ

BANQUETING RELIEFS

A.D. 220–240

89. FRAGMENT OF BANQUETING RELIEF

DATABASE NUMBER: PM590.
LOCATION: Palmyra, Palmyra Museum, inv. no. A86 (?).
CONTEXT: South-west necropolis. Hypogeum of Julius Aurelius Malê.
ACQUISITION HISTORY: —
MEASUREMENTS: —
MATERIAL: Limestone.
PRESERVATION: The right and the upper side of the object are broken off. Only part of the torso, left arm, and left upper leg is preserved. The surface of the waist is chipped.
TECHNICAL DESCRIPTION: —
DATE: A.D. 220–240.
REFERENCES: Ingholt Archives, PS 983.

OBJECT DESCRIPTION

The object is rectangular in shape and depicts a reclining male. It has an outer, plain frame and an inner frame composed of a leaf-and-dart pattern. Beneath the figure is a mattress: it is decorated with a vertical band with leaves on a stem. Curving grooves indicate the texture of the fabric. The figure rests on a round cushion. The cushion is decorated with a band: it is composed of squares separated with narrow bands, with alternating centred rosettes and flowers. The petals of the rosettes are hollowed. Curving grooves indicate the texture of the fabric.

PORTRAIT

The figure is shown in three-quarter view. The left arm is bent in front of the torso, and rests on a cushion.

He wears a ›Parthian-style‹ tunic and a himation. The tunic has a round neckline decorated with a beaded band. The tunic has long, tight-fitting sleeves, and the cuffs are decorated with a wide band with floral motif, and at the hem a beaded band. The tunic has a wide band with a running scroll and rosettes, set between two beaded bands, extending downwards from the middle of the neckline. The folds of the tunic are rendered by curving grooves. He also wears a plain band belt, knotted at the centre with the ends looped under on either side of the waist. Over the tunic, he wears a himation: it falls over his left upper arm, is wrapped around the left arm, and continues along the left side of the body. The himation appears to have been folded across the waist. A large, folded edge of the himation falls under the left arm onto the mattress. The folds of the himation are indicated with curving grooves.

In his left hand, he holds a skyphos. The foot of the skyphos is conical. The body is decorated with a horizontal, incised

Cat. 89

line, and a wide band with crescent-shaped elements oriented towards a central, round object. The rim is indicated with a horizontal, incised line. The right handle is indicated. The left index and the little fingers are extended.

A.D. 108–273

HYPOGEUM OF YARḤAÎ

SARCOPHAGI

A.D. 240–273

90. COMPLETE SARCOPHAGUS RELIEF WITH BANQUETING SCENE AND PORTRAIT BUSTS

DATABASE NUMBER: NMD063.
LOCATION: Damascus, National Museum of Damascus, inv. no. unknown.
CONTEXT: West necropolis. Valley of the Tombs. Hypogeum of Yarḥaî, west exedra. Excavated Nov. 1934 – Feb. 1935.
ACQUISITION HISTORY: Moved and reconstructed at the National Museum of Damascus in 1936.

MEASUREMENTS: —
MATERIAL: Limestone.
PRESERVATION: Portrait A: The surface of the headdress is slightly chipped. The right ring and little fingers are broken off. Portrait B: The upper edge of the headdress has broken off. Portrait C: The head is broken off horizontally at the base of the neck. Portrait D: There are a few cracks on the surface. Portrait E: The nose and a part of the mouth are chipped. Portrait I: The area around the left eye is chipped.
TECHNICAL DESCRIPTION: —
DATE: A.D. 240–273 (Tanabe 1986: A.D. 237–255).
REFERENCES: Ingholt Archives, PS 890+PS 892; Amy – Seyrig 1936, 247 f. pl. 46, 1. 2; Seyrig 1937, 5 n. 9; Seyrig 1940, 307 fig. 17; Gawlikowski 1970a, 112 fig. 63; Colledge 1976a, 60. 133. 155 pl. 60; Browning 1979, 30. 37 f. fig. 4; Makowski 1985a, 95–100 fig. 11, a. c; Tanabe 1986, 31 pls. 237–240; Schmidt-Colinet 1996, 369 481. fig. 208; Parlasca 1998, 311 f.; Yon 2002, 133 fig. 37; Zanker 2010, 183 fig. 107; Krag – Raja 2017, 199 n. 24; 204 n. 72. 73; 205 n. 75; 206 n. 87; 207 n. 94; 208 n. 99; 209 n. 100. 102; 211 n. 117; 217 cat. 23 fig. 9; Raja 2017i, 121 f. figs. 12. 17; Raja 2017a, 213 f. fig. 19, 12. 17; Raja 2017f, 83 f. fig. 10; Raja 2017g, 83 f. fig. 10; Raja 2017j, 421 fig. 6; Raja 2018c, 91 fig. 4; Krag 2018, 28 n. 9; 32 n. 63; 41 n. 143; 53 n. 258; 56 n. 288. 290; 58 n. 300; 59 n. 323. 325; 62 n. 349. 352. 353; 66 n. 382. 385; 88 n. 193. 195; 103 n. 74; 104 n. 83; 391 f. cat. 846; Silver et al. 2018, 188 figs. 9.44. 9.45.

OBJECT DESCRIPTION

The sarcophagus is rectangular in shape and depicts a seated female, a standing priest, a standing male, and two reclining priests. Beneath these figures is a box in the shape of a kline with a female bust, two busts of priests, and a female bust between the kline legs. Above the kline are two mattresses. The thin mattress at the top is decorated with an intersecting lozenge pattern with flowers in the lozenges. The lower mattress has three bands decorated with vegetal motifs (details unclear). Curving grooves indicate the texture of the lower mattress. The reclining figure to the right rests his arm against a cushion. It is decorated with a wide band with serrated leaves in an opposite arrangement on the stem, set between beaded bands. The reclining figure to the left rests the arm against a cushion. It is decorated with a running scroll with rosettes set between beaded bands. On the left side of the kline, a fulcrum is shown. It is decorated with a small, armless bust (portrait J). From it, an animal head, possibly of a lion, protrudes (details unclear). The central stretcher of the kline is decorated. The wide, rectangular central panel is divided by a horizontal line. On either end are two rectangular indentations. On each side of these are two square inlays or appliqués with animals. The kline legs are turned. They are composed of a plinth, and above is a convex quarter, a long, reversed concave quarter, a scotia, a ball, a torus, and above the stretcher is a biconical finial. The seated female sits on two cushions.

The object was found next to objects cat. 91 and cat. 92.

SARCOPHAGUS LID

PORTRAIT A: SEATED FEMALE

The figure is shown frontally. The body appears stocky. The right arm is bent and rests on her right thigh. The left arm is raised to the neck. Her legs are bent with the knees rendered

Cat. 90

under the drapery. Her feet are obscured by the right foot of the reclining figure to her left.

She wears three headdresses: a headband, a turban, and a veil. The band is placed high on the forehead and is divided into rectangular, undecorated panels separated by vertical grooves. The turban is coiled. It is rendered in three twisting layers by horizontal grooves, indicating the coiling of the fabric. She wears a heavy veil that falls over her right shoulder, proceeds in a curving fold across the chest, and falls back over her left shoulder. Part of the hair is covered by the headdresses. Several strands of hair on the sides of the face and above the ears are pushed back over the edge of the turban and disappear under the veil. A curving lock falls on her right shoulder. The individual strands of hair are rendered by incised lines. Her face is oval. Her eyebrows are curving, rendered as thin ridges. The eyes are almond-shaped, with thick upper eyelids that extend beyond the end of the lower ones. The irises are indicated by incised circles and the pupils by punch holes. Only the earlobes are visible under the hair and she is wearing earrings (details unclear). Her nose is straight with the alae carved. The mouth is small with full lips. The cheeks are fleshy, and the chin is prominent, round, and almost double. The neck is wide.

She wears a tunic and a himation. The tunic has a wide, round neckline and short, wide sleeves. The folds of the tunic are rendered by curving grooves. The ankle-length himation crosses her chest diagonally from the left shoulder to the right side and covers the left breast and most of the chest and body. It is fastened at the left shoulder with a brooch shaped as a five-petal rosette (Colledge classification: i). The folds of the himation are rendered by curving and oblique grooves.

She rests her right hand on her thigh and holds a fold of the veil that extends downwards. It has a small, oval weight attached at the edge. The index and the middle finger are extended, and the nails are rendered by incised lines. Her left hand is raised next to the shoulder and she holds a fold of the veil with her hand.

PORTRAIT B: STANDING PRIEST

The figure is shown frontally. The head is turned slightly to his left. The arms appear short in relation to the body. The right arm is held along the body. The left arm is bent and held to the torso. The lower body and legs are obscured by the reclining figure to his left.

He wears a plain, high, cylindrical, flat-top headdress divided into three sections by two vertical grooves that covers his hair and most of his forehead: a Palmyrene priestly hat. His face is oval. The eyebrows are rendered by incised lines, starting from the top of the nose. The eyes are almond-shaped, with thick eyelids. The upper eyelids extend beyond the end of the lower ones. The irises are rendered by incised circles. The ears are large and protruding, with the helix depicted. The nose is straight and wide at the tip. The mouth is small, with full lips. The cheeks are fleshy, and the chin is wide and double. The neck is wide, with one horizontal groove.

He wears a tunic and a himation. The tunic has a small, round neckline and long, tight-fitting sleeves. The folds of the tunic are rendered by oblique and curving grooves. Over the tunic, he wears a himation. It covers most of the body and is wrapped around the left shoulder and arm. One end of the himation crosses the torso in a thick fold from the right and is folded under the left arm. The folds are indicated by oblique and curving grooves.

His right hand is extended along the thigh. With his left hand, he holds a fold of the himation and the end that is wrapped around his body.

PORTRAIT C: STANDING MALE

The figure is shown frontally. The right arm is bent and held to the chest. The left arm is held along the body. The lower body and legs are obscured by the reclining figure.

He wears a tunic and a himation. The tunic has a wide, round neckline. The folds of the tunic are rendered by curving and oblique grooves. Over the tunic, he wears a himation. It is wrapped around the right shoulder and arm, leaving only part of the chest and the hand free. One end of the himation crosses the chest diagonally and falls over the left shoulder (›arm-sling‹ type). The folds of the himation are rendered by vertical, oblique, and curving grooves.

With his right hand, he lightly holds a fold of the himation.

PORTRAIT D: RECLINING PRIEST

The figure is shown in frontal to three-quarter view. The right arm is slightly bent and rests on his raised right knee. The left arm is bent and held to the torso. His right leg is bent, and his foot is resting on the mattress. The left leg is bent under the right with the knee pointing forwards. The lower left leg is obscured by the right leg.

He wears a high, cylindrical, flat-top headdress divided into three sections by two vertical grooves: a Palmyrene priestly hat. A wreath with the leaves pointing towards a bust of a male figure with short hair is depicted at the lower part of the headdress. The midribs of the leaves are incised. His face is oval. The eyebrows are curving, rendered as thin ridges. The eyes are almond-shaped with sharply rendered eyelids. The upper eyelids extend beyond the end of the lower ones. The irises are indicated by incised circles and the pupils by punch holes. The ears are large and protruding with the helix, scapha, and lobe depicted. The nose is straight with carved alae. The mouth is small with a full lower lip. The cheeks are fleshy and the chin is round and almost double. The neck is wide.

He wears a ›Parthian-style‹ tunic, a chlamys, and ›Parthian-style‹ trousers. The tunic has a wide, round neckline decorated with a beaded band and long, tight-fitting sleeves. The cuffs of the sleeves are decorated with serrated leaves in an opposite arrangement on the stem. At the middle, the tunic has a wide band decorated with serrated leaves in an opposite arrangement on the stem, extending downwards. The tunic ends above the knees and has a decorated border with a floral motif (details unclear). The folds of the tunic are rendered by curving, wide grooves. He wears a plain band belt across the lower torso. It is knotted at the centre with the ends looped under on either side of the waist. Along the right thigh he has an object with a pointed end, a rectangular main body and a lateral rectangular: a sheathed dagger. Over the tunic, he wears a chlamys that falls over both shoulders and is wrapped around the left arm. It is fastened at the right shoulder with a circular brooch with an outer beaded border (Colledge classification: f). A zigzag-shaped fold falls from under the brooch. Two wide, zigzag-shaped folds, separated by a deep groove fall down from under the left arm, across the cushion and over the mattress. Each end of the folds is tied in a small knot. The folds of the chlamys are indicated by narrow, deep grooves. The trousers are visible from above the knee. Each trouser leg is decorated in the middle with a wide band with vegetal motif set between beaded bands, extending downwards. The folds of the trousers are indicated by wide, curving grooves. The trousers are tucked into his pointed boots. The boots have an upper edge decorated with a pattern of incised triangles. The plain shoelaces are knotted at the centre with a button from where two laces extend downwards. The boot is further decorated with a beaded band that starts with a circle at the ankle and extends to the toes.

The right hand is resting on his knee. The nails are rendered by incised lines. He holds a skyphos in his left hand. It has a conical foot, and the lower body is decorated with a tongues pattern. The body of the skyphos is decorated with vine leaves and miniature bunches of grapes that meander across the surface, set between horizontal lines. The index and the little fingers are extended. He also wears a ring on his left little finger with a wide, thick hoop and an oval bezel. The nails are indicated by incised lines.

PORTRAIT E: RECLINING PRIEST

The figure is shown in frontal to three-quarter view. The head appears small in relation to the body. The right arm is extended behind the reclining figure to his right. The left arm is bent and held to the torso. The legs are extended behind the reclining figure to his right.

He wears a high, cylindrical, flat-top headdress divided into three sections by two vertical grooves: a Palmyrene priestly hat. A wreath with the leaves pointing towards a bust of a male figure with short hair is depicted at the lower part of the headdress. The midribs of the leaves are incised. His face is oval. The eyebrows are curving, depicted as incised lines, starting from the top of the nose. The eyes are almond-shaped, with sharply rendered eyelids. The upper eyelids extend beyond the end of the lower ones. The irises are indicated by incised circles and the pupils by punch holes. The ears are large and protruding with the helix, scapha, and the lobe depicted. The mouth is small. The chin is round and almost double. The neck is wide.

He wears a tunic and a himation. The tunic has a wide, v-shaped neckline. The folds of the tunic are rendered by vertical and curving grooves. Over the tunic, he wears a himation. It is folded around his left shoulder and arm and proceeds along the left side of his torso. A zigzag-shaped fold falls from under his left arm across the cushion and over the mattress. The edge of the fold ends in a small knot. The folds of the himation are rendered by diagonal, curving grooves.

With the upturned palm of the left hand, he holds a wide, plain bowl with his fingertips. The nails are indicated by fine, incised lines.

Cat. 90

SARCOPHAGUS BOX

PORTRAIT F: ARMLESS FEMALE BUST
The figure is shown frontally. The head appears large.

She wears three headdresses: a headband, a turban, and a veil. The band is placed high on the forehead (details unclear). The turban is coiled. It is divided into three layers and the upper two layers are looped into each other creating a knot in the middle. Curving grooves indicate the coiling of the fabric. The veil is heavy. It falls over her right shoulder and proceeds in a curving fold across the chest and falls back at her left shoulder. Part of the hair is covered by the headdresses. Several strands of hair above the ears are brushed back over the edge of the turban and disappear under the veil. The individual locks of hair are rendered by incised lines. The folds of the veil are indicated by oblique grooves. Her face is oval. The eyebrows are curving. The eyes are close-set and almond-shaped, with thick upper eyelids. The eyeballs appear blank. Only the earlobes are visible, and she is wearing earrings (details unclear). The nose is large and the mouth small, with a full lower lip. The chin is wide, and the neck is short.

She wears a tunic with a small, round neckline. The folds are indicated by curving, wide grooves.

PORTRAIT G: ARMLESS BUST OF A PRIEST
The figure is shown frontally. The head appears large.

He wears a plain, high, cylindrical, flat-top headdress divided into two sections by a vertical groove that covers his hair and most of his forehead: a Palmyrene priestly hat. His face is diamond-shaped. The eyebrows are slightly curving, rendered by incised lines. The eyes are close-set and almond-shaped, with heavy upper eyelids. The eyeballs appear blank. The ears are large and protruding with the helix and concha depicted. The nose is straight and wide at the tip. The mouth is small with thin lips. The chin is pointed, and the neck is short.

He wears a tunic and a chlamys. The tunic has a small, round neckline. The folds are rendered by curving grooves on the chest and oblique grooves on the sleeves. The chlamys is folded from behind and over his left shoulder and runs across his chest and over the right shoulder, where it is fastened with a circular brooch (Colledge classification: i). A zigzag-shaped fold falls from under the brooch. The folds of the chlamys are rendered by curving grooves.

PORTRAIT H: ARMLESS BUST OF A PRIEST
The figure is shown frontally. The head appears large.

He wears a plain, high, cylindrical, flat-top headdress divided into two sections by a vertical groove that covers his hair and most of his forehead: a Palmyrene priestly hat. His face is oval. The eyebrows are slightly curving. The eyes are almond-shaped, with heavy upper eyelids. The pupils are indicated by incised circles. The ears are large and protruding. The nose is straight and wide, and the alae are carved. The mouth is small, with a full lower lip. The chin is pointed, and the neck is short.

He wears a tunic and a chlamys. The tunic has a wide, v-shaped neckline. The folds are rendered by curving grooves on the chest and oblique grooves on the sleeves. The chlamys is folded from behind and over his left shoulder. It is fastened at the right shoulder with a circular brooch (Colledge classification: i). A zigzag-shaped fold falls from under the brooch. The folds of the chlamys are indicated by curving grooves.

PORTRAIT I: ARMLESS FEMALE BUST
The figure is shown frontally. The head appears large.

She wears three headdresses: a headband, a turban, and a veil. The band is placed high on the forehead and is divided into plain, rectangular panels by vertical grooves (details unclear). The turban is coiled. It is rendered in two twisted layers, with horizontal grooves indicating the coiling of the fabric. The veil is heavy. It falls over her right shoulder, proceeds in a curving fold across the chest, and falls back at her left shoulder. Part of the hair is covered by the headdresses. Several strands of hair above the ears are brushed back over the edge of the turban and disappear under the veil. The individual locks of hair are rendered by incised lines. The folds of the veil are indicated by oblique folds. His face is oval. The eyebrows are curving. The eyes are close-set and almond-shaped. The eyeballs appear blank. Only the earlobes are visible, and she is wearing earrings (details unclear). The nose is large with carved alae. The mouth is small, with a full lower lip. The chin is wide, and the neck is short.

She wears a tunic with a small, round neckline. The folds are indicated by curving, wide grooves.

PORTRAIT J: ARMLESS BUST IN FULCRUM
The figure is shown frontally.

91. COMPLETE SARCOPHAGUS RELIEF WITH BANQUETING SCENE AND PORTRAIT BUSTS

DATABASE NUMBER: NMD064.
LOCATION: Damascus, National Museum of Damascus, inv. no. unknown.
CONTEXT: West necropolis. Valley of the Tombs. Hypogeum of Yarḥaî, west exedra. Excavated Nov. 1934 – Feb. 1935.
ACQUISITION HISTORY: Moved and reconstructed at the National Museum of Damascus in 1936.
MEASUREMENTS: —
MATERIAL: Limestone.
PRESERVATION: A part of the upper mattress is chipped. The object is weathered. Portrait A: A part of the veil and turban, and the lower part of her face including the nose, cheeks, mouth, and chin are badly chipped. Portrait D: The upper right part of the headdress has broken off. Portrait E: Areas of the face are chipped. The torso is weathered. Portrait G: Areas of the headdress are chipped.
TECHNICAL DESCRIPTION: —
DATE: A.D. 240–273 (Tanabe 1986: A.D. 237–255).

Cat. 91

REFERENCES: Ingholt Archives, PS 891; Amy – Seyrig 1936, 248 f. pl. 47, 1; Cantineau 1938, 157 cat. d; Tanabe 1986, 31 pls. 241–244; Parlasca 1998, 312; Krag – Raja 2017, 199 n. 24; 204 n. 72. 73; 205 n. 75. 76; 206 n. 87; 208 n. 99; 209 n. 100. 102; 217 f. cat. 24 fig. 6; Krag 2018, 23 n. 160; 28 n. 9; 32 n. 63; 41 n. 143; 53 n. 258; 58 n. 300; 59 n. 323; 62 n. 349. 352. 353; 65 n. 369; 66 n. 382. 385; 67 n. 4; 87 n. 182; 88 n. 193. 195; 89 n. 210; 103 n. 74; 392 cat. 847. Inscription: Cantineau 1938, 157 cat. d; Stark 1971, 39; Tanabe 1986, 31 pl. 244: Parlasca 1998, 312; Krag 2018, 392 cat. 847.

OBJECT DESCRIPTION

The sarcophagus lid is rectangular in shape and depicts a seated female, two standing priests, and a reclining priest. Beneath these figures is a box in the shape of a kline with three busts between the kline legs: a priest, a female, and a priest. Above the kline are two mattresses. The thin mattress at the top is decorated with an intersecting lozenge pattern with flowers in the lozenges. The lower mattress has three bands decorated with vegetal motifs. The central band is decorated with a running scroll with rosettes. The bands on either side are decorated with serrated leaves in an opposite arrangement on the stem. Curving grooves indicate the texture of the lower mattress. The reclining figure rests his left arm against two cushions. The lower cushion has a deep oblique groove, indicating that it is folded at the middle. The lower cushion has two decorated bands, the upper cushion has a wide, decorated band (details unclear). On the left side of the kline, a fulcrum is shown. It is decorated with a small, armless bust of a priest rendered in a clipeus (portrait H). From the fulcrum, is a protruding element, possibly a lion head (details unclear). The central stretcher of the kline is decorated. The wide, rectangular panel at the centre is divided into two horizontal sections by a line. On either side of the central panel are two rectangular indentations decorated with a crisscross pattern. On each side of these are two square inlays or appliqués with four-petal flowers. The kline legs are turned. They are composed of a plinth, and above is a convex quarter, a reversed, long, concave neck, a scotia, a ball, a torus, and above the stretcher is a biconical finial. All elements are decorated with a tongues pattern.

The object was found next to objects cat. 90 and cat. 92.

INSCRIPTION

SCRIPT: Palmyrene Aramaic.
LOCATION ON RELIEF: On the mattress below the foot of the reclining priest.
TRANSCRIPTION: ṢLMT NṢ' BRT TYPYLS | 'TT BWN' TYMRṢW | ḤBL.

TRANSLATION: Image of Neṣâ daughter of Theophilos, wife of Bônnê Taîmarṣû, alas.

CIS no. —; PAT no. 2787.

COMMENTS: L.1: NṢ' Cantineau 1938; NḤ' Stark 1971. Both readings are possible, as the shapes of Ṣ and Ḥ are almost identical in this inscription (compare first letter of l. 1 and l. 3), but there is another example of NṢ' in the same tomb (PAT 2790). TYPYLS is Greek Θεόφιλος.

SARCOPHAGUS LID

PORTRAIT A: SEATED FEMALE, NEṢÂ

The figure is shown frontally. The body appears short. The right arm is bent and held at the waist. The left arm is raised to the neck. Her legs are bent with the knees rendered under the drapery. Her feet are obscured by the leg of the reclining figure to her left.

She wears three headdresses: a headband, a turban, and a veil. The band is placed high on the forehead (details unclear). The turban is coiled. The veil is heavy. It falls over her shoulders, and is wrapped around her right arm and falls over the back of her left shoulder. Part of the hair is covered by the headdresses. Several strands of hair above the ears are pushed back over the edge of the band and disappear under the veil. Her eyebrows are curving, rendered as thin ridges. The eyes are close-set and almond-shaped, with thick upper eyelids that extend beyond the end of the lower ones. The irises and pupils are indicated by concentric, incised circle. The neck is wide.

She wears a tunic and a himation. The ankle-length tunic has a small, round neckline and short, wide sleeves. The folds of the tunic are indicated by curving grooves. The himation crosses her chest diagonally from the left shoulder to the right side and covers the left breast and the lower part of the chest. The folds of the himation are rendered by vertical and curving grooves.

She rests her right hand across her thighs and lightly holds a fold of the himation worn by the reclining priest to her left. Her left hand is raised next to the shoulder and with it, she pulls a fold of the veil.

PORTRAIT B: STANDING PRIEST

The figure is shown in three-quarter view, turned slightly to the right. Both arms are bent and held to the torso. His legs are obscured by the reclining figure to his left.

He wears a plain, high, cylindrical, flat-top headdress divided into two sections by one vertical groove that covers his hair and most of his forehead: a Palmyrene priestly hat. His face is oval. The eyebrows are curving. The eyes are close-set and almond-shaped, with thick upper eyelids. The upper eyelids extend beyond the end of the lower ones. The irises are indicated by incised circles. The ears are large and protruding, with the helix, concha, scapha, and the earlobe depicted. The nose is large. The mouth is small, with thin lips. The cheeks are fleshy, and the chin is wide. The neck is wide.

He wears a tunic and a himation. The tunic has a low, round neckline. The folds of the tunic are rendered by curving grooves. Over the tunic, he wears a himation. The himation covers most of his body. It is wrapped around his right shoulder and arm, leaving the upper part of the chest and the hand free. One end of the himation crosses the chest diagonally and falls over the left shoulder (›arm-sling‹ type). Another end of the himation is wrapped around his left arm leaving the hand free. The folds of the himation are indicated by oblique and curving grooves.

With the upturned palm of the right hand, he holds a bowl with his fingertips. The left hand is held flat to his himation.

PORTRAIT C: STANDING PRIEST

The figure is shown frontally. The right arm is bent and held to the torso. The lower left arm and the legs are obscured by the reclining figure to his left.

He wears a plain, high, cylindrical, flat-top headdress divided into three sections by two vertical grooves that covers his hair and most of his forehead: a Palmyrene priestly hat. His face is round. The eyebrows are rendered by incised lines starting from the root of the nose. The eyes are close-set and almond-shaped, with thick upper eyelids. The upper eyelids extend beyond the end of the lower ones. The irises are indicated by incised circles and the pupils by punch holes. The nose is large, with the alae carved. The ears are large and protruding, with the helix, scapha, and the lobe depicted. The mouth is small, with a full lower lip. The cheeks are fleshy, and the chin is wide. The neck is wide.

He wears a tunic and a himation. The tunic has a low, round neckline. The folds of the tunic are rendered by curving grooves. Over the tunic, he wears a himation. It is wrapped around his right shoulder and arm, leaving the upper part of the chest and the hand free. One end of the himation crosses the chest diagonally and falls over the left shoulder (›arm-sling‹ type). The folds of the tunic are rendered by vertical and curving grooves.

He holds the diagonal fold of the himation with his right hand.

PORTRAIT D: RECLINING PRIEST

The figure is shown in frontal to three-quarter view. The head appears small in relation to the body. The right arm is slightly bent and rests on his right raised knee. The left arm is bent and held to the torso. His right leg is bent, and he rests his foot on the kline. The left leg is bent under the right, with the knee pointing outwards. The lower left leg is obscured by the right leg.

He wears a high, cylindrical, flat-top headdress divided into three sections by two vertical grooves: a Palmyrene priestly hat. A wreath with the leaves pointing towards the bust of a male figure, with short hair is depicted at the lower part of the headdress. The midribs of the leaves are incised. A narrow, horizontal band is depicted under the headdress suggesting a liner. His face is oval. The eyebrows are curving, depicted as thin ridges. The eyes are close-set and almond-shaped with thick upper eyelids. The upper eyelids extend beyond the end of the lower ones. The irises are indicated by incised circles. The ears are large and protruding, with helix, scapha, and lobe depicted. The nose is straight, with carved alae. The mouth is large, with thick lips. The chin is round, and the neck is short.

He wears a >Parthian-style< tunic and a himation. The tunic has a wide, round neckline decorated with a beaded band. The tunic has long, tight-fitting sleeves. The cuffs of the sleeves are decorated with serrated leaves in an opposite arrangement on the stem. At the middle, the tunic has a wide band decorated with a running scroll with rosettes extending downwards. The folds of the tunic are rendered by vertical and curving grooves. Over the tunic, he wears a himation. It is wrapped around his left shoulder and arm and falls along the left side of his torso. It is folded over the tunic, across his waist, and covers the legs. A zigzag-shaped fold falls from under his left hand. The folds of the himation are rendered by diagonal, curving grooves. He wears a round-toe boot that is knotted, with laces at the bridge of the foot.

He rests his right hand on the knee, and is holding a branch. The outline of the leaves is rendered by incised lines. He holds a skyphos in his left hand. It has a conical foot, and the lower body is decorated with a tongues pattern. The body of the skyphos is undecorated and the lip has small, looped handles. The index and the little finger are extended.

SARCOPHAGUS BOX

PORTRAIT E: ARMLESS BUST OF A PRIEST

The figure is shown frontally. The head appears large. The head is turned slightly to his right.

He wears a plain, high, cylindrical, flat-top headdress divided into three sections by two vertical grooves that covers his hair and most of his forehead: a Palmyrene priestly hat. His face is oval. The eyebrows are slightly curving, rendered by incised lines, starting from the root of the nose. The eyes are close-set and almond-shaped, with heavy upper eyelids. The irises are indicated (details unclear). The ears are large and protruding. The nose is straight and wide at the base with carved alae. The mouth is small, with thin lips. The cheeks are fleshy, and the chin is prominent and oval. The neck is short.

He wears a tunic and a chlamys. The folds are rendered by curving grooves. The chlamys covers both shoulders, proceeds across his chest, and is fastened at the right shoulder with a circular brooch (details unclear). The folds of the chlamys are indicated by curving grooves.

PORTRAIT F: ARMLESS FEMALE BUST

The figure is shown frontally. The head appears large.

She wears three headdresses: a headband, a turban, and a veil. The band is placed low on the forehead (details unclear). The turban is coiled. It is rendered in three twisted layers by horizontal grooves indicating the coiling of the fabric. The veil is heavy. It falls over her right shoulder, proceeds in a curving fold across the chest, and falls back at her left shoulder. Part of the hair is covered by the headdresses: several strands of hair above the ears are brushed back over the edge of the headband and disappear under the veil. The individual locks of hair are rendered by incised lines. Her face is diamond-shaped. The eyebrows are curving, rendered by incised lines, starting from the root of her nose. The eyes are close-set and almond-shaped, with thick eyelids. The irises are indicated (details unclear). Only the earlobes are visible, and she wears earrings (details unclear). The nose is large, with carved alae. The mouth is small, with a full lower lip. The chin is prominent and oval, and the neck is short. A sequence of round elements is visible at the base of the neck, possibly a necklace (details unclear).

She wears a tunic with a small, round neckline. The folds are indicated by curving, wide grooves.

PORTRAIT G: ARMLESS BUST OF A PRIEST

The figure is shown frontally. The head appears large. The head is turned slightly to his left.

He wears a plain, high, cylindrical, flat-top headdress divided into three sections by two vertical grooves that covers his hair and most of his forehead: a Palmyrene priestly hat. His face is long. The eyebrows are slightly curving, rendered as thin ridges. The eyes are close-set and almond-shaped, with heavy upper eyelids. The irises are indicated (details unclear). The ears are large and protruding, with the helix, scapha, tragus, and the lobe depicted. The nose is straight and wide at the base, with carved alae. The mouth is small, with thin lips. The chin is oval, and the neck is short.

He wears a tunic and a chlamys. The tunic has a low, round neckline. The folds of the tunic are rendered by curving grooves. The chlamys covers both shoulders, proceeds across his chest, and is fastened at the right shoulder with a circular brooch with an incised border (Colledge classification: h). A zigzag-shaped fold falls from under the brooch. The folds of the chlamys are indicated by curving grooves.

PORTRAIT H: ARMLESS BUST OF A PRIEST IN FULCRUM

The figure is shown frontally, rendered in a clipeus.

He wears a plain, high, cylindrical, flat-top headdress that covers his hair and most of his forehead: a Palmyrene priestly hat. His face is round.

He wears a tunic and a himation. The folds of the tunic are rendered by oblique grooves. The himation covers most of the chest. It falls in a curving line from his left shoulder to his right side. Another fold extends downwards from his left shoulder. The folds of the himation are rendered by curving and vertical grooves.

92. COMPLETE SARCOPHAGUS RELIEF WITH BANQUETING SCENE AND PORTRAIT BUSTS

DATABASE NUMBER: NMD065.
LOCATION: Damascus, National Museum of Damascus, inv. no. unknown.
CONTEXT: West necropolis. Valley of the Tombs. Hypogeum of Yarḥaî, west exedra. Excavated in Nov. 1934 – Feb. 1935.

ACQUISITION HISTORY: Moved and reconstructed at the National Museum of Damascus in 1936.
MEASUREMENTS: —
MATERIAL: Limestone.
PRESERVATION: Portrait B: Parts of the forehead, the eyes, and the headdress are chipped on the left side of the face. Portrait D: The tip of the nose is chipped.
TECHNICAL DESCRIPTION: —
DATE: A.D. 240–273 (Tanabe 1986: A.D. 237–255).
REFERENCES: Ingholt Archives, PS 893; Tanabe 1986, 31 pls. 245. 246; Parlasca 1998, 311 f.; Krag – Raja 2017, 199 n. 24; 204 n. 72. 73; 205 n. 75; 206 n. 87; 208 n. 99; 209 n. 100. 102; 218 cat. 25; Krag 2018, 28 n. 9; 32 n. 63; 41 n. 143; 53 n. 258; 58 n. 300; 59 n. 316. 320. 323. 325; 62 n. 349. 352. 353; 65 n. 369; 66 n. 382. 385; 88 n. 193. 195; 103 n. 74; 106 n. 106; 393 cat. 848.

OBJECT DESCRIPTION

The sarcophagus lid relief is rectangular in shape and depicts a seated female, two standing priests, and a reclining priest. Beneath these figures, is a box relief in the shape of a kline with three busts between the kline legs: a priest, a female, and a priest. Above the kline are two mattresses. The thin mattress at the top is decorated with an intersecting lozenges pattern with flowers inside the lozenges. The lower mattress has three bands. The central band is decorated with serrated leaves in an opposite arrangement on the stem. The bands on either side are decorated with running scrolls with rosettes. Curving grooves indicate the texture of the lower mattress. The reclining figure rests the left arm against a cushion. The right side of the kline is decorated with a fulcrum with a five-petal rosette. The central stretcher of the kline is decorated. The wide, rectangular, central panel is flanked by two square inlays. On either side are two rectangular indentations decorated with an incised wave pattern. On each side of these are two squares, decorated inlays or appliqués (details unclear). The kline legs are turned. They are composed of a plinth, and above is a convex quarter, a reversed long, concave neck, a scotia, a ball, a torus, and above the stretcher is a biconical finial. All elements are decorated with a tongues pattern.

The object was found next to objects cat. 90 and cat. 91.

SARCOPHAGUS LID

PORTRAIT A: SEATED FEMALE

The figure is shown frontally. The head appears large in relation to the body. The head is turned slightly to her right. The right arm is bent and rests on her right thigh. The left is bent and held to the chest. Her legs are bent with the knees rendered under the drapery. Her right foot rests on the mattress. The left foot is obscured by the reclining figure to her left.

She wears three headdresses: a headband, a turban, and a veil. The undecorated headband is placed high on the forehead. The turban is coiled. It is rendered in three twisting layers looped into each other creating a knot in the middle. Horizontal grooves indicate the coiling of the fabric. The veil is heavy. It falls over her shoulders and it is wrapped around her right arm, and it covers the left upper arm and runs back at her waist. Part of the hair is covered by the headdresses: several strands of hair on the sides of the head and above the ears are brushed back over the edge of the headband and turban and disappear under the veil. The individual locks of hair are rendered by incised lines. Her face is oval. Her eyebrows are curving, rendered by incised lines starting from the root of the nose. The eyes are close-set and almond-shaped, with thick upper eyelids that extend beyond the lower ones. The irises are indicated by incised circles. The nose is straight and wide at the base. The mouth is small, with full lips. The cheeks are fleshy, and the chin is wide. The neck is wide.

She wears a tunic and a himation. The tunic has a small, round neckline. The folds of the tunic are indicated by curving grooves. The himation reached to the ankles. It crosses her chest diagonally from the left shoulder to the right side, and covers most of the lower chest, body, and legs. It is fastened at the left shoulder with a circular brooch, with an incised border (Colledge classification: h). The folds of the himation are rendered by curving grooves, and between the legs they are rendered by diagonal and curving grooves.

She rests her right hand on the thigh, lightly pulling a fold of the himation. With her left hand, she lightly holds a fold of the veil.

PORTRAIT B: STANDING PRIEST

The figure is shown frontally. The right arm is bent and held to the chest. The left is bent and held to the torso. The legs are obscured by the reclining figure.

He wears a plain, high, cylindrical, flat-top headdress divided into three sections by two vertical grooves: a Palmyrene priestly hat. His face is round. The eyebrows are curving. The eyes are close-set and almond-shaped with thick upper eyelids. The irises are indicated (details unclear). The ears are large and protruding, with helix, scapha, and the lobe depicted. The nose is small. The mouth is small, with a full lower lip. The cheeks are fleshy, and the chin is wide. The neck is wide.

He wears a tunic and a himation. The tunic has a wide, round neckline. The folds of the tunic are rendered by curving grooves. Over the tunic, he wears a himation. It is wrapped around the right shoulder and arm, leaving the upper part of the chest and the hand free. One end of the himation crosses the chest diagonally and falls over the left shoulder (>arm-sling< type). The folds of the himation are rendered by diagonal and curving grooves.

He holds the diagonal fold of the himation with his right hand. The left hand is held to the torso, and he lightly holds a fold of the himation. The index and the middle finger are extended.

PORTRAIT C: STANDING PRIEST

The figure is shown frontally. The right arm appears short in relation to the body. The right arm is bent and held to the torso. The lower left arm and the legs are obscured by the reclining figure.

He wears a plain, high, cylindrical, flat-top headdress divided into three sections by two vertical grooves: a Palmyrene priestly hat. His face is round. The eyebrows are curving. The eyes are close-set and almond-shaped, with thick upper eyelids. The irises are indicated (details unclear). The ears are large and protruding, with the helix, scapha, and the lobe depicted. The nose is straight and wide at the base, with the alae carved. The mouth is wide, with a full lower lip. The cheeks are fleshy, and the chin is wide. The neck is wide.

He wears a tunic and a himation. The tunic has a wide, round neckline. The folds of the tunic are rendered by curving grooves. Over the tunic, he wears a himation. It is wrapped around his right shoulder and arm, leaving the upper part of the chest and the hand free. One end of the himation crosses the chest diagonally and falls over the left shoulder (>arm-sling< type). The folds of the himation are rendered by diagonal and curving grooves.

He holds the diagonal fold of the himation with his right hand.

PORTRAIT D: RECLINING PRIEST

The figure is shown in frontal to three-quarter view. The head appears small in relation to the body. The right arm is extended and rests on his raised right knee. The left arm is bent and held to the torso. His right leg is bent, and his foot is resting on the mattress. The left leg is bent under the right leg with the knee pointing forwards. The lower left leg is obscured by the right leg.

He wears a high, cylindrical, flat-top headdress divided into three sections by two vertical grooves: a Palmyrene priestly hat. A wreath is rendered at the lower part of the priestly hat. It is composed of three rows of wide leaves that point towards an armless bust. The bust is that of a beardless, male figure with a Palmyrene priestly hat. A narrow, horizontal band is depicted under the headdress suggesting a liner. His face is oval. The eyebrows are curving. The eyes are close-set and almond-shaped, with thick upper eyelids. The upper eyelids extend beyond the end of the lower ones. The irises are indicated by incised circles. The ears are large and protruding, with helix, scapha, anti-helix, and lobe depicted. The nose is straight. The mouth is small, with a full lower lip. The chin is round, and the neck is short.

He wears a >Parthian-style< tunic and a himation. The tunic has a small, round neckline decorated with a beaded band. The tunic has long, tight-fitting sleeves. The cuffs of the sleeves are decorated with a band with a vegetal motif. At the middle, the tunic has a wide band decorated with a running scroll with rosettes, extending downwards. The folds of the tunic are rendered by vertical and curving grooves. Over the tunic, he wears a himation. It is wrapped around his left shoulder and arm, leaving the chest and the hand free. It falls along the left side of his torso, where it is folded over the tunic, across his waist and legs. A wide fold falls from under his left hand, across the cushion and down the mattress. The fold divides into two zigzag-shaped folds, with each end tied into a small knot. The folds of the himation are rendered by diagonal, curving grooves. He wears a round-toe plain boot.

He rests his right hand on the right knee. The nails are indicated by fine, incised lines. He holds a skyphos in his left hand. It has a conical foot and lower body decorated with a tongues pattern. The body of the skyphos and the lip are straight and the skyphos has small, looped handles. The index and the little fingers are extended.

Cat. 92

SARCOPHAGUS BOX

PORTRAIT E: ARMLESS BUST OF A PRIEST

The figure is shown frontally. The head appears large.

He wears a plain, high, cylindrical, flat-top headdress divided into three sections by two vertical grooves: a Palmyrene priestly hat. His face is oval. The eyebrows are slightly curving. The eyes are close-set and almond-shaped, with thick upper eyelids. The eyeballs are blank. The ears are large and protruding, with the helix, concha, scapha, and the lobe depicted. The nose is straight and wide at the base. The mouth is small, with a full lower lip. The cheeks are fleshy, and chin is oval. The neck is short.

He wears a tunic and a chlamys. The tunic has a wide, round neckline. The folds are rendered by oblique grooves. The chlamys is folded from behind and over his left shoulder. It falls in a curving fold across his chest and over the right shoulder, where it is pinned with a circular brooch (details unclear). The folds of the chlamys are indicated by curving grooves.

PORTRAIT F: ARMLESS FEMALE BUST

The figure is shown frontally. The head appears large.

She wears two headdresses: a turban and a veil. The turban is coiled. It is rendered in twisted layers, with horizontal and curving grooves indicating the coiling of the fabric. The veil is heavy. It falls over her right shoulder, falls in a curving fold across the chest, and falls back at her left shoulder. The hair is parted in the middle of the forehead and brushed away to each side of the face, back over the edge of the turban, and disappears under the veil. The individual locks of hair are rendered by incised lines. The folds of the veil are indicated by oblique grooves. Her face is oval. The eyebrows are curving. The eyes are close-set and almond-shaped, with thick upper eyelids. The eyeballs are blank. The nose is thin, with carved alae. The mouth is small, with thin lips. The chin is prominent and oval. The neck is short.

She wears a tunic, with a small, round neckline. The folds are indicated by curving grooves.

PORTRAIT G: ARMLESS BUST OF A PRIEST

The figure is shown frontally. The head appears large.

He wears a plain, high, cylindrical, flat-top headdress divided into three sections by two vertical grooves that covers his hair: a Palmyrene priestly hat. His face is square. The eyebrows are slightly curving. The eyes are close-set, with heavy upper eyelids. The eyeballs appear blank. The ears are large and protruding, with the helix, concha, scapha, and the lobe depicted. The nose is straight, with carved alae. The mouth is small, with thin lips. The cheeks are fleshy, and the chin is wide. The neck is short.

He wears a tunic and a chlamys. The tunic has a wide, round neckline. The folds are rendered by curving grooves. The chlamys falls over his left shoulder, proceeds across his chest in a curving fold, and is pinned with a circular brooch at the right shoulder (details unclear). The folds of the chlamys are indicated by curving grooves.

SARCOPHAGUS LIDS

A.D. 108–150

93. SARCOPHAGUS LID RELIEF WITH BANQUETING SCENE

DATABASE NUMBER: NMD067.
LOCATION: Damascus, National Museum of Damascus, inv. no. unknown.
CONTEXT: West necropolis. Valley of the Tombs. Hypogeum of Yarḥaî, south exedra. Excavated in Nov. 1934 – Feb. 1935.
ACQUISITION HISTORY: Moved and reconstructed at the National Museum of Damascus in 1936.
MEASUREMENTS: —
MATERIAL: Limestone.
PRESERVATION: Portrait A: The area around her feet is weathered. Some damage on the right side on the right shoulder and hand. The nose is chipped.
TECHNICAL DESCRIPTION: The background has a rough finishing. It is reconstructed.
DATE: A.D. 108–150.
REFERENCES: Ingholt Archives, PS 888; Amy – Seyrig 1936, pl. 36, 1. 2; Seyrig 1937, 14 n. 3; Seyrig 1951, 36 fig. 3; Böhme – Schottroff 1979, 31 fig. 25; Tanabe 1986, 32 pl. 255; Curtis 2017, 60 fig. 11; Krag – Raja 2017, 199 n. 23–25; 201 n. 28. 29; 203 n. 43. 48–51. 55; 213 cat. 2; Krag 2018, 33 n. 75. 77. 80–82; 41 n. 142. 143; 51 n. 240; 66 n. 382; 88 n. 193. 195. 197; 241 cat. 281; Silver et al. 2018, 188 fig. 9.47.

OBJECT DESCRIPTION

The sarcophagus lid relief is rectangular in shape and depicts a seated female, a standing male, two standing females, and a reclining male. Beneath the figures is a mattress decorated with a running scroll with four-petal rosettes. The seated female sits in a chair with a central stretcher with a rectangular indentation. The front legs of the chair are turned and composed of a conical element, a neck, a ball, and an abacus. The lower part of the left leg of the chair is obscured by the foot of the reclining male. She rests her feet on a footstool. It is rectangular in shape and has two short legs. The reclining figure rests the left arm on a cushion. Large, raised grooves at the centre indicate that the cushion is folded. Curving grooves indicate the texture of the fabric.

PORTRAIT A: SEATED FEMALE

The figure is shown frontally, the head is turned slightly to the left. The right arm is bent and held to the shoulder. The left arm is bent and held to the lap. Her legs are bent at the knees and rendered under the drapery.

She wears three headdresses: a headband, a turban, and a veil. The band is placed low on her forehead and is divided into rectangular decorated panels separated by vertical bands. The central panel has a flower. The turban is coiled. Curving grooves indicate the coiling of the fabric. The veil is heavy. It falls over her shoulders and is wrapped around her arms

Cat. 93

leaving the hands free. Her hair is partly visible under the veil. Thick locks above the ears are brushed back over the headband and disappear under the veil. Her face is long. Her eyebrows are slightly curving, rendered by incised lines, starting from the root of the nose. The eyes are close-set and round, with thick eyelids. The irises are indicated. The ears are visible under the headdress, and she is wearing earrings shaped like a miniature bunch of grapes (Colledge classification: E). Her nose is straight. The mouth is wide, with thin lips. The cheeks are fleshy, and the chin is round. The neck is wide.

She wears a tunic and a himation. The tunic has a wide, round neckline and long, tight-fitting sleeves. It ends at her feet. The folds of the tunic are indicated by vertical and curving grooves. The himation falls to the ankles. It crosses her chest diagonally from the left shoulder to the right side, and covers the lower chest, body, and legs. It is fastened at the left shoulder with a trapezoidal brooch with a rosette finial (Colledge classification: b). The folds of the himation are rendered by diagonal and curving grooves. The folds between the legs are rendered by curving grooves.

Her right hand is raised to the shoulder, where she holds a fold of the veil. She rests her left hand on her thigh, where she holds a fold of the himation.

PORTRAIT B: STANDING BOY/MALE

The figure is shown frontally. The right arm is bent and held to the torso. The left is extended towards the reclining figure to the left. The lower part of the legs is obscured by the reclining figure.

His hair is voluminous and straight. The individual strands of hair are indicated by incised lines. His face is diamond-shaped. The eyebrows are rendered by incised lines, starting from the root of the nose. The eyes are close-set and round, with thick eyelids. The irises are indicated (details unclear). The nose is straight and wide at the tip. The ears are protruding. The mouth is small, with a full lower lip. The chin is wide. The neck is long.

He wears a tunic with a wide, v-shaped neckline and short, wide sleeves. It has a band on either side of the neckline extending downwards (clavi). He wears a band belt at the waist. The folds of the tunic are rendered by oblique and curving grooves.

With his right hand, he holds an object with globular elements, possibly a branch or dates. He rests his left hand on the right thigh of the reclining figure.

PORTRAIT C: STANDING FEMALE

The figure is shown frontally, her head is turned slightly to the left. The right arm is bent and held to the neck. The left is bent and held to the torso. The lower body is obscured by the reclining figure.

She wears three headdresses: a headband, a turban, and a veil. The headband is placed low on her forehead and is divided into rectangular, decorated panels separated by vertical bands (details unclear). The turban is coiled. It is divided into two layers and the ends are looped into each other creating a knot in the middle. Curving grooves indicate the coiling of the fabric. The veil is heavy. It falls over her shoulders and is wrapped around her right arm leaving the hand free. Her face is oval. Her eyebrows are slightly curving, rendered by incised lines, starting from the root of the nose. The eyes are close-set and round, with thick upper eyelids. The irises are indicated (details unclear). The ears are visible under the headdress and she is wearing earrings in a square shape (details unclear). Her nose is straight. The mouth is small, with thin lips. The cheeks are fleshy, and the chin is round. The neck is wide.

She wears a tunic and a himation. The tunic has a wide, round neckline and long, tight-fitting sleeves. The folds of the tunic are indicated by vertical and curving grooves. The himation crosses her chest diagonally from the left shoulder to the right side and covers the lower chest and body. It is fastened at the left shoulder with a triangular brooch (Colledge classification: c). The folds of the himation are rendered by diagonal and curving grooves.

Her right hand is raised to the chest where she holds a fold of the veil. With the left hand, she holds a fold of the himation.

PORTRAIT D: STANDING FEMALE

The figure is shown frontally. The right arm is bent and held to the shoulder. The left arm is bent and held to the torso. The lower body is obscured by the reclining figure.

She wears three headdresses: a headband, a turban, and a veil. The headband is placed low on her forehead and is divided into rectangular, decorated panels separated by vertical bands (details unclear). The turban is coiled. Curving grooves indicate the coiling of the fabric. The veil is heavy. It falls over her shoulders and is wrapped around her left arm leaving the hand free. Her face is oval. Her eyebrows are slightly curving, rendered by incised lines, and starting from the root of the nose. The eyes are close-set and round, with thick upper eyelids. The irises are indicated (details unclear). The ears are visible under the headdress, and she is wearing earrings in a square shape (details unclear). Her nose is straight. The mouth is small, with thin lips. The cheeks are fleshy, and the chin is round. The neck is wide. She wears one necklace composed of a string of round beads at the base of the neck.

She wears a tunic and a himation. The tunic has a wide, round neckline and long, tight-fitting sleeves. The folds of the tunic are indicated by vertical and curving grooves. The himation crosses her chest diagonally from the left shoulder to the right side and covers the lower chest and body. The folds of the himation are rendered by diagonal and curving grooves.

Her right hand is raised to the shoulder where she holds a fold of the veil. With the left hand, she holds a fold of the himation. She wears a wide hoop bracelet at the left wrist. It is decorated with a vegetal motif.

PORTRAIT E: RECLINING MALE

The head and the body are shown in a frontal to three-quarter view. The head appears small in relation to the body. The head is turned slightly to the left. The right arm is extended and rests on his raised leg, the left arm is bent in front of the torso. His right leg is bent, and his foot is resting on the mattress. The left is bent under the right leg and the lower left leg is obscured by the right leg.

His hair is arranged in three rows of snail-shell curls around the head. The individual strands of hair are indicated by incised lines. His face is diamond-shaped. The eyebrows are curving, rendered by thin ridges. The eyes are close-set and almond-shaped, with thick eyelids. The upper eyelids extend beyond the end of the lower ones. The irises are indicated (details unclear). The ears are protruding. The nose is straight and wide at the base. The mouth is large with a full lower lip. The chin is round, and the neck is long.

He wears a ›Parthian-style‹ tunic, a chlamys, ›Parthian-style‹ trousers, and over-trousers. The tunic has a wide, round neckline and long, tight-fitting sleeves. The cuffs of the sleeves are decorated with a band with a vegetal motif with an upper border of a line of squares. The folds of the tunic are rendered by curving and oblique grooves. Over the tunic, he wears a chlamys that falls over both shoulders and covers most of the chest and body. It falls along the left side of the torso. It is fastened at the right shoulder with a circular brooch enclosing a hexagon (Colledge classification: e). A zigzag-shaped fold with a border decorated with a beaded band falls from under the brooch. One edge of the chlamys has a scalloped border, decorated with running scroll with rosettes, visible on the fold across the chest. The chlamys ends above the knees and has a decorated border with a running scroll with rosettes. Along the right thigh, he has an object with a round end, rectangular main body, and lateral round elements: a sheathed dagger. The folds of the chlamys are rendered by curving and oblique grooves. He wears a band belt with laces across the waist. The belt is divided by one horizontal groove, and the laces are knotted at the centre, with the ends of the laces looped under the strap on either side of the waist. The trousers are visible above the knees, and they have a central band extending downwards decorated with a rosette and a border decorated with a line of squares. The over-trousers are visible under the knees and their folds are indicated by wide, vertical grooves. He wears a pointed shoe.

He holds a skyphos in his left hand. It has a conical foot and a conical lower body. The neck is concave and decorated with horizontal grooves. It has small, looped handles.

94. SARCOPHAGUS LID RELIEF WITH BANQUETING SCENE

DATABASE NUMBER: NMD066.
LOCATION: Damascus, National Museum of Damascus, inv. no. unknown.
CONTEXT: West necropolis. Valley of the Tombs. Hypogeum of Yarḥaî, south exedra. Excavated in Nov. 1934 – Feb. 1935.
ACQUISITION HISTORY: Moved and reconstructed at the National Museum of Damascus in 1936.
MEASUREMENTS: —
MATERIAL: Limestone.
PRESERVATION: There are a few cracks on the surface. The surface on the lower right side of the relief is weathered. Portrait A: Her feet are weathered. Small areas on the legs are chipped. Portrait B: The nose and small areas on the chest are chipped. Portrait C: Small parts on the hand and the lower torso are chipped.
TECHNICAL DESCRIPTION: —
DATE: A.D. 108–150.
REFERENCES: Amy – Seyrig 1936, pl. 36, 1; Böhme – Schottroff 1979, 31 fig. 25; Tanabe 1986, 32 pl. 254; Krag 2018, 33 n. 75. 77. 80. 81; 41 n. 142. 143; 66 n. 382; 241 cat. 280; Silver et al. 2018, 188 fig. 9.47.

OBJECT DESCRIPTION

The sarcophagus lid relief is rectangular in shape and depicts a seated female and two reclining males. Beneath the figures is a mattress decorated with a running scroll with four-petal rosettes. The female sits on a chair. It has a central stretcher with a rectangular indentation on the left side. The front legs of the chair are turned (details unclear). Both reclining males rest their left arm on two cushions. They are decorated with a band with a vegetal motif set between beaded bands. Curving grooves indicate the texture of the fabric.

PORTRAIT A: SEATED FEMALE

The figure is turned slightly to the left. The hands appear large in relation to the body. The right arm is bent and raised to the neck. The left arm is bent and rests on the left thigh. Her legs are bent, and the knees are rendered under the drapery.

She wears a veil. It falls over her shoulders and is wrapped around her left arm. Her hair is visible under the veil. It is arranged in thick locks, brushed back over the ears, and disappears under the veil. Her face is round. Her eyebrows are slightly curving, rendered by incised lines, starting from the root of the nose. The eyes are close-set and round, with thick eyelids. The irises are indicated (details unclear). She wears earrings (details unclear). Her nose is small with carved nostrils. The mouth is small, with thin lips. The cheeks are fleshy, and the chin is round. The neck is wide. At the chest, she wears a necklace with a central, round pendant (details unclear).

She wears a tunic and a himation. The tunic has a wide, v-shaped neckline. The folds of the tunic are indicated by curving grooves. The himation falls to the ankles. It crosses her chest diagonally from the left shoulder to the right side, and covers the lower chest, body, and legs. It is fastened at the left shoulder with a trapezoidal brooch with a rosette finial (Colledge classification: b). The folds of the himation are rendered by diagonal and curving grooves. The folds between the legs are rendered by curving grooves.

Her right hand is raised to the shoulder, where she pulls a fold of the veil. She rests her left hand on her thigh, where she holds a fold of the himation.

PORTRAIT B: RECLINING MALE

The head and the body are shown in frontal view, while the right leg is shown in profile. The arms and hands appear large in relation to the body. The right arm is bent and rests on his raised knee; the left is bent in front of the torso. The right leg is bent with the foot resting on the mattress, while the left leg is bent under the right leg with the knee pointing forwards. The left lower leg is obscured by the right leg.

His hair is curly, arranged in snail-shell curls around the head. The individual strands of hair are indicated by incised lines. His face is diamond-shaped. The eyebrows are curving, rendered by incised lines, and starting from the root of the nose. The eyes are close-set and almond-shaped, with thick eyelids. The upper eyelids extend beyond the end of the lower ones. The irises are indicated by incised circles. The ears are protruding, with the helix, tragus, and the lobe depicted. The nose is straight and wide at the base. The mouth is large, with a full lower lip. The chin is round, and the neck is long.

He wears a ›Parthian-style‹ tunic, a chlamys, ›Parthian-style‹ trousers, and over-trousers. The tunic has a small, round neckline and long, tight-fitting sleeves. The cuffs of the sleeves are decorated with a band with a vegetal motif set between beaded bands. The folds of the tunic are rendered by curving and oblique grooves. He wears a band belt with laces across the lower torso. The belt has an undecorated strap and a central panel. The strap is divided by one horizontal groove, while the central panel is circular. The ends of the laces are fastened by the central panel, where the ends are looped under the belt on either side of the waist. Over the tunic, he wears a chlamys that falls over both shoulders, and covers most of the chest and body. It falls along the left side of the torso, where the border is decorated with a running scroll with rosettes. It is fastened at the right shoulder with a circular brooch (Colledge classification: i). A zigzag-shaped fold falls from under the brooch. The chlamys ends above the knees and has a decorated border with a running scroll with rosettes. The folds of the chlamys are rendered by curving and oblique grooves. The trousers are visible above the knees, and they have a central band extending down, decorated with a vegetal motif. The over-trousers are visible under the knees and have an upper border, decorated with a vegetal motif. The folds of the over-trousers are indicated by wide, vertical grooves.

The right hand rests on the knee. He holds a skyphos in his left hand. It has a conical foot and a conical lower body. The neck is concave and decorated with two horizontal grooves. It has small, looped handles. The left thumb, the index, and the little fingers are extended. He wears a thick hoop ring with an incised line on his little finger.

PORTRAIT C: RECLINING MALE

The head and the body are shown frontally. The hand appears large in relation to the body. The right arm is extended behind the reclining figure to the right. The left is bent in front of the torso.

His hair is curly, arranged in crescent-shaped curls around the head. The individual strands of hair are indicated by incised lines. His face is diamond-shaped. The eyebrows are curving, rendered by incised lines, starting from the root of the nose. The eyes are close-set and almond-shaped, with thick eyelids. The upper eyelids extend beyond the end of the lower ones. The irises are indicated, with incised lines. The ears are protruding. The nose is large and wide at the base. The mouth is large, with a full lower lip. The chin is round, and the neck is long.

He wears a ›Parthian-style‹ tunic and a chlamys. The tunic has a small, round neckline and long, loose sleeves. The cuffs of the sleeves are decorated with a band with a vegetal motif. The folds of the tunic are rendered by curving and oblique grooves. Over the tunic, he wears a chlamys that falls over both shoulders, and covers most of the chest and body. It falls along the left side of the torso, where the border is decorated with a beaded band. It is fastened at the right shoulder with a circular brooch with an incised border (Colledge classification: h). A zigzag-shaped fold falls from under the brooch. The folds of the chlamys are rendered by curving and oblique grooves.

He holds a skyphos in his left hand. It has a conical foot and a conical lower body. The neck is concave and decorated with horizontal grooves. It has small, looped handles. The index and the little fingers are extended.

FRAGMENTS OF LIDS, LID RELIEFS, OR BANQUETING RELIEFS

A.D. 108–120

95. FRAGMENT OF BANQUETING RELIEF

DATABASE NUMBER: NMD094.
LOCATION: Damascus, National Museum of Damascus, inv. no. 3634/8380.
CONTEXT: West necropolis. Valley of the Tombs. Hypogeum of Yarḥaî, east exedra.
ACQUISITION HISTORY: —
MEASUREMENTS: Height: 47.7 cm. Width: 25 cm.
MATERIAL: Limestone, white.
PRESERVATION: The lower right and the left corners of the plinth are broken off. The background is broken off, except for the areas under the stool.
TECHNICAL DESCRIPTION: It is reconstructed.
DATE: A.D. 108–120.
REFERENCES: Ingholt Archives, PS 648; Amy – Seyrig 1936, 251 pl. 49; Kitzinger 1938, 205 pl. 73, 6; Parlasca 1982a, 195 cat. 176; Zouhdi 1983, 315 no. 7; Makowski 1985b, 123 fig. 2, A; Parlasca 1985, 395 cat. 188; Krag 2018, 39 n. 128. 129; 107 n. 110; 115 n. 63; 238 cat. 269.

OBJECT DESCRIPTION

The object depicts a female seated on a stool. The stool has concave legs with conical feet and round finials that project over the seat. On the seat of the stool, a cushion is depicted, with curving grooves indicating the fabric.

PORTRAIT

The figure is shown frontally with the head turned slightly to her right. The left hand appears small in relation to the body. The head and left arm appear large. The right arm is bent and held in front of the chest. The left arm is bent and held in front of the torso. She sits with her legs apart; the knees are visible under the drapery. Both feet rest on a protruding plinth.

She wears three headdresses: a headband, a turban, and a veil. The headband is placed low on her forehead, and is decorated with rectangular vertical panels with floral motifs, separated by vertical beaded bands. The central panel is decorated with a four-petal flower with incised veins. The turban is coiled. It is in a single layer with diagonal grooves indicating the coiling of the fabric. The veil is heavy. It falls over her shoulders and is wrapped around her arms. The hair is visible over her ears, where it is brushed back under the headband. Two wavy locks of hair fall on each of her shoulders. Individual strands of hair are indicated with incised lines. Her face is oval. The eyebrows are curving. The eyes are round, with thick eyelids. The irises are indicated by incised circles and the pupils by punch holes. The ears are slightly protruding, and the tail of the helix and earlobe are depicted. She wears earrings in the shape of two horizontal bars with two round pendants suspended by vertical bars (Colledge classification: F). The nose is short and wide, with incised alae and carved nostrils. The mouth is small, with full lips. The cheeks are fleshy. The chin is pointed. The neck is wide and long. The sternocleidomastoid muscles are indicated by a v-shaped depression.

She wears a tunic and a himation. The tunic falls to the ankles. It has a wide, v-shaped neckline. The folds of the tunic are rendered by v-shaped grooves on the chest. The himation crosses the chest diagonally from the left shoulder to the right side and covers the left breast. It is fastened at the left shoulder with a trapezoidal brooch with a feline head (Colledge classification: a). The himation covers the lower body and legs and ends at the shins, revealing the tunic underneath. The folds of the himation are rendered by oblique grooves on

OBJECTS FROM HYPOGEA 305

Cat.95

the body and curving grooves on the lower legs. She has bare feet, or wears sandals: the toes are indicated by incised lines.

Her right hand is held in front of her chest with the palm forward and the fingers extended. The left hand is in front of her torso and the fingers are slightly bent.

With his left hand, he holds a skyphos. It has a conical foot and lower body. The middle part of the body is undecorated. The lip is straight with opposing, vertical, looped handles. The thumb and the index finger are extended. The nails are rendered by fine, incised lines.

A.D. 120–140

96. FRAGMENT OF BANQUETING RELIEF

DATABASE NUMBER: NMD076.
LOCATION: Damascus, National Museum of Damascus, inv. no. unknown.
CONTEXT: West necropolis. Valley of the Tombs. Hypogeum of Yarḥaî, south exedra. Excavated in Nov. 1934 – Feb. 1935.
ACQUISITION HISTORY: Moved and reconstructed at the National Museum of Damascus in 1936.
MEASUREMENTS: Height: 57 cm.
MATERIAL: Limestone.
PRESERVATION: There are few small cracks on the surface. The lower right arm is broken off at the elbow.
TECHNICAL DESCRIPTION: —
DATE: A.D. 120–140 (Amy – Seyrig 1936: A.D. 100–150).
REFERENCES: Ingholt Archives, PS 1127; Amy – Seyrig 1936, 242 cat. 6 pl. 39, 2; Makowski 1985b, 122–124 fig. 2b.

OBJECT DESCRIPTION
The object depicts a reclining male figure. He rests the left arm against a cushion. It is decorated with a band with running scroll with rosettes between bands with squares. Curving grooves indicate the texture of the fabric.

PORTRAIT
The figure is shown frontally, the head is turned slightly to the left. The left arm is bent and held in front of the torso.

His hair is arranged in two rows of crescent-shaped curls around the head. The individual strands of hair are indicated by incised lines. His face is long. The eyebrows are curving, rendered by incised lines, starting from the root of the nose. The eyes are close-set and almond-shaped, with thick eyelids. The upper eyelids extend beyond the end of the lower ones. The irises and pupils are indicated by concentric, incised circles. The ears are small, with the helix, scapha, and lobe depicted. The nose is straight, with carved nostrils. The mouth is small, with thin lips. The chin is square, and the neck is long.

He wears a tunic and a himation. The tunic has a wide, v-shaped neckline and short, wide sleeves. The folds of the tunic are rendered by curving grooves. Over the tunic, he wears a himation. It is wrapped around the left shoulder and arm, leaving most of the torso and the hand free. The folds of the himation are indicated by diagonal grooves.

Sheet with photographs of the south exedra of the hypogeum of Yarḥaî during excavation.

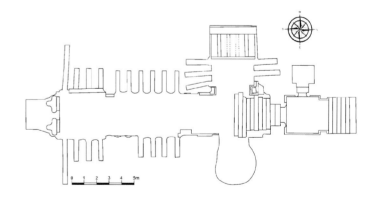

Plan of the hypogeum of Yarḥaî.

Cat. 96

308 CATALOGUE

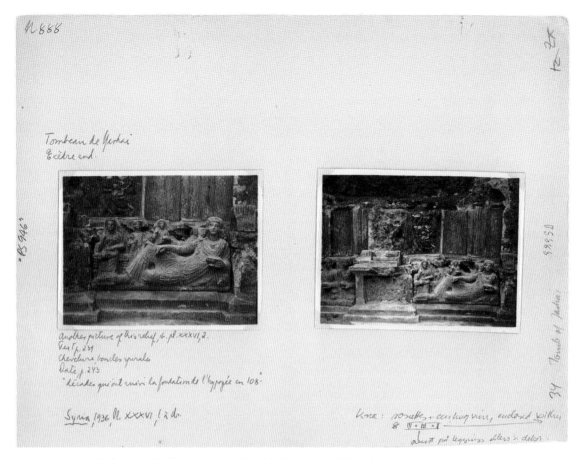

Cat. 96. Sheet with photographs of the south exedra of the hypogeum of Yarḥaî during excavation.

Cat. 96. Sheet with photographs of the south exedra of the hypogeum of Yarḥaî during excavation.

BANQUETING RELIEFS

A.D. 108–150

97. BANQUETING RELIEF

DATABASE NUMBER: NMD096.
LOCATION: Damascus, National Museum of Damascus, inv. no. unknown.
CONTEXT: West necropolis. Valley of the Tombs. Hypogeum of Yarḥaî, west exedra.
ACQUISITION HISTORY: —
MEASUREMENTS: Height: 42 cm. Width: 56 cm.
MATERIAL: Limestone.
PRESERVATION: The lower right corner is broken off. The lower edge appears to be broken off. Portrait A: The feet are chipped. Portrait B: Small areas of the forehead are chipped. Portrait C: The nose and the surface of left hand are chipped.
TECHNICAL DESCRIPTION: —

DATE: A.D. 108–150.
REFERENCES: Ingholt Archives, PS 604; Amy – Seyrig 1936, 250 f. pl. 48, 1; Colledge 1976, 74 f. fig. 40; Makowski 1985b, 127 fig. 4.

OBJECT DESCRIPTION

The relief is rectangular in shape and depicts a standing male and two reclining males. Both reclining males rest their left arm on a cushion. Curving grooves indicate the texture of the fabric.

PORTRAIT A: STANDING MALE

The figure is shown in frontal view. The head appears large. The right arm is held along his body. The left arm is bent and held to his torso. He stands with the feet on the relief ground.

His hair is arranged in three rows of crescent-shaped curls around his head. Each lock of hair is indicated by incised lines. His face is oval. The eyebrows are curving. The eyes are almond-shaped, with thick upper eyelids. The irises are indicated by incised lines. The nose is short and wide, with

Cat. 97

incised alae and nostrils. The mouth is small, with thin lips. Nasolabial lines are indicated by incised lines. The chin is square. The neck is wide, with two curving grooves.

He wears a tunic. The tunic has a wide, round neckline and long, tight-fitting sleeves. The tunic covers his body and legs and continues to the ankles. The folds of the tunic are rendered by curving grooves on the torso and at the legs, and vertical grooves on the sleeves and between the legs. He wears a plain band belt at the waist. A long rectangular object runs diagonally from his left side of the belt to under the left hand (details unclear).

His right hand is held at his right side, the fingers are extended. The left hand is in front of the torso and holds a skyphos. The skyphos has a conical foot and the body is plain. His index finger is extended.

PORTRAIT B: RECLINING MALE

The figure is shown in frontal view, with the head turned slightly to the left. The head appears small. Both arms are bent in front of the torso.

His hair is arranged in two rows of crescent-shaped curls around his head, each row pointing a different direction. Each lock of hair is indicated by incised lines. His face is oval. There is a furrow on the forehead, indicated by a horizontal, incised line. The eyebrows are curving. The eyes are almond-shaped, with thick eyelids. The irises are indicated by incised circles. The ears are protruding, and the helix, tragus, concha, scapha, and lobe are depicted. The nose is short and wide, with incised alae and carved nostrils. The mouth is small, with thin lips. Nasolabial lines are indicated by incised lines. The chin is square. The neck is wide, with two curving grooves.

He wears a tunic and a himation. The tunic has a wide, v-shaped neckline and short, loose sleeves. The folds of the tunic are rendered by curving grooves along the middle of the torso, and oblique grooves on the sleeve. The himation is falling over his left shoulder and left arm and is wrapped around the left wrist. The himation falls along the left side of his body. The folds of the himation are rendered by oblique grooves.

With his right hand, he holds a skyphos. The skyphos has a round base, a concave body without decoration and the rim is indicated by a horizontal, incised line. The right thumb and the index finger are extended. His left hand is relaxed beneath the skyphos, with the thumb and the index finger extended.

PORTRAIT C: RECLINING MALE

The figure is shown in frontal view, with the head turned slightly to the left. The head appears small. The right arm is obscured by the reclining figure to his right. The left arm is bent in front of the lower torso.

His hair is arranged in three rows of crescent-shaped curls around his head. Each lock of hair is indicated by incised lines. His face is oval. There is a furrow on the forehead, indicated by a horizontal, incised line. The eyebrows are curving. The eyes are almond-shaped, with thick upper eyelids. The irises are indicated by incised circles. The ears are protruding, and the helix, tragus, concha, scapha, and lobe are depicted. The nose is short. The mouth is small, with thin lips. Nasolabial lines are indicated by incised lines. The chin is oval. The neck is wide and long, with two curving grooves. There is a vertical groove at the centre of the neckline, indicating the chest musculature.

He wears a tunic and a himation. The tunic has a wide, v-shaped neckline. The folds of the tunic are rendered by curving grooves along the middle of the torso. The himation is falling over his left shoulder and left arm and is wrapped around the left wrist. The himation continues along the left side of his body and is wrapped across the waist. A fold of the himation is rendered under his left hand, on the cushion. The folds of the himation are rendered by oblique and vertical grooves.

The outline of a skyphos is visible in his left hand.

A.D. 113–240

TOMB H, HYPOGEUM OF TAÎBBÔL

SARCOPHAGI

A.D. 200–240

---

98. COMPLETE SARCOPHAGUS RELIEF WITH BANQUETING SCENE AND PORTRAIT BUSTS

DATABASE NUMBER: InSitu099.
LOCATION: Palmyra, in situ.
CONTEXT: South-east necropolis. Tomb H, hypogeum of Taîbbôl, north exedra.
ACQUISITION HISTORY: —
MEASUREMENTS: —
MATERIAL: Limestone, white/yellow.
PRESERVATION: The surface is weathered. Portrait B: The left hand is chipped. Portrait C: The right hand is chipped.
TECHNICAL DESCRIPTION: —
DATE: A.D. 200–240.
REFERENCES: Saito 2007, 84 f. fig. 16; Miyashita 2016, 132 figs. 11–14; Krag – Raja 2017, 199 n. 24; 204 n. 72. 73; 205 n. 75; 206 n. 87; 207 n. 94; 208 n. 99; 209 n. 100; 211 n. 117. 122; 220 cat. 39; Krag 2018, 28 n. 9; 32 n. 63; 53 n. 258. 259; 58 n. 300. 304; 59 n. 323; 61 n. 332; 62 n. 349. 352. 353; 65 n. 369; 66 n. 382. 385; 88 n. 193–195; 103 n. 74; 396 cat. 855; <https://www.facebook.com/permalink.php?story_fbid=758083210919790&id=103105249750926> (06.05.2022).

OBJECT DESCRIPTION

The sarcophagus lid is rectangular in shape and depicts a seated female, a standing boy/male, two reclining males, and a seated female. Beneath these figures is a box in the shape of a kline with four busts between the kline legs: a female, a male, a female, and a male. On top of the kline are two mattresses. The upper mattress is thin and undecorated. The lower mattress has three, possibly decorated, bands (details unclear). Curving grooves indicate the texture of the lower mattress. The reclining figure to the right rests the left arm against two cushions, possibly decorated with a wide band (details unclear). The other reclining figure rests the left arm against two cushions. The lower cushion is decorated with a wide band with lanceolate leaves in an opposite arrangement on the stem. The lower cushion is decorated (details unclear). On the left side of the kline, a fulcrum is shown. It is decorated with a four-petal rosette. The central stretcher of the kline is decorated with two rectangular indentations on either side. The legs are turned. They are composed of a plinth, and above is a convex quarter, a long, reversed concave quarter, a convex quarter, a reversed bell-shaped element, a ball, a torus, and above the stretcher is a biconical finial.

The object is located next to objects cat. 99 and 100.

SARCOPHAGUS LID

PORTRAIT A: SEATED FEMALE

The figure is shown frontally. The arms appear short in relation to the body. The right arm is bent and raised to her neck. The left arm is bent and rests on her lap. Her legs are bent with the knees rendered under the drapery. Her feet are obscured by the right foot of the reclining male to her left.

She wears two headdresses: a turban and a veil. The turban is coiled. It is rendered in three twisting layers with horizontal grooves, indicating the coiling of the fabric. The veil is heavy. It falls over her shoulders and is wrapped around her left arm, where it falls back on the left side of her waist. It falls along the right side of her body and is folded around her right lower arm. Her hair is centrally parted and brushed away on each side of the forehead. Part of the hair is covered by the headdresses. Several strands of hair above the ears are pushed back over the edge of the turban and disappear under the veil. The individual locks of hair are rendered by incised lines. Her face is oval. Her eyebrows are curving, and the eyes are almond-shaped. The irises are indicated by incised lines. Only the earlobes are visible under the hair, and she is wearing dumbbell-shaped earrings (Colledge classification: H). Her cheeks are fleshy. Her nose is short and straight. The mouth is small, with thin lips. The chin is oval and almost double. The neck is slender.

She wears a tunic and a himation. The tunic has a small, round neckline and wide sleeves ending above the elbows. The folds of the tunic are rendered by curving grooves. The himation falls to the ankles. It crosses her chest diagonally from the left shoulder to the right side and covers most of the lower chest and body. It is fastened at her left shoulder with a large, circular brooch (details unclear). A zigzag-shaped fold falls from under her left hand. At the lower edge, a weight is attached. The folds of the himation are rendered by curving grooves.

With her right hand, she holds a fold of the veil. With the left hand, she holds a fold of the veil. The index and the little fingers are extended.

PORTRAIT B: STANDING BOY/MALE

The figure is shown frontally. The arms appear short in relation to the body. Both arms are bent and held to the torso. His legs are obscured by the reclining male to his left.

The hair is arranged in three rows of snail-shell curls around the head. The individual locks of hair are rendered by incised lines. His face is oval. The eyebrows are curving. The eyes are close-set and almond-shaped. The eyeballs appear blank. The ears are large and protruding, with the helix, scapha, and earlobe depicted. The nose is straight and narrow. The mouth is small, with thin lips. The cheeks are fleshy. The chin is oval, and the neck is wide.

He wears a tunic and a himation. The tunic has a small, angular neckline. The folds of the tunic are rendered by curving grooves. Over the tunic, he wears a himation that covers most of his body. It is wrapped around the right shoulder and arm, leaving the chest and the hand free. One end of the himation crosses the chest diagonally and falls over the left shoulder (>arm-sling< type). The folds of the himation are indicated by diagonal and vertical grooves.

With his right hand, he holds the diagonal fold of the himation. He appears to be holding a round object in his left hand (details unclear).

PORTRAIT C: RECLINING MALE

The figure is shown in frontal to three-quarter view. The arms appear short in relation to the body. The left hand appears large. The right arm is bent and resting on his raised right knee. The left arm is bent and held to the chest. His right leg is bent, and he rests his foot on the mattress. The left leg is bent under the right leg with the knee pointing outwards. The lower left leg is obscured by the right leg.

The hair is arranged in crescent-shaped curls around the head. The individual locks of hair are rendered by incised lines. His face is oval. The eyebrows are curving, starting from the root of the nose. The eyes are close-set and almond-shaped, with thick upper eyelids. The eyeballs appear blank. The ears are large and protruding, with the helix, scapha, tragus, and earlobe rendered. His nose is short and narrow. The mouth is small, with thin lips. The chin is oval and almost double. The neck is long.

He wears a tunic and a himation. The tunic has a wide, v-shaped neckline and long, loose sleeves. The folds of the tunic are indicated by diagonal, curving grooves. The himation falls to the ankles. It is folded around his left shoulder and arm and is wrapped around the left wrist. It falls along the left side of the body, is folded across the waist, and covers his legs. A wide, zigzag-shaped fold falls from under his left hand, onto the cushions and the mattress. The folds of the himation are rendered by oblique, curving grooves. He also wears plain boots.

With his right hand, he holds an oblong object, possibly a pinecone or branch. With the upturned palm of the left hand, he holds a wide bowl with his fingertips. It is decorated with a pattern of hollowed-out lozenges.

PORTRAIT D: RECLINING MALE

The figure is shown in frontal to three-quarter view. The head is turned slightly to the left. The left arm appears short in relation to the body. The left hand appears large. The right arm is extended behind the reclining figure to his right. The left arm is bent and held to the chest. The lower body and legs are obscured by the reclining figure to his right.

The hair is arranged in two rows of crescent-shaped curls around the head. His face is oval. The eyebrows are slightly curving ridges, starting from the root of the nose. The eyes are narrow and slanting, with thick eyelids. The irises are indicated (details unclear). The ears are large and protruding, with the helix, scapha, tragus, and the earlobe rendered. His nose is small and wide at the base. The mouth is small, with a full lower lip. The chin is wide and almost double. The neck is short.

He wears a tunic and a himation. The tunic has a wide, v-shaped neckline. The folds of the tunic are indicated by diagonal, curving grooves. He also wears a himation. It is folded around his left shoulder and arm and is wrapped around the wrist. It falls along the left side of his body and proceeds across his waist. A large, zigzag-shaped fold falls from under his left hand. The folds of the himation are rendered by oblique, curving grooves.

With the upturned palm of the left hand, he holds a wide bowl with his fingertips. It is decorated with a pattern of hollowed-out lozenges.

PORTRAIT E: SEATED FEMALE

The figure is shown frontally. The head is turned slightly to the left. The arms appear short in relation to the body. The right upper arm is obscured by the reclining figure to her right. The lower right arm rests on her right thigh. The left arm is bent and raised to her neck. Her legs are bent, with the knees rendered under the drapery. Her feet are rendered resting on the mattress.

She wears two headdresses: a turban and a veil. The turban is coiled. It is rendered in three twisting layers by horizontal grooves, indicating the coiling of the fabric. The veil is heavy. It falls over her shoulders and is wrapped around her left upper arm. Part of the hair is visible under the headdresses. Several strands of hair above the ears are pushed back over the edge of the turban and disappear under the veil. Her face is oval. The eyebrows are rendered by curving, incised lines, starting at the root of her nose. The eyes are close-set and almond-shaped. The eyeballs appear blank. Only the earlobes are visible under the hair and she is wearing dumbbell-shaped earrings (Colledge classification: H). Her cheeks are fleshy. Her nose is straight and wide at the base. The mouth is small, with thin lips. The chin is pointed. The neck is wide. She wears a necklace composed of round beads at the base of the neck.

She wears a tunic and a himation. The tunic has a small, v-shaped neckline. The folds are indicated by oblique and curving grooves. The ankle-length himation crosses her chest diagonally from the left shoulder to the right side and covers most of the lower chest and body. The folds are rendered by curving grooves.

With the right hand she holds a fold of the veil. A zigzag-shaped fold falls from under her right hand. At the lower edge, a weight is attached. The index finger is extended. Her left arm is raised next to the shoulder and she holds a fold of the veil with her hand.

SARCOPHAGUS BOX

PORTRAIT F: ARMLESS FEMALE BUST

The figure is shown frontally.

She wears two headdresses: a turban and a veil. The turban is coiled. It is rendered in twisting layers with horizontal grooves indicating the coiling of the fabric. The veil is heavy and falls over her shoulders. From the right shoulder, the veil proceeds in a curving fold across the chest and falls back over her left shoulder. The hair is centrally parted and brushed away on both sides of the forehead. Part of the hair is covered by the headdresses. Several strands of hair above the ears are pushed back over the edge of the turban and disappear under the veil. Her face is oval. The eyebrows are heavy and curving. The eyes are close-set and slanting. The eyeballs appear blank. She is wearing dumbbell-shaped earrings (Colledge classification: H). The nose is small, and the mouth is narrow with a full lower lip. The chin is oval, and the neck is short.

She wears a tunic with a low, angular neckline. The folds of the tunic are indicated by curving, wide grooves.

PORTRAIT G: ARMLESS MALE BUST

The figure is shown frontally.

The hair is voluminous and the individual strands of hair around the forehead are indicated by incised lines. His face is diamond-shaped. His eyebrows are slightly curving. The eyes are close-set and almond-shaped. The irises are indicated (details unclear). The ears are large and protruding, with the helix and the earlobe rendered. The nose is narrow. The mouth is small, with a full lower lip. The chin is pointed, and the neck is wide.

He wears a tunic and a himation. The tunic has a wide, v-shaped neckline. The folds of the tunic are rendered by curving grooves. Over the tunic, he wears a himation. It is wrapped around his left shoulder and proceeds in a curving fold across the chest. Another wide fold falls vertically from the left shoulder. The folds of the himation are indicated by wide oblique and vertical grooves.

PORTRAIT H: ARMLESS FEMALE BUST

The figure is shown frontally.

She wears two headdresses: a turban and a veil. The turban is coiled. It is rendered in twisting layers with horizontal grooves indicating the coiling of the fabric. The veil is heavy and falls over her shoulders. From the right shoulder, the veil proceeds in a curving fold across the chest and falls back over her left shoulder. Part of the hair is covered by the headdresses. Several strands of hair above the ears are pushed back over the edge of the turban and disappear under the veil. Her face is oval. The eyebrows are heavy and slightly curving. The eyes are small and close-set. The eyeballs appear blank. Only the earlobes are visible, and she is wearing dumbbell-shaped earrings (Colledge classification: H). The nose is small and the mouth narrow, with thin lips. The chin is oval, and the neck is short.

She wears a tunic with a wide, round neckline. The folds of the tunic are indicated by curving, wide grooves.

PORTRAIT I: ARMLESS MALE BUST

The figure is shown frontally.

The hair is arranged in three rows of round curls around the head. His face is oval. His eyebrows are heavy and slightly curving. The eyes are close-set and almond-shaped. The eyeballs appear blank. The ears are large and protruding, with the helix rendered. The nose is thin and slightly crooked. The mouth is small, with thin lips. The chin is wide, and the neck is long.

He wears a tunic and a himation. The tunic has a wide, v-shaped neckline. The folds of the tunic are rendered by curving grooves. Over the tunic, he wears a himation. It is folded over his left shoulder and falls diagonally across the chest. Another fold falls vertically from the left shoulder. The folds of the himation are rendered by wide, oblique, and vertical grooves.

99. COMPLETE SARCOPHAGUS RELIEF WITH BANQUETING SCENE AND PORTRAIT BUSTS

DATABASE NUMBER: InSitu112.
LOCATION: Palmyra, in situ.
CONTEXT: South-east necropolis. Tomb H, hypogeum of Taîbbôl, north exedra.
ACQUISITION HISTORY: —
MEASUREMENTS: —
MATERIAL: Limestone, white/yellow.
PRESERVATION: Portrait D: A crack runs diagonally across the left side of the face. The turban is slightly chipped. Portrait E: A part of the lower left side is broken off. Portrait F: A small crack is visible on the left breast of the figure.
TECHNICAL DESCRIPTION: —
DATE: A.D. 200–240.
REFERENCES: Saito 2007, 83–94 fig. 16; Miyashita 2016, 132 figs. 11. 12; Krag – Raja 2017, 199 n. 24; 204 n. 72. 73; 205 n. 75; 208 n. 99; 209 n. 100; 220 cat. 40; Krag 2018, 28 n. 9; 32 n. 63; 53 n. 258. 259; 58 n. 300. 304; 59 n. 323; 61 n. 332; 62 n. 349. 353; 66 n. 382. 385; 88 n. 193. 197; 103 n. 74; 396 cat. 856.

OBJECT DESCRIPTION

The sarcophagus lid is rectangular in shape and depicts a seated female, a standing boy/male, and a reclining male. Beneath these figures is a box in the shape of a kline with three busts between the kline legs: a female, a male, and a female. Above the kline are two mattresses. The thin mattress at the top is decorated with an intersecting lozenge pattern with flowers inside them. The lower mattress has three bands. The bands at either end are decorated with serrated leaves in an opposite arrangement on the stem. Curving grooves indicate the texture of the lower mattress. The reclining figure rests the left arm against a cushion. A fulcrum is shown on the left side of the kline. It is decorated with a six-petal rosette, and a branch protrudes from it. The central stretcher of the kline is decorated. The central, rectangular part is divided into two sections by a horizontal line. The upper section is decorated with oblique grooves and framed by an animal head on the right side and a vegetal motif on the left. The lower panel is decorated with palm leaves cavetto moulding. On either side are two rectangular indentations with a wave pattern. Framing these are two square inlays or appliqués with four-petal flowers. The legs are turned. They are composed of a plinth, and above is a convex quarter, a long, reversed, concave quarter, a convex quarter, a reversed bell-shaped element, a ball, a torus, and above the stretcher is a biconical finial.

The object is located next to objects cat. 98 and 100.

SARCOPHAGUS LID

PORTRAIT A: SEATED FEMALE

The figure is shown frontally. The arms appear short in relation to the body. The right arm is bent and rests on her right thigh. The left arm is raised to the neck. Her legs are bent, with the knees rendered under the drapery. Her left foot is obscured by the reclining priest.

She wears two headdresses: a turban and a veil (details unclear). The veil is heavy. It falls over her shoulders and it is wrapped around her right arm and falls back the left shoulder. Her face is oval. The neck is wide.

She wears a tunic and a himation. The tunic has a small, round neckline and short, wide sleeves. The folds of the tunic are indicated by oblique grooves. The himation falls to the ankles. It crosses her chest diagonally from the left shoulder to the right side and covers the left breast and the body. The folds of the himation are indicated by curving grooves. The folds between the legs are indicated by curving grooves.

She rests her right hand on her right knee. The left hand is raised to the neck, and she is lightly pulling a fold of the veil. She wears a bracelet at her left wrist (details unclear).

PORTRAIT B: STANDING BOY

The figure is shown frontally. The arms appear short in relation to the body. The right arm is bent and held to the chest. The left is extended to the left. The legs are obscured by the reclining figure to his left.

The hair is long, covering the ears and reaching the neck. His face appears oval.

He wears a tunic and a himation. The tunic is visible at the upper part of the chest. Over the tunic, he wears a himation that covers most of his body. It is wrapped around the right shoulder and arm, leaving the chest and the hand free. One end of the himation crosses the chest diagonally and falls over the left shoulder (›arm-sling‹ type). The folds of the himation are indicated by oblique grooves.

The right hand is held to the chest. The left hand appears to rest on the shoulder of the reclining figure.

PORTRAIT C: RECLINING PRIEST

The figure is shown in frontal to three-quarter view. The left arm appears short in relation to the body. The right arm is slightly bent and rests on his right raised knee. The left arm is bent and held to the torso. His right leg is bent, and his foot is resting on the kline. The left is bent under the right leg, with the knee pointing forwards. The lower leg is obscured by the right leg.

He is wearing a cylindrical headdress: a Palmyrene priestly hat (details unclear). His face appears oval. The chin is pointed, and the neck is long.

He wears a tunic, an over-garment, possibly a himation or chlamys, and trousers. The tunic has a small, round neckline and long sleeves. The tunic ends above the knees. The folds of the tunic are indicated by oblique and curving grooves. The over-garment is folded around his left shoulder and falls across the chest and along the left side of his body. The trousers are visible from above the knees. The trousers are tucked into his ankle boots.

He rests his right hand on his knee. With the upturned palm of the left hand, he holds a bowl with his fingertips.

SARCOPHAGUS BOX

PORTRAIT D: ARMLESS FEMALE BUST

The figure is shown frontally.

She wears two headdresses: a turban and a veil. The turban is coiled. It is rendered in three twisted layers with horizontal grooves indicating the coiling of the fabric. The veil is heavy. It falls over her right shoulder, proceeds in a curving fold across the chest, and falls back at her left shoulder. The folds of the veil are indicated by oblique folds. Her hair is centrally parted and brushed to each side of the forehead. Part of the hair is covered by the headdresses. Several strands of hair above the ears are brushed back over the edge of the turban and disappear under the veil. The individual locks of hair are rendered by incised lines. Her face is oval. The eyebrows are curving. The eyes are close-set and round, with thick upper eyelids. The eyeballs are blank. Only the earlobes are visible, and she is wearing dumbbell-shaped earrings (Colledge classification: H). The nose is wide. The mouth small, with full lips. The cheeks are fleshy. The chin is pointed, with a cleft. The neck is wide. She wears a necklace composed of round beads at the base of the neck.

She wears a tunic with a small, round neckline. The folds are indicated by curving, wide grooves.

PORTRAIT E: ARMLESS MALE BUST

The figure is shown frontally. The head appears large.

The hair is arranged in three rows of crescent-shaped curls around the head. The individual locks of hair are indicated by incised lines. His face is square. The eyebrows are curving. The eyes are close-set and almond-shaped. The eyeballs are blank. The ears are small and protruding, with the helix and scapha depicted. The nose is straight and wide at the base. The mouth is small, with a full lower lip. The corners of the mouth are accentuated by two oblique grooves. The cheeks are fleshy. The chin is small, and the neck is wide.

He wears a tunic and a himation. The tunic has a low, v-shaped neckline. The folds of the tunic are rendered by curving and oblique grooves. Over the tunic, he wears a himation. It is folded over his left shoulder and falls in a diagonal fold across the chest. Another wide fold falls vertically over the left shoulder. The folds of the himation are indicated by wide, oblique grooves.

PORTRAIT F: ARMLESS FEMALE BUST

The figure is shown frontally.

She wears two headdresses: a turban and a veil. The turban is coiled. It is rendered in three twisted layers with horizontal grooves indicating the coiling of the fabric. The veil is heavy. It falls over her right shoulder, proceeds in a curving fold across the chest, and falls back over her left shoulder. Her hair is centrally parted and brushed to each side of the forehead. Part of the hair is covered by the headdresses. Several strands of hair on the sides of the face and above the ears are brushed back over the edge of the turban and disappear under the veil. The individual locks of hair are rendered by incised lines. The folds of the veil are indicated by oblique grooves. Her face is diamond-shaped. The eyebrows are curving. The eyes are close-set and almond-shaped. The eyeballs are blank. Only the earlobes are visible, and she is wearing dumbbell-shaped earrings (Colledge classification: H). The nose is large with the alae carved. The mouth is narrow with full lips. The chin is pointed, with a cleft. The neck is wide. She wears a necklace composed of round beads at the base of the neck.

She wears a tunic with a wide, round neckline. The folds are indicated by curving, wide grooves.

100. COMPLETE SARCOPHAGUS RELIEF WITH BANQUETING SCENE AND PORTRAIT BUSTS

DATABASE NUMBER: InSitu113.
LOCATION: Palmyra, in situ.
CONTEXT: South-east necropolis. Tomb H, hypogeum of Taîbbôl, north exedra.
ACQUISITION HISTORY: —
MEASUREMENTS: —
MATERIAL: Limestone, white/yellow.
PRESERVATION: The sarcophagus is well preserved. All portraits are weathered.
TECHNICAL DESCRIPTION: —
DATE: A.D. 200–240.
REFERENCES: Saito 2007, 83–94 fig. 16; Miyashita 2016, 132 figs. 11. 12; Krag – Raja 2017, 199 n. 24; 204 n. 72. 73; 205 n. 75; 208 n. 99; 209 n. 100; 220 cat. 41; Krag 2018, 28 n. 9; 32 n. 63; 53 n. 258. 259; 58 n. 300. 304; 59 n. 323; 61 n. 332; 62 n. 349. 353; 66 n. 382. 385; 88 n. 193. 195; 103 n. 74; 397 cat. 857;

<https://www.facebook.com/103105249750926/photos/pcb.758083210919790/758082824253162/?type=1&theater> (06.05.2022).

OBJECT DESCRIPTION

The sarcophagus lid is rectangular in shape and depicts a seated female and a reclining male. Beneath these figures is a box in the shape of a kline with three busts between the kline legs: two males and one female. On top of the kline are two mattresses; a thin mattress at the top and a thick one underneath. Curving grooves indicate the texture of the lower mattress. The reclining male rests on a cushion. The left side of the kline is decorated with a fulcrum. The central stretcher of the kline is decorated with two rectangular indentations at either end. The legs are turned. They are composed of a plinth, and above is a convex quarter, a long, reversed concave quarter, a convex quarter, a reversed bell-shaped element, a ball, a torus, and above the stretcher is a biconical finial.

The object is located next to objects cat. 98 and 99.

SARCOPHAGUS LID

PORTRAIT A: SEATED FEMALE

The figure is shown frontally. The left arm is bent and held to the body. Her legs are bent at the knees and rendered under the drapery.

She wears two headdresses: a turban and a veil. Her face is oval. The nose is straight, and the cheeks are fleshy.

She wears a tunic.

PORTRAIT B: RECLINING MALE

The figure is shown reclining. The left arm is bent and held to the torso. His right leg is bent, and his foot is resting on the kline. The left is bent under the right leg.

His hair is arranged in curls around the head. His face is oval. His eyebrows are curving, rendered by incised lines starting from the root of the nose. The nose is straight, and the cheeks are fleshy.

He wears a tunic and a himation. A zigzag-shaped fold falls from under his left hand.

He holds a bowl in his left hand.

SARCOPHAGUS BOX

PORTRAIT C: ARMLESS MALE BUST

The figure is shown frontally.

The hair is arranged in curls around the head. His face is square. His eyebrows are curving, rendered by incised lines, starting from the root of the nose. The nose is small. The chin is small, and the neck is long.

He wears a himation. It is folded over his left shoulder and falls in a diagonal fold across the chest. Another wide fold falls vertically from the left shoulder. The folds are indicated by wide, oblique grooves.

PORTRAIT D: ARMLESS MALE BUST

The figure is shown frontally.

The hair is arranged in curls around the head. His face is oval. His eyebrows are curving, rendered by incised lines, starting from the root of the nose. The nose is small. The chin is small, and the neck is long.

He wears a himation. It is folded over his left shoulder and falls in a diagonal fold across the chest. Another wide fold falls vertically from the left shoulder. The folds are indicated by wide, oblique grooves.

PORTRAIT E: ARMLESS FEMALE BUST

The figure is shown frontally.

She wears two headdresses: a turban and a veil. The veil is heavy. It falls over her right shoulder and proceeds in a curving fold across the chest and falls back over her left shoulder. Her face is oval. The nose is small, and the chin is small. The neck is long.

BANQUETING RELIEFS

A.D. 113–150

101. BANQUETING RELIEF

DATABASE NUMBER: InSitu100.
LOCATION: Palmyra, in situ.
CONTEXT: South-east necropolis. Tomb H, hypogeum of Taîbbôl, inner (west) exedra, over cat. 102.
ACQUISITION HISTORY: —
MEASUREMENTS: —
MATERIAL: Limestone, white/yellow.
PRESERVATION: Restored in 2005 and placed in original location. A large crack runs diagonally from the left side of the relief and through the elbow of portrait D. The surface is weathered.
TECHNICAL DESCRIPTION: —
DATE: A.D. 113–150.
REFERENCES: Miyashita 2016, 132 fig. 8; Krag – Raja 2017, 199 n. 23–25; 201 n. 28. 29; 203 n. 45. 46. 48. 50; 204 n. 73; 205 n. 75; 214 cat. 8; Krag 2018, 58 n. 311; 73 n. 47; 87 n. 182; 88 n. 193. 195; 103 n. 73; 378 cat. 794; <https://www.facebook.com/103105249750926/photos/pcb.758083210919790/758083057586472/?type=1&theater> (06.05.2022).

OBJECT DESCRIPTION

The relief is rectangular in shape and depicts two standing females, a standing male, and a reclining male. This object is located above cat. 102.

INSCRIPTIONS

INSCRIPTION 1

SCRIPT: Palmyrene Aramaic.

LOCATION ON RELIEF: To the left of the standing female.
TRANSCRIPTION: ʿLYT | BRTH.
TRANSLATION: ʿAliyat his daughter.

INSCRIPTION 2
SCRIPT: Palmyrene Aramaic.
LOCATION ON RELIEF: To the left of the standing girl.
TRANSCRIPTION: TDMR? | BRTH.
TRANSLATION: Tadmor his daughter.

INSCRIPTION 3
SCRIPT: Palmyrene Aramaic.
LOCATION ON RELIEF: To the left of the standing boy.
TRANSCRIPTION: YRḤY? | BRH.
TRANSLATION: Iarḥaî his son.

INSCRIPTION 4
SCRIPT: Palmyrene Aramaic.
LOCATION ON RELIEF: To the right of the reclining male.
TRANSCRIPTION: ṢLM BWLNʾ? BR | YRḤY? | ḤBL?
TRANSLATION: Image of Bôlnâ son of Iarḥaî, alas!

CIS no. —; PAT no. —.
COMMENT: Very uncertain readings.

PORTRAIT A: STANDING FEMALE, ʿALIYAT
The figure is shown frontally. The left arm appears short in relation to the body. The right arm is slightly bent and held to the torso. The left arm is bent and held to the chest. Her right leg is slightly bent. The left leg is obscured by the reclining figure to her left.

Her hair is straight and brushed away on each side of the face. The individual strands of hair are rendered by incised lines. Her face is round. The eyebrows are curving. The eyes are close-set, small, and round. Only the earlobes are visible under the hair. She wears large drop-shaped earrings, possibly miniature bunches of grapes (Colledge classification: E). The nose is small and straight. The cheeks are fleshy. The mouth is small, with thin lips. The chin is round and almost double. The neck is wide, with two curving grooves. At the base of the neck, she wears a necklace composed of a plain, wide hoop with a central, round pendant.

She wears a tunic and a himation. The ankle-length tunic has a wide, round neckline and long, wide sleeves. The folds of the tunic are rendered by curving and oblique grooves. The himation falls over both shoulders and across the chest in a wide, curving fold. The folds of the himation are rendered by curving grooves.

With the right hand she lightly pulls the tunic, creating an overfold running diagonally from her lower right leg to the left side of the waist. The thumb, the index, and the little fingers are extended. With the left hand, she holds the wide fold of the himation.

PORTRAIT B: STANDING FEMALE, TADMOR
The figure is shown frontally. The left arm appears short in relation to the body. The right arm is bent and held out from the body. The left arm is bent and held to the chest. Her lower torso and legs are obscured by the reclining figure to her left.

Her hair is straight and brushed away on each side of the face. The individual strands of hair are rendered by incised lines. Her face is round. The eyebrows are curving. The eyes are close-set and small. Only the earlobes are visible under the hair. She wears large drop-shaped earrings, possibly miniature bunches of grapes (Colledge classification: E). The nose is small. The cheeks are fleshy, and the mouth is very small with thin lips. The chin is round and almost double. The neck is wide.

She wears a tunic and a himation. The tunic has a small, round neckline. The folds of the tunic are rendered by curving and oblique grooves. The himation falls over both shoulders and across the chest in a wide, curving fold. The folds of the himation are rendered by curving grooves.

Her right hand rests in the left shoulder of the standing female to her right. With the left hand, she holds the wide fold of the himation. The index finger is extended.

PORTRAIT C: STANDING MALE, IARḤAÎ
The figure is shown frontally. The head is slightly turned to his left. The right arm is bent and held to the torso. The left arm is held along the body. His lower body and legs are obscured by the reclining figure to his left.

His hair is straight and brushed away on each side of the head. The individual strands of hair are rendered by incised lines. His face is oval. The eyebrows are curving. The eyes are close-set and small. The ears are large with the helix depicted. The nose is small. The cheeks are fleshy, and the mouth is small. The chin is round, and the neck is wide.

He wears a tunic and a himation. The tunic has a wide, round neckline. The folds of the tunic are rendered by curving grooves. Over the tunic he wears a himation. The himation covers most of the body: it is wrapped around the right shoulder and arm, leaving only part of the upper chest and the hand free. One fold of the himation crosses the chest diagonally and falls over the left shoulder (>arm-sling< type). The folds of the himation are indicated by diagonal grooves.

With his right hand he holds lightly the fold of the himation. The thumb, the index, and the middle fingers are extended.

PORTRAIT D: RECLINING MALE, BÔLNÂ
The figure is shown in frontal to three-quarter view. The arms appear short in relation to the body. The hands and the head appear large. The right arm is slightly bent and rests on his right leg. The left arm is bent and rests against a cushion. The right leg is bent with the foot resting on the mattress. The left leg is bent under the right with the knee pointing outwards.

His hair is arranged in flame-shaped curls around the head. The individual strands of hair are rendered by incised lines. His face is oval. The eyebrows are curving and plastically rendered, with oblique, incised lines indicating individual hairs. The eyes are close-set and almond-shaped, with thick upper eyelids. The irises and pupils are indicated by concentric, incised circles. The ears are large and protruding, with the helix, concha, scapha, and lobes depicted. The nose is large and wide at the base. He has a beard that starts from the temples and covers his cheeks, upper lip, and chin. The facial hair is rendered by oblique, incised lines. The mouth is small, with a full lower lip. The chin is round. The neck is wide.

He wears a ›Parthian-style‹ tunic, a himation, and ›Parthian-style‹ trousers. The tunic has a wide, round neckline decorated with a beaded band, and long, tight-fitting sleeves. The cuffs of the sleeves are decorated with a band with lobed leaves. The tunic has a wide band decorated with vines extending downwards from the middle of the neckline. The folds of the tunic are rendered by deep, oblique grooves. He wears a himation that is folded around his left shoulder and wrist. It continues in a wide fold along his left side and crosses his lower abdomen and covers his legs and ends at his ankles. A wide fold falls from under his left wrist and over the cushions and ends in two s-shaped folds. The folds of the himation are rendered by curving and oblique grooves. He also wears trousers visible at the ankles. Each trouser leg is decorated in the middle with a beaded band extending downwards. The folds of the garment are indicated by oblique grooves. He wears shoes. They are tied by a single lace running around the ankle.

His right hand rests on his raised right knee. The nails are indicated by fine, incised lines. With the left hand, he holds the left handle of a cup with a disc-shaped foot and a straight body and lip. The body of the cup has a fluted decoration and two-ledged handles. His index and little finger are extended. The nails are indicated by fine, incised lines.

102. BANQUETING RELIEF

DATABASE NUMBER: InSitu037.
LOCATION: Palmyra, in situ.
CONTEXT: South-east necropolis. Tomb H, hypogeum of Taîbbôl, inner (west) exedra, below cat. 101.
ACQUISITION HISTORY: —
MEASUREMENTS: —
MATERIAL: Limestone.
PRESERVATION: The surface is weathered. Portrait B: The top of the head is broken off. Portrait D: A crack runs diagonally from his right ear to the left shoulder. The surface of his left hand is chipped.
TECHNICAL DESCRIPTION: —
DATE: A.D. 113–150.
REFERENCES: Miyashita 2016, 132 fig. 10; Krag 2018, 28 n. 9; 53 n. 259; 62 n. 353; 88 n. 193. 195; 378 cat. 795; <https://www.facebook.com/103105249750926/photos/pcb.758083210919790/758082824253162/?type=1&theater> (06.05.2022).

OBJECT DESCRIPTION

The relief is rectangular in shape and depicts a seated female, a standing male, and two reclining males. The first of the reclining males (portrait C) rests against a round cushion. The cushion is decorated with a central band with a running scroll with rosettes set between beaded bands. Beneath these figures, is a mattress.
This object is located below cat. 101.

PORTRAIT A: SEATED FEMALE

The figure is shown frontally. The head is turned slightly to her left. The arms and legs appear short in relation to the body. The right arm is bent and rests on her right thigh. The left arm is bent and raised to the neck. Her legs are bent with the knees visible in the drapery. Her feet are obscured by the reclining figure to her left.

She wears two headdresses: a turban and a veil. The turban is coiled with horizontal grooves indicating the coiling of the fabric. The veil is heavy. It falls over the shoulders, and is wrapped around her right arm and falls over the back of her left shoulder. Part of the hair is covered by the headdress: several strands of hair above the ears are pushed back over the headband and the edge of the turban and disappear under the veil. Her face is oval. The eyebrows are curving. The eyes are close-set (details unclear). The nose is straight. The earlobes are visible, and she may wear earrings (details unclear). The cheeks are fleshy, and the mouth is small. The neck is wide.

She wears a tunic and a himation. The tunic has short, loose sleeves. The folds of the tunic are rendered by curving grooves. Over the tunic, she wears a himation. The himation crosses the chest diagonally from the left shoulder to the right side and covers the left breast and falls over the legs. The folds of the himation are rendered by curving and oblique grooves.

She may hold an object in her right hand (details unclear). With the left hand, she lightly pulls the edge of the veil.

PORTRAIT B: STANDING MALE

The figure is shown frontally. The right arm is bent and held in front of the chest. The lower left arm and lower body are obscured by the reclining figure to his left.

The hair is voluminous and brushed away on each side of the head, covering the ears. His face is long. The eyebrows are curving and rendered by thin ridges. The eyes are close-set and almond-shaped. No details are visible. The nose is straight and wide at the tip. The mouth is small, and the chin is round. The neck is wide.

He wears a tunic. The tunic has a round neckline and short, loose sleeves. The folds of the tunic are rendered by curving grooves.

He holds a cylindrical and oblong object (details unclear) in his hands. The right hand is placed on top of the object. The index finger is extended.

PORTRAIT C: RECLINING MALE

The figure is shown in frontal to three-quarter view. The head is turned slightly to his left. The right arm appears short in

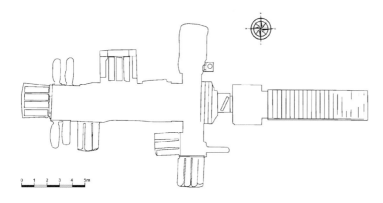

Plan of Tomb no. H, hypogeum of Taîbbôl.

relation to the body. The right arm is slightly bent and rests on his right leg. The left arm is bent and rests against a cushion. The right leg is bent, and the foot is resting on the mattress. The left leg is bent under the right with the knee pointing outwards.

His hair is straight, brushed away on each side of the head. The individual strands of hair are rendered by incised lines. The eyebrows are curving, rendered by thin ridges. The eyes are close-set and almond-shaped, with thick upper eyelids. The irises are rendered by incised circles. The ears are small, with the helix and concha depicted. The nose is straight and wide at the base. He has a beard that starts from the temples and covers the cheeks, the upper lip, and the chin. The facial hair is rendered by flame-shaped curls arranged in rows. The mouth is small with thin lips. The chin is round, and the neck is wide.

He wears a ›Parthian-style‹ tunic, a ›Parthian-style‹ chlamys, and trousers. The tunic has a small, round neckline decorated with round elements and long, tight-fitting sleeves. The tunic has a wide band with a running scroll with a rosette pattern between two beaded bands extending downwards from the middle of the neckline. The tunic ends above the knees and has a decorated border with serrated leaves in an opposite arrangement on the stem. The folds of the tunic are rendered by curving and oblique grooves. Over the tunic, he wears a chlamys that falls over both shoulders, and covers most of the chest. It is wrapped around his left shoulder and arm, leaving the hand free. A wide fold falls from under the hands, over the cushion, and ends in two s-shaped folds. The chlamys is fastened at the right shoulder with a circular brooch (details unclear). The folds of the chlamys are rendered by curving and oblique grooves. He wears a plain band belt, knotted at the centre with the ends looped under on either side of the waist. He also wears trousers. Each trouser leg is decorated in the middle with a wide band (details unclear) extending downwards. The folds of the trousers are indicated by wide, curving grooves. He wears plain round-toe boots.

He rests his right hand on his raised knee. The thumb and the index finger are extended. With the left hand he holds a skyphos. It has a conical foot and body, a straight lip, and small, looped handles. The foot and the body of the skyphos are decorated with a tongues pattern. The thumb, the index, and the little fingers are extended.

PORTRAIT D: RECLINING MALE

The figure is shown frontally. The head is turned slightly to his right. The left arm appears short in relation to the body. The left hand appears large. His right arm is extended behind the reclining figure to his right. The left arm is bent and rests against a cushion. His lower body and legs are obscured by the reclining figure to his left.

His hair is straight and brushed away on each side of the head. The eyebrows are curving. The eyes are close-set and almond-shaped. The ears are large, with the helix depicted. The nose is large and wide at the base. He has a beard that starts from the temples and covers the cheeks, the upper lip, and the chin. The facial hair is rendered by flame-shaped curls arranged in rows. The mouth is small, with thin lips. The chin is round, and the neck is wide.

He wears a tunic. The tunic has a small, round neckline decorated with a beaded band. The tunic has a wide band decorated with leaves in an opposite arrangement on the stem and set between two beaded bands extending downwards from the middle of the neckline. The folds of the tunic are rendered by oblique grooves. The outline of another garment is visible at his left shoulder. The details are unclear.

The outline of a round object, possibly a skyphos, is visible at the centre of his chest.

A.D. 123–250

HYPOGEUM OF ḤENNIBEL

SARCOPHAGUS BOXES

A.D. 220–250

103. SARCOPHAGUS BOX WITH BANQUETING SCENE

DATABASE NUMBER: PM538.
LOCATION: Palmyra, Palmyra Museum, inv. no. unknown.
CONTEXT: South-west necropolis. Hypogeum of Ḥennibel.
ACQUISITION HISTORY: —
MEASUREMENTS: —
MATERIAL: Limestone, white/yellow.
PRESERVATION: The right side and the upper left corner are chipped.
TECHNICAL DESCRIPTION: Partly uncarved: A large rectangle has been left uncarved on the right side of the sarcophagus. Portrait B: The right hand is undercut. Traces of red pigment in the inscription.
DATE: A.D. 220–250.
REFERENCES: al-Asʿad 2013, 19 fig. 9; Krag 2018, 28 n. 9; 32 n. 63; 58 n. 304; 62 n. 353; 63 n. 355; 87 n. 182; 88 n. 197; 397 cat. 860; Silver et al. 2018, 173 fig. 9.6; <https://

Cat. 103, Pl. 46

virtual-museum-syria.org/palmyra/sarcophagus-of-malko-and-his-wife-rabna/> (06.05.2022). Inscription: al-Asʿad 2013, 19; Krag 2018, 397 cat. 860.

OBJECT DESCRIPTION

The sarcophagus box is rectangular in shape and depicts three figures: a seated female, a reclining male, and a standing male. Beneath the figures, is a mattress. The texture is indicated by wide, curving grooves. The seated female sits on two round cushions. The fabric and material of the cushions are indicated by wide, curving grooves. The reclining priest rests on a round cushion with a wide band decorated with a vegetal pattern. A continuous vine tendril with trefoil leaves is carved at the upper part of the relief ground over the three figures and to the left of the standing male.

INSCRIPTION

SCRIPT: Palmyrene Aramaic.
LOCATION ON RELIEF: Between the seated female and the reclining priest.
TRANSCRIPTION: MLKW BR TYMʾ | ḤNBL ḤMṬWŠ | WʾTTH RBNʾ.
TRANSLATION: Malkû son of Taîmê Ḥennibel Ḥamaṭûš and his wife Rabbanê.

CIS no. —; PAT no. —.
COMMENT: RBNʾ was previously considered a masculine name.

PORTRAIT A: SEATED FEMALE, RABBANÊ

The figure is shown in profile, the head in three-quarter view. Her arms are bent; the right resting on her thigh, the left raised to the height of the shoulder. Her feet are obscured by the reclining figure.

She wears three headdresses: a headband, a turban, and a veil. The headband is placed high on her forehead (details unclear). The turban is coiled. The veil falls over the shoulders, and is wrapped around her right arm. It continues to the ground, visible along the side of her right leg. Most of her hair is covered by the headdresses, except for several strands over the ears that are pushed back over the headband and disappear under the veil. Her face is square. The eyebrows are low and curving. The eyes are almond-shaped, and the eyeballs are blank. She wears dumbbell-shaped earrings (Colledge classification: H). The nose is straight. The mouth is small. The neck is short.

She wears a tunic and a himation. The tunic has a wide neckline. The himation is fastened at the left shoulder with a brooch (details unclear). It covers the left side of the chest, falls diagonally down the torso, and covers the legs. The folds of the himation are indicated by oblique grooves.

Her right hand rests in her lap and holds a fold of the veil. With her left hand, she pulls a fold of the veil. The index finger is extended.

PORTRAIT B: RECLINING PRIEST, MALKÛ

His head is shown in a three-quarter view, his torso frontally, his arms and right leg in profile, and his left leg frontally. His right arm is extended to the side. His left arm is bent in front of the torso. His right leg is bent and raised with the foot resting on the mattress. His left leg is bent backwards under the right leg, and the lower leg is thereby obscured.

He wears a tall, cylindrical, flat-top headdress: a Palmyrene priestly hat. A wreath with three rows of leaves pointing towards a central oval decoration is depicted at the middle of the headdress. The face is square. The eyebrows are low and curving. The eyes are almond-shaped, and the eyeballs are blank. The ears are large and protruding. The nose is straight. The mouth is small. The chin is round. The neck is long and wide.

He wears a ›Parthian-style‹ tunic, a chlamys, and ›Parthian-style‹ trousers. The tunic has long, tight-fitting sleeves and is decorated at the cuffs and at the hem with a wide band. At the centre, a band extends downwards (details unclear). The tunic ends above the knees. The folds of the tunic are indicated by oblique, wide grooves. He wears a chlamys over the tunic. It is folded over the chest and is wrapped over the left upper arm and elbow, and it falls below the lower arm and over the cushion in two zigzag-shaped folds. It is fastened at the right shoulder with a round brooch (Colledge classification: h) (details unclear). The folds of the tunic are indicated by diagonal grooves over the arms. He wears loose trousers that are decorated with a central band that extends downwards. The folds of the trousers are indicated by curving grooves. He wears boots.

His right hand rests on his right knee. With the upturned palm of the left hand, he holds a bowl with his fingertips. The bowl has a flat bottom and slightly curving sides. A raised line marks the bottom and the rim of the bowl.

PORTRAIT C: STANDING MALE

The figure is shown frontally. The head is turned to his right. The right arm falls along the side, the left hand is bent in front of the torso.

He has short hair arranged in snail-shell curls. His face is round. The eyebrows are curving. The eyes are almond-shaped, and the eyeballs are blank. The nose is straight and wide. The mouth is small. The chin is pointed. The neck is short and wide.

He wears a ›Parthian-style‹ tunic and ›Parthian-style‹ trousers. The tunic has long, tight-fitting sleeves, and a small, round neckline. It is decorated with a central wide band that extends downwards from the neckline, and another wide band at the lower hem at the knees. The folds of the tunic are indicated by wide, oblique grooves. He wears trousers with the folds indicated by curving grooves. He wears shoes.

In the lowered right hand, he holds a round bowl or patera seen in frontal view. In his left hand, he holds a large rhyton with a ribbed surface. His thumb and the index finger are extended.

BANQUETING RELIEFS

A.D. 123–140

104. BANQUETING RELIEF

DATABASE NUMBER: PM537.
LOCATION: Palmyra, Palmyra Museum, inv. no. unknown.
CONTEXT: South-west necropolis. Hypogeum of Ḥennibel.
ACQUISITION HISTORY: —
MEASUREMENTS: —
MATERIAL: Limestone.
PRESERVATION: The corners and the upper and left sides of the relief are broken off. The surface of the upper edge is chipped. Portrait A: The surface of the face is chipped. Portrait B: The surface of the face is chipped. Portrait C: The forehead, the nose, and the mouth are chipped.
TECHNICAL DESCRIPTION: —
DATE: A.D. 123–140.
REFERENCES: al-Asʿad 2013, 19 f. fig. 8; Krag – Raja 2017, 199 n. 23–25; 201 n. 28; 203 n. 43. 47. 48. 50; 213 cat. 1; Krag 2018, 33 n. 75. 77. 80; 41 n. 142. 143; 66 n. 382; 87 n. 182; 88 n. 190. 195; 240 f. cat. 279.

OBJECT DESCRIPTION

The relief was originally rectangular in shape and depicts a seated female, a standing male, and a reclining male. The reclining figure rests against a round cushion. The cushion is decorated with narrow vertical bands. Curving grooves indicate the fabric of the cushion.

INSCRIPTION

SCRIPT: Palmyrene Aramaic.
LOCATION ON RELIEF: Between standing male and reclining male.
TRANSCRIPTION: ṢLMʾ D[NH] WʾWNʾ | TḤTWH [ʿBD?] | KTBY BR ḤNBL | LḤNBL ʾBWHY | LYQRH | ḤBL.
TRANSLATION: This image and the sarcophagus which is below was made by Kutbaî, son of Ḥennibel, for Ḥennibel his father in his honour alas!

CIS no. —; PAT no. —.

PORTRAIT A: SEATED FEMALE

The body of the figure is shown frontally, the legs are turned to the left. The head appears large. The right arm is bent and held to the chest. The left arm is bent and held to the torso. She sits with her legs set apart. Her left foot is obscured by the feet of the reclining male to her right.

She wears two headdresses: a turban and a veil. The turban is coiled. The veil is heavy and falls back over her right shoulder. It falls over the left shoulder and is wrapped around the left arm. The neck is wide.

She wears a tunic and a himation. The tunic is ankle-length. The himation crosses the chest diagonally from the left shoulder to the right and covers the left breast. It is fastened at the right shoulder with a trapezoidal brooch with possibly an animal head finial (Colledge classification: a) (details unclear). The himation covers the lower body and ends at the shins, revealing the tunic underneath. The folds of the himation are rendered by curving grooves. A large fold runs across the waist.

The right hand holds a fold of the veil. The fingers on the left hand are slightly bent; she is possibly holding a spindle and distaff (details unclear).

PORTRAIT B: STANDING MALE, KUTBAÎ

The figure is shown in frontal view. His head appears large. Both arms are bent and held in front of the torso. The lower body and legs are obscured by the reclining figure to his left.

His hair curls around his head, each lock of hair indicated with incised lines. The ears are protruding, and the helix, tragus, concha, and earlobe are depicted.

He wears a tunic and a himation. The tunic has a wide, round neckline. The folds of the tunic are depicted by curving grooves on the chest. The himation covers most of the body: it is wrapped around the right shoulder and arm, leaving only part of the upper chest and hands free. One fold of the himation crosses the chest diagonally and falls over the left shoulder (>arm-sling< type). The folds of the himation are indicated by diagonal and vertical grooves.

His right hand lightly holds the diagonal fold of the himation, with the index finger extended. He holds an object with his left hand (details unclear).

PORTRAIT C: RECLINING MALE, ḤENNIBEL

The body is shown in frontal view; the head is turned slightly to the left. The head appears large. The arms appear short in relation to the body. The right arm is extended and rests on his raised right knee. The left arm is bent in front of the chest, and rests on a cushion. His right leg is bent. The left leg is slightly bent and rests on the relief ground, obscuring the right foot. The left knee is visible under the drapery.

His hair is arranged in two rows of crescent-shaped curls around his head. The individual strands of hair are indicated with incised lines. His face is oval, and the eyebrows are slightly curving. The eyes are almond-shaped, with thick upper eyelids (details unclear). The ears are large and protruding, and rendered with the tail of the helix and earlobe. The nose has a wide base. The mouth is small with full lips. The chin is square.

He wears a tunic and himation. The tunic has a v-shaped neckline and short, loose sleeves. The right sleeve has a scalloped edge. The folds of the tunic are depicted by oblique grooves on the arm and curving grooves on the body. The himation is folded around his left shoulder and arm, falls along the left side of his body, and is wrapped across the waist. It covers the lower body and legs until the ankles. A folded edge of the himation falls from under the left hand onto the mattress in two zigzag-shaped folds. The folds of the himation are rendered by curving grooves on the legs and vertical grooves on the arm and shoulder.

He rests his right hand on his right knee. His left hand is in front of his chest, and he holds a skyphos. The skyphos has a conical foot, a plain body, and small, looped handles. The left thumb, the little, and the index fingers are extended.

Cat. 104, Pl. 47

A.D. 128–200

HYPOGEUM F

SARCOPHAGI

A.D. 128–150

105. COMPLETE SARCOPHAGUS WITH BANQUETING SCENE AND PORTRAIT BUSTS

DATABASE NUMBER: InSitu058.
LOCATION: Palmyra, in situ.
CONTEXT: South-east necropolis. Hypogeum F, east side of main exedra.
ACQUISITION HISTORY: —
MEASUREMENTS: Lid: Height: 85 cm. Width: 168 cm. Depth: 30 cm. Box: Height: 86 cm. Width: 178 cm. Depth: 20 cm.
MATERIAL: Limestone, yellow/white.
PRESERVATION: Portrait A: The thumb has broken off. Portrait C: The nose is chipped. Portrait D: Small fragments are chipped from his right hand.
TECHNICAL DESCRIPTION: —
DATE: A.D. 128–150.
REFERENCES: Higuchi – Saito 2001, 34 f. pls. 3. 4. 5, 3. 11. 12 appendix 10; Miyashita 2016, 132 fig. 3, 2; Saito 2016, 350 f. fig. 3; Krag 2018, 30 n. 80; 32 n. 63; 66 n. 382; 87 n. 185; 89 n. 199; 105 n. 85. 87; 243 cat. 287; Saito 2018, 191.

OBJECT DESCRIPTION

The sarcophagus lid is rectangular in shape and depicts three reclining male figures. Beneath the figures is a box in the shape of a kline with a male, a female, and a male figure between the kline legs. Above the kline is a mattress. The mattress has two bands decorated with running scrolls with rosettes set between beaded bands. Curving grooves indicate the texture of the fabric. The reclining figures all rest their left arms on cushions. The cushion by the right figure is twisted and folded into itself, creating a depression in the middle. The cushion by the central figure is decorated with a band with a crisscross pattern. The cushion by the left figure is decorated with a band with four-petal rosettes. The left side of the kline is decorated with a fulcrum, where an armless bust of a priest is rendered in a clipeus (portrait G). Next to the bust is an indentation with a four-petal rosette. From it, a lion head protrudes. The central stretcher of the kline is decorated with a rectangular indentation on either end. On each side of these is a square inlay or appliqué (details unclear). The kline has turned legs. They are composed of a plinth, and above is a small, thick torus, a concave quarter, a bell-shaped element, a scotia, a convex neck, a torus, a thick torus, a torus, and above the stretcher is a horizontal, biconvex element.

The sarcophagus is located next to cat. 106 and cat. 107.

SARCOPHAGUS LID

PORTRAIT A: RECLINING MALE

The figure is shown frontally. The arms appear short in relation to the torso. The right arm is bent and held to the torso. The left arm is bent. The legs are not rendered.

His hair is arranged in crescent-shaped curls, brushed from the top of the head and down to the forehead. The individual locks of hair are rendered by incised lines. His face is oval. The eyebrows are curving. The eyes are large and almond-shaped, with thick eyelids. The irises and pupils are rendered by concentric, incised circles. His ears are large and protruding, with the helix, scapha, tragus, and earlobe depicted. The nose is wide, with carved nostrils. The mouth is small, with straight lips. The chin is oval, and the neck is wide.

He wears a tunic and a himation. The tunic has a wide, round neckline. The folds of the tunic are rendered by curving grooves. Over the tunic, he wears a himation. It is wrapped around the left shoulder and arm, covering the left part of the chest, and leaving the hand free. The himation proceeds in a curving fold across his lower torso. The folds of the himation are rendered by oblique and curving grooves.

He is holding a skyphos in his right hand. It has an offset ring base, a straight body, straight rim, and small looped handles. His index and the little finger are extended. His left hand is held downwards, and he lightly holds a fold of the himation.

PORTRAIT B: RECLINING MALE

The figure is shown frontally. The arms appear short in relation to the body. The right arm is extended behind the figure to his right. The left arm is bent. The legs are obscured by the figure to his right.

His hair is arranged in crescent-shaped curls, brushed from the top of the head and down to the forehead. The individual locks of hair are rendered by incised lines. His face is oval. The eyebrows are curving. The eyes are large and almond-shaped, with thick eyelids. The upper eyelids extend beyond the end of the lower ones. The irises and pupils are rendered by concentric, incised circles. His ears are large and protruding, with the helix, scapha, concha, and earlobe depicted. The nose is wide and straight. The mouth is small, with a full lower lip. The chin is prominent, and the neck is wide.

He wears a tunic and a himation. The tunic has a wide, round neckline. The folds of the tunic are rendered by curving grooves. Over the tunic, he wears a himation. It is wrapped around the left shoulder and arm, covering the left part of the chest, and leaving the hand free. The himation proceeds in a curving fold across his lower torso. The folds of the himation are rendered by oblique and curving grooves.

He is holding a skyphos in his left hand. It has an offset ring base, a straight body, straight rim, and small, looped handles. The index and the little fingers are extended. The nails are rendered by fine, incised lines.

PORTRAIT C: RECLINING PRIEST

The figure is shown frontally. The arms appear short in relation to the body. The right arm is extended behind the figure to his right. The left arm is bent. The legs are obscured by the figure to his right.

He wears a plain, high, cylindrical, flat-top headdress divided into three sections by two vertical grooves that cover his hair and most of his forehead: a Palmyrene priestly hat. His face is round. The eyebrows are curving. His eyes are large and almond-shaped, with thick eyelids. The irises and pupils are rendered by concentric, incised circles. The ears are small and protruding, with the helix, scapha, tragus, and the lobe depicted. The mouth is small, with thin lips. The chin prominent and wide. The neck is wide.

He wears a tunic and a himation. The tunic has a wide, round neckline. The folds of the tunic are rendered by curving grooves. Over the tunic, he wears a himation. It is wrapped around the left shoulder and arm, covering the left part of the chest, and leaving the hand free. The himation proceeds in a curving fold across his lower torso. The folds of the himation are rendered by oblique and curving grooves.

He is holding a skyphos in his left hand. It has an offset ring base, a straight body, straight rim, and small, looped handles. His index finger is extended. The nail is rendered by fine, incised lines. He wears a ring with an oval bezel on the left little finger.

SARCOPHAGUS BOX

PORTRAIT D: MALE BUST

The figure is shown frontally. The arms appear short in relation to the body. Both arms are bent and held to the torso.

His hair is arranged in crescent-shaped curls, brushed from the top of the head and down to the forehead. The individual locks of hair are rendered by incised lines. His face is oblong. The eyebrows are curving. The eyes are large and almond-shaped, with thick eyelids. The upper eyelids extend beyond the end of the lower ones. The irises and pupils are rendered by concentric, incised circles. His ears are large and protruding, with the helix, scapha, concha, tragus, and the lobe depicted. The nose is long and straight, and the alae are carved. The mouth is small, with a full lower lip. The chin is oval. The neck is wide.

He wears a tunic and a himation. The tunic has a wide, round neckline and long, wide sleeves. The folds of the tunic are rendered by curving grooves. Over the tunic, he wears a himation. The himation covers most of the body: it is wrapped around the right shoulder and arm, leaving only the upper part of the chest and the hand free. One fold of the himation crosses the chest diagonally and falls over the left shoulder (›arm-sling‹ type). The folds of the himation are rendered by curving, diagonal, and oblique grooves.

With his right hand, he holds the diagonal fold of the himation. With his left hand, he holds two small objects, one composed of two rectangles at an angle, and one thin, rectangular object next to it, possibly a double schedula.

PORTRAIT E: FEMALE BUST

The figure is shown frontally. The arms appear short in relation to the body. Both arms are bent and held to the body.

She wears three headdresses: a headband, a turban, and a veil. The band is placed low on the forehead and is divided into rectangular panels separated by beaded bands. The central panel is decorated with a flower with two lanceolate leaves on either side of the broad stem. The panels on either side are decorated with serrated leaves pointing downwards. The turban is coiled. It is rendered in two layers, with the ends looped into each other creating a knot in the middle. Horizontal grooves indicate the coiling of the fabric. The veil is heavy. It falls over her shoulders and is wrapped around her arms, leaving the hands free. Part of the hair is covered by the headdresses: several strands of hair above the ears are pushed back over the headband and the edge of the turban and disappear under the veil. Two thick, wavy locks of hair fall down her neck and shoulders. The individual strands of hair are indicated by incised lines. Her face is oval. The eyebrows are curving. The eyes are large and almond-shaped, with thick eyelids. The irises and pupils are rendered by concentric, incised circles. The nose is wide, with carved alae and drilled nostrils. Only the earlobes are visible under the headdress, and she wears earrings shaped like a miniature bunch of grapes (Colledge classification: E). The mouth is small, with a full lower lip. The chin is oval, and the neck is long and wide.

She wears a tunic and a himation. The tunic has a wide, round neckline. The folds of the tunic are rendered by curving grooves. The himation crosses the chest diagonally from the left shoulder to the right side and covers the left breast. It is fastened at the shoulder with a triangular brooch with serrated leaves within it and an animal finial (Colledge classification: a). An object is attached to a lace falling from under the brooch. The reversed, P-shaped object has an incised cross on the lower edge and a circular depression on the upper edge. The folds are indicated by vertical and oblique, wide grooves.

The right hand is held to the torso. The thumb, the index, and the middle fingers are extended. The nails are rendered by fine, incised lines. With the left hand, she holds a conical object incised with fine, wavy lines, with a bowl-shaped tip, and a thick, short staff topped by a polygonal mass, with a pattern of oblique, incised lines, and a small cylinder. These are reduced versions of a spindle and a distaff. The left index and the middle finger are extended. She wears two rings: one on her ring and one on her little finger. Each ring is composed of thick hoops.

PORTRAIT F: MALE BUST

The figure is shown frontally. The arms appear short in relation to the body. Both arms are bent and held to the body.

His hair is arranged in thick, crescent-shaped locks around the head, covering the ears. The individual locks of hair are rendered by incised lines. His face is oblong. The eyebrows are curving. The eyes are close-set and almond-shaped, with thick eyelids. The irises and pupils are rendered by concentric, incised circles. The nose is large. The mouth is small, with thin lips. The chin is wide and oval. The neck is wide.

He wears a tunic and a himation. The tunic has a wide, round neckline and long, loose sleeves. The folds of the tunic are rendered by curving grooves. Over the tunic, he wears a himation. The himation covers most of the body: it is wrapped around the right shoulder and arm, leaving only the upper part of the chest and the hand free. One end of the himation crosses the chest diagonally and falls over the left shoulder (›arm-sling‹ type). The folds of the himation are rendered by curving, diagonal, and oblique grooves.

With his right hand, he holds the diagonal fold of the himation. With his left hand, he holds two small, thin, rectangular objects placed next to each other, possibly a double schedula.

PORTRAIT G: ARMLESS BUST OF A PRIEST IN FULCRUM

The figure is shown frontally, rendered in a clipeus.

He wears a plain, high, cylindrical, flat-top headdress divided into three sections by two vertical grooves that covers his hair and most of his forehead: a Palmyrene priestly hat. His face is oval. The eyebrows are slightly curving. The eyeballs are blank. The ears are large and protruding, with the helix rendered. The nose is straight and wide. The mouth is narrow, with thin lips. The chin is oval, and the neck is wide.

He wears a tunic and a chlamys. The tunic has a wide, round neckline. The folds of the tunic are rendered by curving grooves. Over the tunic, he wears a chlamys that falls over both shoulders and covers most of the chest. It is fastened at the right shoulder with a circular brooch with an incised border (Colledge classification: h). A zigzag-shaped fold falls from under the brooch. The folds of the chlamys are indicated by curving and oblique grooves.

106. COMPLETE SARCOPHAGUS WITH BANQUETING SCENE AND PORTRAIT BUSTS

DATABASE NUMBER: InSitu059.
LOCATION: Palmyra, in situ.
CONTEXT: South-east necropolis. Hypogeum F, west side of main exedra.
ACQUISITION HISTORY: —
MEASUREMENTS: Lid: Height: 85 cm. Width: 168 cm. Depth: 30 cm. Box: Height: 86 cm. Width: 178 cm. Depth: 20 cm.
MATERIAL: Limestone, yellow/white.
PRESERVATION: Portraits A and B: The heads are broken off horizontally through the neck. Portrait C: The surface is weathered. The surface of the nose and mouth are chipped. There is a large crack running horizontally across the neck.
TECHNICAL DESCRIPTION: Portrait E: The locks of hair on either side of the neck are undercut by a drill.
DATE: A.D. 128–150.
REFERENCES: Higuchi – Saito 2001, 35 f. pls. 3. 4. 5, 1; 6. 7 appendix 12; Miyashita 2016, 132 fig. 3, 3; Saito 2016, 350 f. fig. 3; Krag 2018, 30 n. 80; 32 n. 63; 66 n. 382; 87 n. 185; 89 n. 199; 98 n. 23; 105 n. 85. n. 87; 244 cat. 288; Saito 2018, 191.

OBJECT DESCRIPTION

The sarcophagus lid is rectangular in shape and depicts two reclining male figures and a reclining priest. Beneath the figures is a box with a male, a female, and a male bust between the kline legs. Above the kline is a mattress. The mattress has two bands, decorated with a running scroll with rosettes set between bands with squares. Curving grooves indicate the texture of the mattress. All the reclining figures rest their left arm on a cushion. The cushion by the right figure is decorated with a narrow band with a vegetal motif (details unclear). The cushion by the central figure is decorated with a running scroll with rosettes. The cushion by the figure to the left is decorated with a running scroll with rosettes. The left side of the kline is decorated with a fulcrum. It has a small armless bust of a male shown in a clipeus (portrait G). From it, a lion head protrudes. The central stretcher of the kline is decorated with a rectangular indentation on either side. These are followed by plain and narrow panels, and then followed by rectangular panels decorated with a floral motif. The kline has turned legs. They are composed of a plinth and above is a small, thick torus, a concave quarter, a bell-shaped element, a scotia, a convex neck, a torus, a thick torus, a torus, and above the stretcher is a horizontal, biconvex element.

The sarcophagus is located next to cat. 105 and cat. 107.

SARCOPHAGUS LID

PORTRAIT A: RECLINING MALE

The figure is shown frontally. The arms appear short in relation to the torso. The right arm is bent and held to the torso. The left arm is bent. The legs are not rendered.

He wears a tunic and a himation. The tunic has a wide, round neckline and long, tight-fitting sleeves. The folds of the tunic are rendered by curving and oblique grooves. Over the tunic, he wears a himation. It is wrapped around his left shoulder and arm, leaving most of the chest and the hand free. The himation proceeds in a curving fold across his abdomen and falls back under his right arm.

He holds a skyphos in his right hand. It has an offset ring base, a straight body, straight rim, and small looped handles. His index finger is extended. The left hand is held downwards. The index and the little finger are extended. He wears a ring on his little finger; a thin hoop with an oval bezel. The nails are rendered by incised lines.

PORTRAIT B: RECLINING MALE

The figure is shown frontally. The arm appears short in relation to the torso. The right arm is extended behind the figure to his right. The left arm is bent. The legs are obscured by the figure to his right.

He wears a tunic and a himation. The tunic has a wide, round neckline. The folds of the tunic are rendered by curving and oblique grooves. Over the tunic, he wears a himation. It is wrapped around his left shoulder and arm, leaving most of the chest and the hand free. The himation proceeds in a curving fold across his abdomen and falls back at his right side.

He holds a skyphos in his left hand. It has an offset ring base, a straight body, straight rim, and small, looped handles.

PORTRAIT C: RECLINING PRIEST

The figure is shown frontally. The arm appears short in relation to the torso. The head appears large. The right arm is extended behind the figure to his right. The left arm is bent. The legs are obscured by the figure to his right.

He wears a plain, high, cylindrical, flat-top headdress divided into three sections by two vertical grooves that covers his hair and most of his forehead: a Palmyrene priestly hat. His face is round. The eyebrows are curving. His eyes are large and almond-shaped with thick eyelids. The irises and pupils are rendered by concentric, incised circles. The ears are small and protruding with the helix, scapha, tragus, and the lobe depicted. The neck is wide.

He wears a tunic and a himation. The tunic has a wide, round neckline. The folds of the tunic are rendered by curving grooves. Over the tunic he wears a himation. It is wrapped around the left shoulder and arm, covering the left part of the chest and leaving the hand free. The himation proceeds in a curving fold across his lower torso. The folds of the himation are rendered by oblique and curving grooves.

He holds a skyphos in his left hand. It has an offset ring base, a straight body, straight rim, and small, looped handles. The index and the little finger are extended.

SARCOPHAGUS BOX

PORTRAIT D: MALE BUST

The figure is shown frontally. The arms appear short in relation to the torso. The head appears large. Both arms are bent to the torso.

His hair is arranged in four large snail-shell curls around the head. His face is oblong. The eyebrows are curving. The eyes are close-set and almond-shaped with thick eyelids. The upper eyelids extend beyond the end of the lower ones. The irises and pupils are indicated by concentric, incised circles. The ears are placed high on the head and are protruding with helix, scapha, tragus, and the lobe depicted. The nose is long with carved alae. The mouth is wide with thin lips. The chin is wide and oval. The neck is wide.

He wears a tunic and a himation. The tunic has a wide, round neckline and long, loose sleeves. The folds of the tunic are rendered by curving grooves. Over the tunic, he wears a himation. It is wrapped around the right shoulder and arm, leaving only the upper part of the chest and the hand free. One end of the himation crosses the chest diagonally and falls over the left shoulder (›arm-sling‹ type). The folds of the himation are rendered by curving, diagonal, and oblique grooves.

With his right hand he holds the diagonal fold of the himation. With his left hand, he holds a half tubular object, possibly a book-roll.

PORTRAIT E: FEMALE BUST

The figure is shown frontally. The arms appear short in relation to the torso. The head appears large. Both arms are bent to the torso.

She wears three headdresses: a headband, a turban, and a veil. The band is placed low on the forehead and is divided into several rectangular panels, separated by beaded bands. The central panel is decorated with a flower with one lanceolate leaf on either side of the broad stem. The panels on either side are decorated with a floral motif (details unclear). The turban is rendered in one layer, indicated by a horizontal groove. The veil is heavy. It falls over her shoulders and is wrapped around her arms, leaving the hands free. The folds of the veil are rendered by vertical and curving grooves. Part of the hair is covered by the headdresses: several strands of hair above the ears are pushed back over the headband and the edge of the turban, and disappear under the veil. Two thick, wavy locks of hair fall down her neck and shoulders. The individual strands of hair are indicated by incised lines. Her face is oval. The eyebrows are arched. The eyes are large and almond-shaped with thick eyelids. The irises and pupils are rendered by concentric, incised circles. The nose is wide with carved alae. Only the earlobes are visible under the headdress and she wears earrings with a single round bead (Colledge classification: J). The mouth is small with a full lower lip. The chin is oval, and the neck is long.

She wears a tunic and a himation. The tunic has a wide, round neckline. The folds of the tunic are rendered by curving grooves. The himation crosses the chest diagonally from the left shoulder to the right side, and covers the left breast. It is fastened at the shoulder with a triangular brooch with an incised border and a rosette finial (Colledge classification: b). A P-shaped key is attached to the brooch by a ribbon. It has a v-shaped incision. The folds of the himation are indicated by vertical and oblique, wide grooves.

The right hand is raised to the chest and she lightly pulls a fold of the veil. With the left hand, she holds a conical object incised with fine, wavy lines, with a pointed tip, and a thick, short staff topped by a polygonal mass with a pattern of oblique, incised lines, and a small cylinder. These are reduced versions of a spindle and a distaff. The index finger is extended. She wears a ring on her little finger; a wide hoop. The nail is rendered by a fine, incised line.

PORTRAIT F: MALE BUST

The figure is shown frontally. The arms appear short in relation to the torso. The head appears large. Both arms are bent to the torso.

The hair is arranged in one row of crescent-shaped locks around the head and covers the upper part of the ear. His face is oval. The eyebrows are curving. The eyes are large and almond-shaped with thick eyelids. The upper eyelids extend beyond the end of the lower ones. The irises and pupils are rendered by concentric, incised circles. Only the earlobes are visible. The nose is large with carved alae. The philtrum is shown over the wide mouth with full lips. The chin is oval, and the neck is long.

He wears a tunic and a himation. The tunic has a wide, round neckline, leaving a part of the upper chest bare. A vertical depression at the neckline indicates the musculature of the chest. The folds of the tunic are rendered by curving and oblique grooves. Over the tunic, he wears a himation. The himation covers most of the body. It is wrapped around the right shoulder and arm, leaving only the upper part of the chest and the hand free. One fold of the himation crosses the chest diagonally and falls over the left shoulder (>arm-sling< type). The folds of the himation are rendered by curving, diagonal, and oblique grooves.

His right hand holds the diagonal fold of the himation. The nail of the thumb is rendered by a fine, incised line. With his left hand, he holds a rectangular object with an incised rectangle at the top, possibly a tablet.

PORTRAIT G: ARMLESS BUST OF A PRIEST IN FULCRUM

The figure is shown frontally, rendered in a clipeus.

He wears a headcloth rendered in two layers by a horizontal groove. At the centre of the cloth, a round medallion is rendered. The cloth covers his hair and the upper part of the ears. His face is oval. The eyebrows are slightly curving. The eyes are large and almond-shaped. The eyeballs are blank. The nose is straight and wide at the base. The mouth is narrow with full lips. The chin is oval, and the neck is wide.

He wears a tunic and a chlamys. The tunic has a wide, round neckline. The folds of the tunic are rendered by curving grooves. Over the tunic, he wears a chlamys that falls over both shoulders, and covers most of the chest. It is fastened at the right shoulder with a circular brooch (Colledge classification: i). A zigzag-shaped fold falls from under the brooch. The folds of the chlamys are indicated by curving and oblique grooves.

107. COMPLETE SARCOPHAGUS WITH BANQUETING SCENE AND PORTRAIT BUSTS

DATABASE NUMBER: InSitu046.
LOCATION: Palmyra, in situ.
CONTEXT: South-east necropolis. Hypogeum F, centre of main exedra.
ACQUISITION HISTORY: —
MEASUREMENTS: Lid: Height: 128 cm. Width: 235 cm. Depth: 40 cm. Box: Height: 53 cm; Width: 185 cm. Depth: 185 cm.
MATERIAL: Limestone, yellow/white.
PRESERVATION: Portrait A: The head is broken off horizontally through the neck. The surface around her chest and around her hands are slightly weathered. A crack runs diagonally below her knees. Portrait B: The head is broken off horizontally through the neck. The left hand is chipped. The surface is weathered. Portrait C: The head is chipped. Portrait D: It is weathered and the left side of the face is chipped. Portrait E: The head is broken off horizontally through the neck. Portrait F: A crack runs horizontally through the neck. The nose is chipped. Portrait I: A small fragment is missing from the right eye.
TECHNICAL DESCRIPTION: —
DATE: A.D. 128–150.
REFERENCES: Colledge 1976a, 247 f. 255 f.; Higuchi – Saito 2001, 31–35 pls. 3. 4. 5, 2; 8–10 appendix 11; Stauffer 2012, 90–95 fig. 4; Wadeson 2014, 50 f. 53 pl. 6a-b; Miyashita 2016, 131 f. figs. 2. 3; Wielgosz-Rondolino 2016a, 74 f. fig. 12; Krag – Raja 2017, 199 n. 24; 204 n. 72. 73; 205 n. 75; 205 n. 84; 206 n. 85. 87; 208 n. 97. 99; 209 n. 100; 210 n. 109. 110; 215 cat. 11; Krag 2018, 32 n. 63; 33 n. 77. n. 80. n. 82–83; 44 n. 174–175; 45 n. 193; 46 n. 194–196; 47 n. 208; 55 n. 238; 65 n. 379; 66 n. 382; 87 n. 180. n. 183; 88 n. 193. n. 195–197; 105 n. 85. n. 87; 243 cat. 286; Saito 2018, 191 fig. 3.

OBJECT DESCRIPTION

The sarcophagus lid is rectangular in shape and depicts a seated female, a standing male, a seated boy, a standing priest, a standing male, and a reclining priest. Beneath these figures is a box in the shape of a kline with two male busts flanked by two female busts between the kline legs. The kline has a mattress decorated with three bands. The central band is decorated with serrated leaves in an opposite arrangement on a stem. The bands on either side are decorated with a running scroll with rosettes, set between beaded bands. Curving grooves indicate the texture of the mattress. The reclining figure is the largest figure on the lid, and he rests his left arm against a cushion. The cushion is decorated with a wide band with a running scroll with rosettes, set between narrow bands with squares. On the left side of the kline, a fulcrum is shown. It is decorated with an armless bust of a male (portrait K). The body of the fulcrum is decorated with a five-petal rosette, and its lower part with the head of a lion. The central stretcher of the kline is decorated with a rectangular indentation on either side. These are followed by plain, narrow panels, then followed by a larger rectangular panel decorated with a floral motif. The kline has turned legs. They are composed of a plinth and above is a small, thick torus, a concave quarter, a bell-shaped element, a scotia, a convex neck, a torus, a thick torus, a torus, and above the stretcher is a horizontal, biconvex element. The seated female is sitting on a cushion in a high-backed chair. The cushion is decorated with a band (details unclear).

The sarcophagus is located next to cat. 105 and cat. 106.

SARCOPHAGUS LID

PORTRAIT A: SEATED FEMALE

The figure is shown frontally. The arms appear short in relation to the body. The arms are bent. The right arm is raised to the neck. The left is held to the torso. Her legs are bent, and the knees are rendered under the drapery. Her feet are pointing forward.

She wears a veil that falls over her shoulders. It is wrapped around her left arm, leaving the hand free.

She wears a tunic and a himation. The tunic has a wide, round neckline and long, tight-fitting sleeves. The folds are indicated by curving, wide grooves. The floor-length himation crosses the chest diagonally from the left shoulder to the right side and covers the left breast. It is fastened at the shoulder with a triangular brooch (Colledge classification: c). The folds are indicated by curving, deep grooves on the upper body, and broad, vertical grooves between the legs. She is wearing round-toe shoes.

The right hand is raised to the neck and she lightly pulls a fold of the veil. With the left hand, she holds a conical object incised with fine, wavy lines, possibly a spindle. The middle finger is extended.

PORTRAIT B: STANDING MALE

The figure is shown frontally. The arms appear short in relation to the body. Both arms are bent and held to the torso. His lower body and legs are obscured by the small figure in front of him.

He wears a tunic and a himation. The tunic has a wide, round neckline. The folds are rendered by curving grooves. Over the tunic, he wears a himation. It is wrapped around his right shoulder and arm, leaving the hand free. One fold of the himation crosses the chest diagonally and falls over the left shoulder (›arm-sling‹ type). The folds of the himation are indicated by diagonal grooves.

With his right hand, he holds lightly the fold of the himation.

PORTRAIT C: SEATED BOY

The figure is shown frontally. The right arm is bent and held to his chest. The left arm is extended in a horizontal line towards the reclining figure. His legs are bent, and the knees point to either side. The feet are crossed.

He wears a ›Parthian-style‹ tunic, ›Parthian-style‹ trousers, and over-trousers. The tunic has a small, round neckline and long, tight-fitting sleeves. The folds of the tunic are rendered by curving and oblique grooves. He wears a plain band belt, knotted at the centre. The trousers are visible at the knees, and they are decorated with a band with a running scroll and rosettes motif. The over-trousers cover the shins and their folds are indicated by wide, curving grooves. He is wearing round-toe shoes.

He holds a bunch of grapes in his right hand. They are gathered in a circular bunch with oblong individual grapes. His left hand lies below the hand of the reclining priest resting on his knee.

PORTRAIT D: STANDING PRIEST

The figure is shown frontally. The head appears large, and the arms appear short in relation to the body. Both arms are bent to the torso. The lower body and legs are obscured by the reclining figure.

He wears a plain, high, cylindrical, flat-top headdress divided into three sections by two vertical grooves that covers his hair and most of his forehead: a Palmyrene priestly hat. His face is square. The eyebrows are slightly curving, rendered as thin ridges. His eyes are close-set and almond-shaped, with thick eyelids. The irises and pupils are indicated by concentric, incised circles. The ears are rendered with the helix, scapha, and concha are depicted. The mouth is small, and the chin is wide. The neck is long.

He wears an undergarment, a ›Parthian-style‹ tunic, and a chlamys. The undergarment has a wide, round neckline. The tunic on top has short, wide sleeves and a wide, round neckline decorated with a line of hollowed-out squares. The folds of the tunic are rendered by curving, wide grooves. Over the tunic, he wears a chlamys that falls over both shoulders and covers most of the chest. The broad upper edge of the chlamys is decorated with a band with a wave-line. The chlamys is fastened at the right shoulder with a circular brooch with incised border (Colledge classification: h). A zigzag-shaped fold falls from under the brooch. The folds of the chlamys are indicated by deep, curving grooves. He also wears a band belt across the lower torso. It has an undecorated strap and a central panel. The strap is divided by a horizontal groove, while the panel is rectangular and decorated with a rosette.

In his right hand, he holds a libation pitcher that has a circular, offset base and a circular rim. The body is ellipse-shaped and tilted to his left side. He is holding a bowl in his left hand. It is circular in shape and decorated with a wide band with a vegetal motif. The thumb, the index, and the middle finger are extended.

PORTRAIT E: STANDING MALE

The figure is shown frontally. The arms appear short in relation to the body. Both arms are bent and held to the torso. The lower part of the torso and legs are obscured by the reclining figure.

He wears a tunic and a himation. The tunic has a wide, round neckline. The folds are rendered by curving grooves. Over the tunic, he wears a himation. It is wrapped around his right shoulder and arm, leaving the hand free. One fold of the himation crosses the chest diagonally and falls over the left shoulder (›arm-sling‹ type). The folds of the himation are indicated by diagonal grooves.

With his right hand, he lightly holds the fold of the himation. With his left hand, he holds a rectangular object, possibly a schedula.

PORTRAIT F: RECLINING PRIEST

Seen in a three-quarter to frontal view. The head appears large. The arms and legs appear shortened in relation to the body. The right arm is slightly bent and rests on his right leg. The left arm is bent and held to the torso. The right leg is bent, and he rests his foot on the mattress. The left leg is bent under the right, with the knee pointing forwards. The lower left leg is obscured by the right leg.

He wears a high, cylindrical, flat-top headdress divided into three sections by two vertical grooves: a Palmyrene priestly hat. A wreath is depicted at the lower part of the headdress. The midribs of the leaves are rendered by incised lines. The leaves point towards the armless bust of a beardless, male figure with a chlamys and a Palmyrene priestly hat. His face is oblong. The eyebrows are curving, rendered by thin ridges. The eyes are almond-shaped, with thick eyelids. The irises and pupils are indicated by concentric, incised circles.

The ears are large and protruding with the helix, scapha, and concha depicted. The mouth is small with a full lower lip. The chin is oval and almost double. The neck is slender with two horizontal grooves.

He wears an undergarment, a ›Parthian-style‹ tunic, a chlamys, ›Parthian-style‹ trousers, and over-trousers. The undergarment is visible high on his chest and it has a wide, round neckline. The folds are rendered by curving grooves. The tunic has a wide, round neckline decorated with a sequence of hollowed-out squares, and long, tight-fitting sleeves. The cuffs of the sleeves are decorated with a running scroll with rosettes set between beaded bands. The tunic ends above his knees and has a lower border decorated with a running scroll with alternating four-petal rosettes and flowers with pointed leaves. The folds of the tunic are rendered by curving and oblique grooves. He wears a plain band belt, knotted at the centre with the ends looped under on either side of the waist. The edges of the laces have fringes. Over the tunic, he wears a chlamys that falls over both shoulders and covers most of the chest. One edge of the chlamys has a border with a running scroll and rosettes pattern, visible on the fold across the chest. It is fastened at the right shoulder with a circular brooch with an incised border (Colledge classification: h). A zigzag-shaped fold falls from under the brooch. A wide fold of the chlamys falls from under the left arm, across the cushion, and along his left side. The folds of the chlamys are rendered by curving and oblique grooves. The trousers are visible at the knees. At the middle, each trouser leg has a wide, decorated band with a running scroll with vines and miniature bunches of grapes set between beaded bands, extending downwards. The over-trousers cover his shins, leaving the knees free. The folds of the over-trousers are rendered by curving and oblique grooves. He also wears shoes with a round toe pointing upwards. At the right thigh, he has an object with a pointed end, a rectangular main body, and a lateral rectangle: a sheathed dagger. Another dagger is shown at the left thigh: depicted with a pointed end, rectangular main body and a lateral rectangle decorated with oblique grooves.

He rests his right hand on his raised right knee. The fingers of the child's left hand are visible above his thumb. The nails are rendered by fine, incised lines. He holds a skyphos in his left hand. It has an offset ring base, a tall, straight body, a straight rim, and small looped handles. The index and the little finger are extended. The nails are rendered by incised lines.

SARCOPHAGUS BOX

PORTRAIT G: FEMALE BUST

The figure is shown frontally. The arms appear short in relation to the torso. The head appears large. Both arms are bent to the torso.

She wears three headdresses: a headband, a turban, and a veil. The band is placed low on the forehead and is divided into a central rectangular panel followed by a beaded line on either side and further followed by narrow, vertical lines with squares on either side. The central panel is decorated with a flower with one serrated leaf on either side of the stem. The panels on either side are decorated with a floral motif (details unclear). The turban is rendered in two layers, indicated by horizontal grooves. The veil is heavy. It falls over her shoulders and is wrapped around her arms, leaving the hands free. The folds of the veil are rendered by vertical and curving grooves. Part of the hair is covered by the headdresses: several strands of hair above the ears are pushed back over the headband and the edge of the turban, and disappear under the veil. Two thick, wavy locks of hair fall down her neck and shoulders. The individual strands of hair are indicated by incised lines. Her face is oval. The eyebrows are curving, rendered as thin ridges. The eyes are large, almond-shaped with thick eyelids. The upper eyelids extend beyond the end of the lower ones. The irises and pupils are rendered by concentric, incised circles. The nose is wide with carved alae. Only the earlobes are visible under the headdress and she wears earrings shaped like a miniature bunch of grapes (Colledge classification: E). The mouth is small with a full lower lip. The chin is oval, and the neck is long with two curving grooves.

She wears a tunic and a himation. The tunic has a wide, round neckline. The folds of the tunic are rendered by curving grooves. The himation crosses the chest diagonally from the left shoulder to the right side, and covers the left breast. It is fastened at the shoulder with a triangular brooch with a serrated leaf within (Colledge classification: i). A P-shaped key is attached to the himation by a ribbon. The folds of the himation are rendered by curving grooves.

The right hand is raised to the chest and she lightly pulls a fold of the veil. The index and the little finger are extended. With the left hand, she holds a conical object incised with fine, wavy lines and a pointed tip, and a thick, short staff topped by a polygonal mass with a pattern of oblique, incised lines, and a small cylinder. These are reduced versions of a spindle and a distaff. The index and the middle finger are extended. She wears two wide hoop rings: one on her ring and one on her little finger. The nails are rendered by fine, incised lines.

PORTRAIT H: BUST OF A PRIEST

The figure is shown frontally. The arms appear short in relation to the body. The head appears large. Both arms are bent to the torso.

He wears a plain, high, cylindrical, flat-top headdress divided into three sections by two vertical grooves: a Palmyrene priestly hat. His face is oval. The eyebrows are curving, rendered as thin ridges. The eyes are large and almond-shaped with thick eyelids. The upper eyelids extend beyond the end of the lower ones. The irises and pupils are rendered by concentric, incised circles. The ears are large and protruding with the helix, scapha, tragus, and concha depicted. The nose is large with carved alae and nostrils. The mouth is small with thin lips. The chin is prominent and oval. The neck is short with two horizontal grooves.

He wears an undergarment, a ›Parthian-style‹ tunic, and a chlamys. The undergarment has a wide, round neckline. The folds of the undergarment are rendered by curving grooves.

The tunic has short, wide sleeves and a wide, round neckline decorated with a band of squares. The folds of the tunic are rendered by curving, wide grooves. Over the tunic, he wears a chlamys that falls over both shoulders, and covers most of the chest. One fold of the chlamys, visible across the chest and on the right shoulder, is decorated with a border with a wave-line. The chlamys is fastened at the right shoulder with a circular brooch with an outer beaded border (Colledge classification: f). A zigzag-shaped fold falls from under the brooch. The folds of the chlamys are indicated by deep grooves.

In his right hand, he holds a libation pitcher that has a circular, offset base and a circular rim. The body is ellipse-shaped, and tilted to his left side. The index finger is extended. He is holding a bowl in his left hand. It is circular in shape and is decorated with a running scroll with rosettes. Two rows of small, grain-like elements are shown in the bowl. The thumb, the index, and the middle finger are extended.

PORTRAIT I: MALE BUST

The figure is shown frontally. The arms appear short in relation to the body. The head appears large. Both arms are bent and held to the torso.

His hair is arranged in s-shaped curls around the head. The individual locks of hair are rendered by incised lines. His face is oblong. The eyebrows are curving, rendered as thin ridges. The eyes are large and almond-shaped with thick eyelids. The upper eyelids extend beyond the ends of the lower ones. The irises and pupils are rendered by concentric, incised circles. His ears are large and protruding with the helix, scapha, concha, and tragus depicted. The nose is long with the alae and nostrils carved. The mouth is small with a full lower lip. The chin is oval. The neck is wide.

He wears a tunic and a himation. The tunic has a wide, round neckline leaving the upper part of the chest free, and long, wide sleeves. The folds of the tunic are rendered by curving grooves. Over the tunic, he wears a himation. The himation covers most of the body: it is wrapped around the right shoulder and arm, leaving only the upper part of the chest and the hand free. One fold of the himation crosses the chest diagonally and falls behind the left shoulder (>arm-sling< type). The folds of the himation are rendered by curving, diagonal, and oblique grooves.

His right hand is clenched around the diagonal fold of the himation. With his left hand, he holds a small, rectangular object with an incised rectangle at the top, possibly a tablet.

PORTRAIT J: FEMALE BUST

The figure is shown frontally. The head is turned slightly to her right. The arms appear short in relation to the body. The right arm is bent and held to the chest. The left arm is bent and held to the torso.

She wears three headdresses: a headband, a turban, and a veil. The headband is placed low on the forehead and is divided into a central rectangular panel followed by three vertical bands on either side. The first band is decorated with a beaded line, then followed by a wave-line, and then followed by a sequence of squares. The central panel is decorated with a flower with serrated leaves. The turban is coiled. It is rendered in two layers. Horizontal grooves indicate the texture of the fabric. The veil is heavy. It falls over her shoulders and is wrapped around her arms, leaving the hands free. The folds of the veil are rendered by vertical and curving grooves. Part of the hair is covered by the headdresses: several strands of hair above the ears are pushed back over the headband and the edge of the turban, and disappear under the veil. Two thick, wavy locks of hair fall down her neck and shoulders. The individual strands of hair are indicated by incised lines. Her face is oval. The eyebrows are curving, rendered as thin ridges. The eyes are large and almond-shaped with thick eyelids. The irises and pupils are rendered by concentric, incised circles. The nose is wide with carved alae and nostrils. Only the earlobes are visible under the headdress and she wears earrings shaped like a miniature bunch of grapes (Colledge classification: E). The mouth is small with thin lips. The chin is oval, and the neck is wide with two curving grooves. She wears three necklaces: one composed of square and oval elements, worn at the base of the neck. One thick twisted chain, worn high on the chest. One composed of round pendants with incised borders linked by beaded elements, worn high on the chest.

She wears a tunic and a himation. The tunic has long, tight-fitting sleeves. A band with serrated leaves in an opposite arrangement on the stem is shown on the right side of the chest. The folds of the tunic are rendered by curving grooves. The himation crosses the chest diagonally from the left shoulder to the right side and covers the left breast. It is fastened at the shoulder with a brooch (details unclear). The folds are indicated by vertical and oblique, wide grooves.

The right hand is raised to the neck. She lightly pulls a fold of the veil. The index and the little finger are extended. With the left hand, she holds a conical object incised with fine, wavy lines, and a bowl-shaped tip, and a thick, short staff topped by a polygonal mass with a pattern of oblique, incised lines, and a small cylinder. These are reduced versions of a spindle and a distaff. Above her left hand, an object, possibly a key, is attached to a ribbon falling from under the brooch. The reversed L-shaped object has an incised cross on the lower edge and a circular depression on the upper edge.

PORTRAIT K: ARMLESS BUST OF A MALE IN FULCRUM

The figure is shown frontally.

His hair is straight, rendered by fine, incised lines. His face is oval. The eyebrows are curving. The eyes are round with thick upper eyelids. The pupils are rendered by punch holes. The ears are large and protruding, with the helix and lobe depicted. The nose is wide and the mouth is narrow with thin lips. The neck is wide.

He wears a tunic and a chlamys. The tunic has a wide, round neckline. The folds of the tunic are rendered by curving and oblique grooves. Over the tunic, he wears a chlamys that falls over both shoulders, and covers most of the chest. It is fastened at the right shoulder with a circular brooch with an incised border (Colledge classification: h). The folds of the chlamys are rendered by curving and oblique grooves.

SARCOPHAGUS RELIEFS

A.D. 170–200

108. COMPLETE SARCOPHAGUS WITH BANQUETING SCENE AND PORTRAIT BUSTS

DATABASE NUMBER: InSitu045.
LOCATION: Palmyra, in situ.
CONTEXT: South-east necropolis. Hypogeum F, east niche.
ACQUISITION HISTORY: —
MEASUREMENTS: —
MATERIAL: Limestone, white/yellow.
PRESERVATION: A large fragment of the relief ground is missing between the portraits. A crack runs vertically through the left side of the object. Portrait D: The right cheek has been restored. Portrait F: The surface is weathered. The surface at the head is chipped.
TECHNICAL DESCRIPTION: There are traces of red pigment in the inscription.
DATE: A.D. 170–200.
REFERENCES: Higuchi – Saito 2001, 24 f. pls. 20–22 appendix 8; Edwell 2008, fig. 2.2; Saito 2016, 350 f. fig. 3; Saito 2018, 191 f. fig. 3. Inscriptions: Higuchi – Saito 2001, 24; Yon 2013, 353 cat. 102.

OBJECT DESCRIPTION

The sarcophagus lid relief is rectangular in shape and depicts a standing male and a reclining male. Beneath these two figures is a box rendered as a kline, with three male busts between the kline legs. On top of the kline is a mattress decorated with three bands. The bands on either side are decorated with a running scroll with rosettes, set between beaded bands, the details of the central band are unclear. Curving grooves indicate the texture of the mattress. The reclining figure rests the left arm against a cushion. The cushion is decorated with a wide band with a crisscross pattern set between beaded bands. On the left side of the kline a fulcrum is shown. It is decorated with a male figure (portrait F) at the lower part and a branch at the body. The upper part of the fulcrum is decorated with a lion head seen frontally. The central stretcher of the kline is decorated with two rectangular indentations at either end. On each side of these are two square inlays or appliqués with a geometric pattern. The legs are turned. They are composed of a reversed bell-shaped element and above is a bell-shaped element, a convex quarter, a thin torus, a ball, a thin torus, and above the stretcher is a torus finial.

INSCRIPTIONS

SCRIPT: Palmyrene Aramaic.
LOCATION: To the left of the right knee of the reclining male.
TRANSCRIPTION: [Ḥ]BL | HR[MS].
TRANSLATION: Alas, Hermes.
INSCRIPTION 2
SCRIPT: Palmyrene Aramaic.
LOCATION: To the left of the right knee of the reclining male.
TRANSCRIPTION: [BR] ḤRY BLḤ BR | MLKW BR ʿGYLW.
TRANSLATION: Freedman of Bôlḥâ son of Malkû son of ʿOgeîlû.
INSCRIPTION 3
SCRIPT: Palmyrene Aramaic.
LOCATION: On the corniche above the niche.
TRANSCRIPTION: GBʾ DY YMYNʾ MDNḤYʾ ʿRṢʾ WṢLMH DY TMLʾ WGWMḤYN TRN MN TMLʾ MDNḤYʾ WMN BNY QRṢY MDNḤ GWMḤYN | ḤMŠʾ BNN | BḤWRTʾ WʿRṢʾ BRYTʾ WṢLMH | WMN RBWʿTʾ DY ʾḤRWHY BʾKSDRʾ GWMḤYN TMNYʾ BM LMNTʾ DH WKTBʾ DY MNTʾ [- - -].
TRANSLATION: The side of the right, eastern couch, and the statue of the platform, and two loculi of the eastern platform, and five loculi of between the east arches in the HWRT, and the exterior couch and the statue, and from the quarter of his others in the exedra eight loculi, by what this part and the part of the inscription …

CIS no. —; PAT no. —.

COMMENT: In the first part, note the word separation. | indicates the different parts of the inscription (sides of the middle pilaster; no text on the inner side of the pilaster).

SARCOPHAGUS LID

PORTRAIT A: STANDING BOY/MALE
The figure is shown frontally. The head appears large in relation to the body. The right arm is held along the body. The left arm is bent and held to the torso. He stands with the legs set slightly apart.

His hair is arranged in thick, crescent-shaped curls around the head, reaching the neck. His face is square. The eyebrows are curving, rendered as thin ridges. The eyes are close-set and almond-shaped with thick upper eyelids. The pupils are indicated by incised circles. The ears are large and protruding with the helix depicted. The nose is large, with the alae and nostrils carved. The cheeks are fleshy and the mouth is wide with a full lower lip. The corners of the mouth are accentuated by an oblique groove. The chin is round and almost double. The neck is wide with one curving groove.

He wears a ›Parthian-style‹ tunic, ›Parthian-style‹ trousers, and over-trousers. The tunic has a wide, round neckline that leaves the upper part of the chest bare and long, tight-fitting sleeves. The tunic ends above the knees and is rendered in a curving line across the thighs. The edge is decorated with a beaded band. The folds of the tunic are rendered by vertical and curving grooves. The trousers are visible above the knees. In the middle, each trouser leg is decorated with a band extending downwards with squares separated by horizontal lines. The over-trousers are fastened on each side of the waist and run in a curving line across the thighs. The upper edges are decorated with a beaded band. The folds of the garment are rendered by curving grooves. He wears round-toe shoes. He wears a plain band belt, knotted at the centre with the ends looped under on either side of the waist.

With the right hand, he lightly pulls the upper edge of the over-trousers. His left hand is clenched around an object, possibly a branch.

PORTRAIT B: RECLINING MALE, HERMES

The figure is shown in frontal to three-quarter view. The head is turned slightly to the right. His arms appear short in relation to the body. The right arm is slightly bent and held along the body. The left arm is bent and held to the chest. The right leg is bent with the foot resting on the mattress. The left leg is bent under the right with the knee pointing outwards. The left foot is obscured by the right leg.

His hair is rendered in three rows of snail-shell curls. The individual strands of hair are rendered by incised lines. His face is square. The eyebrows are curving, rendered as thin ridges. The eyes are close-set and almond-shaped with thick upper eyelids. The irises and pupils are rendered by concentric, incised circles. The ears are large and protruding with the helix, scapha, tragus, and the lobe depicted. The nose is large and straight with the alae and nostrils carved. The mouth is wide with full lips. The chin is oval and almost double. The neck is long. A v-shaped depression indicates the jugular notch.

He wears a >Parthian-style< tunic, a chlamys, >Parthian-style< trousers, and over-trousers. The tunic has a wide, round neckline, which leaves the upper part of the chest bare. The tunic has long, tight-fitting sleeves and the cuffs of the sleeves are decorated with rows of three, oval-shaped leaves, set between beaded bands. The tunic ends above the knees and has a lower border decorated with three, oval-shaped leaves followed by a beaded band. The folds of the tunic are rendered by curving and oblique grooves. He also wears a plain band belt. Over the tunic, he wears a chlamys. It falls over his shoulders and proceeds in a curving line across the chest. One edge of the chlamys has a border decorated with rows of oval-shaped leaves followed by a beaded band. It is fastened at the right shoulder with a circular brooch with an incised border (Colledge classification: h). The folds of the chlamys are rendered by curving grooves. A zigzag-shaped fold falls from under the brooch. The trousers are visible above the knees. At the middle, each trouser leg has a band extending downwards decorated with a running scroll with rosettes and set between beaded bands. The over-trousers have an upper beaded border. The folds of the garments are rendered by curving and oblique folds. He wears plain boots. He wears a plain band belt, knotted at the centre with the tasselled ends looped under on either side of the waist.

He holds a branch downwards with his right hand. With the left hand, he holds a skyphos. It has a concave foot, the body is conical, the lip is rectangular, and it has small loop-handles. The index and little finger are extended.

SARCOPHAGUS BOX

PORTRAIT C: ARMLESS MALE BUST

The figure is shown frontally. The head is turned slightly to his left. The head and eyes appear large.

The hair is arranged in three rows of crescent-shaped curls around the head. The individual locks of hair are rendered by incised lines. His face is square. His eyebrows are curving, rendered by grooves starting from the root of the nose. The eyes are close-set and almond-shaped with thick upper eyelids. The upper eyelids extend beyond the end of the lower ones. The pupils are rendered by incised circles. The ears are large and protruding with the helix, scapha, tragus, and the lobe depicted. The nose is large with carved alae. The cheeks are fleshy, and the chin is round. The neck is wide.

He wears a tunic and a himation. The tunic has a wide, round neckline that leaves part of the upper chest bare. The folds of the tunic are rendered by vertical and curving grooves. Over the tunic, he wears a himation. It is wrapped around his left shoulder and arm. Another fold of the himation comes from his lower right side, falls in a curving fold across the chest, and is folded under the left arm. The folds of the himation are rendered by oblique and curving grooves.

PORTRAIT D: ARMLESS MALE BUST

The figure is shown frontally. The head appears large.

His hair is arranged in three rows of crescent-shaped curls around the head. The direction of the curls alternates each row. His face is square. The eyebrows are curving, rendered as thin ridges. The right eye is placed slightly higher than the left. The eyes are close-set and almond-shaped with thick upper eyelids. The pupils are rendered by incised circles. The ears are large and protruding with the helix, scapha, tragus, and the lobe depicted. The nose is large with the alae carved. The cheeks are fleshy, and the mouth is wide with thin lips. The chin is oval, and the neck is wide.

He wears a tunic and a himation. The tunic has a wide, round neckline that leaves the upper part of the chest bare. A v-shaped depression indicates the jugular notch. The folds of the tunic are rendered by vertical and curving grooves. Over the tunic, he wears a himation. It is wrapped around his left shoulder and arm. Another fold of the himation comes from his lower right side, proceeds in a curving fold across the chest, and is folded under the left arm. The folds of the himation are rendered by oblique and curving grooves.

PORTRAIT E: ARMLESS MALE BUST

The figure is shown frontally. The head appears large.

His hair is arranged in three rows of crescent-shaped curls around the head. The direction of the curls alternates each row. His face is square. The eyebrows are curving, rendered as thin ridges. The right eye is placed slightly higher than the left. The eyes are close-set and almond-shaped with thick upper eyelids. The pupils are rendered by incised circles. The ears are large and protruding with the helix, scapha, tragus, and the lobe depicted. The nose is large with the alae carved. The cheeks are fleshy, and the mouth is wide with thin lips. The chin is oval, and the neck is wide.

He wears a tunic and a himation. The tunic has a wide, round neckline that leaves the upper part of the chest bare. A v-shaped depression indicates the jugular notch. The folds of the tunic are rendered by vertical and curving grooves. Over the tunic, he wears a himation. It is wrapped around his left shoulder and arm. Another fold of the himation comes from his lower right side, proceeds in a curving fold across the chest, and is folded under the left arm. The folds of the himation are rendered by oblique and curving grooves.

PORTRAIT F: MALE BUST IN FULCRUM
The figure is shown frontally.

The figure is tilted slightly to the left and appears not to wear garments. The arms are raised to the height of the head with the palms of the hands turned outwards.

109. COMPLETE SARCOPHAGUS WITH BANQUETING SCENE AND PORTRAIT BUSTS

DATABASE NUMBER: InSitu047.
LOCATION: Palmyra, in situ.
CONTEXT: South-east necropolis. Hypogeum F, west niche.
ACQUISITION HISTORY: —
MEASUREMENTS: —
MATERIAL: Limestone, white/yellow.
PRESERVATION: A large part of the relief ground between the portraits has broken off. The object is weathered.
TECHNICAL DESCRIPTION: —
DATE: A.D. 170–200.
REFERENCES: Higuchi – Saito 2001, 25 f. pls. 23–25 appendix 9; Saito 2016, 350 f. fig. 3; Dirven 2018, 120 fig. 2; Saito 2018, 191 f. fig. 3. Inscription: Higuchi – Saito 2001, 25; Yon 2013, 353 cat. 103.

OBJECT DESCRIPTION

The sarcophagus lid relief is rectangular in shape and depicts a standing boy/male and a reclining male. Beneath these two figures is a box in the shape of a kline, with three male busts between the legs. On top of the kline is a mattress decorated with three vertical bands. The band to the right is decorated with rows of three lanceolate leaves, set between beaded bands. The band in the middle is decorated with a running scroll with rosettes, set between beaded bands. The band to the left is decorated with a crisscross pattern, set between beaded bands. Curving grooves indicate the texture of the fabric. The reclining figure rests the arm against a cushion decorated with a crisscross pattern, set between beaded bands. On the left side of the kline a fulcrum is shown. It is decorated with a small armless bust of a male (portrait F) at the lower end and a branch at the body. The upper part of the fulcrum is decorated with a lion head seen frontally. The central stretcher of the kline is decorated with two rectangular indentations on either end. On each side of these are two square inlays or appliqués with a geometric pattern. The legs are turned. They are composed of a reversed bell-shaped element and above is a bell-shaped element, a convex quarter, a thin torus, a ball, a thin torus, and above the stretcher is a torus finial.

INSCRIPTIONS
INSCRIPTION 1
SCRIPT: Palmyrene Aramaic.
LOCATION ON RELIEF: Next to the head of the standing male.
TRANSCRIPTION: ḤRMS | YLYDH.
TRANSLATION: Hermes - - -.

INSCRIPTION 2
SCRIPT: Palmyrene Aramaic.
LOCATION ON RELIEF: To the left of the reclining male's left knee.
TRANSCRIPTION: ṢLM ḤRMS BR ḤRY | MLKW ʿGYLW | KDLY?.
TRANSLATION: Image of Hermes freedman of ʿOgeîlû son of Malkû KDLY.

CIS no. —; PAT no. —.
COMMENTS: Inscription 1: L.2. Uncertain reading. Inscription 2: L.3. Uncertain reading. The second letter could be R, the third is uncertain.

SARCOPHAGUS LID

PORTRAIT A: STANDING BOY/MALE
The figure is shown frontally. The head appears large in relation to the body. The right arm is held along the body. The left arm is bent and held to the torso. He stands with the legs set slightly apart.

His hair is arranged in thick crescent-shaped curls around the head, reaching the neck. His face is square. The eyebrows are curving, rendered by thin ridges. The eyes are close-set and almond-shaped with thick upper eyelids. The pupils are indicated by punch holes. The ears are large and protruding with the helix depicted. The nose is large, with the alae and nostrils carved. The cheeks are fleshy and the mouth is wide with a full lower lip. The corners of the mouth are accentuated by an oblique groove. The chin is round and almost double. The neck is wide with one curving groove.

He wears a ›Parthian-style‹ tunic, ›Parthian-style‹ trousers, and over-trousers. The tunic has a wide, round neckline decorated with a plain band, which leaves part of the upper chest bare and long, tight-fitting sleeves. The tunic ends above the knees and is rendered in a curving line across the thighs. The edge is decorated with a beaded band. The folds of the tunic are rendered by vertical and curving grooves. The trousers are visible above the knees. In the middle, each trouser leg has a band extending downwards decorated with squares separated by horizontal lines. The over-trousers are fastened on each side of the waist and run in a curving line across the thighs. The upper edges are decorated with a beaded band. The folds of the garment are rendered by curving grooves. He wears a plain band belt, knotted at the centre with the ends looped under on either side of the waist. He wears round-toe shoes.

With the right hand, he lightly pulls the upper edge of the over-trousers. His left hand is clenched around an object, possibly a branch.

PORTRAIT B: RECLINING MALE, HERMES

The figure is shown in frontal to three-quarter view. The head appears large and the legs appear short in relation to the body. The right arm is extended and rests on the right thigh. The left arm is bent and held to the torso. The right leg is bent with the foot resting on the mattress. The left leg is bent under the right leg, with the knee pointing outwards. The left foot is obscured by the right leg.

The hair is arranged in two rows of crescent-shaped curls around the head. The direction of the curls alternates each row. The individual locks of hair are rendered by incised lines. His face is oval. The eyebrows are curving, rendered as thin ridges. The eyes are close-set and almond-shaped with thick upper eyelids. The upper eyelids extend beyond the end of the lower ones. The irises and pupils are rendered by concentric, incised circles. The ears are large and protruding with the helix, scapha, tragus, and the lobe depicted. The nose is large with the alae and nostrils carved. The mouth is wide with a full lower lip. The chin is oval. The neck is slender.

He wears a ›Parthian-style‹ tunic, a chlamys, ›Parthian-style‹ trousers, and over-trousers. The tunic has a wide, round neckline, which leaves part of the upper chest bare. The tunic has long, tight-fitting sleeves, and the cuffs of the sleeves are decorated with rows of three oval-shaped leaves, set between beaded bands. The tunic ends above the knees and has a lower border decorated with three oval-shaped leaves followed by a beaded band. The folds of the tunic are rendered by curving and oblique grooves. Over the tunic, he wears a chlamys. It falls over his shoulders and proceeds in a curving line across the chest. One edge of the chlamys has a border decorated with rows of oval-shaped leaves followed by a beaded band. The chlamys is fastened at the right shoulder with a circular brooch with an incised border (Colledge classification: h). One edge of the chlamys is wrapped around his left wrist and two zigzag-shaped folds proceed downwards, across the cushion and mattress. A zigzag-shaped fold falls from under the brooch. The folds of the chlamys are rendered by

Cat. 109

curving grooves. The trousers are visible above the knees. At the middle, each trouser leg has a band extending downwards and decorated with a running scroll with rosettes set between beaded bands. The over-trousers are visible from the knees. The upper border is decorated with a beaded band. The folds of the garments are rendered by curving and oblique folds. He wears a plain band belt, knotted at the centre with the tasselled ends looped under on either side of the waist. He wears plain round-toe boots.

He holds a branch with his right hand. With the left hand, he holds a skyphos. It has a concave foot, conical body, the lip is rectangular, and it has small loop-handles. The thumb, the index, and the little finger are extended.

SARCOPHAGUS BOX

PORTRAIT C: ARMLESS MALE BUST

The figure is shown frontally. The head and eyes appear large. The head is turned slightly to his left.

The hair is arranged in two rows of crescent-shaped curls around the head. The direction of the curls alternates each row. The individual locks of hair are rendered by incised lines. His face is round. His eyebrows are curving, rendered by curving grooves starting from the root of the nose. The eyes are close-set and almond-shaped with thick upper eyelids. The upper eyelids extend beyond the end of the lower ones. The pupils are rendered by incised circles. The ears are large and protruding with the helix, scapha, tragus, and the lobe depicted. The nose is large with the alae carved. The cheeks are fleshy, and the chin is round. The neck is wide.

He wears a tunic and a himation. The tunic has a wide, round neckline that leaves the upper part of the chest bare. The folds of the tunic are rendered by vertical and curving grooves. Over the tunic, he wears a himation. It is wrapped around his left shoulder and arm. Another fold of the himation comes from his lower right side, proceeds in a curving fold across the chest, and is folded under the left arm. The folds of the himation are rendered by oblique and curving grooves.

PORTRAIT D: ARMLESS MALE BUST

The figure is shown frontally. The head and eyes appear large. The head is turned slightly to his right.

The hair is arranged in three rows of snail-shell curls around the head. His face is round. His eyebrows are curving, rendered by grooves starting from the top of the nose. The eyes are close-set and almond-shaped with thick upper eyelids. The upper eyelids extend beyond the end of the lower ones. The pupils are rendered by incised circles. The ears are large and protruding with the helix, scapha, concha, and the lobe depicted. The nose is large with the alae carved. The cheeks are fleshy, and the chin is round. The neck is wide.

He wears a tunic and a himation. The tunic has a wide, round neckline that leaves an upper part of the chest bare. The folds of the tunic are rendered by vertical and curving grooves. Over the tunic, he wears a himation. It is wrapped around his left shoulder and arm. Another fold of the himation comes from his lower right side, proceeds in a curving fold across the chest, and is folded under the left arm. The folds of the himation are rendered by oblique and curving grooves.

PORTRAIT E: ARMLESS MALE BUST

The figure is shown frontally. The head and eyes appear large. The head is turned slightly to his right.

The hair is arranged in two rows of crescent-shaped curls around the head. The direction of the curls alternates each row. His face is round. His eyebrows are curving, rendered by grooves starting from the root of the nose. The eyes are close-set and almond-shaped with thick upper eyelids. The upper eyelids extend beyond the end of the lower ones. The pupils are rendered by incised circles. The ears are large and protruding with the helix, scapha, concha, and the lobe depicted. The nose is large with the alae carved. The cheeks are fleshy, and the chin is round. The neck is wide.

He wears a tunic and a himation. The tunic has a wide, round neckline that leaves the upper part of the chest bare. The folds of the tunic are rendered by vertical and curving grooves. Over the tunic, he wears a himation. It is wrapped around his left shoulder and arm. Another fold of the himation comes from his lower right side, proceeds in a curving fold across the chest, and is folded under the left arm. The folds of the himation are rendered by oblique and curving grooves.

PORTRAIT F: ARMLESS BUST OF A MALE, IN FULCRUM

The figure is shown frontally, rendered in a clipeus. The head is turned slightly to his left.

His hair is rendered in two rows of round curls around the head and covers the ears. His face is oval. The eyes are close-set. The nose is large and the mouth is small with thin lips. The neck is wide.

He wears a tunic and a chlamys. The tunic has a small, round neckline. The folds of the tunic are rendered by curving grooves. Over the tunic, he wears a chlamys. It falls over his shoulders and covers most of his chest. A round object, possibly a brooch is recognizable at his right shoulder (details unclear). The folds of the chlamys are rendered by curving and oblique grooves.

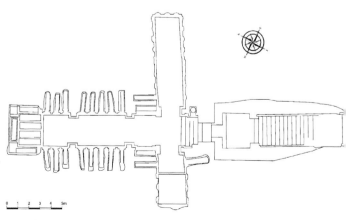

Plan of hypogeum F.

A.D. 130–220

HYPOGEUM OF ŠALAMALLAT

SARCOPHAGI

A.D. 200–220

110. COMPLETE SARCOPHAGUS RELIEF WITH BANQUETING SCENE AND PORTRAIT BUSTS

DATABASE NUMBER: PM395.
LOCATION: Palmyra, Palmyra Museum, inv. no. 1785/6608 and 1786/6609.
CONTEXT: West necropolis. Valley of the Tombs. Hypogeum of Šalamallat, vestibule, south wall. Excavation no. 37.
ACQUISITION HISTORY: —
MEASUREMENTS: Height: 187 cm. Width: 172 cm. Depth: 27 cm.
MATERIAL: Limestone, white/yellow.
PRESERVATION: Portrait A: The nose is chipped. Portrait B: The surface of the left eye is chipped. The head appears to have been reattached. Portrait C: The head appears to have been reattached. Portrait D: The head appears to have been reattached. The thumb and the upper phalanx of the index finger are broken off.
TECHNICAL DESCRIPTION: Portrait C: There are traces of a black pigment in the eyes.
DATE: A.D. 200–220 (Sadurska – Bounni 1994: A.D. 180–220).
REFERENCES: Bounni – Saliby 1957, 34–36 cat. 38 figs. 11. 12; Tanabe 1986, 41 pls. 396–399; Sadurska – Bounni 1994, 170 f. cat. 231 fig. 237; Albertson 2000, 166; Audley-Miller 2016, 557 f. fig. 1; Miyashita 2016, 133 fig. 16; Krag – Raja 2017, 199 n. 24; 204 n. 72. 73; 205 n. 75; 207 n. 94; 208 n. 99; 209 n. 100; 211 n. 117; 217 cat. 20; Krag 2018, 28 n. 9; 32 n. 63; 53 n. 258; 58 n. 300; 59 n. 323. 325; 61 n. 332; 62 n. 349. 351. 353; 66 n. 382. 385; 88 n. 193. 195; 103 n. 74; 390 cat. 842.

OBJECT DESCRIPTION

The sarcophagus lid is rectangular in shape and depicts a seated female, a standing male, a reclining priest, and a reclining male. Beneath these figures is a box in the shape of a kline with four busts between the kline legs: a female, two males, and a female. Above the kline are two mattresses. The thin mattress at the top is decorated with an intersecting lozenges pattern with flowers in the lozenges. The lower mattress has three bands decorated with vegetal motifs (details unclear). Curving grooves indicate the texture of the mattress. The reclining figure to the right rests the arm against two cushions. The upper cushion is decorated with a band with a running scroll with rosettes. The cushion beneath is decorated with four-petal flowers in squares. The other reclining figure rests the left arm against two cushions. They are decorated with a wide band with floral motifs. On the left side of the kline, a fulcrum is shown. The fulcrum is decorated with a small armless bust of a male rendered in a clipeus (portrait I). A head of a horse protrudes from the fulcrum. The stretcher of the kline is decorated. The central part is divided into two sections by a horizontal thin line. The upper section is decorated with a crisscross pattern and the lower with a tongues pattern. On either side of the stretcher is a rectangular indentation decorated with a wave pattern. On either side of these are two square inlays or appliqués (details unclear). The kline legs are turned. They are composed of a plinth, and above is a concave quarter, a reversed bell-shaped element, a scotia, a ball, a torus, and above the stretcher is a biconical finial. All elements are decorated with a tongues pattern, rendered diagonally on the ball.

SARCOPHAGUS LID

PORTRAIT A: SEATED FEMALE

The figure is shown frontally. The head is turned slightly to her left. The right arm is bent and raised to the neck. The left is bent and rests on her left thigh. Her legs are bent with the knees rendered under the drapery. The left foot is obscured by the foot of the reclining figure to her left.

She wears three headdresses: a headband, a turban, and a veil. The band is placed high on the forehead and divided into rectangular panels separated by vertical beaded bands. The central panel is decorated with a rosette. The outer panels are decorated with a crisscross pattern. The turban is coiled. It is rendered in three twisting layers with horizontal and oblique grooves indicating the coiling of the fabric. The veil is heavy. It falls over the shoulders and is wrapped around her left arm. It falls over the back of her right shoulder, is wrapped around her right elbow, and proceeds in a wide fold over her right thigh. Part of the hair is covered by the headdresses: several strands of hair above the ears are pushed back over the headband and the edge of the turban and disappear under the veil. The individual locks of hair are rendered by fine, incised lines. Her face is oval. The eyebrows are curving, rendered by thin ridges. The eyes are almond-shaped, with thick eyelids. The upper eyelids extend beyond the end of the lower ones. The irises and the pupils are indicated by concentric, incised circles. The nose is straight with carved nostrils. Only the earlobes are visible under the hair. She is wearing dumbbell-shaped earrings (Colledge classification: H). The cheeks are fleshy, and the mouth is large with full lips. The chin is pointed, and the neck is slender. She wears one necklace composed of small, round beads at the base of the neck.

She wears a tunic and a himation. The tunic has a small, round neckline and wide sleeves ending at the elbows. The folds of the tunic are rendered by curving grooves. The ankle-length himation crosses the chest diagonally from the left shoulder to the right side, and covers the left breast, lower body, and legs. It is fastened at the left shoulder with a circular brooch with a geometrical outer border (Colledge classification: i). The outer border is a polygon with curving sides meeting in flat ends with round elements between the curving sides. The inner oval of the brooch has a beaded border. The folds are indicated by vertical and oblique, wide grooves.

She holds a fold of the veil with her right hand. With the left hand, she holds the lower part of the veil, crossing her thigh. A zigzag-shaped fold falls from under her hand. She wears a ring on her left little finger. It is composed of a wide hoop divided into three sections by incised lines.

PORTRAIT B: STANDING MALE

The figure is shown frontally. The arms appear short in relation to the body. The right arm is bent and held to the chest. The left arm is bent and held to the body. The legs are obscured by the reclining figure to his left.

His hair is arranged in three rows of snail-shell curls around the head. His face is oval. The eyebrows are curving, depicted by thin ridges. The eyes are close-set and almond-shaped with thick eyelids. The irises are rendered by incised circles. The ears are protruding with the helix, scapha, and lobe depicted. The nose is straight. The mouth is small with a full lower lip. The cheeks are fleshy, and the chin is round. The neck is wide.

He wears a tunic and a himation. The tunic has a small, v-shaped neckline. The folds of the tunic are rendered by angular grooves. Over the tunic, he wears a himation. The himation covers most of the body. It is wrapped around the right shoulder and arm, leaving only part of the chest and the hand free. One end of the himation crosses the chest diagonally and falls over the left shoulder (›arm-sling‹ type). The part of the himation that crosses the chest is decorated with a pleated band. The folds of the himation are indicated by diagonal grooves.

With his right hand, he lightly holds the diagonal fold of the himation. With his left hand he holds a fold of the himation. The index and the little finger are extended.

PORTRAIT C: RECLINING PRIEST

The figure is shown in frontal to three-quarter view. The body appears large. The head appears small in relation to the body. The right arm is bent and rests on his right thigh. The left is bent and held to the torso. His right leg is bent, and his foot is resting on the mattress. The left leg is bent under the right leg with the knee pointing forwards. The lower left leg is obscured by the right foot.

He wears a high, cylindrical, flat-top headdress divided into three sections by two vertical grooves: a Palmyrene priestly hat. A wreath is depicted at the lower part of the headdress. It has three rows of leaves pointing towards the armless bust of a beardless, male figure. The midribs of the leaves are incised. His face is oval. The eyebrows are curving, depicted by thin ridges. The eyes are close-set and almond-shaped with thick eyelids. The upper eyelids extend beyond the end of the lower ones. The irises are painted. The nose is straight and wide at the tip, with the alae carved. The ears are small with the helix and concha depicted. The mouth is large with a full lower lip. The chin is wide, and the neck is slender. The jugular notch is indicated by a v-shaped depression.

He wears a tunic and a himation. The tunic has a wide, v-shaped neckline and short, wide sleeves. The folds of the tunic are rendered by oblique and curving grooves. Over the tunic, he wears a himation. It is wrapped around his left shoulder and arm, leaving the hand free. A wide fold of the himation falls across the cushions and the mattress. It divides into two zigzag-shaped folds with each end tied into a knot. A wide, curving fold of the himation crosses the hips, covers his legs, and falls back at his right side. The folds of the himation are rendered by oblique and curving grooves. He wears a pointed boot. The laces are rendered by fine, incised lines and knotted at the centre.

He holds an oval pinecone with his right hand. The outline of the individual scales of the pinecone are rendered by incised lines. With the upturned palm of the left hand, he holds a circular bowl in front of the chest with his fingertips. The bowl is decorated with hollowed-out lozenges. The nails are rendered by fine, incised lines. He wears a bracelet at the wrist (details unclear).

PORTRAIT D: RECLINING MALE

The figure is shown frontally. The right arm is extended behind the reclining figure to his right. The left arm is bent and held to the torso. His legs are extended behind the reclining figure to his right.

His hair is arranged in s-shaped curls around the head. The individual strands of hair are rendered by incised lines. He wears a wreath high on the forehead with the leaves pointing towards a central armless bust. His face is oval. The eyebrows are curving, depicted as thin ridges. The eyes are close-set and almond-shaped with thick eyelids. The upper eyelids extend beyond the end of the lower ones. The pupils are rendered by incised circles. The ears are large and protruding with the helix, scapha, and lobe depicted. The nose is thin with the alae carved. He has a beard that starts from the temples and covers the cheeks and the chin. The facial hair is rendered by small, s-shaped curls arranged in rows. The moustache is rendered with narrow, oblique, incised lines: they are centred over the philtrum and curve downwards where they are twisted into a small knot on either side. The mouth is small with a full lower lip. The chin is wide, and the neck is wide.

He wears a tunic and a himation. The tunic has a wide, v-shaped neckline. The jugular notch is indicated by a v-shaped depression. The folds of the tunic are rendered by curving grooves. Over the tunic, he wears a himation. It is wrapped around his left shoulder and arm, leaving the hand free. Two s-shaped folds fall from under his arm and over the cushions. The folds of the himation are rendered by oblique and curving grooves.

With the upturned palm of the left hand, he holds a circular bowl in front of the chest with his fingertips. The bowl is decorated with hollowed-out lozenges. The nails are rendered by fine, incised lines. He wears a plain hoop bracelet around his left wrist.

SARCOPHAGUS BOX

PORTRAIT E: ARMLESS FEMALE BUST

The figure is shown frontally.

Cat. 110

She wears three headdresses: a headband, a turban, and a veil. The decorated band is placed low on her forehead (details unclear). The turban is coiled. It is rendered in two twisting layers with horizontal and oblique grooves indicating the coiling of the fabric. The veil is heavy. It falls from the right shoulder in a curving fold across the chest and back over her left shoulder. Part of the hair is covered by the headdresses: several strands of hair above the ears are pushed back over the headband and disappear under the veil. Her face is oval. The eyebrows are curving. The eyes are small and almond-shaped. The irises are indicated (details unclear). The nose is straight and wide at the base. The earlobes are visible under the hair and she appears to wear dumbbell-shaped earrings (Colledge classification: H). The mouth is small and the chin is wide.

She wears a tunic. The folds of the tunic are rendered by oblique and curving grooves.

PORTRAIT F: ARMLESS MALE BUST

The figure is shown frontally. The head is turned slightly to his left.

The hair is arranged in two rows of snail-shell curls around the head. His face is oval. The eyebrows are curving. The eyes are almond-shaped. The eyeballs appear blank. The nose is small, and the mouth is small. The chin is wide.

He wears a tunic and a himation. The tunic has a wide, v-shaped neckline. The folds of the tunic are rendered by vertical and curving grooves. Over the tunic, he wears a himation. It is wrapped around his left shoulder and covers only a part of the chest. The folds of the himation are rendered by oblique and curving grooves.

PORTRAIT G: ARMLESS MALE BUST

The figure is shown frontally.

The hair is arranged in rows of snail-shell curls around the head. His face is oval. The eyebrows are curving. The eyes are almond-shaped, with thick eyelids. The eyeballs appear blank. The nose is straight and wide at the base. The mouth is small. The chin is wide.

He wears a tunic and a himation. The tunic has a wide, v-shaped neckline. The folds of the tunic are rendered by vertical and curving grooves. Over the tunic, he wears a himation. It is wrapped around his left shoulder and covers only a part of the chest. The folds of the himation are rendered by oblique and curving grooves.

PORTRAIT H: ARMLESS FEMALE BUST

The figure is shown frontally.

She wears three headdresses: a headband, a turban, and a veil. The band is placed low on the forehead and is divided into rectangular decorated panels separated by vertical, beaded lines. The central panel is further divided into four sections by a vertical and horizontal line. Each section is decorated with a serrated leaf. The outer panels are decorated with a crisscross pattern. The turban is coiled. It is rendered in three twisting layers with horizontal and oblique grooves indicating the coiling of the fabric. The veil is heavy with a scalloped edge. It falls from the right shoulder in a curving fold across the chest and back over her left shoulder. Part of the hair is covered by the headdresses: several strands of hair above the ears are pushed back over the headband and disappear under the veil. The individual strands of hair are indicated by incised lines. Her face is oval. The eyebrows are curving, depicted as thin ridges. The eyes are close-set and almond-shaped with thick upper eyelids. The eyeballs appear blank. Only the earlobes are visible under the headdress and she is wearing dumbbell-shaped earrings (Colledge classification: H). The nose is large, with carved alae. The chin is wide. The neck is slender. At the base of the neck, she wears a necklace composed of a string with round beads.

She wears a tunic with a small, round neckline. The folds of the tunic are rendered by curving grooves.

PORTRAIT I: ARMLESS MALE BUST IN FULCRUM

The figure is shown frontally, rendered in a clipeus.

BOX RELIEFS

A.D. 130–150

111. SARCOPHAGUS BOX RELIEF WITH PORTRAIT BUSTS

DATABASE NUMBER: PM382.
LOCATION: Palmyra, Palmyra Museum, inv. no. 1780/6603.
CONTEXT: West necropolis. Valley of the Tombs. Hypogeum of Šalamallat, vestibule, north wall, under sarcophagus box relief cat. 98. Excavation no. 34.
ACQUISITION HISTORY: —
MEASUREMENTS: Height: 55 cm. Width: 93 cm. Depth: 11 cm.
MATERIAL: Limestone.
PRESERVATION: The upper right corner, a small part at the top centre, and the lower left side of the relief are broken off. The lower side of the relief, as well as parts of the clipeus around the female bust are lightly chipped.
TECHNICAL DESCRIPTION: The finish is quite smooth with light tool marks visible.
DATE: A.D. 130–150 (Sadurska – Bounni 1994: A.D. 130–160).
REFERENCES: Ingholt Archives, PS 1281/1282; Bounni – Saliby 1957, 37 fig. 10; Tanabe 1986, 45 pl. 472; Sadurska – Bounni 1994, 169 cat. 228 fig. 226; Krag – Raja 2017, 199 n. 24; 204 n. 72. 73; 207 n. 95; 208 n. 98; 209 n. 102; 221 cat. 47; Krag 2018, 32 n. 63; 47 n. 214; 51 n. 241; 98 n. 23; 103 n. 74; 111 n. 8; 245 cat. 293.

OBJECT DESCRIPTION

The sarcophagus box relief is rectangular in shape and depicts three busts in clipei: two large busts of a priest and a female, and a smaller bust of a priest between the two. The clipei are carved in low relief and formed by six concentric grooves. Below the busts is a projecting plinth.

Cat. 111

PORTRAIT A: ARMLESS BUST OF PRIEST

The figure is shown frontally.

He wears low on the forehead a tall, cylindrical, flat-top headdress divided into three sections by two vertical grooves: a Palmyrene priestly hat. A wreath is depicted at the lower part of the headdress. It has three rows of narrow leaves pointing towards the armless bust of a male figure with short hair. A narrow, horizontal band at the bottom of the headdress suggests a liner. His face is triangular. The eyebrows are low and curving, indicated by incised lines. The eyes are wide-set and almond-shaped with thick eyelids. The irises are indicated by incised circles. The ears are small and protruding, with the helix indicated. The nose is thin and straight. The mouth is small with thin lips. The chin is pointed. The neck is slender with two curving grooves.

He wears a tunic and a chlamys. The tunic has a small, scalloped neckline and short, wide sleeves. The folds of the tunic are indicated by oblique grooves in the area of the arms. He wears a chlamys over the tunic. It covers most of the chest and falls over the left shoulder. It is fastened at the right shoulder with a circular brooch enclosing a hexagon (Colledge classification: e). A zigzag-shaped fold falls down from under the brooch. The folds of the chlamys are indicated by wide, curving grooves.

PORTRAIT B: ARMLESS BUST OF PRIEST

The figure is shown frontally. The head is turned to his left.

He wears low on the forehead a tall, cylindrical, flat-top headdress divided into three sections by two vertical grooves: a Palmyrene priestly hat. A narrow, horizontal band at the bottom of the headdress suggests a liner. His face is round. The eyebrows are low and curving. The eyes are large, and the irises are indicated by incised circles. The ears are protruding, with helix indicated. The nose is wide and straight. The mouth is small. The neck is short and wide.

He wears a tunic and a chlamys. The tunic has a wide, v-shaped neckline and short, wide sleeves. The folds of the tunic are indicated by oblique grooves in the area of the arms. He wears a chlamys over the tunic. It covers most of the chest and falls over the left shoulder. It is fastened at the right shoulder with a circular brooch (details unclear). A zigzag-shaped fold falls down from under the brooch. The folds of the chlamys are indicated by wide, curving grooves.

PORTRAIT C: ARMLESS FEMALE BUST

The figure is shown frontally. The head is turned slightly to her left.

She wears three headdresses: a headband, a turban, and a veil. The headband is decorated with rectangular panels with floral decoration. The turban is coiled. It is rendered in a single layer and oblique, incised lines indicate the coiling of the fabric. The veil has a scalloped edge. The veil falls over the shoulders, crosses the chest in a curving fold, and falls behind the left shoulder. Most of the hair is covered by the headdresses, except for several strands pushed back over the ears, and a lock of hair on either side of the neck. Her face is round. The eyebrows are curving, indicated by incised lines. The eyes are large and round with thick eyelids. The irises are indicated by incised circles. The earlobes are visible. She wears earrings shaped like a miniature bunch of grapes (Colledge classification: E). The nose is long with a wide base. The mouth is wide with thin lips. The chin is square, with a cleft. The neck is short and wide. She wears a necklace composed of small, round beads at the middle of the neck (choker), and one composed of alternating large, round beads and smaller beaded elements at the base of the neck.

She wears a tunic. The folds of the tunic are indicated by angular grooves in the area of the upper chest, oblique grooves over the arms, and oblique and curving grooves in the area of the breasts.

112. SARCOPHAGUS BOX RELIEF WITH PORTRAIT BUSTS

DATABASE NUMBER: PM332.
LOCATION: Palmyra, Palmyra Museum, inv. no. 1776/6602.
CONTEXT: West necropolis. Valley of the Tombs. Hypogeum of Šalamallat, vestibule, north wall. Excavation no. 33.
ACQUISITION HISTORY: —
MEASUREMENTS: Height: 57 cm. Width: 96 cm. Depth: 9 cm.
MATERIAL: Limestone.
PRESERVATION: The top left corner is broken off. Two cracks run vertically between the busts. Portrait A: There may be a repair on the headdress. Portrait C: There is some surface damage at the top right of the head.
TECHNICAL DESCRIPTION: The background is fairly smooth with tool marks visible. Portrait A: The finish is smooth.
DATE: A.D. 130–150 (Sadurska – Bounni 1994: A.D. 130–160).
REFERENCES: Bounni – Saliby 1957, 36 f.; Tanabe 1986, 45 pl. 473; Sadurska – Bounni 1994, 169 cat. 227 fig. 225; Krag – Raja 2017, 199 n. 24; 204 n. 72. 73; 207 n. 95; 208 n. 98; 209 n. 102; 221 cat. 48; Krag 2018, 32 n. 63; 47 n. 214; 51 n. 240–241; 98 n. 23; 103 n. 74; 246 cat. 294.

OBJECT DESCRIPTION

The sarcophagus box relief is rectangular in shape and depicts three armless busts in clipei: two large busts of a priest and a female, and a smaller bust of a priest between the two. The clipei are carved in low relief and formed by six concentric grooves. Below the busts is a projecting plinth.

PORTRAIT A: ARMLESS BUST OF PRIEST

The figure is shown frontally.

He wears low on the forehead a tall, cylindrical, flat-top headdress divided into three sections by two vertical grooves: a Palmyrene priestly hat. A wreath is depicted at the lower part of the headdress. It has three rows of narrow leaves pointing towards a central object (rosette?). His face is triangular. The eyebrows are low and curving. The eyes are wide-set and almond-shaped with thick eyelids. The irises are indicated by incised circles. The ears are large and protruding, with helix, scapha, and lobe indicated. The nose is thin and straight. The mouth is wide with thin lips. The chin is pointed. The neck is slender.

He wears a tunic and a chlamys. The tunic has a small, scalloped neckline and wide, short sleeves. The folds of the tunic are indicated by oblique grooves in the area of the arms. He wears a chlamys over the tunic. It covers most of the chest and falls over the left shoulder. It is fastened at the right shoulder with a circular brooch enclosing a hexagon (Colledge classification: e). A zigzag-shaped fold falls down from under the brooch.

PORTRAIT B: ARMLESS BUST OF PRIEST

The figure is shown frontally.

He wears low on the forehead a tall, cylindrical, flat-top headdress divided into three sections by two vertical grooves:

a Palmyrene priestly hat. A wreath is depicted at the lower part of the headdress. It has three rows of leaves pointing towards a central object (details unclear). His face is triangular. The eyebrows are low and curving. The eyes are wide-set and almond-shaped, with thick eyelids. The irises are indicated by incised circles. The ears are large and protruding, with helix, scapha, and lobe indicated. The nose is wide and straight. The mouth is small with full lips. The chin is pointed. The neck is wide and has horizontal grooves.

He wears a tunic and a chlamys. The tunic has a wide, scalloped neckline and short, wide sleeves. The folds of the tunic are indicated by oblique grooves in the area of the arms. He wears a chlamys over the tunic. It covers most of the chest and falls over the left shoulder. It is fastened at the right shoulder with a circular brooch (details unclear). A zigzag-shaped fold falls down from under the brooch.

PORTRAIT C: ARMLESS FEMALE BUST
The figure is shown frontally.

She wears three headdresses: a headband, a turban, and a veil. The headband is decorated with a floral motif (details unclear). The turban is coiled. It is rendered in a single layer and oblique, incised lines indicate the coiling of the fabric. The veil has a scalloped edge. It falls over the right shoulder, crosses the chest in a curving fold, and falls behind the left shoulder. Most of the hair is covered by the headdresses, except for several strands pushed back over the ears, and a lock of hair on either side of the neck. Her face is oval. The eyebrows are curving, rendered by incised lines starting from the root of the nose. The eyes are large, wide-set, and almond-shaped with thick eyelids. The irises are indicated by incised circles. The earlobes are visible. She wears earrings in the shape of a miniature bunch of grapes (Colledge classification: E). The nose is short and wide. The mouth is wide with thin lips. The chin is square, with a cleft. The neck is short and wide. She wears a necklace composed of small, round beads with a crescent-shaped pendant suspended from the centre at the middle of the neck (choker), and another composed of alternating large, round beads and smaller beaded elements at the base of the neck.

She wears a tunic. The folds of the tunic are indicated by v-shaped grooves in the area of the upper chest, oblique grooves over the arms, and oblique and curving grooves in the area of the breasts.

Cat. 112

HEADS: FEMALES

21–30 CM

113. FEMALE HEAD

DATABASE NUMBER: PM380.
LOCATION: Palmyra, Palmyra Museum, inv. no. 1749/6573. Excavation no. 35.
CONTEXT: West necropolis. Valley of the Tombs. Hypogeum of Šalamallat, staircase.
ACQUISITION HISTORY: —
MEASUREMENTS: Height: 30 cm. Width: 22 cm. Depth: 18 cm.
MATERIAL: Limestone, white.
PRESERVATION: The background is broken off. The lower part of the figure is broken off at the neck. The lower left edge of the veil is broken off. The top of the veil and of the turban are chipped. The nose and most of the mouth are broken off.
TECHNICAL DESCRIPTION: —
DATE: A.D. 170–200.
REFERENCES: Bounni – Saliby 1957, 52 cat. 34; Sadurska – Bounni 1994, 169 f. cat. 229 fig. 238; Krag 2018, 293 cat. 470.

OBJECT DESCRIPTION
The object depicts a female head.

PORTRAIT
The figure is shown frontally.
She wears three headdresses: a headband, a turban, and a veil. The headband is placed and is divided into rectangular, undecorated panels by thick, undecorated bands. The turban is coiled and rendered in one layer. The folds are indicated by oblique grooves. The veil is heavy with a scalloped edge. It falls over the back of the head. Part of the hair is covered by the headdress: several strands of hair above the ears are brushed back over the headband and the edge of the turban and disappear under the veil. The individual strands of hair are indicated by incised lines. Her face is round. The eyebrows are curving, rendered by thin ridges. The eyes are close-set, almond-shaped, with thick, upper eyelids. The upper eyelids extend beyond the end of the lower ones. The irises are indicated by incised circles and the pupils by punch holes. Only the earlobes are visible under the hair. She wears earrings composed of two round beads joined by a calyx-shaped element (Colledge classification: L). The nose is straight with incised alae. The mouth is small with full lips. The chin is square. The neck is long and slender with three curving grooves.

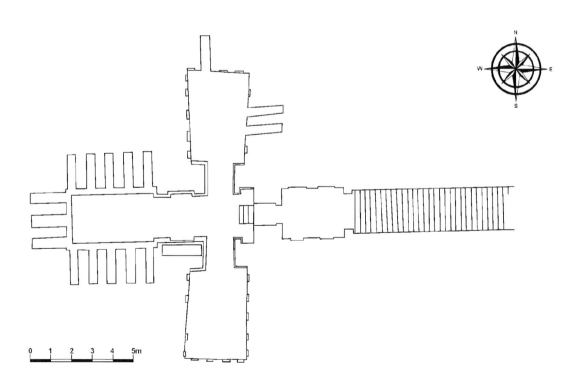

Plan of the hypogeum of Šalamallat (Sadurska – Bounni 1994, pl. 13).

A.D. 131–240

HYPOGEUM OF ZABD'ATEH AND MOQÎMÛ

SARCOPHAGUS BOXES

A.D. 200–240

114. SARCOPHAGUS BOX RELIEF WITH PORTRAIT BUSTS

DATABASE NUMBER: PM319.
LOCATION: Palmyra, Palmyra Museum, inv. no. unknown.
CONTEXT: South-east necropolis. Hypogeum of Zabd'ateh and Moqîmû.
ACQUISITION HISTORY: —
MEASUREMENTS: Height: 75 cm. Width: 170 cm. Depth: 30 cm.
MATERIAL: Limestone.
PRESERVATION: The left, right, and bottom edges of the relief are heavily chipped. There are multiple scratches on the relief background and the portraits. Portrait A: Multiple scratches on the surface. The right side of the face, the right eyebrow, nose, cheek, and the chin are chipped. Portrait B: Multiple scratches on the surface. The left side of the face, nose, and the upper lip are chipped. Portrait C: Multiple scratches on the surface. The nose and part of the chin are broken off.
TECHNICAL DESCRIPTION: —
DATE: A.D. 200–240 (Tanabe 1986: A.D. 200–250).

REFERENCES: Tanabe 1986, 42 f. pl. 427; Krag 2018, 32 n. 63; 53 n. 258; 58 n. 300. 304; 59 n. 323; 62 n. 349; 103 n. 74; 399 cat. 867.

OBJECT DESCRIPTION

The sarcophagus relief box is rectangular in shape and is rendered as a kline. Three busts in clipei are depicted between the kline legs: two busts of priests on either side of a female bust. Above the kline is a mattress decorated by three wide bands with floral motifs. Curving grooves indicate the texture of the fabric. There is a fulcrum on the left side of the kline with a bust of a priest (portrait D). The stretcher has a long, rectangular panel that is framed by two rectangular panels on either side. The central long panel is decorated: the upper section of the central panel has diagonal, incised lines that continue out to the left and right from the centre, the lower section has a tongue or palm leaf motif. The legs are turned. They are composed of a plinth, and above is a convex quarter, a reversed bell-shaped element, a convex quarter, a long concave quarter, a torus, a ball, a torus, and above the stretcher is a biconical finial. All elements are decorated with a tongues pattern, rendered diagonally on the ball.

PORTRAIT A: ARMLESS BUST OF PRIEST

The figure is shown frontally. The head appears large in relation to the body.

He wears low on the forehead a tall, cylindrical, flat-top headdress, divided into three sections by two vertical grooves: a Palmyrene priestly hat. A wreath is depicted at the lower

Cat. 114, Pl. 48

part of the headdress. It has three rows of leaves pointing towards a central decoration (details unclear). A horizontal line at the bottom of the headdress suggests a liner. His face is square. The eyebrows are low and curving. The eyes are wide-set and almond-shaped with thick upper eyelids. The irises are indicated by incised circles. The ears are large and protruding with the helix and scapha depicted. The neck is short and wide.

He wears a tunic and a chlamys. The folds of the tunic are indicated by wide, oblique grooves over the arms. The chlamys covers most of the chest. It is fastened at the right shoulder with a brooch (details unclear). A small zigzag-shaped fold falls under the brooch.

PORTRAIT B: ARMLESS FEMALE BUST

The figure is shown frontally. The head appears large in relation to the body.

She wears three headdresses: a headband, a turban, and a veil. The headband is placed high on the forehead and is undecorated. Over the headband, she wears a coiled turban. The layers of fabric are indicated by wide, curving grooves. The veil is heavy and has a scalloped edge. It falls over both shoulders, crosses the chest in a curving fold, and back over the left shoulder. She wears a head-chain composed of round elements joined by beaded elements: it is attached under the centre of the headband and falls to either side of the forehead. The headdresses cover part of the hair: several strands of hair above the ears are pushed back over the headband and the edge of the turban and disappear under the veil. Her face is oval and fleshy. The eyebrows are low. The eyes are wide-set and almond-shaped with thick upper eyelids. The irises are indicated by incised circles. The ears are not visible under the hair and she wears dumbbell-shaped earrings (Colledge classification: H). The mouth is small with full lips. The chin is square.

She wears a tunic (details unclear).

PORTRAIT C: ARMLESS BUST OF PRIEST

The figure is shown frontally. The head appears large in relation to the body.

He wears low on the forehead a tall, cylindrical, flat-top headdress, divided into three sections by two vertical grooves: a Palmyrene priestly hat. A wreath is depicted at the lower part of the headdress. It has three rows of leaves pointing towards a central decoration. A horizontal line at the bottom of the headdress suggests a liner. His face is square. The eyebrows are low and curving. The eyes are wide-set and almond-shaped with thick upper eyelids. The irises are indicated (details unclear). The ears are large and protruding with the helix and scapha depicted. The mouth is wide with a full lower lip. The chin is square. The neck is short and wide.

He wears a tunic and a chlamys. The folds of the tunic are indicated by wide, oblique grooves over the arms. The chlamys covers most of the chest. It is fastened at the right shoulder with a brooch (details unclear). A small, zigzag-shaped fold falls under the brooch.

PORTRAIT D: ARMLESS BUST OF PRIEST IN FULCRUM

The outline of an armless figure is recognizable in a clipeus.

He wears a tall, cylindrical, flat-top headdress (visible only in outline): a Palmyrene priestly hat.

He wears a garment with short sleeves (details unclear).

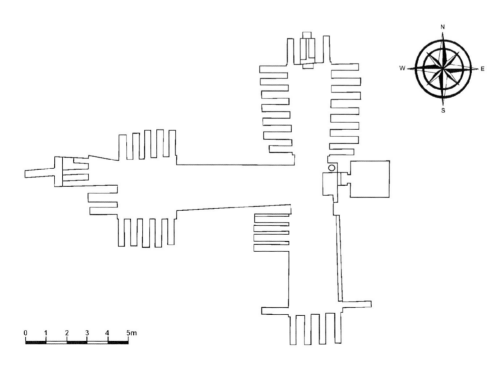

Plan of hypogeum of Zabd'ateh and Moqîmû (Sadurska – Bounni 1994, pl. 10).

SARCOPHAGUS RELIEFS

A.D. 131–150

115. COMPLETE SARCOPHAGUS RELIEF WITH BANQUETING SCENE AND PORTRAIT BUSTS

DATABASE NUMBER: PM113 (115a) + PM114 (115b) + PM116 (115c).
LOCATION: Palmyra, Palmyra Museum, inv. no. 2152/7614, 2157/7619, 2156/7621.
CONTEXT: South-east necropolis. Hypogeum of Zabd'ateh and Moqîmû, north exedra niche, section 35. 115a excavation no: 16. 115b excavation no: 20. 115c excavation no: 21.
ACQUISITION HISTORY: —
MEASUREMENTS: 115a: Height: 27 cm. Width: 16 cm. Depth: 16 cm. Field depth: 1.3 cm. 115b: Height: 47 cm. Width: 66 cm. Depth: 12 cm. 115c: Height: 46 cm. Width: 89 cm. Depth: 6 cm. Depth (relief): 1.5 cm.
MATERIAL: Limestone.
PRESERVATION: 115a: The upper right corner is chipped. The upper left corner and both lower corners are broken off. The left side of forehead is chipped. 115b: The surface is weathered. The lower right corner is broken off. 115c: The upper left corner of the kline is chipped. Portrait F: The surface of the head is chipped. Portrait G: The surface is weathered.
TECHNICAL DESCRIPTION: The figure of the seated female has been restored where the diagonal crack across the torso was. There are traces of red in the inscriptions on the skyphoi.
DATE: A.D. 131–150.
REFERENCES: 115a: al-Asʿad – Taha 1965, 44 cat. 16 pls. 4. 5; Gawlikowski 1974b, 295 cat. 67; Makowski 1985b, 120 f.; Tanabe 1986, 34. 43 pls. 276. 428; Sadurska – Bounni 1994, 134 f. cat. 181 figs. 217–219; Yon 2001b, 355 cat. 191; Clauss 2002, 90 cat. 103; Krag 2018, 47 n. 208; 239 cat. 274. 115b: Gawlikowski 1974b, 296 cat. 71; Tanabe 1986, 43 pl. 428; Sadurska – Bounni 1994, 134 f. cat. 181 figs. 217–219. 115c: al-Asʿad – Taha 1965, 45 cat. 20 pls. 4. 5; Gawlikowski 1974b, 296 cat. 71 pl. 3; Tanabe 1986, 43 pl. 428; Sadurska – Bounni 1994, 134–145 cat. 181 figs. 217–219; Krag – Raja 2017, 199 n. 24; 204 n. 72. 73; 205 n. 76; 207 n. 95; 208 n. 97; 221 cat. 49; Krag 2018, 32 n. 63; 43 n. 164; 50 n. 236; 51 n. 240; 87 n. 182; 89 n. 208–209; 98 n. 23; 111 n. 8; 245 cat. 292. Inscriptions: Gawlikowski 1974b, 295 cat. 67; 296 f. cat. 72; 296 cat. 71; Sadurska – Bounni 1994, 134 f.; Krag 2018, 239 cat. 274; 245 cat. 292.

OBJECT DESCRIPTION

The sarcophagus lid relief is preserved in two fragments. 115a depicts a female sitting in a chair. The chair has a round back, decorated with a beaded band that continues along the edges to the feet of the chair. The back of the chair supports the figure up to the height of her head. The back of the chair is decorated with an incised crisscross pattern. The seat of the chair has a cushion, where curving grooves indicate the fabric. The lower edge of the seat is decorated with a beaded band. The area behind her legs is decorated with an incised crisscross pattern. The crisscross pattern could possibly indicate a wicker chair. At the lower edge there is a protruding plinth. 115b depicts two reclining males. Both figures rest their left arm on a cushion. The cushions are decorated with a beaded band. Curving grooves indicate the texture of the fabric. The sarcophagus box relief (115c) is rectangular in shape and is rendered as a kline. Three figures are depicted between the kline legs: a standing boy/male, a bust of a female, and a standing girl. The central band is decorated with a running scroll with rosettes set between beaded bands. The bands on either side are decorated with leaves in an opposite arrangement between beaded bands. Curving grooves indicate the texture of the mattress. The left side of the kline is decorated with a fulcrum with a small armless bust of a priest (portrait G). The central stretcher of the kline is decorated with two rectangular indentations on either end. The indentations are followed by two rectangular ones followed by two appliques with vegetal motifs. The legs of the kline are turned. They are composed of a scotia, and above is a bell-shaped element, a torus, a neck, a ball, a neck, a bell-shaped element, and above the stretcher is a biconical finial. All elements are decorated with a tongues pattern, rendered diagonally on the ball.

INSCRIPTION ON 115A
INSCRIPTION 1
SCRIPT: Palmyrene Aramaic.
LOCATION ON RELIEF: On the plinth.
TRANSCRIPTION: ʾṬNYʾ ḤBL.
TRANSLATION: Antonia, alas!

CIS no. —; PAT no. 1859.
COMMENT: Latin name Antonia.

INSCRIPTIONS ON 115B
INSCRIPTION 2
SCRIPT: Palmyrene Aramaic.
LOCATION ON RELIEF: On the cup to the right.
TRANSCRIPTION: MRQWS | ḤBL.
TRANSLATION: Marcus, alas!

INSCRIPTION 3
SCRIPT: Palmyrene Aramaic.
LOCATION ON RELIEF: On the cup to the left.
TRANSCRIPTION: WLS ḤBL.
TRANSLATION: Valens, alas!

CIS no. —; PAT no. 1864.
COMMENT: Inscription 2: Latin name Marcus. Inscription 3: Latin name Valens.

INSCRIPTIONS ON 115C
INSCRIPTION 4
SCRIPT: Palmyrene Aramaic.

LOCATION ON RELIEF: To the left of the boy.
TRANSCRIPTION: ʿBDʿSTWR | BRH | ḤBL.
TRANSLATION: ʿAbdʿastôr, her son, alas!

INSCRIPTION 5
SCRIPT: Palmyrene Aramaic.
LOCATION ON RELIEF: To the left of the female.
TRANSCRIPTION: MRTʾ | ʾMHWN | ḤBL.
TRANSLATION: Martâ their mother, alas!

INSCRIPTION 6
SCRIPT: Palmyrene Aramaic.
LOCATION ON RELIEF: To the left of the girl.
TRANSCRIPTION: BʿŠGʾ | BRTH | ḤBL.
TRANSLATION: Baʿašegâ her daughter, alas!

CIS no. —; PAT no. 1863.
COMMENT: Inscription 6: The reference of the pronoun could be to the father (»his daughter«) but as for the son ʿAbdʿastôr, it may be more straightforward to think of a reference to the mother who is portrayed alongside the two children.

SARCOPHAGUS LID

PORTRAIT A: SEATED FEMALE, ANTONIA

The figure is shown frontally, with the head turned slightly to her left. The arms appear short in relation to the body. The left hand and the lower legs appear large. The right arm is bent and raised to her shoulder. The left arm is bent and rests on her left thigh. She sits with her legs apart with both feet resting on a protruding plinth.

She wears three headdresses: a headband, a turban, and a veil. The headband is placed low on the forehead (details unclear). The turban is coiled. It is divided into two layers, and horizontal grooves indicate the coiling of the fabric. The veil is heavy. It falls behind her shoulders, is folded around the upper arms, and continues along the sides of her body until the relief ground. The veil is wrapped around the left wrist. Part of the hair is covered by the headdress: a few strands of hair above the ears are pushed back over the headband and disappear under the veil. Her face is square. The eyebrows are curving. The eyes are almond-shaped, with thick upper eyelids. The irises are indicated (details unclear). The ears are depicted with the tail of the helix and earlobe, and an oval irregular object is depicted below, possibly earrings shaped like a miniature bunch of grapes (Colledge classification: E). The nose is straight and the nasal bridge narrow. The alae are incised, and the nostrils are carved. The mouth is small with a full lower lip. The chin is square. The neck is short and wide.

She wears a tunic and a himation. The tunic has a wide, v-shaped neckline and long, tight-fitting sleeves. The folds of the tunic are rendered by oblique and vertical grooves. The himation crosses the chest diagonally from the left shoulder to the right side and covers the left breast. It is fastened at the left shoulder with a trapezoidal brooch with a rosette finial

Cat. 115

(Colledge classification: b). A large fold is depicted by a deep, horizontal groove across the knees. The himation covers the lower body and legs and ends at the ankles. The folds of the himation are rendered by curving grooves on the body and legs, and vertical grooves between the legs. She wears round-toe shoes, and the opening of the shoes is rendered by incised, v-shaped lines.

Cat. 115

The right hand pulls a fold of the veil from her back. She wears a plain, wide hoop bracelet around her right wrist. The right index and the little finger are extended. With the left hand, she holds a fold of the veil. The left thumb, index, and the middle finger are extended.

PORTRAIT B: RECLINING MALE, MARCUS

The figure is shown frontally. The arms appear short in relation to the torso. The eyes appear large. The right arm is bent and held to the torso. The left arm is bent and held to the chest.

His hair is arranged in flame-shaped curls around the head. The individual strands of hair are indicated by incised lines. His face is square. The eyebrows are curving, rendered by incised lines starting from the root of the nose. The eyes are close-set and almond-shaped with thick eyelids. The upper eyelids extend beyond the end of the lower ones. The irises are indicated by incised circles and the pupils by punch holes. The ears are large and protruding with the helix and scapha depicted. The nose is straight with incised alae and carved nostrils. The mouth is small with a full lower lip. The cheeks are fleshy, and the chin is round and almost double. The neck is wide.

He wears a tunic and a himation. The tunic has a wide, v-shaped neckline leaving the upper part of the chest bare. A vertical, incised line at the neckline indicates the chest musculature. The tunic has wide, short sleeves. The folds of the tunic are rendered by curving grooves at the chest and oblique grooves on the sleeve. Over the tunic, he wears a himation. It is wrapped around the left shoulder and arm, leaving most of the upper torso and hand free. It proceeds in a curving fold across the lower torso and falls over the right side. The folds of the himation are rendered by oblique and curving grooves.

He holds an oblong object with a diamond pattern, possibly a branch, in his right hand. With his left hand, he holds the handle of a skyphos. It has a conical foot and body. The lower body has a tongues pattern, and the upper body carries an inscription. The lip is straight with opposing vertical, looped handles.

PORTRAIT C: RECLINING MALE, VALENS

The figure is shown frontally. The left forearm appears short in relation to the torso. The eyes appear large. The right arm is extended behind the figure to the right. The left arm is bent and held to the chest. The legs are obscured by the other reclining figure.

His hair is arranged in flame-shaped curls around the head. The individual strands of hair are indicated by incised lines. His face is round. The eyebrows are curving, rendered by incised lines starting from the root of the nose. The eyes are close-set and almond-shaped with thick eyelids. The upper eyelids extend beyond the end of the lower ones. The irises are indicated by incised circles and the pupils by punch holes. The ears are large and protruding with the helix and scapha depicted. The nose is straight with carved nostrils. The mouth is small with full lips. The cheeks are fleshy, and the chin is wide and almost double. The neck is wide.

He wears a tunic and a himation. The tunic has a wide, v-shaped neckline leaving the upper part of the chest bare. A vertical, incised line at the neckline indicates the chest musculature. The tunic has wide, short sleeves. The folds of the tunic are rendered by curving grooves. Over the tunic, he wears a himation. It is wrapped around the left shoulder and arm, leaving most of the upper torso and hand free. It proceeds in a curving fold across the lower torso and falls over the right side. The folds of the himation are indicated by vertical grooves on the arm and curving grooves on the body.

With his left hand, he holds the handle of a skyphos. It has a conical foot and body. The lower body has a tongues pattern, and the upper body carries an inscription. The lip is straight with opposing vertical, looped handles.

SARCOPHAGUS BOX

PORTRAIT D: STANDING BOY/MALE, ʿABDʿASTÔR

The figure is shown frontally. The head appears large in relation to the body. The legs appear short in relation to the body. The right arm is bent and held out from the body. The left arm is bent and held to the torso. The legs are set apart and he rests his weight on his left leg.

His hair is voluminous arranged in one row of s-shaped curls around the head. The individual strands of hair are indicated by incised lines. His face is oval. The eyebrows are curving, depicted by thin ridges. The eyes are wide-set and round with thick upper eyelids. The eyeballs are blank. The nose is straight. The cheeks are fleshy, and the chin is wide. The neck is wide.

He wears a tunic and trousers. The tunic has a wide, v-shaped neckline that leaves the upper part of the torso bare, and short, wide sleeves. He wears a plain band belt at the waist, which creates an overfold. The tunic ends at the knees and reveals the lower part of the trousers. The folds of the tunic are rendered by oblique and curving grooves. He wears closed-toe boots.

With his right hand, he holds an oblong object: the object widens behind his hand and ends with large lobed elements; possibly a bunch of dates or grapes. He wears a plain hoop bracelet at the wrist. He holds a small bird in his left hand. The beak is pointed to the right and is large, while the head is small. The body is long, and a few feathers are indicated by grooves. The index and the ring finger are extended.

Cat. 115

PORTRAIT E: BUST OF A FEMALE, MARTÂ
The figure is shown frontally. Her head is turned slightly to her left. The arms appear short in relation to the body. The right arm is bent and raised to the chest. The left arm is bent and held to the torso.

She wears three headdresses: a headband, a turban, and a veil. The band is placed low on the forehead and is divided into panels: the central panel is decorated with a flower, and on either side, it is decorated with a crisscross pattern. The turban is coiled. It is divided into three layers and the upper two layers are looped into each other creating a knot in the middle. Curving grooves indicate the coiling of the fabric. The veil is heavy. It falls over the shoulders and it is wrapped around her left arm and falls over the back of her right shoulder. The headdresses cover part of the hair: several strands of hair above the ears are pushed back over the headband and the edge of the turban and disappear under the veil. One thick, wavy lock of hair falls down the left side of her neck and over the shoulder. The individual strands of hair are indicated by incised lines. Her face is round. The eyebrows are curving, depicted as thin ridges. The eyes are wide-set and almond-shaped with thick upper eyelids. The eyeballs are blank. The upper eyelids extend beyond the end of the lower ones. Only the earlobes are visible under the hair. She wears earrings shaped like a miniature bunch of grapes (Colledge classification: E). The nose is straight with carved nostrils. The mouth is straight with a full lower lip. The cheeks are fleshy, and the chin is oval. The neck is wide with two horizontal grooves.

She wears a tunic and a himation. The tunic has a wide, v-shaped neckline and short, wide sleeves. The folds are indicated by curving, wide grooves. The himation crosses the chest diagonally from the left shoulder to the right side and covers the left breast. It is fastened at the left shoulder with a trapezoidal brooch with a rosette finial (Colledge classification: b). The folds of the himation are indicated by vertical and oblique, wide grooves.

Her right arm is raised next to the shoulder. The thumb, the index, and the middle finger are extended. She pulls the edge of the veil over the shoulder with her hand. With the left hand, she holds a fold of the veil. The thumb, the index, and the little finger are extended.

PORTRAIT F: STANDING GIRL, BAʿAŠEGÂ
The figure is shown frontally. The head appears large, and the legs appear short in relation to the body. The right arm is bent and held out from the body. The left arm is bent and held to the torso. She stands with her legs set apart.

Her hair is voluminous, arranged in one row of s-shaped curls around the head. The individual strands of hair are indicated by incised lines. Her face is round. The eyebrows are curving, rendered by thin ridges. The eyes are wide-set and round with thick upper eyelids. The eyeballs appear blank. The ears are large and protruding. The neck is wide. She wears a necklace composed of large, oval beads at the base of the neck.

She wears a tunic with a round neckline and short, wide sleeves. The tunic proceeds to her feet. The folds of the tunic are rendered by curving, oblique grooves and vertical grooves between the legs.

With her right hand, she holds a large curving element with many globular elements underneath; a bunch of grapes. She holds a small bird in her left hand. The bird is turned to the right. It has a small head and a large oval body. The outline of the wing is indicated with an incised line.

PORTRAIT G: ARMLESS BUST OF A PRIEST, IN FULCRUM
The figure is shown frontally, rendered in a clipeus.

He wears a tall, cylindrical flat-top headdress: a Palmyrene priestly hat.

He wears a tunic and a himation. The folds of the tunic are rendered by oblique grooves. Over the tunic, he wears a himation. It is wrapped around the left shoulder, leaving only part of the chest free. One fold of the himation crosses the chest diagonally.

A.D. 140–160

HYPOGEUM 31/E

BANQUETING RELIEF

A.D. 140–160

116. FRAGMENT OF A BANQUETING RELIEF

DATABASE NUMBER: PM576.
LOCATION: Palmyra, Palmyra Museum, inv. no. unknown.
CONTEXT: South-west necropolis. Hypogeum 31/E. Excavated by Ingholt in 1924.
ACQUISITION HISTORY: —
MEASUREMENTS: Height: 79 cm. Width: 35 cm.
MATERIAL: —
PRESERVATION: The head is broken off at the shoulders. The left elbow, the knees, and the feet are chipped.
TECHNICAL DESCRIPTION: —
DATE: A.D. 140–160.
REFERENCES: Ingholt Archives, PS 646B; Ingholt 1928, 128; Krag 2018, 33 n. 75; 39 n. 129; 44 n. 174–175; 45 n. 193; 46 n. 194–195; 238 cat. 270; Raja et al. 2021a, Diary 1, 103. 131 f.

OBJECT DESCRIPTION
The object depicts a seated female. The armrests and legs of the chair are depicted. They are undecorated.

PORTRAIT
The figure is shown in frontal view. The arms appear short in relation to the body. The right arm is bent and held in front of the chest. The left arm is bent and held in front of the torso. She sits with her legs apart with both feet resting on a protruding plinth. The knees are rendered under the drapery.

Cat. 116

She wears a veil. The veil is heavy. It falls over both her shoulders and is folded around her arms. Two circular incised elements are depicted at the base of the neck: they are pendants of a necklace.

She wears a tunic and a himation. The tunic has a small round neckline and two plain bands extending downwards on the chest. The folds of the ankle-length tunic are rendered by oblique grooves on the chest, and vertical grooves over the feet. The himation crosses the chest diagonally from the left shoulder to the right side and covers the left breast. It is pinned on the left shoulder with a trapezoidal brooch with a feline finial (Colledge classification: a). The body is decorated with a vegetal pattern. The himation covers the lower body and legs and ends at the shins, revealing the tunic underneath. The folds of the himation are rendered by oblique grooves on the body and thighs, and curving grooves on the lower legs.

The right hand is held in front of the chest with the palm turned outwards. The fingers are extended. With the left hand, she holds a conical object incised with fine wavy lines, with a bowl-shaped tip, and a thick, short staff topped by a polygonal mass with a pattern of crisscrossing, incised lines, and a small cylinder. These are reduced versions of a spindle and a distaff.

SARCOPHAGI

A.D. 150–200

117. FRAGMENT OF BANQUETING RELIEF

DATABASE NUMBER: PM953.
LOCATION: Palmyra, Palmyra Museum, inv. no. unknown.
CONTEXT: South-west necropolis, Hypogeum 31/E. Excavated by Ingholt in 1924.
ACQUISITION HISTORY: —
MEASUREMENTS: —
MATERIAL: Limestone.
PRESERVATION: The surface is weathered. The head and the right hand are missing. The torso is chipped.
TECHNICAL DESCRIPTION: —
DATE: A.D. 150–200.
REFERENCES: Ingholt Archives, PS 978.

OBJECT DESCRIPTION

The object depicts a male, possibly reclining. It was part of a larger banqueting scene on a sarcophagus lid.

PORTRAIT:

The figure is shown frontally. The arms are bent in front of the torso.

He wears a tunic and a himation. The tunic has a small round neckline and long tight-fitting sleeves. The folds of the tunic are indicated by wide, curving grooves over the chest and oblique ones over the arms. Over the tunic, he wears a himation. The himation is wrapped around the left shoulder and arm. The folds of the himation are rendered by oblique grooves.

His left hand rests against the side of the cushion.

Cat. 117

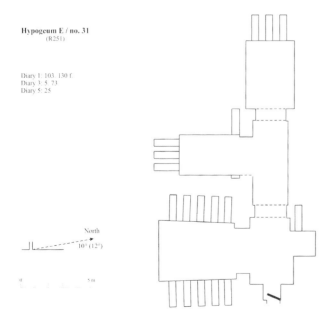

Plan of hypogeum 31/E.

HYPOGEUM NO. 33

SARCOPHAGI

A.D. 140–160

118. COMPLETE SARCOPHAGUS WITH BANQUETING SCENE AND PORTRAIT BUSTS

DATABASE NUMBER: PM771.
LOCATION: Palmyra, Palmyra Museum, inv. no. unknown.
CONTEXT: South-west necropolis. Hypogeum no. 33, right lateral chamber. Excavated by Ingholt in 1924.
ACQUISITION HISTORY: —
MEASUREMENTS: —
MATERIAL: Limestone.
PRESERVATION: The surface of the mattress is chipped. Portrait A: The upper part is broken off horizontally at the waist. Portrait B: The upper part is broken off horizontally at the waist. Portrait C: The head is broken off horizontally at the base of the neck. The surface at the lower left arm is chipped. Portrait D: The surface of the head is weathered and chipped. Portrait E: The surface of the head is weathered and chipped. Portrait F: The surface is weathered. Portrait G: The surface of the face is chipped.
TECHNICAL DESCRIPTION: —
DATE: A.D. 140–160 (Ingholt 1928: A.D. 100–150).
REFERENCES: Ingholt Archives, PS 58; Ingholt 1928, 94; Krag 2018, 32 n. 63; 33 n. 77. n. 80; 66 n. 382; 98 n. 23; 243 cat. 285; Raja et al. 2021a, Diary 1, 109, Diary 5, 108 f.

OBJECT DESCRIPTION

The sarcophagus lid is rectangular in shape and depicts a seated female and a reclining male. Beneath these figures is a box in the shape of a kline, with two female busts and two male busts between the legs. On top of the kline are two mattresses. The thin mattress at the top is decorated (details unclear). The lower mattress has three vertical decorated panels (details unclear). Curving grooves indicate the texture of the mattress. The reclining figure rests the left arm against two cushions. The left side of the kline is decorated with a fulcrum (details unclear). The central stretcher of the kline is decorated with two rectangular indentations on either side. The legs of the kline are turned. They are composed of a plinth, and above is a v-shaped neck, a torus, a concave quarter, a convex quarter, a torus, a ball, and a thin torus. The seated female sits in a chair with a rectangular, undecorated stretcher and a cylindrical, undecorated leg that cuts through the stretcher. The back of the chair is not rendered.

SARCOPHAGUS LID

PORTRAIT A: SEATED FEMALE

The figure is shown frontally. She rests her left hand on the left thigh. The legs are bent with the knees rendered under the drapery.

She wears an ankle-length garment. The folds are rendered by curving grooves. She holds a fold of another cloth, possibly from a veil, in her left hand. A wide fold extends downwards from her hand and along her left leg.

PORTRAIT B: STANDING FIGURE
The figure is shown frontally.

Only the lower part of the figure is preserved. The figure seems to be wearing a long garment that covers the legs.

PORTRAIT C: RECLINING MALE
The figure is shown in frontal to three-quarter view. The right arm is bent and rests on his raised right leg. The left arm is bent and held to the chest. The right leg is bent, and he rests his foot on the mattress. The left leg is bent under the right leg with the knee pointing outwards. The left foot is obscured by the right leg.

He wears a ›Parthian-style‹ tunic, a chlamys, and ›Parthian-style‹ trousers. The tunic has a small, round neckline and long, tight-fitting sleeves. The cuffs of the sleeves are decorated with a band (details unclear). The tunic ends above the knees and has a decorated lower border (details unclear). The folds of the tunic are indicated by curving and oblique grooves. Over the tunic, he wears a chlamys that falls over both shoulders, and covers most of the chest. It is folded around his lower left arm and falls down along his left side and over the cushions. The chlamys is fastened at the right shoulder with a circular brooch (details unclear). A zigzag-shaped fold falls from under the brooch. The folds of the chlamys are indicated by narrow, deep grooves. He wears a plain band belt, knotted at the centre with the ends looped under on either side of the waist. Each trouser leg is decorated in the middle with a wide band extending downwards (details unclear). The folds are indicated by curving grooves.

His right hand rests on his right knee.

SARCOPHAGUS LID

PORTRAIT D: FEMALE BUST
The figure is shown frontally. The left hand appears large in relation to the torso. The right arm is raised to the chest. The left arm is bent and held to the torso.

She wears a veil that falls over the shoulders. It is wrapped around her left arm and falls over the back of her right shoulder.

Cat. 118

She wears one necklace. It is composed of round beads and a central pendant (other details unclear), worn high on the chest.

She wears a tunic and a himation. The tunic has a wide, round neckline. The folds of the tunic are rendered by curving grooves. The himation crosses the chest diagonally from the left shoulder to the right side and covers the left breast. The folds are indicated by vertical and oblique, wide grooves.

With her right hand, she holds the edge of the veil. She wears a bracelet with a wide hoop and oval bezels at her right wrist. The index and the middle finger are extended. Her left hand is clenched around two round objects (details unclear). The index and the middle finger are extended.

PORTRAIT E: FEMALE BUST

The figure is shown frontally. The right arm is raised to the chest. The left arm is bent and held to the torso.

She wears a veil that falls over the shoulders. It is wrapped around her left arm and falls over the back of her right shoulder.

She wears a tunic and a himation. The tunic has a wide, round neckline. The folds of the tunic are rendered by curving grooves. The himation crosses the chest diagonally from the left shoulder to the right side and covers the left breast. The folds of the himation are indicated by vertical and oblique, wide grooves.

With her right hand, she lightly holds the edge of the veil. She wears a ring with a large oval bezel on her ring finger. She wears a bracelet with a wide hoop at her right wrist. The index, the middle, and the little finger are extended. Her left hand is clenched around two objects, possibly a spindle and a distaff (details unclear). The index and the middle finger are extended.

PORTRAIT F: MALE BUST

The figure is shown frontally. The arms are bent and held to the torso.

His hair is arranged in rows of crescent-shaped curls around the head. His face is oval. The eyebrows are depicted by thin ridges. The ears are protruding with the helix and scapha rendered. The mouth is wide with thin lips. The chin is oval. The neck is wide.

He wears a tunic and a himation. The tunic has a wide, round neckline that leaves the upper part of the torso bare. The folds of the tunic are rendered by curving, wide grooves. Over the tunic, he wears a himation. The himation covers most of the body. It is wrapped around the right shoulder and arm, leaving only the upper part of the chest and the hand free. One end of the himation crosses the chest diagonally and falls over the left shoulder (›arm-sling‹ type).

With his right hand, he holds the diagonal fold of the himation. The thumb, the index, and the middle finger are extended. With his left hand, he holds a small, rectangular object, possibly a schedula.

PORTRAIT G: MALE BUST

The figure is shown frontally. The arms are bent and held to the torso.

The outline of the face is recognizable (other details unclear). The neck is wide.

He wears a tunic and a himation. The tunic has a wide, round neckline that leaves the upper part of the torso bare. The folds of the tunic are rendered by curving, wide grooves. Over the tunic, he wears a himation. The himation covers most of the body. It is wrapped around the right shoulder and arm. One end of the himation crosses the chest diagonally and falls over the left shoulder (›arm-sling‹ type).

With his right hand, he holds the diagonal fold of the himation and a book-roll. He is holding the other side of the book-roll with his left hand, displaying a part of its content. The middle and index finger are extended.

A.D. 140–220

HYPOGEUM OF THE THREE BROTHERS

SARCOPHAGI

A.D. 200–220

119. COMPLETE SARCOPHAGUS WITH BANQUETING SCENE AND PORTRAIT BUSTS

DATABASE NUMBER: InSitu040.
LOCATION: Palmyra, in situ.
CONTEXT: South-west necropolis. Hypogeum of the Three Brothers, north exedra. Excavation nos. 1–3.
ACQUISITION HISTORY: —
MEASUREMENTS: Height: 190 cm. Width: 200 cm.
MATERIAL: Limestone, white.
PRESERVATION: Multiple fragments are broken off the sarcophagus and the background of the lid is almost not preserved. Portrait A: Only a small part of the lower torso, the legs, and one foot are preserved. Portrait B: The face is

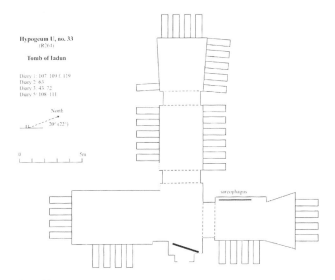

Plan of hypogeum no. 33.

Cat. 119

badly chipped and multiple fragments are broken off from the torso and the left arm. Portrait C: The upper part is broken off across the waist. Portrait D: The head is broken off at the base of the neck. A large crack runs from the left shoulder, diagonally to the waist, proceeding vertically down through the mattress. Portrait E: A large part of the left shoulder and of the elbow are broken off. The left hand is badly chipped. A large crack runs diagonally across the face. Portrait F: The face is badly chipped. Portrait J: The face is badly chipped.

TECHNICAL DESCRIPTION: There are traces of black pigment in the irises and eyelids of portrait E.

DATE: A.D. 200–220 (Sadurska – Bounni 1994: A.D. 160–190).

REFERENCES: Ingholt Archives, PS 1066; Will 1951, 86 fig. 5; Tanabe 1986, 31 pls. 221. 223; Sadurska – Bounni 1994, 119 f. cat. 161 figs. 240. 242. 244; al-Asʿad – Schmidt-Colinet 1995, 40 fig. 47; Parlasca 1998, 312; Palaz Erdemir 2013, 510 f. 514 fig. 6; Wielgosz-Rondolino 2016a, 75 fig. 13; Krag – Raja 2017, 199 n. 24; 204 n. 72. 73; 205 n. 75; 206 n. 87; 207 n. 94; 209 n. 100; 211 n. 117; 217 cat. 19; Krag 2018, 32 n. 63; 53 n. 258; 58 n. 300; 59 n. 323; 62 n. 349. 352–353; 66 n. 382. 385; 88 n. 193; 103 n. 74; 390 cat. 841; Silver et al. 2018, 188 fig. 9.49; <https://www.loc.gov/item/mpc2004002226/PP/> (15.11.2022).

OBJECT DESCRIPTION

The sarcophagus is placed on a high plinth. The sarcophagus lid is rectangular in shape and depicts a seated female, a standing male, a standing figure, and two reclining figures. Beneath these figures is a box in the shape of a kline with two male busts flanked by two female busts between the kline legs. On the right lateral side of the sarcophagus box is a reclining figure, who rests the left arm against a cushion. On top of the kline are two mattresses. The thin mattress at the top is decorated with an intersecting lozenge pattern with flowers in the lozenges. The lower mattress is decorated with three bands with vegetal motifs (details unclear). Curving grooves indicate the texture of the lower mattress. The reclining figure is the largest figure on the lid, and he rests the left arm against a cushion. The cushion is decorated with a band with a vegetal motif, separated by horizontal beaded bands. On the left side of the kline, a fulcrum is shown. It is decorated with a small armless bust of a male (portrait K). Another figure, possibly an animal is rendered to the left of the bust. The central stretcher of the kline is decorated. On either end are two rectangular indentations. On each side of these are two square inlays or appliqués. The legs of the kline are turned. They are composed of a plinth, a long scotia, a scotia, a ball, a bell-shaped element, and above the stretcher is a torus finial.

Cat. 119

The object is located next to cat. 119 and cat. 120.

SARCOPHAGUS LID

PORTRAIT A: SEATED FEMALE

The figure is shown frontally. The left arm is bent and raised towards her neck. Her legs are bent with the left knee rendered in the drapery. Her left foot is obscured by the right foot of the reclining figure to her left.

She wears a garment, possibly a himation, which covers her body and legs. The folds are indicated by oblique and curving grooves. She wears a plain, round-toe shoe on her right foot.

PORTRAIT B: STANDING MALE

The figure is shown frontally. The right arm is held along the body. The left arm is bent and held to the torso. The legs are obscured by the reclining figure to his left.

The outline of his face and hair is recognizable. Two snail-shell curls are rendered on the left side of his face, covering the ears.

He wears a tunic and a himation. The tunic has a small, round neckline and long, tight-fitting sleeves. Over the tunic he wears a himation that covers most of his body. It is wrapped around his left shoulder and arm. Another fold of the himation comes from his right waist and covers his lower body. The folds of the himation are rendered by vertical and oblique grooves.

He holds a round object with his right hand (details unclear). He is holding a fold of the himation with his left hand.

PORTRAIT C: STANDING FIGURE

The figure is shown frontally. The legs are obscured by the reclining figure to the left.

The figure is wearing a garment, possibly a tunic, which covers the lower body and legs. The folds are indicated by curving grooves. The figure also wears a plain band belt at the waist, knotted at the centre.

PORTRAIT D: RECLINING MALE

The figure is shown in frontal to three-quarter view. The right arm is slightly bent and rests on his right raised knee. The left arm is bent and held to the torso. The figure's right leg is bent, and he rests his foot on the mattress. The left leg is bent under the right leg with the knee pointing outwards.

He wears a ›Parthian-style‹ tunic and a himation. The tunic has long, tight-fitting sleeves and a small, round neckline decorated with a beaded band. At the middle, the tunic has a wide band with a running scroll with rosettes extending downward. The folds are indicated by diagonal, curving grooves. He also wears a himation. It is folded around his left upper arm, leaving most of the body and the hand free. It proceeds along the left part of the torso and is folded around the waist and covers his legs. A zigzag-shaped fold falls from under his left hand across the cushion and mattress. The folds of the himation are rendered by oblique, curving grooves. His boot is decorated with vine leaves on a stem.

He rests his right hand at the right knee. He holds an oblong object, possibly a pinecone in his hand. The individual scales are rendered by fine, incised lines. At the centre of the chest, the outline of an object, possibly a bowl is recognizable in his left hand.

PORTRAIT E: RECLINING MALE

The body is shown in frontal to three-quarter view. The right arm is extended beyond the reclining figure to his right. The left arm is bent and held to the torso. The lower part of his body and legs are obscured by the reclining figure to his right.

His hair is arranged in three rows of snail-shell curls around the head. His face is square. The eyebrows are curving. The eyes are close-set and almond-shaped. The irises and pupils are indicated by concentric, incised circles. The ears are large and protruding with helix, scapha, and concha depicted. His nose is straight and wide at the base. He has a beard that starts from the temples and covers the cheeks and the chin. The facial hair is rendered by small, snail-shell curls. The mouth is wide with thin lips. The chin is wide, and the neck is wide.

He wears a ›Parthian-style‹ tunic and a himation. The tunic has long, tight-fitting sleeves and a small, round neckline. At the middle, the tunic has a wide band with a floral motif extending downwards. He also wears a himation. It is folded around his left shoulder and is wrapped around the wrist. A zigzag-shaped fold falls from under his left hand. The folds of the himation are rendered by oblique, curving grooves.

The outline of an object, possibly a bowl is recognizable at the centre of the chest. He holds the object in his left hand.

SARCOPHAGUS BOX

PORTRAIT F: ARMLESS FEMALE BUST

The figure is shown frontally.

She wears a garment, possibly a veil, which falls over her right shoulder and proceeds in a curving fold across the chest and falls back over her left shoulder. The folds are rendered by curving grooves.

PORTRAIT G: ARMLESS MALE BUST

The figure is shown frontally.

He wears a tunic and a himation. The folds of the tunic are indicated by curving grooves. Over the tunic, he wears a himation. It is folded from over his left shoulder and falls in a diagonal fold across the chest. A wide fold falls vertically from the left shoulder. The folds are indicated by wide, oblique grooves.

PORTRAIT H: ARMLESS MALE BUST

The figure is shown frontally.

He wears a tunic and a himation. The tunic has a wide, round neckline. The folds of the tunic are rendered by curving grooves. Over the tunic he wears a himation. It is folded over his left shoulder and falls in a diagonal fold across the chest. A wide fold falls vertically from the left shoulder. The folds are indicated by wide, oblique grooves.

PORTRAIT I: ARMLESS FEMALE BUST
The figure is shown frontally.

She wears a garment, possibly a veil, which falls over her right shoulder and proceeds in a curving fold across the chest and falls back over her left shoulder. The folds are rendered by curving grooves.

PORTRAIT J: RECLINING MALE
The figure is shown in frontal to three-quarter view. His right leg is bent, and his foot is resting on a mattress. The left leg is bent under the right with the knee pointing outwards.

Curving grooves, possibly a rendering of a himation, are visible across the legs.

PORTRAIT K: MALE BUST IN FULCRUM
The figure is shown frontally.

120. COMPLETE SARCOPHAGUS WITH BANQUETING SCENE AND PORTRAIT BUSTS

DATABASE NUMBER: InSitu039.
LOCATION: Palmyra, in situ.
CONTEXT: South-west necropolis. Hypogeum of the Three Brothers, north exedra. Excavation nos. 1–3.
ACQUISITION HISTORY: —
MEASUREMENTS: Height: 192 cm. Width: 198 cm.
MATERIAL: Limestone, white.
PRESERVATION: Portrait A: The head has broken off. Both hands are broken off and the veil is chipped. Portrait B: The head is broken off at the base of the neck. The hands are chipped. Portrait C: The head is broken off at the base of the neck. Portrait D: The head is broken off at the base of the neck. The left hand and the right foot are slightly chipped. Portrait E: The head has broken off at the base of the neck. The attribute and the left hand are badly chipped. Portrait F: The face and veil are badly chipped. Portrait G: The head is badly chipped. Portrait H: The head is badly chipped. Portrait I: The face, the veil, and the left shoulder are badly chipped. Portrait J: The surface of the head is chipped.
TECHNICAL DESCRIPTION: —
DATE: A.D. 200–220 (Sadurska – Bounni 1994: A.D. 200–225).
REFERENCES: Ingholt Archives, PS 1066; Strzygowski 1901, 18 f. fig. 4; Chabot 1922, 98 pls. 17, 1; Kammerer 1929, 310 pl. 120, 2; Will 1951, 86 fig. 5; Tanabe 1986, 31 pls. 221. 222; Sadurska – Bounni 1994, 119 f. cat. 161 figs. 240. 241. 245; al-Asʿad – Schmidt-Colinet 1995, 40 fig. 47; al-Asʿad – Schmidt-Colinet 2005, 42 f. fig. 59; Parlasca 1998, 312; Wielgosz-Rondolino 2016a, 75 fig. 13; Krag – Raja 2017, 199 n. 24; 204 n. 72. 73; 205 n. 75; 206 n. 87; 207 n. 94; 208 n. 97. 99; 209 n. 100; 211 n. 117; 216 cat. 18; Krag 2018, 28 n. 9; 32 n. 63; 53 n. 258; 58 n. 300; 59 n. 323; 62 n. 349. 353; 65 n. 369; 66 n. 382. 385; 88 n. 193. 195; 103 n. 74; 384 cat. 839; Silver et al. 2018, 188 fig. 9.49; <https://www.loc.gov/item/mpc2004002226/PP/> (15.11.2022).

OBJECT DESCRIPTION
The sarcophagus lid is rectangular in shape and depicts a seated female, a standing female, a standing male, and two reclining males. Beneath these figures is a box in the shape of a kline with a female bust, two male busts, and a female bust between the kline legs. Above the kline are two mattresses. The thin mattress at the top is decorated with an intersecting lozenge pattern with flowers inside them. The lower mattress is decorated with three bands with vegetal motifs (details unclear). Curving grooves indicate the texture of the lower mattress. The largest reclining figure rests the left arm against a cushion. It is decorated with a band with a running scroll with five-petal rosettes set between beaded bands. The other reclining figure (portrait E) rests on two cushions. The cushions are decorated with a broad band with a floral motif. The left side of the kline is decorated with a fulcrum with a small armless male bust (portrait J). The central stretcher of the kline is decorated. The wide, rectangular, central panel is decorated with a vegetal motif divided by a horizontal groove. On either end are two rectangular indentations. On each side of these are two square inlays or appliqués. The legs of the kline are turned. They are composed of a plinth, a long scotia, a scotia, a ball, a bell-shaped element, and above the stretcher is a biconical finial.

The object is located next to cat. 118 and cat. 120.

SARCOPHAGUS LID

PORTRAIT A: SEATED FEMALE
The figure is shown frontally. The right arm is bent and rests on her right thigh. The left arm is bent and raised to the neck. Her legs are bent with the knees rendered under the drapery. Her left foot is obscured by the right foot of the reclining figure to her left.

She wears a heavy veil. It falls over her shoulders and it is wrapped around her right arm and falls over the back of her left shoulder. Her neck is slender and long.

She wears a tunic and a himation. The tunic has a small, round neckline and short, wide sleeves. The folds of the tunic are indicated by curving grooves. The himation falls to the ankles. It crosses her chest diagonally from the left shoulder to the right side and covers the left breast and most of the lower chest and body. The folds of the himation are rendered by vertical and curving grooves. The folds between the legs are indicated by curving grooves.

PORTRAIT B: STANDING FEMALE
The figure is shown frontally. Both of her arms are bent and held to the torso. The legs are obscured by the reclining figure to her left.

She wears a tunic with a small, round neckline. The folds are rendered by vertical and curving grooves.

She holds a bird in her hands. It has a round head and a pointed beak. The neck is small and the body oblong.

PORTRAIT C: STANDING MALE

The figure is shown frontally. The right arm is bent and held to the torso. The left arm is held along the body. His lower left arm and legs are obscured by the reclining figure to his left.

He wears a tunic and a himation. The tunic has a small, round neckline. The folds of the tunic are rendered by curving, wide grooves. Over the tunic, he wears a himation. The himation covers most of the body. It is wrapped around the right shoulder and arm, leaving only part of the upper chest and the hand free. One end of the himation crosses the chest diagonally and falls over the left shoulder (›arm-sling‹ type). The folds of the himation are rendered by oblique and curving grooves.

He holds a fold of the himation with his right hand.

PORTRAIT D: RECLINING MALE

The figure is shown in frontal to three-quarter view. The right arm is bent and rests on his raised right knee. The left arm is bent and held to the chest. His right leg is bent, and his foot is resting on the mattress. The left leg is bent under the right leg with the knee pointing outwards. The lower left leg is obscured by the right leg, but the end of his left foot is visible next to the right foot.

He wears a ›Parthian-style‹ tunic and a himation. The tunic has a small, round neckline decorated with a beaded band. The tunic has long, tight-fitting sleeves and the cuffs appear decorated (details unclear). At the middle, the tunic has a wide band extending downwards and decorated with serrated leaves in an opposite arrangement on the stem. The folds of the tunic are rendered by diagonal, curving grooves. Over the tunic, he wears a himation. It is folded around his left upper arm and is wrapped around the left wrist. It falls along the left part of the torso, is folded around the waist, and covers his legs. A zigzag-shaped fold falls from under his left hand. The folds of the himation are rendered by oblique,

Cat. 120

curving grooves. He also wears a plain band belt knotted at the centre with the ends looped under the left side of the waist. The boot is decorated with circular rosettes.

He holds a skyphos in his left hand and a branch with his right.

PORTRAIT E: RECLINING MALE

The body is shown in frontal to three-quarter view. The right arm is extended behind the reclining figure to his right. The left arm is bent and held to the torso. The lower body and legs are obscured by the reclining figure to his right.

He wears a ›Parthian-style‹ tunic and a himation. The tunic has long, tight-fitting sleeves and a small, round neckline decorated with a beaded band. At the middle, the tunic has a wide band with a floral pattern extending downwards. The folds of the tunic are rendered by curving grooves. He also wears a himation. It is folded around his left shoulder and is wrapped around the left wrist. A zigzag-shaped fold falls from under his left hand. The folds of the himation are rendered by oblique, curving grooves.

SARCOPHAGUS BOX

PORTRAIT F: ARMLESS FEMALE BUST

The figure is shown frontally.

She wears a heavy veil that falls over her right shoulder, proceeds in a curving fold across the chest and falls back over her left shoulder.

She wears a tunic. The folds are indicated by curving, wide grooves.

PORTRAIT G: ARMLESS MALE BUST

The figure is shown frontally.

He wears a tunic and a himation. The tunic has a wide, round neckline. The folds of the tunic are rendered by curving grooves. Over the tunic, he wears a himation. It is folded over his left shoulder and falls in a diagonal fold across the chest. Another wide fold falls vertically from the left shoulder. The folds are indicated by wide, oblique grooves.

PORTRAIT H: ARMLESS MALE BUST

The figure is shown frontally.

He wears a tunic and a himation. The tunic has a wide, round neckline. The folds of the tunic are rendered by curving grooves. Over the tunic, he wears a himation. It is folded over his left shoulder and falls in a diagonal fold across the chest. Another wide fold falls vertically from the left shoulder. The folds are indicated by wide, oblique grooves.

PORTRAIT I: ARMLESS FEMALE BUST

The figure is shown frontally.

She wears a heavy veil that falls over her right shoulder, proceeds in a curving fold across the chest, and falls back over her left shoulder.

She wears a tunic. The folds are indicated by curving, wide grooves.

PORTRAIT J: ARMLESS BUST OF A MALE IN FULCRUM

The figure is shown frontally.

He wears a tunic and a himation. The folds of the tunic are rendered by oblique grooves. The himation covers most of the chest. It falls in a curving line from his left shoulder to his right side. Another fold extends downwards from his left shoulder. The folds of the himation are rendered by curving and vertical grooves.

121. COMPLETE SARCOPHAGUS WITH BANQUETING SCENE AND PORTRAIT BUSTS

DATABASE NUMBER: InSitu041.
LOCATION: Palmyra, in situ.
CONTEXT: South-west necropolis. Hypogeum of the Three Brothers, north exedra. Excavation nos. 1–3.
ACQUISITION HISTORY: —
MEASUREMENTS: Height: 190 cm. Width: 200 cm.
MATERIAL: Limestone, white.
PRESERVATION: Multiple fragments are broken off from the sarcophagus. The kline is chipped on the left side. Portrait A: The head and the right side of the torso are broken off. The forearms and the feet are chipped. Portrait B: Only a small part of the figure is preserved. Portrait C: The head, the right forearm, and the left forearm are broken off. Most of the torso is broken off. Portrait D: The head has broken off. The hands are badly chipped. Portrait E: The head and a large piece of the chest have broken off. Portrait F: Most of the head is broken off. Portrait G: The head is chipped. Portrait I: The head is chipped. Portrait J: The head and the body are chipped.
TECHNICAL DESCRIPTION: —
DATE: A.D. 200–220 (Sadurska – Bounni 1994: A.D. 200–225).
REFERENCES: Ingholt Archives, PS 1066; Tanabe 1986, 31 pl. 221; Sadurska – Bounni 1994, 119 f. cat. 161 figs. 240. 243; Parlasca 1998, 312; Wielgosz-Rondolino 2016a, 75 fig. 13; Krag 2018, 32 n. 63; 53 n. 258; 58 n. 300; 59 n. 323; 62 n. 349. 352–353; 66 n. 382. 385; 88 n. 193; 103 n. 74; 389 cat. 840; Silver et al. 2018, 188 fig. 9.49; <https://www.loc.gov/item/mpc2004002226/PP/> (15.11.2022).

OBJECT DESCRIPTION

The sarcophagus is placed on a high plinth. The sarcophagus lid is rectangular in shape and depicts a seated female, a standing figure, and two reclining males. Beneath these figures is a box in the shape of a kline with two male busts flanked by two female busts between the kline legs. On the left lateral side of the sarcophagus box is a reclining figure who rests on a cushion, and a standing figure. On top of the kline are two mattresses. The thin mattress at the top is decorated with an intersecting lozenges pattern with flowers in the lozenges. The lower mattress is decorated with three bands (details unclear). Curving grooves indicate the texture of the lower mattress. The seated female sits on two cushions. The right reclining figure rests on a cushion. The cushion is decorated with a band with a floral motif. The left reclining figure is resting against two cushions. They are decorated with a central panel with a floral motif (details unclear). The central and side stretchers of the kline are decorated. On either end are two rectangular indentations. On either side of these there are two square inlays or appliqués. The legs of the kline are turned. They are composed of a plinth, a long scotia, a scotia, a ball, a bell-shaped element, and above the stretcher is a torus finial.

The object is located next to cat. 118 and cat. 119.

SARCOPHAGUS LID

PORTRAIT A: SEATED FEMALE
The figure is shown frontally. The left arm is bent. Her legs are bent, and the knees set apart, rendered in the drapery. Her left foot is obscured by the right foot of the reclining figure.

She wears a veil.

She wears a tunic and a himation. The folds of the tunic are rendered by curving grooves. She wears an ankle-length himation. The folds are indicated by oblique and curving grooves. She wears a plain shoe on her right foot.

She holds a fold of the veil in the left hand.

PORTRAIT B: STANDING FIGURE
Only a small part of the figure has been preserved (details unclear).

PORTRAIT C: RECLINING MALE
The figure is shown in frontal to three-quarter view. The right arm is held along the body. The left is bent. His right leg is bent, and his foot is resting on the kline. The left leg is bent under the right leg.

He wears a tunic and a himation. The folds of the tunic are rendered by curving grooves. He also wears a himation. It is folded around his left side and lower body. The folds of the himation are rendered by oblique, curving grooves.

PORTRAIT D: RECLINING MALE
The figure is shown in frontal to three-quarter view. The arms appear short in relation to the body. The lower body and legs are obscured by the reclining figure to his right.

Cat. 121

He wears a tunic and a himation. The folds of the tunic are rendered by curving grooves. Over the tunic he wears a himation (details unclear).

SARCOPHAGUS BOX

PORTRAIT E: ARMLESS FEMALE BUST
The figure is shown frontally.

She wears a heavy veil that falls over her right shoulder, proceeds in a curving fold across the chest, and falls back over her left shoulder.

She wears a tunic. The folds are indicated by curving, wide grooves.

PORTRAIT F: ARMLESS MALE BUST
The figure is shown frontally.

He wears a tunic and a himation. The tunic has a low, round neckline. The folds of the tunic are rendered by curving grooves. Over the tunic he wears a himation. It is folded from over his left shoulder and falls in a diagonal fold across the chest. A wide fold falls vertically from the left shoulder. The folds are indicated by wide, oblique grooves.

PORTRAIT G: ARMLESS MALE BUST
The figure is shown frontally.

He wears a tunic and a himation. The tunic has a low, round neckline. The folds of the tunic are rendered by curving grooves. Over the tunic he wears a himation. It is folded from over his left shoulder and falls diagonally across the chest. A wide fold falls vertically from the left shoulder. The folds are indicated by wide, oblique grooves.

PORTRAIT H: ARMLESS FEMALE BUST
The figure is shown frontally.

She wears a heavy veil that falls over her right shoulder, proceeds in a curving fold across the chest and back over her left shoulder.

She wears a tunic. The folds are indicated by curving, wide grooves.

PORTRAIT I: STANDING FIGURE
The figure is shown frontally. The arms are bent to the torso. The legs are set apart.

The figure wears a tunic. The folds are rendered by curving grooves.

PORTRAIT J: RECLINING MALE
The figure is shown in frontal to three-quarter view. The left arm is bent. His right leg is bent, and his foot is resting on the mattress. The left leg is bent under the right leg.

The figure wears a tunic and a himation. The folds of the tunic are rendered by curving grooves. The figure also wears a himation. It is folded around the left side and lower body. The folds of the himation are rendered by oblique, curving grooves.

FRAGMENTS OF LIDS, LID RELIEFS, OR BANQUETING RELIEFS

A.D. 140–160

122. FRAGMENT OF BANQUETING SCENE

DATABASE NUMBER: InSitu213.
LOCATION: Palmyra, in situ.
CONTEXT: South-west necropolis. Hypogeum of the Three Brothers, south exedra, loculus bay 58.
ACQUISITION HISTORY: —
MEASUREMENTS: —
MATERIAL: Limestone, white.
PRESERVATION:
TECHNICAL DESCRIPTION: —
DATE: A.D. 140–160.
REFERENCES: Vibert-Guigue 2019, 74 pl. 81.5.

OBJECT DESCRIPTION
The fragment shows part of a reclining figure. He rests the left arm against a cushion. The cushion is decorated with a band with a vegetal motif, separated by horizontal beaded bands.

PORTRAIT
The figure is shown in frontal to three-quarter view. The left arm is bent and held to the torso.

He wears a tunic and a himation. The tunic has a wide, round neckline. He also wears a himation. It is folded around his left upper arm, leaving most of the body and the hand free. It proceeds along the left part of the torso and is folded around the waist. The folds of the himation are rendered by oblique, curving grooves.

At the centre of the chest, the outline of an object, possibly a bowl is recognizable in his left hand.

A.D. 150–170

HYPOGEUM OF ʿAQRABAN

SARCOPHAGUS LIDS OR LID RELIEFS

A.D. 150–170

123. BANQUETING RELIEF

DATABASE NUMBER: PM545.
LOCATION: Palmyra, Palmyra Museum, inv. no. unknown.
CONTEXT: South-west necropolis. Hypogeum of ʿAqraban (found in 2007).
ACQUISITION HISTORY: —
MEASUREMENTS: Height: 115 cm. Width: 182 cm.
MATERIAL: Limestone, white/yellow.
PRESERVATION: The relief is lightly chipped at the sides. Portrait A: The lower part of the figure is weathered. Portrait B: Several cracks run through the portrait. Portrait C: Several cracks run through the portrait. Portrait D: The front of the torso and the lower part of the figure are weathered. Several cracks run through the portrait.
TECHNICAL DESCRIPTION: Partly carved. Portrait A: The portrait is roughly carved and only a vague outline of a female figure is visible. Partly carved. Portrait B: The portrait is roughly and partly carved. Portrait C: The portrait is roughly and partly carved. Portrait D: The face and headdress are roughly carved. The bowl is undercut.
DATE: A.D. 150–170.
REFERENCES: al-Hariri 2013, 150 f. fig. 11; Krag – Raja 2017, 199 n. 23–25; 201 n. 28. 29; 203 n. 43. 48. 50. 51. 53; 214 cat. 6; Krag 2018, 58 n. 304; 62 n. 353; 88 n. 193. 195; 380 cat. 800.

OBJECT DESCRIPTION

The relief is rectangular in shape and depicts a seated female to the right, two male figures at the centre of the relief, and a reclining male figure on the left side of the relief. The texture of the cushion is indicated by wide, curving grooves.

Cat. 123, Pl. 49

PORTRAIT A: SEATED FEMALE

The figure is shown frontally. Her arms are bent, the right arm raised to the height of the neck, the left arm across her lap. Her left foot is obscured by the foot of the reclining figure.

She wears three headdresses: a headband, a turban, and a veil. The veil falls over the shoulders. The details of the headdresses are not carved. Her face is square. The eyebrows are curving. The eyes are almond-shaped. The nose is straight. The mouth is small. The chin is square. The neck is wide.

The details of the garments are not carved.

With her right hand, she appears to hold the edge of the veil.

PORTRAIT B: STANDING PRIEST

The figure is shown frontally. His left arm is bent in front of his chest.

He wears a tall, cylindrical, flat-top headdress: a Palmyrene priestly hat. A triangular mass is carved at the lower part of the headdress, possibly indicating the location of a wreath with a central decoration. His face is square. The eyebrows are curving. The ears are protruding. The nose is straight. The chin is square.

He holds a bowl in the left hand.

PORTRAIT C: STANDING PRIEST

The figure is shown frontally. His arms are bent in front of the torso.

He wears a tall, cylindrical, flat-top headdress: a Palmyrene priestly hat. A triangular mass is carved at the lower part of the headdress, indicating the location of a wreath with a central decoration. His face is square. The eyebrows are curving. The ears are protruding. The nose is straight. The mouth is small. The chin is square. The neck is short and wide.

He wears a tunic and a himation. The tunic is only visible below the neck. The himation covers most of the body: it is wrapped around the right shoulder and arm, leaving only part of the upper chest and the hand free. One fold of the himation crosses the chest diagonally and falls over the left shoulder (>arm-sling< type). The left arm is wrapped in the himation, leaving the hand free. The himation falls over the lower body, covering the legs.

With his right hand, he holds the fold of the himation crossing the chest. With his left hand, he holds an object with an ovoid body and a conical mouth, possibly a libation pitcher. The thumb, the index, and the little finger are extended.

PORTRAIT D: RECLINING PRIEST

The figure is shown reclining. His face and torso are shown frontally, his arms and right leg in profile and his left leg frontally. His right leg is raised; his left leg is extended backwards under the right leg and is obscured by the right leg. His right arm is extended to the side and slightly bent; his left arm is bent in front of the torso.

He wears a tall, cylindrical, flat-top headdress: a Palmyrene priestly hat. Two triangular masses pointing towards the bust of a male figure are depicted at the lower part of the headdress. His face is square and fleshy. The eyebrows are curving. The ears are small and slightly protruding. The nose is straight. The mouth is small. The chin is round. The neck is short and wide.

He wears a tunic, a chlamys, and >Parthian-style< trousers. The tunic has a round neckline and long, tight-fitting sleeves. The tunic ends above the knees. It is tied at the waist with a thin band belt, with the ends looped around it. The folds of the tunic are indicated by curving grooves. Over the tunic, he wears a chlamys. The chlamys is folded over the chest, falls over the left upper arm, and is wrapped around the lower arm, under which it falls over the cushion in two zigzag-shaped folds. It is fastened at the right shoulder with a round brooch (details unclear). The folds of the himation are indicated by wide, oblique grooves. He wears loose-fitting trousers. The folds of the trousers are indicated by curving grooves. He wears boots.

With the upturned palm of the left hand, he holds a bowl with his fingertips. It has a flat bottom and slightly curving sides. His right hand rests on his raised knee.

124. BANQUETING RELIEF

DATABASE NUMBER: PM544.
LOCATION: Palmyra, Palmyra Museum, inv. no. unknown.
CONTEXT: South-west necropolis. Hypogeum of 'Aqraban (found in 2007).
ACQUISITION HISTORY: —
MEASUREMENTS: Height: 115 cm. Width: 182 cm.
MATERIAL: Limestone, white/yellow.
PRESERVATION: The upper part of the relief is broken off between the figures. Portrait A: The portrait is weathered. Portrait B: The portrait is weathered.
TECHNICAL DESCRIPTION: Partly carved. Portrait A: The lower eyelids are not carved and generally the portrait is roughly carved. Portrait B: The lower eyelids are not carved and generally the portrait is roughly cut.
DATE: A.D. 150–170.
REFERENCES: al-Hariri 2013, 150 f. fig. 10; Krag – Raja 2017, 199 n. 23–25; 201 n. 28. 29; 203 n. 43. 48. 50; 214 cat. 7; Krag 2018, 58 n. 304; 62 n. 353; 65 n. 369; 66 n. 385; 380 cat. 801.

OBJECT DESCRIPTION

The relief is rectangular in shape and depicts a seated female on the right side of the relief. A reclining male figure resting against two round cushions is shown on the left side of the relief. The cushions are decorated with a central wide band. The texture of the cushions is indicated by wide, curving grooves. There are two roughly carved rectangular objects behind the reclining priest, indicating the location for two more portraits of standing figures.

PORTRAIT A: SEATED FEMALE

The figure is shown frontally. Her arms are bent: the right arm is across her lap, and the left arm is raised to the height of the face. Her left foot is obscured by the foot of the reclining figure.

She wears three headdresses: a headband, a turban, and a veil. The veil falls over the right shoulder. The details of the band and turban are not carved. Locks of hair are depicted pushed back over the sides of the forehead and the headband. Her face is oval. The eyebrows are curving. The eyes are almond-shaped. The nose is straight. The mouth is small. The chin is pointed. The neck is slender.

She wears a tunic and a himation that crosses the chest diagonally.

With her left hand, she holds the edge of the veil. With the right hand, she holds a fold of the veil.

PORTRAIT B: RECLINING PRIEST

His face and torso are shown frontally, his arms and right leg in profile, and his left leg frontally. His right leg is raised; his left leg is extended backwards under the right leg and is obscured by the right leg. His right arm is extended to the side and slightly bent; his left arm is bent in front of the torso.

He wears a high, cylindrical, flat-top headdress: a Palmyrene priestly hat. Two triangular masses pointing towards the armless bust of a male figure are depicted at the lower part of the headdress. His face is oval. The eyebrows are curving. The ears are small and protruding. The nose is straight. The mouth is small. The chin is round. The neck is short and slender.

He wears a tunic and a himation. The tunic has a round neckline and short, wide sleeves that reach to the elbow. The folds of the tunic are indicated by curving grooves over the body and oblique ones over the arms. Over the tunic, he wears a himation. One side of the himation is wrapped over the left shoulder and arm and falls below the lower arm and over the cushion in two zigzag-shaped folds. Another side is wrapped over the lower waist and covers both legs. The folds of the himation are indicated by wide, oblique grooves. He wears boots.

His right hand is placed on his right knee and he holds an oblong object, possibly a pinecone in his hand. With the upturned palm of the left hand, he holds a bowl with his fingertips.

Cat. 124, Pl. 50

A.D. 150–240

HYPOGEUM AN

SARCOPHAGI

A.D. 150–200

125. FRAGMENTS OF COMPLETE SARCOPHAGUS WITH BANQUETING SCENE AND PORTRAIT BUSTS

DATABASE NUMBER: Insitu178.
LOCATION: Palmyra, in situ.
CONTEXT: South-west necropolis. Hypogeum AN.
ACQUISITION HISTORY: —
MEASUREMENTS: —
MATERIAL: Limestone.
PRESERVATION: The left side of the sarcophagus lid and the right side of the sarcophagus box are broken off. The surface is weathered. Portrait A: Well-preserved. Portrait B: A crack runs horizontally across the neck, suggesting the head has been broken off. Portrait C: Most of the figure is broken off. Only the lower body and right arm are preserved. The upper and lower sides of the sarcophagus box are broken off. The right side of the box is fragmented. The surface is weathered. Portrait D: The left side of the headdress is chipped. Portrait E: The tip of the nose is broken off. Portrait F: Well-preserved.
TECHNICAL DESCRIPTION: —
DATE: A.D. 150–200.
REFERENCES: Ingholt Archives, IA_NCG_Portrait2016_085_sarcophagi; IA_NCG_Portrait2016_124.

OBJECT DESCRIPTION

The sarcophagus lid is rectangular in shape and depicts a seated female, a standing priest, and a reclining figure (portraits A–C). Beneath these figures is a box in the shape of a kline depicting a bust of a priest, a female bust, and another bust of a priest between the kline legs. The kline has turned legs (visible only on the left side, and with the lower part broken). The leg is composed of a long, concave quarter, a bell-shaped element, a reversed bell-shaped element, a ball, a square torus, and a neck. All the elements are decorated with vertical reeding. The finial is broken off.

Cat. 125

Cat. 125

SARCOPHAGUS LID

PORTRAIT A: SEATED FEMALE

The figure is shown frontally. Her head is turned to her right. Her right arm is bent and rests on her lap while her left arm is bent and held in front of her chest. Her legs are bent, and the knees are rendered beneath the drapery of her clothes.

She wears three headdresses: a headband, a turban, and a veil. The headband is placed low on the forehead (details unclear). The turban is coiled. It is rendered in twisting layers with horizontal and oblique grooves indicating the coiling of the fabric. The veil is heavy and falls over both shoulders and covers the upper arms. The folds of the veil are indicated by oblique grooves. Part of the hair is covered by the headdresses. Several strands of hair above the ears are brushed back over the headband and the edge of the turban and disappear under the veil. Her face is round and fleshy. The eyebrows are curving, rendered by incised lines, and starting from the root of the nose. The eyes are wide-set and almond-shaped with thick eyelids. Only the earlobes are visible under the hair. She appears to wear earrings (details unclear). The nose is small and narrow. The nasolabial lines are faintly indicated. The mouth is small with thin lips. The chin is round. She possibly has a double chin. The neck is short and wide.

She wears a tunic and a himation. The tunic has a wide, v-shaped neckline that leaves the upper part of the torso bare. The folds of the tunic are rendered by narrow, curving grooves. Over the tunic she wears a himation. The folds of the himation are indicated by oblique and curving grooves. It is fastened at the left shoulder by a circular brooch enclosing a polygon with a central, circular bezel (Colledge classification: i).

She holds a loop of fabric in her right hand, possibly a fold of the veil or the himation. The index, middle, ring, and little fingers are slightly extended. With her left hand, she holds the edge of the veil. The index, middle, ring, and little fingers are extended. She possibly wears a ring on her left little finger (details unclear).

PORTRAIT B: STANDING PRIEST

The figure is shown frontally. His head is turned slightly to his left. His arms are bent and held in front of his chest.

He wears a high, plain, cylindrical, flat-top headdress divided into three sections by two vertical grooves that covers his hair and most of his forehead: a Palmyrene priestly hat. A narrow, horizontal band at the bottom of the priestly hat suggests a liner.

His face is oval and fleshy. The eyebrows are curving, rendered by incised lines, and starting from the root of the nose. The eyes are small and close-set with thick eyelids. The ears are large and protruding. The nose is small and narrow. The chin is round. He has a double chin. The neck is short and wide.

He wears a tunic and a himation. The tunic has a wide, round neckline. Over the tunic he wears a himation. The himation is wrapped around the right shoulder and arm, leaving only part of the upper torso and the right hand free. One fold of the himation crosses the chest diagonally and falls over the left shoulder (>arm-sling< type), covering the left arm. One fold of the himation is draped over the left wrist. The folds of the himation are rendered by oblique and curving grooves.

With his right hand, he holds the diagonal fold of the himation. The index, middle, ring, and little fingers are slightly extended. With his left hand, he lightly holds a fold of the himation. The index, middle, and little fingers are extended. He possibly wears a ring on the ring finger (details unclear).

PORTRAIT C: RECLINING FIGURE

The figure is shown in a three-quarter to frontal view. The figure is probably a male.

The figure wears a tunic. The cuff of the sleeve is decorated with a pattern, possibly a rosette and running scroll pattern (details unclear). The folds of the tunic are rendered by oblique grooves.

The right hand rests on the figure's knee. All the fingers are extended and are very long.

SARCOPHAGUS BOX

PORTRAIT D: ARMLESS BUST OF A PRIEST

The figure is shown frontally.

He wears a high, plain, cylindrical, flat-top headdress divided into three sections by two vertical grooves that covers his hair and most of his forehead: a Palmyrene priestly hat. A narrow, horizontal band at the bottom of the priestly hat suggests a liner.

The priest's face is square. The eyebrows are curving, rendered by incised lines, and starting from the root of the nose. The eyes are large, wide-set, and almond-shaped with thick upper eyelids and indicated lower eyelids. The upper eyelids extend beyond the end of the lower ones. The ears are protruding with the helix and lobe depicted. The nose is short with a wide base. The mouth is small with thin lips. The chin is round, possibly with a cleft. The neck is short and wide.

He wears a tunic and a chlamys. The tunic has a wide, v-shaped neckline. The folds of the tunic are rendered by deep, curving grooves. Over the tunic, he wears a chlamys that falls over both shoulders and covers most of the chest. The folds of the chlamys are rendered by curving grooves. It is fastened at the right shoulder with a circular brooch with a central, circular bezel (details unclear). A zigzag-shaped fold falls from under the brooch.

PORTRAIT E: ARMLESS BUST OF A FEMALE

The figure is shown frontally.

She wears three headdresses: a headband, a turban, and a veil. The headband is placed low on the forehead. It is divided into panels by vertical grooves. The central panel is decorated (details unclear). The turban is coiled. It is rendered in three twisting layers with horizontal and oblique grooves indicating the coiling of the fabric. The veil is heavy and falls over both shoulders. The folds of the veil are indicated by oblique grooves. Part of the hair is covered by the headdresses. Several strands of hair above the ears are brushed back over the headband and the edge of the turban and disappear under the veil. Her face is oval. The eyebrows are curving, rendered by incised lines, and starting from the root of the nose. The eyes are close-set and almond-shaped, with thick eyelids. The irises are indicated by incised circles. Only the lobes are visible from under her hair. She wears dumbbell-shaped earrings (Colledge classification: H). The nose is large and wide. The mouth is small with thin lips. The chin is round and wide. The neck is short and slender. She wears a necklace composed of a string of round beads at the base of her neck.

She wears a tunic and a himation. The tunic has a deep, v-shaped neckline. Over the tunic she wears a himation. It falls over both shoulders. The folds of the himation are indicated by deep, curving grooves. It is possibly fastened at the right shoulder with a brooch (details unclear).

PORTRAIT F: ARMLESS BUST OF A PRIEST

The figure is shown frontally.

He wears a high, plain, cylindrical, flat-top headdress divided into three sections by two vertical grooves that covers his hair and most of his forehead: a Palmyrene priestly hat.

The priest's face is square. The eyebrows are curving, rendered by incised lines, and starting from the root of the nose. The eyes are close-set, almond-shaped, and slanting with thick upper eyelids. The irises are indicated by incised circles. The ears are large and protruding with the helix, scapha, and lobe depicted. The nose is short with a wide base. The mouth is small with thick lips. The chin is round with a cleft. The neck is short and wide.

He wears a tunic and a chlamys. The tunic has a wide, v-shaped neckline. The folds of the tunic are rendered by deep, curving grooves. Over the tunic, he wears a chlamys that falls over both shoulders and covers most of the chest. The folds of the chlamys are rendered by curving grooves. It is fastened at the right shoulder with a circular brooch with a central, circular bezel (details unclear). A zigzag-shaped fold falls from under the brooch.

A.D. 200–240

126. COMPLETE SARCOPHAGUS WITH BANQUETING SCENE AND PORTRAIT BUSTS

DATABASE NUMBER: Insitu179.
LOCATION: Last known location: Palmyra, in situ.
CONTEXT: South-west necropolis. Hypogeum AN.
ACQUISITION HISTORY: —
MEASUREMENTS: —
MATERIAL: Limestone.
PRESERVATION: Portrait A: Well-preserved. Portrait B: Well-preserved. Portrait C: Well-preserved. Portrait D: The head is broken off. A crack runs through the body, splitting the object in half. The right hand and the bowl are fragmented. Portrait E: The head is broken off. The left lower arm and hand are fragmented. Portrait F: The head is fragmented. Portrait G: The head is fragmented. Portrait H: The head is fragmented. Portrait I: The head is fragmented. Portrait J: Fragmented.
TECHNICAL DESCRIPTION: —
DATE: A.D. 200–240.
REFERENCES: Ingholt Archives, IA_NCG_Portrait2016_065.

OBJECT DESCRIPTION

The sarcophagus lid is rectangular in shape and depicts a seated female, two standing individuals, and two reclining males (portraits A–E). Beneath these figures is a box in the shape of a kline with a female, two priests, and another female bust between the kline legs (portraits F–I). Three rosettes are depicted between the portraits on the relief background. The central one has six pointed petals with incised midribs and six petals between them. The other two have six round petals. Above these figures is a kline and two mattresses. The thin mattress at the top is decorated with an intersecting lozenge pattern with four-petal flowers with serrated petals in the lozenges. The midribs of the petals are rendered by incised lines. The lower mattress has three vertical panels. The central panel is decorated with serrated flowers in an opposite arrangement on the stem and set between beaded bands. The panels on either side are decorated with a running scroll with rosettes set between beaded bands. Oblique grooves indicate the texture of the mattress. The female sits on a cushion (details unclear). The reclining males rest on a round cushion. The right one is decorated with a panel with a running scroll and rosettes set between beaded bands. The left one is decorated with a panel with leaves arranged in an opposite arrangement on the stem, set between beaded bands. The central stretcher of the kline is decorated. The central part is divided into two sections by a horizontal, thin line. The upper section is decorated with diagonal lines. The lower section is decorated with a tongues pattern. On the left side of the kline, a fulcrum is shown. It is decorated with an armless bust of a male (portrait J). The kline has turned legs. They are composed of a plinth and above is a small torus, a concave quarter, a ball, a second, shorter concave quarter, a torus, and another bell-shaped element. All the elements are decorated with vertical fluting, except for the torus that is decorated with diagonal fluting. The finial is broken off.

SARCOPHAGUS LID

PORTRAIT A: SEATED FEMALE

The figure is shown in three-quarter view. The right arm is bent and resting on the right leg, while the left arm is bent and raised to the height of the shoulder. Her legs are bent, and the knees are rendered under the drapery. Her right foot points forward. The left foot is obscured by the reclining male. The right index finger is very long.

She wears a veil that falls over both of her shoulders, falling down to the ground. She wears four necklaces: The first necklace is composed of large, round beads, worn at the base of the neck. The second necklace is composed of alternating round and rectangular bezels linked by beaded elements, worn right below the neckline. The third necklace is composed of a string of round beads and a central pendant (details unclear). The fourth necklace consists of a chain and a central oval pendant, worn high on the chest (details unclear).

She wears a tunic and a himation. The tunic has a wide, round neckline and short, loose-fitting sleeves. The folds are indicated by wide, curving grooves. Over the tunic, she wears a himation. It falls over the left shoulder, crosses the chest diagonally, and covers the left breast. The folds of the himation are indicated by curving grooves on the torso and knees. It ends at the knees. It is fastened at the left shoulder with a brooch (details unclear). She wears round-toe shoes.

She lightly holds the edge of the veil with her right hand. The index finger is extended. With her left hand, she holds the edge of the veil as well.

PORTRAIT B: STANDING FEMALE (?)

The figure is shown frontally. The right arm is stretched and held to the side, while the left arm is bent and raised to the height of the neck. The lower part of the body and the legs are obscured by the legs of the reclining male.

She wears a veil that falls down to both shoulders and down her body on both sides.

She wears a tunic with a round neckline. The folds of the tunic are indicated by curving grooves.

She holds a fold of the veil with her right hand. The index finger is extended.

PORTRAIT C: STANDING MALE

The figure is shown frontally. Both arms are bent and held to the torso, the right above the left. The lower body and legs are obscured by the reclining figure. His left index finger is very long.

He wears a tunic and a himation. It has long, loose-fitting sleeves. The tunic is decorated in the centre with a band that extends downwards (details unclear). The folds of the tunic are rendered by oblique grooves. Over the tunic he wears a himation that is wrapped around his left side (details unclear).

Cat. 126

With his right hand, palm turned upward, he holds a small bowl in his fingertips (details unclear). With his left hand, he is holding a fold of the himation. The index finger is extended.

PORTRAIT D: RECLINING MALE

The figure is seen in three-quarter to frontal view. The right arm is slightly bent and rests on his right leg, while the left arm is bent and held in front of the torso. The right leg is bent, and he rests his foot on the mattress. The left leg is bent under the right with the knee pointing forwards. The lower left leg is obscured by the right leg.

He wears a ›Parthian-style‹ tunic, a chlamys, and ›Parthian-style‹ trousers. The tunic has a wide, round neckline (details unclear), and long, tight-fitting sleeves. The cuffs of the sleeves are decorated with a lozenge pattern with five-petal flowers in the lozenges set between beaded bands. A central wide band extends downwards from the middle of the neckline decorated with a running scroll with five-petal rosettes between beaded bands. The tunic ends above his knees. The hem is decorated with a wide band, possibly decorated (details unclear). The folds of the tunic are rendered by curving, oblique, and pointed grooves. He wears a plain band belt, knotted at the centre with the ends looped under on either side of the waist. At the right thigh, he has an object with a pointed end, a rectangular main body, and a lateral rectangle: a sheathed dagger. Over the tunic, he wears a chlamys that falls over both shoulders and covers most of the chest. One fold of chlamys has a scalloped edge and a decorated border (details unclear). The folds of the chlamys are rendered by curving and oblique grooves. It is fastened at the right shoulder with a circular brooch (details unclear). A zigzag-shaped fold falls from under the brooch. A wide fold of the chlamys falls from under the left arm, across the cushion, and along his left side. The trousers are visible at the shanks. At the middle, each trouser leg has a wide decorated band with a running scroll with six-petal rosettes set between beaded bands, extending downwards. The folds of the trousers are rendered by oblique and horizontal grooves. He also wears shoes with a round toe pointing upwards. The plain shoelaces are knotted at the centre from where two laces extend downwards.

His right hand rests on his right knee. All fingers are slightly bent. With his right hand, palm turned upward, he holds a small bowl in his fingertips (details unclear).

PORTRAIT E: RECLINING MALE

The figure is seen in three-quarter to frontal view. The right arm is held bent in front of the torso, while the left arm is bent and held in front of the chest. The lower part of the body is obscured by the reclining male to his right.

He wears a tunic and a chlamys. The tunic has short sleeves. Over the tunic, he wears a chlamys that falls over both shoulders and covers most of the chest. The folds of the chlamys are indicated by wide, curving grooves. It is most likely fastened at the right shoulder with a brooch (details unclear).

With his right hand, he holds a small branch of oblong leaves. The thumb and index finger are extended. The other fingers are not indicated but the hand remains in a square shape.

SARCOPHAGUS BOX

PORTRAIT F: ARMLESS FEMALE BUST

The figure is shown frontally, rendered in a clipeus.

She wears a veil. It falls over the back of her head and over both shoulders in a curving fold, and is wrapped around her upper body. The veil has a scalloped edge. The neck is wide with one curving groove. She wears a necklace composed of a plain thin hoop and a central round pendant.

She wears a tunic. The tunic has a wide, round neckline. The folds of the tunic are rendered by curving grooves.

PORTRAIT G: ARMLESS BUST OF A PRIEST

The figure is shown frontally, rendered in a clipeus.

He wears a high, cylindrical, flat-top headdress (visible in outline): a Palmyrene priestly hat.

He wears a tunic and a chlamys. The tunic has a wide, round neckline. The folds of the tunic are rendered by curving and oblique grooves. Over the tunic, he wears a chlamys that falls over both shoulders and covers the chest. The folds of the chlamys are indicated by curving grooves. It is fastened at the right shoulder with a round brooch with a raised centre (Colledge classification: j). A zigzag-shaped fold falls from under the brooch.

PORTRAIT H: ARMLESS BUST OF A PRIEST

The figure is shown frontally, rendered in a clipeus.

He wears a high, cylindrical, flat-top headdress (visible in outline): a Palmyrene priestly hat.

He wears a tunic and a chlamys. The tunic has a wide, round neckline. The folds of the tunic are rendered by curving and oblique grooves. Over the tunic, he wears a chlamys that falls over both shoulders and covers the chest. The folds of the chlamys are indicated by curving grooves. It is fastened at the right shoulder with a round brooch with a raised centre (Colledge classification: j). A zigzag-shaped fold falls from under the brooch.

PORTRAIT I: ARMLESS FEMALE BUST

The figure is shown frontally, rendered in a clipeus.

She wears a veil. It falls over the back of her head and over both shoulders in a curving fold, and is wrapped around her upper body. The veil has a scalloped edge.

She wears a tunic. The tunic has a wide, round neckline. The folds of the tunic are rendered by curving grooves.

PORTRAIT J: ARMLESS BUST OF A PRIEST IN FULCRUM

The figure is shown frontally, rendered in a clipeus.

He wears a high, cylindrical, flat-top headdress (details unclear): a Palmyrene priestly hat.

SARCOPHAGUS LIDS

A.D. 200–240

127. SARCOPHAGUS LID WITH BANQUETING SCENE

DATABASE NUMBER: InSitu183.
LOCATION: Palmyra, in situ.
CONTEXT: South-west necropolis. Hypogeum AN.
ACQUISITION HISTORY: —
MEASUREMENTS: —
MATERIAL: Limestone.
PRESERVATION: Well-preserved.
TECHNICAL DESCRIPTION: The lid is in large parts only partly carved. The figure next to the seated female is only outlines, without any details. There are one or two bosses that could have been carved into standing figures behind the reclining male. The faces and hands of the seated female and the reclining male are not finished. The headdresses and the lower part of the seated female are only roughly finished. Details on both figures are missing: the female's necklaces and bracelets are only outlined and the bowl the male is holding is left in a rough form. The cushions are left in a rough stage as well. Traces of a tooth chisel and a flat chisel are visible all over the lid. Traces of a pick are visible on the one or two bosses in the background.
DATE: A.D. 200–240.
REFERENCES: Ingholt Archives, IA_NCG_Portrait2016_066.

OBJECT DESCRIPTION

The sarcophagus lid is rectangular in shape and depicts a seated female, two or three standing individuals, and a reclining male (portraits A–D). Beneath these figures is a mattress. The female sits on two round cushions and the male reclines on one round cushion.

PORTRAIT A: SEATED FEMALE

The figure is shown in frontal to three-quarter view. Her lower body is turned towards her left. The right arm is held to the side and rests on the cushion, while the left arm is bent and raised to the shoulder. The feet are obscured by the reclining figure.

She wears a veil and possibly further headdresses (left unfinished). The veil is heavy with a scalloped edge. It falls over the back of her head and over both shoulders. Her face round with the eyes and nose indicated. Her neck is long and slender. She wears two unfinished necklaces: the first necklace is composed of a plain hoop with a central, crescent-shaped pendant. The second necklace is composed of a plain hoop and an oval pendant. Some uncarved stone below it shows that the carver had intended to depict suspended bars or twisted wires below it.

She wears a tunic and a himation. The tunic has a wide, round neckline and short, loose sleeves. The folds of the tunic are indicated by oblique grooves. Over the tunic, she wears a himation. The himation falls over the left shoulder, crosses the chest diagonally, and covers the left breast and the lower torso. The diagonal fold of the himation is decorated with a scalloped band. The himation has a short overfold, indicated by a thin incised line across her waist. It falls across her legs (left unfinished). It is fastened at the left shoulder with a brooch (details unclear, most likely left unfinished).

Her right hand rests on her right knee. With her left hand, she holds the edge of the veil. She wears a bracelet on each wrist.

PORTRAIT B: STANDING MALE

The figure is shown frontally. The arms are held to the side.

The hair is short. The face and body are only roughed out.

PORTRAIT C: STANDING FIGURE(S)

One or two bosses for further standing individuals.

PORTRAIT D: RECLINING MALE

The figure is shown in frontal to three-quarter view. The right arm is extended to the side and rests on the knee, while the left arm is bent and held in front of the torso. The right leg is bent and the foot rests on the mattress (left unfinished). The left leg is bent under the right and the lower part is obscured by the right leg.

He wears a ›Parthian-style‹ tunic, a chlamys, and trousers. The tunic has a wide, round neckline with a beaded band and long loose-fitting sleeves. A central wide band extends downwards from the middle of the neckline, left blank. The cuffs are decorated with a wide band, also left plain. The folds of the tunic are indicated by oblique grooves. He also wears a plain band belt, knotted at the centre with the ends looped under on either side of the waist. Over the tunic, he wears a chlamys that falls over the left shoulder, along the left side of his body and is wrapped around his legs. It is wrapped around the left arm and falls below the arm and over the cushion in an s-shaped fold. The folds of the chlamys are indicated by curving and oblique grooves. The trousers are visible at the ankle (left unfinished).

The right hand is curled around the knee, and the individual fingers are not indicated. He holds a fold of the chlamys. With his left hand, palm turned upward, he holds the bowl in his fingertips (both left unfinished).

Cat. 127

A.D. 220–240

128. SARCOPHAGUS LID RELIEF

DATABASE NUMBER: NMD058.
LOCATION: Damascus, National Museum of Damascus, inv. no. 4946.
CONTEXT: South-west necropolis. Hypogeum AN.
ACQUISITION HISTORY: —
MEASUREMENTS: Height: 105 cm. Width: 208 cm.
MATERIAL: Limestone.
PRESERVATION: The lower right and left corners, and the upper left corner of the relief are broken off. Part of the background between portraits A and B is missing. The mattress underneath the feet of portrait A and the lower left edge of the relief have been chipped and filled with another material (later restoration). The surface is lightly chipped. Portrait A: The face is heavily chipped. The pendant of the last necklace, the garment under the left arm, and the left edge of the garment are chipped. Portrait B: A few scratches on the surface of the right leg. Portrait D: The surface of the right elbow is lightly chipped. Portrait E: The decoration on the Palmyrene priestly hat is broken off. There are a few scratches on the surface of the nose and neck. The surface of the left palm and the left thigh is lightly chipped.
TECHNICAL DESCRIPTION: Several areas on the object appear partly carved: the two cushions on the right side of the relief, the end of the fold of the himation that falls down the female's right thigh, and the lozenge at the far right end of the mattress. Portrait A: The lower necklace is partly carved. Portrait B: The lower eyelids, the details of the ears, and the earrings are partly carved. Portrait C: The lower eyelids are partly carved. The hem of the tunic is roughly finished. Portrait D: The lower eyelids are partly carved. Portrait E: The lower eyelids are partly carved. The right handle of the cup and the lower decorations of the wide band on the tunic are partly carved.
DATE: A.D. 220–240 (Abdul-Hak – Abdul-Hak 1951: A.D. 180–200).
REFERENCES: Abdul-Hak – Abdul-Hak 1951, 42 cat. 37 pl. 19, 1; Ambler 1961, 85 fig. 3; Tanabe 1986, 42 pls. 410–415; Parlasca 1987b, 114 cat. 5; Finlayson 2004, 60. 65 figs. 1. 2; Krag – Raja 2017, 199 n. 24; 204 n. 72. 73; 205 n. 75; 208 n. 99; 209 n. 100. 102; 210 n. 110; 219 cat. 35; Krag 2018, 28 n. 9; 39 n. 122; 41 n. 143; 58 n. 311; 59 n. 315; 61 n. 336. 337; 62 n. 350. 353; 63 n. 355. 358. 359; 69 n. 304; 73 n. 47. 51; 74 n. 57; 88 n. 193. 195. 197; 102 n. 66; 103 n. 73; 108 n. 125; 388 cat. 837.

OBJECT DESCRIPTION

The sarcophagus lid is rectangular in shape and depicts a seated female, a standing female, two standing priests, and a reclining priest on a thin mattress. The mattress is decorated with an intersecting lozenge pattern with alternating six-petal rosettes and four-petal cruciform flowers inside them. There are round elements where the lozenges intersect. The female sits on two

Cat. 128, Pl. 51

round cushions, one placed on top of the other. The priest on the left side of the relief reclines on a round cushion with a central, wide band decorated with a branch with serrated leaves in alternating arrangement between beaded bands. The texture of the cushion is indicated by wide, curving grooves.

PORTRAIT A: SEATED FEMALE

The figure is shown in a three-quarter view. Her arms are bent, the right resting on the right thigh, the left arm raised to the height of the shoulder. The knees are slightly parted, with the right leg crossing under the left leg. The arms appear short in relation to the body. The feet are obscured by the reclining figure.

She wears a veil that falls behind the neck and covers the shoulders and upper arms. She wears a head-chain running from the centre of the forehead to the side, composed of circular bezels with incised borders linked together by beaded elements. The hair is rendered as a series of overlapping locks, with the individual strands indicated by narrow, oblique, incised lines. The neck is long and slender. She wears four necklaces: a necklace composed of small, round beads at the base of the neck, a necklace composed of alternating round, rhomboid, and square elements, all with beaded borders, joined together by beaded elements. Over the top of the breasts, she wears a necklace composed of larger, round beads with a central, crescent-shaped pendant with a round bead between the horns, suspended by a narrow sleeve, and between the breasts she wears a necklace composed of a plain, thick chain with a large, oval pendant in the middle.

She wears a tunic and a himation. The tunic has a wide, v-shaped neckline and short, wide sleeves that reach below the elbow. The fabric of the tunic under the right armpit is pushed upwards by the himation. It falls to the ground and covers the legs and feet completely. The folds of the tunic are rendered by narrow, oblique grooves as well as two curving grooves over the right breast. Over the tunic she wears a himation. One side falls diagonally across the chest and passes under the right arm. It is fastened at the left shoulder with a plain, round brooch (Colledge classification: i). The himation covers the lower body and legs, diagonally crossing the right thigh and leg. One edge of the himation is decorated with a pleated band.

With the right hand, she holds a fold of the himation. With the left hand, she holds a fold of the veil. She wears a wide bracelet composed of twisted beaded and plain wires on the right wrist and a plain, wide, and thick hoop bracelet on the left wrist.

PORTRAIT B: STANDING FEMALE

The figure is shown frontally. Her head is turned slightly to her right. Her right arm falls along the right thigh, the left arm is bent and raised in front of the chest. She stands on the left leg, and the right is relaxed. The feet are obscured by the reclining figure.

The hair is gathered upwards in a series of plaits indicated by vertical grooves with diagonal incised, wavy lines on either side. At the top, the hair is gathered in a twisted plait. A wavy lock with individual strands of hair indicated by four incised grooves runs from the centre of the forehead to the ears. She wears a head ornament that extends downwards from the middle of the top plait to the forehead. A round pendant with an incised circle at the centre is placed near the top of the head. A bead on either side of the pendant joins it with a larger round pendant with a beaded border. A beaded element joins this pendant to a rectangular one with a beaded border. Five narrow, rectangular elements with round ends hang from the oval pendant, possibly indicating chains ending in pearls. Her face is square. The eyebrows are indicated by almost straight ridges. The eyes are large and almond-shaped, with thick upper eyelids. The eyeballs are blank. The ears are small, close to the head, and she wears earrings (details not carved). The nose is straight with a flat tip. The alae are carved. The mouth is wide with thin lips. Two small grooves are carved at the corners of the mouth. The chin is square. The neck is short and wide. She wears a plain, wide hoop necklace with a round pendant with an incised border suspended by a wide sleeve.

She wears a tunic and a himation. The tunic has a wide, round neckline and falls to the ground, covering the feet completely. The folds of the tunic are indicated by wide, curving grooves over the upper chest and left leg, and slightly oblique ones between the legs. Over the tunic, she wears a himation. It is folded over the upper chest, covers the shoulders, right arm, upper left arm, torso, waist, and falls between the legs in a triangular fold. The edge of the himation is decorated with a pleated band.

With the right hand, she holds a fold of the himation. The thumb and the index finger are extended. The nails are indicated by incised lines. With the left hand, she holds the curving fold of the himation over the left breast. The thumb, the index, and the little finger are extended. She wears a wide bracelet composed of twisted beaded and plain strands on the left wrist.

PORTRAIT C: STANDING PRIEST

The figure is shown frontally. His head is slightly turned to his left. His arms are bent in front of the chest. The left leg and feet are obscured by the reclining figure.

He wears a tall, cylindrical, flat-top headdress divided into three sections by two vertical grooves low on the forehead: a Palmyrene priestly hat. A wreath is depicted at the lower part of the hat. It has three rows of long, narrow leaves pointing towards an oval with a raised centre. Two round objects, berries(?), are shown on either side of the leaf on the central row next to the oval. The midribs of the leaves are incised. A narrow, horizontal band at the bottom of the hat suggests a liner. His face is square. The eyebrows are indicated by almost straight ridges. The eyes are large and almond-shaped, with thick upper eyelids. The eyeballs are blank. The ears are small and protruding, with helix, scapha, and lobe indicated. The nose is straight and wide. The alae are carved. The mouth is wide with a full upper lip. Two small grooves are carved at the corners of the mouth. The chin is square. The neck is long and wide.

He wears a ›Parthian-style‹ tunic. The tunic has a wide, round neckline decorated with a beaded border. A wide band framed by beaded borders extends downwards from the centre of the neckline. It is decorated with a branch with serrated leaves in opposite arrangement. The tunic has long, tight-fitting sleeves and the cuffs are decorated with rosettes inside a running scroll. The folds of the tunic are indicated by curving grooves on the arms and oblique grooves on the body. At the waist, he wears a thin band belt tied with a double knot and the ends of the belt looped under on either side of the waist.

His right hand rests on top of a bird's body. In the upturned palm of the left hand, he holds the bird, which is shown in profile. Its body turns towards the left, and its head towards the right. It has short legs, a small body, a long neck, and a hooked beak. The bird's wing is indicated by a curving groove.

PORTRAIT D: STANDING PRIEST

The figure is shown frontally. His head is slightly turned to his left. His arms are bent, the right in front of the chest and the left to the side. The lower part of the body is obscured by the reclining figure.

He wears a tall, cylindrical, flat-top headdress divided into three sections by two vertical grooves low on the forehead: a Palmyrene priestly hat. A wreath is depicted at the lower part of the hat. It has three rows of long, narrow leaves pointing towards an oval with a raised centre. Two round objects, berries (?), are shown on either side of the leaf on the central row next to the oval. The midribs of the leaves are incised. A narrow, horizontal band at the bottom of the hat suggests a liner. His face is square. The eyebrows are indicated by curving ridges. The eyes are large and almond-shaped, with thick upper eyelids. The left eye is narrower than the right. The eyeballs are blank. The ears are small and protruding, with helix, scapha, and lobe indicated. The nose is straight and wide. The alae are carved. The philtrum is carved. The mouth is wide with thin lips. Two small grooves are carved at the corners of the mouth. The chin is square. The neck is short and wide.

He wears a tunic and a himation. The tunic has a wide, v-shaped neckline decorated with a narrow, pleated band. The folds of the tunic are rendered by curving grooves. Over the tunic he wears a himation that falls over both shoulders and covers most of the body: it is wrapped around the right shoulder and arm, leaving only the upper part of the chest and the hand free. One fold of the himation crosses the chest diagonally and falls over the left shoulder (›arm-sling‹ type). The edge of the himation that crosses the chest is decorated with a pleated band. The folds of the himation are indicated by oblique grooves.

With the right hand, he holds the diagonal fold of the himation. His left hand rests on the reclining priest's upper right arm.

PORTRAIT E: RECLINING PRIEST

The head, torso, upper left arm, and upper left leg of the figure are shown frontally, the right arm, lower left arm, right leg, and lower left leg are shown in profile. The head is slightly turned to his left. The right arm is extended to the side, and the left is bent in front of the torso. The right leg is bent and the foot rests on the mattress. The left leg is bent under the right leg, with the left foot obscured by it.

He wears a tall, cylindrical, flat-top headdress divided into three sections by two vertical grooves low on the forehead: a Palmyrene priestly hat. A wreath is depicted at the lower part of the hat. It has three rows of serrated leaves pointing towards an oval with a medallion with an armless bust. The bust has short hair and wears a tunic and a himation that crosses the chest diagonally. The midribs of the leaves are incised. A narrow, horizontal band at the bottom of the hat suggests a liner. His face is square. The eyebrows are rendered by ridges that meet over the root of the nose in an upward curve. The eyes are large and almond-shaped with thin upper eyelids. The eyeballs are blank. The ears are small and protruding, with helix, scapha, and lobe indicated. The nose is straight and wide. The alae are carved. The mouth is wide with thin lips. Two small grooves are carved at the corners of the mouth. The chin is square with a cleft. The neck is long and wide.

He wears a ›Parthian-style‹ tunic, a chlamys, and ›Parthian-style‹ trousers. The tunic has a small, round neckline decorated with a narrow, beaded band and a wider band with alternating circles and lozenges with incised borders. A wide band framed by two beaded borders extends downwards from the centre of the neckline. The band is decorated with a series of vegetal motifs: a trilobed leaf with a tendril on either side, a serrated leaf with a serrated leaf in profile and a tendril on either side. The upper tendrils are filled with rosettes with four, five, or six petals, pomegranates, and pinecones. The tunic has long, slightly loose sleeves and the cuffs are decorated with a wide band with a branch with serrated leaves in opposite arrangement, and a beaded border. The lower hem of the tunic is decorated with a wide band with a branch with serrated leaves shown frontally in opposite arrangement, and a beaded border. The tunic has a slit on either side, and the slit edges are decorated with a beaded band. The end of the slit on the right side of the tunic is turned, showing the same pattern of beaded band on the inside of the fabric. A thin band belt is tied with a double knot at the waist with the ends of the belt looped under on either side. The folds of the tunic are indicated by curving and oblique grooves. An object with narrow, trapezoidal main body and two round protrusions near the centre is visible against the left thigh: a sheathed dagger in profile. He wears a chlamys over the tunic. It is folded over the chest, covers both shoulders, the left upper arm, and falls under the left elbow and over the cushion and mattress in two zigzag-shaped folds. It is fastened at the right shoulder with a round brooch with a beaded border (Colledge classification: f). A small, zigzag-shaped fold falls under the brooch. One edge of the chlamys is decorated with a pleated band with a beaded border. The folds of the chlamys that fall under the arm are decorated with a wide band with a running scroll with six-petal rosettes and a beaded border. He wears loose-fitting trousers decorated with a wide band framed by beaded borders that extend downwards. The wide band is decorated with a branch with serrated leaves in opposite arrangement on a stem. The trousers are tucked into the shoes (visible at the right foot). The shoe is pointed. The topline of the shoe is below the ankle, and the shoe is tied at the instep with a thin band or cord forming a double knot and attached to a wide strap that covers the heel.

The right hand rests on the right knee. With his left hand, he holds a cup: the base is conical and decorated with a tongues pattern. The lower body is conical, with a tongues pattern, a narrow, plain band with a straight edge, a narrow, plain band with a flaring edge, a wide band decorated with beads between six-petal rosettes, a narrow, plain band with a flaring edge, and a narrow, plain band with a straight edge at the rim. The right handle is angular. The index and the little finger of the left hand are extended. He wears a ring on the little finger of the left hand: it is a wide, thick hoop with an oval bezel. The fingernails and the cuticles are indicated by fine, incised lines.

A.D. 170–200

HYPOGEUM OF BARÎKÎ

SARCOPHAGUS LIDS

A.D. 170–200

129. SARCOPHAGUS LID RELIEF WITH BANQUETING SCENE

DATABASE NUMBER: PM958.
LOCATION: Palmyra, Palmyra Museum, inv. no. unknown.
CONTEXT: South-east necropolis. Hypogeum of Barîkî, gallery, west wall, south of section 21. Excavation no. 16.
ACQUISITION HISTORY: —
MEASUREMENTS: Height: 83 cm. Width: 135 cm. Depth: 19 cm.
MATERIAL: Limestone, white/yellow.
PRESERVATION: The surface of the sarcophagus lid is weathered. The lower mattress has been reconstructed with two fragments. Portrait A: It is weathered, and fragments are missing from her right arm and forehead. Portrait B: The right eye is chipped. The surface is slightly weathered. Portrait C: The surface is slightly weathered. Portrait D: The lower part of the nose and a part of the right cheek are chipped.
TECHNICAL DESCRIPTION: —
DATE: A.D. 170–200 (Sadurska – Bounni 1994: A.D. 150–180).
REFERENCES: Sadurska – Bounni 1994, 111 f. cat. 153 fig. 228; Krag – Raja 2017, 199 n. 24; 204 n. 72. 73; 205 n. 75. 76. 78; 208 n. 99; 209 n. 100. 102; 215 cat. 12; Krag 2018, 28 n. 9; 33 n. 76. 82. 84; 46 n. 198; 52 n. 249; 66 n. 382; 87 n. 182; 88 n. 193. 195; 98 n. 28; 314 cat. 560. Inscription: Sadurska – Bounni 1994, 111; Krag 2018, 314 cat. 560.

OBJECT DESCRIPTION

The sarcophagus lid relief is rectangular in shape and depicts a seated female, two standing males, and a reclining male. Beneath these figures are two mattresses. The thin mattress at the top is decorated with a chevron pattern. Curving grooves indicate the texture of the lower mattress. The reclining figure rests the left arm on a cushion. It is decorated with a band with curving, incised lines. Curving grooves indicate the texture of the fabric.

INSCRIPTION

SCRIPT: Palmyrene Aramaic.
LOCATION ON RELIEF: To the left of the seated female.
TRANSCRIPTION: ḤBL [- - -] | ʾQMʾ B[RT] | BRʾ BRYK[Y] Rʾʾ | [S]Y D | YKN BR | MQYMW.
TRANSLATION: Alas, Aqmê daughter of Barâ Barîkaî - - - son of Moqîmû.

CIS no. —; PAT no. 2707.

COMMENT: The inscription is not visible on the only available photograph. L.3–5 may have presented the name of at least one male individual, son of Moqîmû. The proposal to read YKN (unknown name) as the name of the husband of Aqmê is dubious.

PORTRAIT A: SEATED FEMALE, AQMÊ

The figure is shown frontally. The head is large, and the body seems stocky. The right arm is bent and raised to the neck. The left is bent and rests on the left thigh. Her legs are bent, and the knees are rendered under the drapery. Her right foot is covered by the foot of the reclining male.

She wears three headdresses: a headband, a turban, and a veil. The band is placed low on the forehead and is divided into panels separated by vertical, beaded bands (details unclear). The turban is coiled. It is rendered in three twisting layers with horizontal grooves, indicating the coiling of the fabric. The veil is heavy. It falls over her shoulders and is wrapped around her left arm and falls over the back of her right shoulder. Most of the hair is covered by the headdresses: several strands of hair above the ears are pushed back over the edge of the band and disappear under the veil. The individual strands of hair are rendered by incised lines. Her face is oval. Her eyebrows are rendered by curving, incised lines starting from the root of the nose. The eyes are close-set and almond-shaped with thick upper eyelids that extend beyond the lower ones. The irises are indicated. Only the earlobes are visible under the hair and she is wearing dumbbell-shaped earrings (Colledge classification: H). Her nose is straight and the mouth small with full lips. The chin is wide and almost double. The neck is wide. She wears two necklaces: one composed of small, round beads worn at the base of the neck and one composed of small, round beads with a central, circular pendant with a hollowed centre as indication of an inlay, worn below the collarbone.

She wears a tunic and a himation. The tunic has a small, round neckline. The folds are indicated by curving grooves.

The himation falls to the ankles. It crosses her chest diagonally from the left shoulder to the right side, and covers most of the lower chest and body. It is fastened at the left shoulder with a trapezoidal brooch with a rosette finial (Colledge classification: b). The folds between the legs are rendered by curving grooves.

With her right hand, she pulls a fold of the veil with her hand. She rests her left hand on her thigh and holds another edge of the veil. It has an oval weight attached to it. The left index finger is extended.

PORTRAIT B: STANDING MALE

The figure is shown frontally. The head is large. Both arms are bent and held to the torso. The left leg and lower part of right leg are obscured by the reclining figure.

The hair is arranged in vertical rows of curls around the head. His face is square. The eyebrows are curving, starting from the root of the nose. The eyes are close-set and almond-shaped with thick eyelids. The eyeballs appear blank. The ears are large and protruding with the helix, scapha, and lobe depicted. The nose is straight and wide at the base with carved nostrils. The mouth is small with thin lips. The cheeks are fleshy and the chin is wide. The neck is wide.

He wears a tunic and a himation. The tunic has a small, round neckline. The folds are indicated by curving grooves. Over the tunic, he wears a himation that covers most of his body. It is wrapped around the right shoulder and arm, leaving the chest and the hand free. A fold of the himation crosses the chest diagonally and falls over the left shoulder (›arm-sling‹ type). The folds are indicated by oblique and curving grooves.

With his right hand, he holds the diagonal fold of the himation. All fingers are extended. With his left hand, he holds a fold of the himation. The index finger is extended.

PORTRAIT C: STANDING MALE

The figure is shown frontally. The head is large. The right arm appears short in relation to the body. The right arm is bent and held to the torso. The lower part of the body is obscured by the reclining figure.

The hair is arranged in horizontal rows of curls around the head. His face is square. The eyebrows are curving, starting from the root of the nose. The eyes are close-set and almond-shaped with thick upper eyelids. The eyeballs appear blank. The nose is straight and wide at the base with carved nostrils. The ears are large and protruding with the helix and lobe depicted. The mouth is small with thin lips. The cheeks are fleshy, and the chin is wide. The neck is wide.

He wears a tunic and a himation. The tunic has a small, v-shaped neckline. The folds are indicated by curving grooves. Over the tunic, he wears a himation that covers most of his body. It is wrapped around the right shoulder and arm, leaving the chest and the hand free. A fold of the himation crosses the chest diagonally and falls over the left shoulder (›arm-sling‹). Another fold of the himation runs vertically down his left side. The folds of the himation are indicated by oblique and curving grooves.

With his right hand, he holds the diagonal fold of the himation.

PORTRAIT D: RECLINING MALE

The head and the body are shown in frontal to three-quarter view. The legs and arms appear short in relation to the body. The right arm is extended and rests on his raised knee, the left arm is bent in front of the torso. His right leg is bent, and his foot is resting on the mattress. The left leg is bent under the right leg, and the lower part is obscured by the right leg.

His hair is arranged in snail-shell curls around the head. He wears a wreath high on the head with a central oval. His face is round. The eyebrows are slightly curving ridges rendered by incised lines. His eyes are close-set, almond-shaped, and slanting with thick upper eyelids that extend beyond the end of the lower ones. The eyeballs are blank. The ears are large with helix and lobe depicted. The nose is small. He has a beard that starts at the temples and covers the cheeks and the chin. The facial hair is rendered by small snail-shell curls. The mouth is small with thin lips. The neck is long.

He wears a tunic and a himation. The tunic has long, slightly loose sleeves and a small, round neckline decorated with a beaded band. The folds of the tunic are rendered by vertical and curving grooves. Over the tunic, he wears a himation. It is folded around his left shoulder and wrist and falls along the left side of his torso where it is folded around his waist and legs. A zigzag-shaped fold falls from under his left hand. The folds of the himation are rendered by diagonal, curving grooves. He also wears pointed boots with laces or a strap that runs around his ankle and heel.

He holds a globular object with an incised pattern on scales in his right hand, possibly a pinecone. With the upturned palm of his left hand, he holds a bowl with a narrow body with his fingertips. It is decorated with a pattern of hollowed-out lozenges.

FRAGMENTS OF LIDS, LID RELIEFS, OR BANQUETING RELIEFS

A.D. 170–200

130. FRAGMENT OF BANQUETING RELIEF

DATABASE NUMBER: PM085.
LOCATION: Palmyra, Palmyra Museum, inv. no. unknown.
CONTEXT: South-east necropolis. Hypogeum of Barîkî, east wall, to the south of section 7. Excavation no. 18.
ACQUISITION HISTORY: —
MEASUREMENTS: Height: 71 cm. Width: 34 cm. Depth: 10 cm.
MATERIAL: Limestone, yellow.
PRESERVATION: The entire left side of the object is broken off. The right side is slightly chipped. The portrait is broken at the lower right arm, and the lower part of the right foot. A part of the veil and the left side of the chest are chipped. A crack runs from the right shoulder to the

lower left side of the torso. Another crack runs vertically through the base of the neck. The surface at the left foot and mattress is weathered.

TECHNICAL DESCRIPTION: The head has been reattached to the body.

DATE: A.D. 170–200 (Sadurska – Bounni 1994: A.D. 150–180).

REFERENCES: Sadurska – Bounni 1994, 112 cat. 155 fig. 229; Krag 2018, 28 n. 9; 47 n. 212; 51 n. 243; 101 n. 58; 105 n. 85. 87; 313 cat. 555. Inscription: Sadurska – Bounni 1994, 112 cat. 155; Krag 2018, 313 cat. 555.

OBJECT DESCRIPTION

The object depicts a seated female. Beneath the figure is a mattress. The mattress is decorated with an incised chevron pattern.

INSCRIPTION

SCRIPT: Palmyrene Aramaic.
LOCATION ON RELIEF: To the right of the head.
TRANSCRIPTION: [- - - | BR]YKY | BR ZBYDʾ | BR [- - -].
TRANSLATION: [Bar]îkaî, son of Zebîdâ, son of - - -.

CIS no. —; PAT no. 2709.

PORTRAIT

The figure is shown frontally with the feet resting on the mattress. The head is turned slightly to her right. The arms are bent; the right resting on her lap, the left raised to the neck.

She wears three headdresses: a headband, a turban, and a veil. The band is placed low on the forehead and is divided into rectangular panels separated by vertical bands. The central panel is decorated with a crisscross pattern. The turban is coiled. It is divided into two layers and the ends are looped into each other creating a knot in the middle. Curving grooves indicate the coiling of the fabric. The veil is heavy. It falls over the shoulders and is wrapped around her upper left arm. Part of the hair is covered by the headdress: several strands of hair above the ears are pushed back over the headband and the edge of the turban and disappear under the veil. Her face is round. The eyebrows are curving, rendered by incised lines starting from the root of the nose. The eyes are close-set and almond-shaped with thick eyelids. The upper eyelids extend beyond the end of the lower ones. The irises are indicated by incised circles. Only the earlobes are visible under the hair. She wears bell-shaped earrings (Colledge classification: D). The nose is large with carved nostrils. The cheeks are fleshy, and the mouth is small with thin lips. The chin is round and pointed. The neck is wide with horizontal grooves. She wears two necklaces: one composed of small, round beads on a string, worn at the base of the neck. One composed of round beads on a string with a central, round pendant, worn high on the chest.

She wears a tunic and a himation. The tunic has a small, v-shaped neckline and sleeves reaching just below the elbows. The folds of the tunic are rendered by curving and oblique grooves. The himation crosses the chest diagonally from the left shoulder to the right side and covers the left breast. It is fastened at the left shoulder with a trapezoidal brooch (details unclear). The folds are indicated by vertical and oblique, wide grooves.

She holds a fold of the veil in her right hand. The fold continues underneath the hand and ends with a tassel. The index and the little finger are extended. With her left hand, she holds a fold of the veil. She wears a thin hoop ring with a round bezel on her little finger.

HYPOGEUM OF BARÎKÎ (SOUTH-WEST NECROPOLIS)

SARCOPHAGUS BOXES

A.D. 170–200

131. SARCOPHAGUS BOX WITH PORTRAIT BUSTS

DATABASE NUMBER: PM738.
LOCATION: Palmyra, Palmyra Museum, inv. no. unknown.
CONTEXT: South-west necropolis. Found (1990) in the south-west necropolis, hypogeum of the Barîkî family.
ACQUISITION HISTORY: —
MEASUREMENTS: —
MATERIAL: Limestone, grey/yellow.
PRESERVATION: Well preserved.
TECHNICAL DESCRIPTION: The inscriptions have traces of red pigment.
DATE: A.D. 170–200.
REFERENCES: Degeorge 2001, 238 f.; Degeorge 2002, 198 f.; al-Asʿad 2018, 25 fig. 6; Krag 2018, 32 n. 63; 36 n. 112; 47 n. 214; 51 n. 241; 103 n. 74; 318 cat. 568; <https://virtual-museum-syria.org/palmyra/facade-of-a-sarcophagus-from-breki-family-tomb/> (06.05.2022). Inscription: Yon 2013, 355 cat. 113; Krag 2018, 318 cat. 568.

OBJECT DESCRIPTION

The sarcophagus box is rectangular in shape and is rendered as a kline. Four armless busts are depicted between the kline legs: two of females framing two of male priests. A cloth secured by two rosettes at the height of the chin is placed behind the third portrait. A palm branch with narrow leaves extends upwards and inwards from the rosettes. The fabric is indicated by slightly oblique grooves. The kline has a mattress with three wide bands: the two on either side have a running scroll with rosettes motif, and the central one has a continuous vegetal motif. Curving grooves indicate the texture of the fabric. The stretcher of the kline is decorated with a central, rectangular panel divided horizontally into two sections, the lower one is decorated with a tongues pattern. On either side of the panel are two small, square decorated panels followed by rectangular ones.

INSCRIPTIONS

INSCRIPTION 1
SCRIPT: Palmyrene Aramaic.
LOCATION ON RELIEF: On the projecting plinth under portrait A.
TRANSCRIPTION: 'T'M BRT ḤGGW BR BRYKY | 'MRŠ' 'TT MLKW BR YRḤBWL'.
TRANSLATION: 'Ateêm daughter of Ḥagegû son of Barîkaî Amrishâ, wife of Malkù son of Yarḥibôlâ.

INSCRIPTION 2
SCRIPT: Palmyrene Aramaic.
LOCATION ON RELIEF: On the projecting plinth under portrait B.
TRANSCRIPTION: ḤGGW BR BRYKY 'MRŠ'.
TRANSLATION: Ḥagegù son of Barîkaî Amrišâ.

INSCRIPTION 3
SCRIPT: Palmyrene Aramaic.
LOCATION ON RELIEF: On the projecting plinth under portrait C.
TRANSCRIPTION: ḤBL MQYMW BR ḤGGW | BR BRYKY 'MRŠ'.
TRANSLATION: Alas, Moqîmù son of Ḥagegù son of Barîkaî Amrišâ.

INSCRIPTION 4
SCRIPT: Palmyrene Aramaic.
LOCATION ON RELIEF: On the projecting plinth under portrait D.
TRANSCRIPTION: ŠLM BRT NŠ' | - - - 'TT ḤGGW.
TRANSLATION: Šalam daughter of Nešâ - - -, wife of Ḥagegù.

CIS no. —; PAT no. —.

PORTRAIT A: ARMLESS FEMALE BUST
The figure is shown frontally.

She wears two headdresses: a turban and a veil. The turban is coiled, with horizontal grooves indicating the coiling of the fabric. The veil has a scalloped edge, and it falls over the neck and shoulders with the right end of the veil folded over the upper torso and falling behind the left shoulder. The hair is centrally parted and several locks over the ear cover the sides of the turban and disappear under the veil. A single, flame-shaped lock falls down at the centre of the forehead. Her face is oval. The eyebrows are indicated by low curving grooves. The eyes are large and almond-shaped with thick upper eyelids. The irises are indicated by incised circles that touch the upper eyelids. The earlobes are visible under the hair. She wears dumbbell-shaped earrings (Colledge classification: H). The nose is straight. The mouth is small with full lips. The chin is pointed. The neck is short and slender with three curving grooves. She wears a necklace composed of large, round beads at the base of the neck. A vertical, incised line at the neckline of the clothing indicates the jugular notch.

She wears a tunic with a small, v-shaped neckline. The folds of the tunic are indicated by wide, curving grooves.

PORTRAIT B: ARMLESS BUST OF PRIEST
The figure is shown frontally.

He wears low on the forehead a tall, cylindrical, flat-top headdress divided into three sections by two vertical grooves: a Palmyrene priestly hat. A wreath is depicted at the lower part of the headdress. It has three rows of leaves pointing towards an armless bust of a priest in a chlamys. A horizontal groove under the headdress suggests a liner. His face is oval. The eyebrows are depicted as curving grooves. The eyes are large and almond-shaped. The irises are indicated (details unclear). The ears are large and protruding. The nose is long and straight. The mouth is small with a full lower lip. The chin is round. The neck is short and wide. A depression above the neckline of the tunic indicates the jugular notch.

He wears a tunic and a chlamys. The tunic has a small, v-shaped neckline and short, wide sleeves. The neckline is

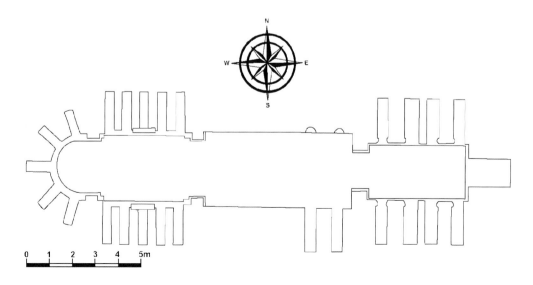

Plan of the hypogeum of Barîkî.

scalloped. The folds of the tunic are rendered by curving grooves in the area of the chest and oblique grooves in the area of the arms. Over the tunic, he wears a chlamys that falls over both shoulders, and covers most of the chest. It is fastened at the right shoulder with a round brooch decorated with a geometrical motif (Colledge classification: i). A zigzag-shaped fold falls from under the brooch. The folds of the chlamys are indicated by deep curving grooves.

PORTRAIT C: ARMLESS BUST OF PRIEST
The figure is shown frontally.

He wears low on the forehead a tall, cylindrical, flat-top headdress divided into three sections by two vertical grooves: a Palmyrene priestly hat. A wreath is depicted at the lower part of the headdress. It has three rows of leaves pointing towards an armless bust of a priest in a chlamys. A horizontal groove under the headdress suggests a liner. His face is oval. The eyebrows are depicted as curving grooves. The eyes are large and almond-shaped. The eyeballs appear blank. The ears are large and protruding. The nose is long and straight. The mouth is small with a full lower lip. The chin is round. The neck is short and wide. A depression above the neckline of the tunic indicates the jugular notch.

He wears a tunic and a chlamys. The tunic has a small, v-shaped neckline and short, wide sleeves. The neckline is scalloped. The folds of the tunic are rendered by curving grooves in the area of the chest and oblique grooves in the area of the arms. Over the tunic, he wears a chlamys that falls over both shoulders, and covers most of the chest. It is fastened at the right shoulder with a round brooch decorated with a geometrical motif (Colledge classification: i). A zigzag-shaped fold falls from under the brooch. The folds of the chlamys are indicated by deep, curving grooves.

PORTRAIT D: ARMLESS FEMALE BUST
The figure is shown frontally.

She wears three headdresses: a headband, a turban, and a veil. The headband is decorated with rectangular panels separated by vertical, incised lines. The turban is coiled, with horizontal grooves indicating the coiling. The veil has a scalloped edge, and it falls over the neck and shoulders with the right end of the veil folded over the upper torso and falling behind the left shoulder. The headdresses hide most of the hair: several locks over the ears are combed backwards and disappear under the veil. Her face is oval. The eyebrows are indicated by low, curving grooves. The eyes are large and almond-shaped with thick upper eyelids. The irises are indicated by incised circles. The nose is straight. The mouth is small with full lips. The chin is pointed. The neck is short and slender with curving grooves. A vertical, incised line at the neckline of the tunic indicates the jugular notch.

She wears a tunic with a small, v-shaped neckline. The folds of the tunic are indicated by wide, curving grooves.

HYPOGEUM OF YARḤAÎ, ʿATENÛRÎ, AND ZABDIBÔL

SARCOPHAGUS LIDS OR LID RELIEFS

A.D. 170–200

132. BANQUETING RELIEF

DATABASE NUMBER: PM777.
LOCATION: Palmyra, Palmyra Museum, inv. no. unknown.
CONTEXT: South-west necropolis. Hypogeum of Yarḥaî, ʿAtenûrî, and Zabdibôl, first central chamber.
ACQUISITION HISTORY: —
MEASUREMENTS: Height: 56 cm. Width: 130 cm.
MATERIAL: Limestone, yellow.
PRESERVATION: Portrait D: The surface of the left hand and of the face is chipped.
TECHNICAL DESCRIPTION: Portrait A: Partly carved. The head, arms, and knees are indicated. Portraits B–D: Partly carved. Portrait E: Partly carved. The head, arms, and a few features are indicated.
DATE: A.D. 170–200 (Ingholt 1938: A.D. 150–200).
REFERENCES: Ingholt Archives, PS 976; Ingholt 1938, 99 f. pl. 36, 1; Krag – Raja 2017, 199 n. 24; 204 n. 72. 73; 205 n. 75; 208 n. 99; 209 n. 100; 211 n. 122; 215 cat. 13 fig. 12; Krag 2018, 33 n. 82. 84; 46 n. 198; 66 n. 382; 98 n. 28; 314 f. cat. 562; Raja et al. 2021a, Diary 5, 2.

OBJECT DESCRIPTION
The object is rectangular in shape and depicts a seated female, two standing figures, and two reclining males. Beneath the figures is a plinth, possibly the outline for a mattress.

PORTRAIT A: SEATED FEMALE
The figure is shown in frontal view. The head appears large. The arms appear short in relation to the body. The right arm is bent and rests on the right thigh. The left arm is bent and raised to the neck. She sits with the legs apart.

She wears a veil. It is heavy and falls over both her shoulders. The neck is wide. A horizontal fold is depicted across her chest, possibly indicating a himation.

The right hand rests on her right thigh. The left hand lightly holds the edge of the veil.

PORTRAIT B: STANDING FEMALE
The figure is shown in frontal view. The head appears large. The arms appear short in relation to the body. The right arm is extended along the right side of the body. The left arm is bent and held to the chest. The legs are obscured by the reclining figure to his left.

A horizontal fold is depicted along the outline of the head and across the chest, possibly indicating a himation.

Cat. 132

PORTRAIT C: STANDING MALE

The figure is shown in frontal view. Head and arms are indicated. The head appears large. The right arm is bent and raised to the neck. The left arm, the lower body, and the legs are obscured by the reclining figure to his left.

The figure wears a tunic and a himation. The tunic has a round neckline. The himation is rendered by a diagonal fold across the chest.

PORTRAIT D: RECLINING MALE

The figure is shown in frontal view. The left hand appears large. The right arm is extended and rests on the right knee. The left arm is bent in front of his chest, and rests on a cushion. Curving grooves indicate the texture of the fabric. The right leg is bent and raised. The left leg is bent under the right leg. The left knee is visible under the drapery.

The neck is short.

He wears a >Parthian-style< tunic and a himation. The tunic has a round neckline decorated with a beaded band, and long, tight-fitting sleeves. The cuffs of the sleeves are decorated with a wide, plain band. The tunic is decorated with a wide, plain band extending downwards from the middle of the neckline. The folds of the tunic are rendered by oblique and curving grooves on the sleeve. He also wears a plain band belt, knotted at the centre with the ends looped under on each side. The himation falls over the left shoulder and arm, is wrapped around the left wrist, and continues down the left side of his body. Two folded edges of the himation fall under the left hand, onto the cushion and mattress in two zigzag-shaped folds. The himation is folded across the waist and covers the legs. The folds of the tunic are rendered by oblique grooves.

The right hand rests on the right knee. In his hand he holds an oval object, possibly a pinecone or a small wreath. The right thumb and the index finger are extended. With the upturned palm of the left hand, he holds a bowl with his fingertips.

PORTRAIT E: RECLINING MALE

The figure is shown in frontal view. The head appears large. The arms appear short in relation to the body. The left arm is bent and rests on a cushion. The lower body and legs are obscured by the reclining figure to his right.

His face is round. The eyes are round (details unclear). The mouth is wide. The neck is short and wide.

He wears a tunic with a round neckline.

In his left hand, he holds a bowl, and the left index finger is extended.

133. BANQUETING RELIEF

DATABASE NUMBER: PM778.
LOCATION: Palmyra, Palmyra Museum, inv. no. unknown.
CONTEXT: South-west necropolis. Hypogeum of Yarḥaî, ʿAtenûrî, and Zabdibôl, first central chamber.
ACQUISITION HISTORY: —
MEASUREMENTS: Height: 100 cm. Width: 225 cm.
MATERIAL: Limestone, white/yellow.
PRESERVATION: The upper part of the right side and the lower part of the left side is broken off. Portrait A: The upper part is broken off horizontally at the waist. Portrait B: The head is broken off at the base of the neck. The surface of the arms is chipped. Portrait C: The upper part is broken

Cat. 133

off diagonally from the left shoulder to the upper right arm. The surface at the left arm is chipped.
TECHNICAL DESCRIPTION: —
DATE: A.D. 170–200 (Ingholt 1938: ca. A.D. 200).
REFERENCES: Ingholt 1938, 100–103 pl. 37, 1; Krag 2018, 58 n. 304; 62 n. 353; 66 n. 382; 87 n. 182. 184. 185; 89 n. 206. 210; 384 cat. 825; Raja et al. 2021a, Diary 3, 9. Inscription: Ingholt 1938, 101–103 pl. 37, 2–5; Krag 2018, 384 cat. 825.

OBJECT DESCRIPTION
The sarcophagus lid is rectangular in shape and depicts a seated female and two reclining males. The figures are resting on a mattress. It is decorated with an intersecting lozenges pattern with flowers in the lozenges. The mattress is decorated with three bands (other details unclear). The female is sitting on two cushions. Curving grooves indicate the texture of the fabric. Both reclining males rest their left arm on a cushion. The right cushion has a wide band decorated with a running scroll with rosettes. The texture of both cushions is indicated by curving grooves.

INSCRIPTIONS
INSCRIPTION 1
SCRIPT: Palmyrene Aramaic.
LOCATION ON RELIEF: On the mattress, under her right foot.
TRANSCRIPTION: ṢLMT | ʾMTʾ | ʾTTH.
TRANSLATION: Image of Amatâ, his wife.

INSCRIPTION 2
SCRIPT: Palmyrene Aramaic.
LOCATION ON RELIEF: Above the hem of the tunic of the central figure.
TRANSCRIPTION: ṢLM BSʾ | NQBʾ.
TRANSLATION: Image of Bassus Naqbâ.

INSCRIPTION 3
SCRIPT: Palmyrene Aramaic.
LOCATION ON RELIEF: The fold of the himation falling onto the cushion, under the left figure.
TRANSCRIPTION: ṢLM | MLKWʾ ḤBL.
TRANSLATION: Image of Malôkâ, alas!

Inscription 1: CIS no. —; PAT no. 0070.
Inscription 2: CIS no. —; PAT no. 0068.
Inscription 3: CIS no. —; PAT no. 0069.

PORTRAIT A: SEATED FEMALE, AMATÂ
The right hand is resting on her right thigh. The legs are bent, and the knees are rendered under the drapery. The right foot rests on the mattress; the left foot is obscured by the reclining figure to her left.

She wears a garment that reaches her ankles, possibly a tunic. Her shoes are pointed.

She holds a fold of a garment in her right hand, possibly the veil. The index finger is extended.

PORTRAIT B: RECLINING MALE, BASSUS NAQBÂ
The figure is shown in frontal to three-quarter view. The right arm is bent and rests on his raised right knee. The left arm is bent in front of the chest. The right leg is bent and the foot rests on the mattress. The left leg is bent under the right leg

with the knee pointing forwards. The left foot is obscured by the right leg.

He wears a ›Parthian-style‹ tunic, a chlamys, and ›Parthian-style‹ trousers. The tunic has a small, round neckline and long, slightly loose sleeves. The tunic ends above the knees and has a decorated lower border with a vegetal motif between beaded bands. The folds of the tunic are rendered by curving, wide grooves. He wears a plain band belt, knotted at the centre with the ends looped under on either side of the waist. Along his right thigh is an object with a pointed end, a rectangular main body, and two lateral elements: a sheathed dagger. Over the tunic, he wears a chlamys that falls over both shoulders, and covers most of the chest. It is wrapped around his lower left arm and proceeds in a wide fold along his left side and over the cushions where it ends in two s-shaped folds. It is fastened at the right shoulder with a circular brooch with an incised border (Colledge classification: h). The folds of the chlamys are indicated by narrow, deep grooves. Each trouser leg has a wide band that extends downwards decorated with leaves in an opposite arrangement. The folds of the garment are indicated by wide, curving grooves. The trousers are tucked into his pointed boots, which have a raised area around the heel.

With the upturned palm of his left hand, he holds a bowl with his fingertips.

PORTRAIT C: RECLINING MALE, MALÔKÂ

The figure is shown in frontal view. The right arm is bent and held to the torso. The left is bent in front of the chest. The legs are obscured by the reclining figure to his right.

He wears a tunic and a himation. The tunic has a small, round neckline and short, loose sleeves. The folds of the tunic are rendered by curving grooves. Over the tunic, he wears a himation. The himation covers most of the body: it is wrapped around the left shoulder and arm, leaving the upper torso free. The folds of the himation are indicated by diagonal grooves.

With his right hand, he lightly holds a fold of the himation. The index finger is extended. The outline of a vessel is visible at the centre of the chest.

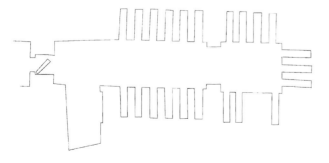

Plan of the hypogeum of Yarḥaî, ʿAtenûrî, and Zabdibôl.

A.D. 180–240

HYPOGEUM OF ʿALAÎNÊ

SARCOPHAGI

A.D. 220–240

134. COMPLETE SARCOPHAGUS WITH BANQUETING SCENE AND PORTRAIT BUSTS

DATABASE NUMBER: PM229 (134a) + PM270 (134b).
LOCATION: Palmyra, Palmyra Museum, inv. no. 2285/8277, H 37/71.
CONTEXT: West necropolis. Valley of the Tombs. Hypogeum of ʿAlaînê, central exedra, on the podium, at the centre. 134a excavation no. H23/70, H134/70, H66/70, H107/70, H68/70, H106/70.
ACQUISITION HISTORY: —
MEASUREMENTS: 134a: Height: 114 cm. Width: 225 cm. Depth: 33 cm. 134b: Height: 98 cm. Width: 245 cm. Depth: 98 cm.
MATERIAL: Limestone, white.
PRESERVATION: 134a: Most of the background of the relief is broken off. Portrait A: The left side is broken off at the left shoulder and chest. Portrait B: The head is broken off at the base of the neck. Portrait C: The surface is weathered. Portrait D: The surface of the head and of the hands is weathered. Portrait E: The head is broken off at the top of the neck. Portrait F: The surface of the face, of the headdress, and of the left edge of the himation is chipped. 134b: The surface of the sarcophagus box is weathered and chipped at the central part of the mattress and on the left side. All the heads and torsos of the portraits are chipped.
TECHNICAL DESCRIPTION: There are traces of a red pigment.
DATE: A.D. 220–240 (Sadurska 1977: A.D. 180–240, probably A.D. 210–230; Sadurska – Bounni 1994: A.D. 210–240).
REFERENCES: 134a: Ingholt Archives, PS 1432; Sadurska 1976, 25–29 figs. 11. 12; Sadurska 1977, 76–95 cat. 1 figs. 18–35 pl. 11; Taha 1982, 121 fig. 4; Parlasca 1984, 290–292 fig. 10; Tanabe 1986, 41 pls. 374–384; Sadurska 1988, 17 fig. 2; Sadurska – Bounni 1994, 174–176 cat. 232 fig. 248; Fortin 1999, 296 cat. 331; Stauffer 2012, 92–94 fig. 3; Stauffer 2013, 128 f. fig. 2; Miyashita 2016, 132 fig. 5; Krag – Raja 2017, 199 n. 24; 204 n. 72. 73; 205 n. 75; 207. 208 n. 99; 209 n. 100. 102; 218 cat. 28 fig. 8; Long 2017, 72 f. fig. 4; Krag 2018, 28 n. 9; 62 n. 351. 353; 65 n. 369; 66 n. 385; 68 n. 384; 88 n. 193. 195; 101 n. 65; 388 cat. 836. 134b: Sadurska 1976, 24 f.; Sadurska 1977, 107–111 cat. 6 fig. 48 pl. 11; Krag 2018, 32 n. 63; 53 n. 258; 58 n. 300. 304; 59 n. 323; 62 n. 349; 103 n. 74; 400 cat. 876.

OBJECT DESCRIPTION

The sarcophagus lid (134a) is rectangular in shape and depicts a seated female, a seated male, two standing boys, a reclining figure, and a standing male. Beneath the figures is a mattress decorated with an intersecting lozenges pattern with alternating six-petal rosettes and four-petal flowers with serrated leaves

OBJECTS FROM HYPOGEA 383

Fig. 11. — Banquet central du *triclinium*.
Calcaire blanc dur. H : 0 m 96 ; L : 2 m 22.
Photographie W. Jerke.

Cat. 134

Cat. 134

in the lozenges. The reclining figure rests on a large, round cushion with a central band decorated with a motif of six-petal rosettes inside a running scroll. The band is framed by two beaded bands, a band with alternating round and rhomboid patterns, a narrow, plain band, and a running wave motif. The fabric of the cushion is indicated by wide, curving grooves. The sarcophagus box (134b) is rendered as a kline. Five figures are depicted inside clipei between the kline legs: a female bust, a male bust, a bust of a priest, a bust of possibly a male, and a female bust. Eight rosettes are depicted between the portraits on the relief ground. Above the kline is a mattress. Curving grooves, visible above portrait A, indicate the texture of the fabric. The central stretcher of the kline is decorated with a rectangular indentation on the far left side, followed by a square inlay. The left leg of the kline is preserved. The leg is turned. The details of the foot of the leg are unclear, but a reversed bell-shaped element, a torus, and a concave quarter is preserved under the stretcher. All the elements are decorated with a tongues pattern.

SARCOPHAGUS LID

PORTRAIT A: SEATED FEMALE

She is shown in three-quarter view, turned towards her left. Both arms are bent; the right one resting on her thigh, the left along her side. Her left foot is obscured by the reclining figure.

She wears three headdresses: a veil, a turban, and a headband. The headband is placed high on the forehead. The headband is decorated with a central, rectangular panel with a flower with serrated petals, framed by two beaded bands. Over the headband, she wears a high turban rendered in three twisting layers. The two upper layers are twisted into each other, creating a central knot. Wide horizontal grooves indicate the coiling of the fabric. The veil is heavy. It falls over the head, covers the shoulders, and continues behind her. The veil falls over the right shoulder and upper arm. The edge of the veil is scalloped and decorated with a thin, plain band. She also wears a head-chain, fastened under the centre of the turban and running to each side of the forehead. The head-chain is composed of round elements with an incised border joined by narrow, beaded elements. Four locks of hair above the forehead and the ears are pushed back over the headband and disappear under the veil. The individual locks of hair are indicated by wavy, incised lines. Her face is oval and fleshy. The eyebrows are indicated by low, curving, incised lines. The eyes are almond-shaped, with thick eyelids. The end of the upper eyelids extends beyond that of the lower ones. The eyeballs are blank. The earlobes are visible under the hair. She wears earrings with two juxtaposed beads; an upper round bead and a lower biconical bead, suspended from the ear with a distinct element, possibly a hook (Colledge classification: L). The nose is thin and straight. The mouth is small with thin lips. The chin is square. The neck is long with three horizontal grooves. She wears three necklaces: a string of small, round beads at the base of the neck, a string of large, oval beads with a central, crescent-shaped pendant with an oval bead between the horns, and a necklace that falls over the breasts composed of an interwoven loop-in-loop chain with a central oval pendant. The large oval pendant has an outer beaded border and three spirally wrapped wires ending in leaf-shaped pendants are suspended from it.

She wears a tunic and a himation. The tunic has a small, v-shaped neckline and short, wide sleeves that reach to the elbows. The folds of the tunic are indicated by oblique grooves. Over the tunic, she wears a himation. The himation crosses the chest diagonally from the left shoulder to the right side, where it passes under the sleeve of the tunic. It covers the left breast and her lower torso, falls over the right thigh, and down the side of the right leg with a wide, zigzag-shaped fold. It is fastened at the left shoulder. The brooch is not preserved. The edge of the himation that crosses the chest is decorated with a pleated band.

With her right hand, she holds a fold of the veil. She wears a thick hoop bracelet on her right wrist.

PORTRAIT B: STANDING MALE

The figure is shown frontally. His right arm falls to the side; the left arm is bent in front of the waist. The lower part of the legs is obscured by the reclining figure.

Over the collarbone, he wears a necklace composed of large, round pendants with an incised border linked by beaded elements.

He wears a ›Parthian-style‹ tunic and a himation. The tunic has a wide, round neckline, and is decorated with two wide bands extending downwards from the sides of the neckline (clavi). The bands are decorated with leaves on a stem set between beaded bands. The tunic has long, tight-fitting sleeves. The cuff of the right sleeve is decorated with a wide band with a rosette inside a running scroll motif. The folds of the tunic are indicated by narrow, alternating curving grooves over the torso, and wide curving grooves over the arm. Over the tunic, he wears a himation. It is wrapped around the left shoulder and arm and is folded over at the waist. The folds of the himation are depicted by curving grooves on the lower body and vertical fold on the left shoulder.

With his right hand, he holds a libation pitcher. It has a disc-shaped foot, an ovoid body, a cylindrical, narrow neck decorated with a beaded band where it joins the shoulder, and a slightly wide mouth. With his left hand, he holds a fold of the himation. The fabric falls under his hand in three oblique folds. The index finger is extended. The nails are indicated by fine, incised lines.

PORTRAIT C: STANDING MALE

The figure is shown frontally. His head is turned to his left. Both arms are bent; the right in front of the chest, the left at the waist. The lower part of the body is obscured by the reclining figure.

He wears a tight-fitting cap composed of rectangular panels. His face is square. The eyebrows are indicated by incised lines. The eyes are almond-shaped, with thick upper eyelids. The irises are marked. The ears are large and protruding with the helix and scapha depicted. The nose is straight and long. The mouth is small with a full lower lip. The chin is square. The neck is long. He wears a plain hoop necklace with a wide, oval pendant with an incised border suspended from the centre, possibly a bulla.

He wears a tunic and an over-garment. The tunic has wide, short sleeves that reach below the elbows. The over-garment has a wide, round neckline and is sleeveless. The folds of the over-garment are rendered by oblique and curving grooves.

In his right hand, he holds a libation pitcher. It has a disc-shaped foot, an ovoid body, a cylindrical, narrow neck decorated with a plain band where it joins the shoulder, and a slightly wide mouth. In his left hand, he holds an object with a small, rectangular tip and a wide, trapezoidal lower part that projects below the hand, possibly a fold of clothing. His index finger is extended.

PORTRAIT D: STANDING MALE

The figure is shown frontally. His head is turned to his right. Both arms are bent; the right in front of the chest, the left at the waist. The lower body is obscured by the reclining figure.

He wears a tight-fitting cap composed of rectangular panels. His face is square. The eyebrows are indicated by incised lines. The eyes are almond-shaped, with thick upper eyelids. The irises are indicated (details unclear). The ears are large and protruding with the helix and scapha depicted. The nose is straight and long. The mouth is small with a full lower lip. The chin is square. The neck is long and wide, with four horizontal grooves. He wears a plain hoop necklace with a wide, oval pendant with an incised border suspended from the centre, possibly a bulla.

He wears a tunic and an over-garment. The tunic has wide, short sleeves that reach below the elbows. The over-garment has a wide, round neckline and is sleeveless. The folds of the over-garment are rendered by oblique and curving grooves.

In his right hand, he holds a libation pitcher. It has a disc-shaped foot, an ovoid body, a cylindrical, narrow neck decorated with a plain band where it joins the shoulder, and a slightly wide mouth. In his left hand, he holds an object with a small, rectangular tip, possibly a fold of the garment. His index finger is extended.

PORTRAIT E: RECLINING MALE

His right leg is shown in profile, his left leg and torso are shown frontally, and the arms are shown in profile. The right arm is extended to the side and rests on the knee, the left arm is bent in front of the torso. The right leg is bent and the foot rests on the mattress. The left leg is slightly bent behind the right leg, and the left ankle is obscured.

Over the collarbone, he wears a necklace composed of large, round pendants with incised borders, linked by beaded elements.

He wears a ›Parthian-style‹ tunic, a himation, and ›Parthian-style‹ trousers. The tunic has a wide, round neckline with a narrow, undecorated band and long, slightly loose sleeves. Two wide bands extend downwards from either side of the middle of the neckline and the shoulder (clavi). They are decorated with a vine scroll, from which small clusters of grapes and vine leaves hang. The vine branches create small hexagonal shapes; in each hexagon a small bird is seen trying to eat the grapes. The plumage of the birds is indicated by incised lines. Each wide band is framed by two narrow bands decorated with alternating lozenges, squares, and circles; all with incised borders and separated by beaded elements. The cuffs of the tunic are decorated with a wide band with a similar motif of interlocking vines with clusters of grapes and vine leaves, but inside the hexagonal shapes, there are small, naked, short-haired figures with a bow in one hand, taking aim at the birds. The wide bands on the cuffs are framed by a band with alternating lozenges and circles with incised borders and a raised centre, separated by beaded elements, and a narrower beaded band. The tunic ends at the middle of the lower legs. The side of the tunic has a slit. The folds of the tunic are indicated by curving grooves over the torso, and oblique ones over the arms. He wears a band belt around his waist composed of a thin piece of fabric, tied with a double knot at the centre. At the side there are round elements with incised borders linked together with three wide bands. He wears a himation over the tunic. It is wrapped around the left arm and elbow and falls below the arm and over the cushion in two wide, zigzag-shaped folds. The edges of the himation that fall over the cushion are decorated with a plain band, a band of six-petal rosettes within circles and a beaded band. The himation is also decorated with a rectangular panel with two projecting narrow, rectangular edges on the area across the left knee: it is decorated with interlocking vine branches, from which hang clusters of grapes and vine leaves, with a bird trying to eat the grapes in each panel created by the branches. Each of the projecting edges is decorated with vine tendrils and a cluster of grapes. The edge of the himation is turned over below the knee, revealing a hemline with an incised border. The folds of the himation are indicated by wide, oblique grooves around the legs and curving ones around the waist and elbow. The trousers are visible from below the knee: they are decorated with a wide, central band with a pattern of interlocking vine branches, from which hang clusters of grapes and vine leaves, with a bird trying to eat the grapes in each panel created by the branches. The band is framed by a beaded band. The folds of the trousers are indicated by narrow, deep, oblique grooves. He wears boots that reach slightly above the ankles. They are decorated with beaded bands around the ankle and along the foot, and alternating sunbursts within or without a beaded border. A wide band fastened with a circle with a six-petal rosette runs around the ankle.

With his right hand, he holds a libation pitcher. It has a disc-shaped foot, an ovoid body, a cylindrical, narrow neck decorated with a beaded band where it joins the shoulder, and a slightly wide mouth. With the upturned palm of his left hand, he holds a skyphos with his fingertips. It has a conical foot decorated with a tongues pattern, and a round body whose decoration is divided into four zones: a zone of upwards pointing palm leaf or tongues pattern with an incised border, a band with three narrow grooves, a band of six-petal rosettes within circles, and a band with three narrow grooves. The handles are looped, topped by a rectangular panel. He wears a bracelet on each wrist composed of large, round elements with incised borders, linked by beaded elements.

PORTRAIT F: STANDING PRIEST

The figure is shown frontally. His head is turned to his right. The right arm is slightly bent at the side of the thigh, the left arm is bent to the waist.

He wears a tall, cylindrical, flat-top headdress: a Palmyrene priestly hat. A wreath is depicted at the lower part of the hat. It has three rows of leaves pointing towards a central decoration (details unclear). His face is square. The eyebrows are curving, indicated by incised lines. The eyes are almond-shaped, with thick upper eyelids. The pupils are marked. The nose is long with a curving ridge. The mouth is small. The chin is square. The neck is long and wide.

He wears a tunic and a himation. The tunic has a wide, round neckline and long, tight-fitting sleeves. Two wide bands extend downwards from either side of the middle of the neckline and the shoulder. They are decorated with alternating pairs of rosettes and leaves, framed by beaded bands. The cuffs of the sleeves are decorated with wide bands with rosettes inside circles framed by beaded bands. The folds of the tunic are indicated by curving grooves. Over the tunic, he wears a himation. It is wrapped around the left shoulder, arm, and wrist. The himation is folded over at the waist. He wears sandals: they have a strap around the ankle, a strap before the toes, and one connecting the two. The sole is indicated by a horizontal groove.

With his right hand, he holds a libation pitcher. It has a disc-shaped foot, an ovoid body, a cylindrical, narrow neck decorated with a beaded band where it joins the shoulder, and a slightly wide mouth. With his left hand, he holds a fold of the himation. The fabric falls under his hand in three oblique folds. The index finger is extended. He wears a ring on the left little finger: it has a plain hoop and a circular bezel. The nails are indicated by fine, incised lines.

SARCOPHAGUS BOX

PORTRAIT G: ARMLESS FEMALE BUST

The figure is shown frontally, rendered in a clipeus.

She wears a veil. It falls over both shoulders and in a curving fold across the chest. She wears a necklace composed of round beads at the base of the neck.

She wears a tunic with a v-shaped neckline.

PORTRAIT H: ARMLESS MALE BUST

The figure is shown frontally, rendered in a clipeus (details unclear).

PORTRAIT I: ARMLESS BUST OF A PRIEST

The figure is shown frontally, rendered in a clipeus.

The outline of a tall cylindrical headdress is recognizable: a Palmyrene priestly hat.

He wears a tunic with a v-shaped neckline.

PORTRAIT J: ARMLESS BUST OF A PRIEST

The figure is shown frontally, rendered in a clipeus (details unclear).

The outline of a tall cylindrical headdress is recognizable: a Palmyrene priestly hat.

He wears a tunic and a chlamys. The folds of the clothing are indicated by oblique grooves.

PORTRAIT K: ARMLESS FEMALE BUST

The figure is shown frontally, rendered in a clipeus (details unclear).

She wears a veil: it falls in a curving fold across the chest.

135. COMPLETE SARCOPHAGUS WITH BANQUETING SCENE AND PORTRAIT BUSTS

DATABASE NUMBER: PM227 (135a) + PM271 (135b).
LOCATION: Palmyra, Palmyra Museum, inv. no. 2284/8276, H 39/71.
CONTEXT: West necropolis. Valley of the Tombs. Hypogeum of ʿAlaînê, central exedra, on the podium, to the right. 135a excavation no. H 22/70, H 70/70, H 67/70.
ACQUISITION HISTORY: —
MEASUREMENTS: 135a: Height: 114 cm. Width: 164 cm. Depth: 34 cm. 135b: Height: 96 cm. Width: 225 cm. Depth: 98 cm.
MATERIAL: Limestone, white.
PRESERVATION: 135a: The right side and the background are broken off. The surface of the mattress is chipped. Portrait A: The lower part is broken off diagonally across the thighs. The upper part of the headdress is broken off. The surface is chipped at the left shoulder and at the hand. Portrait B: The surface is chipped at the left hand and across the torso. 135b: The surface of the sarcophagus box is weathered and chipped on the right side of the mattress and on the upper left side. All portraits are chipped at the heads.
TECHNICAL DESCRIPTION: There are traces of red pigment on the box.
DATE: A.D. 220–240 (Sadurska 1977: A.D. 180–240, probably A.D. 210–230; Sadurska – Bounni 1994: A.D. 210–240).
REFERENCES: 135a: Sadurska 1977, 101–105 cat. 4 figs. 42–45 pl. 14; Tanabe 1986, 41 pls. 389–392; Sadurska – Bounni 1994, 176 f. cat. 234 fig. 250; Yon 2001a, 343 f. cat. 148; Dentzer 2002, 50. 52 cat. 44; Kingley 2002, 4; Stauffer 2013, 130 fig. 4. 135b: Sadurska 1976, 24 f. pl. 3 fig. 10; Sadurska 1977, 111–114 cat. 7 fig. 50 pl. 14; Krag 2018, 32 n. 63; 53 n. 258; 58 n. 300. 304; 59 n. 323; 62 n. 349; 103 n. 74; 113 n. 6; 400 cat. 875.

OBJECT DESCRIPTION

The sarcophagus lid is rectangular in shape and depicts two figures resting on a thin mattress. The mattress is decorated with an intersecting lozenge pattern with rosettes in the lozenges.

Cat. 135

Both figures rest their left arm on a cushion. Both cushions have a band: the band of the right cushion is decorated with a vine scroll, the band of the left cushion is decorated with a running scroll with rosettes. Curving grooves indicate the texture of the fabric. The sarcophagus box is rendered as a kline. Five busts are depicted in clipei between the kline legs: a bust of a male, a bust of a female, a bust of a priest, a bust of a female, and a bust of a male. At the upper and lower part of the relief ground, between each portrait, there are two six-petal rosettes. Above the kline is a mattress. The mattress is decorated with three bands with vegetal motifs. Curving grooves indicate the texture of the fabric. The central stretcher of the kline is decorated with a row of oval elements. The kline legs are turned. They are composed of a plinth, a concave quarter, a reversed bell-shaped element, a scotia, a reversed bell-shaped element, and a torus. All elements are decorated with a tongues pattern.

SARCOPHAGUS LID

PORTRAIT A: RECLINING PRIEST

The figure is shown in frontal to three-quarter view. The eyes and the torso appear large. His head is turned to his left. The right arm is bent and rests on the right thigh. The left arm is bent and held to the chest. The left leg is bent with the knee pointing outwards.

He wears a high, cylindrical, flat-top headdress divided into three sections by two vertical grooves: a Palmyrene priestly hat. A wreath is depicted at the lower part of the hat. It has three rows of leaves pointing towards an armless male bust. The midribs of the leaves are incised. His face is oblong. The eyebrows are curving, depicted by thin ridges. The eyes are close-set and almond-shaped with thick upper eyelids that extend beyond the end of the lower ones. The irises are indicated by incised circles. The ears are large and protruding with the helix, scapha, concha, and lobe depicted. The nose is thin with carved alae. The mouth is small with a thin upper lip and a full lower lip. The chin is pointed with a cleft. The neck is wide.

He wears a ›Parthian-style‹ tunic, a chlamys, and ›Parthian-style‹ trousers. The tunic has a wide, round neckline decorated with a band with vines and long, tight-fitting sleeves. The cuffs of the sleeves are decorated with a beaded band. On either side of the chest, the tunic has two wide bands extending downwards and decorated with a running scroll with rosettes, set between beaded bands. The tunic ends above the knees and has a decorated lower border with a running scroll with rosettes and a beaded band at the hem. The folds of the tunic are rendered by oblique and curving grooves. He also wears a plain band belt knotted at the centre with the ends looped under either side of the waist. Along his right thigh is an object with a pointed end, a rectangular main body, and two lateral round elements: a sheathed dagger. Over the tunic, he wears a chlamys that falls from the right shoulder across the chest. It is wrapped around his left lower arm where two s-shaped folds extend downwards and falls over the cushion. The chlamys is fastened at the right shoulder with a circular brooch with a rosette within it (Colledge classification: g). A zigzag-shaped fold falls from under the brooch. The folds of the chlamys are indicated by narrow, deep grooves. The trousers are visible above the knee. At the middle, the trouser leg is decorated with a band with a floral motif between beaded bands. The folds are indicated by curving grooves.

The outline of a vessel, possibly a bowl, is recognizable at the centre of the chest.

PORTRAIT B: RECLINING PRIEST

The figure is shown frontally. The eyes appear large. The arms appear short in relation to the body. His head is turned to his left. The right arm is extended behind the figure to his right. The left arm is bent and held to the chest. The legs are obscured by the reclining figure to his right.

He wears a high, cylindrical, flat-top headdress divided into three sections by two vertical grooves: a Palmyrene priestly hat. A wreath is depicted at the lower part of the hat. It has three rows of leaves pointing towards an armless male bust. The midribs of the leaves are incised. His face is oval. The eyebrows are curving, depicted by thin ridges. The eyes are close-set and almond-shaped with thick upper eyelids that extend beyond the end of the lower ones. The irises are indicated by incised circles. The ears are large and protruding with the helix, scapha, tragus, concha, and lobe depicted. The nose is long with carved nostrils. Nasolabial lines are indicated by incised lines. The mouth is small with thin lips. The chin is pointed. The neck is wide.

He wears a ›Parthian-style‹ tunic and a himation. The tunic has a wide, round neckline decorated with a band with squares and rhombi divided by vertical lines. On either side of the chest, the tunic has two wide bands extending downwards and decorated with a running scroll with rosettes, set between beaded bands. The folds of the tunic are rendered by oblique and vertical grooves. Over the tunic, he wears a himation. It is wrapped around both shoulders and his left arm. A wide fold of the himation falls across the cushion and onto the mattress. It is divided into two zigzag-shaped folds. The folds of the himation are rendered by oblique and curving grooves.

The outline of a vessel, possibly a bowl, is recognizable at the centre of the chest.

SARCOPHAGUS BOX

PORTRAIT C: ARMLESS MALE BUST

The figure is shown frontally.

The contour of the head is recognizable. The neck appears slender.

He wears a tunic and a chlamys. The tunic has a wide, round neckline and the edge is scalloped. The folds of the tunic are rendered by curving grooves. Over the tunic, he wears a chlamys that falls over both shoulders, and covers the chest. It is fastened at the right shoulder with a brooch (details unclear). An s-shaped fold falls from under the brooch. The folds of the chlamys are indicated by narrow, deep grooves.

PORTRAIT D: ARMLESS FEMALE BUST

The figure is shown frontally.

She wears a veil. It falls over the shoulders and across the chest in a curving fold. The neck is wide. She wears a plain hoop necklace with a central, round pendant at the base of the neck.

She wears a tunic with a wide, round neckline and the edge is scalloped. The folds of the tunic are rendered by curving and oblique grooves.

PORTRAIT E: ARMLESS BUST OF A PRIEST

The figure is shown frontally.

The contour of the head and the headdress is recognizable, suggesting a Palmyrene priestly hat. The neck is wide.

He wears a tunic and a chlamys. The tunic has a wide, slightly v-shaped neckline. The folds of the tunic are rendered by curving grooves. Over the tunic, he wears a chlamys that falls over both shoulders and covers the chest. It is fastened at the right shoulder with a brooch (details unclear). An s-shaped fold falls from under the brooch. The folds of the chlamys are indicated by narrow, deep grooves.

PORTRAIT F: ARMLESS FEMALE BUST

The figure is shown frontally.

She wears a veil. It falls over the shoulders and across the chest in a curving fold. The veil has a woolly fringe. She wears a plain hoop necklace with a central round pendant at the base of the neck.

She wears a tunic with a wide, v-shaped neckline. The folds of the tunic are rendered by curving and oblique grooves.

PORTRAIT G: ARMLESS MALE BUST

The figure is shown frontally.

The neck is wide.

He wears a tunic and a chlamys. The tunic has a wide, slightly v-shaped neckline. The folds of the tunic are rendered by curving grooves. Over the tunic, he wears a chlamys that falls over both shoulders and covers the chest. It is fastened at the right shoulder with a brooch (details unclear). An s-shaped fold falls from under the brooch. The folds of the chlamys are indicated by narrow, deep grooves.

136. COMPLETE SARCOPHAGUS WITH BANQUETING SCENE AND PORTRAIT BUSTS

DATABASE NUMBER: PM228 (136a) + PM272 (136b).
LOCATION: Palmyra, Palmyra Museum, inv. no. 2283/8275.
CONTEXT: West necropolis. Valley of the Tombs. Hypogeum of ʿAlaînê, central exedra, on the podium, to the left. 136a excavation no. H 21/70, H 65/70, H 108/70.
ACQUISITION HISTORY: —

MEASUREMENTS: 136a: Height: 121 cm. Width: 168 cm. Depth: 25 cm. 136b: Height: 98 cm. Width: 240 cm. Depth: 100 cm.
MATERIAL: Limestone, white.
PRESERVATION: 136a: Most of the background of the relief is broken off. Portrait A: The lower part of her face is chipped. The veil is broken off. Portrait B: A small fragment is chipped from his neck. Portrait C: The head is broken off at the shoulders. Portrait D: The head is broken off at the base of the neck. 136b: The surface of the sarcophagus box is weathered and chipped. Portrait E: The surface of the face is chipped. Portrait F: The surface of the face is chipped. Portrait G: The surface is chipped.
TECHNICAL DESCRIPTION: There are traces of red pigment on the box.
DATE: A.D. 220–240 (Sadurska 1977: A.D. 180–240, probably A.D. 210–230; Sadurska – Bounni 1994: A.D. 210–240).
REFERENCES: 136a: Ingholt Archives, PS 1434/1435; Sadurska 1976, 25 pls. 6, 13; Sadurska 1977, 95–99 cat. 2 figs. 36–40 pl. 12; Tanabe 1986, 41 pls. 385–388; Sadurska – Bounni 1994, 176 cat. 233 fig. 249; Stauffer 2013, 128–130 fig. 3; Miyashita 2016, 133. 142 fig. 17; Krag 2018, 28 n. 9; 53 n. 259; 54 n. 263. 264; 59 n. 316. 324. 325; 61 n. 335; 62 n. 351. 353; 63 n. 355. 357; 65 n. 304; 88 n. 195. 197; 387 cat. 833. 136b: Sadurska 1977, 114 cat. 8 fig. 51 pl. 40; Krag – Raja 2017, 199 n. 24; 204 n. 72. 73; 205 n. 75; 208 n. 99; 209 n. 100. 102; 210 n. 109. 110. 112. 114; 218 cat. 27; Krag 2018, 32 n. 63; 53 n. 258; 58 n. 300. 304; 59 n. 323; 62 n. 349; 103 n. 74; 400 cat. 874.

OBJECT DESCRIPTION

The sarcophagus lid is rectangular in shape and depicts a seated female, two standing males, and a reclining male figure. There is a mattress decorated with an intersecting lozenge pattern with four-petal rosettes inside each lozenge. The female sits on two round cushions, one on top of the other. The cushions are decorated with a central band with vegetal motifs framed by a beaded band; each band has a different vegetal motif (details unclear). The reclining figure rests on a large, round cushion decorated with a central band with a

Cat. 136

continuous vegetal motif framed by two beaded bands. The fabric of the cushion is indicated by wide, curving grooves. The sarcophagus box is rendered as a kline. Four busts in clipei are depicted between the kline legs: a bust of a female, a bust of a male, a bust of unknown gender, and a female bust. Above the kline is a mattress. The mattress is decorated with three bands with vegetal motifs (details unclear). Curving grooves indicate the texture of the fabric. The kline is decorated with a fulcrum on the left side (details unclear). The central stretcher of the kline is decorated with a rectangular indentation on the right side. The kline legs are turned. They are composed of a plinth, and above is a long, reversed, concave quarter, a reversed bell-shaped element, a ball, a torus, and above the stretcher is a biconical element. All elements are decorated with a tongues pattern.

SARCOPHAGUS LID

PORTRAIT A: SEATED FEMALE

Her lower body is turned towards her left, her torso and head are shown frontally. The right arm falls along the body and rests on the cushion. The left arm is bent and raised to the shoulder. The feet are obscured by the reclining figure.

She wears three headdresses: a veil, a turban, and a headband. The headband is placed low on the forehead and is decorated. The details are unclear. The turban is coiled and rendered with three wide, horizontal grooves indicating the coiling of the fabric. The veil is heavy with a scalloped edge. She also wears head ornaments; a central head ornament and a head-chain. The central head ornament runs from the middle of the turban, and is composed of oval and rectangular elements with beaded borders, and from the rectangular element four round beads are suspended by small bars. The head-chain runs from either side of the square pendant and disappears under the veil. The chain is composed of round elements linked by beaded elements. Most of the hair is covered by the headdress, but several strands of hair above the ears are pushed back over the headband and the edge of the turban and disappear under the veil. The veil falls over the right shoulder and upper arm. Her face is oval and fleshy. The eyebrows are indicated by curving grooves. The eyes are almond-shaped, with thick upper eyelids. The eyeballs are blank. The earlobes are visible under the hair. She wears earrings with three juxtaposed beads: two larger round beads above and below a smaller central, round bead (Colledge classification: K). Her neck is long and slender. She wears three necklaces: a plain hoop with a central, round pendant worn below at the base of the neck, a necklace composed of alternating round and square pendants joined by beaded elements, and a necklace with small, round beads and a central crescent-shaped pendant.

She wears a tunic and a himation. The tunic has a wide, round neckline and short, wide sleeves. The folds of the tunic are indicated by oblique grooves. Over the tunic, she wears a himation. The himation crosses the chest diagonally from the left shoulder to the right side and covers the left breast. It is fastened at the left shoulder with a circular brooch with an outer beaded border (Colledge classification: f). The edge of the himation that crosses the chest is decorated with a pleated band. The himation has a short overfold. It falls across her legs, leaving only part of the tunic visible at her right side.

Her right hand rests on the cushion. With her left hand, she pulls a fold of the veil. She wears a bracelet on each wrist, composed of twisted plain and beaded wires. She wears a round ring on the little finger of the left hand; a thick and wide hoop.

PORTRAIT B: STANDING PRIEST

The figure is shown frontally. The head is slightly turned to his left. The right arm falls along the side; his left arm is bent to the torso. The lower part of the body is obscured by the reclining figure.

He wears a tall, cylindrical, flat-top headdress divided into three sections by two vertical grooves: a Palmyrene priestly hat. A wreath with three rows of leaves pointing towards a central oval with an incised border is depicted at the lower part of the hat. His face is square. The eyebrows are rendered by low curving ridges that start from the root of the nose. The eyes are large and round, and the eyeballs are blank. The ears are large and protruding with the helix, scapha, and the lobe depicted. The nose is long with a wide base. The alae are indicated by incised lines. The mouth is small with a full lower lip. The chin is pointed. The neck is short and wide with a horizontal groove.

He wears a tunic and a himation. The tunic has a wide, v-shaped neckline and long, tight-fitting sleeves. The folds of the tunic are indicated by wide, curving grooves in the area of the chest and arms, and oblique grooves at the sides. Over the tunic, he wears a himation. It is wrapped around the left shoulder and arm and his waist, falling down his legs. The folds of the himation are indicated by vertical and curving grooves.

The right hand rests on the seated female's knee. With the left hand, he holds a fold of the himation, which continues under the hand in a wide, zigzag-shaped fold. The index finger is extended.

PORTRAIT C: STANDING MALE

The figure is shown frontally. The right arm is bent in front of the chest. The left arm is held at the side. The lower part of the body is obscured by the reclining figure.

He wears a tunic and a himation. The tunic has a wide, v-shaped neckline and long, tight-fitting sleeves. The folds of the tunic are indicated by curving grooves in the area of the chest. Over the tunic, he wears a himation that covers most of his body, leaving only a part of the upper torso and the right hand exposed. It covers the back of the right shoulder and is wrapped over the right arm. An end crosses the chest diagonally and falls over the left shoulder (›arm-sling‹ type). The end that crosses the chest is decorated with a pleated band. The folds of the himation are indicated by oblique grooves over the right arm and torso, and curving ones over the left arm.

With his right hand, he holds the diagonal fold of the himation.

Cat. 136

PORTRAIT D: RECLINING MALE

His right leg is shown in profile, his left leg and torso are shown frontally, the arms are shown in profile. The right arm is extended to the side and resting on the knee, the left arm is bent in front of the torso. The right leg is bent and the foot rests on the mattress. The left leg is bent under the right, and the lower part is obscured by the right leg.

He wears a ›Parthian-style‹ tunic, a chlamys, and ›Parthian-style‹ trousers. The tunic has a wide, round neckline with a wide band. The band is decorated by alternating squares and lozenges with incised borders with beads between. A central wide band extends downwards from the middle of the neckline decorated with a running scroll with rosettes between beaded bands. The tunic has long, loose sleeves with decorated cuffs. The cuffs and the lower hem of the tunic are decorated with a wide band with a vegetal pattern between two beaded bands. The folds of the tunic are indicated by oblique grooves. A thin band belt is tied with a double knot at the waist, with the ends of the belt looped under on either side of the knot. Along the right thigh there is an object with a rectangular main body and a square lateral element; a sheathed dagger. The chlamys falls over both shoulders, covers the upper part of the chest, is wrapped around the left arm, and falls below the arm and over the cushion in two wide, zigzag-shaped folds. It is fastened at the right shoulder with a circular brooch with an outer beaded border (Colledge classification: f). A small, zigzag-shaped fold falls down from the brooch. The edge of the chlamys that crosses the shoulder is scalloped and decorated with a beaded border. The folds of the chlamys are indicated by oblique grooves. The trousers are visible from above the knee: they are decorated with a wide, central band with a vegetal motif between two narrow, beaded bands, extending downwards. The folds are indicated by wide oblique grooves. He wears boots that reach slightly above the ankles (visible at the right foot). A wide band is visible across the ankles, as well as two more bands that cross diagonally the upper part of the foot.

The right hand rests on the knee. With the upturned palm of the left hand, he holds a plain bowl with his fingertips. The rim and base of the bowl are indicated by a horizontal, incised line.

SARCOPHAGUS BOX

PORTRAIT E: ARMLESS FEMALE BUST

The figure is shown frontally, rendered in a clipeus.

The outline of the head is recognizable. She wears a veil. It falls from the right shoulder in a curving fold across the chest and falls back over her left shoulder. The edge of the veil has a pleated band. The neck is wide. She wears a loop-in-loop chain necklace with a crescent-shaped pendant suspended from the centre.

She wears a tunic with a small, v-shaped neckline. The folds of the tunic are rendered by curving grooves.

PORTRAIT F: ARMLESS MALE BUST

The figure is shown frontally, rendered in a clipeus.

The outline of the head is recognizable.

He wears a tunic and a chlamys. The tunic has a wide, round neckline. The folds of the tunic are rendered by curving grooves. Over the tunic, he wears a chlamys that falls over both shoulders and covers the chest. It is fastened at the right shoulder with a brooch (details unclear). A diamond-shaped fold falls from under the brooch. The folds of the chlamys are indicated by narrow, deep grooves.

PORTRAIT G: ARMLESS BUST

The figure is shown frontally, rendered in a clipeus.

Almost no details are preserved. Curving grooves, indicating the folds of a garment, are visible at the lower part of the chest.

PORTRAIT H: ARMLESS FEMALE BUST

The figure is shown frontally, rendered in a clipeus.

She wears a veil. It falls on either side of her neck and across the chest. The edge of the veil is pleated. She wears a plain hoop necklace with a central, oval pendant.

She wears a tunic with a v-shaped neckline.

137. COMPLETE SARCOPHAGUS WITH BANQUETING SCENE AND PORTRAIT BUSTS

DATABASE NUMBER: PM741 (137a) + PM273 (137b).
LOCATION: Palmyra, Palmyra Museum, inv. no. H 24/70, H 36/71.
CONTEXT: West necropolis. Valley of the Tombs. Hypogeum of 'Alaînê. 137a: Found (29.09.1970) at the central axis of the tomb, near the base of the podium. 137b: Found (14.09.1971) at the gallery, near the east wall next to the funerary chamber.
ACQUISITION HISTORY: —
MEASUREMENTS: 137a: Height: 90 cm. Width: 174 cm. Depth: 37 cm. 137b: Height: 98 cm. Width: 230 cm. Depth: 95 cm.
MATERIAL: Limestone, white.
PRESERVATION: 137a: Broken on all sides. Heavily weathered, only the outlines of the figures are recognizable. Portrait A: Only the torso and the legs are preserved. Portraits B and C: The heads are broken off at the shoulders. Portrait D: The head is broken off at the base of the neck and the left arm is broken off at the shoulder. 137b: Broken on all sides. The surface of the sarcophagus box is weathered and chipped. The surface of all the portraits is chipped.
TECHNICAL DESCRIPTION: There are traces of red pigment on the box.
DATE: A.D. 220–240 (Sadurska 1977: A.D. 180–240, probably A.D. 210–230).
REFERENCES: 137a: Sadurska 1977, 99–101 cat. 3 fig. 41 pl. 13; Krag 2018, 58 n. 304; 62 n. 353; 384 cat. 824. 137b: Sadurska 1977, 116 cat. 9 fig. 52 pl. 13; Krag 2018, 32 n. 63; 53 n. 258; 58 n. 300. 304; 59 n. 323; 62 n. 349; 103 n. 74; 400 cat. 873.

OBJECT DESCRIPTION

The sarcophagus lid is rectangular in shape and depicts a seated female, two standing figures, and a reclining male. The figures are resting on a thin mattress (details unclear). The sarcophagus box is rendered as a kline. Four busts are depicted between the kline legs: two male busts flanked by two female busts. Above the kline is a mattress. Curving grooves indicate the fabric of the mattress. The kline legs are turned, but only partially preserved. They are composed of a plinth and above is a long, reversed concave quarter (further details unclear).

SARCOPHAGUS LID

PORTRAIT A: SEATED FEMALE

The figure is shown in frontal view. Her feet are obscured by the reclining figure to her left.

PORTRAIT B: STANDING FIGURE

The figure is shown frontally. The lower part of the body is obscured by the reclining figure.

PORTRAIT C: STANDING FIGURE

The figure is shown frontally. The lower part of the body is obscured by the reclining figure.

PORTRAIT D: RECLINING MALE

The figure is shown in frontal to three-quarter view. The right arm is extended and rests on his right leg. The right leg is bent and the foot rests on the mattress. The left leg is bent under the right, with the knee pointing outwards. The lower left leg is obscured by the right leg.

SARCOPHAGUS BOX

PORTRAIT E: ARMLESS FEMALE BUST

The figure is rendered in a clipeus and shown frontally.

She wears a veil that crosses her chest in a curving fold. She wears a necklace composed of round beads at the base of the neck.

She wears a tunic with a wide, v-shaped neckline.

PORTRAIT F: ARMLESS MALE BUST

The figure is rendered in a clipeus and shown frontally.

He wears a tunic and a chlamys. The tunic is indicated by oblique grooves at the chest. The chlamys falls over both shoulders and proceeds in a curving fold across the chest. It is fastened at the right shoulder with a brooch (details unclear). A zigzag-shaped fold falls from under the brooch. The folds are indicated by curving grooves.

PORTRAIT G: ARMLESS MALE BUST

The figure is rendered in a clipeus and shown frontally.

He wears a tunic and a chlamys. The tunic has a v-shaped neckline. The folds are rendered by narrow, curving grooves. Over the tunic, he wears a chlamys. It falls over both shoulders and proceeds in a curving fold across the chest. It is fastened at the right shoulder with a brooch (details unclear). A zigzag-shaped fold falls from under the brooch. The folds are indicated by curving grooves.

Cat. 137

PORTRAIT H: ARMLESS FEMALE BUST
The figure is rendered in a clipeus and shown frontally.

She wears a veil, visible with a curving fold across the chest. She wears a necklace composed of round beads at the base of the neck.

She wears a tunic with a v-shaped neckline.

FRAGMENTS OF LIDS, LID RELIEFS, OR BANQUETING RELIEFS

A.D. 200–240

138. FRAGMENT OF FEMALE FIGURE

DATABASE NUMBER: PM742.
LOCATION: Palmyra, Palmyra Museum, inv. no. H 19/70.
CONTEXT: West necropolis. Valley of the Tombs. Hypogeum of ʿAlaînê, found (01.10.1970) at the main gallery.
ACQUISITION HISTORY: —
MEASUREMENTS: Height: 40 cm. Width: 23 cm. Depth: 15 cm.
MATERIAL: Limestone, white.
PRESERVATION: The upper and left side are broken off horizontally at the right upper arm and the lower part is broken off diagonally through the left torso and legs. The surface is weathered.
TECHNICAL DESCRIPTION: —

DATE: A.D. 200–240 (Sadurska 1977: A.D. 180–240, probably A.D. 210–230).
REFERENCES: Sadurska 1977, 145 cat. 52 fig. 92; Krag 2018, 43 n. 164; 238. 313 cat. 553.

OBJECT DESCRIPTION
The object depicts a seated female.

PORTRAIT
The figure is shown frontally. The right arm is bent and rests on the right thigh. The leg is bent and the knee is visible through the drapery.

She wears a veil. It falls under her right arm and alongside the right leg.

She wears a tunic with short sleeves. Over the tunic, she wears a himation that covers the chest and legs. The folds of the himation are rendered by oblique and curving grooves.

She holds a fold of the veil with her right hand. She wears a wide, thick hoop bracelet on her right wrist.

139. FRAGMENT OF FEMALE FIGURE

DATABASE NUMBER: PM917.
LOCATION: Palmyra, Palmyra Museum, inv. no. CD 35/69.
CONTEXT: West necropolis. Valley of the Tombs. Hypogeum of ʿAlaînê, found (24.10.1969) in the gallery. Excavation no. 46/69 229/71, 232/71.

ACQUISITION HISTORY: —
MEASUREMENTS: Height: 15 cm. Width: 15 cm. Depth: 7 cm.
MATERIAL: Limestone, white.
PRESERVATION: The object is broken off on all four sides. Only the torso is preserved.
TECHNICAL DESCRIPTION: —
DATE: A.D. 200–240.
REFERENCES: Sadurska 1977, 117–119 cat. 12 fig. 55.

OBJECT DESCRIPTION

The object depicts the torso of a female figure.

PORTRAIT

The figure is shown frontally. The right arm is bent and raised (details unclear).

She wears a tunic and an over-garment, possibly a himation. The tunic has short sleeves that end at the elbows. The folds of the tunic are indicated by curving grooves. The over-garment comes from under the right arm, crosses the chest diagonally, and falls back over the left shoulder. The edge of the garment is scalloped. The folds of the garment are indicated by curving grooves.

140. FRAGMENT OF MALE FIGURE

DATABASE NUMBER: PM739.
LOCATION: Palmyra, Palmyra Museum, inv. no. 36/69.
CONTEXT: West necropolis. Valley of the Tombs. Hypogeum of ʿAlaînê, found (24.10.1969) in the gallery.
ACQUISITION HISTORY: —
MEASUREMENTS: Height: 18 cm. Width: 26 cm. Depth: 11 cm.
MATERIAL: Limestone, white with red veins.
PRESERVATION: The upper part of the figure is broken off at the base of the neck. The arms are broken off. The lower part of the figure is broken off at the middle of the chest, following the line of the chlamys folds. A deep crack runs diagonally across the chest. The upper part of the chest is heavily chipped.
TECHNICAL DESCRIPTION: —
DATE: A.D. 200–240.
REFERENCES: Myśliwiec 1974, 89 fig. 7; Sadurska 1977, 116 f. cat. 10 fig. 53.

OBJECT DESCRIPTION

The fragment depicts a male bust.

PORTRAIT

The figure is shown frontally.

He wears a tunic and a chlamys. The tunic has a wide neckline and sleeves. Over the tunic he wears a chlamys. It falls in a curving fold across the chest. It is fastened at the right shoulder with a round brooch with an incised border (Colledge classification: h). A zigzag-shaped fold falls from under the brooch.

141. FRAGMENT OF MALE FIGURE

DATABASE NUMBER: PM740.
LOCATION: Palmyra, Palmyra Museum, inv. no. CD 19a/69.
CONTEXT: West necropolis. Valley of the Tombs. Hypogeum of ʿAlaînê, found (22.10.1969) to the left of the door at the entrance of the gallery.
ACQUISITION HISTORY: —
MEASUREMENTS: Height: 20 cm. Width: 23 cm. Depth: 9 cm.
MATERIAL: Limestone, white/yellow.
PRESERVATION: The background is broken off. The surface is weathered. The upper part of the figure is broken off at the base of the neck. Part of the chlamys at the centre of the chest is chipped.
TECHNICAL DESCRIPTION: —
DATE: A.D. 200–240 (Sadurska 1977: A.D.: 180–240).
REFERENCES: Sadurska 1977, 117 f. cat. 11 fig. 54.

OBJECT DESCRIPTION

The object depicts a male bust.

PORTRAIT

The figure is shown frontally.

He wears a tunic and a chlamys. The tunic has a small, round neckline. The folds of the tunic are rendered by curving grooves. Over the tunic, he wears a chlamys. The chlamys is fastened over the right shoulder with a round brooch (Colledge classification: h). A small, zigzag-shaped fold falls from under the brooch. The chlamys is folded over the chest and falls over the left shoulder. The edge of the chlamys is decorated with a pleated band.

HEADS: PRIESTS

0–10 CM

A.D. 200–240

142. FRAGMENT OF HEAD OF A PRIEST

DATABASE NUMBER: PM869.
LOCATION: Palmyra, Palmyra Museum, inv. no. H 41/71.
CONTEXT: West necropolis. Valley of the Tombs. Hypogeum of ʿAlaînê, found in the debris of the funerary chamber.
ACQUISITION HISTORY: —
MEASUREMENTS: Height: 6 cm. Width: 17 cm. Depth: 11 cm.
MATERIAL: Limestone, pink.
PRESERVATION: The portrait is broken off at the height of the eyebrows. The upper part of the Palmyrene priestly hat is broken off.
TECHNICAL DESCRIPTION: —
DATE: A.D. 200–240.
REFERENCES: Sadurska 1977, 134 cat. 35 fig. 75.

OBJECT DESCRIPTION

The fragment depicts the head of priest.

PORTRAIT

He wears a tall, cylindrical, flat-top headdress divided into three sections by two vertical grooves: a Palmyrene priestly hat. A wreath is depicted at the lower part of the hat. It is composed of three rows of long, narrow leaves at the sides and elliptical ones at the centre, pointing towards a central, oval decoration. The oval has a beaded border. Two round elements, perhaps berries, are on either side of the central leaf next to the oval. The midribs of the leaves are incised. The eyebrows are curving, rendered by incised lines. The eyes are almond-shaped with thick upper eyelids.

143. FRAGMENT OF PALMYRENE PRIESTLY HAT

DATABASE NUMBER: PM868.
LOCATION: Palmyra, Palmyra Museum, inv. no. H 19/71.
CONTEXT: West necropolis. Valley of the Tombs. Hypogeum of ʿAlaînê, found in front of the sarcophagus cat. 134, at the side of the entrance (15.09.1971).
ACQUISITION HISTORY: —
MEASUREMENTS: Height: 8 cm. Width: 15 cm. Depth: 13 cm.
MATERIAL: Limestone, pink.
PRESERVATION: The object is broken off at the height of the forehead. The upper part of the Palmyrene priestly hat is broken off.
TECHNICAL DESCRIPTION: —
DATE: A.D. 200–240.
REFERENCES: Sadurska 1977, 134 f. cat. 36 fig. 76.

OBJECT DESCRIPTION

The fragment depicts a Palmyrene priestly hat.

PORTRAIT

Tall, cylindrical, flat-top headdress divided into three sections by two vertical grooves: a Palmyrene priestly hat. A wreath is depicted at the lower part of the hat. It is composed of three rows of long, narrow leaves at the sides and elliptical ones at the centre, pointing towards a central, oval decoration. The oval has a beaded border. Two round elements, perhaps berries, are on either side of the central leaf next to the oval. The midribs of the leaves are incised.

144. FRAGMENT OF PALMYRENE PRIESTLY HAT

DATABASE NUMBER: PM870.
LOCATION: Palmyra, Palmyra Museum, inv. no. H 17/71.
CONTEXT: West necropolis. Valley of the Tombs. Hypogeum of ʿAlaînê, found behind sarcophagus cat. 136 (15.09.1971).
ACQUISITION HISTORY: —
MEASUREMENTS: Height: 6 cm. Width: 13 cm. Depth: 10 cm.
MATERIAL: Limestone, pink.
PRESERVATION: Only the upper part of the Palmyrene priestly hat is preserved.
TECHNICAL DESCRIPTION: —
DATE: A.D. 200–240.
REFERENCES: Sadurska 1977, 135 f. cat. 37 fig. 77.

OBJECT DESCRIPTION

The fragment depicts a Palmyrene priestly hat.

PORTRAIT

Tall, cylindrical, flat-top headdress divided into three sections by two vertical grooves: a Palmyrene priestly hat. A wreath is depicted at the lower part of the hat. It is composed of three rows of long serrated leaves pointing towards a central, oval decoration. The oval has a beaded border. The midribs of the leaves are incised.

145. FRAGMENT OF PALMYRENE PRIESTLY HAT

DATABASE NUMBER: PM871.
LOCATION: Palmyra, Palmyra Museum, inv. no. H 14/71.
CONTEXT: West necropolis. Valley of the Tombs. Hypogeum of ʿAlaînê, found between the sarcophagi cat. 133 and cat. 134 (14.09.1971).
ACQUISITION HISTORY: —
MEASUREMENTS: Height: 10 cm. Width: 14 cm. Depth: 7 cm.
MATERIAL: Limestone, pink.
PRESERVATION: Only the upper part of the Palmyrene priestly hat is preserved.
TECHNICAL DESCRIPTION: —
DATE: A.D. 200–240.
REFERENCES: Sadurska 1977, 136 cat. 38 fig. 78.

OBJECT DESCRIPTION

The fragment depicts a Palmyrene priestly hat.

PORTRAIT

Tall, cylindrical, flat-top headdress divided into three sections by two vertical grooves: a Palmyrene priestly hat. A wreath is depicted at the lower part of the hat. It is composed of three rows of long serrated leaves pointing towards a central, oval decoration. The oval has a beaded border. The midribs of the leaves are incised.

146. FRAGMENT OF PALMYRENE PRIESTLY HAT

DATABASE NUMBER: PM872.
LOCATION: Palmyra, Palmyra Museum, inv. no. H 16/71.
CONTEXT: West necropolis. Valley of the Tombs. Hypogeum of ʿAlaînê, found (14.09.1971) between the sarcophagi cat. 133 and cat. 134.
ACQUISITION HISTORY: —
MEASUREMENTS: Height: 10 cm. Width: 13 cm. Depth: 13 cm.
MATERIAL: Limestone, pink.

PRESERVATION: Only the upper part of the Palmyrene priestly hat is preserved.
TECHNICAL DESCRIPTION: —
DATE: A.D. 200–240.
REFERENCES: Sadurska 1977, 136 f. cat. 39 fig. 79.

OBJECT DESCRIPTION
The fragment depicts a Palmyrene priestly hat.

PORTRAIT
He wears a tall, cylindrical, flat-top headdress divided into three sections by two vertical grooves: a Palmyrene priestly hat. A wreath is depicted at the lower part of the hat. It is composed of three rows of long serrated leaves pointing towards a central, oval decoration. The oval has a beaded border. The midribs of the leaves are incised. A narrow, horizontal band at the bottom of the hat suggests a liner.

147. FRAGMENT OF PALMYRENE PRIESTLY HAT

DATABASE NUMBER: PM891.
LOCATION: Palmyra, Palmyra Museum, inv. no. H 24/71.
CONTEXT: West necropolis. Valley of the Tombs. Hypogeum of ʿAlainê, found at the north side of the sarcophagus cat. 136 (15.09.1971).
ACQUISITION HISTORY: —
MEASUREMENTS: Height: 7 cm. Width: 11 cm. Depth: 4 cm.
MATERIAL: Limestone, white with red veins.
PRESERVATION: Only the lower part of the Palmyrene priestly hat is preserved.
TECHNICAL DESCRIPTION: —
DATE: A.D. 200–240.
REFERENCES: Sadurska 1977, 137 cat. 40 fig. 80.

OBJECT DESCRIPTION
The fragment depicts a Palmyrene priestly hat.

PORTRAIT
Tall, cylindrical, flat-top headdress divided into three sections by two vertical grooves: a Palmyrene priestly hat. A wreath is depicted at the lower part of the hat. It is composed of three rows of long serrated leaves pointing towards a central medallion. The medallion has a beaded border. The midribs of the leaves are incised.

148. FRAGMENT OF PALMYRENE PRIESTLY HAT

DATABASE NUMBER: PM893.
LOCATION: Palmyra, Palmyra Museum, inv. no. H 114/70.
CONTEXT: West necropolis. Valley of the Tombs. Hypogeum of ʿAlainê, aisle 18 (found 6.10.1970).
ACQUISITION HISTORY: —
MEASUREMENTS: Height: 6 cm. Width: 13.5 cm. Depth: 11 cm.
MATERIAL: Limestone, white.

PRESERVATION: Only the lower part of the Palmyrene priestly hat is preserved.
TECHNICAL DESCRIPTION: —
DATE: A.D. 200–240.
REFERENCES: Sadurska 1977, 137 f. cat. 41 fig. 81.

OBJECT DESCRIPTION
The fragment depicts a Palmyrene priestly hat.

PORTRAIT
Tall, cylindrical, flat-top headdress divided into three sections by two vertical grooves: a Palmyrene priestly hat. A wreath is depicted at the lower part of the hat, composed of three rows of long narrow leaves pointing towards a central, oval decoration with an incised border. The midribs of the leaves are incised.

149. FRAGMENT OF PALMYRENE PRIESTLY HAT

DATABASE NUMBER: PM894.
LOCATION: Palmyra, Palmyra Museum, inv. no. H 6/70.
CONTEXT: West necropolis. Valley of the Tombs. Hypogeum of ʿAlainê, central niche (found 29.09.1970).
ACQUISITION HISTORY: —
MEASUREMENTS: Height: 6 cm. Width: 12 cm. Depth: 10 cm.
MATERIAL: Limestone, white.
PRESERVATION: Only part of the Palmyrene priestly hat is preserved.
TECHNICAL DESCRIPTION: —
DATE: A.D. 200–240.
REFERENCES: Sadurska 1977, 138 cat. 42 fig. 82.

OBJECT DESCRIPTION
The fragment depicts a Palmyrene priestly hat.

PORTRAIT
Tall, cylindrical, flat-top headdress: a Palmyrene priestly hat. A wreath is depicted at the lower part of the hat. It is composed of three rows of leaves pointing towards a central, oval decoration with an incised border. The midribs of the leaves are incised.

11–20 CM

A.D. 180–200

150. FRAGMENT OF HEAD OF A PRIEST

DATABASE NUMBER: PM236.
LOCATION: Palmyra, Palmyra Museum, inv. no. H 23/71.
CONTEXT: West necropolis. Valley of the Tombs. Hypogeum of ʿAlainê, found near sarcophagus cat. 136.
ACQUISITION HISTORY: —
MEASUREMENTS: Height: 18 cm. Width: 11 cm. Depth: 10 cm.

MATERIAL: Limestone, white.
PRESERVATION: The head is broken off at the neck. The upper and front part of the head is broken off, including the Palmyrene priestly hat, forehead, eyebrows, right eye, right ear, and most of the nose.
TECHNICAL DESCRIPTION: —
DATE: A.D. 180–200.
REFERENCES: Sadurska 1977, 132–134 cat. 34 fig. 74.

OBJECT DESCRIPTION
The object depicts the head of a priest.

PORTRAIT
The figure is shown frontally.
He wears a cylindrical headdress suggesting a Palmyrene priestly hat. His face is square. The eyes are almond-shaped. The end of the upper eyelid extends beyond that of the lower one. The irises are indicated by incised circles. Nasolabial lines are depicted by two grooves extending downwards from either side of the base of the nose. The mouth is small with a full lower lip. The chin is square. The neck is wide.

A.D. 200–240

151. HEAD OF A PRIEST

DATABASE NUMBER: PM232.
LOCATION: Palmyra, Palmyra Museum, inv. no. CD 20/69.
CONTEXT: West necropolis. Valley of the Tombs. Hypogeum of ʿAlaînê, found in the gallery (22.10.1969).
ACQUISITION HISTORY: —
MEASUREMENTS: Height: 19 cm. Width: 12 cm. Depth: 19 cm.
MATERIAL: Limestone, white.
PRESERVATION: The body of the figure is broken off at the middle of the neck. The upper and front part of the Palmyrene priestly hat, the nose, and the left ear are broken off. It is heavily weathered. A crack runs across the middle of the face.
TECHNICAL DESCRIPTION: The lower eyelids have not been carved.
DATE: A.D. 200–240.
REFERENCES: Myśliwiec 1974, 87 fig. 5; Sadurska 1977, 128 f. cat. 30 fig. 70.

OBJECT DESCRIPTION
The fragment depicts the head of a priest.

PORTRAIT
The figure is shown frontally. The head is turned slightly towards his left.
He wears a tall, cylindrical, flat-top headdress divided into three sections by two vertical grooves low on the forehead: a Palmyrene priestly hat. A wreath is depicted at the lower part of the hat. It has three rows of serrated leaves pointing towards a central decoration (oval?). A narrow, horizontal band at the bottom of the hat suggests a liner. His face is square and fleshy. The eyebrows are low, curving ridges. The eyes are close-set and almond-shaped with thick upper eyelids. The ears are large and slightly protruding, with the helix and scapha depicted. The mouth is small with full lips. The chin is pointed. The neck is wide with a curving groove.

152. HEAD OF A PRIEST

DATABASE NUMBER: PM233.
LOCATION: Palmyra, Palmyra Museum, inv. no. CD 21/69.
CONTEXT: West necropolis. Valley of the Tombs. Hypogeum of ʿAlaînê, found in front of the right exedra (23.10.1969).
ACQUISITION HISTORY: —
MEASUREMENTS: Height: 20 cm. Width: 12 cm. Depth: 11 cm.
MATERIAL: Limestone, white.
PRESERVATION: The body of the figure is broken off at the neck. The surface is weathered and chipped, especially the Palmyrene priestly hat, temple, and eyebrow, and the eyes and nose. There are cracks running horizontally across the face.
TECHNICAL DESCRIPTION: The lower eyelids are not carved.
DATE: A.D. 200–240.
REFERENCES: Myśliwiec 1974, 87 fig. 4; Sadurska 1977, 129–131 cat. 31 fig. 71.

OBJECT DESCRIPTION
The fragment depicts the head of a priest.

PORTRAIT
The figure is shown frontally. The head is turned slightly towards his left.
He wears a tall, cylindrical, flat-top headdress divided into three sections by two vertical grooves low on the forehead: a Palmyrene priestly hat. A wreath is depicted at the lower part of the hat. It has three rows of serrated leaves pointing towards a medallion with a beaded border enclosing a circle with a diamond shape in the middle. A narrow, horizontal band at the bottom of the hat indicates a liner. His face is square and fleshy. The eyebrows are low, curving ridges. The eyes are deep-set and almond-shaped. The eyeballs are blank. The ears are small and slightly protruding, with helix, scapha, and concha depicted. The ears are placed asymmetrically on the head, with the left ear placed lower than the right one. The mouth is small with a full lower lip. The chin is round. The neck is wide.

153. HEAD OF A PRIEST

DATABASE NUMBER: PM231.
LOCATION: Palmyra, Palmyra Museum, inv. no. H 12/71.

CONTEXT: West necropolis. Valley of the Tombs. Hypogeum of ʿAlaînê, found between sarcophagi cat. 133 and cat. 134 (14.09.1971).
ACQUISITION HISTORY: —
MEASUREMENTS: Height: 17 cm. Width: 14 cm. Depth: 16 cm.
MATERIAL: Limestone, white.
PRESERVATION: The head is broken off at the neck. The upper and central part of the Palmyrene priestly hat and the nose are broken off. The surface is heavily weathered. An oblique crack runs across the middle of the face, and a vertical crack runs along the left side of the face.
TECHNICAL DESCRIPTION: —
DATE: A.D. 220–240.
REFERENCES: Sadurska 1977, 127 cat. 29 figs. 68. 69.

OBJECT DESCRIPTION
The fragment depicts the head of a priest.

PORTRAIT
The figure is shown frontally.

He wears a cylindrical headdress low on the forehead, suggesting a Palmyrene priestly hat. His face is oval and fleshy. The eyebrows are curving, rendered by incised lines. The eyes are large and almond-shaped with thick upper eyelids. The eyeballs are blank. The ears are large and protruding, with helix, scapha, and concha depicted. The mouth is small with a full lower lip. The chin is pointed, and he has a double chin. The neck is wide.

21–30 CM
A.D. 200–240

154. HEAD OF A PRIEST

DATABASE NUMBER: PM234.
LOCATION: Palmyra, Palmyra Museum, inv. no. CD 19/69.
CONTEXT: West necropolis. Valley of the Tombs. Hypogeum of ʿAlaînê, found in the gallery (22.10.1969).
ACQUISITION HISTORY: —
MEASUREMENTS: Height: 22 cm. Width: 15 cm. Depth: 16 cm.
MATERIAL: Limestone, white.
PRESERVATION: The body of the figure is broken off at the neck. The surface is heavily weathered. The upper left part of the Palmyrene priestly hat, the eyes, and the nose are chipped.
TECHNICAL DESCRIPTION: —
DATE: A.D. 200–240.
REFERENCES: Myśliwiec 1974, 87 fig. 3; Daszewski 1972, 146 fig. 10; Sadurska 1977, 131 f. cat. 32 fig. 72.

OBJECT DESCRIPTION
The fragment depicts the head of a priest.

PORTRAIT
The head is turned slightly towards his left.

He wears a tall, cylindrical, flat-top headdress divided into three sections by two vertical grooves low on the forehead: a Palmyrene priestly hat. A wreath is depicted at the lower part of the hat. It has three rows of serrated leaves pointing towards a medallion. The medallion has a beaded border enclosing an oval with an incised border, indicating an inlay. The midribs of the leaves are incised. His face is square. The eyebrows are depicted by low, curving ridges. They curve upwards over the root over the nose, creating a frowning expression. The eyes are deep-set and almond-shaped (details unclear). The ears are large and protruding, with helix, scapha, and concha depicted. The ears are placed asymmetrically on the head, with the left ear placed lower than the right one. Nasolabial lines are indicated by two grooves extending downwards from the base of the nose. The mouth is small with thin lips. Two wide lines extend downwards from the corners of the mouth (›marionette‹ lines). The chin is square. The neck is wide.

31–40 CM
A.D. 200–240

155. HEAD OF A PRIEST

DATABASE NUMBER: PM235.
LOCATION: Palmyra, Palmyra Museum, inv. no. H 9/71.
CONTEXT: West necropolis. Valley of the Tombs. Hypogeum of ʿAlaînê, found behind sarcophagus cat. 134 (14.10.1971).
ACQUISITION HISTORY: —
MEASUREMENTS: Height: 31 cm. Width: 13 cm. Depth: 13 cm.
MATERIAL: Limestone, white.
PRESERVATION: The body of the figure is broken off at the neck. The top of the Palmyrene priestly hat and the ears are broken off. A scratch runs diagonally across his face. The nose and ears are chipped.
TECHNICAL DESCRIPTION: The lower eyelids are not carved.
DATE: A.D. 200–240.
REFERENCES: Sadurska 1977, 132 cat. 33 fig. 73.

OBJECT DESCRIPTION
The object depicts the head of a priest.

PORTRAIT
The head is turned slightly towards his right.

He wears a tall, cylindrical, flat-top headdress divided into three sections by two vertical grooves low on the forehead: a Palmyrene priestly hat. A wreath is depicted at the lower part of the hat. It has three rows of elliptical leaves pointing towards an oval with an incised border, indicating an inlay. The midribs of the leaves are incised. A narrow, horizontal band at the bottom of the hat suggests a liner. His face is oval. The eyebrows are depicted by low, curving ridges. The eyes are almond-shaped, with thick upper eyelids. The nose is straight with a wide base. The alae are indicated by incised lines. The mouth is small with full lips. The chin is square with a round depression, perhaps indicating a cleft. The neck is wide.

HEADS: MALES

11–20 CM

A.D. 200–240

156. MALE HEAD

DATABASE NUMBER: PM230.
LOCATION: Palmyra, Palmyra Museum, inv. no. H 105/70.
CONTEXT: West necropolis. Valley of the Tombs. Hypogeum of ʿAlaînê, found in section 28 (05.10.1970).
ACQUISITION HISTORY: —
MEASUREMENTS: Height: 20 cm. Width: 17 cm. Depth: 20 cm.
MATERIAL: Limestone, white.
PRESERVATION: The head is broken off at the neck. The upper part of the hair is chipped. The surface is weathered.
TECHNICAL DESCRIPTION: —
DATE: A.D. 200–240.
REFERENCES: Sadurska 1977, 125 f. cat. 28 figs. 66. 67.

OBJECT DESCRIPTION
The object depicts a male figure.

PORTRAIT
His hair is arranged in two rows of snail-shell curls around his head. The individual strands of hair are indicated by incised lines. His face is round. The eyebrows are curving and rendered by incised lines. The eyes are large and almond-shaped with thick eyelids. The upper eyelids extend beyond the end of the lower ones. The eyeballs are blank. The ears are protruding with the helix, scapha, and earlobe indicated. The nose is wide, with the alae incised and the nostrils carved. The mouth is small with thin lips. The chin is pointed. The neck is long.

HEADS: FEMALES

0–10 CM

A.D. 200–240

157. FRAGMENT OF A FEMALE HEAD

DATABASE NUMBER: PM922.
LOCATION: Palmyra, Palmyra Museum, inv. no. H 2/71.
CONTEXT: West necropolis. Valley of the Tombs. Hypogeum of ʿAlaînê. Found in the left exedra, in the rubble (11.09.1971), excavation no. 162/71.
ACQUISITION HISTORY: —
MEASUREMENTS: Height: 8 cm. Width: 11 cm. Depth: 4.5 cm.
MATERIAL: Limestone, white.
PRESERVATION: The object is broken off on all sides.
TECHNICAL DESCRIPTION: —
DATE: A.D. 200–240.
REFERENCES: Sadurska 1977, 152 f. cat. 60 fig. 100.

OBJECT DESCRIPTION
The object depicts the upper part of a female head.

PORTRAIT
The hair is brushed from the centre of the head to the sides. At the sides, above the ears, two rows of large snail-shell curls are rendered. The individual locks of hair are indicated by incised, wavy lines. A small part of the forehead is preserved.

158. FRAGMENT OF A FEMALE HEAD

DATABASE NUMBER: PM862.
LOCATION: Palmyra, Palmyra Museum, inv. no. 15/71.
CONTEXT: West necropolis. Valley of the Tombs. Hypogeum of ʿAlaînê, found between the sarcophagi cat. 133 and 134 (14.09.1971).
ACQUISITION HISTORY: —
MEASUREMENTS: Height: 9 cm. Width: 12 cm. Depth: 9 cm.
MATERIAL: Limestone, pink.
PRESERVATION: The lower part of the figure is broken off diagonally at the left side of the head. The upper part of the figure is broken off at the top of the head.
TECHNICAL DESCRIPTION: —
DATE: A.D. 200–240 (Sadurska 1977: A.D. 180–250).
REFERENCES: Sadurska 1977, 148 f. cat. 55 fig. 95; Krag 2018, 270 cat. 383.

OBJECT DESCRIPTION
The fragment depicts the head of a female figure.

PORTRAIT
The figure is shown frontally.
She wears three headdresses: a headband, a turban, and a veil. The headband is placed low on the forehead (other details unclear). The turban is coiled (other details unclear). The veil is heavy with a scalloped edge. It falls over the back of her head. She also wears head ornaments: a head-chain. The head-chain is composed of round bezels linked by beaded elements. Part of the hair is covered by the headdress: several strands of hair above the ears are brushed back over the headband and the edge of the turban and disappear under the veil. The eyebrows are indicated by thin, curving grooves. The eyes are large, almond-shaped with thick upper eyelids. The irises are indicated by incised circles.

159. FRAGMENT OF A FEMALE HEAD

DATABASE NUMBER: PM918.
LOCATION: Palmyra, Palmyra Museum, inv. no. H 42/71.
CONTEXT: West necropolis. Valley of the Tombs. Hypogeum of ʿAlainê, found in the debris of the funerary chamber (18.09.1971).
ACQUISITION HISTORY: —
MEASUREMENTS: Height: 6 cm. Width: 13.5 cm. Depth: 11 cm.
MATERIAL: Limestone, white.
PRESERVATION: The portrait is broken off at the top of the head.
TECHNICAL DESCRIPTION: —
DATE: A.D. 200–240.
REFERENCES: Sadurska 1977, 148 cat. 54 fig. 94.

OBJECT DESCRIPTION
The object depicts the upper part of a female head.

PORTRAIT
The figure is shown frontally.
She wears two headdresses: a turban and a veil. The veil is heavy, and the edge is scalloped. The turban is coiled. It is composed of a single layer, and the coiling of the fabric is indicated by curving, incised lines. Over the turban she wears a head ornament that extends downwards from the middle of the top of the head from under the veil. The ornament is composed of two square bezels with beaded borders linked by beaded elements.

160. FRAGMENT OF A FEMALE HEAD

DATABASE NUMBER: PM919.
LOCATION: Palmyra, Palmyra Museum, inv. no. H 11/71.
CONTEXT: West necropolis. Valley of the Tombs. Hypogeum of ʿAlainê, found behind the sarcophagus cat. 133 (11.09.1971).
ACQUISITION HISTORY: —
MEASUREMENTS: Height: 8 cm. Width: 15 cm. Depth: 12 cm.
MATERIAL: Limestone, white.
PRESERVATION: The portrait is broken off at the top of the head.
TECHNICAL DESCRIPTION: —
DATE: A.D. 200–240.
REFERENCES: Sadurska 1977, 150 f. cat. 57 fig. 97.

OBJECT DESCRIPTION
The object depicts the upper part of a female head.

PORTRAIT
She wears two headdresses: a turban and a veil. The veil is heavy, and the edge is scalloped. The turban is coiled. It is composed of a single layer, and the coiling of the fabric is indicated by curving, incised lines. The hair is parted in the centre of the forehead and brushed to the sides. Above the ears, it is brushed back over the turban, and disappears under the veil. The individual strands of hair are indicated by incised, wavy lines.

161. FRAGMENT OF A FEMALE HEAD

DATABASE NUMBER: PM921.
LOCATION: Palmyra, Palmyra Museum, inv. no. H 109/70.
CONTEXT: West necropolis. Valley of the Tombs. Hypogeum of ʿAlainê, section 28 (05.10.1970).
ACQUISITION HISTORY: —
MEASUREMENTS: Height: 10 cm. Width: 16.5 cm. Depth: 14 cm.
MATERIAL: Limestone, white.
PRESERVATION: The portrait is broken off at the top of the head.
TECHNICAL DESCRIPTION: —
DATE: A.D. 200–240 (Sadurska 1977: A.D. 200–250).
REFERENCES: Sadurska 1977, 151 cat. 58 fig. 98.

OBJECT DESCRIPTION
The object depicts the upper part of a female head.

PORTRAIT
She wears two headdresses: a turban and a veil. The veil is heavy. The turban is coiled. It is composed of two twisted layers. The coiling of the fabric is indicated by curving, incised lines. The hair is parted in the centre of the forehead and brushed to the sides. Above the ears, it is brushed back over the turban, and disappears under the veil. The individual strands of hair are indicated by incised, wavy lines. A diamond-shaped lock of hair is depicted in the middle of the forehead, under the central parting of the hair.

11–20 CM

A.D. 200–220

162. FRAGMENT OF A FEMALE HEAD

DATABASE NUMBER: PM743.
LOCATION: Palmyra, Palmyra Museum, inv. no. H 13/71.
CONTEXT: West necropolis. Valley of the Tombs. Hypogeum of ʿAlainê, found between sarcophagi cat. 133 and cat. 134 (14.09.1971).
ACQUISITION HISTORY: —
MEASUREMENTS: Height: 16 cm. Width: 14 cm. Depth: 8 cm.
MATERIAL: Limestone.
PRESERVATION: The body of the figure is broken off at the middle of the neck. The upper part of the head is broken off. The surface of the face is heavily chipped.
TECHNICAL DESCRIPTION: —
DATE: A.D. 200–220.
REFERENCES: Sadurska 1977, 151 f. cat. 59 fig. 99; Krag 2018, 350 cat. 694.

OBJECT DESCRIPTION
The fragment depicts the head of a female figure.

PORTRAIT

She wears three headdresses: a headband, a turban, and a veil. The turban is coiled. The coiling is rendered by horizontal, incised lines. The veil is heavy. Part of the hair is covered by the headdress: several strands of hair above the ears are pushed back over the headband and disappear under the veil. The individual locks of hair are rendered by waving, incised lines.

A.D. 200–240

163. FRAGMENT OF A FEMALE HEAD

DATABASE NUMBER: PM907.
LOCATION: Palmyra, Palmyra Museum, inv. no. 25/71.
CONTEXT: West necropolis. Valley of the Tombs. Hypogeum of ʿAlaînê, found at the north side of cat. 136 (14.09.1971).
ACQUISITION HISTORY: —
MEASUREMENTS: Height: 14 cm. Width: 14 cm. Depth: 16 cm.
MATERIAL: Limestone, pink.
PRESERVATION: The lower part of the figure is broken off diagonally at the right side of the head and the left side of the face. The edge of the veil is broken off. The head is broken off below the left eyebrow.
TECHNICAL DESCRIPTION: —
DATE: A.D. 200–240.
REFERENCES: Sadurska 1977, 149 f. cat. 56 fig. 96; Krag 2018, 270 cat. 384.

OBJECT DESCRIPTION

The fragment depicts the head of a female figure.

PORTRAIT

The figure is shown frontally.

She wears three headdresses: a headband, a turban, and a veil. The headband is placed low on the forehead and is divided into rectangular, decorated panels separated by vertical, beaded bands. The central panel has a vegetal motif (other details unclear). The turban is coiled. It is divided into two layers and the ends are looped into each other creating a knot in the middle. Curving grooves indicate the coiling of the fabric. The veil is heavy with a scalloped edge. It falls over the back of her head. She also wears head ornaments: a head-chain. The head-chain is composed of round bezels with an incised border linked together by beaded elements. The chain is attached under the turban and runs to either side of the head, disappearing under the veil. Part of the hair is covered by the headdress: several strands of hair above the ears are brushed back over the headband and disappear under the veil. The individual strands of hair are indicated by incised lines. The eyebrows are indicated by curving grooves.

21–30 CM

A.D. 200–240

164. FEMALE HEAD

DATABASE NUMBER: PM261.
LOCATION: Palmyra, Palmyra Museum, inv. no. CD 38/69.
CONTEXT: West necropolis. Valley of the Tombs. Hypogeum of ʿAlaînê, found behind the threshold to the gallery (24.10.2018).
ACQUISITION HISTORY: —
MEASUREMENTS: Height: 22 cm. Width: 15 cm. Depth: 13 cm.
MATERIAL: Limestone, white.
PRESERVATION: The body of the figure is broken off at the base of the neck. The nose is broken off. The edge of the veil, the mouth, and the chin are chipped.
TECHNICAL DESCRIPTION: —
DATE: A.D. 200–240 (Sadurska 1977: A.D. 180–240, probably A.D. 210–230).
REFERENCES: Myśliwiec 1974, 87 fig. 6; Sadurska 1977, 145–148 cat. 53 fig. 93; Krag 2018, 108 n. 125; 351 cat. 700.

OBJECT DESCRIPTION

The fragment depicts the head of a female figure.

PORTRAIT

The figure is shown frontally.

She wears three headdresses: a headband, a turban, and a veil. The headband is placed high on her forehead, is wide and undecorated. The turban is coiled and composed of a single layer. The coiling is rendered by curving grooves. The veil is heavy, and the edge is scalloped. Over the band, she wears a head-chain that is attached under the centre of the turban and runs to the sides disappearing under the veil. It is composed of circular bezels joined by beaded elements. Another head ornament is fastened under the veil, at the centre of the head, and extends downwards over the middle of the forehead. It is composed of an oval and a square bezel, both with an incised border, joined by a beaded element. Three thin, rectangular elements, probably indicating chains, ending in large beads are suspended from the lower edge of the square bezel and fall over the centre of the forehead. Part of the hair is covered by the headdress: several strands of hair at the sides are brushed back under the head-chain, over the headband and corners of the turban, and disappear under the veil. The individual strands of hair are indicated by incised lines. Her face is oval. The eyes are large and almond-shaped. The upper eyelids are indicated by an incised line (details unclear). She wears dumbbell-shaped earrings (Colledge classification: H). The nose is wide. The mouth is small with full lips. The chin is oval. The neck has three curving grooves.

BANQUETING RELIEFS

A.D. 200–240

165. FRAGMENT OF A BANQUETING RELIEF

DATABASE NUMBER: PM867.
LOCATION: Palmyra, Palmyra Museum, inv. no. H 7/10, H 111/70.
CONTEXT: West necropolis. Valley of the Tombs. Hypogeum of 'Alaînê.
ACQUISITION HISTORY: —
MEASUREMENTS: Height: 22.5 cm. Length: 25 Cm. Depth: 10 cm.
MATERIAL: Limestone, white.
PRESERVATION: The relief is broken in two. Most of the background is broken off. The lower right corner with part of the mattress and part of the tunic, trousers, shoe, and arm of the reclining figure is preserved. The arm and tunic have been chipped.
TECHNICAL DESCRIPTION: —
DATE: A.D. 200–240.
REFERENCES: Sadurska 1977, 165 f. cat. 71 fig. 112.

OBJECT DESCRIPTION

Fragment of banqueting relief. The relief has a plain frame. The inner left side of the frame is decorated with leaves. The object depicts part of a mattress and the lower part of a male reclining on it. The mattress is decorated with wide bands with floral and vegetal motifs between two beaded bands. The texture of the mattress is indicated by wide, curving grooves.

PORTRAIT

The figure is shown in frontal to three-quarter view. The right arm is extended. The right foot is resting on the mattress.

He wears a >Parthian-style< tunic and trousers. The tunic ends above the knees and has a decorated border at the hem (details unclear). The folds of the trousers are indicated by wide, curving grooves. The trousers are tucked into his boots. The boots are rounded and closed-toe.

A.D. 220–240

166. FRAGMENT OF A BANQUETING RELIEF

DATABASE NUMBER: PM267.
LOCATION: Palmyra, Palmyra Museum, inv. no. H7/71 (torso), H115/70 (head).
CONTEXT: West necropolis. Valley of the Tombs. Hypogeum of 'Alaînê (13.09.1971 and 06.10.1971).
ACQUISITION HISTORY: —
MEASUREMENTS: Height: 37 cm. Width: 21 cm. Depth: 11 cm.
MATERIAL: Limestone.
PRESERVATION: The object is composed of two pieces. The right, upper, and lower sides of the relief are broken off. The surface of the forehead and of the nose is chipped. The left hand is chipped. The lower part of the figure is broken off from the right shoulder and waist.
TECHNICAL DESCRIPTION: —
DATE: A.D. 220–240 (Sadurska 1977: A.D. 180–240).
REFERENCES: Sadurska 1977, 162–164 cat. 69 fig. 109.

OBJECT DESCRIPTION

The fragment depicts a reclining male. The relief has a frame with a leaf-and-dart pattern and a beaded band. At the lower edge is a plain band frame. Beneath the figure is a mattress. Curving grooves indicate the texture of the fabric. The figure rests against a cushion. Curving grooves indicate the texture of the fabric.

PORTRAIT

The figure is shown frontally. The arms appear short in relation to the body. The left arm is bent in front of the chest, and rests against a cushion.

His hair is arranged in two rows of flame-shaped curls around his head. The individual strands of hair are indicated by incised lines. His face is diamond-shaped. The eyebrows are curving. The eyes are almond-shaped, with thick upper eyelids. The eyeballs are blank. Only the tail of the helix, tragus, and earlobe are depicted under the hair. The nose has a wide base, and the alae are incised. He has a beard that starts at the temples and covers the outer side of the cheeks, the chin, and the upper lip. The facial hair is rendered by vertical, incised lines. The mouth is small with a full lower lip. The chin is pointed and prominent. The neck is wide.

He wears a >Parthian-style< tunic and a himation. The tunic has a small, round neckline, decorated with a beaded band. It has long, tight-fitting sleeves and the cuffs are decorated with two beaded bands. The tunic has a band decorated with rosettes extending downwards from the middle of the neckline. The folds of the himation are rendered by oblique grooves. He also wears a plain band belt. The himation covers his left shoulder and upper arm and continues along the left side of the body. A folded edge of the himation falls under his left arm onto the cushion and mattress. The folds of the himation are indicated by oblique grooves.

With the upturned palm of the left hand, he holds a bowl (visible in outline) with his fingertips.

OBJECTS FROM HYPOGEA 403

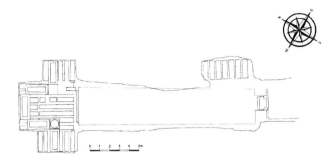

Plan of hypogeum of ʿAlaînê.

A.D. 186–200

HYPOGEUM OF BARʿÂ BONNÛR

SARCOPHAGUS BOXES

167. SARCOPHAGUS BOX WITH PORTRAIT BUSTS

DATABASE NUMBER: InSitu181.
LOCATION: Palmyra, in situ.
CONTEXT: South-west necropolis. Hypogeum of Barʿâ Bonnûr.
ACQUISITION HISTORY: —
MEASUREMENTS: —
MATERIAL: Limestone.
PRESERVATION: Portrait A: The face and the headdress are fragmented. Portrait B: The face is fragmented. Portrait C: The face is fragmented. Portrait D: The face and the headdress are fragmented.
TECHNICAL DESCRIPTION: —
DATE: A.D. 186–200.
REFERENCES: Ingholt Archives, IA_NCG_Portrait2016_029 + portraits. Ingholt 1935, 116.

OBJECT DESCRIPTION

The sarcophagus box is rectangular in shape and depicts a female, two males, and another female bust in clipei between the kline legs. Above these figures, is a kline and a mattress. The mattress has three decorated, vertical panels (details unclear). Oblique grooves indicate the texture of the mattress. The central stretcher of the kline is decorated with incised rectangles. The kline has turned legs. They are composed of a plinth and above is a small torus, a concave quarter, a ball, a second, shorter concave quarter, a torus, and another bell-shaped element. All the elements are decorated with vertical fluting, except for the torus, which is decorated with diagonal fluting.

PORTRAIT A: ARMLESS FEMALE BUST

The figure is shown frontally, rendered in a clipeus.
She wears a veil. It falls over the back of her head and over both shoulders in a curving fold, and is wrapped around her upper body. She probably also wears a coiled turban (details unclear). The left eye is almond-shaped, with thick eyelids. The neck is slender.
She wears a tunic. It has a wide, v-shaped neckline. The folds of the tunic are rendered by curving grooves.

PORTRAIT B: ARMLESS MALE BUST

The figure is shown frontally, rendered in a clipeus.
The neck appears slender.
He wears a tunic and a chlamys. The tunic has a wide, v-shaped neckline. The folds of the tunic are rendered by curving grooves. Over the tunic, he wears a himation that falls over the left shoulder and diagonally over the chest. The folds of the himation are indicated by vertical and oblique grooves.

PORTRAIT C: ARMLESS MALE BUST

The figure is shown frontally, rendered in a clipeus.
The neck appears slender.
He wears a tunic and a chlamys. The tunic has a wide, v-shaped neckline. The folds of the tunic are rendered by curving grooves. Over the tunic, he wears a himation that falls over the left shoulder and diagonally over the chest. The folds of the himation are indicated by vertical and oblique grooves.

PORTRAIT D: ARMLESS FEMALE BUST

The figure is shown frontally, rendered in a clipeus.
She wears a veil. It falls over the back of her head and over both shoulders in a curving fold, and is wrapped around her upper body. She probably also wears a coiled turban (details unclear). The neck is slender.
She wears a tunic. It has a wide, v-shaped neckline. The folds of the tunic are rendered by curving grooves.

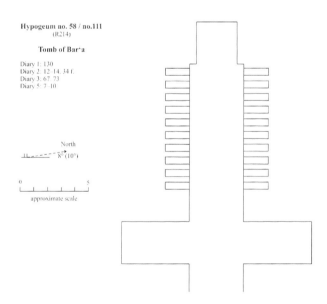

Plan of hypogeum of Barʿâ Bonnûr.

Cat. 167

OBJECTS FROM HYPOGEA

A.D. 200–220

TOMB NO. 7, HYPOGEUM OF BÔLḤÂ

SARCOPHAGI

A.D. 200–220

168. COMPLETE SARCOPHAGUS RELIEF WITH BANQUETING SCENE AND PORTRAIT BUSTS

DATABASE NUMBER: InSitu075.
LOCATION: Palmyra, in situ.
CONTEXT: South-east necropolis. Tomb no. 7, hypogeum of Bôlḥâ, north exedra, niche on the back wall. Excavation no. 28.
ACQUISITION HISTORY: —
MEASUREMENTS: Height: 170 cm. Width: 182 cm. Depth: 18 cm.
MATERIAL: Limestone, white/yellow.
PRESERVATION: The surface is slightly weathered. Portrait C: The left side of the face is slightly weathered. Portrait F: Slightly weathered. Portrait G: Slightly weathered. A fragment is chipped from the forehead. Portrait H: Slightly weathered. Portrait I: Slightly weathered.
TECHNICAL DESCRIPTION: There are traces of red pigment in the inscription. Portrait E: The left hand is undercut.
DATE: A.D. 200–220 (Sadurska – Bounni 1994: A.D. 180–220).
REFERENCES: Bounni 1967, 49; al-Asʿad – Taha 1968, 101–106 cat. 28; Tanabe 1986, 29 pls. 188–191; Sadurska 1994, 15 fig. 9; Sadurska – Bounni 1994, 86–88 cat. 120 figs. 231–232; Audley-Miller 2016, 575. 579 f. fig. 7; Krag – Raja 2017, 199 n. 24; 204 n. 72. 73; 205 n. 75. 76. 79. 83; 206 n. 87; 207 n. 94. 95; 208 n. 99; 209 n. 100. 101. 105; 210 n. 107; 211 n. 117. 119; 216 cat. 17; Krag 2018, 14 n. 58; 23 n. 160; 28 n. 9; 32 n. 63; 33 n. 79. 82; 36 n. 112; 41 n. 143; 46 n. 198; 51 n. 241; 56 n. 284; 65 n. 377; 66 n. 382; 67 n. 4; 87 n. 182–185. 187; 88 n. 190. 193; 89 n. 204–207; 90 n. 210; 103 n. 74; 106 n. 106; 317 cat. 566. Inscription: Gawlikowski 1974b, 307 f. cat. 101; Sadurska – Bounni 1994, 87 f.; Krag 2018, 317 cat. 566.

OBJECT DESCRIPTION

The sarcophagus lid is rectangular in shape and depicts a seated female, two standing males, a reclining priest, and a reclining male. Beneath these figures is a box in the shape of a kline with four busts between the kline legs: a male, two females, and a priest. Above the kline are two mattresses. The thin mattress at the top is decorated with an intersecting lozenges pattern with flowers in the lozenges. The lower mattress is decorated with three bands with vegetal motifs (other details unclear). The reclining priest rests his left arm against a cushion. It is decorated with a panel with leaves between beaded bands. The other reclining figure, rests against a cushion. The central stretcher of the kline is decorated with one rectangular indentation between two square ones on either end. The kline has turned legs. They are composed of a plinth and above is a reversed bell-shaped element, a convex quarter, a reversed bell-shaped element, a thin torus, a horizontal biconical element, a thin torus, a scotia, and above the stretcher is a horizontal biconical finial. All the elements are decorated with a diagonal tongues pattern.

INSCRIPTIONS

INSCRIPTION 1
SCRIPT: Palmyrene Aramaic.
LOCATION ON RELIEF: On the mattress under the seated female.
TRANSCRIPTION: ṢLMT ʿTʾ BRT NBWDʿ | BR MQY ʾTT MLKW.
TRANSLATION: Image of ʿAttâ daughter of Nabûdʿa son of Maqqaî, wife of Malkû.

INSCRIPTION 2
SCRIPT: Palmyrene Aramaic.
LOCATION ON RELIEF: To the left of the boy standing closest to the seated female.
TRANSCRIPTION: ṢLM | NBWDʿ | BR MLKW BR | ʿGYLW.
TRANSLATION: Image of Nabûdʿa son of Malkû son of ʿOgeîlû.

INSCRIPTION 3
SCRIPT: Palmyrene Aramaic.
LOCATION ON RELIEF: To the left of the boy standing to the closest to the reclining priest.
TRANSCRIPTION: ṢLM ʿGYLW | BR MLKW BR | ʿGYLW.
TRANSLATION: Image of ʿOgeîlû son of Malkû son of ʿOgeîlû.

INSCRIPTION 4
SCRIPT: Palmyrene Aramaic.
LOCATION ON RELIEF: On the mattress, under the reclining priest.
TRANSCRIPTION: ṢLMʾ DNH DY MLKW BR ʿGYLW NBWŠWR.
TRANSLATION: This image (is that) of Malkû son of ʿOgeîlû Nabûšûr.

INSCRIPTION 5
SCRIPT: Palmyrene Aramaic.
LOCATION ON RELIEF: On the mattress, under the reclining male.
TRANSCRIPTION: ṢLM ʿGYLW BR ZBDBWL BR | BWLḤʾ NBWŠWR ḤBL.
TRANSLATION: Image of ʿOgeîlû son of Zabdibôl son of Bôlḥâ Nabûšûr, alas!

INSCRIPTION 6
SCRIPT: Palmyrene Aramaic.
LOCATION ON RELIEF: Under the kline, to the left of the male bust.
TRANSCRIPTION: QRBLʾ | BR MLKW | BR ʿGYLW.
TRANSLATION: Corbulo son of Malkû son of ʿOgeîlû.

INSCRIPTION 7
SCRIPT: Palmyrene Aramaic.

LOCATION ON RELIEF: To the right of the male bust on the right side.
TRANSCRIPTION: ṢLMT BʿDʾ | BRT MLKW BR | ʿGYLW.
TRANSLATION: Image of Baʿadâ daughter of Malkû son of ʿOgeîlû.

INSCRIPTION 8
SCRIPT: Palmyrene Aramaic.
LOCATION ON RELIEF: Between the two female busts.
TRANSCRIPTION: ṢLMT TMʾ | BRT ḤWRʾ BR | BWLḤʾ ḤBL.
TRANSLATION: Image of Tammê daughter of Ḥûrâ son of Bôlḥâ, alas!

CIS no. —; PAT no. 1893.
COMMENTS: Inscription 6: L.1: QRBLʾ is the Latin name Corbulo. Inscription 8: L.2: It may be possible to read ḤYRʾ »Ḥaîrâ«, due to the similar shape of Y and W. No reading possible from the photograph.

The sarcophagus is adjacent to cat. 169 and cat. 170.

SARCOPHAGUS LID

PORTRAIT A: SEATED FEMALE, ʿATTÂ
The figure is shown frontally. The head appears large. The legs appear short in relation to the body. The right arm is bent and rests on the knee. The left arm is raised to the neck. Her legs are bent, and the knees are rendered under the drapery. Her feet are obscured by the right foot of the reclining priest to her left.

She wears two headdresses: a turban and a veil. The turban is coiled. It is rendered in three twisting layers with horizontal grooves indicating the coiling of the fabric. The veil is heavy. It falls over her shoulders and is wrapped around her right arm and falls back over her left shoulder. Her hair is centrally parted and brushed away on each side of the forehead, proceeds above the ears, and is pushed back over the edge of the turban and disappears under the veil. The individual strands of hair are rendered by curving, incised lines. Her face is oval. Her eyebrows are curving, rendered as thin ridges. The eyes are close-set and almond-shaped with thick upper eyelids that extend beyond the lower ones. The irises are indicated by incised circles. Only the earlobes are visible under the hair, and she wears earrings with three juxtaposed beads (Colledge classification: K): the upper bead is circular, the central bead is hyperboloid, and the lowest is circular. Her nose is straight and wide at the base. Her mouth is small with a thin upper lip and a full lower lip. Her cheeks are fleshy, and her chin and neck are wide. She is wearing a necklace composed of a string of round beads at the base of the neck.

She wears a tunic and a himation. The tunic has a small, round neckline and wide sleeves ending at the elbows. The folds are indicated by curving grooves. The ankle-length himation crosses her chest diagonally from the left shoulder to the right side and covers most the left breast and the body. It is fastened at the left shoulder with a circular brooch. The outer border is a geometrical polygon with curved sides meeting in flat ends, with round elements between the curving sides. The centre of the brooch has an incised border (Colledge classification: i). The folds of the himation are rendered by curving and oblique grooves. The folds between the legs are rendered by curving grooves.

She rests her right hand on her right thigh. The left hand is raised to the neck and she lightly pulls a fold of the veil. She is wearing a round ring on her left little finger; a wide, thick hoop with a circular bezel. She also wears a bracelet around her left wrist with a wide hoop with a circular bezel. It is wide with indications of a central inlay.

PORTRAIT B: STANDING MALE, NABÛDʿA
The figure is shown frontally. The head appears large. The arms appear short, and the shoulders narrow in relation to the body. The arms are bent and held to the torso. The elbow of the right arm is obscured by the seated female to his right, and the lower body and legs by the reclining figure.

The hair is arranged in two rows of crescent-shaped curls around the head and covers the ears. The individual strands of hair are indicated by incised lines. His face is square. The eyebrows are slightly curving. The eyes are close-set and almond-shaped with thick upper eyelids. The irises are indicated by incised circles and the pupils by punch holes. The nose is thin with a wide base. The mouth is small with thin, straight lips. The cheeks are fleshy. The chin is wide and almost double, indicated by a deep groove on the right side. The neck is wide.

He wears a tunic and a himation. The tunic has a small, v-shaped neckline. The folds of the tunic are rendered by curving, wide grooves. Over the tunic, he wears a himation that covers most of his body. It is wrapped around the right shoulder and arm, leaving the chest and the hand free. One fold of the himation crosses the chest diagonally and falls over the left shoulder (›arm-sling‹ type). The left lower arm is wrapped in a thick fold of the himation.

He is holding the diagonal fold of the himation with his right hand. With his left hand, he is holding a fold of the himation. The index finger is extended.

PORTRAIT C: STANDING MALE, ʿOGEÎLÛ
The figure is shown frontally. The head appears large. The arms appear short in relation to the body. The right arm is bent and held to the torso. The left arm and lower body are obscured by the reclining figure to his left.

The hair is arranged in rows of crescent-shaped locks around the head. The individual locks of hair are indicated by incised lines. His face is round. His eyebrows are slightly curving. The eyes are close-set and almond-shaped with thick upper eyelids. The irises are indicated by incised circles and the pupils by punch holes. The ears are small and protruding with the helix and concha depicted. The nose is wide, and the mouth is small with thin straight lips. The cheeks are fleshy. The chin is wide and almost double. The neck is wide.

He wears a tunic and a himation. The tunic has a small, round neckline. The folds of the tunic are rendered by curving, wide grooves. Over the tunic, he wears a himation. The himation covers most of his body. It is wrapped around the right shoulder and arm, leaving the chest and the hand free. One fold of the himation crosses the chest diagonally and falls over the left shoulder (>arm-sling< type).

He is holding the diagonal fold of the himation with his right hand.

PORTRAIT D: RECLINING PRIEST, MALKÛ

The figure is shown in frontal to three-quarter view. The head appears large. The legs and arms appear short in relation to the body. The right arm is bent and rests on his raised right knee. The left arm is bent and held to the torso. His right leg is bent, and his foot is resting on the kline. The left leg is bent under the right leg with the knee pointing forwards, and the lower leg is obscured by the right leg.

He wears a high, cylindrical, flat-top headdress divided into three sections by two vertical grooves: a Palmyrene priestly hat. A wreath is depicted at the centre of the headdress. It has three rows of leaves pointing towards an armless bust of a beardless, male figure with a chlamys and a Palmyrene priestly hat. The midribs of the leaves are incised. His face is square. The eyebrows are slightly curving, rendered by thin ridges. His eyes are almond-shaped, with thick upper eyelids that extend beyond the end of the lower ones. The irises are indicated by incised circles. The ears are large and protruding with the helix, concha, and the lobe depicted. His nose is straight with carved alae and nostrils. The mouth is small with thin lips. The corners of the mouth are rendered with oblique grooves. The cheeks are modelled, and the chin is pointed with a cleft. The neck is long. A v-shaped depression indicates the jugular notch.

He wears a tunic and a himation. The tunic has a wide, v-shaped neckline. The folds of the tunic are rendered by curving and oblique grooves. Over the tunic, he wears a himation. It is folded around his left upper arm and over his left wrist where it proceeds downwards across the cushion and alongside the torso. It proceeds across his waist, covers his legs, and ends at the ankles. The folds of the himation are rendered by vertical and oblique grooves. The fold across the cushion is rendered in a zigzag-shape. He wears a plain boot.

He rests his right hand on his raised right knee. With his left hand, he holds a skyphos. The skyphos has a conical foot and a lower body that is decorated with a tongues pattern. The body is straight and has a decorated band with a vine scroll that meanders across the surface, set between fluted lines. It has small, looped handles. The index and the little finger are extended. The nails are rendered by fine, incised lines. He is wearing a ring with a wide hoop and a circular bezel on his left little finger.

PORTRAIT E: RECLINING MALE, ʿOGEÎLÛ

The figure is shown in frontal to three-quarter view. The head and left hand appear large. The right arm is extended behind the reclining figure to his right. The left arm is bent and held to the chest. The lower body and legs are behind the reclining figure to his left.

The hair is arranged in rows of flame-shaped curls around the head. The individual locks of hair are indicated by incised lines. His face is oval. The eyebrows are curving, rendered as thin ridges. The eyes are close-set and almond-shaped with thick upper eyelids. The upper eyelids extend beyond the end of the lower ones. The irises and pupils are indicated by concentric, incised circles. The ears are large and protruding with the helix, scapha, tragus, and the concha depicted. The nose is straight and wide at the base. The mouth is wide with thin lips. Nasolabial lines are rendered by two diagonal grooves that start above the alae. The chin is wide, and the neck is long.

He wears a tunic and a himation. The tunic has a wide, v-shaped neckline. The folds of the tunic are rendered by curving grooves. Over the tunic, he wears a himation. It is folded around his left lower arm and over his left wrist where it falls alongside his torso. It proceeds over the cushion and across his lower torso. The folds of the himation are rendered by vertical and oblique folds across the torso and zigzag-shaped folds across the cushion.

With the upturned palm of the left hand, he holds a wide bowl with his fingertips. The bowl is decorated with a pattern of raised zigzag lines. The nails are rendered by incised lines.

SARCOPHAGUS BOX

PORTRAIT F: ARMLESS MALE BUST, CORBULO

The figure is shown frontally. The head appears large. The head is turned slightly to his right.

The hair is arranged in rows of crescent-shaped curls around the head. The individual locks of hair are indicated by incised lines. His face is oval. His eyebrows are curving. The eyes are close-set and almond-shaped with thick eyelids. The pupils are indicated by punch holes. Only the protruding earlobes are visible. His nose is thin and the mouth small with a thin upper lip and a full lower lip. The chin is pointed, and the neck is wide.

He wears a tunic and a himation. The tunic has a low, v-shaped neckline, leaving the upper part of the chest bare. The folds of the tunic are rendered by curving grooves. Over the tunic, he wears a himation. It is folded over his left shoulder, falls in a diagonal fold across the chest, and falls back at his right side.

PORTRAIT G: ARMLESS FEMALE BUST, BAʿADÂ

The figure is shown frontally. The head appears large.

She wears three headdresses: a headband, a turban, and a veil. The headband is undecorated. The turban is coiled. It is rendered in two twisting layers with horizontal grooves indicating the coiling of the fabric. She wears a heavy veil that falls over her right shoulder, proceeds in a curving fold across the chest, and falls back over her left shoulder. Part of the hair is covered by the headdresses. Several strands of hair above the ears are pushed back at the edge of the headband and turban and disappear under the veil. The individual strands of hair are rendered by incised lines. Her face is square. The eyebrows are curving. The eyes are close-set and almond-shaped. The

Cat. 168

eyeballs appear blank. Only the earlobes are visible, and she is wearing circular earrings (details unclear). The nose is small and the mouth wide with thin lips. The chin is very wide, and the neck is short.

She wears a tunic with a small, round neckline. The folds are indicated by curving, wide grooves.

PORTRAIT H: ARMLESS FEMALE BUST, TAMMÊ

The figure is shown frontally. The head appears large.

She wears two headdresses: a turban and a veil. The turban is coiled. It is rendered in one broad layer by a horizontal groove. She wears a heavy veil that falls over her right shoulder, proceeds in a curving fold across the chest, and falls back over her left shoulder. Her hair is centrally parted and brushed to each side of the forehead. Above the ears it is brushed back over the edge of the turban and disappears under the veil. The individual locks of hair are rendered by incised lines. Her face is oval. The eyebrows are curving. The eyes are close-set and almond-shaped. The eyeballs appear blank. Only the earlobes are visible, and she is wearing earrings (details unclear). The nose is small, and the mouth is narrow with thin lips. The chin is very wide, and the neck is short.

She wears a tunic with a small, round neckline. The folds are indicated by curving, wide grooves.

PORTRAIT I: ARMLESS BUST OF A PRIEST

The figure is shown frontally. The head appears large.

He wears a high, cylindrical, flat-top headdress divided into three sections by two vertical grooves: a Palmyrene priestly hat. A wreath is depicted on the lower part of the headdress. It has three rows of leaves pointing towards a bust figure (details unclear). His face is round. The eyebrows are slightly curving. The eyes are almond-shaped, with thick upper eyelids. The pupils are indicated by punch holes. The ears are large and protruding. The nose is small and the mouth small with a thin upper lip and a full lower lip. The chin is wide, and the neck is short.

He wears a tunic and a chlamys. The tunic has a wide, round neckline. The folds are rendered by curving grooves. The chlamys is folded from behind and over his left shoulder, and proceeds across his chest and over the right shoulder where it is pinned with a circular brooch (Colledge classification: i).

169. COMPLETE SARCOPHAGUS RELIEF WITH BANQUETING SCENE AND PORTRAIT BUSTS

DATABASE NUMBER: InSitu060.
LOCATION: Palmyra, in situ.
CONTEXT: South-east necropolis. Tomb no. 7, hypogeum of Bôlḥâ, north exedra, niche on the back wall. Excavation no. 29.
ACQUISITION HISTORY: —
MEASUREMENTS: Height: 166 cm. Width: 120 cm. Depth: 14 cm. Depth 2 cm (relief).
MATERIAL: Limestone, white/yellow.
PRESERVATION: The surface is weathered. Portrait F: A crack runs vertically across the left side of her face. The surface is chipped.
TECHNICAL DESCRIPTION: The right hand of portrait E is undercut.
DATE: A.D. 200–220 (Sadurska – Bounni 1994: A.D. 180–220).
REFERENCES: Bounni 1967, 49; al-Asʿad – Taha 1968, 101–106 cat. 29; Tanabe 1986, 30 pl. 193; Sadurska – Bounni 1994, 86–88 cat. 120 figs. 234. 236; Audley-Miller 2016, 575. 579 f. fig. 9; Krag – Raja 2017, 199 n. 24; 204 n. 72. 73; 205 n. 75. 76. 78; 206 n. 87; 208 n. 99; 209 n. 100. 105. 106; 210 n. 107; 216 cat. 16; Krag 2018, 14 n. 58; 23 n. 160; 28 n. 9; 32 n. 63; 33 n. 79. n. 82; 36 n. 112; 46 n. 198; 47 n. 214; 51 n. 241; 56 n. 284; 66 n. 382; 67 n. 4; 87 n. 182. 184. 186. 187; 88 n. 192. 193; 89 n. 204; 90 n. 210; 98 n. 28; 103 n. 74; 317 cat. 565. Inscription: Gawlikowski 1974b, 308 f. cat. 102; Sadurska – Bounni 1994, 88; Krag 2018, 317 cat. 565.

OBJECT DESCRIPTION

The sarcophagus lid is rectangular in shape and depicts a seated female, three standing figures, and a reclining male. Beneath these figures is a box in the shape of a kline with two busts between the kline legs: a female and a male. On top of the kline are two mattresses. The thin mattress at the top is decorated with an intersecting lozenge pattern. The thick mattress beneath is decorated with two bands. They are decorated with vine leaves on a stem, set between beaded bands. Curving grooves indicate the texture of the fabric. The reclining figure rests against a cushion. The cushion is decorated with a wide band with vine leaves on a stem, set between beaded bands. The midribs of the leaves are rendered by incised lines. On the left side, a fulcrum is shown. It is decorated with a six-petal rosette, the middle section is decorated with a branch and the upper section is decorated with the head of a horse. The central stretcher of the kline is decorated with rectangular indentations on either side. They are decorated with an incised wave pattern. On either side of the indentations are two square inlays decorated with a four-petal flower. The legs are turned. They are composed of a plinth, and above is a concave quarter, a reverse bell-shaped element, a concave quarter, a reversed concave quarter, a torus, a ball, a torus, and above the stretcher is a biconical finial. The legs are decorated with a tongues pattern.

INSCRIPTIONS
INSCRIPTION 1
SCRIPT: Palmyrene Aramaic.
LOCATION ON RELIEF: On the upper mattress, under the seated female.
TRANSCRIPTION: ṢLMT BʿDYʾ BRT BWLḤʾ | NBWŠWR ʾTT ʿGYLW BR ZBDBWL.
TRANSLATION: Image of Baʿadiyâ daughter of Bôlḥâ (son of) Nebôshûr wife of ʿOgeîlû son of Zabdibôl.

INSCRIPTION 2
SCRIPT: Palmyrene Aramaic.

LOCATION ON RELIEF: Between the seated female and standing boy, at the height of their heads.
TRANSCRIPTION: ʿGYLW | BR MLKW | BR ʿGYLW | ḤBL.
TRANSLATION: ʿOgeîlû son of Malkû son of ʿOgeîlû, alas!

INSCRIPTION 3
SCRIPT: Palmyrene Aramaic.
LOCATION ON RELIEF: Between the two standing boys, at the height of their heads.
TRANSCRIPTION: YRḤY BR | MLKW BR | ʿGYLW | ḤBL.
TRANSLATION: Yarḥai son of Malkû son of ʿOgeîlû, alas!

INSCRIPTION 4
SCRIPT: Palmyrene Aramaic.
LOCATION ON RELIEF: On the mattress, under the reclining male.
TRANSCRIPTION: ṢLM HRMS BR ḤRY MLKW WBLḤʾ ʾḤWH.
TRANSLATION: Image of Hermes freedman of Malkû, and of Belḥâ his brother.

CIS no. —; PAT no. 1894.

The sarcophagus is adjacent to cat. 168 and cat. 170.

SARCOPHAGUS LID

PORTRAIT A: SEATED FEMALE, BAʿADIYÂ

The figure is seen in frontal view. The head is turned to her right. Her head is large, and the right arm appears short in relation to the body. The right arm is bent and rests on her right thigh. The left arm is bent and raised to the neck. She sits with the legs apart. The left leg is obscured by the reclining figure to her left.

She wears three headdresses: headband, a turban, and veil. The band is placed high on her forehead and is divided into rectangular panels (details unclear). The turban is coiled, rendered in twisting layers. The veil is heavy. It falls over the shoulders and is wrapped around her right arm and falls over the back of her left shoulder. Part of the hair is covered by the headdresses: several strands of hair above the ears are pushed back over the headband and the edge of the turban and disappear under the veil. Her face is oval. The eyebrows are slightly curving. The eyes are large and almond-shaped with thin upper eyelids. The upper eyelids extend beyond the ends of the lower ones. The irises are rendered by incised circles.

Cat. 169

Cat. 169

She wears earrings with a single ball (Colledge classification: J). The nose is large with the alae carved. The mouth is small with full lips. The cheeks are fleshy, and the chin is oval and almost double. The neck is wide.

She wears a tunic and a himation. The tunic has a wide, v-shaped neckline and long, tight-fitting sleeves. The folds of the tunic are rendered by curving grooves. The himation crosses the chest diagonally from the left shoulder to the right side, and covers the left breast, the lower body, and the legs. It is fastened at the left shoulder with a triangular brooch with a lower, beaded border (Colledge classification: c). The folds of the himation are rendered by oblique and curving grooves.

The right hand rests on her right thigh and she holds a fold, possibly from the veil, in her hand. The index finger is extended. Her left arm is raised next to the shoulder where she holds a fold of the veil with her hand.

PORTRAIT B: STANDING MALE, ʿOGEÎLÛ

The figure is shown frontally. His lower body is obscured by the figures on either side.

His hair is arranged in two rows of crescent-shaped curls around the head, covering the ears. The individual locks of hair are rendered by incised lines. His face is round. The eyebrows are curving. The eyes are round, with thick upper eyelids. The eyeballs appear blank. The nose is small with the alae carved. The mouth is narrow with full lips. The cheeks are fleshy, and the chin is wide. The neck is wide.

He wears a tunic and a himation. The tunic has a wide, v-shaped neckline. The folds of the tunic are rendered by curving grooves. The himation is wrapped around his left shoulder. Another fold comes from his lower right side, proceeds in a curving line across the chest, and is folded under the left arm. The folds of the himation are rendered by vertical and oblique grooves.

The left hand is placed on the left shoulder of the standing figure to his left.

PORTRAIT C: STANDING BOY, BELḤÂ

The figure is shown frontally. The head appears large. The right arm is obscured by the seated female to his right. The left arm and lower body are obscured by the reclining figure.

His hair is arranged in thick, flame-shaped curls around the head. The individual locks of hair are rendered by incised lines. His face is round. The eyebrows are curving. The eyes are close-set with thick upper eyelids. The eyeballs appear blank. The nose is small with the alae carved. The cheeks are fleshy, and the mouth is wide with a full lower lip. The chin is oval, and the neck is short.

He wears a tunic and a himation. The folds of the tunic are rendered by curving grooves. The himation emerges from his lower right side, proceeds in a curving line across the chest, and falls back at his left shoulder. The folds of the himation are rendered by oblique and curving grooves.

PORTRAIT D: STANDING MALE, YARḤAÎ

The figure is shown frontally. The head appears large. The lower right arm is obscured by the standing boy to his right. The lower left arm and body is obscured by the reclining figure.

His hair is arranged in small, round curls around the head, covering the ears. The individual locks of hair are rendered by incised lines. His face is round. The eyebrows are slightly curving. The eyes are close-set and almond-shaped with thick upper eyelids. The upper eyelids extend beyond the end of the lower ones. The eyeballs appear blank. The nose is large. The cheeks are fleshy, and the chin is wide. The neck is wide.

He wears a tunic and a himation. The tunic has a wide, v-shaped neckline. The folds of the tunic are rendered by curving grooves. The himation is wrapped around his left shoulder and upper arm, leaving most of the chest free. The folds of the himation are rendered by curving grooves.

PORTRAIT E: RECLINING MALE, HERMES

The figure is shown in frontal to three-quarter view. The head appears large, and the arms appear short in relation to the body. The right arm is bent and held to the chest. The left arm is bent. The right leg is bent, and he rests the foot on the mattress. The left leg is bent under the right, with the knee pointing outwards. The lower left leg is obscured by the right leg.

His hair is arranged in large, flame-shaped curls around the head. The individual strands of hair are rendered by incised lines. His face is oval. The eyebrows are curving, rendered as thin ridges. The eyes are almond-shaped, with thick upper eyelids. The irises are rendered by incised circles and the pupils by punch holes. The ears are large with the helix, concha, and the lobe depicted. The nose is large with the alae carved. The mouth is small with a full lower lip. An oblique groove accentuates the corners of the mouth. The chin is oval, and the neck is wide.

He wears a ›Parthian-style‹ tunic and a himation. The tunic has a wide, round neckline decorated with a beaded band. At the middle, the tunic has a wide, decorated band extending downwards (details unclear). The folds of the tunic are rendered by oblique and curving grooves. The himation is folded around his shoulders and arms, leaving the chest and the hands free. A wide fold of the himation is wrapped around his right wrist, proceeds in a curving line across the torso, and is folded around the left wrist. It proceeds from under the wrist, across the cushion and the mattress. A deep groove divides the edge into two zigzag-shaped folds. The himation covers his lower body and legs. The lower edge, visible at the ankles, has a scalloped edge. The folds of the himation are rendered by oblique and curving grooves. He wears a plain shoe.

With the palm of the right hand turned upwards, he holds a bowl with his fingertips. It is decorated with hollowed-out lozenges. The nails are rendered by fine, incised lines. The left hand is held relaxed on the cushion, over the wide folds of the himation. The nails are rendered by fine, incised lines.

SARCOPHAGUS BOX

PORTRAIT F: ARMLESS FEMALE BUST

The figure is shown frontally. The head appears large.

She wears two headdresses: a turban and a veil. The turban is coiled. It is rendered in twisting layers by horizontal, curving grooves. The veil is heavy. It falls over her shoulders, proceeds in a curving fold across the chest, and falls back at the left shoulder. Her hair is centrally parted and brushed to each side of the forehead. On the sides of the head, the hair is pushed back over the edge of the turban and disappears under the veil. Her face is oval. The eyebrows are slightly curving, rendered as thin ridges. The eyes are almond-shaped, with thick upper eyelids. The irises and pupils are rendered by concentric, incised circles. Only the earlobes are visible under the hair and she wears dumbbell-shaped earrings (Colledge classification: H). The nose is large with the alae carved. The mouth is wide with thin lips. The chin is wide and oval. The neck is wide. At the base of the neck, she wears a necklace composed of round beads.

She wears a tunic with a small, round neckline. The folds of the tunic are rendered by curving grooves.

PORTRAIT G: ARMLESS MALE BUST

The figure is shown frontally. The head appears large. The head is slightly turned to the left.

His hair is arranged in large, crescent-shaped curls around the head. The individual locks of hair are rendered by incised lines. His face is oval. The eyebrows are slightly curving, rendered as thin ridges. The eyes are almond-shaped, with thick upper eyelids. The irises are rendered by incised circles. The ears are large and protruding with the helix, concha, and the lobe depicted. The nose is straight and wide at the base with the alae carved. The mouth is small with thin lips. The chin is wide and oval. The neck is wide.

He wears a tunic and a himation. The tunic has a wide, v-shaped neckline, which leaves the upper part of the chest bare. The folds of the tunic are rendered by curving and vertical grooves. The himation is wrapped around his left shoulder, proceeds in a curving line across the chest, and falls back at his right side. The folds of the himation are rendered by oblique grooves.

170. COMPLETE SARCOPHAGUS RELIEF WITH BANQUETING SCENE AND PORTRAIT BUSTS

DATABASE NUMBER: InSitu076.
LOCATION: Palmyra, in situ.
CONTEXT: South-east necropolis. Tomb no. 7, hypogeum of Bôlḥâ, north exedra, on the back wall. Excavation no. 27.
ACQUISITION HISTORY: —
MEASUREMENTS: Height: 161 cm. Width: 114 cm. Depth: 17 cm.
MATERIAL: Limestone, white/yellow.
PRESERVATION: The sarcophagus is weathered. Areas on the mattress and on the kline legs are chipped.
TECHNICAL DESCRIPTION: —
DATE: A.D. 200–220 (Sadurska – Bounni 1994: A.D. 180–220).
REFERENCES: Bounni 1967, 49; al-Asʿad – Taha 1968, 101–106 cat. 27; Gawlikowski 1974b, 307 cat. 100; Tanabe 1986, 29 pl. 192; Sadurska – Bounni 1994, 86–88 cat. 120 figs. 233. 235; Audley-Miller 2016, 575. 579 f. fig. 8; Krag 2018, 14 n. 58; 23 n. 160; 32 n. 63; 36 n. 112; 46 n. 198; 47 n. 214; 51 n. 241; 56 n. 284; 66 n. 382; 67 n. 4; 87 n. 182. 184; 88 n. 190. 193; 89 n. 204. 207. 210; 106 n. 106; 103 n. 74; 317 f. cat. 567. Inscriptions: Sadurska – Bounni 1994, 88; Krag 2018, 317 f. cat. 567.

Cat. 170

OBJECT DESCRIPTION
The sarcophagus lid is rectangular in shape and depicts two reclining males and a standing male/boy. Beneath these figures is a box in the shape of a kline with two busts between the kline legs: a male and female. On top of the kline are two mattresses. The thin mattress at the top is decorated with an intersecting lozenges pattern with flowers in the lozenges. The lower one is decorated with three bands. The central one is decorated with serrated leaves in an opposite arrangement on the stem, set between beaded bands. The bands on either side are decorated with lanceolate leaves in an opposite arrangement on the stem, set between beaded bands. Curving grooves indicate the texture of the lower mattress. Both figures rest their left arm on a cushion; the right cushion is decorated with a band with serrated leaves in an opposite arrangement on the stem, set between beaded bands, the details of the left cushion are unclear. On the right side of the kline, a fulcrum is shown. It is decorated with a six-petal rosette. The upper section is decorated with a branch. The central stretcher of the kline is decorated. The rectangular, central part is divided into two horizontal sections by a groove. On either side is a rectangular indentation decorated with an incised wave pattern. On either side of these are two square inlays decorated with four-petal flowers. The legs are turned. They are composed of a plinth, and above is a cyma recta, a reversed concave quarter, a concave quarter, a reversed concave quarter, a torus, a ball, a torus, and above the stretcher is a biconical finial. All elements are decorated with a tongues pattern.

INSCRIPTIONS
INSCRIPTION 1
SCRIPT: Palmyrene Aramaic.
LOCATION ON RELIEF: On the mattress, under the reclining male to the right.
TRANSCRIPTION: ṢLM ZBDBWL QRBLʾ BR ʿGYLW | BR ZBDBWL NBWŠWRY ḤBL.
TRANSLATION: Image of Zabdibôl Corbulo son of ʿOgeîlû son of Zabdibôl Nabûšûrî, alas!

Cat. 170

INSCRIPTION 2
SCRIPT: Palmyrene Aramaic.
LOCATION ON RELIEF: To the left of the standing boy.
TRANSCRIPTION: ʿGYLW | BR ZBDBWL | QRBLʾ | ḤBL.
TRANSLATION: ʿOgeîlû son of Zabidbôl Corbulo, alas!

INSCRIPTION 3
SCRIPT: Palmyrene Aramaic.
LOCATION ON RELIEF: On the mattress, under the reclining male to the left.
TRANSCRIPTION: ṢLM BWLḤʾ BR ʿGYLW BR ZBDBWL | NBWŠWR ḤBL.
TRANSLATION: Image of Bôlḥâ son of ʿOgeîlû son of Zabdibôl Nabûšûr, alas!

CIS no. —; PAT no. 1892.

COMMENT: The sarcophagus is adjacent to cat. 168 and cat. 169.

SARCOPHAGUS LID

PORTRAIT A: RECLINING MALE, ZABDIBÔL CORBULO

The figure is shown in frontal view. The right hand appears large in relation to the body. The right arm is bent and held to the torso. The left arm is bent. The legs of the figure are not rendered.

The hair is arranged in three rows of snail-shell curls around the head, covering the upper part of the ears. His face is square. The eyebrows are slightly curving. The eyes are close-set and almond-shaped with thick eyelids. The upper eyelids extend beyond the end of the lower ones. The pupils are rendered by incised circles. The ears are large and protruding with the tail of the helix and scapha depicted. The nose is straight and wide at the base. The philtrum is rendered by a vertical groove. The mouth is small with thin lips. The cheeks are fleshy, and the chin is wide. The neck is long.

He wears a tunic and a himation. The tunic has a wide, round neckline that leaves the upper part of the chest bare. The folds of the tunic are rendered by curving grooves. Over the tunic, he wears a himation that covers most of his body. It falls in a wide, vertical fold from the left shoulder. It is wrapped around the right shoulder and arm, leaving the hand free. One end of the himation crosses the torso in a curving line and is folded around the left wrist. Two zigzag-shaped folds, separated by a deep, vertical groove, fall from under the wrist and onto the cushion and mattress. The folds of the himation are rendered by vertical and curving grooves.

With the palm of the right hand turned upwards, he holds a wide bowl with his fingertips. It is decorated with a pattern of hollowed-out lozenges. The left hand is relaxed along the cushion. Nails are indicated by incised lines.

PORTRAIT B: STANDING MALE/BOY, ʿOGEÎLÛ

The figure is shown frontally. The head appears large in relation to the body. Both arms are bent and held to the torso. The lower body and legs are obscured by the reclining figures.

The hair is arranged in crescent-shaped curls around the head that covers his ears. The individual strands of hair are indicated by incised lines. His face is square. The eyebrows are curving, rendered by incised lines starting from the top of his nose. The eyes are close-set and almond-shaped. The eyeballs are blank. The nose is straight and wide at the tip. The mouth is small with thin lips. The cheeks are fleshy, and the chin is wide. The neck is wide.

He wears a tunic and a himation. The tunic has a small, v-shaped neckline. The folds of the tunic are rendered by curving, wide grooves. Over the tunic, he wears a himation. The himation covers most of his body. It is wrapped around the right shoulder and arm, leaving the chest and the hand free. He is holding the diagonal fold of the himation with his right hand where it crosses the chest diagonally and falls over the left shoulder (>arm-sling< type).

With the right hand, he holds the diagonal fold of the himation. He holds another fold of the himation with his left hand. The left index and the middle finger are extended.

PORTRAIT C: RECLINING MALE, BÔLḤÂ

The figure is shown in frontal view. The left hand appears large in relation to the body. The right arm is obscured by the other reclining figure. The left arm is bent. The legs are extended behind the reclining figure to his right.

The hair is arranged in three rows of snail-shell curls around the head, covering the upper part of the ears. His face is oval. The eyebrows are curving. The eyes are close-set and almond-shaped with thick eyelids. The upper eyelids extend beyond the end of the lower ones. The irises are rendered by incised circles. The ears are large and protruding with helix and scapha depicted. The nose is thin with the alae carved. The mouth is small with a full lower lip. The chin is oval, and the neck is wide. The neck is long, and a v-shaped groove indicates the sternocleidomastoid muscles.

He wears a tunic and a himation. The tunic has a wide, v-shaped neckline. The folds of the tunic are rendered by curving grooves. Over the tunic, he wears a himation. It is folded around his left shoulder, falls along his left torso, and is wrapped around his left wrist. The folds are indicated by oblique, curving grooves.

He holds a skyphos in his left hand. It has a conical foot and lower body, decorated with a tongues pattern. The body of the skyphos is decorated with a running scroll with rosettes. The skyphos has small, looped handles. The index and the little finger are extended.

SARCOPHAGUS BOX

PORTRAIT D: ARMLESS MALE BUST

The figure is shown frontally. The head appears large.

The hair is arranged in straight rows of crescent-shaped curls around the head. The individual strands of hair are indicated by incised lines. His face is square. His eyebrows are curving. The eyes are close-set and almond-shaped with thick eyelids. The eyeballs are blank. The ears are small and protruding with helix, scapha, and concha depicted. His nose is straight and wide at the base. The mouth is small with a thin upper lip and a full lower lip. The chin is wide and the neck short.

He wears a tunic and a himation. The tunic has a wide, round neckline. The folds of the tunic are rendered by curving grooves. Over the tunic, he wears a himation. It is folded over his left shoulder and falls in a diagonal fold across the chest.

PORTRAIT E: ARMLESS FEMALE BUST

The figure is shown frontally. The head appears large.

She wears two headdresses: a turban and a veil. The turban is coiled. It is rendered by two twisting layers. The veil is heavy. It falls over the shoulders. It is wrapped around her left shoulder and falls back over her right shoulder. Her hair is centrally parted and brushed to each side of the forehead. Part of the hair is covered by the headdresses. Several strands of hair above the ears are brushed back over the edge of the turban and disappear under the veil. The individual strands of hair are rendered by incised lines. Her face is square. The eyebrows are curving. The eyes are close-set and almond-shaped. The eyeballs are blank. Only the earlobes are visible, and she is wearing earrings (details unclear). The nose is straight and wide at the base. The mouth is small with a thin upper lip and a full lower lip. The chin is wide, and the neck is short. She wears a necklace composed of round beads, at the base of her neck.

She wears a tunic with a small, round neckline. The folds are indicated by curving grooves.

171. COMPLETE SARCOPHAGUS RELIEF WITH BANQUETING SCENE AND PORTRAIT BUSTS

DATABASE NUMBER: InSitu074.
LOCATION: Palmyra, in situ.
CONTEXT: South-east necropolis. Tomb no. 7, hypogeum of Bôlḥâ, the podium at the end of the exedra. Excavation no. 30.
ACQUISITION HISTORY: —
MEASUREMENTS: Height: 181 cm. Width: 204 cm. Depth: 25 cm.
MATERIAL: Limestone, white/yellow.
PRESERVATION: The surface is slightly weathered.
TECHNICAL DESCRIPTION: There are traces of red pigment in the inscriptions. Portrait E: The left hand is undercut.
DATE: A.D. 200–220 (Sadurska – Bounni 1994: A.D. 200–230).
REFERENCES: Ingholt Archives, PS 1374; al-Asʿad – Taha 1968, 106–108 cat. 30; Tanabe 1986, 30 pls. 209–212; Sadurska – Bounni 1994, 89 f. cat. 121 fig. 246; Audley-Miller 2016, 575. 579. 580. fig. 10; Krag – Raja 2017, 199 n. 24; 204 n. 72. 73; 205 n. 75. 76. 80. 83; 206 n. 87; 207 n. 94. 95; 208 n. 99; 209 n. 100. 101. 105; 210 n. 107. 109. 110. 112. 115; 211 n. 117. 119; 217 cat. 21; Krag 2018, 28 n. 9; 32 n. 63; 53 n. 258; 54 n. 262; 58 n. 300; 59 n. 323–325; 61 n. 332. 335; 62 n. 349. 352. 353; 63 n. 356; 66 n. 382; 67 n. 4; 87 n. 182. 184. 186; 88 n. 189. 193. 195. 197; 89 n. 201. 204. 208; 90 n. 210; 103 n. 74; 106 n. 105. 106; 390 f. cat. 843. Inscription: Gawlikowski 1974b, 347 f. cat. 103; Sadurska – Bounni 1994, 89 f. cat. 121; Krag 2018, 390 f. cat. 843.

OBJECT DESCRIPTION

The sarcophagus lid is rectangular in shape and depicts a seated female, a standing female, a standing male, a reclining priest, and a reclining male. Beneath these figures is a box in the shape of a kline with four busts inside clipei between the kline legs: a female, a male, a priest, and a female. Above the kline are two mattresses. The thin mattress at the top is decorated with an intersecting lozenge pattern with flowers in the lozenges. The lower mattress is decorated with three bands. The bands on either side are decorated with serrated leaves in an opposite arrangement on the stem. The central band is decorated with a floral motif (details unclear). Curving grooves indicate the texture of the lower mattress. The reclining priest rests his left arm against a cushion. It is decorated with a band with a running scroll with five-petal rosettes, set between beaded bands. The other reclining figure rests his arm on two cushions. The lower cushion is decorated with a broad band (details unclear). The left side of the kline is decorated with a fulcrum with a six-petal rosette. The central stretcher of the kline is decorated. The wide, rectangular central panel is divided into two sections by a horizontal line. The upper section is decorated with miniature bunches of grapes. The lower section is decorated with vine leaves on a stem. On either side, the stretcher is decorated with two rectangular indentations set between two square inlays or appliqués with animals (details unclear). The kline has turned legs. They are composed of a plinth, and above is a long, reversed concave quarter, a torus, a reversed concave quarter, a concave quarter, a ball, a torus, and above the stretcher is a biconical finial. The elements are decorated with a tongues pattern.

INSCRIPTIONS

INSCRIPTION 1
SCRIPT: Palmyrene Aramaic.
LOCATION ON RELIEF: To the left of the seated female, at the height of the head.
TRANSCRIPTION: ṢLM ʾQMʾ | BT BRʿTH.
TRANSLATION: Image of Aqmê daughter of Barʿateh

INSCRIPTION 2
SCRIPT: Palmyrene Aramaic.
LOCATION ON RELIEF: To the right of the reclining priest.
TRANSCRIPTION: ṢLM NBWŠWR | BR ʿGYLW BR | ʿGYLW.
TRANSLATION: Image of Nabûšûr son of ʿOgeîlû son of ʿOgeîlû.

INSCRIPTION 3
SCRIPT: Palmyrene Aramaic.
LOCATION ON RELIEF: To the right of the reclining male.
TRANSCRIPTION: ṢLM ʿGYLW BR | ʿGYLW BR ʿGYLW | DYʿB<D> LH NBWŠWR | BRH BTR MWTH | ŠNYN ŠTYN.
TRANSLATION: Image ʿOgeîlû son of ʿOgeîlû son of ʿOgeîlû, which was made for him by Nabûšûr his son, after his death (at the age of) sixty years.

INSCRIPTION 4
SCRIPT: Palmyrene Aramaic.
LOCATION ON RELIEF: To the right of the female bust at the outer right side.
TRANSCRIPTION: ṢLMT ʾQMʾ BT | ʿGʾ ʾQML | ʾMH DY | NBWŠWR.
TRANSLATION: Image of Aqmê daughter of ʿOggâ Aqqamal, mother of Nabûšûr.

INSCRIPTION 5
SCRIPT: Palmyrene Aramaic.
LOCATION ON RELIEF: To the right of the female bust to the outer left side.
TRANSCRIPTION: ṢLMT HGʾ | BT ʿGYLW.
TRANSLATION: Image of Haggâ daughter of ʿOgeîlû.

CIS no. —; PAT no. 1895.

COMMENT: Inscription 3: L.3: ʿBLH on the stone.

SARCOPHAGUS LID

PORTRAIT A: SEATED FEMALE, AQMÊ

The figure is shown in three-quarter view. The head appears large. The head is turned to her left. The right arm is bent and rests on the right thigh. The left arm is raised to the neck. Her legs are bent, and the knees are rendered under the drapery. Her feet are obscured by the right foot of the reclining priest.

She wears two headdresses: a turban and a veil. The turban is coiled. It is rendered in three twisting layers by horizontal grooves, indicating the coiling of the fabric. The veil is heavy with a scalloped edge. It falls over her shoulders and it is wrapped around her right shoulder and arm. It crosses her chest in a curving fold and falls back over her left shoulder. It proceeds in a zigzag-shaped fold along her right leg. Her hair is centrally parted and brushed to each side of the forehead. These strands of hair above the ears are pushed back over the edge of the turban and disappear under the veil. The individual locks of hair are rendered by incised lines. Her face is long. Her eyebrows are curving. The eyes are close-set and almond-shaped with thick upper eyelids that extend beyond the lower ones. The eyeballs are blank. Only the earlobes are visible under the hair and she is wearing earrings (details unclear). Her nose is thin with carved alae. The mouth is small with a full lower lip. The chin is oval, and almost double. The neck is wide. She wears three necklaces: one composed of round beads, worn at the base of the neck. Worn at the upper chest is a loop-in-loop chain with a circular pendant with an incised border, suspended by a narrow sleeve from the centre. One composed of large, round beads with a circular pendant with an incised border, suspended by a narrow sleeve from the centre of the necklace, worn at the chest.

She wears a tunic and a himation. The tunic has a wide, round neckline and short, wide sleeves. The folds of the tunic are indicated by curving grooves. The himation falls to the ankles. It crosses her chest diagonally from the left shoulder to the right side and covers the left breast and most of the lower

Cat. 171

chest. It proceeds across her body and ends at the ankles. It is fastened at the left shoulder with a circular brooch with a beaded border along the outer edge (Colledge classification: f). The folds of the himation are rendered by diagonal and curving grooves. The folds between the legs are rendered by curving grooves.

Her right hand rests on her thigh and she holds a fold of the veil. The index finger is extended. She wears a bracelet on her right wrist, composed of twisted, beaded wires. Her left hand is raised next to the shoulder. She holds the edge of the veil with her hand. She is wearing an oval ring on her left little finger with indications of a central inlay. She also wears a bracelet around her wrist. It is composed of beaded and plain strands wound spirally.

PORTRAIT B: STANDING FEMALE

The figure is shown frontally. The head appears large. The right arm is obscured by the left arm of the seated female to her right. The left arm is bent and held to the chest. Her legs are obscured by the reclining figure to her left.

She wears three headdresses: A headband, a turban, and a veil. The headband is placed low on the forehead and is divided into decorated panels separated by vertical grooves (details unclear). The turban is coiled. It is rendered in three twisting layers by horizontal grooves, indicating the coiling of the fabric. The veil is heavy. It falls over her right shoulder and arm, proceeds in a curving fold across the chest, and falls back at her left shoulder. The veil covers the body. Part of the hair is covered by the headdresses. Several strands of hair on each side of the face and above the ears are pushed back over the edge of the turban and disappear under the veil. The individual strands of hair are rendered by incised lines. Her face is oval. Her eyebrows are curving. The eyes are close-set and large, with thick upper eyelids. The eyeballs are blank. Only the earlobes are visible under the hair and she is wearing earrings (details unclear). Her nose is straight and wide at the base. The cheeks are fleshy. The mouth is small with a thin upper lip and a full lower lip. The chin is pointed and almost double. The neck is wide. She wears a necklace composed of large round beads at the base of the neck.

She wears a tunic with a wide, round neckline. The folds of the tunic are rendered by oblique grooves.

With the left hand, she holds a fold of the veil. She wears a wide bracelet around her left wrist composed of a wide hoop with a circular bezel.

PORTRAIT C: STANDING MALE

The figure is shown frontally. His head is turned slightly upwards. The head appears large. The right arm is bent and held to the chest. The left is bent and held out from the body, towards the reclining priest to his left.

The hair is arranged in rows of snail-shell curls around the head. The individual locks of hair are indicated by incised lines. His face is long. The eyebrows are curving. The eyes are close-set and round with thick eyelids. The eyeballs are blank. The nose is thin and slightly crooked. The mouth is small with full lips. The cheeks are fleshy. The chin is wide and almost double. The neck is long.

He wears a tunic and a himation. The tunic has a small, v-shaped neckline and long, wide sleeves. The folds of the tunic are rendered by curving and oblique, wide grooves. Over the tunic, he wears a himation that covers most of his body. It is wrapped around the right upper arm, leaving a part of the chest and the hand free. One end of the himation crosses the chest diagonally and falls over the left shoulder (>arm-sling< type). The folds of the himation are rendered by diagonal and vertical grooves.

He holds a fold of the himation with his right hand. His left hand is placed on the right shoulder of the reclining figure to his left.

PORTRAIT D: RECLINING PRIEST, NABÛŠÛR

The figure is shown in frontal to three-quarter view. The head appears large. The arms appear short in relation to the body. The right arm is bent and rests along his right thigh. The left arm is bent and held to the chest. His right leg is bent, and his foot is resting on the mattress. The left leg is bent under the right leg, with the knee pointing forwards. The lower left leg is obscured by the right leg.

He wears a high, cylindrical, flat-top headdress divided into three sections by two vertical grooves: a Palmyrene priestly hat. A wreath with the leaves pointing towards a bust of a male figure is depicted at the centre of the headdress (details unclear). His face is oval. The eyebrows are slightly curving. Two oblique grooves at the root of the nose accentuates the inner edges of the eyebrows. His eyes are close-set and almond-shaped with thick upper eyelids that extend beyond the end of the lower ones. The irises are indicated by incised circles. The ears are large with the helix, scapha, tragus, and the earlobe rendered. His nose is narrow. The cheeks are modelled by two curving grooves on each side of the nose. The mouth is small with thin lips. Nasolabial lines are rendered by deep grooves. The chin is prominent and round. The neck is long. A v-shaped groove indicates the sternocleidomastoid muscles.

He wears a >Parthian-style< tunic, a chlamys, and >Parthian-style< trousers. The tunic has a small, round neckline decorated with a band with leaves on a stem. The tunic has long, tight-fitting sleeves. The cuffs of the sleeves are decorated with a band with a floral motif (details unclear). At the middle, the tunic has a wide band with a floral pattern, set between two beaded bands extending downwards. The tunic ends above the knees and has a decorated lower border with a floral motif (details unclear). The folds of the tunic are rendered by curving, wide grooves. Over the tunic, he wears a chlamys that falls over the right shoulder and the left upper arm. It covers most of the chest. The upper edge of the chlamys has a scalloped border. It is fastened at the right shoulder with a circular brooch with a beaded border along the outer edge (Colledge classification: f). A zigzag-shaped fold falls from the brooch. Two wide zigzag-shaped folds of the chlamys, separated by a deep, oblique groove, fall across the cushion and onto the mattress. The folds of the chlamys are indicated by oblique and curving grooves. He wears a plain band belt across the lower torso. It is knotted at the centre with the ends looped under on either side of the waist. He also wears trousers. Each trouser leg is decorated in the middle with a wide band with a vegetal motif that extends downwards. The trousers are tucked into his plain boots. The folds of the garment are indicated by wide, curving grooves.

He holds a round object, possibly a pinecone in his right hand (details unclear). He holds a skyphos in his left hand. The conical foot and the lower body are decorated with a tongues pattern. The body of the skyphos is decorated with a zigzag line with floral motifs in the spacing, set between fluted lines. The index and the little finger are extended. On his left little finger, he wears a ring with a wide hoop and a circular bezel.

PORTRAIT E: RECLINING MALE, ʿOGEÎLÛ

The figure is shown in three-quarter view. The head appears large. The arms appear short in relation to the body. The right arm is extended behind the reclining figure to his right. The left arm is bent and held to the torso. The legs are extended behind the reclining figure to his right.

The hair is arranged in small snail-shell curls around the head. His face is long. The eyebrows are curving. Two oblique grooves at the base of the nose accentuate the inner edges of the eyebrows. The eyes are close-set and almond-shaped with thick eyelids. The irises are indicated by incised circles and the pupils by punch holes. The ears are large and protruding with the helix depicted. The nose is thin, long, and slightly crooked. He has a beard that starts at the temples, covers the cheeks and the chin, as well as a moustache that covers the upper lip and reaches the beard. The facial hair is rendered by small curls arranged in rows. The moustache is rendered by flame-shaped curls with incised lines indicating individual hairs. The mouth is small with a full lower lip. The chin is wide, and the neck is long. A v-shaped groove indicates the sternocleidomastoid muscles.

He wears a >Parthian-style< tunic and a himation. The tunic has a low, round neckline decorated with a band with leaves on a stem and long tight-fitting sleeves. The musculature of the chest is rendered by a vertical depression at the neckline. At the middle, the tunic has a wide band with serrated leaves in an opposite arrangement on the stem, extending downwards. The folds of the tunic are rendered by vertical and curving grooves. Over the tunic, he wears a himation. It is folded around his left shoulder and arm. It proceeds downwards along the left side of his torso and across the cushions. A zigzag-shaped fold falls from under his left hand. The folds of the himation are rendered by diagonal, curving grooves. He also wears a plain band belt across his lower torso.

With the upturned palm of the left hand, he holds a wide bowl with his fingertips. It is decorated with a pattern of hollowed-out lozenges with circular elements in the centre of the lozenges.

SARCOPHAGUS BOX

PORTRAIT F: ARMLESS BUST OF A FEMALE, AQMÊ

The figure is shown frontally, rendered in a clipeus. The head appears large.

She wears three headdresses: a headband, a turban, and a veil. The band is placed low on the forehead (details unclear). The turban is coiled. It is rendered in three twisted layers with horizontal grooves indicating the coiling of the fabric. The veil is heavy. It falls over her right shoulder, proceeds in a curving fold across the chest, and falls back over her left shoulder. Part of the hair is covered by the headdresses. Several strands of hair on either side of the face and above the ears are brushed back over the headband and the edge of the turban and disappear under the veil. Her face is oval. The eyebrows are curving. The eyes are close-set and almond-shaped. The irises are indicated (details unclear). Only the earlobes are visible, and she is wearing earrings (details unclear). The nose is small, and the mouth is small with thin lips. The chin is very wide, and the neck is short. She wears a necklace of round beads at the base of the neck.

She wears a tunic with a small, round neckline. The folds are indicated by curving, wide grooves.

PORTRAIT G: ARMLESS BUST OF A MALE

The figure is shown frontally, rendered in a clipeus. The head appears large.

The hair is arranged in slightly curving curls brushed from the top of the head and to the forehead. The individual locks of hair are indicated by incised lines. His face is long. His eyebrows are curving. The eyes are close-set and almond-shaped with thick eyelids. The irises are indicated (details unclear). The nose is straight and wide at the base. The mouth is small with thin lips. The chin is square, and the neck is long. The jugular notch is indicated by a v-shaped depression.

He wears a tunic and a himation. The tunic has a low, v-shaped neckline. The folds of the tunic are rendered by oblique, curving grooves. Over the tunic, he wears a himation. It is wrapped around his left shoulder and falls in a diagonal fold across the chest. The edge of the diagonal fold is scalloped. The folds are indicated by curving grooves.

PORTRAIT H: ARMLESS BUST OF A PRIEST

The figure is shown frontally, rendered in a clipeus. The head appears large.

He wears a high, cylindrical, flat-top headdress divided into two sections by one vertical groove: a Palmyrene priestly hat. A wreath with the leaves pointing towards a central oval is depicted at the centre of the headdress. His face is oval. The eyebrows are slightly curving, rendered as thin ridges. The eyes are close-set and almond-shaped with heavy upper eyelids.

The irises are indicated by incised circles. The ears are large and protruding with helix, concha, and scapha rendered. The nose is large and wide at the base with the alae carved. The mouth is small with thin lips. The chin is prominent, and the neck is long with two horizontal grooves.

He wears a tunic and a chlamys. The tunic has a wide, round neckline. The folds are rendered by curving grooves. The chlamys is folded from behind and wrapped around his left shoulder. It crosses the chest in a curving fold and is fastened at the right shoulder by a circular brooch with a beaded outer border (Colledge classification: f.). The folds of the chlamys are indicated by curving grooves.

PORTRAIT I: ARMLESS BUST OF A FEMALE, HAGGÂ

The figure is shown frontally, rendered in a clipeus.

She wears two headdresses: a turban and a veil. The turban is coiled. It is divided into two layers and the ends are looped into each other creating a knot in the middle. Curving grooves indicate the coiling of the fabric. The veil is heavy with a scalloped edge. It falls over her right shoulder, proceeds in a curving fold across the chest, and falls back over her left shoulder. The hair is centrally parted and brushed to each side of the forehead. The locks on either side of the face and above the ears are brushed back over the edge of the turban and disappear under the veil. The individual locks of hair are rendered by incised lines. Her face is oval. The eyebrows are curving, rendered as thin ridges. The eyes are close-set and almond-shaped. The irises are indicated by incised circles. Only the earlobes are visible, and she is wearing earrings with a suspended circular bead (Colledge classification: L). The nose is small with the alae carved. The mouth is narrow with a thin upper lip and a full lower lip. The cheeks are fleshy. The chin is wide and oval. The neck is short. She wears a necklace composed of round beads at the base of the neck.

She wears a tunic with a small, round neckline. The folds are indicated by curving, wide grooves.

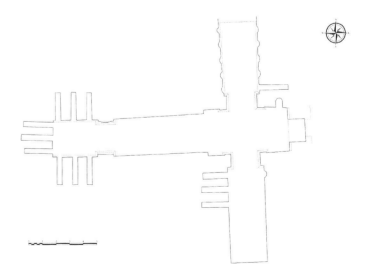

Plan of hypogeum of Bôlḥâ.

HYPOGEUM AG

FRAGMENTS OF LIDS, LID RELIEFS, OR BANQUETING RELIEFS

A.D. 200–220

172. FRAGMENT OF BANQUETING RELIEF

DATABASE NUMBER: PM438.
LOCATION: Palmyra, Palmyra Museum, inv. no. A 71.
CONTEXT: South-west necropolis. Hypogeum AG, main gallery.
ACQUISITION HISTORY: —
MEASUREMENTS: Height: 24 cm. Width: 74 cm.
MATERIAL: Limestone, white/yellow.
PRESERVATION: Portrait A: The head is broken off at the base of the neck and the right side is broken off at the right upper arm. The surface is chipped at the lower left arm, at the waist, at the left leg, and at the feet. Portrait B: The right side is broken off at the waist. The lower part is broken off at the ankles. The right lower arm is chipped.
TECHNICAL DESCRIPTION: —
DATE: A.D. 200–220.
REFERENCES: Ingholt Archives, PS 1005; Tanabe 1986, 42 pl. 419; Raja et al. 2021a, Diary 3, 23. 72, Diary 5, 128–134.

OBJECT DESCRIPTION
The object depicts a seated boy in front of the legs of a reclining figure.

PORTRAIT A: SEATED BOY
The figure is shown in three-quarter view. The left arm is bent and held out from the body. The legs are bent, and the knees are rendered under the drapery.

He wears a knee-length tunic. The tunic has a wide, round neckline and long sleeves. The folds of the tunic are rendered by oblique and curving grooves. He is wearing shoes (details unclear).

A bunch of grapes is depicted at his right lower leg.

PORTRAIT B: RECLINING FIGURE
The figure is shown in three-quarter view. The legs are bent, and the knees are rendered under the drapery. The right arm is bent and rests partly on his raised right knee and partly on the right shoulder of the boy.

The figure wears an ankle-length garment. The folds are rendered by curving, wide grooves.

Cat. 172

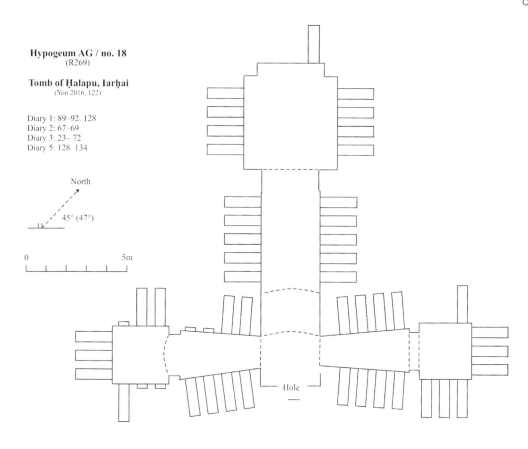

Hypogeum AG / no. 18
(R269)

Tomb of Ḥalapu, Iarḥai
(Yon 2016, 122)

Diary 1: 89–92, 128
Diary 2: 67–69
Diary 3: 23–72
Diary 5: 128–134

A.D. 200–240

HYPOGEUM ANONYMOUS

SARCOPHAGUS BOXES

A.D. 200–240

173. SARCOPHAGUS BOX WITH PORTRAIT BUSTS

DATABASE NUMBER: PM822.
LOCATION: Palmyra, Palmyra Museum, inv. no. A1239/6332.
CONTEXT: South-east necropolis. Hypogeum anonymous, by the north wall.
ACQUISITION HISTORY: —
MEASUREMENTS: Height: 93 cm. Width: 202 cm. Depth: 87 cm.
MATERIAL: Limestone, white/yellow.
PRESERVATION: The surface is weathered, and multiple cracks are running horizontally across the surface. Portrait A: The nose is chipped.
TECHNICAL DESCRIPTION: —
DATE: A.D. 200–240 (Sadurska – Bounni 1994: A.D. 180–220).
REFERENCES: Gawlikowski 1970b, 77–81 figs. 7–11; Sadurska 1982, 271 fig. 152; Parlasca 1984, 290 fig. 11; Sadurska – Bounni 1994, 12 f. cat. 3 fig. 239; Albertson 2000, 166; <https://virtual-museum-syria.org/palmyra/a-sarcophagus-with-six-half-figures-of-four-men-and-two-women/> (06.05.2022).

Inscription: Gawlikowski 1970b, 79–81; Sadurska – Bounni 1994, 13 cat. 3.

OBJECT DESCRIPTION

The sarcophagus box is rectangular in shape and is rendered as a kline. Six figures are depicted between the kline legs: three males, a female, a male, and a female. Above the kline is a mattress. The mattress is decorated with three bands. The band in the middle is decorated with serrated leaves in an opposite arrangement on the stem, set between beaded bands. The bands on either side are decorated with a running scroll with rosettes, set between beaded bands. Curving grooves indicate the texture of the fabric. On the left side of the kline is a fulcrum. It is decorated with a rosette in a clipeus. A branch with three leaves decorates the main body of the fulcrum. The central stretcher of the kline is decorated. The central part of the stretcher is divided into two parts. The upper section is decorated with oblique grooves. The lower section is decorated, possibly with geometric patterns separated by vertical lines. The sections on either side of the central part are decorated with rectangular indentations flanked by two square inlays or appliques. The rectangular indentations are decorated with miniature bunches of grapes and the square inlays with rosettes. The kline legs are turned. They are composed of a plinth, and above is a scotia, a convex quarter, a scotia, a torus, a ball, a bell-shaped element, and above the stretcher is a biconical finial. All elements are decorated with a tongues pattern.

INSCRIPTIONS
INSCRIPTION 1
SCRIPT: Palmyrene Aramaic.
LOCATION ON RELIEF: Plinth below busts.
TRANSCRIPTION: ʾWN' DNH DY ʿBDW ŠRYKW BR BLḤZY MLKW.
TRANSLATION: This sarcophagus was made by Šoraikû son of Belḥazaî Malkû.

INSCRIPTION 2
SCRIPT: Palmyrene Aramaic.
LOCATION ON RELIEF: To the left of the bust.
TRANSCRIPTION: BWLNʾ BR | ŠRYKW BR | BLḤZY | ḤBL.
TRANSLATION: Bôlnâ son of Šoraikû son of Belḥazaî, alas!

INSCRIPTION 3
SCRIPT: Palmyrene Aramaic.
LOCATION ON RELIEF: To the left of the bust.
TRANSCRIPTION: YDYʿBL BR | BLḤZY MLKW | ḤBL.
TRANSLATION: Yedîʿbel son of Belḥazaî Malkû, alas!

INSCRIPTION 4
SCRIPT: Palmyrene Aramaic.
LOCATION ON RELIEF: To the left of bust.
TRANSCRIPTION: BLḤZY BR | ML[K]W | TYM[Ḥʾ] | ḤBL.
TRANSLATION: Belḥazaî son of Malkû Taîmaḥâ, alas!

INSCRIPTION 5
SCRIPT: Palmyrene Aramaic.
LOCATION ON RELIEF: To the left of bust.
TRANSCRIPTION: ŠLMT BRT | ŠRYKW | ḤBL.
TRANSLATION: Šalmat daughter of Šoraikû, alas!

INSCRIPTION 6
SCRIPT: Palmyrene Aramaic.
LOCATION ON RELIEF: To the left of the bust.
TRANSCRIPTION: ŠRYKW BR | BLḤZY ML[KW] | ḤBL.
TRANSLATION: Šoraikû son of Belḥazaî Malkû, alas!

INSCRIPTION 7
SCRIPT: Palmyrene Aramaic.
LOCATION ON RELIEF: To the left of bust.
TRANSCRIPTION: MRTY BRT | TYMḤʾ MLKW | ḤBL.
TRANSLATION: Martî daughter of Taîmaḥâ Malkû, alas!

Inscription 1: CIS no.—; PAT no. 0121.
Inscription 2: CIS no. —; PAT no. 0122.
Inscription 3: CIS no. —; PAT no. 0123.
Inscription 4: CIS no. —; PAT no. 0124.
Inscription 5: CIS no. —; PAT no. 2638.
Inscription 6: CIS no. —; PAT no. 0125.
Inscription 7: CIS no. —; PAT no. 0126.

COMMENT: Inscription 5: »Illisible« Gawlikowski 1970b, 80. Reading Makowski in Sadurska and Bounni 1994. Inscription 6: L1: [ML]KW Gawlikowski 1970b, 80. Corr. Makowski in Sadurska and Bounni 1994.

PORTRAIT A: ARMLESS MALE BUST, BÔLNÂ
The figure is shown frontally. Behind the figure there is a cloth rendered by incised vertical and oblique lines. It is hanging from two six-petal rosettes at the height of the cheeks. A branch of leaves projects upwards and inwards from each rosette.

His hair is arranged in two rows of snail-shell curls around the head. The individual strands of hair are indicated by incised lines. His face is round. The eyebrows are curving. The eyes

Cat. 173, Pl. 52

are close-set and almond-shaped with thick upper eyelids. The eyeballs appear blank. The ears are protruding with the helix and scapha depicted. The cheeks are fleshy, and the mouth is small with a full lower lip. The chin is round and almost double. The neck is wide.

He wears a tunic and a himation. The tunic has a wide, v-shaped neckline. The folds of the tunic are rendered by curving and oblique grooves. Over the tunic, he wears a himation. It is folded from his lower right side and continues in a curving fold across the chest. At the left shoulder, a wide fold of the himation falls downwards and covers the curving fold coming from the right side. Curving and vertical grooves render the folds of the himation.

PORTRAIT B: ARMLESS MALE BUST, YEDÎʿBEL

The figure is shown frontally. Behind the figure there is a cloth rendered by incised vertical and oblique lines. It is hanging from a rosette at the height of the cheeks, visible on the right side. A branch of leaves projects upwards and inwards from the rosette.

His hair is rendered in two rows of snail-shell curls around the head. The individual strands of hair are indicated by incised lines. His face is oval. The eyebrows are curving. The eyes are close-set and round. The eyeballs appear blank. His ears are large with the helix, concha, and scapha depicted. The nose is large and wide. He has a beard that starts from the temples and covers the cheeks, the upper lip, and the chin. The facial hair is rendered by oblique, incised lines. The mouth is small with a full lower lip. The chin is round, and the neck is wide.

He wears a tunic and a himation. The tunic has a wide, v-shaped neckline. The folds of the tunic are rendered by curving and oblique grooves. Over the tunic, he wears a himation. It is folded from his lower right side and continues in a curving fold across the chest. At the left shoulder, a wide fold of the himation falls downwards and covers the curving fold coming from the right side. Curving and vertical grooves render the folds of the himation.

PORTRAIT C: ARMLESS MALE BUST, BELḤAZAÎ

The figure is shown frontally.

His hair is rendered in rows of crescent-shaped curls around the head, and it covers the ears. The individual strands of hair are indicated by incised lines. His face is oval. The eyebrows are curving, rendered by thin ridges. The eyes are close-set and almond-shaped. The eyeballs appear blank. The nose is straight and wide at the base. The chin is pointed, and the neck is wide.

He wears a tunic and a himation. The tunic has a wide, v-shaped neckline. The folds of the tunic are rendered by curving and oblique grooves. Over the tunic, he wears a himation. It is folded from his lower right side and continues in a curving fold across the chest. At the left shoulder, a wide fold of the himation falls downwards and covers the curving fold coming from the right side. Curving and vertical grooves render the folds of the himation.

PORTRAIT D: ARMLESS FEMALE BUST, ŠALMAT

The figure is shown frontally.

She wears three headdresses: a headband, a turban, and a veil. The band is placed high on the forehead and is divided into rectangular panels (details unclear). The turban is coiled. Horizontal grooves indicate the coiling of the fabric. The veil is heavy. It falls over her right shoulder, proceeds in a curving fold across the chest, and falls back at the left shoulder. Her face is oval. The eyebrows are curving. The eyes are close-set. The eyeballs appear blank. The nose is thin. Only the earlobes are visible under the headdresses and she wears dumbbell-shaped earrings (Colledge classification: H). The mouth is small with thin lips. The neck is wide.

She wears a tunic with a wide, round neckline. The folds of the tunic are rendered by curving grooves.

PORTRAIT E: ARMLESS BUST OF A MALE, ŠORAÎKÛ

The figure is shown frontally.

His hair is straight and covers the ears. He wears a wreath high on the head with the leaves pointing towards a central armless bust of a male. His face is oval. The eyebrows are curving, rendered by thin ridges. The eyes are close-set and almond-shaped. The eyeballs appear blank. The nose is straight and wide at the base. He has a beard that starts from the temples and covers the cheeks, the upper lip, and the chin. The facial hair is rendered by oblique, incised lines. The mouth is small with thin lips. The chin is round, and the neck is wide. A v-shaped groove indicates the jugular notch.

He wears a tunic and a himation. The tunic has a wide, v-shaped neckline. The folds of the tunic are rendered by curving and oblique grooves. Over the tunic, he wears a himation. It is folded from his lower right side and continues in a curving fold across the chest. Curving and vertical grooves render the folds of the himation.

PORTRAIT F: ARMLESS FEMALE BUST, MARTÎ

The figure is shown frontally.

She wears two headdresses: a turban and a veil. The turban is coiled. Horizontal grooves indicate the coiling of the fabric. The veil is heavy. It falls over her shoulders and falls in two thick folds. The two thick folds cross each other at the chest. The headdress covers part of the hair: several strands of hair above the ears are pushed back over the headband and the edge of the turban and disappear under the veil. Her face is oval. The eyebrows are curving, rendered by thin ridges. The eyes are close-set and almond-shaped. The eyeballs appear blank. The nose is straight with carved nostrils. Only the earlobes are visible under the headdresses and she wears earrings with a round bead suspended by a bar (Colledge classification: L). The mouth is small with thin lips. The chin is pointed, and the neck is wide. She wears a necklace composed of a plain hoop with a central, circular pendant. The necklace is worn at the base of the neck.

She wears a tunic. The tunic has a v-shaped neckline. The folds are rendered by curving grooves.

Cat. 174

HYPOGEUM OF ʿABDʿASTÔR

SARCOPHAGI

A.D. 200–240

174. COMPLETE SARCOPHAGUS WITH BANQUETING SCENE AND PORTRAIT BUSTS

DATABASE NUMBER: InSitu133.
LOCATION: Palmyra, in situ.
CONTEXT: South-west necropolis. Hypogeum of ʿAbdʿastôr, exedra to the left of the main chamber.
ACQUISITION HISTORY: —
MEASUREMENTS: Height: 88 cm. Width: 210 cm. Depth: 96 cm.
MATERIAL: Limestone.
PRESERVATION: The upper part of the sarcophagus lid is broken off. The upper left corner of the sarcophagus box is broken off. Portrait E: The upper part of the figure is broken off at the height of the shoulders.
TECHNICAL DESCRIPTION: —
DATE: A.D. 200–240 (Ingholt 1938: A.D. 200–273).
REFERENCES: Ingholt 1938, 138–140 pl. 50, 1; Gawlikowski 1970a, 118 n. 47.

OBJECT DESCRIPTION

The sarcophagus lid is rectangular in shape and depicts a seated female, two standing children, and two reclining men. Beneath the figures is a box in the shape of a kline with five busts placed inside clipei between the kline legs. The legs appear turned (details unclear). Above the kline are two mattresses, decorated with different patterns. The upper mattress is thin, the lower mattress is thick (details unclear). The reclining male on the left rests on two round cushions.

The object is located next to objects cat. 175 and cat. 176.

SARCOPHAGUS LID

PORTRAIT A: SEATED FEMALE

The figure is shown frontally. Her right arm is bent and rests on her thigh. According to Ingholt (1938, 139), her left arm is bent and raised to the neck.

She wears a veil that covers her upper body and a tunic.

Ingholt (1938, 139) writes that with her left hand, she pulls the edge of the veil.

PORTRAIT B: STANDING MALE FIGURE

According to Ingholt (1938, 139), the figure is a boy wearing a chiton and a himation.

PORTRAIT C: STANDING MALE FIGURE

According to Ingholt (1938, 139), the figure is a boy wearing a chiton and a himation.

OBJECTS FROM HYPOGEA 425

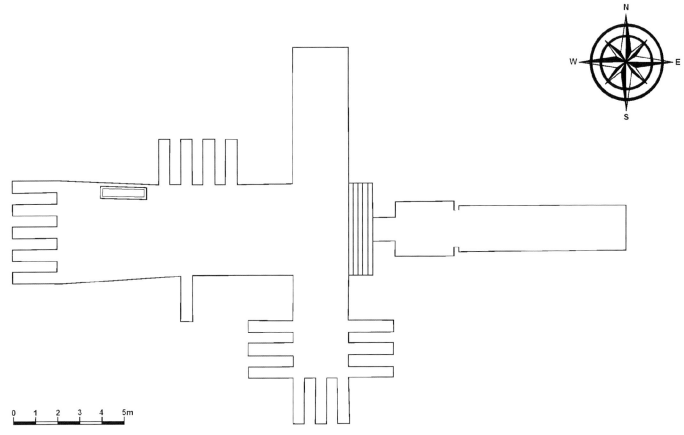

Plan of hypogeum anonymous.

PORTRAIT D: RECLINING MALE FIGURE
According to Ingholt (1938, 139), he wears a ›Parthian-style‹ tunic decorated with a band that extends downward from the neckline and a band at the lower hem. Both bands are decorated with running scrolls with rosettes. He wears a chlamys that is folded over the chest, falls over the left shoulder and arm, and falls under the left lower arm onto the cushion. He wears trousers decorated with »bands with an oak leaf design«.

In his left hand he holds a bowl against his chest, and in his right hand, resting against the raised right knee, he holds a floral wreath.

PORTRAIT E: RECLINING MALE FIGURE
According to Ingholt (1938, 139), the figure is wearing a chiton and a himation.

SARCOPHAGUS BOX
PORTRAIT F: Bust of figure.
PORTRAIT G: Bust of figure.
PORTRAIT H: Bust of figure.
PORTRAIT I: Bust of figure.
PORTRAIT J: Bust of figure.

Ingholt (1938, 139) writes that there are five busts, but it is not possible to ascertain their position based on the image.

175. COMPLETE SARCOPHAGUS WITH BANQUETING SCENE AND PORTRAIT BUSTS

DATABASE NUMBER: InSitu128.
LOCATION: Palmyra, in situ.
CONTEXT: South-west necropolis. Hypogeum of ʿAbdʿastôr, exedra to the left of the main chamber.
ACQUISITION HISTORY: —
MEASUREMENTS: —
MATERIAL: Limestone.
PRESERVATION: The upper part of the sarcophagus lid is broken off. The upper, right corner of the sarcophagus box is broken off. Portrait A: The upper part of the figure is broken off at the height of the shoulders.
TECHNICAL DESCRIPTION: —
DATE: A.D. 200–240 (Ingholt 1938: A.D. 200–273).
REFERENCES: Ingholt 1938, 139 f. pl. 50, 1; Gawlikowski 1970a, 118.

OBJECT DESCRIPTION
The sarcophagus lid is rectangular in shape and depicts a seated female, two standing children, and two reclining men. Beneath the figures is a box in the shape of a kline with four busts between the kline legs: two male busts and two female busts, placed inside clipei. The left kline leg is visible and is turned. Visible are three torus and above the stretcher a biconical finial. Above the kline are two mattresses with

Cat. 175

different patterns (details unclear). The female sits on two round cushions decorated with a wide band. The fabric of the cushions is indicated by curving grooves.

The object is located next to objects cat. 174 and cat. 176.

SARCOPHAGUS LID

PORTRAIT A: SEATED FEMALE

The figure is shown frontally. Her right hand is bent and rests on her thigh. According to Ingholt (1938, 139), her left arm is bent and raised. The feet are obscured by the reclining figure.

She wears a veil that covers her upper body and a tunic. Ingholt (1938, 139) writes that with her left hand she grasps the edge of the veil.

PORTRAIT B: STANDING MALE FIGURE

The lower body and legs are obscured by the reclining figure. According to Ingholt (1938, 139), the figure is a boy wearing a chiton and himation.

PORTRAIT C: STANDING MALE FIGURE

The lower body and legs are obscured by the reclining figure. According to Ingholt (1938, 139), the figure is a boy wearing a chiton and himation.

PORTRAIT D: RECLINING MALE FIGURE

According to Ingholt (1938, 139), he wears a ›Parthian-style‹ tunic decorated with a band that extends downward from the neckline and a band at the lower hem. Both bands are decorated with running scrolls with rosettes. He wears a chlamys that is folded over the chest, falls over the left shoulder and arm, and falls under the left lower arm onto the cushion. He wears trousers decorated with »bands with an oak leaf design«.

In his left hand he holds a bowl against his chest, and in his right hand, resting against the raised right knee, he holds a floral wreath.

PORTRAIT E: RECLINING MALE FIGURE

The legs are obscured by the reclining figure. According to Ingholt (1938, 139), the figure is wearing a chiton and himation.

SARCOPHAGUS BOX

PORTRAIT F: Armless male bust (?).
PORTRAIT G: Armless male bust (?).
PORTRAIT H: Armless female bust (?).
PORTRAIT I: Armless female bust (?).

Ingholt (1938, 139) writes that there are four busts of two men and two women, but it is not possible to ascertain their position based on the image.

176. COMPLETE SARCOPHAGUS WITH BANQUETING SCENE AND PORTRAIT BUSTS

DATABASE NUMBER: InSitu132.
LOCATION: Palmyra, in situ.
CONTEXT: South-west necropolis. Hypogeum of ʿAbdʿastôr, exedra to the left of the main chamber.
ACQUISITION HISTORY: —
MEASUREMENTS: —
MATERIAL: Limestone.
PRESERVATION: The upper part of the sarcophagus lid is broken off. The surface of the sarcophagus box is lightly chipped. The head of all the figures on the lid are broken off at the neck. The busts on the box are all heavily chipped.
TECHNICAL DESCRIPTION: —
DATE: A.D. 200–240 (Ingholt 1938: A.D. 200–273).
REFERENCES: Ingholt 1938, 139 f. pl. 50, 1; Gawlikowski 1970a, 118.

OBJECT DESCRIPTION

The sarcophagus lid is rectangular in shape and depicts a seated female, two standing children, and two reclining men. Beneath the figures is a box in the shape of a kline with four busts between the kline legs: two of male busts and two female busts, placed inside clipei. The kline legs are obscured by the sarcophagi on either side. Above the kline are two mattresses with different patterns: the upper mattress has a pattern with intersecting lozenges and the lower one is decorated with wide bands. The reclining male to the right (portrait D) rests on a large round cushion decorated with a wide band.

The object is located next to objects cat. 174 and cat. 175.

SARCOPHAGUS LID

PORTRAIT A: SEATED FEMALE

The figure is shown frontally. Her right hand is bent and resting on her thigh. Her left hand is bent and raised to the height of the chest.

She is dressed.

Ingholt (1938, 139) writes that she grasps the edge of the veil with her left hand.

PORTRAIT B: STANDING MALE FIGURE

The figure is shown frontally. According to Ingholt (1938, 139), the figure is a boy.

He wears a himation that is wrapped around the right shoulder, crosses the chest diagonally, and falls over the left shoulder and arm, covering the lower body. According to Ingholt, he wears a chiton as well.

With his right hand, he holds folds of the himation in front of the chest.

PORTRAIT C: STANDING MALE FIGURE

The figure is shown frontally. According to Ingholt (1938, 139), this is a boy.

He wears a himation that is wrapped around the right shoulder, crosses the chest diagonally, and falls over the left shoulder and arm, covering the lower body. According to Ingholt, he wears a chiton as well.

With his right hand, he holds folds of the himation in front of the chest.

PORTRAIT D: RECLINING MALE FIGURE

The figure's torso is shown frontally, the arms and the right leg are in profile, the upper left leg is shown frontally, and the lower left leg in three-quarter view. His arms are bent: the left one in front of the chest, and the right is held to the side. The right leg is bent and raised. The left leg rests on the mattress and is bent under the right leg. The left foot is obscured by the right leg.

He wears a ›Parthian-style‹ tunic, a chlamys, and ›Parthian-style‹ trousers. The tunic has long, loose sleeves, and is tied at the waist with a thin band belt. The chlamys is fastened over the right shoulder with a round (?) brooch, with a small fold falling under the brooch. The chlamys is folded across the chest, covers the left shoulder and arm, and falls under the left lower arm in two zigzag-shaped folds onto the cushion.

According to Ingholt (1938, 139), the tunic is decorated with a band that extends downward from the neckline and a band at the lower hem. Both bands are decorated with running scrolls with rosettes. The trousers are decorated with »bands with an oak leaf design«.

In his left hand he holds a bowl against his chest, and in his right hand, resting against the raised right knee, he holds a floral wreath.

PORTRAIT E: RECLINING MALE FIGURE

The figure's torso is shown frontally, the arms and the right leg are in profile, the upper left leg is shown frontally, and the lower left leg in three-quarter view. His arms are bent. The left is held in front of the chest, and the right is held to the side. The right leg is bent and raised. The left leg rests on the mattress and crosses under the right leg.

According to Ingholt (1938, 139), he wears a chiton and himation.

SARCOPHAGUS BOX

PORTRAIT F: Bust of male figure (?).
PORTRAIT G: Bust of male figure (?).
PORTRAIT H: Bust of female figure (?).
PORTRAIT I: Bust of female figure (?).

Ingholt (1938, 139) writes that there are four busts of two men and two women, but it is not possible to ascertain their position based on the image.

Cat. 176

OBJECTS FROM HYPOGEA 429

Cat. 176

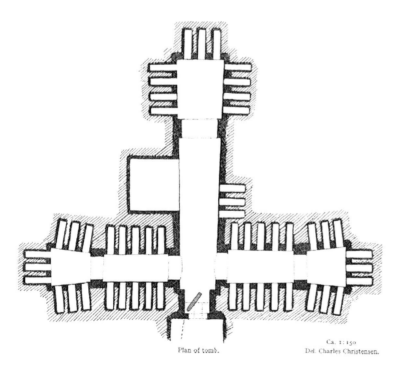

Plan of hypogeum of ʿAbdʿastôr.

A.D. 220–240

HYPOGEUM OF ḤATRAI

SARCOPHAGI

A.D. 220–240

177. COMPLETE SARCOPHAGUS RELIEF WITH BANQUETING SCENE AND PORTRAIT BUSTS

DATABASE NUMBER: PM539.
LOCATION: Palmyra, Palmyra Museum, inv. no. unknown.
CONTEXT: North-west necropolis. Hypogeum of Ḥatrai.
ACQUISITION HISTORY: —
MEASUREMENTS: —
MATERIAL: Limestone, white/yellow.
PRESERVATION: The surface is weathered. The upper right corner, the upper edge of the relief, and the upper left side of the relief are broken off. A large crack runs vertically the sarcophagus relief. An oblique crack runs to the right of portrait J. Portrait A: A large crack runs vertically through the right shoulder and body of portrait A. Portrait B: The left side of the face is broken off. Portrait E: A vertical crack runs through its thighs. Portrait I: The face is chipped. Portrait L: A vertical crack runs through its chest.
TECHNICAL DESCRIPTION: The left hand of portrait F is undercut.
DATE: A.D. 220–240.
REFERENCES: al-Asʿad 2013, 19 fig. 9; Krag – Raja 2017, 199 n. 24; 204 n. 72. 73; 205 n. 75; 206 n. 86; 207 n. 94; 208 n. 99; 209 n. 100; 210 n. 109. 110; 211 n. 117. 122; 219 cat. 30; Krag 2018, 28 n. 9; 32 n. 63; 82 n. 304; 53 n. 258; 58 n. 300; 59 n. 323; 62 n. 349. 352. 353; 66 n. 382; 86 n. 177; 87 n. 183; 88 n. 193. 195. 197; 103 n. 74; 394 cat. 850; <https://virtual-museum-syria.org/palmyra/funeral-banquet-scene-of-a-palmyrene-man-with-his-family/> (06.05.2022).

OBJECT DESCRIPTION

The relief is rectangular in shape and depicts a kline. A seated female, two reclining males, a standing male, two reclining males, and a seated female are depicted resting on a mattress, and six armless busts are depicted between the legs of the kline. The mattress is decorated with four bands (details unclear). Curving grooves indicate the texture of the fabric. The seated females at either end of the kline (portraits A and G) sit on two round cushions (details unclear). Two of the reclining males (portraits B and E) rest on a round cushion decorated with wide bands with rosettes (details unclear). The central stretcher of the kline has a decorated section on the far left side. It is decorated with a wide, rectangular panel flanked by two narrower, rectangular panels. The legs are turned. They are composed of a plinth, a convex quarter, a long, reversed concave quarter, a torus, a ball, a torus, and a concave quarter. All elements are decorated with a tongues pattern.

SARCOPHAGUS LID RELIEF

PORTRAIT A: SEATED FEMALE
The figure is shown frontally. The head is turned slightly to her left. The right arm is bent, and she rests the arm on her right thigh. The left arm is bent and raised to the height of the neck. She sits with the legs set apart with the knees visible under the drapery. Her feet rest on the mattress.

She wears three headdresses: a headband, a turban, and a veil. The band is placed high on her forehead (details unclear). The turban is coiled and is divided into two layers with curving grooves indicating the coiling of the fabric. The veil is heavy. It falls over the shoulders and is wrapped around her left arm and falls over the back of her right shoulder. Part of the hair is covered by the headdress: several strands of hair above the ears are pushed back over the headband and the edge of the turban and disappear under the veil. Her face is oval. The eyebrows are slightly curving. The eyes are close-set and almond-shaped. Only the earlobes are visible under the hair and she wears earrings (details unclear). The nose is large and narrow, with the alae carved. The mouth is small with thin lips. The chin is oval, and the neck is slender and long.

She wears a tunic and a himation. The tunic has a wide, angular neckline and short, loose sleeves. The folds are indicated by curving, wide grooves. The ankle-length himation crosses the chest diagonally from the left shoulder to the right side, covers the left breast, falls over the body, and covers her legs. The himation is fastened at the right shoulder with a circular brooch (details unclear). The folds of the himation are indicated by curving and oblique grooves. She wears round shoes.

She holds a fold of the veil in her right hand. A zigzag-shaped fold falls from her hand and along the right leg across the cushions. The index finger is extended. Her left arm is raised next to the shoulder. She holds a fold of the veil with her hand.

PORTRAIT B: RECLINING MALE
The figure is shown in frontal to three-quarter view. The arms are bent and held to the torso. He rests the arm against a cushion. His lower legs are obscured by the seated female to his right.

His hair is straight and brushed away from the face. The eyebrow is slightly curving, and the eye is round (details unclear). The neck is wide.

He wears a tunic and a himation. The tunic has a wide, round neckline. The folds of the tunic are rendered by curving grooves. Over the tunic he wears a himation. It is wrapped around his left shoulder and arm, leaving most of the chest, body, and hand free. It falls across the left side of his body and is folded across his lower abdomen. A wide, zigzag-shaped fold falls from under his left hand, across the cushion and the mattress. The edge of the fold is tied into two knots. The folds of the himation are indicated by vertical and curving grooves.

He holds a skyphos in his right hand. It has a conical foot and lower body. The body is decorated with two horizontal grooves. The skyphos has small, looped handles. The index and the little finger are extended. With the left hand he holds the wide fold of the himation. The index finger is extended.

Cat. 177, Pl. 53

PORTRAIT C: RECLINING MALE

The figure is shown in frontal to three-quarter view. The head is turned to his left. The right arm is obscured by the reclining male to his right. The left arm is bent and held to the chest. He rests the arm against two cushions. His legs are obscured by the male figure at his right.

His hair is arranged in crescent-shaped curls around the head, covering the ears and reaching the neck. The individual locks of hair are indicated by curving, incised lines. His face is oval. His eyebrows are slightly curving. The eyes are almond-shaped (details unclear). The nose is narrow and large. He has a beard that starts from his temples and covers his cheeks, upper lip, and chin (details unclear). The neck is wide.

He wears a >Parthian-style< tunic and a himation. The tunic has a wide, round, decorated neckline. The tunic has a wide, decorated band (details unclear) extending downwards from the middle of the neckline. The folds of the tunic are indicated by oblique grooves. Over the tunic he wears a himation. It is wrapped around his left shoulder and arm, leaving most of the chest, body, and hand free. It falls along the left side of his body and is folded across his lower abdomen. A wide, zigzag-shaped fold falls from under his left hand, across the cushion and mattress. The folds of the himation are indicated by vertical and curving grooves.

With the upturned palm of the left hand, he holds a wide bowl with his fingertips.

PORTRAIT D: STANDING MALE

The figure is shown frontally. The right arm is bent and held to the chest. The left arm is bent and extended towards the reclining figure to his left. The legs are obscured by the reclining figure to his left.

His hair is straight, covering the ears and brushed away from the face. His face is oval. The eyebrows are curving. The eyes are close-set (details unclear). The nose is narrow and long. The mouth is small, and the chin is oval. The neck is wide.

He wears a tunic and a himation. The tunic has a wide, round neckline. The folds of the tunic are indicated by oblique grooves. Over the tunic he wears a himation. The himation covers most of the body: it is wrapped around the right shoulder and arm, leaving only part of the upper chest and the hand free. One fold of the himation crosses the chest diagonally and falls over the left shoulder (>arm-sling< type). The folds of the himation are indicated by diagonal grooves.

With his right hand he holds lightly the fold of the himation. The left hand lies flat on the upper right arm of the reclining figure to his left.

PORTRAIT E: RECLINING MALE

The figure is shown in frontal to three-quarter view. The head is turned to his left. The right arm is slightly bent, and he rests the hand on the raised right knee. The left arm is bent and held to the chest. He rests the arm against a cushion. It is decorated with a53wide band with a running scroll with rosettes. The right leg is bent, and he rests the foot on the mattress. The left leg is bent under the right, with the knee pointing outwards.

His hair is arranged in one row of round curls around the head. His face is oval. The eyebrows are slightly curving, rendered as thin ridges. The eyes are close-set and almond-shaped. Only the earlobes are visible under the hair. The nose is large and straight with the alae carved. He has a beard that starts from his temples and covers the cheeks, the upper lip, and the chin. The facial hair is rendered by small snail-shell curls arranged in rows. His mouth is narrow with a full lower lip. The chin is round, and the neck is wide.

He wears a ›Parthian-style‹ tunic, a chlamys, and ›Parthian-style‹ trousers. The tunic has a round neckline and long sleeves. The cuffs of the sleeves are decorated with a band (details unclear). The tunic has a wide, decorated band (details unclear) extending downwards from the middle of the neckline. The tunic ends above the knees and has a decorated hem (details unclear). The folds of the tunic are indicated by curving and oblique grooves. Over the tunic he wears a chlamys that falls over both shoulders and covers most of the chest. It is fastened at the right shoulder with a circular brooch (details unclear). A wide, zigzag-shaped fold falls from under the left arm, across the cushion and the mattress. The folds of the chlamys are indicated by narrow, deep grooves. He wears a plain band belt, knotted at the centre, with the ends looped under either side of the waist. He also wears trousers. In the middle, each trouser leg is decorated with a wide band (details unclear) extending downwards. The folds of the trousers are indicated by oblique and curving grooves. He also wears plain, round boots.

The right hand lies on the right knee. He holds an oblong object, possibly a pinecone in his hand. With the upturned palm of the left hand, he holds a bowl with his fingertips. It is decorated with a pattern of hollowed-out lozenges.

PORTRAIT F: RECLINING MALE

The figure is shown in frontal to three-quarter view. The head and the left hand appear large in relation to the body. The head is turned to his left. The right arm is bent and held to the torso. The left arm is bent and held to the chest. He rests the arm against two cushions. His legs are obscured by the reclining figure to his right.

His hair is straight and brushed away on each side of the face. His face is oval. The eyebrows are curving, and the eyes are almond-shaped (details unclear). Only the earlobes are visible under the hair. The nose is narrow and long with carved alae. He has a beard that starts from his temples and covers the cheeks, the upper lip, and the chin. The chin is round, and the neck is wide.

He wears a tunic and a himation. The tunic has a wide, round neckline and short sleeves. The folds of the tunic are indicated by curving and oblique grooves. Over the tunic he wears a himation. It is wrapped around his left shoulder and arm, leaving most of the chest, body, and hand free. It falls along the left side of his body and is folded across his lower abdomen. A wide, zigzag-shaped fold falls from under his left hand, across the cushion and mattress. The folds of the himation are indicated by vertical and curving grooves.

With the right hand he holds a fold of the himation. With the upturned palm of the left hand, he holds a bowl with his fingertips.

PORTRAIT G: SEATED FEMALE

The figure is shown in frontal to three-quarter view. The head is turned to the left. The right hand is raised to the height of the neck. The left arm is held to the torso. The right leg is obscured by two cushions to the right of the figure. The left leg is bent with the knee visible under the drapery. She rests her foot on the mattress.

She wears three headdresses: a headband, a turban, and a veil. The band is placed low on her forehead. The turban is rendered in two layers by a horizontal groove. The veil is heavy. It falls over the shoulders and is wrapped around her right arm and falls over the back of her left shoulder. Part of the hair is covered by the headdress: several strands of hair above the ears are pushed back over the headband and the edge of the turban and disappear under the veil. Her face is oval. The eyes are almond-shaped (details unclear). The nose is narrow and large. Only the earlobes are visible under the hair and she wears earrings (details unclear). The mouth is small, and the chin is oval. The neck is wide.

She wears a tunic and himation. The tunic has a round neckline and short sleeves. The folds of the tunic are indicated by curving grooves. The ankle-length himation crosses the chest diagonally from the left shoulder to the right side, across the left breast, and over the body and legs. The upper end of the himation has a pleated band. The himation is fastened at the right shoulder with a circular brooch (details unclear). The folds of the himation are indicated by curving and oblique grooves. She does not wear shoes.

The right hand is raised to the neck and she holds the edge of the veil in her hand. The left hand is placed on top of two cushions. The cushions are decorated with two wide bands (details unclear). A zigzag-shaped fold of the veil falls from under her left hand.

SARCOPHAGUS BOX RELIEF

PORTRAIT H: ARMLESS BUST OF A MALE

The figure is shown frontally.

His hair is straight and combed around the head. His face is oval. The eyebrows are curving, and the eyes are close-set and almond-shaped (details unclear). The ears are large and protruding with the helix rendered. The nose is narrow and long. The mouth is narrow with thin lips. The chin is oval, and the neck is wide.

He wears a tunic and a himation. The tunic has a wide, round neckline. The folds of the tunic are indicated by curving and oblique grooves. Over the tunic he wears a himation. It is wrapped around his left shoulder. Another fold comes from his lower right side and falls in a curving fold across the chest and under the left shoulder.

PORTRAIT I: ARMLESS BUST OF A FEMALE
The figure is shown frontally.

She wears three headdresses: a headband, a turban, and a veil. The band is placed high on her forehead. The details of the band are unclear. The turban is coiled, it is rendered in two twisting layers by horizontal grooves. The veil is heavy. It falls over her shoulder and continues in a curving fold across the chest and falls back over her left shoulder. The edge of the veil crossing the left shoulder is pleated. Part of the hair is covered by the headdress: several strands of hair above the ears are pushed back over the headband and the edge of the turban and disappear under the veil. Her face is oval. The neck is wide.

She wears a tunic with a round neckline. The folds of the tunic are rendered by curving grooves.

PORTRAIT J: ARMLESS BUST OF A MALE
The figure is shown frontally. The top of the head reaches the central stretcher of the kline.

His hair is straight and combed around the head. His face is oval. The eyebrows are slightly curving, and the eyes are close-set and almond-shaped (other details unclear). The nose is narrow and slightly crooked. He has a beard that starts from the temples and covers the cheeks, the upper lip, and chin. The mouth is small with a full lower lip. The chin is oval, and the neck is wide.

He wears a tunic and a himation. The tunic has a wide, angular neckline. The folds of the tunic are indicated by curving and oblique grooves. Over the tunic he wears a himation. It is wrapped around his left shoulder and falls in a curving line across the chest and falls back at his right shoulder. The folds of the himation are indicated by oblique grooves.

PORTRAIT K: ARMLESS BUST OF A MALE
The figure is shown frontally.

His hair is straight and combed around the head. His face is oval. The eyebrows are slightly curving, and the eyes are close-set and almond-shaped (details unclear). The nose is narrow and long with carved alae. He has a beard that starts from his temples and covers the cheeks, the upper lip, and the chin. The mouth is small with a full lower lip. The chin is oval, and the neck is wide.

He wears a tunic and a himation. The tunic has a wide, angular neckline. The folds of the tunic are indicated by curving and oblique grooves. Over the tunic he wears a himation. It is wrapped around his left shoulder and falls in a curving fold across the chest and falls back at his right shoulder. The folds of the himation are indicated by oblique grooves.

PORTRAIT L: ARMLESS BUST OF A FEMALE
The figure is shown frontally. The top of the head reaches the central stretcher of the kline.

She wears three headdresses: a headband, a turban, and a veil. The band is placed high on her forehead. The details of the band are unclear. The turban is coiled: it is rendered in one layer by horizontal grooves. The veil is heavy. It falls over her shoulder and continues in a curving fold across the chest and falls back over her left shoulder. The edge of the veil crossing the left shoulder is pleated. Part of the hair is covered by the headdress: several strands of hair above the ears are pushed back over the headband and the edge of the turban and disappear under the veil. Her face is oval. The eyebrows are slightly curving. The neck is wide.

She wears a tunic with a round neckline. The folds of the tunic are rendered by curving grooves.

PORTRAIT M: ARMLESS BUST OF A MALE
The figure is shown frontally.

His hair is arranged in two rows of round curls around the head. His face is oval. The eyebrows are curving, and the eyes are close-set and almond-shaped (details unclear). The ears are large and protruding with the helix and lobe rendered. The nose is narrow and long with the alae carved. The mouth is narrow with thin lips. The chin is oval, and the neck is wide.

He wears a tunic and a himation. The tunic has a wide, round neckline. The folds of the tunic are indicated by curving and oblique grooves. Over the tunic he wears a himation. It is wrapped around his left shoulder. Another fold comes from his lower right side and falls in a curving fold across the chest and under the left shoulder.

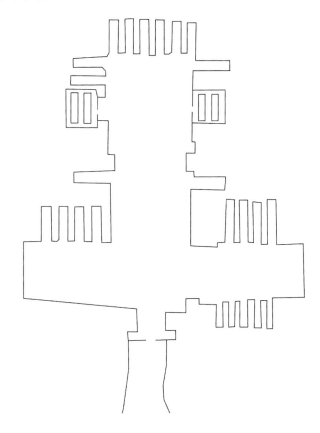

Plan of hypogeum of Ḥatrai.

HYPOGEUM OF MALKÛ

SARCOPHAGI

A.D. 220–240

178. COMPLETE SARCOPHAGUS RELIEF WITH BANQUETING SCENE AND PORTRAIT BUSTS

DATABASE NUMBER: NMD057.
LOCATION: Damascus, National Museum of Damascus, inv. no. 10.941.
CONTEXT: South-west necropolis. Hypogeum of Malkû, eastern wall of recess sold to Julius Aurelius ʿOgeilu.
ACQUISITION HISTORY: —
MEASUREMENTS: Height: 192 cm. Width: 201 cm.
MATERIAL: Limestone.
PRESERVATION: The lower edge of the sarcophagus box is chipped.
TECHNICAL DESCRIPTION: There are traces of black pigment in the outlining of the eyes and the eyebrows of the figures. Portrait D: The left hand is undercut. Portrait E: The left hand is undercut.
DATE: A.D. 220–240 (Abdul-Hak – Abdul-Hak 1951: A.D. 200–220).
REFERENCES: Ingholt Archives, PS 1094; Abdul-Hak – Abdul-Hak 1951, 46 cat. 51 pl. 19, 2; Ghirshman 1962, 80 fig. 92; Ingholt 1962, 104 f. 118 f. pl. 2, 2; Colledge 1967, 92. 154 pl. 46; Colledge 1976a, 74–76. 120. 124 f. 131. 135 f. 155. 157 f. 212. 216. 240 f. pl. 100; Colledge 1977, 98 pl. 30b; Exhibition of Treasures 1977, cat. 184; Colledge 1986, 20 f. 25. 42 pl. 35c; Tanabe 1986, 41 f. pls. 404–409; Equini Schneider 1993, 113 fig. 22; Schmidt-Colinet 1996, 369 f. 481 fig. 209; Finlayson 2008, 113 fig. 6, 6; Cussini 2016b, 48; Miyashita 2016, 133 fig. 16; Krag – Raja 2017, 199 n. 24; 204 n. 72. 73; 205 n. 75. 76; 206 n. 87; 207 n. 94; 208 n. 99; 209 n. 100; 210 n. 109. 110. 112; 211 n. 117; 219 cat. 36 fig. 11; Krag 2018, 28 n. 9; 32 n. 63; 42 n. 153. 154; 53 n. 258; 58 n. 300; 59 n. 315. 323; 61 n. 332. 336; 62 n. 349. 350–353; 63 n. 355. 359; 64; 65 n. 369; 66 n. 382. 385; 83 n. 304; 87 n. 182. 183; 88 n. 193. 195. 197; 103 n. 74; 394 cat. 851. Inscription: Abdul-Hak – Abdul-Hak 1951, 46 cat. 51; Cussini 2016b, 48; Krag 2018, 394 cat. 851.

OBJECT DESCRIPTION

The sarcophagus lid is rectangular in shape and depicts a seated female, two standing males, and two reclining males. Beneath these figures is a box in the shape of a kline with four busts inside clipei between the kline legs: two males flanked by two females. On top of the kline are two mattresses. The thin mattress at the top is decorated with an intersecting lozenge pattern with five-petal flowers in the lozenges. The central veins of the flower petals are rendered by incised lines.

The lower mattress is decorated with three bands. The band in the middle is decorated with a continuous motif of three serrated leaves and two buds or fruits on a stem that originate from a round element with three holes. The pattern is placed between two beaded bands. The bands on either side are decorated with leaves in an opposite arrangement, placed between beaded bands. Curving grooves indicate the texture of the lower mattress. The reclining figure to the right rests on a cushion. It is decorated with a band with a running scroll with six-petal rosettes. The other reclining figure rests on a cushion. The cushion is decorated with a band with lobed leaves. The left side of the kline is decorated with a fulcrum with a six-petal rosette at the lower end, body decorated with vine leaves on a stem, and a horned animal head at the upper end. The central stretcher of the kline is decorated. The wide, rectangular central panel is divided into two parts by a horizontal line. The upper section is decorated with a row of oblique grooves, while the lower section is decorated with a receding moulding with a tongues pattern. On either side of this are two rectangular plain indentations. On each side of these are two square inlays or appliqués with animals. The legs are turned. They are composed of a plinth, and above is a cyma recta, a reversed bell-shaped element, a concave quarter, a reversed bell-shaped element, a ball, a concave quarter, and above the stretcher is a biconical finial. The legs are decorated with a tongues pattern, but it is rendered diagonally on the concave quarters and the ball. A part of the right side of the sarcophagus box is preserved where the left side of a cloth is preserved. It is hanging from a six-petal rosette. A branch of leaves projects upwards and inwards from the rosette. The folds of the cloth are indicated by oblique and curving grooves. At the lower part of the field part of a mattress is preserved. Curving, wide grooves indicate the texture of the fabric. The seated female sits on two cushions. The uppermost cushion is decorated with a band with leaves in an opposite arrangement, placed between beaded bands. The lower one is decorated with lobed leaves with incised midribs.

INSCRIPTION

SCRIPT: Palmyrene Aramaic.
LOCATION ON RELIEF: In the upper right corner of the short side of the sarcophagus.
TRANSCRIPTION: ḤRMS | ḤBL.
TRANSLATION: Hermes, alas!

CIS no. —; PAT no. 0986.

COMMENT: L.1: Greek name Ἑρμῆς.

SARCOPHAGUS LID

PORTRAIT A: SEATED FEMALE

The figure is shown in three-quarter view. The head is shown frontally. The head appears large and the arms short in relation to the body. The right arm is held along the body. The left arm is raised to the neck. Her legs are bent at the knees and rendered under the drapery. Her feet are obscured by the right foot of the reclining male.

Cat. 178

She wears three headdresses: a headband, a turban, and a veil. The headband is placed high on her forehead and is divided into rectangular, decorated panels separated by vertical, beaded bands. The central panel has a motif with leaves arranged in an opposite arrangement. The outer panels have a crisscross pattern. The turban is coiled. It is divided into three layers and the upper two layers are looped into each other creating a knot in the middle. Curving grooves indicate the coiling of the fabric. The veil is heavy with a scalloped edge. It falls over her shoulders. One fold of the veil falls down onto her right side and over the cushions. She also wears a head-chain that is attached under the centre of the turban and runs to the sides disappearing under the veil. It is composed of circular elements with incised borders linked by beaded elements. Her hair is centrally parted and brushed to each side of the forehead. Several strands of hair above the ears are pushed back over the edge of the headband and disappear under the veil. A wavy lock of hair falls on her right shoulder. The individual strands of hair are rendered by incised lines. Her face is oval. Her eyebrows are rendered by curving, incised lines. The eyes are close-set and almond-shaped with thick upper eyelids that extend beyond the lower ones. The irises are indicated by black pigment. Only the earlobes are visible under the hair and she is wearing earrings with three juxtaposed beads (Colledge classification: K): a round upper bead, a biconical bead at the centre, and a round bead ending the earring. Her nose is wide with carved nostrils. The mouth is large, and the upper lip has an accentuated curving while the lower is thin. The chin is round and almost double. The neck is long with three horizontal grooves. She wears four necklaces: a string of round beads worn at the base of the neck. One composed of alternating rectangular and two juxtaposed circular elements with incised borders, joined by beaded elements worn at the collarbone. One composed of oval beads with a central, crescent-shaped pendant with a round bead between the horns, worn below the collarbone. The lower necklace is composed of a wide loop-in-loop chain with a large, oval pendant at the centre. The pendant has a beaded border.

She wears a tunic and a himation. The tunic has a small, v-shaped neckline and loose sleeves ending at the elbows. The folds of the tunic are indicated by curving grooves. The himation falls to the ankles. It crosses her chest diagonally from the left shoulder to the right side, and covers the lower chest, body, and the legs. It is fastened at the left shoulder with a circular brooch with a beaded border (Colledge classification: f). From the left shoulder it is wrapped around her left upper arm. An edge of the himation is folded over her right upper arm and tucked in at the upper edge below the breast. It falls under her lower right arm in a diagonal line towards her ankles. The edge is scalloped. The folds of the himation are rendered by diagonal and curving grooves. The folds between the legs are rendered by curving grooves.

Her right hand rests on a fold of the veil on the cushions. She wears a bracelet with twisted, beaded and plain wires. With her left hand, she holds a fold of the veil. She is wearing an oval ring on her left little finger with a wide, thick hoop and an oval bezel. She wears two bracelets around her left wrist. The uppermost one is composed of twisted beaded and plain wires and the lower one of twisted plain wires with a bell-shaped pendant attached. The nails are rendered by fine, incised lines.

PORTRAIT B: STANDING MALE

The figure is shown frontally. The head appears large and the arms short. The right arm is held along the body. The left is bent and held to the torso. The left leg and lower part of the right leg are obscured by the reclining figure to his left.

His hair is arranged in rows of s-shaped curls around the head. The individual strands of hair are indicated by incised lines. His face is oval. The eyebrows are rendered by incised lines, starting from the root of the nose. The eyes are close-set and almond-shaped with thick eyelids. The irises and pupils are indicated by black pigment. The nose is wide with carved nostrils. The ears are large and protruding, with the helix, scapha, and the earlobe depicted. The mouth is small with full lips. The cheeks are fleshy, and the chin is wide. The neck is wide.

He wears a tunic and a himation. The tunic has a wide, v-shaped neckline and short, wide sleeves. The folds of the tunic are rendered by curving grooves. Over the tunic, he wears a himation. It falls over his left shoulder and is folded around his arm, leaving the upper part of the chest and the hand free. One end of the himation crosses the waist horizontally and falls along his lower body. The folds of the himation are rendered by diagonal and curving grooves.

He rests his right hand on the left thigh of the seated female. With his left hand, he holds a fold of the himation. The index finger is extended.

PORTRAIT C: STANDING MALE

The figure is shown frontally. The head appears large and the arms short in relation to the body. The right arm is bent and held to the chest. The left leg is bent and held to the torso. The lower body and legs are obscured by the reclining figure to his left.

His hair is arranged in two rows of snail-shell curls around the head. His face is oval. The eyebrows are rendered by incised lines starting from the root of the nose. The eyes are close-set and almond-shaped with thick eyelids. The irises are indicated by black pigment. The nose is large with carved nostrils. The ears are protruding with the helix, scapha, and the earlobe depicted. The mouth is small with thin lips. The cheeks are fleshy, and the chin is pointed. The neck is short and wide.

He wears a tunic and a himation. The tunic has a low, v-shaped neckline. The folds of the tunic are rendered by curving grooves. Over the tunic, he wears a himation. It is wrapped around his right shoulder and arm, leaving the upper part of the chest and the hand free. One end of the himation with a scalloped edge crosses the chest diagonally and falls over the left shoulder (›arm-sling‹ type). The folds of the himation are rendered by diagonal and curving grooves.

With his right hand, he holds the diagonal fold of the himation. With his left hand, he holds a fold of the himation. The index finger is extended.

PORTRAIT D: RECLINING MALE

The head and the body are shown in frontal to three-quarter view. His head is turned slightly to the right. The head appears small in relation to the body. The right arm is slightly bent and rests on his raised knee, the left rests on the cushion. His right leg is bent, and his foot is resting on the kline. The left leg is bent under the right leg, and the lower left leg is obscured.

His hair is arranged in rows of s-shaped curls around the head. The individual strands of hair are indicated by incised lines. His face is oval. The eyebrows are depicted by thin ridges that meet above the root of the nose. The eyes are close-set and almond-shaped with thick eyelids. The upper eyelids extend beyond the end of the lower ones. The irises and pupils are indicated by a black pigment. The ears are large and protruding with the helix, concha, and the earlobe depicted. The nose is large with carved nostrils. He has a beard that starts from the temples as well as a moustache that covers his upper lip and reaches the beard. The facial hair is rendered by flame-shaped curls arranged in rows. The moustache is rendered with diagonal, incised lines. The mouth is small with a thin upper lip and a full lower lip. The chin is wide, and the neck is slender.

He wears a tunic and a himation. The tunic has a low, v-shaped neckline and short, wide sleeves. The border of the tunic has a scalloped edge. The folds of the tunic are rendered by curving grooves. Over the tunic, he wears a himation. It is wrapped around his left shoulder and arm and falls along the left side of his torso where it is folded over the tunic, across his waist and legs. A zigzag-shaped fold falls from under his left arm. The folds of the himation are rendered by diagonal, curving grooves. He wears a plain, round-toe boot tied with laces around the ankles.

He rests the right hand on the knee. With the upturned palm of the left hand, he holds a bowl with his fingertips. The body is convex and the base flat. A horizontal, incised line indicates the rim. Fine, incised lines indicate the nails.

PORTRAIT E: RECLINING MALE

The head and the body are shown in frontal to three-quarter view. The head and the right arm appear short in relation to the body. The right upper arm and legs are obscured by the reclining figure to his right. The right arm is bent and held to the torso. The left arm is bent.

His hair is arranged in three rows of snail-shell curls around the head. The individual strands of hair are indicated by incised lines. His face is square. The eyebrows are depicted as thin ridges that meet above the root of the nose. The eyes are close-set and almond-shaped with thick eyelids. The upper eyelids extend beyond the end of the lower ones. The irises and pupils are indicated by a black pigment. The ears are protruding with the helix, concha, and the earlobe depicted. The nose is large with carved nostrils. He has a beard that starts from the temples as well as a moustache that covers the upper lip and reaches the beard. The facial hair is rendered by flame-shaped curls. The moustache is rendered with diagonal, incised lines. The mouth is large with thin lips. The upper lip has an accentuated curving. The chin is wide, and the neck is slender.

He wears a tunic and a himation. The tunic has a wide, v-shaped neckline and short, wide sleeves. The folds of the tunic are rendered by curving grooves. Over the tunic, he wears a himation. It is wrapped around his left shoulder and arm and falls along the left side of his torso. A zigzag-shaped fold falls from under his left arm. The folds of the himation are rendered by diagonal, curving grooves.

He holds a pinecone in his right hand with incised scales. With the upturned palm of the left hand, he holds a bowl with his fingertips. The rim, the body, and the base are indicated by incised lines. The body is decorated with rows of circular depressions. The nails are rendered by fine, incised lines.

SARCOPHAGUS BOX

PORTRAIT F: ARMLESS FEMALE BUST

The figure is rendered in a clipeus and shown frontally. The head is turned to the left and appears large.

She wears three headdresses: a headband, a turban, and a veil. The headband is placed high on her forehead and is divided into rectangular decorated panels separated by vertical, beaded bands. The central panel has a motif with leaves arranged in an opposite arrangement. The outer panels have a crisscross pattern. The turban is coiled. It is divided into three layers and the upper two layers are looped into each other creating a knot in the middle. Curving grooves indicate the coiling of the fabric. She wears a heavy veil with a scalloped edge that falls over her right shoulder, proceeds in a curving fold across the chest, and falls back over her left shoulder. Part of the hair is covered by the headdresses. Several strands of hair above the ears are pushed back over the edge of the headband and disappear under the veil. The individual strands of hair are rendered by incised lines. Her face is oval. Her eyebrows are depicted as thin ridges. The eyes are close-set and almond-shaped with thick upper eyelids that extend beyond the lower ones. The irises are indicated by a black pigment. Only the earlobes are visible under the hair and she is wearing earrings with three juxtaposed beads (Colledge classification: K): an upper, round bead, a central, oval bead, and a lower, round bead. Her nose is wide at the base and the nostrils are carved. The mouth is small, and the upper lip has an accentuated curving, the lower is full. The chin is wide, and the neck is wide. She wears one necklace composed of a string of round beads at the base of her neck.

She wears a tunic with a small, round neckline. The folds of the tunic are indicated by curving grooves.

PORTRAIT G: ARMLESS MALE BUST

The figure is rendered in a clipeus and shown frontally. The head is turned slightly to the right. The head appears large.

His hair is arranged in rows of snail-shell curls around the head. The individual strands of hair are indicated by incised lines. His face is oval. The eyebrows are depicted as thin ridges, which meet at the root of the nose. The eyes are close-set and almond-shaped with thick eyelids. The upper eyelids extend beyond the end of the lower ones. The pupils are indicated by a black pigment. The ears are large and protruding with the helix, scapha, concha, and the earlobe depicted. The nose is straight and wide at the base and the nostrils are carved. He has a beard that starts from the temples, as well as a moustache that covers the upper lip. The facial hair is rendered by snail-shell curls arranged in rows that cover the cheeks and the lower part of the chin. The individual hairs under the lip are rendered with narrow, oblique lines. The moustache is rendered with narrow, oblique lines. The mouth is wide with a thin upper lip and full lower lip. The chin is wide, and the neck is wide.

He wears a tunic and a himation. The tunic has a wide, v-shaped neckline that leaves the upper part of the torso bare. The folds of the tunic are rendered by oblique and curving grooves. Over the tunic, he wears a himation. It is folded over his left shoulder. One end of the himation is folded from behind, crosses the chest diagonally, and runs under the left shoulder. One edge of the himation is scalloped. The folds of the himation are rendered by diagonal and vertical grooves.

PORTRAIT H: ARMLESS MALE BUST

The figure is rendered in a clipeus and shown frontally. The head appears large.

His hair is arranged in rows of s-shaped curls around the head. The individual strands of hair are indicated by incised lines. His face is oval. The eyebrows are depicted as thin ridges, which meet above the root of the nose. The eyes are close-set and almond-shaped with thick eyelids. The upper eyelids extend beyond the end of the lower ones. The pupils are indicated by a black pigment. The ears are large and protruding with the helix, scapha, and lobe depicted. The nose is wide at the base and the nostrils are carved. He has a beard that starts from the temples, as well as a moustache that covers the upper lip. The facial hair is rendered by snail-shell curls arranged in rows that cover the lower parts of the cheeks and the chin. The moustache is rendered with narrow, oblique lines. The mouth is wide with a thin upper lip that has an accentuated curving and full lower lip. The chin is wide, and the neck is wide.

He wears a tunic and a himation. The tunic has a wide, v-shaped neckline. The folds of the tunic are rendered by oblique and curving grooves. Over the tunic, he wears a himation. It is folded over his left shoulder. One end of the himation is folded from behind, crosses the chest diagonally, and runs under the left shoulder. The folds of the himation are rendered by diagonal and vertical grooves.

Cat. 178, Pl. 54

PORTRAIT I: ARMLESS FEMALE BUST

The figure is rendered in a clipeus and shown in frontally. The head appears large.

She wears two headdresses: a turban and a veil. The turban is coiled. It is rendered in three twisting layers with horizontal grooves indicating the coiling of the fabric. The veil is heavy with a scalloped edge. A curving fold falls from her right shoulder and over the back of her left shoulder and covers the breast. Her hair is centrally parted and brushed to each side of the forehead. Several strands of hair above the ears are pushed back and disappear under the veil. The individual strands of hair are rendered by incised lines. Her face is square. Her eyebrows are indicated by curving grooves. The eyes are close-set and almond-shaped with thick upper eyelids that extend beyond the lower ones. The irises are indicated by a black pigment. Only the earlobes are visible under the hair and she is wearing dumbbell-shaped earrings (Colledge classification: H). Her nose is wide at the base and the nostrils are carved. The mouth is small, and the upper lip has an accentuated curving, the lower lip is full. The chin is wide and the neck short and wide. She wears one necklace composed of a string of round beads at the base of the neck.

She wears a tunic with a small, round neckline. The folds of the tunic are indicated by curving grooves.

For the plan of the hypogeum of Malkû, see cat. 10.

A.D. 240–273

HYPOGEUM OF THE BÔLBARAK FAMILY

BANQUETING RELIEFS

A.D. 240–273

179. BANQUETING RELIEF

DATABASE NUMBER: PM092.
LOCATION: Palmyra, Palmyra Museum, inv. no. 1793/6642.
CONTEXT: West necropolis. Valley of the Tombs. Hypogeum of the Bôlbarak family, main exedra.
ACQUISITION HISTORY: —
MEASUREMENTS: Height: 42 cm. Width: 48 cm. Depth: 5 cm.
MATERIAL: Limestone, white.
PRESERVATION: The upper right and the left corner are broken off. The left and the right side are chipped.
TECHNICAL DESCRIPTION: The edges of the relief are roughly worked.
DATE: A.D. 240–273 (Sadurska – Bounni 1994: after A.D. 239).
REFERENCES: Tanabe 1986, 43 pl. 437; Sadurska – Bounni 1994, 145 f. cat. 193 fig. 253; Long 2017, 79 f. fig. 10; Raja 2017a, 219. 221. 226 cat. 16; Raja 2017h, 63–65. 73 cat. 16.

OBJECT DESCRIPTION

The relief is rectangular in shape and depicts a standing male next to a reclining male. It has a frame along its upper, left, and right side composed of a leaf-and-dart moulding, a narrow, undecorated band, and a beaded band. Beneath the figures is a mattress divided into four sections by three wide bands: two bands decorated with vegetal motifs (serrated leaves) inside lozenges at the sides, and a band with a continuous vegetal motif (serrated leaves). The reclining male rests on a round cushion decorated with a central band decorated with a vegetal motif. The folds of the cushion are indicated by wide, curving grooves.

PORTRAIT A: STANDING PRIEST

The figure is shown in a three-quarter view, his body turned towards the left, his head turned towards his right. The arms are bent in front of the torso. The head appears large and the arms small in relation the body. The left leg and the right foot are obscured by the right leg of the reclining male.

His hair is arranged in alternating rows of snail-shell curls that reach the nape. His face is oval. The eyebrows are depicted as thin, curving ridges. The eyes are small and almond-shaped with thick upper eyelids. The eyeballs are blank. The nose is short. The mouth is small with a full lower lip. The chin is round. The neck is short and wide.

He wears a ›Parthian-style‹ tunic and ›Parthian-style‹ trousers. The tunic has a small, round neckline decorated with a beaded band and long, tight-fitting sleeves. A central beaded band extends downwards from the middle of the neckline. The cuffs of the sleeves are decorated with beaded bands. A thin band belt is tied with a double knot at the waist, with the ends of the belt secured on either side of the knot. The hem of the tunic is decorated with a band with a vegetal motif. The folds of the tunic are indicated by wide, oblique grooves. The trousers are decorated in the middle with a beaded band extending downwards.

In his hands, he holds a tall, cylindrical, flat-top headdress that is divided into three sections by two vertical grooves: a Palmyrene priestly hat. A wreath is depicted at the lower part of the headdress. It has three rows of pointed leaves pointing towards a central oval. There is a horizontal, incised line at the bottom of the headdress suggesting a liner. Below the headdress is a curving object followed by a narrow band, probably a piece of fabric with curving and falling folds.

PORTRAIT B: RECLINING MALE

The figure is shown reclining with his right leg in profile, the left leg, torso, and head in three-quarter view turned slightly to his right. The right arm is slightly bent downwards and rests against the right knee, the left arm is bent in front of the chest. The right leg is bent, with the foot on the ground, and the left is bent towards the back under the raised right leg. The left lower leg and foot are obscured by the right leg.

His hair is arranged in three rows of small snail-shell curls. His face is triangular and fleshy. The eyebrows are depicted as thin, arched ridges. The eyes are almond-shaped, with thick eyelids. The upper eyelids extend beyond the end of the lower ones. The eyeballs are blank. The nose is straight. He has a beard that starts from the temples, covers the outer cheeks and the side of the chin, and the upper lip. Small, incised lines render the facial hair. The mouth is small with thin lips. The chin is pointed. The neck is short and wide.

He wears a ›Parthian-style‹ tunic, a chlamys, and ›Parthian-style‹ trousers. The tunic has a wide, round neckline decorated with a beaded border. A central, wide band extends downwards from the middle of the neckline decorated with a continuous vegetal motif. The tunic has long, tight-fitting sleeves with cuffs decorated with a wide band with a floral pattern. The chlamys falls over both shoulders and falls over the upper part of the chest in a curving fold. It is wrapped around the left arm and falls below the arm and onto the cushion and the mattress in two wide, zigzag-shaped folds. It is fastened at the right shoulder with a circular brooch with an incised border (Colledge classification: h). A small, zigzag-shaped fold falls down from the brooch. The folds of the chlamys are indicated by oblique grooves. A thin band belt is tied with a double knot at the waist, with the ends of the belt secured on either side of the knot. Along his right thigh he has an object with a rectangular main body and two angular lateral protrusions: a sheathed dagger. The trousers are visible from above the knee: they are decorated in the middle with a wide central band with a continuous vegetal motif extending downwards. The folds of the trousers are indicated by wide, oblique grooves. He wears a plain boot.

With his right hand, he holds a small, round object (probably fruit). With the upturned palm of his left hand, he holds an undecorated bowl with his fingertips in front of his chest.

Cat. 179

Objects from Temple Tombs

A.D. 140–273

TEMPLE TOMB NO. 186 (›TOMBEAU DE L'AVIATION‹ / ›TOMB DUVAUX‹)

SARCOPHAGI

A.D. 220–240

180. COMPLETE SARCOPHAGUS WITH BANQUETING SCENE AND PORTRAIT BUSTS

DATABASE NUMBER: InSitu216.
LOCATION: Palmyra, in situ.
CONTEXT: South-east necropolis. Temple tomb no. 186 (›Tombeau de l'aviation‹/›Tomb Duvaux‹).
ACQUISITION HISTORY: —
MEASUREMENTS: —
MATERIAL: Limestone.
PRESERVATION: The surface of the sarcophagus is weathered. The upper part of the sarcophagus is broken off. The upper right side and the lower right side of the sarcophagus box are chipped. Portrait A: The head is broken off horizontally at the base of the neck. The surface around the abdomen, right and left arm, and knees are chipped. Portrait B: The head is broken off horizontally at the base of the neck. The right arm has broken off. The tip of the left foot has broken off. The surface of the right leg is chipped. Portrait C: The head is broken off horizontally at the base of the neck. The surface of the lower left arm and attribute is chipped. A large crack runs diagonally from the right side of the neck and through the right arm. Portrait D: The head of the figure is chipped. Portrait E: The head of the figure is chipped. Portrait F: The head of the figure is chipped. Portrait G. The head of the figure is chipped.
TECHNICAL DESCRIPTION: —
DATE: A.D. 220–240 (Schmidt-Colinet 1992: A.D. 200–250).
REFERENCES: Watzinger – Wulzinger 1932, 70 figs. 68. 69; Schmidt-Colinet 1992, 107 n. 380g, 2. n. 383b; 108 n. 389; 110 n. 403. n. 404d; 121 n. 440g; 125 n. 473. n. 476; 130 n. 479; 135 n. 517; pls. 72, d; 73, b; Krag – Raja 2017, 199 n. 24; 204 n. 72. 73; 205 n. 75; 207 n. 94; 209 n. 100; 212 n. 126; 220 cat. 37; Krag 2018, 28 n. 9; 32 n. 63; 45 n. 193; 46 n. 194. 196; 53 n. 258; 58 n. 300–301. 303. 307; 59 n. 323. 325; 61 n. 334; 62 n. 349. 351–353; 63 n. 354; 64 n. 361. 362; 65 n. 375. 376. 379; 66 n. 381. 382; 84 n. 304; 89 n. 203; 101 n. 54; 102 n. 69; 103 n. 74; 105 n. 95; 394 f. cat. 852; Raja – Yon 2022, 219–221 cat. 37. Inscription: Watzinger – Wulzinger 1932, 70 fig. 69; du Mesnil du Buisson 1962, 32–33; Parlasca 1988, 220; SEG 41, 1535, no. 6; Yon 2012, 400, no. 534; Raja – Yon 2022, 219.

OBJECT DESCRIPTION:
The sarcophagus lid is rectangular in shape and depicts a seated female, a reclining female, and a reclining male. The reclining female rests on a round cushion decorated with a band with a running scroll with rosettes, set between beaded bands. The reclining male rests on a round cushion decorated with a band with leaves arranged in an opposite arrangement on the stem, set between beaded bands. Beneath these figures is a box in the shape of a kline with two mattresses. Between the legs of the kline are four busts; two males, a female, and a male. The thin mattress at the top is decorated with an intersecting lozenges pattern with four-petal flowers with serrated petals in the lozenges. The centre of the petals is rendered by incised lines. On the right side of the kline a fulcrum is shown. The fulcrum is decorated with a four-petal rosette. The lower mattress has three bands. The central band is decorated with a running scroll with rosettes set between beaded bands. The bands on either side are decorated with serrated flowers in an opposite arrangement on the stem and set between beaded bands. Curving grooves indicate the texture of the mattress. The central stretcher of the kline is decorated. The central part is divided into two sections by a horizontal thin line. The upper section is decorated with miniature bunches of grapes. The lower section is decorated with vine leaves on a stem. On either side of the stretcher is a rectangular indentation decorated with a wave pattern. On either side of these are two squared inlays or appliqués. The kline legs are turned. They are composed of a plinth, and above is a convex quarter, a reversed bell-shaped element, a bell-shaped element, a small torus, a ball, a torus, and above the stretcher is a biconical finial. All elements are decorated with a tongues pattern, rendered diagonally on the ball.

According to Watzinger and Wulzinger (1932, 70 fig. 69) one of the figures held three keys in their hand, two of them inscribed.

Cat. 180

INSCRIPTIONS

INSCRIPTION 1
SCRIPT: Ancient Greek.
LOCATION ON RELIEF: On key to the left.
TRANSCRIPTION: Τάφος.
TRANSLATION: Tomb.

INSCRIPTION 2
SCRIPT: Ancient Greek.
LOCATION ON RELIEF: On central key.
TRANSCRIPTION: ΤΥΤΗ.
TRANSLATION: —

CIS no. —; PAT no. —.

COMMENTS: Inscription 1: ΠΑΡΟ or ΤΑΡΟ according to the drawing. ΠΑΡΟ du Mesnil du Buisson (followed by Yon). Inscription 2: No clear meaning. Perhaps, misspelling for Τύχη »Fortune«. Not visible on the photograph. Reading from drawing in Watzinger and Wulzinger 1932, 70 fig. 69. See Yon 2012, 400, no. 534, with reference to du Mesnil du Buisson 1962, 32–33 and 283 (and Parlasca 1988, 220, with SEG 41, 1535, no. 6). According to Parlasca, two different objects have been mixed (by Watzinger and Wulzinger or by du Mesnil du Buisson?), »In dieser Skizze sind aber vermutlich zwei Klinengruppen kontaminiert«. Indeed, the hand with the key is not visible either on the drawing fig. 68 of Watzinger and Wulzinger 1932, 70.

SARCOPHAGUS LID

PORTRAIT A: SEATED FEMALE
The figure is shown frontally. The left arm is bent and held in front of the torso. Her legs are bent. The left foot is obscured by the right foot of the reclining figure to her left.

She wears six necklaces: One composed of small, round beads, worn at the base of the neck. One composed of a loop-in-loop chain with a central oval pendant, worn against the collarbone. Below that, she wears a necklace composed of a thick hoop with a central, crescent-shaped pendant. Directly below that, she wears a necklace composed of small, round beads. Above the breasts she wears an interwoven loop-in-loop chain with a large, central oval pendant with a beaded border.

The sixth necklace falls over the breasts: it is composed of large, round beads and has a round medallion with a beaded border and possibly a bust at the centre (details unclear) that falls over the right breast. According to Watzinger and Wulzinger (1932, 70 fig. 68), there is another medallion with a bust on the last necklace.

She wears a tunic and a himation. The tunic has short, wide sleeves and ends at the ankles. The folds of the tunic are rendered by curving and oblique grooves. The himation falls diagonally over the torso and covers the legs. She wears a shoe with a round end.

PORTRAIT B: RECLINING FEMALE

The torso and the upper arms of the figure are shown in frontal view. The right leg is bent and raised. The right arm is bent and rests on the right leg. The left arm rests against a cushion. The left leg is slightly bent, extending along the mattress.

She wears a veil with a scalloped edge. It falls over her right shoulder and upper arm. She wears two necklaces: One composed of large, round beads, worn at the base of the neck. The second is composed of alternating round and square bezels with an incised border. The square bezels have attached round beads at their lower side.

She wears a tunic and a himation. The tunic has a wide, round neckline and short, wide sleeves with a scalloped edge. On the right side of the chest, the tunic has a band decorated with a vegetal motif extending downwards. The folds of the tunic are rendered by curving and oblique grooves. Over the tunic she wears a himation. It is wrapped around her left shoulder and upper arm. It crosses the chest diagonally and covers the left breast. The upper border of the himation has a scalloped edge. The himation covers her body and ends at her ankles. It is fastened at the left shoulder with a circular brooch with a beaded border (details unclear) (Colledge classification: i). A wide fold of the himation extends downwards from the left arm and across the cushion and mattress. At the edge, the fold is divided into two s-shaped folds which end with two triangular-shaped tassels or weights. The folds of the himation are rendered by wide, curving and oblique grooves.

PORTRAIT C: RECLINING MALE

The upper torso of the figure is shown in frontal view and the lower torso and arms in three-quarter view. The right arm is bent and held to the torso. The left arm is bent and rests against a cushion. The legs of the figure are not rendered.

He wears a tunic and a himation. The tunic has a wide, v-shaped neckline and short, wide sleeves. On the right side of the chest, the tunic has a band decorated with a floral motif between two beaded bands extending downwards. The folds of the tunic are rendered by curving and oblique grooves. Over the tunic he wears a himation. It is wrapped around his left shoulder and arm. It falls in a curving fold across the lower abdomen and covers the lower body. The upper edge is scalloped. A wide fold extends downwards from the left arm and across the cushion and mattress. At the edge, the fold is divided into two s-shaped folds which ends with two triangular-shaped tassels or weights. The folds of the himation are rendered by wide, curving and oblique grooves.

The right hand lightly pulls the upper edge of the himation. The thumb and the index finger are extended. The outline of a circular object, possibly a drinking bowl, is recognizable at the centre of the chest.

SARCOPHAGUS BOX

PORTRAIT D: ARMLESS BUST OF PRIEST

The figure is shown frontally, rendered in a clipeus.

He wears a tall, cylindrical, flat-top headdress: a Palmyrene priestly hat (visible in outline).

He wears a tunic and a chlamys. The tunic has a wide, round neckline. The folds of the tunic are rendered by curving grooves. Over the tunic he wears a chlamys that falls over both shoulders and covers the chest. It is fastened at the right shoulder with a circular brooch with a beaded band along the outer border (Colledge classification: f). An s-shaped fold falls from under the brooch. The folds of the chlamys are indicated by narrow, deep grooves.

PORTRAIT E: ARMLESS BUST OF PRIEST

The figure is shown frontally, rendered in a clipeus.

He wears a tall, cylindrical, flat-top headdress: a Palmyrene priestly hat (visible in outline).

He wears a tunic and a chlamys. The tunic has a small, round neckline. The folds of the tunic are rendered by curving grooves. Over the tunic he wears a chlamys that falls over both shoulders and covers the chest. It is fastened at the right shoulder with a circular brooch with a beaded band along the outer border (Colledge classification: f). The folds of the chlamys are indicated by narrow, deep grooves.

PORTRAIT F: ARMLESS BUST OF A FEMALE

The figure is shown frontally, rendered in a clipeus.

She wears a veil. It falls over the shoulders in a semicircular fold.

She wears a thick hoop necklace with a central, round pendant with an incised border at the base of the neck.

She wears a tunic. The tunic has a wide, v-shaped neckline. The folds of the tunic are rendered by curving and oblique grooves.

PORTRAIT G: ARMLESS BUST OF PRIEST

The figure is shown frontally, rendered in a clipeus.

He wears a tall, cylindrical, flat-top headdress: a Palmyrene priestly hat (visible in outline).

He wears a tunic and a chlamys. The tunic has a small, round neckline. The folds of the tunic are rendered by curving grooves. Over the tunic he wears a chlamys that falls over both shoulders and covers the chest. It is fastened at the right shoulder with a circular brooch with a beaded band along the outer border (Colledge classification: f). The folds of the chlamys are indicated by narrow, deep grooves.

181. COMPLETE SARCOPHAGUS WITH BANQUETING SCENE AND PORTRAIT BUSTS

DATABASE NUMBER: InSitu217 (181a) + InSitu218 (181b).
LOCATION: Palmyra, in situ.
CONTEXT: South-east necropolis. Temple tomb no. 186 (>Tombeau de l'aviation</>Tomb Duvaux<).
ACQUISITION HISTORY: —
MEASUREMENTS: —
MATERIAL: Limestone.
PRESERVATION: The upper right side of the sarcophagus lid has broken off. The right side and the far left side of the lower kline mattress are chipped. The central area of the box has broken off. Portrait A: The head is broken off at the base of the neck. The lower part of the arms is broken off at the right elbow and at the left wrist. The surface at the right knee is chipped. Portrait B: The head is broken off at the base of the neck. The surface is chipped at the right hand. Portrait C: The head is broken off at the base of the neck. Portrait D: The head is broken off at the base of the neck. The surface is chipped at the right lower leg, at the right hand, and at the left shoulder and arm. Portrait E: The head is broken off at the base of the neck. The surface is chipped at the left side of the waist and at the legs. The right lateral side of the sarcophagus lid (as photographed by Parlasca 1984): The left and right sides of the lid are broken off. The surface is weathered. Portrait F: The head and right side of the chest are broken off. A horizontal crack runs along the head and chest. Portrait G: The head and upper chest are broken off. The surface is weathered. Portrait H: The head and left shoulder are chipped. The right side of the central stretcher of the kline has broken off. Portrait I: The surface of the head is chipped. When the sarcophagus was photographed by Ingholt, the armless bust in the centre of the box (portrait J) was preserved. Portrait K: The figure is chipped.
TECHNICAL DESCRIPTION: The background is roughly finished. The right arm in portrait D is undercut.
DATE: A.D. 220–240 (Schmidt-Colinet 1992: A.D. 200–250).

Cat. 181

REFERENCES: 181a: Ingholt Archives, PS 896; Seyrig 1937, 9. 20 f. fig. 12; Will 1951, 87 f. fig. 8; Parlasca 1984, 290–292 fig. 7; Schmidt-Colinet 1992, 107 n. 380g; 110 f. n. 404d. 405. 406a; 125 n. 473. 476; 130 n. 479; 134 n. 505. 511 fig. 63; pl. 73, a; Wielgosz 1997, 71 pl. 4, 1; Krag – Raja 2017, 199 n. 24; 204 n. 72. 73; 205 n. 75; 208 n. 99; 209 n. 100; 210 n. 109. 110; 220 cat. 38; Raja 2017a, 220. 222. 226 cat. 18 fig. 19.26; Raja 2017h, 64 f. 75 cat. 18 fig. 10; Krag 2018, 28 n. 9; 32 n. 63; 48 n. 215; 53 n. 258; 58 n. 300; 59 n. 323; 60 n. 330; 61 n. 333; 62 n. 349. 351–353; 63 n. 355; 66 n. 382; 87 n. 183. 195. 197; 101 n. 54; 102 n. 69; 103 n. 74; 395 cat. 853. 181b: Parlasca 1984, 290–292 figs. 7–8; Schmidt-Colinet 1992, 107 n. 380g; 110 f. n. 405. 406a; 125 n. 473. 476; 130 n. 479; 134 n. 505. 511 fig. 63; pl. 69 c; Wielgosz 1997, 71 pl. 4, 1; Krag 2018, 53 n. 258; 58 n. 304; 103 n. 74; 398 cat. 863.

OBJECT DESCRIPTION

The sarcophagus is rectangular in shape and the lid depicts a seated female, two standing males, a reclining male, and a standing male. The right lateral side of the sarcophagus box depicts three busts rendered in clipei. Beneath these figures is a box in the shape of a kline with two female busts between the kline legs. On top of the kline are two mattresses. The thin mattress at the top, visible under the reclining figure, is decorated with an intersecting lozenge pattern with flowers in the lozenges. The lower mattress has three bands. The seated female sits on two tall cushions. The central band is decorated with rosettes set in rhombi. The bands on either side are decorated with a running scroll with rosettes. Curving grooves indicate the texture of the mattress. Both ends of the kline are decorated with a fulcrum. The fulcrum on the right side is curving up and slightly projecting outwards. The fulcra are decorated with running scrolls with rosettes.

At the right lateral side of the sarcophagus lid, there is a large panel. At the top there is a long, rectangular panel divided into two horizontal sections: the upper section is decorated with a series of oblique grooves that fan out from the centre towards the right and left. A wide frame with alternating narrow, rectangular, and square panels is depicted below; the square

Cat. 181

panels are decorated each with a rosette with four serrated petals, and the rectangular panels are decorated with a rosette with four serrated petals inside a lozenge, and serrated leaves at the corners of the lozenge.

There are three armless busts in clipei at the lower part of the box: two busts of priests and a female bust. The clipei are carved in low relief and are formed by six concentric grooves. There is a six-petal rosette between each bust at the height of their heads, with a small, round edge between each petal.

The central stretcher of the kline is decorated. The central part is divided into two sections by a horizontal, thin line. The upper section is decorated with a crisscross pattern and the lower with a tongues pattern. On either side of the central section is a square inlay decorated with an animal. These inlays are followed by rectangular indentations decorated with a wave pattern, and again followed by a square inlay decorated with an animal. One leg of the kline is depicted on the right side. The leg is turned and composed of a plinth, and above this is a concave quarter, a long, reversed concave quarter, a reversed bell-shaped element, a ball, and a bell-shaped element. All elements are decorated with a tongues pattern. The sarcophagus box is further decorated with three animal heads. Each of them has a thick ring gripped in their mouth. Three garlands are fastened to the rings. The central garland is composed of lobed leaves pointing towards a central rosette. The garlands on either side are composed of lanceolate leaves pointing towards a central rosette. The lower part of the box is decorated with four circular elements set between the garlands.

SARCOPHAGUS LID

PORTRAIT A: SEATED FEMALE

The figure is shown in three-quarter view. The left arm is bent and raised to the chest. Her legs are bent with the knees rendered under the drapery. Her feet are obscured by the right foot of the reclining figure to her left.

She wears a veil that falls over her shoulders. It falls back at her right upper arm and appears again below her waist where it proceeds in a wide fold over the cushions and the mattress. She wears two necklaces. One composed of a loop-in-loop chain with a central, circular pendant, worn high on the chest. One composed of an interwoven loop-in-loop chain with three circular pendants decorated with armless busts. The two upper pendants are placed on either side of the breasts and the central one at the stomach.

She wears a tunic and a himation. The tunic has a small, round neckline and short, wide sleeves. The folds of the tunic are rendered by curving grooves. The ankle-length himation crosses the chest diagonally from the left shoulder, leaving the right side of the chest free. The himation covers her lower body and legs. The folds of the himation are rendered by oblique and curving grooves.

She wears a bracelet on her left wrist, composed of a wide hoop.

PORTRAIT B: STANDING MALE

The figure is shown frontally. The arms appear short in relation to the body. The right arm is slightly bent and held in front of the body. The left arm is held along the body. His lower body and legs are obscured by the right leg of the reclining figure.

He wears a tunic with a small, round neckline and long, wide sleeves. An overfold, possibly created by a belt, is visible at the waist. The folds of the tunic are rendered by oblique and curving grooves.

The outline of a round vessel, possibly a bowl, is visible at his right hand. A vessel, possibly a rhyton, with a flat top and a cylindrical body is visible in front of his left arm (details unclear).

PORTRAIT C: STANDING MALE

The figure is shown frontally. The arms appear short in relation to the body. The right arm is bent and held to the torso. The left arm is bent and held out in front of the body. His legs are obscured by the reclining figure to his left.

He wears a tunic with a small, round neckline and long, wide sleeves. The folds of the tunic are rendered by oblique and curving grooves.

He holds the ends of a wreath with his hands. The wreath has a small loop visible above the right hand. The contours of the leaves are incised.

PORTRAIT D: RECLINING MALE

The figure is shown in frontal to three-quarter view. The arms appear short in relation to the body. The right arm is slightly bent and resting on his raised right knee. His right leg is bent, and his foot is resting on the kline. The left leg is bent under the right leg.

He wears a >Parthian-style< tunic, a chlamys, and trousers. The tunic has a small, round neckline and long, wide sleeves. The cuffs of the sleeves are decorated with two bands separated by a thin band. The tunic ends above his knees and has a border decorated with triangles. It is slit at either side. The borders are decorated with large arrows right before the slits. The folds of the tunic are rendered by oblique and curving grooves. Over the tunic, he wears a chlamys that falls over his left shoulder and covers his upper chest. The edge of the chlamys, visible across the chest, has tassels. The chlamys is fastened at the right shoulder with a circular brooch (details unclear). The folds of the chlamys are rendered by narrow, curving grooves. The trousers are visible from the knees. The folds are indicated by oblique and curving grooves.

With his right hand, he holds a round object, possibly fruit, with three circular depressions at the middle. The outline of a large object, possibly a bowl, is recognizable at his chest.

PORTRAIT E: STANDING PRIEST

The figure is shown frontally. The arms appear short in relation to the body. Both arms are slightly bent and held out in front of the body. The right leg is obscured by the reclining figure to his right.

He wears a tunic with a small, round neckline and long, wide sleeves. The tunic covers his legs, and the folds are rendered by oblique and curving grooves.

He holds a plain, high, cylindrical, flat-top headdress divided into three sections by two vertical grooves (Palmyrene priestly hat) with his hands. A wreath is depicted at the lower part of the headdress. It has three rows of leaves pointing towards a central oval decoration. A piece of cloth is attached at the lower edge of the headdress, extending downwards.

RIGHT LATERAL SIDE OF SARCOPHAGUS LID

PORTRAIT F: ARMLESS BUST OF A PRIEST
The figure is shown frontally.

He wears a cylindrical, flat-top headdress: a Palmyrene priestly hat (the outline is visible). The neck is short and wide.

He wears a tunic and a himation. The tunic has a wide, round neckline. The folds are indicated by curving grooves. The himation falls in a curving fold across the chest. The folds of the himation are indicated by wide, curving grooves.

PORTRAIT G: ARMLESS BUST OF A PRIEST
The figure is shown frontally.

He wears a cylindrical, flat-top headdress: a Palmyrene priestly hat (the outline is visible). The neck is short and wide.

He wears a tunic and a himation. The tunic has a wide, round neckline. The folds are indicated by curving grooves. The himation falls in a curving fold across the chest. The folds of the himation are indicated by wide, curving grooves.

PORTRAIT H: ARMLESS FEMALE BUST
The figure is shown frontally.

The outline of a veil is visible. It has a scalloped edge. It falls over both shoulders and crosses the chest in a curving fold, falling behind the left shoulder. She wears a necklace composed of large, round beads around the base of the neck.

She wears a tunic with a small, v-shaped neckline. The folds of the tunic are indicated by wide, curving grooves.

SARCOPHAGUS BOX

PORTRAIT I: ARMLESS FEMALE BUST
The figure is shown frontally, rendered in a clipeus.

She wears a veil with a scalloped edge. It falls over her shoulders in two wide folds that are looped under each other at the centre of the chest. At the base of the neck, she wears a necklace composed of round beads.

She wears a tunic. The folds are indicated by curving grooves.

PORTRAIT J: ARMLESS MALE BUST
The figure is shown frontally, rendered in a clipeus.

He wears a tunic and a himation. The tunic has a wide, v-shaped neckline. The folds of the tunic are rendered by curving grooves. Over the tunic, he wears a himation. It is wrapped around his left shoulder, leaving most of the chest free. The folds of the himation are rendered by oblique and curving grooves.

PORTRAIT K: ARMLESS FEMALE BUST
The figure is shown frontally, rendered in a clipeus.
The figure wears a garment, possibly a veil (details unclear).

SARCOPHAGUS LIDS

A.D. 140–160

182. SARCOPHAGUS LID WITH BANQUETING SCENE

DATABASE NUMBER: PM912.
LOCATION: Palmyra, Palmyra Museum, inv. no. unknown.
CONTEXT: South-east necropolis. Temple tomb no. 186 (>Tombeau de l'aviation</>Tomb Duvaux<).
ACQUISITION HISTORY: —
MEASUREMENTS: —
MATERIAL: Limestone.
PRESERVATION: Portrait A: The head is broken off horizontally at the base of the neck. The right hand is broken off. The surface around the left hand is chipped. Portrait B: The head is broken off horizontally at the base of the neck. The right hand is broken off. The surface of the left hand, of the left elbow, and of the feet is chipped.
TECHNICAL DESCRIPTION: —
DATE: A.D. 140–160.
REFERENCES: Ingholt Archives PS 895; Gabriel 1926, 90–92 fig. 7; Krag 2018, 33 n. 77. 78; 66 n. 382; 242 cat. 283.

OBJECT DESCRIPTION
The object is rectangular in shape and depicts a seated female and a reclining male. The female sits in a high-backed wicker chair, indicated by a crisscross pattern on the stool. The reclining male rests the left arm against a cushion decorated with a wide band with a running scroll. Curving grooves indicate the texture of the fabric.

PORTRAIT A: SEATED FEMALE
The figure is shown in three-quarter view. The right arm is bent and raised to the shoulder. The left arm is bent and held to the chest. The legs are bent with the knees visible under the drapery. The left foot is obscured by the reclining figure.

She wears a veil. It falls over both shoulders and is wrapped around her left arm and falls over the back of her right shoulder.

She wears a tunic and a himation. The tunic has a wide, round neckline and short sleeves. The folds of the tunic are rendered by curving grooves. The himation crosses the chest diagonally from the left shoulder to the right side, and covers the left breast, lower torso, and legs, ending at the ankles. The himation is fastened at the left shoulder with a trapezoidal

Cat. 182

brooch and a round finial (Colledge classification: i). The folds are indicated by vertical and oblique, wide grooves.

PORTRAIT B: RECLINING MALE
The figure is shown in frontal to three-quarter view. The right arm is extended and rests on the right leg. The left arm is bent and held in front of the torso. The right leg is bent and raised. The left leg is extended.

He wears a tunic and a himation. The tunic has a wide, v-shaped neckline and short, wide sleeves. The folds are indicated by curving grooves. Over the tunic, he wears a himation. It is folded over his left shoulder and arm where it continues in a wide fold across the lower torso, covering the legs, and ends at the ankles in a thick fold. Two s-shaped folds fall from under the left hand. The folds of the himation are rendered by curving and oblique grooves.

He holds a skyphos in his left hand. It has a conical foot and body. The foot is decorated with fluting and the body with oblique grooves. The lip is straight and the skyphos has small, looped handles.

A.D. 220–240

183. SARCOPHAGUS LID WITH BANQUETING SCENE

DATABASE NUMBER: PM761.
LOCATION: Palmyra, Palmyra Museum, inv. no. unknown.
CONTEXT: South-east necropolis. Temple tomb no. 186 (>Tombeau de l'aviation</>Tomb Duvaux<).
ACQUISITION HISTORY: —
MEASUREMENTS: —
MATERIAL: Limestone.
PRESERVATION: Broken at left and right side, and the lower corners are broken off. Portrait A: The head is broken off at the base of the neck and the hand is broken off at the left wrist. The surface of the right lower arm and of the hand is chipped. Portrait B: The upper part is broken off diagonally from the upper right side of the chest and to the left side. Portrait C: The upper part is broken off horizontally through the right shoulder and neck, and vertically through the left shoulder and side. The surface of the upper chest, of the right hand, of the left hand, and of the attribute is chipped.
TECHNICAL DESCRIPTION: —
DATE: A.D. 220–240.
REFERENCES: Ingholt Archives, PS 897; Seyrig 1937, 17. 29 fig. 10; Krag – Raja 2017, 199 n. 24; 204 n. 72. 73; 205 n. 75; 208 n. 99; 209 n. 100; 219 cat. 31; Krag 2018, 59 n. 315. 320; 60 n. 330; 61 n. 333; 62 n. 304; 62 n. 353; 66 n. 382; 101 n. 54; 102 n. 69; 385 cat. 829.

OBJECT DESCRIPTION
The sarcophagus lid is rectangular in shape and depicts a seated female, a standing male, and a reclining male. The figures are resting on a mattress. It is decorated with an intersecting lozenges pattern with flowers in the lozenges and three bands. The band to the right is decorated with a vegetal motif between beaded bands. The left and the central bands are decorated with a running scroll with rosettes between beaded bands. The reclining male rests the left hand on a cushion. The texture of the fabric of the cushion is indicated by curving grooves.

PORTRAIT A: SEATED FEMALE
The figure is shown frontally. The right arm is bent, and the left arm is raised to the height of the neck. The legs are bent,

and the knees are rendered under the drapery. The feet are obscured by the reclining figure.

She wears a veil. It falls over her right shoulder and upper arm and is wrapped around her left arm. Three necklaces are preserved. A necklace composed of small, round beads are rendered at the centre of the chest. A necklace at the lower part of the chest; an interwoven loop-in-loop chain with a central, oval pendant. Three long elements are suspended from the pendant (details unclear). The third necklace is composed of two strings of small, round beads with two circular pendants at either side of the chest. The pendants have armless busts wearing cylindrical, flat-top headdresses. There may be more necklaces, but the details are unclear.

She wears a tunic and himation. The tunic falls to the ankles and has a small, round neckline. The folds of the tunic are rendered by curving grooves. The himation crosses the chest diagonally from the left shoulder to the right side and covers most of the chest. It is fastened at the left shoulder with a circular brooch (Colledge classification: i). The folds of the himation are rendered by curving grooves.

PORTRAIT B: STANDING MALE

The figure is shown frontally. The right arm is held along the body. The left arm and legs are obscured by the reclining figure.

He wears a tunic. The folds are rendered by curving grooves. A wide fold is wrapped around his right wrist, possibly from another garment (details unclear).

He holds a fold of the garment in his right hand. The index finger is extended.

PORTRAIT C: RECLINING MALE

The figure is shown in frontal to three-quarter view. The right hand appears large in relation to the body. The right arm is extended and rests on his raised knee. The left arm is bent in front of the chest. His right leg is bent, and his foot is resting on the mattress. The left leg is bent under the right. The lower left leg is obscured by the right leg.

He wears a ›Parthian-style‹ tunic, a chlamys, and ›Parthian-style‹ trousers. The tunic has long, tight-fitting sleeves. The cuffs of the sleeves are decorated (details unclear). On each side of the chest are two bands decorated with running scrolls with rosettes between beaded bands, extending downwards (clavi). The tunic ends above the knees and has a decorated lower border with flowers separated by beaded bands. The folds of the tunic are rendered by curving, wide grooves. He wears a plain band belt, knotted at the centre with the ends looped under on either side of the waist. Along his right thigh is an object with a round end, a rectangular main body, and a round lateral element: a sheathed dagger. Over the tunic, he

Cat. 183

wears a chlamys. A zigzag-shaped fold falls on the right side of the chest. Two wide folds of the chlamys fall along his left side where it is further divided into two s-shaped folds. The border of the chlamys is decorated with six-petal rosettes. The folds of the chlamys are indicated by narrow, deep grooves. The trousers are visible from above the knees, and each trouser leg is decorated in the middle with a wide band with vegetal motifs set between beaded bands that extend downwards. The folds of the garments are indicated by wide, curving grooves. The trousers are tucked into his boot. The boot is decorated with rosettes and the upper edge is decorated with three beaded lines.

With his right hand, he holds a round object with a diamond-shaped pattern around a circle placed at its centre, possibly a pinecone with the top facing outwards, between his thumb and index finger.

SARCOPHAGUS BOXES

A.D. 150–200

184. SARCOPHAGUS BOX WITH TWO BUSTS OF PRIESTS

DATABASE NUMBER: InSitu180.
LOCATION: Palmyra, in situ.
CONTEXT: South-east necropolis. Central niche of temple tomb no. 186 (>Tombeau de l'aviation</>Tomb Duvaux<).
ACQUISITION HISTORY: —
MEASUREMENTS: —
MATERIAL: Limestone.
PRESERVATION: The sarcophagus box is well preserved. The top edge is chipped. The surface is weathered. Portrait A: The face does not appear to be rendered. The hands appear to be fragmented. The surface is weathered. The bottom of the bust is chipped. Portrait B: The face does not appear to be rendered. The hands appear to be fragmented. The surface is weathered. The bottom of the bust is chipped.

Cat. 184

TECHNICAL DESCRIPTION: —
DATE: A.D. 150–200.
REFERENCES: Ingholt Archives, IA_NCG_Architecture2016_020; Gawlikowski 1970a, 136 f. figs. 83–84.

OBJECT DESCRIPTION
The sarcophagus box is in the shape of a kline and depicts two busts of priests between the kline legs. The kline has a mattress and central stretcher (details unclear). The kline has turned legs. Only the left kline leg is visible. It is composed of trapezoidal elements (details unclear).

PORTRAIT A: BUST OF A PRIEST
The figure is shown frontally. The arms are bent and held in front of the torso. The arms appear small in relation to the body.

He wears a high, cylindrical, flat-top headdress: a Palmyrene priestly hat (visible in outline, details unclear).

The neck is wide and long.

He wears a tunic and a chlamys. The tunic has a wide, round neckline and short, loose-fitting sleeves (details unclear). Over the tunic, he wears a chlamys. It covers both shoulders. It appears to be fastened at the right shoulder, possibly by a circular brooch (details unclear).

With his right hand, he possibly holds an object (details unclear).

PORTRAIT B: BUST OF A PRIEST
The figure is shown frontally. The arms are bent and held in front of the torso. The arms appear small in relation to the body.

He wears a high, cylindrical, flat-top headdress: a Palmyrene priestly hat (visible in outline, details unclear).

The neck is slender and long.

He wears a tunic and a chlamys. The tunic has a wide, round neckline and short, loose-fitting sleeves. The folds of the tunic are rendered by oblique grooves over the arms. Over the tunic, he wears a chlamys. It covers both shoulders. The folds of the chlamys are indicated by oblique and curving grooves. It appears to be fastened at the right shoulder, possibly by a circular brooch (details unclear).

With his right hand, he possibly holds a vessel with a conical top and an ovoid body (details unclear). With his left hand, he possibly holds a small, round bowl (details unclear).

Cat. 184

A.D. 200–240

185. SARCOPHAGUS BOX WITH RELIGIOUS SCENE

DATABASE NUMBER: PM955.
LOCATION: Palmyra, Palmyra Museum, inv. no. unknown.
CONTEXT: South-east necropolis. Temple tomb no. 186 (>Tombeau de l'aviation</>Tomb Duvaux<).
ACQUISITION HISTORY: —
MEASUREMENTS: Height: 84 cm.
MATERIAL: Limestone.
PRESERVATION: The left side of the sarcophagus box has broken off. The upper part of the left kline leg has broken off. The upper edge is only preserved above portraits C and D. The surface is weathered. Portrait A: Broken diagonally from the right arm to the left shoulder. The surface of the chest and of the left arm are chipped. Portrait B: The head has broken off. The surface at the chest is chipped. Portrait C: The surface of the face and of the right hand is chipped. Portrait D: The surface of the face is chipped. Portrait E: The surface of the face and of the left hand is chipped. Portrait F: The surface of the face and of the right hand is chipped.
TECHNICAL DESCRIPTION: A large round and protruding block of unworked stone is visible at the lower left side of portrait D.
DATE: A.D. 200–240.
REFERENCES: Ingholt Archives, PS 900; Ingholt 1935, 73 pl. 34, 1; Seyrig 1937, 17 n. 4; Will 1951, 97 figs. 13–15; Colledge 1976, 63. 78. 125 f. 129. 132. 147. 240 f. pl. 106; Makowski 1985a, 71 fig. 1; <https://www.loc.gov/item/mpc2004002224/PP/> (15.11.2022).

OBJECT DESCRIPTION

The sarcophagus box is rectangular in shape and is rendered as a kline. Six standing males are depicted between the kline legs. The left kline leg is preserved and is turned. It is composed of a plinth, and above is a torus, a concave quarter, a small neck, a reversed bell-shaped element, and a concave quarter (other details unclear).

PORTRAIT A: STANDING MALE

The figure is shown in three-quarter view, turned to the right. The right arm is slightly bent and held out from the body. He stands with the legs set slightly apart.

He wears an undergarment and a tunic. The edge of the undergarment is visible at his legs falling in a diagonal line from above the left knee and over the right. The tunic has short, wide sleeves and ends above the knees. The tunic has an overfold at the waist. The folds of the tunic are rendered by curving and oblique grooves.

He holds a patera in his right hand. He holds an object in the left hand (details unclear).

PORTRAIT B: STANDING MALE

The figure is shown in three-quarter view, turned to the left. The right arm is slightly bent and held to the waist. The left arm is slightly bent and held out from the body. He stands with the legs set slightly apart.

He wears an undergarment and a tunic. The fringed edge of the undergarment is visible at his legs falling in a diagonal line from above the left knee and over the right. The folds of the garment are rendered by horizontal grooves. The tunic has short, wide sleeves. On either side of the neckline, a wide undecorated band extends downwards (clavi). The tunic ends at the knees. The tunic has an overfold across the waist. The folds of the tunic are rendered by curving and oblique grooves.

He holds a jug in his right hand. It has a conical lower body and neck. At the base of the neck, the jug is decorated with a beaded line. The thumb and the index finger are extended. With the left hand, he holds a patera with a long handle. The patera has a circular decoration at the tondo.

PORTRAIT C: STANDING MALE

The figure is shown in three-quarter view, turned to the right. The right arm is bent and held at his side. The left arm is bent and held to the chest. He stands with the legs set slightly apart. The left leg is slightly bent.

Only the outline of the head is visible.

He wears an undergarment, a tunic, and a mantle. The fringed edge of the undergarment is visible at his legs falling in a diagonal line from above the left knee and over the right. The folds of the garment are rendered by oblique grooves. He wears a tunic with a round neckline and short, wide sleeves. The tunic ends at the knees. The tunic has an overfold across the waist. The folds of the tunic are rendered by curving and oblique grooves. The himation is wrapped around his left shoulder and upper arm and covering the left side of the torso. The folds of the himation are rendered by oblique and vertical grooves.

He holds a large undecorated bowl in his right hand. The bowl is filled with round objects, possibly fruit. With the left hand, he holds an object (details unclear). The thumb and the index finger are extended.

PORTRAIT D: STANDING MALE

The figure is shown in three-quarter view, turned to the left. The right arm is held along the body. The left arm is bent. He stands with the legs set slightly apart. The right leg is slightly bent, with the knee visible in the drapery.

Only the outline of the head is visible.

He wears an undergarment and a tunic. The fringed edge of the undergarment is visible at his legs falling in a diagonal line from above the left knee and over the right. The folds of the garment are rendered by oblique grooves. He wears a tunic with a round neckline and short, wide sleeves. The tunic has an overfold at the waist. The tunic ends at the knees. The folds of the tunic are rendered by curving and oblique grooves. He does not wear shoes.

He holds a jug in his right hand. It has a disc-shaped ring base and a conical, oblong body. He holds an object in his left hand (details unclear).

PORTRAIT E: STANDING MALE

The figure is shown in three-quarter view, turned to the right. The right arm is slightly bent and held out from the body. The left arm is bent and held to the torso. He stands with the legs set slightly apart.

Only the outline of the head is visible.

He wears an undergarment, a tunic, and a mantle. The fringed edge of the undergarment is visible at his legs, falling in a diagonal line from above the left knee and over the right. The folds of the garment are rendered by oblique grooves. He wears a tunic with a wide, round neckline and short, wide sleeves. On the right side of the chest, the tunic has a wide undecorated band extending downwards (clavus). The tunic ends at the knees. The tunic has an overfold at the waist. The folds of the tunic are rendered by curving and oblique grooves. The mantle is wrapped around his left shoulder and arm and covers the left side of the torso. The folds are rendered by oblique and vertical grooves.

His right hand is clenched around the stems of two cylindrical and oblong objects. The surface is decorated with an incised scale pattern, and a band falls from under one of the objects. It is perhaps a wreath of leaves. He holds the edge of the himation with his left hand. The index finger is extended.

PORTRAIT F: STANDING MALE

The figure is shown in three-quarter view, turned sharply to the left. The right arm is bent and held to the torso. He stands with his legs set slightly apart.

The outline of the head is visible.

He wears an undergarment, a tunic, and a mantle. The fringed edge of the undergarment is visible at his legs falling in a diagonal line from above the left knee and over the right. The folds of the garment are rendered by oblique grooves. He wears a tunic with a wide, round neckline and short, wide sleeves. The tunic ends at the knees. The tunic has an overfold at the waist. The folds of the tunic are rendered by curving and oblique grooves. The chlamys falls over the left shoulder and along the left side.

Cat. 185

186. SARCOPHAGUS BOX WITH RELIGIOUS SCENE

DATABASE NUMBER: PM952.
LOCATION: Palmyra, Palmyra Museum, inv. no. unknown.
CONTEXT: South-east necropolis. Temple tomb no. 186 (›Tombeau de l'aviation‹/›Tomb Duvaux‹).
ACQUISITION HISTORY: —
MEASUREMENTS: —
MATERIAL: Limestone.
PRESERVATION: The left side and upper part of the sarcophagus box are broken off. Portrait A: The head is broken off at the base of the neck. The surface of the left attribute is chipped. Portrait B: The head is broken off at the base of the neck. The surface at the right hand is chipped. Portrait C: The head is broken off at the base of the neck. The surface of the right and left arm and of the hands is chipped. The front of the right foot has broken off.
TECHNICAL DESCRIPTION: —
DATE: A.D. 200–240.
REFERENCES: Ingholt Archives, PS 901; Ingholt 1935, 73 pl. 34, 2.

OBJECT DESCRIPTION

The sarcophagus box is rectangular in shape and is rendered as a kline. Three standing male figures are depicted between the kline legs. The kline leg is turned. It is composed of a high plinth, a convex quarter, a long, reversed concave quarter, a concave quarter, a ball, a reversed bell-shaped element, and a concave quarter (further details unclear). The turnings are decorated with a tongues pattern.

PORTRAIT A: STANDING MALE

The figure is shown frontally. The right arm is bent and held along the body. He stands with the legs slightly apart. He rests his weight on the right leg and the left leg is slightly bent, resulting in a slight s-curve of the body.

He wears an undergarment and a tunic. The undergarment is visible across his left knee where it proceeds in a slight curve from the edge of the tunic. The folds of the garment are rendered by oblique grooves. Over the garment, he wears a tunic with short, wide sleeves. An overfold is rendered at the waist. The tunic ends at the knees. The folds of the tunic are rendered by curving and oblique grooves. He does not wear shoes; the toes are rendered by incised lines.

Cat. 186

With the palm turned outwards, he holds a round patera with the rim indicated by an incised line in his right hand. A curving vessel, possibly a rhyton, is depicted at his left side at the height of the shoulder (details unclear).

PORTRAIT B: STANDING MALE

The figure is shown in three-quarter view. The right arm is held along the body. The left arm is slightly bent and held out from the body. He stands with the legs slightly apart. The right leg is slightly bent with the knee rendered in the drapery. He rests his weight on the left leg.

He wears an undergarment and a tunic. The undergarment is visible across his right knee where it proceeds in a slight curve from the edge of the tunic. The folds of the garment are rendered by oblique grooves. Over the garment, he wears a tunic with short, wide sleeves. An overfold is rendered at the waist. The tunic ends at the knees. The folds of the tunic are rendered by curving and oblique grooves. He does not wear shoes; the toes are indicated.

The outline of an oblong object is recognizable next to his right leg (details unclear). With the palm turned outwards, he holds the long handle of a round patera with the rim indicated by an incised line in his left hand.

PORTRAIT C: STANDING MALE

The figure is shown frontally. He stands with the legs set slightly apart. The right leg is slightly bent with the knee rendered in the drapery. He rests his weight on his left leg resulting in a slight s-curve of the body.

He wears an undergarment, a tunic, and a chlamys. The undergarment is visible across his right knee where it proceeds in a slight curve from the edge of the tunic. The folds of the garment are rendered by oblique grooves. Over the garment, he wears a tunic with short, wide sleeves. An overfold is rendered at the waist. The tunic ends at the knees. The folds of the tunic are rendered by curving and oblique grooves. The chlamys falls over the left shoulder and along his side, until the overfold. He does not wear shoes.

The outline of a round object is recognizable on the right side of his torso. He also holds an object in the left hand (details unclear).

A.D. 220–240

187. SARCOPHAGUS BOX WITH PORTRAIT BUSTS

DATABASE NUMBER: InSitu219.
LOCATION: Palmyra, in situ.
CONTEXT: South-east necropolis. Temple tomb no. 186 (›Tombeau de l'aviation‹/›Tomb Duvaux‹) (found 1923).
ACQUISITION HISTORY: —
MEASUREMENTS: —
MATERIAL: Limestone.
PRESERVATION: The left side of the sarcophagus box is chipped. The heads of the winged figures are chipped. The surface of the sarcophagus is weathered. Portrait A: The surface of the head is chipped. Portrait B: The surface of the head is chipped.
TECHNICAL DESCRIPTION: —
DATE: A.D. 220–240 (Schmidt-Colinet 1992: A.D. 200–250).
REFERENCES: Ingholt Archives, PS 899; Sadurska 1975, 124 f.; Colledge 1976, 76. 123. 128. 135. 158. 212. 216. 240. pl. 101; Parlasca 1984, 290 fig. 12; Schmidt-Colinet 1992, 107 n. 384f; 130 n. 479. n. 481; pl. 75, a. b; Krag 2018, 32 n. 63; 48 n. 215; 53 n. 258; 58 n. 300. 304; 59 n. 323. 325; 62 n. 349; 103 n. 74; 398 cat. 864.

OBJECT DESCRIPTION

The sarcophagus box is rectangular in shape and is rendered as a kline. Two winged figures carrying wreaths with portrait busts, a male and a female one, are depicted at the front of the box. They are possibly representations of Victories, and they are rendered horizontally wearing ankle-length chitons. The folds of the garments are rendered by curving grooves. The figures step on small round objects, possibly globes. The wings of the figures are seen in profile and the feathers are rendered by incised lines. The wreaths are composed of lanceolate leaves, rendered by incised lines. Between the busts is a large rosette. Above the kline is a mattress. The mattress is decorated with five bands. The bands at the outer sides are decorated with vines between beaded bands. The subsequent two bands are decorated with rosettes within circles originating from a floral stem. The central band is decorated with rosettes within oval-shaped wreaths. Curving grooves indicate the fabric of the mattress. On the left side of the kline, a fulcrum is shown: it is decorated with a small armless bust (portrait C). The central stretcher of the kline is decorated with two rectangular indentations on either end. The indentations are followed by two square inlays decorated with animals (other details unclear). The central part of the stretcher is divided into two panels by a thin, horizontal line. The upper panel is decorated with a scroll with miniature bunches of grapes protruding from a floral element on either side. The panel below is decorated with leaves in an opposite arrangement pointing towards a central rosette. The legs are turned. They are composed of a plinth, and above is a concave quarter, a long, reversed concave quarter, a torus, a reversed bell-shaped element, a ball, a torus, a concave quarter, and above the stretcher is a biconical finial.

PORTRAIT A: ARMLESS MALE BUST

The figure is shown frontally.
He wears a tunic and a chlamys. The folds of the tunic are rendered by curving grooves. Over the tunic he wears a chlamys that falls over both shoulders, over the chest in a curving fold, and covers most of the chest. It is fastened at the right shoulder with a brooch (details unclear).

Cat. 187

PORTRAIT B: ARMLESS FEMALE BUST
The figure is shown frontally.
The outline of a veil is visible. It falls on her shoulders and across her chest in a curving fold. She wears one necklace at the base of the neck. It is composed of a plain hoop with a large, round pendant suspended from the centre.
She wears a tunic. The folds of the tunic are indicated by curving grooves.

PORTRAIT C: ARMLESS BUST IN FULCRUM
The outline of a figure rendered in a clipeus is recognizable.

A.D. 240–273

188. SARCOPHAGUS BOX WITH PORTRAIT BUSTS

DATABASE NUMBER: PM786.
LOCATION: Palmyra, Palmyra Museum, inv. no. unknown.
CONTEXT: South-east necropolis. Temple tomb no. 186 (>Tombeau de l'aviation</>Tomb Duvaux<).
ACQUISITION HISTORY: —
MEASUREMENTS: —
MATERIAL: Limestone.
PRESERVATION: The central stretcher of the kline is chipped on the right side. Portrait A: The surface of the face is chipped. Portrait B: The surface of the face is chipped. Portrait C: Broken diagonally through the top of the head.
TECHNICAL DESCRIPTION: —
DATE: A.D. 240–273.
REFERENCES: Ingholt Archives, PS 896; Krag 2018, 32 n. 63; 48 n. 215; 53 n. 258; 58 n. 300. 304; 59 n. 323; 62 n. 349; 103 n. 74; 399 cat. 866.

OBJECT DESCRIPTION
The sarcophagus box is rectangular in shape and is rendered as a kline. Three busts in clipei are depicted between the kline legs: a female, a male, and a female. Above the kline is a mattress. The mattress is decorated with five bands. The band at the far right is decorated with serrated leaves on a stem set between beaded bands. The band following to the left is decorated with a running scroll with rosettes set between bands with squares. The following is decorated with serrated leaves in an opposite arrangement on the stem, set between beaded bands. The two bands on the left side are also decorated (details unclear). The central stretcher of the kline is divided into two parts by a horizontal line. The upper section is decorated with a row of miniature bunches of grapes and the lower is decorated with a tongues pattern. On either side of the central panel is a square inlay or applique with the depiction of an animal.

These are followed by rectangular indentations, again followed by square inlays with depictions of animals. The left side of the kline is decorated with a fulcrum. The kline has turned legs. They are composed of a plinth, and above is a cyma recta, a long reversed concave quarter, a concave quarter, a bell-shaped element, a torus, a ball, a torus, a neck, and above the stretcher is a biconical finial. All elements are decorated with a ridged tongues pattern. Between each portrait, the box is further decorated with four animal heads with pointy ears seen frontally and rendered within a circle with surrounding leaves. Each animal is carrying a ring in the mouth. From each ring a garland is fastened. The garlands hanging in semicircles under portraits A and C, are composed of lanceolate leaves pointing towards a central six-petal rosette. The garland under portrait B is composed of lobed leaves pointing towards a central bunch of grapes. The lower section of the sarcophagus box is further decorated with four flowers: two rosettes and two with pointed petals.

PORTRAIT A: ARMLESS FEMALE BUST

The figure is rendered frontally, in a clipeus.

She wears a veil. It falls over her right shoulder, continues in a curving fold across the chest, and falls back at the left shoulder. She wears a necklace composed of round beads with a circular pendant suspended from the centre, at the base of her neck.

She wears a tunic with a scalloped neckline.

PORTRAIT B: ARMLESS MALE BUST

The figure is shown frontally, rendered in a clipeus.

He wears a tunic and a himation. The tunic has a wide, scalloped neckline. The folds of the tunic are rendered by oblique grooves. Over the tunic, he wears a himation. It is folded over his left shoulder and falls back at his right shoulder (details unclear).

PORTRAIT C: FEMALE BUST

The figure is shown frontally, rendered in a clipeus.

She wears a veil. It falls over her left shoulder, continues in a curving fold across the chest, and falls behind her left shoulder. Only the earlobes are visible under the headdress and she wears earrings with a single round bead (Colledge classification: J). The mouth is small, and the chin is round. The neck is long with two horizontal grooves. She wears a necklace composed of round beads with a round pendant suspended from the centre. The necklace is worn at the base of the neck.

She wears a tunic with a small, scalloped neckline. The edge is scalloped. The folds of the tunic are rendered by curving grooves.

Cat. 188

189. SARCOPHAGUS BOX WITH PORTRAIT BUSTS

DATABASE NUMBER: InSitu220.
LOCATION: Palmyra, in situ.
CONTEXT: South-east necropolis. Temple tomb no. 186 (>Tombeau de l'aviation</>Tomb Duvaux<).
ACQUISITION HISTORY: —
MEASUREMENTS: —
MATERIAL: Limestone.
PRESERVATION: The upper corners of the sarcophagus box are chipped. The right section of the central stretcher has broken off. The heads of the portraits are chipped.
TECHNICAL DESCRIPTION: The finish around the busts is rough.
DATE: A.D. 240–273 (Schmidt-Colinet 1992: A.D. 200–250).
REFERENCES: Ingholt Archives, PS 903; Brykczynski 1975, 98 fig. 17, a–b; Schmidt-Colinet 1992, 107. 130; pl. 74, a–c; Krag 2018, 32 n. 63; 48 n. 215; 53 n. 258; 58 n. 300. 304; 59 n. 323; 62 n. 349; 103 n. 74; 399 cat. 869.

OBJECT DESCRIPTION

The sarcophagus box is rectangular in shape and is rendered as a kline. Four armless busts are depicted between the kline legs. On top of the kline is a mattress. The mattress is decorated with five bands. The outer bands are decorated with serrated leaves in an opposite arrangement on the stem, set between beaded bands. The central band is decorated with a row of branches with three leaves and small berries. The bands on either side of the central one are decorated with running scrolls and leaves. Curving grooves indicate the fabric of the mattress. On the left side of the kline a fulcrum is shown. The fulcrum is decorated with a small armless bust rendered in a clipeus (portrait E). The central stretcher of the kline is decorated. The central part is divided into two sections by a horizontal thin line. The upper section is decorated with miniature bunches of grapes. The lower section is decorated with leaves on a stem pointing towards a central rosette. On either side of the stretcher is a rectangular indentation decorated with a wave pattern. On either side of these are two squared inlays or appliqués decorated with an animal figure. The legs are turned. They are composed of a plinth, and above is a scotia, a reversed bell-shaped element, a concave quarter, a thin torus, a ball, a torus, a concave quarter, and above the stretcher is a biconical finial. All elements are decorated with a tongues pattern.

PORTRAIT A: ARMLESS FEMALE BUST

The figure is shown frontally, rendered in a clipeus with three bands: a plain outer border, a pointed leaf band in the middle, and a beaded band on the inside.

She wears a veil. It falls over her shoulders and across the chest in a curving fold. She wears two necklaces: one at the base of the neck is composed of a plain hoop with an oval pendant with an incised border, suspended by a narrow sleeve at the centre. Another necklace composed of a loop-in-loop chain with a biconical pendant suspended by a narrow sleeve from the centre.

She wears a tunic with a wide, v-shaped neckline. The folds of the tunic are rendered by curving and oblique grooves.

Cat. 189

PORTRAIT B: ARMLESS MALE PRIEST

The figure is shown frontally, rendered in a clipeus with three bands: a plain outer border, a pointed leaf band in the middle, and a beaded band on the inside.

He wears a tunic and a chlamys. The tunic has a wide, v-shaped neckline. The folds of the tunic are rendered by curving grooves. Over the tunic, he wears a chlamys that falls over both shoulders and covers the chest (details unclear).

PORTRAIT C: ARMLESS MALE PRIEST

The figure is shown frontally, rendered in a clipeus with three bands: a plain outer border, a pointed leaf band in the middle, and a beaded band on the inside.

He wears a tunic and a chlamys. The folds of the tunic are rendered by curving grooves. Over the tunic, he wears a chlamys that falls over both shoulders and covers the chest. It is fastened at the right shoulder with a circular brooch with an outer beaded outer border (Colledge classification: f). The folds of the chlamys are indicated by narrow, deep grooves.

PORTRAIT D: ARMLESS FEMALE BUST

The figure is shown frontally, rendered in a clipeus with three bands: a plain outer border, a pointed leaf band in the middle, and a beaded band on the inside.

She wears a veil. The veil has a scalloped edge and falls over the shoulders in a large, curving fold. She wears two necklaces: one at the base of the neck is composed of a plain hoop with an oval pendant with an incised border, suspended by a narrow sleeve at the centre. Another necklace composed of a loop-in-loop chain with a biconical pendant suspended by a narrow sleeve from the centre.

She wears a tunic with a v-shaped neckline. The folds of the tunic are rendered by curving and oblique grooves.

PORTRAIT E: ARMLESS BUST IN FULCRUM

The outline of an armless bust rendered in a clipeus is recognizable.

190. SARCOPHAGUS BOX WITH PORTRAIT BUSTS

DATABASE NUMBER: InSitu134.
LOCATION: Palmyra, in situ.
CONTEXT: South-east necropolis. Temple tomb no. 186 (>Tombeau de l'aviation</>Tomb Duvaux<).
ACQUISITION HISTORY: —
MEASUREMENTS: —
MATERIAL: Limestone.
PRESERVATION: The upper left corner of the sarcophagus box has broken off. The right section of the central stretcher as well as the surface around portrait A are broken off. A large crack runs vertically through the right side of the mattress. Portrait B: The surface of the face is chipped. Portrait C: The surface is weathered.

TECHNICAL DESCRIPTION: —
DATE: A.D. 240–273.
REFERENCES: Ingholt Archives, PS 898; Krag 2018, 32 n. 63; 48 n. 215; 53 n. 258; 58 n. 300. 304; 59 n. 323. 325; 62 n. 349; 87 n. 182; 103 n. 74; 399 cat. 868. Inscription: Ingholt 1951, 177 cat. 8; Yon 2013, 339 cat. 4 fig. 1; Krag 2018, 399 cat. 868.

OBJECT DESCRIPTION

The sarcophagus box is rectangular in shape and is rendered as a kline. Two busts are depicted between the kline legs. Above the kline is a mattress. The mattress is decorated with three bands. The two bands on either side are decorated with serrated leaves in an opposite arrangement on the stem, set between two beaded bands. The central band is decorated with a running scroll with rosettes, set between beaded bands. Curving grooves indicate the texture of the fabric. On the left side, the kline is decorated with a fulcrum. The fulcrum is decorated with a small armless male bust rendered in a clipeus (portrait C). A motif, possibly an animal, is protruding from the clipeus. The central stretcher of the kline is decorated. The central part is divided into sections by a horizontal, thin line. The upper part is decorated with a row of half-circles, possibly miniature bunches of grapes. The lower part is decorated with a wavy line, possibly vines. On the left side, the stretcher is decorated with a square inlay with an animal depicted. At the far left side is a rectangular decorated indentation (details unclear). Between the portraits, the box is further decorated with animal heads with pointy ears seen frontally and rendered within a circle with surrounding leaves. A thick garland composed of lanceolate leaves pointing towards a central rosette is hanging from the mouth of the animal and continues under portrait B. The surface of the garland under portrait A is weathered. Only the left ear of the animal head on the left side of portrait A is preserved. Two rosettes are rendered at the lower part of the box on each side of portrait B. The left kline leg is preserved and is turned. It is composed of a round plinth, and above is a convex quarter, a reversed bell-shaped element, a concave quarter, a reversed bell-shaped element, a ball, a torus, a concave quarter, and above the stretcher is a biconical finial. All elements are decorated with a tongues pattern.

INSCRIPTION

SCRIPT: Palmyrene Aramaic.
LOCATION ON RELIEF: On the bottom right side.
TRANSCRIPTION: 'G' | MRQL' | Y'T.
TRANSLATION: 'Oggâ Marcellus Ya'ut.

CIS no. —; PAT no. —.

The photograph above is the only one known to the Palmyra Portrait Project. It is possible that only the left side of the sarcophagus box is photographed, and that the object had more portraits on its surface.

PORTRAIT A: ARMLESS BUST. GENDER UNCERTAIN

The lower part of a bust is visible. The details are unclear.

Cat. 190

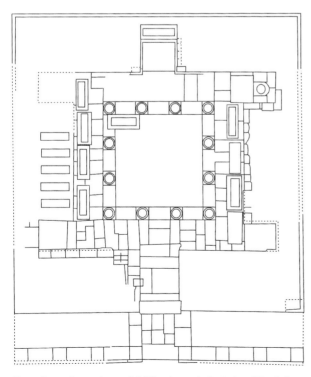

Plan of temple tomb no. 186 (›Tombeau de l'aviation‹/›Tomb Duvaux‹).

PORTRAIT B: ARMLESS FEMALE BUST

The figure is shown frontally.

She wears a veil. It falls over the right shoulder, proceeds in a curving fold across the chest, and falls over her left shoulder. She wears dumbbell-shaped earrings (Colledge classification: H). She wears a necklace composed of a plain hoop at the base of the neck.

She wears a tunic with a v-shaped neckline.

PORTRAIT C: ARMLESS BUST IN FULCRUM

The outline of an armless bust is rendered in a clipeus on the fulcrum. The details are unclear.

OBJECTS FROM TEMPLE TOMBS

A.D. 150–200

TEMPLE TOMB NO. 146

SARCOPHAGUS BOXES

191. SARCOPHAGUS BOX WITH PORTRAIT BUSTS

DATABASE NUMBER: InSitu008.
LOCATION: Palmyra, in situ.
CONTEXT: North necropolis. Temple tomb no. 146.
ACQUISITION HISTORY: —
MEASUREMENTS: —
MATERIAL: Limestone.
PRESERVATION: The upper part of the sarcophagus box is broken off. The surface is chipped and weathered.
TECHNICAL DESCRIPTION: —
DATE: A.D. 150–200.
REFERENCES: al-Asʿad 2013, 17 fig. 4.

OBJECT DESCRIPTION
The sarcophagus box is rectangular in shape and is rendered as a kline. Four busts are depicted between the kline legs. The kline legs appear to be turned and to be on a plinth (details unclear).

PORTRAIT A: BUST (GENDER UNCLEAR)
All details are unclear.

PORTRAIT B: BUST (GENDER UNCLEAR)
All details are unclear.

PORTRAIT C: BUST (GENDER UNCLEAR)
All details are unclear.

PORTRAIT D: BUST (GENDER UNCLEAR)
All details are unclear.

A.D. 150–225

TEMPLE TOMB NO. 3, ›QASR ABJAD / WHITE CASTLE‹

FRAGMENTS OF LIDS, LID RELIEFS, OR BANQUETING RELIEFS

192. FRAGMENT OF A FEMALE FIGURE

DATABASE NUMBER: InSitu168.
LOCATION: Last known location: Palmyra, in situ.
CONTEXT: West necropolis. Valley of the Tombs. Temple tomb Q280, ›Qasr Abjad / White castle‹.
ACQUISITION HISTORY: —

Cat. 192

MEASUREMENTS: —
MATERIAL: Limestone, white/yellow.
PRESERVATION: The upper part of the figure is broken off at the waist. The left knee and the edge of the himation are broken off. The right knee, the left lower leg, and the lower edge of the garment are chipped. The feet are broken off.
TECHNICAL DESCRIPTION: —
DATE: A.D. 150–225.
REFERENCES: Ingholt Archives, PS 1001; Raja – Sørensen 2015a, 447. 449. fig. 10.

OBJECT DESCRIPTION

The object depicts a seated female. The figure could also come from a sculpture in the round.

PORTRAIT

The figure is seen in frontal view. She sits with the legs parted.

She wears a tunic and a himation. The tunic falls to the ankles. It covers the legs completely. The folds of the tunic are indicated by curving grooves at the lower legs and oblique grooves at the upper legs. Over the tunic she wears a himation. It falls in a thick, zigzag-shaped fold over the left thigh and between the legs.

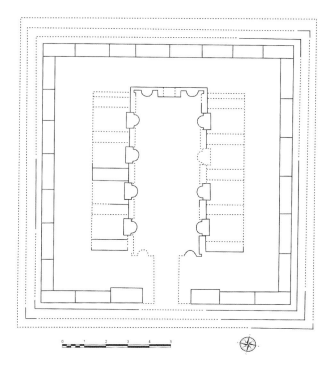

Plan of ›Qasr Abjad / White castle‹.

A.D. 150–240

TEMPLE TOMB NO. 85B, TOMB OF AʿAÎLAMÎ AND ZEBÎDÂ (›TOMB CANTINEAU‹)

SARCOPHAGUS LIDS OR LID RELIEFS

A.D. 170–190

193. SARCOPHAGUS LID WITH BANQUETING SCENE

DATABASE NUMBER: InSitu212.
LOCATION: Palmyra, in situ.
CONTEXT: West necropolis. Valley of the Tombs. Temple tomb no. 85b, tomb of Aʿaîlamî and Zebîdâ (›Tomb Cantineau‹).
ACQUISITION HISTORY: —
MEASUREMENTS: Height: 85 cm.
MATERIAL: Limestone, white.
PRESERVATION: All sides are chipped. Portrait A: The upper part is broken off at the base of the neck and at the left wrist. The right arm is chipped. Portrait B: The upper part is broken off at the base of the neck. Heavily chipped and weathered. Portrait C: The upper part is broken off at the base of the neck. Heavily chipped and weathered. Portrait D: The upper part is broken off horizontally across the shoulders. The left arm is broken off. The surface of the chest is chipped. Portrait E: The head is broken off at the base of the neck.
TECHNICAL DESCRIPTION: The necklaces of the female figures are partly carved.
DATE: A.D. 170–190.
REFERENCES: Ingholt Archives, PS 529A. IA_NCG_Miscellaneous2016_077_PM780; Cantineau 1929, pl. 2 fig. 1; 6 fig. 3; Makowski 1983, 186 cat. 1 pl. 49, b; Krag 2018, 32 n. 62; 58 n. 304; 62 n. 353; 63 n. 354; 64 n. 361. 362; 65 n. 375. 378; 66 n. 382; 88 n. 193. 195; 89 n. 203; 397 cat. 858; Raja – Yon 2022, 187–190 cat. 12. Inscription: Cantineau 1930a, 38–40 cat. 14; Milik 1972, 250; Yon 2012, 333 f. cat. 434.

OBJECT DESCRIPTION

The sarcophagus lid is rectangular in shape and depicts a seated female, two standing figures, a reclining female, and a reclining male. Beneath the figures is a mattress. The female sits on two cushions. The reclining female to the right rests the left arm on two cushions; the lower cushion is decorated with a wide band (details unclear). The reclining male rests the left arm on a single cushion. The texture of all cushions is indicated by curving grooves. The fulcrum is party carved and it depicts several figures, each one placed over the previous figure (possibly mythological figures).

According to Makowski (1983) the following inscription belongs to the relief. The inscription is now in the National Museum of Damascus (Yon 2012, 333 f. cat. 434).

Cat. 193

INSCRIPTION
SCRIPT: Ancient Greek.
LOCATION ON RELIEF: On the base of the relief.
TRANSCRIPTION: [Βωλανος Ζ]ηνοβίου [τοῦ Αιρανοῦ τ]οῦ Μοκιμου τοῦ Μαθθα ΑΚ[- - αἱρεθεὶ]ς συνποσιάρχης ἱερέων [... Δι]ὸς Βή[λου καὶ - - -] [- - -]ς αὐτῷ[- - - ἀδε]λφὴ [τοῦ?] Μουκιανοῦ κ[αὶ - - -] Καλλίστη θυγάτηρ Ηρ[- - -] ΥΜΟΥ [- - -].
TRANSLATION: Bôlanos son of Zenobios son of Airanes son of Mokimos son of Mattha - - - chosen as symposiarches of the priests of Zeus Belos and - - - for him - - - sister of Mucianus and - - - Kalliste the daughter - - -.

CIS no. —; PAT no. —.

COMMENT: The location of the inscription is according to Cantineau 1930a.

PORTRAIT A: SEATED FEMALE
The figure is shown in three-quarter view. The right arm is bent and rests on her right thigh. The left arm is raised to the neck. Her legs are bent, and the knees are rendered under the drapery. Her feet are obscured by the reclining figure to her left.

She wears a veil that is wrapped around her right shoulder. She wears a necklace with a central, rectangular pendant below the collarbone.

She wears a tunic and a himation. The folds of the tunic are indicated with oblique grooves. The himation crosses the chest diagonally from the left shoulder to the right side and covers the left breast. It is fastened with a brooch on her left shoulder (details unclear). The folds of the himation are rendered by curving grooves.

With the right hand, she holds a fold, possibly the edge of the veil. The left hand is raised to the height of the neck.

PORTRAIT B: STANDING FIGURE
The figure is shown frontally. They are wearing a garment (other details unclear).

PORTRAIT C: STANDING FIGURE
The figure is shown frontally. They are wearing a garment (other details unclear).

PORTRAIT D: RECLINING FEMALE
The figure is shown in three-quarter view. The right arm is extended and rests on his right knee. The outline of the left arm is visible, and she holds the arm in front of the chest. The right leg is bent, but the foot is obscured by the left leg. The left leg is slightly bent, and the foot is seen in frontal view.

She wears a veil. It falls over the right shoulder.

She wears three necklaces. The first is worn below the collarbone. It has a wide oval central decoration with an incised border. Its centre is oval-shaped and raised. The second is worn over the breasts. It is composed of a wide, hoop and has a crescent-shaped pendant at the centre suspended by a wide sleeve. Below that she wears a necklace composed of a thick chain with a central oval decoration with a beaded border. Rectangular elements are suspended under the pendant.

She wears a tunic and a himation. The tunic has short, wide sleeves that fall to the elbows. The folds of the tunic are rendered by curving grooves. Over the tunic she wears a himation that is wrapped under the breasts and covers the body. Part of the himation falls over the cushion in two zigzag-shaped folds.

With her right hand, she holds a round object, possibly fruit. She wears a wide, thick hoop bracelet at the wrist.

PORTRAIT E: RECLINING MALE

The figure is shown in three-quarter view. The arms appear short in relation to the body. The right arm is bent and held to the torso. The left arm is bent in front of the chest. His legs are obscured by the reclining figure to his right.

He wears a tunic and a chlamys. The tunic is long-sleeved. The folds of the tunic are rendered by curving grooves. Over the tunic, he wears a chlamys that falls over the left shoulder and covers most of the chest. It is folded around his left arm. A wide fold falls from under the arm along his left side and over the cushions.

His right hand rests on his stomach, the index and the little finger are extended. He holds a bowl in his left hand. The index and the little finger are extended.

194. FRAGMENT OF BANQUETING RELIEF

DATABASE NUMBER: PM551.
LOCATION: Palmyra, Palmyra Museum, inv. no. unknown.
CONTEXT: West necropolis. Valley of the Tombs. Temple tomb no. 85b, tomb of Aʿailamî and Zebîdâ (›Tomb Cantineau‹).
ACQUISITION HISTORY: —
MEASUREMENTS: Height: 88 cm. Width: 40 cm. Depth: 19 cm.
MATERIAL: Limestone, white/yellow.
PRESERVATION: The head is broken off horizontally at the base of the neck, the lower part is broken off vertically at the lower part of the legs. The right arm and left lower arm are broken off. The knees are chipped. Multiple cracks run through the figure.
TECHNICAL DESCRIPTION: —
DATE: A.D. 170–190.
REFERENCES: Ingholt Archives, PS 529A; Makowski 1983, 186 cat. 2 pl. 50, a; Schmidt-Colinet 1992, 110 n. 404c. 477; pl. 72, a; Krag 2018, 56 n. 290; 58 n. 304; 59 n. 325; 62 n. 353; 64 n. 361. 362; 65 n. 374; 384 cat. 821; Raja – Yon 2022, 190 cat. 13. Inscription: Cantineau 1930a, 38 cat. 13; Milik 1972, 250; Yon 2012, 332 f. cat. 432; Krag 2018, 384 cat. 821.

OBJECT DESCRIPTION

The object depicts a reclining female. She rests on a thin mattress. It is decorated with an intersecting lozenges pattern with flowers in the lozenges. She rests the left arm against two cushions. The cushions are decorated with bands with vegetal motifs set between beaded bands. Curving grooves indicate the texture of the fabric.

INSCRIPTION

SCRIPT: Ancient Greek.
LOCATION ON RELIEF: On the edges of the mattress.
TRANSCRIPTION: [- - -κ]αὶ Αμαθαης Μουκιανοῦ σύνβιος αὐτοῦ καὶ Βωλ[ανος- - -].
TRANSLATION: [- - -] Amathaes, daughter of Mukianus, her husband and Bolanos [their son?].

CIS no. —; PAT no. —.

COMMENT: According to Milik 1972 this inscription joins with Cantineau 1930a, 38 cat. 13: Yon 2012, 332 f. cat. 433.

PORTRAIT

The figure is shown in frontal to three-quarter view. The left arm is bent and raised to the neck. The left leg is bent under the right leg.

She wears a veil. It is wrapped around her left shoulder and falls over the back of her right shoulder. A wavy lock of hair falls down the right side of her neck and shoulder. She wears four necklaces. The first is composed of small, round beads, worn at the base of the neck. The second is composed of alternating round and square pendants with beaded borders linked by beaded elements, worn high on the chest. The third is composed of round beads and a central crescent-shaped pendant, worn on the chest. The fourth is composed of a double loop-in-loop chain with a central oval pendant with a beaded border. Three spirally wrapped wires with trefoil-shaped beads at the ends are suspended from the oval pendant. It is worn below the chest.

She wears a tunic and a himation. The tunic has a small, round neckline. The folds of the tunic are rendered by curving and oblique grooves. Over the tunic, she wears a himation. It is folded from behind and falls vertically across the torso in a fold with a scalloped edge. The himation is folded around her left arm. Two s-shaped folds fall from under her left arm and proceed downwards at her left side. The himation is rendered as resembling a toga. The folds of the himation are rendered by curving and vertical grooves.

The left arm is bent to the chest. She wears a bracelet at her wrist (details unclear).

Cat. 194

A.D. 180–200

195. FRAGMENT OF BANQUETING RELIEF

DATABASE NUMBER: PM762.
LOCATION: Palmyra, Palmyra Museum, inv. no. unknown.
CONTEXT: West necropolis. Valley of the Tombs. Temple tomb no. 85b, tomb of Aʿaîlamî and Zebîdâ (›Tomb Cantineau‹).
ACQUISITION HISTORY: —
MEASUREMENTS: Height: 86 cm. Width: 88 cm. Depth: 33 cm.
MATERIAL: Limestone.
PRESERVATION: The upper part of the right and left side, and the background is broken off. A large crack runs vertically through the lid at the thighs of the reclining figure, thereby separating the figures. Portrait A: The upper part is broken off horizontally through the waist and the lower left arm. The surface of the right leg is chipped. Portrait B: The head is broken off at the base of the neck. The right hand and the left lower arm are broken off. The surface of the right foot, of the left knee, and of the left shoulder is chipped.
TECHNICAL DESCRIPTION: —
DATE: A.D. 180–200 (Makowski 1983: A.D. 170–190).
REFERENCES: Ingholt Archives, PS 885; Cantineau 1929, 8–10 pl. 2, 2; Makowski 1983, 186 cat. 5 pl. 51, b; Krag 2018, 59 n. 325; 63 n. 304; 62 n. 353; 66 n. 382; 87 n. 182; 89 n. 210; 386 cat. 830. Inscription: Cantineau 1930a, 41 cat. 15; Krag 2018, 386 cat. 830.

Cat. 195

OBJECT DESCRIPTION
The sarcophagus lid is rectangular in shape and depicts a seated female and a reclining male. The figures are resting on a mattress. It is decorated with an intersecting lozenges pattern with flowers in the lozenges. The centre of the flowers is rendered by incised lines. The reclining figure rests the left arm against two cushions. They are decorated with two bands with floral motifs set between beaded bands. Curving grooves indicate the texture of the fabric.

INSCRIPTION
SCRIPT: Palmyrene Aramaic.
LOCATION ON RELIEF: On the drapery.
TRANSCRIPTION: ṢLM ⁾ʿYLMY BR ZBYDʾ | ḤYRN ḤBL.
TRANSLATION: Image of Aʿaîlamî, son of Zebîdâ Ḥaîran, alas!

CIS no. —; PAT no. 1139.

COMMENT: The location of the inscription is according to Cantineau 1930a.

PORTRAIT A: SEATED FEMALE
The figure is shown frontally. The left lower arm rests on her left thigh. The legs are bent, and the knees are rendered under the drapery. Her feet are obscured by the reclining figure to her left.

She wears an ankle-length garment. The folds are indicated by curving, wide grooves.

Her right hand is resting on a piece of cloth falling downwards at her right side. She holds a fold of a cloth, possibly a himation with her left hand.

PORTRAIT B: RECLINING MALE, AʿAÎLAMÎ
The figure is shown in frontal to three-quarter view. The right arm is extended. The left arm is bent and is held in front of the chest. The right leg is bent, and the foot is resting on the mattress. The left leg is bent under the right, with the knee pointing outwards. The lower left leg is obscured by the right leg.

He wears a ›Parthian-style‹ tunic, a chlamys, and ›Parthian-style‹ trousers. The tunic has a wide, v-shaped neckline and long, loose sleeves. At the middle, the tunic has a wide band with a floral pattern between two beaded bands extending downwards. The tunic ends above the knees and has a decorated border with a running scroll with rosettes and a beaded band at the hem. The folds of the tunic are rendered by curving, wide grooves. He wears a plain band belt, knotted at the centre with the ends looped under on either side of the waist. Over the tunic, he wears a chlamys that falls over his right shoulder. At the left shoulder, a thick fold of the chlamys extends downwards. It is wrapped around his left arm and falls in a thick, s-shaped fold along his left side and over the cushions. The chlamys is fastened at the right shoulder with a circular brooch (details unclear). A zigzag-shaped fold falls from under the brooch. The folds of the chlamys are indicated by narrow, deep grooves. Each trouser leg is decorated in the middle with a beaded band that extends downwards. The folds of the trousers are indicated by wide, curving grooves. The trousers are tucked into his boots.

An outline of a bowl is visible at the centre of his chest.

A.D. 220–240

196. SARCOPHAGUS LID WITH BANQUETING SCENE

DATABASE NUMBER: PM779.
LOCATION: Palmyra, Palmyra Museum, inv. no. unknown.
CONTEXT: West necropolis. Valley of the Tombs. Temple tomb no. 85b, tomb of Aʿaîlamî and Zebîdâ (›Tomb Cantineau‹).
ACQUISITION HISTORY: —
MEASUREMENTS: Height: 100 cm. Width: 190 cm. Depth: 42 cm.
MATERIAL: Limestone.
PRESERVATION: Portrait A: The upper part is broken off at the middle of the torso. The right lower leg is chipped. Portrait B: The head is broken off at the neck. The surface of chest, of the right hand, and the toes of the right foot is chipped. The left hand is broken off.
TECHNICAL DESCRIPTION: —
DATE: A.D. 220–240 (Makowski 1983: A.D. 170–190).
REFERENCES: Ingholt Archives, PS 887; Cantineau 1929, 12 pl. 2, 1; Makowski 1983, 186 cat. 4 pl. 51, a; Krag 2018, 61 n. 304; 62 n. 353; 66 n. 382; 385 cat. 828.

OBJECT DESCRIPTION
The relief is rectangular in shape and depicts a seated female and a reclining male. Beneath the figures is a mattress decorated with an intersecting lozenges pattern with four-petal flowers at the centre. The male rests against two cushions. The upper cushion is decorated with a vertical band with running scroll and rosettes set between bands of incised squares. The lower cushion is decorated with a wide band with a floral motif set between bands of incised squares. Curving grooves indicate the fabric of the cushion.

PORTRAIT A: SEATED FEMALE
The figure is shown in frontal view. The arms appear small in relation to the body. The left arm is bent and rests on the left thigh. She sits with the legs set apart with the knees rendered under the drapery. The lower left leg and the feet are obscured by the reclining figure to her left.

She wears a veil that falls across her body.

Cat. 196

She wears a tunic and a himation. The tunic ends at the ankles, and the folds are indicated with vertical grooves. The himation covers her lower body and legs. It is folded around the left arm, and a large fold of the himation falls beneath the left hand. The himation ends at the shins, revealing the tunic underneath. The folds of the himation are rendered by oblique and curving grooves.

She rests her left hand on her left thigh. She holds a fold of the veil. The thumb and the index finger are extended.

PORTRAIT B: RECLINING MALE

The body is shown in three-quarter view. The arms appear short in relation to the body. The right arm is slightly bent and rests on his raised right knee. The left arm is bent in front of the chest, and rests on two cushions. His right leg is bent and the right foot rests on the mattress. The left leg is bent under the right, and the knee is rendered pointing forwards. The left lower leg is obscured by the right leg.

He wears a ›Parthian-style‹ tunic, a chlamys, and ›Parthian-style‹ trousers. The tunic has a round neckline and long, tight-fitting sleeves. The cuffs are decorated with a wide band with floral motif. The tunic has a wide band decorated with a running scroll and rosettes, set between two beaded bands, extending downwards from the middle of the neckline. The tunic ends at the middle of the thighs, and the lower border is decorated with a wide band of rosettes with an outer beaded band. The folds of the tunic are rendered by curving grooves. He also wears a plain band belt, knotted at the centre with the ends looped under on either side of the waist. The chlamys falls over both shoulders and the left arm, and continues under the left arm. The folded edge of the chlamys falls onto the cushions and mattress in a large zigzag-shaped fold. The chlamys is fastened at the right shoulder with a circular brooch with an incised circle (Colledge classification: h). A narrow fold falls underneath the brooch. The folds of the chlamys are rendered by oblique, v-shaped grooves. He wears trousers: each trouser leg is decorated in the middle with a wide band of floral motifs set between beaded bands extending downwards. The folds of the trousers are rendered by curving grooves. He wears ankle boots, and a strap with circular attachment is depicted around the ankle.

He rests his right hand on the right knee, and an oblong object with drop-shaped elements is rendered underneath, possibly a branch or a small wreath. The outline of a bowl is visible just above the chipped part of the left hand.

197. FRAGMENT OF A BANQUETING RELIEF

DATABASE NUMBER: InSitu151.
LOCATION: Palmyra, in situ.
CONTEXT: West necropolis. Valley of the Tombs. Temple tomb no. 85b, tomb of Aʿaîlamî and Zebîdâ (›Tomb Cantineau‹).
ACQUISITION HISTORY: —
MEASUREMENTS: —
MATERIAL: Limestone.
PRESERVATION: Broken at the right and upper side. The surface is weathered. Portrait A: The figure is broken off

Cat. 197

diagonally above the feet. Portrait B: The head, part of the left hand, the right arm, and the right knee are broken off.

TECHNICAL DESCRIPTION: —
DATE: A.D. 220–240.
REFERENCES: Ingholt Archives, PS 886; Cantineau 1929, pl. 2, 2; Seyrig 1937, 22 n. 2; Makowski 1983, 186 cat. A pl. 51c; Krag 2018, 64 n. 304; 62 n. 353; 66 n. 382. 385; 386 cat. 831.

OBJECT DESCRIPTION

The sarcophagus lid is rectangular in shape and depicts a foot belonging to a seated female, and a reclining male. Beneath the figures is a mattress. It is decorated with six-petal rosettes alternating with acanthus leaves with tendrils. The reclining figure rests the left arm against two cushions. They are decorated with two bands with six-petal rosettes between beaded bands. Curving grooves indicate the texture of the fabric.

PORTRAIT A: SEATED FEMALE

The figure is shown frontally. Her legs are parted, and her left foot is obscured by the reclining figure to her left.

She wears an ankle-length garment. The folds are indicated by curving, wide grooves.

PORTRAIT B: RECLINING MALE

The figure is shown in three-quarter view. The right arm is bent, and the hand is resting on the right knee. The left arm is bent in front of the torso. The right leg is bent, and the foot is resting on the mattress. The left leg is bent under the right, with the knee pointing outwards. The left foot is obscured by the right leg.

He wears a ›Parthian-style‹ tunic, a chlamys, and ›Parthian-style‹ trousers. The tunic has a round neckline, long, tight-fitting sleeves, and ends above the knees. It has a band that extends downwards from the middle of the neckline to the border of the tunic decorated with acanthus leaves. The cuffs and the hem of the tunic are decorated with borders of six-petal rosettes inside circles and beaded bands: one beaded band below the border at the hem, and two beaded bands framing the border at the cuffs. The folds of the tunic are rendered by oblique and curving grooves. Over the tunic he wears a chlamys: it is folded over the chest and falls back over the left shoulder, covering the upper left arm and then falling over the cushions in two zigzag-shaped folds. It is fastened at the right shoulder with a circular brooch with a beaded border (other details unclear) (Colledge classification: i). A small fold of the chlamys falls under the brooch in a zigzag-shaped fold. He wears a thin band belt knotted at the centre with the ends looped under on either side of the waist. In the middle, the trouser legs are decorated with a band with acanthus leaves that extends downwards.

The folds of the garment are rendered by wide, curving grooves. The trousers are tucked into his boots. The boots are decorated with a beaded band at the cuff, and six-petal rosettes inside circling tendrils on the vamp. A thin, tied band is depicted over the ankle.

The right hand rests on the right knee. With the upturned fingertips of his left hand, he holds a bowl (visible only in outline).

198. FRAGMENT OF A BANQUETING RELIEF

DATABASE NUMBER: InSitu166.
LOCATION: Palmyra, in situ.
CONTEXT: West necropolis. Valley of the Tombs. Temple tomb no. 85b, tomb of Aʿaîlamî and Zebîdâ (›Tomb Cantineau‹).
ACQUISITION HISTORY: —
MEASUREMENTS: —
MATERIAL: Limestone.
PRESERVATION: Broken at the right and left side. The surface is weathered. Portrait A: The upper part is broken off diagonally from the upper right side of the chest and to the lower right side. The right leg is chipped. The surface of the torso, of the lower right arm, and of the left leg is chipped. Portrait B: The upper part is broken off horizontally through the chest. The surface of the lower part of the chest and of the right hand is chipped. Portrait C: The upper part is broken off diagonally through the torso. The right arm and tip of the right foot are broken off. The surface around his right side and of the left knee is chipped.
TECHNICAL DESCRIPTION: —
DATE: A.D. 220–240.
REFERENCES: Ingholt Archives, PS 883/829A.

OBJECT DESCRIPTION

The sarcophagus lid is rectangular in shape and depicts two standing males and a reclining male. Beneath the figures is a mattress. It is decorated with an intersecting lozenges pattern with flowers in the lozenges.

PORTRAIT A: STANDING MALE

The figure is shown frontally.

He wears a ›Parthian-style‹ tunic and ›Parthian-style‹ trousers. The tunic has a wide band extending downwards along the middle (details unclear). The tunic ends above the knees and has a decorated lower border at the hem (details unclear). The folds of the tunic are rendered by oblique grooves. He wears a plain band belt, knotted at the centre with the ends looped under on either side of the waist. At the middle, each trouser leg has a wide band extending downwards and decorated with a running scroll with rosettes. The folds of the garment are rendered by oblique grooves.

PORTRAIT B: STANDING MALE

The left arm is held out from the body. The legs of the figure are obscured by the right leg of the reclining figure to his left.

He wears a tunic. The edge of the tunic is visible at his right side. He also wears a band belt, the plain strap is visible at his right side (details unclear).

The outline of the left hand is recognizable and appears to rest on the right knee of the reclining figure.

Cat. 198

PORTRAIT C: RECLINING MALE

The figure is shown in three-quarter view. The right leg is bent, and the foot is resting on the mattress. The left leg is bent under the right, with the knee pointing outwards. The left foot is obscured by the right leg.

He wears a ›Parthian-style‹ tunic and ›Parthian-style‹ trousers. The tunic has a band on the left side of the torso decorated with a running scroll with rosettes set between beaded bands. The tunic ends above the knees and has a decorated lower border with a running scroll with rosettes and a beaded band. The folds of the tunic are rendered by oblique and curving grooves. Along his right thigh is an object with a rectangular main body and two lateral, rectangular elements: a sheathed dagger. In the middle, each trouser leg has a band extending downwards and decorated with a running scroll with rosettes. The folds of the garment are rendered by wide, curving grooves. The trousers are tucked into his boots. The edge of the boot is visible above the ankles (details unclear). At his left side, a wide fold with a beaded edge lies on the mattress. The folds are possibly from another garment, either a himation or chlamys.

199. FRAGMENT OF A SARCOPHAGUS LID WITH BANQUETING SCENE

DATABASE NUMBER: InSitu153.
LOCATION: Palmyra, in situ.
CONTEXT: West necropolis. Valley of the Tombs. Temple tomb no. 85b, tomb of Aʿaîlamî and Zebîdâ (›Tomb Cantineau‹).
ACQUISITION HISTORY: —
MEASUREMENTS: Height: 55 cm. Width: 174 cm. Depth: 22 cm.
MATERIAL: Limestone.
PRESERVATION: Broken on right, left, and upper side. Portrait A: Only a part of the lower legs is preserved. Portrait B: The surface at the entire right side, at the right leg, at the foot, and of the upper chest is badly chipped.
TECHNICAL DESCRIPTION: —
DATE: A.D. 220–240 (Makowski 1983: A.D. 200–230).
REFERENCES: Ingholt Archives, PS 884; Makowski 1983, 187 cat. 8 pl. 52, b; Krag 2018, 64 n. 304; 62 n. 353; 386 cat. 832.

OBJECT DESCRIPTION
The sarcophagus lid is rectangular in shape and depicts a seated female and a reclining male. The figures are resting on a mattress. It is decorated with an intersecting lozenges pattern with flowers in the lozenges.

PORTRAIT A: SEATED FEMALE
She wears an ankle-length garment.

PORTRAIT B: RECLINING MALE
The figure is shown in three-quarter view. The right leg is bent with the foot resting on the mattress. The left leg is bent under the right with the knee pointing outwards. The left foot is obscured by the right leg.

He wears a ›Parthian-style‹ tunic and ›Parthian-style‹ trousers. At the middle, the tunic has a wide band with a floral pattern between two beaded bands extending downwards. The tunic ends above the knees and has a decorated lower border (details unclear). He wears a plain band belt, knotted at the centre with the ends looped under on either side of the waist. The trousers are visible from above the knees and each trouser leg is decorated in the middle with a wide band (details unclear). The folds of the trousers are indicated by curving grooves. He wears a pointed boot.

Cat. 199

SARCOPHAGI BOXES

A.D. 180–200

200. SARCOPHAGUS BOX RELIEF WITH BANQUETING SCENE

DATABASE NUMBER: PM951.
LOCATION: Palmyra, Palmyra Museum, inv. no. unknown.
CONTEXT: West necropolis. Valley of the Tombs. Temple tomb no. 85b, tomb of Aʿaîlamî and Zebîdâ (>Tomb Cantineau<).
ACQUISITION HISTORY: —
MEASUREMENTS: —
MATERIAL: Limestone.
PRESERVATION: The right and left sides of the relief are broken off. The right leg of the kline is broken off. The surface is weathered. Portrait A: The head, right upper side of the torso, and left arm are broken off. The surface is weathered. Portrait B: The headdress and head, the right hand, and the object on the left hand are broken off. The surface is weathered.
TECHNICAL DESCRIPTION: —
DATE: A.D. 180–200.
REFERENCES: Will 1951, 87 fig. 9.

OBJECT DESCRIPTION

The box is rectangular in shape and is rendered in the shape of a kline: the outline of the right leg is visible at the side of the relief, indicating that it was turned. Two figures are depicted between the kline legs: a seated female figure next to a reclining priest. Beneath the figures is a thick mattress. The priest rests on a cushion at his left side. The texture and fabric of the cushion are rendered by curving grooves.

PORTRAIT A: SEATED FEMALE

The figure is shown seated in a three-quarter view. Her left arm is bent and raised to the height of the shoulder; her right arm falls to the side.

The figure wears a veil that falls over the left shoulder.

She wears a tunic that falls to the ankles. Over the tunic she wears another garment, visible over the legs, possibly a himation. The folds of the garment are indicated by curving grooves between the legs.

With the left hand she holds the edge of the veil.

PORTRAIT B: RECLINING PRIEST

The figure's head and torso are shown frontally, the arms and legs in profile. The left arm is bent and raised in front of the chest, the right arm is extended to the side, and the hand rests on the left knee. The left leg is raised and bent under the right leg, with the foot obscured under the right leg.

He wears a tall, cylindrical, flat-top headdress: a Palmyrene priestly hat (visible in outline).

He wears a >Parthian-style< tunic, a >Parthian-style< coat, and >Parthian-style< trousers. The tunic has long sleeves and ends at the middle of the thighs. The folds of the tunic are indicated by curving grooves. Over the tunic he wears a long over-garment that is open in front of the chest and falls under the left elbow in two wide folds. Under the tunic he wears loose-fitting trousers that are tucked into boots (visible on the right foot). Curving grooves indicate the folds of the trousers.

A.D. 200–240

201. SARCOPHAGUS BOX RELIEF WITH BANQUETING SCENE

DATABASE NUMBER: InSitu149.
LOCATION: Palmyra, in situ.
CONTEXT: West necropolis. Valley of the Tombs. Temple tomb no. 85b, tomb of Aʿaîlamî and Zebîdâ (>Tomb Cantineau<).
ACQUISITION HISTORY: —
MEASUREMENTS: Height: 83 cm. Width: 205 cm.
MATERIAL: Limestone.
PRESERVATION: The surface is weathered. The left side and most of the right side of the sarcophagus are broken off. Portrait A: The upper part of the head and the face, as well as a part of the right leg are broken off. Portrait B: The face and the headdress are broken off. The left hand is chipped. Portrait C: The head and the headdress are broken off. Portrait D: The head is broken off. The right hand and the shoulders are chipped.
TECHNICAL DESCRIPTION: —
DATE: A.D. 200–240 (Makowski 1983: A.D. 200–230).
REFERENCES: Ingholt Archives, PS 531a/882; Cantineau 1929, 12 pl. 2, 2; 6, 4; Will 1951, 88 f. fig. 9; Makowski 1983, 187 cat. 7 pl. 52, a; Krag 2018, 28 n. 9; 32 n. 63; 58 n. 304; 62 n. 349. 353; 63 n. 355; 397 cat. 859.

OBJECT DESCRIPTION

The sarcophagus box is rectangular in shape and depicts four figures: a seated female, two reclining men, and a seated female. The figures are framed by a projecting edge. Each female sits on two round cushions, one placed on top of the other. The fabric of the cushions is indicated by curving grooves. Each of the reclining males rests on a round cushion decorated with a central band (details unclear). The fabric of the cushions is indicated by curving, incised lines.

PORTRAIT A: SEATED FEMALE

The head of the figure is shown frontally, while the torso, right arm, and the legs are shown in a three-quarter view. The left arm is shown in profile. The left arm is bent and raised to the height of the shoulder, while the right falls to the side. The feet are obscured by the reclining figure to her left.

She wears a veil that falls down the back of the head and over the shoulders and falls down along her right side.

She wears a tunic and a himation. The tunic has short, wide sleeves. Over the tunic, she wears a himation that falls from the left shoulder, crosses the chest diagonally, and covers the legs.

Cat. 201

Her right hand rests on the cushion. She possibly wears a thick, plain band bracelet on the right wrist. With the left hand, she pulls the edge of the veil.

PORTRAIT B: RECLINING PRIEST

The head, torso, and left leg of the figure are shown frontally, the arms and the right leg in profile. The right arm is extended; the left arm is bent in front of the chest. The left lower leg is bent under the right raised leg and the foot is obscured.

He wears a high, cylindrical, flat-top headdress: a Palmyrene priestly hat (visible only in outline). His face is fleshy. The neck is short and wide.

He wears a ›Parthian-style‹ tunic, a ›Parthian-style‹ coat, and ›Parthian-style‹ trousers. The tunic has a wide, round neckline decorated with three narrow bands. A wide band framed by two beaded bands extends downwards from the middle of the neckline. The tunic has long, tight-fitting sleeves decorated at the cuffs with a wide band. The lower hem of the tunic is also decorated with a wide band. At the waist, a narrow band belt is tied with a knot at the centre with the ends looped under on either side. He wears a coat: it is sleeveless, reaching to the middle of the thighs, and falls open to the left and right of the torso. The edges are scalloped. The trousers are loose and decorated with a beaded and a wide band that extends downwards. He wears boots.

With the right hand, he holds an elliptical-shaped object with a diamond-shaped pattern on its surface, possibly a pinecone. With the upturned palm of the left hand, he holds a round bowl with his fingertips.

PORTRAIT C: RECLINING PRIEST

The head, torso, left arm, and left leg of the figure are shown frontally, the right arm and right leg in profile. The right arm is bent to the chest; the left arm is bent and held along his side. The left leg is bent under the raised right leg and thereby obscured.

He wears a high, cylindrical, flat-top headdress: a Palmyrene priestly hat (visible only in outline). The neck is short and wide.

He wears a >Parthian-style< tunic, a chlamys, and trousers. The tunic has a wide, round neckline decorated with two narrow bands. A wide band with a vegetal motif framed by two beaded bands extends downwards from the middle of the neckline. The tunic has long, tight-fitting sleeves decorated at the cuffs with a wide band. At the waist, a narrow band belt is tied with a knot at the centre with the ends looped under on either side of the waist. He wears a chlamys that is folded over the chest and is wrapped over the left shoulder and arm. It is fastened at the right shoulder with a circular brooch with an incised border (Colledge classification: h). The chlamys falls from under the left arm and over the side of the cushion in two zigzag-shaped folds. He wears trousers (details unclear).

With his right hand, he holds a cup in front of the chest: it has a conical foot, a hemispherical body, and a large handle. The thumb, the ring, and the little finger are extended. In his left hand, he holds a fold of the chlamys. The thumb and the index finger are extended.

PORTRAIT D: SEATED FEMALE

The torso, right arm, and legs are shown in a three-quarter view. The left arm is shown in profile. The right arm is bent and raised to the neck, while the left falls along the side. The right leg is obscured by the reclining figure to her right.

She wears a veil that falls down the back of her head, over the shoulders, and along her right side.

She wears a tunic and a himation. The tunic has short sleeves. Over the tunic, she wears a himation that falls from the left shoulder, crosses the chest diagonally, and covers the legs. She wears pointed shoes.

With the right hand, she pulls the edge of the veil. Her left hand rests on the cushion and pulls the veil aside.

202. SARCOPHAGUS BOX RELIEF WITH STANDING FIGURES

DATABASE NUMBER: InSitu136.
LOCATION: Palmyra, in situ.
CONTEXT: West necropolis. Valley of the Tombs. Temple tomb no. 85b, tomb of Aʿaîlamî and Zebîdâ (>Tomb Cantineau<).
ACQUISITION HISTORY: —
MEASUREMENTS: Height: 85 cm. Width: 195 cm.
MATERIAL: Limestone.
PRESERVATION: The surface of all the figures is heavily chipped.
TECHNICAL DESCRIPTION: —
DATE: A.D. 200–240 (Makowski 1983: A.D. 200–230).
REFERENCES: Cantineau 1929, 12 pls. 2, 2. 3, 2; Makowski 1983, 187 cat. 6; Raja 2019e, 98. 131. 132 cat. 53.

Cat. 202

OBJECT DESCRIPTION

The sarcophagus box relief is rectangular in shape and depicts six standing figures. The figures are framed by a plain projecting edge on all four sides. According to Cantineau (1929, 12) the object depicts six caryatids.

PORTRAIT A: STANDING FIGURE

The figure is shown frontally. The right arm falls along the body. The figure wears a garment that reaches the ankles. Further details are unclear.

PORTRAIT B: STANDING FIGURE

The figure is shown frontally, the head is turned slightly to the left.

The hair is short and voluminous (details unclear).

The figure wears a garment with short sleeves, and that reaches the ankles. The folds of the garment are indicated by oblique grooves on the chest. Further details are unclear.

PORTRAIT C: STANDING FIGURE

The figure is shown frontally. The arms appear bent and held to the torso. Further details are unclear.

PORTRAIT D: STANDING FIGURE

The figure is shown frontally.

The figure wears a garment that reaches the ankles. Further details are unclear.

PORTRAIT E: STANDING FIGURE

The figure is shown frontally. The arms appear bent and held to the waist.

The figure wears a garment that reaches the knees. Oblique grooves on the chest and thighs indicate the folds of the garment.

PORTRAIT F: STANDING FIGURE

The figure is shown frontally.

The figure wears a garment that reaches the knees. Oblique grooves on the chest indicate the folds of the garment.

A.D. 220–240

203. SARCOPHAGUS BOX WITH PORTRAIT BUSTS

DATABASE NUMBER: InSitu158.
LOCATION: Palmyra, in situ.
CONTEXT: West necropolis. Valley of the Tombs. Temple tomb no. 85b, tomb of Aʿaîlamî and Zebîdâ (›Tomb Cantineau‹).
ACQUISITION HISTORY: —
MEASUREMENTS: Height: 48 cm. Width: 226 cm. Depth: 79 cm.
MATERIAL: Limestone.

Cat. 203

Cat. 204

PRESERVATION: The upper part of the sarcophagus box has broken off. The surface of the figures is chipped and weathered.
TECHNICAL DESCRIPTION: —
DATE: A.D. 220–240 (Makowski 1983: A.D. 230–273).
REFERENCES: Ingholt Archives, PS 531b; Makowski 1983, 187 cat. 13 pl. 50, d; Krag 2018, 32 n. 63; 53 n. 258; 58 n. 300. 304; 59 n. 323; 62 n. 349; 103 n. 74; 399 cat. 870.

OBJECT DESCRIPTION
The sarcophagus box is rectangular in shape and depicts four armless busts rendered in clipei. The box appears to be in the shape of a kline with legs, but only the plinth of the legs is preserved.

PORTRAIT A: ARMLESS FEMALE BUST
The figure is shown frontally.

The figure appears to wear a garment with a wide curving fold across the chest, possibly a veil.

PORTRAIT B: ARMLESS BUST
The figure is shown frontally.

PORTRAIT C: ARMLESS BUST
The figure is shown frontally.

PORTRAIT D: ARMLESS FEMALE BUST
The figure is shown frontally.

The figure appears to wear a garment with a wide, curving fold across the chest, possibly a veil.

FRAGMENTS OF LIDS, LID RELIEFS, OR BANQUETING RELIEFS

A.D. 180–200

204. FRAGMENT OF MALE FIGURE

DATABASE NUMBER: PM373.
LOCATION: Last known location: Palmyra, Palmyra Museum.
CONTEXT: West necropolis. Valley of the Tombs. Temple tomb no. 85b, tomb of Aʿaîlamî and Zebîdâ (›Tomb Cantineau‹).
ACQUISITION HISTORY: —
MEASUREMENTS: —
MATERIAL: Limestone.
PRESERVATION: The upper part of the figure is broken off across the torso, and the lower part is broken off at the height of the knees. The background is broken off on all sides.
TECHNICAL DESCRIPTION: —
DATE: A.D. 180–200 (Ingholt: A.D. 170–190).
REFERENCES: Ingholt Archives, PS 880; Seyrig 1937, 9. 16 fig. 1.

OBJECT DESCRIPTION
The object depicts the torso of a male figure.

PORTRAIT
The figure is shown frontally. The right arm is slightly bent and held next to the torso. He stands with the legs parted.

He wears a ›Parthian-style‹ tunic and ›Parthian-style‹ trousers. The tunic has long, tight-fitting sleeves and falls to the middle of the thighs. The tunic has a wide band that extends downwards from the middle of the neckline and is decorated with acanthus leaves. The cuffs of the tunic are decorated with wide bands with acanthus leaves. The hem is decorated with a band with a running scroll with five-petal rosettes. The folds of the tunic are indicated by oblique grooves. He wears a thin band belt around his waist. It is tied with a double knot and the ends are looped under on either side. He wears ›Parthian-style‹ trousers under the tunic. The trousers are loose. They have a wide band that extends downwards, decorated with a scales pattern. The trousers end in tight bands around the knees. The folds of the trousers are indicated by oblique grooves.

A.D. 200–220

205. FRAGMENT OF MALE FIGURE

DATABASE NUMBER: PM843.
LOCATION: Palmyra, Palmyra Museum, inv. no. unknown.
CONTEXT: West necropolis. Valley of the Tombs. Temple tomb no. 85b, tomb of Aʿaîlamî and Zebîdâ (›Tomb Cantineau‹).
ACQUISITION HISTORY: —
MEASUREMENTS: Height: 52 cm. Width: 29 cm. Depth: 23 cm.
MATERIAL: Limestone.
PRESERVATION: The upper part is broken off diagonally through the upper chest; the right side is broken off vertically through the right side of the torso; the lower part is broken off horizontally through the upper thigh.
TECHNICAL DESCRIPTION: —
DATE: A.D. 200–220 (Makowski 1983: A.D. 200–230).
REFERENCES: Makowski 1983, 187 cat. 9 pl. 52, c.

OBJECT DESCRIPTION
The object depicts a standing male.

PORTRAIT
The figure is shown in frontal view. The left arm is held along the body.

He wears a ›Parthian-style‹ tunic and trousers. The tunic has long, tight-fitting sleeves. At the middle, the tunic has a band decorated with a geometric pattern extending downwards (details unclear). The tunic ends above the knees and has a decorated lower border with a geometric pattern between beaded bands. The folds of the tunic are rendered by curving grooves. He wears a plain band belt, knotted at the centre with the ends looped under on either side of the waist. He also wears trousers. The folds are rendered by oblique and curving grooves.

He holds a branch with lanceolate leaves in his left hand. The midribs of the leaves are rendered by incised lines.

478 CATALOGUE

Cat. 205

A.D. 200–240

206. FRAGMENT OF A BANQUETING RELIEF

DATABASE NUMBER: InSitu152.
LOCATION: Palmyra, in situ.
CONTEXT: West necropolis. Valley of the Tombs. Temple tomb no. 85b, tomb of Aʿaîlamî and Zebîdâ (›Tomb Cantineau‹).
ACQUISITION HISTORY: —
MEASUREMENTS: —
MATERIAL: Limestone.
PRESERVATION: The head is broken off at the base of the neck, and the lower part is broken off at the waist. Both arms are broken off.
TECHNICAL DESCRIPTION: —
DATE: A.D. 200–240 (Makowski 1983: A.D. 170–190; Schmidt-Colinet 1992: A.D. 200–273).
REFERENCES: Ingholt Archives PS 881; Starcky 1941, 36 fig. 29; Makowski 1983, 186 cat. D pl. 50 fig. b; Schmidt-Colinet 1992, 110 n. 404c; 120 n. 440d pl. 72, c; Krag 2018, 56 n. 290; 58 n. 304; 62 n. 353; 64 n. 361. 362; 65 n. 374; 102 n. 69; 384 cat. 822. Inscription: Cantineau 1930a, 41 cat. 17; Krag 2018, 384 cat. 822.

OBJECT DESCRIPTION
The object depicts a reclining female. She rests the left arm against a cushion. It is decorated with a band with a vegetal motif set between beaded bands.

PORTRAIT
The figure is shown frontally. The left arm is bent.

She wears a veil. It is wrapped around her left lower arm and falls back over the right shoulder. Two wavy locks of hair fall down the right side of the neck and shoulder. The individual strands of hair are rendered by incised lines. She wears five necklaces: one composed of round beads worn at the base of the neck. One composed of a thin loop-in-loop chain with a central, circular pendant with an incised border, worn high on the chest. One composed of round beads with a central, oval pendant with a beaded border, where three spirally wrapped wires ending in round beads are suspended from the pendant. This is worn below the chest. Two necklaces composed of round beads and round pendants decorated with armless

Cat. 206

busts encircled by beaded edges are worn low on the chest and the pendants are placed at the sides, below each breast.

She wears a tunic and a himation. The tunic has a small, v-shaped neckline and short, wide sleeves. The folds of the tunic are rendered by curving and oblique grooves. Over the tunic, she wears a himation that crosses her chest in a curving fold from the right shoulder to the left side and covers the left breast. It is fastened at the left shoulder with a circular brooch with a polygon with curved sides meeting at flat ends, and an inner beaded border (Colledge classification: i). Three s-shaped folds fall from under her left arm and proceed downwards. The folds of the himation are rendered by curving and oblique grooves.

She wears an armlet on her right upper arm. It is composed of two entwining wires and is decorated with a large round element.

207. FRAGMENT OF A BANQUETING RELIEF

DATABASE NUMBER: InSitu150.
LOCATION: Palmyra, in situ.
CONTEXT: West necropolis. Valley of the Tombs. Temple tomb no. 85b, tomb of Aʿaîlamî and Zebîdâ (›Tomb Cantineau‹).
ACQUISITION HISTORY: —
MEASUREMENTS: Height: 61 cm. Width: 100 cm. Depth: 28 cm.
MATERIAL: Limestone.
PRESERVATION: The upper part is broken off at the waist and the feet are broken off. The right hand and the lower left corner of the mattress are chipped.
TECHNICAL DESCRIPTION: —
DATE: A.D. 200–240 (Makowski 1983: A.D. 170–190).
REFERENCES: Cantineau 1929, 12 pl. 2, 2. pl. 3, 2; Makowski 1983, 186 cat. 3 pl. 50, c; Krag 2018, 58 n. 304; 62 n. 353; 64 n. 361. 362; 65 n. 374; 88 n. 193. 195; 384 cat. 819. Inscription: Cantineau 1930a, 41 cat. 17; Krag 2018, 384 cat. 819; Inv IV. cat. 9e.

OBJECT DESCRIPTION
The object depicts a reclining figure. The figure rests on a thin mattress decorated with an intersecting lozenges pattern with four-petal flowers in the lozenges. The left side of the mattress is decorated with a wide band with a vegetal motif between beaded bands.

Cat. 207

INSCRIPTION

SCRIPT: Palmyrene Aramaic.
LOCATION ON RELIEF: On the folds of the garment.
TRANSCRIPTION: [- - -]NWR ZBYD᾽ | BYD[- - -].
TRANSLATION: - - - Zebîdâ - - -.

CIS no. —; PAT no. —.

COMMENT: Alternatively NWD (l. 1) and BYR (l. 2).

PORTRAIT: ZEBÎDÂ

The legs are bent, and the knees are rendered under the drapery. The figure wears a himation that covers his legs. The folds are rendered by curving and oblique folds.

208. FRAGMENT OF A BANQUETING RELIEF

DATABASE NUMBER: PM956.
LOCATION: Palmyra, Palmyra Museum, inv. no. unknown.
CONTEXT: West necropolis. Valley of the Tombs. Temple tomb no. 85b, tomb of Aʿaîlamî and Zebîdâ (›Tomb Cantineau‹).
ACQUISITION HISTORY: —
MEASUREMENTS: —
MATERIAL: Limestone.
PRESERVATION: The right and left side of the object are broken off. The head and neck are broken off. The surface is weathered.
TECHNICAL DESCRIPTION: —
DATE: A.D. 200–240.
REFERENCES: Will 1951, 87 fig. 6.

OBJECT DESCRIPTION

The object depicts a reclining male figure. He rests on a cushion at his left side. The texture and fabric of the cushion are rendered by curving grooves. The relief ground is preserved above the figure. There is a protruding plinth at the upper side.

PORTRAIT

The figure is shown frontally. The arms are bent in front of the torso.

He wears a tunic and a himation. The tunic has a wide, v-shaped neckline. The folds of the tunic are rendered by oblique grooves. The himation is wrapped over the edge of the right shoulder, over the left shoulder, and both arms, leaving most of the torso and the hands free.

A.D. 200–273

209. FRAGMENT OF A BANQUETING RELIEF

DATABASE NUMBER: PM851.
LOCATION: Palmyra, Palmyra Museum, inv. no. unknown.
CONTEXT: West necropolis. Valley of the Tombs. Temple tomb no. 85b, tomb of Aʿaîlamî and Zebîdâ (›Tomb Cantineau‹).
ACQUISITION HISTORY: —
MEASUREMENTS: —
MATERIAL: Limestone.
PRESERVATION: The object is broken on all sides. The head is broken off horizontally at the base of the neck and the lower part is broken off vertically at the right elbow and lower torso.
TECHNICAL DESCRIPTION: —
DATE: A.D. 200–273.
REFERENCES: Cantineau 1929, pl. 2, 1.

OBJECT DESCRIPTION

The object possibly depicts a reclining figure resting the arm on a cushion (details unclear).

PORTRAIT

The figure is shown in three-quarter view. The right arm is held out from the body. The left is bent.

210. FRAGMENT OF A BANQUETING RELIEF

DATABASE NUMBER: InSitu157.
LOCATION: Palmyra, in situ.
CONTEXT: West necropolis. Valley of the Tombs. Temple tomb no. 85b, tomb of Aʿaîlamî and Zebîdâ (›Tomb Cantineau‹).
ACQUISITION HISTORY: —
MEASUREMENTS: —
MATERIAL: Limestone.
PRESERVATION: The head is broken off horizontally at the base of the neck. The arms are broken off.
TECHNICAL DESCRIPTION: —
DATE: A.D. 200–273 (Makowski 1983: A.D. 230–273).
REFERENCES: Cantineau 1929, pl. 3, 1; Makowski 1983, 187 cat. E.

OBJECT DESCRIPTION

The object depicts a seated female (details unclear).

PORTRAIT

The figure is shown in three-quarter view. The legs are bent with the knees visible under the drapery.

She wears a long garment that covers her body and legs, possibly a himation. The folds are indicated by curving and oblique grooves.

211. FRAGMENT OF A BANQUETING RELIEF

DATABASE NUMBER: InSitu162.
LOCATION: Palmyra, in situ.
CONTEXT: West necropolis. Valley of the Tombs. Temple tomb no. 85b, tomb of Aʿaîlamî and Zebîdâ (>Tomb Cantineau<).
ACQUISITION HISTORY: —
MEASUREMENTS: —
MATERIAL: Limestone.
PRESERVATION: The relief is broken off on all sides. The head is broken off horizontally at the base of the neck.
TECHNICAL DESCRIPTION: —
DATE: A.D. 200–273.
REFERENCES: <https://www.loc.gov/item/mpc2005008584/PP/> (15.11.2022).

OBJECT DESCRIPTION
The object depicts a male bust. Below the figure is a band with oblique incised lines. The lower part of the lid is decorated with squares with lozenges that frame an arched niche.

PORTRAIT
The figure is shown in frontal view. The arms are bent and held in front of the lower torso.

He wears a tunic and a himation. The tunic has short, wide sleeves that reach below the elbows. It is decorated with two wide bands (clavi) extending downwards from the sides of the neckline. The folds of the tunic are rendered by curving grooves. Over the tunic he wears a himation that covers the left shoulder and arm. The folds of the himation are rendered by oblique grooves.

He holds an attribute in each hand (details unclear).

A.D. 220–240

212. FRAGMENT OF A BANQUETING RELIEF

DATABASE NUMBER: InSitu161.
LOCATION: Palmyra, Palmyra Museum, inv. no. unknown.
CONTEXT: West necropolis. Valley of the Tombs. Temple tomb no. 85b, tomb of Aʿaîlamî and Zebîdâ (>Tomb Cantineau<).
ACQUISITION HISTORY: —
MEASUREMENTS: —
MATERIAL: Limestone.
PRESERVATION: Portrait: The head is broken off horizontally at the base of the neck and the lower part is broken off diagonally at the lower torso. The hands are broken off. The attribute in the right hand is broken off.
TECHNICAL DESCRIPTION: —
DATE: A.D. 220–240 (Cantineau 1929: A.D. 200–273).
REFERENCES: Cantineau 1929, 10 pl. 3, 2; Makowski 1983, 186 cat. C; <https://www.loc.gov/item/mpc2005008584/PP/> (15.11.2022).

OBJECT DESCRIPTION
The object depicts a reclining male. He rests his left hand on a round cushion. The texture and fabric of the cushion are indicated by curving grooves.

PORTRAIT
The figure is shown frontally. The left arm is bent in front of the chest. His legs are obscured by the reclining figure to his right.

He wears a tunic and a himation. The folds of the tunic are rendered by curving grooves. Over the tunic, he wears a himation. It is wrapped around his left shoulder and upper arm. A wide fold of the himation falls downwards and over the cushion. The folds of the himation are rendered by oblique and curving grooves.

The outline of an object, possibly a bowl, is visible at the centre of his chest.

Cat. 211

OBJECTS FROM TEMPLE TOMBS 483

Cat. 212

213. FRAGMENT OF A BANQUETING RELIEF

DATABASE NUMBER: InSitu154.
LOCATION: Palmyra, in situ.
CONTEXT: West necropolis. Valley of the Tombs. Temple tomb no. 85b, tomb of Aʿaîlamî and Zebîdâ (›Tomb Cantineau‹).
ACQUISITION HISTORY: —
MEASUREMENTS: Height: 52 cm. Width: 82 cm.
MATERIAL: Limestone.
PRESERVATION: The head is broken off at the base of the neck and the lower and right side is broken off diagonally through the right arm and waist. The surface is weathered. The hands and the attribute are chipped.
TECHNICAL DESCRIPTION: Tool marks are visible on the background and frame.
DATE: A.D. 220–240 (Makowski 1983: A.D. 230–273).
REFERENCES: Cantineau 1929, 12 pl. 2, 1; Makowski 1983, 187 cat. 10 pl. 53, a.

OBJECT DESCRIPTION

The fragment depicts the torso of a reclining male. The figure rests on a mattress. It is decorated with an intersecting lozenges pattern with flowers in the lozenges. He rests the left arm against a cushion. It is decorated with a band with a running scroll with rosettes set between beaded bands.

Cat. 2013

PORTRAIT

The figure is shown in three-quarter view. The right arm is bent and held to the chest. The left is bent and rests along his side.

He wears a tunic and a himation. The tunic has a wide, v-shaped neckline that leaves a part of the upper torso bare. The folds are rendered by curving grooves. Over the tunic, he wears a himation. The himation covers most of the body: it is wrapped around the shoulders and right arm. It proceeds in a curving fold across the lower torso and is folded around his left wrist. A wide fold of the himation falls from under his left hand. The folds of the himation are rendered by vertical and curving grooves.

With his right hand he holds a cup (visible only in outline, other details unclear). His left hand rests on the cushion. He holds a looped fold of the himation with his thumb and index finger. All the fingers are extended. He appears to be wearing five thick hoop finger rings: one in the upper phalanx of the index, middle, and ring finger, and two on the little finger.

214. FRAGMENT OF A BANQUETING RELIEF

DATABASE NUMBER: InSitu156.
LOCATION: Palmyra, in situ.
CONTEXT: West necropolis. Valley of the Tombs. Temple tomb no. 85b, tomb of Aʿaîlamî and Zebîdâ (›Tomb Cantineau‹).
ACQUISITION HISTORY: —
MEASUREMENTS: Height: 24 cm. Width: 146 cm.
MATERIAL: Limestone.
PRESERVATION: The right, left, and upper side are broken off. The surface is very weathered. Only the right leg of the figure, from thigh to foot, is preserved.
TECHNICAL DESCRIPTION: There are traces of tool marks from a tooth chisel on the plinth and the plaque itself.
DATE: A.D. 220–240 (Makowski 1983: A.D. 230–273).
REFERENCES: Makowski 1983, 187 cat. 12 pl. 53, d.

OBJECT DESCRIPTION

The fragment depicts a standing figure. There is a protruding edge on the right side and the relief ground between the figure and the plinth is preserved.

PORTRAIT

The leg is slightly bent with the knee visible in the drapery. The foot is extended.

The figure is wearing an ankle-length garment. The folds are rendered by curving and oblique grooves.

215. FRAGMENT OF A MALE FIGURE

DATABASE NUMBER: InSitu163.
LOCATION: Palmyra, in situ.
CONTEXT: West necropolis. Valley of the Tombs. Temple tomb no. 85b, tomb of Aʿaîlamî and Zebîdâ (›Tomb Cantineau‹).
ACQUISITION HISTORY: —
MEASUREMENTS: —
MATERIAL: Limestone.
PRESERVATION: The relief is broken off on all sides. The figure survives in two joining fragments. The feet, the right part of the legs, and the upper part of the figure are broken off.
TECHNICAL DESCRIPTION: —
DATE: A.D. 220–240.
REFERENCES: <https://www.loc.gov/item/mpc2010000996/PP/> (07.07.2022).

OBJECT DESCRIPTION

The object depicts the legs of a reclining male figure.

PORTRAIT

The figure is shown in three-quarter view. Both legs are bent and raised, the right one higher than the left. The right hand touches the right knee.

He wears a himation. The himation covers both legs. The folds of the himation are rendered by wide oblique grooves.

The fingers of the right hand are extended.

216. FRAGMENT OF A MALE FIGURE

DATABASE NUMBER: InSitu164.
LOCATION: Palmyra, in situ.
CONTEXT: West necropolis. Valley of the Tombs. Temple tomb no. 85b, tomb of Aʿaîlamî and Zebîdâ (›Tomb Cantineau‹).
ACQUISITION HISTORY: —
MEASUREMENTS: —
MATERIAL: Limestone.
PRESERVATION: The relief is broken off on all sides. The figure survives in two non-joining fragments. Fragment A: Only part of the left arm and left side of the torso, and the cushions survive. Fragment B: Part of the torso.
TECHNICAL DESCRIPTION: —
DATE: A.D. 220–240.
REFERENCES: <https://www.loc.gov/item/mpc2010000996/PP/> (15.11.2022).

OBJECT DESCRIPTION

The object depicts part of the torso of a reclining male figure. He rests his right arm on two round cushions, placed one on top of the other. The texture of the cushions is indicated by curving grooves.

Cat. 215

Cat. 216

PORTRAIT

The figure is shown in three-quarter view. The right arm is bent and held in front of the chest.

He wears a tunic and a chlamys. The tunic has two bands that extend downwards (clavi). They are decorated with a floral motif (details unclear). Over the tunic he wears a chlamys that covers the left side of the chest, the left shoulder, and left arm. The edge of the chlamys is decorated with a band with a running scroll with six-petal rosettes inside. The inner part of the petals is hollowed out. Part of the chlamys falls across the cushions in two zigzag-shaped folds.

He holds a bowl in front of his chest with his left hand (other details unclear).

Cat. 217

217. FRAGMENT OF A MALE FIGURE

DATABASE NUMBER: InSitu165.
LOCATION: Palmyra, in situ.
CONTEXT: West necropolis. Valley of the Tombs. Temple tomb no. 85b, tomb of Aʿaîlamî and Zebîdâ (›Tomb Cantineau‹).
ACQUISITION HISTORY: —
MEASUREMENTS: —
MATERIAL: Limestone.
PRESERVATION: The relief is broken off on all sides. Only part of the lower left body of the figure survives. The relief is heavily chipped and weathered.
TECHNICAL DESCRIPTION: —
DATE: A.D. 220–240.
REFERENCES: <https://www.loc.gov/item/mpc2010000996/PP/> (15.11.2022).

OBJECT DESCRIPTION

The object depicts part of the lower left body of a reclining male figure. Next to him is a round cushion, decorated with a wide band between beaded bands.

PORTRAIT

The figure is shown in three-quarter view.

He wears a garment (details unclear) and a chlamys. Part of the chlamys falls across the cushion in a zigzag-shaped fold.

218. FRAGMENT OF A MALE FIGURE

DATABASE NUMBER: InSitu160.
LOCATION: Palmyra, in situ.
CONTEXT: West necropolis. Valley of the Tombs. Temple tomb no. 85b, tomb of Aʿaîlamî and Zebîdâ (›Tomb Cantineau‹).
ACQUISITION HISTORY: —
MEASUREMENTS: —
MATERIAL: Limestone.
PRESERVATION: The head is broken off horizontally at the base of the neck and the lower part is broken off at the waist.
TECHNICAL DESCRIPTION: —
DATE: A.D. 220–240 (Makowski 1983: A.D. 200–230).
REFERENCES: Makowski 1983, pl. 52, c.

OBJECT DESCRIPTION

The object depicts the torso of a male figure.

PORTRAIT

The figure is shown frontally. Both arms are bent and held to the chest.

He wears a tunic and a himation. The tunic has a wide, v-shaped neckline and long, tight-fitting sleeves. The folds of the tunic are rendered by curving and oblique grooves. Over the tunic, he wears a himation. It is folded over his left shoulder and proceeds across the torso and right side. The folds of the himation are rendered by curving and oblique grooves.

He holds a rectangular object in his left hand (details unclear). With the right hand, he lightly touches the upper part of the object with his extended index and middle finger.

Cat. 218

A.D. 240–273

219. FRAGMENT OF A BANQUETING RELIEF

DATABASE NUMBER: InSitu155.
LOCATION: Palmyra, in situ.
CONTEXT: West necropolis. Valley of the Tombs. Temple tomb no. 85b, tomb of Aʿaîlamî and Zebîdâ (›Tomb Cantineau‹).
ACQUISITION HISTORY: —
MEASUREMENTS: Height: 42 cm. Width: 70 cm. Depth: 61 cm.
MATERIAL: Limestone.
PRESERVATION: Broken on all sides. Only a small part of the torso and left arm is preserved.
TECHNICAL DESCRIPTION: —
DATE: A.D. 240–273 (Makowski 1983: A.D. 230–273).
REFERENCES: Makowski 1983, 187 cat. 11 pl. 53, b.

OBJECT DESCRIPTION

The object depicts a reclining figure. He rests the left arm against a cushion. The cushion is folded into itself and is decorated with three bands. The uppermost band is decorated with flowers with lobed petals and separated by horizontal bands. The other two bands are decorated with serrated leaves. Curving grooves indicated the texture of the cushion.

PORTRAIT

The left arm rests along his side.

He wears a ›Parthian-style‹ tunic decorated with a band extending downwards with four-petal flowers with serrated leaves with incised midribs rendered in lozenges. He wears a plain band belt, with one end looped under the central strap. Another garment is folded around his wrist and continues in a wide fold over the cushion. One edge of the garment is scalloped. The folds of the garment are rendered by deep grooves.

The outline of an oblong object is recognizable under his hand (details unclear).

FRAGMENTS OF BOXES, BOX RELIEFS, OR BANQUETING RELIEFS

A.D. 200–220

220. FRAGMENT OF A FEMALE FIGURE

DATABASE NUMBER: PM844.
LOCATION: Palmyra, Palmyra Museum, inv. no. unknown.
CONTEXT: West necropolis, Valley of the Tombs. Temple tomb no. 85b, tomb of Aʿaîlamî and Zebîdâ (›Tomb Cantineau‹).
ACQUISITION HISTORY: —
MEASUREMENTS: Height: 52 cm. Width: 29 cm. Depth: 23 cm.
MATERIAL: Limestone.
PRESERVATION: The object is broken on all four sides. The head is broken off (visible in outline) and most of the legs are broken off.
TECHNICAL DESCRIPTION: —
DATE: A.D. 200–220 (Makowski 1983: A.D. 200–230).
REFERENCES: Makowski 1983, 187 pl. 52, c.

OBJECT DESCRIPTION

Fragment of sarcophagus with female figure.

PORTRAIT

The figure is shown in frontal to three-quarter view. Her arms are bent; the right arm is held in front of the chest, and the left arm is held on the right hip.

She wears a tunic and a himation. The tunic has a wide, v-shaped neckline. Over the tunic, she wears a himation. The himation is pulled over her head, covering the back of the head and is wrapped around the right shoulder, arm, and most of the lower body, covering most of the body. One fold of the himation crosses the chest diagonally and falls over the left shoulder (›arm-sling‹ type), covering the left arm.

The right hand holds the diagonal fold of the himation. With the left hand, she touches her right hip. All the fingers are extended.

Car. 220

SARCOPHAGUS FRAGMENTS

A.D. 200–273

221. FRAGMENT OF A SARCOPHAGUS LID

DATABASE NUMBER: PM782.
LOCATION: Palmyra, Palmyra Museum, inv. no. unknown.
CONTEXT: West necropolis, Valley of the Tombs. Temple tomb no. 85b, tomb of Aʿaîlamî and Zebîdâ (›Tomb Cantineau‹).
ACQUISITION HISTORY: —
MEASUREMENTS: Height: 50 cm. Width: 80 cm. Depth: —.
MATERIAL: Limestone.
PRESERVATION: Only a small fragment of the sarcophagus lid has been preserved. The surface is weathered and chipped.
TECHNICAL DESCRIPTION: —
DATE: A.D. 200–273.
REFERENCES: Ingholt Archives, PS 550; Cantineau 1929, 13 pl. 4, 1; Makowski 1983, pl. 52c; Krag 2018, 32 n. 63; 58 n. 304; 103 n. 74; 401 cat. 877.

OBJECT DESCRIPTION

The object is irregular in shape and depicts a standing female. She is shown on a plinth in a niche that is framed by two columns and an arch that has the form of a shell. To her sides, diamond-shaped forms that contain vegetal decorations are depicted. Above her, a wide band of twisted wires is indicating a kline.

PORTRAIT

The figure is shown frontally. Her right arm is stretched and held to the body. Her left arm is bent and raised to the height of the neck.

She wears two headdresses: a turban and a veil. The veil falls over both shoulders and is wrapped around her arms. Her face is round; details cannot be described due to the weathering. She wears a tunic that is falling all the way down to her feet. She holds the fold of the veil with her right hand at the height of her thigh. With the left hand, she holds the veil at the height of her neck.

Cat. 221

490 CATALOGUE

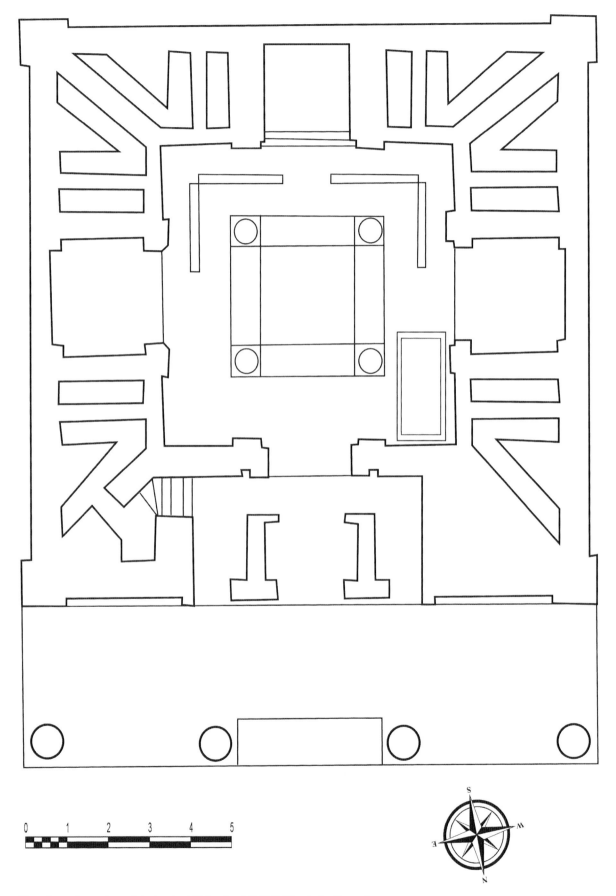

Plan of temple tomb no. 85b, tomb of Aʿaîlamî and Zebîdâ (›Tomb Cantineau‹).

OBJECTS FROM TEMPLE TOMBS 491

Temple tomb no. 85b, tomb of Aʿaîlamî and Zebîdâ (›Tomb Cantineau‹). Interior of the tomb. American Colony. Photo Dept, photographer. (1929) Palmyra, May. Syria Tadmur, 1929. May. [Photograph] Retrieved from the Library of Congress <https://www.loc.gov/item/mpc2005008584/PP/> (15.11.2022).

Temple tomb no. 85b, tomb of Aʿaîlamî and Zebîdâ (›Tomb Cantineau‹). Interior of the tomb. American Colony, P. D., photographer. (1920) Palmyra. Remains of a tomb temple. Palmyrene type of reclining figures. Syria Tadmur, 1920. [Approximately to 1933] [Photograph] Retrieved from the Library of Congress <https://www.loc.gov/item/mpc2010000996/PP/> (15.11.2022).

Cat. 222

A.D. 200–240

TEMPLE TOMB NO. 173D

SARCOPHAGUS LIDS OR LID RELIEFS

A.D. 200–240

222. FRAGMENT OF A SARCOPHAGUS LID RELIEF WITH BANQUETING SCENE

DATABASE NUMBER: InSitu144.
LOCATION: Palmyra, in situ.
CONTEXT: West necropolis. Temple tomb no. 173d.
ACQUISITION HISTORY: —
MEASUREMENTS: —
MATERIAL: Limestone.
PRESERVATION: Most of the background is broken off. The lower right side of the relief is broken off. The surface is weathered. Portrait A: The upper part of the figure is broken off at the waist. Portrait B: The head is broken off at the base of the neck. The lower left arm is broken off. The right arm is chipped. The surface is weathered.
TECHNICAL DESCRIPTION: —
DATE: A.D. 200–240.

REFERENCES: Schmidt-Colinet 1996, 370. 487 fig. 222.

OBJECT DESCRIPTION

The sarcophagus lid is rectangular in shape and depicts a standing male and a reclining male. Between them, there are traces of either another standing figure, or an altar. The figures rest on a mattress decorated with an intersecting lozenges pattern with four-petal flowers in the lozenges. There is a round element at the point where the lozenges intersect. The reclining figure rests on a round cushion decorated with a wide band with rosettes inside circles or a running scroll. The band is framed by a beaded band. The texture of the cushion is indicated by wide, curving grooves.

PORTRAIT A: STANDING MALE

The figure is shown frontally. He is standing with the legs apart. His left arm falls to the side. The left leg and right foot are obscured by the reclining figure.

He wears a >Parthian-style< tunic and >Parthian-style< trousers. The tunic is decorated with a wide band at the hem (details unclear). The trousers are decorated with a wide band that extends downwards (details unclear).

He holds an object in his left hand (details unclear).

Cat. 223

PORTRAIT B: RECLINING MALE

The figure's torso and upper left leg are shown frontally, the arms and legs are shown in profile. The arms are bent; the right in front of the chest, the left is held at the side. The right leg is bent and raised with the foot resting on the mattress; the left leg is bent under the right leg. The lower part of the left leg is obscured by the right leg.

He wears a tunic and himation. The tunic has a wide, round neckline. The folds of the tunic are indicated by curving grooves in the area of the torso and legs, and oblique ones at the arms. Over the tunic, he wears a himation that is wrapped around the left arm, crosses the chest diagonally, and falls over the left shoulder and arm (following the >arm-sling< type). It covers the torso and lower body completely. The folds of the himation are indicated by oblique grooves, except in the area of the lower torso, where they are indicated by curving grooves. He wears sandals (visible at the right leg). They cover the heel with a wide strap that stretches across the top of the foot.

With his right hand, he holds the diagonal fold of the himation.

A.D. 200–273

TEMPLE TOMB NO. 174

SARCOPHAGUS BOXES

A.D. 200–273

223. SARCOPHAGUS BOX WITH PORTRAIT BUSTS

DATABASE NUMBER: PM784.
LOCATION: Palmyra, Palmyra Museum, inv. no. unknown.
CONTEXT: North necropolis. Temple tomb no. 174.
ACQUISITION HISTORY: —
MEASUREMENTS: —
MATERIAL: Limestone.
PRESERVATION: The sarcophagus box has broken in two between portraits C and D. The surface of the sarcophagus and portraits is very weathered and chipped.
TECHNICAL DESCRIPTION: —
DATE: A.D. 200–273.
REFERENCES: Ingholt Archives, PS 874; Gawlikowski 1970a, 133 fig. 77; al-Asʿad 2013, 18; Krag 2018, 32 n. 63; 53 n. 258; 58 n. 300. 304; 59 n. 323; 62 n. 349; 103 n. 74; 399 cat. 784.

OBJECT DESCRIPTION

The sarcophagus box is rectangular in shape and is rendered as a kline. Six busts are rendered in clipei between the kline legs. Above the kline is a mattress. The mattress is decorated with four bands (details unclear). The texture of the fabric is indicated by curving grooves. The kline has two turned legs (details unclear). Between each portrait, an animal head is shown, each carrying a ring in the mouth.

Cat. 224

PORTRAIT A: ARMLESS BUST OF PRIEST

The figure is shown frontally, rendered in a clipeus.

The outline of a tall, cylindrical headdress with a flat top is visible: a Palmyrene priestly hat.

He wears a tunic and a chlamys. The tunic has a wide, v-shaped neckline. Over the tunic, he wears a chlamys. It is fastened at the left shoulder with a brooch (details unclear).

PORTRAIT B: ARMLESS FEMALE BUST

The figure is shown frontally, rendered in a clipeus.

The outline of a veil is visible, and it falls in a wide, curving fold across the chest.

PORTRAIT C: ARMLESS BUST. GENDER UNCERTAIN

The figure is shown frontally, rendered in a clipeus.

The figure wears a garment with a wide fold across the chest, possibly a himation.

PORTRAIT D: ARMLESS BUST. GENDER UNCERTAIN

The figure is shown frontally, rendered in a clipeus. Possibly a male.

The details are unclear.

PORTRAIT E: ARMLESS FEMALE BUST

The figure is shown frontally, rendered in a clipeus.

The outline of a veil is visible, and it falls over her shoulders and crosses her chest in a curving fold.

PORTRAIT F: ARMLESS BUST. GENDER UNCERTAIN

The figure is shown frontally.

The details are unclear.

A.D. 220–240

TEMPLE TOMB NO. 75

SARCOPHAGUS FRAGMENTS

A.D. 220–240

---

224. FRAGMENT OF A MALE FIGURE

DATABASE NUMBER: InSitu194.
LOCATION: Last known location: Palmyra.
CONTEXT: West necropolis. Temple tomb no. 75.
ACQUISITION HISTORY: —
MEASUREMENTS: —
MATERIAL: Limestone.
PRESERVATION: Only the figure and its immediate, surrounding background are preserved. The head and neck of the figure are broken off. The left foot is broken off. The right arm, the jug, and the legs are heavily chipped.
TECHNICAL DESCRIPTION: —
DATE: A.D. 220–240.

REFERENCES: Ingholt Archives PS 1280; Seyrig 1933c, 372 n. 1. 379 fig. 3; Seyrig 1937, 43 n. 1.

OBJECT DESCRIPTION
The object depicts a standing male on a projecting plinth.

PORTRAIT
The figure is shown frontally. His left arm is bent and raised to the height of the chest, the right falls to the side. The legs are slightly parted, and the feet are at an angle.

He wears a >Parthian-style< tunic, and >Parthian-style< trousers. The tunic has a wide, round neckline with a beaded border. A band extends downwards from the middle of the neckline; it is decorated with a vegetal motif. The sides of the tunic are slit, and the hem is decorated with a border with a vegetal motif. He wears a plain band belt at the waist, tied at the centre with a knot and with the ends looped over the sides. Against the right hip he has an object with a rectangular main body and two protrusions in the shape of a quarter-circle: a sheathed dagger. A second plain band belt crosses the hips: it is fastened with a round buckle, from which one end falls down. An object with a rectangular main body with two rectangular protrusions at the upper part is fastened to the belt: a sheathed sword. He wears trousers (other details unclear). He also wears undecorated, round-toe boots that reach up to the ankles.

With his left hand he holds the bottom of a jug. With his right hand he holds a handle or the body of the vase.

TEMPLE TOMB NO. 159

FRAGMENTS OF LIDS, LID RELIEFS, OR BANQUETING RELIEFS

A.D. 220–240

225. FRAGMENT OF A BANQUETING RELIEF

DATABASE NUMBER: InSitu186.
LOCATION: Palmyra, in situ.
CONTEXT: North necropolis. Temple tomb no. 159.
ACQUISITION HISTORY: —
MEASUREMENTS: —
MATERIAL: Limestone, white/yellow.
PRESERVATION: The head is broken off at the base of the neck, and the lower part is broken off at the waist. Both the right and left lower arm are broken off. The surface is very fragmented.
TECHNICAL DESCRIPTION: —
DATE: A.D. 220–240 (Schmidt-Colinet 1992: A.D. 200–273).

Cat. 225

REFERENCES: Watzinger – Wulzinger 1932, 65; Schmidt-Colinet 1992, 110 n. 404 e; pl. 72, e; Henning 2013b, 272; Krag 2018, 58 n. 304; 62 n. 353; 64 n. 361. 362; 65 n. 374; 384 cat. 823.

OBJECT DESCRIPTION

The object depicts a reclining female. She rests the left arm against a cushion. It is decorated with a band with a vegetal motif between beaded bands. Curving grooves indicate the texture of the fabric.

PORTRAIT

The figure is shown frontally. The left arm is bent and raised to the neck.

She wears a veil. It falls over her shoulders. She wears three necklaces. The first is composed of a thin loop-in-loop chain with a central pendant worn low on the neck. The second is composed of round beads and a central, crescent-shaped pendant, worn on the chest. The third is composed of a loop-in-loop chain with a central, oval pendant, worn at the chest.

She wears a tunic and a himation. The tunic has a small, v-shaped neckline. The folds of the tunic are rendered by curving and oblique grooves. Over the tunic, she wears a himation. It is folded from behind and across the torso in a curving fold that is wrapped around her left arm. The folds of the himation are rendered by curving and vertical grooves.

TEMPLE TOMB NO. 173B

SARCOPHAGUS LIDS OR LID RELIEFS

A.D. 220–240

226. FRAGMENT OF A SARCOPHAGUS LID WITH BANQUETING SCENE

DATABASE NUMBER: InSitu173.
LOCATION: Palmyra, in situ.
CONTEXT: West necropolis. Temple tomb 173b.
ACQUISITION HISTORY: —
MEASUREMENTS: —
MATERIAL: Limestone.
PRESERVATION:
TECHNICAL DESCRIPTION: —
DATE: A.D. 220–240.
REFERENCES: Seyrig 1937, 17 n. 4. 24 fig. 16; Schmidt-Colinet 1992, 111 n. 412d.

OBJECT DESCRIPTION

The object depicts a reclining male on a mattress. He rests his left arm on a round cushion decorated with a band at the centre. According to Seyrig the band is decorated with animals inside medallions. The mattress is decorated with an intersecting lozenges pattern with cruciform, four-petal flowers in the lozenges, and two wide bands with vegetal motifs framed by beaded bands.

PORTRAIT

The torso of the figure is shown frontally, with the left arm and lower left leg in three-quarter view, and the right arm and leg in profile. The left arm is bent and held in front of the torso. The right arm is bent and resting on the cushion. His right leg is bent. The left leg is extended.

He wears a ›Parthian-style‹ tunic, and a himation. The tunic has a wide, round neckline, and two wide bands extend downwards from the sides of the neckline. The bands are decorated with geometrical patterns (other details unclear). The folds of the tunic are rendered by curving grooves. Over the tunic he wears a himation. It is wrapped over both shoulders and arms and covers the lower body. One fold of the himation passes under the lower left arm, crosses the torso, is wrapped around the right wrist, and falls across the cushion in two zigzag-shaped folds. The himation is decorated with a wide panel with two projecting rectangles on one side at the area over the left knee. The panel is decorated (other details unclear).

With his left hand he holds a pinecone in front of his chest. The thumb, index finger, and little finger are extended. With his right hand he holds a looped fold of the himation.

TEMPLE TOMB NO. 173C

FRAGMENTS OF SARCOPHAGUS LIDS, LID RELIEFS, OR BANQUETING RELIEFS

A.D. 220–240

227. FRAGMENT OF A BANQUETING RELIEF

DATABASE NUMBER: InSitu195.
LOCATION: Palmyra, in situ.
CONTEXT: South-west necropolis. Temple tomb 173c.
ACQUISITION HISTORY: —
MEASUREMENTS: —
MATERIAL: Limestone.
PRESERVATION: Broken on the right, upper, and the left side. The upper part of the figure is broken horizontally at the base of the neck and the lower part is broken off diagonally through the legs. The surface of the lower right arm, of the right and left knee, and of the left hand is chipped.
TECHNICAL DESCRIPTION: —
DATE: A.D. 220–240 (Seyrig 1937: A.D. 150–200).
REFERENCES: Ingholt Archives, PS 975; Seyrig 1937, 16 n. 2. 29 fig. 7.

OBJECT DESCRIPTION

The object depicts a reclining male. The figure is resting on a mattress. It is decorated with an intersecting lozenges pattern with four-petal flowers in the lozenges. The centre of the

OBJECTS FROM TEMPLE TOMBS 497

Cat. 227

petals is rendered by incised lines. The left arm rests against a cushion. The cushion is folded into itself and is decorated with a band with a floral motif set between beaded bands.

PORTRAIT
The figure is shown in three-quarter view. The right arm is extended. The left arm is bent and held to the chest. The right leg is bent.

He wears a ›Parthian-style‹ tunic, a chlamys, and trousers. The tunic has a wide, round neckline leaving the uppermost part of the chest free. A vertical groove at the neckline indicates the chest musculature. The tunic has long, slightly loose sleeves and ends above the knees. The lower border of the tunic is decorated with a running dog motif. The folds of the tunic are rendered by oblique and curving grooves. He wears a band belt, knotted in the centre with the ends looped under on either side. Along his right thigh is an object with a round end, a rectangular main body, and a round lateral element: a sheathed dagger. Over the tunic, he wears a chlamys that falls over both shoulders, and covers most of the chest. One edge of the chlamys has a scalloped border visible across the chest. It is fastened at the right shoulder with a triangular brooch (Colledge classification: c). An s-shaped fold falls from under the brooch. A wide fold of the chlamys falls from under the left hand, proceeds along his left side, and ends in an s-shaped fold. The folds of the chlamys are rendered by oblique and curving grooves. The folds of the trousers are rendered by wide, curving folds.

A.D. 220–273

TEMPLE TOMB NO. 36

SARCOPHAGI

A.D. 220–240

228. FRAGMENTS OF A COMPLETE SARCOPHAGUS WITH BANQUETING SCENE AND CARAVAN SCENE

DATABASE NUMBER: PM491 (228a) + PM886 (228b) + PM471 (228c) + PM864 (228d).
LOCATION: Palmyra, Palmyra Museum, inv. no. 652–653, I.d.5/II.a.5–7; 16–19; 23/II.d.5, II.d.3–4, II.15–16, 83.12.2, II.a.11.
CONTEXT: West necropolis. Valley of the Tombs. Temple tomb no. 36.
ACQUISITION HISTORY: —
MEASUREMENTS: 228a: Height: 88 cm. Width: 134 cm. 228b: Fragment A: Height: 90 cm (reconstructed). Width: 135 cm (reconstructed). Fragment B: Height: 11 cm. Fragment C: Height: 11 cm. Fragment D: Height: 6.5 cm. Length: 36 cm. Fragment E: Height: 11 cm. Length: 17 cm. 228c: Height: 25 cm. 228d: Height: 5 cm.

MATERIAL: Limestone.
PRESERVATION: Two non-joining fragments possibly from same lid, and joining fragments along with two non-joining fragments from the box. 228a: The object is broken vertically on the left side. The relief ground is broken off. Portrait A: The upper part is broken off horizontally at the base of the neck and diagonally from the left shoulder to the left side. The right hand is chipped. Portrait B: The head is broken off horizontally at the base of the neck. The tip of the right foot and the upper right thigh and knee are broken off. 228b: Fragment A: The left, right, lower sides of the relief are broken off. Most of the background is broken off. Horse at right side of relief: the head and neck, top of back, front legs and left, back leg are broken off. The camel on the left side of the relief: part of the object on its back and the legs are broken off. Fragments B and C: Only the lower leg is preserved. Fragment D: Fragment of a kline frame. Fragment E: The fragment is broken on all sides. Portrait C: The head, lower right arm, and legs from above the knees are broken off. The neck, left arm, upper right arm, and thighs are chipped. 228c: The head is broken off at the neck. The top and upper right side of the headdress, the right ear, and the tip of the nose are chipped. 228d: The portrait is broken off diagonally at the

Cat. 228

height of the nose. The upper part of the head is broken off. Cracks run across the surface.

TECHNICAL DESCRIPTION: —
DATE: A.D. 220–240 (Schmidt-Colinet 1992: A.D. 210–240).
REFERENCES: 228a: Schmidt-Colinet 1992, 13. 23. 105. 109. 111 f. 120. 125. 133–135. 138. 139 f. 148 cat. B 2 figs. 54. 55. 57. 61; pl. 35, d; 36; Krag 2018, 28 n. 9; 58 n. 298; 59 n. 315; 62 n. 351. 353; 65 n. 369; 66 n. 384. 385; 101 n. 65; 387 cat. 834. 228b: Schmidt-Colinet 1992, 13. 23. 105. 106. 108 f. 130. 133–135. 138 f. 146–148. cat. S 5 figs. 59. 61; 32, b. h; 33. Schmidt-Colinet 2018b, 66 fig. 1; 229c: al-Asʿad – Schmidt-Colinet 1985, 34 pl. 11, d; Schmidt-Colinet 1992, 112. 122. 137. 152 cat. K 1 fig. 52; pl. 47, a. b. 229d: Schmidt-Colinet 1992, 137 f. 154 cat. K 26 fig. 53; pl. 49, i.

OBJECT DESCRIPTION

The sarcophagus lid (228a) is rectangular in shape and depicts a seated female and a reclining male. Beneath the figures is a thin mattress. It is decorated with an intersecting lozenge pattern with four-petal flowers in the lozenges. The midribs of the leaves are incised. The female sits in two large cushions (details unclear). The male rests the left arm against a cushion. It has a band decorated with a running scroll with rosettes within circles, between beaded bands. Curving grooves indicate the texture of the fabric on the left cushion. The box (228b) is in the shape of a kline with turned legs. The foot of the leg is not preserved, but above is a reversed bell-shaped element, a concave quarter, a torus, a concave quarter, a ball, a reversed concave quarter, and a bell-shaped element. All the elements are decorated with a tongues pattern, rendered diagonally on the ball. The frame of the kline is decorated with two square panels with a rosette, framing a rectangular panel with a running scroll. The lower end of the fulcrum is decorated with a six-petal rosette. The texture of the mattress is indicated by curving grooves. A figure leading a camel and a horse shown in profile is depicted to the right of the kline leg. The horse on the right side moves towards the left. A wide band decorated with a running scroll crosses under the horse's belly. A cylindrical object decorated with two bands with beaded borders with objects composed of narrow shafts with a pointed tip is depicted behind the band: quiver with arrows. A side-strap is depicted crossing the horse's rump. The rein of the horse is depicted as a thin band. The camel on the left side moves towards the right. A small, round shield decorated with small circles is depicted over the camel's left back thigh. A square saddlecloth with a crisscross pattern, a beaded border, and a tassel at the lower right corner is depicted over the camel's back. Three ropes secure an object on the camel's back. They are fastened on a hook of a strap that crosses under the belly. Two more ropes cross the rump of the animal, and another

Cat. 228

Cat. 228

Cat. 228

strap is at the base of the camel's neck. The rein of the camel is depicted as a thick rope secured around the top of the camel's neck. 228c depicts the head of a priest (portrait C) and belongs to the sarcophagus lid (according to Schmidt-Colinet 1992).

Several other fragments belong together with this sarcophagus. Fragments B and C: Leg of a figure wearing ›Parthian-style‹ trousers. The trousers are loose fitting and decorated with a wide, central band that extends downwards. The band is decorated with squares with four-petal flowers divided by beaded bands. Fragment D: Kline frame. Decorated with running dog pattern, rosettes, acanthus leaf, over horizontal lines. Fragment E: Mattress fragment. Wide band from the decoration of the mattress with a vine scroll with leaves and cluster of grapes framed by beaded border. 228d depicts the head of a male figure (portrait E) and belongs to the box (according to Schmidt-Colinet 1992).

SARCOPHAGUS LID

PORTRAIT A: SEATED FEMALE

The figure is shown in three-quarter view. The right arm is bent, resting on her right thigh. The left arm is bent and raised to the shoulder. Her legs are bent, and the right knee is visible in the drapery. Her feet are obscured by the reclining figure.

She wears a veil. It falls over her right shoulder and is folded around the left lower arm. She wears four necklaces: one composed of small, round beads on a string worn at the base of the neck. One composed of alternating square and round pendants with incised borders, joined by vertical beaded elements, worn high on the chest. One composed of small, round beads with a central, crescent-shaped pendant suspended by a wide sleeve, worn at the middle of the chest. One composed of a wide loop-in-loop chain with a central, oval pendant with an outer beaded border. Three small loop-in-loop chains ending in trefoil-shaped pendants are suspended from the oval pendant. The necklace is worn below the breasts.

She wears a tunic and a himation. The tunic has a small, round neckline and sleeves reaching the elbows. The folds of the tunic are rendered by curving and oblique grooves. Over the tunic, she wears a himation. The himation crosses the chest diagonally from the left shoulder to the right side and covers the left breast and proceeds over her legs. The folds of the himation are rendered by oblique and curving grooves.

With her right hand, she holds an end of the veil. Her thumb and the index finger are extended. She wears a bracelet on her right wrist. It is composed of twisted plain and beaded wires. She also wears a bracelet around her left wrist (details unclear).

PORTRAIT B: RECLINING MALE

The figure is shown in frontal to three-quarter view. The right arm is bent and held to the chest. The left arm is bent and rests at his side. The right leg is bent, and he rests his foot on the mattress. The left leg is bent under the right leg, and the lower part is obscured by the right leg.

Cat. 228

Cat. 228

He wears a ›Parthian-style‹ tunic, a himation, and ›Parthian-style‹ trousers. The tunic has a wide, round neckline decorated with alternating round and square elements. The tunic has long, tight-fitting sleeves. The cuffs of the sleeves are decorated with a wide band with flowers in lozenges, followed by a beaded band. At the middle, the tunic has a wide band decorated with serrated leaves in an opposite arrangement between two beaded bands extending downwards. The folds of the tunic are rendered by curving, wide grooves. Over the tunic, he wears a himation. It is wrapped around his left upper arm, folded around his wrist, and proceeds in a curving fold over the waist and falling back at his right side. The himation covers his legs and ends at his ankles and has a scalloped edge. Two wide, s-shaped folds fall from under his left wrist. The folds of the himation are rendered by oblique and curving grooves. He wears a plain band belt, knotted at the centre with the ends looped under on either side of the waist. The trousers are visible above his ankles. They are decorated in the middle with a band set between beaded bands (details unclear). The folds of the trousers are rendered by curving grooves. The trousers are tucked into his boots visible on the right foot. The boot is decorated with a geometric pattern with four-petal flowers in squares, separated by beaded bands. The midribs of the leaves are rendered by incised lines. The upper edge of the boot is decorated with a beaded band followed by panels decorated with a wave pattern. The boot is fastened at the ankles by a round button with one lace extending down from it.

He holds a skyphos in his right hand. It has a conical foot and lower body, while the upper body is trapezoidal. The foot is decorated with a tongues pattern. The body of the vessel is decorated with rosettes within circles. The lip is rectangular, and it has small, looped handles. The thumb, index, and the little finger are extended. With his left hand he lightly holds a fold of the himation. The thumb and the middle finger are extended. On the surface of the left hand, veins are plastically rendered.

PORTRAIT C: HEAD OF PRIEST

The figure is shown frontally. The head is turned slightly towards his left.

He wears a tall, cylindrical, flat-top headdress divided into three sections by two vertical grooves low on the forehead: a Palmyrene priestly hat. A wreath is depicted at the lower part of the hat. It has three rows of elliptical leaves pointing towards an oval with an incised border, indicating an inlay. The midribs of the leaves are incised. A narrow, horizontal band under the bottom of the hat suggests a liner. His face is oval and fleshy. The eyebrows are depicted by low, curving, incised lines. The eyes are almond-shaped, with thick upper eyelids. The end of the upper eyelids extends downwards

Cat. 228

and beyond that of the lower ones. The irises are indicated by incised arches and the pupils by punch holes. The irises touch the upper eyelids. The nose is straight with a wide base. The alae are indicated by incised lines. The mouth is small with a full lower lip. The chin is round with a flattened tip. The neck is wide with two curving grooves.

The head joins with the sarcophagus lid: it can either belong to a third figure between the two preserved figures, or it could belong to the reclining figure.

SARCOPHAGUS BOX

PORTRAIT D: STANDING MALE

The figure's torso and lower body are shown in a three-quarter view. The arms are shown in profile. The arms are bent, the right to the waist, the left to the side.

He wears a >Parthian-style< tunic. The tunic has a small, round neckline with a beaded border and short, wide sleeves that reach over the elbows. It is decorated with a wide band that extends downwards from the middle of the neckline and is framed by beaded borders. The band is decorated with a vine scroll. The hem of the tunic is decorated with a wide band and a beaded border. The band is decorated with circles with incised borders separated by rows of beads. The tunic is tied with a belt at the waist: the belt is depicted as a narrow band knotted at the centre.

PORTRAIT E: MALE HEAD

The hair is short and arranged in rows of crescent-shaped curls. He wears a wreath with rows of long, narrow leaves. The midribs of the leaves are incised. The eyebrows are arched and plastically rendered, with oblique, incised lines above a diagonal, incised line indicating individual hairs. The eyes are almond-shaped, with thick eyelids. The eyeballs are blank. The ears are small and close to the head. He has a beard that starts from the right temple.

229. FRAGMENTS OF A COMPLETE SARCOPHAGUS RELIEF WITH BANQUETING SCENE AND PORTRAIT BUSTS

DATABASE NUMBER: PM483 (229a) + PM484 (229b) + PM485 (229c) + PM887 (229d).
LOCATION: Palmyra, Palmyra Museum, inv. no. 688/I.c.3/6/9, inv. no. I.a.1/702/704, inv. no. II.c.6, inv. no. II.a.22/679.
CONTEXT: West necropolis. Valley of the Tombs. Temple tomb no. 36.
ACQUISITION HISTORY: —
MEASUREMENTS: Fragment A: Height: 104 cm. Length: 40 cm. Fragment B: Height: 41 cm. Length: 48 cm. Fragment C: Height: 28 cm. Fragment D: Height: 32 cm. Width: 32 cm.
MATERIAL: Limestone.
PRESERVATION: Broken on all sides. Portrait A: A crack runs horizontally at the base of the neck. The head has been reattached. The nose and the eyes are chipped. A crack

Cat. 229

runs horizontally at her right wrist and thigh. The torso appears to have been reattached. The surface is weathered. Portrait B: Broken diagonally from the right side of face and through the torso. Only a part of the head, of the upper chest, and of the left arm is preserved. Portrait C: Broken

Cat. 229

diagonally through the base of the neck. The surface around the lower abdomen is chipped. Fragment D: The relief is broken off on all sides, with a part of the kline, mattress, and two heads surviving.
TECHNICAL DESCRIPTION: The figures are partly carved.
DATE: A.D. 220–240.
REFERENCES: 229a: Schmidt-Colinet 1992, 105. 119. 149 f. cat. B 8b; pl. 40, e. 229b: Schmidt-Colinet 1992, 105. 119. 149 f. cat. B 8; pl. 40, f; Krag 2018, 28 n. 9; 58 n. 304; 62 n. 353; 88 n. 193. 195; 103 n. 74; 382 f. cat. 814. 229c: Schmidt-Colinet 1992, 105. 119. 149 f. cat. B 8a; pl. 41, d; Krag 2018, 28 n. 9; 58 n. 304; 62 n. 353; 88 n. 193. 195; 103 n. 74; 382 f. cat. 814. 229d: Schmidt-Colinet 1992, 105. 108. 133. 147 cat. S 6; pl. 32, c. d.

OBJECT DESCRIPTION

The object was originally rectangular in shape. The object is composed of several fragments. Fragment A (229b) depicts a seated female and possibly part of a reclining figure. She rests her feet on a protruding element. She sits on two round cushions. An oblong element, the foot of another figure, obscures her left foot. Fragment B (229c) depicts a standing female and a standing male. Fragment C (229a) depicts a male head. Fragment D (229d) depicts a sarcophagus box rectangular in shape and rendered as a kline. Two figures are depicted between the kline legs. The frame of the kline is decorated with rectangular panels with incised borders separated by square panels. Above the kline is a mattress decorated with a wide band with a vegetal motif between two beaded bands. The texture of the mattress is indicated by wide, curving grooves. The survival of three heads depicted under the frame of the kline and two fragments of torsos suggests that the sarcophagus box was decorated with a series of busts. Several other fragments belong together with this sarcophagus box fragment (according to Schmidt-Colinet 1992): fragment B depicts the head of a figure and a part of the mattress, fragment C depicts the head of a figure, fragment D depicts a part of the kline leg, fragment E depicts a female torso, and fragment F depicts a male torso.

SARCOPHAGUS LID

PORTRAIT A: SEATED FEMALE

The figure is shown frontally. The right arm is bent and rests on her right thigh. The left arm is bent and raised to the neck. Her legs are bent, and the knees are rendered under the drapery. The arms appear short in relation to the body.

She wears a turban and a veil. The turban is rendered in one layer. The veil falls over the shoulders and it is folded under her right arm. Part of the hair is covered by the headdress: the hair is centrally parted and brushed away on each side of the forehead and covers the ears. An s-shaped lock of hair falls on her right shoulder. Her face is oval. The eyebrows are rendered by thin ridges. The mouth is small with a full lower lip. The cheeks are fleshy and the chin wide. The neck is wide.

She wears a tunic and a himation. The tunic has a wide, round neckline and sleeves reaching the elbows. The folds of the tunic are rendered by curving grooves. The ankle-length himation crosses the chest diagonally from the left shoulder to the right side and covers the left breast and her legs. It is fastened at the left shoulder with a circular brooch (Colledge classification: i). The folds of the himation are rendered by diagonal and curving grooves.

Her left arm is raised next to the shoulder where she holds a fold of the veil with her hand. She wears a wide and thick hoop bracelet, and a thick hoop ring on the little finger. With the right hand, she holds another fold of the veil. A fold of the

Cat. 229

Cat. 229

veil falls from under her hand. A round element, possibly a bell is attached to the fold with a string.

PORTRAIT B: FEMALE FIGURE

The figure is only schematically rendered. The figure is shown frontally. The head is turned slightly to her left.

She wears two headdresses: a turban and a veil. The turban is divided into two layers. Her face is oval, and the neck is short.

The left arm is slightly bent and held to the torso.

PORTRAIT C: MALE FIGURE

The figure is shown frontally. The right arm is bent and held to the torso.

He wears a tunic and a himation. The tunic has a wide, round neckline. The folds are indicated by curving grooves. Over the tunic he wears a himation. It is wrapped around his right shoulder and arm, leaving most of the upper torso free. One fold of the himation crosses the chest diagonally and falls over the left shoulder (possibly a variation of ›arm-sling‹ type).

PORTRAIT D: MALE HEAD

His head is turned slightly to the left.

His face is oval and fleshy. The hair is rendered as one mass. A triangular mass around the head indicates the location where a wreath would have been carved. The eyebrows are curving. The ears are small and slightly protruding. The nose is straight, and the mouth is small. The chin is square, and the neck is long with two curving grooves.

PORTRAIT E: RECLINING MALE

The foot is shown in profile.

SARCOPHAGUS BOX

PORTRAIT F: MALE

The figure is depicted frontally.

He has short hair indicated by curving, incised lines, suggesting tousled locks. His face is round and fleshy. The eyebrows are indicated by curving ridges. The eyes are small. The eyeballs are blank. The nose is straight. Nasolabial lines are indicated by the carving of the planes of the face. The mouth is small with full lips. Two small grooves are carved starting from the corners of the mouth.

PORTRAIT G: FEMALE

The figure is depicted frontally.

Curving grooves at the top of the head indicate that the portrait belonged to a female wearing a turban and a veil.

A.D. 240–273

230. FRAGMENTS OF A COMPLETE SARCOPHAGUS WITH BANQUETING SCENE AND RELIGIOUS SCENE

DATABASE NUMBER: InSitu221 (230a) + InSitu222 (230b).
LOCATION: Palmyra, Palmyra Museum, inv. no. 301, 284/402/403, 83.28.1.
CONTEXT: West necropolis. Valley of the Tombs. Temple tomb no. 36.
ACQUISITION HISTORY: —
MEASUREMENTS: Box: Height: 75.5 cm. Width: 170 cm. Depth: 42 cm. Lid: Height: 86 cm. Width: 170 cm.
MATERIAL: Limestone.
PRESERVATION: Lid: The piece is broken into several fragments. The right and left edges, the central part of the lower side, and the upper part of the lid are broken off. The surface is weathered. Portrait A: The figure is broken off at the lower legs. Portrait B: The upper part of the figure is broken off at the head, neck, upper torso, and upper arms, and the lower part is broken off at the lower legs. Portrait C: The upper part of the figure is broken off at the head, neck, and the upper torso. The arms of the figure are broken off. Portrait D: The upper part of the figure is broken off at the head, neck, and right upper arm. The left leg of the figure is broken off. The right lower arm, the left arm, the torso, and the right leg of the figure are chipped. Box: The surface is heavily weathered.
TECHNICAL DESCRIPTION: —
DATE: A.D. 240–273 (Schmidt-Colinet: A.D. 230–260).
REFERENCES: 230a: Schmidt-Colinet 1992, 23. 105. 106. 108. 135. 147 cat. S 4 fig. 65; 135. 149 cat. B 6; pl. 40, a. b. d. 230b: Schmidt-Colinet 1992, 105. 122. 138. 149. 153. 156 cat. K 11 fig. 53; pl. 49, g.

OBJECT DESCRIPTION

The sarcophagus lid is rectangular in shape and depicts a seated female, two standing male figures, and one reclining male. Another fragment belongs to the lid: A tall, cylindrical, flat-top headdress divided into three sections by two vertical grooves: a Palmyrene priestly hat. It has a wreath rendered at the lower part of the hat. It has three rows of short leaves, elliptical at the centre and narrow at the sides, pointing towards a central oval decoration. The midribs of the leaves are incised. The headdress has a narrow, horizontal band at the bottom. It is placed over a series of deep, vertical grooves: swathes of fabric. Beneath the figures is a box in the shape of a kline with five standing figures and an animal between the kline legs. The legs appear turned (details unclear). Above the kline is a mattress decorated with two wide bands with a crisscross pattern, each set between beaded bands. The fabric and the texture of the mattress are indicated by wide, curving grooves. The male reclines on a round cushion decorated with a wide band (details unclear).

Cat. 230

SARCOPHAGUS LID

PORTRAIT A: SEATED FEMALE

The figure is shown frontally.

She wears a long garment that covers the feet. The folds of the garment are indicated by vertical grooves.

PORTRAIT B: STANDING MALE

The figure is shown frontally. The right arm falls to the side, the left is bent in front of the waist. The lower body and legs are obscured by the reclining figure.

He wears a tunic and a himation. The tunic has long sleeves. The tunic is decorated with two bands that extend downwards from the side of the neckline (clavi). The bands have a crisscross pattern, and they are set between beaded bands. The cuffs of the sleeves are also decorated with a wide band with a crisscross pattern. Over the tunic, he wears a himation that covers the left side of the torso, is wrapped around the waist, and falls down covering the legs. One edge of the himation falls down at the left side of the torso.

He holds a vessel with an ovoid body, a conical neck, and a wide mouth with his right hand.

PORTRAIT C: STANDING MALE

The figure is shown frontally.

He wears a garment that covers his torso, and its folds are depicted with wide, vertical grooves.

PORTRAIT D: RECLINING MALE

The figure's torso is shown frontally. The arms and the right leg are shown in profile.

He wears a tunic, a himation, and shoes. The tunic's folds are indicated by wide, curving grooves over the torso. Over the tunic, he wears the himation. It covers the left shoulder and arm, falls diagonally across the torso, and covers the legs. It falls under the left lower arm in two zigzag-shaped folds that fall over the cushion and the mattress.

With his left hand, he holds an object visible in outline, possibly a cup.

Cat. 230

SARCOPHAGUS BOX

PORTRAIT E: STANDING MALE
The figure is shown frontally. The arms fall to the side. The legs are slightly parted.
    He is dressed.
    He holds a vessel in the right hand.

PORTRAIT F: STANDING MALE
The figure is shown frontally.
    He is dressed.

PORTRAIT G: STANDING FIGURE
The figure is shown frontally.

PORTRAIT H: STANDING FIGURE
The figure is shown frontally.

PORTRAIT I: STANDING FIGURE
The figure is shown frontally.

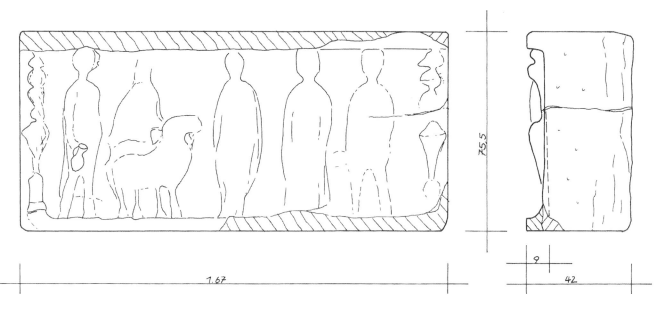

Cat. 230

SARCOPHAGUS LIDS

A.D. 220–240

231. FRAGMENTS OF A BANQUETING RELIEF

DATABASE NUMBER: PM487.
LOCATION: Palmyra, Palmyra Museum, inv. no. 607/I.d.2/II.c.5/II.d.7, inv. no. II.b.4.
CONTEXT: West necropolis. Valley of the Tombs. Temple tomb 36.
ACQUISITION HISTORY: —
MEASUREMENTS: Lid: Height: 117 cm. Width: 176 cm. Fragment: Height: 20 cm.
MATERIAL: Limestone.
PRESERVATION: Most of the background is broken off. Portrait A: The head is broken off at the base of the neck. Part of the lower right arm and the wrist is chipped. Portrait B: The right lower arm is broken off. The top of the Palmyrene priestly hat and the central part of the face are chipped. A crack runs across the waist. Portrait C: The upper part of the figure is broken off at the waist. Portrait D: The head is broken off at the base of the neck. The left lower arm, hand, left foot, and bowl are chipped. Portrait E: Only a part of the torso and attribute is preserved.
TECHNICAL DESCRIPTION: —
DATE: A.D. 220–240 (Schmidt-Colinet: A.D. 210–240).
REFERENCES: al-Asʿad – Schmidt-Colinet 1985, 33 f. pl. 10, c; 11, a; Schmidt-Colinet 1987, 243 fig. 20; Schmidt-Colinet 1992, 23 f. 105. 108. 111 f. 118. 120. 130. 133–137. 148 cat. B 1 figs. 52. 53. 54. 57; pls. 34; 35, a. b; 38, c; Krag – Raja 2017, 199 n. 24; 204 n. 72. 73; 205 n. 75; 208 n. 99; 209 n. 100. 102; 219 cat. 34; Raja 2017a, 220. 222. 227 cat. 21; Raja 2017h, 64 f. 76 cat. 21; Krag 2018, 28 n. 9; 54 n. 263; 59 n. 315. 325; 60 n. 330; 61 n. 333; 62 n. 351. 353; 65 n. 369; 66 n. 385; 88 n. 193. 195; 101 n. 65; 387 cat. 835.

OBJECT DESCRIPTION

The sarcophagus lid is rectangular in shape and depicts a seated female, a standing priest, a standing figure, and a reclining male. A fragment belongs to the lid: it depicts a standing figure. At the upper left side of the relief there is a tall, cylindrical, flat-top headdress divided into three sections by two vertical grooves: a Palmyrene priestly hat. A wreath is depicted at the lower part of the hat. It has three rows of long leaves pointing towards an oval with an incised border. A piece of fabric is looped under the left side of the priestly hat and falls down from its centre. Beneath the figures there is a mattress: it is decorated with an intersecting lozenges pattern with six-petal rosettes and flowers with four elliptical petals between the lozenges. A small bead is depicted at the points where the lozenges cross. The female sits on two cushions placed on top of each other. The upper cushion has a wide, decorated band. The material and texture of the cushions are indicated by wide, curving folds. The reclining male also leans on a cushion decorated with a wide band with floral motifs between two narrow beaded bands. The material and texture of the cushion are indicated by wide, curving folds.

PORTRAIT A: SEATED FEMALE

The figure is shown frontally. Both arms are bent: the right is held at the height of the shoulder, the left rests on the left thigh. The hands appear large in relation to the body. Her left foot is obscured by the reclining figure.

She wears a veil that falls over the right shoulder and side and covers her left shoulder and upper arm. She wears five necklaces, each one slightly below the other. The first is a string of small, round beads around the base of the neck. The next is composed of a series of round and square pendants with incised borders joined by beaded elements. The third is a necklace of small, round beads with an oval pendant with an incised border suspended from the centre. The fourth is composed of an interwoven loop-in-loop chain with an oval pendant with a beaded border. Three spirally wrapped wires ending in clover-shaped pendants are suspended from the central pendant. The last necklace is composed of two loop-in-loop chains that fall parallel to each other. Three round medallions with beaded borders and armless busts are suspended between the chains; two below the breasts and one at the centre, at the height of the navel. The right and central busts depict two priests with priestly hats, tunic, and chlamys, and the one at the left a veiled female with a tall, cylindrical, flat-top headdress.

She wears a tunic and a himation. The tunic has a wide, round neckline, and short sleeves that reach below the elbow. The folds of the tunic are depicted by wide, curving grooves. Over the tunic she wears a himation. It is fastened at the left shoulder with a round brooch enclosing two rows of round beads, one composed of large beads at the outer border, and one of smaller beads. The centre has an incised circle, indicating an inlay (Colledge classification: i). The himation falls across the left side and covers her waist and legs. The edge of the himation visible across the waist is decorated with a pleated band. She wears open-toe sandals. The soles are rendered by a horizontal line.

With the right hand, she pulls the edge of the veil. With the left hand, she holds a fold of the veil at her lap. The index finger is extended. She wears a bracelet composed of twisted beaded and plain wires on each wrist.

PORTRAIT B: STANDING PRIEST

The figure is shown frontally. His head is turned towards his left. The left arm is bent and held at the waist; the right arm falls to the side. The legs are obscured by the reclining figure.

He wears a tall, cylindrical, flat-top headdress low on the forehead: a Palmyrene priestly hat. A wreath is depicted at the lower part of the hat. It has three rows of long leaves pointing towards a central armless bust. A narrow, horizontal band at the bottom of the hat suggests a liner. His face is oval. The eyebrows are curving. The eyes are almond-shaped, with thick upper eyelids. The eyeballs are blank. The mouth is small. The neck is long and slender.

He wears a tunic and a himation. The tunic has a wide, v-shaped neckline. The folds of the tunic are rendered by curving, wide grooves. Over the tunic he wears a himation. It covers both shoulders and arms, the waist, and the legs. The edges of the himation are decorated with pleated bands. The folds of the tunic are indicated by oblique grooves on the upper body and curving grooves on the lower body.

He holds a fold of the himation with his left hand. The index finger is extended. With his right hand he holds an oblong shape with curving sides decorated with a pattern of scales, possibly a pinecone. The index finger and thumb are extended.

PORTRAIT C: STANDING FIGURE

The figure is shown frontally. The lower part of the body is obscured by the reclining figure.

Part of the lower torso of a standing dressed figure is visible.

PORTRAIT D: RECLINING MALE

The torso and the left leg of the figure are shown frontally. The arms and the right leg are shown in profile. The right arm is extended and rests on his raised right leg. The right leg is bent and raised; the left leg is slightly bent and rests along the mattress. The right foot is obscured by the left leg.

He wears a >Parthian-style< tunic and a himation. The tunic has a wide, v-shaped neckline and short, wide sleeves that reach to the elbows. It is decorated with two wide bands that start from the sides of the neckline, next to the shoulders, and extend downwards. The bands are decorated with rosettes inside a running scroll. The folds of the tunic are indicated by curving grooves on the body and oblique grooves on the arms. He wears a thin band belt around his waist. It is tied with a double knot and the ends are looped under on either side. Over the tunic, he wears a himation. It covers his left shoulder and arm, and is wrapped around the left wrist. From the wrist, one part falls across the waist and covers the legs, another part falls over the cushion in two wide, zigzag-shaped folds. The edge of the himation, visible over the waist, is decorated with a pleated band. The folds of the himation are indicated by curving grooves. The feet are bare.

With his right hand, he holds a small, round object with a central depression, possibly fruit. With the upturned palm of his left hand, he holds a bowl (only the outline now visible) with his fingertips.

PORTRAIT E: STANDING FIGURE

The figure wears a tunic. The folds of the tunic are rendered by vertical and oblique grooves.

In the right hand, the figure holds a jug. The jug is decorated with a beaded band between the neck and the body.

Cat. 231

OBJECTS FROM TEMPLE TOMBS 511

Cat. 231

232. FRAGMENTS OF A SARCOPHAGUS LID WITH BANQUETING SCENE

DATABASE NUMBER: PM481.
LOCATION: Palmyra, Palmyra Museum, inv. no. 695/III.a.1, II.b.15.
CONTEXT: West necropolis. Valley of the Tombs. Temple tomb no. 36.
ACQUISITION HISTORY: —
MEASUREMENTS: Height: 117 cm. Width: 84 cm. Fragment C: Height: 20 cm.
MATERIAL: Limestone, white.
PRESERVATION: Broken on all sides. Portrait A: The upper part is broken off horizontally at the shoulders. The right foot and left knee are chipped. Portrait B: The head has been reattached. The surface of the nose, mouth, and lower body is chipped. Portrait C: The left side is broken diagonally through the thigh. The end of the shoe is chipped.
TECHNICAL DESCRIPTION: —
DATE: A.D. 220–240 (Schmidt-Colinet: A.D. 210–240).
REFERENCES: Schmidt-Colinet 1992, 111 f. 118 f. 121–123. 125. 134 f. 137 f. 148 f. cat. B 4 figs. 54. 56. 57. 61; pl. 38, a; 39, a. b; 40, c; Krag – Raja 2017, 199 n. 24; 204 n. 72. 73; 209 n. 100; 210 n. 109. 110. 112; 221 cat. 46; Krag 2018, 28 n. 9; 58 n. 304; 59 n. 320; 62 n. 350. 353; 88 n. 193. 195. 197; 89 n. 201; 102 n. 67; 103 n. 74; 383 cat. 818.

OBJECT DESCRIPTION
The object depicts a seated female, a standing female, and a reclining male. Beneath the figures is a thin mattress. It is decorated with an intersecting lozenges pattern with flowers in the lozenges. Schmidt-Colinet (1992) describes several fragments as belonging to the object. Fragment A: Depicts a male figure. Fragment B: Three cushion fragments. Fragment D: Part of the torso from the reclining figure (not seen).

PORTRAIT A: SEATED FEMALE
The figure is shown in three-quarter view. The left arm appears short in relation to the body. The right arm is bent and held to the chest. The left arm is held at the side of the body. The legs are bent, and the knees are rendered under the drapery.

She wears a veil with a scalloped edge. It falls over her shoulders, is folded around her left arm and wrist and proceeds

Cat. 232

in a curving fold down to her ankles. One end of the veil is folded under her right arm at the elbow. She wears three necklaces: the first is composed of alternating square and round pendants with incised borders, linked by beaded elements. The necklace is worn high on the chest. The second is composed of large, round beads on a string with a central, oval pendant suspended from the centre, worn over the breasts. The third is composed of a loop-in-loop chain, worn below the breasts.

She wears a tunic. It falls to the ankles, has a wide, round neckline and short, wide sleeves. There is an overfold at her thighs. The folds of the tunic are rendered by curving and oblique grooves.

With the right hand, she lightly pulls the edge of the veil from the opposite side. She wears a bracelet composed of twisted beaded and plain wires on her right wrist. Her left hand rests next to her waist.

PORTRAIT B: STANDING FEMALE

The figure is shown frontally. The head is turned slightly to her left. The right arm is bent and held out from the body. The left arm is bent and held to the chest.

She wears two headdresses: a turban and a veil. The turban is coiled. It is rendered in three twisting layers with horizontal grooves indicating the coiling of the fabric. The veil falls over the shoulders and proceeds in a curving fold across the chest. It is wrapped around the left wrist. She also wears a central head ornament and a head-chain. The head ornament runs from under the central part of the veil down to the forehead and is composed of an upper, round and a lower, square pendant.

Cat. 232

The pendants have an incised border and are joined by beaded elements. The head-chain runs from the square pendant to the sides of the head, under the veil. The chain is composed of round elements with incised borders, linked by beaded elements. Part of the hair is covered by the headdress, and several strands of hair above the ears are pushed back over the headband and the edge of the turban and disappear under the veil. Her face is round. The eyebrows are curving, depicted as thin ridges. The eyes are close-set and almond-shaped with heavy upper eyelids. The eyeballs appear blank. Only the earlobes are visible under the hair. She wears earrings with three juxtaposed balls; a central, oval bead with a smaller, round bead above and below it (Colledge classification: K). The cheeks are fleshy, and the chin is pointed. The neck is wide. She wears a necklace composed of a plain hoop with a central, round pendant with a hollowed centre, worn high on the chest.

She wears a tunic with a small, round neckline and short sleeves.

PORTRAIT C: RECLINING MALE

The figure is wearing a garment that proceeds to the ankles and has a scalloped edge. The figure is also wearing a boot. The boot is decorated with a geometric pattern of lozenges with four-petal flowers within, separated by beaded bands. The upper edge of the boot has a beaded band.

A fragment (fragment C) depicts the hand of the reclining figure. A part of the garment is depicted to the left of the hand in curving folds. The veins are rendered plastically on the back of the hand. He wears a ring: a thick hoop ring with an oval bezel on the left little finger.

233. FRAGMENTS OF A BANQUETING RELIEF

DATABASE NUMBER: PM489 (233a) + PM490 (233b).
LOCATION: Palmyra, Palmyra Museum, inv. no. 401/525,VI.5.
CONTEXT: West necropolis. Valley of the Tombs. Temple tomb no. 36.
ACQUISITION HISTORY: —
MEASUREMENTS: Height: 105 cm. Together: min. width: 150 cm. Fragment A: Width: 33 cm. Fragment B: Height: 14 cm.
MATERIAL: Limestone.
PRESERVATION: Two non-joining fragments of the same object. Portrait A: The surface is weathered. The head, left hand, and the lower part of the legs and feet are broken off. The brooch, right arm, and drapery are chipped. Portrait B: The lower part is broken off under the knees; the head is broken off at the middle of the neck. The right upper arm is broken off. Most of the left hand is chipped. The left corner of the cushion and of the mattress are chipped. Fragment A: Only the lower arm and hand and knee are preserved. Fragment B: The lower part of the animal is broken off at the neck. The upper part of the head and the mule are chipped.
TECHNICAL DESCRIPTION: —
DATE: A.D. 220–240 (Schmidt-Colinet: A.D. 220–250).
REFERENCES: 233a: al-Asʿad – Schmidt-Colinet 1985, 33 f. pl. 10, a; Schmidt-Colinet 1992, 108. 112. 119 f. 122. 125. 130. 135. 148 cat. B 3 figs. 55. 57–60; pls. 37. 35, c. e; al-Asʿad – Schmidt-Colinet 1995, 54. 56 fig. 78; Krag 2018, 28 n. 9; 54 n. 262. 263; 58 n. 304; 62 n. 353; 63 n. 355; 383 cat. 815;

Cat. 233

Cat. 233

Cat. 233

<https://virtual-museum-syria.org/palmyra/a-man-with-a-persian-dress-holding-a-skyphos/> (06.05.2022). 233b: al-Asʿad – Schmidt-Colinet 1985, 33 f. pl. 10, a; Schmidt-Colinet 1992, 148 cat. B 3 figs. 55. 57–60; pls. 37. 35, c. e; al-Asʿad – Schmidt-Colinet 1995, 54. 56 fig. 78; Krag 2018, 28 n. 9; 54 n. 262. 263; 58 n. 304; 62 n. 353; 63 n. 355; 383 cat. 815.

OBJECT DESCRIPTION

The sarcophagus lid depicts a seated female and a reclining male. Beneath the figures is a mattress. Under the female it is decorated with a head of a bald male figure rendered in profile within a circle, and the mattress under the reclining male is decorated with an intersecting lozenges pattern with four-petal flowers with serrated leaves in the lozenges. The lozenges are decorated with beaded bands. The mattress is also decorated with wide bands set between beaded bands. A beaded band at the right edge of the mattress suggests the presence of a wide band that has not been preserved. The central band is decorated with lobed leaves set on a stem. The left band is decorated with a vine scroll. The seated female sits on two cushions decorated with four-petal flowers in squares. The reclining figure rests the left arm on a cushion. It is decorated with a running scroll with vines set between bands made up of squares and rhombi, which have an outer, beaded band. Curving grooves indicate the texture of the fabric. Fragment A depicts the lower right arm and hand, as well as knee, of the reclining figure. Fragment B depicts the head of an animal, possibly a donkey or horse. A fragment belonging to the object depicts part of a veil (according to Schmidt-Colinet 1992).

PORTRAIT A: SEATED FEMALE

The figure is shown in three-quarter view. The right arm is held along the body. The left arm is bent and raised to the height of the neck. Her legs are bent, and the knees are rendered under the drapery.

She wears a veil. It falls over the shoulders, is wrapped around her left arm, and falls over the back of her right shoulder. Two s-shaped locks fall on her shoulders. The neck is slender. She wears five necklaces. The first is composed of large, round beads worn at the base of the neck. The second is composed of a thick hoop with an oval pendant with an incised border suspended from the centre by a narrow sleeve, worn at the base of the neck. The third is composed of rectangular pendants and a central pendant in the shape of a six-point star, worn high on the chest. The fourth is composed of tubular beads

Cat. 233

and a thin element suspended from the centre, worn at the chest. The fifth is composed of a double loop-in-loop chain with a central, oval pendant with a beaded border, worn under the chest.

She wears a tunic and a himation. The tunic has short, wide sleeves. The folds of the tunic are rendered by oblique and curving grooves. The himation crosses the chest from the left shoulder to the right side, and covers the left breast, lower body, and legs. The himation is fastened at the right shoulder with a circular brooch with an outer, geometrical border with curving sides meeting in flat ends, with circular elements between the curving sides. The brooch has an inner beaded border and a raised circular centre (Colledge classification: i). The folds of the himation are rendered by oblique and curving grooves.

Her right hand rests on the cushion. She wears two rings, one on her middle and one on her index finger. They are wide hoops with rectangular bezels. She wears a bracelet made of twisted plain wires. Two long folds of the veil fall from under her right hand.

PORTRAIT B: RECLINING MALE

The figure is shown frontally. The left arm appears short in relation to the body. The right arm is extended. The left arm is bent and held in front of the chest.

He wears a >Parthian-style< tunic, a chlamys, and >Parthian-style< trousers. The tunic has a small, round neckline decorated with a band with rhombi and squares and long, loose sleeves. The cuffs of the sleeves are decorated with a scroll with encircled flowers. At the middle, the tunic has a wide band that extends downwards. It is decorated with a scroll with leaves and rosettes between beaded bands. The tunic ends above the knees and has a decorated border with three or four-petal flowers between beaded bands. The folds of the tunic are rendered by oblique and curving grooves. He also wears a plain band belt across the lower torso. It is knotted at the centre with the ends looped under either side of the waist. Over the tunic, he wears a chlamys that falls over both shoulders, and covers the upper chest. The edge of the chlamys has a scalloped border decorated with rosettes and a beaded band, visible on the fold at the left shoulder and under the left arm. The chlamys is folded around his left arm and proceeds in two s-shaped folds over the cushions and his left side. Another edge of the chlamys has a scalloped border and a band with a vegetal motif, visible on top of the cushions. The folds of the chlamys are rendered by oblique and curving grooves. At the middle, the trouser leg is decorated with a scroll with vines between beaded bands.

He holds an ovoid object with a scales pattern in his right hand, possibly a pinecone. Under the right lower arm, an object with a rectangular main body and a round, lateral element is depicted, possibly a dagger. The nails are indicated by incised lines. With the upturned palm of his left hand, he holds an object, possibly a bowl, with his fingertips.

234. FRAGMENTS OF A BANQUETING RELIEF

DATABASE NUMBER: PM486.
LOCATION: Palmyra, Palmyra Museum, inv. no. 682–683, III.b.6, IV.12.
CONTEXT: West necropolis. Valley of the Tombs. Temple tomb no. 36.
ACQUISITION HISTORY: —
MEASUREMENTS: Height: 65 cm. Width: 102 cm.
MATERIAL: Limestone.
PRESERVATION: Four non-joining fragments belong to the same relief. Fragment A: The background is broken off around the figure. A large crack runs across the waist, one on the thighs, and one on the cushion. The surface is weathered. The head is broken off at the base of the neck and at the right shoulder; the lower part is broken off at the thighs. The cushion, attribute, and areas on the clothing are chipped.
TECHNICAL DESCRIPTION: —
DATE: A.D. 220–240 (Schmidt-Colinet: A.D. 230–260).
REFERENCES: Schmidt-Colinet 1992, 105. 110. 130. 135. 150 cat. B 10 figs. 60. 61 pl. 41, b. c. e.

OBJECT DESCRIPTION

The object depicts the torso and a part of the lower body of a reclining male figure. He rests on a thin mattress with an intersecting lozenge pattern with four-petal flowers in the lozenges. He rests the left arm on a cushion. The texture of the fabric is indicated by curving grooves. Schmidt-Colinet (1992) describes several fragments as belonging to the object. Fragment B: Hand and wrist of the figure. Fragment C: Hand fragment. Fragment D: Foot fragment.

PORTRAIT

The figure is shown frontally. The left arm is bent in front of the torso.

He wears a >Parthian-style< tunic and a himation. The tunic has a small, round neckline decorated with a band with circles and squares separated by vertical beaded bands. At the middle, the tunic has a wide band extending downwards. It is decorated with miniature depictions of a griffin, a lion, a dog, or a pig, which are encircled. The folds of the tunic are rendered by oblique and curving grooves. He also wears a plain band belt across the lower torso. It is knotted at the centre with the ends looped under either side of the waist. Over the tunic, he wears a himation. It is folded around his left arm and proceeds in a thick fold along his left side and across the waist. The folds of the himation are rendered by curving grooves.

OBJECTS FROM TEMPLE TOMBS 517

Cat. 234

235. FRAGMENTS OF A BANQUETING RELIEF

DATABASE NUMBER: PM482 (235a) + PM897 (235b).
LOCATION: Palmyra, Palmyra Museum, inv. no. I.c.7/8, VI.3.
CONTEXT: West necropolis. Valley of the Tombs. Temple tomb no. 36.
ACQUISITION HISTORY: —
MEASUREMENTS: 235a: Height: 56 cm. Width: 77 cm. 235b: Height: 23 cm.
MATERIAL: Limestone, yellow.
PRESERVATION: Two non-joining fragments possibly from same object. 235a: Broken on the lower, right, and left side. The object is cracked vertically between the figures. The surface is weathered. Portrait A: The lower part is broken off horizontally at the lower torso and diagonally on the right side. The left hand is chipped. Portrait B: The lower part is broken off horizontally through the lower torso. The nose, central part of headdress, and the mouth are chipped. 235b: The head is broken off at the top of the neck. The upper part of the head, the back of the head, the outer shell of the ears, and most of the face are broken off.
TECHNICAL DESCRIPTION: —
DATE: A.D. 220–240 (Schmidt-Colinet: A.D. 210–240).
REFERENCES: 235a: Schmidt-Colinet 1992, 121. 133–135. 137 f. 149 cat. B 5 figs. 56. 57 pl. 38, b. 39, c. d; Krag – Raja 2017, 199 n. 24; 204 n. 72. 73; 205 n. 75; 209 n. 100; 220 f. cat. 45; Krag 2018, 28 n. 9; 58 n. 304; 59 n. 320; 88 n. 193. 195; 108 n. 125; 383 cat. 817. 235b: Schmidt-Colinet 1992, 112. 122 f. 137 f. 153 cat. K 12 fig. 53 pl. 50, a. d.

OBJECT DESCRIPTION

235a depicts two female figures in two fragments. Schmidt-Colinet (1992) describes two fragments more as belonging to the same object: Fragment A: Depicts the right wrist from a reclining figure. Fragment B: Boot fragment. 235b depicts the head of a male figure, from the same sarcophagus lid.

PORTRAIT A: FEMALE

The figure is shown frontally. The head is turned slightly to her right. The left arm is bent and raised to the shoulder.

She wears three headdresses: a headband, a turban, and a veil. The band is placed high on the forehead and has a central rectangular panel (details unclear). The turban is coiled. It is rendered in three twisting layers with horizontal grooves indicating the coiling of the fabric. The veil is heavy. It is wrapped around her right shoulder and upper arm and covers the right breast. It proceeds across the chest in a curving fold and falls back at her left shoulder. She also wears a head-chain. It is attached under the centre of the turban and runs to the sides disappearing under the veil. It is composed of circular pendants with incised borders joined by beaded elements. Part of the hair is covered by the headdress: several strands of hair above the ears are pushed back over the headband and the edge of the turban and disappear under the veil. Her face is oval. The eyes are close-set and almond-shaped with thick upper eyelids. The irises are indicated by incised circles. Only the earlobes are visible under the hair and she wears earrings with three juxtaposed beads; an upper, circular bead, a central, triangular bead, and a lower, round bead (Colledge classification: K).

The cheeks are fleshy. The neck is long with two horizontal grooves. She wears four necklaces: one composed of round beads on a string, worn at the base of the neck. One where only a square pendant with an incised border and a bead on each side is preserved, worn high in the chest. One worn below the chest, composed of small, round beads on a string with a crescent-shaped pendant with a round bead between the horns, suspended from the centre by a narrow sleeve. One composed of a wide chain with a central, oval pendant with a beaded border, worn below the chest. The pendant and chain are linked by semicircular terminals.

She wears a tunic with a small, round neckline. The folds of the tunic are rendered by curving and oblique grooves. She also wears a circular brooch with a geometrical outer border. The outer border has curving sides meeting in flat ends with round beads between the curving sides (Colledge classification: i).

PORTRAIT B: FEMALE

The figure is shown frontally. The head is turned slightly to her right. The right arm is held along the body. The left arm is bent and raised to the chest.

Cat. 235

She wears two headdresses: a turban and a veil. The turban is coiled. It is rendered in three twisting layers with horizontal and oblique grooves indicating the coiling of the fabric. The veil is heavy. It falls over her right shoulder and continues across the chest in a curving fold and back at her left shoulder. It is wrapped around the left wrist. She also wears a central head ornament and a head-chain. The head ornament has a circular element at the centre of the turban, and a lower, square element. The two elements have incised borders and are linked by smaller, beaded elements. Three round beads are suspended from the square element. The head-chain runs from the square element of the head ornament to either side of the head and disappears under the veil. It is composed of circular elements with incised borders linked by smaller, beaded elements. Part of the hair is covered by the headdresses: several strands of hair above the ears are pushed back over the headband and the edge of the turban and disappear under the veil. Her face is oval. The eyebrows are curving, rendered as thin ridges. The eyes are close-set and almond-shaped. Only the earlobes are visible under the hair. She wears dumbbell-shaped earrings (Colledge classification: H). The cheeks are fleshy, and the mouth is small. The chin is pointed, and the neck is long. She wears a necklace composed of a twisted chain with a central, round pendant suspended by a narrow sleeve, worn at the base of the neck. The pendant has an incised border.

She wears a tunic with wide sleeves reaching the elbows. The folds of the tunic are rendered by curving grooves.

She lightly holds the curving fold of the veil with her left hand. The index and the little finger are extended.

PORTRAIT C: MALE

The hair is short and arranged in rows of snail-shell curls. He wears a wreath with three rows of long, narrow leaves. The midribs of the leaves are incised. His face is square. The ears are small and slightly protruding. He has a beard that starts from the temples and covers the outer side of the cheeks and the chin. The facial hair is arranged in three rows of snail-shell curls.

236. FRAGMENTS OF A BANQUETING RELIEF

DATABASE NUMBER: PM488.
LOCATION: Palmyra, Palmyra Museum, inv. no. 657/686/II.d.8.
CONTEXT: West necropolis. Valley of the Tombs. Temple tomb no. 36.
ACQUISITION HISTORY: —
MEASUREMENTS: Height: 86 cm. Width: 119 cm. Fragment: Height: 11 cm. Width: 16.5 cm.
MATERIAL: Limestone, white/grey.
PRESERVATION: A large crack runs diagonally at the thighs of the figure. The lower part is broken off under the knees; the head is broken off at the base of the neck. The right lower arm and the left lower arm is broken off. The surface is weathered and chipped. Fragment: Only the upper part of the hair and headdress is preserved.
TECHNICAL DESCRIPTION: —
DATE: A.D. 220–240 (Schmidt-Colinet: A.D. 220–250).
REFERENCES: Schmidt-Colinet 1992, 105. 110. 122. 125. 135. 151 f. cat. B 17 fig. 57 pl. 45, a. b. e; Krag 2018, 58 n. 304; 59 n. 325; 62 n. 353; 64 n. 361. 362; 65 n. 374; 384 cat. 820.

OBJECT DESCRIPTION

The object depicts a reclining female. She rests on a thin mattress decorated with an intersecting lozenges pattern with rosettes in the lozenges. She rests the left arm on two cushions: the upper one is decorated with a wide band with a vegetal motif between beaded bands. The lower one is decorated with a running scroll with rosettes between beaded bands. Curving grooves indicate the texture of the fabric. A fragment belonging to the object depicts part of a cushion (according to Schmidt-Colinet 1992).

PORTRAIT

The figure is shown frontally. The right arm is bent and held in front of the torso. The left arm is bent and raised to the shoulder. The left leg is bent under the right leg.

She wears a coiled turban. The coiling of the fabric is indicated by curving grooves. She wears a heavy veil. The hair is parted at the centre of her forehead and brushed to the sides. Individual strands of hair are indicated by incised lines. She wears four necklaces. The first is composed of small,

Cat. 235

Cat. 236

Cat. 236

Cat. 237

Cat. 237

round beads worn at the base of the neck. The second, also worn at the base of the neck, is composed of a twisted hoop with an oval pendant with an incised border, suspended from the centre by a narrow sleeve. The third is composed of alternating circular and square pendants with beaded borders linked together by beaded elements, worn high on the chest. The fourth is composed of a double loop-in-loop chain with a central, oval pendant. The pendant has a beaded border, and five rectangular bars are suspended from it.

She wears a tunic and a himation. The tunic has a small, round neckline and short, wide sleeves. The sleeves have a pleated edge. The folds of the tunic are rendered by curving and oblique grooves. Over the tunic, she wears a himation. It is folded over her right shoulder and arm, and is wrapped around the left arm. Two s-shaped folds fall from under her left arm and proceed over the cushions where a small weight is fastened to the left fold. The folds of the himation are rendered by curving grooves.

237. SARCOPHAGUS LID RELIEF WITH BANQUETING SCENE

DATABASE NUMBER: PM479.
LOCATION: Palmyra, Palmyra Museum, inv. no. 536/II.b.18, 646/661.
CONTEXT: West necropolis, Valley of the Tombs. Temple tomb no. 36.
ACQUISITION HISTORY: —
MEASUREMENTS: Fragment A: Height: 33 cm. Width: 52 cm. Fragment B: Height: 80 cm. Width: 106 cm.
MATERIAL: Limestone, white.
PRESERVATION: The relief ground is mostly broken off. The surface is weathered. Portrait A: The upper part is broken off above the knees. The right knee is chipped. Portrait B: The head is broken off at the base of the neck and the lower part is broken off at the ankles. The hands and the left knee are chipped.
TECHNICAL DESCRIPTION: —
DATE: A.D. 220–240 (Schmidt-Colinet: A.D. 230–260).
REFERENCES: Schmidt-Colinet 1992, 110. 135. 150 cat. B 9 pl. 43, a. b.

OBJECT DESCRIPTION

The two fragments depict a standing figure (fragment A) and a reclining figure (fragment B). Beneath the figures is a thin mattress. It is decorated with an intersecting lozenges pattern. The reclining figure rests the left arm on a cushion. It is decorated with a band with leaves set between beaded bands. Curving grooves indicate the texture of the fabric.

PORTRAIT A: STANDING MALE

The legs are slightly parted, with the feet in three-quarter view. He wears a garment that reaches to the knees, where the lower hem falls in an s-shape.

PORTRAIT B: RECLINING MALE

The body is shown in frontal to three-quarter view. The arms appear short in relation to the body. The right arm is bent to the chest. The left is bent and rests at his side. His right leg is bent. The left leg is bent under the right leg, and the lower part is obscured by the right leg.

He wears a tunic and a himation. The tunic has a wide, v-shaped neckline. The folds of the tunic are rendered by curving and oblique grooves. The himation is folded around both shoulders. It is wrapped around the right arm leaving the hand free. An end of himation runs horizontally from the right arm across the torso and is folded around his left lower arm. An s-shaped fold falls from under the left hand and along the cushion. The folds of the himation are rendered by vertical and curving grooves.

SARCOPHAGUS BOXES

A.D. 220–240

238. SARCOPHAGUS BOX WITH STANDING FIGURES

DATABASE NUMBER: InSitu223.
LOCATION: Palmyra, in situ.
CONTEXT: West necropolis. Valley of the Tombs. Temple tomb no. 36.
ACQUISITION HISTORY: —
MEASUREMENTS: Height: 87.5 cm. Width: 208 cm. Depth: 83 cm.
MATERIAL: Limestone.
PRESERVATION: The right and lower edges of the front of the sarcophagus box are broken off. The upper part of the sarcophagus box is broken off, except for the left corner. Several cracks run across the surface. The surface is weathered, and the figures are heavily chipped.
TECHNICAL DESCRIPTION: —
DATE: A.D. 220–240.
REFERENCES: Schmidt-Colinet 1992, 23. 105–108. 146 cat. S 1 pl. 31, c. d.

OBJECT DESCRIPTION

The sarcophagus box is rectangular in shape and is rendered as a kline. Six figures are depicted standing on a projecting plinth between the kline legs. The kline has turned legs on a plinth (details unclear). The stretcher of the kline is decorated with rectangular panels, one of which has several small circles (rosettes?). The fulcrum has a tondo with a bust at its lower end (portrait G).

PORTRAIT A: STANDING FIGURE

The figure is shown frontally.

OBJECTS FROM TEMPLE TOMBS 523

Cat. 238

Cat. 238

PORTRAIT B: STANDING FIGURE
The figure is shown frontally.

PORTRAIT C: STANDING FIGURE
The figure is shown frontally.

PORTRAIT D: STANDING FIGURE
The figure is shown frontally.

PORTRAIT E: STANDING FIGURE
The figure is shown frontally. The legs are slightly parted. He is dressed (details unclear).

PORTRAIT F: STANDING PRIEST
The figure is shown frontally.
He wears a tall, cylindrical, flat-top hat: a Palmyrene priestly hat. He is dressed (details unclear).

PORTRAIT G: ARMLESS BUST IN FULCRUM
The figure is shown frontally.

239. SARCOPHAGUS BOX WITH STANDING FIGURES

DATABASE NUMBER: InSitu224
LOCATION: Palmyra, Palmyra Museum, inv. no. B.
CONTEXT: West necropolis. Valley of the Tombs. Temple tomb no. 36.
ACQUISITION HISTORY: —
MEASUREMENTS: Height: 87 cm. Width: 210 cm. Depth: 93 cm.
MATERIAL: Limestone.
PRESERVATION: Broken into two parts. The surface is heavily weathered, and the figures are chipped.
TECHNICAL DESCRIPTION: —
DATE: A.D. 220–240.
REFERENCES: Schmidt-Colinet 1992, 106. 108. 146 cat. S 2 pl. 31, c. e.

OBJECT DESCRIPTION

The sarcophagus box is rectangular in shape and is rendered as a kline. According to Schmidt-Colinet (1992), there are

Cat. 239

six standing figures between the kline legs. Several other fragments belong with this sarcophagus box according to Schmidt-Colinet (1992) and two of these fragments depict parts of the kline frame. Another fragment depicts a part of the kline decorated with a running dog motif.

PORTRAIT A: STANDING FIGURE
The figure is shown frontally.

PORTRAIT B: STANDING FIGURE
The figure is shown frontally.

PORTRAIT C: STANDING FIGURE
The figure is shown frontally.

PORTRAIT D: STANDING FIGURE
The figure is shown frontally.

PORTRAIT E: STANDING FIGURE
The figure is shown frontally.

PORTRAIT F: STANDING FIGURE
The figure is shown frontally.

FRAGMENTS OF LIDS, LID RELIEFS, OR BANQUETING RELIEFS

A.D. 220–240

240. FRAGMENT OF A BANQUETING RELIEF

DATABASE NUMBER: PM480.
LOCATION: Palmyra, Palmyra Museum, inv. no. 662/II.c.7.
CONTEXT: West necropolis. Valley of the Tombs. Temple tomb no. 36.
ACQUISITION HISTORY: —
MEASUREMENTS: Height: 101 cm.
MATERIAL: Limestone.
PRESERVATION: The feet are broken off horizontally at the ankles. The surface of the right arm and of the left hand are chipped. The head has been broken off at the neck and reattached. The face is chipped.
TECHNICAL DESCRIPTION: —
DATE: A.D. 220–240 (Schmidt-Colinet: A.D. 210–240).
REFERENCES: Schmidt-Colinet 1992, 112. 133–135. 137 f. 152 cat. B 19 fig. 52 pl. 43, d; 44, c. d.

OBJECT DESCRIPTION
The object depicts a standing priest. Small areas of the relief background are preserved at either side of the figure.

PORTRAIT
The figure is shown frontally. The left arm appears short in relation to the body. The head appears large in relation to the body. The head is turned slightly to the left. The right arm is held along the body. The left is bent and held to the torso. The legs are slightly set apart and he rests his weight on the right leg.

He wears a high, cylindrical, flat-top headdress divided into three sections by two vertical grooves: a Palmyrene priestly hat. A wreath with the leaves pointing towards a central oval is depicted at the lower part of the hat. The midribs of the leaves are incised. His face is square. The upper left eyelids extend beyond the end of the lower one. The ears are protruding with helix, tragus, and earlobe depicted. The cheeks are fleshy, and the chin is round. The neck is wide.

He wears a tunic and a himation. The tunic has a wide, v-shaped neckline and long, slightly loose sleeves. On either side of the neckline is a band extending downwards and decorated with serrated leaves in an opposite arrangement on the stem, set between beaded bands (clavi). The folds of the tunic are rendered by curving grooves. Over the tunic, he wears a himation. The himation covers most of his body. It is wrapped around his left shoulder and arm, leaving most of the chest and the hand free. One end of the himation crosses the body at the waist and covers his legs. An s-shaped fold falls from under the left hand. The folds of the himation are rendered by oblique and curving grooves.

He holds a fold of the himation with his left hand.

241. MALE AND FEMALE FIGURE

DATABASE NUMBER: PM883.
LOCATION: Palmyra, Palmyra Museum, inv. no. III.b.8, I.c4/83.4.3.
CONTEXT: West necropolis. Valley of the Tombs. Temple tomb no. 36.
ACQUISITION HISTORY: —
MEASUREMENTS: Fragment A: Height: 23 cm. Width: 25 cm. Fragment B: Height: 11 cm. Width: 27 cm.
MATERIAL: Limestone.
PRESERVATION: Fragment A: Most of the background is broken off, except for a small piece to the left of the figure. The upper part of the figure is broken off at middle of the chest, and the lower part is broken off at the middle of the shins. The surface is weathered. Fragment B: The surface is weathered. The relief ground is preserved on both sides of the figure. The upper part is broken off at the neck and shoulders, and the lower body of the figure is broken off at the waist. The attribute is chipped.
TECHNICAL DESCRIPTION: —
DATE: A.D. 220–240.
REFERENCES: Schmidt-Colinet 1992, 105. 118. 152 cat. B 18 fig. 61 pl. 45, c. d.

OBJECT DESCRIPTION
The two fragments depict a seated female and a standing male.

Cat. 240

PORTRAIT A: SEATED FEMALE

The figure is shown frontally. The arms are bent; the right rests on her right thigh, the left is raised to the height of the shoulder. The legs are parted with the knees rendered under the drapery.

She wears a veil and a himation. The veil is wrapped around the arms.

The himation crosses the chest diagonally and covers the torso and the lower body. The edge of the himation that crosses the chest is decorated with a pleated band. The folds of the himation are indicated by oblique grooves.

With the right hand, she holds a fold of the veil; it continues down in a wide fold. The corner has a round ending, suggesting a tassel or even a weight. The thumb and the index finger are extended.

PORTRAIT B: STANDING MALE

The figure is depicted frontally. The arms are bent in front of the torso.

The figure wears a ›Parthian-style‹ tunic. The tunic has long, tight-fitting sleeves and a small, round neckline decorated with a beaded border. It has wide band that extends downwards from the middle of the neckline decorated with a series of squares with a hollowed. The cuffs are decorated with a wide band with a branch with elliptical leaves in opposite arrangement. The folds of the tunic are indicated by oblique grooves.

In the upturned palm of the left hand, he holds an object. Schmidt-Colinet (1992) writes that he holds a bird, perhaps dove.

242. FRAGMENT OF A BANQUETING RELIEF

DATABASE NUMBER: PM882.
LOCATION: Palmyra, Palmyra Museum, inv. no. I.3.
CONTEXT: West necropolis. Valley of the Tombs. Temple tomb no. 36.
ACQUISITION HISTORY: —
MEASUREMENTS: Height: 27 cm.
MATERIAL: Limestone.
PRESERVATION: The head is broken off at the base of the neck, and the lower part is broken off at the waist. The right lower arm and the left hand are broken off. The surface of the chest is chipped, and several cracks run across the surface.
TECHNICAL DESCRIPTION: —
DATE: A.D. 220–240 (Schmidt-Colinet: A.D. 220–250).
REFERENCES: Schmidt-Colinet 1992, 122. 135. 151 cat. B 15 fig. 57 pl. 44, a.

OBJECT DESCRIPTION

The object depicts a female.

PORTRAIT

The figure is depicted frontally. The arms are bent, and the left is held to the side.

She wears a veil that covers the back of the right shoulder and arm. She wears five necklaces: a string of small, round

OBJECTS FROM TEMPLE TOMBS 527

Cat. 241

Cat. 241

Cat. 242

ACQUISITION HISTORY: —
MEASUREMENTS: Height: 93 cm. Length: 134 cm.
MATERIAL: Limestone.
PRESERVATION: Only part of the torso and the left arm is preserved. The surface is weathered.
TECHNICAL DESCRIPTION: —
DATE: A.D. 220–240 (Schmidt-Colinet: A.D. 220–250).
REFERENCES: Schmidt-Colinet 1992, 110. 135. 151 cat. B 16 pl. 44, b.

OBJECT DESCRIPTION

The object is rectangular in shape and depicts one reclining figure. Beneath the figure is a mattress, decorated with an intersecting lozenges pattern with a round element at the intersections. The decoration inside the lozenges alternates between a four-petal cruciform flower and a six-petal rosette. The figure rests on two round cushions: the lower cushion is decorated with a wide band with a running scroll and flowers, framed by beaded borders. The upper cushion is decorated with a wide band with a branch with serrated leaves seen in profile, framed by beaded borders. The texture of the cushions is indicated by wide, curving grooves. According to Schmidt-Colinet (1992) there is a fragment belonging to the object depicting a foot wearing a sandal.

beads worn at the base of the neck. Below that, she wears a plain, thick hoop necklace with a teardrop-shaped pendant with an incised border, suspended by a narrow sleeve at the centre. Over the breasts, she wears a necklace composed of alternating round and rhomboid pendants joined by beaded elements. The round pendants have a beaded border, while the rhomboid pendants have an incised border, linked by beaded elements. Under this, she wears a loop-in-loop chain with a teardrop-shaped pendant with an incised border suspended by a narrow sleeve at the centre. Below the breasts, she wears a necklace composed of an interwoven loop-in-loop chain with a central, oval pendant. The oval pendant has a beaded border and from its lower edge, three spirally wrapped wires are suspended ending in trefoil pendants. The chain and the pendant are linked by terminals decorated with a beaded band.

She wears a tunic with a wide, v-shaped neckline and short, wide sleeves.

243. FRAGMENT OF A BANQUETING RELIEF

DATABASE NUMBER: PM879.
LOCATION: Palmyra, Palmyra Museum, inv. no. 339/510.
CONTEXT: West necropolis. Valley of the Tombs. Temple tomb no. 36.

Cat. 243

PORTRAIT

Reclining figure. The figure is shown in a three-quarter view. The left arm is bent and raised towards the neck.

The figure wears a himation. Several curving folds over the waist indicate that he either wears an undecorated tunic or that the himation covers the torso. The himation is wrapped around the left elbow, and two edges fall below the arm and over the cushion and the mattress in two zigzag-shaped folds.

Schmidt-Colinet (1992) writes that the figure is female.

244. FRAGMENT OF A BANQUETING RELIEF

DATABASE NUMBER: PM492.
LOCATION: Palmyra, Palmyra Museum, inv. no. 635/IV.b.5.
CONTEXT: West necropolis. Valley of the Tombs. Temple tomb no. 36.
ACQUISITION HISTORY: —
MEASUREMENTS: Height: 48 cm. Width: 71 cm.
MATERIAL: Limestone.
PRESERVATION: The right side is broken off at the right elbow, the left side is broken at the left shoulder, and the lower part is broken off at the lower part of the torso. The nose, mouth, and attribute are chipped. The relief ground is weathered.
TECHNICAL DESCRIPTION: —
DATE: A.D. 220–240 (Schmidt-Colinet: A.D. 210–240).
REFERENCES: Schmidt-Colinet 1992, 23 f. 105. 133–135. 151 cat. B 13 pl. 43, c.

OBJECT DESCRIPTION

The object depicts the head and upper part of the torso of a male figure. A part of the relief ground is preserved above his shoulders on either side of his head. Schmidt-Colinet (1992) describes another fragment as belonging to the object: it depicts a hand with a pinecone.

PORTRAIT

The figure is shown frontally. The head is turned slightly to the left.

Cat. 244

His hair is short and rendered in one thick whole. His face is oval. There are two furrows along his forehead. The eyebrows are curving, depicted as thin ridges. The eyes are close-set and almond-shaped with thick eyelids. The eyeballs are blank. The ears are small with the helix and scapha depicted. He has a beard that starts from the temples and covers the cheeks and the chin. The facial hair is rendered by small, flame-shaped curls arranged in rows. The neck is wide. A v-shaped groove indicates the sternocleidomastoid muscles.

He wears a tunic with a wide, v-shaped neckline. The folds of the tunic are rendered by curving and oblique grooves.

245. FRAGMENTS OF A RELIEF

DATABASE NUMBER: PM881 (245a) + PM900 (245b).
LOCATION: Palmyra, Palmyra Museum, inv. no. VII.7, II.c.12, no II.d.9.
CONTEXT: West necropolis. Valley of the Tombs. Temple tomb no. 36.
ACQUISITION HISTORY: —
MEASUREMENTS: 245a: Fragment B: Height: 42 cm. Width: 43 cm. Fragment E: Height: 38 cm. Width: 24 cm. Fragment F: Height: 40 cm. 245b: Height: 26 cm.
MATERIAL: Limestone.
PRESERVATION: Two joining and three non-joining fragments possibly from same relief. 245a: Fragment A: Composed of several pieces. Fragment B: Only a part of the torso, lower left arm, and the cushion survives. 245b: The portrait is broken off at the neck. The upper left side of the portrait is broken off. The surface is weathered.
TECHNICAL DESCRIPTION: —
DATE: A.D. 220–240 (Schmidt-Colinet: A.D. 230–260).
REFERENCES: 245a: Schmidt-Colinet 1992, 110. 112. 135. 150 f. cat. B 11 figs. 53. 54 pl. 42, a. b. f. 245b: Schmidt-Colinet 1992, 122. 139. 154 cat. K 16 pl. 50, c. f.

OBJECT DESCRIPTION

The sarcophagus lid depicts a figure reclining on a mattress decorated with an intersecting lozenges pattern with cruciform, four-petal flowers in the lozenges. There is a bead at the point where the lozenges meet. He rests on a round cushion decorated with a wide band with a vegetal motif and a beaded band. Curving grooves indicate the texture of the fabric. Schmidt-

Cat. 245

Cat. 245

Colinet (1992) describes several fragments as belonging to the object. Fragment A: Fragment of a seated figure and the foot of a reclining figure. Fragment C: Hand fragment. Fragment D: Shoulder fragment with hand. Fragment G: Fragment of upper torso. The relief had multiple figures; however, it is not possible to say if the fragments can be joined or if they reflect the number of figures. 245b joins with the objects (according to Schmidt-Colinet 1992), and it depicts the head of a male figure. As it is, only the following portraits can be deduced with certainty:

PORTRAIT A: STANDING FIGURE (FRAGMENT F)

The figure is depicted frontally. The right arm falls along the side, the left arm is bent in front of the torso.

The figure wears a tunic and a himation. The tunic has short sleeves. The folds of the tunic are indicated by wide, curving grooves. Over the tunic, he wears a himation that is wrapped around the waist and covers the left side and arm of the figure. The end of the himation that covers the waist is wrapped around the lower left arm and wrist and falls down.

With his right hand, he holds an object with a thick stem, against which are seven narrow leaves with incised midribs in opposite arrangement; either a branch or a palm leaf. With his left hand, he holds a fold of the himation.

PORTRAIT B: RECLINING MALE (FRAGMENT B)

The figure is dressed. Wide curving grooves over the lower torso may indicate he was wearing a tunic. He also wears a himation that covers the waist, is wrapped around the lower left arm, and falls in two zigzag-shaped folds over the cushion and the mattress.

PORTRAIT C: MALE HEAD

The figure is shown frontally.

The hair is short and arranged in rows of flame-shaped curls. The ear is small and slightly protruding. The helix, scapha, and concha are depicted. The eyebrow is arched and plastically rendered, with oblique, incised lines above a diagonal, incised line indicating individual hairs. The eye has thick eyelids.

Cat. 245

Cat. 245

246. FRAGMENTS OF BANQUETING RELIEF

DATABASE NUMBER: PM473 (246a) + PM466 (246b).
LOCATION: Palmyra, Palmyra Museum, inv. no. II.b.1/2, II.a.1.
CONTEXT: West necropolis. Valley of the Tombs. Temple tomb no. 36.
ACQUISITION HISTORY: —
MEASUREMENTS: 246a: Height: 27 cm. 246b: Height: 15 cm.
MATERIAL: Limestone.
PRESERVATION: Two non-joining fragments possibly from same relief. 246a: The lower part of the figure is broken off diagonally from the right shoulder to the left upper arm. A crack runs vertically through the head under the ears. The nose and the mouth are chipped. 246b: The portrait is broken off at the lower part of the head. The veil is chipped.
TECHNICAL DESCRIPTION: —
DATE: A.D. 220–240 (Schmidt-Colinet: A.D. 210–240).
REFERENCES: 246a: Schmidt-Colinet 1992, 118–120. 122 f. 136 f. 153 cat. K 4 fig. 52 pl. 49, a. b. 246b: Schmidt-Colinet 1992, 136 f. 154 f. cat. K 29 fig. 56 pl. 53, c. d; Krag 2018, 108 n. 125. 127; 352 cat. 708.

OBJECT DESCRIPTION
246a depicts the head of a priest. 246b depicts a female head. The fragments probably come from figures on a banqueting relief.

PORTRAIT A: HEAD OF PRIEST
The figure is shown frontally. The head is turned slightly to the left.

He wears a high, cylindrical, flat-top headdress divided into three sections by two vertical grooves: a Palmyrene priestly hat. A wreath with narrow, pointed leaves in three rows pointing towards a central, raised oval is depicted at the lower part of the hat. The midribs of the leaves are incised.

His face is square. The eyebrows are curving, rendered by incised lines, starting from the root of the nose. The eyes are almond-shaped, with thick upper eyelids. The end of the upper eyelids extends beyond that of the lower ones. The irises are indicated by incised circles and touch the upper eyelids. The ears are protruding with the helix and lobe depicted. The mouth is small with a full lower lip. The chin is round and almost double. The neck is wide with two curving grooves.

He wears a tunic. The folds are rendered by oblique grooves. Another garment, possibly a himation or chlamys is rendered on his left shoulder.

Cat. 246

Cat. 246

PORTRAIT B: FEMALE HEAD

The figure is shown frontally.

She wears three headdresses: a headband, turban, and a veil. The headband is decorated with rectangular panels and a beaded border at its lower edge. The turban is coiled, with curving grooves indicating the coiling of the fabric. Over the headband, she wears a heavy veil that falls down the back of the head. Over the turban, she wears a central head ornament and a head-chain. The central head ornament has an upper, oval bezel with a beaded border and a lower, rectangular bezel with a beaded border, joined by a beaded element composed of five round beads. Four round beads are suspended from the lower edge of the rectangular bezel. It runs from under the veil to the centre of the forehead. The head-chain is fastened under the oval bezel and runs to either side of the head. It is composed of large, round elements joined by small, round beaded elements. The hair is visible at the sides of the forehead; it is slightly wavy and combed backwards, with individual strands of hair indicated by s-shaped grooves. It covers the sides of the headband and of the turban. Her face is oval. The eyebrows are rendered by thin, curving grooves that start from the root of the nose. The eyes are large and almond-shaped, with thick upper eyelids. The upper eyelids extend downwards and beyond the end of the lower eyelids. The irises touch the upper eyelids; they are rendered by incised circles and the pupils by punch holes. The earlobes are visible, and she wears earrings composed of three juxtaposed biconical beads (Colledge classification: L). The nose is straight.

247. FRAGMENTS OF A BANQUETING RELIEF

DATABASE NUMBER: PM467 (247a) + PM468 (247b).
LOCATION: Palmyra, Palmyra Museum, inv. no. II.c.4, III.b.2.
CONTEXT: West necropolis. Valley of the Tombs. Temple tomb no. 36.
ACQUISITION HISTORY: —
MEASUREMENTS: Portrait A: Height: 23 cm. Width: 20 cm. Height of head: 13 cm. Portrait B: Height: 19 cm. Width: 15 cm. Height of head: 13 cm.
MATERIAL: Limestone.
PRESERVATION: Two non-joining fragments from the same relief. Portrait A: The lower part of the figure is broken diagonally from the right shoulder. The nose and mouth are chipped. Portrait B: The background around the figure is broken off. The lower part is broken off at the neck. The veil is broken off. The nose and mouth are chipped.
TECHNICAL DESCRIPTION: The lower eyelids are not carved.
DATE: A.D. 220–240 (Schmidt-Colinet: A.D. 220–250).
REFERENCES: 247a: Schmidt-Colinet 1992, 121–123 137. 152 cat. B 20a fig. 54 pl. 46, a. b. 247b: Schmidt-Colinet 1992, 152 cat. B 20b pl. 46, c. d; Krag 2018, 73 n. 47. 51; 373 cat. 781.

OBJECT DESCRIPTION

The object was originally rectangular in shape and depicts the head and right shoulder of a male figure, and the head of a female figure. The relief ground is preserved on the right side of his head.

PORTRAIT A: MALE FIGURE

The figure is shown frontally.

His hair is arranged in three rows of flame-shaped curls around the head. A thick braid runs in a semicircle from the crown of the head to the right side. The individual strands

Cat. 247

Cat. 247

of hair are indicated by incised lines. His face is oval. The eyebrows are curving, depicted as thin ridges. The eyes are deep-set and almond-shaped, with thick upper eyelids. The eyeballs are blank. His ears are protruding and partly covered by his hair, with the helix and lobe depicted. The cheeks are fleshy. The mouth is small, with full lips. The chin is round and almost double. The neck is wide.

He wears a tunic with a wide, round neckline. The folds of the tunic are rendered by curving and vertical grooves.

PORTRAIT B: FEMALE FIGURE
The figure is shown frontally.

She wears a veil that falls on either side of her head. The hair is centrally parted and arranged in rows. Oblique grooves indicate the individual strands of hair. A series of curved grooves at the top of the head indicate either a plait at the top of the head or a turban. She wears a drop-shaped pendant on the hair over the left ear. The face is oval and fleshy. The eyebrows are curving. The upper eyelids are thick. The eyeballs are blank. The ears are small and close to the head. She wears dumbbell-shaped earrings (Colledge classification: H). The nose is straight. Nasolabial lines are indicated by incised grooves. The mouth is small, with full lips. The chin is square. The neck is slender and long, with a curving groove.

248. FRAGMENTS OF A RELIEF

DATABASE NUMBER: PM895 (248a) + PM476 (248b).
LOCATION: Palmyra, Palmyra Museum, inv. no. II.b.3, III.b.7.
CONTEXT: West necropolis. Valley of the Tombs. Temple tomb no. 36.
ACQUISITION HISTORY: —
MEASUREMENTS: 248a: Height: 13 cm. 248b: Height: 11 cm.
MATERIAL: Limestone.
PRESERVATION: Two non-joining fragments possibly from same relief. 248a: The head is broken off at the height of the top of the nose. The upper and the left part of the priestly hat are broken off. 248b: The portrait is broken off at the top of the neck. The nose and the lips are broken off. The hair and cheeks are chipped. A crack runs across the lower part of the face. The surface is weathered.
TECHNICAL DESCRIPTION: —
DATE: A.D. 220–240 (Schmidt-Colinet: A.D. 220–250).
REFERENCES: 248a: Schmidt-Colinet 1992, 122. 137 f. 153 cat. K 7 pl. 49, c. 248b: Schmidt-Colinet 1992, 122. 137 f. 154 cat. K 27 pl. 49, h.

OBJECT DESCRIPTION
248a depicts a priest and 248b depicts the head of a male figure.

PORTRAIT A: HEAD OF PRIEST
He wears a tall, cylindrical, flat-top headdress divided into three sections by two vertical grooves: a Palmyrene priestly hat. A wreath is depicted at the lower part of the hat. It has three rows of small, elliptical leaves pointing towards an oval

Cat. 248

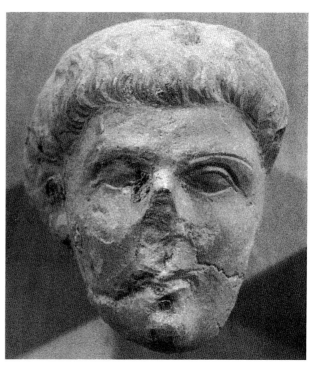

Cat. 248

decoration with an incised centre. A narrow, horizontal band at the bottom of the hat suggests a liner. The eyebrows are arched, rendered by incised lines. The eyes are almond-shaped, with thick eyelids. The irises are indicated by incised arches that touch the upper eyelids.

PORTRAIT B: MALE HEAD
The figure is shown frontally.

The hair is short and arranged in alternating rows of crescent-shaped curls. His face is oval. The eyebrows are curving and indicated by incised lines. The eyes are almond-shaped, with thin upper eyelids. The end of the upper eyelids extends downwards and beyond that of the lower ones. The eyeballs are blank. The mouth is small. The chin is pointed.

249. FRAGMENTS OF A BANQUETING RELIEF

DATABASE NUMBER: PM877.
LOCATION: Palmyra, Palmyra Museum, inv. no II.a.20/I.4, inv. no II.c.15/18, inv. no II.a.4, inv. no VI.10/13/16.
CONTEXT: West necropolis. Valley of the Tombs. Temple tomb no. 36.
ACQUISITION HISTORY: —
MEASUREMENTS: Fragment A: Height: 30 cm. Width: 40 cm. Fragment B: Width: 26 cm. Fragment C: Height: 26 cm. Fragment D: Height: 43 cm.
MATERIAL: Limestone.
PRESERVATION: Fragment A: Part of the foot of a reclining figure on a mattress. The surface of the foot is chipped. Composed of several pieces. Fragment B: Part of right upper arm. Fragment C: The figure is broken off at the waist and the middle of the thighs. The area of the waist and the hands are chipped. Composed of several fragments. Fragment D: Part of cushion. Composed of several fragments.
TECHNICAL DESCRIPTION: —
DATE: A.D. 220–240 (Schmidt-Colinet: A.D. 210–240).
REFERENCES: Schmidt-Colinet 1992, 130. 133–135. 151 cat. B 12 fig. 61 pl. 42, c. d. e. g.

OBJECT DESCRIPTION
The relief was rectangular and depicts one reclining figure and at least two standing figures. The figure reclines on a mattress, decorated with an intersecting lozenges pattern. There is a round, raised element at the intersections. Each lozenge is decorated with a four-petal cruciform flower. The reclining figure rests on a round cushion: it is decorated with a wide band between two beaded bands. The wide band has a running scroll motif with flowers. Two of the flowers have round, flat petals, one of the flowers has round raised petals, another has serrated and twisting petals and two have rhomboid petals.

PORTRAIT A: RECLINING MALE
The foot is shown in profile.

He wears a garment that falls over the cushion in several folds, either a chlamys or a himation, and >Parthian-style< trousers. The trousers are loose-fitting and tucked into boots. The folds of the trousers are indicated by curving grooves. The boot is decorated with a beaded band at the top, a band with a running scroll with five-petal rosettes and circles, and a hexagon with beaded border. Each circle encloses a flower; the flowers all have different petals: one has round ones with an incised border and a depression at the centre, one has long, narrow ones, and one has serrated and twisted ones. The hexagon encloses a flower with serrated petals. The space between the circles and the hexagon is decorated with tendrils and serrated leaves.

Fragment B probably belongs to this portrait: it shows the upper right arm of a figure, dressed in a sleeved tunic (not seen).

PORTRAIT B: STANDING FIGURE
The remains of a hand across the upper arm of a figure suggest a standing figure behind the reclining one (fragment B). Schmidt-Colinet (1992) proposes it is that of a child.

PORTRAIT C: STANDING FEMALE FIGURE
The figure is shown frontally. The arms fall to the sides.

The figure wears a tunic and a second garment over it, a himation or a veil. The tunic covers the legs. The folds of the tunic are rendered by oblique grooves on either side of the leg and a curving groove over the thigh. She wears a garment over the tunic, a himation or a veil that falls diagonally across the lower body and the left leg. The edge of the garment is decorated with a pleated band. The folds of the garment are rendered by curving grooves. The thumb, index, and the little fingers of the right hand are extended.

Cat. 249

Cat. 249

Cat. 249

Cat. 249

250. FRAGMENTS OF A RELIEF

DATABASE NUMBER: PM873 (250a) + PM460 (250b).
LOCATION: Palmyra, Palmyra Museum, inv. no. VI.4, VI.2.
CONTEXT: West necropolis. Valley of the Tombs. Temple tomb no. 36.
ACQUISITION HISTORY: —
MEASUREMENTS: 250a: Height: 13 cm. Length: 23 cm. 250b: Height: 20 cm.
MATERIAL: Limestone.
PRESERVATION: Two non-joining fragments possibly from same object. 250a: The head is broken off at the middle of the neck. The upper part of the head, including the face, is broken off. The left side of the face is broken off. 250b: The head is broken off at the top of the neck. The upper part of the head, the forehead, and the right eye are broken off. The nose, the mouth, and the chin are chipped. A part of the relief background is preserved above the left side of the head.
TECHNICAL DESCRIPTION: —
DATE: A.D. 220–240 (Schmidt-Colinet: A.D. 220–250).
REFERENCES: 250a: Schmidt-Colinet 1992, 122. 137 f. 154 cat. K 32 pl. 54, b. 250b: Schmidt-Colinet 1992, 122. 136 f. 154 cat. K 22 pl. 52, e.

OBJECT DESCRIPTION
250a depicts the head of a female figure and 250b depicts the head of a male figure. According to Schmidt-Colinet (1992), the objects join together.

PORTRAIT A: FEMALE
The figure is shown frontally.

She wears a headdress: a veil. The veil is thick and falls down on either side of the face. Several strands of hair are pushed back over the ears. Individual strands of hair are indicated by incised lines.

The face is oval and fleshy. She wears earrings composed of three juxtaposed beads: two large round ones on either side of a small, biconical one (Colledge classification: L).

PORTRAIT B: MALE
His hair is rendered in four rows of snail-shell curls around the head. The individual strands of hair are indicated by incised lines. The face is oval. The eyes are almond-shaped, with thick upper eyelids. The end of the upper eyelids extends beyond that of the lower ones. The eyeballs are blank. Only the earlobe is visible under the hair. The nose is narrow. The mouth is small, with full lips. The chin is oval.

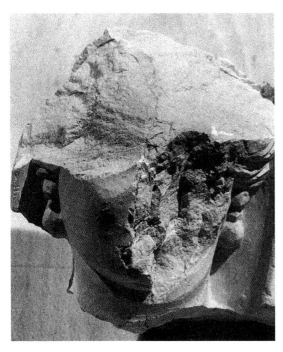

Cat. 250

Cat. 250

A.D. 240–273

251. FRAGMENTS OF BANQUETING RELIEF

DATABASE NUMBER: PM880 (251a) + PM899 (251b).
LOCATION: Palmyra, Palmyra Museum, inv. no. 346/361/83.13.3, II.19.
CONTEXT: West necropolis. Valley of the Tombs. Temple tomb no. 36.
ACQUISITION HISTORY: —
MEASUREMENTS: 251a: Height: 56 cm. Width: 77 cm. 251b: Height: 25 cm.
MATERIAL: Limestone.
PRESERVATION: 251a: The left, upper, and lower sides of the lid are broken off. The head and neck of the figure, the right arm, and part of the upper left arm are broken off. The surface is weathered and heavily chipped, especially at the lower left arm, the waist, and the legs. 251b: Only a small part of a wreath is preserved.
TECHNICAL DESCRIPTION: —
DATE: A.D. 240–273 (Schmidt-Colinet: A.D. 220–250).
REFERENCES: 251a: Schmidt-Colinet 1992, 108. 112. 125. 130. 135. 149 cat. B 7 fig. 60 pl. 38, d. 41, a. f. 251b: Schmidt-Colinet 1992, 153 cat. K 14 fig. 53.

OBJECT DESCRIPTION

The object (251a) depicts a reclining male. He rests on a round cushion decorated with a wide band with a branch with serrated leaves in opposite arrangement, framed by beaded bands. The texture of the cushion is rendered by wide, curving grooves. Behind the left shoulder of the figure is a priestly headdress. It is tall, cylindrical, with a flat top and divided into three sections by two vertical grooves. A wreath with three rows of small, elliptical leaves is depicted at the lower part of the headdress. The leaves point towards a medallion with an armless bust of a male in tunic and a chlamys fastened at the right shoulder by a round brooch (details unclear). A series of grooves curving in opposite directions is depicted under the headdress, probably indicating swathes of fabric. 251b depicts part of a wreath, composed of two rows of serrated leaves.

PORTRAIT

The figure is depicted frontally.

He wears a >Parthian-style< tunic and a himation. The tunic has a wide, round neckline. The tunic is decorated with two wide bands that extend downwards from the sides of the neckline. The bands are decorated with two vine scrolls with small leaves and tendrils, and they are framed by beaded bands. The folds of the tunic are indicated by curving grooves. The himation covers the left lower arm and is wrapped around the left elbow and lower arm. It falls down from under the arm over the cushion and the mattress in two zigzag-shaped folds. The edges of the himation are decorated with a wide band framed by beaded borders. The folds of the himation are indicated by oblique folds.

Cat. 251

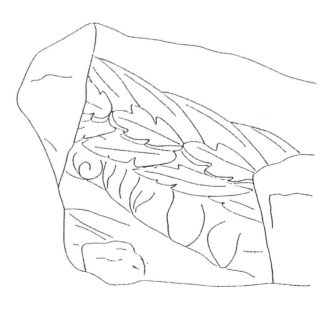

Cat. 251

FRAGMENTS OF BOXES, BOX RELIEFS, OR BANQUETING RELIEFS

A.D. 220–240

252. FRAGMENTS OF A SARCOPHAGUS BOX

DATABASE NUMBER: PM888.
LOCATION: Palmyra, Palmyra Museum, inv. no. unknown.
CONTEXT: West necropolis. Valley of the Tombs. Temple tomb no. 36.
ACQUISITION HISTORY: —
MEASUREMENTS: Fragment A: Height: 20 cm. Width: 21 cm. Fragment B: Height 9 cm. Width: 23 cm.
MATERIAL: Limestone.
PRESERVATION: The surface is weathered. Fragment A: Fragments from a sarcophagus box broken on all sides. Fragment B: Part of frame of a kline. Portrait: The upper part of the head and the torso are broken off.
TECHNICAL DESCRIPTION: —
DATE: A.D. 220–240.
REFERENCES: Schmidt-Colinet 1992, 108. 147 f. cat. S 7 pl. 32, e. f. g.

OBJECT DESCRIPTION
The fragments depict a sarcophagus box in the shape of a kline. Fragment A depicts two clipei, rendered as concentric, incised circles. A bust inside a clipeus is also depicted. Fragment B depicts a part of the kline's stretcher, decorated with a rectangular, raised frame. Inside, there is a running dog pattern.

PORTRAIT
The figure is depicted frontally.
The face is oval. The neck is slender.

Cat. 252

Cat. 252

Cat. 252

HEADS: PRIESTS

1–10 CM

A.D. 210–273

253. FRAGMENT OF HEAD OF A PRIEST

DATABASE NUMBER: PM896.
LOCATION: Palmyra, Palmyra Museum, inv. no. III.1.
CONTEXT: West necropolis. Valley of the Tombs. Temple tomb no. 36.
ACQUISITION HISTORY: —
MEASUREMENTS: Height: 7 cm.
MATERIAL: Limestone.
PRESERVATION: The upper and the lower part of the priestly hat are broken off.
TECHNICAL DESCRIPTION: —
DATE: A.D. 210–273.
REFERENCES: Schmidt-Colinet 1992, 122. 153 cat. K 9 fig. 52.

OBJECT DESCRIPTION
The fragment depicts a Palmyrene priestly hat. According to Schmidt-Colinet (1992), the fragment possibly comes from the same relief as cat. 255.

PORTRAIT
Tall, cylindrical, flat-top headdress divided into three sections by two vertical grooves: a Palmyrene priestly hat. A wreath is depicted at the lower part of the hat. It has three rows of small, elliptical leaves pointing towards an oval with an incised border. Two berries are on either side of the central leaf next to the oval.

A.D. 220–240

254. HEAD OF A PRIEST

DATABASE NUMBER: PM474.
LOCATION: Palmyra, Palmyra Museum, inv. no. 83.38.3.
CONTEXT: West necropolis. Valley of the Tombs. Temple tomb no. 36.
ACQUISITION HISTORY: —
MEASUREMENTS: Height: 9.5 cm.
MATERIAL: Limestone.
PRESERVATION: The head is broken off at the neck. The upper left part of the Palmyrene priestly hat is broken off. The oval decoration on the Palmyrene priestly hat and the lower part of the hat, the forehead, the right ear, the nose, the right cheek, and the chin are chipped.
TECHNICAL DESCRIPTION: —

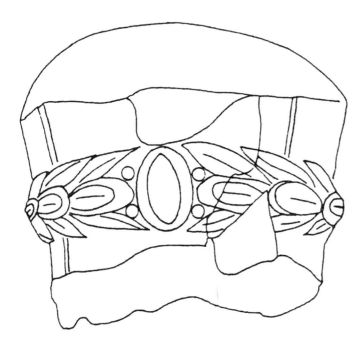

Cat. 253

Cat. 254

OBJECTS FROM TEMPLE TOMBS 541

DATE: A.D. 220–240.
REFERENCES: Schmidt-Colinet 1992, 122. 138. 153 cat. K 6 fig. 52 pl. 49, d.

OBJECT DESCRIPTION
The fragment depicts a priest.
According to Schmidt-Colinet (1992), this head is possibly from the same relief as cat. 257.

PORTRAIT
He wears a tall, cylindrical, flat-top headdress divided into three sections by two vertical grooves low on the forehead: a Palmyrene priestly hat. A wreath, with three rows of long, elliptical leaves pointing towards an oval, is depicted at the lower part of the hat. The midribs of the leaves are incised. A narrow, horizontal band under the bottom of the hat suggests a liner. His face is oval. The eyebrows are depicted by low, curving, incised lines. The eyes are almond-shaped, with thick upper eyelids. The eyeballs are blank. The ears are small and protruding, with the helix, anti-helix, and lobe depicted. The nose is wide. The mouth is small, with full lips. The chin is pointed.

11–20 CM

A.D. 220–240

255. HEAD OF A PRIEST

DATABASE NUMBER: PM475.
LOCATION: Palmyra, Palmyra Museum, inv. no. III.d.1/IV.a.1.
CONTEXT: West necropolis. Valley of the Tombs. Temple tomb no. 36.
ACQUISITION HISTORY: —
MEASUREMENTS: Height: 15 cm.
MATERIAL: Limestone.
PRESERVATION: The head is broken off at the neck. The upper part and the lower left side of the Palmyrene priestly hat, the upper left side of the face, the left ear, the nose, the right cheek, and the tip of the chin are broken off. A large crack runs horizontally across the face under the nose.
TECHNICAL DESCRIPTION: —
DATE: A.D. 220–240.
REFERENCES: Schmidt-Colinet 1992, 122. 153 cat. K 8 fig. 52 pl. 49, e.

OBJECT DESCRIPTION
The fragment depicts a priest.
According to Schmidt-Colinet (1992), this head is possibly from the same relief as cat. 253.

PORTRAIT
The figure is shown frontally. The head is slightly turned to his right.

Cat. 255

He wears a tall, cylindrical, flat-top headdress divided into three sections by two vertical grooves low on the forehead: a Palmyrene priestly hat. A wreath, with three rows of long, elliptical leaves pointing towards an oval with an incised border, is depicted at the lower part of the hat. The midribs of the leaves are incised. A narrow, horizontal band under the bottom of the hat suggests a liner. His face is oval. The eyebrows are depicted by low, curving, incised lines. The eyes are almond-shaped, with thick upper eyelids. The eyeballs are blank. The ears are small and protruding, with the helix, anti-helix, and lobe depicted. The mouth is small, with a full lower lip. The chin is pointed. The neck is long.

256. FRAGMENT OF HEAD OF A PRIEST

DATABASE NUMBER: PM477.
LOCATION: Palmyra, Palmyra Museum, inv. no. 83.27.1.
CONTEXT: West necropolis. Valley of the Tombs. Temple tomb no. 36.
ACQUISITION HISTORY: —
MEASUREMENTS: Height: 17 cm.
MATERIAL: Limestone.
PRESERVATION: The head is broken off at the neck. The upper part of the face, including the nose, and the Palmyrene

Cat. 256

257. HEAD OF A PRIEST

DATABASE NUMBER: PM478.
LOCATION: Palmyra, Palmyra Museum, inv. no. 83.38.2.
CONTEXT: West necropolis. Valley of the Tombs. Temple tomb no. 36.
ACQUISITION HISTORY: —
MEASUREMENTS: Height: 17 cm.
MATERIAL: Limestone.
PRESERVATION: The head is broken off at the neck. The upper part of the Palmyrene priestly hat, the ears, and the tip of the nose are broken off. Two cracks run horizontally across the head, one across the lower part of the hat, and one in the middle of the face.
TECHNICAL DESCRIPTION: —
DATE: A.D. 220–240.
REFERENCES: Schmidt-Colinet 1992, 122. 137. 153 K 5 fig. 52 pl. 48, c. d.

OBJECT DESCRIPTION
The fragment depicts a priest.
According to Schmidt-Colinet (1992), this head is possibly from the same relief as cat. 254.

priestly hat are broken off. The centre of the upper lip is chipped.
TECHNICAL DESCRIPTION: —
DATE: A.D. 220–240.
REFERENCES: Schmidt-Colinet 1992, 122. 137. 152 cat. K 2 pl. 48, a. b.

OBJECT DESCRIPTION
The fragment depicts a priest.

PORTRAIT
The figure is shown frontally.
He wears a tall, cylindrical headdress: a Palmyrene priestly hat. It has a wreath projecting out of a tubular band that runs across the side of the hat. His face is oval. The eyebrows are depicted by low, curving, incised lines. The eyes are large and round, with thick upper eyelids. The ears are large and protruding, with helix, anti-helix, and lobe depicted. The nose has a wide base. Nasolabial lines are indicated by incised lines. The mouth is small, with full lower lip. Two incised lines project downwards from the corners of the mouth. The chin is pointed, and he has a double chin. The neck is wide.

Cat. 257

OBJECTS FROM TEMPLE TOMBS 543

PORTRAIT

The figure is shown frontally. The head is turned slightly to his right.

He wears a tall, cylindrical, flat-top headdress divided into three sections by two vertical grooves low on the forehead: a Palmyrene priestly hat. A wreath is depicted at the lower part of the hat. It has three rows of long, elliptical leaves pointing towards a medallion with an incised centre. A narrow, horizontal band under the bottom of the hat suggests a liner. His face is square and fleshy. The eyebrows are depicted by low, curving, incised lines. The eyes are large and round, with thick upper eyelids. The end of the upper eyelids extends downwards and beyond that of the lower ones. The irises are indicated by incised arches and they touch the upper eyelids. The nose is straight. Nasolabial lines are indicated by the carving of the planes of the face. The mouth is small, with a full lower lip. The chin is round, with a cleft. The neck is wide.

21–30 CM

A.D. 220–240
---

258. HEAD OF A PRIEST

DATABASE NUMBER: PM472.
LOCATION: Palmyra, Palmyra Museum, inv. no. II.a.2.
CONTEXT: West necropolis. Valley of the Tombs. Temple tomb no. 36.
ACQUISITION HISTORY: —
MEASUREMENTS: Height: 25 cm.
MATERIAL: Limestone.
PRESERVATION: The head is broken off at the neck, with only a small piece of the background preserved behind the right shoulder. The top of the Palmyrene priestly hat, part of the left side of the wreath next to the oval decoration, the lower left side of the forehead, the left side of the forehead and left eyebrow, the bridge of the nose, and the alae, the left cheek, and chin, are chipped.
TECHNICAL DESCRIPTION: —
DATE: A.D. 220–240 (Schmidt-Colinet: A.D. 210–240).
REFERENCES: Schmidt-Colinet 1992, 136 f. 152 f. cat. K 3 fig. 52 pl. 47, c. d.

OBJECT DESCRIPTION

The fragment depicts a priest.

PORTRAIT

The figure is shown frontally.

He wears a tall, cylindrical, flat-top headdress divided into three sections by two vertical grooves low on the forehead: a Palmyrene priestly hat. A wreath is depicted at the lower part of the hat. It has three rows of long, elliptical leaves pointing towards an oval with a beaded border and an incised central oval, indicating an inlay. The wreath projects from a

Cat. 258

tubular band that runs across the side of the hat. The midribs of the leaves are incised. A narrow, horizontal band under the bottom of the hat suggests a liner. His face is oval. The eyebrows are depicted by low curving, incised lines. The eyes are almond-shaped, with thick upper eyelids. The left eye is positioned slightly higher on the head than the right one. The lower eyelids are indicated by incised lines. The upper eyelids extend downwards and beyond the end of the lower ones. The irises are indicated by incised lines, and the pupils by punch holes. The irises touch the upper eyelids. The ears are small and protruding, with the helix, anti-helix, and lobe depicted. The left ear is positioned slightly higher at the head than the right one. The nose is straight with a wide base. The nostrils are drilled. The mouth is small, with full lips. Two grooves extend downwards from the corners of the mouth. The chin is round. The neck is long and slender, with two curving grooves.

Cat. 259

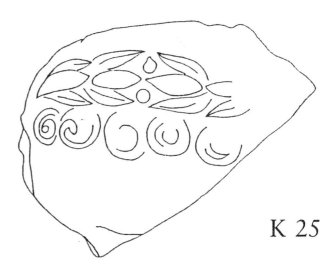

Cat. 260

HEADS: MALES

0–10 CM

A.D. 220–240

259. FRAGMENT OF A MALE HEAD

DATABASE NUMBER: PM866.
LOCATION: Palmyra, Palmyra Museum, inv. no. 83.6.2.
CONTEXT: West necropolis. Valley of the Tombs. Temple tomb no. 36.
ACQUISITION HISTORY: —
MEASUREMENTS: Height: 4 cm.
MATERIAL: Limestone.
PRESERVATION: The portrait is broken off diagonally at the middle of the face. The upper part of the head is broken off.
TECHNICAL DESCRIPTION: —
DATE: A.D. 220–240.
REFERENCES: Schmidt-Colinet 1992, 154 cat. K 28 pl. 49, k.

OBJECT DESCRIPTION
The fragment depicts the head of a male figure.
According to Schmidt-Colinet (1992), it probably comes from a sarcophagus.

PORTRAIT
The figure is shown frontally.
The hair is short and rendered by a series of oblique, incised lines. The eyebrows are low, curving and indicated by incised lines. The eyes are round, with thick eyelids. The irises are hollowed out.

260. FRAGMENT OF A MALE HEAD

DATABASE NUMBER: PM863.
LOCATION: Palmyra, Palmyra Museum, inv. no. 83.2.6.
CONTEXT: West necropolis. Valley of the Tombs. Temple tomb no. 36.
ACQUISITION HISTORY: —
MEASUREMENTS: Height: 10 cm.
MATERIAL: Limestone.
PRESERVATION: Only a part of the head with the wreath survives.
TECHNICAL DESCRIPTION: —
DATE: A.D. 220–240.
REFERENCES: Schmidt-Colinet 1992, 122. 154 cat. K 25 fig. 53.

OBJECT DESCRIPTION
The fragment depicts a male head.

PORTRAIT
The hair is arranged in rows of snail-shell curls. He wears a wreath, with three rows of narrow leaves pointing towards two round elements.

11–20 CM

A.D. 210–220

261. MALE HEAD

DATABASE NUMBER: PM459.
LOCATION: Palmyra, Palmyra Museum, inv. no. VI.2.
CONTEXT: West necropolis. Valley of the Tombs. Temple tomb no. 36.
ACQUISITION HISTORY: —
MEASUREMENTS: Height: 20 cm.
MATERIAL: Limestone.

OBJECTS FROM TEMPLE TOMBS 545

Cat. 261

PRESERVATION: The head is broken off at the base of the neck. The chin is slightly chipped.
TECHNICAL DESCRIPTION: —
DATE: A.D. 210–220.
REFERENCES: Schmidt-Colinet 1992, 122. 136. 137 n. 530. 154 cat. K 22 pl. 52, c–d.

OBJECT DESCRIPTION
The fragment depicts the head of a male figure.

PORTRAIT
His hair is rendered in three rows of snail-shell curls around the head. The individual strands of hair are indicated by incised lines. His face is round. The eyebrows are curving and rendered, with incised lines starting at the root of the nose. The eyes are almond-shaped, with a thick upper eyelid. The end of the upper eyelids extends beyond that of the lower ones. The irises are indicated by incised circles. The nose is short and wide. The mouth is small, with full lips. The chin is oval. The neck is wide.

A.D. 220–240
---

262. MALE HEAD

DATABASE NUMBER: PM457.
LOCATION: Palmyra, Palmyra Museum, inv. no. III.3.

CONTEXT: West necropolis. Valley of the Tombs. Temple tomb no. 36.
ACQUISITION HISTORY: —
MEASUREMENTS: Height: 20 cm.
MATERIAL: Limestone.
PRESERVATION: The head is broken off at the base of the neck. The nose and the right ear are chipped.
TECHNICAL DESCRIPTION: —
DATE: A.D. 220–240.
REFERENCES: Schmidt-Colinet 1992, 137 n. 534. 154 cat. K 19 pl. 51, c. d.

OBJECT DESCRIPTION
The fragment depicts the head of a male figure. Part of the relief background is preserved at the left side of the head.

PORTRAIT
The figure is shown frontally. He turns his head slightly to the left.

His hair is rendered in two rows of flame-shaped curls around the head. The individual strands of hair are indicated by incised lines. His face is oval. The eyebrows are curving and plastically rendered, with oblique, incised lines indicating individual hairs, and meeting above the root of the nose in a v-shaped groove. The eyes are almond-shaped, with a thick

Cat. 262

upper eyelid. The end of the upper eyelids extends beyond that of the lower ones. The irises are depicted by incised circles and the pupils by punch holes. The ears are protruding, and the helix, scapha, tragus, and earlobe are depicted. The nose is wide. The alae are incised, and the nostrils are carved. He has a beard: it starts at the temples and covers the outer side of the cheeks, the chin, and the upper lip. The facial hair is rendered by comma-shaped curls in the beard, and vertical, incised lines on the moustache. The mouth is small, with full lips. The chin is oval.

263. FRAGMENT OF A MALE HEAD

DATABASE NUMBER: PM458.
LOCATION: Palmyra, Palmyra Museum, inv. no. III.3.
CONTEXT: West necropolis. Valley of the Tombs. Temple tomb no. 36.
ACQUISITION HISTORY: —
MEASUREMENTS: Height: 15 cm.
MATERIAL: Limestone.
PRESERVATION: The head is broken off at the mouth. The lower half of the left ear is broken off.
TECHNICAL DESCRIPTION: —
DATE: A.D. 220–240 (Schmidt-Colinet: A.D. 220–250).
REFERENCES: Schmidt-Colinet 1992, 138. 139 n. 547. 154 cat. K 20 pl. 52, a–b.

OBJECT DESCRIPTION
The fragment depicts the head of a male figure.

PORTRAIT
His hair is rendered in comma-shaped curls around the head. The individual strands of hair are indicated by incised lines. His face is oval. The eyebrows are curving and rendered as narrow ridges, starting from the root of the noose. The eyes are almond-shaped, with a thick upper eyelid. The end of the upper eyelids extends beyond that of the lower ones. The eyeballs are blank. The ears are protruding, and the helix, scapha, tragus, and earlobe are depicted. The nose is straight and wide. The alae are incised, and the nostrils carved. He has a nasolabial fold on each side of the nose. He has a beard: it starts at the temples and covers the outer side of the cheeks, the chin, and the upper lip. The facial hair is rendered by comma-shaped curls in the beard, and vertical, incised lines on the moustache. The mouth is large, with a full lower lip.

According to Schmidt-Colinet (1992), it could belong to a loculus relief.

264. FRAGMENT OF A MALE HEAD

DATABASE NUMBER: PM465.
LOCATION: Palmyra, Palmyra Museum, inv. no. II.a.12.
CONTEXT: West necropolis. Valley of the Tombs. Temple tomb no. 36.
ACQUISITION HISTORY: —
MEASUREMENTS: Height: 17 cm.
MATERIAL: Limestone.
PRESERVATION: The lower part of the figure is broken off at the chin. The tip of the nose is chipped. The crown of the head is broken off.
TECHNICAL DESCRIPTION: —
DATE: A.D. 220–240 (Schmidt-Colinet: A.D. 210–240).

Cat. 263

Cat. 264

REFERENCES: Schmidt-Colinet 1992, 136 f. 154 cat. K 21 pl. 53, a. b.

OBJECT DESCRIPTION
The fragment depicts the head of a male figure.

PORTRAIT
His hair is rendered in two rows of flame-shaped curls around the head. The individual strands of hair are indicated by incised lines. His face is oval. The eyebrows are curving and rendered with incised lines starting at the root of the nose. The eyes are almond-shaped, with a thick upper eyelid. The end of the upper eyelids extends beyond that of the lower ones. The irises are indicated by incised circles. The ears are protruding, and the helix, scapha, tragus, and earlobe are depicted. The nose is straight, with a wide base. The alae are incised. He has a beard: it starts at the temples and covers the outer side of the cheeks, the chin, and the upper lip. The facial hair is rendered by flame-shaped curls; the individual strands of hair are rendered by incised lines. The mouth is large, with full lips. The upper lip curves highly.

265. FRAGMENT OF A MALE HEAD

DATABASE NUMBER: PM903.
LOCATION: Palmyra, Palmyra Museum, inv. no. I.c.2.
CONTEXT: West necropolis. Valley of the Tombs. Temple tomb no. 36.
ACQUISITION HISTORY: —
MEASUREMENTS: Height: 11 cm.
MATERIAL: Limestone.
PRESERVATION: The lower part of the portrait is broken off at the height of the chin. The hair and face are chipped.
TECHNICAL DESCRIPTION: —

DATE: A.D. 220–240 (Schmidt-Colinet: A.D. 220–250).
REFERENCES: Schmidt-Colinet 1992, 122. 137 f. 154 cat. K 23 pl. 52, f.

OBJECT DESCRIPTION
The fragment depicts the head of a male figure. It probably comes from a figure on a banqueting relief.

PORTRAIT
The figure is shown frontally.
The hair is short and voluminous, arranged in three rows of snail-shell curls. His face is oval. The eyebrows are rendered by thin, curving, incised lines that start from the root of the nose. The left eyebrow is at a higher level than the right one. The eyes are large and almond-shaped, with thick upper eyelids. The end of the upper eyelids extends downwards and beyond that of the lower eyelids. The left eye is at a higher level than the right one, and the left eyelid is thicker. The eyeballs are blank. The mouth is wide, with thin lips.

A.D. 240–273

266. FRAGMENT OF A MALE HEAD

DATABASE NUMBER: PM901.
LOCATION: Palmyra, Palmyra Museum, inv. no. I.d.2.
CONTEXT: West necropolis. Valley of the Tombs. Temple tomb no. 36.
ACQUISITION HISTORY: —
MEASUREMENTS: Height: 13 cm.
MATERIAL: Limestone.

Cat. 265

Cat. 266

PRESERVATION: The portrait is broken off at the height of the eyes. The back of the head is broken off. The surface is weathered.
TECHNICAL DESCRIPTION: –
DATE: A.D. 240–273 (Schmidt-Colinet: A.D. 230–260).
REFERENCES: Schmidt-Colinet 1992, 138. 139 n. 546. 154 cat. K 17 pl. 50 g. h.

OBJECT DESCRIPTION
The fragment depicts the head of a male figure. According to Schmidt-Colinet (1992) it probably belongs to cat. 229.

PORTRAIT
The figure is shown frontally.

The hair is short and arranged in rows of flame-shaped curls, giving the appearance of tousled hair. The ears are small and slightly protruding. The helix, scapha, and concha are depicted. The eyebrows are arched and plastically rendered, with oblique, incised lines above a diagonal, incised line indicating individual hairs. The eyes have thick upper eyelids.

21–30 CM

A.D. 220–240

267. MALE HEAD

DATABASE NUMBER: PM898.
LOCATION: Palmyra, Palmyra Museum, inv. no. II.a.15.
CONTEXT: West necropolis. Valley of the Tombs. Temple tomb no. 36.
ACQUISITION HISTORY: —
MEASUREMENTS: Height: 25 cm.
MATERIAL: Limestone.
PRESERVATION: The lower part of the portrait is broken off at the neck. The upper part of the head, the back of the head, and the face are broken off. The surface is weathered.
TECHNICAL DESCRIPTION: —
DATE: A.D. 220–240 (Schmidt-Colinet: A.D. 220–250).
REFERENCES: Schmidt-Colinet 1992, 122. 137 f. 153 cat. K 13; pl. 50, b. e.

OBJECT DESCRIPTION
The fragment depicts the head of a male figure.

PORTRAIT
The hair is short and arranged in rows of flame-shaped curls. He wears a wreath with three rows of long, narrow leaves. The midribs of the leaves are incised. At the sides, the wreath projects out of a tubular band decorated with diagonal lines. His face is oval. The ears are small and slightly protruding. The helix, scapha, and concha are depicted.

Cat. 267

268. MALE HEAD

DATABASE NUMBER: PM456.
LOCATION: Palmyra, Palmyra Museum, inv. no. II.d.6.
CONTEXT: West necropolis, Valley of the Tombs. Temple tomb no. 36.
ACQUISITION HISTORY: —
MEASUREMENTS: Height: 27 cm.
MATERIAL: Limestone.
PRESERVATION: The lower part of the figure is broken off at the base of the neck. The forehead, the right eye, the nose, and the right ear are chipped.
TECHNICAL DESCRIPTION: —
DATE: A.D. 220–240 (Schmidt-Colinet: A.D. 220–250).
REFERENCES: al-Asʿad – Schmidt-Colinet 1985, 34 pl. 11, c; Schmidt-Colinet 1992, 122 f. 137 f. 153 cat. K 15 pl. 51, a. b.

OBJECT DESCRIPTION
The fragment depicts the head of a male figure. Remains of the relief background are visible behind the neck.

PORTRAIT
The figure is shown frontally.

His hair is rendered in flame-shaped curls around the head, some of them ending in a snail-shell curl at the forehead. The

OBJECTS FROM TEMPLE TOMBS

individual strands of hair are indicated by incised lines. His face is oval, and there is a horizontal groove on the forehead. The eyebrows are curving and plastically rendered, with oblique, incised lines indicating individual hairs, meeting at the root of the nose. The eyes are almond-shaped, with a thick upper eyelid. The end of the upper eyelids extends beyond that of the lower ones. The eyeballs are blank. The ears are protruding, and the helix, scapha, tragus, and earlobe are depicted. The nose is wide. He has a beard: it starts at the temples and covers the outer side of the cheeks, the chin, and the upper lip. The facial hair is rendered by crescent-shaped curls. The mouth is small, with thin lips. The chin is oval. A v-shaped groove indicates the sternocleidomastoid muscles.

Cat. 268

HEADS: FEMALES

11–20 CM

A.D. 220–240

269. FEMALE HEAD

DATABASE NUMBER: PM461.
LOCATION: Palmyra, Palmyra Museum, inv. no. II.c.3.
CONTEXT: West necropolis. Valley of the Tombs. Temple tomb no. 36.
ACQUISITION HISTORY: —
MEASUREMENTS: Height: 19 cm.
MATERIAL: Limestone.
PRESERVATION: The lower part of the figure is broken off at the chin. The frontal, upper part of the head, and the edge of the veil are broken off. The nose, the mouth, and the chin are chipped.
TECHNICAL DESCRIPTION: —
DATE: A.D. 220–240 (Schmidt-Colinet: A.D. 230–260).
REFERENCES: Schmidt-Colinet 1992, 138. 155 cat. K 31 pl. 54, a. d; Krag 2018, 342 cat. 655.

OBJECT DESCRIPTION
The fragment depicts the head of a female figure.

PORTRAIT
The figure is shown frontally.

She wears two headdresses: a turban and a veil. The turban is coiled. Horizontal grooves indicate the coiling of the fabric. The veil is heavy and has a scalloped edge. The hair is parted in the centre and brushed to the sides. It is brushed back above the ears. The hair covers the sides of the turban and disappears under the veil. The individual strands of hair are indicated by incised lines. Her face is oval. The eyebrows are curving and depicted by incised lines, starting at the root of the nose. The eyes are almond-shaped, with thick eyelids. The end of the upper eyelids extends beyond that of the lower ones. The irises are indicated by incised circles (details unclear). She wears

Cat. 269

earrings composed of three juxtaposed round beads (Colledge classification: K). The nose is wide. The alae are incised. The mouth is small, with full lips, the upper lip is curving.

270. FEMALE HEAD

DATABASE NUMBER: PM462.
LOCATION: Palmyra, Palmyra Museum, inv. no. VII.1.
CONTEXT: West necropolis. Valley of the Tombs. Temple tomb no. 36.
ACQUISITION HISTORY: —
MEASUREMENTS: Height: 20 cm.
MATERIAL: Limestone, white/yellow.
PRESERVATION: The lower part of the portrait is broken off at the top of the neck. The surface of the left and right sides of the upper part of the head, and most of the face are heavily weathered. A crack runs across the right side of the head. The upper part of the head is chipped.
TECHNICAL DESCRIPTION: —
DATE: A.D. 220–240.
REFERENCES: Schmidt-Colinet 1992, 119. 123. 155 cat. K 33 fig. 56 pl. 54, e; Krag 2018, 276 cat. 407.

OBJECT DESCRIPTION
The fragment depicts a female head. It probably comes from a figure on a banqueting relief (Schmidt-Colinet 1992).

PORTRAIT
The figure is shown frontally.

She wears a headdress, a turban, and a veil. The headdress is placed high on the forehead. It is decorated with three rectangular panels with geometric motifs separated by beaded bands. The turban is coiled: curving grooves indicate the coiling of the fabric. Over the turban, she wears a heavy veil that falls down the sides of the head. Her face is oval and fleshy. The eyebrows are rendered by curving grooves. The eyes are almond-shaped, with thick upper eyelids (details unclear). The mouth is wide, with thin lips. The chin is pointed.

21–30 CM

A.D. 220–240

271. FEMALE HEAD

DATABASE NUMBER: PM464.
LOCATION: Palmyra, Palmyra Museum, inv. no. 83.38.1.
CONTEXT: West necropolis. Valley of the Tombs. Temple tomb no. 36.
ACQUISITION HISTORY: —
MEASUREMENTS: Height: 24 cm.
MATERIAL: Limestone, white.

Cat. 270

Cat. 271

PRESERVATION: The lower part is broken off at the base of the neck. The tip of the nose is broken off. Parts of the hair on the right side of the head, the right eyebrow, the mouth, and the chin are chipped. There are cracks running across the lower part of the face and the left side of the neck.
TECHNICAL DESCRIPTION: The back of the head is roughly carved.
DATE: A.D. 220–240 (Schmidt-Colinet: A.D. 210–240).
REFERENCES: Schmidt-Colinet 1992, 122. 124. 136 f. 155 cat. K 34 pl. 55, c. d; Krag 2018, 310 cat. 532.

OBJECT DESCRIPTION
The fragment depicts a female head. Part of the background is preserved on the lower left side and the back of the fragment.

PORTRAIT
The figure is shown frontally.
The hair is centrally parted and brushed away on each side of the head in five thick locks separated by deep grooves and reaching the neck. The hair is knotted at the top of the head with a ribbon. Two locks of hair curl upwards from the ribbon. An s-shaped lock of hair extends downwards at the centre of the forehead. The individual strands of hair are rendered by incised lines. Her face is oval. The eyebrows are curving, rendered by incised lines, and starting from the root of the nose. The eyes are close-set and almond-shaped, with thick upper eyelids. The end of the upper eyelids extends beyond that of the lower ones. The irises are indicated by incised circles, and the pupils by punch holes. The irises touch the upper eyelids. The nostrils are carved, and the alae are incised. Only the earlobes are visible under the hair. The mouth is small, with a full lower lip. The chin is round, and the neck is wide.

272. FEMALE HEAD

DATABASE NUMBER: PM463.
LOCATION: Palmyra, Palmyra Museum, inv. no. III.b.1.
CONTEXT: West necropolis. Valley of the Tombs. Temple tomb no. 36.
ACQUISITION HISTORY: —
MEASUREMENTS: Height: 27 cm.
MATERIAL: Limestone.
PRESERVATION: The lower part of the figure is broken off at the base of the neck. Part of the background is preserved behind the head and the neck. The lower parts of the veil are broken off. The left eye, the nose, the cheeks, and the chin are chipped.
TECHNICAL DESCRIPTION: —
DATE: A.D. 220–240 (Schmidt-Colinet: A.D. 230–260).
REFERENCES: Schmidt-Colinet 1992, 124. 138 f. 155 cat. K 30 fig. 56 pl. 55, a. b; Krag 2018, 106 n. 105; 346 cat. 678.

OBJECT DESCRIPTION
The fragment depicts the head of a female figure.

Cat. 272

PORTRAIT
The figure is shown frontally.
She wears two headdresses: a turban and a veil. The turban is coiled and composed of a single layer. Curving grooves indicate the coiling of the fabric. The veil is heavy and has a scalloped edge. Incised lines indicate the folds of the fabric. The hair is parted in the centre of the forehead and is brushed to the sides in waves. The individual locks of hair are indicated by incised lines. Her face is oval. The eyebrows are curving and depicted by narrow ridges, starting at the root of the nose. The eyes are almond-shaped, with thick eyelids. The end of the upper eyelids extends beyond that of the lower ones. The irises are indicated by incised circles, and the pupils by punch holes. She wears earrings composed of two beads and a crescent-shaped pendant (Colledge classification: L). The nose has a wide base. The alae are incised. Nasolabial lines are indicated by oblique grooves. The mouth is straight, with thin lips. The chin is oval, with a small, round depression in the middle. The neck is wide.
Two oblique grooves on the right side of the neck indicate a garment.

273. FEMALE HEAD

DATABASE NUMBER: PM874.
LOCATION: Palmyra, Palmyra Museum, inv. no. II.b.9.
CONTEXT: West necropolis. Valley of the Tombs. Temple tomb no. 36.
ACQUISITION HISTORY: —
MEASUREMENTS: Height: 27 cm.
MATERIAL: Limestone.
PRESERVATION: The lower part of the figure is broken off at the base of the neck. The top of the head and the face are broken off. Cracks run across the head.
TECHNICAL DESCRIPTION: —
DATE: A.D. 220–240.
REFERENCES: Schmidt-Colinet 1992, 136. 155 cat. K 35 pl. 54, c. f.

OBJECT DESCRIPTION
The fragment depicts the head of a female figure.

PORTRAIT
The figure is shown frontally.

The hair is centrally parted and combed backwards in a series of wavy locks. Part of the hair was pulled upwards at the top of the head. The individual strands of hair are indicated by incised lines. The neck is long and slender, with two curving grooves. She wears a necklace composed of small, round beads at the base of the neck.

Cat. 273

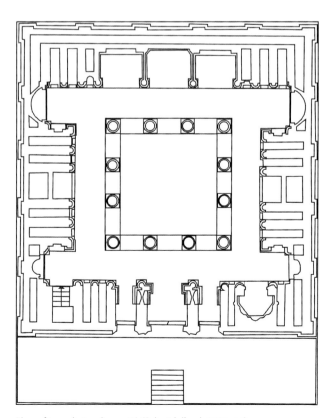

Plan of temple tomb no. 36 (Schnädelbach 2010, 95).

A.D. 236–273

TEMPLE TOMB NO. 150, TOMB OF MARONA

SARCOPHAGUS BOX RELIEF

A.D. 236–273

274. FRAGMENT OF SARCOPHAGUS BOX RELIEF WITH TRADE SCENE

DATABASE NUMBER: PM597.
LOCATION: Palmyra, Palmyra Museum, inv. no. 1046/2249.
CONTEXT: North necropolis. Temple tomb no. 150, tomb of Marona.
ACQUISITION HISTORY: —
MEASUREMENTS: Height: 85 cm.
MATERIAL: Limestone.
PRESERVATION: A large crack runs vertically through the object. The right side of the figure is broken off diagonally from the left shoulder to his right side. The surface is chipped and weathered.
TECHNICAL DESCRIPTION: —
DATE: A.D. 236–273 (Equini Schneider 1993: A.D. 200–273).
REFERENCES: Ingholt Archives, PS 1440; Colledge 1976, 20. 158 fig. 103; Equini Schneider 1993, 128 fig. 32; Stoneman 1999, 48 pl. 19; Sartre 2001, 862. 865; Hvidberg-Hansen 2002, 40 fig. 9; Seland 2010, 58; Seland 2016, 71 n. 445 fig. 14; van der Lans et al. 2017, 10; Silver et al. 2018, 26 fig. 2, 21; <https://virtual-museum-syria.org/palmyra/bas-relief-depicting-a-palmyrene-ship-with-a-standing-warrior/> (06.05.2022).

OBJECT DESCRIPTION
The object is rectangular in shape. A panel, possibly the central stretcher of the kline, is preserved in the upper left corner. It has a square indentation with a rosette and a plaque with a tongues pattern. The rear legs of a camel are rendered in the right lower corner. To the left of the standing figure, a ship is depicted. The boom of the mast is rendered in an oblique angle. A trapezoidal sail falls from the boom. Wide lines, possibly a rendering of the ropes, creates a square pattern across the sail. The central and upper parts of the hull are rectangular, while the stern is oblong and narrow towards the top. A large rudder is attached to the central part of the hull. The plinth under the ship is rendered by wide grooves.

PORTRAIT
The figure is shown frontally. The left arm is bent. His legs are set slightly apart. The left foot points forward and the right to the side.

He wears a tunic. The tunic ends at the knees. The folds are rendered by curving and oblique grooves.

He grasps the stern of the ship, with his left hand. With his right hand, he holds the reins, possibly connected with the animal to the right.

Cat. 274

A.D. 240–273

HEXAGONAL TOMB

HEADS: MALES

31–40 CM

A.D. 240–273

275. MALE HEAD

DATABASE NUMBER: PM448.
LOCATION: Palmyra, Palmyra Museum, inv. no. B 2726/9163.
CONTEXT: North necropolis. Hexagonal tomb.
ACQUISITION HISTORY: —
MEASUREMENTS: Height: 38 cm. Width: 25 cm.
MATERIAL: Limestone, yellow.
PRESERVATION: The body of the figure is broken off at the base of the neck. The chin is broken off.
TECHNICAL DESCRIPTION: The nose is reconstructed.
DATE: A.D. 240–273 (Parlasca 2001b: A.D. 100–273).
REFERENCES: Parlasca 2001b, 367 cat. 252; Gawlikowski 2010c, 69 fig. 2; Wielgosz-Rondolino 2016a, 75 fig. 14.

OBJECT DESCRIPTION

The fragment depicts a male head.

PORTRAIT

The head is turned slightly to the left.

His hair is plastically rendered in two rows of snail-shell curls around the head. The individual strands of hair are indicated by incised lines. He wears a wreath high on the head, with the leaves pointing towards a central bust. The midribs of the leaves are indicated by incised lines. The small bust depicts a male figure wearing a tunic and himation, with the folds of the clothing rendered by curving grooves. The figure's face is oval. There is a horizontal groove on the forehead. The eyebrows are curving and plastically rendered, with oblique, incised lines indicating individual hairs, and they meet in a pointed groove above the root of the nose. The eyes are almond-shaped, with thick eyelids. The end of the upper eyelids extends beyond that of the lower ones. The irises were indicated by circular inlays. A horizontal groove is indicated under each eye. The ears are small, and the helix, scapha, tragus, and earlobe are depicted. The nose is wide. The alae are incised, and the nostrils are carved. There is a nasolabial fold on each side of the nose. He has a beard: it starts at the temples and covers the outer side of the cheeks and the chin. He also has a moustache, which continues down past the corners of the mouth, and a goatee. The facial hair is rendered by snail-shell curls in the beard, and vertical, incised lines on the moustache and goatee. The mouth has a full lower lip. The neck is long, with a protrusion indicating the Adam's apple. A v-shaped groove indicates the sternocleidomastoid muscles.

NO MEASUREMENTS

A.D. 240–273

276. MALE HEAD

DATABASE NUMBER: PM889.
LOCATION: Palmyra, Palmyra Museum, inv. no. unknown.
CONTEXT: North necropolis. Hexagonal tomb.
ACQUISITION HISTORY: —
MEASUREMENTS: —
MATERIAL: Limestone, yellow.
PRESERVATION: The body of the figure is broken off at the base of the neck. The top of the head is broken off. The right side of the head, the left eyebrow, and the cheeks are chipped. The surface is weathered.
TECHNICAL DESCRIPTION: The nose appears restored. The irises were indicated by inlays.
DATE: A.D. 240–273.
REFERENCES: Gawlikowski 2010c, 70 fig. 2; Wielgosz-Rondolino 2016a, 75 fig. 14.

OBJECT DESCRIPTION

The fragment depicts a male head.

PORTRAIT

The head is turned slightly to the left.

His hair is plastically rendered in two rows of snail-shell curls around the head. The individual strands of hair are indicated by incised lines. He wears a wreath high on the head, with three rows of serrated leaves pointing towards a central, oval decoration with an incised border. The midribs of the leaves are incised. His face is oval. There is a long furrow on the forehead. The eyebrows are curving and plastically rendered, with oblique, incised lines indicating individual hairs, and they meet in a pointed groove above the root of the nose. The eyes are almond-shaped, with thick upper eyelids. The end of the upper eyelids extends beyond that of the lower ones. The lower eyelids are indicated by two curving, incised lines. The right iris was indicated by a circular inlay, and the left iris by an arched inlay. The ears are small, and the helix, scapha, tragus, and earlobe are depicted. The nose is wide. The alae are incised, and the nostrils are drilled. There is a nasolabial fold on each side of the nose. He has a beard: it starts at the temples and covers the outer side of the cheeks and the chin. He also has a moustache, which continues down past the corners of the mouth, and a goatee. The facial hair is rendered by snail-shell curls in the beard, and vertical, incised lines on the moustache and goatee. The mouth has a full lower lip. The neck is long, with a protrusion indicating the Adam's apple. A v-shaped groove indicates the sternocleidomastoid muscles.

277. MALE HEAD

DATABASE NUMBER: PM890.
LOCATION: Palmyra, Palmyra Museum, inv. no. B 2726/9163.
CONTEXT: North necropolis. Hexagonal tomb.
ACQUISITION HISTORY: —
MEASUREMENTS: Height: 45 cm. Width: 24 cm. Depth: 27 cm.
MATERIAL: Limestone, yellow.
PRESERVATION: The body of the figure is broken off at the base of the neck. The top of the head is broken off. The right side of the head, the left eyebrow, and the cheeks are chipped. The surface is weathered.
TECHNICAL DESCRIPTION: The irises were indicated by inlays.
DATE: A.D. 240–273.
REFERENCES: Fortin 1999, 114 cat. 64; Eisenberg 2000, 15 fig. 26; Gawlikowski 2010c, 69 fig. 2; Wielgosz-Rondolino 2016a, 75 fig. 14; <https://commons.wikimedia.org/wiki/File:Odenaethus_bust.jpg> (06.05.2022); <https://virtual-museum-syria.org/palmyra/head-of-a-statue-of-king-odainat/> (06.05.2022).

OBJECT DESCRIPTION
The fragment depicts a male head.

PORTRAIT
The head is turned slightly to the left.

His hair is plastically rendered in two rows of snail-shell curls around the head. The individual strands of hair are indicated by incised lines. He wears a wreath high on the head with three rows of serrated leaves pointing towards an armless central bust. The bust depicts a male, dressed figure. The midribs of the leaves are incised. His face is oval. There is a long furrow on the forehead. The eyebrows are curving and plastically rendered, with oblique, incised lines indicating individual hairs, and they meet in a pointed groove above the root of the nose. The eyes are almond-shaped, with thick upper eyelids. The end of the upper eyelids extends beyond that of the lower ones. The lower eyelids are indicated by two curving, incised lines. The right iris was indicated by an arched inlay, and the left by a circular inlay. The ears are small, and the helix, scapha, tragus, and earlobe are depicted. The nose is wide. The alae are incised, and the nostrils are drilled. There is a nasolabial fold on each side of the nose. He has a beard: it starts at the temples and covers the outer side of the cheeks and the chin. He also has a moustache, which continues down past the corners of the mouth, and a goatee. The facial hair is rendered by snail-shell curls in the beard, and vertical, incised lines on the moustache and goatee. The mouth has a full lower lip. The neck is long, with a protrusion indicating the Adam's apple. A v-shaped groove indicates the sternocleidomastoid muscles.

Text Image Credits

Figure 1 (E. Heldaas Seland): © Eivind Heldaas Seland. Basemap copyright ESRI 2014.

Figure 2 (K. Schnädelbach): © Klaus Schnädelbach.

Figure 3 (author not known): © Andreas Schmidt-Colinet. Schmidt-Colinet 1996, 366 f. cat. 62 fig. 197.

Figure 4 (author not known): New York, Metropolitan Museum of Art, acc. no. 55.11.5. Purchase, Joseph Pulitzer Bequest, 1955. <https://www.metmuseum.org/art/collection/search/254819> (09.05.2022). Licensed under CC0 1.0.

Figure 5 (author not known): New York, Metropolitan Museum of Art, acc. no. 2005.258. Purchase, Ruth E. White Bequest and Leon Levy Foundation, Philodoroi, Renée E. and Robert A. Belfer, the Concordia Foundation, Dr Lewis M. Dubroff, Roger and Susan Hertog, and the Joseph Rosen Foundation Inc. Gifts, 2005. <https://www.metmuseum.org/art/collection/search/257781> (09.05.2022). Licensed under CC0 1.0y.

Figure 6 (author not known): Los Angeles, J. P. Getty Museum, inv. no. 95.AA.80.1. Image in the public domain: <https://www.getty.edu/art/collection/objects/32301/unknown-maker-made-in-an-attic-workshop-sarcophagus-roman-ad-180-220/> (09.05.2022).

Figure 7 (author not known): New York, Metropolitan Museum of Art, acc. no. 74.51.2453. The Cesnola Collection, Purchased by subscription, 187476. <https://www.metmuseum.org/art/collection/search/242006> (09.05.2022). Licensed under CC0 1.0.

Figure 8 (A. Sune Berg): Copenhagen, Ny Carlsberg Glyptotek, IN 1033. © Ny Carlsberg Glyptotek, Copenhagen / Anders Sune Berg.

Figure 9 (author not known): New York, Metropolitan Museum of Art, acc. no. 01.25.1. Purchase, 1901. <https://www.metmuseum.org/art/collection/search/322367> (09.05.2022). Licensed under CC0 1.0.

Figure 10 (author not known): © Rubina Raja and Palmyra Portrait Project, Ingholt Archive at Ny Carlsberg Glyptotek, PS 877.

Figure 11 (author not known): Damascus, National Museum of Damascus, inv. no. C4024. © Rubina Raja and Palmyra Portrait Project, Ingholt Archive at Ny Carlsberg Glyptotek, PS 1129 C.

Figure 12 (author not known): © Rubina Raja and Palmyra Portrait Project, Ingholt Archive at Ny Carlsberg Glyptotek, PS 1143.

Figure 13 (author not known): Damascus, National Museum of Damascus, inv. no. C4129. © Rubina Raja and Palmyra Portrait Project, Ingholt Archive at Ny Carlsberg Glyptotek.

Figure 14. Damascus, National Museum of Damascus, inv. no. C4021. © Rubina Raja and Palmyra Portrait Project, Ingholt Archive at Ny Carlsberg Glyptotek, PS 1131B.

Figure 15 (Philippe Fuzeau): Paris, Musée du Louvre, inv. no. AO 2344. © 2016 Musée du Louvre / Philippe Fuzeau: <https://collections.louvre.fr/en/ark:/53355/cl010121762> (15.11.2022).

Figure 16 (author not known): New York, Metropolitan Museum of Art, acc. no. 30.4.105. Rogers Fund, 1930. <https://www.metmuseum.org/art/collection/search/557771> (09.05.2022). Licensed under CC0 1.0.

Figure 17 (author not known): New York, Metropolitan Museum of Art, acc. no. 30.4.78. Rogers Fund, 1930. <https://www.metmuseum.org/art/collection/search/557623> (09.05.2022). Licensed under CC0 1.0.

Figure 18 (A. Sune Berg): Copenhagen, Ny Carlsberg Glyptotek, IN 2771. © Ny Carlsberg Glyptotek, Copenhagen / Anders Sune Berg.

Figure 19 (Stéphane Maréchalle): Paris, Musée du Louvre, inv. no. LP 2597. © 2012 RMN-Grand Palais (musée du Louvre) / Stéphane Maréchalle: <https://collections.louvre.fr/en/ark:/53355/cl010275224> (15.11.2022).

Figure 20 (author not known): J. P. Getty Museum, inv. no. 73.AA.11. Image in the public domain: <https://www.getty.edu/art/collection/objects/7021/unknown-maker-kline-monument-with-a-reclining-girl-roman-ad-120-140/> (25.11.2021).

Figure 21 (author not known): New York, Metropolitan Museum of Art, acc. no. 1970.6. Harris Brisbane Dick Fund, 1970. <https://www.metmuseum.org/art/collection/search/326007> (09.05.2022). Licensed under CC0 1.0.

Figure 22 (author not known): New Haven, Yale University Art Gallery, inv. no. 1931.386. Yale University Art Gallery. Image in the public domain: <https://artgallery.yale.edu/collections/objects/4961> (10.05.2022).

Figure 23 (Katarína Mokránová): © Palmyra Portrait Project, Rubina Raja, Olympia Bobou, and Katarína Mokránová.

TEXT IMAGE CREDITS

Based on extended Topographia Palmyrena (Schnädelbach 2010) data, provided courtesy of Deutsches Archäologisches Institut (Orient-Abteilung, AS Damaskus).

Figure 24 (R. Raja): © Rubina Raja.

Figure 25 (Katarína Mokránová): © Palmyra Portrait Project, Rubina Raja, Olympia Bobou, and Katarína Mokránová. Based on extended Topographia Palmyrena (Schnädelbach 2010) data, provided courtesy of Deutsches Archäologisches Institut (Orient-Abteilung, AS Damaskus).

Figure 26 (Katarína Mokránová): © Palmyra Portrait Project, Rubina Raja, Olympia Bobou, and Katarína Mokránová. Based on extended Topographia Palmyrena (Schnädelbach 2010) data, provided courtesy of Deutsches Archäologisches Institut (Orient-Abteilung, AS Damaskus).

Figure 27 (Katarína Mokránová): © Palmyra Portrait Project, Rubina Raja, Olympia Bobou, and Katarína Mokránová. Based on extended Topographia Palmyrena (Schnädelbach 2010) data, provided courtesy of Deutsches Archäologisches Institut (Orient-Abteilung, AS Damaskus).

Figure 28 (A. Henning): © Agnes Henning.

Figure 29 (R. Raja): © Rubina Raja.

Figure 30 (author not known): London, British Museum, inv. no. BM 125206. Ingholt 1928, pl. 1 PS 1.

Figure 31 (A. Sune Berg): Copenhagen, Ny Carlsberg Glyptotek, inv. no. IN 2816. © Ny Carlsberg Glyptotek, Copenhagen / Anders Sune Berg.

Figure 32 (A. Sune Berg): Copenhagen, Ny Carlsberg Glyptotek, inv. no. IN 1079. © Ny Carlsberg Glyptotek, Copenhagen / Anders Sune Berg.

Figure 33 (A. Sune Berg): Copenhagen, Ny Carlsberg Glyptotek, inv. no. IN 1049. © Ny Carlsberg Glyptotek, Copenhagen / Anders Sune Berg.

Figure 34 (author not known): Beirut, American University Museum, inv. no. 2739. © Rubina Raja and Palmyra Portrait Project, Ingholt Archive at Ny Carlsberg Glyptotek, PS 43.

Figure 35 (author not known): St Petersburg, State Hermitage Museum, inv. no. ДВ-8841. Ingholt 1928, pl. 3 PS 9.

Figure 36 (author not known): Istanbul, İstanbul Arkeoloji Müzesi, inv. no. 3783/O.M.242. Ingholt 1928, pl. 8 PS 23.

Figure 37 (author not known): Oslo, Kulturhistorisk museum, Universitetet i Oslo, inv. no. C42237. Ingholt 1928, pl. 16 PS 53.

Figure 38 (Katarína Mokránová): © Palmyra Portrait Project, Rubina Raja, Olympia Bobou, and Katarína Mokránová. Based on extended Topographia Palmyrena (Schnädelbach 2010) data, provided courtesy of Deutsches Archäologisches Institut (Orient-Abteilung, AS Damaskus).

Figure 39 (Katarína Mokránová): © Palmyra Portrait Project, Rubina Raja, Olympia Bobou, and Katarína Mokránová. Based on extended Topographia Palmyrena (Schnädelbach 2010) data, provided courtesy of Deutsches Archäologisches Institut (Orient-Abteilung, AS Damaskus).

Figure 40 (Katarína Mokránová): © Palmyra Portrait Project, Rubina Raja, Olympia Bobou, and Katarína Mokránová. Based on extended Topographia Palmyrena (Schnädelbach 2010) data, provided courtesy of Deutsches Archäologisches Institut (Orient-Abteilung, AS Damaskus).

Figure 41 (author not known): © Rubina Raja and Palmyra Portrait Project.

Figure 42 (author not known): © Rubina Raja and Palmyra Portrait Project, Ingholt Archive at Ny Carlsberg Glyptotek, PS1107.

Figure 43 (R. Raja): © Rubina Raja.

Figure 44 (R. Raja): © Rubina Raja and Palmyra Portrait Project.

Figure 45 (author not known): © Rubina Raja and Palmyra Portrait Project.

Figure 46 (R. Raja): © Rubina Raja.

Figure 47 (J.-B. Yon): Palmyra, Palmyra Museum, inv. no. A 910/10. © Jean-Baptiste Yon, 2010.

Figure 48 (M. and P. Chuzeville): Paris, Musée du Louvre, inv. no. Ma 1428. Vue d'ensemble © Musée du Louvre / Maurice et Pierre Chuzeville: <https://collections.louvre.fr/en/ark:/53355/cl010275541> (15.11.2022).

Figure 49 (M. Beck-Coppola): Paris, Musée du Louvre, inv. no. TH 48. © Musée du Louvre / Martine Beck-Coppola: <https://collections.louvre.fr/en/ark:/53355/cl010099017> (15.11.2022).

Figure 50 (R.-G. Ojéda): Paris, Musée du Louvre, inv. no. Ma 2119. © 1993 RMN-Grand Palais (musée du Louvre) / René-Gabriel Ojéda: <https://collections.louvre.fr/en/ark:/53355/cl010276117> (15.11.2022).

Figure 51 (P. Lebaube): Paris, Musée du Louvre, inv. no. Ma 165. Face, recto, avers, avant © 1996 Musée du Louvre / Patrick Lebaube: <https://collections.louvre.fr/en/ark:/53355/cl010252192> (15.11.2022).

Figure 52 (author not known): © Rubina Raja and Palmyra Portrait Project, courtesy of Mary Ebba Underdown.

Catalogue Image Credits

Cat. 1 (A. Henning): © Agnes Henning.

Cat. 1 (A. Henning): © Agnes Henning.

Cat. 1 (A. Henning): © Agnes Henning.

Cat. 1 (N. Sauer): © Palmyra Portrait Project, Rubina Raja, and Nikoline Sauer.

Cat. 2 (author not known): Gawlikowski 1970b, fig. 13.

Cat. 2 (N. Sauer): © Palmyra Portrait Project, Rubina Raja, and Nikoline Sauer.

Cat. 3 (A. Henning): © Agnes Henning.

Cat. 3 (A. Henning): © Agnes Henning.

Cat. 3 (N. Sauer): © Palmyra Portrait Project, Rubina Raja, and Nikoline Sauer.

Cat. 4 (W. al-Asʿad): © Walid al-Asʿad.

Cat. 4 (W. al-Asʿad): © Walid al-Asʿad.

Cat. 5 (A. Sartre): © Annie Sartre.

Cat. 6 (R. Raja): © Rubina Raja.

Cat. 6 (S. Bruuns): © Palmyra Portrait Project, Rubina Raja, and Signe Bruuns.

Cat. 7 (A. Sune Berg): © Ny Carlsberg Glyptotek/Anders Sune Berg.

Cat. 8 (S. Hoss and A. Paetz gen. Schieck): © DAI – Orient-Abteilung.

Cat. 9 (author not known): Metropolitan Museum of Art, acc. no. 02.29.1. Purchase, 1902. <https://www.metmuseum.org/art/collection/search/322375> (23.05.2022). Licensed under CC0 1.0.

Cat. 10 (author not known): © Rubina Raja and Palmyra Portrait Project, Ingholt Archive at Ny Carlsberg Glyptotek, PS 1391.

Cat. 10 (S. Bruuns): © Palmyra Portrait Project, Rubina Raja, and Signe Bruuns.

Cat. 11 (author not known): © Rubina Raja and Palmyra Portrait Project, Ingholt Archive at Ny Carlsberg Glyptotek, PS 1262/1264.

Cat. 11 (S. Bruuns): © Palmyra Portrait Project, Rubina Raja, and Signe Bruuns.

Cat. 12 (A. Henning): © Agnes Henning.

Cat. 12 (N. Sauer): © Palmyra Portrait Project, Rubina Raja, and Nikoline Sauer.

Cat. 13 (T. Biniewski): Courtesy of the Polish Centre of Mediterranean Archaeology of the University of Warsaw.

Cat. 14 (T. Biniewski): Courtesy of the Polish Centre of Mediterranean Archaeology of the University of Warsaw.

Cat. 15 (T. Biniewski): Courtesy of the Polish Centre of Mediterranean Archaeology of the University of Warsaw.

Cat. 16 (T. Biniewski): Courtesy of the Polish Centre of Mediterranean Archaeology of the University of Warsaw.

Cat. 17 (T. Biniewski): Courtesy of the Polish Centre of Mediterranean Archaeology of the University of Warsaw.

Cat. 18 (T. Biniewski): Courtesy of the Polish Centre of Mediterranean Archaeology of the University of Warsaw.

Cat. 18 (S. Bruuns): © Palmyra Portrait Project, Rubina Raja, and Signe Bruuns.

Cat. 19 (A. Henning): © Agnes Henning.

Cat. 19 (N. Sauer): © Palmyra Portrait Project, Rubina Raja, and Nikoline Sauer.

Cat. 20 (T. Biniewski): Courtesy of the Polish Centre of Mediterranean Archaeology of the University of Warsaw.

Cat. 20 (S. Bruuns): © Palmyra Portrait Project, Rubina Raja, and Signe Bruuns.

Cat. 21 (A. Henning): © Agnes Henning.

Cat. 21 (S. Bruuns): © Palmyra Portrait Project, Rubina Raja, and Signe Bruuns.

Cat. 22 (A. Henning): © Agnes Henning.

Cat. 23 (A. Henning): © Agnes Henning.

Cat. 24 (A. Henning): © Agnes Henning.

Cat. 25 (A. Henning): © Agnes Henning.

Cat. 26 (A. Henning): © Agnes Henning.

Cat. 27 (A. Henning): © Agnes Henning.

Cat. 28 (P. Grunwald): German Institute of Archaeology, DAI Damascus Inst.-Neg. 85/554. 85/552. 85/555.

Cat. 29 (P. Grunwald): German Institute of Archaeology, DAI Damascus Inst.-Neg. 85/553.

Cat. 30 (P. Grunwald): German Institute of Archaeology, DAI Damascus Inst.-Neg. 85/556.

Cat. 31 (A. Henning): © Agnes Henning.

Cat. 32 (A. Henning): © Agnes Henning.

CATALOGUE IMAGE CREDITS

Cat. 33 (A. Henning): © Agnes Henning.

Cat. 34 (P. Grunwald): German Institute of Archaeology, DAI Damascus Inst.-Neg. 85/523.

Cat. 35 (A. Henning): © Agnes Henning.

Cat. 36 (P. Grunwald): German Institute of Archaeology, DAI Damascus Inst.-Neg. 85/529.

Cat. 37 (P. Grunwald): German Institute of Archaeology, DAI Damascus Inst.-Neg. 85/543.

Cat. 38 (P. Grunwald): German Institute of Archaeology, DAI Damascus Inst.-Neg. 85/559.

Cat. 39 (P. Grunwald): German Institute of Archaeology, DAI Damascus Inst.-Neg. 85/535.

Cat. 40 (P. Grunwald): German Institute of Archaeology, DAI Damascus Inst.-Neg. 85/531.

Cat. 41 (P. Grunwald): German Institute of Archaeology, DAI Damascus Inst.-Neg. 85/568.

Cat. 42 (A. Henning): © Agnes Henning.

Cat. 43 (A. Henning): © Agnes Henning.

Cat. 44 (A. Henning): © Agnes Henning.

Cat. 45 (A. Henning): © Agnes Henning.

Cat. 46 (P. Grunwald): German Institute of Archaeology, DAI Damascus Inst.-Neg. 85/546.

Cat. 47 (P. Grunwald): German Institute of Archaeology, DAI Damascus Inst.-Neg. 85/521.

Cat. 48 (A. Henning): © Agnes Henning.

Cat. 49 (A. Henning): © Agnes Henning.

Cat. 50 (A. Henning): © Agnes Henning.

Cat. 51 (A. Henning): © Agnes Henning.

Cat. 52 (A. Henning): © Agnes Henning.

Cat. 53 (A. Henning): © Agnes Henning.

Cat. 54 (A. Henning): © Agnes Henning.

Cat. 55 (A. Henning): © Agnes Henning.

Cat. 56 (A. Henning): © Agnes Henning.

Cat. 57 (A. Henning): © Agnes Henning.

Cat. 58 (A. Henning): © Agnes Henning.

Cat. 58 (N. Sauer): © Palmyra Portrait Project, Rubina Raja, and Nikoline Sauer.

Cat. 59 (A. Henning): © Agnes Henning.

Cat. 60 (P. Grunwald): German Institute of Archaeology, DAI Inst.-Neg. 88.2335, Sadurska – Bounni 1994, fig. 208.

Cat. 61 (P. Grunwald): German Institute of Archaeology, DAI Inst.-Neg. 88.2334, Sadurska – Bounni 1994, fig. 209.

Cat. 62 (P. Grunwald): German Institute of Archaeology, DAI Inst.-Neg. 88.2463, Sadurska – Bounni 1994, fig. 211.

Cat. 63 (P. Grunwald): German Institute of Archaeology, DAI Inst.-Neg. 88.2455, Sadurska – Bounni 1994, fig. 210.

Cat. 64 (P. Grunwald): German Institute of Archaeology, DAI Inst.-Neg. 88.2454, Sadurska – Bounni 1994, fig. 212.

Cat. 65 (P. Grunwald): German Institute of Archaeology, DAI Inst.-Neg. 88.2458, Sadurska – Bounni 1994, fig. 213.

Cat. 66 (P. Grunwald): German Institute of Archaeology, DAI Inst.-Neg. 88.2456, Sadurska – Bounni 1994, fig. 215.

Cat. 67 (P. Grunwald): German Institute of Archaeology, DAI Inst.-Neg. 88.2457 Sadurska – Bounni 1994, fig. 214.

Cat. 68 (P. Grunwald): German Institute of Archaeology, DAI Inst.-Neg. 88.2333, Sadurska – Bounni 1994, fig. 252.

Cat. 69 (P. Grunwald): German Institute of Archaeology, DAI Inst.-Neg. 88.2329, Sadurska – Bounni 1994, fig. 251.

Cat. 69 (S. Bruuns): © Palmyra Portrait Project, Rubina Raja, and Signe Bruuns.

Cat. 70 (author not known): © Rubina Raja and Palmyra Portrait Project, Ingholt Archive at Ny Carlsberg Glyptotek, PS 1008.

Cat. 70 (K. Schnädelbach): © K. Schnädelbach.

Cat. 71 (P. Grunwald): German Institute of Archaeology, DAI Inst.-Neg. 2326, Sadurska – Bounni 1994, fig. 221.

Cat. 71 (author not known): © Rubina Raja and Palmyra Portrait Project, Ingholt Archive at Ny Carlsberg Glyptotek, PS 1378.

Cat. 71 (S. Bruuns): © Palmyra Portrait Project, Rubina Raja, and Signe Bruuns.

Cat. 72 (P. Grunwald): German Institute of Archaeology, DAI Inst.-Neg. 88.2563–88.2569, Sadurska – Bounni 1994, figs. 222–223.

Cat. 73 (P. Grunwald): German Institute of Archaeology, DAI Inst.-Neg. 88.2548, Sadurska – Bounni 1994, fig. 227.

Cat. 73 (S. Bruuns): © Palmyra Portrait Project, Rubina Raja, and Signe Bruuns.

Cat. 74 (author not known): © Rubina Raja and Palmyra Portrait Project, Ingholt Archive at Ny Carlsberg Glyptotek.

Cat. 74 (author not known): © Rubina Raja and Palmyra Portrait Project, Ingholt Archive at Ny Carlsberg Glyptotek.

Cat. 74 (author not known): © Rubina Raja and Palmyra Portrait Project, Ingholt Archive at Ny Carlsberg Glyptotek.

Cat. 74 (S. Bruuns): © Palmyra Portrait Project, Rubina Raja, and Signe Bruuns.

Cat. 77 (S. Hoss and A. Paetz gen. Schieck): Courtesy of DAI – Orient-Abteilung.

Cat. 78 (S. Hoss and A. Paetz gen. Schieck): Courtesy of DAI – Orient-Abteilung.

Cat. 78 (S. Bruuns): © Palmyra Portrait Project, Rubina Raja, and Signe Bruuns.

Cat. 79 (S. Hoss and A. Paetz gen. Schieck): Courtesy of DAI – Orient-Abteilung.

Cat. 81 (author not known): © Rubina Raja and Palmyra Portrait Project, Ingholt Archive at Ny Carlsberg Glyptotek, PS 1048.

Cat. 81 (author not known): © Rubina Raja and Palmyra Portrait Project, Ingholt Archive at Ny Carlsberg Glyptotek, PS 985.

Cat. 82 (author not known): © Rubina Raja and Palmyra Portrait Project, Ingholt Archive at Ny Carlsberg Glyptotek, PS 984.

Cat. 83 (author not known): © Rubina Raja and Palmyra Portrait Project, Ingholt Archive at Ny Carlsberg Glyptotek, PS 986.

Cat. 84 (author not known): © Rubina Raja and Palmyra Portrait Project, Ingholt Archive at Ny Carlsberg Glyptotek, PS 987.

Cat. 85 (author not known): © Rubina Raja and Palmyra Portrait Project, Ingholt Archive at Ny Carlsberg Glyptotek, PS 988.

Cat. 86 (author not known): © Rubina Raja and Palmyra Portrait Project, Ingholt Archive at Ny Carlsberg Glyptotek, PS 564.

Cat. 87 (author not known): © Rubina Raja and Palmyra Portrait Project, Ingholt Archive at Ny Carlsberg Glyptotek, PS 989. Cat. 93.

Cat. 88 (author not known): © Rubina Raja and Palmyra Portrait Project, Ingholt Archive at Ny Carlsberg Glyptotek, PS 989.

Cat. 88 (S. Bruuns): © Palmyra Portrait Project, Rubina Raja, and Signe Bruuns.

Cat. 89 (author not known): © Rubina Raja and Palmyra Portrait Project, Ingholt Archive at Ny Carlsberg Glyptotek, PS 983.

Cat. 90 (author not known): © Rubina Raja and Palmyra Portrait Project, Ingholt Archive at Ny Carlsberg Glyptotek, PS 890.

Cat. 90 (author not known): © Rubina Raja and Palmyra Portrait Project, Ingholt Archive at Ny Carlsberg Glyptotek, PS 892.

Cat. 91 (author not known): © Rubina Raja and Palmyra Portrait Project, Ingholt Archive at Ny Carlsberg Glyptotek, PS 891.

Cat. 92 (author not known): © Rubina Raja and Palmyra Portrait Project, Ingholt Archive at Ny Carlsberg Glyptotek, PS 893.

Cat. 93 (author not known): © Rubina Raja and Palmyra Portrait Project, Ingholt Archive at Ny Carlsberg Glyptotek, PS 888.

Cat. 95 (author not known): © Rubina Raja and Palmyra Portrait Project, Ingholt Archive at Ny Carlsberg Glyptotek, PS 648.

Cat. 96 (author not known): © Rubina Raja and Palmyra Portrait Project, Ingholt Archive at Ny Carlsberg Glyptotek, PS 1127.

Cat. 96 (author not known): © Rubina Raja and Palmyra Portrait Project, Ingholt Archive at Ny Carlsberg Glyptotek, PS 888.

Cat. 96 (author not known): © Rubina Raja and Palmyra Portrait Project, Ingholt Archive at Ny Carlsberg Glyptotek.

Cat. 96 (author not known): © Rubina Raja and Palmyra Portrait Project, Ingholt Archive at Ny Carlsberg Glyptotek, PS 889.

Cat. 96 (S. Bruuns): © Palmyra Portrait Project, Rubina Raja, and Signe Bruuns.

Cat. 97 (author not known): © Rubina Raja and Palmyra Portrait Project, Ingholt Archive at Ny Carlsberg Glyptotek, PS 604.

Cat. 102 (S. Bruuns): © Palmyra Portrait Project, Rubina Raja, and Signe Bruuns.

Cat. 103 (J. Aliquot): © Jean-Baptiste Yon and J. Aliquot, 2009.

Cat. 104 (W. al-Asʿad): © Walid al-Asʿad.

Cat. 109 (J.-B. Yon): © Jean-Baptiste Yon, 2002.

Cat. 109 (S. Bruuns): © Palmyra Portrait Project, Rubina Raja, and Signe Bruuns.

Cat. 110 (P. Grunwald): German Institute of Archaeology, DAI Inst.-Neg. 88.2413, Sadurska – Bounni 1994, fig. 237.

Cat. 111 (author not known): © Rubina Raja and Palmyra Portrait Project, Ingholt Archive at Ny Carlsberg Glyptotek, PS 1281.

Cat. 112 (P. Grunwald): German Institute of Archaeology, DAI Inst.-Neg. 88.2548, Sadurska – Bounni 1994, fig. 227.

Cat. 113 (S. Bruuns): © Palmyra Portrait Project, Rubina Raja, and Signe Bruuns.

Cat. 114 (J.-B. Yon): © Jean-Baptiste Yon, 2010.

Cat. 114 (S. Bruuns): © Palmyra Portrait Project, Rubina Raja, and Signe Bruuns.

Cat. 115 (P. Grunwald): German Institute of Archaeology, DAI Inst.-Neg. 88.2497, Sadurska – Bounni 1994, fig. 218.

Cat. 115 (P. Grunwald): German Institute of Archaeology, DAI Inst.-Neg. 88.2495, Sadurska – Bounni 1994, fig. 217.

Cat. 115 (P. Grunwald): German Institute of Archaeology, DAI Inst.-Neg. 88.2494, Sadurska – Bounni 1994, fig. 219.

Cat. 116 (author not known): © Rubina Raja and Palmyra Portrait Project, Ingholt Archive at Ny Carlsberg Glyptotek, PS 646B.

Cat. 117 (author not known): © Rubina Raja and Palmyra Portrait Project, Ingholt Archive at Ny Carlsberg Glyptotek, PS 978.

Cat. 117 (K. Schnädelbach): © K. Schnädelbach.

Cat. 118 (author not known): © Rubina Raja and Palmyra Portrait Project, Ingholt Archive at Ny Carlsberg Glyptotek, PS 58.

Cat. 118 (S. Bruuns): © Palmyra Portrait Project, Rubina Raja, and Signe Bruuns.

C145_ cat. 119 (P. Grunwald): German Institute of Archaeology, DAI Inst.-Neg. 88.2620, Sadurska – Bounni 1994, fig. 242.

C146_ cat. 119 (P. Grunwald): German Institute of Archaeology, DAI Inst.-Neg. 88.2617, Sadurska – Bounni 1994, fig. 244.

C147_ cat. 120 (P. Grunwald): German Institute of Archaeology, DAI Inst.-Neg. 88.2618, Sadurska – Bounni 1994, fig. 241.

C148_ cat. 121 (R. Raja): © Rubina Raja.

Cat. 123 (M. Gawlikowski): Courtesy of Michał Gawlikowski.

Cat. 124 (M. Gawlikowski): Courtesy of Michał Gawlikowski.

Cat. 125 (author not known): © Rubina Raja and Palmyra Portrait Project, Ingholt Archive at Ny Carlsberg Glyptotek, IA_NCG_Portrait2016_085_sarcophagi.

Cat. 125 (author not known): © Rubina Raja and Palmyra Portrait Project, Ingholt Archive at Ny Carlsberg Glyptotek, IA_NCG_Portrait2016_124.

Cat. 126 (author not known): © Rubina Raja and Palmyra Portrait Project, Ingholt Archive at Ny Carlsberg Glyptotek, IA_NCG_Portrait2016_065.

Cat. 127 (author not known): © Rubina Raja and Palmyra Portrait Project, Ingholt Archive at Ny Carlsberg Glyptotek, IA_NCG_Portrait2016_066.

Cat. 128 (S. Hoss and A. Paetz gen. Schieck): Courtesy of DAI – Orient-Abteilung.

Cat. 131 (S. Bruuns): © Palmyra Portrait Project, Rubina Raja, and Signe Bruuns.

Cat. 132 (author not known): © Rubina Raja and Palmyra Portrait Project, Ingholt Archive at Ny Carlsberg Glyptotek.

Cat. 133 (author not known): © Rubina Raja and Palmyra Portrait Project, Ingholt Archive at Ny Carlsberg Glyptotek.

Cat. 133 (S. Bruuns): © Palmyra Portrait Project, Rubina Raja, and Signe Bruuns.

Cat. 134 (author not known): © Rubina Raja and Palmyra Portrait Project, Ingholt Archive at Ny Carlsberg Glyptotek, PS 1433.

Cat. 134 (author not known): © Rubina Raja and Palmyra Portrait Project, Ingholt Archive at Ny Carlsberg Glyptotek, IA_NCG_Miscellaneous2016_076picF.

Cat. 135 (author not known): © Rubina Raja and Palmyra Portrait Project, Ingholt Archive at Ny Carlsberg Glyptotek, IA_NCG_Miscellaneous2016_076picA.

Cat. 136 (author not known): © Rubina Raja and Palmyra Portrait Project, Ingholt Archive at Ny Carlsberg Glyptotek, IA_NCG_Miscellaneous2016_076picD.

Cat. 136 (author not known): © Rubina Raja and Palmyra Portrait Project, Ingholt Archive at Ny Carlsberg Glyptotek, IA_NCG_Miscellaneous2016_076picG.

Cat. 137 (author not known): © Rubina Raja and Palmyra Portrait Project, Ingholt Archive at Ny Carlsberg Glyptotek, IA_NCG_Miscellaneous2016_076picE.

Cat. 166 (N. Sauer): © Palmyra Portrait Project, Rubina Raja, and Nikoline Sauer.

Cat. 167 (author not known): © Rubina Raja and Palmyra Portrait Project, Ingholt Archive at Ny Carlsberg Glyptotek, IA_NCG_Portrait2016_029 + portraits.

Cat. 167 (K. Schnädelbach): © K. Schnädelbach.

Cat. 168 (P. Grunwald): German Institute of Archaeology, DAI Inst.-Neg. 88.2576, Sadurska – Bounni 1994, fig. 231.

Cat. 169 (P. Grunwald): German Institute of Archaeology, DAI Inst.-Neg. 88.2604, Sadurska – Bounni 1994, fig. 234.

Cat. 169 (P. Grunwald): German Institute of Archaeology, DAI Inst.-Neg. 88.2608, Sadurska – Bounni 1994, fig. 236.

Cat. 170 (P. Grunwald): German Institute of Archaeology, DAI Inst.-Neg. 88.2605, Sadurska – Bounni 1994, fig. 233.

Cat. 170 (P. Grunwald): German Institute of Archaeology, DAI Inst.-Neg. 88.2607, Sadurska – Bounni 1994, fig. 235.

Cat. 171 (author not known): © Rubina Raja and Palmyra Portrait Project, Ingholt Archive at Ny Carlsberg Glyptotek, PS 1374.

Cat. 171 (N. Sauer): © Palmyra Portrait Project, Rubina Raja, and Nikoline Sauer.

Cat. 172 (author not known): © Rubina Raja and Palmyra Portrait Project, Ingholt Archive at Ny Carlsberg Glyptotek, PS 1005.

Cat. 172 (K. Schnädelbach): © K. Schnädelbach.

Cat. 173 (M. Gawlikowski): Courtesy of Michal Gawlikowski.

Cat. 173 (S. Bruuns): © Palmyra Portrait Project, Rubina Raja, and Signe Bruuns.

Cat. 174 (author not known): © Rubina Raja and Palmyra Portrait Project, Ingholt Archive at Ny Carlsberg Glyptotek, IA_NCG_Portrait2016_021.

Cat. 175 (author not known): © Rubina Raja and Palmyra Portrait Project, Ingholt Archive at Ny Carlsberg Glyptotek, IA_NCG_Portrait2016_021.

Cat. 176 (author not known): © Rubina Raja and Palmyra Portrait Project, Ingholt Archive at Ny Carlsberg Glyptotek, IA_NCG_Portrait2016_021.

Cat. 176 (author not known): © Rubina Raja and Palmyra Portrait Project, Ingholt Archive at Ny Carlsberg Glyptotek, IA_NCG_Portrait2016_021.

Cat. 176 (C. Christensen): Ingholt 1938, pl. 45.

Cat. 177 (W. al-Asʿad): © Walid al-Asʿad.

Cat. 177 (N. Sauer): © Palmyra Portrait Project, Rubina Raja, and Nikoline Sauer.

Cat. 178 (author not known): © Rubina Raja and Palmyra Portrait Project, Ingholt Archive at Ny Carlsberg Glyptotek, PS 1094.

Cat. 178 (S. Hoss and A. Paetz gen. Schieck): Courtesy of DAI – Orient-Abteilung.

Cat. 179 (P. Grunwald): German Institute of Archaeology, DAI Inst.-Neg. 88.2388, Sadurska – Bounni 1994, fig. 253.

Cat. 180 (A. Schmidt-Colinet): © Andreas Schmidt-Colinet. Schmidt-Colinet 1992, pl. 73, b.

Cat. 181 (A. Schmidt-Colinet): © Andreas Schmidt-Colinet. Schmidt-Colinet 1992, pl. 73, a.

Cat. 181 (A. Schmidt-Colinet): © Andreas Schmidt-Colinet. Schmidt-Colinet 1992, pl. 69, c.

Cat. 182 (author not known): © Rubina Raja and Palmyra Portrait Project, Ingholt Archive at Ny Carlsberg Glyptotek, PS 895.

Cat. 183 (author not known): © Rubina Raja and Palmyra Portrait Project, Ingholt Archive at Ny Carlsberg Glyptotek, PS 897.

Cat. 184 (author not known): © Rubina Raja and Palmyra Portrait Project, Ingholt Archive at Ny Carlsberg Glyptotek, PS IA_NCG_Architecture2016_020.

Cat. 185 (author not known): © Rubina Raja and Palmyra Portrait Project, Ingholt Archive at Ny Carlsberg Glyptotek, PS 900.

Cat. 186 (author not known): © Rubina Raja and Palmyra Portrait Project, Ingholt Archive at Ny Carlsberg Glyptotek, PS 901.

Cat. 187 (author not known): © Rubina Raja and Palmyra Portrait Project, Ingholt Archive at Ny Carlsberg Glyptotek, PS 899.

Cat. 188 (author not known): © Rubina Raja and Palmyra Portrait Project, Ingholt Archive at Ny Carlsberg Glyptotek, PS 896.

Cat. 189 (author not known): © Rubina Raja and Palmyra Portrait Project, Ingholt Archive at Ny Carlsberg Glyptotek, PS 903.

Cat. 190 (author not known): © Rubina Raja and Palmyra Portrait Project, Ingholt Archive at Ny Carlsberg Glyptotek, PS 898.

Cat. 190 (N. Sauer): © Palmyra Portrait Project, Rubina Raja, and Nikoline Sauer.

Cat. 192 (author not known): © Rubina Raja and Palmyra Portrait Project, Ingholt Archive at Ny Carlsberg Glyptotek, PS 1001.

Cat. 192 (N. Sauer): © Palmyra Portrait Project, Rubina Raja, and Nikoline Sauer.

Cat. 193 (author not known): © Rubina Raja and Palmyra Portrait Project, Ingholt Archive at Ny Carlsberg Glyptotek, PS 529A.

Cat. 194 (author not known): © Rubina Raja and Palmyra Portrait Project, Ingholt Archive at Ny Carlsberg Glyptotek, PS 529A.

Cat. 195 (author not known): © Rubina Raja and Palmyra Portrait Project, Ingholt Archive at Ny Carlsberg Glyptotek, PS 885.

Cat. 196 (author not known): © Rubina Raja and Palmyra Portrait Project, Ingholt Archive at Ny Carlsberg Glyptotek, PS 887.

Cat. 197 (author not known): © Rubina Raja and Palmyra Portrait Project, Ingholt Archive at Ny Carlsberg Glyptotek, PS 886.

Cat. 198 (author not known): © Rubina Raja and Palmyra Portrait Project, Ingholt Archive at Ny Carlsberg Glyptotek, PS 883/829A.

Cat. 199 (author not known): © Rubina Raja and Palmyra Portrait Project, Ingholt Archive at Ny Carlsberg Glyptotek, PS 884.

Cat. 201 (author not known): © Rubina Raja and Palmyra Portrait Project, Ingholt Archive at Ny Carlsberg Glyptotek, PS 531a/882.

Cat. 202 © Library of Congress, <www.loc.gov/item/2019703531/> (01.12.2021).

Cat. 203 (author not known): © Rubina Raja and Palmyra Portrait Project, Ingholt Archive at Ny Carlsberg Glyptotek, PS 531b.

Cat. 204 (author not known): © Rubina Raja and Palmyra Portrait Project, Ingholt Archive at Ny Carlsberg Glyptotek, PS 880.

Cat. 205 (author not known): © Rubina Raja and Palmyra Portrait Project, Ingholt Archive at Ny Carlsberg Glyptotek.

Cat. 206 (author not known): © Rubina Raja and Palmyra Portrait Project, Ingholt Archive at Ny Carlsberg Glyptotek, PS 881.

Cat. 207 (American Colony (Jerusalem). Photo Department, photographer): © Library of Congress, <www.loc.gov/item/2019703531/> (01.12.2021).

Cat. 211 (American Colony (Jerusalem). Photo Department, photographer): © Library of Congress, <www.loc.gov/item/2019703531/> (01.12.2021).

Cat. 212 (American Colony (Jerusalem). Photo Department, photographer): © Library of Congress, <www.loc.gov/item/2019703531/> (01.12.2021).

Cat. 213 (American Colony (Jerusalem). Photo Department, photographer): © Library of Congress, <www.loc.gov/item/2019703531/> (01.12.2021).

Cat. 215 (American Colony (Jerusalem). Photo Department, photographer): © Library of Congress, <www.loc.gov/item/2019706277/> (01.12.2021).

Cat. 216 (American Colony (Jerusalem). Photo Department, photographer): © Library of Congress, <www.loc.gov/item/2019706277/> (01.12.2021).

Cat. 217 (American Colony (Jerusalem). Photo Department, photographer): © Library of Congress, <www.loc.gov/item/2019706277/> (01.12.2021).

Cat. 218 (author not known): © Rubina Raja and Palmyra Portrait Project, Ingholt Archive at Ny Carlsberg Glyptotek.

Cat. 220 (author not known): © Rubina Raja and Palmyra Portrait Project, Ingholt Archive at Ny Carlsberg Glyptotek.

Cat. 221 (author not known): © Rubina Raja and Palmyra Portrait Project, Ingholt Archive at Ny Carlsberg Glyptotek, PS 550.

Cat. 221 (N. Sauer): © Palmyra Portrait Project, Rubina Raja, and Nikoline Sauer.

Cat. 221 (American Colony (Jerusalem). Photo Department, photographer): © Library of Congress, <www.loc.gov/item/2019703531/> (01.12.2021).

Cat. 221 (American Colony (Jerusalem). Photo Department, photographer): © Library of Congress, <www.loc.gov/item/2019706277/> (01.12.2021).

Cat. 222 (A. Schmidt-Colinet): © Andreas Schmidt-Colinet. Schmidt-Colinet 1996, fig. 222.

Cat. 223 (author not known): © Rubina Raja and Palmyra Portrait Project, Ingholt Archive at Ny Carlsberg Glyptotek, PS 874.

Cat. 224 (author not known): © Rubina Raja and Palmyra Portrait Project, Ingholt Archive at Ny Carlsberg Glyptotek, PS 1280.

CATALOGUE IMAGE CREDITS

Cat. 225 (A. Schmidt-Colinet): © Andreas Schmidt-Colinet. Schmidt-Colinet 1992, pl. 72, e.

Cat. 227 (author not known): © Rubina Raja and Palmyra Portrait Project, Ingholt Archive at Ny Carlsberg Glyptotek, PS 975.

Cat. 228 (A. Schmidt-Colinet): © Andreas Schmidt-Colinet. Schmidt-Colinet 1992, pl. 36, a.

Cat. 228 (J. Zbinden): © Andreas Schmidt-Colinet. Schmidt-Colinet 1992, pl. 32, h.

Cat. 228 (J. Zbinden): © Andreas Schmidt-Colinet. Schmidt-Colinet 1992, pl. 33, b.

Cat. 228 (A. Schmidt-Colinet): © Andreas Schmidt-Colinet. Schmidt-Colinet 1992, pl. 32, b.

Cat. 228 (J. Zbinden): © Andreas Schmidt-Colinet. Schmidt-Colinet 1992, pl. 47, a.

Cat. 228 (J. Zbinden): © Andreas Schmidt-Colinet. Schmidt-Colinet 1992, pl. 49, i.

Cat. 228 (A. Schmidt-Colinet): © Andreas Schmidt-Colinet. Schmidt-Colinet 1992, pl. 33, a.

Cat. 229 (A. Schmidt-Colinet): © Andreas Schmidt-Colinet. Schmidt-Colinet 1992, pl. 40, f.

Cat. 229 (A. Schmidt-Colinet): © Andreas Schmidt-Colinet. Schmidt-Colinet 1992, pl. 41, d.

Cat. 229 (J. Zbinden): © Andreas Schmidt-Colinet. Schmidt-Colinet 1992, pl. 40, e.

Cat. 229 (J. Zbinden): © Andreas Schmidt-Colinet. Schmidt-Colinet 1992, pl. 32, c.

Cat. 230 (A. Schmidt-Colinet): © Andreas Schmidt-Colinet. Schmidt-Colinet 1992, pl. 40, a.

Cat. 230 (A. Schmidt-Colinet): © Andreas Schmidt-Colinet. Schmidt-Colinet 1992, pl. 40, b.

Cat. 230 (C. Müting-Zimmer – A. Schmidt-Colinet): © Andreas Schmidt-Colinet. Schmidt-Colinet 1992, fig. 65.

Cat. 231 (J. Zbinden): © Andreas Schmidt-Colinet. Schmidt-Colinet 1992, pl. 34, a.

Cat. 231 (A. Schmidt-Colinet): © Andreas Schmidt-Colinet. Schmidt-Colinet 1992, pl. 38, c.

Cat. 232 (J. Zbinden): © Andreas Schmidt-Colinet. Schmidt-Colinet 1992, pl. 38, a.

Cat. 232 (J. Zbinden): © Andreas Schmidt-Colinet. Schmidt-Colinet 1992, pl. 40, c.

Cat. 233 (J. Zbinden): © Andreas Schmidt-Colinet. Schmidt-Colinet 1992, pl. 37, b.

Cat. 233 (J. Zbinden): © Andreas Schmidt-Colinet. Schmidt-Colinet 1992, pl. 35, c.

Cat. 233 (J. Zbinden): © Andreas Schmidt-Colinet. Schmidt-Colinet 1992, pl. 35, e.

Cat. 233 (J. Zbinden): © Andreas Schmidt-Colinet. Schmidt-Colinet 1992, pl. 37, a.

Cat. 234 (J. Zbinden): © Andreas Schmidt-Colinet. Schmidt-Colinet 1992, pl. 41, e.

Cat. 235 (J. Zbinden): © Andreas Schmidt-Colinet. Schmidt-Colinet 1992, pl. 38, b.

Cat. 235 (J. Zbinden): © Andreas Schmidt-Colinet. Schmidt-Colinet 1992, pl. 50, a.

Cat. 236 (J. Zbinden): © Andreas Schmidt-Colinet. Schmidt-Colinet 1992, pl. 45, a.

Cat. 236 (A. Schmidt-Colinet): © Andreas Schmidt-Colinet. Schmidt-Colinet 1992, pl. 45, e.

Cat. 237 (J. Zbinden): © Andreas Schmidt-Colinet. Schmidt-Colinet 1992, pl. 43, b.

Cat. 237 (J. Zbinden): © Andreas Schmidt-Colinet. Schmidt-Colinet 1992, pl. 43, a.

Cat. 238 (K. Anger): © Andreas Schmidt-Colinet. Schmidt-Colinet 1992, pl. 31, c.

Cat. 238 (J. Zbinden): © Andreas Schmidt-Colinet. Schmidt-Colinet 1992, pl. 31, d.

Cat. 239 (J. Zbinden): © Andreas Schmidt-Colinet. Schmidt-Colinet 1992, pl. 31, e.

Cat. 240 (J. Zbinden): © Andreas Schmidt-Colinet. Schmidt-Colinet 1992, pl. 44, c.

Cat. 241 (J. Zbinden): © Andreas Schmidt-Colinet. Schmidt-Colinet 1992, pl. 45, c.

Cat. 241 (J. Zbinden): © Andreas Schmidt-Colinet. Schmidt-Colinet 1992, pl. 45, d.

Cat. 242 (A. Schmidt-Colinet): © Andreas Schmidt-Colinet. Schmidt-Colinet 1992, pl. 44, a.

Cat. 243 (J. Zbinden): © Andreas Schmidt-Colinet. Schmidt-Colinet 1992, pl. 44, b.

Cat. 244 (J. Zbinden): © Andreas Schmidt-Colinet. Schmidt-Colinet 1992, pl. 43, c.

Cat. 245 (J. Zbinden): © Andreas Schmidt-Colinet. Schmidt-Colinet 1992, pl. 42, b.

Cat. 245 (A. Schmidt-Colinet): © Andreas Schmidt-Colinet. Schmidt-Colinet 1992, pl. 42, a.

Cat. 245 (J. Zbinden): © Andreas Schmidt-Colinet. Schmidt-Colinet 1992, pl. 50, c.

Cat. 245 (J. Zbinden): © Andreas Schmidt-Colinet. Schmidt-Colinet 1992, pl. 42, f.

Cat. 246 (J. Zbinden): © Andreas Schmidt-Colinet. Schmidt-Colinet 1992, pl. 49, a.

Cat. 246 (J. Zbinden): © Andreas Schmidt-Colinet. Schmidt-Colinet 1992, pl. 53, c.

Cat. 247 (J. Zbinden): © Andreas Schmidt-Colinet. Schmidt-Colinet 1992, pl. 46, a.

Cat. 247 (J. Zbinden): © Andreas Schmidt-Colinet. Schmidt-Colinet 1992, pl. 46, c.

Cat. 248 (J. Zbinden): © Andreas Schmidt-Colinet. Schmidt-Colinet 1992, pl. 49, c.

Cat. 248 (J. Zbinden): © Andreas Schmidt-Colinet. Schmidt-Colinet 1992, pl. 49, h.

Cat. 249 (A. Schmidt-Colinet): © Andreas Schmidt-Colinet. Schmidt-Colinet 1992, pl. 42, c.

Cat. 249 (A. Schmidt-Colinet): © Andreas Schmidt-Colinet. Schmidt-Colinet 1992, pl. 42, g.

Cat. 249 (A. Schmidt-Colinet): © Andreas Schmidt-Colinet. Schmidt-Colinet 1992, pl. 42, d.

Cat. 249 (J. Zbinden): © Andreas Schmidt-Colinet. Schmidt-Colinet 1992, pl. 42, e.

Cat. 250 (J. Zbinden): © Andreas Schmidt-Colinet. Schmidt-Colinet 1992, pl. 54, b.

Cat. 250 (J. Zbinden): © Andreas Schmidt-Colinet. Schmidt-Colinet 1992, pl. 52, e.

Cat. 251 (A. Schmidt-Colinet): © Andreas Schmidt-Colinet. Schmidt-Colinet 1992, pl. 41, a.

Cat. 251 (C. Müting-Zimmer – A. Schmidt-Colinet): © Andreas Schmidt-Colinet. Schmidt-Colinet 1992, fig. 53.

Cat. 252 (J. Zbinden): © Andreas Schmidt-Colinet. Schmidt-Colinet 1992, pl. 32, g.

Cat. 252 (A. Schmidt-Colinet): © Andreas Schmidt-Colinet. Schmidt-Colinet 1992, pl. 32, e.

Cat. 252 (J. Zbinden): © Andreas Schmidt-Colinet. Schmidt-Colinet 1992, pl. 32, f.

Cat. 253 (C. Müting-Zimmer – A. Schmidt-Colinet): © Andreas Schmidt-Colinet. Schmidt-Colinet 1992, fig. 52.

Cat. 254 (J. Zbinden): © Andreas Schmidt-Colinet. Schmidt-Colinet 1992, pl. 49, d.

Cat. 255 (A. Schmidt-Colinet): © Andreas Schmidt-Colinet. Schmidt-Colinet 1992, pl. 49, e.

Cat. 256 (J. Zbinden): © Andreas Schmidt-Colinet. Schmidt-Colinet 1992, pl. 48, a.

Cat. 257 (J. Zbinden): © Andreas Schmidt-Colinet. Schmidt-Colinet 1992, pl. 48, c.

Cat. 258 (J. Zbinden): © Andreas Schmidt-Colinet. Schmidt-Colinet 1992, pl. 47, c.

Cat. 259 (J. Zbinden): © Andreas Schmidt-Colinet. Schmidt-Colinet 1992, pl. 49, k.

Cat. 260 (C. Müting-Zimmer – A. Schmidt-Colinet): © Andreas Schmidt-Colinet. Schmidt-Colinet 1992, fig. 53.

Cat. 261 (J. Zbinden): © Andreas Schmidt-Colinet. Schmidt-Colinet 1992, pl. 52, c.

Cat. 262 (J. Zbinden): © Andreas Schmidt-Colinet. Schmidt-Colinet 1992, pl. 51, c.

Cat. 263 (J. Zbinden): © Andreas Schmidt-Colinet. Schmidt-Colinet 1992, pl. 52, a.

Cat. 264 (J. Zbinden): © Andreas Schmidt-Colinet. Schmidt-Colinet 1992, pl. 53, a.

Cat. 265 (J. Zbinden): © Andreas Schmidt-Colinet. Schmidt-Colinet 1992, pl. 52, f.

Cat. 266 (J. Zbinden): © Andreas Schmidt-Colinet. Schmidt-Colinet 1992, pl. 50, g.

Cat. 267 (J. Zbinden): © Andreas Schmidt-Colinet. Schmidt-Colinet 1992, pl. 50, b.

Cat. 268 (J. Zbinden): © Andreas Schmidt-Colinet. Schmidt-Colinet 1992, pl. 51, a.

Cat. 269 (J. Zbinden): © Andreas Schmidt-Colinet. Schmidt-Colinet 1992, pl. 54, a.

Cat. 270 (J. Zbinden): © Andreas Schmidt-Colinet. Schmidt-Colinet 1992, pl. 54, e.

Cat. 271 (J. Zbinden): © Andreas Schmidt-Colinet. Schmidt-Colinet 1992, pl. 55, c.

Cat. 272 (J. Zbinden): © Andreas Schmidt-Colinet. Schmidt-Colinet 1992, pl. 55, a.

Cat. 273 (J. Zbinden): © Andreas Schmidt-Colinet. Schmidt-Colinet 1992, pl. 54, c.

Cat. 273 (N. Sauer): © Palmyra Portrait Project, Rubina Raja, and Nikoline Sauer.

Cat. 274 (author not known): © Rubina Raja and Palmyra Portrait Project, Ingholt Archive at Ny Carlsberg Glyptotek, PS 1440.